UNIVERSITY CASEBOOK SERIES

EDITORIAL BOARD

ROBERT C. CLARK
DIRECTING EDITOR
Dean & Royall Professor of Law
Harvard University

DANIEL A. FARBER
Henry J. Fletcher Professor of Law
University of Minnesota

OWEN M. FISS
Sterling Professor of Law
Yale University

GERALD GUNTHER
William Nelson Cromwell Professor of Law, Emeritus
Stanford University

THOMAS H. JACKSON
President
University of Rochester

HERMA HILL KAY
Dean & Barbara Nachtrieb Armstrong Professor of Law
University of California, Berkeley

DAVID W. LEEBRON
Dean & Lucy G. Moses Professor of Law
Columbia University

SAUL LEVMORE
William B. Graham Professor of Law
University of Chicago

ROBERT L. RABIN
A. Calder Mackay Professor of Law
Stanford University

CAROL M. ROSE
Gordon Bradford Tweedy Professor of Law & Organization
Yale University

DAVID L. SHAPIRO
William Nelson Cromwell Professor of Law
Harvard University

THE LAW OF DEMOCRACY

LEGAL STRUCTURE OF THE POLITICAL PROCESS

by

SAMUEL ISSACHAROFF
Charles Tilford McCormick Professor of Law
The University of Texas School of Law

PAMELA S. KARLAN
Professor of Law and Roy L. and Rosamond Woodruff Morgan Research Professor
The University of Virginia School of Law

RICHARD H. PILDES
Professor of Law and Roy F. and Jean Humphrey Profitt Research Professor
The University of Michigan Law School

WESTBURY, NEW YORK

THE FOUNDATION PRESS, INC.

1998

COPYRIGHT © 1998 By THE FOUNDATION PRESS, INC.
615 Merrick Ave.
Westbury, N.Y. 11590–6607
(516) 832–6950

All rights reserved
Printed in the United States of America

ISBN 1–56662–462–2

 TEXT IS PRINTED ON 10% POST CONSUMER RECYCLED PAPER

For my family — SI

For Beth and Art, Peter, Nathan and Louise, and Jim and Lani — PSK

For Robert and Rosita, inspirational parents — RHP

*

PREFACE

The foundations of democracy are being thrown open for examination today as they have been at only a few previous moments in political history. Internationally, more new democracies have been formed in the last decade than at any previous time, as countries ranging from South Africa, to the former Soviet Union, to Eastern and Central Europe, to less visible places like Nepal, are all moving to regimes of constitutional democracy. As democratic governments are constructed in diverse political, historical, and cultural contexts, the basic questions in democratic theory and practice are being confronted anew: what is the most appropriate conception of political representation, and should the answer vary depending on the specific contexts of different polities? What is the range of electoral structures different democracies might adopt, and what is at stake in the choice among them? How much can institutions shape a country's formal politics and political culture?

At the same time, assumptions about democratic structures long taken for granted in the United States are now facing pressure along several fronts. Some of these challenges stem from the way the Voting Rights Act, first enacted in 1965, has been reshaping the political process to seek greater inclusion of racial and ethnic minorities. Struggles over racial redistricting now regularly dominate the Supreme Court docket and are the site of some of the most contentious confrontations in constitutional law. In turn, these conflicts have raised questions about the most basic structures of American democracy, such as electing individual officeholders from geographically defined election districts. Technology has placed new pressures on the democratic process, where computers now allow a manipulation of district boundaries that no one foresaw at the outset of the Reapportionment Revolution. Alternative voting systems, such as cumulative voting, limited voting, and preference voting, are generating considerable interest as possible new directions for American democracy. How do these alternatives work; what are the advantages and disadvantages of each; what does experience show about how they work in practice? Other challenges stem from the role of money in politics. Agitation for campaign-finance reform is greater now than at any time since the 1970s, at least, and the possible directions for such reforms—as well as the constitutional constraints on possible reforms—differ dramatically. Still other challenges are emerging from the striking recent upsurge in the use of direct democracy to bypass the institutions of representative government. Does direct democracy contribute to good democratic politics or undermine it? If major policies are increasingly going to be adopted this way, are there techniques through which the process of direct citizen participation in politics can be improved?

Given the prevalence of these and similar questions—and given the longstanding centrality of democratic politics to all aspects of public law—it is something of a mystery that law schools have not typically taught courses in the law of democracy. Conceptions of democratic politics provide the backdrop for many courses, but that is where they remain. There is little systematic exploration of the historical struggles over the structure of democratic institutions, or of the theoretical principles that underlie the choice of different democratic forms, or of the practical consequences that follow from different institutional arrangements, or of the way in which the law shapes the kind of democratic politics we experience.

This casebook tries to address those absences. We examine an array of specific issues currently posing challenges to the practice of democratic politics in the United States: issues involving the individual right to vote, partisan and racial gerrymandering, the relationship of the state to political parties, campaign-finance reform, and the fair representation of minorities in democratic bodies. We look at both the constitutional framework for democratic politics and the approaches that have emerged through major legislative initiatives, such as the Voting Rights Act. Although we do not draw on the experiences of other democracies at each point in the book, we do also provide a comprehensive overview of alternatives to the traditional American approach for structuring electoral politics, including a look at consociational forms of democracy, proportional representation, and lottery voting. We attempt to bring historical perspective to the way specific issues have developed in the legal context of the United States. In addition, we develop certain theoretical themes that we believe run throughout nearly all the specific issues we explore, and that go to the foundational questions in the application of democratic theory to particular problems in democratic politics. If nothing else, our aim is to open the minds of readers to other ways of conceiving democratic institutions than those that are reflected in current arrangements.

The wealth of issues makes it unlikely that any one-semester course will cover the entire book. The tradeoff between breadth and depth might depend in part on the configuration of the course: a three-hour survey course for students with a relatively general interest in the political system might seek to expose students to a broad range of issues, while a weekly seminar might pick only a few topics for more extensive discussion. We have taught parts of these materials in settings ranging from seminars with a dozen students, where participants were expected to do substantial outside reading and short papers to focus the discussion, to large classes of 150; while the precise coverage varied, we found in each case that students were excited about discussing the doctrinal, philosophical, and practical aspects of voting rights law. There are a variety of ways to use this book. One course might concentrate on democratic theory and devote greater attention to Chapters 1, 4, 10, and 11. Another might focus more on questions relating to race, and accordingly spend more time with Chapters 2, 5, 6, 7, and 8. Yet another might focus more heavily on the regulation of partisan politics and campaigns; it would emphasize the materials in Chapters 3, 4, 8, and 9. Moreover, although each chapter works somewhat as a contained unit, the book's pervasive themes make it possible to "mix and match" materials from different chapters. For example, some professors might want to include the historical materials from Chapter 11 about the emergence of single-member congressional districts with earlier discussions of congressional districting in Chapter 3 (one person, one vote) or Chapter 8 (political gerrymandering and race-conscious redistricting); others might find it interesting to teach the materials on write-in voting and the development of the secret ballot that appear in Chapter 4 along with the materials in Chapter 2 on the formal right to participate. In working on this project, we found that the order in which the chapters appeared changed many times. One of the exciting aspects of this field is the multiplicity of connections among the materials; discussion can flow from one issue to another along many different paths, depending on the interests and expertise of the professor and students.

We would first like to express appreciation for our students who worked with earlier versions of this material in courses at the University of Chicago Law School, Harvard Law School, the University of Michigan Law School, New York University School of Law, Stanford Law School, the University of Texas School of Law, the University of Virginia School of Law, and Yale Law School. Not only did they offer numerous ideas we incorporated in terms of presentation of the material, but in many cases they wrote papers which deepened our understanding of the relevant issues and from which we borrowed in constructing this casebook. Their enthusiasm about the issues and material convinced us this book was worth doing.*

Over the years, our views on the issues discussed here have developed in conversation or collaboration with too many people to mention, but some of them include Alex Aleinikoff, Jim Blacksher, Richard Briffault, Bruce Cain, Norman Chachkin, Chandler Davidson, Richard Engstrom, Cynthia Estlund, David Estlund, Lani Guinier, Bernie Grofman, Gerry Hebert, Roderick Hills, Jr., Sherrilyn Ifill, Morgan Kousser, Douglas Laycock, Daryl Levinson, Sandy Levinson, Allan Lichtman, Daniel Lowenstein, David Lublin, Eben Moglen, Peyton McCrary, Dan Ortiz, Frank Parker, George Rutherglen, and Ed Still. Justice Holmes once stated that "it is required of a man that he should share the action and passion of his time at peril of

---

* In excerpting materials from cases and secondary sources, we have used the following conventions. Insertions are indicated with brackets and deletions with either ellipses or asterisks, depending on their length. We have not indicated the deletions of citation material or footnotes, but we have retained the original numbering of notes that we include. Notes that we have written are indicated by letters rather than numbers.

being judged not to have lived." Oliver Wendell Holmes, *Memorial Day* in The Occasional Speeches of Justice Oliver Wendell Holmes 6-7 (Mark Howe ed. 1962). Each of us has participated, not only as a scholar but also as a litigator, in shaping some of the legal doctrine covered in this book. We do not indicate at each point in the book when one of us has been involved in the underlying litigation, and instead rely on this general disclaimer to warn readers that we are not disinterested observers of all the events chronicled here. We would also like to thank our co-counsel, expert witnesses, even some of our opposing counsel, and, especially, our clients, for the many practical insights they provided into the operation and effects of the American law of democracy.

For reading or teaching sections of the manuscript and commenting, we would like to thank Cynthia Estlund, Elizabeth Garrett, Barack Obama, Dan Ortiz, Nate Persily, Scot Powe, Judith Reed, and David Strauss. For document assistance: David Gunn. For research assistance: Jeff Costello, Sally Dworak-Fisher, Alexandra Foster, Jeffrey Fisher, Gary Gansle, Jeff Gitchel, Tom Goldstein, Deborah Hamilton, Chris Herren, Chris Hoffman, David Horan, Bruce Itchkawitz, Daryl Levinson, Laura Mate, Alex Romain, Johanna Schneider, Anne Showalter, Paul Speaker, Sara Stadler, Elana Tyrangiel, and Heather Way. For copy editing: Ann Estlund. For manuscript production: Diane Cronk, Juli Martin, Sylvia Sexton. Finally, for a wealth of intellectual and material support, we thank the law schools at the Universities of Michigan, Texas, and Virginia, and our Deans: Jeffrey Lehman; Michael Sharlot; and Bob Scott.

ACKNOWLEDGMENTS

We gratefully acknowledge the permission extended by the following authors or publishers to reprint excerpts from the works indicated:

Bruce A. Ackerman, *Beyond* Carolene Products, 98 Harv. L. Rev. 713 (1985) (reprinted by permission of the author)

Lynn A. Baker, *Direct Democracy and Discrimination: A Public Choice Perspective*, 67 Chi.-Kent L. Rev. 707 (1992) ("Reprinted with the permission of the Chicago Kent Law Review.")

Lynn A. Baker and Samuel H. Dinkin, *The Senate: An Institution Whose Time Has Gone?*, 13 J.L. & Pol. 21 (1997) (reprinted by permission of the Journal of Law and Politics)

Jonathan Bourne, Jr., *Functions of the Initiative, Referendum and Recall*, 43 Annals of the Am. Acad. Pol. & Soc. Sci. 3 (1912) (© The American Academy of Political and Social Science; reprinted by permission of Sage Publications, Inc.)

Thomas M. Boyd and Stephen J. Markman, *The 1982 Amendments to the Voting Rights Act: A Legislative History*, 40 Wash. & Lee L. Rev. 1347 (1983) (reprinted by permission of the authors)

Richard Briffault, *Lani Guinier and the Dilemmas of American Democracy*, 95 Colum. L. Rev. 418 (1995) ("This article originally appeared at 95 Colum. L. Rev. 418 (1995). Reprinted by permission.")

Richard Briffault, *Who Rules at Home?:One Person/One Vote and Local Governments*, 60 U. Chi. L. Rev. 339 (1993) (reprinted by permission of the Columbia Law Review)

Bruce E. Cain, *Moralism and Realism in Campaign Finance Reform*, 1995 U. Chi. Legal F. 111 (reprinted by permission of the author)

Thomas Christiano, The Rule of the Many: Fundamental Issues in Democratic Theory (1996) (reprinted by permission of the Westview Press)

David Cole, *First Amendment Antitrust: The End of Laissez-Faire in Campaign Finance*, 9 Yale L. & Pol'y Rev. 236 (1991) (reprinted by permission of the Yale Law and Policy Review)

Ronald Dworkin, *The Curse of American Politics,* New York Review of Books, Oct. 17, 1996, at 23 ("Reprinted with permission from *The New York Review of Books.* Copyright © 1996, NYREV, Inc.")

Richard L. Engstrom and Michael McDonald, *Quantitative Evidence in Vote Dilution Litigation: Political Participation and Polarized Voting*, 17 Urb. Law. 369 (Summer 1995) (reprinted by permission of the authors)

Richard L. Engstrom, *The Supreme Court and Equipopulous Gerrymandering: A Remaining Obstacle in the Quest for Fair and Effective Representation*, 1976 Ariz. St. L.J. 277 (reprinted by permission of the author and the Arizona State Law Journal)

Julian Eule, *Promoting Speaker Diversity: Austin and Metro Broadcasting*, 1990 Sup. Ct. Rev. 105 (reprinted by permission of Carole L. Eule)

Owen M. Fiss, *Free Speech and Social Structure*, 71 Iowa L. Rev. 1405 (1986) (reprinted by permission of the Iowa Law Review)

Gerald Frug, *Decentering Decentralization,* 60 U. Chi. L. Rev. 253 (1993) (reprinted by permission of the author)

Joel Garreau, Edge City: Life on the Frontier (1991) (reprinted by permission of Doubleday)

Thomas Geoghegan, *The Infernal Senate*, The New Republic, Nov. 21, 1995 (reprinted by permission of The New Republic)

Lani Guinier, *[E]racing Democracy*, 108 Harv. L. Rev. 109 (1994) (reprinted by permission of the author)

Lani Guinier, The Tyranny of the Majority (1994) (reprinted by permission of the author)

Roderick M. Hills, Jr., *A Defense of State Constitutional Limits on Federal Congressional Terms*, 53 U. Pitt. L. Rev. 97 (1991) (reprinted by permission of the University of Pittsburgh Law Review and the author)

Richard Hofstader, The Age of Reform (1955) ("© Vintage Books. Reprinted by permission of Alfred A. Knopf, Inc.")

J. Morgan Kousser, The Shaping of Southern Politics: Suffrage Restrictions and the Establishment of the One-Party South (1974) (reprinted by permission of the author)

Michael J. Klarman, *Majoritarian Judicial Review: The Entrenchment Problem*, 85 Geo. L.J. 491 (1997) ("Reprinted with permission of the publisher, Georgetown University and Georgetown Law Journal. © 1997.")

Michael J. Klarman, *The Puzzling Resistance to Political Process Theory*, 77 Va. L. Rev. 747 (1991) (reprinted by permission of the Virginia Law Review)

Eric Lipton, *Democracy Can Stop Traffic*, Washington Post, Jan. 8, 1995 at A1 ("© 1997 Washington Post Writers Group. Reprinted with permission.")

Daniel H. Lowenstein, *Associational Rights of Major Political Parties: A Skeptical Inquiry*, 71 Tex. L. Rev. 1741 (1993) (reprinted by permission of the author)

David Lublin, *Representation and Redistricting*, in Classifying by Race (Paul Peterson ed. 1996) (reprinted by permission of the author and the Princeton University Press)

David Magleby, *Let the Voters Decide? An Assessment of the Initiative and Referendum Process*, 66 U. Colo. L. Rev. 13 (1995) ("Reprinted with permission of the University of Colorado Law Review.")

Bernard Manin, The Principles of Representative Government (1997) (reprinted by permission of Cambridge University Press)

Abner J. Mikva and Jeff Bleich, *Civil Rights Legislation in the 1990s: When Congress Overrules the Court*, 79 Calif. L. Rev. 729 (1991) ("© 1991 by The California Law Review, Inc.; reprinted by permission.")

James A. Morone, The Democratic Wish (1990) (reprinted by permission of Harpercollins Publishers)

Michael Pertschuk, Giant Killers (W.W. Norton & Co. 1986) (reprinted by permission of the author)

Richard Pildes, *Gimme Five: Non-Gerrymandering Racial Justice*, The New Republic, March 1995, at 16 (reprinted by permission of The New Republic)

Frances Fox Piven and Richard Cloward, Why Americans Don't Vote (1989) (reprinted by permission of the authors)

J.R. Pole, Political Representation in England & Origins of the American Republic ("© J.R. Pole. Reprinted with permission of St. Martin's Press, Inc.")

Jane S. Schacter, *The Pursuit of "Popular Intent": Interpretative Dilemmas in Direct Democracy*, 105 Yale. L.J. 107 (1995) ("Reprinted by permission of The Yale Law Journal Company and Fred B. Rothman & Company from The Yale Law Journal, Vol. 105, pages 107-176.")

Peter Schrag, *Take the Initiative, Please: Referendum Madness in California*, 28 American Prospect 61 (1996) (reprinted by permission of The American Prospect and "© Peter Schrag".)

Bradley Smith, *Faulty Assumptions and Undemocratic Consequences to Campaign Finance Reform*, 105 Yale L.J. 1049 ("Reprinted by permission of The Yale Law Journal Company and Fred B. Rothman & Company from The Yale Law Journal, Vol. 105, pages 1049-91.")

Frank J. Sorauf, Inside Campaign Finance (1992) (reprinted by permission of the author and Yale University Press)

David A. Strauss, *Corruption, Equality, and Campaign Finance Reform*, 94 Col. L. Rev. 1369 (1994) (reprinted by permission of the author)

Adam Winkler, Note, *Expressive Voting*, 68 N.Y.U. L. Rev. 330 (1993) (reprinted by permission of the New York University Law Review)

Jerry Wilson, Demonstrative Redistricting Exercise (reprinted by permission of Jerry Wilson)

Gordon Wood, The Radicalism of the American Revolution (1992) (reprinted by permission of Alfred A. Knopf, Inc.)

SUMMARY OF CONTENTS

PREFACE v
ACKNOWLEDGMENTS ix
TABLE OF CASES xxiii

CHAPTER 1 An Introduction to the Selection of Democratic Institutions 1

CHAPTER 2 The Right to Participate 17

A. Constitutional Text and Structure 21
B. The Modern Constitutional Framework 40
C. The Struggle for Black Enfranchisement 68
   1. Techniques for Outright Disenfranchisement 78
   2. The White Primary Cases 79
   3. The Demise of Discretion 95
   4. Redrawing District Boundaries 102
D. Voter Registration and Participation 107

CHAPTER 3 The Reapportionment Revolution 116

A. The Political Thicket 117
B. Local Governance 157
C. The Senate, Republican Theory, and Interest Representation 177

CHAPTER 4 The Role of Political Parties 186

A. The Ballot: Political Parties as Gatekeepers 189
   1. Restrictions on Whom Voters Can Vote For 193
   2. Restrictions on Who Appears on the Ballot 203
B. Who Can Participate in a Party's Activities? 212
   1. Both the Party and the State Seek to Exclude Citizen X From Participating 213
   2. The Party Seeks to Exclude Citizen X from Participating But the State Demands That the Party Permit Him to Participate 224
   3. The Party Wishes to Permit Citizen X to Participate But the State Demands Her Exclusion 230
C. When Can the Government Regulate a Party's Internal Affairs? 237
D. Does the Existing Legal Regime Improperly Entrench the Existing Two–Party System? 244
   1. Challenges to Ballot Access by Independent and Third–Party Candidates 245

2. The Interaction of Ballot Access and Other Electoral Regulations in Perpetuating the Two–Party System 254

CHAPTER 5 Preclearance and the Voting Rights Act 264

A. Congressional Power to Enact the Special Provisions of the Voting Rights Act 266
B. What Is a "Covered Change"? 285
C. What Constitutes a Discriminatory Purpose or Effect? 313
D. The Administrative Process 324
E. Preclearance: A Case Study 336

CHAPTER 6 Majority Rule and Minority Vote Dilution: Constitutional and Legislative Approaches 367

A. Defining the Harm 368
B. The Rise of the Intent Requirement 388
C. The 1982 Amendments to Section 2 of the VRA 410
   1. Section 2 as amended in 1982: 411
   2. The Legislative Process leading to Section 2 411
   3. Excerpts From the Senate Judiciary Committee Report 424

CHAPTER 7 Racial Vote Dilution Under the Voting Rights Act 441

A. Judicial Modulation of the "Results" Standard: The Three–Part Test for Challenges to Multimember Districts 443
   1. *Gingles'* First Prong: "Sufficiently Large and Geographically Compact" 472
   2. *Gingles'* Second Prong: "Political Cohesion": The Special Problem of Coalition Lawsuits 481
   3. *Gingles'* Third Prong: "White Bloc Voting" 489
B. The Reemergence of a "Totality of the Circumstances Approach" .. 499
C. Beyond Dilution Through Submergence 519

CHAPTER 8 Redistricting and Representation 546

A. Partisan Gerrymandering 547
B. Racial Gerrymandering 566
C. A Redistricting Exercise 612

CHAPTER 9 Money and Politics 616

A. Regulating Contributions and Expenditures 618
B. Do Concerns Over Corruption Justify Campaign Finance Regulation? 632
C. Equality and Liberty in Political Campaigns 647
D. Has Campaign Finance Regulation Worked? 658

E. A Caution on Public Financing 660
F. Proposals for Reform 662

CHAPTER 10 Direct Democracy 665

A. Constitutional Underpinnings and Concerns 666
B. Direct Democracy and Rights of Political Participation 677
   1. Popular Lawmaking and Unpopular Groups 677
   2. Popular Lawmaking and Problems of Entrenchment 695

CHAPTER 11 Alternative Democratic Structures 713

A. Types of Electoral Systems 719
B. Cumulative Voting 722
C. Preference Voting or the Single–Transferrable Vote (STV) 748
D. Limited Voting 756
E. The Lot Versus the Election 765
F. The History of Territorial Districting 769
G. The Debate Between Majoritarian Systems and Proportional Representation 773
H. Consociational Democracy 780

INDEX 785

TABLE OF CONTENTS

PREFACE	v
ACKNOWLEDGMENTS	ix
TABLE OF CASES	xxiii

CHAPTER 1 An Introduction to the Selection of Democratic Institutions 1

Lucas v. The Forty–Fourth General Assembly of the State of Colorado	3
Notes and Questions	11

CHAPTER 2 The Right to Participate 17

A.	Constitutional Text and Structure	21
	Minor v. Happersett	22
	Notes and Questions	27
	Richardson v. Ramirez	33
	Notes and Questions	36
B.	The Modern Constitutional Framework	40
	Lassiter v. Northampton County Board of Elections	40
	Harper v. Virginia Board of Elections	42
	Kramer v. Union Free School District No. 15	47
	Notes and Questions	53
C.	The Struggle for Black Enfranchisement	68
	Giles v. Harris	69
	Notes and Questions	71
	1. Techniques for Outright Disenfranchisement	78
	A Note on the Contemporaneous Effect of the Poll Tax	78
	2. The White Primary Cases	79
	Nixon v. Herndon	79
	Notes and Questions	80
	Smith v. Allwright	82
	Terry v. Adams	85
	Notes and Questions	92
	3. The Demise of Discretion	95
	4. Redrawing District Boundaries	102
	Gomillion v. Lightfoot	103
	Notes and Questions	106
D.	Voter Registration and Participation	107
	Notes and Questions	113

CHAPTER 3 The Reapportionment Revolution 116

A.	The Political Thicket	117
	Colegrove v. Green	117
	Notes and Questions	121

      Baker v. Carr 122
      Notes and Questions 133
      Reynolds v. Sims 135
      Notes and Questions 144
      Karcher v. Daggett 150
      Notes and Questions 154
  B. Local Governance 157
      Board of Estimate v. Morris 158
      Notes and Questions 163
      Ball v. James 164
      Notes and Questions 169
      Fumarolo v. Chicago Board of Education 173
      Notes and Questions 177
  C. The Senate, Republican Theory, and Interest Representation 177
      Gray v. Sanders 182
      Notes and Questions 184

CHAPTER 4   The Role of Political Parties 186

  A. The Ballot: Political Parties as Gatekeepers 189
    1. Restrictions on Whom Voters Can Vote For 193
      Burdick v. Takushi 193
      Notes and Questions 200
    2. Restrictions on Who Appears on the Ballot 203
      Bullock v. Carter 204
      Notes and Questions 209
  B. Who Can Participate in a Party's Activities? 212
    1. Both the Party and the State Seek to Exclude Citizen X From Participating 213
      Nader v. Schaffer 213
      Notes and Questions 216
      Duke v. Massey 218
      Republican Party of Texas v. Dietz 220
      Notes and Questions 223
    2. The Party Seeks to Exclude Citizen X from Participating But the State Demands That the Party Permit Him to Participate 224
      Democratic Party of the United States v. Wisconsin 224
      Notes and Questions 229
    3. The Party Wishes to Permit Citizen X to Participate But the State Demands Her Exclusion 230
      Tashjian v. Republican Party of Connecticut 230
      Notes and Questions 235
  C. When Can the Government Regulate a Party's Internal Affairs? 237
      Eu v. San Francisco County Democratic Central Committee 237
      Notes and Questions 242
  D. Does the Existing Legal Regime Improperly Entrench the Existing Two–Party System? 244

1. Challenges to Ballot Access by Independent and Third-Party Candidates 245
   Munro v. Socialist Workers Party 249
   Notes and Questions 252
2. The Interaction of Ballot Access and Other Electoral Regulations in Perpetuating the Two-Party System 254
   Timmons v. Twin Cities Area New Party 254
   Notes and Questions 260

CHAPTER 5 Preclearance and the Voting Rights Act 264

A. Congressional Power to Enact the Special Provisions of the Voting Rights Act 266
   South Carolina v. Katzenbach 266
   Notes and Questions 274
B. What Is a "Covered Change"? 285
   Allen v. State Board of Elections 286
   Notes and Questions 293
   Dougherty County Board of Education v. White 295
   Presley v. Etowah County Commission 299
   Notes and Questions 304
   McDaniel v. Sanchez 309
   Notes and Questions 312
C. What Constitutes a Discriminatory Purpose or Effect? 313
   Beer v. United States 313
   Notes and Questions 316
D. The Administrative Process 324
   Morris v. Gressette 325
   Notes and Questions 329
   Miller v. Johnson 329
   Notes and Questions 333
E. Preclearance: A Case Study 336
   Major v. Treen 359
   Notes and Questions 366

CHAPTER 6 Majority Rule and Minority Vote Dilution: Constitutional and Legislative Approaches 367

A. Defining the Harm 368
   Whitcomb v. Chavis 369
   White v. Regester 380
   Notes and Questions 383
   Note on Purpose Versus Effects 387
B. The Rise of the Intent Requirement 388
   City of Mobile v. Bolden 388
   Notes and Questions 405
C. The 1982 Amendments to Section 2 of the VRA 410
   1. Section 2 as amended in 1982: 411
   2. The Legislative Process leading to Section 2 411

Thomas M. Boyd and Stephen J. Markman, The 1982 Amendments to the Voting Rights Act: A Legislative History, 40 Wash. & Lee L. Rev. 1347 (1983) 412
    3. Excerpts From the Senate Judiciary Committee Report 424
    Senate Report No. 97–417 (1982) 425
        Notes and Questions on the Substance of the 1982 Amendments 434
        Notes and Questions on the Political Process and the 1982 Amendments 437

CHAPTER 7 Racial Vote Dilution Under the Voting Rights Act 441

A. Judicial Modulation of the "Results" Standard: The Three-Part Test for Challenges to Multimember Districts 443
    Thornburg v. Gingles 443
    Notes and Questions 464
      1. *Gingles'* First Prong: "Sufficiently Large and Geographically Compact" 472
        Dillard v. Baldwin County Board of Education 476
        Notes and Questions 478
      2. *Gingles'* Second Prong: "Political Cohesion": The Special Problem of Coalition Lawsuits 481
        Nixon v. Kent County 481
        Notes and Questions 486
      3. *Gingles'* Third Prong: "White Bloc Voting" 489
        League of United Latin American Citizens (LULAC) v. Clements 489
        Notes and Questions 496
B. The Reemergence of a "Totality of the Circumstances Approach" 499
    Johnson v. De Grandy 500
    Notes and Questions 506
    Rural West Tennessee African–American Affairs Council v. McWherter 511
    Notes and Questions 517
C. Beyond Dilution Through Submergence 519
    Holder v. Hall 519
    Notes and Questions 535

CHAPTER 8 Redistricting and Representation 546

A. Partisan Gerrymandering 547
    Gaffney v. Cummings 548
    Karcher v. Daggett 550
    Notes and Questions 554
    Davis v. Bandemer 554
    Notes and Questions 560
    Badham v. Eu 561
    Notes and Questions 563

B.	Racial Gerrymandering	566
	United Jewish Organizations of Williamsburgh v. Carey	567
	Shaw v. Reno	573
	Notes and Questions	581
C.	A Redistricting Exercise	612

CHAPTER 9 Money and Politics ... 616

A.	Regulating Contributions and Expenditures	618
	Colorado Republican Federal Campaign Committee v. Federal Election Commission	620
	Notes and Questions	629
B.	Do Concerns Over Corruption Justify Campaign Finance Regulation?	632
	First National Bank of Boston v. Bellotti	633
	Notes and Questions	643
C.	Equality and Liberty in Political Campaigns	647
	Austin v. Michigan Chamber of Commerce	649
	Notes and Questions	655
D.	Has Campaign Finance Regulation Worked?	658
E.	A Caution on Public Financing	660
F.	Proposals for Reform	662

CHAPTER 10 Direct Democracy ... 665

A.	Constitutional Underpinnings and Concerns	666
	Pacific States Telephone & Telegraph Company v. Oregon	669
	Notes and Questions	670
	Note on Money and the Initiative Process	675
B.	Direct Democracy and Rights of Political Participation	677
	1. Popular Lawmaking and Unpopular Groups	677
	Hunter v. Erickson	677
	Notes and Questions	680
	Evans v. Romer	686
	Notes and Questions	688
	Note on Improving the Processes of Direct Lawmaking	693
	2. Popular Lawmaking and Problems of Entrenchment	695
	U.S. Term Limits, Inc. v. Thornton	695
	Notes and Questions	705

CHAPTER 11 Alternative Democratic Structures ... 713

A.	Types of Electoral Systems	719
B.	Cumulative Voting	722
	John Dillard v. Chilton County Board of Education and Chilton County Commission	726
	Notes and Questions	729

	Richard H. Pildes and Kristen A. Donoghue, Cumulative Voting in the United States	730
	Notes and Questions	739
	Cane v. Worcester County, Md.	741
	Notes and Questions	745
C.	Preference Voting or the Single–Transferrable Vote (STV)	748
	Notes and Questions	754
D.	Limited Voting	756
	McGhee v. Granville County Board of Commissioners	758
	Notes and Questions	762
E.	The Lot Versus the Election	765
F.	The History of Territorial Districting	769
G.	The Debate Between Majoritarian Systems and Proportional Representation	773
H.	Consociational Democracy	780
Index		785

TABLE OF CASES

Principal cases are in bold type. Non-principal cases are in roman type. References are to Pages.

Abrams v. Johnson, 591
Addy v. Newton County, 611
Adkins v. Children's Hospital of the District of Columbia, 32, 33
Alabama, United States v., 102
Allen v. State Bd. of Elections, 286, 293, 294, 442, 534
American Party of Texas v. White, 248
Anderson v. Celebrezze, 229, 248, 249
Andress v. Reed, 212
Arizona Farmworkers Union v. Agricultural Employment Relations Bd., 171
Arizonans for Fair Representation v. Symington, 488
Arlington Heights, Village of v. Metropolitan Housing Development Corp., 323
Armour v. Ohio, 474, 475, 488
Association of Citizens Councils of La., Inc., United States v., 467
Association of Community Organizations for Reform Now (ACORN) v. Edgar, 114
Auerbach v. Rettaliata, 60
Austin v. Michigan Chamber of Commerce, 649, 655, 656, 657
Avery v. Midland County, 406 S.W.2d 422, p. 157, 158
Avery v. Midland County, Tex., 88 S.Ct. 1114, p. 157

Badham v. Eu, 561, 563
Badillo v. City of Stockton, Cal., 486
Baker v. Carr, 3, 11, **122,** 133, 134, 135, 147, 148, 536, 548, 561
Baker v. Pataki, 39
Baldwin v. G.A.F. Seelig, Inc., 282
Ball v. James, 164, 169, 170, 171, 172, 177
Bates v. Jones, 706
Beer v. United States, 313, 319, 321, 322, 334, 340
Bencomo v. Phoenix Union High School Dist. No. 10, p. 740
Benner v. Oswald, 173
Berea College v. Kentucky, 73
Board of Election Commissioners v. Chicago/Gary Area Union of the Homeless, 61
Board of Estimate of City of New York v. Morris, 158, 163, 164, 177
Boerne, City of v. Flores, 264, 284, 409, 437

Bolden v. City of Mobile, Ala., 405, 406, 407, 408, 409, 410, 411, 413, 418, 419, 421, 425, 426, 427, 430, 431, 434, 440, 441, 442
Bonilla v. City Council of City of Chicago, 307
Bradwell v. Illinois, 29
Breedlove v. Suttles, 44
Brown v. Board of Com'rs of City of Chattanooga, Tenn., 61
Brown v. Board of Ed. of Topeka, Shawnee County, Kan., 281, 285
Brown v. Hartlage, 644
Brown v. Thomson, 145
Buckley v. Valeo, 618, 620, 631, 632, 644, 646, 647, 648, 656, 663
Bullock v. Carter, 204, 209
Burdick v. Takushi, 193, 202, 210, 716
Burns v. Richardson, 145
Burson v. Freeman, 189
Busbee v. Smith, 333, 557, 592
Bush v. Vera, 436, 582, 584, 593, 595, 597
Butts v. City of New York, 536, 537, 538

Cabell v. Chavez–Salido, 54
California Democratic Party v. Lungren, 244
California Med. Ass'n v. Federal Elec. Com'n, 630
Campos v. City of Baytown, Tex., 486
Cane v. Worcester County, Md., 57 F.3d 1065, p. 741
Cane v. Worcester County, Md., 874 F.Supp. 687, p. **741**
Cantwell v. Hudnut, 172
Carolene Products Co., United States v., 124, 134
Carrington v. Rash, 37, 58, 59
Carver v. Nixon, 658
Chapman v. Meier, 590
Chisom v. Roemer, 436
Cipriano v. City of Houma, 67
Citizens Against Rent Control/Coalition for Fair Housing v. Berkeley, Cal., 630, 647, 675
City of (see name of city)
Clark v. Roemer, 308
Classic, United States v., 82, 212, 546
Cleburne, City of v. Cleburne Living Center, 53

xxiii

Cleveland County Ass'n for Government by the People v. Cleveland County Bd. of Com'rs, 763
Coalition for Economic Equity v. Wilson, 110 F.3d 1431, p. 692
Coalition for Economic Equity v. Wilson, 946 F.Supp. 1480, p. 691, 692
Colegrove v. Green, 77, **117,** 121, 133, 134, 169, 536, 674, 709
Collier v. Menzel (Santa Barbara County), 61
Collins v. Brennan, 172
Collins v. Town of Goshen, 172
Colorado Republican Federal Campaign Committee v. Federal Election Com'n, 620, 629, 631, 663, 664
Concerned Citizens of Hardee County v. Hardee County Bd. of Com'rs, 486
Condon v. Reno, 115
Connor v. Johnson, 308
Cooper v. Aaron, 217
Cousins v. Wigoda, 229
Crawford v. Board of Educ. of City of Los Angeles, 682, 684, 685, 691
Creel v. Freeman, 62
Cruikshank, United States v., 17, 68
Cumming v. Richmond County Board of Ed., 73

Davis v. American Tel. & Tel. Co., 173
Davis v. Bandemer, 116, 517, 547, **554,** 560, 561, 563, 564, 565
Davis v. Beason, 94
Davis v. Schnell, 98
Day v. Holahan, 660
DeBaca v. County of San Diego, 474
Democratic Party of United States v. Wisconsin, 217, **224,** 229, 235, 236
DeWitt v. Wilson, 568, 608, 610
Dillard v. Baldwin County Bd. of Educ., 476, 478, 479
Dillard v. Chilton County Bd. of Educ., 726, 740, 741
Dillard v. Crenshaw County, 203
Dixon v. Maryland Bd. of Election Laws, 201
Doenges v. Salt Lake City, 172
Dougherty County, Georgia, Bd. of Ed. v. White, 276, **295,** 304, 305
Duke v. Massey, 218, 224
Duke, United States v., 224
Dunn v. Blumstein, 56, 58

East Lake Water Ass'n v. Rogers, 172
Edwards v. California, 282
Employment Div., Dept. of Human Resources of Oregon v. Smith, 264, 284
Eu v. San Francisco County Democratic Cent. Committee, 237, 243
Evans v. Romer, 670, **686,** 689, 691, 692
Ex parte (see name of party)

Federal Election Com'n v. Massachusetts Citizens for Life, Inc., 648
Federal Election Com'n v. National Conservative Political Action Committee, 631
Federation for American Immigration Reform v. Klutznick, 146
First Nat. Bank of Boston v. Bellotti, 633, 675
Fortson v. Dorsey, 383
Foster v. Sunnyside Valley Irr. Dist., 171
Franklin v. Massachusetts, 772
Frontier Acres Community Development Dist. Pasco County, State v., 171
Fullerton Joint Union High School Dist. v. State Bd. of Educ., 173
Fumarolo v. Chicago Bd. of Educ., 173, 177

Gaffney v. Cummings, 262, 263, 547, **548,** 561
Garza v. Los Angeles County Board of Supervisors, 145, 472, 475, 476
Gaston County, N. C. v. United States, 276
Gaunt v. Brown, 55
Georgia v. United States, 294
Giles v. Harris, 69, 71, 72, 73, 74, 75, 76, 77, 78, 80, 674
Giles v. Teasley, 72, 74
Gillard v. Estrella Dells I Imp. Dist., 172
Glisson v. Mayor and Councilmen of Town of Savannah Beach, Tybee Island, Ga., 62
Goldstein v. Mitchell, 171
Gomez v. City of Watsonville, 480
Gomillion v. Lightfoot, 65, 77, **103,** 203, 682
Gordon v. Lance, 155, 156, 691
Gray v. Sanders, 59, **182,** 184, 383
Green v. Board of Elections of City of New York, 37
Greene County Racing Com'n v. City of Birmingham, 304
Grovey v. Townsend, 82, 83, 84
Growe v. Emison, 312, 474, 481, 508
Guinn v. United States, 75, 76, 78
Guy v. Hickel, 488

Hadley v. Junior College Dist. of Metropolitan Kansas City, Mo., 158
Hadnott v. Amos, 294
Hardy v. Wallace, 306, 307
Harman v. Forssenius, 78, 114, 275
Harper v. Virginia Bd. of Elections, 42, 53, 78, 275
Hastert v. State Bd. of Elections, 474
Hathorn v. Lovorn, 294
Hays, United States v., 560, 596, 597, 598
Hayward v. Clay, 172
Hedge v. Lyng, 173
Hellebust v. Brownback, 173
Hernandez v. Texas, 487

Hirabayashi v. United States, 487
Hogencamp v. Lee County Bd. of Educ. of Lee County, 62
Holder v. Hall, 478, **519,** 535, 536, 593
Holt Civic Club v. City of Tuscaloosa, 62, 65
Humane Soc. of United States, New Jersey Branch, Inc. v. New Jersey State Fish and Game Council, 173
Humble, City of v. Metropolitan Transit Authority, 172
Hunter v. Erickson, 498, **677,** 680, 681, 682, 683, 685, 688, 689, 691
Hunter v. Underwood, 38, 39, 408

Igartua De La Rosa v. United States, 66

Jeffers v. Clinton, 538, 539, 540
Jenness v. Fortson, 246, 248
Johnson v. De Grandy, 319, 474, 488, **500,** 506, 508, 511
Johnson v. Miller, 590, 607, 608, 610
Jones v. Lubbock, 727 F.2d 364, p. 436
Jones v. Lubbock, 640 F.2d 777, p. 426

Kansas City v. Whipple, 203
Karcher v. Daggett, 148, **150,** 154, 155, **550,** 554
Katzenbach v. Morgan, 264, 277, 284, 333, 436, 487
King County Water Dist. No. 54 v. King County Boundary Review Bd., 173
Kirkpatrick v. Preisler, 144, 547
Kirksey v. City of Jackson, Mississippi, 496
Knox v. Milwaukee County Bd. of Election Com'rs, 486
Kramer v. Union Free School Dist. No. 15, 47, 53, 55, 63, 66, 67, 148, 157, 169, 546

Lampkin v. Connor, 22
Lane v. Town of Oyster Bay, 172
Lane v. Wilson, 76, 78
Lassiter v. Northampton Election Board, 40, 53, 78, 277, 280, 437
Latino Political Action Committee, Inc. v. Boston, 784 F.2d 409, p. 474
Latino Political Action Committee, Inc. v. Boston, 609 F.Supp. 739, p. 473
Lawyer v. Department of Justice, 568, 608, 610
League of United Latin American Citizens, Council No. 4434 v. Clements, 489, 496, 536, 540, 543
Lightfoot v. Eu, 212
Lochner v. People of State of New York, 32
Lockhart, City of v. United States, 317

Louisiana, State of, United States v., 78, 95, 96, 467
Louisville, N.O. & T. Ry. Co. v. Mississippi, 73
Lower Valley Water and Sanitation Dist., Petition of, 172
Lubin v. Panish, 209, 210
Lucas v. Forty-Fourth General Assembly of State of Colorado, 3, 11, 12, 13, 14, 15, 16, 149, 691, 692, 709

Mahan v. Howell, 144, 145
Major v. Treen, 336, 351, **359,** 442, 468
Marbury v. Madison, 217
Marengo County Com'n, United States v., 436
Marston v. Lewis, 58, 113
McCain v. Lybrand, 308
McDaniel v. Sanchez, 309
McElveen, United States v., 264
McGhee v. Granville County, N.C., 758
McIntyre v. Ohio Elections Com'n, 201
McLaughlin v. City of Canton, Miss., 39
McNeil v. Springfield Park Dist., 466, 473
Meek v. Metropolitan Dade County, 488
Meyer v. Grant, 655, 656, 675
Miller v. Johnson, 321, **329,** 333, 336, 496, 589, 590, 591, 592, 597, 763
Mills v. Green, 73
Minor v. Happersett, 22, 27, 28, 29, 31, 32, 54
Mississippi State Chapter, Operation Push v. Allain, 114
Mobile, Ala., City of v. Bolden, 322, **388,** 425, 434, 436, 439, 441, 465, 680, 784
Moores v. Edelbrock, 171
Moorman v. Wood, 172
Morris v. Gressette, 325, 333
Morse v. Republican Party of Virginia, 93, 94, 244, 276
Muller v. Oregon, 33
Munro v. Socialist Workers Party, 249, 253, 254, 260

N.A.A.C.P. v. Hampton County Election Com'n, 294, 305
Nader v. Schaffer, 213, 217, 230
Nevett v. Sides, 434, 441, 442
New York v. State, 172
New York Times Co. v. Sullivan, 617
Nixon v. Condon, 81, 83, 95, 224
Nixon v. Herndon, 79, 80, 81, 83, 94, 95
Nixon v. Kent County, 481, 486, 487, 488, 535

Opinion of the Justices, 173
Oregon v. Mitchell, 54, 280, 284, 333, 436
Ortiz v. City of Philadelphia Office of City Com'rs Voter Registration Div., 543, 545
Overton v. City of Austin, 473
Oyama v. California, 487

Pacific States Telephone & Telegraph Co. v. State of Oregon, 669, 671, 672, 674
Perkins v. Matthews, 294, 307, 318
Petersburg, Va., City of v. United States, 468
Petition of (see name of party)
Phillips v. Andress, 62
Phoenix v. Kolodziejski, 67
Pitts v. Black, 61
Pleasant Grove, City of v. United States, 321
Plessy v. Ferguson, 281
Porterfield v. Van Boening, 171
Potter v. Washington County, Fla., 479
Powell v. McCormack, 659, 707, 708
Presley v. Etowah County Com'n, 112 S.Ct. 820, pp. **299,** 304, 306, 307, 747
Presley v. Etowah County Com'n, 869 F.Supp. 1555, p. 304
Printz v. United States, 106, 114
Provance v. Shawnee Mission Unified School Dist. No. 512, 173

Quilter v. Voinovich, 509
Quinn v. Millsap, 173

Ray v. Blair, 218
Reese, United States v., 68
Reno v. Bossier Parish School Bd., 322, 323
Republican Party of North Carolina v. Hunt, 565
Republican Party of North Carolina v. Martin, 563, 565
Republican Party of North Carolina v. North Carolina State Bd. of Elections, 565
Republican Party of Texas v. Dietz, 94, **220**
Reynolds v. Sims, 3, 134, **135,** 144, 145, 146, 147, 148, 149, 157, 169, 285, 367, 383, 384, 547, 548, 561, 617
Richardson v. Ramirez, 33, 38, 39, 55
Richmond, City of v. J.A. Croson Co., 297, 320
Richmond, Virginia, City of v. United States, 317, 319, 321
Rockefeller v. Powers, 211
Rogers v. Lodge, 385, 386, 408, 409
Rome, City of v. United States, 277, 437
Romer v. Evans, 53, 689, 692
Romero v. City of Pomona, 473
Rosario v. Rockefeller, 211, 236
Rosenstiel v. Rodriguez, 663
Rural West Tennessee African–American Affairs Council, Inc. v. McWherter, 511, 475, 509, 510, 517, 518

Sailors v. Board of Ed. of Kent County, 157, 158
Saint Francis College v. Al–Khazraji, 487

Salyer Land Co. v. Tulare Lake Basin Water Storage Dist., 66, 67, 172, 177
Scott v. Sandford, 29, 31
Scott v. United States Dept. of Justice, 568, 609
Seattle, City of v. State, 172
Shaare Tefila Congregation v. Cobb, 487
Shaw v. Hunt, 597
Shaw v. Reno, 321, 406, 479, 496, 508, 509, **573,** 581, 582, 589, 591, 593, 596, 597, 598, 605, 608, 610, 611, 612, 763
Sheffield Board of Commissioners, United States v., 275
Shepherd v. Trevino, 37
Shrink Missouri Government PAC v. Maupin, 659
Simi Val. Recreation and Park Dist. v. Local Agency Formation Commission of Ventura County, 172
Sims v. Baggett, 285
Slaughter–House Cases, 29
Slisz v. Western Regional Off–Track Betting Corp., 173
Smith v. Allwright, 82, 93, 94, 95, 96
Smith v. Paris, 285, 467
Solomon v. Liberty County, Florida, 499
South Carolina v. Katzenbach, 266, 280, 436
Spahos v. Mayor and Councilmen of Town of Savannah Beach, Tybee Island, Ga., 62
Sparf and Hansen v. United States, 29
State v. _____ (see opposing party)
State of (see name of state)
Stelzel v. South Indian River Water Control Dist., 171
Storer v. Brown, 246, 248
Sullivan v. Farmers Home Admin., 173

Tashjian v. Republican Party of Connecticut, 217, **230,** 235, 236
Taxpayers to Limit Campaign Spending v. Fair Political Practices Com'n, 673
Terry v. Adams, 85, 92, 93, 94, 95, 216, 224
The Florida Bar re Amendments to the Rules Regulating the Florida Bar (Reapportionment), 173
Theriot v. Parish of Jefferson, 568, 612
Thornburg v. Gingles, 322, **443,** 464, 465, 466, 468, 471, 472, 473, 474, 475, 476, 478, 480, 481, 488, 489, 499, 506, 507, 510, 543, 582, 603, 605, 608
Timmons v. Twin Cities Area New Party, 252, **254,** 260, 261, 262

United Jewish Organizations of Williamsburgh, Inc. v. Carey, 473, **567**
United States v. _____ (see opposing party)

Table of Cases

United States Term Limits, Inc. v. Thornton, 670, **695,** 706, 707, 708, 709, 711, 712

Valley Forge Christian College v. Americans United for Separation of Church and State, Inc., 598
Vera v. Bush, 607, 608, 610, 611
Village of (see name of village)
Virginia Soc. for Human Life, Inc. v. Caldwell, 660
Voinovich v. Quilter, 474, 508, 513
Voting Rights Coalition v. Wilson, 114

Washington v. Davis, 321, 405, 434, 441, 442, 681
Washington v. Seattle School Dist. No. 1, 682, 683, 684, 685, 691
Wells v. Edwards, 163
Wesberry v. Sanders, 144, 146, 148, 592
Wesley v. Collins, 40

West Virginia State Board of Education v. Barnette, 15, 16, 203
Whitcomb v. Chavis, 368, **369,** 383, 384, 385, 387, 388, 405, 427, 496
White v. Regester, 322, 368, **380,** 384, 385, 386, 387, 388, 405, 413, 420, 424, 425, 426, 427, 431, 436, 465
Williams v. Rhodes, 16, 245, 246
Williams v. Salerno, 60
Williams v. Mississippi, 68
Williams v. Wallace, 266
Wilson v. Eu (Assembly of State of Cal.), 312
Wisconsin v. City of New York, 155
Wise v. Lipscomb, 309, 590
Wood v. Broom, 772
Wooley v. Maynard, 203

Yarbrough, Ex parte, 546

Zimmer v. McKeithen, 385, 386, 388, 405, 409, 420, 436, 465

*

The Law of Democracy

Legal Structure of the Political Process

*

CHAPTER 1

AN INTRODUCTION TO THE SELECTION OF DEMOCRATIC INSTITUTIONS

Before the first vote is cast or the first ballot counted, the possibilities for democratic politics are already constrained and channeled. The election process is well under way before the formal stage of voting, for elections do not take place in a legal vacuum. Rather, the election process emerges from previously fixed—and often carefully orchestrated—institutional arrangements that influence the range of possible outcomes that formal elections and subsequent policymaking can achieve. Thus a paradox rests at the core of democratic politics: this politics is in part a contest over the structure of state institutions, and yet those very institutions define the terms in which the contest of democratic politics proceeds.

The central focus of this book is this complex interaction between democratic politics and the formal institutions of the state. On one view of democracy, politics should be a domain autonomous of existing state institutions. Democratic politics provides the arena in which private preferences and collective deliberation should be free to develop without state interference or constraint; indeed, a democratic political system is largely defined by the relative liberty of citizens to criticize existing distributions of political power and institutional arrangements. This is probably the most conventional understanding of democracy: democratic deliberation *creates* public offices, officials, institutions, and policies, and these arrangements are justified to the extent they are responsive to democratic decisionmaking. In this view, democracy exists in some sense prior to and independent of the specific institutional forms in which it happens to be embodied at any particular time and place.

But this vision of democratic politics as autonomous from existing state institutions is, in our view, misconceived and perhaps even unintelligible. At the heart of a democratic political order lies a process of collective decisionmaking that must operate through pre-existing laws, rules, and institutions. The kind of democratic politics we have is always and inevitably itself a product of institutional forms and legal structures. There are many possible forms democracy can take, many different institutional embodiments of democratic politics. Should we have representative or direct democracy? If we employ electoral politics, should elections be from single-member geographical districts, through cumulative voting, or through one of the many forms of proportional representation? Who is eligible to participate in politics, and who decides that question? These institutional structures all limit and define the decisions available through democratic politics itself. In turn, these institutional arrangements are either the inherited product of prior democratic choice or of inertia—or perhaps some combination of the two. That is one central point we hope to convey: there is no "We the People" independent of the way the law constructs democracy.

That perspective leads to the second central point this book will emphasize throughout. Because democratic politics is not autonomous of existing law and institutions, those who control existing arrangements have the capacity to shape, manipulate, and distort democratic processes. Historical experience provides convincing reasons to believe that those who currently hold power will deploy that power to try to preserve their control. Thus, democratic politics constantly confronts the prospect of law being used to freeze existing political arrangements into place, a phenomenon we will refer to as a political lockup. Yet there is no way to take the law "out" of democracy. The question, then, is what the law might contribute to mediating or resolving this tension. Can institutional arrangements be developed that both reflect the inevitable role of law in shaping democracy and at the same time prevent that role from being manipulated by existing office holders for self-interested aims? That is the other side of the mutual relationship between law and democracy we stress: the need to find techniques and theories that prevent the capture of democratic politics by existing distributions of political power.

Any inquiry into institutional arrangements leads inevitably to the question of the relationship between courts, legislatures, executive officials, and voters in overseeing democratic processes. At some points, we will see legislatures play a leading role, as when we explore Congress' enactment of the Voting Rights Act of 1965 and its subsequent amendments. At other points, the courts will assume center stage, invoking the tools of constitutional law. When courts become central players, that will raise some of the most difficult questions about institutional role in all of constitutional theory. On the one hand, courts will become embroiled in partisan political struggles, not over specific enactments, but over the very political framework through which the electorate exercises its political will. This is most starkly posed when courts act to set aside the choices that emerge from pre-existing electoral arrangements. At that point, the pressure on the judiciary to articulate a coherent vision of properly functioning politics is most acute if the electoral will is to be deemed unlawful or unconstitutional. On the other hand, if the courts refuse to oversee the process, we risk leaving the power to shape the fundamental ground rules of politics in the largely unaccountable hands of existing officeholders. In many instances, we shall see that the judiciary emerges as the sole branch of government capable of destabilizing an apparently unshakable lockup of the political process.

We turn now to an opening case. Although less well-known than its contemporaries, *Baker v. Carr*, 369 U.S. 186 (1962), and *Reynolds v. Sims*, 377 U.S. 533 (1964), the *Lucas* case should be seen as one of the dramatic moments in American constitutional history. In one stroke of breathtaking sweep, the Supreme Court invalidated the fundamental structure of democracy in nearly every state. The case presents in a particularly striking form the difficult issues of both how democratic bodies should be structured and how the role of various institutions of the state in addressing that question, including courts, should be understood.

Lucas v. The Forty-Fourth General Assembly of the State of Colorado

377 U.S. 713 (1964).

■ MR. CHIEF JUSTICE WARREN delivered the opinion of the Court.

Involved in this case is an appeal from a decision of the Federal District Court for the District of Colorado upholding the validity, under the Equal Protection Clause of the Fourteenth Amendment to the Federal Constitution, of the apportionment of seats in the Colorado Legislature pursuant to the provisions of a constitutional amendment ["Amendment No. 7"] approved by the Colorado electorate in 1962.

* * *

II.

[...] The 1953 apportionment scheme ... in effect immediately prior to the adoption of Amendment No. 7, was contained in several statutory provisions which provided for a 35-member Senate and a 65-member House of Representatives. Section 63-1-2 of the Colorado Revised Statutes established certain population "ratio" figures for the apportionment of Senate and House seats among the State's 63 counties. One Senate seat was to be allocated to each senatorial district for the first 19,000 population, with one additional senator for each senatorial district for each additional 50,000 persons or fraction over 48,000. One House seat was to be given to each representative district for the first 8,000 population, with one additional representative for each House district for each additional 25,000 persons or fraction over 22,400. Sections 63-1-3 and 63-1-6 established 25 senatorial districts and 35 representative districts, respectively, and allocated the 35 Senate seats and 65 House seats among them according to the prescribed population ratios. No counties were divided in the formation of senatorial or representative districts, in compliance with the constitutional proscription. Thus, senators and representatives in those counties entitled to more than one seat in one or both bodies were elected at large by all of the county's voters. The City and County of Denver was given eight Senate seats and 17 House seats, and Pueblo County was allocated two Senate seats and four House seats. Other populous counties were also given more than one Senate and House seat each. Certain counties were entitled to separate representation in either or both of the houses, and were given one seat each. Sparsely populated counties were combined in multicounty districts.

Under the 1953 apportionment scheme, applying 1960 census figures, 29.8% of the State's total population lived in districts electing a majority of the members of the Senate, and 32.1% resided in districts electing a majority of the House members. Maximum population-variance ratios of approximately 8-to-1 existed between the most populous and least populous districts in both the Senate and the House. One senator represented a district containing 127,520 persons, while another senator had only 17,481 people in his district. The smallest representative district had a population of only 7,867, while another district was given only two House seats for a population of 127,520. . . .

Amendment No. 7 provides for the establishment of a General Assembly composed of 39 senators and 65 representatives, with the State divided geographically into 39 senatorial and 65 representative districts, so that all seats in both houses are apportioned among singlemember districts. Responsibility for creating House districts "as nearly equal in population as may be" is given to the legislature. Allocation of senators among the counties follows the existing scheme of districting and apportionment, except that one sparsely populated county is detached from populous Arapahoe County and joined with four others in forming a senatorial district, and one additional senator is apportioned to each of the counties of Adams, Arapahoe, Boulder and Jefferson. Within counties given more than one Senate seat, senatorial districts are to be established by the legislature "as nearly equal in population as may be." Amendment No. 7 also provides for a revision of representative districts, and of senatorial districts within counties given more than one Senate seat, after each federal census, in order to maintain conformity with the prescribed requirements. Pursuant to this constitutional mandate, the Colorado Legislature, in early 1963, enacted a statute establishing 65 representative districts and creating senatorial districts in counties given more than one Senate seat. Under the newly adopted House apportionment plan, districts in which about 45.1% of the State's total population reside are represented by a majority of the members of that body. The maximum population-variance ratio, between the most populous and least populous House districts, is approximately 1.7-to-1. The court below concluded that the House was apportioned as nearly on a population basis as was practicable, consistent with Amendment No. 7's requirement that "(n)o part of one county shall be added to another county or part of another county" in the formation of a legislative district, and directed its concern solely to the question of whether the deviations from a population basis in the apportionment of Senate seats were rationally justifiable.

Senatorial apportionment, under Amendment No. 7, involves little more than adding four new Senate seats and distributing them to four populous counties in the Denver area, and in substance perpetuates the existing senatorial apportionment scheme. Counties containing only 33.2% of the State's total population elect a majority of the 39-member Senate under the provisions of Amendment No. 7. Las Animas County, with a 1960 population of only 19,983, is given one Senate seat, while El Paso County, with 143,742 persons, is allotted only two Senate seats. Thus, the maximum population-variance ratio, under the revised senatorial apportionment, is about 3.6-to-1. Denver and the three adjacent suburban counties contain about one-half of the State's total 1960 population of 1,753,947, but are given only 14 out of 39 senators. The Denver, Pueblo, and Colorado Springs metropolitan areas, containing 1,191,832 persons, about 68%, or over two-thirds of Colorado's population, elect only 20 of the State's 39 senators, barely a majority. The average population of Denver's eight senatorial districts, under Amendment No. 7, is 61,736, while the five least populous districts contain less than 22,000 persons each. Divergences from population-based representation in the Senate are growing continually wider, since the underrepresented districts in the Denver, Pueblo, and Colorado Springs metropolitan areas are rapidly gaining in population, while many of the overrepresented rural districts have tended to decline in population continuously in recent years.

III.

[... T]he Colorado scheme of legislative apportionment here attacked is one adopted by a majority vote of the Colorado electorate almost contemporaneously with the District Court's decision on the merits in this litigation. Thus, the plan at issue did not result from prolonged legislative inaction.

As appellees have correctly pointed out, a majority of the voters in every county of the State voted in favor of the apportionment scheme embodied in Amendment No. 7's provisions, in preference to that contained in proposed Amendment No. 8, which, subject to minor deviations, would have based the apportionment of seats in both houses on a population basis. However, the choice presented to the Colorado electorate, in voting on these two proposed constitutional amendments, was hardly as clear-cut as the court below regarded it. One of the most undesirable features of the existing apportionment scheme was the requirement that, in counties given more than one seat in either or both of the houses of the General Assembly, all legislators must be elected at large from the county as a whole. Thus, under the existing plan, each Denver voter was required to vote for eight senators and 17 representatives. Ballots were long and cumbersome, and an intelligent choice among candidates for seats in the legislature was made quite difficult. No identifiable constituencies within the populous counties resulted, and the residents of those areas had no single member of the Senate or House elected specifically to represent them.... Amendment No. 8 ... would have perpetuated, for all practical purposes, this debatable feature of the existing scheme.... Thus, neither of the proposed plans was, in all probability, wholly acceptable to the voters in the populous counties, and the assumption of the court below that the Colorado voters made a definitive choice between two contrasting alternatives and indicated that 'minority process in the Senate is what they want' does not appear to be factually justifiable.

Finally, ... the initiative device provides a practicable political remedy to obtain relief against alleged legislative malapportionment in Colorado. An initiated measure proposing a constitutional amendment or a statutory enactment is entitled to be placed on the ballot if the signatures of 8% of those voting for the Secretary of State in the last election are obtained. No geographical distribution of petition signers is required. Initiative and referendum has been frequently utilized throughout Colorado's history....

IV.

[...] Except as an interim remedial procedure, justifying a court in staying its hand temporarily, we find no significance in the fact that a nonjudicial, political remedy may be available for the effectuation of asserted rights to equal representation in a state legislature. Courts sit to adjudicate controversies involving alleged denials of constitutional rights. While a court sitting as a court of equity might be justified in temporarily refraining from the issuance of injunctive relief in an apportionment case in order to allow for resort to an available political remedy, such as initiative and referendum, individual constitutional rights cannot be deprived, or denied judicial effectuation, because of the existence of a nonjudicial remedy through which relief against the alleged malapportionment, which the individual voters seek, might be achieved. An individual's constitutionally protected right to cast an equally weighted vote cannot be denied even by a vote of a majority of a State's electorate, if the apportionment scheme adopted by the voters fails to measure up to the requirements of the Equal Protection Clause. Manifestly, the fact that an apportionment plan is adopted in a popular referendum is insufficient to sustain its constitutionality or to induce a court of equity to refuse to act. As stated by this Court in *West Virginia State Bd. of Educ. v. Barnette,* 319 U.S. 624, 638 (1943), "One's right to life, liberty, and property ... and other fundamental rights may not be submitted to vote; they depend on the outcome of no elections." A citizen's constitutional rights can hardly be infringed simply because a majority of the people choose that it be. We hold that the fact that a challenged legislative apportionment plan was approved by the electorate is without federal constitutional significance, if the scheme adopted fails to satisfy the basic requirements of the Equal Protection Clause....

Since the apportionment of seats in the Colorado Legislature, under the provisions of Amendment No. 7, fails to comport with the requirements of the Equal Protection Clause, the decision below must be reversed....

■ Mr. Justice Clark, dissenting.

[...] I would refuse to interfere with this apportionment for several reasons. First, Colorado enjoys the initiative and referendum system which it often utilizes and which, indeed, produced the present apportionment. As a result of the action of the Legislature and the use of initiative and referendum, the State Assembly has been reapportioned eight times since 1881. This indicates the complete awareness of the people of Colorado to apportionment problems and their continuing efforts to solve them. The courts should not interfere in such a situation.... Next, as my Brother Stewart has pointed out, there are rational and most persuasive reasons for some deviations in the representation in the Colorado Assembly. The State has mountainous areas which divide it into four regions, some parts of which are almost impenetrable. There are also some depressed areas, diversified industry and varied climate, as well as enormous recreational regions and difficulties in transportation. These factors give rise to problems indigenous to Colorado, which only its people can intelligently solve. This they have done in the present apportionment.

Finally, I cannot agree to the arbitrary application of the "one man, one vote" principle for both houses of a State Legislature. In my view, if one house is fairly apportioned by population (as is admitted here) then the people should have some latitude in providing, on a rational basis, for representation in the other house. The Court seems to approve the federal arrangement of two Senators from each State on the ground that it was a compromise reached by the framers of our Constitution and is a part of the fabric of our national charter. But what the Court overlooks is that Colorado, by an overwhelming vote, has likewise written the organization of its legislative body into its Constitution,* and our dual federalism requires that we give it recognition. After all, the Equal Protection Clause is not an algebraic formula. Equal protection does not rest on whether the practice assailed "results in some inequality" but rather on whether "any state of facts reasonably can be conceived that would sustain it".... Certainly Colorado's arrangement is not arbitrary. On the contrary, it rests on reasonable grounds which, as I have pointed out, are peculiar to that State. It is argued that the Colorado apportionment would lead only to a legislative stalemate between the two houses, but the experience of the Congress completely refutes this argument. Now in its 176th year, the federal plan has worked well. It is further said that in any event Colorado's apportionment would substitute compromise for the legislative process. But

---

* The Court says that the choice presented to the electorate was hardly "clear-cut." The short answer to this is that if the voters had desired other choices, they could have accomplished this easily by filing initiative petitions, since in Colorado 8% of the voters can force an election.

most legislation is the product of compromise between the various forces acting for and against its enactment.

In striking down Colorado's plan of apportionment, the Court, I believe, is exceeding its powers under the Equal Protection Clause; it is invading the valid functioning of the procedures of the States, and thereby is committing a grievous error which will do irreparable damage to our federal-state relationship. I dissent.

■ MR. JUSTICE STEWART, whom MR. JUSTICE CLARK joins, dissenting.

It is important to make clear at the outset what these cases are not about. They have nothing to do with the denial or impairment of any person's right to vote. Nobody's right to vote has been denied. Nobody's right to vote has been restricted. Nobody has been deprived of the right to have his vote counted....

The question involved in these cases is quite a different one. Simply stated, the question is to what degree, if at all, the Equal Protection Clause of the Fourteenth Amendment limits each sovereign State's freedom to establish appropriate electoral constituencies from which representatives to the State's bicameral legislative assembly are to be chosen. The Court's answer is a blunt one, and, I think, woefully wrong. The Equal Protection Clause, says the Court, "requires that the seats in both houses of a bicameral state legislature must be apportioned on a population basis."

After searching carefully through the Court's opinions in these and their companion cases, I have been able to find but two reasons offered in support of this rule. First, says the Court, it is "established that the fundamental principle of representative government in this country is one of equal representation for equal numbers of people...." With all respect, I think that this is not correct, simply as a matter of fact. It has been unanswerably demonstrated before now that this "was not the colonial system, it was not the system chosen for the national government by the Constitution, it was not the system exclusively or even predominantly practiced by the States at the time of adoption of the Fourteenth Amendment, it is not predominantly practiced by the States today." Secondly, says the Court, unless legislative districts are equal in population, voters in the more populous districts will suffer a "debasement" amounting to a constitutional injury. As the Court explains it, "To the extent that a citizen's right to vote is debased, he is that much less a citizen." We are not told how or why the vote of a person in a more populated legislative district is "debased," or how or why he is less a citizen, nor is the proposition self-evident. I find it impossible to understand how or why a voter in California, for instance, either feels or is less a citizen than a voter in Nevada, simply because, despite their population disparities, each of these States is represented by two United States Senators.

To put the matter plainly, there is nothing in all the history of this Court's decisions which supports this constitutional rule. The Court's draconian pronouncement, which makes unconstitutional the legislatures of most of the 50 States, finds no support in the words of the Constitution, in any prior decision of this Court, or in the 175-year political history of our Federal Union.... The rule announced today ... stifles values of local individuality and initiative vital to the character of the Federal Union which it was the genius of our Constitution to create.

I.

What the Court has done is to convert a particular political philosophy into a constitutional rule, binding upon each of the 50 States, from Maine to Hawaii, from Alaska to Texas, without regard and without respect for the many individualized and differentiated characteristics of each State, characteristics stemming from each State's distinct history, distinct geography, distinct distribution of population, and distinct political heritage. My own understanding of the various theories of representative government is that no one theory has ever commanded unanimous assent among political scientists, historians, or others who have considered the problem. But even if it were thought that the rule announced today by the Court is, as a matter of political theory, the most desirable general rule which can be devised as a basis for the make-up of the representative assembly of a typical State, I could not join in the fabrication of a constitutional mandate which imports and forever freezes one theory of political thought into our Constitution, and forever denies to every State any opportunity for enlightened and progressive innovation in the design of its democratic institutions, so as to accommodate within a system of representative government the interests and aspirations of diverse groups of people, without subjecting any group or class to absolute domination by a geographically concentrated or highly organized majority.

Representative government is a process of accommodating group interests through democratic institutional arrangements. Its function is to channel the numerous opinions, interests, and abilities of the people of a State into the making of the State's public policy. Appropriate legislative apportionment, therefore, should ideally be designed to insure effective representation in the State's legislature, in cooperation with other organs of political power, of the various groups and interests making up the electorate. In practice, of course, this ideal is approximated in the particular apportionment system of any State by a realistic accommodation of the diverse and often conflicting political forces operating within the State.

I do not pretend to any specialized knowledge of the myriad of individual characteristics of the several States, beyond the records in the cases before us today. But I do know enough to be aware that a system of legislative apportionment which might be best for South Dakota, might be unwise for Hawaii with its many islands, or Michigan with its Northern Peninsula. I do know enough to realize that Montana with its vast distances is not Rhode Island with its heavy concentrations of people. I do know enough to be aware of the great variations among the several States in their historic manner of distributing legislative power—of the Governors' Councils in New England, of the broad powers of initiative and referendum retained in some States by the people, of the legislative power which some States give to their Governors, by the right of veto or otherwise of the widely autonomous home rule which many States give to their cities. The Court today declines to give any recognition to these considerations and countless others, tangible and intangible, in holding unconstitutional the particular systems of legislative apportionment which these States have chosen. Instead, the Court says that the requirements of the Equal Protection Clause can be met in any State only by the uncritical, simplistic, and heavy-handed application of sixth-grade arithmetic.

But legislators do not represent faceless numbers. They represent people, or, more accurately, a majority of the voters in their districts— people with identifiable needs and interests which require legislative representation, and which can often be related to the geographical areas in which these people live. The very fact of geographic districting, the constitutional validity of which the Court does not question, carries with it an acceptance of the idea of legislative representation of regional needs and interests. Yet if geographical residence is irrelevant, as the Court suggests, and the goal is solely that of equally 'weighted' votes, I do not understand why the Court's constitutional rule does not require the abolition of districts and the holding of all elections at large.

The fact is, of course, that population factors must often to some degree be subordinated in devising a legislative apportionment plan which is to achieve the important goal of ensuring a fair, effective, and balanced representation of the regional, social, and economic interests within a State. And the further fact is that throughout our history the apportionments of State Legislatures have reflected the strongly felt American tradition that the public interest is composed of many diverse interests, and that in the long run it can better be expressed by a medley of component voices than by the majority's monolithic command. What constitutes a rational plan reasonably designed to achieve this objective will vary from State to State, since each State is unique, in terms of topography, geography, demography, history, heterogeneity and concentration of population, variety of social and economic interests, and in the operation and interrelation of its political institutions. But so long as a State's apportionment plan reasonably achieves, in the light of the State's own characteristics, effective and balanced representation of all substantial interests, without sacrificing the principle of effective majority rule, that plan cannot be considered irrational.

II.

This brings me to what I consider to be the proper constitutional standards to be applied in these cases.... I think that the Equal Protection

Clause demands but two basic attributes of any plan of state legislative apportionment. First, it demands that, in the light of the State's own characteristics and needs, the plan must be a rational one. Secondly, it demands that the plan must be such as not to permit the systematic frustration of the will of a majority of the electorate of the State. I think it is apparent that any plan of legislative apportionment which could be shown to reflect no policy, but simply arbitrary and capricious action or inaction, and that any plan which could be shown systematically to prevent ultimate effective majority rule, would be invalid under accepted Equal Protection Clause standards. But, beyond this, I think there is nothing in the Federal Constitution to prevent a State from choosing any electoral legislative structure it thinks best suited to the interests, temper, and customs of its people.

NOTES AND QUESTIONS

1. In conjunction with related cases decided the same day, *Lucas* helped invalidate the basic institutional structure of representative government in nearly all 50 states—a structure that had governed in those states more or less since their admission. *Lucas* is the culmination of a line of cases that begins with *Baker v. Carr*, 369 U.S. 186 (1962); the full development of that line is presented in Chapter 3. *Lucas* itself, though, directly raises central philosophical, political, and institutional questions concerning the appropriate conception of American representative government. These questions are raised here by way of introduction to the themes that run throughout this book.

2. Procedurally, which institutional arrangements should be used for resolving these substantive questions? What considerations should determine whether the authority to resolve these substantive questions ought to lie with the current legislators of Colorado, or the voters of Colorado, or some administrative body, or, as *Lucas* concludes, with the judicial system? Several striking features stand out regarding the institutional and procedural context in which the plan challenged in *Lucas* was adopted: (a) the plan had been recently adopted; (b) it had been adopted by the voters, rather than the legislature; (c) it had been approved by a majority of voters in every county in the State, not just by a statewide majority. A recurrent theme throughout this book will be the proper relationship between courts and other actors—legislatures, administrative bodies, independent commissions, and voters—in the design of democratic institutions. Given these particular features of the process in Colorado, does the Court make a persuasive case as to why "the fact that a challenged legislative apportionment plan was approved by the electorate is without federal constitutional significance?" Note that in many political struggles over democratic institutional design, the process will be controlled by political insiders. When politicians who have been elected under one set of rules are asked to change the existing rules, there might be good reason to distrust their incentives. We will also see that for long periods of American history, legislators refused to redistrict legislatures even when they were legally obligated to do so; inertia was politically advantageous to those elected under the pre-existing rules. In both these situations, arguments for judicial intervention might be thought particularly powerful. By contrast, does the fact of recent popular enactment militate against judicial intervention?

3. The first three words in the United States Constitution, "We the People," purport to claim as a source of authority an already established background fact: an entity known as "the People" that has expressed its will in advance of the design of political institutions, including the institution of the Constitution itself. In this rhetorical structure, "the People" is a recognizable entity that can act as the creator of the Constitution. But as *Lucas* intimates, many possible versions of "We the People" exist. Perhaps the most important task of any constitution is picking among these versions and giving effect, through specific institutions, to one version rather than another of "the People." Can "We the People" pre-exist the Constitution, as opposed to being created by it? Indeed, are not "the People" the most important legal creation of any constitution? Consider the following view:

> [Some theorists imagine that "democracy" involves] a collective will already in existence, lying in wait for democratic institutions to discover. Before institutions are formed, however, no such collective will exists. Political institutions and decision procedures must create the conditions out of which, for the first time, a political community can forge for itself a collective will. Those institutions and procedures specify whose views will be counted in determining the collective will and define the means by which the collective will can be recognized. No uniquely "rational" institutional architecture exists for constructing that will. Each bundle of institutions and practices represents a distinct social constitution of the collective will.

Richard H. Pildes and Elizabeth S. Anderson, *Slinging Arrows at Democracy: Social Choice Theory, Value Pluralism, and Democratic Politics*, 90 Colum. L. Rev. 2121, 2197–98 (1990). Is there some unique version of "We the People" that democracy itself or the Constitution should be understood to require? If not, what values and considerations should be looked to in determining which version of "We the People" to incorporate into the design of democratic political institutions?

4. *Lucas* is not the place where the Court justifies constitutional adoption of the one-vote, one-person rule; the decision addresses whether this rule must be adhered to regardless of contemporaneous majoritarian preferences for other forms of representation. But consider the reasons that might be marshalled on behalf of the one-person, one-vote rule, particularly in light of Justice Stewart's powerful dissent. Does the Court's result rest on an individualist philosophy of representation, namely, that legislators must be conceived as representing individuals? Justice Stewart argues that "[r]epresentative government is a process of accommodating group interests through democratic institutional arrangements." Why isn't this "group interest" vision of representation more accurate, or at least, an acceptable option for states to choose? Colorado's system recognizes distinct, minority political interests that the state (the majority of initiative voters) fears might get discounted in a strict majoritarian system. As Justice Stewart describes it, the purpose is to avoid subjecting "any group or class to absolute domination by a geographically concentrated or highly organized majority." In this case, the protected minority is rural voters. But, as we shall see, every act of institutional design carries a purpose. What is wrong with designing political institutions with these aims? Suppose Colorado had decided to design its Senate to protect other kinds of minority interests, such as economic ones? Or, what if Colorado's objective had been to protect "discrete and insular" minority groups, such as racial or ethnic ones? Or consider still a broader justification, based on parallels to the United States Senate. If the existence of a distinctly elected upper branch of the legislature can be justified at the national level, why is that same type of justification not available here? Does the Court's decision hold, in effect, that strict majority rule is constitutionally required?

5. Justice Stewart argues that the Court's decision in *Lucas* is inconsistent with "the very fact of geographic districting, the constitutional validity of which the Court does not question." Many American representative institutions, such as the United States House, use single-member geographic districts to elect legislators. This electoral structure first was mandated for congressional elections in 1842; that requirement lapsed in 1927, but was re-enacted by Congress in 1967 and remains in effect today. For the full history of territorial districting for Congress, see Chapter 11. Even during periods when no federal statute required single-member congressional districts, many states followed this practice. In what way is *Lucas* purportedly inconsistent with this long-established practice? Stewart argues that, like the Colorado Senate plan, the very *raison d'être* of districting itself "carries with it an acceptance of the idea of legislative representation of regional needs and interests." Consider the possible purposes for basing elections to representative institutions on geographic districts. Are the purposes that motivate or justify the use of districted elections ultimately the same as those behind Colorado's Senate plan? If so, is Justice Stewart right that the rationale for invalidating that plan applies with as much force to the long-established practice of geographically based election districts? If Justice Stewart is persuasive, which way should the tension be resolved: by concluding that *Lucas* is wrong, or by concluding that geographic-based districting is equally unconstitutional? If districting were abandoned, what would replace it? Consider the alternatives presented in Chapter 11.

6. What constitutional standard would the dissents have applied to evaluate the structure of democratic institutions? Justice Stewart would impose only two requirements: First, the plan must be a "rational one" in light of a particular State's characteristics and needs—it must reflect some intelligible policy. Second, the plan must not "systematically" prevent effective majority rule. Let us accept that legal rules need not be crystalline clear to perform the task asked of them; they need only be clear enough for the particular context. With that functional view of "clear" in mind, would the dissent's standards enable courts to apply these requirements appropriately? Do these two standards provide the right kind of guidance to those with the power in the first instance to design political institutions—typically, political actors, responsive to partisan pressures, who redistrict states every ten years? Is it relatively clear what kinds of redistricting plans the dissenters would rule out?

7. What latitude does the Constitution give to states seeking to protect minority rights? Does the Court actually object to the purposes the dissent offers to justify Colorado's Senate plan? Or is *Lucas* better understood as objecting to the means used to pursue these purposes? Perhaps the problem is not Colorado's aim of diffusing majoritarian power to enhance the political influence of minority interests, but rather pursuing that aim through the design of election districts. Why might the means chosen be particularly troubling? Consider possible alternative approaches to protecting minority voting power. One such approach might focus on voting rules. Colorado could require supermajority support to enact legislation, or to enact specific types of legislation that have particularly significant effects on certain minority interests. Or Colorado could give certain regions or interests in the state a legislative veto over some designated areas of legislation: for example, no legislation affecting water rights may be enacted without approval of representatives from the rural counties. Would these rules be equally effective at protecting the minority interests Colorado purports to care about? If so, would they be unconstitutional under *Lucas*? If not, what differs about building special concern for minority representation into voting rules rather than the underlying architecture of political institutions?

Perhaps voting rules embed these special protections in a more visible, and hence more publicly accountable, form. Unlike obscure features of institutional design, these kind of voting rules announce their presence each and every time policy is being made. Some political theorists have argued that the basic principles on which political power is organized must satisfy the condition of publicity: they must be capable of being publicly articulated and accepted. *See* John Rawls, A Theory of Justice 133, 177–183 (1971). Can a case be made that minority preferences in voting rules satisfy this requirement better than disproportional numbers of voters allocated to districts? That the voting rule preference is more likely to be continually revisited than the latter? Consider other means that might be available for Colorado to protect minority interests. Rather than manipulating numbers of voters per district, the state might manipulate the location of districts. For example, if the state wanted to assure some special voice for farmers in its legislature, it could place equal numbers of voters in districts, but draw certain districts so that they were dominated by farmers. Would this be unconstitutional under *Lucas*? How would it fare under the publicity standard?

8. What exactly is the underlying substantive injury in *Lucas*? The substantive concern might be that the Senate plan overrepresents the interests of smaller counties relative to their population; thus, it is voters in more urban areas who are disadvantaged by the apportionment plan. In some circumstances, that might raise troubling concerns. Here, however, the majority in each county voted to cede a bit of its power to voters in smaller counties. Is there any reason to distrust political processes in which majorities vote to give greater voice to the interests of political minorities? Notice the general attitude of skepticism the Court conveys about the initiative process, and the Court's willingness to discount the meaningfulness of the voters' approval of Amendment 7. Contrast this attitude with that in more recent cases we will examine concerning voter initiatives in Chapter 10.

9. The Court's response to the procedural questions raised in *Lucas* ultimately appears to lie in its quotation of the magisterial flag salute case. In *West Virginia State Bd. of Educ. v. Barnette,* 319 U.S. 624, 638 (1943), the Court says: "One's right to life, liberty, and property . . . and other fundamental rights may not be submitted to vote; they depend on the outcome of no elections." Individual constitutional rights cannot be denied simply because political majorities desire to do so. Such a principle makes sense in contexts like *Barnette*; when personal constitutional liberties, such as the right to the integrity of one's own conscience, are at stake, the very nature of the constitutional right precludes political majorities from invading that right. These types of individual rights might well be understood as meriting protections from the temporary preferences of political majorities. *See* Ronald Dworkin, Taking Rights Seriously 184–205 (1977) (developing conception of legal rights as trumps over routine policy considerations). But is the aspect of "the right to vote" recognized in *Lucas* a personal or individual right in the same sense as the right to freedom of conscience? As Justice Stewart observes, no one in Colorado is denied the right to vote or to have that vote counted. And of course, no one has a right to have his or her preferred candidate elected. Instead, isn't the concern that the voters as a group in certain areas of the state have less overall political influence in the Senate than the same number of voters have as a group in other areas of the state? The question in *Lucas* is the relative distribution of political power within the state; but distributional questions require comparisons of the political power of different voting groups. As the Supreme Court subsequently noted, the right at issue in the reapportionment cases is not so much a question of casting a ballot as "the right of qualified voters regardless of their political persuasion, to cast their votes effectively...." *Williams v. Rhodes,* 393 U.S. 23, 30 (1968). Consider the following argument, that the recognition of a right of effective participation takes the law of elections decidedly away from a conception of individual rights:

> [T]he right to cast an effective ballot implie[s] more than simply the equal weighting of all votes, as per the one-person, one-vote rule. To be effective, a voter's ballot must stand a meaningful chance of effective aggregation with those of like-minded voters to claim a just share of electoral results. For this reason, any sophisticated right to genuinely meaningful electoral participation must be evaluated and measured as a group right, that of groups of voters seeking the outcomes promised to them through the electoral system.

Samuel Issacharoff, *Groups and the Right to Vote,* 44 Emory L.J. 869, 883–84 (1995). Many aspects of voting rights are best understood in terms unfamiliar in other areas of constitutional law. For example, as we shall develop in later chapters, one of the inevitable effects and aims of apportionment is to treat voters as members of groups. That will raise questions about which dimensions of "group" identity should be considered relevant for this purpose, and which institutions should be empowered to decide that issue. Can economic interest provide a proper basis for attributions of group identity in the design of political institutions? Can racial or ethnic identity? Finally, legal regulation of the electoral process must recognize the unique blend of state action and constitutionally protected private conduct that voting implicates. *See* Pamela S. Karlan & Daryl J. Levinson, *Why Voting is Different,* 84 Cal. L. Rev. 1201 (1996). Accordingly, rather than being viewed through the prism of traditional personal or individual rights, voting rights are frequently better understood as group-based rights. They focus on whether one group's political power is being inappropriately diluted or enhanced at the expense of other groups. If the "right to vote" in cases like *Lucas* is best understood as a group right, is the Court's reliance on *Barnette* justified? Or should the Court have been more willing to accept the contemporaneous decision of the majority in Colorado to grant its political minorities more influence than they otherwise would have had?

These themes constitute the fundamental building blocks of the law of democracy, and we will return to them throughout.

CHAPTER 2

THE RIGHT TO PARTICIPATE

Constitutions are often viewed today as constraints on majoritarian power in the service of minority interests. But constitutional ground rules also create the possibility of ongoing democratic self-government; constitutions establish relatively stable and non-negotiable precommitments that enable generally accepted structures of political competition to emerge and endure.

Despite the centrality of this role for the American Constitution, however, there is paradoxically little that the text or its history offers in the way of directly relevant guidance. In part, this results from the great silences of the Constitution regarding the structure of electoral politics—a silence that often reflects America's peculiar federal structure, in which so much regarding the ground rules of political competition was left to be settled at the state level. Thus, as the first cases in this Chapter will reveal, neither the original Constitution nor the Fourteenth Amendment secured even the basic right to vote.

In its original form, the Constitution contained scant mention of voting. The only organ of the national government that was elected directly was the House of Representatives, and Article I, section 2, clause 1 provided simply that "The House of Representatives shall be composed of Members chosen every second Year by the People of the several States, and the Electors in each State shall have the Qualifications requisite for Electors of the most numerous Branch of the State Legislature." Thus, the entitlement to vote in the only popular federal election was entirely dependent on a state's grant of the franchise, and all states limited the right to vote to only a subset of the population. The most widespread limitations involved age, sex, race, property ownership, and length of residence within the jurisdiction, but there were others as well. Nonetheless, the franchise was extended more widely among white males than in any other country at the time. *See* Chilton Williamson, American Suffrage: From Property to Democracy, 1760–1860, at 21–39 (1960) (American electorate in late 18th century included 50 to 75 percent of adult white males, as compared to 20 to 25 percent in England). In a series of nineteenth century cases, the Supreme Court reiterated that "the Constitution of the United States has not conferred the right of suffrage upon any one," *United States v. Cruikshank*, 92 U.S. 542, 555 (1875). And yet, since the Civil War, a majority of the ratified constitutional amendments have dealt in whole or in part with voting and they have marked a consistent expansion of the franchise. Not only has voting come to occupy a more prominent place in the written Constitution; it has also come to be treated by the Supreme Court as a central, and fundamental, right of citizenship.

As with the right to vote, the Constitution is also silent about much else regarding the structure of democratic politics. The text does speak in quite general terms about the terms of federal elected officials and even more generally about qualifications for election. But in addition to voting rights, the Constitution also does not explicitly address most other important issues regarding elections—from how ballots are to be cast, to the electoral system for all public offices save the president and Senate, to issues of how elections are to be run and financed, and so forth.

The failure of the Constitution to offer much specific guidance also reflects the premodern world of democratic practice and the long-since rejected assumptions of that world on which the Constitution rests. Most importantly for present purposes, the Constitutional structure was specifically intended to preclude the rise of political parties, which were considered the quintessential form of "faction."[1] Yet as we will examine in Chapter 4, political parties have long become the principal organizational form through which mass democracy can be mobilized and effectively pursued. No constitutional framework for enabling modern democratic self-government can neglect the role of political parties, yet the Constitution not only is silent about parties, it was designed to preclude their emergence. Similarly, the original Constitution reflected a particularly elite conception of democratic politics, one in which, as the leading historian of the period puts it, "Madison hoped that the new federal government might restore some aspect of monarchy that had been lost in the Revolution."[2]

---

1. As the classic study of shifting concepts of political representation in the 18th century puts it, "when [Madison] discussed the problem of interests in the tenth number of *The Federalist,* he was occupied immediately with the problem of so dividing the government as to resist the formation of political parties. No doubt influenced by his great Irish fellow-Whig, Burke, Madison anticipated the division of the country into conflicting and competing economic interests, and maintained that the chief cause of conflict would be between those with and those without property. The political organization of these interests he called factions, a disparaging name for parties—but he hoped that parties would merely come and go as their temporary objects dictated. By an irony which he cannot have either anticipated or enjoyed, Madison himself soon became one of the leading agents in the process by which interests were consolidated into parties...."

J.R. Pole, Political Representation in England & the Origins of the American Republic 530-31 (1966).

2. Gordon S. Wood, The Radicalism of the American Revolution 255 (1992). As Wood elaborates: "With the 'purest and noblest characters' of the society in power, Madison expected the new national government to play the same suprapolitical neutral role that the British king had been supposed to play in the empire." Id. Bernard Manin argues that the debate between Federalists and Anti-Federalists was, as the Anti-Federalists argued, essentially a debate over how aristocratic political leadership should be, or whether it should mirror the electorate. Bernard Manin, The Principles of Representative Government 121 (1997) ("The Federalists, however, all agreed that representatives should not be like their constituents. Whether the difference was expressed in terms of wisdom, virtue, talents, or sheer wealth and

But this more aristocratic conception of democracy was already being displaced by the 1790s, and was utterly supplanted as early as the Jacksonian era—developments that led virtually all the Framers who lived that long to a pervasive but underappreciated pessimism because democracy had fallen "into the hands of the young and ignorant and needy part of the community."[3] This transformation in the conception of democracy eventually culminates in certain structural changes, such as the Seventeenth Amendment's shift to direct senatorial elections, and the various franchise-expanding amendments. But these changes are layered onto a document and set of institutional structures that reflected the pre-modern vision of democratic politics.[4] For example, while voting for public officeholders was the quintessential attribute of representative government, the act of voting quickly changed its social meaning and significance from what the Framers originally envisioned. Initially, the open ballot played the role of ratifying social and political hierarchies; as another important historian notes, "leaders still assumed political office as their right and instructed the

property, they all expected and wished the elected to stand higher than those who elected them.").

3. The characterization of pervasive pessimism is from Wood, *supra*, at 365; the complaint about commoner control of democracy is Benjamin Rush's, a signer of the Declaration of Independence, id., at 366. Wood quotes a similar view of George Washington's from 1799, who bemoaned that the rising spirit of party politics had displaced character as the touchstone for electability: members of one party or another could "set up a broomstick" as a candidate, call it "a true son of Liberty," or a "Democrat" or "any other epithet that will suit their purpose," and the broomstick would still "command their votes in toto!" Id., at 366. Similarly, J.R. Pole reports that in Virginia by the 1820s, "[t]he open electioneering of the candidates would certainly have struck anyone bred in the habits of the eighteenth century as a debasement of the dignity of the legislature and a corruption of the freedom and purity of elections." J.R. Pole, Political Representation in England & the Origins of the American Republic 165 (1966).

4. In what Gordon Wood characterizes as "maybe the crucial moment" in "the history of American politics," Wood, *supra*, at 256, Wood reproduces the attack on the first Bank of the United States launched by William Findley in 1786. Findley, an ex-weaver from Western Pennsylvania and defender of paper-money interests and debtor-relief laws, was the kind of common and backcountry legislator whom "gentry like Madison," id., at 256, considered too narrowly self-interested to be worthy legislators. Findley argued not only that the elite political leaders were just as interested as anyone else in political outcomes, but that there was nothing wrong or suspect about the promotion of private interests through politics—indeed, that the promotion of private interests was exactly what democratic politics was about. As Wood sees it, Findley's attack on the Bank in 1786 anticipated "all of the modern democratic political developments of the *succeeding generation:* the increased electioneering and competitive politics, the open promotion of private interests in legislation, the emergence of parties, the extension of the actual and direct representation of particular groups in government, and the eventual weakening, if not the repudiation, of the classical republican ideal that legislators were supposed to be disinterested umpires above the play of private interests." Id., at 258 (emphasis added). The point is that all these developments that characterize modern conceptions of democratic politics and that emerge in the culture and politics of the early 19th century are at odds in the most fundamental respects with the conception of democracy that underlay the original Constitution and Bill of Rights.

people as their duty."[5] Elections focused on personal qualities, not political issues; a striking example was that in the elections to the Virginia ratifying Convention for the Constitution, many districts would elect their two leading men—even though they held opposing opinions on whether the Constitution should be embraced.[6] Already by the early 19th century, though, the open ballot had come to symbolize a kind of political equality and independent choice of citizens, with genuine sovereign power, that had not been originally contemplated in the election-as-ratification conception.[7]

With respect to democratic politics, then, the American Constitution is a curious amalgam of textual silences, archaic assumptions that subsequent developments quickly undermined, and a small number of narrowly targeted more recent amendments that reflect more modern conceptions of politics. Particularly in this arena of democratic institutional design, the American Constitution reveals its age. More modern constitutions invariably devote considerable space to the institutional framework for politics and tend to reflect the structures now associated with democracy, such as political parties.

---

5. Robert H. Wiebe, Self-Rule: A Cultural History of American Democracy 29 (1995). For a similar view of the historical distinction between voting as the genuine collective choice between competing candidates in competitive contests, and voting as "a ritual of acclamation, a public act that recognizes (and reconstitutes) the superior status of the candidate," Don Herzog, Happy Slaves 197 (1989), see Mark Kishlansky, Parliamentary Selection: Social and Political Choice in Early Modern England (1986). For a similar view of the role of deference in English elections in the eighteenth century, see Bernard Manin, The Principles of Representative Government 96 (1997) ("[Before the English civil war] returning a Member was a way of honoring the 'natural leader' of the local community. Elections were seldom contested. It was seen as an affront to the man or to the family of the man who customarily held the seat for another person to compete for that honor. Electoral contests were then feared, and avoided as much as possible.... This distinctive feature of British political culture later came to be termed 'deference.' The term was coined by Walter Bagehot in the late nineteenth-century, but the phenomenon to which it referred had long been typical of English social and political life.").

6. Pole, *supra*, at 151. Referring to the colonial period, but in a pattern Pole argues continued after the Revolution, Pole concludes that "[i]ssues seldom entered elections, and even when they did it was often agreed that the natural leaders were the best men to entrust with the decisions." Id.

7. Wiebe, *supra*, at 29–30. Carrying on with the significance of the view of democratic politics and political representation he sees reflected in William Findley's speech from 1786, supra, Wood argues that within one generation following the Constitution's formation, the original views on these practices had changed dramatically: "In the generation following the formation of the Constitution, the Anti-Federalist conception of actual or interest representation in government—the William Findley conception of representation—came to dominate the realities, if not the rhetoric, of American political life. ...Elected officials were to bring the partial, local interests of the society, and sometimes even their own interests, right into the workings of government. Partisanship and parties became legitimate activities in politics. And all adult white males, regardless of their property holdings or their independence, were to have the right to vote. By 1825, every state but Rhode Island, Virginia, and Louisiana had achieved universal white manhood suffrage." Wood, *supra*, at 294.

In light of this history, American courts facing contemporary questions of democratic principles today often have to construct a conception of democracy with less textual and historical foundation than in some other areas of constitutional law. Yet the pressure on courts to do so is great, given the self-interest existing powerholders have in manipulating the ground rules of democracy in furtherance of their own partisan, ideological, and personal interests. Throughout, we will see the problems facing the Supreme Court as it struggles to work out a democratic theory of the Constitution to deal with numerous specific issues. To what extent should the Constitution's pre-modern assumptions preclude the Court from taking on this task itself? To what extent do those assumptions instead require that the Court assume this role?

This Chapter looks at the development of the right to formal political participation in the election process. Who is entitled to cast a ballot, in which elections? What restrictions can states impose on the franchise? How and why does the Court generate answers to these questions in light of the Constitution's silence with respect to the right to vote?

A. Constitutional Text and Structure

Most of the constitutional provisions dealing with the right to vote are phrased in the negative: they prohibit states from using specified grounds to deny the right to vote. The Fifteenth and Nineteenth Amendments, for example, provide that "the right of citizens of the United States to vote shall not be denied or abridged ... on account of" race and sex, respectively, and the Twenty-Sixth Amendment contains parallel language regarding the right of citizens "who are eighteen years of age or older." Similarly, the Twenty-Fourth Amendment provides that the right to vote cannot be denied "by reason of failure to pay any poll tax or other tax," but it too simply identifies one forbidden basis for restricting the vote, potentially leaving all sorts of bases for disenfranchisement undisturbed. None of these amendments contains an affirmative grant of voting rights. Even the Seventeenth Amendment, which provides for the popular election of senators, directs only that states permit participation by voters who are qualified to vote for the most numerous branch of the state legislature, without explicitly regulating in any way who falls into that class.

With the exception of the Fifteenth Amendment, there has been little litigation over the amendments that explicitly regulate voting. The major source of constitutional voting rights litigation has been the Fourteenth Amendment. The amendment's specific voting rights provision—section 2, which provides that representation in Congress is to be apportioned among the states by population, but that a state shall lose a proportionate share of its seats if "the right to vote at any election [for federal or state office] is denied to any of the male inhabitants of the States, being twenty-one years of age, and citizens of the United States, or in any way abridged except for participation in rebellion, or other crime"—has been essentially a dead letter. *See Lampkin v. Connor*, 360 F.2d 505 (D.C.Cir.1966). Instead, litigation has focused largely on section 1 of the Fourteenth Amendment, which prohibits states from abridging the privileges or immunities of citizens of the United States and from denying due process or equal protection to any person within their jurisdiction.

Minor v. Happersett
88 U.S. 162 (1875).

■ THE CHIEF JUSTICE [WAITE] delivered the opinion of the court.

The question is presented in this case, whether, since the adoption of the fourteenth amendment, a woman, who is a citizen of the United States and of the State of Missouri, is a voter in that State, notwithstanding the provision of the constitution and laws of the State, which confine the right of suffrage to men alone....

It is contended that the provisions of the constitution and laws of the State of Missouri which confine the right of suffrage and registration therefor to men, are in violation of the Constitution of the United States, and therefore void. The argument is, that as a woman, born or naturalized in the United States and subject to the jurisdiction thereof, is a citizen of the United States and of the State in which she resides, she has the right of suffrage as one of the privileges and immunities of her citizenship, which the State cannot by its laws or constitution abridge.

There is no doubt that women may be citizens. They are persons, and by the fourteenth amendment "all persons born or naturalized in the United States and subject to the jurisdiction thereof" are expressly declared to be "citizens of the United States and of the State wherein they reside." But, in our opinion, it did not need this amendment to give them that position. Before its adoption the Constitution of the United States did not in terms prescribe who should be citizens of the United States or of the several States, yet there were necessarily such citizens without such provision. There cannot be a nation without a people. The very idea of a political community, such as a nation is, implies an association of persons for the promotion of their general welfare. Each one of the persons associated becomes a member of the nation formed by the association. He owes it allegiance and is entitled to its protection. Allegiance and protection are, in this connection, reciprocal obligations. The one is a compensation for the other; allegiance for protection and protection for allegiance.

* * *

The Constitution does not, in words, say who shall be natural-born citizens. Resort must be had elsewhere to ascertain that. At common-law, with the nomenclature of which the framers of the Constitution were familiar, it was never doubted that all children born in a country of parents who were its citizens became themselves, upon their birth, citizens also. These were natives, or natural-born citizens, as distinguished from aliens or foreigners.... The words "all children" are certainly as comprehensive, when used in this connection, as "all persons," and if females are included in the last they must be in the first. That they are included in the last is not denied. In fact the whole argument of the plaintiffs proceeds upon that idea.

* * *

But if more is necessary to show that women have always been considered as citizens the same as men, abundant proof is to be found in the legislative and judicial history of the country. Thus, by the Constitution, the judicial power of the United States is made to extend to controversies between citizens of different States. Under this it has been uniformly held that the citizenship necessary to give the courts of the United States jurisdiction of a cause must be affirmatively shown on the record. Its existence as a fact may be put in issue and tried. If found not to exist the case must be dismissed. Notwithstanding this the records of the courts are full of cases in which the jurisdiction depends upon the citizenship of women, and not one can be found, we think, in which objection was made on that account.

* * *

Other proof of like character might be found, but certainly more cannot be necessary to establish the fact that sex has never been made one of the elements of citizenship in the United States. In this respect men have never had an advantage over women. The same laws precisely apply to both. The fourteenth amendment did not affect the citizenship of women any more than it did of men. In this particular, therefore, the rights of Mrs. Minor do not depend upon the amendment. She has always been a citizen from her birth, and entitled to all the privileges and immunities of citizenship....

If the right of suffrage is one of the necessary privileges of a citizen of the United States, then the constitution and laws of Missouri confining it to men are in violation of the Constitution of the United States, as amended, and consequently void. The direct question is, therefore, presented whether all citizens are necessarily voters.

The Constitution does not define the privileges and immunities of citizens. For that definition we must look elsewhere. In this case we need not determine what they are, but only whether suffrage is necessarily one of them.

It certainly is nowhere made so in express terms. The United States has no voters in the States of its own creation. The elective officers of the United States are all elected directly or indirectly by State voters. The members of the House of Representatives are to be chosen by the people of the States, and the electors in each State must have the qualifications requisite for electors of the most numerous branch of the State legislature. Senators are to be chosen by the legislatures of the States, and necessarily the members of the legislature required to make the choice are elected by the voters of the State. Each State must appoint in such manner, as the legislature thereof may direct, the electors to elect the President and Vice-President....

The amendment did not add to the privileges and immunities of a citizen. It simply furnished an additional guaranty for the protection of such as he already had. No new voters were necessarily made by it. Indirectly it may have had that effect, because it may have increased the number of citizens entitled to suffrage under the constitution and laws of the States, but it operates for this purpose, if at all, through the States and the State laws, and not directly upon the citizen.

It is clear, therefore, we think, that the Constitution has not added the right of suffrage to the privileges and immunities of citizenship as they existed at the time it was adopted. This makes it proper to inquire whether suffrage was coextensive with the citizenship of the States at the time of its adoption. If it was, then it may with force be argued that suffrage was one of the rights which belonged to citizenship, and in the enjoyment of which every citizen must be protected. But if it was not, the contrary may with propriety be assumed.

When the Federal Constitution was adopted, all the States, with the exception of Rhode Island and Connecticut, had constitutions of their own. These two continued to act under their charters from the Crown. Upon an examination of those constitutions we find that in no State were all citizens permitted to vote. Each State determined for itself who should have that power. Thus, [for example,] in New Hampshire, "every male inhabitant of each town and parish with town privileges, and places unincorporated in the State, of twenty one years of age and upwards, excepting paupers and persons excused from paying taxes at their own request," were its voters; ... in New York "every male inhabitant of full age who shall have personally resided within one of the counties of the State for six months immediately preceding the day of election ... if during the time aforesaid he shall have been a freeholder, possessing a freehold of the value of twenty pounds within the county, or have rented a tenement therein of the yearly value of forty shillings, and been rated and actually paid taxes to the State;" in New Jersey "all inhabitants ... of full age who are worth fifty pounds, proclamation-money, clear estate in the same, and have resided in the county in which they claim a vote for twelve months immediately preceding the election;" ... [and] in South Carolina "every free white man of the age of twenty-one years, being a citizen of the State and having resided therein two years previous to the day of election, and who hath a freehold of fifty acres of land, or a town lot of which he hath been legally seized and possessed at least six months before such election, or (not having such freehold or town lot), hath been a resident within the election district in which he offers to give his vote six months before said election, and hath paid a tax the preceding year of three shillings sterling towards the support of the government"....

In this condition of the law in respect to suffrage in the several States it cannot for a moment be doubted that if it had been intended to make all citizens of the United States voters, the framers of the Constitution would not have left it to implication. So important a change in the condition of citizenship as it actually existed, if intended, would have been expressly declared.

But if further proof is necessary to show that no such change was intended, it can easily be found both in and out of the Constitution.... [B]y the very terms of the amendment we have been considering (the fourteenth),

> "Representatives shall be apportioned among the several States according to their respective numbers, counting the whole number of persons in each State, excluding Indians not taxed. But when the right to vote at any election for the choice of electors for President and Vice-President of the United States, representatives in Congress, the executive and judicial officers of a State, or the members of the legislature thereof, is denied to any of the male inhabitants of such State, being twenty-one years of age and citizens of the United States, or in any way abridged, except for participation in the rebellion, or other crimes, the basis of representation therein shall be reduced in the proportion which the number of such male citizens shall bear to the whole number of male citizens twenty-one years of age in such State."

Why this, if it was not in the power of the legislature to deny the right of suffrage to some male inhabitants? And if suffrage was necessarily one of the absolute rights of citizenship, why confine the operation of the limitation to male inhabitants? Women and children are, as we have seen, "persons." They are counted in the enumeration upon which the apportionment is to be made, but if they were necessarily voters because of their citizenship unless clearly excluded, why inflict the penalty for the exclusion of males alone? Clearly, no such form of words would have been selected to express the idea here indicated if suffrage was the absolute right of all citizens.

And still again, after the adoption of the fourteenth amendment, it was deemed necessary to adopt a fifteenth.... The fourteenth amendment had already provided that no State should make or enforce any law which should abridge the privileges or immunities of citizens of the United States. If suffrage was one of these privileges or immunities, why amend the Constitution to prevent its being denied on account of race, & c.? Nothing is more evident than that the greater must include the less, and if all were already protected why go through with the form of amending the Constitution to protect a part?

It is true that the United States guarantees to every State a republican form of government.... The guaranty necessarily implies a duty on the part of the States themselves to provide such a government. All the States had governments when the Constitution was adopted. In all the people participated to some extent, through their representatives elected in the manner specially provided. These governments the Constitution did not change. They were accepted precisely as they were, and it is, therefore, to be presumed that they were such as it was the duty of the States to provide. Thus we have unmistakable evidence of what was republican in form, within the meaning of that term as employed in the Constitution.

As has been seen, all the citizens of the States were not invested with the right of suffrage. In all, save perhaps New Jersey, this right was only bestowed upon men and not upon all of them. Under these circumstances it is certainly now too late to contend that a government is not republican, within the meaning of this guaranty in the Constitution, because women are not made voters.

* * *

But we have already sufficiently considered the proof found upon the inside of the Constitution. That upon the outside is equally effective.

The Constitution was submitted to the States for adoption in 1787, and was ratified by nine States in 1788, and finally by the thirteen original States in 1790. Vermont was the first new State admitted to the Union, and it came in under a constitution which conferred the right of suffrage only upon men of the full age of twenty-one years, having resided in the State for the space of one whole year next before the election, and who were of quiet and peaceable behavior. This was in 1791. The next year, 1792, Kentucky followed with a constitution confining the right of suffrage to free male citizens of the age of twenty-one years who had resided in the State two years or in the county in which they offered to vote one year next before the election. Then followed Tennessee, in 1796, with voters of freemen of the age of twenty-one years and upwards, possessing a freehold in the county wherein they may vote, and being inhabitants of the State or freemen being inhabitants of any one county in the State six months immediately preceding the day of election. But we need not particularize further. No new State has ever been admitted to the Union which has conferred the right of suffrage upon women, and this has never been considered a valid objection to her admission. On the contrary, as is claimed in the argument, the right of suffrage was withdrawn from women as early as 1807 in the State of New Jersey, without any attempt to obtain the interference of the United States to prevent it. Since then the governments of the insurgent States have been reorganized under a requirement that before their representatives could be admitted to seats in Congress they must have adopted new constitutions, republican in form. In no one of these constitutions was suffrage conferred upon women, and yet the States have all been restored to their original position as States in the Union.

Besides this, citizenship has not in all cases been made a condition precedent to the enjoyment of the right of suffrage. Thus, in Missouri, persons of foreign birth, who have declared their intention to become citizens of the United States, may under certain circumstances vote. The same provision is to be found in the constitutions of Alabama, Arkansas, Florida, Georgia, Indiana, Kansas, Minnesota, and Texas.

Certainly, if the courts can consider any question settled, this is one. For nearly ninety years the people have acted upon the idea that the Constitution, when it conferred citizenship, did not necessarily confer the right of suffrage. If uniform practice long continued can settle the construction of so important an instrument as the Constitution of the United States confessedly is, most certainly it has been done here. Our province is to decide what the law is, not to declare what it should be.

We have given this case the careful consideration its importance demands. If the law is wrong, it ought to be changed; but the power for that is not with us. The arguments addressed to us bearing upon such a view of the subject may perhaps be sufficient to induce those having the power, to make the alteration, but they ought not to be permitted to influence our judgment in determining the present rights of the parties now litigating before us. No argument as to woman's need of suffrage can be considered. We can only act upon her rights as they exist. It is not for us to look at the hardship of withholding. Our duty is at an end if we find it is within the power of a State to withhold.

Being unanimously of the opinion that the Constitution of the United States does not confer the right of suffrage upon any one, and that the constitutions and laws of the several States which commit that important trust to men alone are not necessarily void, we affirm the judgment.

NOTES AND QUESTIONS

1. The insertion of the word "male" into Section 2 of the Fourteenth Amendment was the first textual reference to gender in the Constitution. On one view, this insertion might be seen as a substantial setback for women's rights; the provision would almost certainly be used to argue, as the Court invoked it in *Minor*, that the Fourteenth Amendment did not intend to extend the suffrage to women. On the other hand, perhaps the very fact that the Framers of the Fourteenth Amendment perceived the need to make gender distinctions *express* is, paradoxically, itself a sign of the growing political power of the movement for women's rights. Before the Amendment, rights granted in universal terms could nonetheless sometimes be understood to extend to men but not women. (Thus, Blackstone noted that women could not serve on juries despite the requirement that juries be composed of "liber et legalis homo;" Blackstone acknowledged that the word "homo" was common to both sexes, but concluded nonetheless "the female is however excluded, propter defectum sexus"—on account of defect of sex. 3 William Blackstone, Commentaries *362.). By 1866, this background assumption was being called into question through political movements pressing for equal rights for women. The increasing success of that effort might be evidenced in the Framers' perceived need to make gender distinctions explicit for the first time to ensure that the franchise remained conditioned on gender. *See* Nina Morais, Note, *Sex Discrimination and the Fourteenth Amendment: Lost History*, 97 Yale L.J. 1153 (1988) (arguing that the absence of similar gender qualification in the first section of the Fourteenth Amendment is evidence that the Framers might have intended the equal protection clause to apply to gender discrimination with respect to rights other than "political rights," such as voting).

2. The first stage leading to *Minor* was mobilized resistance among women suffragists to Section 2's inclusion of "male." As Elizabeth Cady Stanton put it, "If that word 'male' be inserted [into the Constitution], it will take us a century at least to get it out." She and Susan B. Anthony sparked a nationwide debate in newspapers and the floor of Congress. More than 10,000 supporters of women's rights wrote in protest to their Congressmen. Petitions protesting this aspect of Section 2 were presented on the floor of Congress on at least five occasions. Nonetheless, Congress adopted Section 2 with the word "male." According to Stanton, a friend with access to the congressional deliberations reported that when one committee member proposed substituting "persons" for "males," another replied "That will never do, it would enfranchise wenches." Note, *supra*, at 1159.

3. The second stage was the effort to have Congress use its new powers under Section 5 of the Fourteenth Amendment to eliminate gender distinctions in state franchise laws. In 1870, supportive members in the House and Senate presented a memorial to Congress from the suffragist Victoria Woodhull, who testified on behalf of such legislation. The House and Senate Judiciary Committees issued reports, over dissenting views, concluding that denying women the vote did not violate the Fourteenth Amendment. To some, Woodhull's credibility was undermined because she was a well-known advocate of "free love." Part of the congressional response was to tell women suffragists that if they were right that the Fourteenth Amendment did grant the franchise, then they were already entitled to vote and could go to the courts to prove it.

4. Having lost these congressional battles, the suffrage movement then did turn to the courts. The plaintiff in *Minor*, Virginia L. Minor, had grown up in Charlottesville, Virginia, where she married a graduate of the University of Virginia School of Law. The couple moved to St. Louis in 1845; after being active in relief work during the Civil War, Mrs. Minor (a follower of Susan B. Anthony) had organized the Woman Suffrage Association of Missouri in 1867. Minor's husband, Francis, urged resort to the courts as a means of gaining credibility and supportive publicity for the Women's Suffrage Association. *See* The Oxford Companion to the Supreme Court of the United States 329 (ed. Kermit Hall 1992). Her petition, brought in the Circuit Court of St. Louis County, Missouri, had to be signed by her husband under Missouri law to be valid.

In 1872, the same year that Minor sought to register, Susan B. Anthony had actually voted in the New York congressional elections. She was indicted for violating the federal Enforcement Act of 1870, designed to protect blacks against electoral corruption in the Reconstruction South, on the grounds that she did "knowingly ... vote without having a lawful right to vote." New York limited the suffrage to males. In a jury trial, the presiding federal judge ordered that a directed verdict of guilty be entered against her; a fine of $100 was imposed. The Supreme Court some years later held that "a judge may not direct a verdict of guilty no matter how conclusive the evidence." *Sparf and Hansen v. United States*, 156 U.S. 51, 105 (1895).

Minor's suit was not only rejected unanimously by the Court, but it was considered frivolous even in "progressive" circles. Consider the following editorial excerpt from The Nation, Oct. 14, 1875: "Considering the crowded condition of the Supreme Court docket, and the vast number of really important cases which are delayed by such suits as this," the editorial asked whether in "giving up precious time to the consideration of such arguments" the Court was not vulnerable to being charged with "delay of justice." In light of the context, is the most exceptional feature of Chief Justice Waite's opinion that it treats the claim with such respect and detailed analysis?

5. *Minor v. Happersett* completes the process begun in the *Slaughter-House Cases*, 83 U.S. 36 (1873), of essentially reading the privileges and immunities clause out of the Fourteenth Amendment. (Two years before *Minor*, the Court had decided its first case addressing issues of gender distinctions, *Bradwell v. Illinois*, 83 U.S. 130 (1872), in which the Court had found no violation of the privileges and immunities clause in Illinois' refusal to admit an otherwise qualified woman to the practice of law.) All subsequent Fourteenth Amendment cases depended on either the equal protection or due process clauses. As you read the later cases, consider whether the Court hasn't *sub silentio* revived a kind of privileges of citizenship analysis.

6. Note the different sorts of arguments in Chief Justice Waite's opinion. How does he use the explicit text of the Constitution? What sorts of "originalist" arguments does he make?

7. At the time of *Minor* and before, the relationship between citizenship and the franchise was more complicated than today. Consider, for example, the different perspectives taken in the notorious *Dred Scott v. Sandford*, 60 U.S. 393 (1856). As you may remember, the precise holding of the case was that African Americans could not bring suit in federal court because, enslaved or free, they could never become citizens.

Justice Curtis raised the argument that black enfranchisement in several states at the time of the ratification of the Constitution proved their citizenship:

> At the time of the ratification of the Articles of Confederation, all free native-born inhabitants of the States of New Hampshire, Massachusetts, New York, New Jersey, and North Carolina, though descended from African slaves, were not only citizens of those States, but such of them as had the other necessary qualifications possessed the franchise of electors, on equal terms with other citizens.

* * *

> Th[e] Constitution was ordained and established by the people of the United States, through the action, in each State, of those persons who were qualified by its laws to act thereon, in behalf of themselves and all other citizens of that State. In some of the States, as we have seen, colored persons were among those qualified by law to act on this subject. These colored persons were not only included in the body of "the people of the United States," by whom the Constitution was ordained and established, but in at least five of the States they had the power to act, and doubtless did act, by their suffrages, upon the question of its adoption. It would be strange, if we were to find in that instrument anything which deprived of their citizenship any part of the people of the United States who were among those by whom it was established.

To Justice Curtis, the fact that most of those states later restricted black enfranchisement—New York's 1820 Constitution required black voters to meet additional prerequisites not required of whites and New Jersey disenfranchised them entirely—was irrelevant since any changes "can have no other effect upon the present inquiry, except to show, that before they were made, no such restrictions existed; and colored in common with white persons, were not only citizens of those States, but entitled to the elective franchise on the same qualifications as white persons, as they now are in New Hampshire and Massachusetts."

By contrast, Chief Justice Taney downplayed entirely the relevance of the franchise:

> But it is said that a person may be a citizen, and entitled to that character, although he does not possess all the rights which may belong to other citizens; as, for example, the right to vote, or to hold particular offices; and that yet, when he goes into another State, he is entitled to be recognized there as a citizen, although the State may measure his rights by the rights which it allows to

persons of a like character or class resident in the State, and refuse to him the full rights of citizenship.

* * *

Undoubtedly, a person may be a citizen, that is, a member of the community who form the sovereignty, although he exercises no share of the political power, and is incapacitated from holding particular offices. Women and minors, who form a part of the political family, cannot vote; and when a property qualification is required to vote or hold a particular office, those who have not the necessary qualification cannot vote or hold the office, yet they are citizens.

So, too, a person may be entitled to vote by the law of the State, who is not a citizen even of the State itself. And in some of the States of the Union foreigners not naturalized are allowed to vote. And the State may give the right to free negroes and mulattoes, but that does not make them citizens of the State, and still less of the United States.

8. Both *Minor* and *Scott v. Sandford* mention restrictions on the franchise based on property. One of the seeming historical oddities in the movement toward broader suffrage rules was the exclusion of "paupers"—those receiving poor relief—from the vote. Many states amended their constitutions to add this exclusion during the nineteenth century; by the end of that century, 14 states excluded paupers. As of 1934, these states still excluded paupers from the vote. While these restrictions might be thought to be associated with more general property-holding qualifications on the franchise, the historical pattern is just the opposite: most states adopted "pauper" exclusions around the time those states were moving toward elimination of property qualifications. In some states, property qualifications were being replaced with taxpayer qualifications, but even in states that adopted universal white "manhood" suffrage, pauper exclusions were adopted.

An intriguing exploration of this phenomenon, which sheds much light on the relationship between conceptions of political community and the right to vote, can be found in Robert J. Steinfeld, *Property and Suffrage in the Early American Republic*, 41 Stan. L. Rev. 335 (1989). Steinfeld argues that pauper exclusions were integral to a new way of conceiving membership in a republican political community that emerged in the nineteenth century. As the franchise was extended and property qualifications replaced, American political thought still asserted that the "selves" with the requisite capacity for self-government had to have sufficient "independence;" those dependent on others would too easily be manipulated or corrupted in the exercise of the franchise. While before this time, that conception had been understood to require property holding to ensure independence, during this period wage earners succeeded in pressing their claim to the franchise. But the antithesis of such persons were those who had no legal right to dispose of their own labor. This included women, children, and paupers. As Steinfeld puts it, "[i]ncreasingly, political rights were being linked ... to self-ownership rather than to property ownership." Id. at 367. Paupers, whom towns were obligated to support with poor relief, were also legally obligated to work for the towns. Thus, the same reasons that justified expansion of the franchise to those without land, such as wage earners, were also used to justify denying the franchise to paupers. Note how a political theory of voting and "self-government" informed judgments on to whom the franchise should be extended.

9. Minor was overturned by the Nineteenth Amendment. The movement for women's equality is typically traced to the 1848 Woman's Rights Convention in Seneca Falls, New York, which issued the Declaration of Sentiments similar to the Declaration of Independence. The first item of proof of men's "tyranny" over women was: "He has never permitted her to exercise her inalienable right to the elective franchise." 1 History of Woman Suffrage 70 (Elizabeth Cady Stanton et al. eds., 1985) (reprinting Declaration of Sentiments). Women were first enfranchised in the Western territories, starting with Wyoming in 1869, Utah in 1870, Washington in 1883, and Colorado in 1893. The success of the suffrage movement in the West is sometimes attributed to the shared rigors of frontier life making men more willing to perceive women as legal equals. See Eleanor Flexner, Century of Struggle: The Woman's Rights Movement in the United States 159–66 (rev. ed. 1975). After victories in several states, the movement succeeded in having the Nineteenth Amendment ratified on August 26, 1920. The Amendment proclaims: "The right of citizens of the United States to vote shall not be denied or abridged by the United States or by any State on account of sex."

The Nineteenth Amendment has generated virtually no litigation. A potentially interesting interpretive contest has now largely been lost to history. Like many political movements that culminate in specific legal change, there is a question as to how broadly or narrowly to interpret the specific legal manifestation of this larger political movement. Should the Nineteenth Amendment be seen as only a discrete legal change addressing the one specific issue of voting? Or as reflecting a broader principle of political equality—or even more general equality—for women? Might the courts have invoked this Amendment as a basis for reading the Fourteenth Amendment to require equal protection along gender lines much earlier than the 1970's, when the Court first began to strike down gender distinctions?

In one striking example, the Supreme Court signalled such a willingness. Three years after the Nineteenth Amendment, in the Lochner-era case of Adkins v. Children's Hospital, 261 U.S. 525 (1923), the Court struck down a Washington, D.C. minimum wage law that applied only to women. Before Adkins, the Court had refused to extend Lochner's liberty of contract principle to labor laws that singled women out for "special protection;" thus in *Muller v. Oregon*, 208 U.S. 412 (1908), the Court had upheld maximum hours laws only for women on the theory that the role of women as childbearers justified such legislation. *Adkins* struck down women-specific labor laws on the basis of a broad reading of the equality the Nineteenth Amendment established:

> "[T]he ancient inequality of the sexes, otherwise than physical, as suggested in the *Muller* Case, has continued with 'diminishing intensity.' In view of the great—not to say revolutionary—changes which have taken place since that utterance, in the contractual, political and civil status of women, culminating in the Nineteenth Amendment, it is not unreasonable to say that these differences have now come almost, if not quite, to the vanishing point."

Adkins, 261 U.S. at 553. As one commentator has put it, "Whatever its merits as a labor law decision, the *Adkins* case presented a view of women's history that credited the suffrage amendment as a virtual declaration of women's equality—at least in most spheres." Jennifer K. Brown, Note, *The Nineteenth Amendment and Women's Equality*, 102 Yale L. J. 2175, 2192 (1993). By the time of the famous "switch in time" decision upholding the New Deal reforms, however, the Court returned to the earlier view that special legislation for women was constitutionally proper. *See* West Coast Hotel Co. v. Parrish, 300 U.S. 379 (1937).

The Court, however, never further developed *Adkins*' suggestion that the Nineteenth Amendment stood for a broader equality principle than the specific legal change it incorporated. The only other cases in which the Amendment came into play were a series of state court decisions involving jury service. The question here was whether state jury-service provisions that limited jury service to "men" or to "electors" (written at a time when only men were understood to be electors) should be understood to be modified by the Nineteenth Amendment. Was jury service a form of political participation analogous to voting so that the same constitutional concepts of equality should be read into both, notwithstanding specific state laws to the contrary? The state courts divided on the significance of the Nineteenth Amendment for this question. *See* Note, *supra*, at 2182–91 (contrasting cases taking an "incremental" view of the Amendment versus those taking an "emancipatory" view). How much of the Nineteenth Amendment's limited constitutional role, therefore, is best attributed to its original intent? How much to subsequent judicial interpretations?

Richardson v. Ramirez
418 U.S. 24 (1974).

■ MR. JUSTICE REHNQUIST delivered the opinion of the Court.

The three individual respondents in this case were convicted of felonies and have completed the service of their respective sentences and paroles.

They filed a petition for a writ of mandate in the Supreme Court of California to compel California county election officials to register them as voters. They claimed, on behalf of themselves and others similarly situated, that application to them of the provisions of the California Constitution and implementing statutes which disenfranchised persons convicted of an "infamous crime" denied them the right to equal protection of the laws under the Federal Constitution.

Article XX, § 11, of the California Constitution has provided since its adoption in 1879 that "[l]aws shall be made" to exclude from voting persons convicted of bribery, perjury, forgery, malfeasance in office, "or other high crimes." At the time respondents were refused registration, former Art. II, § 1, of the California Constitution provided in part that "no alien ineligible to citizenship, no idiot, no insane person, no person convicted of any infamous crime, no person hereafter convicted of the embezzlement or misappropriation of public money, and no person who shall not be able to read the Constitution in the English language and write his or her name, shall ever exercise the privileges of an elector in this State."

* * *

II

Unlike most claims under the Equal Protection Clause, for the decision of which we have only the language of the Clause itself as it is embodied in the Fourteenth Amendment, respondents' claim implicates not merely the language of the Equal Protection Clause of § 1 of the Fourteenth Amendment, but also the provisions of the less familiar § 2 of the Amendment:

> "Representatives shall be apportioned among the several States according to their respective numbers, counting the whole number of persons in each State, excluding Indians not taxed. But when the right to vote at any election for the choice of electors for President and Vice President of the United States, Representatives in Congress, the Executive and Judicial officers of a State, or the members of the Legislature thereof, is denied to any of the male inhabitants of such State, being twenty-one years of age, and citizens of the United States, or in any way abridged, except for participation in rebellion, or other crime, the basis of representation therein shall be reduced in the proportion which the number of such male citizens shall bear to the whole number of male citizens twenty-one years of age in such State."

Petitioner contends that the ... language of § 2 expressly exempts from the sanction of that section disenfranchisement grounded on prior conviction of a felony. She goes on to argue that those who framed and adopted the Fourteenth Amendment could not have intended to prohibit outright in § 1 of that Amendment that which was expressly exempted from the lesser sanction of reduced representation imposed by § 2 of the

Amendment. This argument seems to us a persuasive one unless it can be shown that the language of § 2, "except for participation in rebellion, or other crime," was intended to have a different meaning than would appear from its face.

The problem of interpreting the "intention" of a constitutional provision is, as countless cases of this Court recognize, a difficult one. . . . The legislative history bearing on the meaning of the relevant language of § 2 is scant indeed; the framers of the Amendment were primarily concerned with the effect of reduced representation upon the States, rather than with the two forms of disenfranchisement which were exempted from that consequence by the language with which we are concerned here. Nonetheless, what legislative history there is indicates that this language was intended by Congress to mean what it says.

* * *

Further light is shed on the understanding of those who framed and ratified the Fourteenth Amendment, and thus on the meaning of § 2, by the fact that at the time of the adoption of the Amendment, 29 States had provisions in their constitutions which prohibited, or authorized the legislature to prohibit, exercise of the franchise by persons convicted of felonies or infamous crimes.

More impressive than the mere existence of the state constitutional provisions disenfranchising felons at the time of the adoption of the Fourteenth Amendment is the congressional treatment of States readmitted to the Union following the Civil War. For every State thus readmitted, affirmative congressional action in the form of an enabling act was taken, and as a part of the readmission process the State seeking readmission was required to submit for the approval of the Congress its proposed state constitution. . . . [In readmitting the former Confederate states, the enabling legislation provided that each state was]

> entitled and admitted to representation in Congress as one of the States of the Union upon the following fundamental condition: That [its] constitution . . . shall never be so amended or changed as to deprive any citizen or class of citizens of the United States of the right to vote who are entitled to vote by the constitution herein recognized, except as a punishment for such crimes as are now felonies at common law, whereof they shall have been duly convicted, under laws equally applicable to all the inhabitants of said State. . . .

The phrase "under laws equally applicable to all the inhabitants of said State" was introduced . . . by Senator Drake of Missouri. Senator Drake's explanation of his reason for introducing his amendment is illuminating. He expressed concern that without that restriction, [the readmitted states] might misuse the exception for felons to disenfranchise Negroes.

* * *

This convincing evidence of the historical understanding of the Fourteenth Amendment is confirmed by the decisions of this Court which have discussed the constitutionality of provisions disenfranchising felons. Although the Court has never given plenary consideration to the precise question of whether a State may constitutionally exclude some or all convicted felons from the franchise, we have indicated approval of such exclusions on a number of occasions. In two cases decided toward the end of the last century, the Court approved exclusions of bigamists and polygamists from the franchise under territorial laws of Utah and Idaho. *Murphy v. Ramsey*, 114 U.S. 15 (1885); *Davis v. Beason*, 133 U.S. 333 (1890).

* * *

[T]he exclusion of felons from the vote has an affirmative sanction in § 2 of the Fourteenth Amendment, a sanction which was not present in the case of the other restrictions on the franchise which were invalidated in the cases on which respondents rely. We hold that the understanding of those who adopted the Fourteenth Amendment, as reflected in the express language of § 2 and in the historical and judicial interpretation of the Amendment's applicability to state laws disenfranchising felons, is of controlling significance in distinguishing such laws from those other state limitations on the franchise which have been held invalid under the Equal Protection Clause by this Court.

* * *

Pressed upon us by the respondents, and by amici curiae, are contentions that these notions are outmoded, and that the more modern view is that it is essential to the process of rehabilitating the ex-felon that he be returned to his role in society as a fully participating citizen when he has completed the serving of his term. We would by no means discount these arguments if addressed to the legislative forum which may properly weigh and balance them against those advanced in support of California's present constitutional provisions. But it is not for us to choose one set of values over the other. If respondents are correct, and the view which they advocate is indeed the more enlightened and sensible one, presumably the people of the State of California will ultimately come around to that view. And if they do not do so, their failure is some evidence, at least, of the fact that there are two sides to the argument.

* * *

NOTES AND QUESTIONS

1. How persuasive is Justice Rehnquist's textual exegesis? Does the fact that section 2 exempts felon disenfranchisement from reducing a state's congressional seats necessarily mean that felon disenfranchisement cannot violate section 1 of the Amendment? *See* David Shapiro, *Mr. Justice Rehnquist: A Preliminary View*, 90 Harv. L. Rev. 293, 303 (1976) ("[T]here is not a word in the fourteenth amendment suggesting that the exemptions in section two's formula are in any way a barrier to the judicial application of section one in voting rights cases, whether or not they involve the rights of ex-convicts."). Is this simply an argument that a specific constitutional provision trumps a general one or something more?

2. What are the arguments in favor of disenfranchising felons? Are they instrumental or expressive? Are these arguments unique to the disenfranchisement of felons or do they have similar force with regard to other groups? Are there countervailing arguments? *See generally* Note, *The Disenfranchisement of Ex–Felons: Citizenship, Criminality, and "the Purity of the Ballot Box"*, 102 Harv. L. Rev. 1300 (1989). The note's author argues that ultimately the disenfranchisement of felons rests on two philosophical approaches: "Their predominant themes, contract and competence, correspond to the distinct conceptions of citizenship, community, and personal identity associated with the two main currents in American political thought—liberalism and civic republicanism.... The first is that ex-felons should be disenfranchised because they have broken the social contract; the second is that they should be excluded because only the virtuous are morally competent to participate in governing society."

In this light, consider Judge Henry Friendly's analysis in *Green v. Board of Elections*, 380 F.2d 445, 451–52 (2d Cir.1967), *cert. denied*, 389 U.S. 1048 (1968):

> [I]t can scarcely be deemed unreasonable for a state to decide that perpetrators of serious crimes shall not take part in electing the legislators who make the laws, the executives who enforce these, the prosecutors who must try them for further violations, or the judges who are to consider their cases. This is especially so when account is taken of the heavy incidence of recidivism and the prevalence of organized crime.... A contention that the equal protection clause requires New York to allow convicted mafiosi to vote for district attorneys or judges would not only be without merit but as obviously so as anything can be.

How relevant ought it to be that Green's offense was not racketeering but conspiracy to organize the Communist party for the purpose of teaching and advocating the overthrow of the United States government? Compare Judge Friendly's analysis with *Carrington v. Rash*, 380 U.S. 89, 94 (1965), discussed *infra*, which held that " 'fencing out' from the franchise a sector of the population because of the way they may vote is constitutionally impermissible."

How does *Green*'s approach differ from that taken in *Shepherd v. Trevino*, 575 F.2d 1110, 1115 (5th Cir.1978), *cert. denied*, 439 U.S. 1129 (1979), which concluded that the state may exclude ex-offenders because they, "like insane persons, have raised questions about their ability to vote responsibly"?

3. A decade after *Ramirez*, the Supreme Court decided *Hunter v. Underwood*, 471 U.S. 222 (1985). There, Justice Rehnquist delivered a unanimous opinion for the Court striking down section 182 of the Alabama Constitution, which disenfranchised individuals convicted of "any crime ... involving moral turpitude." Under administrative interpretations of the provision, some nonfelony offenses such as presenting a worthless check and petty larceny were covered while more serious misdemeanors such as second-degree manslaughter, assault on a police officer, and mailing pornography were not.

The basis for the Court's ruling was the finding that the crimes selected for inclusion in § 182 were believed by delegates to the 1901 Constitutional Convention that enacted § 182 to be more frequently committed by blacks than whites—and present-day evidence suggesting that blacks were at least 1.7 times as likely as whites to suffer disenfranchisement for the commission of nonprison offenses.

> Although understandably no "eyewitnesses" to the 1901 proceedings testified, testimony and opinions of historians were offered and received without objection. These showed that the Alabama Constitutional Convention of 1901 was part of a movement that swept the post-Reconstruction South to disenfranchise blacks. The delegates to the all-white convention were not secretive about their purpose. John B. Knox, president of the convention, stated in his opening address:
>
>> "And what is it that we want to do? Why it is within the limits imposed by the Federal Constitution, to establish white supremacy in this State."
>
> * * *
>
> In their brief to this Court, appellants maintain on the basis of their expert's testimony that the real purpose behind § 182 was to disenfranchise poor whites as well as blacks. The Southern Democrats, in their view, sought in this way to stem the resurgence of Populism which threatened their power.... Even were we to accept this explanation as correct, it hardly saves § 182 from invalidity. The explanation concedes both that discrimination against blacks, as well as against poor whites, was a motivating factor for the provision and that § 182 certainly would not have been adopted by the convention or ratified by the electorate in the absence of the racially discriminatory motivation.
>
> Appellants contend that the State has a legitimate interest in denying the franchise to those convicted of crimes involving moral turpitude, and that § 182 should be sustained on that ground. The Court of Appeals convincingly demonstrated that such a purpose simply was not a motivating factor of the 1901 convention. In addition to the general catchall phrase "crimes involving moral

turpitude" the suffrage committee selected such crimes as vagrancy, living in adultery, and wife beating that were thought to be more commonly committed by blacks:

> "Most of the proposals disqualified persons committing any one of a long list of petty as well as serious crimes which the Negro, and to a lesser extent the poor whites, most often committed.... Most of the crimes contained in the report of the suffrage committee came from an ordinance by John Fielding Burns, a Black Belt planter. The crimes he listed were those he had taken cognizance of for years in his justice of the peace court in the Burnsville district, where nearly all his cases involved Negroes."

At oral argument in this Court, appellants' counsel suggested that, regardless of the original purpose of § 182, events occurring in the succeeding 80 years had legitimated the provision. Some of the more blatantly discriminatory selections, such as assault and battery on the wife and miscegenation, have been struck down by the courts, and appellants contend that the remaining crimes—felonies and moral turpitude misdemeanors—are acceptable bases for denying the franchise. Without deciding whether § 182 would be valid if enacted today without any impermissible motivation, we simply observe that its original enactment was motivated by a desire to discriminate against blacks on account of race and the section continues to this day to have that effect. As such, it violates [the equal protection clause].

* * *

Is *Hunter* consistent with *Ramirez*? Does it turn on the felony/misdemeanor distinction, the state's inclusion of only some offenses on the list, or simply the presence of a racially discriminatory purpose? Is a state's choice of which crimes, or which criminals to disenfranchise, subject to anything other than cursory review? For example, Mississippi disenfranchises only individuals convicted of murder, rape, bribery, theft, arson, obtaining money or goods under false pretense, perjury, forgery, embezzlement or bigamy, *see* Miss. Const. art. 12, § 241, while New Hampshire law disenfranchises only those convicted of treason, bribery, or election offenses, *see* N.H. Const. Pt. I, art. 11. *See also McLaughlin v. City of Canton*, 947 F.Supp. 954 (S.D.Miss.1995) (holding, inter alia, that Mississippi's disenfranchisement of misdemeanants violates the Fourteenth Amendment's equal protection clause).

4. Suppose felon disenfranchisement statutes generally exclude a higher proportion of the minority community from the franchise. Do they then raise questions under the Voting Rights Act? *See, e.g. Baker v. Pataki*, 85 F.3d 919 (2d Cir.1996) (en banc) (upholding, by an equally divided court, the dismissal of a claim that New York's felon disenfranchisement statute, which bars only incarcerated and paroled felons, but not those on probation, violates the Voting Rights Act); *Wesley v. Collins*, 791 F.2d 1255 (6th Cir.1986) (rejecting a voting rights challenge to Tennessee's disenfranchisement statute). *See generally* Andrew L. Shapiro, Note, *Challenging Criminal Disenfranchisement Under the Voting Rights Act: A New Strategy*, 103 Yale L.J. 537 (1993).

B. THE MODERN CONSTITUTIONAL FRAMEWORK

In the decade between 1959 and 1969, the Supreme Court, which had addressed relatively few voting rights issues in the preceding half century not directly connected with black disenfranchisement (discussed later in this Chapter), entertained a steady stream of voting rights cases. In addition to the Reapportionment Revolution (*see* Chapter 3), the Court also dramatically changed its approach to the formal right to participate. The following three cases illustrate that change.

Lassiter v. Northampton County Board of Elections
360 U.S. 45 (1959).

■ MR. JUSTICE DOUGLAS delivered the opinion of the Court.

* * *

[Lassiter, a "Negro citizen of North Carolina",] applied for registration as a voter. Her registration was denied by the registrar because she refused to submit to a literacy test as required by the North Carolina statute.[1]

* * *

We come then to the question whether a State may consistently with the Fourteenth and Seventeenth Amendments apply a literacy test to all voters irrespective of race or color.... The States have long been held to have broad powers to determine the conditions under which the right of suffrage may be exercised, absent of course the discrimination which the

---

1. This Act, passed in 1957, provides in § 163-28 as follows:

   "Every person presenting himself for registration shall be able to read and write any section of the Constitution of North Carolina in the English language. It shall be the duty of each registrar to administer the provisions of this section." * * *

   [The literacy test was based on a requirement in Art. VI § 4 of the North Carolina Constitution. The literacy requirements was contained in the first sentence of § 4, while the second sentence contained a so-called grandfather clause, which exempted voters and descendants of voters who were registered prior to 1867 (when the Fifteenth Amendment was passed). The state agreed that the grandfather clause contained in Art. VI was invalid under the Fifteenth Amendment and the Court's decision in *Guinn v. United States*, 238 U.S. 347 (1915).]

Constitution condemns. Article I, § 2 of the Constitution in its provision for the election of members of the House of Representatives and the Seventeenth Amendment in its provision for the election of Senators provide that officials will be chosen "by the People." Each provision goes on to state that "the Electors in each State shall have the Qualifications requisite for Electors of the most numerous Branch of the State Legislature." So while the right of suffrage is established and guaranteed by the Constitution, it is subject to the imposition of state standards which are not discriminatory and which do not contravene any restriction that Congress, acting pursuant to its constitutional powers, has imposed....

We do not suggest that any standards which a State desires to adopt may be required of voters. But there is wide scope for exercise of its jurisdiction. Residence requirements, age, previous criminal record are obvious examples indicating factors which a State may take into consideration in determining the qualifications of voters. The ability to read and write likewise has some relation to standards designed to promote intelligent use of the ballot. Literacy and illiteracy are neutral on race, creed, color, and sex, as reports around the world show. Literacy and intelligence are obviously not synonymous. Illiterate people may be intelligent voters. Yet in our society where newspapers, periodicals, books, and other printed matter canvass and debate campaign issues, a State might conclude that only those who are literate should exercise the franchise. It was said last century in Massachusetts that a literacy test was designed to insure an "independent and intelligent" exercise of the right of suffrage.[7] North

---

[7]. Nineteen States, including North Carolina, have some sort of literacy requirement as a prerequisite to eligibility for voting. Five require that the voter be able to read a section of the State or Federal Constitution and write his own name. Five require that the elector be able to read and write a section of the Federal or State Constitution.... Two States require that the voter be able to read and write English.... [Two others] require that the voter read a constitutional provision in English, while [one] requires that the voting application be written in the applicant's hand before the registrar and without aid, suggestion or memoranda. [Another] has the requirement that the voter be able to read and speak the English language.

Georgia requires that the voter read intelligibly and write legibly a section of the State or Federal Constitution. If he is physically unable to do so, he may qualify if he can give a reasonable interpretation of a section read to him. An alternative means of qualifying is provided: if one has good character and understands the duties and obligations of citizenship under a republican government, and he can answer correctly 20 of 30 questions listed in the statute (e.g., How does the Constitution of Georgia provide that a county site may be changed?, what is treason against the State of Georgia?, who are the solicitor general and the judge of the State Judicial Circuit in which you live?) he is eligible to vote. Geo. Code Ann. §§ 34–117, 34–120.

In Louisiana one qualifies if he can read and write English or his mother tongue, is of good character, and understands the duties and obligations of citizenship under a republican form of government. If he cannot read and write, he can qualify if he can give a reasonable interpretation of a section of the State or Federal Constitution when read to him, and if he is attached to the principles of the Federal and State Constitutions. La. Rev. Stat., Tit. 18, § 31.

In Mississippi the applicant must be able to read and write a section of the State Constitution and give a reasonable interpre-

Carolina agrees. We do not sit in judgment on the wisdom of that policy. We cannot say, however, that it is not an allowable one measured by constitutional standards.

Of course a literacy test, fair on its face, may be employed to perpetuate that discrimination which the Fifteenth Amendment was designed to uproot. No such influence is charged here. On the other hand, a literacy test may be unconstitutional on its face. In *Davis v. Schnell*, 81 F.Supp. 872, aff'd 336 U.S. 933, the test was the citizen's ability to "understand and explain" an article of the Federal Constitution. The legislative setting of that provision and the great discretion it vested in the registrar made clear that a literacy requirement was merely a device to make racial discrimination easy. We cannot make the same inference here. The present requirement, applicable to members of all races, is that the prospective voter "be able to read and write any section of the Constitution of North Carolina in the English language." That seems to us to be one fair way of determining whether a person is literate, not a calculated scheme to lay springes for the citizen. Certainly we cannot condemn it on its face as a device unrelated to the desire of North Carolina to raise the standards for people of all races who cast the ballot.

Harper v. Virginia Board of Elections
383 U.S. 663 (1966).

■ Mr. Justice Douglas delivered the opinion of the Court.

These are suits by Virginia residents to have declared unconstitutional Virginia's poll tax[1]....

While the right to vote in federal elections is conferred by Art. I, § 2, of the Constitution, the right to vote in state elections is nowhere expressly mentioned. It is argued that the right to vote in state elections is implicit,

---

tation of it. He must also demonstrate to the registrar a reasonable understanding of the duties and obligations of citizenship under a constitutional form of government. Miss. Code Ann. § 3213.

1. Section 173 of Virginia's Constitution directs the General Assembly to levy an annual poll tax not exceeding $1.50 on every resident of the State 21 years of age and over (with exceptions not relevant here). One dollar of the tax is to be used by state officials "exclusively in aid of the public free schools" and the remainder is to be returned to the counties for general purposes. Section 18 of the Constitution includes payment of poll taxes as a precondition for voting. Section 20 provides that a person must "personally" pay all state poll taxes for the three years preceding the year in which he applies for registration. By § 21 the poll tax must be paid at least six months prior to the election in which the voter seeks to vote.... The poll tax is often assessed along with the personal property tax. Those who do not pay a personal property tax are not assessed for a poll tax, it being their responsibility to take the initiative and request to be assessed. Va. Code § 58–1163. Enforcement of poll taxes takes the form of disenfranchisement of those who do not pay, § 22 of the Virginia Constitution providing that collection of delinquent poll taxes for a particular year may not be enforced by legal proceedings until the tax for that year has become three years delinquent.

particularly by reason of the First Amendment and that it may not constitutionally be conditioned upon the payment of a tax or fee. We do not stop to canvass the relation between voting and political expression. For it is enough to say that once the franchise is granted to the electorate, lines may not be drawn which are inconsistent with the Equal Protection Clause of the Fourteenth Amendment. But the *Lassiter [v.Northampton County Board of Elections]* case does not govern the result here, because, unlike a poll tax, the "ability to read and write ... has some relation to standards designed to promote intelligent use of the ballot."

We conclude that a State violates the Equal Protection Clause of the Fourteenth Amendment whenever it makes the affluence of the voter or payment of any fee an electoral standard. Voter qualifications have no relation to wealth nor to paying or not paying this or any other tax. Our cases demonstrate that the Equal Protection Clause of the Fourteenth Amendment restrains the States from fixing voter qualifications which invidiously discriminate.... Previously we [have] said that neither homesite nor occupation "affords a permissible basis for distinguishing between qualified voters within the State." *Gray v. Sanders*, 372 U.S. 368, 380. We think the same must be true of requirements of wealth or affluence or payment of a fee.

Long ago, the Court referred to "the political franchise of voting" as a "fundamental political right, because preservative of all rights." Recently in *Reynolds v. Sims*, we said, "Undoubtedly, the right of suffrage is a fundamental matter in a free and democratic society. Especially since the right to exercise the franchise in a free and unimpaired manner is preservative of other basic civil and political rights, any alleged infringement of the right of citizens to vote must be carefully and meticulously scrutinized." There we were considering charges that voters in one part of the State had greater representation per person in the State Legislature than voters in another part of the State. We concluded:

> "A citizen, a qualified voter, is no more nor no less so because he lives in the city or on the farm. This is the clear and strong command of our Constitution's Equal Protection Clause. This is an essential part of the concept of a government of laws and not men. This is at the heart of Lincoln's vision of 'government of the people, by the people, [and] for the people.' The Equal Protection Clause demands no less than substantially equal state legislative representation for all citizens, of all places as well as of all races."

We say the same whether the citizen, otherwise qualified to vote, has $1.50 in his pocket or nothing at all, pays the fee or fails to pay it. The principle that denies the State the right to dilute a citizen's vote on account of his economic status or other such factors by analogy bars a system which excludes those unable to pay a fee to vote or who fail to pay.

It is argued that a State may exact fees from citizens for many different kinds of licenses; that if it can demand from all an equal fee for a driver's license, it can demand from all an equal poll tax for voting. But we must remember that the interest of the State, when it comes to voting, is limited to the power to fix qualifications. Wealth, like race, creed, or color, is not germane to one's ability to participate intelligently in the electoral process. Lines drawn on the basis of wealth or property, like those of race are traditionally disfavored. To introduce wealth or payment of a fee as a measure of a voter's qualifications is to introduce a capricious or irrelevant factor. The degree of the discrimination is irrelevant. In this context—that is, as a condition of obtaining a ballot—the requirement of fee paying causes an "invidious" discrimination that runs afoul of the Equal Protection Clause....

We agree, of course, with Mr. Justice Holmes that the Due Process Clause of the Fourteenth Amendment "does not enact Mr. Herbert Spencer's Social Statics" (*Lochner v. New York*, 198 U.S. 45, 75). Likewise, the Equal Protection Clause is not shackled to the political theory of a particular era. In determining what lines are unconstitutionally discriminatory, we have never been confined to historic notions of equality, any more than we have restricted due process to a fixed catalogue of what was at a given time deemed to be the limits of fundamental rights. [Accordingly, *Breedlove v. Suttles*, 302 U.S. 277 (1937), which upheld Georgia's use of a poll tax, is overruled.]

■ MR. JUSTICE BLACK, dissenting.

* * *

Since the *Breedlove* and *Butler* cases [upholding poll taxes against equal protection challenges] were decided the Federal Constitution has not been amended in the only way it could constitutionally have been, that is, as provided in Article V of the Constitution. I would adhere to the holding of those cases. The Court, however, overrules *Breedlove* in part, but its opinion reveals that it does so not by using its limited power to interpret the original meaning of the Equal Protection Clause, but by giving that clause a new meaning which it believes represents a better governmental policy. From this action I dissent.

* * *

I think the interpretation that this Court gave the Equal Protection Clause in *Breedlove* was correct.... All voting laws treat some persons differently from others in some respects. Some bar a person from voting who is under 21 years of age; others bar those under 18. Some bar convicted felons or the insane, and some have attached a freehold or other property qualification for voting. The *Breedlove* case upheld a poll tax which was imposed on men but was not equally imposed on women and minors, and the Court today does not overrule that part of *Breedlove* which approved those discriminatory provisions. And in *Lassiter v. Northampton Election Board*, 360 U.S. 45, this Court held that state laws which disqualified the illiterate from voting did not violate the Equal Protection Clause.

From these cases and all the others decided by this Court interpreting the Equal Protection Clause it is clear that some discriminatory voting qualifications can be imposed without violating the Equal Protection Clause.

A study of our cases shows that this Court has refused to use the general language of the Equal Protection Clause as though it provided a handy instrument to strike down state laws which the Court feels are based on bad governmental policy. The equal protection cases carefully analyzed boil down to the principle that distinctions drawn and even discriminations imposed by state laws do not violate the Equal Protection Clause so long as these distinctions and discriminations are not "irrational," "irrelevant," "unreasonable," "arbitrary," or "invidious." . . . . [I]t would be difficult to say that the poll tax requirement is "irrational" or "arbitrary" or works "invidious discriminations." State poll tax legislation can "reasonably," "rationally" and without an "invidious" or evil purpose to injure anyone be found to rest on a number of state policies including (1) the State's desire to collect its revenue, and (2) its belief that voters who pay a poll tax will be interested in furthering the State's welfare when they vote. Certainly it is rational to believe that people may be more likely to pay taxes if payment is a prerequisite to voting. And if history can be a factor in determining the "rationality" of discrimination in a state law, then whatever may be our personal opinion, history is on the side of "rationality" of the State's poll tax policy. Property qualifications existed in the Colonies and were continued by many States after the Constitution was adopted. Although I join the Court in disliking the policy of the poll tax, this is not in my judgment a justifiable reason for holding this poll tax law unconstitutional. Such a holding on my part would, in my judgment, be an exercise of power which the Constitution does not confer upon me.

* * *

The Court's justification for consulting its own notions rather than following the original meaning of the Constitution, as I would, apparently is based on the belief of the majority of the Court that for this Court to be bound by the original meaning of the Constitution is an intolerable and debilitating evil; that our Constitution should not be "shackled to the political theory of a particular era," and that to save the country from the original Constitution the Court must have constant power to renew it and keep it abreast of this Court's more enlightened theories of what is best for our society. It seems to me that this is an attack not only on the great value of our Constitution itself but also on the concept of a written constitution which is to survive through the years as originally written unless changed through the amendment process which the Framers wisely provided. Moreover, when a "political theory" embodied in our Constitution becomes outdated, it seems to me that a majority of the nine members of this Court are not only without constitutional power but are far less qualified to choose a new constitutional political theory than the people of this country proceeding in the manner provided by Article V.

The people have not found it impossible to amend their Constitution to meet new conditions. The Equal Protection Clause itself is the product of the people's desire to use their constitutional power to amend the Constitution to meet new problems. Moreover, the people, in § 5 of the Fourteenth Amendment, designated the governmental tribunal they wanted to provide additional rules to enforce the guarantees of that Amendment. The branch of Government they chose was not the Judicial Branch but the Legislative. I have no doubt at all that Congress has the power under § 5 to pass legislation to abolish the poll tax in order to protect the citizens of this country if it believes that the poll tax is being used as a device to deny voters equal protection of the laws.

* * *

■ MR. JUSTICE HARLAN, whom MR. JUSTICE STEWART joins, dissenting.

* * *

Is there a rational basis for Virginia's poll tax as a voting qualification? I think the answer to that question is undoubtedly "yes."

Property qualifications and poll taxes have been a traditional part of our political structure. In the Colonies the franchise was generally a restricted one. Over the years these and other restrictions were gradually lifted, primarily because popular theories of political representation had changed. Often restrictions were lifted only after wide public debate. The issue of woman suffrage, for example, raised questions of family relationships, of participation in public affairs, of the very nature of the type of society in which Americans wished to live; eventually a consensus was reached, which culminated in the Nineteenth Amendment no more than 45 years ago.

Similarly with property qualifications, it is only by fiat that it can be said, especially in the context of American history, that there can be no rational debate as to their advisability. Most of the early Colonies had them; many of the States have had them during much of their histories; and, whether one agrees or not, arguments have been and still can be made in favor of them. For example, it is certainly a rational argument that payment of some minimal poll tax promotes civic responsibility, weeding out those who do not care enough about public affairs to pay $1.50 or thereabouts a year for the exercise of the franchise. It is also arguable, indeed it was probably accepted as sound political theory by a large percentage of Americans through most of our history, that people with some property have a deeper stake in community affairs, and are consequently more responsible, more educated, more knowledgeable, more worthy of confidence, than those without means, and that the community and Nation would be better managed if the franchise were restricted to such citizens. Nondiscriminatory and fairly applied literacy tests, upheld by this Court in *Lassiter v. Northampton Election Board*, 360 U.S. 45, find justification on very similar grounds.

These viewpoints, to be sure, ring hollow on most contemporary ears. Their lack of acceptance today is evidenced by the fact that nearly all of the States, left to their own devices, have eliminated property or poll-tax qualifications [and] by the cognate fact that Congress and three-quarters of the States quickly ratified the Twenty–Fourth Amendment. . . .

Kramer v. Union Free School District No. 15

395 U.S. 621 (1969).

■ MR. CHIEF JUSTICE WARREN delivered the opinion of the Court.

[N.Y. Educ. L. § 2012 limited the right to vote in certain school district elections to residents who were otherwise eligible to vote in state and federal elections if they also either (1) owned or leased taxable real property within the district, or (2) were parents or had custody of children enrolled in the local public schools.]

* * *

I.

* * *

Appellant is a 31–year-old college-educated stockbroker who lives in his parents' home in the Union Free School District No. 15, a district to which § 2012 applies. He is a citizen of the United States and has voted in federal and state elections since 1959. However, since he has no children and neither owns nor leases taxable real property, appellant's attempts to register for and vote in the local school district elections have been unsuccessful. . . .

II.

At the outset, it is important to note what is not at issue in this case. The requirements of § 2012 that school district voters must (1) be citizens of the United States, (2) be bona fide residents of the school district, and (3) be at least 21 years of age are not challenged. Appellant agrees that the States have the power to impose reasonable citizenship, age, and residency requirements on the availability of the ballot. The sole issue in this case is whether the additional requirements of § 2012—requirements which prohibit some district residents who are otherwise qualified by age and citizenship from participating in district meetings and school board elections—violate the Fourteenth Amendment's command that no State shall deny persons equal protection of the laws.

"In determining whether or not a state law violates the Equal Protection Clause, we must consider the facts and circumstances behind the law, the interests which the State claims to be protecting, and the interests of those who are disadvantaged by the classification." *Williams v. Rhodes*, 393

U.S. 23, 30 (1968). And, in this case, we must give the statute a close and exacting examination. "Since the right to exercise the franchise in a free and unimpaired manner is preservative of other basic civil and political rights, any alleged infringement of the right of citizens to vote must be carefully and meticulously scrutinized." *Reynolds v. Sims*, 377 U.S. 533, 562 (1964). This careful examination is necessary because statutes distributing the franchise constitute the foundation of our representative society. Any unjustified discrimination in determining who may participate in political affairs or in the selection of public officials undermines the legitimacy of representative government.

* * *

[T]he deference usually given to the judgment of legislators does not extend to decisions concerning which resident citizens may participate in the election of legislators and other public officials. Those decisions must be carefully scrutinized by the Court to determine whether each resident citizen has, as far as is possible, an equal voice in the selections. Accordingly, when we are reviewing statutes which deny some residents the right to vote, the general presumption of constitutionality afforded state statutes and the traditional approval given state classifications if the Court can conceive of a "rational basis" for the distinctions made are not applicable. *See Harper v. Virginia Bd. of Elections*, 383 U.S. 663, 670 (1966). The presumption of constitutionality and the approval given "rational" classifications in other types of enactments[9] are based on an assumption that the institutions of state government are structured so as to represent fairly all the people. However, when the challenge to the statute is in effect a challenge of this basic assumption, the assumption can no longer serve as the basis for presuming constitutionality. And, the assumption is no less under attack because the legislature which decides who may participate at the various levels of political choice is fairly elected. Legislation which delegates decision making to bodies elected by only a portion of those eligible to vote for the legislature can cause unfair representation. Such legislation can exclude a minority of voters from any voice in the decisions just as effectively as if the decisions were made by legislators the minority had no voice in selecting.[10]

The need for exacting judicial scrutiny of statutes distributing the franchise is undiminished simply because, under a different statutory scheme, the offices subject to election might have been filled through appointment. States do have latitude in determining whether certain public officials shall be selected by election or chosen by appointment and whether various questions shall be submitted to the voters. In fact, we have held

---

9. Of course, we have long held that if the basis of classification is inherently suspect, such as race, the statute must be subjected to an exacting scrutiny, regardless of the subject matter of the legislation.

10. Thus, statutes structuring local government units receive no less exacting an examination merely because the state legislature is fairly elected.

that where a county school board is an administrative, not legislative, body, its members need not be elected. However, "once the franchise is granted to the electorate, lines may not be drawn which are inconsistent with the Equal Protection Clause of the Fourteenth Amendment." *Harper v. Virginia Bd. of Elections.*

Nor is the need for close judicial examination affected because the district meetings and the school board do not have "general" legislative powers. Our exacting examination is not necessitated by the subject of the election; rather, it is required because some resident citizens are permitted to participate and some are not....

III.

Besides appellant and others who similarly live in their parents' homes, the statute also disenfranchises the following persons (unless they are parents or guardians of children enrolled in the district public school): senior citizens and others living with children or relatives; clergy, military personnel, and others who live on tax-exempt property; boarders and lodgers; parents who neither own nor lease qualifying property and whose children are too young to attend school; parents who neither own nor lease qualifying property and whose children attend private schools.

Appellant asserts that excluding him from participation in the district elections denies him equal protection of the laws. He contends that he and others of his class are substantially interested in and significantly affected by the school meeting decisions. All members of the community have an interest in the quality and structure of public education, appellant says, and he urges that "the decisions taken by local boards ... may have grave consequences to the entire population." Appellant also argues that the level of property taxation affects him, even though he does not own property, as property tax levels affect the price of goods and services in the community.

We turn therefore to question whether the exclusion is necessary to promote a compelling state interest. First, appellees argue that the State has a legitimate interest in limiting the franchise in school district elections to "members of the community of interest"—those "primarily interested in such elections." Second, appellees urge that the State may reasonably and permissibly conclude that "property taxpayers" (including lessees of taxable property who share the tax burden through rent payments) and parents of the children enrolled in the district's schools are those "primarily interested" in school affairs.

We do not understand appellees to argue that the State is attempting to limit the franchise to those "subjectively concerned" about school matters. Rather, they appear to argue that the State's legitimate interest is in restricting a voice in school matters to those "directly affected" by such decisions. The State apparently reasons that since the schools are financed in part by local property taxes, persons whose out-of-pocket expenses are "directly" affected by property tax changes should be allowed to vote.

Similarly, parents of children in school are thought to have a "direct" stake in school affairs and are given a vote.

Appellees argue that it is necessary to limit the franchise to those "primarily interested" in school affairs because "the ever increasing complexity of the many interacting phases of the school system and structure make it extremely difficult for the electorate fully to understand the whys and wherefores of the detailed operations of the school system." Appellees say that many communications of school boards and school administrations are sent home to the parents through the district pupils and are "not broadcast to the general public"; thus, nonparents will be less informed than parents. Further, appellees argue, those who are assessed for local property taxes (either directly or indirectly through rent) will have enough of an interest "through the burden on their pocketbooks, to acquire such information as they may need."

We need express no opinion as to whether the State in some circumstances might limit the exercise of the franchise to those "primarily interested" or "primarily affected." . . . . [A]ssuming, arguendo, that New York legitimately might limit the franchise in these school district elections to those "primarily interested in school affairs," close scrutiny of the § 2012 classifications demonstrates that they do not accomplish this purpose with sufficient precision to justify denying appellant the franchise.

. . . . [T]he classifications must be tailored so that the exclusion of appellant and members of his class is necessary to achieve the articulated state goal.[14] Section 2012 does not meet the exacting standard of precision we require of statutes which selectively distribute the franchise. The classifications in § 2012 permit inclusion of many persons who have, at best, a remote and indirect interest in school affairs and, on the other hand, exclude others who have a distinct and direct interest in the school meeting decisions.[15]

Nor do appellees offer any justification for the exclusion of seemingly interested and informed residents—other than to argue that the § 2012 classifications include those "whom the State could understandably deem to be the most intimately interested in actions taken by the school board," and urge that "the task of . . . balancing the interest of the community in the maintenance of orderly school district elections against the interest of any individual in voting in such elections should clearly remain with the Legislature." But the issue is not whether the legislative judgments are

---

14. Of course, if the exclusions are necessary to promote the articulated state interest, we must then determine whether the interest promoted by limiting the franchise constitutes a compelling state interest. We do not reach that issue in this case.

15. For example, appellant resides with his parents in the school district, pays state and federal taxes and is interested in and affected by school board decisions; however, he has no vote. On the other hand, an uninterested unemployed young man who pays no state or federal taxes, but who rents an apartment in the district, can participate in the election.

rational. A more exacting standard obtains. The issue is whether the § 2012 requirements do in fact sufficiently further a compelling state interest to justify denying the franchise to appellant and members of his class. The requirements of § 2012 are not sufficiently tailored to limiting the franchise to those "primarily interested" in school affairs to justify the denial of the franchise to appellant and members of his class.

* * *

■ MR. JUSTICE STEWART, with whom MR. JUSTICE BLACK and MR. JUSTICE HARLAN join, dissenting.

* * *

Although at times variously phrased, the traditional test of a statute's validity under the Equal Protection Clause is a familiar one: a legislative classification is invalid only "if it rest[s] on grounds wholly irrelevant to achievement of the regulation's objectives." It was under just such a test that the literacy requirement involved in *Lassiter [v. Northampton County Bd. of Elections*, 360 U.S. 45 (1959)] was upheld. The premise of our decision in that case was that a State may constitutionally impose upon its citizens voting requirements reasonably "designed to promote intelligent use of the ballot." A similar premise underlies the proposition, consistently endorsed by this Court, that a State may exclude nonresidents from participation in its elections. Such residence requirements, designed to help ensure that voters have a substantial stake in the outcome of elections and an opportunity to become familiar with the candidates and issues voted upon, are entirely permissible exercises of state authority. Indeed, the appellant explicitly concedes, as he must, the validity of voting requirements relating to residence, literacy, and age. Yet he argues—and the Court accepts the argument—that the voting qualifications involved here somehow have a different constitutional status. I am unable to see the distinction.

Clearly a State may reasonably assume that its residents have a greater stake in the outcome of elections held within its boundaries than do other persons. Likewise, it is entirely rational for a state legislature to suppose that residents, being generally better informed regarding state affairs than are nonresidents, will be more likely than nonresidents to vote responsibly. And the same may be said of legislative assumptions regarding the electoral competence of adults and literate persons on the one hand, and of minors and illiterates on the other. It is clear, of course, that lines thus drawn cannot infallibly perform their intended legislative function. Just as "illiterate people may be intelligent voters," nonresidents or minors might also in some instances be interested, informed, and intelligent participants in the electoral process. Persons who commute across a state line to work may well have a great stake in the affairs of the State in which they are employed; some college students under 21 may be both better informed and more passionately interested in political affairs than many adults. But such discrepancies are the inevitable concomitant of the line drawing that is essential to law making. So long as the classification is rationally related to a permissible legislative end, therefore—as are residence, literacy, and age requirements imposed with respect to voting—there is no denial of equal protection.

Thus judged, the statutory classification involved here seems to me clearly to be valid. New York has made the judgment that local educational policy is best left to those persons who have certain direct and definable interests in that policy: those who are either immediately involved as parents of school children or who, as owners or lessees of taxable property, are burdened with the local cost of funding school district operations.[6] True, persons outside those classes may be genuinely interested in the conduct of a school district's business—just as commuters from New Jersey may be genuinely interested in the outcome of a New York City election. But unless this Court is to claim a monopoly of wisdom regarding the sound operation of school systems in the 50 States, I see no way to justify the conclusion that the legislative classification involved here is not rationally related to a legitimate legislative purpose....

With good reason, the Court does not really argue the contrary. Instead, it strikes down New York's statute by asserting that the traditional equal protection standard is inapt in this case, and that a considerably stricter standard—under which classifications relating to "the franchise" are to be subjected to "exacting judicial scrutiny"—should be applied. But the asserted justification for applying such a standard cannot withstand analysis.

* * *

I am at a loss to understand how such reasoning is at all relevant to the present case. The voting qualifications at issue have been promulgated, not by Union Free School District No. 15, but by the New York State Legislature, and the appellant is of course fully able to participate in the election of representatives in that body. There is simply no claim whatever here that the state government is not "structured so as to represent fairly all the people," including the appellant.

Nor is there any other justification for imposing the Court's "exacting" equal protection test. This case does not involve racial classifications, which in light of the genesis of the Fourteenth Amendment have traditionally been viewed as inherently "suspect." And this statute is not one that impinges upon a constitutionally protected right, and that consequently can be justified only by a "compelling" state interest. For "the Constitution of

---

6. Presumably the rationale for including lessees and their spouses in the electoral process is that the cost of property taxes is in many instances passed on from owner to lessee.

the United States does not confer the right of suffrage upon any one...."
Minor v. Happersett, 21 Wall. 162, 178.

* * *

NOTES AND QUESTIONS

1. As you probably remember from your constitutional law class, modern equal protection law is said to use three tiers of scrutiny. The most searching is "strict scrutiny," which requires that the government show that the challenged classification is necessary for the achievement of a compelling government interest; this standard has been applied over the years to distinctions based on "suspect classifications" such as race or nationality as well as to laws that impair the exercise of a fundamental right. The most lenient is "rational relationship" scrutiny, in which the court asks only whether the classification is reasonably connected to the achievement of some legitimate, albeit not necessarily compelling, interest. Most distinctions are reviewed using the rational relationship test. Somewhere in between lies "intermediate scrutiny": a distinction can be sustained if the government can show that it is actually and "substantially" related to an "important" purpose. This level of scrutiny has been used primarily to analyze distinctions based on sex. The conventional wisdom is that strict scrutiny is "strict in theory but fatal in fact," while virtually anything goes under rational relationship scrutiny. (The two most notable recent exceptions involve discrimination against retarded persons in *City of Cleburne v. Cleburne Living Center*, 473 U.S. 432 (1985), and the discrimination against gays, lesbians, and bisexuals involved in *Romer v. Evans*, 116 S.Ct. 1620 (1996).)

Lassiter was decided under the rational relationship standard, while *Harper* and *Kramer* were decided using strict scrutiny. Does this factor alone explain their different outcomes? Could literacy tests survive strict scrutiny? Are the challenged distinctions in *Harper* and *Kramer* rationally related to the achievement of a legitimate government interest?

2. Strict scrutiny comes into play either when a suspect classification is used or when a fundamental right is impaired. Which strand of strict scrutiny is responsible for *Harper*? Does *Kramer* follow from *Harper* or does it rest on a different rationale?

Given the tremendous evidence that poll taxes and literacy tests had been adopted and maintained for racially discriminatory purposes, why didn't the plaintiffs argue, or the Court decide, *Lassiter* and *Harper* as race discrimination cases? Note that the plaintiffs in both cases were black.

3. The *Kramer* Court notes that several aspects of the New York statute were not challenged, namely that school district voters be (1) citizens of the United States, (2) at least 21 years of age, and (3) bona fide residents of the school district. Could citizenship, age, and residency requirements withstand strict scrutiny? If not, what explains why they are subject to only rational relationship review?

4. *Citizenship.* For many years, citizenship was not an invariable requirement for voting. *See Minor v. Happersett*, 88 U.S. 162 (1874). In some jurisdictions today, resident aliens are permitted to vote in local elections. *See, e.g.,* Gerald L. Neuman, *"We Are the People": Alien Suffrage in German and American Perspective*, 13 Mich. J. Int'l L. 259 (1992); Jamin B. Raskin, *Legal Aliens, Local Citizens: The Historical, Constitutional, and Theoretical Meanings of Alien Suffrage*, 141 U. Pa. L. Rev. 1391 (1993); Gerald M. Rosberg, *Aliens and Equal Protection: Why Not the Right to Vote?*, 75 Mich. L. Rev. 1092 (1977). For the Supreme Court's view that formal citizenship can be made a prerequisite to full rights of political participation, see *Cabell v. Chavez-Salido*, 454 U.S. 432, 439–40 (1982):

> The exclusion of aliens from basic governmental processes is not a deficiency in the democratic system but a necessary consequence of the community's process of political self-definition. Self-government, whether direct or through representatives, begins by defining the scope of the community of the governed and thus of the governors as well: aliens are by definition outside this community.

If school board positions are at issue, are resident aliens whose children attend public schools any less "interested" members of the community than Kramer was? In as mobile a society as ours what distinguishes citizens from aliens? Ought different rules apply to local as opposed to state or national elections?

For an interesting parallel set of problems from another constitutional system, consider two decisions in 1990 from the Constitutional Court of Germany. There, two states (or *Landër*), had sought to permit foreign residents to vote in municipal elections, as long as their home country extended similar privileges to German nationals. In one, some seven thousand foreign residents, who had to have resided at least five years in the state, including Danes, Irish, Dutch, Norwegians, Swedes, and Swiss became eligible to vote. In the second, foreign nationals were required to have lived eight years in the relevant local government, and the extension added some ninety thousand persons to the voting rolls. The Constitutional Court held unconstitutional these decisions to extend the franchise in local elections, on the ground that the German Constitution *required* that only German citizens be permitted to vote in any election. When treaties of the European Union required that member states extend the franchise to all European Union citizens residing in a member state, the German Basic Law was amended in 1992 to nullify these court decisions and extend the franchise to resident foreign nationals. For discussion, see Donald P. Kommers, The Constitutional Jurisprudence of the Federal Republic of Germany 197–99 (1997).

5. *Age.* In *Oregon v. Mitchell*, 400 U.S. 112 (1970), the Supreme Court struck down a 1970 amendment to the Voting Rights Act which enfranchised 18 year-olds in state and local elections on the grounds that it was beyond Congress' power. (The Court did uphold their enfranchisement in elections for national office.) Soon after, the Twenty–Sixth Amendment was enacted. Section 1 provides:

> The right of citizens of the United States, who are eighteen years of age or older, to vote shall not be denied or abridged by the United States or by any State on account of age.

What, if any, implications does the amendment have for the claims of persons under eighteen? Does it forbid states from granting the right to vote to, for example, sixteen year-olds, who, after all are old enough in many states to drive, to be tried as adults, to consent on their own behalf to medical procedures, or to marry? Would giving them the vote dilute the voting rights of adults?

Does the Twenty–Sixth Amendment implicitly do to the claims of 17 year-olds what section 2 of the Fourteenth Amendment does to the claims of felons, namely, remove them from the ambit of strict scrutiny? Recall that in *Richardson v. Ramirez*, 418 U.S. 24 (1974), the Court held that felon disenfranchisement was contemplated by section 2 of the Fourteenth Amendment.

Kramer reiterated "that the States have the power to impose reasonable ... age ... requirements on the availability of the ballot." The word "reasonable" usually refers to the less exacting "rational basis" scrutiny rather than the strict scrutiny applied to most statutes regarding the franchise. However, the opinion in *Gaunt v. Brown*, 341 F.Supp. 1187 (S.D.Ohio 1972), *aff'd*, 409 U.S. 809 (1972), suggests a third possibility. In *Gaunt*, a group of 17 year-olds brought an action to compel the state of Ohio to permit them to vote in primary elections because they would be eligible to vote by the time of the general election and wanted to participate in the selection of candidates. (By contrast to Ohio law, West Virginia allows 17 year-olds who will turn 18 by the time of the general election to vote in primaries. W. Va. Code § 3–2–2 (1995)). The *Gaunt* court rejected the 17 year-olds' claim: "We hold to the view that in a case where a State is called on to justify its drawing the line for qualifications at 18 years of age no test is required...."

Level of scrutiny aside, what is the justification for age restrictions on the franchise? Consider the following observations by Professor Charles Alan Wright, cited in *Gaunt*:

> I do not think an argument [that the denial of the vote is invidious discrimination] can be convincingly made with regard to age. Age limit on voting necessarily must be arbitrary. There is no single specific day in the life of all citizens in which it can rationally be said that they are suddenly informed members of the electorate though they were not so one day before. It is a problem in drawing

lines and I think the clear meaning ... of the Constitution is that these lines are for the States to draw.

This suggests that perhaps the ability to rationally and intelligently distinguish among candidates and positions is the motive behind prohibiting those below 18 from voting. Such a distinction is inevitably both overinclusive and underinclusive. Does such a justification survive the invalidation of literacy tests and other forms of testing older voters' knowledge or interest? Can states deny the franchise to other classes of citizens who are deemed irrational? *See* Boris Feldman, Note, *Mental Disability and the Right to Vote*, 88 Yale L.J. 1644 (1979) (discussing the disenfranchisement of various groups of mentally disabled voters and arguing that their incapacity to vote rationally provides no basis for barring them from the polls); *cf.* Daniel R. Ortiz, *The Engaged and the Inert: Theorizing Political Personality Under the First Amendment*, 81 Va. L. Rev. 1 (1995) (suggesting that most American voters are "civic slobs" whose votes are cast on the basis of emotion and absent much information).

6. *Residency.* There has been relatively little litigation over citizenship and age restrictions. By contrast, residency restrictions of various sorts have engendered substantially more challenges.

Dunn v. Blumstein, 405 U.S. 330 (1972), involved a challenge to Tennessee's "durational residence" requirement. Durational residency requirements mandate that a citizen have lived in the jurisdiction for some extended period of time before being eligible to vote. *See generally* David Cocanower & David Rich, *Residency Requirements for Voting*, 12 Ariz. L. Rev. 477 (1970); John A. MacLeod & Merle F. Wilmerding, *State Voting Residency Requirements and Civil Rights*, 38 Geo. Wash. L. Rev. 93 (1969).

Tennessee law required that, in addition to being a resident, a would-be voter have been a resident for a year in the State and three months in the county before actually voting. Justice Marshall's opinion for the Court explained that "[a]n appropriately defined and uniformly applied requirement of bona fide residence may be necessary to preserve the basic conception of a political community, and therefore could withstand close constitutional scrutiny." But it held that the additional requirement of a substantial period of residence failed strict scrutiny.

Tennessee offered two justifications for its durational residence requirement: (1) preventing voting fraud through colonization and inability to identify persons offering to vote, and (2) making sure that a voter has "in fact, become a member of the community and that as such, he has a common interest in all matters pertaining to its government and is, therefore, more likely to exercise his right more intelligently."

With regard to the first interest, the Court held that Tennessee's requirement failed the means-ends test. Preventing fraud was clearly a compelling state interest. But durational requirements were not necessary to the achievement of that end: the state's failure to look behind voters' oaths meant that a person bent on fraud would simply swear to the length as well as the fact of his residence; moreover, the state should have ample time to check its registration rolls in the months leading up to an election.

As for the second interest, the Court largely rejected the premises on which it was based:

> The argument that durational residence requirements further the goal of having "knowledgeable voters" appears to involve three separate claims. The first is that such requirements "afford some surety that the voter has, in fact, become a member of the community." But here the State appears to confuse a bona fide residence requirement with a durational residence requirement. As already noted, a State does have an interest in limiting the franchise to bona fide members of the community. But this does not justify or explain the exclusion from the franchise of persons, not because their bona fide residence is questioned, but because they are recent rather than longtime residents.
>
> The second branch of the "knowledgeable voters" justification is that durational residence requirements assure that the voter "has a common interest in all matters pertaining to [the community's] government...." By this, presumably, the State means that it may require a period of residence sufficiently lengthy to impress upon its voters the local viewpoint. This is precisely the sort of argument this Court has repeatedly rejected.... Tennessee's hopes for voters with a "common interest in all matters pertaining to [the community's] government" is impermissible. The fact that newly arrived [Tennesseeans] may have a more national outlook than longtime residents, or even may retain a viewpoint characteristic of the region from which they have come, is a constitutionally impermissible reason for depriving them of their chance to influence the electoral vote of their new home State.[28]

---

[28]. Tennessee may be revealing this impermissible purpose when it observes:

"The fact that the voting privilege has been extended to 18 year old persons ... increases, rather than diminishes, the need for durational residency requirements.... It is so generally known, as to be judicially accepted, that there are many political subdivisions in this state, and other states, wherein there are colleges, universities and military installations with sufficient student body or military personnel over eighteen years of age, as would completely dominate elections in the district, county or municipality so located. This would offer the maximum of opportunity for fraud through colonization, and permit domination by those not knowledgeable or having a common interest in matters of government, as opposed to the interest and the knowledge of permanent members of the community. Upon completion of their schooling, or service tour, they move on, leaving the community bound to a course of political expediency not of its choice and, in fact, one over which its more permanent citizens, who will continue to be affected, had no control."

Finally, the State urges that a longtime resident is "more likely to exercise his right [to vote] more intelligently." To the extent that this is different from the previous argument, the State is apparently asserting an interest in limiting the franchise to voters who are knowledgeable about the issues. In this case, Tennessee argues that people who have been in the State less than a year and the county less than three months are likely to be unaware of the issues involved in the congressional, state, and local elections, and therefore can be barred from the franchise. We note that the criterion of "intelligent" voting is an elusive one, and susceptible of abuse. But without deciding as a general matter the extent to which a State can bar less knowledgeable or intelligent citizens from the franchise,[29] we conclude that durational residence requirements cannot be justified on this basis.

What vision of voting does the *Dunn v. Blumstein* Court embrace? Frank Michelman has argued that the Supreme Court's enfranchisement cases move back and forth between a deliberative, "republican" model of politics and a more strategic, "liberal" view. *See* Frank Michelman, *Conceptions of Democracy in American Constitutional Argument: Voting Rights,* 41 U.Fla.L.Rev. 443 (1989). Is the *Dunn* Court rejecting the idea that political activity will lead to commonly shared beliefs or simply the appropriateness of durational residency requirements in achieving republican ends?

Note that in *Marston v. Lewis*, 410 U.S. 679 (1973), the Supreme Court upheld Arizona's fifty-day durational residency requirement for state and local elections given the administrative necessities of obtaining accurate voting rolls in time for the election.

Federal law, by contrast, establishes a nationwide thirty-day cutoff for voter registration for the presidential election. *See* 42 U.S.C. § 1973aa–1 (1994). Section 1973aa–1 also provides for "gap" voting: if a citizen has begun residence in a new state or political subdivision within the thirty days prior to an election and therefore cannot satisfy the new jurisdiction's registration requirements, he must be permitted to vote either in person or by absentee ballot in the jurisdiction where he previously lived, so long as he had been duly registered there prior to leaving.

7. *Who counts as a "bona fide resident"?* In *Carrington v. Rash*, 380 U.S. 89 (1965), the Supreme Court struck down a provision of the Texas

---

29. In the 1970 Voting Rights Act, which added § 201, 42 U.S.C. § 1973aa, Congress provided that "no citizen shall be denied, because of his failure to comply with any test or device, the right to vote in any Federal, State, or local election...." The term "test or device" was defined to include, in part, "any requirement that a person as a prerequisite for voting or registration for voting (1) demonstrate the ability to read, write, understand, or interpret any matter, (2) demonstrate any educational achievement or his knowledge of any particular subject...." By prohibiting various "test[s]" and "device[s]" that would clearly assure knowledgeability on the part of voters in local elections, Congress declared federal policy that people should be allowed to vote even if they were not well informed about the issues. We upheld § 201 in Oregon v. Mitchell

Constitution that prohibited "any member of the Armed Forces of the United States" who moves his home to Texas during the course of his military duty from ever voting in any state election "so long as he or she is a member of the Armed Forces." Carrington had bought a house in El Paso—from which he commuted to a military post in New Mexico—and had opened a business in Texas as well. Texas defended its rule on two grounds: first, an interest in protecting local elections from bloc voting by military personnel that might overwhelm a small local civilian community and second, an assumption that most servicemen were transients and therefore not permanent members of the community.

The Court responded that although Texas undoubtedly had the power to restrict the franchise to bona fide residents, it could not " 'fenc[e] out' from the franchise a sector of the population because of the way they may vote...." Thus, the fact that residents who were also in the armed services might have different viewpoints from civilian voters provided no basis for excluding them: "The exercise of rights so vital to the maintenance of democratic institutions ... cannot constitutionally be obliterated because of a fear of the political views of a particular group of bona fide residents." Moreover, although Texas could also deny the vote to transients, it had improperly singled out military personnel with essentially an irrebuttable presumption of nonresidence. The Court relied on *Gray v. Sanders*, 372 U.S. 368 (1963), for the proposition that "[t]here is no indication in the Constitution that ... occupation affords a permissible basis for distinguishing between qualified voters within the State." Instead of such an irrebuttable presumption, Texas would have to use a more finely crafted test of residence: "States may not casually deprive a class of individuals of the vote because of some remote administrative benefit to the State."

Notice that *Carrington* was decided before the Supreme Court explicitly applied strict scrutiny to restrictions on the franchise, but nonetheless used a somewhat heightened form of review.

Does Texas's first rationale—that military personnel might overwhelm the civilian community in which a large base is located—ring true with regard to other groups of voters? For example, consider "college towns," in which students, most of whom will likely remain in the community for around four years, outnumber non-student residents. Will students and nonstudents likely have distinctive political preferences? On what sorts of issues? Does it matter that the *average* American moves at least once each decade? What about untenured faculty members? Are they all that likely to remain in the same location?

With regard to student voting, consider New York's scheme. N.Y. Elec. Law § 5-104 (McKinney 1978) established a set of guidelines for determining who was a resident for voting purposes:

> 1. For the purpose of registering and voting no person shall be deemed to have gained or lost a residence by reason of his presence or absence while employed in the service of the United

States, nor while engaged in the navigation of the waters of this state, or of the United States, or of the high seas; nor while a student of any institution of learning; nor while kept at any welfare institution, asylum or other institution wholly or partly supported at public expense or by charity; nor while confined in any public prison.

2. In determining a voter's qualifications to register and vote, the board to which such application is made shall consider, in addition to the applicant's expressed intent, his conduct and all attendant surrounding circumstances relating thereto. The board taking such registration may consider the applicant's financial independence, business pursuits, employment, income sources, residence for income tax purposes, age, marital status, residence of parents, spouse and children, if any, leaseholds, sites of personal and real property owned by the applicant, motor vehicle and other personal property registration, and other such factors that it may reasonably deem necessary to determine the qualifications of an applicant to vote in an election district within its jurisdiction.

The New York statute, which identified certain categories of persons as particularly likely to include transients and subjected members of those classes "to the risk of a more searching inquiry than is applicable to prospective registrants generally" was upheld against a facial challenge in *Auerbach v. Rettaliata*, 765 F.2d 350 (2d Cir.1985). But in *Williams v. Salerno*, 792 F.2d 323 (2d Cir.1986), the Court of Appeals upheld an injunction that forbid the registrars in Westchester County from applying a more stringent substantive standard to the registration applications of students who lived in the dormitories of the State University campus at Purchase. The registrars had essentially determined that a dormitory room could never be a permanent domicile. The court disagreed with this erection of an irrebuttable presumption, since it would "have the effect of completely disenfranchising a person who abandons a former residence in a state other than New York with the intent of becoming a domiciliary of the community in New York where he or she attends school."

Ought it to matter that the decennial census counts college students as living where they attend school? Ought a state be permitted to charge nonresident tuition to persons who are qualified as residents for voting purposes?

8. *The Homeless.* The voting rights of homeless persons have become a topic of substantial interest. *See, e.g.,* Patricia M. Hanrahan, *No Home? No Vote*, 21 Hum. Rts. 8 (Winter 1994); Edward J. Smith, *Disenfranchisement of Homeless Persons*, 31 Wash. U.J. Urb. & Contemp. L. 225 (1987); Suzie Turner, Note, *Recognition of the Voting Rights of the Homeless*, 3 J.L. & Pol. 103 (1986). A critical issue in obtaining the right to vote has been how to define a homeless person's "residence." Although many states allow homeless persons to vote, roughly two-thirds require that homeless persons provide mailing addresses.

In general, courts have held that a fixed address is unnecessary as long as a homeless person can provide sufficient information about his or her usual location to allow assignment to a precinct. *See, e.g., Pitts v. Black*, 608 F.Supp. 696 (S.D.N.Y.1984) (striking down New York's requirement of a fixed address as a violation of the equal protection clause); *Collier v. Menzel*, 221 Cal.Rptr. 110 (Cal.Ct.App.1985) (holding that a Santa Barbara city park could be a place of habitation for voting purposes); *Board of Election Commissioners v. Chicago/Gary Area Union of the Homeless*, No. 86–29 (Ill. Cir. Ct. Sept. 26, 1986) (permitting homeless persons to register if they provided two pieces of identification and an address or location description sufficient to enable assignment to an appropriate voting location).

9. *Nonresidents.* What about voting by nonresidents? Ought jurisdictions to extend the right to vote to persons who live outside their boundaries but are nonetheless affected by the government's decisions? Consider the following cases.

In *Brown v. Chattanooga Board of Commissioners*, 722 F.Supp. 380 (E.D.Tenn.1989), black residents of Chattanooga challenged Tennessee Code Ann. § 2–2–107(a) and section 5.1 of the Chattanooga charter, which permitted nonresident "property qualification" as a basis for voting in municipal elections. The district court found that 547 nonresidents had registered to vote under these provisions, of whom 427 were known to be white (the others were black, other minorities, or of unknown race). About 32% of the city's population was black. Of the assessed real property in the city, 0.05% was owned by nonresidents. The district court began its analysis with the fact that the challenged provisions "expand rather than curtail the franchise." Thus, it determined that it should apply rational basis, rather than strict, scrutiny. Nonetheless, it concluded that the charter provision, although not the state law, was invalid:

> There is no question that city property owners, including nonresident property owners, have an interest in the conduct of municipal affairs, including property taxes, zoning, public services such as sewage and garbage disposal, and other matters that may affect their property. The difficulty, however, with Chattanooga's charter provision is that it contains no limitation of the number of people who can "vote" on a piece of property or no limitation as to any minimum property value required for the exercise of the franchise. The record in this case shows that as many as 23 nonresidents have been registered to vote on a single piece of property in the city. By way of further example, 15 nonresidents are registered to vote as co-owners of one parcel of property which has an assessed

value of $100.[24]

A nonresident who owns a one-fifteenth undivided interest in a lot assessed at $100 does not have a substantial interest in the operation of the city. Since the Chattanooga charter permits a nonresident who owns a trivial amount of property to vote in municipal elections, it does not further any rational governmental interest.... The Court, therefore, concludes that section 5.1 of the Chattanooga city charter violates of the equal protection clause of the Fourteenth Amendment. If Chattanooga wishes to give nonresident property owners the right to vote in municipal elections, the city charter must use means "more finely tailored to achieve the desired goal."

By contrast, other courts have upheld nonresident voting schemes using rational basis review. State law and the relevant municipal charter permitted nonresident property owners to vote in municipal elections in Savannah Beach, Georgia, a resort town, whose population at the time of the decisions in *Glisson v. Mayor and Councilmen of Savannah Beach*, 346 F.2d 135 (5th Cir.1965), and *Spahos v. Mayor and Councilmen of Savannah Beach*, 207 F.Supp. 688 (S.D.Ga.), *aff'd*, 371 U.S. 206 (1962), was 1,385, with a summer population of 2,500. Nonresident property owners owned real estate with an assessed valuation of $2,852,040, while permanent residents owned property assessed at $1,586,485. Nonresident voters were limited to those who owned property in Savannah Beach and who resided in Chatham County. There were 712 resident voters and 467 property qualified nonresident voters. The Georgia legislation under these facts was found to have a "rational" objective and to make a reasonable classification with respect to the right to vote in municipal elections. In addition, Alabama has permitted residents of cities with independent school systems nonetheless to vote in county school board elections. *See Hogencamp v. Lee County Board of Education*, 722 F.2d 720 (11th Cir.1984); *Phillips v. Andress*, 634 F.2d 947 (5th Cir.1981); *Creel v. Freeman*, 531 F.2d 286 (5th Cir.1976), *cert. denied*, 429 U.S. 1066 (1977). In these cases, the equal protection test of validity was whether the city residents had a "substantial interest" in the operation of the county school system.

Holt Civic Club v. City of Tuscaloosa, 439 U.S. 60 (1978), raised a converse claim. There, citizens who lived outside the municipal boundaries, but within the police jurisdiction, of Tuscaloosa, claimed that they were unconstitutionally barred from participating in Tuscaloosa's municipal elections. Justice Rehnquist's opinion for the Court centered on the appropriate standard of review:

24. As plaintiffs have pointed out, the law currently would permit Muammar el-Qaddafi to buy a parcel of land in Chattanooga and deed it to thousands of Libyans who would then be able to control the outcome of Chattanooga's elections.

Appellants focus their equal protection attack on the statute fixing the limits of municipal police jurisdiction and giving extraterritorial effect to municipal police and sanitary ordinances. Citing *Kramer v. Union Free School Dist.*, and cases following in its wake, appellants argue that the section creates a classification infringing on their right to participate in municipal elections. The State's denial of the franchise to police jurisdiction residents, appellants urge, can stand only if justified by a compelling state interest.

* * *

From [*Kramer*] and our other voting qualifications cases a common characteristic emerges: The challenged statute in each case denied the franchise to individuals who were physically resident within the geographic boundaries of the governmental entity concerned.... [O]ur cases have uniformly recognized that a government unit may legitimately restrict the right to participate in its political processes to those who reside within its borders....

Appellants' argument that extraterritorial extension of municipal powers requires concomitant extraterritorial extension of the franchise proves too much. The imaginary line defining a city's corporate limits cannot corral the influence of municipal actions. A city's decisions inescapably affect individuals living immediately outside its borders. The granting of building permits for high rise apartments, industrial plants, and the like on the city's fringe unavoidably contributes to problems of traffic congestion, school districting, and law enforcement immediately outside the city. A rate change in the city's sales or ad valorem tax could well have a significant impact on retailers and property values in areas bordering the city. The condemnation of real property on the city's edge for construction of a municipal garbage dump or waste treatment plant would have obvious implications for neighboring nonresidents. Indeed, the indirect extraterritorial effects of many purely internal municipal actions could conceivably have a heavier impact on surrounding environs than the direct regulation contemplated by Alabama's police jurisdiction statutes. Yet no one would suggest that nonresidents likely to be affected by this sort of municipal action have a constitutional right to participate in the political processes bringing it about.... The line heretofore marked by this Court's voting qualifications decisions coincides with the geographical boundary of the governmental unit at issue, and we hold that appellants' case, like their homes, falls on the farther side.

Thus stripped of its voting rights attire, the equal protection issue presented by appellants becomes whether the Alabama statutes giving extraterritorial force to certain municipal ordinances and powers bear some rational relationship to a legitimate state purpose....

Government, observed Mr. Justice Johnson, "is the science of experiment," *Anderson v. Dunn* (1821), and a State is afforded wide leeway when experimenting with the appropriate allocation of state legislative power....

The extraterritorial exercise of municipal powers is a governmental technique neither recent in origin nor unique to the State of Alabama. In this country 35 States authorize their municipal subdivisions to exercise governmental powers beyond their corporate limits. Although the extraterritorial municipal powers granted by these States vary widely, several States grant their cities more extensive or intrusive powers over bordering areas than those granted under the Alabama statutes.

In support of their equal protection claim, appellants suggest a number of "constitutionally preferable" governmental alternatives to Alabama's system of municipal police jurisdictions. For example, exclusive management of the police jurisdiction by county officials, appellants maintain, would be more "practical." From a political science standpoint, appellants' suggestions may be sound, but this Court does not sit to determine whether Alabama has chosen the soundest or most practical form of internal government possible. Authority to make those judgments resides in the state legislature, and Alabama citizens are free to urge their proposals to that body. Our inquiry is limited to the question whether "any state of facts reasonably may be conceived to justify" Alabama's system of police jurisdictions, *Salyer Land Co. v. Tulare Lake Basin Water Storage Dist.*, and in this case it takes but momentary reflection to arrive at an affirmative answer.

The Alabama Legislature could have decided that municipal corporations should have some measure of control over activities carried on just beyond their "city limit" signs, particularly since today's police jurisdiction may be tomorrow's annexation to the city proper. Nor need the city's interests have been the only concern of the legislature when it enacted the police jurisdiction statutes. Urbanization of any area brings with it a number of individuals who long both for the quiet of suburban or country living and for the career opportunities offered by the city's working environment. Unincorporated communities like Holt dot the rim of most major population centers in Alabama and elsewhere, and state legislatures have a legitimate interest in seeing that this substantial segment of the population does not go without basic municipal services such as police, fire, and health protection. Established cities are experienced in the delivery of such services, and the incremental cost of extending the city's responsibility in these areas to surrounding environs may be substantially less than the expense of establishing wholly new service organizations in each community.

Does *Holt* simply underscore that the standard of review is the entire ballgame?

What do you make of Justice Brennan's argument in dissent that geography was an "entirely arbitrary" bases for distinguishing between the enfranchised and the disenfranchised because the state provided no reason for defining the relevant political unit as the city of Tuscaloosa rather than the city together with its police jurisdiction?

Frank Michelman has argued that the disagreement in *Holt* turns on the majority and dissent's different "normative conception[s] of 'political community.'" Frank Michelman, *Conceptions of Democracy in American Constitutional Argument: Voting Rights*, 41 Fla. L. Rev. 443, 447 (1989). The majority seems to view the formal community as primary, constitutive in some sense of the political participation of its members—that is, republican—while Justice Brennan's view involves the classic liberalism of pluralistic, individualistic politics in which the central value of the right to vote is the ability it gives individuals to pursue their pre-political interests in the governing process. What are the limits, if any, to Justice Brennan's position? If there are limits, aren't they as formalistic, if more expansive, than the Court's?

How tenable is the *Holt* Court's assumption that pre-existing municipal boundaries are neutral phenomena? Remember that Alabama is also the home of *Gomillion v. Lightfoot*, 364 U.S. 339 (1960), to be discussed later in this Chapter. Would *Holt* come out differently if most of the residents of the police jurisdiction were black? What degree of intent to exclude would be required?

Businesses within the Tuscaloosa police jurisdiction paid only one-half the licensing fee charged to businesses within the city limits. We can easily imagine calibrating revenue raised from a fringe area like Holt to the services actually provided. But the "right to vote" has more of an all or nothing quality and isn't as easily parcelled out in more finegrained ways. One might think residents of Holt should have "a bit of a say" but not as much influence over city policy as city residents. Could some form of weighted voting—where, for example, each nonresident got one-half a vote in city elections—capture this intuition?

10. *Overseas voters.* The Uniformed and Overseas Citizens Absentee Voting Act, 42 U.S.C. §§ 1973ff to 1973ff–6 (1994), requires states to permit certain voters to continue to participate by absentee ballot in federal elections, that is, presidential and congressional elections. The Act applies to two groups: military service personnel and "overseas voters"—defined as persons who reside outside the United States and who are or "but for such residence would be" qualified to vote in the last domestic location in which they were domiciled. In light of the previous notes, is the Act justified? Is the Act's restriction to federal elections simply an artifact of Congress' desire to assure constitutionality (since Art. I, § 2, cl. 4 and Art. II, § 1, cl. 4 accord Congress power to regulate federal elections) or does it also reflect a difference between being a member of the national and local communities?

In *Igartua De La Rosa v. United States*, 32 F.3d 8 (1st Cir.1994), *cert. denied*, 514 U.S. 1049 (1995), the court of appeals rejected an equal protection challenge brought under the Act by American citizens living in Puerto Rico who had previously lived, and voted, on the mainland. They claimed that it was unfair that citizens who moved overseas could continue to vote in presidential and congressional elections while citizens who moved to Puerto Rico could not. Their claim was assessed under rational basis scrutiny—because the court found that the Act limited states' rights to disenfranchise former residents, thus expanding the overall right to vote, rather than contracting it—and the court found that it was reasonable for Congress to assume that voters who moved within the United States would continue to vote in federal elections. (Voters in Puerto Rico, for example, vote for the Resident Commissioner, in what is statutorily defined as a "federal election.") That those elections did not include elections for President or members of Congress was a function of the constitutional text, which allocates the selection of presidential electors to the states, Art. II, § 1, cl. 2, and seats in Congress among the states, Art. I, § 2, cl. 1.

11. *Voter Registration*. The final barrier to participation is the existence of registration requirements. This issue is taken up in the final section of the chapter, along with the new National Voter Registration Act of 1993, 42 U.S.C. §§ 1973gg to 1973gg–10 (1994) (the so-called "Motor Voter" law). At this point, consider the following question: could the entire existence of a voter registration regime be justified under strict scrutiny given that one state—North Dakota—has no registration requirement and several other states have long permitted voters to register on election day at the local polling place?

12. *"General" versus "Special Purpose" Elections*. In *Kramer*, the Court applied strict scrutiny despite the fact that, unlike city councils, county commissions, or state legislatures, school boards do not exercise "general legislative powers," that is, their jurisdiction extends only to a limited range of subject matters. Are there some elected governmental bodies whose jurisdiction is so limited and specialized that the franchise can be restricted to a subset of resident, adult citizens? Consider in this regard, for example, *Salyer Land Co. v. Tulare Lake Basin Water Storage District*, 410 U.S. 719 (1973), which is discussed in more detail in Chapter 3. *Salyer* concerned elections for the board of directors for a state-created water storage district. Under California law, only landowners were permitted to vote in water storage district general elections, and votes in those elections were apportioned according to the assessed valuation of the land (a sort of "one acre, one vote" system). In upholding a challenge by non-landowning residents, the Court distinguished *Kramer*, and cases such as *Phoenix v. Kolodziejski*, 399 U.S. 204 (1970), and *Cipriano v. City of Houma*, 395 U.S. 701 (1969), which had dealt with bond elections. One-person, one-vote did not apply, the Court explained:

> The appellee district in this case, although vested with some typical governmental powers, has relatively limited authority. Its primary purpose, indeed the reason for its existence, is to provide for the acquisition, storage, and distribution of water for farming in the Tulare Lake Basin. It provides no other general public services such as schools, housing, transportation, utilities, roads, or anything else of the type ordinarily financed by a municipal body. There are no towns, shops, hospitals, or other facilities designed to improve the quality of life within the district boundaries, and it does not have a fire department, police, buses, or trains.
>
> Not only does the district not exercise what might be thought of as "normal governmental" authority, but its actions disproportionately affect landowners. All of the costs of district projects are assessed against land by assessors in proportion to the benefits received. Likewise, charges for services rendered are collectible from persons receiving their benefit in proportion to the services....
>
> Under these circumstances, it is quite understandable that the statutory framework for election of directors of the appellee focuses on the land benefited, rather than on people as such.... The franchise is extended to landowners, whether they reside in the district or out of it, and indeed whether or not they are natural persons who would be entitled to vote in a more traditional political election. Appellants do not challenge the enfranchisement of nonresident landowners or of corporate landowners for purposes of election of the directors of appellee. Thus, to sustain their contention that all residents of the district must be accorded a vote would not result merely in the striking down of an exclusion from what was otherwise a delineated class, but would instead engraft onto the statutory scheme a wholly new class of voters in addition to those enfranchised by the statute.

How would you explain the difference between school board elections, which *Kramer* seems to view as open to all voters, whatever the objective level of their "interest" and elections such as those involved in *Salyer*? Can you think of other elections which should be similarly limited? Note how *Salyer* conflates the analysis of who can participate (landowners only) with the question of what voting rule should be used (one-acre, one-vote).

C. The Struggle for Black Enfranchisement

The Fifteenth Amendment barred racial discrimination in voting. During the Reconstruction period following the Civil War, and even during the first few years of Redemption, the period of reassertion of state autonomy and white supremacy beginning after the election of 1876, black male turnout (remember that the Reconstruction Amendments did nothing to enfranchise female voters) remained high: in all but two Southern states, a majority of adult black males voted in the presidential election of 1880. Nonetheless, by the first decade of the twentieth century, virtually all black voters had been eliminated from the rolls across the South, through a combination of force and the imposition of restrictive (and often fraudulently administered) voting qualifications. In Louisiana, for example, there were 127,923 black voters and 126,884 white voters on the registration rolls in 1888 (the population of the state was about fifty percent black); by 1910 only 730 blacks (less than 0.5 percent of the adult male population) were still registered. In 27 of the state's sixty parishes, no blacks were registered; in another nine, only one was registered. For extensive accounts of this process across the South, see J. Morgan Kousser, The Shaping of Southern Politics: Suffrage Restrictions and the Establishment of the One-Party South, 1880–1910 (1974); Armand Derfner, *Racial Discrimination and the Right To Vote*, 26 Vand. L. Rev. 523 (1973).

Part of the reason for the decline of black suffrage was Congress' inability or unwillingness to enforce the Reconstruction Amendments' guarantees. During the last decade of the nineteenth century, for example, although the Republican-controlled House refused to seat some southern Democrats on the grounds that their election had been procured by fraud, Congress declined to act on proposals to investigate allegations of black exclusion from the Alabama senatorial election of 1894 or to enforce the provisions of section 2 of the Fourteenth Amendment that provided for a reduction in the size of a state's House delegation if the state discriminated in voting. At the same time, there were a series of proposals by southern senators and representatives to repeal the Fifteenth Amendment outright.

The Supreme Court also played a pivotal role in disenfranchisement, both through decisions striking down and eviscerating various federal protections of black voting rights, see, e.g., *United States v. Cruikshank*, 92 U.S. 542 (1875) (dismissing indictments arising out of the Colfax Massacre, in which a white mob murdered a group of black voters in Louisiana); *United States v. Reese*, 92 U.S. 214 (1875) (striking down other sections of the 1870 Enforcement Act as beyond congressional power), and through decisions upholding various state efforts at disenfranchisement, see, e.g., *Williams v. Mississippi*, 170 U.S. 213 (1898).

Giles v. Harris
189 U.S. 475 (1903).

■ MR. JUSTICE HOLMES delivered the opinion of the court.

This is a bill in equity brought by a colored man, on behalf of himself "and on behalf of more than five thousand negroes, citizens of the county of Montgomery, Alabama, similarly situated and circumstanced as himself," against the board of registrars of that county....

The allegations of the bill may be summed up as follows. The plaintiff.... applied in March, 1902, for registration as a voter, and was refused arbitrarily on the ground of his color, together with large numbers of other duly qualified negroes, while all white men were registered. The same thing was done all over the State. Under section 187 of article 8 of the Alabama constitution persons registered before January 1, 1903, remain electors for life unless they become disqualified by certain crimes, etc., while after that date severer tests come into play which would exclude, perhaps, a large part of the black race. Therefore, by the refusal, the plaintiff and the other negroes excluded were deprived not only of their votes at an election which has taken place since the bill was filed, but of the permanent advantage incident to registration before 1903. The white men generally are registered for good under the easy test and the black men are likely to be kept out in the future as in the past. This refusal to register the blacks was part of a general scheme to disfranchise them, to which the defendants and the State itself, according to the bill, were parties. The defendants accepted their office for the purpose of carrying out the scheme. The part taken by the State, that is, by the white population which framed the constitution, consisted in shaping that instrument so as to give opportunity and effect to the wholesale fraud which has been practised.

* * *

It seems to us impossible to grant the equitable relief which is asked.... The difficulties which we cannot overcome are two, and the first is this: The plaintiff alleges that the whole registration scheme of the Alabama constitution is a fraud upon the Constitution of the United States, and asks us to declare it void. But of course he could not maintain a bill for a mere declaration in the air. He does not try to do so, but asks to be registered as a party qualified under the void instrument. If then we accept the conclusion which it is the chief purpose of the bill to maintain, how can we make the court a party to the unlawful scheme by accepting it and adding another voter to its fraudulent lists?.... It is impossible simply to shut our eyes, put the plaintiff on the lists, be they honest or fraudulent, and leave the determination of the fundamental question for the future....
It is not an answer to say that if all the blacks who are qualified according to the letter of the instrument were registered, the fraud would be cured. In the first place, there is no probability that any way now is open by which more than a few could be registered, but if all could be the difficulty would

not be overcome. If the sections of the constitution concerning registration were illegal in their inception, it would be a new doctrine in constitutional law that the original invalidity could be cured by an administration which defeated their intent. We express no opinion as to the alleged fact of their unconstitutionality beyond saying that we are not willing to assume that they are valid, in the face of the allegations and main object of the bill, for the purpose of granting the relief which it was necessary to pray in order that that object should be secured.

The other difficulty is of a different sort, and strikingly reinforces the argument that equity cannot undertake now, any more than it has in the past, to enforce political rights.... In determining whether a court of equity can take jurisdiction, one of the first questions is what it can do to enforce any order that it may make. This is alleged to be the conspiracy of a State.... The Circuit Court has no constitutional power to control its action by any direct means. And if we leave the State out of consideration, the court has as little practical power to deal with the people of the State in a body. The bill imports that the great mass of the white population intends to keep the blacks from voting. To meet such an intent something more than ordering the plaintiff's name to be inscribed upon the lists of 1902 will be needed. If the conspiracy and the intent exist, a name on a piece of paper will not defeat them. Unless we are prepared to supervise the voting in that State by officers of the court, it seems to us that all that the plaintiff could get from equity would be an empty form. Apart from damages to the individual, relief from a great political wrong, if done, as alleged, by the people of a state and the State itself, must be given by them or by the legislative and political department of the Government of the United States.

* * *

■ MR. JUSTICE BREWER dissenting.

* * *

[I cannot agree with] the proposition that the case presented by the plaintiff's bill is not strictly a legal one and entitling a party to a judicial hearing and decision. He alleges that he is a citizen of Alabama, entitled to vote; that he desired to vote at an election for representative in Congress; that without registration he could not vote, and that registration was wrongfully denied him by the defendants. That many others were similarly treated does not destroy his rights or deprive him of relief in the courts. That such relief will be given has been again and again affirmed in both National and state courts.

[....] I refer to two recent cases which bear directly upon the present question. *Wiley v. Sinkler*, 179 U.S. 58, was an action brought in the Circuit Court of the United States by the plaintiff to recover damages of an election board for wilfully rejecting his vote for a member of the House of Representatives. We held that the court had jurisdiction, and said:

"This action is brought against election officers to recover damages for their rejection of the plaintiff's vote for a member of the House of Representative of the United States. The complaint, by alleging that the plaintiff was at the time, under the constitution and laws of the State of South Carolina and the Constitution and laws of the United States, a duly qualified elector of the State, shows that the action is brought under the Constitution and laws of the United States. The damages are laid at the sum of $2500. What amount of damages the plaintiff shall recover in such an action is peculiarly appropriate for the determination of a jury, and no opinion of the court upon that subject can justify it in holding that the amount in controversy was insufficient to support the jurisdiction of the Circuit Court...."

Again, in *Swafford v. Templeton*, 185 U.S. 487, which, like the former case, was one brought in the Circuit Court of the United States to recover damages for the alleged wrongful refusal by the defendants as election officers to permit the plaintiff to vote at a national election for a member of the House of Representative, it was held that the court had jurisdiction.

* * *

It seems to me nothing need be added to these decisions, and unless they are to be considered as overruled they are decisive of this case.

MR. JUSTICE BROWN also dissents.

■ MR. JUSTICE HARLAN dissenting.

[Justice Harlan's primary argument was that the Supreme Court lacked jurisdiction over Giles's case because nothing in the record showed that the amount in dispute met the then-existing jurisdictional amount of $2000.] Upon this record, I will not formulate and discuss my views upon the merits of this case. But to avoid misapprehension, I may add that my conviction is that upon the facts alleged in the bill (if the record showed a sufficient value of the matter in dispute) the plaintiff is entitled to relief in respect of his right to be registered as a voter. I agree with Mr. Justice Brewer that it is competent for the courts to give relief in such cases as this.

NOTES AND QUESTIONS

1. *Giles* is an extremely important moment in the twentieth-century disenfranchisement of American blacks, for it signalled that, the Fifteenth Amendment notwithstanding, the Supreme Court would not intervene. Jackson W. Giles, born in 1859, had lived and voted in Montgomery, Alabama, where he was a janitor at the courthouse, for nearly 30 years before adoption of the 1901 Alabama Constitution. And in his complaint, he alleged that 75,000 other qualified black voters had been similarly denied the right to register.

2. Is Justice Holmes's opinion disingenuous? Note the Catch–22 he creates. Contemporary constitutional law has a variety of techniques for avoiding the problem he identifies, such as as-applied challenges and affirmative injunctions.

Justice Holmes' opinion might be read to turn on the distinction between equitable and legal relief. Near the end, Holmes suggests that "damages to the individual" for the alleged constitutional violations might be judicially available, even though "equity cannot undertake now, any more than it has in the past, to enforce political rights."

In subsequent litigation, the persistent Giles accepted this seeming invitation and brought a damages action on his own behalf against the board of registrars, seeking $5000 for their refusal to register him. He also brought a petition for mandamus, seeking that the courts order the board of registrars to register him and other eligible black voters.

The Alabama Supreme Court affirmed the dismissal of both complaints on two grounds: (1) that if Giles were right that the provisions of the Alabama Constitution violated the Fourteenth and Fifteenth Amendments, it then followed that the registrars had no authority to register him at all, and "their refusal to do so cannot be made the predicate for a recovery of damages against them;" (2) on the other hand, if the registrars did have authority to register voters, their decisions about who was qualified were judicial acts for which the registrars were legally immune.

In *Giles v. Teasley*, 193 U.S. 146 (1904), the Supreme Court affirmed. The Court held that the first ground cited by the Alabama Supreme Court constituted an independent and adequate state-law basis for dismissing Giles's federal claims. Thus, the Supreme Court held that it had no jurisdiction to review these decisions of the Alabama Supreme Court. Justice Day's opinion acknowledged "the gravity of the statements" of Giles's complaints, but reminded him that *Giles v. Harris* had already explained "[t]he great difficulty of reaching the political action of a State through remedies afforded in the courts, state or federal." Thus, Giles's efforts to seek damages, injunctive relief, or mandamus were all judicially rejected.

3. From another perspective, Holmes's opinion might be thought remarkable not for its disingenuousness, but for its candor. Holmes had several more technical legal grounds available which would have led to the same result of dismissing the complaint for lack of federal jurisdiction, but he chose not to rest on any of them: (1) the complaint failed to allege the requisite amount in controversy necessary for federal jurisdiction (at that time, $2,000)—this is the ground on which Justice Harlan would have dismissed; (2) the statute under which Giles sued protected federal rights against deprivations that arose from state "statutes" and "customs," but did not expressly include state constitutions—Holmes mentioned this problem but did not address it; (3) the claim might have been treated as moot, since the 1902 elections for which Giles sought registration had taken place already—the very approach the Court, before Holmes joined it, had taken in *Mills v. Green*, 159 U.S. 651 (1895), in which the Court dismissed as moot a challenge to South Carolina's disenfranchisement laws of the 1890's.

Instead, Holmes seemed determined to confront head on the problem of racial disenfranchisement—which his opinion itself called a "new and extraordinary situation"—only to proclaim judicial impotence in the face of it. Does *Giles* confirm the theory that "conformity of the law to the wishes of the dominant power in the community was the fundamental tenet of [Holmes'] legal theory?" Gary J. Aichele, Oliver Wendell Holmes, Jr. 145 (1989). Is *Giles* evidence of Holmes "viewing electoral majorities as unanswerable military victors?" David Luban, *Justice Holmes and the Metaphysics of Judicial Restraint*, 44 Duke L.J. 449, 515 (1994). Does it reflect a resigned moral relativism that some attribute to Holmes's experience fighting for the North in the Civil War, from which Holmes drew the lesson that "[d]eep seated preferences [could] not be argued about," Oliver Wendell Holmes, *Natural Law*, 32 Harv. L. Rev. 40, (1918), and that a judge must never "forget that what seem to him to be first principles [are] believed by half his fellow men to be wrong," Oliver Wendell Holmes, *Law and the Court* (1913), in The Essential Holmes 147 (Richard A. Posner, ed., 1992)? Or does *Giles* reflect a belief that "adjudication should and must be result-oriented?" Thomas C. Grey, *Holmes and Legal Pragmatism*, 41 Stan. L. Rev. 787, 847 (1989). Or more starkly, that "[l]aw stands impotent before history?" Owen M. Fiss, History of the Supreme Court of the United States: The Troubled Beginnings of the Modern State, 1888–1910, at 373 (1993). *See generally* Eben Moglen, *Holmes' Legacy and the New Constitutional History*, 108 Harv. L. Rev. 2027, 2039–40, 2043–44 (1995) (suggesting the unexamined importance of the civil war experience to the Court's social thought).

4. The dissents of Justices Brewer and Harlan might be seen as an early recognition of the view, not to be adopted by the Supreme Court until much later, that voting rights are constitutionally "fundamental" and warrant the strictest judicial scrutiny. Justice Brewer had written the opinion in *Berea College v. Kentucky*, 211 U.S. 45 (1908), upholding Kentucky's statute making it a crime for a private school to permit racially-integrated education. Justice Brewer had also written for the Court in *Louisville, New Orleans & Texas Railway v. Mississippi*, 133 U.S. 587 (1890), rejecting a commerce clause challenge to a state law requiring all carriers, including those engaged in interstate transportation, to enforce racial segregation. Similarly, Justice Harlan had upheld the decision of a Georgia school district to close its black high school while maintaining a high school for whites. *Cumming v. Richmond County Board of Education*, 175 U.S. 528 (1899). Thus, in *Giles* Justices Brewer and Harlan appear to have recognized voting as special, distinct in terms of individual rights and the judicial role from areas such as public education and public accommodations.

5. Press reaction to the *Giles* decision recognized its sweep. One publication characterized the Fifteenth Amendment as "suspended in fact." *Recent Discussion of the Fifteenth Amendment*, Harper's Weekly, July 11, 1903, at 1144. A New York Times editorial termed *Giles* a "monstrous denial of justice and a humiliating admission of helplessness by the court," but concluded that "it is well that the court has decided as it has." *The Alabama Decision*, N.Y. Times, May 1, 1903, at 8.

6. *Giles* suggested that enforcement of voting rights was a political function to be handled by Congress. Within a month of the decision in *Giles v. Teasley*, however, Congress demonstrated yet another Catch-22 for black voters.

In the 1902 House elections, Asbury Lever had defeated Alexander Dantzler in South Carolina's Seventh District. Dantzler challenged the results, claiming that Lever's victory was illegitimate because South Carolina's new disenfranchising constitution violated the Reconstruction Act of June 25, 1868. In particular he claimed that "thousands of colored voters" had been disenfranchised under South Carolina's new constitution, in violation of both the 1868 Act and unspecified provisions of the federal constitution. But the House Committee on Elections confirmed Lever's victory, and declined "to put on record its opinion" of Dantzler's constitutional claim. Instead, it explained:

> However desirable it may be for a legislative body to retain control of the decision as to the election and qualification of its members, it is quite certain that a legislative body is not the ideal body to pass judicially upon the constitutionality of the enactments of other bodies. We have in this country a proper forum for the decision of constitutional and other judicial questions. If any citizen of South Carolina who was entitled to vote under the constitution of that state in 1868 is now deprived by the provisions of the present constitution, he has the right to tender himself for registration and for voting, and in case his right is denied, to bring suit in a proper court for the purpose of enforcing his right or recovering damages for its denial.
>
> That suit can be carried by him, if necessary to the Supreme Court of the United States. If the United States Supreme Court shall declare in such case that the "fundamental conditions" in the reconstruction acts were valid and constitutional and that the State constitutions are in violation of those acts, and hence invalid and unconstitutional, every State will be compelled to immediately bow in submission to the decision. The decision of the Supreme Court would be binding and would be a positive declaration of the law of the land which could not be denied or challenged.
>
> On the contrary, the decision of the House of Representatives upon this grave judicial question would not be considered as

binding or effective in any case except the one acted upon or as a precedent for future action in the House itself.

H.R. Rep. No. 1740 at 3 (1904).

7. *Giles* took place against the backdrop of Redemption, the failure to enforce federal civil rights legislation in the 1890's, and a pervasive effort across the South to disenfranchise black, and sometimes also poor white, voters. Given the rising tide of white supremacism, could the Court effectively have enfranchised black voters without federal legislative or executive support? With respect to whether a judicial remedy was available, consider the following plaintive editorial response to the decision from The New York Daily Tribune, April 29, 1908:

> Somewhere, somehow, there must be a way of passing on the constitutionality of State laws which plainly nullify the spirit of the federal Constitution, and it is no more an assumption of the administrative functions of a State government for the court to declare that State authorities cannot deprive negroes of a ballot on pretexts which do not exclude white men than it is for the court to overrule any other action of a State or its officers.

Note that the same paper reported the previous day that an unnamed Justice had asserted "that the legitimate outcome of the power [Giles asked the Court to assume] would be that the court of equity would take charge of the State government and administer it, which is an unheard of proposition." N.Y. Daily Tribune, April 28, 1908.

In this light, consider the Court's decision a decade later in *Guinn v. United States*, 238 U.S. 347 (1915). *Guinn* involved a federal prosecution of two Oklahoma election officers for having conspired to deprive certain black citizens, on account of their race, of the right to vote in the 1910 congressional election. The officials enforced a newly enacted state constitutional amendment that provided that:

> "No person shall be registered as an elector of this State or be allowed to vote in any election herein, unless he be able to read and write any section of the constitution of the State of Oklahoma; but no person who was, on January 1, 1866, or at any time prior thereto, entitled to vote under any form of government, or who at that time resided in some foreign nation, and no lineal descendant of such person, shall be denied the right to register and vote because of his inability to so read and write sections of such constitution."

The United States argued that the so-called "Grandfather Clause," which exempted persons who were eligible to vote on January 1, 1866, and their lineal descendants from the literacy test, violated the Fifteenth Amendment: that date had been picked because it antedated passage of the Fifteenth Amendment and black enfranchisement; thus, virtually all whites, but virtually no blacks, would be exempt from the literacy test. The Supreme Court agreed:

> We have difficulty in finding words to more clearly demonstrate the conviction we entertain that this standard has the characteristics which the Government attributes to it than does the mere statement of the text. It is true it contains no express words of an exclusion from the standard which it establishes of any person on account of race, color, or previous condition of servitude prohibited by the Fifteenth Amendment, but the standard itself inherently brings that result into existence since it is based purely upon a period of time before the enactment of the Fifteenth Amendment and makes that period the controlling and dominant test of the right of suffrage. In other words, we seek in vain for any ground which would sustain any other interpretation but that the provision, recurring to the conditions existing before the Fifteenth Amendment was adopted and the continuance of which the Fifteenth Amendment prohibited, proposed by in substance and effect lifting those conditions over to a period of time after the Amendment to make them the basis of the right to suffrage conferred in direct and positive disregard of the Fifteenth Amendment. And the same result, we are of opinion, is demonstrated by considering whether it is possible to discover any basis of reason for the standard thus fixed other than the purpose above stated. We say this because we are unable to discover how, unless the prohibiting of the Fifteenth Amendment were considered, the slightest reason was afforded for basing the classification upon a period of time prior to the Fifteenth Amendment. Certainly it cannot be said that there was any peculiar necromancy in the time named which engendered attributes affecting the qualification to vote which would not exist at another and different period unless the Fifteenth Amendment was in view.

Id. at 364–65. Can the result in *Guinn* be squared with the result in *Giles* by seeing *Guinn* as judicial enforcement of federal legislative and executive commands? Is Justice Holmes's essential pessimism borne out by the post-*Guinn* experience? After the invalidation of the Grandfather Clause, the Oklahoma Legislature enacted a new registration scheme in 1916. Persons who had voted in the general election of 1914, which had been conducted under the amendment struck down in *Guinn*, automatically remained qualified voters but all other persons had to apply for registration between April 30, 1916 and May 11, 1916, if qualified at that time, or be forever barred from registering. Lane, a black citizen of Oklahoma, did not attempt to register until 1934, at which time registrars used the 1916 law to refuse his application. In *Lane v. Wilson*, 307 U.S. 268 (1939), the Supreme Court struck down Oklahoma's 1916 scheme. The state relied on *Giles*, arguing that Lane's claim that the Oklahoma scheme was invalid meant that there was no Oklahoma statute under which he could register and therefore that no right to registration has been denied. The Court distinguished *Giles* on the ground that Giles had raised an equitable claim, while Lane was advancing a legal one:

> This case is very different from *Giles v. Harris*—the difference having been explicitly foreshadowed by *Giles v. Harris* itself. In that case this Court declared "we are not prepared to say that an action at law could not be maintained on the facts alleged in the bill." That is precisely the basis of the present action, brought under [the prior version of 42 U.S.C. § 1983].... Whosoever "under color of any statute" subjects another to such discrimination thereby deprives him of what the Fifteenth Amendment secures and, under § [1983] becomes "liable to the party injured in an action at law." The theory of the plaintiff's action is that the defendants, acting under color of [the Oklahoma statute] did discriminate against him because that Section inherently operates discriminatorily. If this claim is sustained his right to sue under [§ 1983] follows. The basis of this action is inequality of treatment though under color of law, not denial of the right to vote.

On the merits, the Court concluded that the 1916 law violated the Fifteenth Amendment:

> The Amendment nullifies sophisticated as well as simple-minded modes of discrimination. It hits onerous procedural requirements which effectively handicap exercise of the franchise by the colored race although the abstract right to vote may remain unrestricted as to race. When in *Guinn v. United States*, the Oklahoma "grandfather clause" was found violative of the Fifteenth Amendment, Oklahoma was confronted with the serious task of devising a new registration system consonant with her own political ideas but also consistent with the Federal Constitution. We are compelled to conclude, however reluctantly, that the legislation of 1916 partakes too much of the infirmity of the "grandfather clause" to be able to survive.

Only persons who were beneficiaries of the unconstitutional Grandfather Clause regime were exempted from the onerous 12-day registration window. "We believe that the opportunity thus given negro voters to free themselves from the effects of discrimination to which they should never have been subjected was too cabined and confined. The restrictions imposed must be judged with reference to those for whom they were designed. It must be remembered that we are dealing with a body of citizens lacking the habits and traditions of political independence and otherwise living in circumstances which do not encourage initiative and enterprise."

Does Justice Frankfurter's distinction of *Giles* make sense? Compare his maneuvering around *Giles* here with his attempt in *Gomillion v. Lightfoot*, 364 U.S. 339 (1960), to get around his view in *Colegrove v. Green*, 328 U.S. 549 (1946), that apportionment claims were nonjusticiable.

1. TECHNIQUES FOR OUTRIGHT DISENFRANCHISEMENT

Giles, *Guinn*, *Lane*, *Lassiter*, and *Harper* illustrate the major techniques for black disenfranchisement: force, restrictive and arbitrary registration practices, poll taxes, and literacy tests. Every state in the Deep South adopted a new constitution in the period between 1890 and 1908, and every constitution employed at least one, and often several, of these disenfranchising devices. *See* J. Morgan Kousser, The Shaping of Southern Politics: Suffrage Restrictions and the Establishment of the One–Party South, 1880–1910 (1974); Armand Derfner, *Racial Discrimination and the Right To Vote*, 26 Vand. L. Rev. 523 (1973).

The states were quite explicit about the purpose of these new provisions.

> The Virginia poll tax was born of a desire to disenfranchise the Negro. At the Virginia Constitutional Convention of 1902, the sponsor of the suffrage plan of which the poll tax was an integral part frankly expressed the purpose of the suffrage proposal:
>
> "Discrimination! Why, that is precisely what we propose; that, exactly, is what this Convention was elected for—to discriminate to the very extremity of permissible action under the limitations of the Federal Constitution, with a view to the elimination of every negro voter who can be gotten rid of, legally, without materially impairing the numerical strength of the white electorate."

Harman v. Forssenius, 380 U.S. 528 (1965). *See also United States v. State of Louisiana,* 225 F.Supp. 353 (E.D.La.1963), *aff'd,* 380 U.S. 145 (1965) ("Judge Thomas J. Semmes, Chairman of the Judiciary Committee of the [1898 Louisiana Constitutional] Convention and a former president of the American Bar Association, described the purpose of the Convention: 'We [meet] here to establish the supremacy of the white race, and the white race constitutes the Democratic party of this State.' The Convention of 1898 'interpreted its mandate from the "people" to be, to disfranchise as many Negroes and as few whites as possible.'"). Consider also the account of Alabama's convention offered in *Hunter v. Underwood, supra.*

A NOTE ON THE CONTEMPORANEOUS EFFECT OF THE POLL TAX

1. For detailed information on the original context of the poll tax, see J. Morgan Kousser, The Shaping of Southern Politics: Suffrage Restrictions and the Establishment of the One–Party South, 1880–1910, at 63–72 (1974). By 1904, every ex-Confederate state had adopted the poll tax. How significant economically was a $1 or $2 poll tax at the time? The average per capita income, including non-cash income, in the eleven ex-Confederate states was $86 in 1880 and $100 in 1900; Kousser estimates that the bottom 76 percent of the population averaged only $55–$64 per person. In addition, those who worked the land tended to have little cash at all during the year until crops could be harvested and sold; by 1900 three-fourths of blacks in the South were sharecroppers or tenant farmers. Moreover, in many states the poll tax was cumulative—failure to pay in one year had to be made up in subsequent years (in Georgia and Alabama, the taxes could cumulate indefinitely). Note that the point of the tax was not so much to collect it as to bar voters who did not pay it; Kousser reports finding no recorded prosecutions of non-payers.

2. How effective was the poll tax in disenfranchising blacks? Historians have disagreed on this question. Kousser compares black turnout rates in Presidential elections in two states that had similar black populations during the 1880's: Georgia, when it had the poll tax, and Florida, when it did not. Turnout among black voters in Florida was consistently more than twice that in Georgia. Contemporaries certainly believed the poll tax enormously effective. One knowledgeable observer considered Georgia's cumulative poll tax "the most effective bar to Negro suffrage ever devised." A member of the Mississippi Constitutional Convention argued in 1902 that the tax had proven "the most effective instrumentality of Negro disenfranchisement;" similar statements from political actors can easily be found in other states.

3. Historians differ even more over whether the tax was intended to include whites as well. Some assert that the tax was a principal method for discouraging poorer whites, who tended to be Populists, from challenging the disenfranchisers' control of southern politics. For Alabama, one estimate is that nearly 25 percent of adult white men were disenfranchised solely as a result of the poll tax in 1904; the same figure is estimated for the effect of the Virginia poll tax between 1876 and 1882. Kousser notes that newspapers at the time warned of the effect on whites of the poll tax, but that no grandfather provisions or other means to exempt whites were attached. Although disenfranchising poor whites was far more difficult than disenfranchising blacks to defend publicly at the time, Kousser quotes numerous sources, such as a North Carolina Democratic party paper, which cast the campaign for suffrage restrictions as designed to rid the state of "the danger of the rule of Negroes and the lower classes of whites."

2. THE WHITE PRIMARY CASES

Perhaps the device that occasioned the most litigation in the Supreme Court was the "White Primary."

Nixon v. Herndon
273 U.S. 536 (1927).

■ MR. JUSTICE HOLMES delivered the opinion of the Court.

[A Texas statute regulating primary elections provided that "in no event shall a negro be eligible to participate in a Democratic party primary election held in the State of Texas." Nixon brought suit against the Judges of Elections seeking damages of $5000.]

* * *

The petition alleges that the plaintiff is a negro, a citizen of the United States and of Texas and a resident of El Paso, and in every way qualified to vote, as set forth in detail, except that the statute ... interferes with his right; ... that the plaintiff, being a member of the Democratic party, sought to vote but was denied the right by defendants; and that [the Texas] statute is contrary to the Fourteenth and Fifteenth Amendments to the Constitution of the United States. The defendants moved to dismiss upon the ground that the subject matter of the suit was political and not within the jurisdiction of the Court and that no violation of the Amendments was shown....

The objection that the subject matter of the suit is political is little more than a play upon words. Of course the petition concerns political action but it alleges and seeks to recover for private damage. That private damage may be caused by such political action and may be recovered for in a suit at law hardly has been doubted for over two hundred years....

The important question is whether the statute can be sustained. But although we state it as a question the answer does not seem to us open to a doubt. We find it unnecessary to consider the Fifteenth Amendment, because it seems to us hard to imagine a more direct and obvious infringement of the Fourteenth. That Amendment, while it applies to all, was passed, as we know, with a special intent to protect the blacks from discrimination against them. That Amendment "not only gave citizenship and the privileges of citizenship to persons of color, but it denied to any State the power to withhold from them the equal protection of the laws.... What is this but declaring that the law in the States shall be the same for the black as for the white; that all persons, whether colored or white, shall stand equal before the laws of the States, and, in regard to the colored race, for whose protection the amendment was primarily designed, that no discrimination shall be made against them by law because of their color?" The statute of Texas in the teeth of the prohibitions referred to assumes to forbid negroes to take part in a primary election .... States may do a good deal of classifying that it is difficult to believe rational, but there are limits, and it is too clear for extended argument that color cannot be made the basis of a statutory classification affecting the right set up in this case.

NOTES AND QUESTIONS

1. Can Justice Holmes's positions in *Giles* and *Nixon v. Herndon* be reconciled?

2. Promptly after the decision in *Nixon v. Herndon*, Texas passed a new statute. This statute provided that "every political party in this State through its State Executive Committee shall have the power to prescribe the qualifications of its own members and shall in its own way determine who shall be qualified to vote or otherwise participate in such political party...." The Democratic Party State Executive Committee then adopted a resolution providing that only "white democrats" could participate in the upcoming primaries. Once again, Nixon sued the election judges who refused to give him a ballot. In *Nixon v. Condon*, 286 U.S. 73 (1932), the Supreme Court struck down the new statute. The defendants argued that the Fourteenth Amendment did not apply because here the exclusion was the work of a private actor—the political party—rather than the state. Nixon responded that "if heed is to be given to the realities of political life," the party should be treated as "the instruments by which government becomes a living thing." The Court sidestepped the issue by resting its decision on a technicality: Texas gave party executive committees, rather than party conventions, the power to regulate participation; the executive committee's power thus flowed from the state rather than the party membership:

> The pith of the matter is simply this, that when those agencies are invested with an authority independent of the will of the association in whose name they undertake to speak, they become to that extent the organs of the State itself, the repositories of official power.... What they do in that relation, they must do in submission to the mandates of equality and liberty that bind officials everywhere.... Whether in given circumstances parties or their committees are agencies of government within the Fourteenth or the Fifteenth Amendment is a question which this court will determine for itself....
>
> With the problem thus laid bare and its essentials exposed to view, the case is seen to be ruled by *Nixon v. Herndon*. Delegates of the State's power have discharged their official functions in such a way as to discriminate invidiously between white citizens and black. The Fourteenth Amendment, adopted as it was with special solicitude for the equal protection of members of the Negro race, lays a duty upon the court to level by its judgment these barriers of color.

But the Democrats did not give up in their efforts to bar Nixon and other blacks from primary elections. Three weeks after the decision in *Nixon v. Condon*, the State Democratic Convention passed a resolution "that all white citizens of the State of Texas who are qualified to vote under the Constitution and laws of the state shall be eligible to membership in the Democratic party and as such entitled to participate in its deliberations." Pursuant to this resolution, a county clerk refused to issue an absentee ballot to a black voter who sought to participate in the primary. The voter sued and in *Grovey v. Townsend*, 295 U.S. 45 (1935), the Supreme Court unanimously upheld his exclusion. Although the Court recognized that the use of nominating primaries was required by state law and was pervasively regulated by the state, it held that the party's exclusion of Grovey did not constitute state action subject to the Fourteenth Amendment. As a matter of state constitutional law, political parties possessed the right to determine their membership without state interference and thus Grovey's exclusion was the product of private, perhaps constitutionally protected, activity.

There, it seemed, the matter would rest: the Supreme Court had provided a roadmap for the continued exclusion of blacks from southern politics. But the Court's decision in *United States v. Classic*, 313 U.S. 299 (1941), opened the door to a renewed challenge to the white primary. *Classic* involved the prosecution of several Louisiana election officials who had stuffed ballot boxes and committed other sorts of fraud in a primary election. (As was true in the rest of the South, the primary election was the one that counted, since the state was overwhelmingly Democratic.) The statutes under which they were charged made it a felony either to conspire to interfere with the exercise of a federally protected right or to act under color of state law to deprive individuals of rights guaranteed by the Constitution or federal law. In *Classic*, the government alleged that the federally protected right with which the defendants had interfered was the right to vote. The district court dismissed the indictment on the grounds that the right to vote was not implicated since the defendants' actions occurred during a primary election, rather than a general election. The Supreme Court disagreed. It held that "[t]he primary in Louisiana is an integral part of the procedure for the popular choice of Congressman. The right of qualified voters to vote at the Congressional primary in Louisiana and to have their ballots counted is thus the right to participate in that choice." Buoyed by *Classic*, black voters launched a new challenge to the Texas white primary.

Smith v. Allwright

321 U.S. 649 (1944).

■ Mr. Justice Reed delivered the opinion of the Court.

* * *

We granted the petition for certiorari to resolve a claimed inconsistency between the decision in the *Grovey* case and that of *United States v. Classic*.

.... [Under Texas law,] the Democratic party was required to hold the primary which was the occasion of the alleged wrong to petitioner....

[The state defends its refusal to provide Smith with a ballot for the Democratic primary] on the ground that the Democratic party of Texas is a voluntary organization with members banded together for the purpose of selecting individuals of the group representing the common political beliefs as candidates in the general election. As such a voluntary organization, it was claimed, the Democratic party is free to select its own membership and limit to whites participation in the party primary....

The right of a Negro to vote in the Texas primary has been considered heretofore by this Court [in *Nixon v. Herndon, Nixon v. Condon*, and *Grovey v. Townsend*.].... Since *Grovey v. Townsend* and prior to the present suit, no case from Texas involving primary elections has been before this Court. We did decide, however, *United States v. Classic*. We there held that § 4 of Article I of the Constitution authorized Congress to regulate primary as well as general elections, "where the primary is by law made an integral part of the election machinery.".... The Nixon Cases were decided under the equal protection clause of the Fourteenth Amendment without a determination of the status of the primary as a part of the electoral process. The exclusion of Negroes from the primaries by action of the State was held invalid under that Amendment. The fusing by the *Classic* case of the primary and general elections into a single instrumentality for choice of officers has a definite bearing on the permissibility under the Constitution of excluding Negroes from primaries. This is not to say that the *Classic* case cuts directly into the rationale of *Grovey v. Townsend*. This latter case was not mentioned in the opinion. *Classic* bears upon *Grovey v. Townsend* not because exclusion of Negroes from primaries is any more or less state action by reason of the unitary character of the electoral process but because the recognition of the place of the primary in the electoral scheme makes clear that state delegation to a party of the power to fix the qualifications of primary elections is delegation of a state function that may make the party's action the action of the State. When *Grovey v. Townsend* was written, the Court looked upon the denial of a vote in a primary as a mere refusal by a party of party membership.

* * *

The question as to whether the exclusionary action of the party was the action of the State persists as the determinative factor.

* * *

Texas requires electors in a primary to pay a poll tax. Every person who does so pay and who has the qualifications of age and residence is an acceptable voter for the primary.... [The state] directs the selection of all party officers.

Primary elections are conducted by the party under state statutory authority.

* * *

We think that this statutory system for the selection of party nominees for inclusion on the general election ballot makes the party which is required to follow these legislative directions an agency of the State in so far as it determines the participants in a primary election. The party takes its character as a state agency from the duties imposed upon it by state statutes; the duties do not become matters of private law because they are performed by a political party.... When primaries become a part of the machinery for choosing officials, state and national, as they have here, the same tests to determine the character of discrimination or abridgement should be applied to the primary as are applied to the general election. If the State requires a certain electoral procedure, prescribes a general election ballot made up of party nominees so chosen and limits the choice of the electorate in general elections for state offices, practically speaking, to those whose names appear on such a ballot, it endorses, adopts and enforces the discrimination against Negroes, practiced by a party entrusted by Texas law with the determination of the qualifications of participants in the primary. This is state action within the meaning of the Fifteenth Amendment.

The United States is a constitutional democracy. Its organic law grants to all citizens a right to participate in the choice of elected officials without restriction by any State because of race. This grant to the people of the opportunity for choice is not to be nullified by a State through casting its electoral process in a form which permits a private organization to practice racial discrimination in the election. Constitutional rights would be of little value if they could be thus indirectly denied.

The privilege of membership in a party may be, as this Court said in *Grovey v. Townsend* no concern of a State. But when, as here, that privilege is also the essential qualification for voting in a primary to select nominees for a general election, the State makes the action of the party the action of the State.... *Grovey v. Townsend* is overruled.

■ MR. JUSTICE ROBERTS, dissenting.

* * *

I believe it will not be gainsaid [that *Grovey v. Townsend*] received the attention and consideration which the questions involved demanded and the opinion represented the views of all the justices. It appears that those views do not now commend themselves to the court. I shall not restate them. They are exposed in the opinion and must stand or fall on their merits. Their soundness, however, is not a matter which presently concerns me.

The reason for my concern is that the instant decision, overruling that announced about nine years ago, tends to bring adjudications of this tribunal into the same class as a restricted railroad ticket, good for this day and train only. I have no assurance, in view of current decisions, that the opinion announced today may not shortly be repudiated and overruled by justices who deem they have new light on the subject.

* * *

It is regrettable that in an era marked by doubt and confusion, an era whose greatest need is steadfastness of thought and purpose, this court, which has been looked to as exhibiting consistency in adjudication, and a steadiness which would hold the balance even in the face of temporary ebbs and flows of opinion, should now itself become the breeder of fresh doubt and confusion in the public mind as to the stability of our institutions.

Terry v. Adams

345 U.S. 461 (1953).

■ Mr. Justice Black announced the judgment of the Court and an opinion in which Mr. Justice Douglas and Mr. Justice Burton join.

.... This case raises questions concerning the constitutional power of a Texas county political organization called the Jaybird Democratic Association or Jaybird Party to exclude Negroes from its primaries on racial grounds. The Jaybirds deny that their racial exclusions violate the Fifteenth Amendment. They contend that the Amendment applies only to elections or primaries held under state regulation, that their association is not regulated by the state at all, and that it is not a political party but a self-governing voluntary club....

There was evidence that:

The Jaybird Association or Party was organized in 1889. Its membership was then and always has been limited to white people; they are automatically members if their names appear on the official list of county voters. It has been run like other political parties with an executive committee named from the county's voting precincts. Expenses of the party are paid by the assessment of candidates for office in its primaries. Candidates for county offices submit their names to the Jaybird Committee in accordance with the normal practice followed by regular political parties all over the country. Advertisements and posters proclaim that these candidates are running subject to the action of the Jaybird primary. While there is no legal compulsion on successful Jaybird candidates to enter Democratic primaries, they have nearly always done so and with few exceptions since 1889 have run and won without opposition in the Democratic primaries and the general elections that followed. Thus the party has been the dominant political group in the county since organization, having endorsed every county-wide official elected since 1889.

* * *

[The Fifteenth] Amendment bans racial discrimination in voting by both state and nation. It thus establishes a national policy, obviously applicable to the right of Negroes not to be discriminated against as voters in elections to determine public governmental policies or to select public officials, national, state, or local.

Clearly the Amendment includes any election in which public issues are decided or public officials selected. Just as clearly the Amendment excludes social or business clubs. And the statute shows the congressional mandate against discrimination whether the voting on public issues and officials is conducted in community, state or nation. Size is not a standard.

It is significant that precisely the same qualifications as those prescribed by Texas entitling electors to vote at county-operated primaries are adopted as the sole qualifications entitling electors to vote at the county-wide Jaybird primaries with a single proviso—Negroes are excluded. Everyone concedes that such a proviso in the county-operated primaries would be unconstitutional. The Jaybird Party thus brings into being and holds precisely the kind of election that the Fifteenth Amendment seeks to prevent. When it produces the equivalent of the prohibited election, the damage has been done.

For a state to permit such a duplication of its election processes is to permit a flagrant abuse of those processes to defeat the purposes of the Fifteenth Amendment. The use of the county-operated primary to ratify the result of the prohibited election merely compounds the offense. It violates the Fifteenth Amendment for a state, by such circumvention, to permit within its borders the use of any device that produces an equivalent of the prohibited election.

The only election that has counted in this Texas county for more than fifty years has been that held by the Jaybirds from which Negroes were excluded. The Democratic primary and the general election have become no more than the perfunctory ratifiers of the choice that has already been made in Jaybird elections from which Negroes have been excluded. It is immaterial that the state does not control that part of this elective process which it leaves for the Jaybirds to manage. The Jaybird primary has become an integral part, indeed the only effective part, of the elective process that determines who shall rule and govern in the county. The effect of the whole procedure, Jaybird primary plus Democratic primary plus general election, is to do precisely that which the Fifteenth Amendment forbids—strip Negroes of every vestige of influence in selecting the officials who control the local county matters that intimately touch the daily lives of citizens.

We reverse the Court of Appeals' judgment reversing that of the District Court. We affirm the District Court's holding that the combined Jaybird–Democratic–general election machinery has deprived these petitioners of their right to vote on account of their race and color. The case is remanded to the District Court to enter such orders and decrees as are necessary and proper.... In exercising this jurisdiction, the Court is left free to hold hearings to consider and determine what provisions are essential to afford Negro citizens of Fort Bend County full protection from future discriminatory Jaybird–Democratic-general election practices which deprive citizens of voting rights because of their color.

* * *

■ Mr. Justice Frankfurter

* * *

The evidence, summarized by formal stipulation, shows that.... formal State action, either by way of legislative recognition or official authorization, is wholly wanting.

* * *

This case is for me by no means free of difficulty.

* * *

[V]iolation of [the Fifteenth] Amendment and the enactments passed in enforcement of it must involve the United States or a State. In this case the conduct that is assailed pertains to the election of local Texas officials. To find a denial or abridgment of the guaranteed voting right to colored citizens of Texas solely because they are colored, one must find that the State has had a hand in it.

The State, in these situations, must mean not private citizens but those clothed with the authority and the influence which official position affords. The application of the prohibition of the Fifteenth Amendment to "any State" is translated by legal jargon to read "State action." This phrase gives rise to a false direction in that it implies some impressive machinery or deliberative conduct normally associated with what orators call a sovereign state. The vital requirement is State responsibility—that somewhere, somehow, to some extent, there be an infusion of conduct by officials, panoplied with State power, into any scheme by which colored citizens are denied voting rights merely because they are colored.

As the action of the entire white voting community, the Jaybird primary is as a practical matter the instrument of those few in this small county who are politically active—the officials of the local Democratic party and, we may assume, the elected officials of the county. As a matter of practical politics, those charged by State law with the duty of assuring all eligible voters an opportunity to participate in the selection of candidates at the primary—the county election officials who are normally leaders in their communities—participate by voting in the Jaybird primary. They join the white voting community in proceeding with elaborate formality, in almost all respects parallel to the procedures dictated by Texas law for the primary itself, to express their preferences in a wholly successful effort to withdraw significance from the State-prescribed primary, to subvert the operation of what is formally the law of the State for primaries in this county.

* * *

The State of Texas has entered into a comprehensive scheme of regulation of political primaries, including procedures by which election officials shall be chosen. The county election officials are thus clothed with the authority of the State to secure observance of the State's interest in "fair methods and a fair expression" of preferences in the selection of nominees. If the Jaybird Association, although not a political party, is a device to defeat the law of Texas regulating primaries, and if the electoral officials, clothed with State power in the county, share in that subversion, they cannot divest themselves of the State authority and help as participants in the scheme....

This is not a case of occasional efforts to mass voting strength. Nor is this a case of boss-control, whether crudely or subtly exercised. Nor is this a case of spontaneous efforts by citizens to influence votes or even continued efforts by a fraction of the electorate in support of good government. This is a case in which county election officials have participated in and condoned a continued effort effectively to exclude Negroes from voting. Though the action of the Association as such may not be proscribed by the Fifteenth amendment, its role in the entire scheme to subvert the operation of the official primary brings it within reach of the law.

* * *

It does not follow, however, that the relief granted below was proper. Since the vice of this situation is not that the Jaybird primary itself is the primary discriminatorily conducted under State law but is that the determination there made becomes, in fact, the determination in the Democratic primary by virtue of the participation and acquiescence of State authorities, a federal court cannot require that petitioners be allowed to vote in the Jaybird primary. The evil here is that the State, through the action and abdication of those whom it has clothed with authority, has permitted white voters to go through a procedure which predetermines the legally devised primary.... We cannot tell the State that it must participate in and regulate this primary; we cannot tell the State what machinery it will use. But a court of equity can free the lawful political agency from the combination that subverts its capacity to function. What must be done is that this county be rid of the means by which the unlawful "usage" in this case asserts itself.

■ MR. JUSTICE CLARK, with whom THE CHIEF JUSTICE, MR. JUSTICE REED, and MR. JUSTICE JACKSON join, concurring.

* * *

An old pattern in new guise is revealed by the record. The Jaybird Democratic Association of Fort Bend County was founded in 1889 to promote "good government" in the post-Reconstruction period. During its entire life span the Association has restricted membership to whites. In earlier years, the members at mass meetings determined their choice of candidates to support at forthcoming official elections. Subsequently the

Association developed a system closely paralleling the structure of the Democratic Party.

* * *

The Fifteenth Amendment secures the franchise exercised by citizens of the United States against abridgment by any state on the basis of race or color. In *Smith v. Allwright*, 321 U.S. 649 (1944), this Court held that the Democratic Party of itself, and perforce any other political party, is prohibited by that Amendment from conducting a racially discriminatory primary election. By the rule of that case, any "part of the machinery for choosing officials" becomes subject to the Constitution's restraints. There, as here, we dealt with an organization that took the form of "voluntary association" of unofficial character. But because in fact it functioned as a part of the state's electoral machinery, we held it controlled by the same constitutional limitations that ruled the official general election.

[.... T]he Jaybird Democratic Association is a political party whose activities fall within the Fifteenth Amendment's self-executing ban. Not every private club, association or league organized to influence public candidacies or political action must conform to the Constitution's restrictions on political parties. Certainly a large area of freedom permits peaceable assembly and concerted private action for political purposes to be exercised separately by white and colored citizens alike. More, however, is involved here.

The record discloses that the Jaybird Democratic Association operates as part and parcel of the Democratic Party, an organization existing under the auspices of Texas law.

* * *

Quite evidently the Jaybird Democratic Association operates as an auxiliary of the local Democratic Party organization, selecting its nominees and using its machinery for carrying out an admitted design of destroying the weight and effect of Negro ballots in Fort Bend County. To be sure, the Democratic primary and the general election are nominally open to the colored elector. But his must be an empty vote cast after the real decisions are made. And because the Jaybird-indorsed nominee meets no opposition in the Democratic primary, the Negro minority's vote is nullified at the sole stage of the local political process where the bargaining and interplay of rival political forces would make it count.

The Jaybird Democratic Association device, as a result, strikes to the core of the electoral process in Fort Bend County. Whether viewed as a separate political organization or as an adjunct of the local Democratic Party, the Jaybird Democratic Association is the decisive power in the county's recognized electoral process. Over the years its balloting has emerged as the locus of effective political choice. Consonant with the broad and lofty aims of its Framers, the Fifteenth Amendment, as the Fourteenth, "refers to exertions of state power in all forms." *Shelley v. Kraemer*, 334 U.S. 1, 20 (1948). Accordingly, when a state structures its electoral apparatus in a form which devolves upon a political organization the uncontested choice of public officials, that organization itself, in whatever disguise, takes on those attributes of government which draw the Constitution's safeguards into play.

In sum, we believe that the activities of the Jaybird Democratic Association fall within the broad principle laid down in *Smith v. Allwright, supra*. For that reason we join the judgment of the Court.

■ MR. JUSTICE MINTON, dissenting.

I am not concerned in the least as to what happens to the Jaybirds or their unworthy scheme. I am concerned about what this Court says is state action within the meaning of the Fifteenth Amendment to the Constitution....

As I understand Mr. Justice Black's opinion, he would have this Court redress the wrong even if it was individual action alone. I can understand that praiseworthy position, but it seems to me it is not in accord with the Constitution. State action must be shown.

Mr. Justice Frankfurter recognizes that it must be state action but he seems to think it is enough to constitute state action if a state official participates in the Jaybird primary. That I cannot follow. For it seems clear to me that everything done by a person who is an official is not done officially and as a representative of the State. However, I find nothing in this record that shows the state or county officials participating in the Jaybird primary.

Mr. Justice Clark seems to recognize that state action must be shown. He finds state action in assumption, not in facts. This record will be searched in vain for one iota of state action sufficient to support an anemic inference that the Jaybird Association is in any way associated with or forms a part of or cooperates in any manner with the Democratic Party of the County or State, or with the State. It calls itself the Jaybird Democratic Association because its interest is only in the candidates of the Democratic Party in the county, a position understandable in Texas.

* * *

[....] Surely white or colored members of any political faith or economic belief may hold caucuses. It is only when the State by action of its legislative bodies or action of some of its officials in their official capacity cooperates with such political party or gives it direction in its activities that the Federal Constitution may come into play. A political organization not using state machinery or depending upon state law to authorize what it does could not be within the ban of the Fifteenth Amendment.

* * *

This case does not hold that a group of Democrats, white, black, male, female, native-born or foreign, economic royalists or workingmen, may not caucus or conduct a straw vote. What the Jaybird Association did here was to conduct as individuals, separate and apart from the Democratic Party or the State, a straw vote as to who should receive the Association's endorsement for county and precinct offices. It has been successful in seeing that those who receive its endorsement are nominated and elected. That is true of concerted action by any group. In numbers there is strength. In organization there is effectiveness. Often a small minority of stockholders control a corporation. Indeed, it is almost an axiom of corporate management that a small, cohesive group may control, especially in the larger corporations where the holdings are widely diffused.

* * *

[T]he Jaybird Association's activities ... are confined to one County where a group of citizens have appointed themselves the censors of those who would run for public offices. Apparently so far they have succeeded in convincing the voters of this County in most instances that their supported candidates should win. This seems to differ very little from situations common in many other places far north of the Mason–Dixon line, such as areas where a candidate must obtain the approval of a religious group. In other localities, candidates are carefully selected by both parties to give proper weight to Jew, Protestant and Catholic, and certain posts are considered the sole possession of certain ethnic groups. The propriety of these practices is something the courts sensibly have left to the good or bad judgment of the electorate. It must be recognized that elections and other public business are influenced by all sorts of pressures from carefully organized groups. We have pressure from labor unions, from the National Association of Manufacturers, from the Silver Shirts, from the National Association for the Advancement of Colored People, from the Ku Klux Klan and others. Far from the activities of these groups being properly labeled as state action, under either the Fourteenth or the Fifteenth Amendment, they are to be considered as attempts to influence or obtain state action.

The courts do not normally pass upon these pressure groups, whether their causes are good or bad, highly successful or only so-so. It is difficult for me to see how this Jaybird Association is anything but such a pressure group. Apparently it is believed in by enough people in Fort Bend County to obtain a majority of the votes for its approved candidates. This differs little from the situation in many parts of the "Bible Belt" where a church stamp of approval or that of the Anti-Saloon League must be put on any candidate who does not want to lose the election.

The State of Texas in its elections and primaries takes no cognizance of this Jaybird Association. The State treats its decisions apparently with the same disdain as it would the approval or condemnation of judicial candidates by a bar association poll of its members.

In this case the majority have found that this pressure group's work does constitute state action. The basis of this conclusion is rather difficult to ascertain. Apparently it derives mainly from a dislike of the goals of the Jaybird Association. I share that dislike. I fail to see how it makes state action. I would affirm.

NOTES AND QUESTIONS

1. The following appraisal of the draft opinions in *Terry* was prepared by William H. Rehnquist, who was at the time Justice Robert Jackson's law clerk.

Re: Opinions of Black and FF in *Terry v. Adams*

If you are going to dissent, I should think you might combine the ideas which you expressed last week with an attack on the reasoning of the two "majority opinions."

(1) *Black*—simply assumes the whole point of the issue. The 15th Amendment requires state action, and certainly Congress under its power to "enforce" the amendment cannot drastically enlarge its scope. Yet the Black opinion utterly fails to face the problem of state action. He says rather that the effect of the Fifteenth Amendment is to prevent the states from discriminating against Negroes in official elections; the result here is to accomplish that result "by indirection"; therefore that result is bad. Surely it should not take a quotation from Mr. Justice Holmes to establish the proposition that, especially in the field of constitutional law, differences will be ones of degree and the point at which the constitutional result changes will not be marked by any sharp turn in the road. Surely the justices of this Court do not sit here to ruthlessly frustrate results which they consider undesirable, regardless of the working of the Constitution.

(2) *FF*—places the weight of the decision on the rather skimpy support to be found in his discovery of "state action": the county election officials voted in the Jaybird primary. In the first place, they voted not in their capacity as election officials, but as private citizens. Secondly, it was not their voting which effected the discrimination; it was the previously adopted rules, with which they may have had nothing to do. Thirdly, if this is the vice why not simply enjoin the officials from voting? When one must strain this hard to reach a result, the chances are that something is the matter with the result....

(3) *Your ideas*—the Constitution does not prevent the majority from banding together, nor does it attaint success in the effort. It is about time the Court faced the fact that the white people in the South don't like colored people; the Supreme Court is not a

watchdog to rear up every time private discrimination raises its admittedly ugly head. To the extent that this decision advances the frontier of state action and "social gain", it pushes back the frontier of freedom of association and majority rule. Liberals should be the first to realize, after the past twenty years, that it does not do to push blindly through towards one constitutional goal without paying attention to other equally desirable values that are being trampled on in the process.

This is a position that I am sure ought to be stated; but if stated by Vinson, Minton, or Reed it just won't sound the same way as if you state it.

How would you assess future Chief Justice Rehnquist's criticisms? Note that ultimately Justice Jackson joined Justice Clark's opinion. Also compare Justice Minton's dissent. Does it essentially adopt the Rehnquist position?

2. Is there any limit to the *Terry* position? Suppose that Fort Bend County was run, as a number of other Southern counties were, by a very few "bosses," who were also elected officials (for example, the sheriff and the probate judge). If those officials met every July at the local country club to pick a slate of candidates, and those candidates always won the election, could a voter claim the right to attend their annual lunch? Would it be different if the local Rotary Club or Chamber of Commerce did the picking?

In this regard, consider *Morse v. Republican Party of Virginia*, 116 S.Ct. 1186 (1996). There, a five-justice majority, which was unable to coalesce behind a single opinion, held that the rules governing who could participate in the defendant's party nominating convention involved "voting" within the meaning of the Voting Rights Act of 1965, 42 U.S.C. §§ 1973 *et seq*. The author of the Act's definitional provision, which defined the terms "vote" or "voting" to include "all action necessary to make a vote effective in any primary, special, or general election, including, but not limited to, ... casting a ballot and having such ballot counted properly with respect to candidates for public or party office," 42 U.S.C. § 1973*l*(c)(1), explained that he had "recommended the addition of language which would extend the protections of the bill to the type of situation which arose last year when the regular Democratic delegation from Mississippi to the Democratic National Convention was chosen through a series of Party caucuses and conventions from which Negroes were excluded." 111 Cong. Rec. 16273 (July 9, 1965) (statement of Rep. Jonathan B. Bingham). *Morse* was a statutory interpretation case, but the application of the statute depended on there being state action, since only "states" and "political subdivisions" are bound by the Act.

3. What notion of political parties underlies *Smith* and *Terry*? Does the Court essentially view them as common carriers? How important is the fact that the Democratic or Jaybird winner always won? Would or should the Court's analysis be different for a smaller, or more ideological, party? For example, consider the Black Panther Party of Lowndes County, Alabama, founded in the wake of the 1965 march from Selma to Montgomery. Black voters sought to have a party responsive to their interests. Could white voters insist on participating in the party's nomination process?

4. Would *Smith* and *Terry* extend beyond race? Suppose, for example, that a group of feminist separatists wished to found a local party that excluded men from its nomination process. Would the Nineteenth Amendment bar such discrimination? Similarly, could a party exclude voters based on their exercise of a fundamental right? For example, could a pro-life party open its nomination process only to voters who had never had abortions or who promised never to have or aid anyone else in obtaining one? In *Davis v. Beason*, 133 U.S. 333 (1890), the Supreme Court upheld a territorial statute that provided, among other things, that "No person ... who teaches, advises, counsels, or encourages any person or persons to become bigamists or polygamists, or to commit any other crime defined by law, ... is permitted to vote at any election, or to hold any position or office of honor, trust, or profit within this Territory." Idaho Rev. Stats. § 501. In order to cast a ballot, a voter had to swear that he or she "do[es] not and will not, publicly or privately, or in any manner whatever teach, advise, counsel or encourage any person to commit the crime of bigamy or polygamy, or any other crime defined by law, either as a religious duty or otherwise...."

Do *Smith*, *Terry*, and *Morse* (discussed in a previous note) shed any light on *Republican Party of Texas v. Dietz*, 940 S.W.2d 86 (Tex.Sup.Ct. 1997), discussed *infra* in Chapter 4? The Log Cabin Republicans, a gay and lesbian group, sought to operate a booth at the Texas Republican Party convention. Respondent Dietz, a Democratic state district judge, granted them an injunction, requiring the party to give them access to the convention. His ruling rested on the conclusion that the state party had incorporated the Texas Constitution into its party rules and that denial of the booth and advertising space in the convention program amounted to a "prior restraint" that violated the group's free speech right under the Texas Constitution. The Texas Supreme Court granted an emergency motion to stay Judge Dietz's order, concluding, among other things, that "state action is required for there to have been a violation of the constitutional rights asserted by the Log Cabin Republicans and that such action was not present under the facts of this case."

5. The Texas Democratic Party cases from *Nixon* through *Terry* are collectively referred to as the "White Primary Cases" and generally stand for the proposition that forcible exclusion of black voters from the political process will not be tolerated. Is it possible, however, to distinguish among the cases on different grounds? Consider an argument that focuses on the role of courts as preventing a lockup of the political process. One can begin by asking why it was so important to the Democratic Party to have the State of Texas forbid black voting in its primary elections. Perhaps the

appeal to state intervention was a guarantee that no disgruntled elements of the party would seek to enhance their power by appealing to black voters. Historically, the Texas Democratic Party was a rather diverse and unstable mix of both conservative and populist currents that divided quite sharply over issues such as the New Deal. (This history is chronicled in Chandler Davidson, Race and Class in Texas Politics 155–79 (1990)). When such divisions were particularly sharp, what would discourage a sufficiently disgruntled faction from seeking to secure control of the Party by courting even the relatively small numbers of potential black voters? The answer was a precommitment among the varying factions that no one would appeal to black voters. The role of the state was guarantor of that agreement. In such circumstances, the agreements struck down in *Nixon v. Herndon*, *Nixon v. Condon*, and, although to a lesser extent, *Smith v. Allwright* all shared the critical feature of the Party using the state to secure the racial lockup of the political process. So long as the restrictive covenants of the Party were enshrined through state law, there was no prospect for black voters to serve as potential swing voters who could secure some measure of political redress in exchange for their votes. Under these circumstances, judicial intervention can be justified as the necessary destabilizing element required in order to break the stranglehold on a political system unable to generate change from within. (We shall see a variant of this same argument in the next Chapter in discussing the one-person, one-vote malapportionment cases.) Can the same be said of *Terry v. Adams*? By the time of *Terry*, the element of state enforcement had been removed. Certainly the Jaybirds were all white and held nearly complete power in the Democratic Party. But was this system stable? Was it as immune from change as those state-enforced arrangements struck down in the earlier White Primary Cases? Are competing values of freedom of political association more salient in *Terry* than in the other White Primary Cases? For a fuller analysis of the White Primary Cases as examples of political lockups, see Samuel Issacharoff and Richard Pildes, *Politics as Markets: Partisan Lockups of the Democratic Process*, ___ Stanford L.J. ___ (1998).

3. THE DEMISE OF DISCRETION

With the elimination of the white primary, blacks sought to register in increasing numbers. The potential that black voters might hold the balance of power among competing white factions—the very concern that had motivated white primaries—now led election officials back to long-unused constitutional provisions regarding literacy and good character tests. Louisiana, for example, had had an "interpretation test" since the 1898 disenfranchising convention, but the test was rarely, if ever, applied until the early 1950's. As the district court explained in *United States v. State of Louisiana*, 225 F.Supp. 353 (E.D.La.1963), *aff'd*, 380 U.S. 145 (1965), "[i]t was not needed. The Democratic white primary made registration futile for Negroes ..... The white primary ... effectively kept Negroes from voting in the only election that had any significance in the Louisiana electoral process...." In the wake of *Smith v. Allwright* and increased attempts by blacks to register, partisans of Massive Resistance and white supremacy turned to the interpretation test to keep black voters out. The district court in *United States v. Louisiana* found that:

> The registrar's whim alone determines which applicants will be tested. The Constitution merely states that applicants "shall be able to understand and give a reasonable interpretation" of a section of a constitution. Some registrars, for example, those in LaSalle, Lincoln, and Webster parishes, have interpreted this to mean that the applicant need not actually interpret the constitution, only that he have the ability to do so....
>
> The Louisiana Constitution contains 443 sections, as against 56 sections in the United States Constitution, and is the longest and the most detailed of all state constitutions. The printed copy published by the State, unannotated, contains 600 pages, not counting an index of 140 pages. The evidence clearly demonstrates great abuses in the selection of sections of the constitutions to be interpreted. Some registrars have favorite sections which they apparently use regardless of an applicant's race. Some open a volume containing the United States and Louisiana Constitutions and, like soothsayers seeking divine help from the random flight of birds, require an applicant to interpret the section on the page where the book opens. The Segregation Committee distributed to registrars sets of twenty-four cards, each containing three sections of the Constitution with instructions that they be used in administering the interpretation test....
>
> It is evident from the record that frequently the choice of difficult sections has made it impossible for many Negro applicants to pass. White applicants were more often given easy sections, many of which could be answered by short, stock phrases such as "freedom of speech", "freedom of religion", "States' rights", and so on. Negro applicants, on the other hand, were given [extremely complex parts of the state constitution].

* * *

Registrars were easily satisfied with answers from white voters. In one instance "FRDUM FOOF SPETGH" was an acceptable response to the request to interpret Article 1, § 3 of the Louisiana Constitution [which guarantees freedom of speech].

On the other hand, the record shows that Negroes whose application forms and answers indicate that they are highly qualified by literacy standards and have a high degree of intelligence have been turned down although they had given a reasonable interpretation of fairly technical clauses of the constitution. For example the Louisiana Constitution, Article X, § 16 provides:

"Rolling stock operated in this State, the owners of which have no domicile therein, shall be assessed by the Louisiana Tax Commission, and shall be taxed for State purposes only, at a rate not to exceed forty mills on the dollar assessed value." The rejected interpretation was: "My understanding is that it means if the owner of which does not have residence within the State, his rolling stock shall be taxed not to exceed forty mills on the dollar."

In another instance the registrar rejected the following interpretation of the Search and Seizure provision of the Fourth Amendment: "[Nobody] can just go into a person's house and take their belongings without a warrant from the law, and it had to specify in this warrant what they were to search and seize." Another rejected interpretation of the same Amendment by a Negro applicant was: "To search you would have to get an authorized authority to read a warrant." The Louisiana Constitution Article I, § 5 provides: "The people have the right peaceably to assemble." A registrar rejected the following interpretation: "That one may assemble or belong to any group, club, or organization he chooses as long as it is within the law."

Each of these incidents could conceivably be an isolated event, indicating personal dereliction by one registrar, regrettable, but basically trivial in the general administration of the interpretation test. However, the great number of these and other examples, illustrative of a conscious decision, show conclusively that the discriminatory acts were not isolated or accidental or peculiar to the individual registrar but were part of a pervasive pattern and practice of disfranchisement by discriminatory use of the interpretation test.

The State does not deny that unlimited discretion is vested in the registrars by the laws of Louisiana, but argues that officials must act reasonably and that their decisions are subject to review by district courts. Louisiana, however, provides no effective method whereby arbitrary and capricious action by registrars of voters may be prevented or redressed. Unreviewable discretion was built into the test.

* * *

The statistics demonstrate strikingly the effect of resurrection of the interpretation test. A report of the Louisiana Sovereignty Committee, December 14, 1960, boasts:

"We would like to call your attention to the fact that, during this four year period of time, from 1956 until 1960, 81,241 colored people became of voting age, when the registration figures of colored people actually declined 2,377. Going further during this four year period, we had 114,529 white people who became of voting age and, during this four year period of time, the white registration increased 96,620."

Similarly, *Davis v. Schnell*, 81 F.Supp. 872 (S.D.Ala.), *aff'd,* 336 U.S. 933 (1949), struck down Alabama's Boswell Amendment, which limited registration to persons who could "understand and explain" any article of the Federal Constitution. The district court found that the test was both invalid on its face and invalid as applied:

> "[U]nderstand" may mean to interpret. This meaning requires an exceedingly high, if not impossible, standard. The distinguished Justices of the Supreme Court of the United States have frequently disagreed in their interpretations of various articles of the Constitution. We learn from history that many of the makers of the Constitution did not understand its provisions; many of them understood and believed that its provisions gave the Supreme Court no power to declare an act of Congress unconstitutional. An understanding or explanation given by the Supreme Court a few years ago as to the meaning of the commerce clause does not apply today. Among our most learned judges there are at least four different understandings and explanations of the Fourteenth Amendment to the Constitution as to whether it made the first eight Amendments applicable to state action. Such a rigorous standard ... illustrates the completeness with which any individual or group of prospective electors, whether white or Negro, may be deprived of the right of franchise by boards of registrars inclined to apply this one of the innumerable meanings of such an indefinite phrase.
>
> * * *
>
> It, thus, clearly appears that [the Boswell] Amendment was intended to be, and is being used for the purpose of discriminating against applicants for the franchise on the basis of race or color. Therefore, we are necessarily brought to the conclusion that the Amendment to the Constitution of Alabama, both in its object and the manner of its administration, is unconstitutional, because it violates the Fifteenth Amendment. While it is true that there is no mention of race or color in the Boswell Amendment, this does not save it.

The following example of a typical Alabama literacy test was reprinted in Howard Ball, Dale Krane & Thomas P. Lauth, Compromised Compliance 238–42 (1982). How many questions can you answer? Notice how some questions have ambiguous answers that allow for administrative discretion.

1. Which of the following is a right guaranteed by the Bill of Rights?

    _____ Public Education   _____ Voting
    _____ Employment   _____ Trial by Jury

C. The Struggle for Black Enfranchisement

2. The federal census of population is taken each five years. (True or false)
3. If a person is indicted for a crime, name two rights which he has.
4. A United States senator elected at the general election in November takes office the following year on what date? _____
5. A President elected at the general election in November takes office the following year on what date? _____
6. Which definition applies to the word "amendment?"

   _____ Proposed change, as in a Constitution
   _____ Making of peace between nations at war
   _____ A part of the government

7. A person appointed to the United States Supreme Court is appointed for a term of _____.
8. When the Constitution was approved by the original colonies, how many states had to ratify it in order for it to be in effect?
9. Does enumeration affect the income tax levied on citizens in various states?
10. Persons opposed to swearing in an oath may say, instead: "I solemnly _____."
11. To serve as President of the United States a person must have attained _____ 25, _____ 35, _____ 40, _____ 45 years.
12. What words are required by law to be on all coins and paper currency of the United States?
13. The Supreme Court is the chief lawmaking body of the state. (True or false)
14. If a law passed by a state is contrary to provisions of the United States Constitution, which law prevails?
15. If a vacancy occurs in the United States Senate, the state must hold an election but, meanwhile, the place may be filled by a temporary appointment made by _____.
16. A United States senator is elected for a term of _____ years.
17. Appropriation of money for the armed services can be only for a period limited to _____ years.
18. The chief executive and the administrative officers make up the _____ branch of government.
19. Who passes laws dealing with piracy?
20. The number of representatives which a state is entitled to have in the House of Representatives is based on _____.

21. The Constitution protects an individual against punishments which are _____ and _____.
22. When a jury has heard and rendered a verdict in a case, and the judgment on the verdict has become final, the defendant cannot again be brought to trial for the same case. (True or false)
23. Communism is the type of government in: _____ United States _____ Russia _____ England.
24. Name two levels of government which can levy taxes.
25. Cases tried before a court of law are of two types, civil and _____.
26. By a majority vote of the members of the Congress, the Congress can change provisions of the Constitution of the United States. (True or false)
27. For security, each state has a right to form a _____.
28. The electoral vote for President is counted in the presence of two bodies. Name them.
29. If no candidate for President receives a majority of the electoral vote, who decides who will become President?
30. Of the original 13 states, the one with the largest representation in the first Congress was _____.
31. Of which branch of state government is the Speaker of the House a part? _____ Executive _____ Legislative _____ Judicial
32. Capital punishment is the giving of a death sentence. (True or false)
33. In case the President is unable to perform the duties of his office, who assumes them?
34. "Involuntary servitude" is permitted in the United States upon conviction of a crime. (True or false).
35. If a state is a party to a case, the Constitution provides that original jurisdiction shall be in _____.
36. Congress passes laws regulating cases which are included in those over which the United States Supreme Court has _____ jurisdiction.
37. Which of the following is a right guaranteed by the Bill of Rights of the United States Constitution?

    _____ Public Housing   _____ Education
    _____ Voting   _____ Trial by Jury

38. The Legislatures of the states decide how presidential electors may be chosen. (True or false)
39. If it were proposed to join Alabama and Mississippi to form one state, what groups would have to vote approval in order for this to be done?
40. The Vice President presides over _____.

C. The Struggle for Black Enfranchisement

41. The Constitution limits the size of the District of Columbia to _____.

42. The only laws which can be passed to apply to an area in a federal arsenal are those passed by _____ provided consent for the purchase of the land is given by the _____.

43. In which document or writing is the Bill of Rights found?

44. Of which branch of government is a Supreme Court justice a part?
_____ Executive _____ Legislative _____ Judicial

45. If no person receives a majority of the electoral votes, the Vice President is chosen by the Senate. (True or false)

46. Name two things which the states are forbidden to do by the United States Constitution.

47. If election of the President becomes the duty of the United States House of Representatives it fails to act, who becomes President and when?

48. How many votes must a person receive in order to become President if the election is decided by the United States House of Representatives?

49. How many states were required to approve the original Constitution in order for it to be in effect?

50. Check the offenses below which, if you are convicted of them, disqualify you for voting.

_____ Murder   _____ Petty Larceny
_____ Issuing worthless checks   _____ Manufacturing Whiskey

51. The Congress decides in what manner states elect presidential electors. (True or false)

52. Name two of the purposes of the United States Constitution.

53. Congress is composed of _____.

54. All legislative powers granted in the United States Constitution may legally be used only by _____.

55. The population census is required to be made every _____ years.

56. Impeachments of United States officials are tried by _____.

57. If an effort to impeach the President of the United States is made, who presides at the trial?

58. On the impeachment of the chief justice of the Supreme Court of the United States, who tries the case?

59. Money is coined by order of:

_____ U.S. Congress
_____ The President's Cabinet
_____ State Legislatures

60. Persons elected to cast a state's vote for United States President and Vice President are called presidential _____.

61. Name one power which is exclusively legislative and is mentioned in one of the parts of the United States Constitution above.

62. If a person flees from justice into another state, who has authority to ask for his return?

63. Whose duty is it to keep Congress informed of the state of the Union?

64. If the two houses of Congress cannot agree on adjournment, who sets the time?

65. When the presidential electors meet to cast ballots for President, must all electors in a state vote for the same person for President or can they vote for different persons if they so choose?

66. After the presidential electors have voted, to whom do they send the count of their votes?

67. The power to declare war is vested in _____.

68. Any power and rights not given to the United States or prohibited to the states by the United States Constitution are specified as belonging to whom?

Ultimately, as part of the Voting Rights Act of 1965, Congress abolished all literacy, understanding, and good character tests in the Deep South. In 1970, this ban was extended nationwide.

4. REDRAWING DISTRICT BOUNDARIES

Perhaps the last gasp of disenfranchisement was the notorious Tuskegee gerrymander. Tuskegee was a majority black community in Macon County, Alabama. Blacks in Tuskegee were relatively well educated and independent of the local white power structure because of the presence of two nationally funded employers: the Tuskegee Institute, a black college, and a Veterans' Administration hospital. Beginning in the late 1950's, they sought to participate in the political process. They were met with three responses. First, the Macon County Board of Registrars engaged in a series of evasive maneuvers designed to prevent African Americans from registering to vote. *See United States v. Alabama*, 192 F.Supp. 677 (M.D.Ala.1961), aff'd, 304 F.2d 583 (5th Cir.), aff'd 371 U.S. 37 (1962) (per curiam). Second, through a statewide referendum, Alabama adopted a constitutional amendment permitting the state to abolish Macon County altogether "if the uppity Negroes there continued pestering for the vote." Bernard Taper, Gomillion v. Lightfoot: Apartheid in Alabama 51 (1962). *See* Ala. Const. Amend. No. 132 (1957), *repealed* Ala. Const. Amend. No. 406 (1982). Third, the Alabama Legislature passed Local Act 140, which redrew Tuskegee's municipal boundaries.

Gomillion v. Lightfoot

364 U.S. 339 (1960).

■ MR. JUSTICE FRANKFURTER delivered the opinion of the Court.

This litigation challenges the validity, under the United States Constitution, of Local Act No. 140, passed by the Legislature of Alabama in 1957, redefining the boundaries of the City of Tuskegee. Petitioners, Negro citizens of Alabama who were, at the time of this redistricting measure, residents of the City of Tuskegee, brought an action in the United States District Court for the Middle District of Alabama for a declaratory judgment that Act 140 is unconstitutional.... Petitioners' claim is that enforcement of the statute, which alters the shape of Tuskegee from a square to an uncouth twenty-eight-sided figure, will constitute a discrimination against them in violation of the Due Process and Equal Protection Clauses of the Fourteenth Amendment to the Constitution and will deny them the right to vote in defiance of the Fifteenth Amendment.

* * *

At this stage of the litigation we are not concerned with the truth of the allegations, that is, the ability of petitioners to sustain their allegations by proof. The sole question is whether the allegations entitle them to make good on their claim that they are being denied rights under the United States Constitution. The complaint, charging that Act 140 is a device to disenfranchise Negro citizens, alleges the following facts: Prior to Act 140 the City of Tuskegee was square in shape; the Act transformed it into a strangely irregular twenty-eight-sided figure as indicated in the diagram appended to this opinion. The essential inevitable effect of this redefinition of Tuskegee's boundaries is to remove from the city all save only four or five of its 400 Negro voters while not removing a single white voter or resident. The result of the Act is to deprive the Negro petitioners discriminatorily of the benefits of residence in Tuskegee, including, inter alia, the right to vote in municipal elections.

These allegations, if proven, would abundantly establish that Act 140 was not an ordinary geographic redistricting measure even within familiar abuses of gerrymandering. If these allegations upon a trial remained uncontradicted or unqualified, the conclusion would be irresistible, tantamount for all practical purposes to a mathematical demonstration, that the legislation is solely concerned with segregating white and colored voters by fencing Negro citizens out of town so as to deprive them of their pre-existing municipal vote.

It is difficult to appreciate what stands in the way of adjudging a statute having this inevitable effect invalid in light of the principles by which this Court must judge, and uniformly has judged, statutes that, howsoever speciously defined, obviously discriminate against colored citizens. "The [Fifteenth] Amendment nullifies sophisticated as well as simple-minded modes of discrimination." *Lane v. Wilson*.

The complaint amply alleges a claim of racial discrimination. Against this claim the respondents have never suggested, either in their brief or in oral argument, any countervailing municipal function which Act 140 is designed to serve. The respondents invoke generalities expressing the State's unrestricted power—unlimited, that is, by the United States Constitution—to establish, destroy, or reorganize by contraction or expansion its political subdivisions, to wit, cities, counties, and other local units.

* * *

[A review of our cases] shows that the Court has never acknowledged that the States have power to do as they will with municipal corporations regardless of consequences. Legislative control of municipalities, no less than other state power, lies within the scope of relevant limitations imposed by the United States Constitution.

* * *

[A state's power to define municipal boundaries], extensive though it is, is met and overcome by the Fifteenth Amendment to the Constitution of the United States, which forbids a State from passing any law which deprives a citizen of his vote because of his race. The opposite conclusion, urged upon us by respondents, would sanction the achievement by a State of any impairment of voting rights whatever so long as it was cloaked in the garb of the realignment of political subdivisions. "It is inconceivable that guaranties embedded in the Constitution of the United States may thus be manipulated out of existence."

The respondents find another barrier to the trial of this case in *Colegrove v. Green*, 328 U.S. 549.... [But t]he decisive facts in this case, which at this stage must be taken as proved, are wholly different from the considerations found controlling in *Colegrove*.

That case involved a complaint of discriminatory apportionment of congressional districts. The appellants in *Colegrove* complained only of a dilution of the strength of their votes as a result of legislative inaction over a course of many years. The petitioners here complain that affirmative legislative action deprives them of their votes and the consequent advantages that the ballot affords. When a legislature thus singles out a readily isolated segment of a racial minority for special discriminatory treatment, it violates the Fifteenth Amendment. In no case involving unequal weight in voting distribution that has come before the Court did the decision sanction a differentiation on racial lines whereby approval was given to unequivocal withdrawal of the vote solely from colored citizens. Apart from all else, these considerations lift this controversy out of the so-called "political" arena and into the conventional sphere of constitutional litigation.

In sum, as Mr. Justice Holmes remarked, when dealing with a related situation, in *Nixon v. Herndon*, "Of course the petition concerns political action," but "The objection that the subject matter of the suit is political is little more than a play upon words." A statute which is alleged to have worked unconstitutional deprivations of petitioners' rights is not immune to attack simply because the mechanism employed by the legislature is a redefinition of municipal boundaries. According to the allegations here made, the Alabama Legislature has not merely redrawn the Tuskegee city limits with incidental inconvenience to the petitioners; it is more accurate to say that it has deprived the petitioners of the municipal franchise and consequent rights and to that end it has incidentally changed the city's boundaries. While in form this is merely an act redefining metes and bounds, if the allegations are established, the inescapable human effect of this essay in geometry and geography is to despoil colored citizens, and only colored citizens, of their theretofore enjoyed voting rights. That was not *Colegrove v. Green*.

When a State exercises power wholly within the domain of state interest, it is insulated from federal judicial review. But such insulation is not carried over when state power is used as an instrument for circumventing a federally protected right. ....."Acts generally lawful may become

APPENDIX TO OPINION OF THE COURT.

CHART SHOWING TUSKEGEE, ALABAMA, BEFORE AND AFTER ACT 140

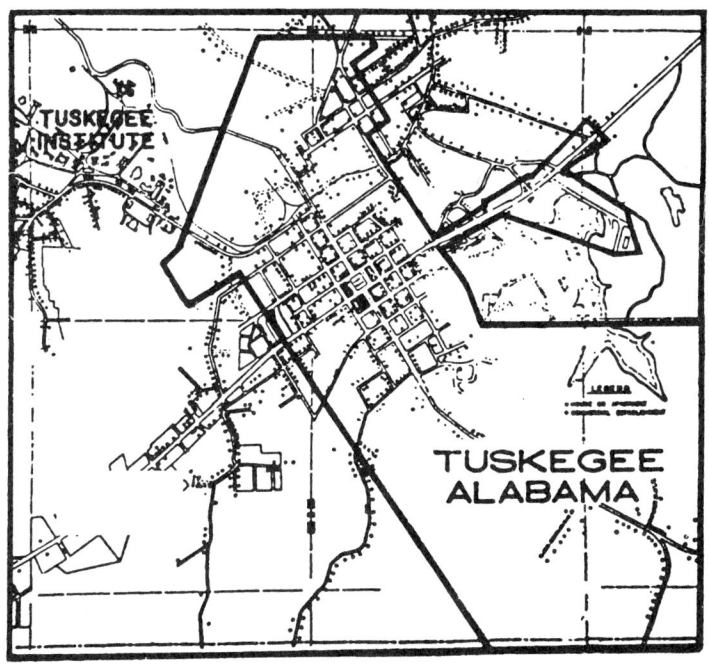

unlawful when done to accomplish an unlawful end, and a constitutional power cannot be used by way of condition to attain an unconstitutional result." The petitioners are entitled to prove their allegations at trial.

■ MR. JUSTICE DOUGLAS, while joining the opinion of the Court, adheres to the dissents in *Colegrove v. Green*, 328 U.S. 549, and *South v. Peters*, 339 U.S. 276.

(The entire area of the square comprised the City prior to Act 140. The irregular black-bordered figure within the square represents the post-enactment city.)

■ MR. JUSTICE WHITAKER, concurring.

I concur in the Court's judgment, but not in the whole of its opinion. It seems to me that the decision should be rested not on the Fifteenth Amendment, but rather on the Equal Protection Clause of the Fourteenth Amendment to the Constitution. I am doubtful that the averments of the complaint, taken for present purposes to be true, show a purpose by Act No. 140 to abridge petitioners' "right ... to vote," in the Fifteenth Amendment sense. It seems to me that the "right ... to vote" that is guaranteed by the Fifteenth Amendment is but the same right to vote as is enjoyed by all others within the same election precinct, ward or other political division. And, inasmuch as no one has the right to vote in a political division, or in a local election concerning only an area in which he does not reside, it would seem to follow that one's right to vote in Division A is not abridged by a redistricting that places his residence in Division B if he there enjoys the same voting privileges as all others in that Division, even though the redistricting was done by the State for the purpose of placing a racial group of citizens in Division B rather than A.

But it does seem clear to me that accomplishment of a State's purpose—to use the Court's phrase—of "fencing Negro citizens out of" Division A and into Division B is an unlawful segregation of races of citizens, in violation of the Equal Protection Clause of the Fourteenth Amendment, *Brown v. Board of Education*, 347 U.S. 483; *Cooper v. Aaron*, 358 U.S. 1; and, as stated, I would think the decision should be rested on that ground—which, incidentally, clearly would not involve, just as the cited cases did not involve, the Colegrove problem.

NOTES AND QUESTIONS

1. For detailed accounts of the political struggle in Tuskegee and its aftermath, see, e.g., Margaret Edds, Free At Last: What Really Happened When Civil Rights Came to Southern Politics (1987); Robert J. Norrell, Reaping the Whirlwind: Change and Conflict in Macon County, Alabama, 1941-1972 (1983).

2. Why does Justice Frankfurter rely on the Fifteenth Amendment rather than the Fourteenth? Were black voters actually disenfranchised or only placed into a "different" electoral jurisdiction—Macon County, rather than the city of Tuskegee? Does the police jurisdiction statute discussed in *Holt Civic Club, supra,* shed any light on this case?

D. VOTER REGISTRATION AND PARTICIPATION

Most Americans don't vote. In 1990, for example, only 33.1 percent of the voting-age population cast ballots for congressional representatives. *See* United States Dep't of Commerce, Bureau of the Census, Projections of the Voting-Age Population, for States, November 1992, tbl. 3, at 13 (1992). And in the 1996 presidential election, only 49.1 percent of the voting-age population went to the polls. See Eric Schmitt, The 1996 Elections: The Presidency—The Voters, N.Y. Times, Nov. 7, 1996, at B6; see also Voter Registration and Turnout—1996 <http://www.fec.gov/pages/96to.htm>. By contrast, the 1992 presidential race represents a recent high-water mark: Census Bureau survey data suggests that 61.3 percent of the voting-age population cast ballots in that election. *See* U.S. Dep't of Commerce, Bureau of the Census, Voting and Registration in the Election of November 1992, at v (1993). But the 1992 figures, and most survey data actually overestimate the level of participation. *See id.* at vii-viii; Allan J. Lichtman & Samuel Issacharoff, *Black/White Voter Registration Disparities in Mississippi: Legal and Methodological Issues in Challenging Bureau of Census Data,* 7 J. L. & Pol. 525 (1991). These data suggest several questions: First, what accounts for the strikingly low turnout? Second, what about the 1992 election stimulated such a notable increase in participation? Was it dissatisfaction with the current administration, the presence of a galvanizing third-party candidate in Ross Perot, or some other factor? Third, what conclusions can we draw from survey respondents' systematic overreporting of their own participation (put simply, people either forget or lie about their failure to vote)?

The exceptionally low level of voter turnout in the United States for presidential elections compared to similar elections in other countries is often taken to raise serious questions about the state of American democracy. But note that while the United States does have the lowest turnout of any democracy, it is also true that the United States has more elections for more levels of government with more elective offices at each level than any other country in the world. *See* Michael Schudson, *Voting Rites: Why We Need a New Concept of Citizenship,* American Prospect, Fall 1994, at 62. For example, even the majority of judges in the United States are elected, rather than appointed, a fact traceable to the Jacksonian era's populist ideology. No other constitutional democracy elects judges on a similar scale; indeed, only Japan and Switzerland appear to have any form of electoral control over judges. Steven P. Croley, *The Majoritarian Difficulty: Elective Judiciaries and the Rule of Law,* 62 U. Chi. L. Rev. 689, 690-91 (1995).

What does the conjunction of these two facts—a multitude of elective offices but low voter turnout—suggest about the relationship between the rhetoric and practice of American democracy? One view might be that the ideology of popular sovereignty, understood as direct electoral participation, became so unchallengeable at various periods, such as the Jacksonian era, that American democracy now suffers from too many offices being elective. Might weak democracy—low turnout—stem, in part, from too much democracy—too many elections for too many offices? Is it clear that the best way to hold public officials accountable is through the electoral mechanism? Assuming it might be a good idea to change some currently elective offices to appointed ones, how politically likely is such a shift, given the power of popular sovereignty rhetoric in American culture? Note that commissions or bar associations in several states have recently proposed replacing elective state judiciaries with merit-selection systems, but none of these reforms has as yet been enacted. In general, what kinds of public offices should be controlled through popular vote as opposed to other selection methods?

A number of commentators and critics have focused on one aspect of the American system—its voter registration practices—as a significant factor in the low levels of turnout.

Frances Fox Piven and Richard Cloward, Why Americans Don't Vote (1989)

[D]espite the importance that political scientists usually attribute to electoral processes in shaping politics, much scholarly opinion does not attribute important political or policy consequences to the constriction of the electorate. In fact, a fair amount of academic work has been directed to explaining why nonvoting should not be considered a problem at all. In one major tradition, nonvoting is defined as a kind of voting, a tacit expression of consent and evidence of satisfaction. Since many people are so satisfied, their abstention actually demonstrates the strength of the democratic polity. Of course, no one has satisfactorily explained why "the politics of happiness" is so consistently concentrated among the least well off.

Another variant on this theme asserts that nonvoting contributes to the health of a democratic polity, not because the abstainers are necessarily so satisfied, but because mass abstention reduces conflict and provides political leaders with the latitude they require to govern responsibly. A functioning democracy, the argument goes, requires a balance between participation and nonparticipation, between involvement and noninvolvement. The "crisis of democracy" theorists, for example, reason that an "excess" of participation endangers democratic institutions by "overloading" them with demands, especially popular economic demands. This rather Olympian view of the democratic "functions" of nonvoting generally fails to deal with the decidedly undemocratic consequences of tempering the demands of some strata of the polity and not others.

* * *

Our answer to the question why people don't vote is informed by a different intellectual tradition focusing on how politics patterns electoral participation. Voting and nonvoting are shaped by institutional arrangements that have been forged by a long history of political conflict, including conflict specifically over the question of who should enjoy the right to vote. That conflict, in turn, was motivated by the recognition that who votes and who does not would have consequences for American politics.

... We think the linchpin of the distorted American democracy in the contemporary period is the distinctive system of voter registration procedures. This requires comment because people rarely give much thought to governmental procedures for certifying voters. Existing registration arrangements are taken for granted as natural and inevitable. In fact, American registration procedures are Byzantine compared with those that prevail in other democracies. The major difference is that governments elsewhere assume an affirmative obligation to register citizens. People are certified as automatically eligible to vote when they come of age and obtain identity cards, or government-sponsored canvassers go from door to door before each election to enlist voters. The United States is the only major democracy where government assumes no responsibility for helping citizens cope with voter registration procedures. In 1980, 39 to 40 percent of the American electorate was unregistered, or more than 60 million in an eligible voting age population of 159 million, and two out of three of the unregistered resided in households with incomes below the median. Furthermore, the significance of low registration is suggested by the fact that once people are registered, they overwhelmingly vote. In 1980, more than 80 percent of registrants went to the polls, and the turnout among those with little education and income was only marginally lower. Consequently, when turnout in the United States is calculated just for registered voters, the rate here is comparable to rates in other democracies with more or less automatic registration systems.

We hasten to say, however, that we do not think voter registration requirements were historically the singular cause of low turnout (nor are they the singular cause today). The changes in electoral politics that converged to produce that result were indeed complicated; they included shifts in the pattern of party competition and in the organization of the parties, as well as in the rules governing access to the ballot. Those complications have provided the empirical grounds for the diverse points of view in the literature. Nevertheless, we think voter registration requirements were more important than is generally acknowledged. On the one hand, these requirements constituted direct barriers to voting. On the other hand, as these procedural obstacles gradually eroded voter participation among working people, the parties turned away from the issues and campaign stratagems needed to win lower-class support, with lasting effects on our politics. The resulting marginalization of working people not only from political influence but from the political culture created by the parties in turn reinforced their tendency to abstain. Finally, the circle was completed when the political parties that had been shaped within this constricted electorate then defended the barriers to electoral participation that worked to limit the electorate.

In other words, voter registration barriers not only restricted the suffrage, but by restricting the suffrage, they transformed the calculus of the political parties, with pervasive consequences for American political development. In principle, parties strive to select candidates and fashion political appeals that will win majorities. And, in principle, electoral competition should stimulate contending parties to mobilize voters, including new voters. Of course, the parties are subject to many other influences in fashioning campaigns, not least the influence of big money contributors. But to the extent that voters and their preferences figure in party calculations, the skewed shape of the American voting universe has decisively influenced the practices of the parties. Except under extremely volatile electoral conditions, party organizers turn away from the candidates, the policies, the campaign language, and the logistics that would reach and appeal to the have-nots. Voter registration procedures are thus a main reason that the American political parties have become unhinged from large portions of the potential electorate.

* * *

[E]arly voter registration laws emerged out of conflicts in which state and local parties were very active contenders, if not the principal contenders. Converse, notwithstanding his general conviction that idealistic reformers were the main political actors in voter registration reform, describes the "heated political controversy" generated by the registration issue in the period from 1860 to 1900:

> Minority groups in the largest urban centers typically used the Democratic Party as a vehicle to challenge the constitutionality of laws that forced them into an elaborate registration procedure but required nothing of their small-town and rural compatriots. Meanwhile, of course, the Republicans were painfully and often explicitly aware of how sharply their rural vote base might shrink with the extension of controls on voting to the countryside, and fought tooth and nail to preserve their artificial legal advantage. Many of the wanderings into and out of statewide registration laws that occurred in some states were a simple reflection of the momentary ascendancy of one or the other of these competing powers.

The sources of these local partisan conflicts are clear. State Republican parties stood to gain from disenfranchising urban and working-class voters, and northern Democratic parties stood to lose, not only because the laws were aimed at the cities where the Democrats were stronger, but because the immigrant and working-class voters who were more likely to be affected were the key to Democratic power in the cities.

* * *

The first observation to be made about these early battles over registration is how aptly they illustrate [the] point that the grand strategy of politics concerns itself above all else with the structure of institutions. It follows that the parties themselves always try to shape the rules under which they compete, including the rules governing voter participation.

* * *

Accordingly, just how the new requirements worked out in practice depended very much on the vigor of local political parties, and particularly on the clientelist parties that dominated electoral politics in the cities where the immigrant working class was concentrated. Whatever the intentions of the registration reformers, where local parties were strong and closely linked to the immigrant working class, ways were discovered to overcome the new restrictions, just as ways had been found to overcome earlier restrictions, such as naturalization laws....

However, after the election of 1896 and the weakening of party competition on the state level throughout most of the country, effective partisan resistance to registration statutes largely dissipated. Registration laws spread rapidly, and became more restrictive.

* * *

.... With these points made, we return to the proposition that rules, once implemented, change politics. As voter registration restrictions took effect little by little, the linkages that bound the parties to their working- and lower-class constituencies withered. Calculations of electoral advantage turned party strategists away from the worse off, who voted less, and toward the better off, who voted more. This tendency meshed nicely with other developments that were changing the local parties, including the contraction of clientelist resources, and the rise of business influence. Once this shift in orientation and constituencies had occurred, the parties tried to sustain it in order to avoid the threats to incumbency and to internal stability that new and unpredictable voters entailed. Consequently, the parties themselves became the defenders of the voter registration procedures that ensured their stability and protected incumbents. As early as 1917, the machine and the reformers switched sides in Chicago, with the machine defending more cumbersome registration procedures against the Chicago Bureau of Public Efficiency's efforts at simplification. Thus, the local parties became the guardians of a contracted electoral universe, using the voter registration restrictions that had helped to create that constricted electorate in the first place. In the late nineteenth century, the local parties helped voters hurdle electoral barriers because they depended on a broad electorate, but as the parties lost ground to the disenfranchisers, they adapted to a narrow electorate by taking up the defense of electoral barriers.

As the connections between the parties and the electorate were reconstituted so that working-class groups were far less important, party appeals changed. In the mid-nineteenth century, clientelist parties employed the boisterous rhetoric of class in building popular support, along with strident ethnic and religious appeals. And in the decades after the Civil War, there were at least some signs of the emergence of appeals based on issues, including economic issues, partly in response to the insurgent third-party challenges that injected broad issue appeals into electoral contests. The campaign of 1896 underlined the possibility of the emergence of issue politics. "Perceptions of 'hard times' dominated ... and strongly influenced the decisionmaking process of large numbers of voters. Older ethno-religious antagonisms did not suddenly evaporate ... [but] as economic worries came increasingly to the forefront of consciousness, they crosscut the older lines of conflict and decreased their salience." As the links that bound the local parties to a working-class constituency became attenuated, however, party appeals based on class identity and class interests gradually disappeared. Electoral contests were eventually neutered of class rhetoric, with the result that the marginalization of working-class voters from electoral politics that resulted in the first instance from the combination of registration barriers and the breakdown of clientelist ties was not overcome by the emergence of electoral contests whose symbols and substance resonated strongly with working-class experience, except under the exceptional conditions of the Great Depression campaigns of the 1930s.

Under these political conditions, voter registration procedures depressed turnout. Without the parties as intermediaries to help voters complete registration procedures, the "costs" of registration rise. And without appeals that resonate with the identity and interests of working-class groups, the benefits of voting shrink. In short, rules do indeed originate in politics, and their implementation is conditioned by complex features of the political situation, including the new political conditions the rules themselves helped to produce. Voter registration arrangements helped to create a party system severed from the working class. In a politics of weak linkages and hollow appeals, registration became a larger barrier to participation.

We argued earlier that a singular emphasis on the crushing of party competition associated with the election of 1896 ultimately fails as an explanation of the long-term decline in turnout, if only because it cannot explain why low turnout became a permanent feature of twentieth-century political life, persisting throughout the twentieth century, long after party competition was restored to most of the country. In our opinion, it was the combined effects of changes in the local parties and the introduction of new rules that marginalized potentially disruptive elements from the electorate. This helped to stabilize the tendency toward one-party sectional domination associated with the election of 1896. Moreover, the changes in the rules and in the parties that secured that result continued to depress turnout, even after party competition intensified in much of the North in the 1930s, and in the South in the 1960s. One-party sectionalism is a thing of the past, to be sure, but other aspects of the system of 1896 persist.

NOTES AND QUESTIONS

1. Courts have never applied strict scrutiny to the requirement that voters register a substantial time before the general election. (Remember *Marston v. Lewis*, 410 U.S. 679 (1973), which upheld closing the rolls in Arizona nearly two months before the election). Why not? Does the fact that some states—Minnesota, Wisconsin, and Wyoming—have election-day registration, and that North Dakota has no registration requirement at all suggest that such systems are unnecessary to achieve any compelling state interest? Note that Minnesota, Wisconsin, and Wyoming rank among the top states in the percent of eligible voters registered.

2. The negative liberty aspect of voting has particular bite with respect to registration requirements. If voting were a positive entitlement, would the states bear more of a burden to assure registration? For example, would they be required to do affirmative outreach?

3. The newly-enacted National Voter Registration Act of 1993, 42 U.S.C. §§ 1973gg to 1973gg–10 (the so-called "motor voter" law) marks the first attempt by Congress to create an affirmative government duty to register voters. (The appointment of federal registrars to enroll voters in particularly recalcitrant southern jurisdictions under the Voting Rights Act of 1965 was a relatively small-scale program and did not involve the enlistment of the states in the effort.) The Act requires states to establish three sorts of registration procedures. First, they must enable individuals to register to vote simultaneously with their application for drivers' licenses. 42 U.S.C. § 1973gg–3. Second, states are required to provide for mail-in voter registration and the forms must be made readily available, essentially so groups can conduct registration drives. *See* 42 U.S.C. § 1973gg–4. Finally, states have to provide in-person registration at various agencies, including all public assistance agencies and agencies that serve primarily the disabled; they are encouraged to provide such assistance at other agencies, such as schools, libraries, and licensing bureaus. 42 U.S.C. § 1973gg–5.

The Act's requirements apply only to registration for federal elections. Why? Is a state's decision to maintain a dual registration system suspicious, particularly if the federal registration system achieves much higher registration among minority groups? Recently, a state court judge ordered Illinois to abandon dual registration. *See* Sue Ellen Christian, *State Ordered To Stop 2–Step on Motor–Voter; Edgar Blasted for Dual System of*

Registration, Chi. Trib., June 22, 1996, at 1 (requiring Illinois to let 160,000 voters who had been registered under the NVRA solely for federal elections to vote in state and local elections as well). *Cf. Harman v. Forssenius,* 380 U.S. 528 (1965); *Mississippi State Chapter, Operation Push v. Allain,* 674 F.Supp. 1245 (N.D.Miss.1987) (holding that Mississippi's dual registration system violated section 2 of the Voting Rights Act because of its disproportionate impact on black citizens).

In addition to these affirmative obligations, the Act restricts states from engaging in certain actions that remove voters from the rolls. Perhaps the most important of these prohibitions is the Act's ban on removing voters simply for failure to vote. 42 U.S.C. § 1973gg–6(b)(2).

The Act has survived a variety of constitutional challenges raised by state governments. *See, e.g., Association of Community Organizations for Reform Now v. Edgar,* 56 F.3d 791 (7th Cir.1995); *Voting Rights Coalition v. Wilson,* 60 F.3d 1411 (9th Cir.1995), *cert. denied,* 116 S.Ct. 815 (1996). But consider whether the NVRA is vulnerable in light of the Supreme Court's recent decision in *Printz v. United States,* 117 S.Ct. 2365 (1997). *Printz* involved a challenge to the Brady Handgun Violence Prevention Act, which required local law enforcement agencies to conduct background checks of firearms buyers. In *Printz,* the Court held that the Federal Government cannot command State officers "to administer or enforce a federal regulatory program." Moreover, "no case-by-case weighing of the burdens or benefits is necessary; such commands are fundamentally incompatible with our constitutional system of dual sovereignty." The NVRA requires state officials in particular state agencies to provide forms permitting people to register to vote and to provide the same assistance in filling out those forms as they do in filling out their own agency's forms. How would you distinguish *Printz?*

The Act took effect on January 1, 1995. Eleven million citizens either enrolled or updated their registrations during the Act's first year: 5.5 million registered in motor vehicle agencies, 1.3 registered in public assistance agencies, and 4.2 million registered by mail. Florida and Texas each registered over 1.2 million voters. *See* National Motor Voter Coalition, First Year Report on the Impact of the National Voter Registration Act, January 1, 1995–December 31, 1995 (1996).

What are the political consequences of increased registration? Initially, many Republicans opposed motor-voter legislation (in fact, President George Bush vetoed a precursor to the NVRA), in part on the assumption that making registration easier would disproportionately benefit the Democratic Party, since its supporters tended to be poorer and less well educated. The early evidence suggests the Act has had mixed effects. *See* Nancy E. Roman, *Motor-Voter Law Gives GOP Unexpected Lift,* Wash. Times, May 13, 1996, at A1 (nearly one-third of new voters have registered as independents and more have registered as Republicans than Democrats across the south). A high percentage of new registrants are younger voters. In the last few presidential elections, voters under 30 made up the strongest age group supporting Republicans. *See* Cokie Roberts & Steven Roberts, *Young Voters Apathetic and Both Parties Like It That Way*, Dallas Morning News, July 7, 1996, at 5J. At the same time, some reports suggest that states have dragged their heels at implementing voter registration in public-assistance and other social service agencies, where the voters most prone to support Democrats are more likely to be found. *See, e.g., Condon v. Reno*, 913 F.Supp. 946 (D.S.C.1995) (gubernatorial executive order required voter registration applications to be provided at the DMV but not at the Department of Social Services, the Department of Disabilities and Special Needs, the Commission for the Blind, the Department of Vocational Rehabilitation, or the Protection and Advocacy System for the Handicapped).

CHAPTER 3

THE REAPPORTIONMENT REVOLUTION

The right of individual citizens to vote freely is undoubtedly one of the defining features of democratic legitimacy. Unfortunately, the act of casting a ballot by itself is insufficient to guarantee a truly meaningful right of democratic participation. Because of the apparent legitimacy that the act of voting gives to government, it has been a hallmark of the twentieth century that repressive regimes of all sorts have claimed the mantle of elected representatives of their citizens. This has given rise to show elections in countries such as the Soviet Union, which not only allowed but oftentimes compelled citizens to vote in state-sponsored elections. Such voting was an electoral device in name only, however, as the exclusive candidates for office were those on the state-approved slate. Clearly, something more than simply casting a ballot for a series of state-prescribed candidates was necessary to define democratic legitimacy.

In searching for a more robust understanding of voting in a democratic society, the inquiry must turn to the act of casting a *meaningful* vote. To be meaningful, a vote must matter in the sense that it is capable of being aggregated with those of like-minded voters in order to pursue common electoral objectives. As soon as the inquiry shifts to effectiveness in securing representation, therefore, our attention must move away from individuals to the capacity to effectively aggregate groups of votes. As expressed by Justice Lewis Powell, "[t]he concept of 'representation' necessarily applies to groups: groups of voters elect representatives, individual voters do not." *Davis v. Bandemer*, 478 U.S. 109, 167 (1986)(Powell, J., concurring in part and dissenting in part).

The search for meaningful electoral opportunity thrust the Supreme Court into one of the most difficult areas of policing the electoral system. In this Chapter, we shall explore the structural dimension of proper electoral opportunity, focusing on the emergence and application of the, by now well-known, one-person/one-vote rule.

A. The Political Thicket

Colegrove v. Green
328 U.S. 549 (1946).

■ Mr. Justice Frankfurter announced the judgment of the Court and an opinion in which Mr. Justice Reed and Mr. Justice Burton concur.

[T]hree qualified voters in Illinois districts which have much larger populations than other Illinois Congressional districts ... brought this suit against the Governor, the Secretary of State, and the Auditor of the State of Illinois, as members ex officio of the Illinois Primary Certifying Board, to restrain them, in effect, from taking proceedings for an election in November 1946, under the provisions of Illinois law governing Congressional districts....

We are of opinion that the appellants ask of this Court what is beyond its competence to grant. This is one of those demands on judicial power which cannot be met by verbal fencing about "jurisdiction." It must be resolved by considerations on the basis of which this Court, from time to time, has refused to intervene in controversies. It has refused to do so because due regard for the effective working of our Government revealed this issue to be of a peculiarly political nature and therefore not meet for judicial determination.

This is not an action to recover for damage because of the discriminatory exclusion of a plaintiff from rights enjoyed by other citizens. The basis for the suit is not a private wrong, but a wrong suffered by Illinois as a polity. Compare *Nixon v. Herndon*, 273 U.S. 536 and *Lane v. Wilson*, 307 U.S. 268, with *Giles v. Harris*, 189 U.S. 475. In effect this is an appeal to the federal courts to reconstruct the electoral process of Illinois in order that it may be adequately represented in the councils of the Nation. Because the Illinois legislature has failed to revise its Congressional Representative districts in order to reflect great changes, during more than a generation, in the distribution of its population, we are asked to do this, as it were, for Illinois.

Of course no court can affirmatively re-map the Illinois districts so as to bring them more in conformity with the standards of fairness for a representative system. At best we could only declare the existing electoral system invalid. The result would be to leave Illinois undistricted and to bring into operation, if the Illinois legislature chose not to act, the choice of members for the House of Representatives on a state-wide ticket. The last stage may be worse than the first. The upshot of judicial action may defeat the vital political principle which led Congress, more than a hundred years ago, to require districting. This requirement, in the language of Chancellor Kent, "was recommended by the wisdom and justice of giving, as far as possible, to the local subdivisions of the people of each state, a due influence in the choice of representatives, so as not to leave the aggregate minority of the people in a state, though approaching perhaps to a majority, to be wholly overpowered by the combined action of the numerical majority, without any voice whatever in the national councils." 1 Kent, Commentaries (12th ed., 1873) * 230–31, n. (c). Assuming acquiescence on the part of the authorities of Illinois in the selection of its Representatives by a mode that defies the direction of Congress for selection by districts, the House of Representatives may not acquiesce. In the exercise of its power to judge the qualifications of its own members, the House may reject a delegation of Representatives-at-large. Article I, § 5, Cl. 1.... Nothing is clearer than that this controversy concerns matters that bring courts into immediate and active relations with party contests. From the determination of such issues this Court has traditionally held aloof. It is hostile to a democratic system to involve the judiciary in the politics of the people. And it is not less pernicious if such judicial intervention in an essentially political contest be dressed up in the abstract phrases of the law.

The appellants urge with great zeal that the conditions of which they complain are grave evils and offend public morality. The Constitution of the United States gives ample power to provide against these evils. But due regard for the Constitution as a viable system precludes judicial correction. Authority for dealing with such problems resides elsewhere. Article I, § 4 of the Constitution provides that "The Times, Places and Manner of holding Elections for ... Representatives, shall be prescribed in each State by the Legislature thereof; but the Congress may at any time by Law make or alter such Regulations...." The short of it is that the Constitution has conferred upon Congress exclusive authority to secure fair representation by the States in the popular House and left to that House determination whether States have fulfilled their responsibility. If Congress failed in exercising its powers, whereby standards of fairness are offended, the remedy ultimately lies with the people. Whether Congress faithfully discharges its duty or not, the subject has been committed to the exclusive control of Congress. An aspect of government from which the judiciary, in view of what is involved, has been excluded by the clear intention of the Constitution cannot be entered by the federal courts because Congress may have been in default in exacting from States obedience to its mandate.

The one stark fact that emerges from a study of the history of Congressional apportionment is its embroilment in politics, in the sense of party contests and party interests. The Constitution enjoins upon Congress the duty of apportioning Representatives "among the several States ... according to their respective Numbers...." Article I, § 2. Yet, Congress has at times been heedless of this command and not apportioned according to the requirements of the Census. It never occurred to anyone that this Court could issue mandamus to compel Congress to perform its mandatory duty to apportion.... Until 1842 there was the greatest diversity among the States in the manner of choosing Representatives because Congress had made no requirement for districting. 5 Stat. 491. Congress then provided for the election of Representatives by districts. Strangely enough, the power to do so was seriously questioned; it was still doubted by a Committee of Congress as late as 1901.... In 1850 Congress dropped the requirement. 9 Stat. 428, 432-33. The Reapportionment Act of 1862 required that the districts be of contiguous territory. 12 Stat. 572. In 1872 Congress added the requirement of substantial equality of inhabitants. 17 Stat. 28. This was reinforced in 1911. 37 Stat. 13, 14. But the 1929 Act, as we have seen, dropped these requirements. 46 Stat. 21. Throughout our history, whatever may have been the controlling Apportionment Act, the most glaring disparities have prevailed as to the contours and the population of districts....

To sustain this action would cut very deep into the very being of Congress. Courts ought not to enter this political thicket. The remedy for unfairness in districting is to secure State legislatures that will apportion properly, or to invoke the ample powers of Congress. The Constitution has many commands that are not enforceable by courts because they clearly fall outside the conditions and purposes that circumscribe judicial action.... The Constitution has left the performance of many duties in our governmental scheme to depend on the fidelity of the executive and legislative action and, ultimately, on the vigilance of the people in exercising their political rights.

Dismissal of the complaint is affirmed.

■ MR. JUSTICE BLACK, dissenting.

The complaint alleges the following facts essential to the position I take: Appellants, citizens and voters of Illinois, live in congressional election districts, the respective populations of which range from 612,000 to 914,000. Twenty other congressional election districts have populations that range from 112,116 to 385,207. In seven of these districts the population is below 200,000. The Illinois Legislature established these districts in 1901 on the basis of the Census of 1900. The Federal Census of 1910, of 1920, of 1930, and of 1940, each showed a growth of population in Illinois and a substantial shift in the distribution of population among the districts established in 1901. But up to date, attempts to have the State Legislature reapportion congressional election districts so as more nearly to equalize their population have been unsuccessful. A contributing cause of this situation, according to appellants, is the fact that the State Legislature is chosen on the basis of state election districts inequitably apportioned in a way similar to that of the 1901 congressional election districts. The implication is that the issues of state and congressional apportionment are thus so interdependent that it is to the interest of state legislators to perpetuate the inequitable apportionment of both state and congressional election districts. Prior to this proceeding a series of suits had been brought in the state courts challenging the State's local and federal apportionment system. In all these cases the Supreme Court of the State had denied effective relief....

It is difficult for me to see why the 1901 State Apportionment Act does not deny appellants equal protection of the laws. The failure of the Legislature to reapportion the congressional election districts for forty years, despite census figures indicating great changes in the distribution of the population, has resulted in election districts the populations of which range from 112,000 to 900,000. One of the appellants lives in a district of more than 900,000 people. His vote is consequently much less effective than that of each of the citizens living in the district of 112,000. And such a gross inequality in the voting power of citizens irrefutably demonstrates a complete lack of effort to make an equitable apportionment. The 1901 State Apportionment Act if applied to the next election would thus result in a wholly indefensible discrimination against appellants and all other voters in heavily populated districts. The equal protection clause of the Fourteenth Amendment forbids such discrimination. It does not permit the States to pick out certain qualified citizens or groups of citizens and deny them the right to vote at all. See *Nixon v. Herndon*, 273 U.S. 536, 541; *Nixon v. Condon*, 286 U.S. 73. No one would deny that the equal protection clause would also prohibit a law that would expressly give certain citizens a half-vote and others a full vote. The probable effect of the 1901 State Apportionment Act in the coming election will be that certain citizens, and among them the appellants, will in some instances have votes only one-ninth as effective in choosing representatives to Congress as the votes of other citizens. Such discriminatory legislation seems to me exactly the kind that the equal protection clause was intended to prohibit.

[...] While the Constitution contains no express provision requiring that congressional election districts established by the States must contain approximately equal populations, the constitutionally guaranteed right to vote and the right to have one's vote counted clearly imply the policy that state election systems, no matter what their form, should be designed to give approximately equal weight to each vote cast. To some extent this implication of Article I is expressly stated by § 2 of the Fourteenth Amendment which provides that "Representatives shall be apportioned among the several States according to their respective numbers...." The purpose of this requirement is obvious: It is to make the votes of the citizens of the several States equally effective in the selection of members of Congress. It was intended to make illegal a nation-wide "rotten borough" system as between the States. The policy behind it is broader than that. It prohibits as well congressional "rotten boroughs" within the States, such as the ones here involved. The policy is that which is laid down by all the constitutional provisions regulating the election of members of the House of Representatives, including Article I which guarantees the right to vote and to have that vote effectively counted: All groups, classes, and individuals shall to the extent that it is practically feasible be given equal representation in the House of Representatives, which, in conjunction with the Senate, writes the laws affecting the life, liberty, and property of all the people....

Had Illinois passed an Act requiring that all of its twenty-six Congressmen be elected by the citizens of one county, it would clearly have amounted to a denial to the citizens of the other counties of their constitutionally guaranteed right to vote. And I cannot imagine that an Act that would have apportioned twenty-five Congressmen to the State's smallest county and one Congressman to all the others, would have been sustained by any court. Such an Act would clearly have violated the constitutional policy of equal representation. The 1901 Apportionment Act here involved violates that policy in the same way. The policy with respect to federal elections laid down by the Constitution, while it does not mean that the courts can or should prescribe the precise methods to be followed by state legislatures and the invalidation of all Acts that do not embody those precise methods, does mean that state legislatures must make real efforts to bring about approximately equal representation of citizens in Congress. Here the Legislature of Illinois has not done so. Whether that was due to negligence or was a wilful effort to deprive some citizens of an effective vote, the admitted result is that the constitutional policy of equality of representation has been defeated. Under these circumstances it is the Court's duty to invalidate the state law....

■ MR. JUSTICE DOUGLAS and MR. JUSTICE MURPHY join in this dissent.

NOTES AND QUESTIONS

1. *Colegrove* is best remembered for Justice Frankfurter's evocative image of the "political thicket." Justice Frankfurter gives a number of justifications for the judiciary staying out of questions of political apportionment. These run a broad gamut from concerns over constitutional structure to the administrability of a potential remedy, should the Court immerse itself in deciding on proper forms of political governance. Among the concerns, we may identify: a) prudential limitations on the Court's jurisdiction (the "political question" doctrine); b) concerns over institutional competence (the Court has little expertise in redressing apportionment imbalances); c) administrability of remedies (embroilment in politics); and d) availability of alternative institutions to remedy any apportionment defects (such as Congress or the state legislature). How persuasive are any of these arguments individually?

2. Are there structural obstacles to the reform of malapportionment through the State political process? Justice Black argues that congressional apportionment is conducted by the state legislature, which in turn is malapportioned along the same lines as the State congressional delegation. Would reform of the State's congressional delegation further the interests of state legislators from similarly malapportioned districts? Would it serve the interests of such legislators' constituents who would have otherwise enjoyed enhanced influence over the election of the State's congressional representatives?

3. Do similar problems present themselves in Congress? Why should representatives from one state be concerned about malapportionment in another state? Is there not reason to believe that the malapportionment found in Illinois was likely replicated in other states? Would this reduce the likelihood that other representatives would lend assistance to underrepresented citizens of Illinois?

4. The malapportionment in Illinois had a clear urban/rural division. The pattern of maldistribution of representatives generally resulted from the increasingly urban nature of American life through the twentieth century. The malapportionment tended to result from the distribution of representatives on a county-by-county basis. As urban areas grew, the malapportionment of representatives increased. Not surprisingly, rural representatives were unwilling to reapportion their states. Not only were rural constituents likely to be adversely affected by the consolidation of urban political power, but rural elected officials likely would be displaced from their jobs by reapportionment. Should rural interests be protected through independent representation even when the urban population is growing? May a state legitimately choose to represent regional interests on a non-population basis?

Baker v. Carr
369 U.S. 186 (1962).

■ Mr. Justice Brennan delivered the opinion of the Court.

* * *

The General Assembly of Tennessee consists of the Senate with 33 members and the House of Representatives with 99 members.... [Under the Tennessee Constitution,] Tennessee's standard for allocating legislative representation among her counties is the total number of qualified voters resident in the respective counties, subject only to minor qualifications. Decennial reapportionment in compliance with the constitutional scheme was effected by the General Assembly each decade from 1871 to 1901.... In 1901 the General Assembly abandoned separate enumeration in favor of reliance upon the Federal Census and passed the Apportionment Act here in controversy. In the more than 60 years since that action, all proposals in both Houses of the General Assembly for reapportionment have failed to pass.

Between 1901 and 1961, Tennessee has experienced substantial growth and redistribution of her population. In 1901 the population was 2,020,616, of whom 487,380 were eligible to vote. The 1960 Federal Census reports the State's population at 3,567,089, of whom 2,092,891 are eligible to vote. The relative standings of the counties in terms of qualified voters have changed significantly. It is primarily the continued application of the 1901 Apportionment Act to this shifted and enlarged voting population which gives rise to the present controversy.

[T]he complaint alleges . . . that "because of the population changes since 1900, and the failure of the Legislature to reapportion itself since 1901," the 1901 statute became "unconstitutional and obsolete." Appellants also argue that, because of the composition of the legislature effected by the 1901 Apportionment Act, redress in the form of a state constitutional amendment to change the entire mechanism for reapportioning, or any other change short of that, is difficult or impossible.[14] The complaint concludes that "these plaintiffs and others similarly situated, are denied the equal protection of the laws accorded them by the Fourteenth Amendment to the Constitution of the United States by virtue of the debasement of their votes."

* * *

IV.

JUSTICIABILITY

In holding that the subject matter of this suit was not justiciable, the District Court relied on *Colegrove v. Green,* and subsequent per curiam cases. . . . We hold that this challenge to an apportionment presents no nonjusticiable "political question." . . .

Of course the mere fact that the suit seeks protection of a political right does not mean it presents a political question. Such an objection "is little more than a play upon words." *Nixon v. Herndon,* 273 U.S. 536, 540. Rather, it is argued that apportionment cases, whatever the actual wording of the complaint, can involve no federal constitutional right except one resting on the guaranty of a republican form of government, and that complaints based on that clause have been held to present political questions which are nonjusticiable.

We hold that the claim pleaded here neither rests upon nor implicates the Guaranty Clause and that its justiciability is therefore not foreclosed by our decisions of cases involving that clause.

* * *

14. The appellants claim that no General Assembly constituted according to the 1901 Act will submit reapportionment proposals either to the people or to a Constitutional Convention. There is no provision for popular initiative in Tennessee. Amendments proposed in the Senate or House must first be approved by a majority of all members of each House and again by two-thirds of the members in the General Assembly next chosen. The proposals are then submitted to the people at the next general election in which a Governor is to be chosen. Alternatively, the legislature may submit to the people at any general election the question of calling a convention to consider specified proposals. Such as are adopted at a convention do not, however, become effective unless approved by a majority of the qualified voters voting separately on each proposed change or amendment at an election fixed by the convention. Conventions shall not be held oftener than once in six years. . . . [The enabling acts for the most recent conventions] . . . provided that delegates . . . were to be chosen from the counties and floterial districts just as are members of the State House of Representatives.

[... I]n the Guaranty Clause cases and in the other "political question" cases, it is the relationship between the judiciary and the coordinate branches of the Federal Government, and not the federal judiciary's relationship to the States, which gives rise to the "political question."

We have said that "In determining whether a question falls within [the political question] category, the appropriateness under our system of government of attributing finality to the action of the political departments and also the lack of satisfactory criteria for a judicial determination are dominant considerations." The nonjusticiability of a political question is primarily a function of the separation of powers.

It is apparent that several formulations which vary slightly according to the settings in which the questions arise may describe a political question, although each has one or more elements which identify it as essentially a function of the separation of powers. Prominent on the surface of any case held to involve a political question is found a textually demonstrable constitutional commitment of the issue to a coordinate political department; or a lack of judicially discoverable and manageable standards for resolving it; or the impossibility of deciding without an initial policy determination of a kind clearly for nonjudicial discretion; or the impossibility of a court's undertaking independent resolution without expressing lack of the respect due coordinate branches of government; or an unusual need for unquestioning adherence to a political decision already made; or the potentiality of embarrassment from multifarious pronouncements by various departments on one question.

Unless one of these formulations is inextricable from the case at bar, there should be no dismissal for nonjusticiability on the ground of a political question's presence. The doctrine of which we treat is one of "political questions," not one of "political cases." ...

[Although] it is argued that this case shares the characteristics of ... cases concerning the Constitution's guaranty, in Art. IV, § 4, of a republican form of government [... we believe] that the nonjusticiability of such claims has nothing to do with their touching upon matters of state governmental organization.

* * *

The question here is the consistency of state action with the Federal Constitution. We have no question decided, or to be decided, by a political branch of government coequal with this Court. Nor do we risk embarrassment of our government abroad, or grave disturbance at home if we take issue with Tennessee as to the constitutionality of her action here challenged. Nor need the appellants, in order to succeed in this action, ask the Court to enter upon policy determinations for which judicially manageable standards are lacking. Judicial standards under the Equal Protection

Clause are well developed and familiar, and it has been open to courts since the enactment of the Fourteenth Amendment to determine, if on the particular facts they must, that a discrimination reflects no policy, but simply arbitrary and capricious action.

This case does, in one sense, involve the allocation of political power within a State, and the appellants might conceivably have added a claim under the Guaranty Clause. Of course ... any reliance on that clause would be futile. But because any reliance on the Guaranty Clause could not have succeeded it does not follow that appellants may not be heard on the equal protection claim which in fact they tender. True, it must be clear that the Fourteenth Amendment claim is not so enmeshed with those political question elements which render Guaranty Clause claims nonjusticiable as actually to present a political question itself. But we have found that not to be the case here.

* * *

When challenges to state action respecting matters of "the administration of the affairs of the State and the officers through whom they are conducted" have rested on claims of constitutional deprivation which are amenable to judicial correction, this Court has acted upon its view of the merits of the claim. For example, ... only last Term, in *Gomillion v. Lightfoot,* we applied the Fifteenth Amendment to strike down a redrafting of municipal boundaries which effected a discriminatory impairment of voting rights, in the face of what a majority of the Court of Appeals thought to be a sweeping commitment to state legislatures of the power to draw and redraw such boundaries.

* * *

We conclude that the complaint's allegations of a denial of equal protection present a justiciable constitutional cause of action upon which appellants are entitled to a trial and a decision. The right asserted is within the reach of judicial protection under the Fourteenth Amendment.

The judgment of the District Court is reversed and the cause is remanded for further proceedings consistent with this opinion.

■ Mr. Justice Douglas, concurring.

[Omitted]

■ Mr. Justice Clark, concurring.

One emerging from the rash of opinions with their accompanying clashing of views may well find himself suffering a mental blindness. The Court holds that the appellants have alleged a cause of action. However, it refuses to award relief here—although the facts are undisputed—and fails to give the District Court any guidance whatever.

* * *

II.

The controlling facts cannot be disputed. It appears from the record that 37% of the voters of Tennessee elect 20 of the 33 Senators while 40% of the voters elect 63 of the 99 members of the House. But this might not on its face be an "invidious discrimination," for a statutory discrimination will not be set aside if any state of facts reasonably may be conceived to justify it.

[... T]he root of the trouble is not in Tennessee's Constitution, for admittedly its policy has not been followed. The discrimination lies in the action of Tennessee's Assembly in allocating legislative seats to counties or districts created by it. Try as one may, Tennessee's apportionment just cannot be made to fit the pattern cut by its Constitution.... The frequency and magnitude of the inequalities in the present districting admit of no policy whatever.... [T]he apportionment picture in Tennessee is a topsy-turvical of gigantic proportions. This is not to say that some of the disparity cannot be explained, but when the entire [system] is examined—comparing the voting strength of counties of like population as well as contrasting that of the smaller with the larger counties—it leaves but one conclusion, namely that Tennessee's apportionment is a crazy quilt without rational basis....

As is admitted, there is a wide disparity of voting strength between the large and small counties. Some samples are: Moore County has a total representation of two with a population (2,340) of only one-eleventh of Rutherford County (25,316) with the same representation; Decatur County (5,563) has the same representation as Carter (23,303) though the latter has four times the population; likewise, Loudon County (13,264), Houston (3,084), and Anderson County (33,990) have the same representation, i. e., 1.25 each.

* * *

The truth is that—although this case has been here for two years and has had over six hours' argument (three times the ordinary case) and has been most carefully considered over and over again by us in Conference and individually—no one, not even the State nor the dissenters, has come up with any rational basis for Tennessee's apportionment statute.

No one ... contends that mathematical equality among voters is required by the Equal Protection Clause. But certainly there must be some rational design to a State's districting. The discrimination here does not fit any pattern—as I have said, it is but a crazy quilt.

* * *

III.

Although I find the Tennessee apportionment statute offends the Equal Protection Clause, I would not consider intervention by this Court into so delicate a field if there were any other relief available to the people of Tennessee. But the majority of the people of Tennessee have no "practical opportunities for exerting their political weight at the polls" to correct the existing "invidious discrimination." Tennessee has no initiative and referendum. I have searched diligently for other "practical opportunities" present under the law. I find none other than through the federal courts. The majority of the voters have been caught up in a legislative strait jacket. Tennessee has an "informed, civically militant electorate" and "an aroused popular conscience," but it does not sear "the conscience of the people's representatives." This is because the legislative policy has riveted the present seats in the Assembly to their respective constituencies, and by the votes of their incumbents a reapportionment of any kind is prevented. The people have been rebuffed at the hands of the Assembly; they have tried the constitutional convention route, but since the call must originate in the Assembly it, too, has been fruitless. They have tried Tennessee courts with the same result, and Governors have fought the tide only to flounder. It is said that there is recourse in Congress and perhaps that may be, but from a practical standpoint this is without substance. To date Congress has never undertaken such a task in any State. We therefore must conclude that the people of Tennessee are stymied and without judicial intervention will be saddled with the present discrimination in the affairs of their state government.

IV.

* * *

In view of all this background I doubt if anything more can be offered or will be gained by the State on remand, other than time. Nevertheless, not being able to muster a court to dispose of the case on the merits, I concur in the opinion of the majority and acquiesce in the decision to remand. However, in fairness I do think that Tennessee is entitled to have my idea of what it faces on the record before us and the trial court some light as to how it might proceed.

* * *

■ Mr. Justice Stewart, concurring.

The separate writings of my dissenting and concurring Brothers stray so far from the subject of today's decision as to convey, I think, a distressingly inaccurate impression of what the Court decides. For that reason, I think it appropriate, in joining the opinion of the Court, to emphasize in a few words what the opinion does and does not say.

* * *

The complaint in this case asserts that Tennessee's system of apportionment is utterly arbitrary—without any possible justification in rationality. The District Court did not reach the merits of that claim, and this

Court quite properly expresses no view on the subject. Contrary to the suggestion of my Brother Harlan, the Court does not say or imply that "state legislatures must be so structured as to reflect with approximate equality the voice of every voter." The Court does not say or imply that there is anything in the Federal Constitution "to prevent a State, acting not irrationally, from choosing any electoral legislative structure it thinks best suited to the interests, temper, and customs of its people." And contrary to the suggestion of my Brother Douglas, the Court most assuredly does not decide the question, "may a State weight the vote of one county or one district more heavily than it weights the vote in another?"

* * *

■ MR. JUSTICE FRANKFURTER, whom MR. JUSTICE HARLAN joins, dissenting.

The Court today reverses a uniform course of decision established by a dozen cases, including one by which the very claim now sustained was unanimously rejected only five years ago. The impressive body of rulings thus cast aside reflected the equally uniform course of our political history regarding the relationship between population and legislative representation—a wholly different matter from denial of the franchise to individuals because of race, color, religion or sex. Such a massive repudiation of the experience of our whole past in asserting destructively novel judicial power demands a detailed analysis of the role of this Court in our constitutional scheme. Disregard of inherent limits in the effective exercise of the Court's "judicial power" not only presages the futility of judicial intervention in the essentially political conflict of forces by which the relation between population and representation has time out of mind been and now is determined. It may well impair the Court's position as the ultimate organ of "the supreme Law of the Land" in that vast range of legal problems, often strongly entangled in popular feeling, on which this Court must pronounce. The Court's authority—possessed of neither the purse nor the sword—ultimately rests on sustained public confidence in its moral sanction. Such feeling must be nourished by the Court's complete detachment, in fact and in appearance, from political entanglements and by abstention from injecting itself into the clash of political forces in political settlements.

* * *

We were soothingly told at the bar of this Court that we need not worry about the kind of remedy a court could effectively fashion once the abstract constitutional right to have courts pass on a state-wide system of electoral districting is recognized as a matter of judicial rhetoric, because legislatures would heed the Court's admonition. This is not only a euphoric hope. It implies a sorry confession of judicial impotence in place of a frank acknowledgment that there is not under our Constitution a judicial remedy for every political mischief, for every undesirable exercise of legislative power. The Framers carefully and with deliberate forethought refused so to enthrone the judiciary. In this situation, as in others of like nature, appeal for relief does not belong here. Appeal must be to an informed, civically militant electorate. In a democratic society like ours, relief must come through an aroused popular conscience that sears the conscience of the people's representatives. In any event there is nothing judicially more unseemly nor more self-defeating than for this Court to make in terrorem pronouncements, to indulge in merely empty rhetoric, sounding a word of promise to the ear, sure to be disappointing to the hope.

* * *

II.

* * *

The Court has been particularly unwilling to intervene in matters concerning the structure and organization of the political institutions of the States. The abstention from judicial entry into such areas has been greater even than that which marks the Court's ordinary approach to issues of state power challenged under broad federal guarantees....

The cases involving Negro disfranchisement are no exception to the principle of avoiding federal judicial intervention into matters of state government in the absence of an explicit and clear constitutional imperative. For here the controlling command of Supreme Law is plain and unequivocal. An end of discrimination against the Negro was the compelling motive of the Civil War Amendments. The Fifteenth expresses this in terms, and it is no less true of the Equal Protection Clause of the Fourteenth.

* * *

The influence of these converging considerations—the caution not to undertake decision where standards meet for judicial judgment are lacking, the reluctance to interfere with matters of state government in the absence of an unquestionable and effectively enforceable mandate, the unwillingness to make courts arbiters of the broad issues of political organization historically committed to other institutions and for whose adjustment the judicial process is ill-adapted—has been decisive of the settled line of cases, reaching back more than a century, which holds that Art. IV, § 4, of the Constitution, guaranteeing to the States "a Republican Form of Government," is not enforceable through the courts.

* * *

III.

The present case involves all of the elements that have made the Guarantee Clause cases non-justiciable. It is, in effect, a Guarantee Clause claim masquerading under a different label. But it cannot make the case more fit for judicial action that appellants invoke the Fourteenth Amendment rather than Art. IV, § 4, where, in fact, the gist of their complaint is the same—unless it can be found that the Fourteenth Amendment speaks with greater particularity to their situation.

* * *

Appellants invoke the right to vote and to have their votes counted. But they are permitted to vote and their votes are counted. They go to the polls, they cast their ballots, they send their representatives to the state councils. Their complaint is simply that the representatives are not sufficiently numerous or powerful—in short, that Tennessee has adopted a basis of representation with which they are dissatisfied. Talk of "debasement" or "dilution" is circular talk. One cannot speak of "debasement" or "dilution" of the value of a vote until there is first defined a standard of reference as to what a vote should be worth. What is actually asked of the Court in this case is to choose among competing bases of representation—ultimately, really, among competing theories of political philosophy—in order to establish an appropriate frame of government for the State of Tennessee and thereby for all the States of the Union.

In such a matter, abstract analogies which ignore the facts of history deal in unrealities; they betray reason. This is not a case in which a State has, through a device however oblique and sophisticated, denied Negroes or Jews or redheaded persons a vote, or given them only a third or a sixth of a vote.... What Tennessee illustrates is an old and still widespread method of representation—representation by local geographical division, only in part respective of population—in preference to others, others, forsooth, more appealing.

* * *

The notion that representation proportioned to the geographic spread of population is so universally accepted as a necessary element of equality between man and man that it must be taken to be the standard of a political equality preserved by the Fourteenth Amendment—that it is, in appellants' words "the basic principle of representative government"—is, to put it bluntly, not true. However desirable and however desired by some among the great political thinkers and framers of our government, it has never been generally practiced, today or in the past. It was not the English system, it was not the colonial system, it was not the system chosen for the national government by the Constitution, it was not the system exclusively or even predominantly practiced by the States at the time of adoption of the Fourteenth Amendment, it is not predominantly practiced by the States today. Unless judges, the judges of this Court, are to make their private views of political wisdom the measure of the Constitution—views which in all honesty cannot but give the appearance, if not reflect the reality, of involvement with the business of partisan politics so inescapably a part of apportionment controversies—the Fourteenth Amendment, "itself a historical product," ... provides no guide for judicial oversight of the representation problem.

* * *

Detailed recent studies are available to describe the present-day constitutional and statutory status of apportionment in the fifty States. They demonstrate a decided twentieth-century trend away from population as the exclusive base of representation. Today, only a dozen state constitutions provide for periodic legislative reapportionment of both houses by a substantially unqualified application of the population standard, and only about a dozen more prescribe such reapportionment for even a single chamber. "Specific provision for county representation in at least one house of the state legislature has been increasingly adopted since the end of the 19th century...." More than twenty States now guarantee each county at least one seat in one of their houses regardless of population, and in nine others county or town units are given equal representation in one legislative branch, whatever the number of each unit's inhabitants. Of course, numerically considered, "These provisions invariably result in over-representation of the least populated areas...." And in an effort to curb the political dominance of metropolitan regions, at least ten States now limit the maximum entitlement of any single county (or, in some cases, city) to one legislative house—another source of substantial numerical disproportion.

* * *

The stark fact is that if among the numerous widely varying principles and practices that control state legislative apportionment today there is any generally prevailing feature, that feature is geographic inequality in relation to the population standard. Examples could be endlessly multiplied. In New Jersey, counties of thirty-five thousand and of more than nine hundred and five thousand inhabitants respectively each have a single senator. Representative districts in Minnesota range from 7,290 inhabitants to 107,246 inhabitants. Ratios of senatorial representation in California vary as much as two hundred and ninety-seven to one. In Oklahoma, the range is ten to one for House constituencies and roughly sixteen to one for Senate constituencies. Colebrook, Connecticut—population 592—elects two House representatives; Hartford—population 177,397—also elects two. The first, third and fifth of these examples are the products of constitutional provisions which subordinate population to regional considerations in apportionment; the second is the result of legislative inaction; the fourth derives from both constitutional and legislative sources. A survey made in 1955, in sum, reveals that less than thirty percent of the population inhabit districts sufficient to elect a House majority in thirteen States and a Senate majority in nineteen States. These figures show more than individual variations from a generally accepted standard of electoral equality. They show that there is not—as there has never been—a standard by which the place of equality as a factor in apportionment can be measured.

Manifestly, the Equal Protection Clause supplies no clearer guide for judicial examination of apportionment methods than would the Guarantee Clause itself. Apportionment, by its character, is a subject of extraordinary complexity, involving—even after the fundamental theoretical issues concerning what is to be represented in a representative legislature have been fought out or compromised—considerations of geography, demography, electoral convenience, economic and social cohesions or divergencies among particular local groups, communications, the practical effects of political institutions like the lobby and the city machine, ancient traditions and ties of settled usage, respect for proven incumbents of long experience and senior status, mathematical mechanics, censuses compiling relevant data, and a host of others. Legislative responses throughout the country to the reapportionment demands of the 1960 Census have glaringly confirmed that these are not factors that lend themselves to evaluations of a nature that are the staple of judicial determinations or for which judges are equipped to adjudicate by legal training or experience or native wit. And this is the more so true because in every strand of this complicated, intricate web of values meet the contending forces of partisan politics. The practical significance of apportionment is that the next election results may differ because of it. Apportionment battles are overwhelmingly party or intra-party contests. It will add a virulent source of friction and tension in federal-state relations to embroil the federal judiciary in them.

* * *

■ Dissenting opinion of MR. JUSTICE HARLAN, whom MR. JUSTICE FRANKFURTER joins.

* * *

II.

The claim that Tennessee's system of apportionment is so unreasonable as to amount to a capricious classification of voting strength [fails] under dispassionate analysis.

* * *

What ... is the basis for the claim made in this case that the distribution of state senators and representatives is the product of capriciousness or of some constitutionally prohibited policy? It is not that Tennessee has arranged its electoral districts with a deliberate purpose to dilute the voting strength of one race ... or that some religious group is intentionally underrepresented. Nor is it a charge that the legislature has indulged in sheer caprice by allotting representatives to each county on the basis of a throw of the dice, or of some other determinant bearing no rational relation to the question of apportionment. Rather, the claim is that the State Legislature has unreasonably retained substantially the same allocation of senators and representatives as was established by statute in 1901, refusing to recognize the great shift in the population balance between urban and rural communities that has occurred in the meantime.

* * *

A Federal District Court is asked to say that the passage of time has rendered the 1901 apportionment obsolete to the point where its continuance becomes vulnerable under the Fourteenth Amendment. But is not this matter one that involves a classic legislative judgment? Surely it lies within the province of a state legislature to conclude that an existing allocation of senators and representatives constitutes a desirable balance of geographical and demographical representation, or that in the interest of stability of government it would be best to defer for some further time the redistribution of seats in the state legislature.

Indeed, I would hardly think it unconstitutional if a state legislature's expressed reason for establishing or maintaining an electoral imbalance between its rural and urban population were to protect the State's agricultural interests from the sheer weight of numbers of those residing in its cities. A State may, after all, take account of the interests of its rural population in the distribution of tax burdens, . . . and recognition of the special problems of agricultural interests has repeatedly been reflected in federal legislation. . . . Does the Fourteenth Amendment impose a stricter limitation upon a State's apportionment of political representatives to its central government? I think not. These are matters of local policy, on the wisdom of which the federal judiciary is neither permitted nor qualified to sit in judgment.

* * *

These conclusions can hardly be escaped by suggesting that capricious state action might be found were it to appear that a majority of the Tennessee legislators, in refusing to consider reapportionment, had been actuated by self-interest in perpetuating their own political offices or by other unworthy or improper motives. Since *Fletcher v. Peck*, [6 Cranch 87, 3 L.Ed. 162 (1810)], was decided many years ago, it has repeatedly been pointed out that it is not the business of the federal courts to inquire into the personal motives of legislators.

* * *

NOTES AND QUESTIONS

1. Between *Colegrove* and *Baker*, the primary issues concerning whether malapportionment stated a cognizable cause of action had largely boiled down to a dispute over the manageability of a constitutional standard for evaluating apportionment systems. Although Justice Brennan is confident that there are no manageability problems in administering judicial review,

Baker is curiously silent as to the exact contours of what courts should do. The opinion is far more noteworthy for its declarations of why the political question doctrine should not preclude judicial review, than for what the nature of that review would be. The opinion does not respond to Justice Frankfurter's argument in dissent that there are no clear standards by which courts can navigate among the competing concerns present in apportionment.

2. *Baker* was perhaps the most profoundly destabilizing opinion in the Supreme Court's history. The patterns of malapportionment found in Tennessee were prevalent throughout the country. Within nine months of the Court's opinion in *Baker*, litigation was underway in 34 states challenging the constitutionality of state legislative apportionment schemes. *Reynolds v. Sims*, 377 U.S. 533, 556 n. 30 (1964). The importance of *Baker* was quite apparent at the time. For example, in an interview conducted just before his retirement, Chief Justice Earl Warren explained that apportionment "is perhaps the most important issue we have had before the Supreme Court. If everyone in this country has the opportunity to participate on equal terms with everyone else and can share in electing representatives who will be representative of the entire community and not of some special interest, then most of these problems that we are now confronted with would be solved through the political process rather than through the courts." N.Y. Times, June 26, 1969 (city ed.), at 17, cols. 4,6,7.

3. Justice Clark in *Baker* offers alternative grounds for judicial intervention based upon process failure. His argument is that the prospect for political resolution of malapportionment, introduced by Justice Frankfurter in *Colegrove*, had effectively collapsed. He viewed the political system in Tennessee as essentially hostage to a self-interested political faction powerful enough to resist all legislative efforts at change. This form of political process failure resonates in the language of the *Carolene Products* footnote's rationale for judicial intervention. *United States v. Carolene Products*, 304 U.S. 144, 152 n.4 (1938). The famous *Carolene Products* footnote is generally remembered for its articulation of a theory of why judicial review needs be more exacting to combat "prejudice against discrete and insular minorities ... which tends seriously to curtail the operation of the political processes ordinarily to be relied upon to protect minorities." However, the same footnote identified a broader rationale for judicial intervention in cases of what may be termed political process failure. Accordingly, court oversight is mandated not only where the political process might be infected by prejudice, but also in the face of challenges to laws that "restrict[] those political processes which can ordinarily be expected to bring about repeal of undesireable legislation." This argument also draws directly from the concerns expressed by James Madison in *The Federalist Papers* of the need to provide mechanisms to check the effects of factionalism in the political process. *See The Federalist* No. 10 (James Madison). Does this provide a sounder basis for judicial intervention?

If the political process succumbs to capture by a self-interested faction, then a "process failure" argument may be called upon to justify judicial intervention. Voting rights is therefore an arena in which deference to the legislative design is improper. On this view, voting cases "involve rights (1) that are essential to the democratic process and (2) whose dimensions cannot safely be left to our elected representatives, who have an obvious vested interest in the status quo." John Hart Ely, Democracy and Distrust 117 (1980). For example, Professor Michael Klarman argues that, "[i]t is difficult to imagine a more compelling case for judicial intervention on political process grounds than *Baker v. Carr*; Tennessee legislators had proven fiercely resistant to reapportioning themselves out of a job, and even a 'civically militant electorate' was not about to budge them." Michael J. Klarman, *The Puzzling Resistance to Political Process Theory*, 77 Va. L. Rev. 747, 757–58 (1991)(quoting *Baker*, 369 U.S. at 270) (Frankfurter, J., dissenting).

Reynolds v. Sims
377 U.S. 533 (1964).

■ Mr. Chief Justice Warren delivered the opinion of the Court.

* * *

Plaintiffs below alleged that the last apportionment of the Alabama Legislature was based on the 1900 federal census, despite the requirement of the State Constitution that the legislature be reapportioned decennially. They asserted that, since the population growth in the State from 1900 to 1960 had been uneven, Jefferson and other counties were now victims of serious discrimination with respect to the allocation of legislative representation. As a result of the failure of the legislature to reapportion itself, plaintiffs asserted, they were denied "equal suffrage in free and equal elections ... and the equal protection of the laws" in violation of the Alabama Constitution and the Fourteenth Amendment to the Federal Constitution. The complaint asserted that plaintiffs had no other adequate remedy, and that they had exhausted all forms of relief other than that available through the federal courts. They alleged that the Alabama Legislature had established a pattern of prolonged inaction from 1911 to the present which "clearly demonstrates that no reapportionment ... shall be effected"; that representation at any future constitutional convention would be established by the legislature, making it unlikely that the membership of any such convention would be fairly representative; and that, while the Alabama Supreme Court had found that the legislature had not complied with the State Constitution in failing to reapport according to population decennially, that court had nevertheless indicated that it would not interfere with matters of legislative reapportionment.

* * *

III.

A predominant consideration in determining whether a State's legislative apportionment scheme constitutes an invidious discrimination violative of rights asserted under the Equal Protection Clause is that the rights allegedly impaired are individual and personal in nature.... While the result of a court decision in a state legislative apportionment controversy may be to require the restructuring of the geographical distribution of seats in a state legislature, the judicial focus must be concentrated upon ascertaining whether there has been any discrimination against certain of the State's citizens which constitutes an impermissible impairment of their constitutionally protected right to vote.... Undoubtedly, the right of suffrage is a fundamental matter in a free and democratic society. Especially since the right to exercise the franchise in a free and unimpaired manner is preservative of other basic civil and political rights, any alleged infringement of the right of citizens to vote must be carefully and meticulously scrutinized....

Legislators represent people, not trees or acres. Legislators are elected by voters, not farms or cities or economic interests. As long as ours is a representative form of government, and our legislatures are those instruments of government elected directly by and directly representative of the people, the right to elect legislators in a free and unimpaired fashion is a bedrock of our political system. It could hardly be gainsaid that a constitutional claim had been asserted by an allegation that certain otherwise qualified voters had been entirely prohibited from voting for members of their state legislature. And, if a State should provide that the votes of citizens in one part of the State should be given two times, or five times, or 10 times the weight of votes of citizens in another part of the State, it could hardly be contended that the right to vote of those residing in the disfavored areas had not been effectively diluted. It would appear extraordinary to suggest that a State could be constitutionally permitted to enact a law providing that certain of the State's voters could vote two, five, or 10 times for their legislative representatives, while voters living elsewhere could vote only once. And it is inconceivable that a state law to the effect that, in counting votes for legislators, the votes of citizens in one part of the State would be multiplied by two, five, or 10, while the votes of persons in another area would be counted only at face value, could be constitutionally sustainable. Of course, the effect of state legislative districting schemes which give the same number of representatives to unequal numbers of constituents is identical. Overweighting and overvaluation of the votes of those living here has the certain effect of dilution and undervaluation of the votes of those living there. The resulting discrimination against those individual voters living in disfavored areas is easily demonstrable mathematically. Their right to vote is simply not the same right to vote as that of those living in a favored part of the State. Two, five, or 10 of them must vote before the effect of their voting is equivalent to that of their favored neighbor. Weighting the votes of citizens differently, by any method or means, merely because of where they happen to reside, hardly seems justifiable. One must be ever aware that the Constitution forbids "sophisticated as well as simple-minded modes of discrimination." *Lane v. Wilson*, 307 U.S. 268, 275; *Gomillion v. Lightfoot*, 364 U.S. 339, 342....

State legislatures are, historically, the fountainhead of representative government in this country.... But representative government is in essence self-government through the medium of elected representatives of the people, and each and every citizen has an inalienable right to full and effective participation in the political processes of his State's legislative bodies. Most citizens can achieve this participation only as qualified voters through the election of legislators to represent them. Full and effective participation by all citizens in state government requires, therefore, that each citizen have an equally effective voice in the election of members of his state legislature. Modern and viable state government needs, and the Constitution demands, no less.

Logically, in a society ostensibly grounded on representative government, it would seem reasonable that a majority of the people of a State could elect a majority of that State's legislators. To conclude differently, and to sanction minority control of state legislative bodies, would appear to deny majority rights in a way that far surpasses any possible denial of minority rights that might otherwise be thought to result. Since legislatures are responsible for enacting laws by which all citizens are to be governed, they should be bodies which are collectively responsive to the popular will. And the concept of equal protection has been traditionally viewed as requiring the uniform treatment of persons standing in the same relation to the governmental action questioned or challenged. With respect to the allocation of legislative representation, all voters, as citizens of a State, stand in the same relation regardless of where they live. Any suggested criteria for the differentiation of citizens are insufficient to justify any discrimination, as to the weight of their votes, unless relevant to the permissible purposes of legislative apportionment. Since the achieving of fair and effective representation for all citizens is concededly the basic aim of legislative apportionment, we conclude that the Equal Protection Clause guarantees the opportunity for equal participation by all voters in the election of state legislators.... Our constitutional system amply provides for the protection of minorities by means other than giving them majority control of state legislatures. And the democratic ideals of equality and majority rule, which have served this Nation so well in the past, are hardly of any less significance for the present and the future.

We are told that the matter of apportioning representation in a state legislature is a complex and many-faceted one. We are advised that States can rationally consider factors other than population in apportioning legislative representation. We are admonished not to restrict the power of the States to impose differing views as to political philosophy on their citizens. We are cautioned about the dangers of entering into political thickets and mathematical quagmires. Our answer is this: a denial of constitutionally protected rights demands judicial protection; our oath and our office require no less of us.... To the extent that a citizen's right to vote is debased, he is that much less a citizen. The fact that an individual lives here or there is not a legitimate reason for overweighting or diluting the efficacy of his vote. The complexions of societies and civilizations change, often with amazing rapidity. A nation once primarily rural in character becomes predominantly urban. Representation schemes once fair and equitable become archaic and outdated. But the basic principle of representative government remains, and must remain, unchanged—the weight of a citizen's vote cannot be made to depend on where he lives. Population is, of necessity, the starting point for consideration and the controlling criterion for judgment in legislative apportionment controversies. A citizen, a qualified voter, is no more nor no less so because he lives in the city or on the farm. This is the clear and strong command of our Constitution's Equal Protection Clause.

* * *

V.

* * *

[W]e find the federal analogy inapposite and irrelevant to state legislative districting schemes....

The system of representation in the two Houses of the Federal Congress is one ingrained in our Constitution, as part of the law of the land. It is one conceived out of compromise and concession indispensable to the establishment of our federal republic. Arising from unique historical circumstances, it is based on the consideration that in establishing our type of federalism a group of formerly independent States bound themselves together under one national government. Admittedly, the original 13 States surrendered some of their sovereignty in agreeing to join together "to form a more perfect Union." But at the heart of our constitutional system remains the concept of separate and distinct governmental entities which have delegated some, but not all, of their formerly held powers to the single national government. The fact that almost three-fourths of our present States were never in fact independently sovereign does not detract from our view that the so-called federal analogy is inapplicable as a sustaining precedent for state legislative apportionments. The developing history and growth of our republic cannot cloud the fact that, at the time of the inception of the system of representation in the Federal Congress, a compromise between the larger and smaller States on this matter averted a deadlock in the Constitutional Convention which had threatened to abort the birth of our Nation.

* * *

Political subdivisions of States—counties, cities, or whatever—never were and never have been considered as sovereign entities. Rather, they have been traditionally regarded as subordinate governmental instrumentalities created by the State to assist in the carrying out of state governmental functions.

* * *

Thus, we conclude that the plan contained in the 67-Senator Amendment for apportioning seats in the Alabama Legislature cannot be sustained by recourse to the so-called federal analogy. Nor can any other inequitable state legislative apportionment scheme be justified on such an asserted basis. This does not necessarily mean that such a plan is irrational or involves something other than a "republican form of government." We conclude simply that such a plan is impermissible for the States under the Equal Protection Clause, since perforce resulting, in virtually every case, in submergence of the equal population principle in at least one house of a state legislature. Since we find the so-called federal analogy inapposite to a consideration of the constitutional validity of state legislative apportionment schemes, we necessarily hold that the Equal Protection Clause requires both houses of a state legislature to be apportioned on a population basis.

* * *

VI.

By holding that as a federal constitutional requisite both houses of a state legislature must be apportioned on a population basis, we mean that the Equal Protection Clause requires that a State make an honest and good faith effort to construct districts, in both houses of its legislature, as nearly of equal population as is practicable. We realize that it is a practical impossibility to arrange legislative districts so that each one has an identical number of residents, or citizens, or voters. Mathematical exactness or precision is hardly a workable constitutional requirement.

In *Wesberry v. Sanders*, the Court stated that congressional representation must be based on population as nearly as is practicable. In implementing the basic constitutional principle of representative government as enunciated by the Court in *Wesberry*—equality of population among districts—some distinctions may well be made between congressional and state legislative representation. Since, almost invariably, there is a significantly larger number of seats in state legislative bodies to be distributed within a State than congressional seats, it may be feasible to use political subdivision lines to a greater extent in establishing state legislative districts than in congressional districting while still affording adequate representation to all parts of the State. To do so would be constitutionally valid, so long as the resulting apportionment was one based substantially on population and the equal-population principle was not diluted in any significant way....

A State may legitimately desire to maintain the integrity of various political subdivisions, insofar as possible, and provide for compact districts of contiguous territory in designing a legislative apportionment scheme. Valid considerations may underlie such aims. Indiscriminate districting, without any regard for political subdivision or natural or historical boundary lines, may be little more than an open invitation to partisan gerrymandering. Single-member districts may be the rule in one State, while another State might desire to achieve some flexibility by creating multimember or floterial districts. Whatever the means of accomplishment, the overriding objective must be substantial equality of population among the various districts, so that the vote of any citizen is approximately equal in weight to that of any other citizen in the State.

History indicates, however, that many States have deviated, to a greater or lesser degree, from the equal-population principle in the apportionment of seats in at least one house of their legislatures. So long as the divergences from a strict population standard are based on legitimate considerations incident to the effectuation of a rational state policy, some deviations from the equal-population principle are constitutionally permissible with respect to the apportionment of seats in either or both of the two houses of a bicameral state legislature. But neither history alone, nor economic or other sorts of group interests, are permissible factors in attempting to justify disparities from population-based representation. Citizens, not history or economic interests, cast votes. Considerations of area alone provide an insufficient justification for deviations from the equal-population principle. Again, people, not land or trees or pastures, vote. Modern developments and improvements in transportation and communications make rather hollow, in the mid–1960's, most claims that deviations from population-based representation can validly be based solely on geographical considerations. Arguments for allowing such deviations in order to insure effective representation for sparsely settled areas and to prevent legislative districts from becoming so large that the availability of access of citizens to their representatives is impaired are today, for the most part, unconvincing.

A consideration that appears to be of more substance in justifying some deviations from population-based representation in state legislatures is that of insuring some voice to political subdivisions, as political subdivisions. Several factors make more than insubstantial claims that a State can rationally consider according political subdivisions some independent representation in at least one body of the state legislature, as long as the basic standard of equality of population among districts is maintained. Local governmental entities are frequently charged with various responsibilities incident to the operation of state government. In many States much of the legislature's activity involves the enactment of so-called local legislation, directed only to the concerns of particular political subdivisions. And a State may legitimately desire to construct districts along political subdivision lines to deter the possibilities of gerrymandering. However, permitting deviations from population-based representation does not mean that each local governmental unit or political subdivision can be given separate representation, regardless of population. Carried too far, a scheme of giving at least one seat in one house to each political subdivision (for example, to each county) could easily result, in many States, in a total subversion of the equal-population principle in that legislative body.

■ Mr. Justice Harlan, dissenting.

* * *

Preliminary Statement

Today's holding is that the Equal Protection Clause of the Fourteenth Amendment requires every State to structure its legislature so that all the members of each house represent substantially the same number of people; other factors may be given play only to the extent that they do not significantly encroach on this basic "population" principle. Whatever may be thought of this holding as a piece of political ideology—and even on that score the political history and practices of this country from its earliest beginnings leave wide room for debate . . .—I think it demonstrable that the Fourteenth Amendment does not impose this political tenet on the States or authorize this Court to do so.

The Court's constitutional discussion . . . is remarkable . . . for its failure to address itself at all to the Fourteenth Amendment as a whole or to the legislative history of the Amendment pertinent to the matter at hand. Stripped of aphorisms, the Court's argument boils down to the assertion that appellees' right to vote has been invidiously "debased" or "diluted" by systems of apportionment which entitle them to vote for fewer legislators than other voters, an assertion which is tied to the Equal Protection Clause only by the constitutionally frail tautology that "equal" means "equal."

Had the Court paused to probe more deeply into the matter, it would have found that the Equal Protection Clause was never intended to inhibit the States in choosing any democratic method they pleased for the apportionment of their legislatures. This is shown by the language of the Fourteenth Amendment taken as a whole, by the understanding of those who proposed and ratified it, and by the political practices of the States at the time the Amendment was adopted. It is confirmed by numerous state and congressional actions since the adoption of the Fourteenth Amendment, and by the common understanding of the Amendment as evidenced by subsequent constitutional amendments and decisions of this Court before *Baker v. Carr* made an abrupt break with the past in 1962.

The failure of the Court to consider any of these matters cannot be excused or explained by any concept of "developing" constitutionalism. It is meaningless to speak of constitutional "development" when both the language and history of the controlling provisions of the Constitution are wholly ignored. Since it can, I think, be shown beyond doubt that state legislative apportionments, as such, are wholly free of constitutional limitations, save such as may be imposed by the Republican Form of Government Clause (Const., Art. IV, § 4), the Court's action now bringing them within the purview of the Fourteenth Amendment amounts to nothing less than an exercise of the amending power by this Court.

So far as the Federal Constitution is concerned, the complaints in these cases should all have been dismissed below for failure to state a cause of action, because what has been alleged or proved shows no violation of any constitutional right.

* * *

It should by now be obvious that these cases do not mark the end of reapportionment problems in the courts. Predictions once made that the courts would never have to face the problem of actually working out an apportionment have proved false. This Court, however, continues to avoid the consequences of its decisions, simply assuring us that the lower courts "can and ... will work out more concrete and specific standards." Deeming it "expedient" not to spell out "precise constitutional tests," the Court contents itself with stating "only a few rather general considerations."

Generalities cannot obscure the cold truth that cases of this type are not amenable to the development of judicial standards. No set of standards can guide a court which has to decide how many legislative districts a State shall have, or what the shape of the districts shall be, or where to draw a particular district line. No judicially manageable standard can determine whether a State should have single-member districts or multimember districts or some combination of both. No such standard can control the balance between keeping up with population shifts and having stable districts. In all these respects, the courts will be called upon to make particular decisions with respect to which a principle of equally populated districts will be of no assistance whatsoever. Quite obviously, there are limitless possibilities for districting consistent with such a principle. Nor can these problems be avoided by judicial reliance on legislative judgments so far as possible. Reshaping or combining one or two districts, or modifying just a few district lines, is no less a matter of choosing among many possible solutions, with varying political consequences, than reapportionment broadside.

The Court ignores all this, saying only that "what is marginally permissible in one State may be unsatisfactory in another, depending on the particular circumstances of the case." It is well to remember that the product of today's decisions will not be readjustment of a few districts in a few States which most glaringly depart from the principle of equally populated districts. It will be a redetermination, extensive in many cases, of legislative districts in all but a few States.

Although the Court—necessarily, as I believe—provides only generalities in elaboration of its main thesis, its opinion nevertheless fully demonstrates how far removed these problems are from fields of judicial competence. Recognizing that "indiscriminate districting" is an invitation to "partisan gerrymandering," the Court nevertheless excludes virtually every basis for the formation of electoral districts other than "indiscriminate districting." In one or another of today's opinions, the Court declares it unconstitutional for a State to give effective consideration to any of the following in establishing legislative districts:

(1) history;

(2) "economic or other sorts of group interests";

(3) area;

(4) geographical considerations;

(5) a desire "to insure effective representation for sparsely settled areas";

(6) "availability of access of citizens to their representatives";

(7) theories of bicameralism (except those approved by the Court);

(8) occupation;

(9) "an attempt to balance urban and rural power";

(10) the preference of a majority of voters in the State.

So far as presently appears, the only factor which a State may consider, apart from numbers, is political subdivisions. But even "a clearly rational state policy" recognizing this factor is unconstitutional if "population is submerged as the controlling consideration...."

I know of no principle of logic or practical or theoretical politics, still less any constitutional principle, which establishes all or any of these exclusions. Certain it is that the Court's opinion does not establish them. So far as the Court says anything at all on this score, it says only that "legislators represent people, not trees or acres"; that "citizens, not history or economic interests, cast votes"; that "people, not land or trees or pastures, vote." All this may be conceded. But it is surely equally obvious, and, in the context of elections, more meaningful to note that people are not ciphers and that legislators can represent their electors only by speaking for their interests—economic, social, political—many of which do reflect the place where the electors live. The Court does not establish, or indeed even attempt to make a case for the proposition that conflicting interests within a State can only be adjusted by disregarding them when voters are grouped for purposes of representation.

NOTES AND QUESTIONS

1. *Reynolds* combined with *Wesberry v. Sanders*, 376 U.S. 1 (1964), to introduce the equipopulation principle to the constitutional law of reapportionment. *Reynolds* read the equal protection clause of the Fourteenth Amendment to impose the one-person/one-vote rule on state apportionment for its legislatures. *Wesberry* found a similar equipopulation principle in Art. I, § 2 of the Constitution, which provides,

> The House of Representatives shall be composed of Members chosen every second Year by the people of the several States, and the Electors in each State shall have the Qualifications requisite for Electors of the most numerous Branch of the State Legislature.

Justice Harlan's dissent in *Reynolds* challenges the use of either constitutional provision as the basis for imposing the equipopulation rule. Does either source better justify judicial oversight of reapportionment? Should state authorities have greater latitude in departing from the equipopulation rule in congressional or state legislative apportionment?

2. How exacting should the equipopulation standard be? The Supreme Court has set different standards for state legislative and congressional redistricting plans. In the congressional context, the Court has long adhered to the principle that one person's vote be worth "as nearly as practicable" the equal of another's to the extent that a State must "make a good-faith effort to achieve precise mathematical equality." *Kirkpatrick v. Preisler*, 394 U.S. 526 (1969)(striking down "a State's preference for pleasingly shaped districts" that yielded districts up to 3.13 percent above and 2.84 percent below the ideal mathematical distribution of population per district). By contrast, in *Mahan v. Howell*, 410 U.S. 315 (1973), the Court upheld a Virginia state redistricting plan whose maximum percentage deviation from the ideal was 16.4 percent. (The maximum percentage deviation is derived by adding the percentage excess of the largest district above the ideal, in this case 6.8 percent, to the percentage under the ideal of the smallest district, in this case 9.6 percent). The Court, per Justice Rehnquist, seemingly retreated from *Reynolds* to find that the State interest in regional representation justified a broader deviation from the congressional standard. The Court grounded its opinion on a distinction between Article I, § 2 of the Constitution on the one hand, and the Equal Protection Clause on the other, as well as a recognition that "there is a significantly larger number of seats in state legislative bodies to be distributed within a State than congressional seats, and that therefore it may be feasible for a State to use political subdivision lines to a greater extent in establishing state legislative districts than congressional districts while still affording statewide representation." As a result, the Court concluded that "the legislature's plan for apportionment of the House of Delegates may reasonably be said to advance the rational state policy of respecting the boundaries of political subdivisions." Does either the constitutional text or the policy argument justify a different standard for congressional as opposed to state legislative redistricting?

While congressional districts are increasingly held to a zero deviation standard (*see Karcher v. Daggett, infra*), state legislative plans with maximum population deviations in the vicinity of 10 percent are considered presumptively valid, while the 16.4 percent figure in *Mahan* "approaches tolerable limits." Curiously, in *Brown v. Thomson*, 462 U.S. 835 (1983), the Court upheld a state legislative redistricting plan with a maximum deviation of 89 percent on the grounds that the complaint challenged only the apportionment of one district, rather than the statewide apportionment scheme. Does it make any sense to speak of a one-person/one-vote challenge to one district when the baseline must of necessity be the statewide apportionment?

3. How should population be measured for apportionment purposes? *Reynolds* appears to emphasize both equality of representation and the equal value of the ballot cast by all voters. Unfortunately, the two concepts are not identical. Simply counting persons does not yield equality of voting power to all voters, even were districts to be perfectly equipopulational. There are predictable groups who may not vote, including minors, convicted felons, immigrants. Should communities with large numbers of children be afforded the same amount of representation as those containing primarily senior citizens, even though the likely level of potential voters may be dramatically different? Is there not a paradox in counting voting-ineligible prisoners in maximum security facilities such as Parchman in Mississippi, or Huntsville in Texas, and then using their numbers to enhance the representation of local communities that will be heavily populated by prison guards and their families? Should illegal aliens be counted among the total population in order to apportion representatives?

In *Burns v. Richardson*, 384 U.S. 73 (1966), the Supreme Court upheld a Hawaii districting plan based on registered voters. The State clearly intended to enhance the voting power of the permanent citizens of Hawaii, while excluding the largely transient but numerically overwhelming military population. The Court held that,

> [T]he Equal Protection Clause does not require the States to use total population figures derived from the federal census as the standard by which [] substantial population equality is to be measured.... Neither in *Reynolds v. Sims* nor in any other decision has this Court suggested that the States are required to include aliens, transients, short-term or temporary residents, or persons denied the vote for conviction of crime in the apportionment base by which their legislators are distributed and against which compliance with the Equal Protection Clause is to be measured.

Does *Burns* survive the subsequent development of voting rights law? Consider *Garza v. County of Los Angeles*, 918 F.2d 763 (9th Cir.1990), *cert.*

denied, 498 U.S. 1028 (1991). In a case that arose out of a challenge to the drawing of county commissioner district lines, the County of Los Angeles attacked a court-ordered remedial plan in part on the grounds that the apparent underrepresentation of Hispanics under alternative proposals was not legally cognizable since many Hispanics were not eligible voters. The court rejected this argument based on:

> [T]he standard enunciated in *Wesberry v. Sanders*, 376 U.S. 1 (1964) that "the fundamental principle of representative government is one of equal representation for equal numbers of people, without regard to race, sex, economic status, or place of residence within a state." This standard derives from the constitutional requirement that members of the House of Representatives are elected "by the people," *Reynolds*, 377 U.S. at 560, from districts "founded on the aggregate number of inhabitants of each state" (James Madison, *The Federalist,* No. 54 at 369 (J. Cooke ed. 1961)); U.S. Const. art. I, § 2. The framers were aware that this apportionment and representation base would include categories of persons who were ineligible to vote—women, children, bound servants, convicts, the insane, and, at a later time, aliens. *FAIR v. Klutznick*, 486 F.Supp. 564, 576 (D.D.C.1980). Nevertheless, they declared that government should represent all the people. In applying this principle, the *Reynolds* Court recognized that the people, including those who are ineligible to vote, form the basis for representative government. Thus population is an appropriate basis for state legislative apportionment.

In a separate dissent and concurrence, Judge Kozinski revisited *Reynolds* to find an equally compelling set of references to the need to preclude the disparate weighting of votes of defined sets of voters simply as a result of the happenstance of where they resided. He concluded that the Supreme Court's pronouncements supported both a principle of equal representation and a principle of equal voting power:

> While apportionment by population and apportionment by number of eligible electors normally yield precisely the same result, they are based on radically different premises and serve materially different purposes. Apportionment by raw population embodies the principle of equal representation; it assures that all persons living within a district—whether eligible to vote or not—have roughly equal representation in the governing body. A principle of equal representation serves important purposes: It assures that constituents have more or less equal access to their elected officials, by assuring that no official has a disproportionately large number of constituents to satisfy. Also, assuming that elected officials are able to obtain benefits for their districts in proportion to their share of the total membership of the governing body, it assures

that constituents are not afforded unequal government services depending on the size of the population in their districts.

Apportionment by proportion of eligible voters serves the principle of electoral equality. This principle recognizes that electors—persons eligible to vote—are the ones who hold the ultimate political power in our democracy. This is an important power reserved only to certain members of society; states are not required to bestow it upon aliens, transients, short-term residents, persons convicted of crime, or those considered too young. *See* J. Nowak, R. Rotunda & J.N. Young, Constitutional Law § 14.31, at 722–23 (3d ed. 1986).

The principle of electoral equality assures that, regardless of the size of the whole body of constituents, political power, as defined by the number of those eligible to vote, is equalized as between districts holding the same number of representatives. It also assures that those eligible to vote do not suffer dilution of that important right by having their vote given less weight than that of electors in another location. Under this paradigm, the fourteenth amendment protects a right belonging to the individual elector and the key question is whether the votes of some electors are materially undercounted because of the manner in which districts are apportioned....

When considered against the Supreme Court's repeated pronouncements that the right being protected by the one person one vote principle is personal and limited to citizens, the various arguments raised by the majority do not carry the day. Thus, the Court's passing reference in *Kirkpatrick v. Preisler*, 394 U.S. 526, 531 (1969), to "prevent[ing] debasement of voting power and diminution of access to elected representatives" suggests only that the Court did not consider the possibility that the twin goals might diverge in some cases. As *Kirkpatrick* contains no discussion of the issue, it provides no clue as to which principle has primacy where there is a conflict between the two.

In cases of conflict, which principle should govern?

4. In *Reynolds*, Chief Justice Warren was able to ground the claims in individual rights to equal treatment by the state. This was clearly facilitated by the remarkable disparities in the population bases of various districts. In *Baker* for example, the divergences reached 23-to-1, while in *Reynolds* they were as high as 41-to-1. However, *Reynolds* expands the scope of the equipopulation principle by invoking the concept of *political fairness*. The Court claimed it was guaranteeing to each citizen "an *equally effective* voice" in the electoral process so as to yield "fair and effective representation" for the electorate as a whole. Since clearly there will always be winners and losers in contested elections, how does an individual voting for a losing candidate assess whether she has realized an "equally effective voice" and secured "fair and effective representation"? If the definition of fairness turns solely on the absence of malapportionment, what do the additional claims of *Reynolds* add? Or, if there is indeed some greater principle than simply equality in apportionment, what does *Reynolds* suggest it is? Can effective representation be measured in terms of individual voters?

One hint of the Court's thinking is its treatment of the comparisons to the U.S. Senate. The Court implies that but for the original political compromise inherited in the Constitution, the constraints on the popular will involved in overrepresentation of small states should violate the principles of political fairness. Is the Court decidedly hostile to the argument that States or local jurisdictions may have their own political compromises that may in turn necessitate a Senate-like arrangement?

5. While *Baker* introduced the concept of the justiciable claim of unconstitutional apportionment of legislative office, it fell to *Reynolds* and *Wesberry* to reduce the constitutional command to the equipopulation rule of one-person, one-vote. As conceived by the Supreme Court in the 1960's, the reliance on numerical standards of apportionment was to have served three purposes. First, numerical standards could be drawn from unassailable empirical data, specifically the decennial Census enumeration of population, and thus could provide an objective basis for measuring political equality. Second, the one-person, one-vote rule based on strict population equality could be readily managed by the courts and thus allowed a justiciable standard for judicial immersion into the "political thicket" of elected institutions. *See Karcher v. Daggett*, 462 U.S. 725, 732 (1983)(Justice Brennan invoking the justiciability argument in favor of strict numerical application of one-person, one-vote standard). Third, the existence of objective measures would defeat attempts to gerrymander districting schemes and would implement the constitutional guarantee that "each resident citizen has, as far as is possible, an equal voice" in the selection of public officials. *See Kramer v. Union Free School Dist. No. 15,* 395 U.S. 621, 627 (1969).

The third feature is untested in the early reapportionment cases. In *Reynolds*, the Court refers to the evils of an imprecise system "as an open invitation to partisan gerrymandering," 377 U.S. at 579, which the one-person, one-vote rule is intended to forestall. To what extent is gerrymandering consistent with an equipopulation scheme? An immediate problem is that districting always involves choices among competing apportionment schemes that may favor one or another political party, incumbent official, regional interest, minority group, etc. *Reynolds* offers very little to resolve these issues. Professor Dixon has commented that the problem is inherent to districting: "The primary difficulty is that in a generic sense all *districting is gerrymandering.* A near-infinite number of sets of 'equal' districts may be drawn in any state; each set, however, having a quite different effect in terms of overall party balance and minority representation."

Robert G. Dixon, Jr., Democratic Representation: Reapportionment in Law and Politics 462 (1968).

6. As the equipopulation command took hold, the intervening considerations identified by both Chief Justice Warren and Justice Harlan receded in importance. *Reynolds* itself left open the possibility that some intervening political considerations might justify departures from the equipopulation principle:

> So long as the divergences from a strict population standard are based on legitimate considerations incident to the effectuation of a rational state policy, some deviations from the equal-population principle are constitutionally permissible with respect to the apportionment of seats in either or both of the two houses of a bicameral state legislature.

However, as Chapter 1 reveals, even as early as *Lucas v. Forty–Fourth General Assembly of Colorado*, 377 U.S. 713 (1964), the Court struck down a county-based apportionment system for Colorado that had been approved in a state-wide referendum by a majority of voters in every county in the State. The Court refused to give any particular weight to the manner of adoption of the non-equipopulous system and held instead that the resulting apportionment violated one-person, one-vote. In dissent, Justice Stewart caustically described the emerging constitutional apportionment standard as resting on "the uncritical, simplistic, and heavy-handed application of sixth-grade arithmetic." Consider the following early assessment of the reliance on numerical standards as the critical factor in reapportionment:

> The Warren Court's reliance on the one person, one vote principle without the development of other judicial restraints on the discretion of districting authorities threatened to transform the celebrated reapportionment revolution into a "gerrymandering revolution." . . . Not only had the Court failed to develop effective checks on the practice of gerrymandering, but in pursuing the goal of population equality to a point of satiety it had actually facilitated that practice. The Court rejected as justifications for even small population deviations the use of established political subdivision boundaries (such as those for counties) in designing districts and the construction of geographically "compact" districts. Although these non-population considerations, frequently required by state constitutions, did not prevent gerrymandering, they at least functioned as minimal restrictions on the cartographic flexibility of districting authorities. The absence of even these minimal restrictions in the districting process increased the already numerous options available for locating district boundaries. This expanded flexibility was conducive to the creation of politically self-serving representational designs.

Richard L. Engstrom, *The Supreme Court and Equipopulous Gerrymandering: A Remaining Obstacle in the Quest for Fair and Effective Representa-*

tion, 1976 Ariz. St. L.J. 277, 278–79. In the two decades since Professor Engstrom sounded this warning, the use of computers has transformed the process of redistricting. *See* Samuel Issacharoff, *Judging Politics: The Elusive Quest for Judicial Review of Political Fairness*, 71 Tex. L. Rev. 1643, 1695–1702 (1993); Michelle H. Browdy, Note, *Computer Models and Post-Bandemer Redistricting*, 99 Yale L.J. 1379, 1387–91 (1990). The increased availability of minutely detailed demographic information has allowed a proliferation of redistricting plans drawn by various interest constituents. It has also allowed for far greater flights of cartographic fancy as an increasingly elaborate set of districting designs could be constructed to accomplish specific political aims. *See* Richard H. Pildes & Richard G. Niemi, *Expressive Harms, "Bizarre Districts," and Voting Rights: Evaluating Election-District Appearances After* Shaw v. Reno, 92 Mich. L. Rev. 483 (1993)(documenting the greater irregularity of districts drawn after the 1990 Census to accommodate minority representation).

Karcher v. Daggett

462 U.S. 725 (1983).

■ JUSTICE BRENNAN delivered the opinion of the Court.

The question presented by this appeal is whether an apportionment plan [the "Feldman plan"] for congressional districts satisfies Art. I, § 2, of the Constitution without need for further justification if the population of the largest district is less than one percent greater than the population of the smallest district.

* * *

I.

After the results of the 1980 decennial census had been tabulated, the Clerk of the United States House of Representatives notified the Governor of New Jersey that the number of Representatives to which the State was entitled had decreased from 15 to 14. [Ultimately, the New Jersey Legislature] . . . passed a bill (S–711) introduced by Senator Feldman . . . which created the apportionment plan at issue in this case. . . .

Like every plan considered by the legislature, the Feldman Plan contained 14 districts, with an average population per district (as determined by the 1980 census) of 526,059. Each district did not have the same population. On the average, each district differed from the "ideal" figure by 0.1384%, or about 726 people. The largest district, the Fourth District, which includes Trenton, had a population of 527,472, and the smallest, the Sixth District, embracing most of Middlesex County, a population of 523,798. The difference between them was 3,674 people, or 0.6984% of the average district. The populations of the other districts also varied. . . .

The legislature had before it other plans with appreciably smaller population deviations between the largest and smallest districts. The one receiving the most attention in the District Court was [one which] had a maximum population difference of 2,375, or 0.4514% of the average figure. . . .

III

Appellants' principal argument in this case is addressed to the first question described above. They contend that the Feldman Plan should be regarded per se as the product of a good-faith effort to achieve population equality because the maximum population deviation among districts is smaller than the predictable undercount in available census data.

A

Kirkpatrick squarely rejected a nearly identical argument. "The whole thrust of the 'as nearly as practicable' approach is inconsistent with adoption of fixed numerical standards which excuse population variances without regard to the circumstances of each particular case." Adopting any standard other than population equality, using the best census data available, would subtly erode the Constitution's ideal of equal representation. . . .

Any standard, including absolute equality, involves a certain artificiality. As appellants point out, even the census data are not perfect, and the well-known restlessness of the American people means that population counts for particular localities are outdated long before they are completed. Yet problems with the data at hand apply equally to any population-based standard we could choose.[] As between two standards—equality or something less than equality—only the former reflects the aspirations of Art. I, § 2.

To accept the legitimacy of unjustified, though small population deviations in this case would mean to reject the basic premise of *Kirkpatrick* and *Wesberry*. We decline appellants' invitation to go that far. The unusual rigor of their standard has been noted several times. Because of that rigor, we have required that absolute population equality be the paramount objective of apportionment only in the case of congressional districts, for which the command of Art. I, § 2, as regards the National Legislature outweighs the local interests that a State may deem relevant in apportioning districts for representatives to state and local legislatures, but we have not questioned the population equality standard for congressional districts. The principle of population equality for congressional districts has not proved unjust or socially or economically harmful in experience. If anything, this standard should cause less difficulty now for state legislatures than it did when we adopted it in *Wesberry*. The rapid advances in computer technology and education during the last two decades make it relatively simple to draw contiguous districts of equal population and at the

APPENDIX A

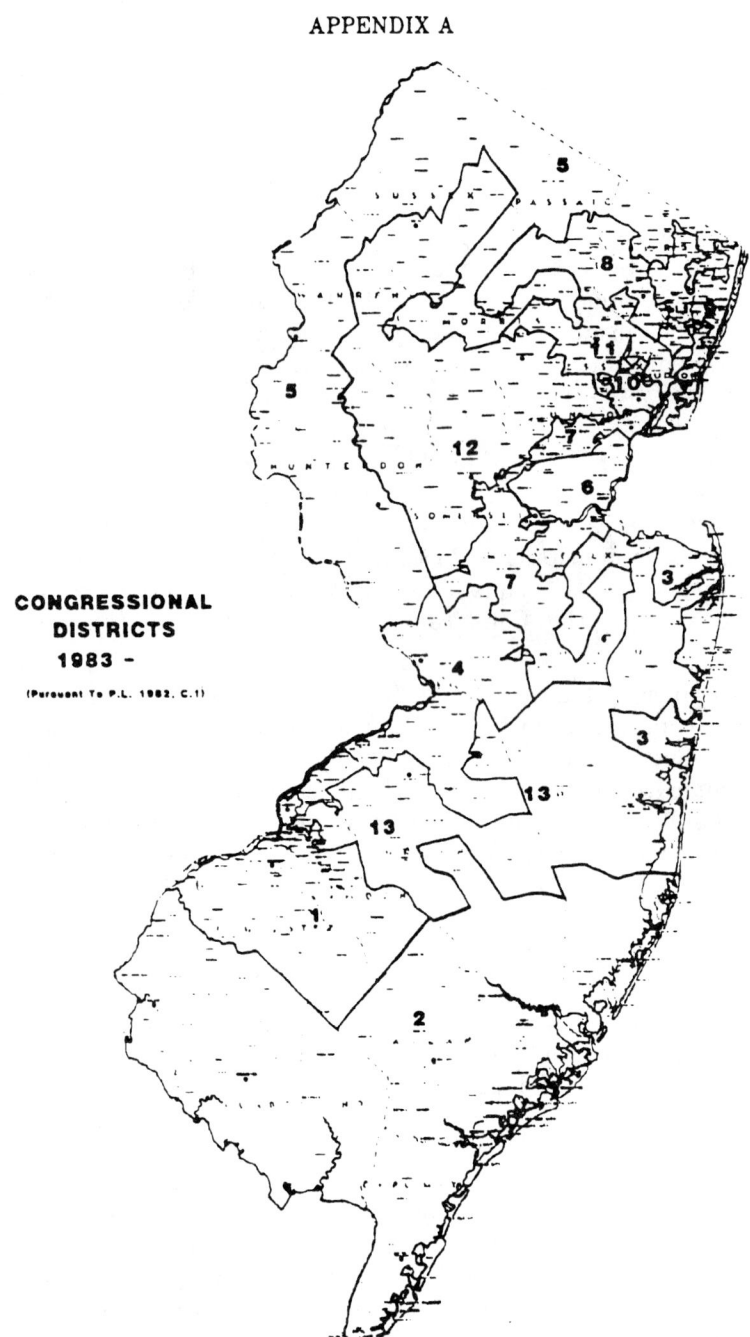

**CONGRESSIONAL
DISTRICTS
1983 –**

(Pursuant To P.L. 1982, C.1)

same time to further whatever secondary goals the State has.... We thus reaffirm that there are no de minimis population variations, which could practicably be avoided, but which nonetheless meet the standard of Art. I, § 2, without justification....

IV

By itself, the foregoing discussion does not establish that the Feldman Plan is unconstitutional. Rather, appellees' success in proving that the Feldman Plan was not the product of a good-faith effort to achieve population equality means only that the burden shifted to the State to prove that the population deviations in its plan were necessary to achieve some legitimate state objective ... [W]e are willing to defer to state legislative policies, so long as they are consistent with constitutional norms, even if they require small differences in the population of congressional districts. Any number of consistently applied legislative policies might justify some variance, including, for instance, making districts compact, respecting municipal boundaries, preserving the cores of prior districts, and avoiding contests between incumbent Representatives. As long as the criteria are nondiscriminatory, these are all legitimate objectives that on a proper showing could justify minor population deviations. The State must, however, show with some specificity that a particular objective required the specific deviations in its plan, rather than simply relying on general assertions. The showing required to justify population deviations is flexible, depending on the size of the deviations, the importance of the State's interests, the consistency with which the plan as a whole reflects those interests, and the availability of alternatives that might substantially vindicate those interests yet approximate population equality more closely. By necessity, whether deviations are justified requires case-by-case attention to these factors....

■ JUSTICE WHITE, with whom the CHIEF JUSTICE, JUSTICE POWELL, and JUSTICE REHNQUIST join, dissenting.

* * *

II.

[... T]here are many, including myself, who take issue with the Court's self-congratulatory assumption that *Kirkpatrick* has been a success. First, a decade of experience with *Kirkpatrick* has shown that "the rule of absolute equality is perfectly compatible with 'gerrymandering' of the worst sort." *Wells v. Rockefeller*, 394 U.S., at 551 (Harlan, J., dissenting)....

In addition to providing a patina of respectability for the equipopulous gerrymander, *Kirkpatrick's* regime assured extensive intrusion of the judiciary into legislative business.... More than a decade's experience with *Kirkpatrick* demonstrates that insistence on precise numerical equality only invites those who lost in the political arena to refight their battles in federal court. Consequently, "[most] estimates are that between 25 percent and 35 percent of current house district lines were drawn by the Courts."

As I have already noted, by extending *Kirkpatrick* to deviations below even the 1% level, the redistricting plan in every State with more than a single Representative is rendered vulnerable to after-the-fact attack by anyone with a complaint and a calculator.

The Court ultimately seeks refuge in stare decisis. I do not slight the respect that doctrine is due, but is it not at least ironic to find stare decisis invoked to protect *Kirkpatrick* as the Court itself proceeds to overrule other holdings in that very decision? ... [T]oday the Court—with no mention of the contrary holdings in *Kirkpatrick*—opines: "Any number of consistently applied legislative policies might justify some variance, including for instance, making districts compact, respecting municipal boundaries, preserving the cores of prior districts, and avoiding contests between incumbent Representatives." I, of course, welcome the Court's overruling of these ill-considered holdings of *Kirkpatrick*. There should be no question but that state legislatures may account for political and geographic boundaries in order to preserve traditional subdivisions and achieve compact and contiguous districts....

NOTES AND QUESTIONS

1. In many ways, Justice Brennan's opinion in *Karcher* marks the end of the road for the one-person, one-vote doctrine. The clear import of *Karcher* was a confrontation with a Democratic Party gerrymander that resulted in what was aptly termed "a flight of cartographic fancy." The only reason for the challenge was the inability of the equipopulation principle to constrain the partisan gerrymander of the New Jersey congressional delegation. While Justice Stevens in concurrence and Justice Powell in dissent would have reached the constitutionality of the gerrymander directly (we shall discuss this issue subsequently in Chapter 8), the plurality adhered only to an ever stricter application of numerical equality, all the while recognizing its increasing disutility in policing the political process. In response to the argument that the deviations were so trivial as to not only fall within the margin of error of the underlying Census enumeration, but so as to make any impact on individual voting strength meaningless, Brennan argued:

> Adopting any standard other than population equality, using the best census data available, would subtly erode the Constitution's ideal of equal representation. If state legislators knew that a certain *de minimis* level of population differences was acceptable, they would doubtless strive to achieve that level rather than equality.... In this case, appellants argue that a maximum deviation of approximately 0.7% would be considered *de minimis*. If we accept that argument, how are we to regard deviations of 0.8%, 0.95%, 1%, or 1.1%?

Recall that the initial identified advantages of the equipopulation rule were its easy calculation, its administrability, and its prophylactic function against gerrymandering. What happens when there are real disputes about the underlying numbers and when the prophylactic effect is significantly diminished? Does administrability by itself justify the strict application of the equipopulation rule in *Karcher*? *See* John Hart Ely, Democracy and Distrust 121 (1980) (the equipopulation rule "is certainly administrable. In fact, administrability is its long suit, and the more troublesome question is what else it has to recommend it.")

2. Given the exacting quality of the equipopulation standard in *Karcher*, should not greater attention be paid to problems of miscounting in the Census enumeration? Alhough the Census has grown increasingly sophisticated, the Census Bureau estimates that millions of Americans are uncounted each decade. In addition, the undercounting is not random. Racial and ethnic minorities are significantly more likely than non-minorities to be left out of the enumeration. *See* Samuel Issacharoff & Allan J. Lichtman, *The Census Undercount and Minority Representation: The Constitutional Obligation of the States to Guarantee Equal Representation*, 13 Rev. Litig. 1, 8 (1993)(reporting that percentage of black Americans missed in Census is steadily about 5 percentage points higher than percentage of white Americans missed from 1940 to 1980). Following the refusal of the Census to statistically adjust the 1990 Census, several cities and states with heavy minority concentrations sued the Department of Commerce claiming that the persistent undercount was unconstitutional. In *Wisconsin v. City of New York*, 116 S.Ct. 1091 (1996), the Supreme Court rejected this claim, primarily on the grounds that the Constitution vests Congress with essentially unreviewable authority to conduct an "actual Enumeration ... in such Manner as they shall by Law direct." Art. I, § 2, cl. 3. In addition, the Court credited the Secretary of Commerce's claim that "distributive accuracy" among the states was a more critical need than "numerical accuracy" in calculating the entire population: "Indeed, a preference for distributive accuracy (even at the expense of some numerical accuracy) would seem to follow from the constitutional purpose of the census, viz., to determine apportionment of the Representatives among the States." 116 S.Ct. at 1101. As this book goes to press, the subject of possible statistical adjustments to the 2000 Census remains unresolved.

3. Should the protection of incumbents be a permissible grounds for departing from the equipopulation command? For arguments that this is an invitation to self-serving behavior by political insiders, *see* Kristen L. Silverberg, Note, *The Illegitimacy of the Incumbent Gerrymander*, 74 Tex. L. Rev. 913 (1996); Sally Dworak–Fisher, Note, *Drawing the Line on Incumbency Protection,* 2 Mich. J. of Race & L. 131 (1996).

4. Does the equipopulation principle require that a majority of voters be able to control electoral outcomes? Consider *Gordon v. Lance*, 403 U.S. 1 (1971), in which the Court reviewed West Virginia requirements that political subdivisions of the state not incur bonded indebtedness or increase tax rates without the approval of 60 percent of the voters in a referendum election. *Gordon* poses the *Baker/Reynolds* problem in reverse. Instead of an entrenched minority having the votes to affirmatively push through its desired legislative agenda, any minority of 40 percent plus 1 has effective veto power over the will of the majority. In any ensuing negotiations, it would be expected that such a minority would be able to secure significant concessions in order to allow the majority's preferred course of action to be realized. Nonetheless, in an opinion by Chief Justice Burger, the Court upheld the West Virginia supermajority requirements:

> Although West Virginia has not denied any group access to the ballot, it has indeed made it more difficult for some kinds of governmental actions to be taken. Certainly any departure from strict majority rule gives disproportionate power to the minority. But there is nothing in the language of the Constitution, our history, or our cases that requires that a majority always prevail on every issue. On the contrary, while we have recognized that state officials are normally chosen by a vote of the majority of the electorate, we have found no constitutional barrier to the selection of a Governor by a state legislature, after no candidate received a majority of the popular vote.
>
> The Federal Constitution itself provides that a simple majority vote is insufficient on some issues; the provisions on impeachment and ratification of treaties are but two examples. Moreover, the Bill of Rights removes entire areas of legislation from the concept of majoritarian supremacy. The constitutions of many States prohibit or severely limit the power of the legislature to levy new taxes or to create or increase bonded indebtedness, thereby insulating entire areas from majority control. Whether these matters of finance and taxation are to be considered as less "important" than matters of treaties, foreign policy, or impeachment of public officers is more properly left to the determination by the States and the people than to the courts operating under the broad mandate of the Fourteenth Amendment. It must be remembered that in voting to issue bonds voters are committing, in part, the credit of infants and of generations yet unborn, and some restriction on such commitment is not an unreasonable demand. That the bond issue may have the desirable objective of providing better education for future generations goes to the wisdom of an indebtedness limitation: it does not alter the basic fact that the balancing of interests is one for the State to resolve.
>
> Wisely or not, the people of the State of West Virginia have long since resolved to remove from a simple majority vote the choice on certain decisions as to what indebtedness may be incurred and what taxes their children will bear.
>
> We conclude that so long as such provisions do not discriminate against or authorize discrimination against any identifiable

class they do not violate the Equal Protection Clause. We see no meaningful distinction between such absolute provisions on debt, changeable only by constitutional amendment, and provisions that legislative decisions on the same issues require more than a majority vote in the legislature. On the contrary, these latter provisions may, in practice, be less burdensome than the amendment process. Moreover, the same considerations apply when the ultimate power, rather than being delegated to the legislature, remains with the people, by way of a referendum. Indeed, we see no constitutional distinction between the 60% requirement in the present case and a state requirement that a given issue be approved by a majority of all registered voters.

That West Virginia has adopted a rule of decision, applicable to all bond referenda, by which the strong consensus of three-fifths is required before indebtedness is authorized, does not violate the Equal Protection Clause or any other provision of the Constitution.

B. LOCAL GOVERNANCE

As should be evident, there is a wide array of non-legislative elected offices in the United States. These range from local bodies that resemble smaller legislatures, such as county commissions or city councils, to specialized bodies, such as water district boards or parks commissions, to specific function bodies that are frequently not even elected, such as school boards. While there is no specific constitutional command that such bodies be elected, the applicability of the equipopulation principle to such bodies as were elected quickly came to occupy the courts. In *Avery v. Midland County*, 390 U.S. 474 (1968), the Court held that the election of the Commissioners Court of a Texas county must satisfy the *Reynolds* standard. Although the Commissioners Court performed functions that were both administrative/executive and legislative, the Court nonetheless found that one-person, one-vote applied because the Commissioner Court served as the immediate "unit of local government with general responsibility and power for local affairs." Should it have made any difference that the Texas Supreme Court had previously held that "[t]he primary function of the commissioners court is the administration of the business affairs of the county. Its legislative functions are negligible and county government is not otherwise comparable to the legislature of the state." *Avery v. Midland County*, 406 S.W.2d 422, 426 (Tex.1966)? Recall that *Kramer v. Union Free School District No. 15*, 395 U.S. 621 (1969), also rejected the attempted distinction between a school board and the state legislature.

By contrast, in *Sailors v. Board of Education of Kent County*, 387 U.S. 105 (1967), the Court upheld an appointive system of selecting members of a local school board. Although an argument could be made that the school board exercised some general responsibilities, the Court held that there was no constitutional requirement that school boards be elected and that the largely administrative function of the board permitted appointment of the county school board by delegates of local school boards.

In *Hadley v. Junior College District*, 397 U.S. 50 (1970), the Court confronted a case falling between the cracks of *Avery* and *Sailors*. Under Missouri law, eight school districts combined to form a Junior College District of Metropolitan Kansas City. The Trustees were apportioned on the basis of school age students residing in each of the eight school districts. Under this formula, the urban Kansas City school district elected 50 percent of the total number of trustees, although it contained 60 percent of the school age population. In order to reach the specific powers over junior colleges alone, however, the Court had to revisit the *Avery* rule that appeared to rely on the exercise of general powers to trigger one-person, one-vote scrutiny:

> Appellants in this case argue that the junior college trustees exercised general governmental powers over the entire district and that under *Avery* the State was thus required to apportion the trustees according to population on an equal basis, as far as practicable. Appellants argue that since the trustees can levy and collect taxes, issue bonds with certain restrictions, hire and fire teachers, make contracts, collect fees, supervise and discipline students, pass on petitions to annex school districts, acquire property by condemnation, and in general manage the operations of the junior college, ... their powers are equivalent, for apportionment purposes, to those exercised by the county commissioners in *Avery*. We feel that these powers, while not fully as broad as those of the Midland County Commissioners ..., certainly show that the trustees perform important governmental functions within the districts, and we think these powers are general enough and have sufficient impact throughout the district to justify the conclusion that the principle which we applied in *Avery* should also be applied here.

What powers of government would not be considered "important governmental functions" after *Hadley*?

Board of Estimate v. Morris
489 U.S. 688 (1989).

■ JUSTICE WHITE delivered the opinion of the Court.

The Board of Estimate of the city of New York consists of three members elected citywide, plus the elected presidents of each of the city's five boroughs. Because the boroughs have widely disparate populations—yet each has equal representation on the board—the Court of Appeals for the Second Circuit held that this structure is inconsistent with the Equal Protection Clause of the Fourteenth Amendment. We affirm.

Appellees, residents and voters of Brooklyn, New York City's most populous borough, commenced this action against the city in December 1981. They charged that the city's charter sections that govern the composition of the Board of Estimate are inconsistent with the Equal Protection Clause of the Fourteenth Amendment as construed and applied in various decisions of this Court dealing with districting and apportionment for the purpose of electing legislative bodies.

* * *

As an initial matter, we reject the city's suggestion that because the Board of Estimate is a unique body wielding non-legislative powers, board membership elections are not subject to review under the prevailing reapportionment doctrine. The equal protection guarantee of "one-person, one-vote" extends not only to congressional districting plans, *see Wesberry v. Sanders*, not only to state legislative districting, see *Reynolds v. Sims*, but also to local government apportionment. Both state and local elections are subject to the general rule of population equality between electoral districts.

* * *

These cases are based on the propositions that in this country the people govern themselves through their elected representatives and that "each and every citizen has an inalienable right to full and effective participation in the political processes" of the legislative bodies of the Nation, State, or locality as the case may be. Since "most citizens can achieve this participation only as qualified voters through the election of legislators to represent them," full and effective participation requires "that each citizen have an equally effective voice in the election of members of his ... legislature." As Daniel Webster once said, "the right to choose a representative is every man's portion of sovereign power." Electoral systems should strive to make each citizen's portion equal. If districts of widely unequal population elect an equal number of representatives, the voting power of each citizen in the larger constituencies is debased and the citizens in those districts have a smaller share of representation than do those in the smaller districts....

That the members of New York City's Board of Estimate trigger this constitutional safeguard is certain. All eight officials become members as a matter of law upon their various elections. The mayor, the comptroller, and the president of the city council, who comprise the board's citywide number, are elected by votes of the entire city electorate. Each of these three cast two votes, except that the mayor has no vote on the acceptance or modification of his budget proposal. Similarly, when residents of the city's five boroughs—the Bronx, Brooklyn, Manhattan, Queens, and Richmond (Staten Island)—elect their respective borough presidents, the elections decide each borough's representative on the board. These five members each have single votes on all board matters.

New York law assigns to the board a significant range of functions common to municipal governments. Fiscal responsibilities include calculating sewer and water rates, tax abatements, and property taxes on urban development projects. The board manages all city property; exercises plenary zoning authority; dispenses all franchises and leases on city property; fixes generally the salaries of all officers and persons compensated through city moneys; and grants all city contracts. This array of powers, which the board shares with no other part of the New York City government, are exercised through the aforementioned voting scheme: three citywide officials cast a total of six votes; their five borough counterparts, one vote each.

In addition, and of major significance, the board shares legislative functions with the city council with respect to modifying and approving the city's capital and expense budgets. The mayor submits a proposed city budget to the board and city council, but does not participate in board decisions to adopt or alter the proposal. Approval or modification of the proposed budget requires agreement between the board and the city council. Board votes on budget matters, therefore, consist of four votes cast by two at-large members; and five, by the borough presidents.

This considerable authority to formulate the city's budget, which last fiscal year surpassed $25 billion, as well as the board's land use, franchise, and contracting powers over the city's 7 million inhabitants, situate the board comfortably within the category of governmental bodies whose "powers are general enough and have sufficient impact throughout the district" to require that elections to the body comply with equal protection strictures.

The city also erroneously implies that the board's composition survives constitutional challenge because the citywide members cast a 6-to-5 majority of board votes and hence are in position to control the outcome of board actions. The at-large members, however, as the courts below observed, often do not vote together; and when they do not, the outcome is determined by the votes of the borough presidents, each having one vote. Two citywide members, with the help of the presidents of the two least populous boroughs, the Bronx and Staten Island, will prevail over a disagreeing coalition of the third citywide member and the presidents of the three boroughs that contain a large majority of the city's population. Furthermore, because the mayor has no vote on budget issues, the citywide members alone cannot control board budgetary decisions.

The city's primary argument is that the courts below erred in the methodology by which they determined whether, and to what extent, the method of electing the board members gives the voters in some boroughs more power than the voters in other boroughs. Specifically, the city focuses on the relative power of the voters in the various boroughs to affect board decisions, an approach which involves recognizing the weighted voting of the three citywide members.

[... T]he method urged by the city to determine an individual voter's power to affect the outcome of a board vote first calculates the power of each member of the board to affect a board vote, and then calculates voters' power to cast the determining vote in the election of that member. This method, termed the Banzhaf Index, applies as follows: 552 possible voting combinations exist in which any one member can affect the outcome of a board vote. Each borough president can cast the determining vote in 48 of these combinations (giving him a "voting power" of 8.7%), while each citywide member can determine the outcome in 104 of 552 combinations (18.8%). A citizen's voting power through each representative is calculated by dividing the representative's voting power by the square root of the population represented; a citizen's total voting power thus aggregates his power through each of his four representatives—borough president, mayor, comptroller, and council president. Deviation from ideal voting power is then calculated by comparing this figure with the figure arrived at when one considers an electoral district of ideal population. Calculated in this manner, the maximum deviation in the voting power to control board outcomes is 30.8% on nonbudget matters, and, because of the mayor's absence, a higher deviation on budget issues.

The Court of Appeals gave careful attention to and rejected this submission. We agree with the reasons given by the Court of Appeals that the population-based approach of our cases from *Reynolds* through *Abate* [*v. Mundt*, 403 U.S. 182 (1971)] should not be put aside in this litigation. We note also that we have once before, although in a different context, declined to accept the approach now urged by the city. *Whitcomb v. Chavis*, 403 U.S. 124 (1971). In that case we observed that the Banzhaf methodology "remains a theoretical one" and is unrealistic in not taking into account "any political or other factors which might affect the actual voting power of the residents, which might include party affiliation, race, previous voting characteristics or any other factors which go into the entire political voting situation."

The personal right to vote is a value in itself, and a citizen is, without more and without mathematically calculating his power to determine the outcome of an election, shortchanged if he may vote for only one representative when citizens in a neighboring district, of equal population, vote for two; or to put it another way, if he may vote for one representative and the voters in another district half the size also elect one representative....

The Court of Appeals also thought that the city's approach ... did not reflect the way the board actually works in practice; rather, the method is a theoretical explanation of each board member's power to affect the outcome of board actions. It may be that in terms of assuring fair and effective representation, the equal protection approach reflected in the *Reynolds v. Sims* line of cases is itself imperfect, but it does assure that legislators will be elected by, and represent citizens in, districts of substantially equal size. It does not attempt to inquire whether, in terms of how the legislature actually works in practice, the districts have equal power to affect a legislative outcome. This would be a difficult and ever-changing task, and its challenge is hardly met by a mathematical calculation that itself stops short of examining the actual day-to-day operations of the legislative body . . . .

Having decided to follow the established method of resolving equal protection issues in districting and apportionment cases, the Court of Appeals then inquired whether the presence of at-large members on the board should be factored into the process of determining the deviation between the more and less populous boroughs. The court decided that they need not be taken into account because the at-large members and the borough presidents respond to different constituencies. The three at-large members obviously represent citywide interests; but, in the Court of Appeals' judgment, the borough presidents represent and are responsive to their boroughs, yet each has one vote despite the dramatic inequalities in the boroughs' populations. Consideration of the citywide members might be different, the court explained, "If the at-large bloc was not simply a majority, but a majority such that it would always and necessarily control the governing body, and the district representatives play a decidedly subsidiary role. . . ."

The Court of Appeals then focused on the five boroughs as single-member districts, electing five representatives to the board, each with a single vote. Applying the formula that we have utilized without exception since 1971, the Court of Appeals agreed with the District Court that the maximum percentage deviation from the ideal population is 132.9% . . . .

We do not agree with the Court of Appeals' approach. . . . Here the voters in each borough vote for the at-large members as well as their borough president, and they are also represented by those members. Hence in determining whether there is substantially equal voting power and representation, the citywide members are a major component in the calculation and should not be ignored.

Because of the approach followed by the District Court and the Court of Appeals, there was no judicial finding concerning the total deviation from the ideal that would be if the at-large members of the board are taken into account. In pleadings filed with the District Court, however, appellees indicated, and the city agreed, that the deviation would then be 78%. And as to budget matters, when only two citywide members participate, the deviation would be somewhat larger. We accept for purposes of this case the figure agreed upon by the parties.

We note that no case of ours has indicated that a deviation of some 78% could ever be justified. At the very least, the local government seeking to support such a difference between electoral districts would bear a very difficult burden, and we are not prepared to differ with the holding of the courts below that this burden has not been carried. The city presents in this Court nothing that was not considered below, arguing chiefly that the board, as presently structured, is essential to the successful government of a regional entity, the city of New York. The board, it is said, accommodates natural and political boundaries as well as local interests. Furthermore, because the board has been effective it should not be disturbed. All of this, the city urges, is supported by the city's history. The courts below, of course, are in a much better position than we to assess the weight of these arguments, and they concluded that the proffered governmental interests were either invalid or were not sufficient to justify a deviation of 132%.... Their analysis is equally applicable to a 78% deviation, and we conclude that the city's proffered governmental interests do not suffice to justify such a substantial departure from the one-person, one-vote ideal.

Accordingly the judgment of the Court of Appeals is

Affirmed.

NOTES AND QUESTIONS

1. In *Wells v. Edwards*, 347 F.Supp. 453 (M.D.La.1972)(three-judge court), *aff'd*, 409 U.S. 1095 (1973) (per curiam), the court found the election of state court judges not to be governed by the one-person, one-vote rule. According to the court,

> The primary purpose of one-man, one-vote apportionment is to make sure that each official member of an elected body speaks for approximately the same number of constituents. But as stated in *Buchanan v. Rhodes*, [249 F.Supp. 860 (N.D.Ohio 1966), appeal dismissed, 385 U.S. 3]: "Judges do not represent people, they serve people." Thus, the rationale behind the one-man, one-vote principle, which evolved out of efforts to preserve a truly representative form of government, is simply not relevant to the makeup of the judiciary.

Wells involved the Louisiana Supreme Court, whose seven Justices were elected from judicial districts with widely varying populations—created directly by the Louisiana Constitution of 1921 and unchanged since that time. Is the equipopulation principle "simply not relevant" to the election of state court judges? Are elected judges truly less "representative" than elected Trustees of a Junior College District? For a discussion of the tension between judicial elections and judicial independence, *see* Hans A. Linde, *The Judge as Political Candidate*, 40 Clev. St. L. Rev. 1 (1992); Steven P. Croley, *The Majoritarian Difficulty: Elective Judiciaries and the Rule of Law,* 62 U.Chi.L.Rev. 689 (1995).

2. *Morris* proved a significant tripwire in New York City. The Board of Estimate served to give enhanced power to the outlying boroughs of New York, primarily Staten Island. This arrangement allayed fears that the concentration of population and wealth in the largest boroughs would result in unfavorable treatment for residents without the same level of political clout. Although the modern borough-based Board of Estimate had not yet been created at the founding of New York City in 1898, it did emerge in 1901 and became a mainstay of the City's development. After *Morris*, strong secessionist sentiments surfaced in Staten Island. *See* Richard Briffault, *Voting Rights, Home Rule, and Metropolitan Governance: The Secession of Staten Island as a Case Study in the Dilemmas of Local Self-Determination*, 92 Colum. L. Rev. 775 (1992). Does regional representation to the least urbanized part of New York City fall within any of the recognized grounds for departure from the strict application of one-person, one-vote?

Ball v. James
451 U.S. 355 (1981).

■ JUSTICE STEWART delivered the opinion of the Court.

This appeal concerns the constitutionality of the system for electing the directors of a large water reclamation district in Arizona, a system which, in essence, limits voting eligibility to landowners and apportions voting power according to the amount of land a voter owns. The case requires us to consider whether the peculiarly narrow function of this local governmental body and the special relationship of one class of citizens to that body releases it from the strict demands of the one-person, one-vote principle of the Equal Protection Clause of the Fourteenth Amendment.

* * *

III

Reynolds v. Sims, supra, held that the Equal Protection Clause requires adherence to the principle of one-person, one-vote in elections of state legislators. *Avery v. Midland County*, 390 U.S. 474, extended the *Reynolds* rule to the election of officials of a county government, holding that the elected officials exercised "general governmental powers over the entire geographic area served by the body." 390 U.S., at 485.[] The Court, however, reserved any decision on the application of *Reynolds* to "a special-purpose unit of government assigned the performance of functions affecting definable groups of constituents more than other constituents." 390 U.S., at 483–484. In *Hadley v. Junior College District*, 397 U.S. 50, the Court extended *Reynolds* to the election of trustees of a community college district because those trustees "exercised general governmental powers" and "perform[ed] important governmental functions" that had significant effect on all citizens residing within the district. 397 U.S., at 53–54. But in that case the Court stated: "It is of course possible that there might be some case in which a State elects certain functionaries whose duties are so far removed from normal governmental activities and so disproportionately affect different groups that a popular election in compliance with *Reynolds* . . . might not be required. . . ."

The Court found such a case in *Salyer* [*Land Co. v. Tulare Lake Basin Water Storage District*, 410 U.S. 719 (1973)]. The Tulare Lake Basin Water Storage District involved there encompassed 193,000 acres, 85% of which were farmed by one or another of four corporations. . . . Under California law, public water districts could acquire, store, conserve, and distribute water, and though the Tulare Lake Basin Water Storage District had never chosen to do so, could generate and sell any form of power it saw fit to support its water operations. *Id.*, at 723–724. The costs of the project were assessed against each landowner according to the water benefits the landowner received. *Id.*, at 724. At issue in the case was the constitutionality of the scheme for electing the directors of the district, under which only landowners could vote, and voting power was apportioned according to the assessed valuation of the voting landowner's property. The Court recognized that the Tulare Lake Basin Water Storage District did exercise "some typical governmental powers," including the power to hire and fire workers, contract for construction of projects, condemn private property, and issue general obligation bonds. *Id.*, at 728, and n. 7. Nevertheless, the Court concluded that the district had "relatively limited authority," because "its primary purpose, indeed the reason for its existence, is to provide for the acquisition, storage, and distribution of water for farming in the Tulare Lake Basin." *Id.*, at 728. . . . The Court also noted that the financial burdens of the district could not but fall on the landowners, in proportion to the benefits they received from the district, and that the district's actions therefore disproportionately affected the voting landowners. *Id.*, at 729. The *Salyer* Court thus held that the strictures of *Reynolds* did not apply to the Tulare District, and proceeded to inquire simply whether the statutory voting scheme based on land valuation at least bore some relevancy to the statute's objectives. The Court concluded that the California Legislature could have reasonably assumed that without voting power apportioned according to the value of their land, the landowners might not have been willing to subject their lands to the lien of the very assessments which made the creation of the district possible. 410 U.S., at 731.

As noted by the Court of Appeals, the services currently provided by the Salt River District are more diverse and affect far more people than those of the Tulare Lake Basin Water Storage District. Whereas the Tulare District included an area entirely devoted to agriculture and populated by only 77 persons, the Salt River District includes almost half the population of the State, including large parts of Phoenix and other cities. Moreover, the Salt River District, unlike the Tulare District, has exercised its statutory power to generate and sell electric power, and has become one of the largest suppliers of such power in the State. Further, whereas all the water delivered by the Tulare District went for agriculture, roughly 40% of the water delivered by the Salt River District goes to urban areas or is used for nonagricultural purposes in farming areas. Finally whereas all operating costs of the Tulare District were born by the voting landowners through assessments apportioned according to land value, most of the capital and operating costs of the Salt River District have been met through the revenues generated by the selling of electric power. Nevertheless, a careful examination of the Salt River District reveals that, under the principles of the *Avery*, *Hadley*, and *Salyer* cases, these distinctions do not amount to a constitutional difference.

First, the District simply does not exercise the sort of governmental powers that invoke the strict demands of *Reynolds*. The District cannot impose ad valorem property taxes or sales taxes. It cannot enact any laws governing the conduct of citizens, nor does it administer such normal functions of government as the maintenance of streets, the operation of schools, or sanitation, health, or welfare services.

Second, though they were characterized broadly by the Court of Appeals, even the District's water functions, which constitute the primary and originating purpose of the District, are relatively narrow. The District and Association do not own, sell, or buy water, nor do they control the use of any water they have delivered. The District simply stores water behind its dams, conserves it from loss, and delivers it through project canals. It is true, as the Court of Appeals noted, that as much as 40% of the water delivered by the District goes for nonagricultural purposes. But the distinction between agricultural and urban land is of no special constitutional significance in this context. The constitutionally relevant fact is that all water delivered by the Salt River District, like the water delivered by the Tulare Lake Basin Water Storage District, is distributed according to land ownership, and the District does not and cannot control the use to which the landowners who are entitled to the water choose to put it. As repeatedly recognized by the Arizona courts, though the state legislature has allowed water districts to become nominal public entities in order to obtain inexpensive bond financing, the districts remain essentially business enterprises, created by and chiefly benefiting a specific group of landowners.... As in *Salyer*, the nominal public character of such an entity cannot transform it into the type of governmental body for which the Fourteenth Amendment demands a one-person, one-vote system of election.

Finally, neither the existence nor size of the District's power business affects the legality of its property-based voting scheme. As this Court has noted in a different context, the provision of electricity is not a traditional element of governmental sovereignty, *Jackson v. Metropolitan Edison Co.*, 419 U.S. 345, 353 [(1974)], and so is not in itself the sort of general or important governmental function that would make the government provider subject to the doctrine of the *Reynolds* case. In any event, since the electric power functions were stipulated to be incidental to the water functions which are the District's primary purpose, they cannot change the character of that enterprise. The Arizona Legislature permitted the District to generate and sell electricity to subsidize the water operations which were the beneficiaries intended by the statute. A key part of the *Salyer* decision was that the voting scheme for a public entity like a water district may constitutionally reflect the narrow primary purpose for which the district is created. In this case, the parties have stipulated that the primary legislative purpose of the District is to store, conserve, and deliver water for use by District landowners, that the sole legislative reason for making water projects public entities was to enable them to raise revenue through interest-free bonds, and that the development and sale of electric power was undertaken not for the primary purpose of providing electricity to the public, but "to support the primary irrigation functions by supplying power for reclamation uses and by providing revenues which could be applied to increase the amount and reduce the cost of water to Association subscribed lands."

The appellees claim, and the Court of Appeals agreed, that the sheer size of the power operations and the great number of people they affect serve to transform the District into an entity of general governmental power. But no matter how great the number of nonvoting residents buying electricity from the District, the relationship between them and the District's power operations is essentially that between consumers and a business enterprise from which they buy. Nothing in the *Avery*, *Hadley*, or *Salyer* cases suggests that the volume of business or the breadth of economic effect of a venture undertaken by a government entity as an incident of its narrow and primary governmental public function can, of its own weight, subject the entity to the one-person, one-vote requirements of the *Reynolds* case.

The functions of the Salt River District are therefore of the narrow, special sort which justifies a departure from the popular-election requirement of the *Reynolds* case. And as in *Salyer*, an aspect of that limited purpose is the disproportionate relationship the District's functions bear to the specific class of people whom the system makes eligible to vote. The voting landowners are the only residents of the District whose lands are subject to liens to secure District bonds. Only these landowners are subject to the acreage-based taxing power of the District, and voting landowners are the only residents who have ever committed capital to the District through stock assessments charged by the Association. The *Salyer* opinion did not say that the selected class of voters for a special public entity must be the only parties at all affected by the operations of the entity, or that their entire economic well-being must depend on that entity. Rather, the question was whether the effect of the entity's operations on them was disproportionately greater than the effect on those seeking the vote.

As in the *Salyer* case, we conclude that the voting scheme for the District is constitutional because it bears a reasonable relationship to its statutory objectives. Here, according to the stipulation of the parties, the subscriptions of land which made the Association and then the District possible might well have never occurred had not the subscribing landowners been assured a special voice in the conduct of the District's business. Therefore, as in *Salyer*, the State could rationally limit the vote to landowners. Moreover, Arizona could rationally make the weight of their vote dependent upon the number of acres they own, since that number reasonably reflects the relative risks they incurred as landowners and the distribution of the benefits and the burdens of the District's water operations.

The judgment of the Court of Appeals is reversed, and the case is remanded for further proceedings consistent with this opinion.

■ JUSTICE POWELL, concurring.

Our cases have recognized the necessity of permitting experimentation with political communities. *E.g., Holt Civic Club v. Tuscaloosa*, 439 U.S. 60, 71–72 (1978). As this case illustrates, it may be difficult to decide when experimentation and political compromise have resulted in an impermissible delegation of those governmental powers that generally affect all of the people to a body with a selective electorate. But state legislatures, responsive to the interests of all the people, normally are better qualified to make this judgment than federal courts.... Given the broad reforms effected by *Reynolds v. Sims*, we should expect that a legislature elected on the rule of one person, one vote will be vigilant to prevent undue concentration of power in the hands of undemocratic bodies. The absence of just such a political safeguard was a major justification for the Court's role in requiring legislative reapportionment. *See Baker v. Carr*, 369 U.S. 186, 258–259 (1962) (Clark, J., concurring).

The Court's opinion convincingly demonstrates that the powers exercised by the Salt River District are not powers that always must be exercised by a popularly elected body.... Both storage and delivery of water are functions that in other areas of the Nation are performed by private or administrative bodies. These tasks sometimes are performed by an elected government entity, because of the aridity of the Southwest, federal water policy, and the historical interest of Arizona landowners in irrigation, not because of their inherent character nor an insistent demand that the people as a whole decide how much water each will receive or how much each will pay for electricity.

Appellees argue that control of water is of prime importance in the Southwest and that many people purchase electricity from the District. These observations raise the question whether this Court should interfere with the constitution of the District, but do not answer it. The Arizona Legislature recently has demonstrated its control over the electoral processes of the District. It has reformed the District to increase the political voice of the small householder at the expense of the large landowner.... This reform no doubt reflects political and demographic changes in Arizona since the District was established.

The authority and will of the Arizona Legislature to control the electoral composition of the District are decisive for me in this case. The District is large enough and the resources it manages are basic enough that the people will act through their elected legislature when further changes in the governance of the District are warranted. We should allow the political process to operate. For this Court to dictate how the Board of the District must be elected would detract from the democratic process we profess to protect.

NOTES AND QUESTIONS

1. Justice Powell's concurrence in *Ball* raises two important questions about the nature of judicial review of how the political process is constituted. He identifies the importance of the *Reynolds v. Sims* line of cases as destabilizing a locked-in legislative distribution of power that was structurally immune from being displaced by the electorate. This argument responds to Justice Frankfurter's initial argument in *Colegrove v. Green* that the resolution of the maldistribution of power should come from within the political process itself. Justice Powell also returns to the theme first encountered in *Kramer v. Union Free School District* that the justification for judicial intervention might turn on whether the voting rules in questions were of sufficient public moment to arouse concerted efforts at reform at the state legislative level. Thus, for Justice Powell, the fact that water issues are of undoubted public salience in the Southwest indicates that maldistributions of political power are remediable through the state legislature. It then follows that the courts should be leery of entrenching upon local decisions about how to order the political process.

There is, however, the real concern that Justice Powell may be substituting one area of judicial non-expertise for another. Do judges really possess the skills necessary to distinguish electoral arrangements over matters that "are basic enough" to elicit popular political mobilizations, from those that are not? Is the composition of water regulatory agencies more or less likely to fall into that category than electoral rules for selecting school boards? How can courts determine when sufficient political safeguards exist to leave claims of political distortion to the political process itself to remedy? Can a line be drawn that would reject remedies that must be directed to the political body that is itself under challenge, as with the redistricting powers of a state legislature over itself?

There is also a strong concern emanating from public choice theory. At its most basic, public choice theory would challenge the ability of a concerned but relatively diffuse majority of the electorate to force an issue squarely onto the legislative arena. Because of the greater investment of what are generally denominated special interest groups, self-interested minorities tend to do disproportionately well in the legislative arena. For example, though most polls routinely show a majority of Americans favoring some form of gun control, the National Rifle Association is relatively successful in frustrating efforts to limit access to firearms. While a majority of the electorate may favor such restrictions if the question were posed in a survey, few are willing to vote exclusively based on that preference. By contrast, the NRA is credibly able to threaten to deliver or withhold some non-trivial number of votes based exclusively on the gun control issue. For a politician therefore, a vote in favor of gun control by itself is unlikely to translate into any votes, but is rather certain to lose votes. There is also the funding, lobbyists, and public relations that come with this type of strong interest group involvement in the political process. Is it credible to argue, as does Justice Powell, that a political monopoly over water policies would be that easy to dislodge at the state legislative level? For an extensive discussion of public choice theory and the political process, see Daniel A. Farber & Philip P. Frickey, Law and Public Choice (1991).

2. What is it that distinguishes the Salt River District from "the normal functions of government"? Can delivery of water to half the population of a parched state such as Arizona really be thought to be outside such normal governmental functions? After all, public works for the delivery of water have long been thought a major activity of government, going back to the Roman aqueducts and even before. A history of the area under consideration in *Ball* raises questions about whether water management can properly be considered a non-central part of government:

> The land around Phoenix is martini-dry. The only reason a city exists there at all is that as long ago as the time of Christ, humans of the Hohokam tribe recognized that by the standards of the Sonoran desert, the Valley of the Sun can be made water rich. These native Americans built a 250–mile canal system that permitted an advanced civilization to support twenty thousand people. For reasons that remain a mystery, the Hohokam disappeared from the valley just before Columbus sailed. A century and a half later, the Spanish showed up and gave the name Rio Salado—Salt River—to the broad gravel bed from which the canals radiated. A miner, scout, and Confederate calvary veteran named Jack Swilling reintroduced canal building to the area in the late 1800s. Then, in 1902, President Teddy Roosevelt championed the National Reclamation Act, which provided government loans to "reclaim" Western lands with irrigation projects. Metropolitan Phoenix rose around the bed of the Salt River because, in 1903, the shadow government called the Salt River Project was born....
>
> In the dry Southwest, water is the linchpin of the universe. With water you can create charming cities, fields of agricultural plenty, thriving industry, or wild rivers that charge the spirit. But there's not enough water to have all four. Who gets what is determined in a highly expensive, complex, and politicized fashion. And in central Arizona, that means the Salt River Project. An

entity like the Salt River Project, which determines the price and availability of electricity, has the power of life and death. In Arizona in the summer, people without air conditioning die, just as surely as do people in Montana without winter heat. When the Salt River Project decides to encourage water conservation—or, conversely, subsidizes water use by making it artificially cheap—or decides to share the cost of a nuclear reactor forty miles upwind of Phoenix or builds a coal-fired generator whose pollution is accused of obscuring the Grand Canyon, it exercises more control over the Arizona environment than virtually any other player.

Joel Garreau, Edge City: Life on the Frontier 192–93 (1991). Consider an alternative analysis focusing on the difference between the proprietary and legislative functions of government:

> Local government as business enterprise gave the Court a new framework for considering questions of local government organization, thereby increasing the discretion accorded the states in the creation of locally representative public entities. If a local government is a business enterprise, then the organizing principles for political bodies—universal adult resident enfranchisement and equal population representation—need not apply. With the proprietary enterprise model as an option, a state may design a local government to be responsive and accountable to just a limited group within the locality without having to prove that the restriction on the franchise or the bias in local representation is narrowly focused on all those interested in the local government and necessary to the furtherance of a compelling state interest. Moreover, although based on the notion that the restrictive franchise is justified by the landowners' stake in the special district enterprise, proprietary governments are not, in turn, subject to a rigid requirement that votes actually reflect the extent of a landowner's potential liability. Proprietary governments may use assessment-based voting, acreage-based voting, or even one owner/one vote for qualified owners.

Richard Briffault, *Who Rules at Home?:One Person/One Vote and Local Governments*, 60 U.Chi. L. Rev. 339, 369 (1993).

3. Following *Ball*, a broad array of governmental bodies were found to be single purpose boards and therefore immune from one-person, one-vote challenge. *See, e.g., State v. Frontier Acres Community Development District Pasco County*, 472 So.2d 455 (Fla.1985)(community development district); *Stelzel v. South Indian River Water Control District*, 486 So.2d 65 (Fla.App.1986)(water control district); *Goldstein v. Mitchell*, 494 N.E.2d 914 (Ill.App.1986)(drainage district); *Moores v. Edelbrock*, 276 Cal. Rptr. 320 (Cal.1990)(water district); *Foster v. Sunnyside Valley Irrigation District*, 687 P.2d 841 (Wash.1984)(irrigation district); *Porterfield v. Van Boening*, 744 P.2d 468 (Ariz.App.1987)(irrigation district); *Arizona Farm-*

workers Union v. Agricultural Employment Relations Board, 712 P.2d 960 (Ariz.Ct.App.1985)(union representation district). *But see Lower Valley Water and Sanitation District v. Public Service Co. of N.M.*, 632 P.2d 1170 (N.M. 1981)(sanitation district not a single purpose body).

4. *Salyer* and *Ball* raise important issues about the nature of individual access to the ballot whenever jurisdictions limit the franchise to property owners, generally referred to as freeholders. For an example of a case upholding limiting the franchise to freeholders, *see Lane v. Town of Oyster Bay*, 603 N.Y.S.2d 53 (Sup.Ct.App.Div.1993) (can limit vote on extension of sanitation collection district to freeholders). A number of issues follow from the restriction of the franchise. First, does the single purpose district ("SPD") exception make it permissible to limit the range of people who can sign the petition asking that a SPD be created in the first place? That is, do non-freeholders have any right to participate before the district exists? The general answer is that the petition can be limited. *See Gillard v. Estrella Dells I Improvement District*, 541 P.2d 932 (Ariz.App.1975); *Lower Valley Water & Sanitation District v. Public Service Co. of N.M.*, 632 P.2d 1170 (N.M. 1981); *City of Humble v. Metro. Transit Auth.*, 636 S.W.2d 484 (Tex.App.1982); *Doenges v. Salt Lake City*, 614 P.2d 1237 (Utah 1980). There is, however, an exception to the general rule. If the result of a successful petition would be a vote by the full electorate, then the one-person, one-vote rule applies because one group cannot be allowed to control the full electorate's ability to vote. *See Hayward v. Clay*, 573 F.2d 187 (4th Cir.), *cert. denied*, 439 U.S. 959 (1978); *City of Seattle v. State*, 694 P.2d 641 (Wash.1985).

A second outgrowth of the SPD cases is whether they recognize any affirmative right in the more directly affected group. For example, while it is clear that the vote in *Salyer* could be limited to freeholders, did it *have* to be limited to freeholders? The answer is clearly no. *Collins v. Town of Goshen*, 635 F.2d 954 (2d Cir.1980); *Cantwell v. Hudnut*, 566 F.2d 30 (7th Cir.1977), *cert. denied*, 439 U.S. 1114 (1979); *East Lake Water Assoc. v. Rogers*, 761 P.2d 627 (Wash.Ct.App.1988). A similar question is whether, even if the directly affected group doesn't have the exclusive right to vote, does it have any right to vote at all? Again, the answer appears to be no. *See Collins v. Brennan*, 456 N.Y.S.2d 931 (Sup.Ct.Tompkins Cty.1982) (referendum election on sewer project not required to include nonresident property owners).

A third question concerns the restriction of the franchise based on geography rather than property-holding, which is also generally upheld. *See Simi Valley Recreation & Park District v. Local Agency Formation Comm'n*, 124 Cal.Rptr. 635 (Cal.App.1975) (permissible to exclude residents who don't live in area to be deannexed; special purpose district doesn't require strict scrutiny); *Moorman v. Wood*, 504 F.Supp. 467 (E.D.Ky.1980) (permissible to limit franchise in deannexation to only those voters in area potentially to be deannexed); *New York v. State*, 556 N.Y.S.2d 823 (Sup.

Ct.), *aff'd* 561 N.Y.S.2d 154 (Ct.App., N.Y., 1990)(permissible to limit vote on Staten Island secession to Staten Island residents); *King County Water District No. 54 v. King County Boundary Review Board*, 554 P.2d 1060 (Wash.1976)(*en banc*)(in taking over water district, city can limit vote to city residents, who are most directly affected); *Provance v. Shawnee Mission Unified School District No. 512*, 648 P.2d 710 (Kan.), *aff'd* 683 P.2d 902 (Kan.1984)(permissible to limit school closing election to residents in vicinity of affected school). *But see Fullerton Joint Union High School Dist. v. State Board of Educ.*, 654 P.2d 168 (Cal.1982) (*en banc*) (cannot limit deannexation vote to voters in deannexation area).

Finally, courts have recognized a category of special purpose bodies that, like special purpose districts, have been held immune from one-person, one-vote challenge. These bodies include: *The Florida Bar re Amendments to the Rules Regulating the Florida Bar (Reapportionment)*, 518 So.2d 251 (Fla.1987)(Florida Bar Association Board of Governors elected from circuits of varying population); *Opinion of the Justices*, 319 So.2d 699 (Ala.1975)(electric company board); *Humane Society v. New Jersey State Fish & Game Council*, 362 A.2d 20 (N.J.1976) (appointed board of state fish and game council); *Slisz v. Western Regional Off-Track Betting Corp.*, 382 F.Supp. 1231 (W.D.N.Y.1974)(appointed board treated as "quasi-elective," but sustained because of limited powers); *Sullivan v. Farmers Home Administration*, 691 F.Supp. 927 (E.D.N.C.1987) (FmHA County Loan Committees upheld despite borrowers and spouses not permitted on loan committees); *Hedge v. Lyng*, 689 F.Supp. 898 (D.Minn.1988) (same); *Benner v. Oswald*, 444 F.Supp. 545 (M.D.Pa.1978), *aff'd*, 592 F.2d 174 (3d Cir.), *cert. denied* 444 U.S. 832 (1979)(university board of trustees); *Davis v. AT & T*, 478 F.2d 1375 (2d Cir.1973) (assuming state action, corporation is a special purpose entity). *But see Quinn v. Millsap*, 491 U.S. 95 (1989) (striking down, under rational relation standard of review, a Missouri statute limiting membership to landholders for advisory board of freeholders appointed by governor); *Hellebust v. Brownback*, 824 F.Supp. 1511 (D.Kan.1993), *aff'd* 42 F.3d 1331 (10th Cir.1994) (striking down on one-person, one-vote grounds a board that regulated milk and meat, had a right to inspect and seize, managed dams, and governed all weights and measures in state).

5. Even if special purpose boards do not violate the constitutional one-person, one-vote command, might they still violate other regulations of the franchise, such as the Voting Rights Act? *See* Glenn P. Smith, Note, *Interest Exceptions to One–Resident, One–Vote: Better Results from the Voting Rights Act?*, 74 Tex. L. Rev. 1153 (1996).

Fumarolo v. Chicago Board of Education
142 Ill.2d 54, 566 N.E.2d 1283 (1990).

■ JUSTICE WARD delivered the opinion of the court:

* * *

The record shows that, as in most large cities, Chicago has serious problems in its public school system. The Chicago School Reform Act was enacted in 1988 in an attempt to resolve certain of the problems. The Act makes significant changes in school governance and administration by decentralizing the school system and by imposing primary responsibility for local school governance on parents, community residents, teachers and school principals. The plaintiffs do not dispute the need for change in the Chicago public school system, but they challenge the constitutionality of the Act, arguing that sections of the statute violate the Federal and State constitutional assurances of equal protection and due process. The plaintiffs, who are registered voters and taxpayers in the City of Chicago, allege that the Act's voting scheme for electing members of the local school councils violates the equal protection clauses of the State and Federal Constitutions because it denies an equal vote in local school council elections to large portions of the electorate.

* * *

Local School Councils

Although the board of education retains many general administrative powers and responsibilities, its powers and responsibilities under the Act have been substantially altered. To place increased authority for individual school decisions at the individual school level, the Act provides for the creation of a local school council for each grammar school and each high school in the Chicago public school system (there are 539 schools in the Chicago public school system). (Ill.Rev.Stat.1989, ch. 122, par. 34–2.1.) The local school council is composed of the school principal and 10 elected members. The elected members are: six parents of currently enrolled students who are elected by parents of currently enrolled students, two residents of the attendance area served by the school who are elected by the residents of that area (except in multiarea districts—districts which draw and admit students from more than a single attendance area—where the community residents to be elected are elected by the parents of currently enrolled students, the principal of the multiarea school and the school staff, and two teachers of the school who are elected by the school staff. Each local school council elects the principal who will serve at the school for a contract period of four years and may retain the principal for another four-year period when the contract expires. Should a principal not be retained, the local school council will select a new principal. The local school council also develops specific performance criteria for its principal and has responsibility for approving the budget plan drawn up and administered by the principal. In addition, the local school council has substantial advisory responsibilities.

Subdistrict Councils

The Act creates 11 subdistrict councils. Each local school council elects one of its parent or nonparent resident members to sit on a subdistrict council. Each subdistrict council performs various advisory functions (e.g., promoting and coordinating communication among local school councils, promoting and coordinating training of local school councils), elects and evaluates for retention the subdistrict school superintendent and is responsible for electing one of its members to sit on the school board nominating commission.

School Board Nominating Commission

The school board nominating commission is composed of 11 members elected from each subdistrict council and five members appointed by the mayor. The nominating commission, in an open public forum, interviews candidates for seats on the board of education and presents the mayor with a slate of three qualified candidates for each vacant seat on the board. The mayor selects one of the candidates for each seat from this list. The Act provides that there are to be 15 members on the board of education. An interim board of education was created by the Act until the mayor should appoint candidates as provided by the Act. A permanent board of education has now been selected under the Reform Act.

* * *

The plaintiffs argue that the Act's differentiated allocation of votes among parents, community residents and teachers in local school council elections impermissibly interferes with their fundamental right to have an equal voice in an election involving a governmental matter of general interest, namely, the operation of local schools. Under the Act, community residents who reside in multiarea districts and do not have children in attendance at the public schools are unable to vote for any local school council members. Community residents in single district attendance centers who do not have children in attendance in a public school are entitled to vote for only two members of the council. Parents, however, who have children in the school, are entitled to vote for six members of the council. The defendants, in response, contend that a voting scheme which results in differentiated treatment of voters will not be found to violate constitutional assurances of equal protection if the voters given the weighted vote have a greater interest in and are more greatly benefited by the particular activities of the governmental unit which is the subject of the election.... [Defendants also argue] that strict scrutiny analysis should not be applied because the local school councils are subordinate panels of tightly limited authority which do not perform "general governmental functions." The local school councils cannot levy taxes, appropriate money, enter into contracts, issue bonds, acquire property, or set basic educational policy at the district level. All of these powers, the defendants point out, are retained by the board of education. The local school councils, the defendants argue, simply implement in the particular school the district-wide policies set by the board.

* * *

The local school councils are readily distinguishable from the water districts at issue in *Ball* and *Salyer*. The local school councils are the cornerstone, in a real sense, of the operation of the city's schools and they play a significant role in the Act's scheme to improve education in the City of Chicago. They have important and multiple powers that affect the whole community.

The administration of education through the operation of our schools is a fundamental governmental activity in which all members of society have an interest. Furthermore, educational activities are financed by and affect virtually every resident. The local school councils perform an indispensable role in administering the board's educational policy at the local level and in carrying out the legislature's intent to create a dominant force at that level. We hold, therefore, that the local school councils exercise general governmental functions, as that term has been defined in *Hadley* and *Kramer*.

A second consideration in *Ball* and *Salyer* was whether the functions of the local water district disproportionately benefited those given the weighted votes. In *Ball* and *Salyer*, the functions performed by the water reclamation districts and the costs associated with the districts were directly linked to land ownership and directly and disproportionately benefited the landowners. Here, the cost of operating the community's schools falls directly or indirectly on virtually all community residents, e.g., property taxes are imposed on all residents regardless of whether they have children attending the schools, and the decisions of the local school council affect virtually every resident of the school's attendance area. The benefits resulting from the election of competent and efficient local school councils are far from limited to parents with children in the public schools. For example, nonparent residents are directly affected by the individual school's performance in that the quality of the community's schools often directly affects the value of their property; parents with children not yet of school age have a proper and direct interest in the quality and operation of the schools their children will soon enter; parents of children who attend private schools also have a direct interest in the school system (improved public schools would allow the parents to re-enroll their children in public school). Furthermore, it is clear that a community school is not judged solely on the basis of the general district-wide policy set by the board. The school is judged, instead, on its individual performance and on its ability to implement effectively general educational policy. Although a parent's interest in the quality of the school his or her child attends is clearly identifiable, it is not an exclusive interest. It simply cannot be said that the activities and the performance of the local school council have a sufficiently disproportionate effect on those parents with children in current attendance at the public school.

We hold, therefore, that because the local school councils perform a general governmental function which affects the entire community, the trial judge erred in applying the rational basis standard in determining whether the voting scheme of the Act violated equal protection. Absent a showing that an elected body serves a special limited purpose, a restriction which operates to dilute a citizen's vote must meet a strict scrutiny test of justification. (*Hill v. Stone*, 421 U.S. 289 (1975)). The Act creates a classification which dilutes the vote of those citizens who do not have children attending the public schools in the year of the local school council election. A rational basis will not justify the classification of voters created by the Act.

* * *

We hold that the Act does not meet the strict scrutiny standard and is violative of the equal protection clauses of the Federal and State Constitutions.

NOTES AND QUESTIONS

1. Do *Ball* and *Salyer* compel the conclusion in *Fumarolo*? Does *Morris* foreclose any possibility of enhancing parental representation in the governance of the educational system?

2. The Illinois Supreme Court relies on the broad impact of educational decisions in striking down the Chicago educational reforms. Recall, however, the discussion by Justice Powell in *Ball* that broad impact of the electoral arrangement might yield viable political checks on any abuses of the franchise. Does the fact that the Chicago School Reform Act was passed by the state legislature as a response to a perceived crisis in the Chicago schools militate in favor of upholding the voting reforms?

C. THE SENATE, REPUBLICAN THEORY, AND INTEREST REPRESENTATION

The most salient feature of the equipopulation revolution in the Court's jurisprudence was its hostility to the claim that allocating representation in a specified manner was necessary to the protection of special interests that risked being numerically overwhelmed. Except in those areas deemed outside the one-person, one-vote rule—such as the special districts in *Salyer* and *Ball*—the demands of equal voting strength clearly outweighed local representational interests. Two issues nonetheless present themselves. The first, which will recur centrally in later chapters of this book, concerns how representational opportunity will be assigned even under the equipopulation principle. The second is to give a fuller accounting of the now anomalous position of the U.S. Senate as the one major elected institution in our political order that remains exempt from the constraints of equal representation.

The distinct features of the Senate emerged at the founding of the American Republic. American political thought in the constitutional period was strongly influenced by the English conception of the constitution as the embodiment of mixed government.

The Concept of Mixed Government at the time of the Constitution— At the time of the American Revolution, the English political structure was widely considered the perfected form of representative government. Montesquieu called it "this beautiful system." Even American revolutionaries, like John Adams and James Wilson, described the English system as "the best model of government that can be framed by Mortals." Gordon Wood, The Creation of the American Republic 11 (1969). The basis for this admiration was the exquisite "balance" the English constitution was thought to embody. This balance was exceptionally intricate, for it operated along two distinct dimensions: the English system of government was thought to incorporate the three principal *forms of government,* as well as the the principal *social orders* within society. This system exerted great influence over the design of the American Constitution.

Since Aristotle, forms of government had been categorized into monarchy, aristocracy, and democracy. In monarchy, the entire ruling power was placed in the discretion of a single figure; in aristocracy, in the hands of a select wise elite; and in democracy, ruling power lay with the people as a whole. Each form was thought to have its own distinct virtues or capacities. For monarchy, it was order, strength, and energy; for aristocracy, it was wisdom; and for democracy, honesty and goodness. But each had dangers as well. Any one of these simple forms, if left to dominate, was thought prone to degenerate into extreme versions of itself as those with power sought to grab more.

Mixed government included each of these types of government within the overall constitutional structure. In "balancing" these simple forms, mixed government was thought to create a stable equilibrium of the virtues and vices of any one form taken in isolation. The King brought the benefits of monarchy; the House of Lords, of aristocracy, and the House of Commons, the benefits of democracy. This balance was the best security for liberty.

At the same time, the English system was though to represent and balance the essential social elements or estates within the state. That is, mixed government was viewed as the political embodiment of society itself. By this period, the King no longer represented all of English society, but one of its distinct estates. The church had lost its status as a separate estate and was merged into the remaining two estates, the nobility and the people. These three orders—King, nobility, and the people—constituted all of English society, and corresponded perfectly to the three forms of government. "This marvellous coincidence between the society and the government, together with its relation to the three simple governments of antiquity, gave the English constitution its awesomeness and Parliament its sovereignty." Wood, id., at 199.

The Transformation of Mixed Government into the United States Senate: But what mixed government meant for republican politics, in a society without a hereditary aristocracy and purportedly committed to egalitarian principles, posed vexing questions. Many of these focused on the issue of bicameral legislatures, particularly on the upper house or Senate. Should the states and the national government adopt a Senate at all, or should the legislature be unicameral? If a Senate was created, on what principles of representation should it be based?

As a general matter, democratic thought of the period was hostile to the representation of particular interests, and by extension to the use of electoral devices aimed at guaranteeing particularized interest representation. The most radical elements in the American Revolution, such as Thomas Paine, advocated unicameral elections. Thus, unicameral legislatures were established in those ex-colonies that were most under the sway of democratic theory: Georgia, Pennsylvania, and Vermont. The upper house of a bicameral legislature was generally associated by supporters and detractors with an aristocratic influence, present from the Roman Senate to the House of Lords; an upper house was thought necessary to check the proclivity for "passion" to hold sway in popular rule. For example, in *The Federalist,* No. 10, Madison discusses the dangers that might be posed by passion serving as the basis for confiscation of property should there not be institutional obstacles to direct majoritarian rule. *See also* Gordon S. Wood, *Interests and Disinterestedness in the Making of the Constitution*, in Beyond Confederation: Origins of the Constitution and American National Identity 69–103 (R. Beeman, S. Botein, and E. Carter II, eds. 1987)(ascribing Madison's aversion to his direct experience observing narrow interest-based legislation in the Virginia state legislature under the Articles of Confederation); Frank G. Bates & Oliver P. Field, State Government 151 (1939). Where large landed interests were able to check the exercise of democratic power, as in Maryland and South Carolina, the system of electors was supplemented by high property qualifications and long terms of office for the Senate. *See* Jackson Turner Main, The Upper House in Revolutionary America, 1763–1788, at 195–205 (1967). Their arguments were summarized by John Adams as providing six reasons why a single assembly was bad. It was "liable to all the vices, follies, and frailties of an individual; subject to fits of humor, starts of passion, flights of enthusiasm, partialities, or prejudice, and consequently productive of hasty results and absurd judgments. And all these errors ought to be corrected and defects applied by some controlling power." Moreover, he opined, "a single assembly is apt to be avaricious, and in time will not scruple to exempt itself from burdens, which it will lay, without compunction, on its constituents." *Id.* at 206, *quoting* Charles Francis Adams, ed. The Works of John Adams 195–96 (1858).

These issues were extensively debated on a state-by-state basis at the time of the Founding of the United States. For example, Thomas Jefferson, the most democratic of the Framers, proposed a draft constitution for Virginia in which he sought to ensure that the "wisest men" would be elected to the senate and would then be "perfectly independent of their electors." Thus he strongly resisted direct popular election and proposed term limits: a single nine-year term for state senators to avoid their "casting their eyes forward to the period of election (however distant) and . . . currying favor with the electors." *Id.* at 213. But in 1776, he lost this battle. The Virginia Constitution provided for direct popular election of the senate, with no special qualifications for either voters or candidates. In other states, higher property-holding requirements were sometimes imposed on candidates or, as Madison favored, on electors.

In struggling to apply the ideology of mixed government to America's republican setting, state constitution makers in the 1780s, the period leading up to the U.S. Constitution, gradually developed an alternative vision. Because America lacked any traditional aristocracy, a substitute was found in the criteria of property and wealth. Considered imperfect, these criteria nonetheless came to be viewed as proxies for eliciting the kind of "wisdom" and "steadiness" that justified the need for bicameralism and upper houses. In the process, the conception of representative government and of republicanism was dramatically transformed.

This transformation is best embodied in the Massachusetts Constitution of 1780. The theory justifying it quickly became widespread in debates over bicameralism. This theory was articulated in the famous *Essex Result*, the publication in 1778 of one county convention in Massachusetts that had met to consider what became the new state constitution:

> The only objects of legislation are the person and property of the individuals which compose the state. If the law affects only the persons of the members, the consent of a majority of any members is sufficient. If the law affects the property only, the consent of those who hold a majority of the property is enough. If it affects, (as it will very frequently, if not always) both the persons and property, the consent of a majority of the members, and of those members also, who hold a majority of the property is necessary.

Thus, upper houses were needed to protect distinct *interests*. One House represented persons; the other, the Senate, should represent property. This reflected a radical change in the way American society was coming to be conceived. First, republican thought had depended on a vision of a largely homogenous society, one with a unity of interests. This new vision acknowledged diverse and clashing economic interests; that vision would come to underlie the U.S. Constitution. Second, a conception of interest representation emerged. Equal *interests* among the society should have equal influence over government. As Madison put it, "persons and property being both essential objects of Government, the most that either can claim, is such a structure of it as will leave a reasonable security for the other." Gordon Wood, The Radicalism of the American Revolution 221(1992). Third, this conception was at odds with the crucial republican view that representatives should be disinterested; instead, it signalled an emerging view that all representatives were interested, and that the task of governmental design was to contain and balance the competing interests.

Thus, the classic ideal of mixed government, with honor and wisdom balancing goodness and honesty, was replaced with an ideal of different chambers representing different interests in a diverse society. Note that this view assumed a permanent, politically separate, and unified property interest in the society. Lest this view be too quickly dismissed as reactionary, recall that American representation was still extraordinarily popular by contemporary standards. When the Constitution was adopted in 1787, the states confined the franchise to property-owning white males. Yet what was seen as remarkable about the early American states was, in fact, the *breadth* of the franchise. By all accounts, the early American electorate was significantly more expansive than that of England. *See* Chilton Williamson, American Suffrage: From Property to Democracy, 1760–1860, at 21–39 (1960)(noting that the American states' electorate ranged from approximately 50–75 percent of adult white males as compared to 20–25 percent in England). That the House represented persons meant, in Massachusetts for example, that no property qualifications applied to those voting for House members; anyone could hold office as long as he had paid taxes for two years in the county; and representation was allocated exactly according to the population in each county. For the state Senate, voting became based on estates and representation was apportioned to counties on the basis of the taxes they paid.

Despite the initial popularity of the mixed governments, some made an argument that has since been often repeated but with little success: that bicameral legislatures and the entire idea of mixed government were unjustified in republican America. Consider the radical populist Thomas Paine, in Common Sense: the "exceedingly complex" English constitution was appropriate only "for the dark and slavish times in which it was erected," but not for the American republics. The English constitution reflected "two ancient tyrannies ... monarchical tyranny in the person of the king," and "aristocratical tyranny in the person of the peers," combined with "new Republican materials, in the persons of the Commons, on whose virtue depends the freedom of England." *Quoted in* Wood, *supra,* at 223–24. Even Alexander Hamilton agreed, at this time, in a "simple legislature" with equal-population based representation.

On this view, American institutions should therefore be pure applications of the republican principle of direct popular participation. In Pennsylvania, this experiment was adopted in the most radical Constitution of the Revolutionary period. Pennsylvania abandoned the theory of mixed government altogether. The legislature was unicameral. Elections for offices took place every year. Term limits of four years were imposed. Suffrage rights were broader than in any other state. This was "simple" democracy in its most pure form. Its opponents attacked the system as "mob rule," and the Pennsylvania experiment quickly unravelled—whether through subversion by its opponents or its own defects remains unclear. This form of government has never since been adopted in any state in America. At present, only Nebraska has a unicameral legislature.

The debates at the Constitutional Convention brought directly to light the tensions that had been building for many years between the emerging equality of republicanism and the inherited tradition of an upper house representing a distinct social class or economic interest. By the time of these debates, the justification for the Senate was obscure, even while virtually all participants agreed on the need for an upper chamber that would lend stability to government. Some wanted a Senate to reproduce the social balance of the English constitution; this view led Hamilton, for example, to argue that Senators should serve for life. Once this view was rejected out of recognition that in republican America the Senate could not be justified as representing a distinct social group, the question of the justification for the Senate became only more acute. In the original Virginia Plan for the Constitution, drafted by Madison, Senators were to be elected by members of the House, in proportion to either the wealth or population of the states. Only after the Virginia Plan was defeated and the Great Compromise (the Connecticut Compromise) was proposed, did a justification for the Senate finally emerge. Now the principle of representation for the upper chamber would be that each state would send two Senators, and the Senate became a means for ensuring that large states did not overrun the interests of the small states. In addition, bicameralism became defended as simply yet another means of fragmenting and diffusing political power. Thus, the Senate became a "kind of perversion of the ancient theory of balanced government," an entity whose structure and justification was invented at the last stage to respond to the perceived need for bicameralism while completely transforming the reasons for it. Gordon S. Wood, The Creation of the American Republic 562 (1969).

In light of the history of the Senate, consider the Court's reasoning in striking down Georgia's county-unit system by which votes for certain statewide offices were aggregated at the county level and then cast as county votes at the state level.

Gray v. Sanders

372 U.S. 368 (1963).

■ MR. JUSTICE DOUGLAS delivered the opinion of the Court.

* * *

This case ... does not involve a question of the degree to which the Equal Protection Clause of the Fourteenth Amendment limits the authority of a State Legislature in designing the geographical districts from which representatives are chosen either for the State Legislature or for the Federal House of Representatives. Nor does it include the related problems of *Gomillion v. Lightfoot,* 364 U.S. 339, where "gerrymandering" was used to exclude a minority group from participation in municipal affairs. Nor does it present the question, inherent in the bicameral form of our Federal Government, whether a State may have one house chosen without regard to population. The District Court, however, analogized Georgia's use of the county unit system in determining the results of a statewide election to phases of our federal system. It pointed out that under the electoral college, ... required by Art. II, § 1, of the Constitution and the Twelfth Amendment in the election of the President, voting strength "is not in exact proportion to population.... Recognizing that the electoral college was set up as a compromise to enable the formation of the Union among the several sovereign states, it still could hardly be said that such a system used in a state among its counties, assuming rationality and absence of arbitrariness in end result, could be termed invidious."

Accordingly the District Court as already noted held that use of the county unit system in counting the votes in a statewide election was permissible "if the disparity against any county is not in excess of the disparity that exists against any state in the most recent electoral college allocation." Moreover the District Court held that use of the county unit system in counting the votes in a statewide election was permissible "if the disparity against any county is not in excess of the disparity that exists ... under the equal proportions formula for representation of the several states in the Congress." The assumption implicit in these conclusions is that since equality is not inherent in the electoral college and since precise equality among blocs of votes in one State or in the several States when it comes to the election of members of the House of Representatives is never possible, precise equality is not necessary in statewide elections.

We think the analogies to the electoral college, to districting and redistricting, and to other phases of the problems of representation in state or federal legislatures or conventions ... are inapposite. The inclusion of the electoral college in the Constitution, as the result of specific historical concerns, validated the collegiate principle despite its inherent numerical inequality, but implied nothing about the use of an analogous system by a State in a statewide election. No such specific accommodation of the latter was ever undertaken, and therefore no validation of its numerical inequality ensued. Nor does the question here have anything to do with the composition of the state or federal legislature.... The present case is only a voting case. Georgia gives every qualified voter one vote in a statewide election; but in counting those votes she employs the county unit system which in end result weights the rural vote more heavily than the urban vote and weights some small rural counties heavier than other larger rural counties.

* * *

NOTES AND QUESTIONS

1. In *Gray*, the Court began the process of narrowing the asserted justifications for malapportionment. Georgia's county unit system greatly enhanced the voting strength of the typical rural voter relative to urban voters living in more populous districts. Justice Douglas sweepingly proclaimed that, "The conception of political equality from the Declaration of Independence, to Lincoln's Gettysburg Address, to the Fifteenth, Seventeenth, and Nineteenth Amendments can mean only one thing—one person, one vote." Does this seem a credible reading of American constitutional history? Is there any difference between the use of the county-based system for state election purposes and the use of the States for elections to the U.S. Senate and the Electoral College? For an argument that the current structure of the Electoral College, particularly the winner-take-all feature of state-by-state elections, violates the Voting Rights Act, see Matthew M. Hoffman, *The Illegitimate President: Minority Vote Dilution and the Electoral College,* 105 Yale L.J. 935 (1996).

2. Consider the Court's argument in *Gray* concerning the disparities in Georgia voting power in light of the following indictment of the Senate:

- The forty senators from the twenty smallest states represent a population base of 10 percent! In the Clinton era, this means even senators who represent 90 percent of the population are not enough by themselves to pass a bill. In the worst case lineup, a mere 10 percent of the population base could be enough to block a bill.

- The fifty senators from the twenty-five smallest states represent a population base of 16 percent. In the same worst case, senators representing just more than 16 percent of the population base could be enough to block a bill.

- Think of what they can *pass*. The sixty senators from the thirty smallest states represent a population base of only 24 percent. Yet senators representing 24 percent of the population have sixty votes. They can bring back the death penalty for sheep-stealing.

Hasn't it always been this bad?

No. In 1789, when the first Senate was sworn in, there were eighteen states, five newly admitted. The senators from the nine smallest states still represented 33 percent of the population. And there was no filibuster. So back then, to block a bill, it took senators representing a population base of 33 percent. Now, in the worst case lineup, it is merely 10 percent. One could also hope that in time the five new states would fill up. In 1789 they were practically empty (although back then, states like New York were pretty empty, too).

Tom Geoghegan, *The Infernal Senate*, The New Republic Nov. 21, 1995, at 17. For an analysis of the impact of the maldistribution of power in the Senate on federal expenditures at the state level, *see* Lynn A. Baker & Samuel H. Dinkin, *The Senate: An Institution Whose Time Has Gone?*, 13 J. of Law & Politics 21 (1997). Baker and Dinkin argue that the existing allocation of representation in the Senate provides small population states disproportionately great coalition-building power relative to their shares of the nation's population, and injects a significant super-majoritarianism into the federal law-making process. Based on a sophisticated statistical model of the relative power of individual actors in being able to shape coalitions (the "Shapley-Shubik Index"), this article concludes that the current allocation of representation causes three systemic distortions in the allocation of constitutional power.

> First, the Senate systematically and unjustifiably redistributes wealth from the large population states to the small ones. Second, it systematically and unjustifiably provides racial minorities a voice in the federal lawmaking process which is disproportionately small relative to their numbers. And finally, it systematically and unjustifiably affords large population states disproportionately little power, relative to their shares of the nation's population, to block federal homogenizing legislation that they consider disadvantageous. *Id.* at 23.

Do the critiques by Geoghegan and Baker & Dinkin call into question the legitimacy of the original constitutional compromise? Could alternative versions of a bicameral legislature serve the original Madisonian purposes without deviating so significantly from competing principles of popular representation?

CHAPTER 4

THE ROLE OF POLITICAL PARTIES

The preceding chapters have focused on the individual's right to participate in the political process by casting a ballot and on the structure of legislative institutions. But as we suggested at the outset of this book, a conception of politics that comprehends only atomistic individuals and governing bodies offers an impoverished account. It ignores the critical questions of how individuals aggregate their preferences to create governing bodies, and, just as important, how governments organize and constrain the political choices available to their citizens.

Since the time of De Tocqueville, observers of American politics have recognized the importance of voluntary intermediate institutions in a pluralist democracy. Most individuals participate in self-governance only through representatives; these organizations—ranging from churches to labor unions to neighborhood associations to contemporary mass-mailing ideological and affinity groups such as NOW, the AARP, and the National Rifle Association—both serve as a vehicle for making their members' voices more effective in the electoral process and in many cases, help to shape their members' preferences.

Perhaps the most significant mediating institutions in the American political system are the political parties. For a comprehensive discussion, see Leon D. Epstein, Political Parties in the American Mold (1986). And, as our dynamic account of the interaction between various actors in the system might suggest, American political parties are both the creators and the creatures of the existing political order. They thus stand in an ambiguous position vis-à-vis legal regulation. On the one hand, the Constitution sometimes constrains party behavior, as in the White Primary cases covered in Chapter 2. And sometimes the government is empowered to regulate party activity, as in the arena of campaign finance covered in Chapter 9. On the other hand, the Constitution sometimes protects parties *against* governmental regulation. In this chapter, we focus on the ambiguous relationship among voters, parties and the state. To what extent can the government use parties or other mechanisms to channel individuals' expression of their political preferences? To what extent do individuals have rights as against political parties? And to what extent do political parties have rights as against individuals, or the state? That is, when do individuals have a right to participate in a party's processes and when does the party have a right to exclude them? And we focus as well on the way in which the electoral system enlists parties as an element of the electoral machinery. To what extent is such delegation permissible or desirable?

An Historical Note on Political Parties

Although today we consider political parties the quintessential organizational form through which democratic politics is structured, the Constitution did not expressly recognize their existence. But this omission did not reflect indifference to political parties or ignorance of their possible existence: the Constitution was explicitly constructed to preclude the rise of political parties. Indeed, this was one of the principal points of the entire constitutional framework. In this respect, then, the Constitution must be considered to have failed—although it is a failure rarely noticed because we now take for granted political parties as the embodiment of democratic politics.[a]

As we consider modern constitutional issues in the relationship of the state to political parties, it is worth keeping this deeper history in mind. How should originalist methods of constitutional interpretation deal with modern issues in state regulation of political parties, given that the Constitution itself was designed to avoid the very existence of parties? How should other methods of interpretation take into account, if at all, the original intent and early practices with respect to political parties? Note that the cases virtually never discuss these issues.

The Constitution was conceived as a "Constitution against parties." Richard Hofstadter, The Idea of a Party System: The Rise of Legitimate Opposition in the United States, 1780–1840, at 40 (1969). When Madison wrote of the problem of "faction," as in *Federalist No. 10,* political parties were one of the paramount forms of faction he had in mind. Similarly, in his famous Farewell Address, George Washington warned against "the baneful effect" of parties:

> The common and continual mischiefs of the spirit of party are sufficient to make it the interest and duty of a wise people to discourage and restrain it.

[a.] More modern constitutions tend to embrace parties expressly as fundamental elements of democracy. Article 21 of the post-World War II German Constitution, or Basic Law, for example, declares that "political parties shall participate in forming the political will of the people." For general discussion, see Donald P. Kommers, The Constitutional Jurisprudence of the Federal Republic of Germany, Ch. 5 (1997). Moreover, the German Constitution, according to its Court, has "raised [political parties] to the rank of constitutional institutions" and defines parties as "constitutionally integral unites of a free and democratic system of government." Id., at 200, 209. Therefore the Court has aggressively acted to protect the equality of political parties and their institutional integrity, and has emphasized the constitutional importance of ensuring, through judicial decisions where necessary, meaningful party competition, which has often led the Court to protect the participatory rights of minor parties and the legislative positions of their members. Id., at 167, 169.

> It serves always to distract the public councils and enfeeble the public administration. It agitates the community with ill-founded jealousies and false alarms; kindles the animosity of one part against another; foments occasionally riot and insurrection. It opens the door to foreign influence and corruption, which find a facilitated access to the government itself through the channels of party passion. Thus the policy and the will of one country are subjected to the policy and will of another.

George Washington, *Farewell Address,* in 1 A Compilation of the Messages and Papers of the Presidents 218–19 (James D. Richardson, ed. 1900).

The Framers viewed "faction" and "party" as interchangeable concepts. Republicanism was widely understood to imply popular sovereignty and the absence of government controlled by party. Party politics was considered the antithesis of the (elite) politics of "the common good" that the Constitution sought to enshrine. *See* Gordon Wood, The Creation of the American Republic 506–518 (1969). The hostility to the role that political parties were thought to play as permanent factions in turn helped shape the institutional forms of the American Republic. Many of the structural features of the new national government, such as bicameralism, separated powers, and federalism were designed to check the rise and effectiveness of party politics.

Despite these efforts, competing political philosophies rather quickly emerged; politicians came to be identified as Federalists or Republicans. But it is a mistake to see these early groupings as modern political parties. For even as the Jeffersonians in the early 1800s became the greatest party organizers that democratic politics had seen, their justification for party organization remained tied to the original Constitutional vision—and was radically different from the modern conception of parties. Thus, they argued their organization was an effort to *eliminate* parties; it was a temporary device made necessary by the corrupt efforts of their opponents to capture the government for party purposes.

This "antiparty" justification for nascent political organization dominated the early nineteenth century. Republicans, for example, did not conceive of themselves as defined through any specific policy commitments; they justified their organization as defined only through its commitment to preserving the constitutional structure and the principle of majority rule—as opposed to rule of the minority aristocratic interests to which, they alleged, their opponents aspired. In the view of some historians, it is not until after the Civil War that political parties come to be understood and justified in the form we now take for granted: as permanent features of democratic politics; as divided over competing policy views rather than standing for the "true" Constitution; as forms of loyal and desirable opposition. For a sophisticated and rich history of the shifting intellectual justifications for political parties, see Gerald Leonard, Partisan Political

Theory and the Unwritten Constitution: The Origins of Democracy in Illinois, 1818–1840 (Ph.D. dissertation 1992).

The early hostility to political parties stands in rather stark contrast to contemporary political science. The Madisonian design for the early Republic hoped to avoid permanent non-governmental organizations standing between the citizenry and a representative government. Government, if properly functioning, would provide the vehicle for the expression of the sober popular will, channelled through the structures of checks and balances that would protect against rash decisions inflamed by "passion." Modern political scientists and legal scholars, by contrast, often argue that political parties are inevitable, given the need for political organization to aggregate the voices of individuals. Rather than seeing these intermediate institutions as antithetical to the ability of citizens to participate effectively in the political process, these scholars view such organizational vehicles as indispensable if lone individuals are to have any meaningful participation in the messy political marketplace. *See, e.g.*, E.E. Schattschneider, Party Government (1942); Maurice Duverger, Political Parties (1963 3rd. ed.); Michael A. Fitts, *The Vices of Virtue: A Political Party Perspective on Civic Virtue Reforms of the Legislative Process*, 136 U. Pa. L. Rev. 1567 (1988); Jonathan R. Macey, *The Role of the Democratic and Republican Parties as Organizers of Shadow Interest Groups*, 89 Mich. L. Rev. 1 (1989). That might be so, but the question remains of how those organizations are justified and understood—particularly how they are reconciled with the constitutional framework. Throughout much of the nineteenth century, the conception of party we now take for granted—and that underlies modern constitutional doctrine—was considered antithetical to the Constitution.

A. THE BALLOT: POLITICAL PARTIES AS GATEKEEPERS

The physical act of voting differs rather dramatically from the way eighteenth and nineteenth century citizens indicated their choices. Early voting was conducted *viva voce,* that is, by a voice vote from among the assembled electorate, or by a show of hands, the traditional European method. Contrary to contemporary mythology, in which the secret ballot occupies a sacred place, these early forms of voting represented a public statement by individual voters of their position. In *Burson v. Freeman*, 504 U.S. 191, 200–02 (1992), the Supreme Court offered the traditional account of the movement toward the secret ballot:

> Within 20 years of the formation of the Union, most States had incorporated the paper ballot into their electoral system. Initially, this paper ballot was a vast improvement. Individual voters made their own handwritten ballots, marked them in the privacy of their homes, and then brought them to the polls for counting. But the effort of making out such a ballot became increasingly more complex and cumbersome.

Wishing to gain influence, political parties began to produce their own ballots for voters. These ballots were often printed with flamboyant colors, distinctive designs, and emblems so that they could be recognized at a distance. State attempts to standardize the ballots were easily thwarted—the vote-buyer could simply place a ballot in the hands of the bribed voter and watch until he placed it in the polling box. Thus, the evils associated with the earlier viva voce system reinfected the election process; the failure of the law to secure secrecy opened the door to bribery and intimidation.[7]

Approaching the polling place under this system was akin to entering an open auction place. As the elector started his journey to the polls, he was met by various party ticket peddlers "who were only too anxious to supply him with their party tickets." Often the competition became heated when several such peddlers found an uncommitted or wavering voter. Sham battles were frequently engaged in to keep away elderly and timid voters of the opposition. In short, these early elections "were not a very pleasant spectacle for those who believed in democratic government."

The problems with voter intimidation and election fraud that the United States was experiencing were not unique. Several other countries were attempting to work out satisfactory solutions to these same problems. Some Australian provinces adopted a series of reforms intended to secure the secrecy of an elector's vote. The most famous feature of the Australian system was its provision for an official ballot, encompassing all candidates of all parties on the same ticket.

* * *

After several failed attempts to adopt the Australian system in Michigan and Wisconsin, the Louisville, Kentucky, municipal government, the Commonwealth of Massachusetts and the State of New York

---

7. According to a report of a committee of the Forty-Sixth Congress, men were frequently marched or carried to the polls in their employers' carriages. They were then furnished with ballots and compelled to hold their hands up with their ballots in them so they could easily be watched until the ballots were dropped into the box. S. Rep. No. 497, 46th Cong., 2d Sess., 9–10 (1880).[One commentator] recounted that intimidation, particularly by employers, was "extensively practiced":

"Many labor men were afraid to vote and remained away from the polls. Others who voted against their employers wishes frequently lost their jobs. If the employee lived in a factory town, he probably lived in a tenement owned by the company, and possibly his wife and children worked in the mill. If he voted against the wishes of the mill-owners, he and his family were thrown out of the mill, out of the tenement, and out of the means of earning a livelihood. Frequently the owner and the manager of the mill stood at the entrance of the polling-place and closely observed the employees while they voted. In this condition, it cannot be said that the workingmen exercised any real choice."

adopted the Australian system in 1888.... The success achieved through these reforms was immediately noticed and widely praised. One commentator remarked of the New York law of 1888:

> "We have secured secrecy; and intimidation by employers, party bosses, police officers, saloonkeepers and others has come to an end.
>
> "In earlier times our polling places were frequently, to quote the litany, 'scenes of battle, murder, and sudden death.' This also has come to an end, and until nightfall, when the jubilation begins, our election days are now as peaceful as our Sabbaths.
>
> "The new legislation has also rendered impossible the old methods of frank, hardy, straightforward and shameless bribery of voters at the polls."

The triumphs of 1888 set off a rapid and widespread adoption of the Australian system in the United States. By 1896, almost 90 percent of the States had adopted the Australian system. This accounted for 92 percent of the national electorate.

For more extensive discussions of the history of ballots and voting, *see* Spencer D. Albright, The American Ballot (1942); Eldon C. Evans, A History of the Australian Ballot System in the United States (1917); L. E. Fredman, The Australian Ballot: The Story of an American Reform (1968).

But the traditional account, which views the secret ballot as an unambiguous improvement, may be at least somewhat incomplete. Morgan Kousser, for example, describes the movement to, and effect of, secret ballots rather differently:

> Until 1888, political parties printed and distributed the ballots in each of the United States. Besides discouraging split-ticket voting and encouraging strong party organization ... the party ballot insured illiterates the right to vote. Nevertheless, reformers, who were more concerned with eliminating fraud than safeguarding the rights of illiterates, instituted the secret ballot in eight Southern and 30 non-Southern states between 1888 and 1900.
>
> The publicly printed ticket required the voter, sometimes without any aid from anyone, to scurry quickly through a maze of names of candidates running for everything from presidential elector to county court clerk, a list which was often arranged by office rather than party. He then had to mark an "X" by the names of the candidates for whom he wished to vote, or, in some states, mark through or erase those he opposed. Such a task demanded not merely literacy, but fluency in the English language. An ingenious lawmaker could make voting all but impossible. Florida totally abolished party designations on the ballot. A Populist or Republican who wished to vote for his presidential electors

had to count down five, ten, or fifteen unfamiliar names before starting to mark. Voters in one Virginia congressional district in 1894 confronted a ballot printed in the German Fraktur script.

J. Morgan Kousser, The Shaping of Southern Politics: Suffrage Restrictions and the Establishment of the One–Party South, 1880–1910, at 51–52 (1974). Kousser identifies the desire to exclude illiterate and foreign-born immigrants in the North, and blacks in the South, as a major consideration behind the adoption of standardized, pre-printed ballots. In this vein, consider the 1892 campaign song of the Arkansas Democratic Party, "Australian Ballot" (sung to the tune of "The Bonnie Blue Flag"):

> The Australian ballot works like a charm,
> It makes them think and scratch,
> And when a negro gets a ballot
> He has certainly got his match.
>
> * * *
>
> They go into the booth alone
> Their ticket to prepare.
> And as soon as five minutes are out
> They have got to git from there.

John William Graves, *Negro Disfranchisement in Arkansas*, 26 Ark. Hist. Q. 199, 212–13 (1967). This element of the secret ballot is no longer upon us. Today, as a statutory matter, a voter is entitled to assistance by the person of her choice, as long as that person is not her employer or an officer or agent of her union. *See* 42 U.S.C. § 1973aa–6 (1994). Nonetheless, in light of the historical context, it is worth at least thinking about the competing advantages and disadvantages of a system of non-anonymous or public voting. Voters who participate in municipal governance at town meetings, for example, still usually vote publicly. And many institutions—for example, law school faculties—vote on important issues publicly (at least in the sense that the relevant electorate is aware of how each member voted).

One of the lasting effects of the secret ballot does persevere. The standardized ballot does have the effect of introducing a strong measure of state regulation *prior to the election* in determining who shall be eligible for inclusion on the ballot. Notice that as soon as the state becomes involved in regulating even a function as simple as printing and distributing ballots, the problems the casebook raises throughout arise here too: will existing political forces, such as the dominant political parties, seek to capture the state processes and use them to perpetuate their hold on power? Is there some distinct role for courts and constitutional law to play in monitoring that process? Prior to the introduction of the standardized ballot, each voter could vote for whomever he preferred, regardless of the candidate's party, or even whether the candidate was publicly seeking a particular office, simply by preparing his personal ballot with that candidate's name on it. But the standardized ballot, at least in the first instance, constrained the voter's choices to the candidates whose names appeared on the ballot. Not until 1992 did the Supreme Court confront the question whether a state could constitutionally limit a voter's choice to a pre-set field of candidates.

1. RESTRICTIONS ON WHOM VOTERS CAN VOTE FOR

Burdick v. Takushi
504 U.S. 428 (1992).

■ JUSTICE WHITE delivered the opinion of the Court.

The issue in this case is whether Hawaii's prohibition on write-in voting unreasonably infringes upon its citizens' rights under the First and Fourteenth Amendments....

I

Petitioner is a registered voter in the city and County of Honolulu. In 1986, only one candidate filed nominating papers to run for the seat representing petitioner's district in the Hawaii House of Representatives. Petitioner wrote to state officials inquiring about Hawaii's write-in voting policy and received a copy of an opinion letter issued by the Hawaii Attorney General's Office stating that the State's election law made no provision for write-in voting.

Petitioner then filed this lawsuit, claiming that he wished to vote in the primary and general elections for a person who had not filed nominating papers and that he wished to vote in future elections for other persons whose names were not and might not appear on the ballot.

* * *

II

Petitioner proceeds from the erroneous assumption that a law that imposes any burden upon the right to vote must be subject to strict scrutiny. Our cases do not so hold.

It is beyond cavil that "voting is of the most fundamental significance under our constitutional structure." It does not follow, however, that the right to vote in any manner and the right to associate for political purposes through the ballot are absolute. The Constitution provides that States may prescribe "the Times, Places and Manner of holding Elections for Senators and Representatives," Art. I, § 4, cl. 1, and the Court therefore has recognized that States retain the power to regulate their own elections. Common sense, as well as constitutional law, compels the conclusion that government must play an active role in structuring elections; "as a practical matter, there must be a substantial regulation of elections if they are to be fair and honest and if some sort of order, rather than chaos, is to accompany the democratic processes."

Election laws will invariably impose some burden upon individual voters. Each provision of a code, "whether it governs the registration and qualifications of voters, the selection and eligibility of candidates, or the voting process itself, inevitably affects—at least to some degree—the individual's right to vote and his right to associate with others for political ends." Consequently, to subject every voting regulation to strict scrutiny and to require that the regulation be narrowly tailored to advance a compelling state interest, as petitioner suggests, would tie the hands of States seeking to assure that elections are operated equitably and efficiently. Accordingly, the mere fact that a State's system "creates barriers ... tending to limit the field of candidates from which voters might choose ... does not of itself compel close scrutiny."

Instead, ... a more flexible standard applies. A court considering a challenge to a state election law must weigh "the character and magnitude of the asserted injury to the rights protected by the First and Fourteenth Amendments that the plaintiff seeks to vindicate" against "the precise interests put forward by the State as justifications for the burden imposed by its rule," taking into consideration "the extent to which those interests make it necessary to burden the plaintiff's rights."

Under this standard, the rigorousness of our inquiry into the propriety of a state election law depends upon the extent to which a challenged regulation burdens First and Fourteenth Amendment rights. Thus, as we have recognized when those rights are subjected to "severe" restrictions, the regulation must be narrowly drawn to advance a state interest of "compelling importance." But when a state election law provision imposes only "reasonable, nondiscriminatory restrictions" upon the First and Fourteenth Amendment rights of voters, "the State's important regulatory interests are generally sufficient to justify" the restrictions. We apply this standard in considering petitioner's challenge to Hawaii's ban on write-in ballots.

A

There is no doubt that the Hawaii election laws, like all election regulations, have an impact on the right to vote, but it can hardly be said that the laws at issue here unconstitutionally limit access to the ballot by party or independent candidates or unreasonably interfere with the right of voters to associate and have candidates of their choice placed on the ballot. Indeed, petitioners understandably do not challenge the manner in which the State regulates candidate access to the ballot.

To obtain a position on the November general election ballot, a candidate must participate in Hawaii's open primary, "in which all registered voters may choose in which party primary to vote." *See* Haw. Rev. Stat. § 12–31 (1985). The State provides three mechanisms through which a voter's candidate-of-choice may appear on the primary ballot.

First, a party petition may be filed 150 days before the primary by any group of persons who obtain the signatures of one percent of the State's registered voters. Then, 60 days before the primary, candidates must file nominating papers certifying, among other things, that they will qualify for the office sought and that they are members of the party that they seek to represent in the general election. The nominating papers must contain the signatures of a specified number of registered voters: 25 for candidates for statewide or federal office; 15 for state legislative and county races. The winner in each party advances to the general election. Thus, if a party forms around the candidacy of a single individual and no one else runs on that party ticket, the individual will be elected at the primary and win a place on the November general election ballot.

The second method through which candidates may appear on the Hawaii primary ballot is the established party route. Established parties that have qualified by petition for three consecutive elections and received a specified percentage of the vote in the preceding election may avoid filing party petitions for 10 years. The Democratic, Republican, and Libertarian Parties currently meet Hawaii's criteria for established parties. Like new party candidates, established party contenders are required to file nominating papers 60 days before the primary.

The third mechanism by which a candidate may appear on the ballot is through the designated nonpartisan ballot. Nonpartisans may be placed on the nonpartisan primary ballot simply by filing nominating papers containing 15 to 25 signatures, depending upon the office sought, 60 days before the primary. To advance to the general election, a nonpartisan must receive 10 percent of the primary vote or the number of votes that was sufficient to nominate a partisan candidate, whichever number is lower. During the 10 years preceding the filing of this action, 8 of 26 nonpartisans who entered the primary obtained slots on the November ballot.

Although Hawaii makes no provision for write-in voting in its primary or general elections, the system outlined above provides for easy access to the ballot until the cutoff date for the filing of nominating petitions, two months before the primary. Consequently, any burden on voters' freedom of choice and association is borne only by those who fail to identify their candidate of choice until days before the primary. But [we have given] little weight to "the interest the candidate and his supporters may have in making a late rather than an early decision to seek independent ballot status." . . . [Thus,] any burden imposed by Hawaii's write-in vote prohibition is a very limited one. "To conclude otherwise might sacrifice the political stability of the system of the State, with profound consequences for the entire citizenry, merely in the interest of particular candidates and their supporters having instantaneous access to the ballot."

Because he has characterized this as a voting rights rather than ballot access case, petitioner submits that the write-in prohibition deprives him of the opportunity to cast a meaningful ballot, conditions his electoral participation upon the waiver of his First Amendment right to remain free from espousing positions that he does not support, and discriminates against him based on the content of the message he seeks to convey through his vote. At bottom, he claims that he is entitled to cast and Hawaii required to count a "protest vote" for Donald Duck, and that any impediment to this asserted "right" is unconstitutional.

Petitioner's argument is based on two flawed premises. First, [our prior cases have rejected the argument that] . . . voting rights cases are distinguishable from ballot access cases, stating that "the rights of voters and the rights of candidates do not lend themselves to neat separation." Second, the function of the election process is "to winnow out and finally reject all but the chosen candidates," not to provide a means of giving vent to "short-range political goals, pique, or personal quarrels." Attributing to elections a more generalized expressive function would undermine the ability of States to operate elections fairly and efficiently.

Accordingly, we have repeatedly upheld reasonable, politically neutral regulations that have the effect of channeling expressive activity at the polls. Petitioner offers no persuasive reason to depart from these precedents. Reasonable regulation of elections does not require voters to espouse positions that they do not support; it does require them to act in a timely fashion if they wish to express their views in the voting booth. And there is nothing content based about a flat ban on all forms of write-in ballots. . . .

[W]e conclude that, in light of the adequate ballot access afforded under Hawaii's election code, the State's ban on write-in voting imposes only a limited burden on voters' rights to make free choices and to associate politically through the vote.

B

We turn next to the interests asserted by Hawaii to justify the burden imposed by its prohibition of write-in voting. Because we have already concluded that the burden is slight, the State need not establish a compelling interest to tip the constitutional scales in its direction. Here, the State's interests outweigh petitioner's limited interest in waiting until the eleventh hour to choose his preferred candidate.

Hawaii's interest in "avoiding the possibility of unrestrained factionalism at the general election" provides adequate justification for its ban on write-in voting in November. The primary election is "an integral part of the entire election process," and the State is within its rights to reserve "the general election ballot . . . for major struggles . . . [and] not a forum for continuing intraparty feuds." The prohibition on write-in voting is a legitimate means of averting divisive sore-loser candidacies. Hawaii further promotes the two-stage, primary-general election process of winnowing out candidates, by permitting the unopposed victors in certain primaries to be designated office holders. This focuses the attention of voters upon contested races in the general election. This would not be possible, absent the write-in voting ban.

Hawaii also asserts that its ban on write-in voting at the primary stage is necessary to guard against "party raiding." Party raiding is generally defined as "the organized switching of blocs of voters from one party to another in order to manipulate the outcome of the other party's primary election." ... Hawaii's system could easily be ... frustrated at the general election by permitting write-in votes for a loser in a party primary or for an independent who had failed to get sufficient votes to make the general election ballot. The State has a legitimate interest in preventing these sorts of maneuvers, and the write-in voting ban is a reasonable way of accomplishing this goal.

We think these legitimate interests asserted by the State are sufficient to outweigh the limited burden that the write-in voting ban imposes upon Hawaii's voters.

III

Indeed, the foregoing leads us to conclude that when a State's ballot access laws pass constitutional muster as imposing only reasonable burdens on First and Fourteenth Amendment rights—as do Hawaii's election laws—a prohibition on write-in voting will be presumptively valid, since any burden on the right to vote for the candidate of one's choice will be light and normally will be counterbalanced by the very state interests supporting the ballot access scheme.

In such situations, the objection to the specific ban on write-in voting amounts to nothing more than the insistence that the State record, count, and publish individual protests against the election system or the choices presented on the ballot through the efforts of those who actively participate in the system. There are other means available, however, to voice such generalized dissension from the electoral process; and we discern no adequate basis for our requiring the State to provide and to finance a place on the ballot for recording protests against its constitutionally valid election laws.

"No right is more precious in a free country than that of having a voice in the election of those who make the laws under which, as good citizens, we must live." But the right to vote is the right to participate in an electoral process that is necessarily structured to maintain the integrity of the democratic system. We think that Hawaii's prohibition on write-in voting, considered as part of an electoral scheme that provides constitutionally sufficient ballot access, does not impose an unconstitutional burden upon the First and Fourteenth Amendment rights of the State's voters.

* * *

■ JUSTICE KENNEDY, with whom JUSTICE BLACKMUN and JUSTICE STEVENS join, dissenting.

* * *

In the election that triggered this lawsuit, petitioner did not wish to vote for the one candidate who ran for state representative in his district. Because he could not write in the name of a candidate he preferred, he had no way to cast a meaningful vote. Petitioner's dilemma is a recurring, frequent phenomenon in Hawaii because of the State's ballot access rules and the circumstance that one party, the Democratic Party, is predominant....

Democratic candidates often run unopposed, especially in state legislative races. In the 1986 general election, 33 percent of the elections for state legislative offices involved single candidate races. The comparable figures for 1984 and 1982 were 39 percent and 37.5 percent. Large numbers of voters cast blank ballots in uncontested races, that is, they leave the ballots blank rather than vote for the single candidate listed. In 1990, 27 percent of voters who voted in other races did not cast votes in uncontested state Senate races. Twenty-nine percent of voters did not cast votes in uncontested state house races. Even in contested races in 1990, 12 to 13 percent of voters cast blank ballots.

Given that so many Hawaii voters are dissatisfied with the choices available to them, it is hard to avoid the conclusion that at least some voters would cast write-in votes for other candidates if given this option. The write-in ban thus prevents these voters from participating in Hawaii elections in a meaningful manner.

* * *

The dominance of the Democratic Party [creates a disincentive for voters to participate in Hawaii's ballot access scheme to generate candidates for specific offices] ... because the primary election is dispositive in so many races. In effect, a Hawaii voter who wishes to vote for any independent candidate must choose between doing so and participating in what will be the dispositive election for many offices. This dilemma imposes a substantial burden on voter choice. It explains also why so few independent candidates secure enough primary votes to advance to the general election. As the majority notes, only eight independent candidates have succeeded in advancing to the general election in the past 10 years. That is, less than one independent candidate per year on average has in fact run in a general election in Hawaii.

The majority's approval of Hawaii's ban is ironic at a time when the new democracies in foreign countries strive to emerge from an era of sham elections in which the name of the ruling party candidate was the only one on the ballot. Hawaii does not impose as severe a restriction on the right to vote, but it imposes a restriction that has a haunting similarity in its tendency to exact severe penalties for one who does anything but vote the dominant party ballot.

Aside from constraints related to ballot access restrictions, the write-in ban limits voter choice in another way. Write-in voting can serve as an important safety mechanism in those instances where a late-developing issue arises or where new information is disclosed about a candidate late in the race. In these situations, voters may become disenchanted with the available candidates when it is too late for other candidates to come forward and qualify for the ballot. The prohibition on write-in voting imposes a significant burden on voters, forcing them either to vote for a candidate whom they no longer support, or to cast a blank ballot. Write-in voting provides a way out of the quandary, allowing voters to switch their support to candidates who are not on the official ballot. Even if there are other mechanisms to address the problem of late-breaking election developments (unsuitable candidates who win an election can be recalled), allowing write-in voting is the only way to preserve the voters' right to cast a meaningful vote in the general election.

* * *

Because Hawaii's write-in ban, when considered in conjunction with the State's ballot access laws, imposes a significant burden on voters such as petitioner, it must put forward the state interests which justify the burden so that we can assess them. I do not think it necessary here to specify the level of scrutiny that should then be applied because, in my view, the State has failed to justify the write-in ban under any level of scrutiny. The interests proffered by the State, some of which are puzzling, are not advanced to any significant degree by the write-in prohibition. I consider each of the interests in turn.

The interest that has the best potential for acceptance, in my view, is that of preserving the integrity of party primaries by preventing sore loser candidacies during the general election.... [But] a write-in ban is a very overinclusive means of addressing the problem; it bars legitimate candidacies as well as undesirable sore loser candidacies. If the State desires to prevent sore loser candidacies, it can implement a narrow provision aimed at that particular problem.

The second interest advanced by the State is enforcing its policy of permitting the unopposed victors in certain primaries to be designated as officeholders without having to go through the general election. The majority states that "this would not be possible, absent the write-in voting ban." This makes no sense. As petitioner's counsel acknowledged during oral argument, "to the degree that Hawaii has abolished general elections in these circumstances, there is no occasion to cast a write-in ballot." If anything, the argument cuts the other way because this provision makes it all the more important to allow write-in voting in the primary elections because primaries are often dispositive....

The State also cites its interest in promoting the informed selection of candidates, an interest it claims is advanced by "flushing candidates into the open a reasonable time before the election." I think the State has it backwards. The fact that write-in candidates often do not conduct visible campaigns seems to me to make it more likely that voters who go to the trouble of seeking out these candidates and writing in their names are well informed. The state interest may well cut the other way.

The State cites interests in combating fraud and enforcing nomination requirements. But the State does not explain how write-in voting presents a risk of fraud in today's polling places. As to the State's interest in making sure that ineligible candidates are not elected, petitioner's counsel pointed out at argument that approximately 20 States require write-in candidates to file a declaration of candidacy and verify that they are eligible to hold office a few days before the election.

* * *

NOTES AND QUESTIONS

1. Most states permit write-in voting. In addition to Hawaii, only Nevada, Oklahoma, and South Dakota refuse to count write-in votes for any office. Several other states prohibit write-in votes for certain offices, or in primary or runoff elections, or in general elections for candidates who lost in the primary. And most states condition the tabulation of a candidate's votes upon his filing a declaration of candidacy prior to the election. *See generally* David Perney, Note, *The Dimensions of the Right to Vote: The Write–In Vote, Donald Duck, and Voting Booth Speech Written–Off*, 58 Mo. L. Rev. 945 (1993). Contrary to the U.S. Supreme Court's approach, most state courts to have faced the question have held that the "general concept of a right to vote" includes the right to cast a write-in ballot. *See id.* at 955.

2. To what extent does the ban on write-in voting entrench the existing political order? When is write-in voting most likely to affect the outcome of a particular election? What bearing, if any, should the fact that a large number of Hawaiian legislative elections had only one official candidate have on the Court's analysis? The Court's opinions make reference to the tremendous power of the state Democratic party, including the fact that Democratic nomination for many offices is considered such a guarantee of electoral success that there is oftentimes no general election held. This fact pattern strongly implies that the prohibition on write-in votes serves to lock in the political power of the Democratic Party. After all, when the opinion speaks of "state policy" underlying the prohibition on write-in votes, who are the state policymakers other than those same Democratic Party elected officials who have reaped the benefits of the current system? Should courts assume some special role in more exacting oversight of the political process when incumbent powers appear to have designed electoral rules that serve to lock in their hold on power? Notice as well that the Court appears to hold out the prospect of forming independent parties as a sufficient vehicle for venting alternative political views. How does this argument compare with the original Madisonian skepticism toward constitutionally entrenching political parties? Should individual claims to self-expression in the political arena be dependent upon the creation of independent intermediate organizations? What if an individual voter wanted to express dissatisfaction with only one candidate in one specific election? Does the formation of an independent political party seem an efficient manner for such expression?

3. The Supreme Court's approach seems to reject the idea of voting as core political speech, since, under well-established doctrine, infringements of political speech are subject to strict scrutiny. Is the Court right? Is the fact that voters cast their ballots anonymously relevant here? In this regard, consider the Court's decision in *McIntyre v. Ohio Elections Commission*, 514 U.S. 334 (1995), striking down, on First Amendment grounds, Ohio's prohibition of anonymous campaign literature. The idea of locating a right to vote in the First Amendment guarantee of free speech has a distinguished pedigree. *See, e.g.*, Alexander Bickel, The Supreme Court and the Idea of Progress 59–61 (1978); Alexander Meiklejohn, Political Freedom 39–40 (1960). Nonetheless, the Supreme Court seems to have rejected that argument. Why?

4. More broadly, is the Court's conception of the right to vote unduly cramped? Why *shouldn't* at least one function of the election process be "to provide a means of giving vent to 'short-range political goals [or] pique'"? Isn't the kind of voter dissatisfaction that prompts casting a "protest vote" for Donald Duck an important piece of data for the political system? Donald Duck has a long and distinguished history as the exasperated voter's candidate of choice. In *Dixon v. Maryland Board of Elections*, 878 F.2d 776, 785 n. 12 (4th Cir.1989), for example, the court of appeals explained that "under appropriate circumstances" a write-in vote for Donald Duck should be constitutionally protected "as serious satirical criticism of the powers that be.... Correcting this problem through censorship of the vote is utterly inconsistent with the principles under which our form of government operates." Consider the argument that free speech jurisprudence could inform our understanding of the right to vote. Broadly speaking, there are two main justifications for free speech:

> The first is instrumentalist: it views the freedom of speech as a tool for achieving certain societal objectives. Thus, philosophers and jurists have argued that free speech is valuable because it enables the search for truth in the marketplace of ideas or because

> it furthers the ability of the people to govern themselves by protecting political information. Under such theories, the freedom of speech is not valuable in itself but only for the results that unfettered dialogue can bring to society, in terms of either the "truth" or good self-government. The ends to which speech is directed determine whether the speech should be constitutionally protected.
>
> The second major theoretical model for free speech focuses on the constitutive value of speech: it argues that freedom of speech is necessary because it is essential to one's dignity or self-fulfillment, vital aspects of one's identity. These aspects of identity are not objectives that can be separated from the underlying freedom but rather are inherently intertwined with it. Most importantly ..., constitutive approaches to the freedom of speech posit that the right has intrinsic value apart from the mere ability to use speech as a method of conveying ideas for external ends.

Adam Winkler, Note, *Expressive Voting*, 68 N.Y.U. L. Rev. 330, 339–40 (1993). Is the Supreme Court's view of voting in *Burdick* entirely instrumental? Does, or should, voting have any function beyond "the societal goal of gauging and institutionalizing the political will"? *Id.* at 331. Should voting be viewed as constitutive? What legal consequences might flow from such a stance?

5. What other constraints on how a voter may mark his ballot are permissible? Consider the longstanding prohibitions in many jurisdictions on "single-shot" (also called "bullet") voting. "Single-shot" voting refers to a practice whereby voters cast fewer than all of their votes for a multi-member office. For example, in an at-large election for four seats on the city council, each voter may be entitled to cast four votes. If she casts only one of those votes, and forgoes casting her other votes—then she has bullet voted. The strategic thinking behind single-shot voting is that members of a numerical minority group can increase the share of the overall vote received by their most preferred candidate by depriving all other candidates of their support. (Thus, voters single shoot when their group is sponsoring only one candidate—because, for example, they lack the resources to run a full slate.) While single-shot voting cannot *guarantee* that the minority will be able to elect a candidate (since a strategic majority could simply limit the number of candidates it supports and outvote the minority for every seat), it can increase the likelihood of minority electoral success:

> Consider [a] town of 600 whites and 400 blacks with an at-large election to choose four council members. Each voter is able to cast four votes. Suppose there are eight white candidates, with the votes of the whites split among them approximately equally, and one black candidate, with all the blacks voting for him and no one else. The result is that each white candidate receives about 300 votes and the black candidate receives 400 votes. The black has

probably won a seat.... Single-shot voting enables a minority group to win some at-large seats if it concentrates its vote behind a limited number of candidates and if the vote of the majority is divided among a number of candidates.

U.S. Commission on Civil Rights, *The Voting Rights Act: Ten Years After* 206–07 (1975). Many states, particularly in the South, banned single-shot voting. Until 1986, Mississippi law provided that if an elector voted for fewer candidates than the number of positions to be filled, none of her votes for that office would be counted. *See* Miss. Code Ann. § 21–11–15 (1972) (repealed by 1986 Miss. Laws ch. 495, § 329). The same state legislator who engineered the Tuskegee gerrymander struck down in *Gomillion v. Lightfoot*, 364 U.S. 339 (1960), covered in Chapter 2, also sponsored Alabama's anti-single-shot law. *See Dillard v. Crenshaw County*, 640 F.Supp. 1347, 1357 (M.D.Ala.1986). Does an anti-single-shot law violate the First Amendment because it compels speech, namely, voting for some candidates one does not prefer in order to have one's votes counted for the candidates one does support? *Cf. Wooley v. Maynard*, 430 U.S. 705 (1977) (striking down New Hampshire's requirement that all license plates display the slogan "Live Free or Die"); *West Virginia State Board of Education v. Barnette*, 319 U.S. 624 (1943) (striking down a compulsory flag salute). Would compulsory voting violate the First Amendment? *Cf. Kansas City v. Whipple*, 38 S.W. 295, 297 (Mo.1896) (striking down a Kansas City penalty tax imposed for failure to vote because "it is obnoxious to the provisions of the organic law which secures to every citizen protection against ... invasion of his sovereign right of suffrage"); Jeffrey A. Blomberg, Note, *Protecting the Right Not to Vote from Voter Purge Statutes*, 64 Fordham L. Rev. 1015 (1995) (arguing that courts should recognize a fundamental right not to vote).

2. RESTRICTIONS ON WHO APPEARS ON THE BALLOT

Although political parties no longer distribute the actual ballots voters use, they still perform a major function in determining who appears on the ballot. When the officially printed, Australian ballot was adopted, states necessarily needed some mechanism for determining who should appear on the ballot. As Professor Bradley Smith explains, "early laws were not restrictive, and there was a broad public consensus that ballot-access laws were not intended to be a substantive barrier"; indeed, some supporters of the Australian ballot had actually argued that it would increase the number of candidates, since it would relieve candidates or minor parties of the expense of printing ballots with their names on them and distributing them to voters. Bradley A. Smith, Note, *Judicial Protection of Ballot–Access Rights: Third Parties Need Not Apply*, 28 Harv. J. Legis. 167, 173 (1991).

Within a few decades, however, states begin using restrictive ballot-access rules that drastically limited the number of candidates who could appear on the ballot. Every state provided essentially automatic access to the general election ballot for certain candidates, essentially those nominated by major political parties. Typically, the statute would place on the general election ballot the names of candidates nominated by parties that had received a specified share of the vote in a previous general election. *See, e.g.,* Mich. Stat. Ann. § 6.1560 (1996) (providing that a "political party the principal candidate of which received at the last preceding general election a vote equal to or more than 1% of the total number of votes cast for the successful candidate for secretary of state at the last preceding election in which a secretary of state was elected is qualified to have its name, party vignette, and candidates listed on the next general election ballot"); Va. Code Ann. § 24.2–101 (1996) (defining as a "political party," entitled to automatic ballot access for its candidates, "an organization of citizens of the Commonwealth which, at either of the two preceding statewide general elections, received at least ten percent of the total vote cast for any statewide office filled in that election"). In most states today, only the Democratic and Republican parties enjoy automatic ballot access; there are some states, however, where additional parties have automatic ballot lines.

Because appearance on the general election ballot is so tightly constrained—an issue to which we shall return later in the chapter—the major winnowing down of candidates occurs in primary elections. But here, too, a variety of regulations limit candidates' ability to get a spot. In general, these restrictions take two forms: filing fees and petition requirements.

Bullock v. Carter

405 U.S. 134 (1972).

■ MR. CHIEF JUSTICE BURGER delivered the opinion of the Court.

Under Texas law, a candidate must pay a filing fee as a condition to having his name placed on the ballot in a primary election....

Appellee Pate met all qualifications to be a candidate in the May 2, 1970, Democratic primary for the office of County Commissioner of Precinct Four for El Paso County, except that he was unable to pay the $1,424.60 assessment required of candidates in that primary. Appellee Wischkaemper sought to be placed on the Democratic primary ballot as a candidate for County Judge in Tarrant County, but he was unable to pay the $6,300 assessment for candidacy for that office. Appellee Carter wished to be a Democratic candidate for Commissioner of the General Land Office; his application was not accompanied by the required $1,000 filing fee.

* * *

Under the Texas statute, payment of the filing fee is an absolute prerequisite to a candidate's participation in a primary election. There is no alternative procedure by which a potential candidate who is unable to pay the fee can get on the primary ballot by way of petitioning voters,[5] and write-in votes are not permitted in primary elections for public office. Any person who is willing and able to pay the filing fee and who meets the basic eligibility requirements for holding the office sought can run in a primary.

Candidates for most district, county, and precinct offices must pay their filing fee to the county executive committee of the political party conducting the primary; the committee also determines the amount of the fee. The party committee must make an estimate of the total cost of the primary and apportion it among the various candidates "as in their judgment is just and equitable." ... In counties with populations of one million or more, candidates for offices of two-year terms can be assessed up to 10% of their aggregate annual salary, and candidates for offices of four-year terms can be assessed up to 15% of their aggregate annual salary. In smaller counties there are no such percentage limitations.[10]

The record shows that the fees required of the candidates in this case are far from exceptional in their magnitude. The size of the filing fees is plainly a natural consequence of a statutory system that places the burden of financing primary elections on candidates rather than on the governmental unit, and that imposes a particularly heavy burden on candidates for local office. The filing fees required of candidates seeking nomination for state offices and offices involving statewide primaries are more closely regulated by statute and tend to be appreciably smaller. The filing fees for candidates for State Representative range from $150 to $600, depending on the population of the county from which nomination is sought. Candidates for State Senator are subject to a maximum assessment of $1,000. Candidates for nominations requiring statewide primaries, including candidates for Governor and United States Senator, must pay a filing fee of $1,000 to the chairman of the state executive committee of the party conducting the primary....

---

5. Texas law does permit the names of independent candidates to appear on the official ballot in the general election if a proper application containing a voter petition is submitted. The number of eligible voters required to sign the petition varies from 1% to 5% depending on the office sought. For district, county, and precinct offices, candidates must obtain the signatures of 5% of the eligible voters with a ceiling of 500 signatures. No person may sign the application of more than one person for the same office, and no person who has voted in a primary may sign the application of a candidate for an office for which a nomination was made at such primary.

No fees are assessed against candidates in general elections.

10. The $6,300 fee required of appellee Wischkaemper, for example, amounts to 32% of the $19,700 annual salary for County Judge in Tarrant County. Similarly, in the May 2, 1970, Democratic primary, candidates for five county offices in Ward County were assessed $6,250 for a filing fee; this fee represented 76.6% of the $8,160 annual salary for four of these offices; for the fifth office, that of County Commissioner, it represented 99.7% of the annual salary of $6,270.

(1)

* * *

The threshold question to be resolved is whether the filing-fee system should be sustained if it can be shown to have some rational basis, or whether it must withstand a more rigid standard of review.

In *Harper v. Virginia Board of Elections,* 383 U.S. 663 (1966), the Court held that Virginia's imposition of an annual poll tax not exceeding $1.50 on residents over the age of 21 was a denial of equal protection. Subjecting the Virginia poll tax to close scrutiny, the Court concluded that the placing of even a minimal price on the exercise of the right to vote constituted an invidious discrimination. The problem presented by candidate filing fees is not the same, of course, and we must determine whether the strict standard of review of the *Harper* case should be applied.

The initial and direct impact of filing fees is felt by aspirants for office, rather than voters, and the Court has not heretofore attached such fundamental status to candidacy as to invoke a rigorous standard of review. However, the rights of voters and the rights of candidates do not lend themselves to neat separation; laws that affect candidates always have at least some theoretical, correlative effect on voters.... In approaching candidate restrictions, it is essential to examine in a realistic light the extent and nature of their impact on voters.

Unlike a filing-fee requirement that most candidates could be expected to fulfill from their own resources or at least through modest contributions, the very size of the fees imposed under the Texas system gives it a patently exclusionary character. Many potential office seekers lacking both personal wealth and affluent backers are in every practical sense precluded from seeking the nomination of their chosen party, no matter how qualified they might be, and no matter how broad or enthusiastic their popular support. The effect of this exclusionary mechanism on voters is neither incidental nor remote. Not only are voters substantially limited in their choice of candidates, but also there is the obvious likelihood that this limitation would fall more heavily on the less affluent segment of the community, whose favorites may be unable to pay the large costs required by the Texas system. To the extent that the system requires candidates to rely on contributions from voters in order to pay the assessments, a phenomenon that can hardly be rare in light of the size of the fees, it tends to deny some voters the opportunity to vote for a candidate of their choosing; at the same time it gives the affluent the power to place on the ballot their own names or the names of persons they favor. Appellants do not dispute that this is endemic to the system. This disparity in voting power based on wealth cannot be described by reference to discrete and precisely defined segments of the community as is typical of inequities challenged under the Equal Protection Clause, and there are doubtless some instances of candidates representing the views of voters of modest means who are able to pay the required fee. But we would ignore reality were we not to recognize that this system falls with unequal weight on voters, as well as candidates, according to their economic status.

Because the Texas filing-fee scheme has a real and appreciable impact on the exercise of the franchise, and because this impact is related to the resources of the voters supporting a particular candidate, we conclude, as in Harper, that the laws must be "closely scrutinized" and found reasonably necessary to the accomplishment of legitimate state objectives in order to pass constitutional muster.

(2)

Appellants contend that the filing fees required by the challenged statutes are necessary both to regulate the ballot in primary elections and to provide a means for financing such elections.

The Court has recognized that a State has a legitimate interest in regulating the number of candidates on the ballot. In so doing, the State understandably and properly seeks to prevent the clogging of its election machinery, avoid voter confusion, and assure that the winner is the choice of a majority, or at least a strong plurality, of those voting, without the expense and burden of runoff elections. Although we have no way of gauging the number of candidates who might enter primaries in Texas if access to the ballot were unimpeded by the large filing fees in question here, we are bound to respect the legitimate objectives of the State in avoiding overcrowded ballots. Moreover, a State has an interest, if not a duty, to protect the integrity of its political processes from frivolous or fraudulent candidacies.

There is no escape from the conclusion that the imposition of filing fees ranging as high as $8,900 tends to limit the number of candidates entering the primaries. However, even under conventional standards of review, a State cannot achieve its objectives by totally arbitrary means; the criterion for differing treatment must bear some relevance to the object of the legislation. To say that the filing fee requirement tends to limit the ballot to the more serious candidates is not enough. There may well be some rational relationship between a candidate's willingness to pay a filing fee and the seriousness with which he takes his candidacy, but the candidates in this case affirmatively alleged that they were unable, not simply unwilling, to pay the assessed fees, and there was no contrary evidence. It is uncontested that the filing fees exclude legitimate as well as frivolous candidates. And even assuming that every person paying the large fees required by Texas law takes his own candidacy seriously, that does not make him a "serious candidate" in the popular sense. If the Texas fee requirement is intended to regulate the ballot by weeding out spurious candidates, it is extraordinarily ill-fitted to that goal; other means to protect those valid interests are available.

Instead of arguing for the reasonableness of the exclusion of some candidates, appellants rely on the fact that the filing-fee requirement is applicable only to party primaries, and point out that a candidate can gain a place on the ballot in the general election without payment of fees by submitting a proper application accompanied by a voter petition. Apart from the fact that the primary election may be more crucial than the general election in certain parts of Texas, we can hardly accept as reasonable an alternative that requires candidates and voters to abandon their party affiliations in order to avoid the burdens of the filing fees imposed by state law. Appellants have not demonstrated that their present filing-fee scheme is a necessary or reasonable tool for regulating the ballot.

In addition to the State's purported interest in regulating the ballot, the filing fees serve to relieve the State treasury of the cost of conducting the primary elections, and this is a legitimate state objective; in this limited sense it cannot be said that the fee system lacks a rational basis. But under the standard of review we consider applicable to this case, there must be a showing of necessity....

More importantly, the costs do not arise because candidates decide to enter a primary or because the parties decide to conduct one, but because the State has, as a matter of legislative choice, directed that party primaries be held. The State has presumably chosen this course more to benefit the voters than the candidates.

Appellants seem to place reliance on the self-evident fact that if the State must assume the cost, the voters, as taxpayers, will ultimately be burdened with the expense of the primaries. But it is far too late to make out a case that the party primary is such a lesser part of the democratic process that its cost must be shifted away from the taxpayers generally. The financial burden for general elections is carried by all taxpayers and appellants have not demonstrated a valid basis for distinguishing between these two legitimate costs of the democratic process. It seems appropriate that a primary system designed to give the voters some influence at the nominating stage should spread the cost among all of the voters in an attempt to distribute the influence without regard to wealth. Viewing the myriad governmental functions supported from general revenues, it is difficult to single out any of a higher order than the conduct of elections at all levels to bring forth those persons desired by their fellow citizens to govern. Without making light of the State's interest in husbanding its revenues, we fail to see such an element of necessity in the State's present means of financing primaries as to justify the resulting incursion on the prerogatives of voters.

(3)

Since the State has failed to establish the requisite justification for this filing-fee system, we hold that it results in a denial of equal protection of the laws.... By requiring candidates to shoulder the costs of conducting primary elections through filing fees and by providing no reasonable alternative means of access to the ballot, the State of Texas has erected a system that utilizes the criterion of ability to pay as a condition to being on the ballot, thus excluding some candidates otherwise qualified and denying an undetermined number of voters the opportunity to vote for candidates of their choice. These salient features of the Texas system are critical to our determination of constitutional invalidity.

NOTES AND QUESTIONS

1. Two years later, in *Lubin v. Panish*, 415 U.S. 709 (1974), the Supreme Court addressed California's filing fee regime. The California fees were far lower—representing either one or two percent of the annual salary of the office sought and ranging from $192 for State Assembly seats up to $982 for Governor. The Court noted that *Bullock* did not completely resolve the case because the Texas filing fees "were so patently exclusionary as to violate traditional equal protection concepts." Chief Justice Burger's opinion for the Court identified two conflicting "means of achieving an effective, representative political system"—the first being the "steady trend toward limiting the size of the ballot in order to 'concentrate the attention of the electorate on the selection of a much smaller number of officials and so afford to the voters the opportunity of exercising more discrimination in their use of the franchise,'" the second being the "increasing pressure" for "expansion of political opportunity" reflected in twentieth-century constitutional amendments, the Voting Rights Act, and the "gradual enlargement of the Fourteenth Amendment's equal protection provision in the area of voting rights." While the Court ultimately struck down California's scheme on equal protection grounds, it also seemed to recognize distinct categories of substantive rights involved in elections. First, the Court acknowledged the importance of weighing the burden on voters' associational rights: "The interests involved are not merely those of parties or individual candidates; the voters can assert their preferences only through candidates or parties or both and it is this broad interest that must be weighed in the balance." Second, the Court identified an independent right of candidates to be on the ballot: "Conversely, if the filing fee is more moderate, as here, impecunious but serious candidates may be prevented from running. Even in this day of high-budget political campaigns some candidates have demonstrated that direct contact with thousands of voters by 'walking tours' is a route to success. Whatever may be the political mood at any given time, our tradition has been one of hospitality toward all candidates without regard to their economic status." *Bullock* and *Lubin* taken together raise the question of precisely which constitutional rights (and whose constitutional rights) render filing fees so constitutionally suspect.

2. Does it seem plausible that someone like Lubin—who claimed he was unable to raise $701.60—is a "serious" candidate for a position on the Los Angeles County Board of Supervisors? If, realistically speaking, someone in his position has no chance of winning, or perhaps even affecting the outcome, what accounts for the Court's special solicitude for his claim? Is this consistent with the Court's perspective in *Burdick*?

3. The Court suggests that the fatal flaw in the filing fee regimes was their failure to provide any alternative mechanism by which indigent but serious candidates could get on the ballot. In *Lubin*, the Court suggested that "a candidate who establishes that he cannot pay the filing fee required for a place on the primary ballot may be required to demonstrate the 'seriousness' of his candidacy by persuading a substantial number of voters to sign a petition in his behalf."

Today, all states provide some petition mechanism for candidates to get on primary (and general election) ballots. Some of the petition requirements, such as Hawaii's (discussed in *Burdick*) are purely nominal, requiring only a few dozen signatures. Hawaii, you may recall, requires candidates seeking nominations for statewide office to submit petitions with the signatures of 25 registered voters and candidates for state legislative nominations to submit petitions with 15 signatures. It is hard to imagine that any "serious" candidate would be unable to meet such a requirement. But other petition requirements seem designed largely, if not entirely, to restrict the field to "insiders." In this regard, consider the New York system. New York Election Law § 6–136 provides, in pertinent part:

> 1. Petitions for any office to be filled by the voters of the entire state must be signed by not less than fifteen thousand or five per centum, whichever is less, of the then enrolled voters of the party in the state (excluding voters in inactive status), of whom not less than one hundred or five per centum, whichever is less, of such enrolled voters shall reside in each of one-half of the congressional districts of the state.
>
> 2. All other petitions must be signed by not less than five per centum, as determined by the preceding enrollment, of the then enrolled voters of the party residing within the political unit in which the office or position is to be voted for (excluding voters in inactive status), provided, however, that for the following public offices the number of signatures need not exceed the following limits:
>
> * * *
>
> (h) For any office to be filled by all the voters of any state senatorial district, one thousand signatures;
>
> (i) For any office to be filled by all voters of any assembly district, five hundred signatures

New York provides no filing fee alternative; thus, all candidates must obtain their ballot positions through indications of voter support. New York's law also contains a large number of technical requirements involving such things as how petitions should be collated and requirements for additional information by signatories. In recent years, New York has accounted for one-half of the ballot access challenges in the nation. *See* Katherine E. Schuelke, Note, *A Call for Reform of New York State's Ballot Access Laws*, 64 N.Y.U.L. Rev. 182 (1989).

Which candidates are benefitted or disadvantaged by New York's system? For one recent example of litigation involving the New York system, see *Rockefeller v. Powers*, 917 F.Supp. 155 (E.D.N.Y.), *aff'd*, 78 F.3d 44 (2d Cir.), *cert. denied*, 116 S.Ct. 1703 (1996), which involved the regulation of candidates on the state's Republican presidential primary ballot. Half of the candidates who ran in other states chose not even to attempt to appear on the New York ballot. Steve Forbes, who spent millions of dollars of his own money on his presidential bid, presumably could have met any filing fee requirement. But he was unable to meet the petition requirements in roughly half of the state's congressional districts. Only Bob Dole satisfied the ballot access requirements statewide. Interestingly, in 1988, when Dole was challenging George Bush (rather than occupying the front-runner's position), he had been unable to satisfy the same requirements.

To appear on the ballot in a particular congressional district (New York's scheme determines access district-by-district rather than statewide), a candidate needed to collect roughly 1250 signatures within the district during a 37-day period in the middle of the winter. Each candidate also faced a host of rules defining what was a valid signature, including rules as to the qualification of witnesses to signings and inclusion of the election or Assembly district numbers of signers. Moreover, a voter could sign only one petition. Can you think of reasons why a voter might want to sign more than one such petition? While the requirement of signatures from each congressional district undoubtedly would measure widespread support, it proved a close to insuperable obstacle to a candidate in districts where it was "easier to find a needle in haystack than an enrolled Republican," such as the 86 percent nonwhite Fifteenth Congressional District centered on Harlem. The district court and court of appeals held that the Republicans' system violated the due process clause because it placed an undue burden on the voting rights of Republicans in heavily Democratic districts; in those districts, the voters' choice was constrained.

Does it seem even remotely plausible that a candidate who cannot afford a filing fee would have the resources to get on the ballot under the sort of petitioning scheme at issue in *Rockefeller*? It turns out that many parties and candidates seeking spots on the ballot turn to paid signature gatherers, who charge fees like $3.50 per signature collected. *See* Rogers Worthington, *Perot Party Goes All Out in Ballot Drive*, Chi. Tribune, Oct. 23, 1995, at 3. Is Bradley Smith right that "[g]iven these numbers, it is ludicrous to suggest that a candidate who could not pay a one dollar filing fee, or even an $8,900 filing fee, could conduct a major petition drive to appear on the ballot"? Smith, *supra*, at 201; *cf. Andress v. Reed*, 880 F.2d 239 (9th Cir.1989) (rejecting a potential candidate's claim that the cost to obtain the required 10,000 signatures would be more than the $1,702 filing fee he could not afford, and therefore violated the equal protection clause).

Whether ludicrous or not, the Supreme Court has devoted substantial attention to the constitutionality of various petition schemes that determine when particular candidates can gain access to the ballot. We will return to this issue in the context of petitions to appear on the general election ballot and the question of entrenchment of the two-party system.

B. WHO CAN PARTICIPATE IN A PARTY'S ACTIVITIES?

Since the mid–1800's, the United States has had two major political parties: the Democrats and the Republicans. For a history of the rise and fall of American political parties, see James L. Sundquist, Dynamics of the Party System (1983). Virtually all successful candidates for national office have been members of one party or the other; today, for example, only one Member of Congress is neither a Republican nor a Democrat. And with a few notable and short-lived exceptions, virtually all state and local officials elected in partisan elections are affiliated with one (or sometimes both) of the major parties. For example, "of over 20,000 elections for state legislatures from 1982 to 1988, only three [were] won by members of a party other than the Democrats or Republicans." Bradley A. Smith, Note, *Judicial Protection of Ballot–Access Rights: Third Parties Need Not Apply*, 28 Harv. J. Legis. 167, 171 (1991).

Thus, as recognized in cases stretching as far back as *United States v. Classic*, 313 U.S. 299 (1941), primary elections and major party nomination processes are "an integral part of the procedure for the popular choice" of elected officials. States closely regulate major-party nomination processes, and a majority of states now require some form of primary elections. The Supreme Court has never squarely addressed the question whether a state can compel a party to use a particular nomination process, but as Professor Lowenstein explains, it is unlikely that the Court would strike down a mandatory primary law. *See* Daniel H. Lowenstein, *Associational Rights of Major Political Parties: A Skeptical Inquiry*, 71 Tex. L. Rev. 1741, 1768–69 (1993). *See also Lightfoot v. Eu*, 964 F.2d 865, 872 (9th Cir.1992) (rejecting a challenge to California's primary requirement), *cert. denied*, 507 U.S. 919 (1993). For an opposing view, see Arthur M. Weisburd, *Candidate-Making and the Constitution: Constitutional Restraints on and Protections of Party Nominating Methods*, 57 S. Cal. L. Rev. 213 (1984); Karl D. Cooper, Note, *Are State–Imposed Political Party Primaries Constitutional? The Constitutional Ramifications of the 1986 Illinois LaRouche Primary Victories*, 4 J.L. & Pol. 343 (1987).

The question of when particular individuals can participate in the nomination process implicates a variety of individual, party, and state interests. The possible legal questions can be represented by the following three pairs of responses to the question: Can Citizen X participate in the "A" Party's nomination process?[b]

Can Citizen X participate in the "A" Party's Nomination Process?		
	The Party's Answer	*The State's Answer*
1.	No	No
2.	No	Yes
3.	Yes	No

The following cases work through these permutations.

1. BOTH THE PARTY AND THE STATE SEEK TO EXCLUDE CITIZEN X FROM PARTICIPATING

Nader v. Schaffer
417 F.Supp. 837 (D.Conn.), summarily aff'd, 429 U.S. 989 (1976).

■ ROBERT P. ANDERSON, CIRCUIT JUDGE:

[The plaintiffs in this case are registered voters who refused to register as members of a political party. Under Connecticut law, this precludes them from voting in any party primary. The case arises on a motion to dismiss by the named defendants: the Secretary of State of Connecticut, and the state Republican and Democratic parties.] Plaintiffs' principal argument is that participation in a primary election is an exercise of the constitutionally protected right to vote and of the constitutionally protected right to associate with others in support of a candidate. They also assert that to the latter there is a constitutionally protected correlative right not to associate, and to be free from coerced associations. They further claim a constitutionally protected right of privacy of association. Plaintiffs wish to exercise both of these claimed sets of rights, but [Connecticut law] limits them to one or the other; that is, in order to vote in a party's primary

---

b. Since individual voters are free not to participate, no cases arise unless an individual seeks to take part. Although it is conceivable that some party members might object if both the party and the state agree to let an interested voter participate, it seems likely that courts would refuse to intervene in that sort of internecine dispute.

election, plaintiffs must enroll in the party, while on the other hand, if they maintain their stand against enrollment, they are precluded.

* * *

Plaintiffs argue that the alternative avenues of political activity open to them under Connecticut law [if they are unable to participate in primary elections] are ineffectual and unrealistic, since in most general elections, only the Democratic and Republican nominees have reasonable probabilities of success.... [But] any dominant position enjoyed by the Democratic and Republican Parties is not the result of improper support, or discrimination in their favor, by the State. Rather, the two Parties enjoy this position because, over a period of time, they have been successful in attracting the bulk of the electorate, so that they now have substantial followings.

* * *

Improper State support for the Democratic and Republican Parties cannot be inferred from the fact that their primary elections are closely regulated by statute. In the past, many political nominations were made by a process ... described as the "smoke-filled room." Many states, such as Connecticut, have enacted statutes calling for nomination by primary election, presumably because they find it beneficial to allow the general party membership a voice in the nominating process.

* * *

With regard to the claimed right not to associate, it is true that, in order to vote in a party's primary, plaintiffs must publicly affiliate with that party. But enrollment in Connecticut imposes absolutely no affirmative party obligations on the voter, in terms of time or money, and it does not even obligate him to vote for the party's positions or candidates or to vote at all. The voter's name, however, may be erased from the party's enrollment list on a proper showing that he does not support the party's principles or candidates. Conn.Gen.Stat. §§ 9-60, 9-61; but in actual practice these statutes are not used. Such limited public affiliation is simply not ... coerced orthodoxy imposed by government officials....

Plaintiffs also claim that the public nature of enrollment violates their right to privacy of association by potentially subjecting them to harassment because of their affiliations with a party. It is insufficient, however, for plaintiffs merely to raise the spectre of harassment; instead, they must make a detailed factual showing of actual threats or incidents of harassment. At least one form of potential harassment suggested by plaintiffs—loss of civil service employment due to political affiliation—cannot necessarily be considered a realistic threat since this practice was recently declared unconstitutional by the Supreme Court, at least as to patronage employees in non-policy-making positions. *Elrod v. Burns*, 427 U.S. 347 (1976).

* * *

Because the political party is formed for the purpose of engaging in political activities, constitutionally protected associational rights of its members are vitally essential to the candidate selection process.... [P]arty members also have a "right to organize a party in the way that will make it the most effective political organization." An attempt to interfere with a party's ability so to maintain itself is simultaneously an interference with the associational rights of its members. The rights of party members may to some extent offset the importance of claimed conflicting rights asserted by persons challenging some aspect of the candidate selection process. More importantly, party members are entitled to affirmative protection of their associational rights.... [T]he state has a legitimate interest in protecting party members' associational rights, by legislating to protect the party "from intrusion by those with adverse political principles."

In addition to protecting the associational rights of party members, a state has a more general, but equally legitimate, interest in protecting the overall integrity of the historic electoral process. This includes preserving parties as viable and identifiable interest groups; insuring that the results of primary elections, in a broad sense, accurately reflect the voting of party members. Parties should be able to avoid primary election outcomes which will confuse or mislead the general electorate to the extent it relies on party labels as representative of certain ideologies; and preventing fraudulent and deceptive conduct which mars the nominating process.

* * *

As we have noted, the phrase "preservation of the integrity of the electoral process" contemplates, in the nominating context, the assurance that primary election results reflect the will of party members, undistorted by the votes of those unconcerned with, if not actually hostile to, the principles, philosophies, and goals of the party. The phrase contemplates the prevention of fraud in the nominating process, and a candidacy determined by the votes of non-party members is arguably a fraudulent candidacy.

* * *

From the party's point of view, enrollment also serves an important housekeeping function. Candidates need to know who is in the electorate, so that they (the candidates) can attempt to persuade those individuals to vote for them. Party members who wish to establish, as party policy, a particular course of conduct through the election of a particular candidate, similarly need to know who their supporters are. It is common experience that direct solicitation of party members—by mail, telephone, or face-to-face contact, and by the candidates themselves or by their active supporters—is part of any primary election campaign. But, without the public list of party members which is provided by the enrollment process, such electioneering would become quite difficult.

* * *

[Plaintiffs' complaint is therefore dismissed.]

NOTES AND QUESTIONS

1. Could a party require more of a voter than public affiliation with the party as a condition of participation in its nominating event? Consider the following state statutes. Ala. Code § 17–16–14(b) (1996) provides that:

> All poll lists for primary elections shall state at the top thereof that by participating in said primary election a voter shall indicate his preference for the party holding said primary, and will support the nominees of that party in the general election, and that he is qualified under the rules of such party to vote in its primary election. No person shall be eligible to participate in said primary unless he signs said poll list and thereby certifies to the truth of said statement.

Minn. Stat. § 200.02, subd. 17 (1996) defines a member of a political party as "an individual who:

> (a) Supports the general principles of that party's constitution;
>
> (b) Voted for a majority of that party's candidates in the last general election; or
>
> (c) Intends to vote for a majority of that party's candidates in the next general election."

Could a party limit voting in its primary to individuals who agree with these sorts of requirements? There are no reported cases involving enforcement of these types of provisions. *See* Arthur M. Weisburd, *Candidate-Making and the Constitution: Constitutional Restraints on and Protections of Party Nominating Methods*, 57 S. Cal. L. Rev. 213, 271 (1984). But if political parties enjoy associational freedom, as the Supreme Court has repeatedly held they do, why shouldn't they be able to exclude "those with adverse political principles"? In that case, who should decide whether an individual is really a member of the party?

Parties have enforced "loyalty oaths" in other nomination settings. Consider the following account of a recent Republican "firehouse primary" in Fairfax County, Virginia. (A "firehouse primary" is a polling process conducted by a party without state supervision. The Jaybird balloting described in *Terry v. Adams*, 345 U.S. 461 (1953), *see supra* Chapter 2, is an example of a firehouse primary.)

> Many were turned off by a requirement that they sign an "intent form" to support the Republican nominee regardless of yesterday's outcome.
>
> Shouting matches erupted at times, as Republican officials tried to block people who had refused to sign the form from voting.

> "My right to vote without coercion has been violated," said Thierry Gaudin, 45, of Reston. "It is a rigging of the game for the political power of a few at the cost of democracy."
>
> Gaudin pressed his point with a half-dozen Republican officials, including party Chairman Patrick Mullins, who had a simple response.
>
> "Sue us. Thank you," Mullins said.
>
> Police were called when Gaudin refused to leave. After an hour, he did so voluntarily.
>
> Supreme Court Justice Antonin Scalia, a Fairfax resident, at first questioned the legality of the oath, but signed after getting an explanation from a party official, said Steve Jennings Jr., who checked Scalia in.

Eric Lipton, *Democracy Can Stop Traffic*, Wash. Post, Jan. 8, 1995, at A1. Should Justice Scalia rely on low-level party officials to tell him what the Constitution means? *Cf. Cooper v. Aaron*, 358 U.S. 1, 18 (1958) (declaring that "the federal judiciary is supreme in the exposition of the law of the Constitution"); *Marbury v. Madison*, 5 U.S. 137, 177 (1803) ("It is emphatically the province and duty of the judicial department to say what the law is."). Is Justice Scalia's deference to party wishes here consistent with his stance in *Tashjian v. Republican Party of Connecticut*, 479 U.S. 208 (1986), discussed later in this Chapter?

2. In a related vein, are the two major political parties in this country organizations with clearly held ideological commitments to which individuals might actually be adverse? Consider Justice Powell's observations in his dissent in *Democratic Party of the United States v. Wisconsin ex rel. LaFollette*, 450 U.S. 107, (1981), discussed *infra* at pages ___:

> If [the national Democratic Party] were an organization with a particular ideological orientation or political mission, perhaps [permitting individuals who did not profess this ideology would] ... interfere with the associational rights of its founders.
>
> The Democratic Party, however, is not organized around the achievement of defined ideological goals. Instead, the major parties in this country "have been characterized by a fluidity and overlap of philosophy and membership." It can hardly be denied that this Party generally has been composed of various elements reflecting most of the American political spectrum. The Party does take positions on public issues, but these positions vary from time to time, and there never has been a serious effort to establish for the Party a monolithic ideological identity by excluding all those with differing views.

3. The court's opinion in *Nader* refers to the state's "interest in protecting the overall integrity of the historic electoral process." How should a court weigh such state declarations of public interest when a) the beneficiaries of the regulation are the two dominant political parties, and b) the decision is made by elected representatives from these two dominant political parties? Does it make sense to speak of a "state interest" in such circumstances? Are there any restrictions or limitations on such claims of "state interest" when the effect of state regulation is to restrict challenges to the preeminent position of the established political parties?

4. Should parties have a greater right to exclude *candidates* from their nomination processes? In *Ray v. Blair*, 343 U.S. 214 (1952), the Supreme Court upheld the exclusion of Edmund Blair's name as a candidate for Democratic Presidential Elector because Blair refused to sign a pledge to aid and support "the nominees of the National Convention of the Democratic Party for President and Vice–President of the United States." Admittedly, the "office" of elector might be a special case; the only function an elector serves is to cast one of his state's votes in the Electoral College. It is inconceivable that more than a handful of voters are even aware of the *names* of the electors for whom they have voted; indeed, in many states the ballot simply allows voters to cast an undivided vote for the entire slate of electors pledged to a particular party's candidates for president and vice president. So Blair's implicit threat to bolt the party and refuse to support the Democratic candidate for president (a not insubstantial risk, perhaps, given the voting behavior of some arch-segregationist Democratic-pledged electors during the period) might be reframed as a threat to deny voters who cast ballots for the Democratic ticket *their* right to vote.

Two more recent examples of exclusion perhaps present the question more squarely.

Duke v. Massey

87 F.3d 1226 (11th Cir.1996).

■ JOSEPH HATCHETT, CIRCUIT JUDGE:

David Duke, a controversial political figure, sought the Republican Party's nomination for President of the United States for the 1992 election. In pursuing the Republican Party nomination, Duke participated in presidential primaries in various states throughout the nation. In December 1991, Georgia's Secretary of State, Max Cleland, prepared and published a list of potential candidates for Georgia's presidential preference primary. Duke's name appeared on the Georgia list of presidential candidates for the Republican Party nomination. The Secretary submitted his initial list of presidential primary candidates to the presidential candidate selection committee (Committee) for the Republican Party....

On December 16, 1991, the Committee, consisting of Georgia's Republican Party Chairperson Alec Poitevint, Senate Minority Leader Tom Phillips, and House Minority Leader Paul Heard . . . deleted Duke's name from the list of potential republican presidential candidates.[1]

* * *

Duke asserts that the Committee's decision and the Georgia statute severely burdened his rights of free speech and association under the First and Fourteenth Amendments to the United States Constitution. Duke contends that because the statute grants the committee members "unfettered discretion" to grant or deny ballot access it is unconstitutional in that it allows the Committee members to exclude candidates based on the content of their speech. Duke argues that the statute also infringes his right to freedom of association.

[. . .] Duke does not have a right to associate with an "unwilling partner," the Republican Party. . . . [T]he Republican Party has a right to "identify the people who constitute the association and to limit the association to those people only." . . . Although Duke is correct in identifying his First and Fourteenth Amendment interests, those interests do not trump the Republican Party's right to identify its membership based on political beliefs nor the state's interests in protecting the Republican Party's right to define itself. Therefore, the Committee, acting as representatives of the Republican Party under O.C.G.A. § 21-2-193, did not heavily burden Duke's First Amendment and Fourteenth Amendment rights when it excluded him from the Republican Party's presidential primary ballot.

* * *

The voters, supporters of Duke, claim that O.C.G.A. § 21-2-193 burdens their associational rights and their right to vote for a candidate of their choice. The voters contend that the right to vote is "heavily burdened" when the choices of candidates on primary ballots are restricted and other persons are "clamoring" to be listed on the election ballot. . . . The Supreme Court has recognized that a free and open debate on the qualifications of candidates is "integral to the operation of the system of government established by our Constitution," and that burdens on candidate access to the ballot directly burden the voters' ability to voice preferences. In this case, however, the voters have failed to offer any authority suggesting that they have a right to vote for their candidate of choice as a republican in a nonbinding primary.[7]

* * *

Although we do not believe that Duke and the voters' rights were heavily burdened as a result of the Committee's decision under O.C.G.A.

---

1. Under Georgia law, "each person designated by the Secretary of State as a presidential candidate shall appear upon the ballot of the appropriate political party or body unless all committee members of the same political party or body as the candidate agree to delete such candidate's name from the ballot." O.C.G.A. § 21-2-193(a).

7. Nothing precludes these voters from supporting Duke as an independent candidate or a third-party candidate in the general election.

§ 21-2-193, we will apply strict scrutiny ... in order to err on the side of caution....

The state has a compelling interest in protecting political parties' right to define their membership.... We believe that O.C.G.A. § 21-2-193 is narrowly tailored to further Georgia's compelling state interests. Under the statute, three party leaders are appointed to serve on the Committee.[8] Although the Committee's decision to exclude a candidate from the presidential primary ballot is unreviewable by the entire membership of the party, these committee members are leaders in the Republican Party and are ultimately held accountable for their decisions by the membership of the Republican Party. Under the terms of O.C.G.A. § 21-2-193, a person cannot serve on the Committee unless the membership of the Republican Party has placed them in a key leadership position. Surely, these persons are aware of the principles and platform of the Republican Party and can decide what presidential candidates are aligned with the party's views. Therefore, as leaders the membership of the party elected, they have been entrusted with the authority to make decisions for the party, and O.C.G.A. § 21-2-193 recognizes that these party leaders are in the best position to decide who should appear on Georgia's Republican Party presidential primary ballot.

* * *

Duke and the voters argue that the operation of the Georgia statute actually undermined its purported interest in protecting a political party's ability to define itself because it allows the committee members to make decisions that the party membership may not review. This argument suggests that the full party should have the right to determine what names appear on the ballot for a presidential primary.... [But] a system that would require a full party vote to put candidates on the presidential primary ballot would likely duplicate the results of the primary itself and also of the Committee. We hold that O.C.G.A. § 21-2-103 is narrowly tailored as it provides the state an efficient and effective means of furthering its compelling interest of protecting a political party's right to exclude persons with "adverse political principles."

Republican Party of Texas v. Dietz
940 S.W.2d 86 (Tex.Sup.Ct.1997).

■ JUSTICE ABBOTT delivered the opinion of the Court.

* * *

---

8. It is difficult to imagine composing a committee of party leaders who are in a better position to determine how a presidential candidate lines up with the views of the party than the State Chairperson of the party and the Majority and Minority leaders of both the state house and senate.

I

The Log Cabin Republicans of Texas and the Texas Log Cabin Republicans, Inc. (collectively LCR) are Texas non-profit corporations of Republicans who support equal civil rights for gay and lesbian individuals. In April 1996, LCR applied for an exhibitor's booth at the 1996 Republican Party of Texas Convention which began on June 20. As part of the booth application, LCR agreed to abide by the rules and regulations issued by the Republican Party of Texas for the convention. One of these rules allowed the Republican Party "the right to restrict exhibits which, because of undue noise, method of operation, material, content, or any other reason, become objectionable."

The Exhibits Chairman for the convention orally informed LCR's President, Dale Carter, that the group's booth application was approved. The Republican Party also cashed the $400 check Carter submitted for the booth. On May 15, 1996, LCR submitted to the Republican Party an advertisement to be included in the convention program along with a $750 check for the cost of the advertisement. The advertisement asserted LCR's beliefs that equal rights should be provided for gay and lesbian individuals. On May 21, 1996, the Republican Party Executive Director sent a letter to LCR rejecting the advertisement and the booth request. The Party returned the $750 check and refunded the cost of the booth.

On May 30, 1996, LCR filed this lawsuit in Travis County seeking injunctive relief. LCR alleged that the Republican Party's actions unconstitutionally infringed upon LCR's rights to free speech, equal rights, and due course of law under the Texas Constitution.... [The district court granted a preliminary injunction essentially requiring the Party to let LCR participate.] ...

II

* * *

The district court's injunction was based on a finding that LCR would probably prevail on its ... its free speech, equal rights, and due course of law claims under the Texas Constitution. The Republican Party urges that LCR's state constitutional claims cannot be maintained because the Party's conduct did not constitute "state action." ...

[We agree with the Party. S]everal decisions have considered the circumstances under which a political party (such as the Republican Party of Texas) is a state actor.

In the White Primary Cases, the Supreme Court ... declared that political parties were state actors when they held primary elections. While state action may exist when political parties exercise the "traditional government function" of conducting elections, it is not true that every act of a political party is state action. As one commentator has observed:

The idea of parties as "public" is in tension not only with the everyday recognition that parties are not government agencies, but also with the need to assure that the party system maintains a basic autonomy from the state so that the parties may serve as vehicles for expressing the public's needs and sentiments. Such autonomy distinguishes democracies from authoritarian systems....

Lowenstein, *Associational Rights of Major Political Parties: A Skeptical Inquiry*, 71 Tex. L. Rev. 1741, 1750 (1993).

Accordingly, federal courts have held that some party activities, such as holding elections, are public state action, while other activities are private.... [T]he normal role of party leaders in conducting internal affairs of their party, other than primary or general elections, does not make their party offices governmental offices or the filling of these offices state action.... [For example, h]olding a presidential candidates' forum [is not state action] because the forum was not an integral part of the election process. Accordingly, the Democratic Party [has] the absolute right to exclude a Democratic presidential candidate from the forum, even [if] the candidate had originally been invited to participate.... [And t]he election of party ward chairmen [is similarly] not state action because there [is] no evidence that the chairmen [play] an "integral part" in the election process.

[...] We hold that the actions of the Republican Party in denying LCR the booth and advertisement were mere internal party affairs. The stated purpose of LCR in attempting to obtain a booth and advertising space was to work toward changing the Party's internal platform. However, a Party's platform is not an element of the electoral process. Party candidates are free to accept in part and reject in part the platform, and there is no requirement that a party member adhere to all portions of the platform....

Because the Republican Party's conduct in denying LCR a booth and advertisement at the convention is an internal party affair rather than an integral part of the election process, the Republican Party is not a state actor under the undisputed facts of this case. Therefore, LCR cannot maintain its state constitutional claims against the Party, and the district court abused its discretion in issuing an injunction based on these claims.

* * *

■ SPECTOR, J., concurring in the judgment.

* * *

Even assuming a state action requirement should apply to the Log Cabin Republicans' claims, the majority does not offer a satisfactory justification for finding an absence of state action here....

Based only on the facts brought to light in a brief hearing on the temporary injunction, the trial court observed that a symbiotic relationship exists between the state and a major political party, and concluded that the Log Cabin Republicans could probably demonstrate a sufficient degree of state involvement to prevail on their constitutional claims....

Political speech, the type of speech that the Log Cabin Republicans sought to exercise at the Party's convention, is integral to our democratic form of government and receives the broadest protection under the First Amendment to assure an open debate on political issues. I cannot join an opinion that precipitately cuts off such a debate....

NOTES AND QUESTIONS

1. Must the Georgia Republican Party have an identifiable ideological character in order legitimately to exclude Duke, or can they exclude him for purely instrumental reasons, such as a belief that his running in the party's primary would repel some voters from the party? Does the court even care?

2. Could the Republican Party of Texas exclude homosexuals from holding party office? Could they exclude from nomination for public office homosexuals or persons who opposed discrimination on the basis of sexual orientation? Although no major party currently has such a policy, the Democratic Party's "Equal Division Rule" requires party delegations to contain equal numbers of men and women, thereby excluding citizens on the basis of sex from some party positions. *See* Mary T. Boyle, Note, *Affirmative Action in the Democratic Party: An Analysis of the Equal Division Rule*, 7 J.L. & Pol. 559 (1991).

3. If the Log Cabin Republicans are undeniably members of the Republican Party of Texas (and no one contested that fact), why don't they have a right to "work toward changing the Party's internal platform"?

4. Who speaks for a party? Elected officials who have received the party's nomination? Party officials? Party members? How, if at all, can rank-and-file members of the Georgia Republican Party hold the party chairman accountable for the Commission's decision? What leverage do they have over the two elected Republican officials? As Professor Lowenstein colorfully observes, "Unlike a chair, or a planet, or a baked potato, a political party is not something that occupies a particular space at a particular time or that can be discerned with the senses.... Although there have been a great many typologies of the varying 'locations' and functions of parties, probably the most common identifies three: the party in the electorate, the party organization, and the party in or running for public office." Daniel H. Lowenstein, *Associational Rights of Major Political Parties: A Skeptical Inquiry*, 71 Tex. L. Rev. 1741, 1759, 1760 (1993); *see also* V. O. Key, Parties, Politics and Pressure Groups (5th ed. 1964); Frank J. Sorauf & Paul A. Beck, Party Politics in America (4th ed. 1980); Larry J. Sabato, The Party's Just Begun: Shaping Political Parties for America's Future (1988).

5. Is *Duke* consistent with the Supreme Court's reasoning in *Nixon v. Condon*, 286 U.S. 73 (1932), the second of the White Primary cases discussed in Chapter 2? Nixon challenged his exclusion pursuant to a resolution enacted by the State Executive Committee of the Democratic Party that white Democrats, "and none other," be allowed to vote in the party's primary. Justice Cardozo's opinion for the Court found that the resolution was state action, rather than protected free association, because the resolution had been passed by the Executive Committee, "not by virtue of any authority delegated by the party, but by virtue of an authority originating or supposed to originate in the mandate of the law."

> To this committee the statute here in controversy has attempted to confide authority to determine of its own motion the requisites of party membership and in so doing to speak for the party as a whole. Never has the State convention made declaration of a will to bar Negroes of the State from admission to the party ranks.... Whatever power of exclusion has been exercised by the members of the committee has come to them, therefore, not as the delegates of the party, but as the delegates of the State.

Leaving aside the question whether *Nixon v. Condon* and *Duke v. Massey* are simply products of different times, is there an intuitive difference between a party excluding *voters* on the basis of their *race*—an immutable status—and a party excluding *candidates* on the basis of their *beliefs*? In fact, following the decisions in the White Primary Cases, several state parties did attempt to exclude black voters on the basis of belief. For example, after federal courts in South Carolina struck down the state's initial attempts to circumvent *Terry v. Adams*, "the party organized itself into clubs open only to white Democrats. Club members and blacks could vote in the primaries, but all voters were required to take an oath as follows: 'I ... solemnly swear that I understand, believe in and will support the principles of the Democratic Party of South Carolina, and that I believe in and will support the social (religious) and educational separation of the races.' Voters also were required to swear their belief in states' rights and their opposition to federal equal employment legislation." Laughlin McDonald, *The 1982 Extension of Section 5 of the Voting Rights Act of 1965: The Continued Need for Preclearance*, 51 Tenn. L. Rev. 1 (1983).

2. THE PARTY SEEKS TO EXCLUDE CITIZEN X FROM PARTICIPATING BUT THE STATE DEMANDS THAT THE PARTY PERMIT HIM TO PARTICIPATE

Democratic Party of the United States v. Wisconsin
450 U.S. 107 (1981).

■ JUSTICE STEWART delivered the opinion of the Court.

* * *

I

Rule 2A of the [National Democratic Party's] Selection Rules for the 1980 National Convention states: "Participation in the delegate selection process in primaries or caucuses shall be restricted to Democratic voters only who publicly declare their party preference and have that preference publicly recorded."

The election laws of Wisconsin allow non-Democrats—including members of other parties and independents—to vote in the Democratic primary without regard to party affiliation and without requiring a public declaration of party preference. The voters in Wisconsin's "open" primary express their choice among Presidential candidates for the Democratic Party's nomination; they do not vote for delegates to the National Convention. Delegates to the National Convention are chosen separately, after the primary, at caucuses of persons who have stated their affiliation with the Party. But these delegates, under Wisconsin law, are bound to vote at the National Convention in accord with the results of the open primary election. Accordingly, while Wisconsin's open Presidential preference primary does not itself violate National Party rules, the State's mandate that the results of the primary shall determine the allocation of votes cast by the State's delegates at the National Convention does.

* * *

II

Rule 2A can be traced to efforts of the National Party to study and reform its nominating procedures and internal structure after the 1968 Democratic National Convention. The Convention, the Party's highest governing authority, directed the Democratic National Committee (DNC) to establish a Commission on Party Structure and Delegate Selection (McGovern/Fraser Commission). This Commission concluded that a major problem faced by the Party was that rank-and-file Party members had been underrepresented at its Convention, and that the Party should "find methods which would guarantee every American who claims a stake in the Democratic Party the opportunity to make his judgment felt in the presidential nominating process." The Commission stressed that Party nominating procedures should be as open and accessible as possible to all persons who wished to join the Party, but expressed the concern that "a full opportunity for all Democrats to participate is diluted if members of other political parties are allowed to participate in the selection of delegates to the Democratic National Convention."

The 1972 Democratic National Convention also established a Commission on Delegate Selection and Party Structure (Mikulski Commission). This Commission reiterated many of the principles announced by the McGovern/Fraser Commission, but went further to propose binding rules directing state parties to restrict participation in the delegate selection process to Democratic voters. The DNC incorporated these recommendations into the Delegate Selection Rules for the 1976 Convention....

In 1975, the Party established yet another commission to review its nominating procedures, the Commission on Presidential Nomination and Party Structure (Winograd Commission). This Commission was particularly concerned with what it believed to be the dilution of the voting strength of Party members in States sponsoring open or "crossover" primaries. Indeed, the Commission based its concern in part on a study of voting behavior in Wisconsin's open primary.

The Adamany study, assessing the Wisconsin Democratic primaries from 1964 to 1972, found that crossover voters comprised 26% to 34% of the primary voters; that the voting patterns of crossover voters differed significantly from those of participants who identified themselves as Democrats; and that crossover voters altered the composition of the delegate slate chosen from Wisconsin.[19] The Winograd Commission thus recommended that the Party strengthen its rules against crossover voting, predicting that continued crossover voting "could result in a convention delegation which did not fairly reflect the division of preferences among Democratic identifiers in the electorate."

* * *

III

The question in this case is not whether Wisconsin may conduct an open primary election if it chooses to do so, or whether the National Party may require Wisconsin to limit its primary election to publicly declared Democrats. Rather, the question is whether, once Wisconsin has opened its Democratic Presidential preference primary to voters who do not publicly declare their party affiliation, it may then bind the National Party to honor

---

19. In 1964, crossovers made up 26% of the participants in the Wisconsin Democratic primary. Seven percent of those identifying themselves as Democrats voted for Governor George Wallace, but 62% of the crossovers voted for him. Three-quarters of Governor Wallace's support in the Democratic primary came from crossover voters.

In 1968, crossovers constituted 28% of the participants in the Wisconsin Democratic primary. Forty-eight percent of those who said they were Democrats voted for Senator Eugene McCarthy, while 39% voted for President Johnson. Of the crossovers, however, 70% voted for Senator McCarthy, while only 14% voted for President Johnson. Participation of crossovers increased Senator McCarthy's margin of victory over President Johnson in Wisconsin by 2 1/2 times.

In 1972, crossovers amounted to 34% of the participants. Fifty-one percent of the self-identified Democrats voted for Senator George McGovern, while only 7% voted for Governor Wallace. Of the crossovers, however, only 33% voted for Senator McGovern, while 29% voted for Governor Wallace. The study figures indicate that two-thirds of Governor Wallace's support in the Democratic primary came from crossover voters. The study found that "the participation of crossover voters will ... alter the composition of national convention delegations."....

the binding primary results, even though those results were reached in a manner contrary to National Party rules.

[We think the answer to this question is "No."]

* * *

Here, the members of the National Party, speaking through their rules, chose to define their associational rights by limiting those who could participate in the processes leading to the selection of delegates to their National Convention. On several occasions this Court has recognized that the inclusion of persons unaffiliated with a political party may seriously distort its collective decisions—thus impairing the party's essential functions—and that political parties may accordingly protect themselves "from intrusion by those with adverse political principles." In *Rosario v. Rockefeller,* for example, the Court sustained the constitutionality of a requirement—there imposed by a state statute—that a voter enroll in the party of his choice at least 30 days before the general election in order to vote in the next party primary. The purpose of that statute was "to inhibit party 'raiding,' whereby voters in sympathy with one party designate themselves as voters of another party so as to influence or determine the results of the other party's primary."

The State argues that its law places only a minor burden on the National Party. The National Party argues that the burden is substantial, because it prevents the Party from "[screening] out those whose affiliation is ... slight, tenuous, or fleeting," and that such screening is essential to build a more effective and responsible Party. But it is not for the courts to mediate the merits of this dispute. For even if the State were correct, a State, or a court, may not constitutionally substitute its own judgment for that of the Party. A political party's choice among the various ways of determining the makeup of a State's delegation to the party's national convention is protected by the Constitution. And as is true of all expressions of First Amendment freedoms, the courts may not interfere on the ground that they view a particular expression as unwise or irrational.

IV

We must consider, finally, whether the State has compelling interests that justify the imposition of its will upon the appellants.... The State asserts a compelling interest in preserving the overall integrity of the electoral process, providing secrecy of the ballot, increasing voter participation in primaries, and preventing harassment of voters. But all those interests go to the conduct of the Presidential preference primary—not to the imposition of voting requirements upon those who, in a separate process, are eventually selected as delegates. Therefore, the interests advanced by the State do not justify its substantial intrusion into the associational freedom of members of the National Party.

V

The State has a substantial interest in the manner in which its elections are conducted, and the National Party has a substantial interest in the manner in which the delegates to its National Convention are selected. But these interests are not incompatible, and to the limited extent they clash in this case, both interests can be preserved. The National Party rules do not forbid Wisconsin to conduct an open primary. But if Wisconsin does open its primary, it cannot require that Wisconsin delegates to the National Party Convention vote there in accordance with the primary results, if to do so would violate Party rules. Since the Wisconsin Supreme Court has declared that the National Party cannot disqualify delegates who are bound to vote in accordance with the results of the Wisconsin open primary, its judgment is reversed.

■ JUSTICE POWELL, with whom JUSTICE BLACKMUN and JUSTICE REHNQUIST join, dissenting.

* * *

It is significant that the Democratic Party of Wisconsin, which represents those citizens of Wisconsin willing to take part publicly in Party affairs, is here defending the state law. Moreover, the National Party's apparent concern that the outcome of the Wisconsin Presidential primary will be skewed cannot be taken seriously when one considers the alternative delegate-selection methods that are acceptable to the Party under its rules. Delegates pledged to various candidates may be selected by a caucus procedure involving a small minority of Party members, as long as all participants in the process are publicly affiliated. While such a process would eliminate "crossovers," it would be at least as likely as an open primary to reflect inaccurately the views of a State's Democrats.[6]

* * *

B

The Court does not dispute that the State serves important interests by its open primary plan. Instead the Court argues that these interests are irrelevant because they do not support a requirement that the outcome of the primary be binding on delegates chosen for the convention. This argument, however, is premised on the unstated assumption that a nonbinding primary would be an adequate mechanism for pursuing the state interests involved. This assumption is unsupportable because the very purpose of a Presidential primary, as enunciated as early as 1903 when Wisconsin passed its first primary law, was to give control over the nomination process to individual voters. Wisconsin cannot do this, and still pursue the interests underlying an open primary, without making the open

---

6. The unrepresentative nature of the delegate selections produced by caucuses is suggested by differences between the results

primary binding.[11]

* * *

NOTES AND QUESTIONS

1. *Democratic Party* involves a conflict between a *national* party and a *state* rule. Thus, one way to understand the case would be to say that single states should not be able to unilaterally regulate nationwide activities. *Cf. Anderson v. Celebrezze*, 460 U.S. 780 (1983) (observing that "in the context of a Presidential election, state-imposed restrictions implicate a uniquely important national interest"). Would the Court's analysis necessarily carry over to similar state regulations on the nomination of officeholders elected entirely within the state? The Court's observation that states have legitimate interests in conducting open primaries suggests that it would not, that is, that a state could mandate open primaries for the nomination of candidates for state and local office. If so, then does the Court's analysis turn on a match between the regulated interest and the regulator? For example, would the Court's analysis have been different if Congress, rather than the Wisconsin legislature, had passed the challenged regulation, so that a national legislature were regulating a national party?

2. Justice Powell's dissent remarks on the fact that the state Democratic Party was aligned with Wisconsin against the national party. In a state like Wisconsin, where the Democratic Party was often in power, the state's laws regulating political parties will usually (although not inevitably) reflect the state party's view. If, therefore, we view the state of Wisconsin as essentially a placeholder for the state Democratic Party, then *Democratic Party* turns out to be a lawsuit between the national and state parties. Reconceptualized in this way, does the Court's opinion provide a sufficient basis for ruling in favor of the former? Ought the Court even to be in the business of adjudicating these sorts of internecine conflicts? *Cf. Cousins v. Wigoda*, 419 U.S. 477 (1975) (holding that the Illinois state courts had no power to force the National Democratic Party to seat an Illinois delegation that violated the party's delegate selection rules). Ought state parties have any associational rights that national parties are obligated to respect?

3. Should courts consider whether there are alternative fora available for the resolution of a conflict between state and national parties before deeming such conflicts justiciable? Consider the dispute between the Wisconsin and the national Democratic parties. Whatever the legal rule an-

---

11. Any argument that a nonbinding primary would be sufficient to allow individual voters a voice in the nomination process is belied by the fact that such a primary often will be ignored in later, nonprimary delegate- of caucuses and nonbinding primaries held in the same State. *See* n. 11, infra.

selection processes. In 1980, for example, Vermont's nonbinding open primary produced a lopsided victory, 74.3% to 25.7%, for President Carter over Senator Kennedy. Party caucuses then produced a state delegation to the Democratic Convention that favored Kennedy over Carter by 7 to 5.

nounced by the Supreme Court, it had relatively little effect at ground zero. In 1988 the national party revised its rules to permit Wisconsin to use an open primary. *See* Leon D. Epstein, *Will American Political Parties Be Privatized?*, 5 J.L. & Pol. 239, 255 n.69 (1989). For a more general account of national parties and "party reform," see Nelson W. Polsby, Consequences of Party Reform (1983).

3. THE PARTY WISHES TO PERMIT CITIZEN X TO PARTICIPATE BUT THE STATE DEMANDS HER EXCLUSION

The Connecticut Republican Party that supported the state's defense of the closed primary in *Nader* executed an about-face a few years later. In 1984, the party's state convention adopted a party rule that would permit "[a]ny elector enrolled as a member of the Republican Party and any elector not enrolled as a member of a party" (that is, an independent voter) to vote in the party's primaries for Congress or statewide office. A major motivation behind the rule seemed to be the party's desire to gauge its candidates' attractiveness to independent voters. At the time, independents outnumbered Republicans roughly 5 to 4, and any successful Republican candidate would either have to appeal to independents or attract substantial Democratic crossover votes. The party's leadership in the state legislature proposed legislation to amend the closed primary law so that independents could vote in primaries when permitted by party rules. The first time the legislation came up for a vote, it was defeated in a party-line vote. In November 1984, the Republicans won a majority of the seats in both houses of the state legislature. This time the bill passed but the governor, who was a Democrat, vetoed the bill. So the Republicans brought a lawsuit.

Tashjian v. Republican Party of Connecticut
479 U.S. 208 (1986).

■ JUSTICE MARSHALL delivered the opinion of the Court.

* * *

II

* * *

The nature of appellees' First Amendment interest is evident. "It is beyond debate that freedom to engage in association for the advancement of beliefs and ideas is an inseparable aspect of the 'liberty' assured by the Due Process Clause of the Fourteenth Amendment, which embraces freedom of speech." The freedom of association protected by the First and Fourteenth Amendments includes partisan political organization. "The right to associate with the political party of one's choice is an integral part of this basic constitutional freedom."

The Party here contends that [the Connecticut statute] impermissibly burdens the right of its members to determine for themselves with whom they will associate, and whose support they will seek, in their quest for political success. The Party's attempt to broaden the base of public participation in and support for its activities is conduct undeniably central to the exercise of the right of association. As we have said, the freedom to join together in furtherance of common political beliefs "necessarily presupposes the freedom to identify the people who constitute the association."

A major state political party necessarily includes individuals playing a broad spectrum of roles in the organization's activities. Some of the Party's members devote substantial portions of their lives to furthering its political and organizational goals, others provide substantial financial support, while still others limit their participation to casting their votes for some or all of the Party's candidates. Considered from the standpoint of the Party itself, the act of formal enrollment or public affiliation with the Party is merely one element in the continuum of participation in Party affairs, and need not be in any sense the most important.

Were the State to restrict by statute financial support of the Party's candidates to Party members, or to provide that only Party members might be selected as the Party's chosen nominees for public office, such a prohibition of potential association with nonmembers would clearly infringe upon the rights of the Party's members under the First Amendment to organize with like-minded citizens in support of common political goals.... The statute here places limits upon the group of registered voters whom the Party may invite to participate in the "basic function" of selecting the Party's candidates. The State thus limits the Party's associational opportunities at the crucial juncture at which the appeal to common principles may be translated into concerted action, and hence to political power in the community.

It is, of course, fundamental to appellant's defense of the State's statute that this impingement upon the associational rights of the Party and its members occurs at the ballot box, for the Constitution grants to the States a broad power to prescribe the "Times, Places and Manner of holding Elections for Senators and Representatives," Art. I, § 4, cl. 1, which power is matched by state control over the election process for state offices. But this authority does not extinguish the State's responsibility to observe the limits established by the First Amendment rights of the State's citizens. The power to regulate the time, place, and manner of elections does not justify, without more, the abridgment of fundamental rights.... We turn then to an examination of the interests which appellant asserts to justify the burden cast by the statute upon the associational rights of the Party and its members.

III

Appellant contends that [the Connecticut statute] is a narrowly tailored regulation which advances the State's compelling interests by ensuring the administrability of the primary system, preventing raiding, avoiding voter confusion, and protecting the responsibility of party government.

A

... Appellant contends that the Party's rule would require the purchase of additional voting machines, the training of additional poll workers, and potentially the printing of additional ballot materials specifically intended for independents voting in the Republican primary. In essence, appellant claims that the administration of the system contemplated by the Party rule would simply cost the State too much.

Even assuming the factual accuracy of these contentions, ... the possibility of future increases in the cost of administering the election system is not a sufficient basis here for infringing appellees' First Amendment rights.... While the State is of course entitled to take administrative and financial considerations into account in choosing whether or not to have a primary system at all, it can no more restrain the Republican Party's freedom of association for reasons of its own administrative convenience than it could on the same ground limit the ballot access of a new major party.

B

Appellant argues that [the Connecticut statute] is justified as a measure to prevent raiding, a practice "whereby voters in sympathy with one party designate themselves as voters of another party so as to influence or determine the results of the other party's primary." While we have recognized that "a State may have a legitimate interest in seeking to curtail 'raiding,' since that practice may affect the integrity of the electoral process," that interest is not implicated here. The statute as applied to the Party's rule prevents independents, who otherwise cannot vote in any primary, from participating in the Republican primary. Yet a raid on the Republican Party primary by independent voters, a curious concept ... is not impeded by [the statute]; the independent raiders need only register as Republicans ... as late as noon on the business day preceding the primary....

C

Appellant's next argument is that the closed primary system avoids voter confusion. Appellant contends that "[the] legislature could properly find that it would be difficult for the general public to understand what a candidate stood for who was nominated in part by an unknown amorphous body outside the party, while nevertheless using the party name." Appellees respond that the State is attempting to act as the ideological guarantor of the Republican Party's candidates, ensuring that voters are not misled by a "Republican" candidate who professes something other than what the State regards as true Republican principles.

As we have said, "[there] can be no question about the legitimacy of the State's interest in fostering informed and educated expressions of the popular will in a general election." To the extent that party labels provide a shorthand designation of the views of party candidates on matters of public concern, the identification of candidates with particular parties plays a role in the process by which voters inform themselves for the exercise of the franchise. Appellant's argument depends upon the belief that voters can be "misled" by party labels. But "[our] cases reflect a greater faith in the ability of individual voters to inform themselves about campaign issues." Moreover, appellant's concern that candidates selected under the Party rule will be the nominees of an "amorphous" group using the Party's name is inconsistent with the facts. The Party is not proposing that independents be allowed to choose the Party's nominee without Party participation; on the contrary, to be listed on the Party's primary ballot continues to require, under a statute not challenged here, that the primary candidate have obtained at least 20% of the vote at a Party convention, which only Party members may attend....

In arguing that the Party rule interferes with educated decisions by voters, appellant also disregards the substantial benefit which the Party rule provides to the Party and its members in seeking to choose successful candidates. Given the numerical strength of independent voters in the State, one of the questions most likely to occur to Connecticut Republicans in selecting candidates for public office is how can the Party most effectively appeal to the independent voter? By inviting independents to assist in the choice at the polls between primary candidates selected at the Party convention, the Party rule is intended to produce the candidate and platform most likely to achieve that goal. The state statute is said to decrease voter confusion, yet it deprives the Party and its members of the opportunity to inform themselves as to the level of support for the Party's candidates among a critical group of electors. "A State's claim that it is enhancing the ability of its citizenry to make wise decisions by restricting the flow of information to them must be viewed with some skepticism." ...

D

Finally, appellant contends that [the Connecticut statute] furthers the State's compelling interest in protecting the integrity of the two-party system and the responsibility of party government....

The relative merits of closed and open primaries have been the subject of substantial debate since the beginning of this century, and no consensus has as yet emerged. Appellant invokes a long and distinguished line of political scientists and public officials who have been supporters of the closed primary. But our role is not to decide whether the state legislature was acting wisely in enacting the closed primary system in 1955, or whether the Republican Party makes a mistake in seeking to depart from the practice of the past 30 years.

[. . .] In the present case, the state statute is defended on the ground that it protects the integrity of the Party against the Party itself.

Under these circumstances, the views of the State, which to some extent represent the views of the one political party transiently enjoying majority power, as to the optimum methods for preserving party integrity lose much of their force. The State argues that its statute is well designed to save the Republican Party from undertaking a course of conduct destructive of its own interests. But on this point "even if the State were correct, a State, or a court, may not constitutionally substitute its own judgment for that of the Party." The Party's determination of the boundaries of its own association, and of the structure which best allows it to pursue its political goals, is protected by the Constitution. "And as is true of all expressions of First Amendment freedoms, the courts may not interfere on the ground that they view a particular expression as unwise or irrational."

* * *

■ JUSTICE SCALIA, with whom THE CHIEF JUSTICE and JUSTICE O'CONNOR join, dissenting.

In my view, the Court's opinion exaggerates the importance of the associational interest at issue, if indeed it does not see one where none exists. There is no question here of restricting the Republican Party's ability to recruit and enroll Party members by offering them the ability to select Party candidates; [Connecticut law] permits an independent voter to join the Party as late as the day before the primary. Nor is there any question of restricting the ability of the Party's members to select whatever candidate they desire. Appellees' only complaint is that the Party cannot leave the selection of its candidate to persons who are not members of the Party, and are unwilling to become members. It seems to me fanciful to refer to this as an interest in freedom of association between the members of the Republican Party and the putative independent voters. The Connecticut voter who, while steadfastly refusing to register as a Republican, casts a vote in the Republican primary, forms no more meaningful an "association" with the Party than does the independent or the registered Democrat who responds to questions by a Republican Party pollster. If the concept of freedom of association is extended to such casual contacts, it ceases to be of any analytic use.

The ability of the members of the Republican Party to select their own candidate, on the other hand, unquestionably implicates an associational freedom—but it can hardly be thought that that freedom is unconstitutionally impaired here. The Party is entirely free to put forward, if it wishes, that candidate who has the highest degree of support among Party members and independents combined. The State is under no obligation, however, to let its party primary be used, instead of a party-funded opinion poll, as the means by which the party identifies the relative popularity of its potential candidates among independents. Nor is there any reason apparent to me why the State cannot insist that this decision to support what might be called the independents' choice be taken by the party membership in a democratic fashion, rather than through a process that permits the members' votes to be diluted—and perhaps even absolutely outnumbered—by the votes of outsiders.

The Court's opinion characterizes this, disparagingly, as an attempt to "[protect] the integrity of the Party against the Party itself." There are two problems with this characterization. The first, and less important, is that it is not true. We have no way of knowing that a majority of the Party's members is in favor of allowing ultimate selection of its candidates for federal and statewide office to be determined by persons outside the Party. That decision was not made by democratic ballot, but by the Party's state convention—which, for all we know, may have been dominated by officeholders and office seekers whose evaluation of the merits of assuring election of the Party's candidates, vis-a-vis the merits of proposing candidates faithful to the Party's political philosophy, diverged significantly from the views of the Party's rank and file. I had always thought it was a major purpose of state-imposed party primary requirements to protect the general party membership against this sort of minority control. Second and more important, however, even if it were the fact that the majority of the Party's members wanted its candidates to be determined by outsiders, there is no reason why the State is bound to honor that desire—any more than it would be bound to honor a party's democratically expressed desire that its candidates henceforth be selected by convention rather than by primary, or by the party's executive committee in a smoke-filled room. In other words, the validity of the state-imposed primary requirement itself, which we have hitherto considered "too plain for argument," presupposes that the State has the right "to protect the Party against the Party itself." Connecticut may lawfully require that significant elements of the democratic election process be democratic—whether the Party wants that or not. It is beyond my understanding why the Republican Party's delegation of its democratic choice to a Republican Convention can be proscribed, but its delegation of that choice to nonmembers of the Party cannot.

* * *

NOTES AND QUESTIONS

1. After *Democratic Party* and *Tashjian* is the rule that, in a conflict between a state and a party over who can participate in the party's nomination process, the party invariably wins? Must Connecticut now apply different rules for voting in the Democratic and Republican primaries, permitting only party members to vote in the former, while permitting party members and independents to vote in the latter? Consider an equal protection claim by an independent voter who argues that independents who want to vote in the Republican primary are able to vote but independents who want to vote in the Democratic primary cannot and thus that the state treats Democratic-leaning independents worse than Republican ones. Would the parties' First Amendment rights trump the voter's equal protection claim? What about a claim by a Republican voter that the state is treating him differently than a Democratic voter because it administers a system in which his primary vote is "diluted" by the votes of outsiders while the Democrat's vote is not? Note that in the White Primary Cases, black voters' equal protection/Fifteenth Amendment claims trumped party First Amendment associational rights. Is Justice Marshall's position as a justice in *Tashjian* entirely consistent with his position as counsel for the plaintiff in *Smith v. Allwright*?

2. Does *Tashjian* overrule *Democratic Party*'s suggestion that Wisconsin was entitled to conduct open primaries?

3. The Court places substantial weight on the fact that the Republican Party was not seeking to permit participation by voters who were registered members of other parties. Why is that fact relevant? Should it be? What would happen if the Court allowed part of the balance to be an individual voter's First Amendment interest in effective political participation? Put somewhat differently, is there any reason to suppose that the Republicans have less of an interest in associating with a Democratic voter who wishes to associate with them than with an independent voter?

4. Professor Lowenstein argues that *Tashjian* represented "a significant and ... unwelcome step beyond the Court's earlier decisions" about the associational rights of parties. Daniel H. Lowenstein, *Associational Rights of Major Political Parties: A Skeptical Inquiry*, 71 Tex. L. Rev. 1741, 1742 (1993). Given that one key element of a political party is party members who are public officials, "a party subject to state legislation operates under rules devised by the elected officials who make up the party in government. They are nominated by a process that, however imperfect, is vastly more democratic than is possible in the case of party officials, and their stake in the electoral success of the party is more immediate and personal than can be the case for party officials." *Id.* at 1770. If this is so, then many "party vs. the state" lawsuits can be recast as "party-organization vs. party-in-government" disputes, thereby lessening the justification for judicial deference to the party organization position. His general position is that "both the substance of the rules affecting parties and the question of who sets these rules should ordinarily be resolved in the give-and-take of the political process, and that extragovernmental party organizations should not enjoy a constitutional position that immunizes them from the results of that give-and-take." *Id.* at 1771.

5. In *Rosario v. Rockefeller*, 410 U.S. 752 (1973), the Supreme Court upheld a New York law that required voters to enroll in the party of their choice at least 30 days before the general election in November in order to vote in the next subsequent, closed, party primary. The cutoff date for enrollment was thus roughly eight months before the presidential, and eleven months before a nonpresidential, primary. The Court held that the statute was a permissible effort to prevent interparty "raiding" and did not unduly burden voters' ability to participate in the affairs of the party of their choice. Connecticut's statute seemed far less onerous, since it allowed voters to affiliate up until right before a party's primary. Thus, it both lowered the burden on voters and lowered its efficacy as a hedge on raiding.

C. When Can the Government Regulate a Party's Internal Affairs?

Parties do more than simply nominate candidates for discrete offices. For example, they promulgate platforms, collect and distribute campaign funds, appoint election judges, and set nomination policies. The party organization is thus in some senses the "intermediary's intermediary," interacting both with the party in the electorate and with the party in government. As we saw in the preceding section, to some extent it may determine the membership of each of the other branches of the party. When can the other branches determine how the party organization is constituted?

Eu v. San Francisco County Democratic Central Committee

489 U.S. 214 (1989).

■ Justice Marshall delivered the opinion of the Court.

* * *

I

A

The State of California heavily regulates its political parties. Although the laws vary in extent and detail from party to party, certain requirements apply to all "ballot-qualified" parties [which includes the Democratic, Republican, American Independent, and Peace and Freedom parties]. The California Elections Code (Code) provides that the "official governing bodies" for such a party are its "state convention," "state central committee," and "county central committees," and that these bodies are responsible for conducting the party's campaigns. At the same time, the Code provides that the official governing bodies "shall not endorse, support, or oppose, any candidate for nomination by that party for partisan office in the direct primary election." It is a misdemeanor for any primary candidate, or a person on her behalf, to claim that she is the officially endorsed candidate of the party.

Although the official governing bodies of political parties are barred from issuing endorsements, other groups are not. Political clubs affiliated with a party, labor organizations, political action committees, other politically active associations, and newspapers frequently endorse primary candidates. With the official party organizations silenced by the ban, it has been possible for a candidate with views antithetical to those of her party nevertheless to win its primary.[4]

In addition to restricting the primary activities of the official governing bodies of political parties, California also regulates their internal affairs. Separate statutory provisions dictate the size and composition of the state central committees; set forth rules governing the selection and removal of committee members; fix the maximum term of office for the chair of the state central committee; require that the chair rotate between residents of northern and southern California; specify the time and place of committee meetings; and limit the dues parties may impose on members. Violations of these provisions are criminal offenses punishable by fine and imprisonment.

* * *

II

A State's broad power to regulate the time, place, and manner of elections "does not extinguish the State's responsibility to observe the limits established by the First Amendment rights of the State's citizens." To assess the constitutionality of a state election law, we first examine whether it burdens rights protected by the First and Fourteenth Amendments. If the challenged law burdens the rights of political parties and their members, it can survive constitutional scrutiny only if the State shows that it advances a compelling state interest, and is narrowly tailored to serve that interest.

A

We first consider California's prohibition on primary endorsements by the official governing bodies of political parties. California concedes that its ban implicates the First Amendment, but contends that the burden is "minuscule." We disagree. The ban directly affects speech which "is at the core of our electoral process and of the First Amendment freedoms." We have recognized repeatedly that "debate on the qualifications of candidates [is] integral to the operation of the system of government established by our Constitution." Indeed, the First Amendment "has its fullest and most

---

4. In 1980, for example, Tom Metzger won the Democratic Party's nomination for United States House of Representative from the San Diego area, although he was a Grand Dragon of the Ku Klux Klan and held views antithetical to those of the Democratic Party.

urgent application" to speech uttered during a campaign for political office. Free discussion about candidates for public office is no less critical before a primary than before a general election. In both instances, the "election campaign is a means of disseminating ideas as well as attaining political office."

California's ban on primary endorsements, however, prevents party governing bodies from stating whether a candidate adheres to the tenets of the party or whether party officials believe that the candidate is qualified for the position sought. This prohibition directly hampers the ability of a party to spread its message and hamstrings voters seeking to inform themselves about the candidates and the campaign issues. A "highly paternalistic approach" limiting what people may hear is generally suspect, but it is particularly egregious where the State censors the political speech a political party shares with its members.

Barring political parties from endorsing and opposing candidates not only burdens their freedom of speech but also infringes upon their freedom of association. It is well settled that partisan political organizations enjoy freedom of association protected by the First and Fourteenth Amendments. Freedom of association means not only that an individual voter has the right to associate with the political party of her choice, but also that a political party has a right to "identify the people who constitute the association," and to select a "standard bearer who best represents the party's ideologies and preferences."

Depriving a political party of the power to endorse suffocates this right. The endorsement ban prevents parties from promoting candidates "at the crucial juncture at which the appeal to common principles may be translated into concerted action, and hence to political power in the community." Even though individual members of the state central committees and county central committees are free to issue endorsements, imposing limitations "on individuals wishing to band together to advance their views on a ballot measure, while placing none on individuals acting alone, is clearly a restraint on the right of association."

Because the ban burdens appellees' rights to free speech and free association, it can only survive constitutional scrutiny if it serves a compelling governmental interest. The State offers two: stable government and protecting voters from confusion and undue influence. Maintaining a stable political system is, unquestionably, a compelling state interest. California, however, never adequately explains how banning parties from endorsing or opposing primary candidates advances that interest. There is no showing, for example, that California's political system is any more stable now than it was in 1963, when the legislature enacted the ban. Nor does the State explain what makes the California system so peculiar that it is virtually the only State that has determined that such a ban is necessary.

The only explanation the State offers is that its compelling interest in stable government embraces a similar interest in party stability. . . . States may regulate elections to ensure that "some sort of order, rather than chaos ... accompanies the democratic processes." ... [But we have never held] that a State may enact election laws to mitigate intraparty factionalism during a primary campaign. To the contrary, [we have stated that] ... [a] primary is not hostile to intraparty feuds; rather it is an ideal forum in which to resolve them....

It is no answer to argue, as does the State, that a party that issues primary endorsements risks intraparty friction which may endanger the party's general election prospects. Presumably a party will be motivated by self-interest and not engage in acts or speech that run counter to its political success. However, even if a ban on endorsements saves a political party from pursuing self-destructive acts, that would not justify a State substituting its judgment for that of the party. Because preserving party unity during a primary is not a compelling state interest, we must look elsewhere to justify the challenged law.

The State's second justification for the ban on party endorsements and statements of opposition is that it is necessary to protect primary voters from confusion and undue influence. Certainly the State has a legitimate interest in fostering an informed electorate. However, "[a] State's claim that it is enhancing the ability of its citizenry to make wise decisions by restricting the flow of information to them must be viewed with some skepticism."

Because the ban on primary endorsements by political parties burdens political speech while serving no compelling governmental interest, we hold that [it] violate[s] the First and Fourteenth Amendment.

B

We turn next to California's restrictions on the organization and composition of official governing bodies, the limits on the term of office for state central committee chair, and the requirement that the chair rotate between residents of northern and southern California. These laws directly implicate the associational rights of political parties and their members....

The laws at issue burden these rights. By requiring parties to establish official governing bodies at the county level, California prevents the political parties from governing themselves with the structure they think best.[20] And by specifying who shall be the members of the parties' official governing bodies, California interferes with the parties' choice of leaders. A party might decide, for example, that it will be more effective if a greater number of its official leaders are local activists rather than Washington-based elected officials. The Code prevents such a change. A party might also decide that the state central committee chair needs more than two years to successfully formulate and implement policy. The Code prevents

20. For example, the Libertarian Party was forced to abandon its region-based organization in favor of the statutorily mandated county-based system.

such an extension of the chair's term of office. A party might find that a resident of northern California would be particularly effective in promoting the party's message and in unifying the party. The Code prevents her from chairing the state central committee unless the preceding chair was from the southern part of the State.

Each restriction thus limits a political party's discretion in how to organize itself, conduct its affairs, and select its leaders. Indeed, the associational rights at stake are much stronger than those we credited in *Tashjian*. There, we found that a party's right to free association embraces a right to allow registered voters who are not party members to vote in the party's primary. Here, party members do not seek to associate with nonparty members, but only with one another in freely choosing their party leaders.

Because the challenged laws burden the associational rights of political parties and their members, the question is whether they serve a compelling state interest. A State indisputably has a compelling interest in preserving the integrity of its election process. Toward that end, a State may enact laws that interfere with a party's internal affairs when necessary to ensure that elections are fair and honest. For example, ... a State may impose restrictions that promote the integrity of primary elections. *See, e.g., American Party of Texas v. White* (limitation on voters' participation to one primary and bar on voters both voting in a party primary and signing a petition supporting an independent candidate); *Rosario v. Rockefeller* (waiting periods before voters may change party registration and participate in another party's primary). None of these restrictions, however, involved direct regulation of a party's leaders. Rather, the infringement on the associational rights of the parties and their members was the indirect consequence of laws necessary to the successful completion of a party's external responsibilities in ensuring the order and fairness of elections.

In the instant case, the State has not shown that its regulation of internal party governance is necessary to the integrity of the electoral process. Instead, it contends that the challenged laws serve a compelling "interest in the democratic management of the political party's internal affairs." This, however, is not a case where intervention is necessary to prevent the derogation of the civil rights of party adherents. *Cf. Smith v. Allwright.* Moreover, as we have observed, the State has no interest in "protecting the integrity of the Party against the Party itself." ...

In sum, a State cannot justify regulating a party's internal affairs without showing that such regulation is necessary to ensure an election that is orderly and fair. Because California has made no such showing here, the challenged laws cannot be upheld.

* * *

NOTES AND QUESTIONS

1. California had argued that strict scrutiny was not required because the major political parties had "consented" to the statutory regime in that the parties could have achieved the statute's repeal through the legislative process had they wished to. Justice Marshall gave that argument short shrift:

> California's consent argument is contradicted by the simple fact that the official governing bodies of various political parties have joined this lawsuit....
>
> Simply because a legislator belongs to a political party does not make her at all times a representative of party interests. In supporting the endorsement ban, an individual legislator may be acting on her understanding of the public good or her interest in reelection. The independence of legislators from their parties is illustrated by the California Legislature's frequent refusal to amend the election laws in accordance with the wishes of political parties. Moreover, the State's argument ignores those parties with negligible, if any, representation in the legislature.

How persuasive is Justice Marshall's response? Why ought we assume that the particular officials who controlled the San Francisco County Democratic Central Committee at the time of this litigation were better "representatives" of the party? Are the legislators "independent" of their parties or simply more responsive to the "party in the electorate" than the "party organization"? In this respect, consider Professor Lowenstein's analysis:

> The question of who speaks for the party was especially embarrassing in *Eu*.... Only if the plaintiffs could speak for the Democratic and Republican parties was the posture of *Eu* comparable to that of *Tashjian*.
>
> * * *
>
> Even if ... one unrealistically exalts the legal status of the California central committees, the handful of county central committees that were plaintiffs in *Eu* cannot be regarded as speaking for the parties as a whole with regard to the statewide associational claims that were asserted. The Court simply swept under the rug the inconvenient fact that neither major-party state central committee was a plaintiff or otherwise had expressed a desire to assert the associational claims. Perhaps the Court believed the Ninth Circuit had dealt adequately with this fact. The lower court had asserted that legislators so dominated the membership of the state central committees that it was wrong for the legislature to benefit from the committees' consequent unwillingness to challenge the constraints under which they labored. Perhaps under these circumstances the silence of the state central committees

should not bar the claim that "the parties" seek freedom from legislative control, but nowhere in its opinion did the Ninth Circuit give any affirmative reason to believe that the scattered individual and county central committee plaintiffs spoke for "the Republicans" or "the Democrats." . . . [168]

Daniel H. Lowenstein, *Associational Rights of Major Political Parties: A Skeptical Inquiry*, 71 Tex. L. Rev. 1741, 1781–82 (1993).

2. There are a variety of reasons why a party might embed particular rules in the law, rather than simply in party rules. Perhaps this represents a precommitment strategy in which the party binds its future self to avoid self-destructive acts. In this sense, a party's seeking statutory regulation might be akin to implanting a particular rule in the constitution rather than in an easy-to-modify or repeal statute. *Eu* might be read to deprive parties of this hands-tying ability. Paradoxically, then, *Eu* might end up denying, rather than protecting, party autonomy. Would the validation of a party's precommitment strategy be consistent with the Court's decisions in the White Primary Cases?

3. Is Justice Marshall correct that California is not intervening "to prevent the derogation of the civil rights of party adherents"? Is racial discrimination the only way in which a party might deny its adherents their civil rights? The party's ambiguous stance as sometimes state actor and sometimes private, specially protected association makes this a difficult question. Suppose, for example, that a party imposed restrictions on its adherents that would, if imposed by the state directly, violate First Amendment rights. Would states be totally disempowered from protecting those members against retaliation for exercising their First Amendment rights?

4. In its discussion of the regulations of party structure, the Court seems to be giving parties heightened First Amendment associational protection. After all, a state could presumably regulate the composition of boards of directors of corporations chartered within the state. For example, many states require boards of directors to be elected by cumulative voting, a semi-proportional representation system. But *Eu* suggests this sort of regulation becomes unconstitutional if the corporation is a political party. Why?

5. As for the anti-endorsement provision, if a "party" picks its candidates through a primary election, how can the "party" endorse a candidate before it has indicated its preference? This paradox highlights the ambiguous definition of the "party." In a related area, after protracted litigation, a

---

168. . . . As between the partisan elected representatives in the state legislature and the ragtag collection of plaintiffs in *Eu*, there seems to me to be very little contest. . . . But if the *Eu* plaintiffs cannot speak for the party, it makes no sense to say that their associational rights as individual members have been infringed. To the contrary, in this view of the case the plaintiffs are simply dissenting members who disagree with the procedures the party (speaking through the medium of state law) has chosen for its self-governance.

federal district court recently struck down California's ban on party endorsement of candidates in nonpartisan elections. See *California Democratic Party v. Lungren,* 919 F.Supp. 1397 (N.D.Cal.1996).

6. Is a political party's decision about how to finance its nomination process subject to governmental oversight? In *Morse v. Republican Party of Virginia,* 116 S.Ct. 1186 (1996), the Supreme Court reviewed the defendants' decision to hold a nominating convention, rather than a primary, to select its candidate for United States Senate, and to charge individuals who wished to attend the convention a $45 registration fee. The Court held that these decisions were covered by section 5 of the Voting Rights Act of 1965, 42 U.S.C. § 1973c (1994), which forbids certain "states" from making any change in their voting laws without receiving prior approval from the Federal Government. (Section 5 is the subject of the next chapter of this book.) Although the majority did not unite behind a single opinion, both Justice Stevens's opinion and Justice Breyer's found that the party was a state actor in performing its nominating function (relying on the White Primary Cases) and both opinions rejected the party's First Amendment claim. According to Justice Stevens, who was joined by Justice Ginsburg, the party never explained how "the registration fee at issue in this case . . . is itself protected by the First Amendment." He also rejected the argument that the requirement that a party obtain federal approval before implementing a new practice was "a 'classic prior restraint.' It imposes no restraint at all on speech. Given the past history of discrimination that gave rise to the preclearance remedy imposed by § 5, the minimal burden on the right of association implicated in this case is unquestionably justified." Similarly, Justice Breyer, joined by Justices O'Connor and Souter, found that the fee "lies . . . well outside the area of greatest 'associational concern.'" Suppose the Republican Party had proclaimed an ideological reason for requiring payment (e.g., because it wanted to measure participants' "commitment to the party"). Would, or should, the Court's response be different then? Moreover, does *Eu* suggest that the First Amendment rights attach to the party's right of self-governance, rather than to the speech value of its particular choices?

D. DOES THE EXISTING LEGAL REGIME IMPROPERLY ENTRENCH THE EXISTING TWO–PARTY SYSTEM?

As we have already seen, every state limits, to some extent, which potential candidates' names appear on the ballot. Candidates nominated by the Democratic or Republican parties appear on the ballot in every state; often they are the *only* candidates on the general election ballot. For most of our history, American politics at the national level has been based on a two-party system. (In certain places, such as the Solid South of the early twentieth century, there was effectively only one political party.) But there is nothing inevitable about a two-party system. Two-party systems are the product of a series of conscious and unconscious choices about how electoral politics ought to be structured. Nor is the presence of two, and only two, parties necessary for a robust democracy. Countries such as Germany, Israel, the Netherlands, and Finland all have multiparty democracies. We will turn to these issues more directly in Chapter 11.

While the United States' two-party politics may in part be the result of historical contingency, this by no means suggests that the survival of the two-party system is accidental. Once a two-party system is in place, the beneficiaries—namely, the parties who achieve electoral success—may engage in a variety of behaviors designed to perpetuate the privileged positions they won, perhaps fortuitously, during an earlier time. By contrast, a party whose candidates are not on the ballot is highly unlikely to win any elections. Concomitantly, a party whose candidates fail to attract substantial support may find its candidates excluded from the ballot in the future. Thus, access to the ballot is a critical juncture for the emergence of new parties. And it is at this juncture that American state legislatures, composed virtually entirely of partisans of the two established parties, have strenuously resisted the recognition of new parties.

1. CHALLENGES TO BALLOT ACCESS BY INDEPENDENT AND THIRD-PARTY CANDIDATES

The Supreme Court first gave serious attention to the influence of ballot access laws in *Williams v. Rhodes*, 393 U.S. 23 (1968). The case concerned placement on the presidential election ballot. Parties whose candidate for governor at the last election received at least 10 percent of the votes cast were automatically given lines on the ballot. Other parties that wanted their candidate's name to appear were required to gather petition signatures from a number of voters equal to 15 percent of the ballots cast in the last gubernatorial election and to file those petitions by early February of the election year (substantially before the major parties had chosen their candidates).

In 1967, George Wallace decided to run for president as a third-party candidate. The Ohio American Independent Party was formed in January 1968, and during the next six months it obtained over 450,000 signatures, which easily exceeded the 15 percent requirement. But the Ohio secretary of state denied the party's request for a place on the ballot because the February deadline had expired. The Court held that Ohio's law violated the equal protection clause because it gave the two established parties a decided advantage over new parties. It found that Ohio's restrictive ballot access procedure heavily burdened the right of individuals to associate for the advancement of political beliefs and the right of qualified voters to cast their votes effectively, and that the state had shown no "compelling interest" justifying those burdens:

[Ohio] claims that the State may validly promote a two-party system in order to encourage compromise and political stability. The fact is, however, that the Ohio system does not merely favor a "two-party system"; it favors two particular parties—the Republicans and the Democrats—and in effect tends to give them a complete monopoly. There is, of course, no reason why two parties should retain a permanent monopoly on the right to have people vote for or against them. Competition in ideas and governmental policies is at the core of our electoral process and of the First Amendment freedoms. New parties struggling for their place must have the time and opportunity to organize in order to meet reasonable requirements for ballot position, just as the old parties have had in the past.

Ohio makes a variety of other arguments to support its very restrictive election laws. It points out, for example, that if three or more parties are on the ballot, it is possible that no one party would obtain 50% of the vote, and the runner-up might have been preferred to the plurality winner by a majority of the voters. Concededly, the State does have an interest in attempting to see that the election winner be the choice of a majority of its voters. But to grant the State power to keep all political parties off the ballot until they have enough members to win would stifle the growth of all new parties working to increase their strength from year to year. *Id.* at 31–32.

While the 15 percent requirement, coupled with the excessively early filing deadline might run afoul of the Constitution, less onerous requirements were permissible. In *Jenness v. Fortson*, 403 U.S. 431 (1971), the Court upheld Georgia's requirement that independent candidates secure supporting signatures amounting to 5 percent of the total registered voters in the last election for filling the office sought by the candidate.

In 1974, the Supreme Court decided another pair of ballot access cases, involving the rights of third-party and independent candidates. *Storer v. Brown*, 415 U.S. 724 (1974), concerned several provisions of the California Election Code. Section 6830 made independent candidates ineligible for placement on the ballot if they had voted in the immediately preceding primary or had been registered members of an existing political party within one year prior to the immediately preceding primary election. Section 6831 required independent candidates to file nomination papers signed by a number of voters between 5 and 6 percent of the entire vote cast in the preceding general election in the area served by the office they were seeking; these signatures had to be obtained during a 24–day period following the primary and ending 60 days prior to the general election, and none of the signatures could be from a person who voted in a primary.

The Court began its analysis by noting that although *Williams v. Rhodes* and the right-to-vote cases such as *Dunn v. Blumstein* and *Kramer v. Union Free School District* (covered in Chapter 2) had applied heightened scrutiny, not every "substantial restriction on the right to vote or to associate" required invalidation of a state statute. "[A]s a practical matter, there must be a substantial regulation of elections if they are to be fair and honest and if some sort of order, rather than chaos, is to accompany the democratic processes":

> It is very unlikely that all or even a large portion of the state election laws would fail to pass muster under our cases; and the rule fashioned by the Court to pass on constitutional challenges to specific provisions of election laws provides no litmus-paper test for separating those restrictions that are valid from those that are invidious under the Equal Protection Clause. The rule is not self-executing and is no substitute for the hard judgments that must be made. Decision in this context, as in others, is very much a "matter of degree," very much a matter of "consider[ing] the facts and circumstances behind the law, the interests which the State claims to be protecting, and the interests of those who are disadvantaged by the classification." What the result of this process will be in any specific case may be very difficult to predict with great assurance. *Id.* at 730.

With regard to the "sore loser" statute, the Court found it legitimate in light of the integral role primary elections played in the state's overall electoral scheme:

> The direct party primary in California is not merely an exercise or warm-up for the general election but an integral part of the entire election process, the initial stage in a two-stage process by which the people choose their public officers. It functions to winnow out and finally reject all but the chosen candidates. The State's general policy is to have contending forces within the party employ the primary campaign and primary election to finally settle their differences. The general election ballot is reserved for major struggles; it is not a forum for continuing intraparty feuds. The provision against defeated primary candidates running as independents effectuates this aim, the visible result being to prevent the losers from continuing the struggle and to limit the names on the ballot to those who have won the primaries and those independents who have properly qualified. The people, it is hoped, are presented with understandable choices and the winner in the general election with sufficient support to govern effectively.
>
> [California's law] protects the direct primary process by refusing to recognize independent candidates who do not make early plans to leave a party and take the alternative course to the ballot. It works against independent candidacies prompted by short-range political goals, pique, or personal quarrel. It is also a substantial barrier to a party fielding an "independent" candidate to capture

and bleed off votes in the general election that might well go to another party.

A State need not take the course California has, but California apparently believes with the Founding Fathers that splintered parties and unrestrained factionalism may do significant damage to the fabric of government. *See The Federalist, No. 10* (Madison). It appears obvious to us that the one-year disaffiliation provision furthers the State's interest in the stability of its political system. We also consider that interest as not only permissible, but compelling and as outweighing the interest the candidate and his supporters may have in making a late rather than an early decision to seek independent ballot status. *Id.* at 735–36.

Note the extent to which the Court's opinion channels the acceptable forms of political sentiment. It puts "short-range political goals" and "pique" outside the boundaries of acceptable reasons for candidates to run and delegitimates these as sources to inform voter choice.

With respect to the signature requirement, the Court remanded for additional factfinding. The disqualification of voters who had participated in primaries was unproblematic. As the Court explained at greater length in another case decided the same day, *American Party of Texas v. White*, 415 U.S. 767 (1974), such a disqualification simply limited each voter to one nominating event for each office on the ballot. But its interaction with the 5 percent requirement might pose problems. In *Jenness*, the Court had intimated that 5 percent was near the high end of the range of permissible measures of support. If most voters had in fact voted in the primaries, then 5 percent of the pool of all voters might be closer to 10 percent of the pool of eligible signatories, and that might unreasonably freeze out new parties.

Storer's acknowledgment of the central indeterminacy of the Court's test was borne out over the next two decades. In *Anderson v. Celebrezze*, 460 U.S. 780 (1983), for example, the Court struck down Ohio's early filing deadline for independent presidential candidates. Although the Court recognized that the right of voters to express their choice for political office was "fundamental," the Court reiterated that "not all restrictions imposed by the States on candidates' eligibility for the ballot impose constitutionally suspect burdens on voters' rights to associate or to choose among candidates." A court faced with a challenge to the restriction of ballot access "must first consider the character and magnitude of the asserted injury to the rights protected by the First and Fourteenth Amendments that the plaintiff seeks to vindicate. It then must identify and evaluate the precise interests put forward by the State as justifications for the burden imposed by its rule. In passing judgment, the Court must not only determine the legitimacy and strength of each of those interests, it also must consider the extent to which those interests make it necessary to burden the plaintiff's rights. Only after weighing all these factors is the reviewing court in a position to decide whether the challenged provision is unconstitutional."

Anderson, taken at its word, appears to impose a searching form of scrutiny on any state infringement on ballot access. It appears unlikely that any of the ballot restrictions covered in this Chapter could withstand a literal application of the standard of review set forth by Justice Stevens in *Anderson.* Perhaps for that reason, *Anderson* is largely disregarded in subsequent court opinions.

What explains the Court's inability to articulate a clear, easy-to-apply test to ballot restrictions? To what extent is the Court asking simply the sort of hypothetical question often at issue in rational-basis scrutiny cases, namely, "can we conceive of a way in which the challenged statute is rationally related to a legitimate governmental purpose"? To what extent is it demanding that the state provide empirical evidence to back up its claims? At what level of specificity or generality is the state's interest assessed? Everyone can agree that protecting the integrity of the electoral system is a compelling government interest, but the Court never defines what "integrity" consists of. Finally, on whose behalf does a state claim to articulate a specific interest in electoral rules? Since state governments are dominated by the two major parties, should courts be more suspicious of state claims to protect the integrity of the two-party system?

The Court's response to Washington State's ballot access scheme underscores these questions. Washington State did not use a filing fee or petition to winnow out nonserious candidates. Instead, the state conducted a "blanket primary" at which registered voters could vote for any candidate of their choice, irrespective of the candidates' political party affiliation. To be placed on the general election ballot, a candidate had to receive at least 1 percent of the votes cast for that office. Each candidate who was seeking a party's nomination had to declare his candidacy for that party's nomination. As to each party, only the name of the candidate who received a plurality of the votes cast for the candidates of his party would appear on the general election ballot.

Dean Peoples (yes, his real name) qualified to be placed on the primary election ballot for a U.S. Senate seat as the nominee of the Socialist Workers Party. Also appearing on that ballot were 32 other candidates seeking the nomination of a variety of other parties. Peoples received approximately 596 of the 681,690 votes cast in the primary (roughly .00009 percent of the total), and thus the secretary of state refused to put his name on the general election ballot.

Munro v. Socialist Workers Party

479 U.S. 189 (1986).

■ JUSTICE WHITE delivered the opinion of the Court.

* * *

While there is no "litmus-paper test" for deciding a case like this, it is now clear that States may condition access to the general election ballot by a minor-party or independent candidate upon a showing of a modicum of support among the potential voters for the office.

* * *

[There] is surely an important state interest in requiring some preliminary showing of a significant modicum of support before printing the name of a political organization's candidate on the ballot—the interest, if no other, in avoiding confusion, deception, and even frustration of the democratic process at the general election.

* * *

The Court of Appeals determined that Washington's interest in insuring that candidates had sufficient community support did not justify the enactment of [this scheme] because "Washington's political history evidences no voter confusion from ballot overcrowding." We accept this historical fact, but it does not require invalidation of [the law.]

We have never required a State to make a particularized showing of the existence of voter confusion, ballot overcrowding, or the presence of frivolous candidacies prior to the imposition of reasonable restrictions on ballot access. In *Jenness v. Fortson*, [for example], we conducted no inquiry into the sufficiency and quantum of the data supporting the reasons for Georgia's 5% petition-signature requirement. In *American Party of Texas v. White*, we upheld the 1% petition-signature requirement, asserting that the "State's admittedly vital interests are sufficiently implicated to insist that political parties appearing on the general ballot demonstrate a significant, measurable quantum of community support." And, in *Storer v. Brown*, we upheld California's statutory provisions that denied ballot access to an independent candidate if the candidate had been affiliated with any political party within one year prior to the immediately preceding primary election. We recognized that California had a "compelling" interest in maintaining the integrity of its political processes, and that the disaffiliation requirement furthered this interest and was therefore valid, even though it was an absolute bar to attaining a ballot position. We asserted that "[it] appears obvious to us that the one-year disaffiliation provision furthers the State's interest in the stability of its political system." There is no indication that we held California to the burden of demonstrating empirically the objective effects on political stability that were produced by the 1–year disaffiliation requirement.

To require States to prove actual voter confusion, ballot overcrowding, or the presence of frivolous candidacies as a predicate to the imposition of reasonable ballot access restrictions would invariably lead to endless court battles over the sufficiency of the "evidence" marshaled by a State to prove the predicate. Such a requirement would necessitate that a State's political system sustain some level of damage before the legislature could take corrective action. Legislatures, we think, should be permitted to respond to potential deficiencies in the electoral process with foresight rather than reactively, provided that the response is reasonable and does not significantly impinge on constitutionally protected rights.

In any event, the record here suggests that revision of [the Washington ballot access regime] was, in fact, linked to the state legislature's perception that the general election ballot was becoming cluttered with candidates from minor parties who did not command significant voter support. In 1976, one year prior to [the revision,] the largest number of minor political parties in Washington's history—12—appeared on the general election ballot. The record demonstrates that at least part of the legislative impetus for revision ... was concern about minor parties having such easy access to Washington's general election ballot.

The primary election in Washington ... is "an integral part of the entire election process ... [that] functions to winnow out and finally reject all but the chosen candidates." We think that the State can properly reserve the general election ballot "for major struggles," by conditioning access to that ballot on a showing of a modicum of voter support. In this respect, the fact that the State is willing to have a long and complicated ballot at the primary provides no measure of what it may require for access to the general election ballot. The State of Washington was clearly entitled to raise the ante for ballot access, to simplify the general election ballot, and to avoid the possibility of unrestrained factionalism at the general election.

Neither do we agree with the Court of Appeals and appellees that the burdens imposed on appellees' First Amendment rights by the 1977 amendments are far too severe to be justified by the State's interest in restricting access to the general ballot. Much is made of the fact that prior to 1977, virtually every minor-party candidate who sought general election ballot position so qualified, while since 1977 only 1 out of 12 minor-party candidates has appeared on that ballot. Such historical facts are relevant, but they prove very little in this case, other than the fact that [the statute] does not provide an insuperable barrier to minor-party ballot access.[11] It is hardly a surprise that minor parties appeared on the general election ballot before [the revision]; for, until then, there were virtually no restrictions on access. Under our cases, however, Washington was not required to afford such automatic access and would have been entitled to insist on a more substantial showing of voter support. Comparing the actual experience before and after 1977 tells us nothing about how minor parties would have

---

11. [The law] apparently poses an insubstantial obstacle to minor-party candidates for nonstatewide offices and independent candidates for statewide offices. Since 1977, 36 out of 40 such minor-party candidates have qualified for the general election ballot and 4 out of 5 independent candidates for statewide office have so qualified.

fared in those earlier years had Washington conditioned ballot access to the maximum extent permitted by the Constitution.

* * *

We also observe that [Washington's system] is more accommodating of First Amendment rights and values than were the statutes we upheld in *Jenness*, *American Party*, and *Storer*. Under each scheme analyzed in those cases, if a candidate failed to satisfy the qualifying criteria, the State's voters had no opportunity to cast a ballot for that candidate and the candidate had no ballot-connected campaign platform from which to espouse his or her views; the unsatisfied qualifying criteria served as an absolute bar to ballot access.... Here, however, Washington virtually guarantees what the parties challenging the Georgia, Texas, and California election laws so vigorously sought—candidate access to a statewide ballot. This is a significant difference. Washington has chosen a vehicle by which minor-party candidates must demonstrate voter support that serves to promote the very First Amendment values that are threatened by overly burdensome ballot access restrictions. It can hardly be said that Washington's voters are denied freedom of association because they must channel their expressive activity into a campaign at the primary as opposed to the general election.

* * *

NOTES AND QUESTIONS

1. Lurking in the Court's opinions on restrictions on ballot access is a concern for the state's interest in preventing unrestrained electoral factionalism. The contexts vary from the virtually uncontested elections in Hawaii in which the Democratic Party holds sway, to rules in Washington that attempt to restrict the election process to a "main arena" bout between the major parties. At what level of generality may a state assert an argument that expanded electoral participation risks "unrestrained factionalism"? Can an assertion that the state seeks to preserve a two-party monopoly suffice to meet the state's burden? Consider Minnesota's defense of ballot restrictions as restraining "factionalism" in *Timmons v. Twin Cities Area New Party*, 117 S.Ct. 1364 (1997), the next principal case.

2. Note that Justice White's opinion does not require empirical proof that a state's restrictions either respond to an actual problem or that they are the most reasonable way of avoiding voter confusion or ensuring the integrity of the process. In traditional terms, then, the Court seems to be applying a sort of rational relationship scrutiny—under which courts often hypothesize a relationship between the challenged classification and a legitimate governmental purpose, rather than requiring any actual proof—rather than any sort of heightened review.

By contrast, Justice Marshall's dissent suggested that some form of more searching judicial review was required because of the connection between the major parties and ballot access legislation: "The necessity for [a higher standard of review] becomes evident when we consider that major parties, which by definition are ordinarily in control of legislative institutions, may seek to perpetuate themselves at the expense of developing minor parties. The application of strict scrutiny to ballot access restrictions ensures that measures taken to further a State's interest in keeping frivolous candidates off the ballot do not incidentally impose an impermissible bar to minor-party access."

In a provocative recent article, Professor Klarman seeks to offer a majoritarian conception of judicial review. He focuses on what he calls problems of "entrenchment," and identifies two sorts: "legislative entrenchment" occurs when legislators act to perpetuate themselves in office; "cross-temporal entrenchment" occurs when a temporary popular majority reorganizes the system to ensure its continued predominance even if it loses its majority status. Professor Klarman analyzes ballot access restrictions as representing the former phenomenon:

> For the most part, ballot access restrictions represent a problem of legislative, rather than intertemporal, entrenchment. There is little reason to suppose that most voters wish to foreclose the option of expressing discontent with the traditional political parties by supporting an occasional third party or independent challenger. To compound the entrenchment problem, not only do incumbents have something to gain by restricting outsider competition; they may have little to lose. If incumbents of both major political parties share a self-interested commitment to imposing onerous ballot access restrictions, how are dissatisfied voters to express their frustration at the poll? The only candidates on the ballot, by hypothesis, have endorsed the restrictions. The Supreme Court on several occasions had explicitly acknowledged that ballot access restrictions warrant close judicial scrutiny because of the potential they create for incumbent self-dealing.

Michael J. Klarman, *Majoritarian Judicial Review: The Entrenchment Problem*, 85 Geo. L.J. 491, 522 (1997).

3. *Munro* offers a noticeably constrained vision of the purpose of general elections: they serve "to winnow out and finally reject all but the chosen candidates" and thus the general election ballot is reserved "for major struggles." Under such a vision, most minor party candidates are irrelevant, since they have little chance of winning.

But suppose minor parties sponsor candidates for reasons beyond the (admittedly minuscule) chance of winning office. What was Peoples' and the SWP's aim in running? Does appearing on the primary ballot satisfy this aim? Consider Richard Hofstader's account of the distinctive aspirations and role of third parties. Hofstader points out that in the United

States no third party has ever replaced one of the existing major parties and thus leaders of minor parties "must look for success in terms different from those that apply to the major parties, for in those terms third parties always fail." Richard Hofstader, The Age of Reform 89 (1955). In contrast to the two major parties, which are more concerned with patronage than principles, third parties are usually ideologically driven. "Their function has not been to win or govern, but to agitate, educate, generate new ideas, and supply the dynamic element in our political life. When a third party's demands become popular enough, they are appropriated by one or both of the major parties and the third party disappears. Third parties are like bees; once they have stung, they die." Id.

4. *Munro* raises the possibility that the general election ballot may be limited essentially to ensure that the winning candidate receives a majority of the votes cast. Consider the ways in which such a practice secures stability in the electoral system. See Richard H. Pildes and Elizabeth S. Anderson, *Slinging Arrows at Democracy: Social Choice Theory, Value Pluralism, and Democratic Politics*, 90 Colum. L. Rev. 2121 (1990) (discussing the social choice theory arguments on behalf of a two-party political system: that such systems guarantee that the winning candidate has majority support, with no competing majority supporting an incompatible choice). What other aspects of the electoral system also strengthen the two-party system?

2. THE INTERACTION OF BALLOT ACCESS AND OTHER ELECTORAL REGULATIONS IN PERPETUATING THE TWO-PARTY SYSTEM

Timmons v. Twin Cities Area New Party
117 S.Ct. 1364 (1997).

■ CHIEF JUSTICE REHNQUIST delivered the opinion of the Court.

Most States prohibit multiple-party, or "fusion," candidacies for elected office.[1] The Minnesota laws challenged in this case prohibit a candidate from appearing on the ballot as the candidate of more than one party. We hold that such a prohibition does not violate the First and Fourteenth Amendments to the United States Constitution.

Respondent is a chartered chapter of the national New Party. Petitioners are Minnesota election officials. In April 1994, Minnesota State Representative Andy Dawkins was running unopposed in the Minnesota Democratic–Farmer–Labor Party's (DFL) primary. That same month, New Party members chose Dawkins as their candidate for the same office in the November 1994 general election. Neither Dawkins nor the DFL objected,

---

1. "Fusion," also called "cross-filing" or "multiple-party nomination," is "the electoral support of a single set of candidates by two or more parties." Fusion is "the nomination by more than one political party of the same candidate for the same office in the same general election."

D. Entrenchment of the Two-Party System

and Dawkins signed the required affidavit of candidacy for the New Party. Minnesota, however, prohibits fusion candidacies. Because Dawkins had already filed as a candidate for the DFL's nomination, local election officials refused to accept the New Party's nominating petition.

* * *

Fusion was a regular feature of Gilded Age American politics. Particularly in the West and Midwest, candidates of issue-oriented parties like the Grangers, Independents, Greenbackers, and Populists often succeeded through fusion with the Democrats, and vice versa. Republicans, for their part, sometimes arranged fusion candidacies in the South, as part of a general strategy of encouraging and exploiting divisions within the dominant Democratic Party.

Fusion was common in part because political parties, rather than local or state governments, printed and distributed their own ballots.... But after the 1888 presidential election, which was widely regarded as having been plagued by fraud, many States moved to the "Australian ballot system." ... During the same period, many States enacted other election-related reforms, including bans on fusion candidacies. Minnesota banned fusion in 1901. This trend has continued and, in this century, fusion has become the exception, not the rule. Today, multiple-party candidacies are permitted in just a few States, and fusion plays a significant role only in New York.

* * *

The New Party's claim that it has a right to select its own candidate is uncontroversial, so far as it goes. That is, the New Party, and not someone else, has the right to select the New Party's "standard bearer." It does not follow, though, that a party is absolutely entitled to have its nominee appear on the ballot as that party's candidate. A particular candidate might be ineligible for office, unwilling to serve, or, as here, another party's candidate. That a particular individual may not appear on the ballot as a particular party's candidate does not severely burden that party's association rights....

[Minnesota's ban on fusion does not involve] regulation of political parties' internal affairs and core associational activities.... The ban, which applies to major and minor parties alike, simply precludes one party's candidate from appearing on the ballot, as that party's candidate, if already nominated by another party. Respondent is free to try to convince Representative Dawkins to be the New Party's, not the DFL's, candidate. Whether the Party still wants to endorse a candidate who, because of the fusion ban, will not appear on the ballot as the Party's candidate, is up to the Party.

The Court of Appeals ... held that Minnesota's laws "keep the New Party from developing consensual political alliances and thus broadening the base of public participation in and support for its activities." The burden on the Party was, the court held, severe because "history shows that minor parties have played a significant role in the electoral system where multiple party nomination is legal, but have no meaningful influence where multiple party nomination is banned." In the view of the Court of Appeals, Minnesota's fusion ban forces members of the new party to make a "no-win choice" between voting for "candidates with no realistic chance of winning, defecting from their party and voting for a major party candidate who does, or declining to vote at all."

But Minnesota has not directly precluded minor political parties from developing and organizing. Nor has Minnesota excluded a particular group of citizens, or a political party, from participation in the election process. The New Party remains free to endorse whom it likes, to ally itself with others, to nominate candidates for office, and to spread its message to all who will listen.

The Court of Appeals emphasized its belief that, without fusion-based alliances, minor parties cannot thrive. This is a predictive judgment which is by no means self-evident.[9] But, more importantly, the supposed benefits of fusion to minor parties does not require that Minnesota permit it. Many features of our political system—e.g., single-member districts, "first past the post" elections, and the high costs of campaigning—make it difficult for third parties to succeed in American politics. But the Constitution does not require States to permit fusion any more than it requires them to move to proportional-representation elections or public financing of campaigns.

* * *

[Because the burden on the New Party's associational rights is not very severe,] the State's asserted regulatory interests need only be "sufficiently weighty to justify the limitation" imposed on the Party's rights.... Minnesota argues here that its fusion ban is justified by its interests in avoiding voter confusion, promoting candidate competition (by reserving limited ballot space for opposing candidates), preventing electoral distor-

---

9. Between the First and Second World Wars, for example, various radical, agrarian, and labor-oriented parties thrived, without fusion, in the Midwest. One of these parties, Minnesota's Farmer–Labor Party, displaced the Democratic Party as the Republicans' primary opponent in Minnesota during the 1930's. As one historian has noted: "The Minnesota Farmer–Labor Party elected its candidates to the governorship on four occasions, to the U. S. Senate in five elections, and to the U. S. House in twenty-five campaigns.... Never less than Minnesota's second strongest party, in 1936 Farmer-Laborites dominated state politics.... The Farmer–Labor Party was a success despite its independence of America's two dominant national parties and despite the sometimes bold anticapitalist rhetoric of its platforms." It appears that factionalism within the Farmer–Labor Party, the popular successes of New Deal programs and ideology, and the gradual movement of political power from the States to the national government contributed to the Party's decline. Eventually, a much-weakened Farmer–Labor Party merged with the Democrats, forming what is now Minnesota's Democratic–Farmer–Labor Party, in 1944.

tions and ballot manipulations, and discouraging party splintering and "unrestrained factionalism."

States certainly have an interest in protecting the integrity, fairness, and efficiency of their ballots and election processes as means for electing public officials. Petitioners contend that a candidate or party could easily exploit fusion as a way of associating his or its name with popular slogans and catchphrases. For example, members of a major party could decide that a powerful way of "sending a message" via the ballot would be for various factions of that party to nominate the major party's candidate as the candidate for the newly-formed "No New Taxes," "Conserve Our Environment," and "Stop Crime Now" parties. In response, an opposing major party would likely instruct its factions to nominate that party's candidate as the "Fiscal Responsibility," "Healthy Planet," and "Safe Streets" parties' candidate.

Whether or not the putative "fusion" candidates' names appeared on one or four ballot lines, such maneuvering would undermine the ballot's purpose by transforming it from a means of choosing candidates to a billboard for political advertising. The New Party responds to this concern, ironically enough, by insisting that the State could avoid such manipulation by adopting more demanding ballot-access standards rather than prohibiting multiple-party nomination. However, as we stated above, because the burdens the fusion ban imposes on the Party's associational rights are not severe, the State need not narrowly tailor the means it chooses to promote ballot integrity....

* * *

States also have a strong interest in the stability of their political systems. This interest does not permit a State to completely insulate the two-party system from minor parties' or independent candidates' competition and influence.... That said, the States' interest permits them to enact reasonable election regulations that may, in practice, favor the traditional two-party system, and that temper the destabilizing effects of party-splintering and excessive factionalism. The Constitution permits the Minnesota Legislature to decide that political stability is best served through a healthy two-party system. And while an interest in securing the perceived benefits of a stable two-party system will not justify unreasonably exclusionary restrictions, States need not remove all of the many hurdles third parties face in the American political arena today.

* * *

■ JUSTICE STEVENS, with whom JUSTICE GINSBURG joins, and with whom JUSTICE SOUTER joins as to Par[t] I ..., dissenting.

* * *

I

The members of a recognized political party unquestionably have a constitutional right to select their nominees for public office and to communicate the identity of their nominees to the voting public. Both the right to choose and the right to advise voters of that choice are entitled to the highest respect.

The Minnesota statutes place a significant burden on both of those rights.... The fact that the Party may nominate its second choice surely does not diminish the significance of a restriction that denies it the right to have the name of its first choice appear on the ballot.

* * *

[A] party's choice of a candidate is the most effective way in which that party can communicate to the voters what the party represents and, thereby, attract voter interest and support.[1]

The State next argues that—instead of nominating a second-choice candidate—the Party could remove itself from the ballot altogether, and publicly endorse the candidate of another party. But the right to be on the election ballot is precisely what separates a political party from any other interest group.

The majority rejects as unimportant the limits that the fusion ban may impose on the Party's ability to express its political views, relying on our decision in *Burdick v. Takushi*, 504 U. S. 428, 445 (1992), in which we noted that "the purpose of casting, counting, and recording votes is to elect public officials, not to serve as a general forum for political expression." But in *Burdick* we concluded simply that an individual voter's interest in expressing his disapproval of the single candidate running for office in a particular election did not require the State to finance and provide a mechanism for tabulating write-in votes. Our conclusion that the ballot is not principally a forum for the individual expression of political sentiment through the casting of a vote does not justify the conclusion that the ballot

---

1. The burden on the Party's right to nominate its first-choice candidate, by limiting the Party's ability to convey through its nominee what the Party represents, risks impinging on another core element of any political party's associational rights—the right to "broaden the base of public participation in and support for its activities." ... A fusion ban burdens the right of a minor party to broaden its base of support because of the political reality that the dominance of the major parties frequently makes a vote for a minor party or independent candidate a "wasted" vote. When minor parties can nominate a candidate also nominated by a major party, they are able to present their members with an opportunity to cast a vote for a candidate who will actually be elected. Although this aspect of a party's effort to broaden support is distinct from the ability to nominate the candidate who best represents the party's views, it is important to note that the party's right to broaden the base of its support is burdened in both ways by the fusion ban.

serves no expressive purpose for the parties who place candidates on the ballot.

* * *

III

* * *

[I would also reject the majority's argument that the ban on fusion protects the state's interest in a healthy two-party system.] In most States, perhaps in all, there are two and only two major political parties. It is not surprising, therefore, that most States have enacted election laws that impose burdens on the development and growth of third parties. The law at issue in this case is undeniably such a law. The fact that the law was both intended to disadvantage minor parties and has had that effect is a matter that should weigh against, rather than in favor of, its constitutionality.

Our jurisprudence in this area reflects a certain tension: on the one hand, we have been clear that political stability is an important state interest and that incidental burdens on the formation of minor parties are reasonable to protect that interest; on the other, we have struck down state elections laws specifically because they give "the two old, established parties a decided advantage over any new parties struggling for existence." Between these boundaries, we have acknowledged that there is "no litmus-paper test for separating those restrictions that are valid from those that are invidious. . . . The rule is not self-executing and is no substitute for the hard judgments that must be made."

Nothing in the Constitution prohibits the States from maintaining single-member districts with winner-take-all voting arrangements. And these elements of an election system do make it significantly more difficult for third parties to thrive. But these laws are different in two respects from the fusion bans at issue here. First, the method by which they hamper third-party development is not one that impinges on the associational rights of those third parties; minor parties remain free to nominate candidates of their choice, and to rally support for those candidates. The small parties' relatively limited likelihood of ultimate success on election day does not deprive them of the right to try. Second, the establishment of single-member districts correlates directly with the States' interests in political stability. Systems of proportional representation, for example, may tend toward factionalism and fragile coalitions that diminish legislative effectiveness. In the context of fusion candidacies, the risks to political stability are extremely attenuated.[8] Of course, the reason minor parties so ardently support fusion politics is because it allows the parties to build up a greater base of support, as potential minor party members realize that a

---

8. Even in a system that allows fusion, a candidate for election must assemble majority support, so the State's concern cannot logically be about risks to political stability in the particular election in which the fusion candidate is running.

vote for the smaller party candidate is not necessarily a "wasted" vote. Eventually, a minor party might gather sufficient strength that—were its members so inclined—it could successfully run a candidate not endorsed by any major party, and legislative coalition-building will be made more difficult by the presence of third party legislators. But the risks to political stability in that scenario are speculative at best.... The fusion candidacy does not threaten to divide the legislature and create significant risks of factionalism, which is the principal risk proponents of the two-party system point to.

* * *

■ JUSTICE SOUTER, dissenting.

* * *

[I would leave open the question whether, in a different case, "preservation of the two-party system" would provide a permissible rationale.] There is considerable consensus that party loyalty among American voters has declined significantly in the past four decades, and that the overall influence of the parties in the political process has decreased considerably. In the wake of such studies, it may not be unreasonable to infer that the two-party system is in some jeopardy.

Surely the majority is right that States "have a strong interest in the stability of their political systems," that is, in preserving a political system capable of governing effectively. If it could be shown that the disappearance of the two-party system would undermine that interest, and that permitting fusion candidacies poses a substantial threat to the two-party scheme, there might well be a sufficient predicate for recognizing the constitutionality of the state action presented by this case....

NOTES AND QUESTIONS

1. For discussions of fusion, see, e.g., Peter H. Argersinger, *"A Place on the Ballot": Fusion Politics and Antifusion Laws*, 85 Am. Hist. Rev. 287 (1980); William R. Kirschner, Note, *Fusion and the Associational Rights of Minor Political Parties*, 95 Colum. L. Rev. 683 (1995); Note, *Fusion Candidacies, Disaggregation, and Freedom of Association*, 109 Harv. L. Rev. 1302 (1996).

2. Does *Timmons* go even further than *Munro* in lifting any empirical burden from the state? The Chief Justice offers a set of quite fanciful hypotheticals. And there may be good reasons to suppose that the major parties will not fracture themselves into several ballot lines. In some states, for example, the party that received the highest number of votes in the last election gets the first spot on the ballot the next time around, with concomitant advantages. *See* Note, *California Ballot Position Statutes: An Unconstitutional Advantage to Incumbents*, 45 S. Cal. L. Rev. 365 (1972);

Mark E. Dreyer, Comment, *Constitutional Problems with Statutes Regulating Ballot Position*, 23 Tulsa L. J. 123 (1987).

3. *Timmons* goes decidedly beyond earlier cases in its endorsement of the two-party system. Note how it links ballot access with other structural aspects of the electoral system, most notably single-member districts.

We shall return to questions of districting in later chapters, but it is worth at least understanding the dimensions of the Court's point. Single-member districts create a series of geographically based, winner-take-all contests. Only blocs of voters who constitute a plurality within a given constituency can elect the candidate they prefer. Thus, a voter who wishes to affect the outcome must vote for a candidate who has a realistic possibility of finishing first within her electoral district. This candidate is likely to be a centrist candidate (with the center being defined relative to the district's electorate). Voters closer to the ideological margins than to the center will not be able to join with like-minded voters in other constituencies.

The standard political science accounts suggest a strong propensity toward a two-party system in jurisdictions that use single-member districting systems. A simple analogy may clarify the point. Consider a town with a single main street one mile long whose residents are equally dispersed along this one-mile stretch. Assuming full choice, the first merchant who comes to town will open a store at the mid-point of the street; such a location is most efficient in terms of providing service to the largest number of customers. What would happen if there were two merchants, however? Ideally, each would open a store one-third of a mile from the town's borders; that too would maximize efficiency in providing customer access to shopping. Unfortunately, if one of the merchants were to choose such a location, the other would set up somewhere between the first merchant and the center of town. From that location, the second merchant could compete for some of the first merchant's market, while holding a preferred position for more than half the town. Because of this strategic dilemma, the resolution seen in markets around the world is for both merchants to establish stores in the center of town, usually across the street from each other. This classic illustration of markets may be found in Harold Hotelling, *Stability in Competition*, 39 Econ. Journal 41 (1929), and Arthur Smithies, *Optimum Location in Spatial Competition*, 49 J. Pol. Econ. 423 (1941).

The American single-member electoral district, also referred to as a "first-past-the-post" system, presents the same pressures toward centrism found in geographic markets. Imagine instead of a town whose population is dispersed along a one-mile stretch, an electorate comparably dispersed from left to right. If there were two political parties, the population's views would be most "efficiently" represented by each party posturing itself one-third of the way in from the respective poles. However, were one party to camp itself one-third of the way in from the left pole, for example, the other party would lay claim to the greatest number of potential voters by positioning itself only slightly to the right of the first party. The first party would be at a tremendous competitive disadvantage unless it were to move more toward the center. The second party would then have to edge to the right to maintain its hold on its base. And so forth. The equilibrium strategy in such a political market would be for each party to hew fairly close to the center, with one perceived as the party of the center-left, and the other the party of the center-right. The analogy of political markets to the town merchants is first set out in Anthony Downs, An Economic Theory of Democracy, at 115–17 (1957).

Now consider the plight of a would-be third party. Imagine this party as a potential party of the right whose ideology would place it to the right of the center-right party. The new party would compete with the center-right party for those voters closest to the right pole. But such a strategy would rarely yield electoral success. The new party of the right and the center-right party would divide voters on the right part of the spectrum, leaving the center-left party in an ideal position. So long as elections were by plurality vote, the center-left party would prevail against the divided partisans of the right. As against charges of being "spoilers" or "guaranteeing" the success of the center-left, the party of the right would be under tremendous pressure to return to the fold of the party of the center-right and agitate from within. Hence the pressure is not only toward centrist parties, but toward two and only two parties.

This then highlights the issues at stake in *Timmons*. As a general rule, there are two strategies available to third parties in a system structurally oriented toward two parties. The first is to displace one of the established parties, an event not successfully accomplished in American history. *See* James L. Sundquist, Dynamics of the Party System (1983). The second is to become a sufficiently credible political force so as to shift the balance of power within one of the established parties. As a historical matter, this has been the classic third party strategy in the U.S. for groups ranging from populists at the turn of the century to the Christian Coalition today. Because of the high cost of organizing a viable electoral vehicle in the face of first-past-the-post elections, ideological third party movements have had their greatest success in creating a sufficient base to influence the major political parties.

Should the Court in *Timmons* have distinguished electoral structures that have the incidental effect of entrenching the two-party system, such as single-member districts, from rules that have as their primary purpose restrictions on third parties, such as antifusion laws? Should the purpose of the restriction be a basis for judging the constitutionality of election laws?

The Supreme Court has been noticeably hostile to claims that districting constitutes impermissible entrenchment of the current two major parties. In *Gaffney v. Cummings*, 412 U.S. 735 (1973), for example, the

Court confronted a challenge to Connecticut's "bipartisan gerrymander." In redrawing the state's legislative districts after the 1970 census, the Apportionment Board followed a policy of "political fairness" for the two major political parties and drew "what was thought to be a proportionate number of Republican and Democratic legislative seats." It rejected the claim that the bipartisan gerrymander unfairly diluted the voting strength of independent voters:

> [J]udicial interest should be at its lowest ebb when a State purports fairly to allocate political power to the parties in accordance with their voting strength and, within quite tolerable limits, succeeds in doing so. There is no doubt that there may be other reapportionment plans for Connecticut that would have different political consequences and that would also be constitutional.... [But we have no] constitutional warrant to invalidate a state plan, otherwise within tolerable population limits, because it undertakes, not to minimize or eliminate the political strength of any group or party, but to recognize it and, through districting, provide a rough sort of proportional representation in the legislative halls of the State.

Note that *Gaffney* presupposes that the decision to provide rough proportional representation to the two major parties does not minimize or cancel out the ability of other groups to elect their preferred candidates.

To what extent is Justice Stevens successful in distinguishing single-member districts from anti-fusion laws?

CHAPTER 5

PRECLEARANCE AND THE VOTING RIGHTS ACT

As the materials in Chapters 2 and 6 illustrate, the guarantees of the Fourteenth and Fifteenth Amendments were essentially disregarded in many states for roughly a century. To a substantial extent, nonenforcement of the amendments was a function of Southern legislators' control of Congress: attempts to eliminate the poll tax, for example, were stymied for decades by Southern senators and representatives, and no civil rights bill of any sort was passed until 1957, when a watered-down voting rights bill was enacted. Among other things, that bill created the Civil Rights Division of the Department of Justice and, along with the Civil Rights Act of 1960, authorized the Department to bring suits on behalf of citizens who were denied the right to vote on account of race.

These lawsuits, however, were extremely time-consuming and often pyrrhic. The formal legal standard was hard to satisfy: in a jurisdiction with a literacy test, like Mississippi, for example, the United States had to prove that the applications of black applicants who had been denied registration were comparable to the applications of whites who had been registered. This meant going county by county, comparing literally thousands of applications. This analysis took hundreds, sometimes thousands, of hours. Local officials engaged in ingenious forms of resistance—"losing" records, resigning (thereby vitiating injunctions against them of any force) and leaving registrar positions vacant so that no applicants could be registered, or purging black voters from the rolls shortly after their enfranchisement. *See, e.g., United States v. McElveen*, 180 F.Supp. 10 (E.D.La.), *aff'd sub nom. United States v. Thomas*, 362 U.S. 58 (1960). Perhaps just as importantly, several federal district court judges were almost equally resistant to the enfranchisement of black voters. Virtually every lawsuit required repeated trips to the Court of Appeals before any relief at all was granted.

Although the Department of Justice had filed 71 voting rights cases in the seven years following the 1957 Act, black registration in the South remained minuscule. Between 1958 and 1964, black registration in Alabama rose from 5.2 to 19.4 percent; in Mississippi, from 1954 to 1964 black registration rose from 4.4 percent to only 6.4 percent. Dallas County, Alabama—whose county seat, Selma, was soon to become nationally famous—offered a textbook illustration of the problems with case-by-case litigation of the disenfranchisement problem. The county had a voting-age population of approximately 29,500, including 15,000 blacks. Although roughly two-thirds of the county's eligible white citizens were registered to vote, only one percent of the black residents—156 out of 15,000—were registered. Nonetheless, it took thirteen months of procedural wrangling before the Department of Justice's lawsuit against the county registrars came to trial. By then, the registrars who had been in office when the suit had been filed had resigned and the district court refused to issue any injunction against the new registrars since it found that they had not discriminated against anyone. On appeal, the Fifth Circuit ordered the district court to enter an injunction against discriminatory practices, but it permitted the continued use of the literacy test. Although in the past, the test had been administered leniently—allowing essentially illiterate white applicants to register—it was now applied to black aspirants with a vengeance: 175 black applicants with high-school diplomas were rejected, along with 21 applicants with college degrees and one who had a master's degree. Moreover, the board added an "understanding" requirement that demanded that applicants interpret an excerpt of the state constitution. As was true in other jurisdictions, black applicants were given far harder passages than their white counterparts; even if they were able to offer a plausible interpretation, the board would often reject them. After additional investigation, the Department of Justice filed a motion for further relief and, four years after the original lawsuit was filed, the district court finally issued a meaningful injunction. In the meantime, only 383 of the nearly 15,000 eligible black citizens had managed to register.

While the lawsuit was wending its way through the courts, grassroots civil rights organizations, such as the Southern Christian Leadership Conference (SCLC) and the Student Nonviolent Coordinating Committee (SNCC) had moved into Selma and launched a registration campaign. In part, they picked Selma because they knew that the Dallas County Sheriff, Jim Clark, was prone to the kind of overreaction that the national media would cover and which would garner support for their cause. *See* David J. Garrow, Protest at Selma: Martin Luther King, Jr., and the Voting Rights Act of 1965 (1978); Michael J. Klarman, Brown, *Racial Change and the Civil Rights Movement*, 80 Va. L. Rev. 7, 147–49 (1994). In February 1965, in nearby Perry County, Alabama, a nighttime voting-rights march was broken up by Alabama state troopers; in the ensuing assault, a trooper shot Jimmie Jackson, who was trying to protect his mother. A few weeks later, on March 7, 1965, SCLC and SNCC began a protest march from Selma to the state capital, Montgomery, to present Governor George Wallace with a list of their grievances. On the Edmund Pettis Bridge outside Selma, they were stopped by state troopers, sheriff's deputies, and "possemen" on horseback. The lawmen fired tear gas into the crowd and charged the marchers, trampling and injuring many of them. The entire scene was captured by television cameras and prompted nationwide revulsion. In the wake of "Bloody Sunday," Judge Frank M. Johnson issued an injunction permitting the march on the grounds that such a march provided one of the only available means for black citizens to petition their government for redress of grievances—since less dramatic political mechanisms such as voting were unavailable—and recognized that troops would be necessary to protect the marchers. *See Williams v. Wallace*, 240 F.Supp. 100 (M.D.Ala. 1965). In the wake of national outrage over the events in Selma, President Lyndon B. Johnson instructed the Department of Justice to propose a more expansive voting rights bill. That bill ultimately became the Voting Rights Act of 1965. Wilson Baker, at the time Selma's Director of Public Safety, later recalled asking then-Attorney General Nicholas Katzenbach, "What do you expect if the Voter [sic] Rights Bill passes?" Katzenbach replied, " 'What do you mean *if* it passes. You people passed that on that bridge. You people in Selma passed that on that bridge that Sunday.' He said, 'You can be sure it will pass, and because of that, if nothing else.' " Howell Raines, My Soul Is Rested: Movement Days in the Deep South Remembered 215 (1977).

A. CONGRESSIONAL POWER TO ENACT THE SPECIAL PROVISIONS OF THE VOTING RIGHTS ACT

South Carolina v. Katzenbach
383 U.S. 301 (1966).

■ MR. CHIEF JUSTICE WARREN delivered the opinion of the Court.

.... South Carolina has filed a bill of complaint, seeking a declaration that selected provisions of the Voting Rights Act of 1965 violate the Federal Constitution, and asking for an injunction against enforcement of these provisions by the Attorney General.

* * *

The Voting Rights Act was designed by Congress to banish the blight of racial discrimination in voting, which has infected the electoral process in parts of our country for nearly a century. The Act creates stringent new remedies for voting discrimination where it persists on a pervasive scale, and in addition the statute strengthens existing remedies for pockets of voting discrimination elsewhere in the country. Congress assumed the power to prescribe these remedies from § 2 of the Fifteenth Amendment, which authorizes the National Legislature to effectuate by "appropriate" measures the constitutional prohibition against racial discrimination in voting. We hold that the sections of the Act which are properly before us are an appropriate means for carrying out Congress' constitutional responsibilities and are consonant with all other provisions of the Constitution. We therefore deny South Carolina's request that enforcement of these sections of the Act be enjoined.

I

The constitutional propriety of the Voting Rights Act of 1965 must be judged with reference to the historical experience which it reflects. Before enacting the measure, Congress explored with great care the problem of racial discrimination in voting.... Two points emerge vividly from the voluminous legislative history of the Act contained in the committee hearings and floor debates. First: Congress felt itself confronted by an insidious and pervasive evil which had been perpetuated in certain parts of our country through unremitting and ingenious defiance of the Constitution. Second: Congress concluded that the unsuccessful remedies which it had prescribed in the past would have to be replaced by sterner and more elaborate measures in order to satisfy the clear commands of the Fifteenth Amendment. We pause here to summarize the majority reports of the House and Senate Committees, which document in considerable detail the factual basis for these reactions by Congress.

* * *

The Fifteenth Amendment to the Constitution was ratified in 1870. Promptly thereafter Congress passed the Enforcement Act of 1870, which made it a crime for public officers and private persons to obstruct exercise of the right to vote. The statute was amended in the following year to provide for detailed federal supervision of the electoral process, from registration to the certification of returns. As the years passed and fervor for racial equality waned, enforcement of the laws became spotty and ineffective, and most of their provisions were repealed in 1894. The remnants have had little significance in the recently renewed battle against voting discrimination.

Meanwhile, beginning in 1890, the States of Alabama, Georgia, Louisiana, Mississippi, North Carolina, South Carolina, and Virginia enacted tests still in use which were specifically designed to prevent Negroes from voting.[9] Typically, they made the ability to read and write a registration qualification and also required completion of a registration form. These laws were based on the fact that as of 1890 in each of the named States, more than two-thirds of the adult Negroes were illiterate while less than one-quarter of the adult whites were unable to read or write. At the same time, alternate tests were prescribed in all of the named States to assure that white illiterates would not be deprived of the franchise. These included grandfather clauses, property qualifications, "good character" tests, and

9. The South Carolina Constitutional Convention of 1895 was a leader in the widespread movement to disenfranchise Negroes. Senator Ben Tillman frankly explained to the state delegates the aim of the new literacy test: "[The] only thing we can do as patriots and as statesmen is to take from [the 'ignorant blacks'] every ballot that we can under the laws of our national government." He was equally candid about the exemption from the literacy test for persons who could "understand" and "explain" a section of the state constitution: "There is no particle of fraud or illegality in it. It is just simply showing partiality, perhaps, [laughter,] or discriminating." He described the alternative exemption for persons paying state property taxes in the same vein: "By means of the $300 clause you simply reach out and take in some more white men and a few more colored men." Senator Tillman was the dominant political figure in the state convention, and his entire address merits examination.

the requirement that registrants "understand" or "interpret" certain matter.

* * *

According to the evidence in recent Justice Department voting suits, the latter stratagem is now the principal method used to bar Negroes from the polls. Discriminatory administration of voting qualifications has been found in all eight Alabama cases, in all nine Louisiana cases, and in all nine Mississippi cases which have gone to final judgment. Moreover, in almost all of these cases, the courts have held that the discrimination was pursuant to a widespread "pattern or practice." White applicants for registration have often been excused altogether from the literacy and understanding tests or have been given easy versions, have received extensive help from voting officials, and have been registered despite serious errors in their answers.[12] Negroes, on the other hand, have typically been required to pass difficult versions of all the tests, without any outside assistance and without the slightest error.[13] The good-morals requirement is so vague and subjective that it has constituted an open invitation to abuse at the hands of voting officials. Negroes obliged to obtain vouchers from registered voters have found it virtually impossible to comply in areas where almost no Negroes are on the rolls.

In recent years, Congress has repeatedly tried to cope with the problem by facilitating case-by-case litigation against voting discrimination. The Civil Rights Act of 1957 authorized the Attorney General to seek injunctions against public and private interference with the right to vote on racial grounds. Perfecting amendments in the Civil Rights Act of 1960 permitted the joinder of States as parties defendant, gave the Attorney General access to local voting records, and authorized courts to register voters in areas of systematic discrimination. Title I of the Civil Rights Act of 1964 expedited the hearing of voting cases before three-judge courts and outlawed some of the tactics used to disqualify Negroes from voting in federal elections.

Despite the earnest efforts of the Justice Department and of many federal judges, these new laws have done little to cure the problem of voting discrimination.

* * *

II

---

12. A white applicant in Louisiana satisfied the registrar of his ability to interpret the state constitution by writing, "FRDUM FOOF SPETGH." United States v. Louisiana, 225 F. Supp. 353, 384. A white applicant in Alabama who had never completed the first grade of school was enrolled after the registrar filled out the entire form for him.

13. In Panola County, Mississippi, the registrar required Negroes to interpret the provision of the state constitution concerning "the rate of interest on the fund known as the 'Chickasaw School Fund.'" United States v. Duke, 332 F. 2d 759, 764. In Forrest County, Mississippi, the registrar rejected six Negroes with baccalaureate degrees, three of whom were also Masters of Arts. United States v. Lynd, 301 F. 2d 818, 821.

The Voting Rights Act of 1965 reflects Congress' firm intention to rid the country of racial discrimination in voting. The heart of the Act is a complex scheme of stringent remedies aimed at areas where voting discrimination has been most flagrant. Section 4 (a)-(d) lays down a formula defining the States and political subdivisions to which these new remedies apply. The first of the remedies, contained in § 4(a), is the suspension of literacy tests and similar voting qualifications for a period of five years from the last occurrence of substantial voting discrimination. Section 5 prescribes a second remedy, the suspension of all new voting regulations pending review by federal authorities to determine whether their use would perpetuate voting discrimination.

* * *

Coverage formula.

The remedial sections of the Act assailed by South Carolina automatically apply to any State, or to any separate political subdivision such as a county or parish, for which two findings have been made: (1) the Attorney General has determined that on November 1, 1964, it maintained a "test or device," and (2) the Director of the Census has determined that less than 50% of its voting-age residents were registered on November 1, 1964, or voted in the presidential election of November 1964. These findings are not reviewable in any court and are final upon publication in the Federal Register. § 4(b). As used throughout the Act, the phrase "test or device" means any requirement that a registrant or voter must "(1) demonstrate the ability to read, write, understand, or interpret any matter, (2) demonstrate any educational achievement or his knowledge of any particular subject, (3) possess good moral character, or (4) prove his qualifications by the voucher of registered voters or members of any other class."§ 4(c).

* * *

South Carolina was brought within the coverage formula of the Act on August 7, 1965, pursuant to appropriate administrative determinations which have not been challenged in this proceeding. On the same day, coverage was also extended to Alabama, Alaska, Georgia, Louisiana, Mississippi, Virginia, 26 counties in North Carolina, and one county in Arizona. Two more counties in Arizona, one county in Hawaii, and one county in Idaho were added to the list on November 19, 1965. Thus far Alaska, the three Arizona counties, and the single county in Idaho have asked the District Court for the District of Columbia to grant a declaratory judgment terminating statutory coverage.

Suspension of tests.

In a State or political subdivision covered by § 4(b) of the Act, no person may be denied the right to vote in any election because of his failure to comply with a "test or device." § 4(a).

On account of this provision, South Carolina is temporarily barred from enforcing the portion of its voting laws which requires every applicant for registration to show that he:

> "Can both read and write any section of [the State] Constitution submitted to [him] by the registration officer or can show that he owns, and has paid all taxes collectible during the previous year on, property in this State assessed at three hundred dollars or more." S.C. Code Ann. § 23–62 (4) (1965 Supp.).

The Attorney General has determined that the property qualification is inseparable from the literacy test, and South Carolina makes no objection to this finding. Similar tests and devices have been temporarily suspended in the other sections of the country listed above.

Review of new rules.

In a State or political subdivision covered by § 4(b) of the Act, no person may be denied the right to vote in any election because of his failure to comply with a voting qualification or procedure different from those in force on November 1, 1964. This suspension of new rules is terminated, however, under either of the following circumstances: (1) if the area has submitted the rules to the Attorney General, and he has not interposed an objection within 60 days, or (2) if the area has obtained a declaratory judgment from the District Court for the District of Columbia, determining that the rules will not abridge the franchise on racial grounds. These declaratory judgment actions are to be heard by a three-judge panel, with direct appeal to this Court. § 5.

South Carolina altered its voting laws in 1965 to extend the closing hour at polling places from 6 p.m. to 7 p.m. The State has not sought judicial review of this change in the District Court for the District of Columbia, nor has it submitted the new rule to the Attorney General for his scrutiny, although at our hearing the Attorney General announced that he does not challenge the amendment. There are indications in the record that other sections of the country listed above have also altered their voting laws since November 1, 1964.

* * *

III

These provisions of the Voting Rights Act of 1965 are challenged on the fundamental ground that they exceed the powers of Congress and encroach on an area reserved to the States by the Constitution.

* * *

[T]he basic question presented by the case [is]: Has Congress exercised its powers under the Fifteenth Amendment in an appropriate manner with relation to the States?

The ground rules for resolving this question are clear. The language and purpose of the Fifteenth Amendment, the prior decisions construing its several provisions, and the general doctrines of constitutional interpretation, all point to one fundamental principle. As against the reserved powers of the States, Congress may use any rational means to effectuate the constitutional prohibition of racial discrimination in voting.

* * *

Section 1 of the Fifteenth Amendment declares that "[the] right of citizens of the United States to vote shall not be denied or abridged by the United States or by any State on account of race, color, or previous condition of servitude." This declaration has always been treated as self-executing and has repeatedly been construed, without further legislative specification, to invalidate state voting qualifications or procedures which are discriminatory on their face or in practice.... The gist of the matter is that the Fifteenth Amendment supersedes contrary exertions of state power....

South Carolina contends that [only the judiciary can] strike down state statutes and procedures—that to allow an exercise of this authority by Congress would be to rob the courts of their rightful constitutional role. On the contrary, § 2 of the Fifteenth Amendment expressly declares that "Congress shall have power to enforce this article by appropriate legislation." By adding this authorization, the Framers indicated that Congress was to be chiefly responsible for implementing the rights created in § 1. "It is the power of Congress which has been enlarged. Congress is authorized to enforce the prohibitions by appropriate legislation. Some legislation is contemplated to make the [Civil War] amendments fully effective." *Ex parte Virginia*, 100 U.S. 339, 345. Accordingly, in addition to the courts, Congress has full remedial powers to effectuate the constitutional prohibition against racial discrimination in voting.

* * *

The basic test to be applied in a case involving § 2 of the Fifteenth Amendment is the same as in all cases concerning the express powers of Congress with relation to the reserved powers of the States. Chief Justice Marshall laid down the classic formulation, 50 years before the Fifteenth Amendment was ratified:

> "Let the end be legitimate, let it be within the scope of the constitution, and all means which are appropriate, which are plainly adapted to that end, which are not prohibited, but consist with the letter and spirit of the constitution, are constitutional."

McCulloch v. Maryland, 4 Wheat. 316, 421.

The Court has subsequently echoed his language in describing each of the Civil War Amendments:

"Whatever legislation is appropriate, that is, adapted to carry out the objects the amendments have in view, whatever tends to enforce submission to the prohibitions they contain, and to secure to all persons the enjoyment of perfect equality of civil rights and the equal protection of the laws against State denial or invasion, if not prohibited, is brought within the domain of congressional power." *Ex parte Virginia,* 100 U.S., at 345–346.

* * *

We therefore reject South Carolina's argument that Congress may appropriately do no more than to forbid violations of the Fifteenth Amendment in general terms—that the task of fashioning specific remedies or of applying them to particular localities must necessarily be left entirely to the courts. Congress is not circumscribed by any such artificial rules under § 2 of the Fifteenth Amendment.

* * *

IV.

Congress exercised its authority under the Fifteenth Amendment in an inventive manner when it enacted the Voting Rights Act of 1965. First: The measure prescribes remedies for voting discrimination which go into effect without any need for prior adjudication. This was clearly a legitimate response to the problem, for which there is ample precedent under other constitutional provisions.... Congress had found that case-by-case litigation was inadequate to combat widespread and persistent discrimination in voting, because of the inordinate amount of time and energy required to overcome the obstructionist tactics invariably encountered in these lawsuits. After enduring nearly a century of systematic resistance to the Fifteenth Amendment, Congress might well decide to shift the advantage of time and inertia from the perpetrators of the evil to its victims.

* * *

Second: The Act intentionally confines these remedies to a small number of States and political subdivisions which in most instances were familiar to Congress by name. This, too, was a permissible method of dealing with the problem. Congress had learned that substantial voting discrimination presently occurs in certain sections of the country, and it knew no way of accurately forecasting whether the evil might spread elsewhere in the future. In acceptable legislative fashion, Congress chose to limit its attention to the geographic areas where immediate action seemed necessary.

* * *

Coverage formula.

.... South Carolina contends that the coverage formula is awkwardly designed in a number of respects and that it disregards various local conditions which have nothing to do with racial discrimination. These arguments, however, are largely beside the point. Congress began work with reliable evidence of actual voting discrimination in a great majority of the States and political subdivisions affected by the new remedies of the Act. The formula eventually evolved to describe these areas was relevant to the problem of voting discrimination, and Congress was therefore entitled to infer a significant danger of the evil in the few remaining States and political subdivisions covered by § 4 (b) of the Act. No more was required to justify the application to these areas of Congress' express powers under the Fifteenth Amendment....

To be specific, the new remedies of the Act are imposed on three States—Alabama, Louisiana, and Mississippi—in which federal courts have repeatedly found substantial voting discrimination. Section 4(b) of the Act also embraces two other States—Georgia and South Carolina—plus large portions of a third State—North Carolina—for which there was more fragmentary evidence of recent voting discrimination mainly adduced by the Justice Department and the Civil Rights Commission. All of these areas were appropriately subjected to the new remedies. In identifying past evils, Congress obviously may avail itself of information from any probative source.

The areas listed above, for which there was evidence of actual voting discrimination, share two characteristics incorporated by Congress into the coverage formula: the use of tests and devices for voter registration, and a voting rate in the 1964 presidential election at least 12 points below the national average. Tests and devices are relevant to voting discrimination because of their long history as a tool for perpetrating the evil; a low voting rate is pertinent for the obvious reason that widespread disenfranchisement must inevitably affect the number of actual voters. Accordingly, the coverage formula is rational in both practice and theory. It was therefore permissible to impose the new remedies on the few remaining States and political subdivisions covered by the formula, at least in the absence of proof that they have been free of substantial voting discrimination in recent years.

* * *

Suspension of tests.

We now arrive at consideration of the specific remedies prescribed by the Act for areas included within the coverage formula. South Carolina assails the temporary suspension of existing voting qualifications, reciting the rule laid down by *Lassiter v. Northampton County Bd. of Elections*, 360 U.S. 45, that literacy tests and related devices are not in themselves contrary to the Fifteenth Amendment. In that very case, however, the Court went on to say, "Of course a literacy test, fair on its face, may be employed to perpetuate that discrimination which the Fifteenth Amendment was designed to uproot." Id., at 53. The record shows that in most of the States covered by the Act, including South Carolina, various tests and devices have been instituted with the purpose of disenfranchising Negroes, have been framed in such a way as to facilitate this aim, and have been administered in a discriminatory fashion for many years. Under these circumstances, the Fifteenth Amendment has clearly been violated.

The Act suspends literacy tests and similar devices for a period of five years from the last occurrence of substantial voting discrimination. This was a legitimate response to the problem, for which there is ample precedent in Fifteenth Amendment cases. Underlying the response was the feeling that States and political subdivisions which had been allowing white illiterates to vote for years could not sincerely complain about "dilution" of their electorates through the registration of Negro illiterates. Congress knew that continuance of the tests and devices in use at the present time, no matter how fairly administered in the future, would freeze the effect of past discrimination in favor of unqualified white registrants. Congress permissibly rejected the alternative of requiring a complete re-registration of all voters, believing that this would be too harsh on many whites who had enjoyed the franchise for their entire adult lives.

Review of new rules.

The Act suspends new voting regulations pending scrutiny by federal authorities to determine whether their use would violate the Fifteenth Amendment. This may have been an uncommon exercise of congressional power, as South Carolina contends, but the Court has recognized that exceptional conditions can justify legislative measures not otherwise appropriate.... Congress knew that some of the States covered by § 4 (b) of the Act had resorted to the extraordinary stratagem of contriving new rules of various kinds for the sole purpose of perpetuating voting discrimination in the face of adverse federal court decrees. Congress had reason to suppose that these States might try similar maneuvers in the future in order to evade the remedies for voting discrimination contained in the Act itself. Under the compulsion of these unique circumstances, Congress responded in a permissibly decisive manner.

... [T]here was nothing inappropriate about limiting litigation under this provision to the District Court for the District of Columbia, and in putting the burden of proof on the areas seeking relief.

* * *

NOTES AND QUESTIONS

1. The core of the 1965 Act is the interaction of three provisions: the triggering formula, the suspension of tests and devices, and the preclearance requirement. The triggering formula is entirely mechanical. Although it was stated in formal, neutral terms, it managed to reach the Deep South and very few other jurisdictions. When the Act was amended and extended in 1970 and 1975, many other jurisdictions, most notably three boroughs of

New York City in 1970, and the entire state of Texas in 1975, were brought within the special provisions of the Act.

Note that the special provisions did not reach either Texas or Arkansas in 1965. Those two states, like the states of the former Confederacy, had a long history of racial discrimination in voting. Remember, for example, the White Primary Cases discussed in Chapter 2. But neither state used a literacy test. Instead, the primary disenfranchising device in use by the 1960's in those two states was the poll tax.

Why didn't Congress use the poll tax as a triggering device as well? Some of the answer probably rests on then-raging arguments over Congress' authority to ban poll taxes through a statute rather than a constitutional amendment. The Twenty–Fourth Amendment, enacted in 1964, banned poll taxes as a qualification for voting in presidential and congressional elections. *See Harman v. Forssenius*, 380 U.S. 528 (1965). Moreover, as we have already seen in Chapter 2, the Supreme Court struck down the use of poll taxes under the Equal Protection Clause in *Harper v. Virginia State Board of Elections*, 383 U.S. 663 (1966). But some of the answer may depend on the identity of the two states involved: by omitting poll taxes from the list of "test[s] or device[s]," the Administration, presided over by a Texan, could sidestep determined opposition by Texas' and Arkansas's powerful legislative delegations.

In 1975, the definition of a "test or device" was amended to include the use of English-only election materials, including ballots, in areas with substantial numbers of non-English speakers. 42 U.S.C. § 1973b(f)(3). This amendment was designed in part to require Texas to provide bilingual election materials but largely to bring the state under the preclearance obligation. It also brought Arizona, New Mexico, and several counties, particularly in California and Colorado, under section 5 coverage.

2. *The identification of "covered jurisdictions."* The statutory formula applied to any "State or political subdivision" which satisfied the two elements of the trigger—use of a test or device and low voter turnout. The Act defined "political subdivision" to mean "any county or parish, except that where registration for voting is not conducted under the supervision of a county or parish, the term shall include any other subdivision of a State which conducts registration for voting." Voting Rights Act § 14(c)(2). Under the initial formulation, which looked at the practices in effect on November 1, 1964, seven full states—Alabama, Alaska, Georgia, Louisiana, Mississippi, South Carolina, and Virginia—were designated for coverage. In addition, 26 counties in North Carolina, three counties in Arizona, one county in Hawaii, and one county in Idaho were included.

The question of what jurisdictions beyond states and counties were covered was taken up in *United States v. Sheffield Board of Commissioners*, 435 U.S. 110 (1978). There, the Court held that the city of Sheffield, Alabama—a municipality within a covered state—was itself a covered jurisdiction despite the fact that the city did not conduct voter registration.

The dispute arose in the context of a section 5 proceeding in which the city argued that it was not required to seek review of its new voting procedures because section 5 applied only to jurisdictions covered by section 4. The Court disagreed: "The language, structure, history, and purposes of the Act persuade us that § 5, like the constitutional provisions it is designed to implement, applies to all entities having power over any aspect of the electoral process within designated jurisdictions, not only to counties or to whatever units of state government perform the function of registering voters." *Id.* at 118. Thus, the city, as a state actor, was covered. Similarly, in *Dougherty County Board of Education v. White*, 439 U.S. 32 (1978), the Court held that a board of education was required to seek preclearance for a personnel rule that might affect candidates for public office. Is coverage under sections 4 and 5 coterminous with the state action doctrine? Do they reach non-governmental entities engaged in state action, for example, political parties? *See Morse v. Republican Party of Virginia*, 116 S.Ct. 1186 (1996) (holding that a state party's decisions about who could participate in its nominating conventions are covered by section 5).

Under the current version of section 4, which uses triggering dates in 1964, 1968, and 1972, nine states, 54 counties (including 40 in North Carolina), and twelve municipalities or townships are covered jurisdictions. *See* 28 C.F.R. Part 51, Appendix (1995).

In addition, the Act poses the question of when changes embodied in judicial decrees are subject to the preclearance requirement. For a discussion of that question, see *infra* pages 308–13.

3. The Act permitted covered jurisdictions to "bail out," that is, to escape from the suspension of tests or devices under section 4 and the preclearance requirement of section 5, by bringing a declaratory judgment action in the United States District Court for the District of Columbia. In that action, the jurisdiction was required to show that no test or device had been used "during the five years preceding the filing of the action for the purpose or with the effect of denying or abridging the right to vote on account of race or color." Voting Rights Act § 4(a). In *Gaston County v. United States*, 395 U.S. 285 (1969), Gaston County, North Carolina, sought such a declaratory judgment. The district court and the Supreme Court denied bailout on the grounds that, regardless of whether the county had administered its literacy test impartially, its maintenance of a *de jure* segregated school system that provided black citizens with an inferior education "in turn deprived them of an equal chance to pass the literacy test." *Id.* at 291. Consider whether this rationale can be applied more broadly. For example, to what extent might racially polarized voting—discussed in Chapters 6 and 7—be a product of prior *de jure* discrimination by the government, either because such discrimination contributed to socioeconomic differences that in turn create different political preferences or because the discrimination affected white voters' willingness to support black-sponsored candidates? *See, e.g.,* Pamela S. Karlan and Daryl J. Levinson, *Why Voting Is Different*, 84 Cal. L. Rev. 1201, 1229–30 (1996).

In *City of Rome v. United States*, 446 U.S. 156 (1980), the Supreme Court held that jurisdictions within a covered jurisdiction (such as cities within a covered state) cannot bail out. Bailout must be accomplished, if at all, by an entire covered jurisdiction.

4. Internal congressional dynamics may also explain another targeted provision of the 1965 Act: § 4(e), which provided in pertinent part that no person who had completed the sixth grade in a public school in, or a private school accredited by, the Commonwealth of Puerto Rico in which the language of instruction was other than English could be denied the right to vote in any election because of his inability to read or write English. (This section rested on Congress' enforcement power under section 5 of the Fourteenth Amendment rather than section 2 of the Fifteenth Amendment, presumably because Congress did not see the problem as one of racial discrimination.) Representative Emanuel Cellar, a Puerto Rican, was chairman of the House Judiciary Subcommittee responsible for the 1965 Act.

New York maintained a literacy test. (Actually, it required that applicants for registration fill out a form which asked them questions regarding their place of residence, citizenship, and the like.) In *Katzenbach v. Morgan*, 384 U.S. 641 (1966), the Court upheld § 4(e). Justice Brennan's opinion for the Court offered the following analysis of congressional power:

> .... A construction of § 5 [of the Fourteenth Amendment] that would require a judicial determination that the enforcement of the state law precluded by Congress violated the Amendment, as a condition of sustaining the congressional enactment, would depreciate both congressional resourcefulness and congressional responsibility for implementing the Amendment. It would confine the legislative power in this context to the insignificant role of abrogating only those state laws that the judicial branch was prepared to adjudge unconstitutional, or of merely informing the judgment of the judiciary by particularizing the "majestic generalities" of § 1 of the Amendment.
>
> Thus our task in this case is not to determine whether the New York English literacy requirement as applied to deny the right to vote to a person who successfully completed the sixth grade in a Puerto Rican school violates the Equal Protection Clause. Accordingly, our decision in *Lassiter v. Northampton Election Bd.*, 360 U.S. 45, sustaining the North Carolina English literacy requirement as not in all circumstances prohibited by the first sections of the Fourteenth and Fifteenth Amendments, is inapposite.... *Lassiter* did not present the question before us here: Without regard to whether the judiciary would find that the Equal Protection Clause itself nullifies New York's English literacy requirement as so applied, could Congress prohibit the enforce-

ment of the state law by legislating under § 5 of the Fourteenth Amendment? In answering this question, our task is limited to determining whether such legislation is, as required by § 5, appropriate legislation to enforce the Equal Protection Clause.

* * *

We therefore proceed to the consideration whether § 4(e) is "appropriate legislation" to enforce the Equal Protection Clause, that is, under the *McCulloch v. Maryland* standard, whether § 4(e) may be regarded as an enactment to enforce the Equal Protection Clause, whether it is "plainly adapted to that end" and whether it is not prohibited by but is consistent with "the letter and spirit of the constitution."[10]

There can be no doubt that § 4 (e) may be regarded as an enactment to enforce the Equal Protection Clause.... [S]pecifically, § 4(e) may be viewed as a measure to secure for the Puerto Rican community residing in New York nondiscriminatory treatment by government—both in the imposition of voting qualifications and the provision or administration of governmental services, such as public schools, public housing and law enforcement.

Section 4(e) may be readily seen as "plainly adapted" to furthering these aims of the Equal Protection Clause. The practical effect of § 4(e) is to prohibit New York from denying the right to vote to large segments of its Puerto Rican community. Congress has thus prohibited the State from denying to that community the right that is "preservative of all rights." *Yick Wo v. Hopkins,* 118 U.S. 356, 370. This enhanced political power will be helpful in gaining nondiscriminatory treatment in public services for the entire Puerto Rican community. Section 4(e) thereby enables the Puerto Rican minority better to obtain "perfect equality of civil rights and the equal protection of the laws." It was well within congressional authority to say that this need of the Puerto Rican minority for the vote warranted federal intrusion upon any state interests served by the English literacy requirement. It was for Congress, as the branch that made this judgment, to assess and weigh the various conflicting considerations—the risk or pervasiveness of the discrimination in governmental services, the effectiveness of eliminating the state restriction on the right to vote as

10. Contrary to the suggestion of the dissent, ... § 5 does not grant Congress power to exercise discretion in the other direction and to enact "statutes so as in effect to dilute equal protection and due process decisions of this Court." We emphasize that Congress' power under § 5 is limited to adopting measures to enforce the guarantees of the Amendment; § 5 grants Congress no power to restrict, abrogate, or dilute these guarantees. Thus, for example, an enactment authorizing the States to establish racially segregated systems of education would not be—as required by § 5—a measure "to enforce" the Equal Protection Clause since that clause of its own force prohibits such state laws.

a means of dealing with the evil, the adequacy or availability of alternative remedies, and the nature and significance of the state interests that would be affected by the nullification of the English literacy requirement as applied to residents who have successfully completed the sixth grade in a Puerto Rican school. It is not for us to review the congressional resolution of these factors. It is enough that we be able to perceive a basis upon which the Congress might resolve the conflict as it did. There plainly was such a basis to support § 4(e) in the application in question in this case. Any contrary conclusion would require us to be blind to the realities familiar to the legislators.

The result is no different if we confine our inquiry to the question whether § 4(e) was merely legislation aimed at the elimination of an invidious discrimination in establishing voter qualifications. We are told that New York's English literacy requirement originated in the desire to provide an incentive for non-English speaking immigrants to learn the English language and in order to assure the intelligent exercise of the franchise. Yet Congress might well have questioned, in light of the many exemptions provided, and some evidence suggesting that prejudice played a prominent role in the enactment of the requirement,[14] whether these were actually the interests being served. Congress might have also questioned whether denial of a right deemed so precious and fundamental in our society was a necessary or appropriate means of encouraging persons to learn English, or of furthering the goal of an intelligent exercise of the franchise. Finally, Congress might well have concluded that as a means of furthering the intelligent exercise of the franchise, an ability to read or understand Spanish is as effective as ability to read English for those to whom Spanish-language newspapers and Spanish-language radio and television programs are available to inform them of election issues and governmental affairs. Since Congress undertook to legislate so as to preclude the enforcement of the state law, and did so in the context of a general appraisal of literacy requirements for voting, ... to which it brought a specially informed legislative competence, it was Congress' prerogative to weigh these competing

---

14. This evidence consists in part of statements made in the Constitutional Convention first considering the English literacy requirement, such as the following made by the sponsor of the measure: "More precious even than the forms of government are the mental qualities of our race. While those stand unimpaired, all is safe. They are exposed to a single danger, and that is that by constantly changing our voting citizenship through the wholesale, but valuable and necessary infusion of Southern and Eastern European races.... The danger has begun.... We should check it."

This evidence was reinforced by an understanding of the cultural milieu at the time of proposal and enactment, spanning a period from 1915 to 1921—not one of the enlightened eras of our history. Congress was aware of this evidence.

considerations. Here again, it is enough that we perceive a basis upon which Congress might predicate a judgment that the application of New York's English literacy requirement to deny the right to vote to a person with a sixth grade education in Puerto Rican schools in which the language of instruction was other than English constituted an invidious discrimination in violation of the Equal Protection Clause.

What Fourteenth Amendment right, precisely, is section 4(e) designed to secure? Is it the right to vote or some more general interest in equal protection?

Footnote 10 of Justice Brennan's opinion offers his now-famous "ratchet theory" of constitutional law: Congress may expand, but not contract, the protections offered by a constitutional amendment. Does Justice Brennan's theory make sense? Where does Congress' authority to go beyond the Court's interpretation of the Fourteenth or Fifteenth Amendments come from? If Congress can disagree with the Court's decision in *Lassiter*—and sections 4 and 5 of the Act did just that by bringing Northampton County within the list of covered jurisdictions whose literacy tests were suspended—why can't it disagree with other decisions? Moreover, is it entirely clear that congressional expansion under section 5 doesn't infringe on *other* constitutional rights or limits, like Article I, § 2's implicit conferral on the states of control over eligibility to vote; or the Tenth Amendment; or even the voting rights of individuals who *are* eligible to vote under New York's literacy requirement who now see their voting power diluted by the enfranchisement of a new class of individuals? Could Congress decide tomorrow that promoting a well-informed electorate was an important national interest and require a literacy or an understanding test like the ones required for naturalization?

5. Originally, the Act suspended literacy tests only in "covered" jurisdictions, and only for a period of five years. In 1970, the Act was amended to ban all literacy tests nationwide. In *Oregon v. Mitchell*, 400 U.S. 112 (1970), the Supreme Court unanimously upheld the nationwide ban. Arizona challenged the ban on the grounds that its literacy test had always been administered fairly, and thus that the state was entitled to continue its use. The case is captioned "Oregon v. Mitchell" because Oregon had challenged a different provision of the 1970 Act relating to the enfranchisement of eighteen year-olds. The challenge to other provisions of the Act produced a deeply fractured Court; thus, the Justices explained their views on the constitutionality of the literacy test suspension in separate opinions.

Justice Black, who had dissented in *South Carolina v. Katzenbach*, largely because he objected to Congress' singling out southern jurisdictions, upheld the nationwide ban on these terms:

In enacting the literacy test ban ... Congress had before it a long history of the discriminatory use of literacy tests to disfranchise voters on account of their race.... Moreover, Congress had before it striking evidence to show that the provisions of the 1965 Act had had in the span of four years a remarkable impact on minority group voter registration. Congress also had evidence to show that voter registration in areas with large Spanish–American populations was consistently below the state and national averages. In Arizona, for example, only two counties out of eight with Spanish surname populations in excess of 15% showed a voter registration equal to the state-wide average. Arizona also has a serious problem of deficient voter registration among Indians. Congressional concern over the use of a literacy test to disfranchise Puerto Ricans in New York State is already a matter of record in this Court. *Katzenbach v. Morgan, supra*. And as to the Nation as a whole, Congress had before it statistics which demonstrate that voter registration and voter participation are consistently greater in States without literacy tests.

Congress also had before it this country's history of discriminatory educational opportunities in both the North and the South. The children who were denied an equivalent education by the "separate but equal" rule of *Plessy v. Ferguson*, 163 U.S. 537 (1896), overruled in *Brown v. Board of Education*, 347 U.S. 483 (1954), are now old enough to vote. There is substantial, if not overwhelming, evidence from which Congress could have concluded that it is a denial of equal protection to condition the political participation of children educated in a dual school system upon their educational achievement. Moreover, the history of this legislation suggests that concern with educational inequality was perhaps uppermost in the minds of the congressmen who sponsored the Act. The hearings are filled with references to educational inequality. Faced with this and other evidence that literacy tests reduce voter participation in a discriminatory manner not only in the South but throughout the Nation, Congress was supported by substantial evidence in concluding that a nationwide ban on literacy tests was appropriate to enforce the Civil War amendments.

Finally, there is yet another reason for upholding the literacy test provisions of this Act. In imposing a nationwide ban on literacy tests, Congress has recognized a national problem for what it is—a serious national dilemma that touches every corner of our land. In this legislation Congress has recognized that discrimination on account of color and racial origin is not confined to the South, but exists in various parts of the country. Congress has decided that the way to solve the problems of racial discrimination is to deal with nationwide discrimination with nationwide legislation.

Justice Brennan's opinion, joined by Justices White and Marshall, also focused on the denial of equal educational opportunity to minorities, as well as interstate movement:

> We need not question Arizona's assertions as to the nondiscriminatory character, past and present, of its educational system. Congressional power to remedy the evils resulting from state-sponsored racial discrimination does not end when the subject of that discrimination removes himself from the jurisdiction in which the injury occurred. "The Constitution was framed under the dominion of a political philosophy less parochial in range. It was framed upon the theory that the peoples of the several states must sink or swim together, and that in the long run prosperity and salvation are in union and not division." *Baldwin v. G.A.F. Seelig, Inc.*, 294 U.S. 511, 523 (1935); *see Edwards v. California*, 314 U.S. 160, 173–176 (1941)....
>
> The legislative history of the 1970 Amendments contains substantial information upon which Congress could have based a finding that the use of literacy tests in Arizona and in other States where their use was not proscribed by the 1965 Act has the effect of denying the vote to racial minorities whose illiteracy is the consequence of a previous, governmentally sponsored denial of equal educational opportunity. The Attorney General of Arizona told the Senate Subcommittee on Constitutional Rights that many older Indians in the State were "never privileged to attend a formal school." Extensive testimony before both Houses indicated that racial minorities have long received inferior educational opportunities throughout the United States. And interstate migration of such persons, particularly of Negroes from the Southern States, has long been a matter of common knowledge.
>
> Moreover, Congress was given testimony explicitly relating the denial of educational opportunity to inability to pass literacy tests in States not covered by the formula contained in the 1965 Act. The United States Commission on Civil Rights reported a survey of the Northern and Western States which concluded that literacy tests have a negative impact upon voter registration which "falls most heavily on blacks and persons of Spanish surname." With regard specifically to Arizona, the Chairman of the Navajo Tribal Council testified that a greater percentage of Navajos are registered in New Mexico, which has no literacy test, than in Arizona.

And Justice Stewart's opinion, joined by Chief Justice Burger and Justice Blackmun, focused on Congress' institutional competence to make the decision to ban nationwide:

Congress has now undertaken to extend the ban on literacy tests to the whole Nation. I see no constitutional impediment to its doing so. Nationwide application reduces the danger that federal intervention will be perceived as unreasonable discrimination against particular States or particular regions of the country. This in turn increases the likelihood of voluntary compliance with the letter and spirit of federal law. Nationwide application facilitates the free movement of citizens from one State to another, since it eliminates the prospect that a change in residence will mean the loss of a federally protected right. Nationwide application avoids the often difficult task of drawing a line between those States where a problem is pressing enough to warrant federal intervention and those where it is not. Such a line may well appear discriminatory to those who think themselves on the wrong side of it. Moreover the application of the line to particular States can entail a substantial burden on administrative and judicial machinery and a diversion of enforcement resources. Finally, nationwide application may be reasonably thought appropriate when Congress acts against an evil such as racial discrimination which in varying degrees manifests itself in every part of the country. A remedy for racial discrimination which applies in all the States underlines an awareness that the problem is a national one and reflects a national commitment to its solution.

Because the justification for extending the ban on literacy tests to the entire Nation need not turn on whether literacy tests unfairly discriminate against Negroes in every State in the Union, Congress was not required to make state-by-state findings concerning either the equality of educational opportunity or actual impact of literacy requirements on the Negro citizen's access to the ballot box. In the interests of uniformity, Congress may paint with a much broader brush than may this Court, which must confine itself to the judicial function of deciding individual cases and controversies upon individual records. *Cf. Lassiter v. Northampton Election Board, supra.* The findings that Congress made when it enacted the Voting Rights Act of 1965 would have supported a nationwide ban on literacy tests. Instead, at that time "Congress chose to limit its attention to the geographic areas where immediate action seemed necessary." *South Carolina v. Katzenbach*, 383 U.S., at 328. Experience gained under the 1965 Act has now led Congress to conclude that it should go the whole distance. This approach to the problem is a rational one; consequently it is within the constitutional power of Congress under § 2 of the Fifteenth Amendment.

Do *Katzenbach v. Morgan* and *Oregon v. Mitchell* essentially abandon any serious constitutional constraint on Congress' ability to regulate the right to vote? Under what circumstances might the Court doubt Congress' institutional competence to regulate the political process?

The Court revisited these questions in *City of Boerne v. Flores,* 117 S.Ct. 2157 (1997). Congress enacted the Religious Freedom Restoration Act of 1993 (RFRA) in response to a Supreme Court decision, *Employment Division v. Smith,* 494 U.S. 872 (1990). *Smith* had upheld Oregon's denial of unemployment benefits to members of the Native American Church who had lost their jobs because they used peyote, a practice forbidden by the state's criminal law. The *Smith* Court rejected the workers' free exercise of religion claim: it held that as long as a generally applicable government policy was not enacted with the purpose of discriminating against religion, it remains constitutional even if its effect is to impose substantial burdens on religious practice.

An overwhelming bipartisan majority in Congress sought to reverse the result in *Smith by* enacting RFRA, which provided that general policies that "substantially burdened" religious practices were illegal unless the government could prove that (1) the policy furthered a compelling governmental interest and (2) the policy chosen was the least restrictive means of furthering that interest.

The right to free exercise is constitutionally guaranteed against congressional infringement through the First Amendment and, via incorporation of the First Amendment into the Fourteenth Amendment, guaranteed against infringement by state and local governments. Congress' power to enact RFRA rested on its claim to be using its Fourteenth Amendment section 5 powers to enforce the Fourteenth Amendment's guarantees of free exercise of religion.

The Court held RFRA unconstitutional for being beyond the scope of Congress' legitimate powers under section 5. The Court distinguished between legislation that provides remedies for acts that the Court would recognize violate the Fourteenth Amendment, and legislation that redefines the meaning of the Fourteenth Amendment. It held that the former was a valid exercise of Congress' powers under section 5 to "enforce" the Fourteenth Amendment but that the latter was invalid.

In *Boerne*, the Court explicitly re-affirmed all of the voting-rights cases in which Congress had legislated on the basis of its section 5 powers. But the Court noted that "[t]here is language in our opinion in *Katzenbach v. Morgan,* 384 U.S. 641 (1966), which could be interpreted as acknowledging a power in Congress to enact legislation that expands the rights contained in Sec. 1 of the Fourteenth Amendment." The Court rejected this interpretation of *Morgan.*

In light of the line *Boerne* now recognizes between remedial and substantive uses of the section 5 powers, reconsider the scope of Congress' power to legislate to protect the right to vote. Is it clear that the cases we just studied all present no more than remedial uses of Congress' powers under section 5? Are there principled grounds for distinguishing the provisions of the Voting Rights Act of 1965 from RFRA, or does the Court in *City of Boerne* simply treat these voting-rights precedents as sacrosanct, without giving persuasive grounds for doing so? Even if the 1965 Voting Rights Act is not in tension with *City of Boerne,* we will have to consider whether the 1982 Amendments to the VRA are constitutional exercises of Congress' enforcement powers in the wake of *City of Boerne.* We postpone that question until after we study the 1982 Amendments in Chapter 6. *See generally* Pamela S. Karlan, *Two Section Twos and Two Section Fives: Voting Rights and Remedies After* Boerne, 39 Wm. & Mary L. Rev. ___ (1998).

B. What Is a "Covered Change"?

Although at first the suspension of literacy tests and the appointment of federal registrars in selected jurisdictions were the most significant aspects of the 1965 Act, once voters were registered attention turned to other electoral practices and to section 5 of the Act, which required covered jurisdictions to seek prior approval—"preclearance"—of any changes in voting practices in effect on the triggering date.

Many Southern jurisdictions responded to the explosive growth in black voter registration with a campaign of "massive resistance" akin to their attempts to evade the mandate of *Brown v. Board of Education*, 347 U.S. 483 (1954). Consider the first post-Act vote-dilution case, *Smith v. Paris*, 257 F.Supp. 901 (M.D.Ala.1966), *modified*, 386 F.2d 979 (5th Cir. 1967). For over thirty years, elections to the Barbour County (Alabama) Democratic Executive Committee were held on a combined at-large and beat (that is, precinct) basis. Prior to the 1965 Act, only a minuscule number of blacks were registered to vote. Once federal examiners were sent to the county, however, black registration skyrocketed, and by March 1966, four beats in Barbour County had majority-black electorates. In each of these beats, black candidates filed to run. That month, the Committee "with little or no debate, without taking any minutes or making any record of its meetings or discussions, and, so far as the record reflects, with little or no discussion among the members of the community," changed the election method, requiring at-large (county-wide) elections for all positions. *Id.* at 904. The district court enjoined the new election method, finding that its purpose and effect "greatly diminish the effectiveness of the Negroes' right to vote." *Id. See also, e.g., Sims v. Baggett*, 247 F.Supp. 96 (M.D.Ala. 1965), the remedial stage of *Reynolds v. Sims*, where the district court rejected Alabama's state House reapportionment on the grounds that "the Legislature intentionally aggregated predominantly Negro counties with predominantly white counties for the sole purpose of preventing the election of Negroes to House membership." *Id.* at 109. *See generally* Frank R. Parker, Black Votes Count: Political Empowerment in Mississippi After

1965, at 34–77 (1990) (describing Mississippi legislation intended to neutralize black registration).

Section 5 of the Act provides, in pertinent part:

Whenever a State or political subdivision [covered by section 4] shall enact or seek to administer any voting qualification or prerequisite to voting, or standard, practice, or procedure with respect to voting different from that in force or effect on November 1, 1964 [or November 1, 1968, or November 1, 1972, for jurisdictions brought within the coverage formula on those dates,] such State or subdivision may institute an action in the United States District Court for the District of Columbia for a declaratory judgment that such qualification, prerequisite, standard, practice, or procedure does not have the purpose and will not have the effect of denying or abridging the right to vote on account of race or color, or in contravention of the guarantees [protecting language minorities,] and unless and until the court enters such judgment no person shall be denied the right to vote for failure to comply with such qualification, prerequisite, standard, practice, or procedure: *Provided,* That such qualification, prerequisite, standard, practice, or procedure may be enforced without such proceeding if the qualification, prerequisite, standard, practice, or procedure has been submitted by the chief legal officer or other appropriate official of such State or subdivision to the Attorney General and the Attorney General has not interposed an objection within sixty days after such submission, or upon good cause shown, to facilitate an expedited approval within sixty days after such submission, the Attorney General has affirmatively indicated that such objection will not be made. Neither an affirmative indication by the Attorney General that no objection will be made, nor the Attorney General's failure to object, nor a declaratory judgment entered under this section shall bar a subsequent action to enjoin enforcement of such qualification, prerequisite, standard, practice, or procedure.

To what extent does section 5 prevent attempts to circumvent the empowerment of minority voters? The following cases raise the question of when preclearance is required.

Allen v. State Board of Elections
393 U.S. 544 (1969).

■ Mr. Chief Justice Warren delivered the opinion of the Court.

These four cases, three from Mississippi and one from Virginia, involve the application of the Voting Rights Act of 1965 to state election laws and regulations.

* * *

In these four cases, the States have passed new laws or issued new regulations. The central issue is whether these provisions fall within the prohibition of § 5 that prevents the enforcement of "any voting qualification or prerequisite to voting, or standard, practice, or procedure with respect to voting" unless the State first complies with one of the section's approval procedures.

No. 25, *Fairley v. Patterson*, involves a 1966 amendment to § 2870 of the Mississippi Code of 1942. The amendment provides that the board of supervisors of each county may adopt an order providing that board members be elected at large by all qualified electors of the county. Prior to the 1966 amendment, all counties by law were divided into five districts; each district elected one member of the board of supervisors. After the amendment, Adams and Forrest Counties adopted the authorized orders, specifying that each candidate must run at large, but also requiring that each candidate be a resident of the county district he seeks to represent.

* * *

No. 26, *Bunton v. Patterson*, concerns a 1966 amendment to § 6271–08 of the Mississippi Code. The amendment provides that in 11 specified counties, the county superintendent of education shall be appointed by the board of education. Before the enactment of this amendment, all these counties had the option of electing or appointing the superintendent....

No. 36, *Whitley v. Williams*, involves a 1966 amendment to § 3260 of the Mississippi Code, which changed the requirements for independent candidates running in general elections. The amendment makes four revisions: (1) it establishes a new rule that no person who has voted in a primary election may thereafter be placed on the ballot as an independent candidate in the general election; (2) the time for filing a petition as an independent candidate is changed to 60 days before the primary election from the previous 40 days before the general election; (3) the number of signatures of qualified electors needed for the independent qualifying petition is increased substantially; and (4) a new provision is added that each qualified elector who signs the independent qualifying petition must personally sign the petition and must include his polling precinct and county. Appellants are potential candidates whose nominating petitions for independent listing on the ballot were rejected for failure to comply with one or more of the amended provisions.

In all three of these cases, the three-judge District Court ruled that the amendments to the Mississippi Code did not come within the purview of and are not covered by § 5, and dismissed the complaints.

No. 3, *Allen v. State Board of Elections*, concerns a bulletin issued by the Virginia Board of Elections to all election judges. The bulletin was an attempt to modify the provisions of § 24–252 of the Code of Virginia of 1950 which provides, inter alia, that "any voter [may] place on the official ballot the name of any person in his own handwriting...." The Virginia

Code (§ 24–251) further provides that voters with a physical incapacity may be assisted in preparing their ballots. For example, one who is blind may be aided in the preparation of his ballot by a person of his choice. Those unable to mark their ballots due to any other physical disability may be assisted by one of the election judges. However, no statutory provision is made for assistance to those who wish to write in a name, but who are unable to do so because of illiteracy. When Virginia was brought under the coverage of the Voting Rights Act of 1965, Virginia election officials apparently thought that the provision in § 24–252, requiring a voter to cast a write-in vote in the voter's own handwriting, was incompatible with the provisions of § 4 (a) of the Act suspending the enforcement of any test or device as a prerequisite to voting. Therefore, the Board of Elections issued a bulletin to all election judges, instructing that the election judge could aid any qualified voter in the preparation of his ballot, if the voter so requests and if the voter is unable to mark his ballot due to illiteracy.

Appellants are functionally illiterate registered voters from the Fourth Congressional District of Virginia.... In the 1966 elections, appellants attempted to vote for a write-in candidate by sticking labels, printed with the name of their candidate, on the ballot. The election officials refused to count appellants' ballots, claiming that the Virginia election law did not authorize marking ballots with labels. As the election outcome would not have been changed had the disputed ballots been counted, appellants sought only prospective relief.... [Their complaint was also dismissed by a three-judge court.]

* * *

IV.

.... [Section 5 applies] to "any voting qualification or prerequisite to voting, or standard, practice, or procedure with respect to voting...." The Act further provides that the term "voting" "shall include all action necessary to make a vote effective in any primary, special, or general election, including, but not limited to, registration, listing ... or other action required by law prerequisite to voting, casting a ballot, and having such ballot counted properly and included in the appropriate totals of votes cast with respect to candidates for public or party office and propositions for which votes are received in an election." § 14(c)(1). Appellees in the Mississippi cases maintain that § 5 covers only those state enactments which prescribe who may register to vote. While accepting that the Act is broad enough to insure that the votes of all citizens should be cast, appellees urge that § 5 does not cover state rules relating to the qualification of candidates or to state decisions as to which offices shall be elective....[29]

* * *

29. Appellees in No. 3 also argue that § 5 does not apply to the regulation in their

We must reject a narrow construction that appellees would give to § 5. The Voting Rights Act was aimed at the subtle, as well as the obvious, state regulations which have the effect of denying citizens their right to vote because of their race.... We are convinced that in passing the Voting Rights Act, Congress intended that state enactments such as those involved in the instant cases be subject to the § 5 approval requirements.

* * *

The weight of the legislative history and an analysis of the basic purposes of the Act indicate that the enactment in each of these cases constitutes a "voting qualification or prerequisite to voting, or standard, practice, or procedure with respect to voting" within the meaning of § 5.

No. 25 involves a change from district to at-large voting for county supervisors. The right to vote can be affected by a dilution of voting power as well as by an absolute prohibition on casting a ballot. *See Reynolds v. Sims*. Voters who are members of a racial minority might well be in the majority in one district, but in a decided minority in the county as a whole. This type of change could therefore nullify their ability to elect the candidate of their choice just as would prohibiting some of them from voting.

In No. 26 an important county officer in certain counties was made appointive instead of elective. The power of a citizen's vote is affected by this amendment; after the change, he is prohibited from electing an officer formerly subject to the approval of the voters. Such a change could be made either with or without a discriminatory purpose or effect; however, the purpose of § 5 was to submit such changes to scrutiny.

The changes in No. 36 appear aimed at increasing the difficulty for an independent candidate to gain a position on the general election ballot. These changes might also undermine the effectiveness of voters who wish to elect independent candidates. One change involved in No. 36 deserves special note. The amendment provides that no person who has voted in a primary election may thereafter be placed on the ballot as an independent candidate in the general election. This is a "procedure with respect to voting" with substantial impact. One must forgo his right to vote in his party primary if he thinks he might later wish to become an independent candidate.

case, because that regulation was issued in an attempt to comply with the provisions of the Voting Rights Act. They argue that if § 5 applies to the Virginia regulation, covered States would be prohibited from quickly complying with the Act. We cannot accept this argument, however. A State is not exempted from the coverage of § 5 merely because its legislation is passed in an attempt to comply with the provisions of the Act. To hold otherwise would mean that legislation, allegedly passed to meet the requirements of the Act, would be exempted from § 5 coverage—even though it would have the effect of racial discrimination. It is precisely this situation Congress sought to avoid in passing § 5.

The bulletin in No. 3 outlines new procedures for casting write-in votes. As in all these cases, we do not consider whether this change has a discriminatory purpose or effect. It is clear, however, that the new procedure with respect to voting is different from the procedure in effect when the State became subject to the Act; therefore, the enactment must meet the approval requirements of § 5 in order to be enforceable.

* * *

■ MR. JUSTICE HARLAN, concurring in part and dissenting in part.

* * *

I.

I shall first consider the Court's extremely broad construction of § 5. It is best to begin by delineating the precise area of difference between the position the majority adopts and the one which I consider represents the better view of the statute. We are in agreement that in requiring federal review of changes in any "standard, practice, or procedure with respect to voting," Congress intended to include all state laws that changed the process by which voters were registered and had their ballots counted. The Court, however, goes further to hold that a State covered by the Act must submit for federal approval all those laws that could arguably have an impact on Negro voting power, even though the manner in which the election is conducted remains unchanged. I believe that this reading of the statute should be rejected on several grounds. It ignores the place of § 5 in the larger structure of the Act; it is untrue to the statute's language; and it is unsupported by the legislative history.

A.

First, and most important, the Court's construction ignores the structure of the complex regulatory scheme created by the Voting Rights Act. The Court's opinion assumes that § 5 may be considered apart from the rest of the Act. In fact, however, the provision is clearly designed to march in lock-step with § 4—the two sections cannot be understood apart from one another. Section 4 is one of the Act's central provisions, suspending the operation of all literacy tests and similar "devices" for at least five years in States whose low voter turnout indicated that these "tests" and "devices" had been used to exclude Negroes from the suffrage in the past. Section 5, moreover, reveals that it was not designed to implement new substantive policies but that it was structured to assure the effectiveness of the dramatic step that Congress had taken in § 4. The federal approval procedure found in § 5 only applies to those States whose literacy tests or similar "devices" have been suspended by § 4.

* * *

As soon as it is recognized that § 5 was designed solely to implement the policies of § 4, it becomes apparent that the Court's decision today permits the tail to wag the dog. For the Court has now construed § 5 to require a revolutionary innovation in American government that goes far beyond that which was accomplished by § 4. The fourth section of the Act had the profoundly important purpose of permitting the Negro people to gain access to the voting booths of the South once and for all. But the action taken by Congress in § 4 proceeded on the premise that once Negroes had gained free access to the ballot box, state governments would then be suitably responsive to their voice, and federal intervention would not be justified. In moving against "tests and devices" in § 4, Congress moved only against those techniques that prevented Negroes from voting at all. Congress did not attempt to restructure state governments. The Court now reads § 5, however, as vastly increasing the sphere of federal intervention beyond that contemplated by § 4, despite the fact that the two provisions were designed simply to interlock.

* * *

The difficulties with the Court's construction increase even further when the language of the statute is considered closely.... Immediately following the statute's description of the federal approval procedure, § 5 proceeds to describe the type of relief an aggrieved voter may obtain if a State enforces a new statute without obtaining the consent of the appropriate federal authorities: "no person shall be denied the right to vote for failure to comply with such qualification, prerequisite, standard, practice, or procedure." This remedy serves to delimit the meaning of the formula in question. Congress was clearly concerned with changes in procedure with which voters could comply. But a law, like that in *Fairley v. Patterson*, No. 25, which permits all members of the County Board of Supervisors to run in the entire county and not in smaller districts, does not require a voter to comply with anything at all, and so does not come within the scope of the language used by Congress....

B.

While the Court's opinion does not confront the factors I have just canvassed, it does attempt to justify its holding on the basis of its understanding "of the legislative history and an analysis of the basic purposes of the Act." Turning first to consider the Act's basic purposes, the Court suggests that Congress intended to adopt the concept of voting articulated in *Reynolds v. Sims*, 377 U.S. 533 (1964), and protect Negroes against a dilution of their voting power.... [T]he fact is that Congress consciously refused to base § 5 of the Voting Rights Act on its powers under the Fourteenth Amendment, upon which the reapportionment cases are grounded. The Act's preamble states that it is intended "to enforce the fifteenth amendment to the Constitution of the United States, and for other purposes." When Senator Fong of Hawaii suggested that the preamble include a citation to the Fourteenth Amendment as well, the Attorney General explained that he "would have quite a strong preference not to," because "I believe that S. 1564 as drafted can be squarely based on the 15th amendment.".....

As the reapportionment cases rest upon the Equal Protection Clause, they cannot be cited to support the claim that Congress, in passing this Act, intended to proceed against state statutes regulating the nature of the constituencies legislators could properly represent. If Congress intended, as it clearly did, to ground § 5 on the Fifteenth Amendment, the leading voting case is not *Reynolds v. Sims*, but *Gomillion v. Lightfoot*, 364 U.S. 339 (1960). While that case establishes the proposition that redistricting done with the purpose of excluding Negroes from a municipality violates the Fifteenth Amendment, it also maintains the distinction between an attempt to exclude Negroes totally from the relevant constituency, and a statute that permits Negroes to vote but which uses the gerrymander to contain the impact of Negro suffrage.

* * *

C.

Section 5, then, should properly be read to require federal approval only of those state laws that change either voter qualifications or the manner in which elections are conducted. This does not mean, however, that the District Courts in the four cases before us were right in unanimously concluding that the Voting Rights Act did not apply. Rather, it seems to me that only the judgment in *Fairley v. Patterson*, No. 25, should be affirmed, as that case involves a state statute which simply gives each county the right to elect its Board of Supervisors on an at-large basis.

In *Whitley v. Williams*, No. 36, however, Mississippi's new statute both imposes new qualifications on independent voters who wish to nominate a candidate by petition and alters the manner in which such nominations are made. Since the Voting Rights Act explicitly covers "primary" elections, see § 14(c)(1), the only significant question presented is whether a petitioning procedure should be considered a "primary" within the meaning of the Act. As the nominating petition is the functional equivalent of the political primary, I can perceive no good reason why it should not be included within the ambit of the Act.

The statute involved in *Bunton v. Patterson*, No. 26, raises a somewhat more difficult problem of statutory interpretation. If one looks to its impact on the voters, the State's law making the office of school superintendent appointive enacts a "voting qualification" of the most drastic kind. While under the old regime all registered voters could cast a ballot, now none are qualified. On the other hand, one can argue that the concept of a "voting qualification" presupposes that there will be a vote. On balance, I would hold that the statute comes within § 5. . . .

Finally, Virginia has quite obviously altered the manner in which an election is conducted when for the first time it has been obliged to issue regulations concerning the way in which illiterate voters shall be processed at the polls. Consequently, I would reverse the lower court's decision in the *Allen* case, No. 3.

* * *

■ Mr. Justice Black, dissenting.

Assuming the validity of the Voting Rights Act of 1965, as the Court does, I would agree with its careful interpretation of the Act, and would further agree with its holding as to jurisdiction and with its disposition of the four cases now before us. But I am still of the opinion that . . . a part of § 5 violates the United States Constitution. Section 5 provides that several Southern States cannot effectively amend either their constitutions or laws relating to voting without persuading the United States Attorney General or the United States District Court for the District of Columbia that the proposed changes in state laws do not have the purpose and will not have the effect of denying to citizens the right to vote on account of race or color. This is reminiscent of old Reconstruction days when soldiers controlled the South and when those States were compelled to make reports to military commanders of what they did. The Southern States were at that time deprived of their right to pass laws on the premise that they were not then a part of the Union and therefore could be treated with all the harshness meted out to conquered provinces. The constitutionality of that doctrine was certainly not clear at that time. And whether the doctrine was constitutional or not, I had thought that the whole Nation had long since repented of the application of this "conquered province" concept, even as to the time immediately following the bitter Civil War. I doubt that any of the 13 Colonies would have agreed to our Constitution if they had dreamed that the time might come when they would have to go to a United States Attorney General or a District of Columbia court with hat in hand begging for permission to change their laws.

* * *

NOTES AND QUESTIONS

1. In addition to deciding important questions about the scope of section 5, *Allen* also resolved a number of important procedural questions. First, it held that affected citizens had a private right of action under section 5: they could sue to enjoin voting practices or procedures that had not received preclearance. The Court recognized that these citizens could serve as "private attorneys general" to ensure compliance with section 5. Particularly in light of the Court's expansive reading of its scope, it was clear the Justice Department alone could not enforce section 5 adequately. Second, *Allen* held that private citizens could bring suit before local three-judge district courts, that is, courts in their home state, for an injunction ordering the jurisdiction seeking to use the new practice to obtain preclearance prior to implementation. (Private plaintiffs may also seek section 5 injunctions in state court. *See Hathorn v. Lovorn*, 457 U.S. 255 (1982).) By contrast, jurisdictions seeking preclearance were required to bring suit only in the United States District Court for the District of Columbia. Finally, *Allen* distinguished between the burden facing private plaintiffs in a so-called coverage lawsuit—simply to show that the defendant jurisdiction was seeking to use a new voting practice, standard, or procedure—and the burden facing plaintiff jurisdictions in so-called "preclearance" lawsuits—in which the jurisdiction was required to prove that the change has neither a discriminatory purpose nor a discriminatory effect. *See infra* Section C.

2. According to a study by the United States Commission on Civil Rights, the electoral changes from Mississippi at issue in *Allen* were only some of at least 30 bills introduced during regular and special legislative sessions in 1966, following passage of the Voting Rights Act in 1965. Twelve of these bills passed, making substantial alterations in the state's election laws. The bill at issue in *Allen* was sponsored by representatives from counties with either potential black majorities or at least one black-majority district. Abigail Thernstrom, Whose Votes Count 23–24 (1987). Why would white representatives from counties with potential black majorities favor at-large elections, if voting was polarized along racial lines in those counties? Would voter registration rates and turnout affect the outcome of at-large elections?

3. What accounts for the difference between Chief Justice Warren's and Justice Harlan's approach? Notice that the Chief Justice's opinion focuses more heavily on the overall purpose of the Act while Justice Harlan concentrates on the Act's structure. Which approach do you find more persuasive? Does Justice Harlan have to stretch his own analysis to reach the result he clearly favors?

4. Between 1965 and 1969, very few jurisdictions sought preclearance of any changes at all. Since then, the number of requests for preclearance has skyrocketed. Each year the Department receives an average of 17,000 preclearance submissions. The question remains, however, of what changes require preclearance. In *Perkins v. Matthews*, 400 U.S. 379 (1971), the Court held that changes in locations of the polling places, changes in municipal boundaries through annexations of adjacent areas which enlarged the number of eligible voters, and a change from ward to at-large election of aldermen were covered. Using the analysis from *Allen*, how would you explain the rationale? Similarly, in *Georgia v. United States*, 411 U.S. 526 (1973), the Court held that reapportionment involved a covered change. And in *Hadnott v. Amos*, 394 U.S. 358 (1969), and *NAACP v. Hampton County Election Commission*, 470 U.S. 166 (1985), the Court held that statutes relating to filing dates and special elections warranted § 5 scrutiny. Can you sketch out an account under which these types of measures would have a discriminatory purpose or effect? Are there any limits to the reach of section 5? Consider the following two cases.

Dougherty County Board of Education v. White
439 U.S. 32 (1978).

■ MR. JUSTICE MARSHALL delivered the opinion of the Court.

* * *

I

The facts in this case are not in dispute. Appellee, a Negro, is employed as Assistant Coordinator of Student Personnel Services by appellant Dougherty County Board of Education (Board). In May 1972, he announced his candidacy for the Georgia House of Representatives. Less than a month later, on June 12, 1972, the Board adopted Rule 58 without seeking prior federal approval. Rule 58 provides:

> "POLITICAL OFFICE. Any employee of the school system who becomes a candidate for any elective political office, will be required to take a leave of absence, without pay, such leave becoming effective upon the qualifying for such elective office and continuing for the duration of such political activity, and during the period of service in such office, if elected thereto."

Appellee qualified as a candidate for the Democratic primary in June 1972, and was compelled by Rule 58 to take a leave of absence without pay. After his defeat in the August primary, appellee was reinstated. Again in June 1974, he qualified as a candidate for the Georgia House and was forced to take leave. He was successful in both the August primary and the November general election. Accordingly, his leave continued through mid-November 1974. Appellee took a third leave of absence in June 1976, when he qualified to run for re-election. When it became clear in September that he would be unopposed in the November 1976 election, appellee was reinstated.[3] As a consequence of those mandatory leaves, appellee lost pay in the amount of $2,810 in 1972, $4,780 in 1974, and $3,750 in 1976.

In June 1976, appellee filed this action in the Middle District of Georgia alleging that Rule 58 was ... subject to the preclearance requirements of § 5 of the [Voting Rights] Act. Appellee averred that he was the first Negro in recent memory, perhaps since Reconstruction, to run for the Georgia General Assembly from Dougherty County. The Board did not contest this fact, and further acknowledged that it was aware of no individual other than appellee who had run for public office while an employee of the Dougherty County Board of Education.

* * *

---

3. The Solicitor General and counsel for appellants advise us that appellee was also on unpaid leave during his participation in the annual 2 1/2–month sittings of the Georgia General Assembly in 1975, 1976, 1977, and 1978. Appellee did not challenge this application of Rule 58 below. We therefore do not consider whether preclearance is required for a policy governing mandatory leaves during the interval in which an employee is actually absent due to legislative responsibilities.

II

.... Although § 14(c)(1) expansively defines the term "voting" to "include all action necessary to make a vote effective," the [Voting Rights] Act itself nowhere amplifies the meaning of the phrase "standard, practice, or procedure with respect to voting." Accordingly, in our previous constructions of § 5, we have sought guidance from the history and purpose of the Act.

A

This Court first considered the scope of the critical language of § 5 in *Allen v. State Board of Elections*.... [T]he *Allen* Court held that the phrase "standard, practice, or procedure" must be given the "broadest possible scope," and construed it to encompass candidate qualification requirements.

* * *

The Attorney General's regulations, in force since 1971, reflect an equally inclusive understanding of the reach of § 5. They provide that "[all] changes affecting voting, even though the change appears to be minor or indirect," must be submitted for prior approval. 28 CFR § 51.4(a) (1977). More particularly, the regulations require preclearance of "[any] alteration affecting the eligibility of persons to become or remain candidates or obtain a position on the ballot in primary or general elections or to become or remain office-holders." § 51.4(c)(4). Pursuant to these regulations, the Attorney General, after being apprised of Rule 58, requested its submission for § 5 clearance. Given the central role of the Attorney General in formulating and implementing § 5, this interpretation of its scope is entitled to particular deference.

B

Despite these consistently expansive constructions of § 5, appellants contend that the Attorney General and District Court erred in treating Rule 58 as a "standard, practice, or procedure with respect to voting" rather than as simply "a means of getting a full days work for a full days pay—nothing more and nothing less." In appellants' view, Congress did not intend to subject all internal personnel measures affecting political activity to federal superintendence.

The Board mischaracterizes its policy. Rule 58 is not a neutral personnel practice governing all forms of absenteeism. Rather, it specifically addresses the electoral process, singling out candidacy for elective office as a disabling activity. Although not in form a filing fee, the Rule operates in precisely the same fashion. By imposing substantial economic disincentives on employees who wish to seek elective office, the Rule burdens entry into elective campaigns and, concomitantly, limits the choices available to Dougherty County voters. Given the potential loss of thousands of dollars by employees subject to Rule 58, the Board's policy could operate as a more substantial inhibition on entry into the elective process than many of the filing-fee changes involving only hundreds of dollars to which the Attorney General has successfully interposed objections.

* * *

We do not, of course, suggest that all constraints on employee political activity affecting voter choice violate § 5. Presumably, most regulation of political involvement by public employees would not be found to have an invidious purpose or effect. Yet the same could be said of almost all changes subject to § 5. According to the most recent figures available, the Voting Rights Section of the Civil Rights Division processes annually some 1,800 submissions involving over 3,100 changes and interposes objections to less than 2%. Approximately 91% of these submissions receive clearance without further exchange of correspondence. Thus, in determining if an enactment triggers § 5 scrutiny, the question is not whether the provision is in fact innocuous and likely to be approved, but whether it has a potential for discrimination.

Without intimating any views on the substantive question of Rule 58's legitimacy as a nonracial personnel measure, we believe that the circumstances surrounding its adoption and its effect on the political process are sufficiently suggestive of the potential for discrimination to demonstrate the need for preclearance. Appellee was the first Negro in recent years to seek election to the General Assembly from Dougherty County, an area with a long history of racial discrimination in voting. Less than a month after appellee announced his candidacy, the Board adopted Rule 58, concededly without any prior experience of absenteeism among employees seeking office. That the Board made its mandatory leave-of-absence requirement contingent on candidacy rather than on absence during working hours underscores the Rule's potential for inhibiting participation in the electoral process.

* * *

■ MR. JUSTICE POWELL, with whom THE CHIEF JUSTICE and MR. JUSTICE REHNQUIST join, dissenting.[a]

* * *

Section 5 requires federal preclearance before a "political subdivision" of a State covered by § 4 of the Act may enforce a change in "any voting qualification or prerequisite to voting, or standard, practice, or procedure with respect to voting...." This provision marked a radical departure from traditional notions of constitutional federalism, a departure several Members of this Court have regarded as unconstitutional.... Congress tem-

---

a. Justice Stewart also joined the relevant portions of the dissent.

pered the intrusion of the Federal Government into state affairs, however, by limiting the Act's coverage to voting regulations.

* * *

The question under this language, therefore, is whether Rule 58 of the Board pertains to voting. Contrary to the suggestion of the Court's opinion, the answer to this question turns neither on the Board's possible discrimination against the appellee, nor on the potential of enactments such as Rule 58 for use as instruments of racial discrimination. Section 5 by its terms is not limited to enactments that have a potential for discriminatory use; rather, it extends to all regulations with respect to voting, regardless of their purpose or potential uses. The affected party's race was conceded by counsel to be irrelevant in determining whether Rule 58 pertains to voting; nor is the timing of the adoption of Rule 58 of any significance. Indeed, in stating his cause of action under the Act, the appellee does not allege any discrimination on the basis of race. Yet the Court, in holding that Rule 58 is subject to the preclearance requirements of § 5, relies on a perceived potential for discrimination. In so doing, the Court simply disregards the explicit scope of § 5 and relies upon factors that the parties have conceded to be irrelevant.

Separated from all mistaken references to racial discrimination, the Court's holding that Rule 58 is a "standard, practice, or procedure with respect to voting" is difficult to understand. It tortures the language of the Act to conclude that this personnel regulation, having nothing to do with the conduct of elections as such, is state action "with respect to voting." No one is denied the right to vote; nor is anyone's exercise of the franchise impaired.

To support its interpretation of § 5, the Court has constructed a tenuous theory, reasoning that, because the right to vote includes the right to vote for whoever may wish to run for office, any discouragement given any potential candidate may deprive someone of the right to vote. In constructing this theory, the Court relies upon *Bullock v. Carter*, 405 U.S. 134 (1972); *Hadnott v. Amos*, 394 U.S. 358 (1969); and *Allen v. State Board of Elections*, 393 U.S. 544 (1969)—cases that involved explicit barriers to candidacy, such as the filing fees held to violate the Fourteenth Amendment in *Bullock*. The Court states that the "reality here is that Rule 58's impact on elections is no different from that of many of the candidate qualification changes for which we have previously required preclearance." But the notion that a State or locality imposes a "qualification" on candidates by refusing to support their campaigns with public funds is without support in reason or precedent.

. . . . [Rule 58] effects no change in an election law or in a law regulating who may vote or when and where they may do so. It is a personnel rule directed to the resolution of a personnel problem: the expenditure of public funds to support the candidacy of an employee whose time and energies may be devoted to campaigning, rather than to counseling schoolchildren.

After extending the scope of § 5 beyond anything indicated in the statutory language or in precedent, the Court attempts to limit its holding by suggesting that Rule 58 somehow differs from a "neutral personnel practice governing all forms of absenteeism," as it "specifically addresses the electoral process." Thus, the Court intimates that it would not require Rule 58 to be precleared if the rule required Board employees to take unpaid leaves of absence whenever an extracurricular responsibility required them frequently to be absent from their duties—whether that responsibility derived from candidacy for office, campaigning for a friend who is running for office, fulfilling civic duties, or entering into gainful employment with a second employer. The Court goes on, however, to give as the principal reason for extension of § 5 to Rule 58 the effect of such rules on potential candidates for office. What the Court fails to note is that the effect on a potential candidate of a "neutral personnel practice governing all forms of absenteeism" is no less than the effect of Rule 58 as enacted by the Dougherty County School Board. Thus, under a general absenteeism provision the appellee would go without pay just as he did under Rule 58; the only difference would be that Board employees absent for reasons other than their candidacy would join the appellee on leave. Under the Court's rationale, therefore, even those enactments making no explicit reference to the electoral process would have to be cleared through the Attorney General or the District Court for the District of Columbia. Indeed, if the Court truly means that any incidental impact on elections is sufficient to trigger the preclearance requirement of § 5, then it is difficult to imagine what sorts of state or local enactments would not fall within the scope of that section.

* * *

Presley v. Etowah County Commission
502 U.S. 491 (1992).

■ JUSTICE KENNEDY delivered the opinion of the Court.

In various Alabama counties voters elect members of county commissions whose principal function is to supervise and control the maintenance, repair, and construction of the county roads. See Ala. Code §§ 11-3-1, 11-3-10 (1975). [The case before us concerns] certain changes in the decisionmaking authority of the elected members on [the Etowah County Commission], and the question to be decided is whether these were changes "with respect to voting" within the meaning of § 5 of the Voting Rights Act of 1965.

* * *

I

To determine whether there have been changes with respect to voting, we must compare the challenged practices with those in existence before they were adopted. Absent relevant intervening changes, the Act requires us to use practices in existence on November 1, 1964, as our standard of comparison.

* * *

On November 1, 1964, commission members were elected at large under a "residency district" system. The entire electorate of Etowah County voted on candidates for each of the five seats. Four of the seats corresponded to the four residency districts of the county. Candidates were required to reside in the appropriate district. The fifth member, the chairman, was not subject to a district residency requirement, though residency in the county itself was a requirement.

Each of the four residency districts functioned as a road district. The commissioner residing in the district exercised control over a road shop, equipment, and road crew for that district. It was the practice of the commission to vote as a collective body on the division of funds among the road districts, but once funds were divided each commissioner exercised individual control over spending priorities within his district. The chairman was responsible for overseeing the solid waste authority, preparing the budget, and managing the courthouse building and grounds.

Under a consent decree issued in 1986, see *Dillard v. Crenshaw County*, No. 85–T–1332–N (MD Ala., Nov. 12, 1986), the commission is being restructured, so that after a transition period there will be a six-member commission, with each of the members elected by the voters of a different district. The changes required by the consent decree were precleared by the Attorney General. For present purposes, it suffices to say that when this litigation began the commission consisted of four holdover members who had been on the commission before the entry of the consent decree and two new members elected from new districts. Commissioner Williams, who is white, was elected from new district 6, and Commissioner Presley, who is black, was elected from new district 5. Presley is the principal appellant in the Etowah County case. His complaint relates not to the elections but to actions taken by the four holdover members when he and Williams first took office.

On August 25, 1987, the commission passed the "Road Supervision Resolution." It provided that each holdover commissioner would continue to control the workers and operations assigned to his respective road shop, which, it must be remembered, accounted for all the road shops the county had. It also gave the four holdovers joint responsibility for overseeing the repair, maintenance, and improvement of all the roads of Etowah County in order to pick up the roads in the districts where the new commissioners resided. The new commissioners, now foreclosed from exercising any authority over roads, were given other functions under the resolution. Presley was to oversee maintenance of the county courthouse and Williams the operation of the engineering department. The Road Supervision Resolution was passed by a 4–2 margin, with the two new commissioners dissenting.

The same day the Road Supervision Resolution was passed, the commission passed a second, the so-called "Common Fund Resolution." It provides in part that

> "all monies earmarked and budgeted for repair, maintenance and improvement of the streets, roads and public ways of Etowah County [shall] be placed and maintained in common accounts, [shall] not be allocated, budgeted or designated for use in districts, and [shall] be used county-wide in accordance with need, for the repair, maintenance and improvement of all streets, roads and public ways in Etowah County which are under the jurisdiction of the Etowah County Commission."

This had the effect of altering the prior practice of allowing each commissioner full authority to determine how to spend the funds allocated to his own district. The Etowah County Commission did not seek judicial or administrative preclearance of either the Road Supervision Resolution or the Common Fund Resolution. The District Court held that the Road Supervision Resolution was subject to preclearance but that the Common Fund Resolution was not. No appeal was taken from the first ruling, so only the Common Fund Resolution is before us in the Etowah County case.

* * *

II

* * *

The principle that § 5 covers voting changes over a wide range is well illustrated by the separate cases we considered in the single opinion for the Court in *Allen*. *Allen* involved four cases. The eponymous *Allen v. State Board of Elections* concerned a change in the procedures for the casting of write-in ballots. In *Whitley v. Williams*, there were changes in the requirements for independent candidates running in general elections. The challenged procedure in *Fairley v. Patterson* resulted in a change from single-district voting to at-large voting. The remaining case, *Bunton v. Patterson*, involved a statute which provided that officials who in previous years had been elected would be appointed. We held that the changes in each of the four cases were covered by § 5.

Our cases since *Allen* reveal a consistent requirement that changes subject to § 5 pertain only to voting. Without implying that the four typologies exhaust the statute's coverage, we can say these later cases fall within one of the four factual contexts presented in the *Allen* cases.

* * *

The first three categories involve changes in election procedures, while all the examples within the fourth category might be termed substantive changes as to which offices are elective. But whether the changes are of procedure or substance, each has a direct relation to voting and the election process.

III

A comparison of the changes at issue here with those in our prior decisions demonstrates that the present cas[e] do[es] not involve changes covered by the Act.

* * *

The Etowah County Commission's Common Fund Resolution is not a change within any of the categories recognized in *Allen* or our later cases. It has no connection to voting procedures: It does not affect the manner of holding elections, it alters or imposes no candidacy qualifications or requirements, and it leaves undisturbed the composition of the electorate. It also has no bearing on the substance of voting power, for it does not increase or diminish the number of officials for whom the electorate may vote. Rather, the Common Fund Resolution concerns the internal operations of an elected body.

* * *

Were we to accept the appellants' proffered reading of § 5, we would work an unconstrained expansion of its coverage. Innumerable state and local enactments having nothing to do with voting affect the power of elected officials. When a state or local body adopts a new governmental program or modifies an existing one it will often be the case that it changes the powers of elected officials. So too, when a state or local body alters its internal operating procedures, for example by modifying its subcommittee assignment system, it "implicates an elected official's decisionmaking authority."

Appellants and the United States fail to provide a workable standard for distinguishing between changes in rules governing voting and changes in the routine organization and functioning of government. Some standard is necessary, for in a real sense every decision taken by government implicates voting. This is but the felicitous consequence of democracy, in which power derives from the people. Yet no one would contend that when Congress enacted the Voting Rights Act it meant to subject all or even most decisions of government in covered jurisdictions to federal supervision. Rather, the Act by its terms covers any "voting qualification or prerequisite to voting, or standard, practice, or procedure with respect to voting." 42 U.S.C. § 1973c. A faithful effort to implement the design of the statute must begin by drawing lines between those governmental decisions that involve voting and those that do not.

A simple example shows the inadequacy of the line proffered by the appellants and the United States. Under the appellants' view, every time a covered jurisdiction passed a budget that differed from the previous year's budget it would be required to obtain preclearance. The amount of funds available to an elected official has a profound effect on the power exercised. A vote for an ill-funded official is less valuable than a vote for a well-funded one.

* * *

Under the view advanced by appellants and the United States, every time a state legislature acts to diminish or increase the power of local officials, preclearance would be required. Governmental action decreasing the power of local officials could carry with it a potential for discrimination against those who represent racial minorities at the local level. At the same time, increasing the power of local officials will entail a relative decrease in the power of state officials, and that too could carry with it a potential for discrimination against state officials who represent racial minorities at the state level. The all but limitless minor changes in the allocation of power among officials and the constant adjustments required for the efficient governance of every covered State illustrate the necessity for us to formulate workable rules to confine the coverage of § 5 to its legitimate sphere: voting.

Changes which affect only the distribution of power among officials are not subject to § 5 because such changes have no direct relation to, or impact on, voting. The Etowah County Commission's Common Fund Resolution was not subject to the preclearance requirement.

* * *

V

Nothing we say implies that the conduct at issue . . . is not actionable under a different remedial scheme. The Voting Rights Act is not an all-purpose antidiscrimination statute. The fact that the intrusive mechanisms of the Act do not apply to other forms of pernicious discrimination does not undermine its utility in combating the specific evils it was designed to address.

Our prior cases hold, and we reaffirm today, that every change in rules governing voting must be precleared. The legislative history we rehearsed in *South Carolina v. Katzenbach* was cited to demonstrate Congress' concern for the protection of voting rights. Neither the appellants nor the United States has pointed to anything we said there or in the statutes reenacting the Voting Rights Act to suggest that Congress meant other than what it said when it made § 5 applicable to changes "with respect to voting" rather than, say, changes "with respect to governance."

If federalism is to operate as a practical system of governance and not a mere poetic ideal, the States must be allowed both predictability and efficiency in structuring their governments. Constant minor adjustments in the allocation of power among state and local officials serve this elemental purpose.

* * *

NOTES AND QUESTIONS

1. What accounts for the difference in result between *Dougherty County* and *Presley*? Is it simply a change in the Court's membership—three of the four Justices who sat in both cases (White, Blackmun, and Stevens) dissented in *Presley*, a change in the Court's attitude due to the passage of time, or something else?

2. To what extent should evidence about the context in which a challenged provision is adopted inform the question whether it affects "voting"? Justice Marshall's opinion in *Dougherty County* seems to weigh these circumstances quite heavily while Justice Kennedy's opinion in *Presley* essentially disregards them. In dissent in *Presley*, Justice Stevens recognized the potential line-drawing problem identified by the majority but responded that "this is a case in which a few pages of history are far more illuminating than volumes of logic and hours of speculation about hypothetical line-drawing problems," and concluded that "[a]t the very least, I would hold that the reallocation of decisionmaking authority of an elective office that is taken (1) after the victory of a black candidate, and (2) after the entry of a consent decree designed to give black voters an opportunity to have representation on an elective body, is covered by § 5." On remand, this perspective prevailed: the district court concluded that the Commission's actions violated the 1986 consent decree. *See Presley v. Etowah County Commission*, 869 F.Supp. 1555 (M.D.Ala.1994).

If context is considered, does this transform section 5 coverage litigation into a full-blown consideration of actual racial discrimination rather than simply an inquiry into whether, under some circumstances, a rule might be discriminatory?

3. The reliance on context poses another question: does the Court's decision in *Dougherty County* mean that *all* similar personnel rules—even if not adopted in similarly suspicious circumstances—require preclearance? One district court has held that "[w]hether a specific change made by a covered political jurisdiction constitutes a change in a 'voting qualification or prerequisite to voting, or standard, or practice, or procedure with respect to voting' that is subject to the preclearance requirement of Section 5 turns on whether such a change has the 'potential for discrimination' against black persons" in light of the facts presented by the plaintiffs in the case before it. *Greene County Racing Commission v. City of Birmingham*, 772 F.Supp. 1207, 1212 (N.D.Ala.1991) (three-judge court), *vacated and re-*

manded sub nom. Harris v. City of Birmingham, 505 U.S. 1201 (1992). Under this approach, for example, a personnel change in an all-white municipality would not require preclearance. Is that conclusion correct? Can any procedural rule, such as preclearance, function mechanically if it sometimes requires a substantive determination, such as the existence of a "potential for discrimination," to decide whether the procedural rule should apply?

Ultimately, this issue comes down to *who* should decide, and with what level of certainty, whether there is a potential for discrimination. Arguably, requiring plaintiffs in section 5 coverage cases to present facts regarding electoral circumstances in specific jurisdictions asks the local district court to do precisely what was forbidden by Congress—that is, to determine whether a change was actually discriminatory. The "potential for discrimination" inquiry may be simply a way of determining, with regard to a previously unaddressed type of statute, whether the change is a change "with respect to voting" (as opposed to a change affecting only things other than voting). *See, e.g., NAACP v. Hampton County Election Commission*, 470 U.S. 166 (1985) (declining to decide whether the change in the particular election date at issue was plausibly discriminatory because preclearance had been required of previous changes in election dates in other jurisdictions).

4. Note the *Dougherty County* Court's deference to the Department of Justice's interpretation of the scope of section 5. The current version of the Department's section 5 regulations, 28 C.F.R. § 51.13 (1995) provides the following examples of changes affecting voting:

(a) Any change in qualifications or eligibility for voting.

(b) Any change concerning registration, balloting, and the counting of votes and any change concerning publicity for or assistance in registration or voting.

(c) Any change with respect to the use of a language other than English in any aspect of the electoral process.

(d) Any change in the boundaries of voting precincts or in the location of polling places.

(e) Any change in the constituency of an official or the boundaries of a voting unit (e.g., through redistricting, annexation, deannexation, incorporation, reapportionment, changing to at-large elections from district elections, or changing to district elections from at-large elections).

(f) Any change in the method of determining the outcome of an election (e.g., by requiring a majority vote for election or the use of a designated post or place system).

(g) Any change affecting the eligibility of persons to become or remain candidates, to obtain a position on the ballot in primary or general elections, or to become or remain holders of elective offices.

(h) Any change in the eligibility and qualification procedures for independent candidates.

(i) Any change in the term of an elective office or an elected official or in the offices that are elective (e.g., by shortening the term of an office, changing from election to appointment or staggering the terms of offices).

(j) Any change affecting the necessity of or methods for offering issues and propositions for approval by referendum.

(k) Any change affecting the right or ability of persons to participate in political campaigns which is effected by a jurisdiction subject to the requirement of section 5.

5. In light of *Presley*, is *Hardy v. Wallace*, 603 F.Supp. 174 (N.D.Ala.1985) (three-judge court), still good law? *Hardy* involved the selection of members to the Greene County Racing Commission. Greene County was 78 percent black. The race track was the major employer in the county and track revenue accounted for 63 percent of the total budget. Under a 1975 law, the commission was appointed by the legislative delegation that represented Greene County in the House and Senate of Alabama. (For an account of the role of local legislative delegations, see Binny Miller, *Who Shall Rule and Govern?: Local Legislative Delegations, Racial Politics, and the Voting Rights Act*, 102 Yale L.J. 105 (1992).)

In 1975, all of the Greene County legislators were white. Under a 1983 reapportionment, however, Greene County was placed in both House and Senate districts likely to elect black candidates. Three days after the reapportionment was approved, the still-sitting, all-white delegation introduced—and obtained passage for—a bill providing for gubernatorial appointment of the Commission (at the time by then-governor George C. Wallace). When the newly elected black legislators took office, they introduced legislation to restore the old form of appointment but in a wholly unprecedented act, the bill was not reported to the Senate.

The three-judge district court held that the change required preclearance:

> The most relevant attribute of the challenged act is its effect on the power of the voters rather than any aspect of the electoral process.... The ordinary or routine legislative modification of the duties or authority of elected officials or changes by law or ordinance in the makeup, authority or means of selection of the vast majority of local appointed boards, commissions and agencies probably are beyond the reach of section 5, even given its broadest interpretation. Without undertaking to define a precise line of demarcation we conclude, however, that Act 507 is fundamentally different from such noncovered legislation. The attributes that

characterize this fundamental difference are: (1) that it reverses a scheme of indirect local control of the Commission that was put in place by a vote of the people themselves; (2) that the Commission's control of over 63% of the total county revenue makes it an agency of unique importance to the voters of Greene County; (3) that although the voters' control of the Commission was indirect, it was nonetheless quite real when the Commission was selected by only the locally elected legislators; and (4) that the transfer of appointment authority to the governor, over 99.7% of whose constituents are not inhabitants of Green County, substantially dilutes the power of the voters in Greene County by effectively eliminating the power of such voters over the Commission.

If you represented the plaintiffs in *Hardy* on appeal in the Supreme Court, how would you approach the question of *Presley*'s weight?

6. Does *Presley*'s analysis apply only to section 5 or does it stand for the more general proposition that reallocations of power cannot be challenged under *any* section of the Voting Rights Act? Consider *Bonilla v. City Council of Chicago*, 809 F.Supp. 590 (N.D.Ill.1992). After the 1990 census, Chicago was required to redistrict its 50 aldermanic wards. Blacks and whites were each about 38 percent of the city's total population and Hispanics were 19.6 percent. The city council could not agree on a plan, and by state law, any 10 aldermen could then propose a redistricting ordinance and have it put before the voters at a referendum. Four aldermen proposed a plan with 9 Hispanic wards, but their proposal was not put on the ballot (since fewer than 10 aldermen supported it). Two other plans did get on the ballot: one proposed by 28 aldermen with Mayor Daley's support and another proposed by black aldermen. The voters approved the 28–alderman plan, which had seven Hispanic wards. The Hispanic aldermen then sued, arguing in part that the "10 aldermen rule" violated section 2. The court dismissed that claim on *Presley* grounds.

7. In most cases, it will be clear whether a challenged practice involves a change: if it differs from the practices in effect on the triggering date for the jurisdiction's coverage, preclearance is required. Under some circumstances, however, the inquiry is slightly more complicated. *Perkins v. Matthews*, 400 U.S. 379 (1971), for example, sought an injunction against Canton, Mississippi's adoption of at-large elections. The change to at-large elections was mandated by a Mississippi statute enacted in 1962, which normally would have meant that at-large elections would have been the practice in effect on November 1, 1964, and their continued use would thus not require preclearance. But Canton ignored the statute in conducting its 1965 municipal elections and, as in 1961, elected aldermen by wards. The city argued that because it had no choice but to comply with the 1962 statute in the 1969 elections, it should not be enjoined from obeying the 1962 requirement. The Supreme Court disagreed, and ordered the city to seek preclearance:

In our view, § 5's reference to the procedure "in force or effect on November 1, 1964," must be taken to mean the procedure that would have been followed if the election had been held on that date. That judgment is necessarily a matter of inference in this case since Canton did not hold a municipal election on November 1, 1964. But in drawing that inference, there is little reason to blind ourselves to relevant evidence in the record by restricting our gaze to events that occurred before that date. Ordinarily we presume that officials will act in accordance with law. If the only available facts showed that Canton conducted its 1961 election by wards but that the Mississippi Legislature had subsequently enacted a statute in 1962 requiring future municipal elections to be held at large, Canton officials would be entitled to the weight of that presumption.

With the benefit of hindsight, however, we know that Canton elected its aldermen by wards in its June 1965 municipal election. The record reflects no relevant change between November 1964 and June 1965 to suggest that a different procedure would have been in effect if the elections had been held seven months earlier. Consequently, we conclude that the procedure in fact "in force or effect" in Canton on November 1, 1964, was to elect aldermen by wards. That sufficed to bring the 1969 change within § 5.... The bearing of the 1962 statute upon the change was for the Attorney General or the District Court for the District of Columbia to decide [in the course of deciding whether to grant preclearance.]

In *McCain v. Lybrand*, 465 U.S. 236, 256 (1984), the Court clarified that "[w]hen a jurisdiction adopts legislation that makes clearly defined changes in its election practices, sending that legislation to the Attorney General merely with a general request for preclearance pursuant to § 5 constitutes a submission of the changes made by the enactment and cannot be deemed a submission of changes made by previous legislation which themselves were independently subject to § 5 preclearance." Thus, in *Clark v. Roemer*, 500 U.S. 646 (1991), the Court reversed the district court's conclusion that preclearance of Louisiana's most recent round of additional judgeships within various at-large judicial electoral districts retroactively operated to preclear earlier increases in the number of positions on the grounds that "when an act provides for a certain number of judicial positions, approval of that act must include all of the judicial positions necessary to reach that number." Instead, those earlier judgeships required preclearance as well.

8. What does it mean to say that a *covered jurisdiction* is seeking to implement a change? *Connor v. Johnson*, 402 U.S. 690, 691 (1971), held that "[a] decree of the United States District Court is not within reach of Section 5 of the Voting Rights Act." But what happens when a change is embodied in a judicial decree? In the mid–1970's, black and Mexican-American plaintiffs successfully challenged Dallas's use of at-large elections to select its city council. The city responded by proposing a mixed plan: some seats would be chosen by district-based elections but several would continue to be elected at large. In *Wise v. Lipscomb*, 437 U.S. 535 (1978), a deeply fractured Supreme Court sustained the proposed remedy. A majority of the Justices concluded that although federal courts must normally use single-member districts when they imposed remedial reapportionment plans, so-called "legislative plans," that is, plans developed by the political authorities, are subject to less stringent standards. The Dallas plan was a "legislative plan," as Justice Powell's opinion for four Members of the Court explained, because "[t]he essential point is that the Dallas City Council exercised a legislative judgment, reflecting the policy choices of the elected representatives of the people, rather than the remedial directive of a federal court," in choosing among potential remedies. *Id.* at 548.

If plans like Dallas's require judicial deference because they are legislative judgments, then do they require preclearance as well? (The plan in *Wise* did not because Texas was not yet a covered jurisdiction at the time Dallas proposed its remedy.) The next case addresses this question.

McDaniel v. Sanchez
452 U.S. 130 (1981).

■ JUSTICE STEVENS delivered the opinion of the Court.

We granted certiorari to decide whether the preclearance requirement of § 5 of the Voting Rights Act applies to a reapportionment plan submitted to a Federal District Court by the legislative body of a covered jurisdiction in response to a judicial determination that the existing apportionment of its electoral districts is unconstitutional.

* * *

In January 1978, four Mexican–American residents of Kleberg County brought this class action against various county officials alleging that the apportionment of the four commissioners' precincts denied individual residents of the larger precincts a vote of equal weight, and unconstitutionally diluted the voting strength of the county's substantial Mexican–American population. After a trial, the District Court rejected the plaintiffs' [racial vote dilution] claim ... but held that individual voters were denied equal representation because of the substantial disparity in the number of residents in each commissioners' precinct. The District Court therefore directed the county officials to submit a proposed reapportionment plan to the court within six weeks, and scheduled a hearing on the validity of the proposal for four weeks thereafter.

Pursuant to the District Court's order, the Commissioners Court undertook the task of devising a new apportionment plan.... Respondents objected to the proposed plan. They challenged the data used by the [architect of the plan], they claimed that the plan diluted the voting strength of Mexican–Americans, and they contended that the Voting Rights Act required the county to obtain preclearance....

* * *

I

* * *

Two polar propositions are perfectly clear. First, the [Voting Rights] Act requires preclearance of new legislative apportionment plans that are adopted without judicial direction or approval. Second, the Act's preclearance requirement does not apply to plans prepared and adopted by a federal court to remedy a constitutional violation. Petitioners contend that the Act does not apply to this reapportionment plan because it is a court-ordered plan, while respondents argue that the Act does apply because the plan was prepared and submitted on behalf of the local legislative body.

In prior reapportionment cases not arising under the Voting Rights Act, we have recognized important differences between legislative plans and court-ordered plans. Because "reapportionment is primarily the duty and responsibility of the State through its legislature or other body, rather than of a federal court," the Court has tolerated somewhat greater flexibility in the fashioning of legislative remedies for violation of the one-person, one-vote rule than when a federal court prepares its own remedial decree.

* * *

III

This is not a case in which the language of the controlling statute unambiguously answers the question presented. The Solicitor General ... contends that a covered jurisdiction "[seeks] to administer" a new voting practice when it submits a redistricting plan to a district court as a proposed remedy for a constitutional violation. This is a plausible but not an obviously correct reading of the statutory language. For there is force to the contrary argument that Kleberg County had no intention to administer any new plan until after it was given legal effect by incorporation in a judicial decree. Arguably, therefore, the statute has no application before the District Court enters its decree, and because the Act does not require the District Court to have its decisions precleared ... once such a decree is entered it is too late for the statute to qualify the county's duty to administer the plan as entered by the District Court. We find sufficient ambiguity in the statutory language to make it appropriate to turn to legislative history for guidance.

In 1975, when Congress adopted the amendments that ultimately brought Texas and Kleberg County within the coverage of the Act, it directed special attention to § 5 and to the redistricting that would be required after the 1980 census. In its Report ..., the Senate Committee on the Judiciary explained "the future need for the Act" by pointing out that redrafting of district lines to correct violations of the one-person, one-vote rule created opportunities to disenfranchise minority voters. "By providing that Section 5 protections not be removed before 1985, S. 1279 would guarantee Federal protection of minority voting rights during the years that the post-census redistrictings will take place."

The Committee unambiguously stated that the statutory protections are to be available even when the redistricting is ordered by a federal court to remedy a constitutional violation that has been established in pending federal litigation. The Committee Report is crystal clear on this point:

"Thus, for example, where a federal district court holds unconstitutional an apportionment plan which predates the effective date of coverage under the Voting Rights Act, any subsequent plan ordinarily would be subject to Section 5 review. In the typical case, the court either will direct the governmental body to adopt a new plan and present it to the court for consideration or else itself choose a plan from among those presented by various parties to the litigation. In either situation, the court should defer its consideration of—or selection among—any plans presented to it until such time as these plans have been submitted for Section 5 review. Only after such review should the district court proceed to any remaining fourteenth or fifteenth amendment questions that may be raised.

"The one exception where Section 5 review would not ordinarily be available is where the court, because of exigent circumstances, actually fashions the plan itself instead of relying on a plan presented by a litigant. This is the limited meaning of the 'court decree' exception recognized in *Connor v. Johnson*, 402 U.S. 690 (1971). Even in these cases, however, if the governmental body subsequently adopts a plan patterned after the court's plan, Section 5 review would be required. Furthermore, in fashioning the plan, the court should follow the appropriate Section 5 standards, including the body of administrative and judicial precedents developed in Section 5 cases."

The view expressed by the Committee is consistent with the basic purposes of the statute and with the well-settled rule that § 5 is to be given a broad construction. The preclearance procedure is designed to forestall the danger that local decisions to modify voting practices will impair minority access to the electoral process. The federal interest in preventing local jurisdictions from making changes that adversely affect the rights of minority voters is the same whether a change is required to remedy a constitutional violation or is merely the product of a community's perception of the desirability of responding to new social patterns.

It is true, of course, that the federal interest may be protected by the federal district court presiding over voting rights litigation, but sound reasons support the Committee's view that the normal § 5 preclearance procedures should nevertheless be followed in cases such as this. The procedures contemplated by the statute reflect a congressional choice in favor of specialized review—either by the Attorney General of the United States or by the United States District Court for the District of Columbia. Because a large number of voting changes must necessarily undergo the preclearance process, centralized review enhances the likelihood that recurring problems will be resolved in a consistent and expeditious way. Moreover, if covered jurisdictions could avoid the normal preclearance procedure by awaiting litigation challenging a refusal to redistrict after a census is completed, the statute might have the unintended effect of actually encouraging delay in making obviously needed changes in district boundaries. The federal interest in evenhanded review of all changes in covered jurisdictions is furthered by the application of the statute in cases such as this.

* * *

As we construe the congressional mandate, it requires that whenever a covered jurisdiction submits a proposal reflecting the policy choices of the elected representatives of the people—no matter what constraints have limited the choices available to them—the preclearance requirement of the Voting Rights Act is applicable. It was, therefore, error for the District Court to act on the county's proposed plan before it had been submitted to the Attorney General or the United States District Court for the District of Columbia for preclearance.

* * *

NOTES AND QUESTIONS

1. Should a federal court defer to a jurisdiction's remedial choices as reflecting the will of the people even when the proposal flouts either procedural or substantive state law that normally would preclude such a choice? Isn't preclearance especially warranted as to remedial proposals since "the vindication of voting rights can hardly be trusted to the very representatives whose election is the result of the alleged vote dilution." Samuel Issacharoff, Note, *Making the Violation Fit the Remedy: Intent and Equal Protection Law*, 92 Yale L.J. 328, 346 (1982).

2. In the 1990 round of redistricting, political deadlock in many states resulted in state courts conducting the reapportionment process. *See, e.g., Growe v. Emison*, 507 U.S. 25 (1993) (Minnesota); *Wilson v. Eu*, 823 P.2d 545 (Cal.1992) (California). In *Growe*, the Supreme Court unanimously held that federal courts must "defer considerations of disputes involving redistricting where the State, through its legislative *or* judicial branch, has begun to address that highly political task itself." 507 U.S. at 33. In a covered jurisdiction, then, should plans adopted by state courts be subject to preclearance as "legislative" rather than "judicial" plans?

C. What Constitutes a Discriminatory Purpose or Effect?

Assuming that preclearance is required because a jurisdiction has made a change with respect to voting, when ought preclearance to be denied? The vast majority of all preclearance decisions are made administratively within the Department of Justice. The standards the Department applies are supposed to mirror those that would be applied if the jurisdiction sought preclearance through a declaratory judgment action in the United States District Court for the District of Columbia. 28 C.F.R. § 51.52 (1995). Moreover, since the Department explains its position largely through relatively pro forma preclearance and objection letters to submitting jurisdictions, see, e.g., Howard Ball, Dale Krane & Thomas Lauth, Compromised Compliance: Implementation of the 1965 Voting Rights Act 258 (1982) (providing an example of an objection letter); Hiroshi Motamura, *Preclearance Under Section 5 of the Voting Rights Act*, 61 N.C.L. Rev. 191, 192 (1983), the most general articulation of standards appears in the relatively sparse case law.

Beer v. United States
425 U.S. 130 (1976).

■ Mr. Justice Stewart delivered the opinion of the Court.

* * *

I

New Orleans is a city of almost 600,000 people. Some 55% of that population is white and the remaining 45% is Negro. Some 65% of the registered voters are white, and the remaining 35% are Negro.[4] In 1954, New Orleans adopted a mayor-council form of government. Since that time the municipal charter has provided that the city council is to consist of seven members, one to be elected from each of five councilmanic districts, and two to be elected by the voters of the city at large. The 1954 charter also requires an adjustment of the boundaries of the five single-member councilmanic districts following each decennial census to reflect population shifts among the districts.

In 1961, the city council redistricted the city based on the 1960 census figures. That reapportionment plan established four districts that stretched

---

4. The difference in the two figures is due in part to the fact that proportionately more whites of voting age are registered to vote than are Negroes and in part to the fact that the age structures of the white and Negro populations of New Orleans differ significantly—72.3% of the white population is of voting age, but only 57.1% of the Negro population is of voting age.

from the edge of Lake Pontchartrain on the north side of the city to the Mississippi River on the city's south side. The fifth district was wedge shaped and encompassed the city's downtown area. In one of these councilmanic districts, Negroes constituted a majority of the population, but only about half of the registered voters. In the other four districts white voters clearly outnumbered Negro voters. No Negro was elected to the New Orleans City Council during the decade from 1960 to 1970.

After receipt of the 1970 census figures the city council adopted a reapportionment plan (Plan I) that continued the basic north-to-south pattern of councilmanic districts combined with a wedge-shaped, downtown district. Under Plan I Negroes constituted a majority of the population in two districts, but they did not make up a majority of registered voters in any district. The largest percentage of Negro voters in a single district under Plan I was 45.2%. When the city submitted Plan I to the Attorney General pursuant to § 5, he objected to it, stating that it appeared to "dilute black voting strength by combining a number of black voters with a larger number of white voters in each of the five districts." He also expressed the view that "the district lines [were not] drawn as they [were] because of any compelling governmental need" and that the district lines did "not reflect numeric population configurations or considerations of district compactness or regularity of shape."

Even before the Attorney General objected to Plan I, the city authorities had commenced work on a second plan—Plan II. That plan followed the general north-to-south districting pattern common to the 1961 apportionment and Plan I. It produced Negro population majorities in two districts and a Negro voter majority (52.6%) in one district. When Plan II was submitted to the Attorney General, he posed the same objections to it that he had raised to Plan I. In addition, he noted that "the predominantly black neighborhoods in the city are located generally in an east to west progression," and pointed out that the use of north-to-south districts in such a situation almost inevitably would have the effect of diluting the maximum potential impact of the Negro vote. Following the rejection by the Attorney General of Plan II, the city brought this declaratory judgment action in the United States District Court for the District of Columbia.

The District Court concluded that Plan II would have the effect of abridging the right to vote on account of race or color.[7] It calculated that if Negroes could elect city councilmen in proportion to their share of the city's registered voters, they would be able to choose 2.42 of the city's seven councilmen, and, if in proportion to their share of the city's population, to choose 3.15 councilmen. But under Plan II the District Court concluded that, since New Orleans' elections had been marked by bloc voting along racial lines, Negroes would probably be able to elect only one councilman—

7. The District Court did not address the question whether Plan II was adopted with such a "purpose."

the candidate from the one councilmanic district in which a majority of the voters were Negroes.

As a separate and independent ground for rejecting Plan II, the District Court held that the failure of the plan to alter the city charter provision establishing two at-large seats had the effect in itself of "abridging the right to vote ... on account of race or color." As the court put it: "[T]he City has not supported the choice of at-large elections by any consideration which would satisfy the standard of compelling governmental interest, or the need to demonstrate the improbability of its realization through the use of single-member districts. These evaluations compel the conclusion that the feature of the city's electoral scheme by which two councilmen are selected at large has the effect of impermissibly minimizing the vote of its black citizens; and the further conclusion that for this additional reason the city's redistricting plan does not pass muster."

The District Court therefore refused to allow Plan II to go into effect. As a result there have been no councilmanic elections in New Orleans since 1970, and the councilmen elected at that time (or their appointed successors) have remained in office ever since.

II

A

The appellants urge, and the United States on reargument of this case has conceded, that the District Court was mistaken in holding that Plan II could be rejected under § 5 solely because it did not eliminate the two at-large councilmanic seats that had existed since 1954. The appellants and the United States are correct in their interpretation of the statute in this regard.

The language of § 5 clearly provides that it applies only to proposed changes in voting procedures. "[D]iscriminatory practices ... instituted prior to November 1964 ... are not subject to the requirement of preclearance [under § 5].". . . .

B

* * *

By prohibiting the enforcement of a voting-procedure change until it has been demonstrated to the United States Department of Justice or to a three-judge federal court that the change does not have a discriminatory effect, Congress desired to prevent States from "undo[ing] or defeat[ing] the rights recently won" by Negroes. Section 5 was intended "to insure that [the gains thus far achieved in minority political participation] shall not be destroyed through new [discriminatory] procedures and techniques.". . . . In other words the purpose of § 5 has always been to insure that no voting-procedure changes would be made that would lead to a retrogression in the position of racial minorities with respect to their effective exercise of the electoral franchise.

It is thus apparent that a legislative reapportionment that enhances the position of racial minorities with respect to their effective exercise of the electoral franchise can hardly have the "effect" of diluting or abridging the right to vote on account of race within the meaning of § 5. We conclude, therefore, that such an ameliorative new legislative apportionment cannot violate § 5 unless the new apportionment itself so discriminates on the basis of race or color as to violate the Constitution.

The application of this standard to the facts of the present case is straightforward. Under the apportionment of 1961 none of the five councilmanic districts had a clear Negro majority of registered voters, and no Negro has been elected to the New Orleans City Council while that apportionment system has been in effect. Under Plan II, by contrast, Negroes will constitute a majority of the population in two of the five districts and a clear majority of the registered voters in one of them. Thus, there is every reason to predict, upon the District Court's hypothesis of bloc voting, that at least one and perhaps two Negroes may well be elected to the council under Plan II. It was therefore error for the District Court to conclude that Plan II "will ... have the effect of denying or abridging the right to vote on account of race or color" within the meaning of § 5 of the Voting Rights Act.

* * *

NOTES AND QUESTIONS

1. The majority's opinion rests on a statutory reading that looks at whether the *change*, as opposed to the standard, practice, or procedure itself, has a discriminatory purpose or effect. Is that reading compelled by the statute itself? What are the arguments in favor of or against such a reading?

2. Note the consequences of drawn-out section 5 litigation: since the city could not implement an unprecleared plan, existing council members remained in office for six years while the case worked its way through the courts. This situation is not atypical. One-person, one-vote, combined with population shifts, surely rendered the pre-existing districts unconstitutional.

3. What do "retrogressive" and "ameliorative" mean? Consider the following questions posed by Justice Marshall in his dissent. What facts would a reviewing court, or the Department of Justice, need to know in order to resolve the question of preclearance? To what extent would resolution depend on questions of political philosophy rather than of fact?

> ... [T]he Court today finds that an increase in the size of the Negro majority in one district, with a concomitant increased

likelihood of electing a delegate, conclusively shows that Plan II is ameliorative. Will that always be so? Is it not as common for minorities to be gerrymandered into the same district as into separate ones? Is an increase in the size of an existing majority ameliorative or retrogressive? When the size of the majority increases in one district, Negro voting strength necessarily declines elsewhere. Is that decline retrogressive? Assuming that the shift from a 50.2% to a 52.6% majority in District B in this case is ameliorative, and is not outweighed by the simultaneous decrease in Negro voting strength in Districts A and C, when would an increase become retrogressive? As soon as the majority becomes "safe"? When the majority is achieved by dividing pre-existing concentrations of Negro voters?

Moreover, the Court implies ... that this preliminary inquiry into the nature of the change is the proper approach to all § 5 cases. The Court's test will prove even more difficult of application outside the redistricting context. Some changes just do not lend themselves to comparison in positive or negative terms; others will always seem negative—or positive—no matter how good or bad the result. For instance, when a city goes from an appointed town manager to an elected council form of government, can the change ever be termed retrogressive, even if the new council is elected at large and Negroes are a minority? Or where a jurisdiction in which Negroes are a substantial minority switches from at-large to ward voting, can that change ever constitute a negative change, no matter how badly the wards are gerrymandered?

Cf. City of Lockhart v. United States, 460 U.S. 125, 135 (1983) (permitting a change that simply perpetuated the existing situation because "[a]lthough there may have been no improvement in their voting strength, there has been no retrogression either").

4. Some changes, such as annexations, raise particularly tricky questions. An annexation of populated territory will always dilute the voting strength of members of the pre-annexation community. Moreover, unless the annexed territory has the same racial composition as the pre-annexation community, it will always alter the relative voting strength of racially identifiable groups. At the same time, although annexations have undeniable consequences for voting, they are often undertaken for reasons independent of those consequences. All these issues were presented in *City of Richmond v. United States*, 422 U.S. 358 (1975).

In May 1969, Richmond, Virginia, annexed approximately 23 square miles of land adjacent to the city in Chesterfield County. Before the annexation, the city was 52 percent black; afterwards, the city was only 42 percent black. Richmond was governed by a nine-member city council, elected at large. In 1968, three candidates endorsed by the Crusade for Voters of Richmond, a black civic organization, were elected to the council.

In the post-annexation, at-large election in 1970, three of the nine members elected had also received the endorsement of the Crusade.

After *Perkins v. Matthews* held that section 5 applied to city annexations, Richmond sought preclearance. The Attorney General objected because he found that the annexation substantially increased the proportion of whites and decreased the proportion of blacks in the city and that the annexation "inevitably tend[ed] to dilute the voting strength of black voters." In his objection letter, however, the Attorney General suggested that "[you] may, of course, wish to consider means of accomplishing annexation which would avoid producing an impermissible adverse racial impact on voting, including such techniques as single-member districts."

Dissatisfied with the Attorney General's objection, Richmond commenced a preclearance declaratory judgment suit in the District of Columbia. While that lawsuit was pending, the city developed and submitted to the Attorney General a series of plans for establishing councilmanic districts. Ultimately, the city and the Attorney General settled on a nine ward proposal under which four of the wards would have substantial black majorities, four wards substantial white majorities, and the ninth a racial division of approximately 59 percent white and 41 percent black. The city and the Attorney General submitted this plan to the District Court for the District of Columbia in the form of a consent judgment.

The district court, however, rejected the plan because it found that the annexation had had an invidious racial purpose—it was intended to prevent blacks from taking over control of the city. Furthermore, the ward system did not minimize the dilution of black voting power to the greatest possible extent, since it would easily have been possible to draw a plan with effective black voting majorities in five out of the nine wards.

In an opinion written by Justice White, the Supreme Court reversed the district court's rejection of the districting plan and remanded for further proceedings.

> It is our view that a fairly designed ward plan [following annexation] ... would not only prevent the total exclusion of Negroes from membership on the council but would afford them representation reasonably equivalent to their political strength in the enlarged community.
>
> We cannot accept the position that such a single-member ward system would nevertheless have the effect of denying or abridging the right to vote because Negroes would constitute a lesser proportion of the population after the annexation than before and, given racial bloc voting, would have fewer seats on the city council. If a city having a ward system for the election of a nine-man council annexes a largely white area, the wards are fairly redrawn, and as a result Negroes have only two rather than the four seats they had before, these facts alone do not demonstrate that the annexation

has the effect of denying or abridging the right to vote. As long as the ward system fairly reflects the strength of the Negro community as it exists after the annexation, we cannot hold, without more specific legislative directions, that such an annexation is nevertheless barred by § 5. It is true that the black community, if there is racial bloc voting, will command fewer seats on the city council; and the annexation will have effected a decline in the Negroes' relative influence in the city. But a different city council and an enlarged city are involved after the annexation. Furthermore, Negro power in the new city is not undervalued, and Negroes will not be underrepresented on the council.

As long as this is true, we cannot hold that the effect of the annexation is to deny or abridge the right to vote. To hold otherwise would be either to forbid all such annexations or to require, as the price for approval of the annexation, that the black community be assigned the same proportion of council seats as before, hence perhaps permanently overrepresenting them and underrepresenting other elements in the community, including the nonblack citizens in the annexed area. We are unwilling to hold that Congress intended either consequence in enacting § 5.

What does Justice White mean when he refers to "overrepresentation" and "underrepresentation"? Is the Court adopting a notion of proportional representation as a ceiling on minority political aspirations? *Cf. Johnson v. DeGrandy*, 512 U.S. 997 (1994) (suggesting that rough proportionality weighs heavily against finding a violation of the Voting Rights Act).

Ultimately, when Richmond finally drew a city council plan that obtained preclearance, blacks (who were apparently by then a majority of the electorate) won five of the nine seats. This was the racial composition of the Richmond City Council that enacted the contract set-aside plan that was held unconstitutional by the Supreme Court in *City of Richmond v. J.A. Croson Co.*, 488 U.S. 469 (1989). In a part of her opinion joined by the Chief Justice and Justices White and Kennedy, Justice O'Connor explained why strict scrutiny was appropriate for Richmond's affirmative action plan:

> Even were we to accept a reading of the guarantee of equal protection under which the level of scrutiny varies according to the ability of different groups to defend their interests in the representative process, heightened scrutiny would still be appropriate in the circumstances of this case. One of the central arguments for applying a less exacting standard to "benign" racial classifications is that such measures essentially involve a choice made by dominant racial groups to disadvantage themselves. If one aspect of the judiciary's role under the Equal Protection Clause is to protect "discrete and insular minorities" from majoritarian prejudice or indifference, see *United States v. Carolene Products Co.*, 304 U.S. 144, 153, n. 4 (1938), some maintain that these concerns are not implicated when the "white majority" places burdens upon itself. See J. Ely, Democracy and Distrust 170 (1980).

In this case, blacks constitute approximately 50% of the population of the city of Richmond. Five of the nine seats on the city council are held by blacks. The concern that a political majority will more easily act to the disadvantage of a minority based on unwarranted assumptions or incomplete facts would seem to militate for, not against, the application of heightened judicial scrutiny in this case. See Ely, The Constitutionality of Reverse Racial Discrimination, 41 U. Chi. L. Rev. 723, 739, n. 58 (1974) ("Of course it works both ways: a law that favors Blacks over Whites would be suspect if it were enacted by a predominantly Black legislature").

Id. at 495–96.

How ought preclearance authorities to treat questions of discriminatory purpose, as opposed to questions of effect? The Court's opinion *City of Richmond* takes the following position:

Accepting the findings ... that the annexation, as it went forward in 1969, was infected by the impermissible purpose of denying the right to vote based on race through perpetuating white majority power to exclude Negroes from office through at-large elections, we are nevertheless persuaded that if verifiable reasons are now demonstrable in support of the annexation, and the ward plan proposed is fairly designed, the city need do no more to satisfy the requirements of § 5.

Is this position defensible, particularly in light of *Beer*'s focus on the change itself? Is it consistent with the general constitutional law principle that strikes down acts taken with a discriminatory purpose? What if the city had mixed motives?

Consider the district court's account of the purpose behind the Richmond annexation:

Richmond's focus in the negotiations was upon the number of new white voters it could obtain by annexation; it expressed no interest in economic or geographic considerations such as tax revenues, vacant land, utilities, or schools. The mayor required assurances from Chesterfield County officials that at least 44,000 additional white citizens would be obtained by the City before he would agree upon [the terms of the annexation].... And the mayor and one of the city councilmen conditioned final acceptance of the settlement agreement on the annexation going into effect in sufficient time to make citizens in the annexed area eligible to vote in the City Council elections of 1970.

If there is no discriminatory effect to an annexation, can a discriminatory purpose nonetheless taint the annexation? *See City of Pleasant Grove v. United States*, 479 U.S. 462 (1987), which involved an all-white municipality's annexation of two empty parcels of land. When the city sought preclearance it was denied, in large part because the Attorney General found that the city's refusal to annex an adjacent black community that had petitioned for inclusion showed that it had applied a wholly different and discriminatory annexation standard. The Supreme Court affirmed the denial of preclearance:

> [The city] relies on the fact that there were no black voters in Pleasant Grove at the time the relevant annexation decisions were made, so that the annexations did not reduce the proportion of black voters or deny existing black voters representation equivalent to their political strength in the enlarged community. [The city] contends that since the annexations could not possibly have caused an impermissible effect on black voting, it makes no sense to say that appellant had a discriminatory purpose. This argument is based on the incorrect assumption that an impermissible purpose under § 5 can relate only to present circumstances. Section 5 looks not only to the present effects of changes, but to their future effects as well, as shown by the fact that annexations of vacant land are subject to preclearance even though no one's right to vote is immediately affected. Likewise, an impermissible purpose under § 5 may relate to anticipated as well as present circumstances.

Is *Pleasant Grove* consistent with either *City of Richmond* or *Beer*?

5. *Beer* held that "an ameliorative new legislative apportionment cannot violate § 5 unless the new apportionment itself so discriminates on the basis of race or color as to violate the Constitution." What does this latter phrase mean? Could the Attorney General or a court refuse to preclear a nonretrogressive or ameliorative plan that involves unacceptable population deviations? Or one that rises to the level of an impermissible political gerrymander?

Consider in this light *Miller v. Johnson*, 515 U.S. 900 (1995), in which the Supreme Court struck down Georgia's post–1990 congressional apportionment because the state's race-conscious creation of two new majority-black congressional districts violated the equal protection clause as interpreted in *Shaw v. Reno*, 509 U.S. 630 (1993). (The post-*Shaw* cases are considered in depth in Chapter 8.) "Taken literally, *Miller* suggests that then the Justice Department might have been correct in objecting to the earlier plans, not because they created one too few majority-black districts but because they created (at least) one too many: the deliberate creation of a second majority-black district (or perhaps even a first) violated the equal protection clause." Pamela S. Karlan, *Still Hazy After All These Years: Voting Rights in the Post–Shaw Era*, 26 Cumb. L. Rev. 287, 306 (1996). See also Pamela S. Karlan, *The Fire Next Time: Reapportionment After the 2000 Census*, 50 Stan. L. Rev. ___ (1998) (discussing post-*Miller* problems with measuring retrogression).

6. *The relationship of section 5 to section 2.* The decision in *Beer* predated the decision in *Washington v. Davis*, 426 U.S. 229 (1976). Under

Davis, a plaintiff seeking to establish an equal protection violation must show both a discriminatory purpose and a discriminatory effect. The constitutional understanding of "effect" extends beyond the statutory understanding expressed in *Beer* in which "effect" is equivalent to "retrogression." At the time *Beer* was decided, however, the law was unclear as to whether discriminatory purpose was an essential element of a claim of unconstitutional racial vote dilution. *See, e.g., White v. Regester*, 412 U.S. 755 (1973); *infra* Chapter 6. Moreover, at the time *Beer* was decided, the statutory language of section 2 of the Voting Rights Act—the general prohibition on racial discrimination in voting—tracked the language of section 1 of the Fifteenth Amendment. *See City of Mobile v. Bolden*, 446 U.S. 55 (1980).

In 1982, however, Congress amended section 2 to forbid the use of any voting practice or procedure that results in denial or dilution of the right to vote, thereby replacing the constitutional discriminatory-purpose test with a disparate impact standard. (For an extensive discussion of the 1982 amendments, see Chapters 6 and 7.)

Should the Attorney General or the district court therefore take into account the fact that a proposed change would violate section 2 of the Act? Note that under the statute itself, the grant of preclearance will not preclude a later lawsuit under section 2, the Fourteenth or Fifteenth Amendment, or any other constitutional or statutory protection of voting rights. *See, e.g., Thornburg v. Gingles*, 478 U.S. 30 (1986).

The Department of Justice's administrative regulations provide in pertinent part that "In those instances in which the Attorney General concludes that, as proposed, the submitted change is free of discriminatory purpose and retrogressive effect, but also concludes that a bar to implementation of the change is necessary to prevent a clear violation of amended section 2, the Attorney General shall withhold section 5 preclearance." 28 C.F.R. § 51.55(b)(2) (1995). Is the administrative regulation consistent with the Court's view in *Beer*? What about congressional intent in amending section 2 in 1982? *See, e.g.*, Senate Report No. 97–417, 97th Cong., 2nd Sess. at 12, n.31 (1982) ("In light of the amendment to section 2, it is intended that a section 5 objection also follow if a new voting procedure itself so discriminates as to violate section 2."). What are the policy arguments in favor of "incorporating" section 2 into section 5? *See, e.g.*, Mark E. Haddad, Note, *Getting Results Under Section 5 of the Voting Rights Act*, 94 Yale L.J. 139 (1984); Heather K. Way, Note, *A Shield or a Sword: Section 5 of the Voting Rights Act and the Argument for the Incorporation of Section 2*, 74 Tex.L.Rev. 1439 (1996).

In *Reno v. Bossier Parish School Board*, 117 S.Ct. 1491 (1997), the Supreme Court rejected the position that preclearance might be denied simply because a proposed change would violate section 2. But the Court held that what it called "§ 2 evidence" might be relevant to whether a jurisdiction possessed the requisite "intent to retrogress":

Evidence is "relevant" if it has "any tendency to make the existence of any fact that is of consequence to the determination of the action more probable or less probable than it would be without the evidence." Fed. Rule Evid. 401. As we observed in [*Arlington Heights v. Metropolitan Housing Development Corp.*, 429 U.S. 252, 266 (1977)], the impact of an official action is often probative of why the action was taken in the first place since people usually intend the natural consequences of their actions. Thus, a jurisdiction that enacts a plan having a dilutive impact is more likely to have acted with a discriminatory intent to dilute minority voting strength than a jurisdiction whose plan has no such impact. A jurisdiction that acts with an intent to dilute minority voting strength is more likely to act with an intent to worsen the position of minority voters—i.e., an intent to retrogress—than a jurisdiction acting with no intent to dilute. The fact that a plan has a dilutive impact therefore makes it "more probable" that the jurisdiction adopting that plan acted with an intent to retrogress than "it would be without the evidence." To be sure, the link between dilutive impact and intent to retrogress is far from direct, but "the basic standard of relevance ... is a liberal one," and one we think is met here.

That evidence of a plan's dilutive impact may be relevant to the § 5 purpose inquiry does not, of course, mean that such evidence is dispositive of that inquiry. In fact, we have previously observed that a jurisdiction's single decision to choose a redistricting plan that has a dilutive impact does not, without more, suffice to establish that the jurisdiction acted with a discriminatory purpose. *Shaw v. Hunt*, 517 U. S. ___, ___, n. 6 ("We doubt that a showing of discriminatory effect under § 2, alone, could support a claim of discriminatory purpose under § 5"). This is true whether the jurisdiction chose the more dilutive plan because it better comported with its traditional districting principles, *see Miller v. Johnson* (rejecting argument that a jurisdiction's failure to adopt the plan with the greatest possible number of majority black districts establishes that it acted with a discriminatory purpose); *Shaw* (same), or if it chose the plan for no reason at all. Indeed, if a plan's dilutive impact were dispositive, we would effectively incorporate § 2 into § 5, which is a result we find unsatisfactory no matter how it is packaged.

Id. at 1502.

In light of the materials on the administrative process contained in the next section, consider how an administration inclined to object on section 2 grounds might "package" its objection.

The Court's opinion in *Bossier Parish* also "le[ft] open for another day the question whether the § 5 purpose inquiry ever extends beyond the search for retrogressive intent." *Id.* at 1501. Is this reservation correct? Does section 5's "purpose" prong extend only to a purpose to retrogress or is any discriminatory purpose a basis for objection? In this regard, consider Justice Stevens's argument in dissent:

> In *Pleasant Grove v. United States*, 479 U.S. 462, 469–472 (1987), for instance, we found that the city had failed to prove that its annexation of certain white areas lacked a discriminatory purpose. Despite the fact that the annexation lacked a retrogressive effect, we found it was subject to § 5 preclearance. Furthermore, limiting the § 5 purpose inquiry to retrogressive intent is inconsistent with the basic purpose of the Act. Assume, for example, that the record unambiguously disclosed a long history of deliberate exclusion of African–Americans from participating in local elections, including a series of changes each of which was adopted for the specific purpose of maintaining the status quo. None of those changes would have been motivated by an "intent to regress," but each would have been motivated by a "discriminatory purpose" as that term is commonly understood. Given the long settled understanding that § 5 of the Act was enacted to prevent covered jurisdictions from "contriving new rules of various kinds for the sole purpose of perpetuating voting discrimination," *South Carolina v. Katzenbach*, 383 U. S., at 335, it is inconceivable that Congress intended to authorize preclearance of changes adopted for the sole purpose of perpetuating an existing pattern of discrimination.

Id. at 1512.

7. When does the need to obtain preclearance override otherwise binding legal requirements? For example, consider a state whose constitution prohibits the splitting of counties among state legislative districts. Can a plan that refuses to split counties and therefore dilutes the voting strength of a Native American community be objected to on the grounds that the refusal to split counties is intentionally discriminatory? Does the need to avoid retrogression permit otherwise unacceptable race consciousness? For example, suppose that in 1980 a state deliberately created a majority-black congressional district. Suppose further that the decision was constitutionally acceptable—because the black community that forms the predominant group within the district lived in a geographically compact neighborhood with traditional boundaries (along, say a river). Between 1980 and 1990, population shifts caused many black residents of the district to move out of the traditional black neighborhood into smaller, still largely black enclaves in the suburbs. Must, or can, the state now draw a majority-black district with less regular boundaries in order to preserve a majority-black seat?

D. THE ADMINISTRATIVE PROCESS

As we have already seen, section 5 provides two alternative paths to preclearance: an administrative mechanism involving submission to the

Attorney General and a declaratory judgment action in the United States District Court for the District of Columbia. The Attorney General has promulgated a set of extensive regulations for the administrative preclearance process. *See* 28 C.F.R. Part 51 (1995). In this section, we consider several issues raised by the administrative preclearance process.

The vast bulk of administrative submissions receive preclearance. Between 1965 and 1980, for example, the Attorney General objected to fewer than three percent of all submissions. *See* Richard Scher & James Button, *Voting Rights Act: Implementation and Impact*, in Implementation of Civil Rights Policy, 21, 34 (Charles S. Bullock, III, & Charles M. Lamb eds. 1984). The administrative process is initially handled by non-lawyer section 5 analysts although their work is reviewed by attorneys before going to the Assistant Attorney General for Civil Rights, to whom the Attorney General has delegated her preclearance authority. For general accounts of this process, see, e.g., Howard Ball, Dale Krane & Thomas Lauth, Compromised Compliance: Implementation of the 1965 Voting Rights Act (1982).

Section 5 provides explicitly that: "Neither an affirmative indication by the Attorney General that no objection will be made, nor the Attorney General's failure to object, nor a declaratory judgment entered under this section shall bar a subsequent action to enjoin enforcement of such qualification, prerequisite, standard, practice, or procedure." Thus, even if the Attorney General declines to object, a private party (or, in fact, the United States) may still sue to enjoin a precleared practice under any other constitutional or statutory provision. Such a lawsuit may differ, though, in several critical respects: the identity of the parties, venue, and the burden of proof. How might these affect the outcome? Can the Attorney General's failure to object be reviewed?

Morris v. Gressette
432 U.S. 491 (1977).

■ MR. JUSTICE POWELL delivered the opinion of the Court.

* * *

[In November 1971, South Carolina reapportioned its State Senate. It submitted the plan to the Attorney General for preclearance but while its submission was still pending, the local federal district court held that the plan violated one-person, one-vote. The court then ordered the state to develop a new plan. The state did, and the district court approved the new plan. The Attorney General then notified South Carolina that he would not interpose an objection to the new plan because he felt "constrained to defer to the . . . determination of the three-judge District Court." In light of the later decision in *Connor v. Waller*, 421 U.S. 656 (1975), such deference was not in fact required.

Objecting to that deference, another set of plaintiffs brought suit in the United States District Court for the District of Columbia challenging the Attorney General's failure to object to the new senate reapportionment plan. That suit was called *Harper v. Kleindienst*. Ultimately, the District Court directed the Attorney General to consider South Carolina's plan without regard to the decision by the South Carolina federal court. The next day the Attorney General interposed an objection because he was "unable to conclude that [the plan] does not have the effect of abridging voting rights on account of race." The Court of Appeals affirmed.]

Armed with the decision of the Court of Appeals and the belated objection interposed by the Attorney General, two South Carolina voters filed the present suit in the United States District Court for the District of South Carolina as a class action under § 5 of the Voting Rights Act. The plaintiffs, appellants here, sought an injunction against implementation of [the challenged plan] on the ground that the Attorney General had interposed an objection and the State had not subsequently obtained a favorable declaratory judgment from the United States District Court for the District of Columbia.

* * *

II

The ultimate issue in this case concerns the implementation of South Carolina's reapportionment plan for the State Senate.... It is conceded that no objection was entered within the 60-day period. But appellants insist that the Attorney General's nunc pro tunc objection of July 20, 1973, is effective under the Act and thus bars implementation of the reapportionment plan. Since that objection was interposed pursuant to the District Court's order in *Harper v. Kleindienst,* its validity depends on whether the *Harper* court had jurisdiction under the Administrative Procedure Act to review the Attorney General's failure to object.

The Administrative Procedure Act stipulates that the provisions of that Act authorizing judicial review apply "except to the extent that—(1) statutes preclude judicial review; or (2) agency action is committed to agency discretion by law." 5 U.S.C. § 701(a). It is now well settled that "judicial review of a final agency action by an aggrieved person will not be cut off unless there is persuasive reason to believe that such was the purpose of Congress." The reviewing court must determine whether "Congress has in express or implied terms precluded judicial review or committed the challenged action entirely to administrative discretion."

As no provision of the Voting Rights Act expressly precludes judicial review of the Attorney General's actions under § 5, it is necessary to determine "whether nonreviewability can fairly be inferred." That inquiry must address the role played by the Attorney General within "the context of the entire legislative scheme."

The nature of the § 5 remedy, which this Court has characterized as an "unusual" and "severe" procedure, strongly suggests that Congress did not intend the Attorney General's actions under that provision to be subject to judicial review. Section 5 requires covered jurisdictions to delay implementation of validly enacted state legislation until federal authorities have had an opportunity to determine whether that legislation conforms to the Constitution and to the provisions of the Voting Rights Act. Section 5 establishes two alternative methods by which covered jurisdictions can comply with this severe requirement of federal preclearance review. First, a covered jurisdiction may file a declaratory judgment action in the District Court for the District of Columbia.... Second, a covered jurisdiction may submit a change in voting laws to the Attorney General and subsequently may enforce the change if "the Attorney General has not interposed an objection within sixty days after such submission."

According to the terms of § 5, a covered jurisdiction is in compliance pursuant to the latter alternative once it has (i) filed a complete submission with the Attorney General, and (ii) received no objection from that office within 60 days. This second method of compliance under § 5 is unlike the first in that implementation of changes in voting laws is not conditioned on an affirmative statement by the Attorney General that the change is without discriminatory purpose or effect. To the contrary, compliance with § 5 is measured solely by the absence, for whatever reason, of a timely objection on the part of the Attorney General....

Although there is no legislative history bearing directly on the issue of reviewability of the Attorney General's actions under § 5, the legislative materials do indicate a desire to provide a speedy alternative method of compliance to covered States....

In light of the potential severity of the § 5 remedy, the statutory language, and the legislative history, we think it clear that Congress intended to provide covered jurisdictions with an expeditious alternative to declaratory judgment actions. The congressional intent is plain: The extraordinary remedy of postponing the implementation of validly enacted state legislation was to come to an end when the Attorney General failed to interpose a timely objection based on a complete submission.[19] Although

---

19. The Attorney General has promulgated regulations providing that the 60-day period shall commence from the time that the Department of Justice receives a submission satisfying certain enumerated requirements. 28 CFR § 51.3(b)-(d) (1976). These regulations were reviewed and found valid by this Court in *Georgia v. United States*. The Court noted that "[t]he judgment that the Attorney General must make is a difficult and complex one, and no one would argue that it should be made without adequate information." To deny the Attorney General the power to suspend the 60-day period until a complete submission was tendered would leave him no choice but to interpose an objection to incomplete submissions, a result which "would only add acrimony to the administration of § 5."

Nothing in our opinion in *Georgia v. United States* suggests that Congress did not intend to preclude judicial review of the Attorney General's failure to interpose an objection within 60 days of a complete submission. The factors relied on in that case are

there was to be no bar to subsequent constitutional challenges to the implemented legislation, there also was to be "no dragging out" of the extraordinary federal remedy beyond the period specified in the statute....

Our conclusions in this respect are reinforced by the fact that the Attorney General's failure to object is not conclusive with respect to the constitutionality of the submitted state legislation.[21] The statute expressly provides that neither "an affirmative indication by the Attorney General that no objection will be made, nor the Attorney General's failure to object ... shall bar a subsequent action to enjoin enforcement" of the newly enacted legislation or voting regulation.... Where the discriminatory character of an enactment is not detected upon review by the Attorney General, it can be challenged in traditional constitutional litigation. But it cannot be questioned in a suit seeking judicial review of the Attorney General's exercise of discretion under § 5, or his failure to object within the statutory period.

* * *

■ MR. JUSTICE MARSHALL, with whom MR. JUSTICE BRENNAN joins, dissenting.

The Court holds today that an Attorney General's failure to object within 60 days to the implementation of a voting law that has been submitted to him under § 5 of the Voting Rights Act, as amended cannot be questioned in any court. Under the Court's ruling, it matters not whether the Attorney General fails to object because he misunderstands his legal duty, as in this case; because he loses the submission; or because he seeks to subvert the Voting Rights Act. Indeed, the Court today grants unreviewable discretion to a future Attorney General to bargain acquiescence in a discriminatory change in a covered State's voting laws in return for that State's electoral votes. *Cf.* J. Randall & D. Donald, The Civil War and Reconstruction 678–701 (2d ed. 1961) (settlement of the election of 1876).

* * *

II

Perhaps out of justifiable embarrassment, the majority never mentions the effect of its ruling. That effect is easy to describe: The Court today upholds a system of choosing members of the South Carolina Senate that

inapplicable once a complete submission has been pending before the Attorney General for 60 days. Indeed, subsequent judicial review of the Attorney General's failure to interpose a timely objection to a complete submission would itself "add acrimony" by denying covered jurisdictions the statutorily prescribed "rapid method of rendering a new state election law enforceable."

21. Similarly, an objection on the part of the Attorney General is not conclusive with respect to the invalidity of the submitted state legislation under the Constitution or the Voting Rights Act. After receiving an objection from the Attorney General, a covered jurisdiction retains the option of seeking a favorable declaratory judgment from the District Court for the District of Columbia.

has prevented the election of any black senators, despite the fact that 25% of South Carolina's population is black. Thus, South Carolina, which was a leader of the movement to deprive the former slaves of their federally guaranteed right to vote, *South Carolina v. Katzenbach,* is allowed to remain as one of the last successful members of that movement. It would take much more evidence than the Court can muster to convince me that this result is consistent with "Congress' firm intention to rid the country of racial discrimination in voting."....

It is true that today's decision does not quite spell the end of all hope that the South Carolina Senate will someday be representative of the entire citizenry of South Carolina. If the Decennial Census in 1980 requires substantial reapportionment, and if the Voting Rights Act is still in effect when that reapportionment takes place, and if the then Attorney General is conscientious, the devices approved today will be rejected under the strict standards of § 5. This highly contingent possibility that the promise of the Fifteenth Amendment will be realized in South Carolina, some 110 years after that Amendment was ratified, is apparently sufficient in the eyes of the majority. It is not sufficient for me, as it was not for Congress, which wrote the Voting Rights Act in 1965 to put an end to what was then "nearly a century of widespread resistance to the Fifteenth Amendment." *South Carolina v. Katzenbach.*

* * *

NOTES AND QUESTIONS

1. Although the Attorney General's preclearance determination is not subject to judicial review, his objection may be overridden as a practical matter, since a jurisdiction may seek a declaratory judgment from the District of Columbia District Court without regard to whether an objection was interposed in the administrative process. That declaratory judgment is an entirely separate proceeding in which the administrative objection plays no role.

As a practical matter, however, few jurisdictions seek judicial preclearance after an administrative objection has been interposed. *See* Abigail M. Thernstrom, Whose Votes Count? Affirmative Action and Minority Voting Rights 158 (1987). Can you identify the practical reasons for this situation? Recently, however, the number of such cases seems to have increased. After considering the Court's account of the Department's preclearance process in the recent decennial reapportionment, can you suggest why this might be so?

Miller v. Johnson
515 U.S. 900 (1995).

■ JUSTICE KENNEDY delivered the opinion of the Court.

* * *

Between 1980 and 1990, one of Georgia's 10 congressional districts was a majority-black district, that is, a majority of the district's voters were black. The 1990 Decennial Census indicated that Georgia's population of 6,478,216 persons, 27% of whom are black, entitled it to an additional eleventh congressional seat, prompting Georgia's General Assembly to redraw the State's congressional districts.... A special session opened in August 1991, and the General Assembly submitted a congressional redistricting plan to the Attorney General for preclearance on October 1, 1991. The legislature's plan contained two majority-minority districts, the Fifth and Eleventh, and an additional district, the Second, in which blacks comprised just over 35% of the voting age population. Despite the plan's increase in the number of majority-black districts from one to two and the absence of any evidence of an intent to discriminate against minority voters, the Department of Justice refused preclearance on January 21, 1992. The Department's objection letter noted a concern that Georgia had created only two majority-minority districts, and that the proposed plan did not "recognize" certain minority populations by placing them in a majority-black district.

The General Assembly returned to the drawing board. A new plan was enacted and submitted for preclearance. This second attempt assigned the black population in Central Georgia's Baldwin County to the Eleventh District and increased the black populations in the Eleventh, Fifth and Second Districts. The Justice Department refused preclearance again, relying on alternative plans proposing three majority-minority districts. One of the alternative schemes relied on by the Department was the so-called "max-black" plan, drafted by the American Civil Liberties Union (ACLU) for the General Assembly's black caucus. The key to the ACLU's plan was the "Macon/Savannah trade." The dense black population in the Macon region would be transferred from the Eleventh District to the Second, converting the Second into a majority-black district, and the Eleventh District's loss in black population would be offset by extending the Eleventh to include the black populations in Savannah. Pointing to the General Assembly's refusal to enact the Macon/Savannah swap into law, the Justice Department concluded that Georgia had "failed to explain adequately" its failure to create a third majority-minority district. The State did not seek a declaratory judgment from the District Court for the District of Columbia.

Twice spurned, the General Assembly set out to create three majority-minority districts to gain preclearance. Using the ACLU's "max-black" plan as its benchmark, the General Assembly enacted a plan that

> "bore all the signs of [the Justice Department's] involvement: The black population of Meriwether County was gouged out of the Third District and attached to the Second District by the narrowest of land bridges; Effingham and Chatham Counties were split to

make way for the Savannah extension, which itself split the City of Savannah; and the plan as a whole split 26 counties, 23 more than the existing congressional districts."

* * *

The Almanac of American Politics has this to say about the Eleventh District: "Geographically, it is a monstrosity, stretching from Atlanta to Savannah. Its core is the plantation country in the center of the state, lightly populated, but heavily black. It links by narrow corridors the black neighborhoods in Augusta, Savannah and southern DeKalb County." M. Barone & G. Ujifusa, Almanac of American Politics 356 (1994). Georgia's plan included three majority-black districts, though, and received Justice Department preclearance on April 2, 1992.

* * *

The Justice Department refused to preclear both of Georgia's first two submitted redistricting plans. The District Court found that the Justice Department had adopted a "black-maximization" policy under § 5, and that it was clear from its objection letters that the Department would not grant preclearance until the State made the "Macon/Savannah trade" and created a third majority-black district. It is, therefore, safe to say that the congressional plan enacted in the end was required in order to obtain preclearance. It does not follow, however, that the plan was required by the substantive provisions of the Voting Rights Act.

We do not accept the contention that the State has a compelling interest in complying with whatever preclearance mandates the Justice Department issues. When a state governmental entity seeks to justify race-based remedies to cure the effects of past discrimination, we do not accept the government's mere assertion that the remedial action is required. Rather, we insist on a strong basis in evidence of the harm being remedied.... Where a State relies on the Department's determination that race-based districting is necessary to comply with the Voting Rights Act, the judiciary retains an independent obligation in adjudicating consequent equal protection challenges to ensure that the State's actions are narrowly tailored to achieve a compelling interest. Were we to accept the Justice Department's objection itself as a compelling interest adequate to insulate racial districting from constitutional review, we would be surrendering to the Executive Branch our role in enforcing the constitutional limits on race-based official action. We may not do so. *See, e.g., United States v. Nixon,* 418 U.S. 683, 704 (1974) (judicial power cannot be shared with Executive Branch); *Marbury v. Madison,* 5 U.S. 137, 1 Cranch 137, 177 (1803) ("It is emphatically the province and duty of the judicial department to say what the law is"); *cf. Baker v. Carr,* 369 U.S. 186, 211 (1962) (Supreme Court is "ultimate interpreter of the Constitution"); *Cooper v.*

Aaron, 358 U.S. 1, 18, (1958) ("permanent and indispensable feature of our constitutional system" is that "the federal judiciary is supreme in the exposition of the law of the Constitution").

* * *

Georgia's drawing of the Eleventh District was not required under the Act because there was no reasonable basis to believe that Georgia's earlier enacted plans violated § 5. Wherever a plan is "ameliorative," a term we have used to describe plans increasing the number of majority-minority districts, it "cannot violate § 5 unless the new apportionment itself so discriminates on the basis of race or color as to violate the Constitution." Georgia's first and second proposed plans increased the number of majority-black districts from 1 out of 10 (10%) to 2 out of 11 (18.18%). These plans were "ameliorative" and could not have violated § 5's non-retrogression principle. Acknowledging as much, the United States now relies on the fact that the Justice Department may object to a state proposal either on the ground that it has a prohibited purpose or a prohibited effect. The Government justifies its preclearance objections on the ground that the submitted plans violated § 5's purpose element. The key to the Government's position, which is plain from its objection letters if not from its briefs to this Court, is and always has been that Georgia failed to proffer a nondiscriminatory purpose for its refusal in the first two submissions to take the steps necessary to create a third majority-minority district.

The Government's position is insupportable.... Although it is true we have held that the State has the burden to prove a nondiscriminatory purpose under § 5, Georgia's Attorney General provided a detailed explanation for the State's initial decision not to enact the max-black plan. The District Court accepted this explanation, and found an absence of any discriminatory intent. The State's policy of adhering to other districting principles instead of creating as many majority-minority districts as possible does not support an inference that the plan [was purposefully discriminatory].

* * *

... [T]he Justice Department's implicit command that States engage in presumptively unconstitutional race-based districting brings the Voting Rights Act, once upheld as a proper exercise of Congress' authority under § 2 of the Fifteenth Amendment, into tension with the Fourteenth Amendment. As we recalled in [*South Carolina v.*] *Katzenbach* itself, Congress' exercise of its Fifteenth Amendment authority even when otherwise proper still must " 'consist with the letter and spirit of the constitution.' " We need not, however, resolve these troubling and difficult constitutional questions today. There is no indication Congress intended such a far-reaching application of § 5, so we reject the Justice Department's interpretation of the statute and avoid the constitutional problems that interpretation raises.

* * *

NOTES AND QUESTIONS

1. Is *Miller* consistent with *Gressette*? Is the Court in effect reviewing the Attorney General's finding that he was unable to conclude the plan had no discriminatory purpose or effect? Is it impermissibly delegating that review to the Georgia district court?

2. How does *Miller* approach the questions of institutional competence addressed in *Katzenbach v. Morgan* and *Oregon v. Mitchell*?

3. To what extent does the Court's discussion reflect public-choice notions of regulatory "capture" by special interest groups? *See* Abigail Thernstrom, Whose Votes Count? Affirmative Action and Minority Voting Rights 235 (1987). Might partisan concerns also affect the Department's use of its preclearance power? In this respect, consider to what extent Democrats or Republicans might embrace "max-black" strategies. *See* Pamela S. Karlan, *Loss and Redemption: Voting Rights at the Turn of a Century*, 50 Vand. L. Rev. 291, 302–03 (1997) (discussing the relationship between partisanship and the creation of black districts); Richard H. Pildes, *The Politics of Race*, 108 Harv. L. Rev. 1359 (1995) (same).

4. How would you assess the Department of Justice's claim that its objection was defensible under the purpose prong of section 5? Would a deliberate failure to maximize the number of majority-black districts be objectionable if it was motivated by a desire to reduce black political power? Would a decision to maximize the political power of groups other than racial minorities be a proper basis for objection? In this regard, consider *Busbee v. Smith*, 549 F.Supp. 494, 517 (D.D.C.1982), *aff'd*, 459 U.S. 1166 (1983), which struck down Georgia's post–1980 reapportionment as intentionally discriminatory:

> The evidence demonstrates that the State attempted to "maximize" the voting strength of [white] persons in other areas whom State officials believe to possess similar communities of interest. For example, the Lieutenant Governor expressly required that the "mountain people" be maintained in one district for the precise reasons that Senator Bond proposed that the black neighborhoods of Fulton–DeKalb be maintained in one district. Thus, although the Voting Rights Act does not require the State to maximize minority voting strength, if the State determines to implement a policy of preserving "communities of interest" it bears a heavy burden under the Act to demonstrate why such a policy would be implemented in white residential areas but not in black residential

areas. "Such unexplained departures from the results that might have been expected to flow from the [State's] own neutral guidelines can lead ... to a charge that the departures are explicable only in terms of a purpose to minimize the voting strength of a minority group." *Connor v. Finch*, 431 U.S. 407, 425 (1977). The evidence here of the divergent utilization of the "community of interest" standard is indicative of racially discriminatory intent.

5. The Court also seems to chide the Department for oscillating between claims that Georgia's plan was purposefully discriminatory and discriminatory in effect. In this light, contrast Georgia's administrative preclearance experience with its post–1980 congressional reapportionment with the district court's treatment of the same redistricting. In January 1982, the state submitted Act No. 5 to the Attorney General for preclearance. On February 11, 1982, the Attorney General interposed an objection because of the way the plan treated the Atlanta metropolitan area. The entire objection letter was only three and a half pages long. The letter noted that the black percentage in proposed district 5 had been increased from roughly 50 percent black prior to 1980 to 57.3 percent black and therefore under *Beer*, "the plan must be considered one which 'enhances the position of minorities ...' and therefore cannot be said to have a racial 'effect' within the meaning of Section 5." Nonetheless, the Attorney General objected under *Beer*'s alternative postulate that "[i]t is possible that a legislative reapportionment could be a substantial improvement over its predecessor in terms of lessening racial discrimination, and nonetheless continue so to discriminate on the basis of race or color as to be unconstitutional." *Beer v. United States*, 425 U.S. at 142 n.14. Relying on this latter principle, the Attorney General found, in the three short paragraphs that represented the whole of the substantive analysis, that the state had split the "apparently cohesive black community of Fulton and DeKalb Counties" between two districts, when it could instead have been placed in a 69 percent black district, in order to dilute minority voting strength, and that its claims that the two-county minority community was not "cohesive" and that the purpose behind the plan was to preserve separate Fulton and DeKalb-based districts were not supported by the evidence. Thus, "[i]n this case, we have not been presented with information sufficient to enable us to reject the claims that the line between districts 4 and 5 was drawn to minimize the voting strength in that area. Under these circumstances, ... I am unable to conclude that the State has satisfied the burden of proof required by Section 5."

Georgia then sought judicial preclearance. The three-judge court unanimously denied the state's request. In contrast to the Department's three-and-a-half page letter, it issued a thirty-page opinion, which made clear that, far from simply failing to carry its burden of proof, the Georgia process had been overtly racist:

Representative Joe Mack Wilson [then Chairman of the Georgia House Permanent Standing Committee on Legislative and Congressional Reapportionment] is a racist. Wilson uses the term "nigger" to refer to black persons. He stated to one Republican member of the Reapportionment Committee that "there are some things worse than niggers and that's Republicans." Wilson opposes legislation of benefit to blacks, which he refers to as "nigger legislation." His views on blacks are well known to members of the General Assembly. From the House reapportionment committee to the Conference committee, Wilson played the instrumental role in 1981 Congressional reapportionment and he was guided by the same racial attitudes throughout the reapportionment process that guided his other legislative work.

* * *

Chairman Wilson stated [at the outset of the reapportionment process] ... that he didn't know "what's going to be the outcome of this [reapportionment] because the Justice Department is trying to make us draw nigger districts and I don't want to draw nigger districts."

* * *

[When a plan with one district with an effective black voting majority was proposed to the Georgia Senate, Senate Reapportionment Committee chairman Perry Hudson] cast the lone vote in opposition, in violation of Georgia Senate rules, which permit the Chairman to vote only in the event of a tie. That action was the first of several that Hudson would take to avoid a reapportionment plan which would allow blacks in the metropolitan Atlanta area a unified district.

* * *

Speaker [of the Georgia House Thomas] Murphy testified that he opposed [creating a black district] because "I was concerned that ... we were gerrymandering a district to create a black district where a black would certainly be elected...." Speaker Murphy's attitude about a majority black district is also reflected in a statement he previously made to several legislators. Speaker Murphy had delivered a speech to a Parents–Teachers Association meeting in DeKalb County. The audience had only two black individuals in attendance. After the speech, Speaker Murphy described the racial composition of the audience to several legislators, and noted, "Wouldn't you love to have a district like that."

* * *

The evidence demonstrates that Speaker Murphy purposefully discriminated on the basis of race in selecting House members to serve on the conference committee [designated to craft a final reapportionment plan]. He selected white persons whom he knew would adamantly oppose the creation of a congressional district in which black voters would be able to elect a candidate of their choice to the United States Congress; and he refused to appoint black persons to the conference committee solely because they might support a plan which would allow black voters, in one district, an opportunity to elect a candidate of their choice.

* * *

[Senate majority leader Allgood explained that a] second reason that Senators cited as the basis for their affirmative vote [on the plan ultimately adopted] ... was they "[didn't] want to have to go home and explain why I [the Senator] was the leader in getting a black elected to the United States Congress."

* * *

What might account for the difference between the language and approach of the preclearance letter and the language and approach of the judicial opinion? What insights does this episode shed on the difference between judicial and executive oversight over voting rights? In light of the post-1980 experience with Georgia, was the Supreme Court perhaps too hasty in concluding that no discriminatory purpose infected Georgia's 1990 round of redistricting?

E. PRECLEARANCE: A CASE STUDY

For the most part, the administrative preclearance process takes place with very little scrutiny from the judicial or legislative branches of the federal government. *Miller* is one salient exception. Another involves the first case to be decided under amended section 2 of the Voting Rights Act, *Major v. Treen*, 574 F.Supp. 325 (E.D.La.1983) (three-judge court), which challenged Louisiana's post–1980 congressional reapportionment. The following materials present the submission analysis prepared by a Department of Justice staff member; the Assistant Attorney General's explanation of his decisionmaking regarding the submission; and the district court's account of the state's activities.

SECTION 5 SUBMISSION ANALYSIS

Reapportionment of Congressional Districts in the State of Louisiana

by

Act No. 20 of the First Extraordinary Session of the Louisiana Legislature of 1981

TIME LIMIT

Received	December 17, 1981
More Information Received	April 19, 1982
Due Out	June 18, 1982

FACTUAL REVIEW AND ANALYSIS

By: Robert N. Kwan

Attorney

Voting Section

I. RELATED LITIGATION

A lawsuit challenging the submitted legislation on Section 5 and constitutional racial vote dilution grounds is currently pending. *Major v. Treen*, C.A. No. 82–1192–H (E.D. La.). Last week, a single-judge court on an uncontested motion for summary judgment ruled that the present Congressional apportionment plan adopted in 1971 violates the "one-person, one-vote" Fourteenth Amendment standard. Discovery is now underway in this litigation on the merits of the 1982 Congressional reapportionment plan. A three-judge court has been designated to hear this action (Circuit Judge Politz and District Judges Collins and Cassibry).

* * *

II. INTRODUCTION

* * *

The Louisiana Legislature recognized in early 1981 that there was a need for Congressional reapportionment and began its proceedings to undertake this legislative responsibility. In January 1981, Senator Thomas H. Hudson, Chairman of the Senate Reapportionment Study Group, advised David C. Treen, Governor of the State of Louisiana, of the need for Congressional and legislative reapportionment and recommended that reapportionment take place outside the regular legislative session to minimize interference with regular legislative business. Governor Treen agreed, and he ordered that a special two-week legislative session to consider reapportionment was scheduled to begin on November 2, 1981.

* * *

Congressional reapportionment did not come before the full Louisiana Legislature until this special 1981 legislative session. Various bills to reapportion the Congressional districts were introduced during this session (i.e., Senate Bills 4, 5, 6 and 28 and House Bills 2, 25 and 26), but of these, only Senate Bill 5, House Bill 2 and their amendments were seriously considered.

.... The Congressional reapportionment plan in Senate Bill 5, known as the "Nunez Plan," provided for a Jefferson Parish based district (72% of the First Congressional District would be in Jefferson Parish) and an Orleans parish based district (94.9% of the Second Congressional District would be in that parish).... Because the Second District under the Nunez Plan would include almost all of Orleans parish, it would be 54.0% black in population.

* * *

[Within a week,] in both houses of the legislature, Congressional reapportionment bills incorporating the Nunez Plan were adopted by both the Senate and the House.[2]

After the House votes on Congressional reapportionment, Governor Treen that evening issued a public statement that "Any bill in that form is unacceptable and without question will be vetoed." Times/Picayune, November 7, 1981. (At the May 31, 1982 conference with Mr. Reynolds, Governor Treen admitted that he publicly threatened to veto any legislation embodying the Nunez Plan.).

* * *

[A few days later,] Governor Treen held a news conference and released his so-called "Reconciliation Plan," which would ... not include a majority black district in New Orleans. Governor Treen also reiterated his threat to veto the Nunez Plan, if further action is made on that plan. Times/Picayune, November 10, 1981.

.... [Inconsistencies between the House and Senate versions of the reapportionment plan] forced the necessity of a conference committee to work out the differences between the two legislative chambers.

5. Negotiations and Adoption of a Plan, November 9–12, 1981

On November 9, after the Senate and House failed to come to an agreement on Congressional reapportionment, Senate President O'Keffe

---

2. This indicates that at the May 31, 1982 conference with Mr. Reynolds, Governor Treen and Speaker of the House of Representatives, John J. Hainkel, Jr., misspoke in stating that the Nunez Bill would not have passed the House of Representatives.

took aside Senator Nunez and Jefferson Parish Assessor Lawrence Chehardy, representing the Jefferson Parish legislative delegation, [and] Victor Bussie of the AFL–CIO, to tell them that unless a compromise on the configuration in Jefferson and Orleans Parishes is worked out, the special legislative session may end without a Congressional reapportionment plan....

A formal conference committee was appointed on Tuesday, November 10, which consisted of Senators Hudson, Nunez and O'Keffe and Representatives Alario, Bruneau and Scott. But the actual work of hammering out a settlement took place in the Senate Computer Room in the State Capitol basement and the Governor's Suite upstairs. In the basement computer room, the Jefferson Parish delegation and Democratic Congressional representatives and the Senate leadership tried to work out their compromise proposal.[10]

According to Senator Nunez and Mr. Chehardy, the Capitol Basement group tried to strike a balance to raise the Jefferson Parish proportion and the black percentage within the parameters of the Governor's requirements. After the plan was agreed upon by that group, it was taken up later that night to the Governor for his examination. Governor Treen was noncommittal on the proposal at that time and indicated to the group that the plan did not look "proper." Chehardy recalled that he responded that the plan had to look that way in order to meet the Governor's requirements.[11] On Wednesday, November 11, the next day, Governor Treen signalled that he could accept the plan and would not veto it.

* * *

10. Participants in the basement working out alternatives on the State computers were Jefferson Parish Assessor Chehardy, State AFL–CIO President Victor Bussie, Senate President O'Keffe, and Senators Nunez and Laurcella, Representative Alario, Congressman Long and aides to Congresswoman Boggs, Long and Tauzin, and members of the Senate administrative services staff. No member of the Louisiana Legislative Black Caucus participated at these sessions, nor were the aides of Governor Treen or of Congressmen Livingston and Moore.

11. Mr. Chehardy stated that Congressman Breaux was concerned because Governor Treen had not given any sign whether he would go along with the compromise and later called the Governor at his mansion later that evening. Mr. Chehardy and Senator Nunez were present when Congressman Breaux made his call to Governor Treen and the Congressman spoke in a way to let the others in the room know what was being said and after the conversation was over, told them the substance of the telephone conversation. According to Mr. Chehardy, Congressman Breaux asked the Governor what his opinion was of the compromise plan. Governor Treen stated that he had serious problems in the Orleans and Jefferson Parishes area because the lines look funny, the "head of a dog." Governor Treen added that he was concerned about dilution of minority voting strength as there would be no potential for minority growth potential in the Second Congressional District. In response, Congressman Breaux pointedly asked Governor Treen then why did the Governor would refuse to sign a plan (i.e., the Nunez Plan) which would increase black political participation. Governor Treen then said that he would discuss the proposal with Congressmen Moore and Livingston at the Governor's mansion and will discuss the plan later with Congressman Breaux. Accord-

The plan which came out of the conference committee became Act No. 20, the submitted legislation. The plan worked out in the negotiations between the Jefferson Parish delegation and the Governor and adopted by the conference committee did not include a majority black district, but did provide for a district which would be 55% Jefferson Parish in population.

* * *

II. DISCUSSION

A. **Racial Effect**

In *Beer v. United States*, 425 U.S. 130, 141 (1976), the Supreme Court held that "[t]he purpose of Section 5 has always been to insure that no voting procedure changes would be made that would lead to a retrogression in the position of racial minorities with respect to their effective exercise of the electoral franchise."

The last valid Congressional apportionment plan under Section 5 is the precleared 1972 Plan. A comparison of the 1972 and 1981 Plans under the 1980 Census indicates that the submitted plan is not retrogressive. The Second Congressional District, which has the highest black population percentage, was 40.7% black under the 1972 Plan, but would be 44.5% black. There is no black population majority district under either plan.

* * *

Under the old plan, the two districts with the highest black percentages were the First and Second Congressional Districts, which were 40.7% and 36.5% black respectively. But under the submitted plan, the two districts with the highest black percentages are the Second and Eighth Congressional Districts which are respectively 44.5% and 38.3% black. The racial proportions in the other districts in the submitted plan remain much the same as under the old plan. Because of the black population increase in the Second District, the black population percentage in the First District drops seven percentage points to 29.5% black and the black percentage in the Sixth District declines about 4.5% to 25.17% black. But the minority

ing to Mr. Chehardy, Congressman Breaux felt that Governor Treen was still holding out for the possibility that the legislature would adopt something closer to his own three proposals.

Later that night, Congressmen Livingston and Moore tried to persuade Governor Treen to accept the compromise. *See* Times/Picayune, November 13, 1981. Apparently, Governor Treen was hesitant about the plan because it placed his Metarie home in Congresswoman Boggs' district. While the Governor issued a denial, the general understanding in the legislature is that this was true. On the morning of Wednesday, November 11, Treen aide John Cade admitted to Senator Nunez that the Governor was not happy that his house was in Congresswoman Boggs' district and asked if the legislature to bring over Congressman Livingston's district into Jefferson Parish to pick up Treen's residence. Senator Nunez answered that since the Governor got his way on everything else on the plan, accommodation of this request would jeopardize the compromise and said that either the compromise plan be adopted or no plan will be enacted this special session.

percentage gains and losses seem to even out, and apparently the change is somewhat ameliorative.

B. **Racial Purpose**

* * *

The sequence of events in the reapportionment process indicate that the role of Governor Treen in the process, particularly in his public threat of a gubernatorial veto, was central in the reversal of the legislature in its adoption of a plan which would incorporate a majority black Congressional district. Thus, it becomes crucial to examine Governor Treen's motivation for his participation in the reapportionment process.

There have been allegations that the Nunez Plan was not adopted and the submitted plan was enacted because of racial reasons. Senators Hudson and Nunez, who had primary responsibility in the Senate for Congressional reapportionment, agreed that it would be fair to say that racial considerations played a role in Congressional reapportionment. Senator Hudson, however, said that Governor Treen's opposition to the Nunez Plan was not racism per se, but that while Governor Treen had a concern over the proposed changes in the First Congressional District represented by Congressman Livingston, the Governor insisted on keeping Orleans and Jefferson Parishes divided in spite of the lack of communities of interest and thus, since the growing predominantly white suburban parishes will dominate, the urban interests in New Orleans will not be represented.

The Louisiana Legislative Black Caucus consisting of the two black senators and the ten black representatives unanimously opposed the submitted plan as a dilution of minority voting strength and blames Governor Treen as the one chiefly responsible. *See* Comment of Louisiana Legislative Black Caucus, January 18, 1982; remarks of Representatives Alphonse Jackson, Johnny Jackson, Jr., and Diana Bajole, Conference Committee hearing, November 11, 1981. The Louisiana Survival Coalition also maintains that the plan was a purposeful dilution of minority voting strength and that Governor Treen was the central figure. The Survival Coalition also alleges that Governor Treen's resistance of a plan creating a majority black Congressional district may be in part explained by his personal history. *See* Comment of the Louisiana Survival Coalition, January 7, 1982.

The initial position of Governor Treen towards any inquiry into his reapportionment intent is that what his motives [were] in Congressional reapportionment simply is not relevant to the determination whether the submitted plan is valid under the requirements of the Voting Rights Act. "It should be kept in mind that the congressional districts now under review were determined by an act of the Legislature, not by act of the chief executive of the State." *See* Memorandum of David C. Treen to William J. Guste, Jr., Louisiana Attorney General, April.l 7, 1982, at 3 and Attachment A, at 1. This position implies that the Governor had no role in Congressional reapportionment.

There is no question that Governor Treen was heavily involved in the Congressional reapportionment process and that his actions determined the outcome of the process.... In the views of Congressman Breaux, Senators Nunez and Hudson and the members of the Louisiana Legislative Black Caucus, the submitted plan is basically the Governor's plan as modified. It is clear that the Governor was involved in the process; to suggest otherwise would be as one commenter said to argue that two plus two is not four.

In the submission review process, Governor Treen has enunciated several reasons for his opposition to the Nunez Plan and in support of the submitted plan. Directly on the question of race and Congressional reapportionment, Governor Treen said:

> What I did do was to question the appropriateness of a deliberate, conscious drawing of congressional district lines for the deliberate purpose of achieving a majority black district. I observed that such motives were inconsistent with our goal of a homogenous society. In fact, it is demeaning to blacks to suggest that they must be in an absolute majority in order to effect the election of a member of their race. It is also demeaning to them that they will always vote along racial lines.

Statement of Governor David C. Treen, Attachment A to Memorandum to William J. Guste, Jr., Louisiana Attorney General, April 7, 1982, at 3.

His first statement in the reapportionment process was apparently made on September 7, 1981 when he commented at a news conference that the idea of drawing a majority black Congressional district "smacks of racism," Baton Rouge Morning Advocate, September 9, 1981. On October 26, 1981 Governor Treen at a news conference in answer to a question why his Congressional reapportionment proposals did not incorporate a majority black district, he stated that there is "no constitutional imperative that that be done, nor do I think there is a policy imperative." Times/Picayune, October 27, 1981. Finally, at a third news conference on November 9, 1981 after the adoption of the submitted plan, Governor Treen stated "I question whether the interests of the black people ... of that city [New Orleans] are better served by concentration in one district, or by having a large and substantial voice, a chance to influence the policy and the decisions of two congressmen, which they would continue to have under this arrangement (referring to my final proposal to the Legislature.)" Attachment A to Memorandum to William J. Guste, April 7, 1982, at 1.

* * *

There are several concerns raised by Governor Treen's views. First, implicit in these statements is the belief that the Nunez Plan had no other legitimate objective other than the intentional creation of a majority black district. In other words, that it was merely an exercise to achieve racial maximization and proportional representation....

While there was discussion in the reapportionment process to the effect that the creation of a majority black district was desirable, the Nunez Plan had other significant objectives. Another primary interest of the legislature, particularly the influential Jefferson Parish delegation, would be the creation of a Congressional district anchored in Jefferson Parish.... The logical by-product of the creation of a Jefferson Parish district would be an Orleans parish based district across the Mississippi River on the East Bank, which would likely be majority black. The main impetus for the Nunez Plan was not the Louisiana Legislative Black Caucus, but the all-white Jefferson Parish legislative delegation. The success of the Nunez Plan is a direct result of the political influence of the Jefferson Parish.

* * *

Aside from giving Jefferson parish control of a Congressional district, the Nunez Plan would recognize divergent communities of interest. First, it would provide heavily black, urban New Orleans with a district, and also predominantly white, suburban Jefferson Parish with a district. Second, the Nunez Plan would be more faithful to the recognition of parish boundaries than the other plans. Third, it would also observe the natural geographic boundary of the Mississippi River.

The key point is the divergence of communities of interest. And there is agreement of the most prominent political leaders of the two parishes on this point of communities of interest, including Ernest Morial, the Mayor of New Orleans; Representative Louis Charbonnet, III, the only black legislative supporter of Governor Treen; Senator Samuel Nunez; and Jefferson Parish Assessor Lawrence Chehardy along with the other minority commenters, the Louisiana Survival Coalition, Representatives Jon Johnson and Johnny Jackson, Jr., and the Louisiana League of Women Voters.

New Orleans is urban, liberal and heavily black; Jefferson Parish is suburban, conservative and white. Their interests are often antagonistic. The commenters were quite candid in stating that many of the Jefferson Parish residents moved there from New Orleans to get away from living with blacks. The New Orleans metropolitan area, in their view, is no different from other American cities as an example of the phenomenon of "white flight," (New Orleans, Orleans Parish is the minority core 55% black) while the surrounding parishes are the white suburban ring, Jefferson, Plaquemines, St. Bernard and St. Tammany (all over 85% white).

* * *

The commenters concluded that they do not see how a member of Congress in the Second Congressional District under the submitted plan could adequately serve two constituencies with diametrically opposed interests and needs. They believe that helping one would displace the other and that given the racial and parish makeup of the district, the urban and black interests in Orleans Parish would lose out to Jefferson parish interests.

* * *

The Louisiana Legislative Black Caucus has stated in its comment that the failure to create a majority black district and the enactment of the submitted plan intentionally dilutes black voting strength. Representative Turnley, the chairman of the Louisiana Legislative Black Caucus, has informed us that the Caucus is sending a letter signed by each black state legislator reaffirming the position against the submitted plan and in support of the Nunez Plan. Even the lone black legislative supporter of Governor Treen, Representative Louis Charbonnet, said that even though he is a Treen supporter, the submitted plan is a "racist" plan. Of the hundred or so letters from minority commenters, not one supports the submitted plan.

One organization, the Louisiana Survival Coalition, has even directly questioned the credibility of Governor Treen's position by referring to his past political history, which evidences in their view hostility to black interests. In its comment, the Coalition discussed Treen's participation in the Louisiana States Rights Party and provide campaign flyers of the States Rights Party for the 1960 presidential election. According to William Quigley, attorney for the Survival Coalition, this campaign literature was found in the States Rights Party file at the Public Library in New Orleans. Governor Treen's participation in the States Rights Party is also acknowledged in his authorized biography by Grover Rees, III.

In 1959, David Treen joined the States Rights Party of Louisiana. He served as the chairman of the party's central committee and ran as a presidential elector candidate in 1960. The main platform of the States Rights Party was preservation of racial segregation in the state and resistance to any federal effort to curtail segregation. Its leadership included the most notorious white supremacists in Louisiana, such as Judge Leander Perez of Plaquemines Parish, who was excommunicated from the Roman Catholic Church for his racist views, and State Senator William Rainach, the most prominent spokesman for racial segregation in the state legislature. Senator Rainach led efforts in the legislature for racially selective enforcement of Louisiana's literacy test requirement for voter registration. *See* Jack Bass and Walter DeVries, Transformation of Southern Politics (1977) at 162 and 166. Along with Judge Perez and Senator Rainach, David Treen was a candidate for presidential elector in 1960 on the States Rights ticket. (In fact, on the campaign flyer submitted by the Survival Coalition, Governor Treen's picture is sandwiched between the two men. The main theme of the flyer to "stop integration by federal force.")

In his authorized biography, Governor Treen explained that his interest in the States Rights Party was "idealistic" due to concern over what he believed was excessive federal intervention in state and local matters, contrary to the letter, if not the spirit of the Tenth Amendment to the United States Constitution. Besides the cry to stop federal civil rights efforts by the federal judiciary and the Congress to desegregate Louisiana public schools and to require racial equality in employment and voting, the campaign flyer also raises legitimate concerns about the relationship between the federal government and the states, many of which are the subject of contemporary debate. But in the context of the history of the state and the period in which the statements were made, the main public appeal of the States Rights Party was clearly its campaign to resist laws for racial equality.

Governor Treen in his biography stated that he was disturbed with the racist tendencies, latent or otherwise, in the party and that he always believed that "all men are created equal" and that there should be equal application of the laws. Yet it is difficult to reconcile these beliefs with his prominent leadership in this party. Another flyer lists Governor Treen as a featured speaker at a "Rally to Save Segregation" with top billing given to Governor Ross Barnett of Mississippi and Judge Leander Perez and Senator William Rainach.

David Treen unsuccessfully attempted to run for Congress in the Second Congressional District against the late Hale Boggs, a southern Democratic liberal and formerly the majority whip of U.S. House of Representatives. Governor Treen ran three times against Congressman Boggs (1962, 1964 and 1968). In 1964 and 1968, Treen's campaign platform was conservative, and one main plank was opposition to federal civil rights measures in voting, education and housing. *See* Treen Congressional campaign flyers in 1964 and 1968, Files of the Tulane University Library. In 1968, Treen almost defeated Boggs by running against the latter's support of federal civil rights legislation. However, the black community in New Orleans bloc voted for Boggs, and according to Governor Treen, the black vote provided the margin of victory. *See* Attachment A to Memorandum of David C. Treen to William J. Guste, Jr., Louisiana Attorney General, April 7, 1982.

While we are somewhat reluctant to probe the racial views of a particular individual, the issue has been raised. Because that individual, the Governor of Louisiana, played the key role in the adoption of the submitted Congressional reapportionment plan and the defeat of a plan which would have created a majority black district, but for his intervention, we believe that the inquiry is relevant to our review pursuant to Section 5. While it may be distasteful to do so, we believe that an inference of racial motivation can be drawn from Governor Treen's background.

Additionally, a racial motivation to continue the division of the minority community in New Orleans, which could be a cohesive voting bloc to substantially influence, if not control, the election of a member of Congress in a New Orleans based district, may be inferred in the fact that Governor

Treen was frustrated in two bids for Congress by the black vote in New Orleans. Governor Treen in the memorandum to Attorney General Guste further noted that the black vote proved decisive in defeating other Congressional candidates in 1976 and 1980. A cursory examination of election returns of the 1979 gubernatorial election reveals that the black community in New Orleans continued to bloc vote for his Democratic opponent.

The Louisiana Legislative Black Caucus also furnished a survey of Governor Treen's legislative record as a member of Congress, which was compiled by the Congressional Black Caucus indicating that he almost always voted against positions supported by the black community (assuming of course that the Congressional Black Caucus represents the black community). For example, in 1975, Congressman Treen voted against the extension of the Voting Rights Act of 1965.

With respect to the other assertions in Governor Treen's statement that "it is demeaning to blacks to suggest that they must be in an absolute majority in order to effect the election of their race. It is also demeaning to them to suggest that they will always vote along racial lines." Attachment A to Memorandum to Attorney General Guste at 3, there are further concerns raised. While it may be "demeaning" to suggest that blacks require a majority to elect someone of their choice, the reality in the State of Louisiana is that the statement is true. In our review of the 1981 Louisiana House of Representatives plan, in elections between 1972 and 1982 we found that no black had ever been elected in a district with less than 63.5% black population, though there had been many black candidates who have tried with less than that percentage.

* * *

While the record has shown that blacks can get elected in New Orleans with only 55% black population and slightly less than a majority in registered voters, there is no evidence that is the case outside of New Orleans, particularly in Jefferson Parish, which constitutes 55% of the new Second Congressional District. According to the views of the commenters, including the most prominent political figures in the area, Mayor Morial of New Orleans and Tax Assessor Chehardy of Jefferson parish, the Second Congressional District will be controlled by Jefferson Parish and that it would be highly unlikely that a black would be elected in that Congressional district.

* * *

The issue of Congressional reapportionment was in part whether to perpetuate the existing fragmentation of the New Orleans black community or not. Apparently, the legislature was resolved to eliminate that condition as the by-product of creating the Jefferson Parish district, but that was all changed.

* * *

Also Governor Treen suggested at his November 9, 1981 news conference that black interests would be better served by having influence in two districts rather than a majority in one district. No state black leader in or out of the Louisiana Legislature supports the Governor's view; in fact, black leaders uniformly and adamantly oppose that view. This would include Mayor Morial, Representative Turnley on behalf of the Legislative Black Caucus, and even the Governor's most steadfast black legislative supporter, Representative Charbonnet....

* * *

There is other evidence of the direct racial purpose of statements made by particular legislators, which are best left discussed in the confidential portion of this memorandum.

IV. CONCLUSION

* * *

[The] Governor, though he initially downplayed his role for whatever reason, had the central role in the reapportionment process. He proposed his own reapportionment bills, used his veto power to achieve a desired objective and did not allow the enactment of a final plan unless it met his requirements.

When Governor Treen threatened his veto, he issued only a terse statement to that effect and did not specify his reasons. The rationale for his actions during the reapportionment process has come forth only slowly. While this may be understandable, given the sensitive political nature of the matter, it is difficult to ascertain what his motivation was at the time those actions occurred. His rationale has come forward in a piecemeal manner, and the reasons have differed, though not necessarily inconsistent with each other.

* * *

While there may have been nonracial considerations in the Governor's deliberations, such as historical boundaries, dilution of voting strength of certain parishes, ripple effect, political rivalries, and incumbency preservation, and it is difficult to weigh them, even if inaccurate or frivolous, it is clear in our view that the Governor was acutely aware of the racial consequences of his actions, and those racial considerations formed the basis of his actions.

We conclude that the State has not met its burden of proving the lack of a racial purpose and recommend the interposition of a Section 5 objection.

CONFIDENTIAL PORTION OF SECTION 5 MEMORANDUM

Lawrence Chehardy, the Tax Assessor of Jefferson Parish, who was integrally involved in Congressional reapportionment as the leader of the Jefferson parish political establishment and one of the architects of the Nunez Plan, alleged that Representative Charles Emile Bruneau of New Orleans told him at the time of the floor debates on Congressional reapportionment on November 5 or 6, 1981 that he is opposing the Jefferson/Nunez Plan because "We already have a nigger mayor [in New Orleans], and we don't need another nigger bigshot." Representative Bruneau was the chairman of the reapportionment subcommittee responsible for the objected-to Louisiana House of Representatives apportionment plan of 1981. He was also one of the six members of the joint plan of 1981. He was also one of the six members of the joint conference committee which was responsible for developing a compromise plan after Governor Treen's veto threat and the House reversal on the Nunez Plan. Representative Bruneau voted against the Nunez Plan in all votes and voted for the submitted plan. He played a prominent role in the adoption of amendments in the Committee on House and Governmental Affairs and on the House floor which would eliminate the Nunez Plan.

There were other racial considerations involved by other legislators in Mr. Chehardy's conversation. I am not sure what weight Mr. Chehardy's remarks are entitled to because he requested confidentiality. Representative Bruneau has not been confronted with these allegations; the confidentiality would be compromised if we were to do so.

* * *

Hearings on the Nomination of William Bradford Reynolds to Be Associate Attorney General of the United States, Sen. Judiciary Comm., 99th Cong., 1st Sess. (1985)

Senator Biden. Mr. Reynolds, this case concerns, as you well know, Congressional redistricting in Louisiana brought about by the 1980 Census. It is known by the name of the court case that it resulted in, *Major v. Treen*, and is sometimes referred to as "the Duck District case" for a simple reason—because in fact, the district, just like we used to learn in grade school, the district as it comes out looks like a duck—the famous gerrymandering that we learned about in eighth or ninth or tenth grade, or whatever it was, we learned what gerrymandering was. And in the case of the Voting Section staff, which concluded that there was discriminatory intent, recommended that you object to the plan. After you overruled your staff and precleared it, private parties filed suit under section 2 of the Voting Rights Act, and a unanimous three-judge Federal District Court found discriminatory results, using the totality of circumstances effects test that was enacted in 1982.

* * *

According to the documents you produced for us in this case, the Voting Section attorneys and analysts who were responsible for giving you recommendations on the Louisiana plan recommended you object. They did not base their recommendation on a finding of discriminatory effect, since the plan submitted to you was no worse than the districting plan that New Orleans had been operating under for the past ten years. But they did find racial intent, primarily on the part of Governor Treen. . . .

* * *

Mr. REYNOLDS: . . . . I would like to preface my remarks by saying that the district court in this case did not find discriminatory intent; indeed, did not disagree at all with the determination made by the Attorney General. In fact, the district court said that it was not reviewing the Attorney General's determination in this regard, because my determination was under section 5, which had a standard that was different from the standard that the district court was using. . . .

The district court used the catalog of factors that Congress had indicated [in the legislative history of amended section 2] it should use to determine whether it was a discriminatory result and did indeed make that finding that it resulted in discrimination. Had I had that factor available to me at the time I did the Louisiana redistricting, I might well have decided the same way. But I did not have that. . . . Congress had not passed section 2 at that time, and I had only the standard of section 5 available. That one says that you must deny or object to a redistricting if it has discriminatory purpose or effect. And the real question here was whether the redistricting was done with the purpose of discriminating or denying minorities an equal opportunity in the voting process.

We went through that discussion. I met—I am not sure how many times. I certainly met with Governor Treen. I met with a large number of representatives on the other side from Louisiana. I met with my staff—

* * *

The major argument was that the redistricting process that had been engaged in was one where the lines were drawn in a way that purposefully intended to deny minorities the opportunity to—the full or equal opportunity—to participate in the electoral process.

And my conclusion was that the line-drawing was one that was indeed very much motivated by political considerations, and indeed, wholly by political considerations, and had not been done in a manner or with a purpose of denying or minimizing minority voting strength, but indeed had been driven very much by a lot of political considerations that were inherent at the time.

Senator BIDEN. Was one of those political considerations to protect the district of a Republican Congressman named Livingston, in your opinion? Had you been told that by the Governor that that was one of the—

Mr. REYNOLDS. I think there was an allegation that—no, I do not believe that the Governor—well, I cannot remember precisely what the Governor said.

Senator BIDEN. Did you have any doubt about that—let me put it that way.

Mr. REYNOLDS. I think that district was one that, for political reasons, was the subject of considerable concentration in the redistricting.

Senator BIDEN. That is not quite what I am asking now Mr. Reynolds. You pointed out that you concluded that there was no racial intent, that it was a political districting that was being done, that it was for political reasons that the district was drawn to look like this. Now I am asking you if, in fact, your view was, was it clear to you, that one of those political reasons to justify this "duck" was to protect a Republican Congressperson—and remember, you are under oath, as I know you do know.

Mr. REYNOLDS. No, I think that Congressman Livingston's district was one that, for political reasons, they drew the way they did.

Senator BIDEN. So when you looked at it, if you are going to put a positive light on it, you said in effect—I am putting words in your mouth now, and I would like to ask you to respond to it—that when your staffers came to you and said, "Look, they are doing this; they are drawing this thing to keep blacks from having power," I assume you essentially said, "No, no. That does not have to do with blacks. That is politics. It has to do with protecting a Republican Congressman."

Is that the essence of the difference of opinion you had with your staff?

Mr. REYNOLDS. Well, it did not occur that way, Senator. Obviously, we went through a rather long, extensive analysis of this, back and forth, and indeed, I think by the time we finished, there was not as much disagreement among myself and the staff as the memoranda that you have been furnished might indicate. But certainly, the difference of opinion that we had was essentially whether the redistricting was done for racial reasons or political reasons.

Senator BIDEN. Well, one of the allegations made in that memorandum concluded that there were allegations, much more blatant evidence of discriminatory intent. For example, they stated an allegation was made by one individual required confidentiality, so I will not mention his name, and it was in the memo, that the legislator was very influential in the majority black district plan, that in fact, he had been told, quote, "We already have a nigger Mayor; we don't need another nigger bigshot," end of quote.

Do you recall whether this allegation or any similar allegations came to your attention through your staff when this matter was in fact before you?

Mr. REYNOLDS. Those allegations certainly were brought to my attention, and they are in the memo, I believe, that you have reference to, and we discussed them at length as to who said them and what was the context, and whether the people who were reportedly saying those statements, whether that could be verified, what their role was in the redistricting process, whether indeed that was made in connection directly with the redistricting process. All of that was explored fully, and we actually had a very long discussion both with people from Louisiana who were opposed to the redistricting, with the Governor and people, officials of Louisiana, and those were indeed aired.

* * *

The Governor's concern was that the Nunez plan, which was not the one that was before us, but that the Nunez plan had been drawn in a way that took race into account to, in essence, make it a majority black district, and his view was that the black community would be better served by having two influence districts, 40 percent or better, rather than having all of the black population packed into a single district.

And what he was concerned about, and I think that's what the Court is saying and I would agree with that, is that as to the Nunez plan it was drawn in a way that was designed really to either have a maximized black district or to put all of the blacks in one district rather than draw it so the would have two influence districts.

Senator BIDEN. Did you agree with the Governor's argument?

Mr. REYNOLDS. Well, it wasn't for me to agree or disagree with his argument as to whether it's better for the community to have one majority district or two influence districts. We really stay away from those kinds of judgments in these section 5 matters.

My only interest was in ascertaining whether the Governor was doing it for racial or nonracial reasons.

* * *

Senator BIDEN. Soon after Governor Treen stated his intention to veto this majority black district plan, or the Nunez plan, the Senate president summoned, quote, "interested parties" to a private meeting in the Senate computer room, in the subbasement of the State capital. From this meeting emerged the plan that was ultimately enacted and sent to Justice.

* * *

Most importantly, in my view, the [district court in *Major v. Treen*] found that black legislators were not invited to attend this meeting, and that:

Because all were aware that the conflicting objectives of the Governor and the black [legislators] with respect to the black majority district could not be harmonized, the latter were deliberately excluded from the final decisionmaking process.

Mr. Reynolds, were you aware of any of the allegation of discrimination along the lines of what I have just read you, at the time you precleared, that is, that the black legislators were excluded from discussions in the final decision here?

Mr. REYNOLDS. I was, Senator. What happened, to try to put it together, is that the legislators decided, when they did the final drawing of the plan, that both of those who were on either side of the arguments for a particular districting would not be included in the room, and therefore, the Governor and his officials, who had indeed been party to most of the redistricting discussions, at that time were excluded, as were the black legislators, and the effort was made in that room, as I understand it, to come up with a kind of a legislative package that would indeed be responsive to the very antidiscrimination concerns that were on the record and not be ones that were put together in the room with the antagonists and the protagonists going at it yet again in the redistricting process.

Senator BIDEN. So the fact that blacks were excluded from the meeting did not in any way concern you in light of the fact that the Governor's people were also excluded?

Mr. REYNOLDS. Well, it concerned me, Senator, in the same way as I've indicated in the other answers to you. We certainly probed that situation along with the others, and my staff and I came to the conclusion that as far as legislative purpose or animus was concerned, we did not feel that there was anything that had been demonstrated to us, that would suggest that the legislature had acted with a racial purpose.

* * *

Senator BIDEN. My understanding from a memo, that I am not sure we are able to put in the record based on our agreement, is that the actual work of hammering out this settlement, according to your staff—an internal memorandum—was that the actual work of hammering out the settlement took place in the Senate computer room in the State capital basement, and the Governor's suite upstairs.

So apparently, the Governor was very much—based on my understanding of the facts, the only parties excluded from these final negotiations were the blacks.

The Governor was deeply involved in hammering out the final solution, or his office was, and, the State legislators were deeply involved in hammering out the solution. Everyone was there but the black folk.

Mr. REYNOLDS. I do not believe that is correct, Senator.

Senator BIDEN. No?

Mr. REYNOLDS. What did happen, as I understand it, is that the compromise was hammered out in the computer room, and was then taken to the Governor's office because there was, again, the question of whether the Governor would veto or would not veto the plan once it had been devised.

It was under those circumstances then, that the Governor's office had to be brought into the matter, once they had reached a compromise, to see whether indeed it was one that he would veto.

Senator BIDEN. Well, it seems to me that's a distinction, not a difference. The final agreement was hammered out between the Governor and the legislators who were white. No black legislators were a part of that hammering out process, right?

Mr. REYNOLDS. I guess that that would be correct.

Senator BIDEN. And that is not a problem? I mean, that did not cause you concern?

Mr. REYNOLDS. Well, Senator, your characterization of what might or might not have caused me concern—I guess I would preface my remark by saying this particular redistricting caused considerable concern. It was one that I was personally involved in from the beginning.

It was one that I wrestled with, I worked at from start to finish. It was one that I had numerous discussions of with my staff; we went through numerous analyses, and certainly, all of these things that you are bringing up caused me concern.

Senator BIDEN. In reading the mind of the legislature and the Governor, did the fact that black legislators did not participate, did that lead you toward the conclusion that there was discriminatory intent here, or, did it lead you away from that, or did it not matter? That is what I am trying to get at.

Mr. REYNOLDS. Senator, I think it did matter. I think it was one of the ingredients that was considered, and considered very carefully. As I say again, it was the considered judgment of the staff, and me, after we had reviewed all of the factors—and we have only touched on but a small number in this complex redistricting—that the legislature was not motivated by racial purpose, and indeed, everybody then focused on whether it was Governor Treen's participation in this that was racially motivated such as to defeat the redistricting.

But I think all of these matters that you have raised were pieces of a larger puzzle. They all were of legitimate and serious concern. I certainly took them seriously, I probed them and I reviewed them all, and the question was, when you put all of that together, in the final analysis, what is your best judgment as to the redistricting activity?

Senator BIDEN. Well, let's talk about another piece. The alleged gerrymandered shape of this duck-shaped district that was precleared.

The court rather dramatically described the alleged shape in the following, when it says:

> Act 20's jagged line dissects a large concentrated community of black voters residing in Orleans Parish, dispersing that community into the First and Second Congressional District. With unerring precision, the line slices through the city's traditional political subunit, the ward, in a racially selective manner, leaving intact predominantly white wards, while carving up those densely populated by blacks. Homogeneous black precincts are separated. White precincts are not.

Now, my question to you is, as you pre-cleared the plan, had you studied in sufficient detail the actual physical makeup of the district, and whether or not the line sliced through, to use the court's words, "in a racially selective manner, leaving intact predominantly white wards, while carving up those in densely populated black wards"?

Mr. REYNOLDS. Well, Senator, I certainly did review the configuration in minute detail, and went over it carefully over and over again, and I think that as to some features of the line drawing, it can be said that that description fits, and I think as to other features, it can be said that it carved up white wards and did not leave them in the same kind of a situation as was described in this particular area.

The problem you have in any redistricting is that you are going to draw lines through population areas, and in doing that, there is going to be some fragmentation and there is going to be division of communities, and my judgment on this has to be, in those circumstances, whether or not that line drawing was done in a way that was designed to deprive the minority population—

Senator BIDEN. But it would cause you alarm, would it not, if in fact you looked down, and all the white wards remained intact, but the black wards were split? I mean, that is enough to send up an alarm bell, is it not?

Mr. REYNOLDS. That is certainly enough to send up an alarm bell. I think that overstates what the situation was as far as the whole redistricting is concerned, but certainly as to certain portions of it, and as the court pointed out, that is a correct characterization.

Senator BIDEN. Put it in another context. Is it not true that black wards were impacted upon in terms of a change in shape and configuration much more than the white wards were in that areas, is that not true?

Mr. REYNOLDS. I think certainly in the New Orleans–Jefferson County area, that was correct, and part of that had to do with the concentration of the community of black voters that resided in that area, and the whole question, really, was one that the court itself pointed out as being a difficult one, and that's whether you are going to have one single majority district where all the black voters are packed into one district, or whether you are going to do some degree of fragmentation in order to give the black voters two influence districts so they can have an opportunity to have an influence for two seats rather than one seat.

Senator BIDEN. See, the problem.... some of us have with that kind of rationale is sort of the old notion that, you know, "We really know what's best for you now. Don't concentrate your power or you're going to dilute that power." And the rationale, by well-intentioned white folks, to say, "You're really better served having 40 percent in two districts than having a predominance in one district and electing a Congressperson."

I mean, that is why a lot of this is so suspect. We have heard that kind of rationale before, and when any white man or woman uses that kind of language with me, it is a little bit like some of my best friends. It sends up alarm bells because history indicates that that is the rationalization that was almost always used to justify discrimination.

* * *

Senator BIDEN. [Jerris Leonard was the Assistant Attorney General for Civil Rights during the Nixon Administration.] Is it your view that Mr. Leonard understands the Voting Rights Act pretty well?

Mr. REYNOLDS. I think he does; yes, sir.

Senator BIDEN. Is it your view that he is qualified to testify as an expert witness in the voting rights case of *Major v. Treen*? Is he qualified as an expert witness, in your view?

Mr. REYNOLDS. I do not know, because I do not know what he would be testifying to. If you mean as an expert witness with regard to the line drawing that was involved in that situation, and so on, I would not want to say no, he was not qualified; but he certainly has a full understanding of the law, and he was in the Department as the Assistant Attorney General, and I think he knows section 5 extraordinarily well.

I think he could be qualified as an expert on that.

Senator BIDEN. The State of Louisiana, under the Governor succeeding Governor Treen, is taking the position that civil rights lawyers in *Major v. Treen*, having won, should get very limited attorneys' fees from the State because it was such an easy case for them to prove, and Mr. Leonard has been retained as an expert witness for the State and I would like to quote from some of the recent testimony. He said, "I think it is fair to characterize what the legislature did, what the State did, as its official act, the legislature, working in concert with the Government as being one of the most egregious and blatant racial gerrymandering that I have seen, and I think it is fair to characterize it as falling into the category of the only two cases that I can think of where legislative bodies intentionally, overtly intentionally went out of its way to disenfranchise black voters."

"Now, what happened out of that basement room on November 10, or 11, 1981, was that the legislature, or at least that committee and subsequently the legislature, abandoned the entire principle of the creation of black majority districting in spite of the fact that they had directed their staff to create such a district previously, in spite of the fact that both Houses have adopted a black majority district. And then under the threat of veto from the Governor for what may have, to him, seemed to be well intentioned reasons, but which were clearly unconstitutional reasons, the legislature backed off and went back creating two districts, neither of which had a black population majority."

"Now, to use the sportsman's vernacular, is a duck, because it walks like a duck and it quacks like a duck, it flies like a duck. In this case, it even looks like a duck. It was referred to as a duck or the duck bill district."

"Now, your Honor, that is blatant gerrymander. You don't have to have been involved in too many voting rights cases to know that that's not a smoking gun; that's a smoking cannon."

I assume you do not agree with Mr. Leonard.

Mr. REYNOLDS. Senator, as I have indicated, my analysis of that redistricting was one where that I came to the conclusion that it was not put in place or devised by reason of racial purposes or retrogression in that situation, and, therefore—

Senator BIDEN. It was done for political reasons?

Mr. REYNOLDS. That was the conclusion I reached, and I believe that the district court, which decided the case under a section 2 theory, which was the other standard under the statute also, ... the district court also made the point that defendant's showing political motivations were.... the primary impetus behind the configuration of the first and second district's did not provide pervasive rebuttable evidence of nondilution—as I say, had we had the section 2 provision available to us at the time of the Louisiana redistricting it might well have been that it would have come out differently; but Congress had not passed that particular provision then, and that was the one that the Court was looking at.

My analysis of it as a careful review as I could undertake, it was indeed political gerrymandering that was involved, and that the actions that were taken were ones that were taken were ones that were driven by politics rather than race.

Senator BIDEN. Now, having said that, assuming section 2 were in effect, would you have changed your judgment? Would you have ruled the same way the Court did, do you think? Would you have decided the same way the Court did?

Mr. REYNOLDS. I believe that if the evidence had been put before me that was before the Court, that I probably would have ruled the same way on the section 2 analysis in the Louisiana case.

Senator BIDEN. That is interesting. For the record, explain to us why the distinction between the standard in section 5 and section 2 was the Court may have—

Mr. REYNOLDS. The section 5 standard is one that is two-pronged. It deals with discriminatory purposes, as we discussed, and the discriminatory effect text has been defined by the Supreme Court in a case that Senator Hatch referred to earlier as the *Beer* decision as one that looks to the retrogressive aspects of the change, and so what you do is you compare the redistricting plan that has been submitted to the particular districting configuration in place at the time of the change to see if indeed that caused any retrogression in the position of the minority voters by reason of a change. Section 2, which Congress passed, actually, I think in July, on July 23, of 1982, which was shortly after this decision went down, was made by us.

Section 2 looks to discriminatory results and what the Congress says was that you evaluate a host of criteria to determine whether they had the result of discriminating against the black electorate in a particular jurisdiction; and in those circumstances, if you can find that it has a discriminatory result, looking at the factors that the district court did indeed examine, then you find it was a violation of the statute even if it was not purposeful or retrogressive.

Senator BIDEN. Which was the higher standard?

Mr. REYNOLDS. Higher in what sense, Senator?

Senator BIDEN. More difficult to prove.

Mr. REYNOLDS. In the abstract?

Senator BIDEN. Yes; is it harder to make a case under section 5 or section 2?

Mr. REYNOLDS. Well, it depends. If you have retrogression, it is a lot easier to make it under section 5 than it is under section 2. If you have a situation where you have your benchmark and compare it to the new change, and you can show there has been some dilution of the vote, then I think that is an easier case.

Under the prong of the intent standard, I think that it probably is a little more difficult to show the intent, although the court in *Rogers v. Lodge* has said that you accumulate the same factors that the Court went through here and you can draw an influence of an intent as a result of those factors. I think it says that is a little bit higher standard than the results test.

Senator BIDEN. When did you make your decision to sign off?

Mr. REYNOLDS. I decided on the *Louisiana* case on June 18, I believe.

Senator BIDEN. June 18, 1982. And discrimination results, section 2, became law in July 1982?

Mr. REYNOLDS. I believe that is the correct date.

* * *

Senator BIDEN. You obviously met with the Governor a couple of times and talked to him a couple of times; is that correct?

Mr. REYNOLDS. I did.

Senator BIDEN. And you say you met with the opponents, or those who opposed what I will refer to as the basement plan. Who were those people with whom you met who were opposed who were arguing with you that you should not sign off?

Mr. REYNOLDS. I do not remember the names of them. I know that there were different representatives of the—some in the civil rights community, some members of the—I believe some of the members of the legislature down in Louisiana. I know that we had a couple of meetings with people who came up to talk to us about it.

Senator BIDEN. And you feel that you in fact investigated this matter sufficiently and pursued the opposition's concerns as vigorously as you pursued the concerns of the Governor?

Mr. REYNOLDS. Oh, absolutely. In fact, the real concern here, on, I think, everybody's part, as I tried to indicate, Senator, was whether the Governor indeed had operated with racial motives and, therefore, part of my meetings with the Governor and conversation with the Governor was to probe very carefully what his motives were and what indeed had been his involvement in this. I think that we certainly did probe it extensively.

Senator BIDEN. One of the reasons why this sort of an air or cloud, at least in the minds of some about this situation was it is alleged by some of your critics that when your staff was studying this matter early in 1982, they sent a letter to the State asking for additional information, including information about statements allegedly attributed to Governor Treen, and it goes on to suggest that after you were made aware of this, you canceled the letter and ordered a new one sent. You did not ask about the Governor's statement.

Is there any truth to this?

Mr. REYNOLDS. That is exactly what did happen, and, indeed, that was done with the concurrence of my deputy and also the chief of the section. The letter that went out originally was one that I thought in tone more than in substance, was not the proper kind of a letter for us to be addressing to a Governor of a State. The drafted letter, the one that we recut that we sent out was one that I really think more than anything else addressed the tone of it, and the substance of the letters were largely identical.

* * *

I think the Governor was called upon to answer the delicate questions in full measure and did so and submitted information to us on those points and came in and talked to me and my staff with regard to those questions and was asked by me and my staff on those quotes, about those quotes.

Major v. Treen

574 F.Supp. 325 (E.D.La.1983) (three-judge court).

■ HENRY POLITZ, Circuit Judge:

* * *

Facts and Procedural History

In November 1981, Act 20 of the Louisiana Legislature's First Extraordinary Session of 1981 apportioned the state into eight single-member congressional districts.... [Act 20 was] submitted to the Attorney General of the United States for preclearance under § 5 of the Voting Rights Act, 42 U.S.C. § 1973c.... On June 18, 1982, Act 20 was precleared by the Attorney General....

Findings of Fact

* * *

During the decade of the 1970s, Orleans Parish (coterminous with the City of New Orleans) experienced a marked change and a slight decline in population. While overall population declined, the black population increased. The city/parish now has a black population of 308,039 persons, which constitutes 55% of the total population, 48.93% of the voting age population, and 44.89% of the registered voters....

By contrast, the predominantly white, suburban parishes of Jefferson and St. Tammany, which flank the central city, have undergone explosive population growth. According to the 1980 census, Jefferson Parish, with a 13.9% black population, a 13.75% black voting age population, and a 10.45% black voter registration, is nearly 87% the size of the ideal congressional district. Unlike Orleans Parish, Jefferson Parish's black population is diffused throughout the parish. Prior to the recent demographic shifts, New Orleans had enough people to form the dominant majority in two congressional districts. Now only 1.06 times the size of the ideal district, as defined by the 1980 census, New Orleans' traditional dominance of two congressional districts is no longer supported by its population.

* * *

Legislative History of Act 20

.... [In 1981, r]ecognizing the need for realignment of the state's congressional districts, the legislature established the Louisiana House and Senate Joint Congressional Reapportionment Committee. In July, at the close of the regular 1981 session, each house appointed legislators to ad hoc congressional reapportionment subcommittees.... There were four black legislators on the joint committee. No black legislator was appointed to either subcommittee.

* * *

Several groups submitted proposals to the joint committee or the two subcommittees, among them Governor Dave Treen.... None of the Governor's three proposed plans, denominated Treen A, B, and C, contemplated a majority black district. During this period the Governor publicly expressed his opposition to the concept of a majority black district, stating that districting schemes motivated by racial considerations, however benign, smacked of racism, and in any case were not constitutionally required.

* * *

... [T]he Senate staff developed a plan which, as the result of the sponsorship of Senator Samuel B. Nunez, Jr. of St. Bernard Parish, would subsequently be referred to as the "Nunez Plan." As drafted, this plan envisaged one black and seven white population majority districts. Nunez's proposed ... Second Congressional District consisted almost entirely of Orleans Parish (94.9%), together with 25 contiguous precincts drawn from east Jefferson Parish.... By allocating separate districts to majority black, urban Orleans Parish and virtually all-white residential Jefferson Parish, Nunez took into account the divergent, frequently antithetical, concerns of city and suburban dwellers, as well as parish lines and the natural geographic barrier erected by the Mississippi River. Utilizing 1980 census figures, Nunez's Second District would be 54% black in population and 43% black in voter registration.

* * *

Members of the Louisiana Black Caucus united with the Jefferson parish forces, led by Nunez and Chehardy, in urging passage of the Nunez Plan. That Nunez and Chehardy were principally concerned with establishing a district controlled by predominantly white Jefferson Parish was of little import to black legislators, who advocated the plan's concomitant formation of a majority black district in Orleans Parish.... [Ultimately, both the Senate and the House rejected attempts to substitute one of Governor Treen's plans for the Nunez plan and b]oth houses of the Louisiana Legislature ... approved reapportionment bills incorporating the Nunez Plan in its entirety, although the House Bill inadvertently left out one precinct. Upon learning of the action of the legislature, Governor Treen announced his intention to veto the Nunez Plan if finally passed.

* * *

Because of his decisive role in the defeat of the Nunez Plan after it had received the overwhelming support of both houses of the legislature, Governor Treen's stated reasons for acting are relevant.... He denounced any legislative scheme which intentionally drew boundary lines so as to consolidate a majority of one race within a single district. He specifically rejected the Nunez Plan, which would create a 55% black district, for this reason. In the state's section 5 submission to the Justice Department, prepared by counsel and approved by the Governor, this plan was characterized as an attempt by the Louisiana Legislature to enact into law the discredited idea of proportional representation.

These concerns were restricted to the aggregation of blacks within one district; the coalescence of whites was not regarded as ominous so long as [Republican] Congressman Livingston's chances for re-election were maximized. An Orleans-based district with a 55% black population was not acceptable to the Governor. As later noted, an Orleans-based district with a 55% white population encountered no objection.

The court finds that the Governor's opposition to the Nunez Plan was predicated in significant part on its delineation of a majority black district centered in Orleans Parish.

* * *

[Various politicians then met to craft an apportionment acceptable to the governor.].... Senate President Michael O'Keefe of New Orleans summoned "interested" parties to a private meeting in the Senate Computer Room, situated in the sub-basement of the State Capitol.... Black legislators were not invited, those responsible for calling the gathering having decided that the goal of crafting a district with a high minority profile would have to be abandoned.

A plethora of factors was considered at the meeting.... [T]he participants determined that the minority's interest in obtaining a predominantly black district would have to be sacrificed in order to satisfy both the Governor and the Jefferson Parish group. As [one participant, Laurence Chehardy] candidly explained:

> ... the feeling in the meeting was that the one group, the one [constituency] group that was not going to come out of the session satisfied was going to be the blacks. The reason for that was that with all of the competing interests ... there was probably going to be virtually no way to satisfy the black members of the Legislature ... insofar as creating a majority black district [was concerned].... They [minority legislators] didn't have enough votes.

Working late into the evening, the sub-basement conferees ultimately arrived at that synthesis of conflicting interests incorporated into Act 20. Jefferson Parish constitutes approximately 55% of the Second District under the Act; portions of Orleans Parish make up the remainder. St. Tammany, St. Bernard and Plaquemines parishes, together with the lakefront, New Orleans east, and Algiers sections of Orleans Parish, are placed within the First District. The jagged line dividing the First and Second Districts commences in the east below the west bank of the Mississippi River, casting Ward 15 and Plaquemines Parish into District One. Traversing the Mississippi, the line runs north for approximately 15 blocks and juts sharply to the east to sever the southern extremities of Wards 8 and 9, gathering predominantly white neighborhoods within District One. Veering north through the midsection of Ward 9, then west through Wards 9, 7, and 8, the line sweeps the densely-populated black community of central New Orleans into District Two, and the adjoining white neighborhoods which border Lake Ponchartrain into District One. Moving south and west, the line fractures Wards 5, 4, 3, and 2 to separate white and black areas into Districts One and Two, respectively. Ward 14, which is 90% white, is aligned within District One. Tracing a northwesterly path along the east bank of the Mississippi, the line extends north to dissect a discrete black concentration on Carrolton, joining one part with an expanse of white population in Jefferson Parish. The total population, percent deviation from the ideal population, percent black population and percent black registered voters for each district created by Act 20 are as follows:

Dist.	Total Pop.	Deviation	% Black Pop.	%Black Reg. Voters
1	525,319	−0.03	29.5	21.5
2	526,605	+0.21	44.5	38.7
3	526,364	+0.17	15.2	12.7
4	525,067	−0.08	31.6	22.3
5	525,668	+0.03	31.2	24.6
6	524,374	−0.21	25.1	18.1
7	525,186	−0.06	20.1	16.9
8	525,389	−0.02	38.3	21.9

District boundaries fixed by Act 20 are clearly racial in character, selectively segregating white and black residents of New Orleans into the majority white First District and the more heterogeneous Second District. When traced on a map of the city, that portion of the Second District which cuts into Orleans Parish resembles the head of a duck, with the bill splintering Ward 9, a contiguous black community of approximately 94,000 people. Ward 8, which also contains a high concentration of blacks, was sliced three ways, with the extreme northern (lakefront) and southern segments assigned to District One and the midsection to District Two. Although other black wards are fragmented, the integrity of predominantly white wards is assured. Of the 31 metropolitan precincts with a black population of 95% or higher, most of which are situated precisely on the duck bill, 17 were placed in District One and 14 were placed in District Two. Act 20's racial boundary line separates cohesive black neighborhoods

APPENDIX B

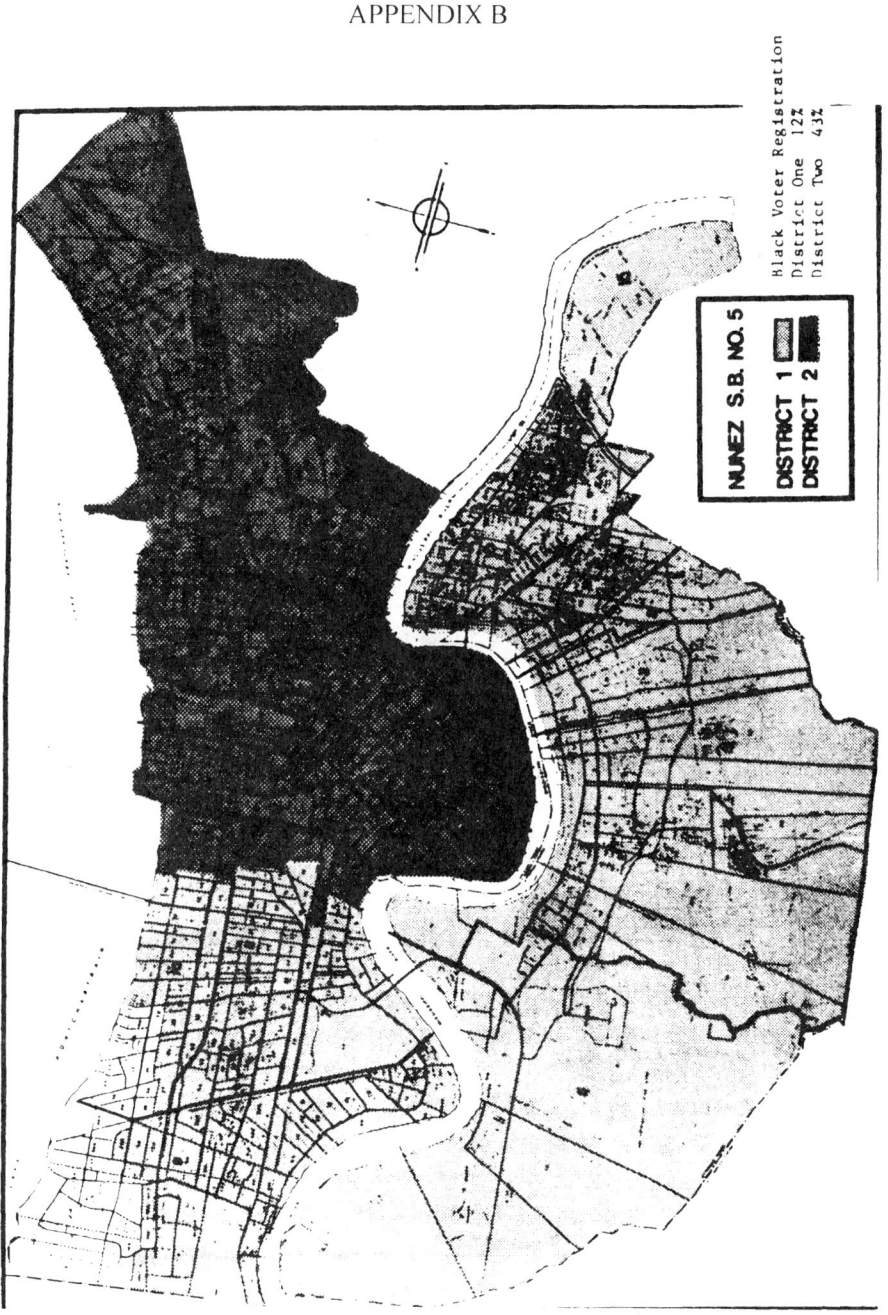

in the inner city which share common political and socio-economic interests premised on income, transportation, education and housing. Similar disruption of white neighborhoods is minimal.

APPENDIX C

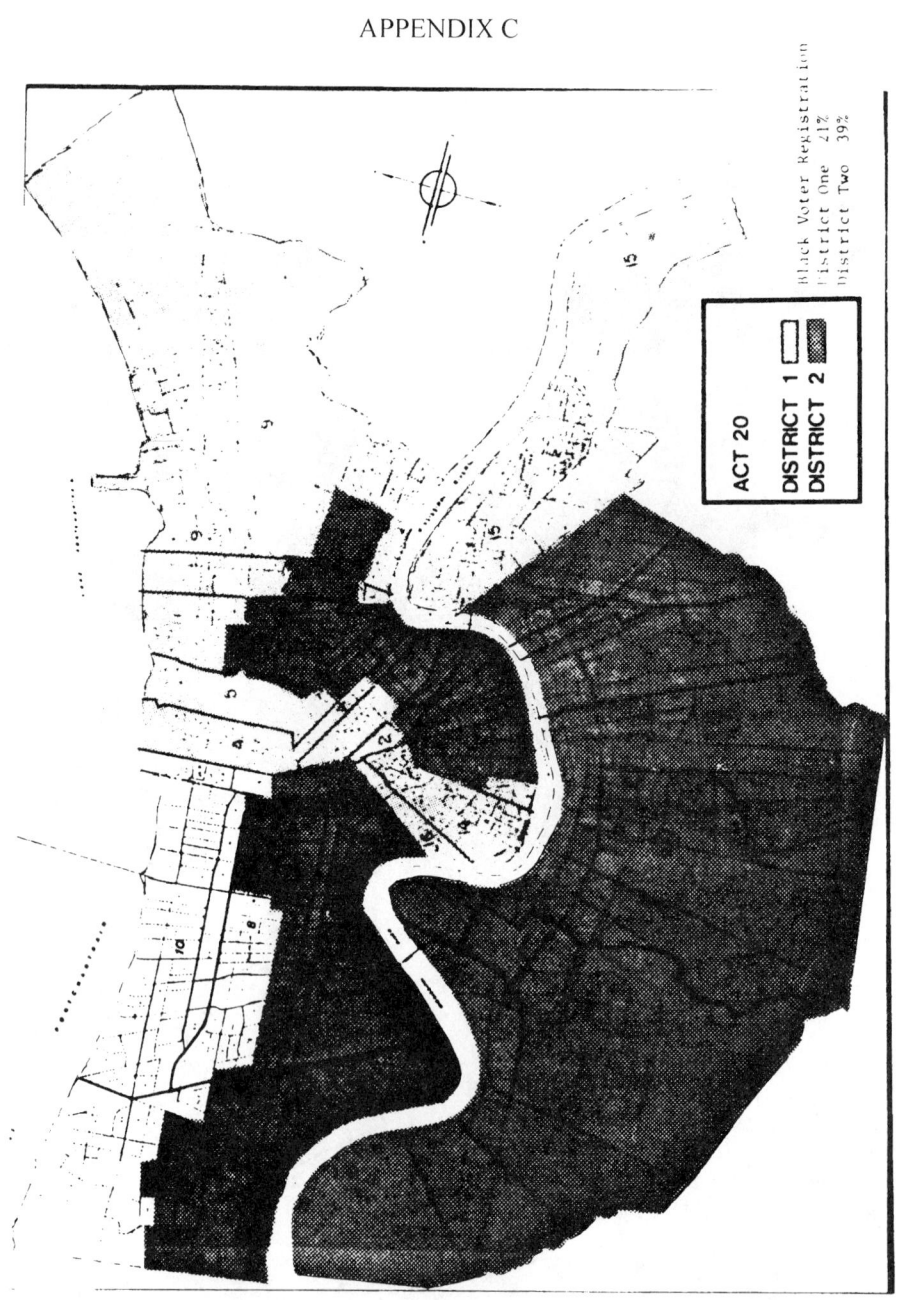

.... Districts One and Two of Act 20, with their distorted shapes and irregular, indented perimeters, are not geographically compact. These unusual configurations are not necessary to ensure adherence to the one-person, one-vote rubric. In contrast to the Nunez Plan, Act 20 deviates from the natural geographic barrier formed by the Mississippi River, which separates an enclave of inner city blacks from whites residing in suburban areas.

New Orleans' traditional political subunit, the ward, has been selectively fragmented by Act 20. Black population concentrations within most of the nine Orleans Parish wards split by the Act have been disrupted, whereas white concentrations remain essentially inviolate. Not a single ward is divided under the Nunez Plan.

By disregarding parish lines and uniting populated segments of Orleans and Jefferson Parishes with mutually exclusive, often discordant needs and concerns, Act 20 effectively ignores both historic boundaries and obvious communities of interest. Since Jefferson Parish comprises the majority of Act 20's Second District, the interests of the more conservative, suburban white populace have effectively eclipsed those of the less conservative, urban blacks who make up only 17.9% of the district's population.

Once completed, the new plan was submitted to Governor Treen for review.... On November 12, 1981, the House and Senate adopted the conference committee report. Governor Treen signed this bill into law on November 19, 1981, and it became Act 20 of the First Extraordinary Session of 1981.

* * *

Application of amended § 2's "results" test to the aggregate of the facts adduced at trial, including Louisiana's history of discrimination and the impact of that history on the present ability of blacks in Orleans Parish to join in the political process, the vestiges of discrimination which take the form of a marked disparity in the socioeconomic conditions under which blacks and whites currently subsist, the parish's racially polarized voting, as exacerbated by the state's majority vote requirement, the tenuousness of the state policy underlying Act 20 and the history of its enactment and the manipulation of district boundary lines so as to fracture a cohesive minority voting bloc, preponderates in favor of the plaintiffs. Circumstantial evidence that race played a role in the confection of Act 20 also figures in the court's calculus, although we have not engaged in the intent analysis permitted by § 2.[39] Based on the totality of relevant circumstances, there-

39. Given our conclusion that Act 20 results in a dilution of black voting strength, we need not draw the ultimate inference of purposeful discrimination from the composite of factors heretofore outlined. The court has nevertheless taken into account, as but one aspect of the totality of circumstances, the evidence that opposition to the creation of majority black district was responsible, to a

fore, the court concludes that the contours of the First and Second Congressional Districts, as established by Act 20, operate to deny or abridge the rights of minority voters, who are accorded less opportunity than other members of the electorate to participate in the political process and to elect representative of their choice.

* * *

NOTES AND QUESTIONS

1. Is this "Rashomon"? What accounts for the different perceptions of the various actors who scrutinized Louisiana's reapportionment process?

2. In light of the evidence it adduced, why was the district court unwilling to strike down Louisiana's plan as purposefully discriminatory? What insight does this shed on Congress' decision to abandon a purpose requirement in section 2 cases?

3. Is it plausible to assume racial and political considerations can be disentangled in the reapportionment process? We return to this question in Chapters 7 and 8.

significant extent, for the defeat of the Nunez Plan and the substitution of Act 20.

CHAPTER 6

MAJORITY RULE AND MINORITY VOTE DILUTION: CONSTITUTIONAL AND LEGISLATIVE APPROACHES

To the extent that courts or others believed that the one-vote, one-person doctrine and the emergence of constitutional constraints on race discrimination in voting would fully integrate various minority groups into the political process, they were disappointed. Indeed, as a matter of political and constitutional theory, one-vote, one-person was distinctly focused on ensuring majority rule and reflected relatively little concern with claims of small, geographically discrete groups of voters. First, the doctrine rested on a strong presumption in favor of majoritarian control and a distrust of minority influence. Although that distrust was overtly directed at rural, largely conservative, white, numerical minorities, the heavy presumption in favor of majority control evinced little concern with political minorities, be they defined racially, ethnically, geographically, or in partisan terms. Second, in its focus on abstract mathematical equality, one-vote one-person downplayed the importance of group representation in the governance process. *See* Lani Guinier and Pamela S. Karlan, *The Majoritarian Difficulty: One Person, One-Vote*, in Reason and Passion: Justice Brennan's Enduring Influence 207 (E. Joshua Rosenkranz & Bernard Schwartz eds. 1997). Ironically, *Reynolds v. Sims*, 377 U.S. 533 (1964), "stripped Alabama's rural, predominantly black counties of their legislative influence virtually on the eve of the massive black enfranchisement brought about by the Voting Rights Act of 1965. Had the 1901 apportionment remained in effect until 1982 [that is, if the state did not change its system as black participation increased], blacks would have controlled a higher percentage of the seats in the Alabama Legislature (18% of the House and 20% of the Senate in a state with a 25% black population) than they controlled as a result of the protections against dilution [under the pre–1982 Voting Rights Act.]" Pamela S. Karlan, *The Rights to Vote: Some Pessimism About Formalism*, 71 Tex. L. Rev. 1705, 1718 n. 54 (1993); *see also* James U. Blacksher and Larry T. Menefee, *From* Reynolds v. Sims *to* City of Mobile v. Bolden: *Have the White Suburbs Commandeered the Fifteenth Amendment?*, 34 Hastings L.J. 1, 39 n.261 (1982).

In this chapter, we explore the rise and fall of constitutional doctrine to deal with the potential that, even once the franchise was extended on fair terms, political majorities could leverage their political power by diluting the political power of minorities. One way of thinking about these issues is that, in the first generation of constitutional litigation, attention focused on access to the ballot box and conditions under which the franchise could be regulated. At that stage, the questions centered on voting as an individual right. Once the franchise was widely available, a second generation of litigation turned to the institutional structures through which these individual votes were aggregated. As you will see, there are many different ways in which election systems can be designed to aggregate the votes cast; the choice between these different structures can dramatically affect the distribution of political power between competing interests, and hence strongly influence the policies political bodies adopt. At this stage, the questions focus less on individual rights and more on the "proper" distribution of political power between competing groups.

This issue is one of the most difficult in political and constitutional theory: how to design political institutions that both reflect the right of "the people" to be self-governing and that also ensure appropriate integration of and respect for the interests of political minorities. In the context we examine, this question has an institutional aspect as well: what distinct role should different institutions, such as courts and legislatures, play in responding to the tension between majority rule and minority interest? There is a recurring doctrinal aspect to the issue as well: should constitutional law address these issues by focusing on when the majority uses its power over institutions for discriminatory purposes, or should it also focus on situations in which the majority uses this power in ways that merely have the effect, however inadvertent, of diminishing minority influence?

A. DEFINING THE HARM

We begin with constitutional approaches, then turn to Congress' intervention via the important 1982 amendments to the Voting Rights Act ("VRA"). The constitutional analysis starts with *Whitcomb v. Chavis,* 403 U.S. 124 (1971), and *White v. Regester,* 412 U.S. 755 (1973). Together *Whitcomb* and *Regester* are of great importance in defining the concept of minority vote dilution, which began to emerge in the 1970s after the VRA was enacted and the first generation litigation had begun to wind down. The cases are important not just for the content they give this concept under the Constitution, but as we will see in Chapter 7, they will also be central to the statutory definition of vote dilution once the Voting Rights Act is amended in 1982. Congress will draw directly on these decisions in amending the statute. Thus, it becomes crucial to determine the content and theory of the line the Court draws between *Whitcomb*, in which the Court rejects the claim of racial vote dilution, and the two contexts in *Regester*, in which the Court accepts this claim.

Whitcomb v. Chavis
403 U.S. 124 (1971).

■ MR. JUSTICE WHITE delivered the opinion of the Court with respect to the validity of the multi-member election district in Marion County, Indiana ... and announced the judgment of the Court....

I

Indiana has a bicameral general assembly consisting of a house of representatives of 100 members and a senate of 50 members. Eight of the 31 senatorial districts and 25 of the 39 house districts are multi-member districts, that is, districts that are represented by two or more legislators elected at large by the voters of the district. Under the statutes here challenged, Marion County is a multi-member district electing eight senators and 15 members of the house.

On January 9, 1969, six residents of Indiana, five of whom were residents of Marion County, filed a suit ... [alleging] that the two statutes invidiously diluted the force and effect of the vote of Negroes and poor persons living within certain Marion County census tracts constituting what was termed "the ghetto area." Residents of the area were alleged to have particular demographic characteristics rendering them cognizable as a minority interest group with distinctive interests in specific areas of the substantive law. With single-member districting, it was said, the ghetto area would elect three members of the house and one senator, whereas under the present districting voters in the area "have almost no political force or control over legislators because the effect of their vote is cancelled out by other contrary interest groups" in Marion County. The mechanism of political party organization and the influence of party chairmen in nominating candidates were additional factors alleged to frustrate the exercise of power by residents of the ghetto area....

The three-judge court ... first determined that a racial minority group inhabited an identifiable ghetto area in Indianapolis. That area, located in the northern half of Center Township and termed the "Center Township ghetto," ... contained a 1967 population of 97,000 nonwhites, over 99% of whom were Negro, and 35,000 whites. The court proceeded to compare [representative census tracts within the ghetto] ... with tract 211, a predominantly white, relatively wealthy suburban census tract in Washington Township contiguous to the northwest corner of the court's ghetto area and with tract 220, also in Washington Township, a contiguous tract inhabited by middle class Negroes. Strong differences were found in terms of housing conditions, income and educational levels, rates of unemployment, juvenile crime, and welfare assistance. The contrasting characteristics between the ... ghetto area and its inhabitants on the one hand and tracts 211 and 220 on the other indicated the ghetto's "compelling interests in such legislative areas as urban renewal and rehabilitation, health care, employment training and opportunities, welfare, and relief of the poor, law enforcement, quality of education, and anti-discrimination measures." These interests were in addition to those the ghetto shared with the rest of the county, such as metropolitan transportation, flood control, sewage disposal, and education.

The court then turned to evidence showing the residences of Marion County's representatives and senators in each of the five general assemblies elected during the period 1960 through 1968. Excluding tract 220, the middle class Negro district, Washington Township, the relatively wealthy suburban area in which tract 211 was located, with an average of 13.98% of Marion County's population, was the residence of 47.52% of its senators and 34.33% of its representatives. The court's Center Township ghetto area, with 17.8% of the population, had 4.75% of the senators and 5.97% of the representatives.... Also, tract 220 alone, the middle class Negro district, had only 0.66% of the county's population but had been the residence of more representatives than had the ghetto area. The ghetto area had been represented in the senate only once—in 1964 by one senator—and the house three times—with one representative in 1962 and 1964 and by two representatives in the 1968 general assembly. The court found the "Negro Center Township Ghetto population" to be sufficiently large to elect two representatives and one senator if the ghetto tracts "were specific single-member legislative districts" in Marion County....

The court's conclusions of law on the merits may be summarized as follows:

1. There exists within Marion County an identifiable racial element, "the Negro residents of the Center Township Ghetto," with special interests in various areas of substantive law, diverging significantly from interests of nonresidents of the ghetto.

2. The voting strength of this racial group has been minimized by Marion County's multi-member senate and house district because of the strong control exercised by political parties over the selection of candidates, the inability of the Negro voters to assure themselves the opportunity to vote for prospective legislators of their choice and the absence of any particular legislators who were accountable for their legislative record to Negro voters.

3. Party control of nominations, the inability of voters to know the candidate and the responsibility of legislators to their party and the county at large make it difficult for any legislator to diverge from the majority of his delegation and to be an effective representative of minority ghetto interests.

4. Although each legislator in Marion County is arguably responsible to all the voters, including those in the ghetto, "partial responsiveness of all legislators is [not] ... equal [to] total responsiveness and the informed concern of a few specific legislators."

5. The apportionment statutes of Indiana as they relate to Marion County operate to minimize and cancel out the voting strength of a minority racial group, namely Negroes residing in the Center Township ghetto, and to deprive them of the equal protection of the laws.

6. As a legislative district, Marion County is large as compared with the total number of legislators, it is not subdistricted to insure distribution of the legislators over the county and comprises a multi-member district for both the house and the senate....

9. ... [Plaintiff] Walker "probably has received less effective representation" than Marion County voters because "he votes for fewer legislators and, therefore, has fewer legislators to speak for him," and, since in theory voting power in multi-member districts does not vary inversely to the number of voters, Marion County voters had greater opportunity to cast tie-breaking or "critical" votes. But the court declined to hold that the latter ground had been proved, absent more evidence concerning Lake County....

III

... The question of the constitutional validity of multi-member districts has been pressed in this Court since the first of the modern reapportionment cases. These questions have focused not on population-based apportionment but on the quality of representation afforded by the multi-member district as compared with single-member districts. In *Lucas v. Colorado General Assembly*, 377 U.S. 713 (1964), decided with *Reynolds v. Sims*, we noted certain undesirable features of the multi-member district but expressly withheld any intimation "that apportionment schemes which provide for the at-large election of a number of legislators from a county, or any political subdivision, are constitutionally defective." Subsequently, when the validity of the multi-member district, as such, was squarely presented, we held that such a district is not per se illegal under the Equal Protection Clause. That voters in multi-member districts vote for and are represented by more legislators than voters in single-member districts has so far not demonstrated an invidious discrimination against the latter. But we have deemed the validity of multi-member district systems justiciable, recognizing also that they may be subject to challenge where the circumstances of a particular case may "operate to minimize or cancel out the voting strength of racial or political elements of the voting population." ... But we have insisted that the challenger carry the burden of proving that multi-member districts unconstitutionally operate to dilute or cancel the voting strength of racial or political elements. We have not yet sustained such an attack.

IV

Plaintiffs level two quite distinct challenges to the Marion County district. The first charge is that any multi-member district bestows on its voters several unconstitutional advantages over voters in single-member districts or smaller multi-member districts. The other allegation is that the Marion County district, on the record of this case, illegally minimizes and cancels out the voting power of a cognizable racial minority in Marion County....

... [O]ur prior cases have ... proceeded on the assumption that the dilution of voting power suffered by a voter who is placed in a district 10 times the population of another is cured by allocating 10 legislators to the larger district instead of the one assigned to the smaller district. Plaintiffs challenge this assumption at both the voter and legislator level. They demonstrate mathematically that in theory voting power does not vary inversely with the size of the district and that to increase legislative seats in proportion to increased population gives undue voting power to the voter in the multi-member district since he has more chances to determine election outcomes than does the voter in the single-member district. This consequence obtains wholly aside from the quality or effectiveness of representation later furnished by the successful candidates. The District Court did not quarrel with plaintiffs' mathematics, nor do we. But like the District Court we note that the position remains a theoretical one[23] and, as plaintiffs' witness conceded, knowingly avoids and does "not take into account any political or other factors which might affect the actual voting power of the residents, which might include party affiliation, race, previous voting characteristics or any other factors which go into the entire political voting situation." The real-life impact of multi-member districts on individ-

---

23. The mathematical backbone of this theory is as follows: In a population of n voters, where each voter has a choice between two alternatives (candidates), there are 2^n possible voting combinations. For example, with a population of three voters, A, B, and C, and two candidates, X and Y, there are eight combinations:

	A	B	C
#1.	X	X	X
#2.	X	X	Y
#3.	X	Y	X
#4.	X	Y	Y
#5.	Y	X	X
#6.	Y	X	Y
#7.	Y	Y	X
#8.	Y	Y	Y

The theory hypothesizes that the true test of voting power is the ability to cast a tie-breaking, or "critical" vote. In the population of three voters as shown above, any voter can cast a critical vote in four situations; in the other four situations, the vote is not critical since it cannot change the outcome of the election. For example, C can cast a tie-breaking vote only in situations 3, 4, 5, and 6. The number of combinations in which a voter can cast a tie-breaking vote is $2 \times (n-1)!/n-\frac{1}{2}! \times n-\frac{1}{2}!$, where n is the number of voters. Dividing this result (critical votes) by 2^n (possible combinations), one arrives at that fraction of possible combinations in which a voter can cast a critical vote. This is the theory's measure of voting power. In District K with three voters, the fraction is 4/8, or 50%. In District L with nine voters, the fraction is 140/512, or 28%. Conventional wisdom would give District K one representative and District L three. But under the theory, a voter in District L is not 1/3 as powerful as the voter in District K, but more than half as powerful. District L deserves only two representatives, and by giving it three the State causes voters therein to be overrepresented. For a fuller explanation of this theory, see Banzhaf,—*Do Multi–Member Electoral Districts They Violate the "One Man, One Vote" Principle*, 75 Yale L. J. 1309 (1966).

ual voting power has not been sufficiently demonstrated, at least on this record, to warrant departure from prior cases.

The District Court was more impressed with the other branch of the claim that multi-member districts inherently discriminate against other districts. This was the assertion that whatever the individual voting power of Marion County voters in choosing legislators may be, they nevertheless have more effective representation in the Indiana general assembly for two reasons. First, each voter is represented by more legislators and therefore, in theory at least, has more chances to influence critical legislative votes. Second, since multi-member delegations are elected at large and represent the voters of the entire district, they tend to vote as a bloc, which is tantamount to the district having one representative with several votes....

We are not ready, however, to agree that multi-member districts, wherever they exist, overrepresent their voters as compared with voters in single-member districts, even if the multi-member delegation tends to bloc voting. The theory that plural representation itself unduly enhances a district's power and the influence of its voters remains to be demonstrated in practice and in the day-to-day operation of the legislature. Neither the findings of the trial court nor the record before us sustains it, even where bloc voting is posited.

... That bloc voting tended to occur is sustained by the record, and defendants' own witness thought it was advantageous for Marion County's delegation to stick together.... [But] Marion County would have no less advantage, if advantage there is, if it elected from individual districts and the elected representatives demonstrated the same bloc-voting tendency, which may also develop among legislators representing single-member districts widely scattered throughout the State. Of course it is advantageous to start with more than one vote for a bill. But nothing before us shows or suggests that any legislative skirmish affecting the State of Indiana or Marion County in particular would have come out differently had Marion County been subdistricted and its delegation elected from single-member districts.

Rather than squarely finding unacceptable discrimination against outstate voters in favor of Marion County voters, the trial court struck down Marion County's multi-member district because it found the scheme worked invidiously against a specific segment of the county's voters as compared with others. The court identified an area of the city as a ghetto, found it predominantly inhabited by poor Negroes with distinctive substantive-law interests and thought this group unconstitutionally underrepresented because the proportion of legislators with residences in the ghetto elected from 1960 to 1968 was less than the ghetto's proportion of the population, less than the proportion of legislators elected from Washington Township, a less populous district, and less than the ghetto would likely have elected had the county consisted of single-member districts. We find major deficiencies in this approach.

First, it needs no emphasis here that the Civil War Amendments were designed to protect the civil rights of Negroes and that the courts have been vigilant in scrutinizing schemes allegedly conceived or operated as purposeful devices to further racial discrimination. There has been no hesitation in striking down those contrivances that can fairly be said to infringe on Fourteenth Amendment rights. But there is no suggestion here that Marion County's multi-member district, or similar districts throughout the State, were conceived or operated as purposeful devices to further racial or economic discrimination. As plaintiffs concede, "there was no basis for asserting that the legislative districts in Indiana were designed to dilute the vote of minorities."

Nor does the fact that the number of ghetto residents who were legislators was not in proportion to ghetto population satisfactorily prove invidious discrimination absent evidence and findings that ghetto residents had less opportunity than did other Marion County residents to participate in the political processes and to elect legislators of their choice. We have discovered nothing in the record or in the court's findings indicating that poor Negroes were not allowed to register or vote, to choose the political party they desired to support, to participate in its affairs or to be equally represented on those occasions when legislative candidates were chosen. Nor did the evidence purport to show or the court find that inhabitants of the ghetto were regularly excluded from the slates of both major parties, thus denying them the chance of occupying legislative seats. It appears reasonably clear that the Republican Party won four of the five elections from 1960 to 1968, that Center Township ghetto voted heavily Democratic and that ghetto votes were critical to Democratic Party success.... [I]t seems unlikely that the Democratic Party could afford to overlook the ghetto in slating its candidates.[30] Clearly, in 1964—the one election that the Democrats won—the party slated and elected one senator and one representative from Center Township ghetto.... Nor is there any indication that the party failed to slate candidates satisfactory to the ghetto in other years. Absent evidence or findings we are not sure, but it seems reasonable to infer that had the Democrats won all of the elections or even most of them, the ghetto would have had no justifiable complaints about representation. The fact is, however, that four of the five elections were won by Republicans, which was not the party of the ghetto and which would not always slate ghetto candidates—although in 1962 it nominated and elected one representative and in 1968 two representatives from that area. If this is the proper view of this case, the failure of the ghetto to have legislative seats in proportion to its population emerges more as a function of losing elections than of built-in bias against poor Negroes. The voting

30. ... For the 1960–1968 period which concerned the District Court, ... the Democratic Party slated one Negro representative in 1960; one in 1962; one senator and two representatives in 1964; three representatives in 1966; and one senator and two representatives in 1968. The Republican Party slated one Negro senator in 1960; two representatives in 1966; and three representatives in 1968....

power of ghetto residents may have been "cancelled out" as the District Court held, but this seems a mere euphemism for political defeat at the polls.

On the record before us plaintiffs' position comes to this: that although they have equal opportunity to participate in and influence the selection of candidates and legislators, and although the ghetto votes predominantly Democratic and that party slates candidates satisfactory to the ghetto, invidious discrimination nevertheless results when the ghetto, along with all other Democrats, suffers the disaster of losing too many elections. But typical American legislative elections are district-oriented, head-on races between candidates of two or more parties. As our system has it, one candidate wins, the others lose. Arguably the losing candidates' supporters are without representation since the men they voted for have been defeated; arguably they have been denied equal protection of the laws since they have no legislative voice of their own. This is true of both single-member and multi-member districts. But we have not yet deemed it a denial of equal protection to deny legislative seats to losing candidates, even in those so-called "safe" districts where the same party wins year after year.

Plainly, the District Court saw nothing unlawful about the impact of typical single-member district elections. The court's own plan created districts giving both Republicans and Democrats several predictably safe general assembly seats, with political, racial or economic minorities in those districts being "unrepresented" year after year. But similar consequences flowing from Marion County multi-member district elections were viewed differently. Conceding that all Marion County voters could fairly be said to be represented by the entire delegation, just as is each voter in a single-member district by the winning candidate, the District Court thought the ghetto voters' claim to the partial allegiance of eight senators and 15 representatives was not equivalent to the undivided allegiance of one senator and two representatives; nor was the ghetto voters' chance of influencing the election of an entire slate as significant as the guarantee of one ghetto senator and two ghetto representatives. As the trial court saw it, ghetto voters could not be adequately and equally represented unless some of Marion County's general assembly seats were reserved for ghetto residents serving the interests of the ghetto majority. But are poor Negroes of the ghetto any more underrepresented than poor ghetto whites who also voted Democratic and lost, or any more discriminated against than other interest groups or voters in Marion County with allegiance to the Democratic Party, or, conversely, any less represented than Republican areas or voters in years of Republican defeat? We think not. The mere fact that one interest group or another concerned with the outcome of Marion County elections has found itself outvoted and without legislative seats of its own provides no basis for invoking constitutional remedies where, as here, there is no indication that this segment of the population is being denied access to the political system....

V

The District Court's holding, although on the facts of this case limited to guaranteeing one racial group representation, is not easily contained. It is expressive of the more general proposition that any group with distinctive interests must be represented in legislative halls if it is numerous enough to command at least one seat and represents a majority living in an area sufficiently compact to constitute a single-member district. This approach would make it difficult to reject claims of Democrats, Republicans, or members of any political organization in Marion County who live in what would be safe districts in a single-member district system but who in one year or another, or year after year, are submerged in a one-sided multi-member district vote. There are also union oriented workers, the university community, religious or ethnic groups occupying identifiable areas of our heterogeneous cities and urban areas. Indeed, it would be difficult for a great many, if not most, multi-member districts to survive analysis under the District Court's view unless combined with some voting arrangement such as proportional representation or cumulative voting aimed at providing representation for minority parties or interests....

We are not insensitive to the objections long voiced to multi-member district plans.... Criticism is rooted in their winner-take-all aspects, their tendency to submerge minorities and to overrepresent the winning party as compared with the party's statewide electoral position, a general preference for legislatures reflecting community interests as closely as possible and disenchantment with political parties and elections as devices to settle policy differences between contending interests. The chance of winning or significantly influencing intraparty fights and issue-oriented elections has seemed to some inadequate protection to minorities, political, racial, or economic; rather, their voice, it is said, should also be heard in the legislative forum where public policy is finally fashioned. In our view, however, experience and insight have not yet demonstrated that multi-member districts are inherently invidious and violative of the Fourteenth Amendment.... [W]e are unprepared to hold that district-based elections decided by plurality vote are unconstitutional in either single-or multi-member districts simply because the supporters of losing candidates have no legislative seats assigned to them. As presently advised we hold that the District Court misconceived the Equal Protection Clause in applying it to invalidate the Marion County multi-member district....

■ Separate opinion of MR. JUSTICE HARLAN.

Earlier this Term I remarked on "the evident malaise among the members of the Court" with prior decisions in the field of voter qualifications and reapportionment.... Today's opinio[n] ... confirm[s] that diagnosis.

I

... [P]ast decisions have suggested that multi-member constituencies would be unconstitutional if they could be shown "under the circumstances of a particular case ... to minimize or cancel out the voting strength of racial or political elements of the voting population." *Fortson v. Dorsey*, 379 U.S. 433, 439 (1965); *Burns v. Richardson*, 384 U.S. 73, 88 (1966). Today the Court holds that a three-judge District Court, which struck down an apportionment scheme for just this reason, "misconceived the Equal Protection Clause."

Prior opinions stated that "once the class of voters is chosen and their qualifications specified, we see no constitutional way by which equality of voting power may be evaded." *Gray v. Sanders*, 372 U.S. 368, 381 (1963); *Hadley v. Junior College District*, 397 U.S. 50, 59 (1970). Today the Court sustains a provision that gives opponents of school bond issues half again the voting power of proponents. *Gordon v. Lance* [403 U.S. 1 (1971)].

II

The Court justifies the wondrous results in these cases by relying on different combinations of factors.... *Gordon v. Lance* relies heavily on the "federal analogy" and the prevalence of similar anti-majoritarian elements in the constitutions of the several States.

To my mind the relevance of such considerations as the foregoing is undeniable and their cumulative effect is unanswerable. I can only marvel, therefore, that they were dismissed, singly and in combination, in a line of cases which began with *Gray v. Sanders*, 372 U.S. 368 (1963)....

That line of cases can best be understood, I think, as reflections of deep personal commitments by some members of the Court to the principles of pure majoritarian democracy.... If this philosophy of majoritarianism had been given its head, it would have led to different results in each of the cases decided today, for it is in the very nature of the principle that it regards majority rule as an imperative of social organization, not subject to compromise in furtherance of merely political ends. It is a philosophy which ignores or overcomes the fact that the scheme of the Constitution is one not of majoritarian democracy, but of federal republics, with equality of representation a value subordinate to many others, as both the body of the Constitution and the Fourteenth Amendment itself show on their face.

III

If majoritarianism is to be rejected as a rule of decision, as the Court implicitly rejects it today, then an alternative principle must be supplied if this earlier line of cases just referred to is still to be regarded as good law. The reapportionment opinions of this Court provide little help. They speak in conclusory terms of "debasement" or "dilution" of the "voting power" or "representation" of citizens without explanation of what these concepts are....

An interesting illustration of the light which a not implausible definition of "voting power" can shed on reapportionment doctrine is provided by the theoretical model created by Professor Banzhaf, to which the Court refers.² This model uses as a measure of voting power the probability that a given voter will cast a tie-breaking ballot in an election. Two further assumptions are made: first, that the voting habits of all members of the electorate are alike; and second, that each voter is equally likely to vote for either candidate before him. On these assumptions, and taking the voting population in Marion County as roughly 300,000, it can be shown that the probability of an individual voter's casting a decisive vote in a given election is approximately .00146. This provides a standard to which "voting power" of residents in other districts may be compared.

However, Professor Banzhaf's model also reveals that minor variations in assumptions can lead to major variations in results. For instance, if the temper of the electorate changes by one-half of one percent,³ each individual's voting power is reduced by a factor of approximately 1,000,000. Or if a few of the 300,000 voters are committed—say 15,000 to candidate A and 10,000 to candidate B—the probability of any individual's casting a tie-breaking vote is reduced by a factor on the rough order of 120,000,000,000,000,000,000. Obviously in comparison with the astronomical differences in voting power which can result from such minor variations in political characteristics, the effects of the 12% and 28% population variations considered in *Abate v. Mundt* and in this case are de minimis, and even the extreme deviations from the norm presented in *Baker v. Carr*, 369 U.S. 186 (1962), and *Avery v. Midland County*, 390 U.S. 474 (1968), pale into insignificance.⁵

It is not surprising therefore that the Court in this case declines to embrace the measure of voting power suggested by Professor Banzhaf. But it neither suggests an alternative nor considers the consequences of its inability to measure what it purports to be equalizing. Instead it becomes enmeshed in the haze of slogans and numerology which for 10 years has obscured its vision in this field....

This case is nothing short of a complete vindication of Mr. Justice Frankfurter's warning nine years ago "of the mathematical quagmire

2. The Court, though stating that it does "not quarrel with plaintiffs' mathematics," nevertheless implies that it may be ignored because "the position remains a theoretical one ... and does 'not take into account any political or other factors which might affect the actual voting power of the residents, which might include party affiliation, race, previous voting characteristics or any other factors which go into the entire political voting situation.'" Precisely the same criticism applies, with even greater force, to the "one man, one vote" opinions of this Court. The only relevant difference between the elementary arithmetic on which the Court relies and the elementary probability theory on which Professor Banzhaf relies is that calculations in the latter field cannot be done on one's fingers.

3. More precisely, the result follows if the second of Professor Banzhaf's assumptions is altered so that the probability of each voter's selecting candidate A over candidate B is 50.5% rather than 50%.

5. "There is something fascinating about science. One gets such wholesale returns of conjecture out of such a trifling investment of fact." Mark Twain, Life on the Mississippi 109 (Harper & Row, 1965).

(apart from divers judicially inappropriate and elusive determinants) into which this Court today catapults the lower courts of the country." *Baker v. Carr*, 369 U.S. 186, 268 (1962) (dissenting opinion).... I would reverse the judgment below and remand the case to the District Court with directions to dismiss the complaint.

■ MR. JUSTICE DOUGLAS, with whom MR. JUSTICE BRENNAN and MR. JUSTICE MARSHALL concur, dissenting in part and concurring in the result in part....

The merits of the case go to the question ... whether a gerrymander can be "constitutionally impermissible." The question of the gerrymander is the other half of *Reynolds v. Sims*, 377 U.S. 533. Fair representation of voters in a legislative assembly—one man, one vote—would seem to require (1) substantial equality of population within each district and (2) the avoidance of district lines that weigh the power of one race more heavily than another. The latter can be done—and is done—by astute drawing of district lines that makes the district either heavily Democratic or heavily Republican as the case may be. Lines may be drawn so as to make the voice of one racial group weak or strong, as the case may be.

The problem of the gerrymander is how to defeat or circumvent the sentiments of the community. The problem of the law is how to prevent it. As MR. JUSTICE HARLAN once said "A computer may grind out district lines which can totally frustrate the popular will on an overwhelming number of critical issues." The easy device is the gerrymander. The District Court found that it operated in this case to dilute the vote of the blacks ...

In *Gomillion v. Lightfoot*, 364 U.S. 339, we dealt with the problem of a State intentionally making a district smaller to exclude black voters. Here we have almost the converse problem. The State's districts surround the black voting area with white voters.

Gomillion, involving the turning of the city of Tuskegee from a geographical square "to an uncouth twenty-eight-sided figure," was only one of our cases which dealt with elevating the political interests of one identifiable group over those of another. Georgia's county unit system was similar, although race was not a factor. Under the Georgia system a farmer in a rural county could have up to 99 times the voting power of his urban-dwelling brother. See *Gray v. Sanders*, 372 U.S. 368. Here the districting plan operates to favor "upper-middle class and wealthy" suburbanites.

A showing of racial motivation is not necessary when dealing with multi-member districts.... In *Burns v. Richardson*, we ... stated that assuming the requirements of *Reynolds v. Sims*, 377 U.S. 533, were satisfied, multi-member districts are unconstitutional "only if it can be shown that 'designedly or otherwise' ... [such a district would operate] to minimize or cancel out the voting strength of racial or political elements of the voting population." 384 U.S., at 88.... [W]e demanded that the invidious effects of multi-member districts appear from evidence in the record. Here that demand is satisfied by (1) the showing of an identifiable voting group living in Center Township, (2) the severe discrepancies of residency of elected members of the general assembly between Center and Washington Townships, ... (3) the finding of pervasive influence of the county organizations of the political parties, and (4) the finding that legislators from the county maintain "common, undifferentiated" positions on political issues....

It is said that if we prevent racial gerrymandering today, we must prevent gerrymandering of any special interest group tomorrow, whether it be social, economic, or ideological. I do not agree. Our Constitution has a special thrust when it comes to voting; the Fifteenth Amendment says the right of citizens to vote shall not be "abridged" on account of "race, color, or previous condition of servitude."

Our cases since *Baker v. Carr* have never intimated that "one man, one vote" meant "one white man, one vote." Since "race" may not be gerrymandered, I think the Court emphasizes the irrelevant when it says that the effect on "the actual voting power" of the blacks should first be known. They may be all Democratic or all Republican; but once their identity is purposely washed out of the system, the system, as I see it, has a constitutional defect. It is asking the impossible for us to demand that the blacks first show that the effect of the scheme was to discourage or prevent poor blacks from voting or joining such party as they chose. On this record, the voting rights of the blacks have been "abridged," as I read the Constitution.

The District Court has done an outstanding job, bringing insight to the problems. One can always fault a lower court by stating theoretical aspects of apportionment plans that may not have been considered. This District Court acted earnestly and boldly to correct a festering electoral system. I would not even vacate and remand ... I would affirm the judgment.

White v. Regester
412 U.S. 755 (1973).

■ Mr. Justice White delivered the opinion of the Court.

This case [concerns] the validity of the reapportionment plan for the Texas House of Representatives adopted in 1970 by the State Legislative Redistricting Board: ... [we must decide] whether the multimember districts provided for Bexar and Dallas Counties were properly found to have been invidiously discriminatory against cognizable racial or ethnic groups in those counties....

III

We affirm the District Court's judgment ... insofar as it invalidated the multimember districts in Dallas and Bexar Counties and ordered those districts to be redrawn into single-member districts. Plainly, under our cases, multimember districts are not per se unconstitutional, nor are they necessarily unconstitutional when used in combination with single-member districts in other parts of the State. But we have entertained claims that multimember districts are being used invidiously to cancel out or minimize the voting strength of racial groups. To sustain such claims, it is not enough that the racial group allegedly discriminated against has not had legislative seats in proportion to its voting potential. The plaintiffs' burden is to produce evidence to support findings that the political processes leading to nomination and election were not equally open to participation by the group in question—that its members had less opportunity than did other residents in the district to participate in the political processes and to elect legislators of their choice.

With due regard for these standards, the District Court first referred to the history of official racial discrimination in Texas, which at times touched the right of Negroes to register and vote and to participate in the democratic processes. It referred also to the Texas rule requiring a majority vote as a prerequisite to nomination in a primary election and to the so-called "place" rule limiting candidacy for legislative office from a multimember district to a specified "place" on the ticket, with the result being the election of representatives from the Dallas multimember district reduced to a head-to-head contest for each position. These characteristics of the Texas electoral system, neither in themselves improper nor invidious, enhanced the opportunity for racial discrimination, the District Court thought. More fundamentally, it found that since Reconstruction days, there have been only two Negroes in the Dallas County delegation to the Texas House of Representatives and that these two were the only two Negroes ever slated by the Dallas Committee for Responsible Government (DCRG), a white-dominated organization that is in effective control of Democratic Party candidate slating in Dallas County. That organization, the District Court found, did not need the support of the Negro community to win elections in the county, and it did not therefore exhibit good-faith concern for the political and other needs and aspirations of the Negro community. The court found that as recently as 1970 the DCRG was relying upon "racial campaign tactics in white precincts to defeat candidates who had the overwhelming support of the black community." Based on the evidence before it, the District Court concluded that "the black community has been effectively excluded from participation in the Democratic primary selection process," and was therefore generally not permitted to enter into the political process in a reliable and meaningful manner. These findings and conclusions are sufficient to sustain the District Court's judgment with respect to the Dallas multimember district and, on this record, we have no reason to disturb them.

IV

The same is true of the order requiring disestablishment of the multimember district in Bexar County. Consistently with *Hernandez v.*

Texas, 347 U.S. 475 (1954), the District Court considered the Mexican–Americans in Bexar County to be an identifiable class for Fourteenth Amendment purposes and proceeded to inquire whether the impact of the multimember district on this group constituted invidious discrimination. Surveying the historic and present condition of the Bexar County Mexican–American community, which is concentrated for the most part on the west side of the city of San Antonio, the court observed, based upon prior cases and the record before it, that the Bexar community, along with other Mexican–Americans in Texas, had long "suffered from, and continues to suffer from, the results and effects of invidious discrimination and treatment in the fields of education, employment, economics, health, politics and others." The bulk of the Mexican–American community in Bexar County occupied the Barrio, an area consisting of about 28 contiguous census tracts in the city of San Antonio. Over 78% of Barrio residents were Mexican–Americans, making up 29% of the county's total population. The Barrio is an area of poor housing; its residents have low income and a high rate of unemployment. The typical Mexican–American suffers a cultural and language barrier that makes his participation in community processes extremely difficult, particularly, the court thought, with respect to the political life of Bexar County. "[A] cultural incompatability ... conjoined with the poll tax and the most restrictive voter registration procedures in the nation have operated to effectively deny Mexican–Americans access to the political processes in Texas even longer than the Blacks were formally denied access by the white primary." The residual impact of this history reflected itself in the fact that Mexican–American voting registration remained very poor in the county and that only five Mexican–Americans since 1880 have served in the Texas Legislature from Bexar County. Of these, only two were from the Barrio area. The District Court also concluded from the evidence that the Bexar County legislative delegation in the House was insufficiently responsive to Mexican–American interests.

Based on the totality of the circumstances, the District Court evolved its ultimate assessment of the multi-member district, overlaid, as it was, on the cultural and economic realities of the Mexican–American community in Bexar County and its relationship with the rest of the county. Its judgment was that Bexar County Mexican–Americans "are effectively removed from the political processes of Bexar [County] in violation of all the *Whitcomb* standards, whatever their absolute numbers may total in that County." Single-member districts were thought required to remedy "the effects of past and present discrimination against Mexican–Americans," and to bring the community into the full stream of political life of the county and State by encouraging their further registration, voting, and other political activities.

The District Court apparently paid due heed to *Whitcomb v. Chavis*, did not hold that every racial or political group has a constitutional right to be represented in the state legislature, but did, from its own special vantage point, conclude that the multimember district, as designed and operated in Bexar County, invidiously excluded Mexican–Americans from effective participation in political life, specifically in the election of representatives to the Texas House of Representatives. On the record before us, we are not inclined to overturn these findings, representing as they do a blend of history and an intensely local appraisal of the design and impact of the Bexar County multimember district in the light of past and present reality, political and otherwise.

V

Affirmed in part, reversed in part, and remanded. MR. JUSTICE BRENNAN, with whom MR. JUSTICE DOUGLAS and MR. JUSTICE MARSHALL join, concurred in this part of the opinion and dissented on other grounds not relevant here.

NOTES AND QUESTIONS

1. The first equal protection challenge to multi-member election districts was brought to the Court in the immediate aftermath of *Reynolds v. Sims*. In *Fortson v. Dorsey*, 379 U.S. 433 (1965), plaintiffs challenged Georgia's system for electing its 54 state senators, which was based on existing counties (compare Georgia's county-unit system struck down in *Gray v. Sanders*, 372 U.S. 368 (1963)). Smaller counties were banded together into one election district and elected one senator. The larger counties, however, used multi-member elections in which they elected more than one senator, up to seven in the largest county. The Court held that equal protection was not violated by this hybrid system in which some counties used multi-member elections and others elected only one senator; at the time, the Court was focused primarily on the one-vote, one-person principle and found no violation of it because approximately equal numbers of voters elected each senator throughout the State. The plaintiffs had also alleged that the multi-member elections had been devised to dilute the political strength of racial and political minorities in the populous urban counties. The Court left that question open for further litigation, suggesting that there might be a constitutional basis for challenging electoral structures that diluted the voting power of certain groups: "It might well be that, designedly or otherwise, a multi-member constituency apportionment scheme, under the circumstances of a particular case, would operate to minimize or cancel out the voting strength of racial or political elements of the voting population." *Id.* at 439.

2. In *Whitcomb*, the Court appears concerned with drawing the line between ordinary interest-group struggles in democratic politics, in which some groups will inevitably lose, and the improper dilution of the voting power of racial or political minorities. Vote dilution under the Constitution cannot become "a mere euphemism for political defeat at the polls."

How is the line between losing fairly versus unconstitutionally to be understood conceptually? Does *Whitcomb* hold that as long as blacks and other ethnic or political minorities are fully able to register and cast a vote, and to participate in politics, then they cannot claim their voting power has been impermissibly diluted when they are unable to elect the candidates they prefer? If so, does the concept of vote dilution have much power or meaning?

The Court holds that black voters in Marion County are losing because they are Democrats, not because they are black. Does that mean that the Court refuses to recognize a concept of partisan vote dilution—that is, a claim that one party has cleverly designed the electoral system to diminish the power of the other party? If the Court is implying such a view, is that view correct, or should the Constitution protect against partisan vote dilution as well as racial vote dilution? And if the Court is drawing a distinction between partisan and racial motivations and effects, how coherent would this line be if black voters were also overwhelmingly Democratic voters—as they likely were in 1971 in Indiana and as they largely are today.

Justice Harlan argues that *Whitcomb* implicitly rejects a philosophy of pure majoritarian democracy, but that the Court's earlier decisions, such as *Reynolds v. Sims*, 377 U.S. 533 (1964), embrace just that philosophy. Is Justice Harlan right to see a fundamental tension between the one-vote, one-person cases and constitutional protections against minority vote dilution?

The three dissenters would have found impermissible vote dilution in *Whitcomb*. Consider whether the four factors they point to as justifying this conclusion ought to be sufficient to find a constitutional violation. The majority asserts that to find vote dilution here would be to endorse the "general proposition that any group with distinctive interests must be represented in legislative halls if it is numerous enough to command at least one seat and represents a majority living in an area sufficiently compact to constitute a single-member district." Is that exactly the proposition underlying the dissent? Why is that general proposition troubling, if indeed it is?

3. In *White*, the Court upholds the vote dilution challenge with respect to two Texas counties. Two comparisons are the most important in coming to terms with the decision: (a) with respect to these two counties, does the Court rely on the same or different theories of vote dilution to strike down the districts in each? (b) given the invalidity of districting in these two counties, what separates the case from *Whitcomb*?

a. With respect to black voters in Dallas County, the Court referred to several specific electoral features internal to the electoral structure. Thus, the Court paid heed to majority-vote requirements, "place" rules, and the powerful slating role of a white-dominated political organization, the Dallas Committee for Responsible Government (recall the *White Pri-*

mary Cases from Texas). The Court also noted racial appeals in recent political campaigns, along with Texas' past history of racial discrimination in voting. With respect to Mexican–American voters in Bexar County, does the Court instead seem focused on factors external to the practice of voting itself—such as the "cultural and economic realities" of this community within Bexar County?

The Court refers to the vote dilution inquiry as one that focuses on "the totality of the circumstances." Does it consider the same *kind* of circumstances relevant to the decisions in Dallas and Bexar counties? More generally, do the Court's two decisions within *White* provide a consistent and coherent approach to identifying unconstitutional vote dilution?

In another case, Justice Stevens argued that a "constitutional standard that gave special protection to political groups identified by racial characteristics would be inconsistent with the basic tenet of the Equal Protection clause." *Rogers v. Lodge*, 458 U.S. 613, 651 (1982) (Stevens, J., dissenting). Is that what the Court has done in *White*?

b. How does *White* square with *Whitcomb*, decided two years earlier? Does *White* persuasively establish that vote dilution in the Texas counties was not "a mere euphemism for defeat at the polls?" Are you persuaded that there are significant differences of constitutional principle between *Whitcomb* and *White*? Do the differences have to do with one case arising from Indiana, which did not have the same history of formal disenfranchisement (and was not a covered jurisdiction under Section 5 of the 1965 VRA) as did Texas? Are the courts, at least in the immediate aftermath of the VRA, simply going to examine electoral structures in the South with more skepticism? Or are there important factual differences that reflect a clear understanding of when vote dilution occurs?

4. In the lower court effort to apply the *Whitcomb/White* principles, the most important touchstone became the en banc Fifth Circuit decision in *Zimmer v. McKeithen*, 485 F.2d 1297 (5th Cir.1973), *aff'd sub nom. East Carroll Parish School Board v. Marshall*, 424 U.S. 636 (1976) (per curiam). *Zimmer* provided more analytical content to the vote dilution inquiry by offering a catalogue of factors that would be deemed relevant. These "*Zimmer* factors" were invoked by many lower courts and by Congress when it amended the VRA in 1982.

In *Zimmer*, black plaintiffs challenged the use of at-large elections for the school board and police jury (the county legislature) in East Carroll Parish, Louisiana. While the black population was nearly 60 percent, blacks were 46 percent of registered voters as of 1971. Plaintiffs argued that the at-large election scheme, which had been adopted in 1968 by federal court order, had the effect of diluting black voting power compared to a district or ward-based system. In upholding this challenge, the Fifth Circuit identified a "panoply of factors" that aided the dilution inquiry:

> [W]here a minority can demonstrate a lack of access to the process of slating candidates, the unresponsiveness of legislators to their particularized interests, a tenuous state policy underlying the preference for multi-member or at-large districting, or that the existence of past discrimination in general precludes the effective participation in the election system, a strong case is made. Such proof is enhanced by a showing of the existence of large districts, majority vote requirements, anti-single shot voting provisions and the lack of provision for at-large candidates from running from particular geographical subdistricts.... [A]ll these factors need not be proved to obtain relief. *Id.* at 1305.

Applying these factors to strike down the at-large scheme, the Fifth Circuit emphasized that from 1922 to 1962, no black had been permitted to register to vote in the Parish, that the State had a general policy against the use of at-large elections from these political bodies up until 1967, and that the Parish employed a majority-vote requirement, as Texas had in *White*.

Consider the different *Zimmer* factors. What might make each of them relevant to a vote dilution inquiry? Are courts likely to have the capacity to decide whether each factor, taken in isolation, is politically significant in particular cases? If they can, are courts likely to be able to apply these factors, taken in combination, in a consistent and principled manner from case to case? If not, is there some alternative way to frame the constitutional inquiry into vote dilution? Should the Court simply read the Constitution to create a bright-line rule against the use of multi-member districts? While rejecting this view as a constitutional matter, Justice Stevens suggested in a 1982 opinion that "[i]t might indeed be wise policy to accelerate the transition of minority groups to a position of political power commensurate with their voting strength by amending the [VRA] to prohibit the use of multimember districts in all covered jurisdictions." *Rogers v. Lodge*, 458 U.S. 613, 632 (1982) (Stevens, J., dissenting).

5. Notice that neither *White* nor *Zimmer* discuss the role of polarized voting. Instead, they address the context under which minority vote dilution most likely occurs (for example, against a backdrop of historic discrimination and in the presence of significant socioeconomic disparities) and the likely outcome of minority underrepresentation (specifically, nonresponsiveness of governmental actors). But neither decision explains *how* an electoral system undervalues minority voting rights. In the absence of a clear operational definition of how dilution worked, *White/Zimmer* invited a free flowing inquiry into the totality of a political jurisdiction's practices. If minority plaintiffs were to claim non-responsiveness in the provision of sanitation services to the black part of town, for example, should not the municipal defendant have been heard to show that fire services were indeed comparable across the entire town? On the other hand, perhaps *White/Zimmer* were sufficient to resolve the cases before the courts in early voting rights challenges in deeply segregated cities such as Selma, Alabama and Jackson, Mississippi:

> We may speculate that, as an evolutionary matter, no great doctrinal clarity emerged from the early case law challenging Deep South, at-large elections because none was needed. Even the crude methodology of *White/Zimmer* sufficiently illustrated that something was wrong when, more than a century after the adoption of the Fifteenth Amendment, blacks were still clustered in great numbers in poverty-stricken neighborhoods, unable to secure any meaningful representation on the councils of state.

Samuel Issacharoff, *Supreme Court Destabilization of Single–Member Districts*, 1995 U. Chi. L. Forum 205, 219. Does this hypothesis explain the different outcomes in *White* and *Whitcomb*?

NOTE ON PURPOSE VERSUS EFFECTS

In all areas of civil-rights law and policy, a central question is whether actions should be considered discriminatory only if they stem from an invidious purpose, or whether discrimination should be considered to be present when actions have sufficiently disadvantageous effects along racial lines. As in other arenas, when it comes to defining the right to vote, this question will occupy a central role. What light do the Court's initial efforts shed on the question of the appropriate legal standard for defining vote dilution?

In *Whitcomb* the Court takes note that the plaintiffs did *not* allege that the multi-member election districts had been designed for the purpose of diluting minority voting power. Does that suggest that plaintiffs must be able to prove an invidious purpose in order to prevail on a constitutional vote-dilution claim? On the other hand, the Court does not stop with this observation, but goes on to analyze the challenge at length before rejecting it. Does that suggest that the Constitution does permit vote dilution claims to be brought merely by proving discriminatory effects, as long as the evidence of such effects is more compelling than that in *Whitcomb*? Note that the dissent wavers on this question too: initially, Justice Douglas strongly states that impermissible motivation is not required to prove vote dilution, but he concludes that the Indiana system is unconstitutional because it has "purposely washed out of the system" the voting power of Marion County's black voters.

When we turn to *White v. Regester*, some language suggests the Court is striking down the districts for reasons of discriminatory purpose, while other language might suggest that discriminatory effects alone are sufficient. Read the opinion carefully and ask whether the Court finds the districts to have been designed out of discriminatory purposes. Or does the Court conclude that the districts are invalid because of their racial effects, without regard to issues of purpose? Another way to put the question is whether the distinction between *Whitcomb* and *White* is that, in the latter, the Court found discriminatory purposes to be present? When *Whitcomb* and *White* are combined, what do we learn about the concept of vote dilution—and about whether discriminatory purposes or effects or both are necessary or sufficient to prove vote dilution?[a]

If you conclude that the decisions are ambiguous on these central questions, what might account for that ambiguity? Lack of analytical clarity or something else? Is intentional ambiguity in Supreme Court opinions ever justifiable? What are the potential costs of such ambiguity in the area of race and politics?

B. THE RISE OF THE INTENT REQUIREMENT

After *Whitcomb* and *Regester*, the next major confrontation in the Supreme Court over the constitutional concept of vote dilution was in a case challenging at-large city council elections in Mobile, Alabama. The divided Court's approach to the question spawned considerable political controversy, leading eventually to major congressional amendments to the VRA. Consider both the substantive issue of how majority rule and minority interests can be accommodated in democratic institutions, as well as the institutional processes by which these questions are decided, as we turn to that dramatic sequence of judicial and congressional interactions.

City of Mobile v. Bolden
446 U.S. 55 (1980).

■ MR. JUSTICE STEWART announced the judgment of the Court and delivered an opinion, in which THE CHIEF JUSTICE, MR. JUSTICE POWELL, and MR. JUSTICE REHNQUIST joined.

The city of Mobile, Ala., has since 1911 been governed by a City Commission consisting of three members elected by the voters of the city at large. The question in this case is whether this at-large system of municipal elections violates the rights of Mobile's Negro voters in contravention of federal statutory or constitutional law. . . .

I

. . . The three Commissioners jointly exercise all legislative, executive, and administrative power in the municipality. They are required after

---

[a] *Zimmer* had held that plaintiffs could win a vote dilution claim under the Constitution by proving either discriminatory purpose or that the electoral scheme "would operate to minimize or cancel out the voting strength of racial or political elements of the voting population." 485 F.2d at 1304.

election to designate one of their number as Mayor, a largely ceremonial office, but no formal provision is made for allocating specific executive or administrative duties among the three. As required by the state law enacted in 1911, each candidate for the Mobile City Commission runs for election in the city at large for a term of four years in one of three numbered posts, and may be elected only by a majority of the total vote. This is the same basic electoral system that is followed by literally thousands of municipalities and other local governmental units throughout the Nation.[7]

II

Although required by general principles of judicial administration to do so, neither the District Court nor the Court of Appeals addressed the complaint's statutory claim—that the Mobile electoral system violates § 2 of the Voting Rights Act of 1965. Even a cursory examination of that claim, however, clearly discloses that it adds nothing to the appellees' complaint.

Section 2 of the Voting Rights Act provides:

"No voting qualification or prerequisite to voting, or standard, practice, or procedure shall be imposed or applied by any State or political subdivision to deny or abridge the right of any citizen of the United States to vote on account of race or color."

Assuming, for present purposes, that there exists a private right of action to enforce this statutory provision, it is apparent that the language of § 2 no more than elaborates upon that of the Fifteenth Amendment, and the sparse legislative history of § 2 makes clear that it was intended to have an effect no different from that of the Fifteenth Amendment itself....

III

... Our decisions ... have made clear that action by a State that is racially neutral on its face violates the Fifteenth Amendment only if motivated by a discriminatory purpose.... In *Gomillion v. Lightfoot*, ... [t]he constitutional infirmity of the state law ... was that in drawing the municipal boundaries the legislature was "solely concerned with segregating white and colored voters by fencing Negro citizens out of town so as to deprive them of their pre-existing municipal vote." The Court made clear that in the absence of such an invidious purpose, a State is constitutionally free to redraw political boundaries in any manner it chooses.

In *Wright v. Rockefeller*, the Court upheld by like reasoning a state congressional reapportionment statute against claims that district lines had been racially gerrymandered, because the plaintiffs failed to prove that the legislature "was either motivated by racial considerations or in fact drew

---

7. According to the 1979 Municipal Year Book, most municipalities of over 25,000 people conducted at-large elections of their city commissioners or council members as of 1977. It is reasonable to suppose that an even larger majority of other municipalities did so.

the districts on racial lines"; or that the statute "was the product of a state contrivance to segregate on the basis of race or place of origin."

... The appellees have argued in this Court that *Smith v. Allwright* and *Terry v. Adams* support the conclusion that the at-large system of elections in Mobile is unconstitutional, reasoning that the effect of racially polarized voting in Mobile is the same as that of a racially exclusionary primary. The only characteristic, however, of the exclusionary primaries that offended the Fifteenth Amendment was that Negroes were not permitted to vote in them. The difficult question was whether the "State [had] had a hand in" the patent discrimination practiced by a nominally private organization.

... [Appellees'] freedom to vote has not been denied or abridged by anyone. The Fifteenth Amendment does not entail the right to have Negro candidates elected, and neither *Smith v. Allwright* nor *Terry v. Adams* contains any implication to the contrary. That Amendment prohibits only purposefully discriminatory denial or abridgment by government of the freedom to vote "on account of race, color, or previous condition of servitude." Having found that Negroes in Mobile "register and vote without hindrance," the District Court and Court of Appeals were in error in believing that the appellants invaded the protection of that Amendment in the present case.

IV

The Court of Appeals also agreed with the District Court that Mobile's at-large electoral system violates the Equal Protection Clause of the Fourteenth Amendment. There remains for consideration, therefore, the validity of its judgment on that score.

A

The claim that at-large electoral schemes unconstitutionally deny to some persons the equal protection of the laws has been advanced in numerous cases before this Court. That contention has been raised most often with regard to multimember constituencies within a state legislative apportionment system. The constitutional objection to multimember districts is not and cannot be that, as such, they depart from apportionment on a population basis in violation of *Reynolds v. Sims* and its progeny. Rather the focus in such cases has been on the lack of representation multimember districts afford various elements of the voting population in a system of representative legislative democracy....

Despite repeated constitutional attacks upon multimember legislative districts, the Court has consistently held that they are not unconstitutional per se. We have recognized, however, that such legislative apportionments could violate the Fourteenth Amendment if their purpose were invidiously to minimize or cancel out the voting potential of racial or ethnic minorities....

This burden of proof is simply one aspect of the basic principle that only if there is purposeful discrimination can there be a violation of the Equal Protection Clause of the Fourteenth Amendment. *See Washington v. Davis; Arlington Heights v. Metropolitan Housing Dev. Corp.; Personnel Administrator of Mass. v. Feeney*....

In only one case has the Court sustained a claim that multimember legislative districts unconstitutionally diluted the voting strength of a discrete group. That case was *White v. Regester*. There the Court upheld a constitutional challenge by Negroes and Mexican–Americans to parts of a legislative reapportionment plan adopted by the State of Texas. The plaintiffs alleged that the multimember districts for the two counties in which they resided minimized the effect of their votes in violation of the Fourteenth Amendment, and the Court held that the plaintiffs had been able to "produce evidence to support findings that the political processes leading to nomination and election were not equally open to participation by the [groups] in question." In so holding, the Court relied upon evidence in the record that included a long history of official discrimination against minorities as well as indifference to their needs and interests on the part of white elected officials. The Court also found in each county additional factors that restricted the access of minority groups to the political process. In one county, Negroes effectively were excluded from the process of slating candidates for the Democratic Party, while the plaintiffs in the other county were Mexican–Americans who "[suffered] a cultural and language barrier" that made "participation in community processes extremely difficult, particularly ... with respect to the political life" of the county.

White v. Regester is thus consistent with "the basic equal protection principle that the invidious quality of a law claimed to be racially discriminatory must ultimately be traced to a racially discriminatory purpose." The Court stated the constitutional question in *White* to be whether the "multimember districts [were] being used invidiously to cancel out or minimize the voting strength of racial groups," strongly indicating that only a purposeful dilution of the plaintiffs' vote would offend the Equal Protection Clause....

We may assume, for present purposes, that an at-large election of city officials with all the legislative, executive, and administrative power of the municipal government is constitutionally indistinguishable from the election of a few members of a state legislative body in multimember districts—although this may be a rash assumption.[15] But even making this assumption, it is clear that the evidence in the present case fell far short of

15. [...] It is noteworthy that a system of at-large city elections in place of elections of city officials by the voters of small geographic wards was universally heralded not many years ago as a praiseworthy and progressive reform of corrupt municipal government....

showing that the appellants "conceived or operated [a] purposeful [device] to further racial ... discrimination."

* * *

[T]he District Court based its conclusion of unconstitutionality primarily on the fact that no Negro had ever been elected to the City Commission, apparently because of the pervasiveness of racially polarized voting in Mobile. The trial court also found that city officials had not been as responsive to the interests of Negroes as to those of white persons. On the basis of these findings, the court concluded that the political processes in Mobile were not equally open to Negroes, despite its seemingly inconsistent findings that there were no inhibitions against Negroes becoming candidates, and that in fact Negroes had registered and voted without hindrance. Finally, with little additional discussion, the District Court held that Mobile's at-large electoral system was invidiously discriminating against Negroes in violation of the Equal Protection Clause.[17]

In affirming the District Court, the Court of Appeals acknowledged that the Equal Protection Clause of the Fourteenth Amendment reaches only purposeful discrimination, but held that one way a plaintiff may establish this illicit purpose is by adducing evidence that satisfies the [*White/Zimmer* criteria.] Thus, because the appellees had proved an "aggregate" of the *Zimmer* factors, the Court of Appeals concluded that a discriminatory purpose had been proved. That approach, however, is inconsistent with our decisions in *Washington v. Davis* and *Arlington Heights*. Although the presence of the indicia relied on in *Zimmer* may afford some evidence of a discriminatory purpose, satisfaction of those criteria is not of itself sufficient proof of such a purpose. The so-called *Zimmer* criteria upon

---

17. The only indication given by the District Court of an inference that there existed an invidious purpose was the following statement: "It is not a long step from the systematic exclusion of blacks from juries ... to [the] present purpose to dilute the black vote as evidenced in this case. There is a 'current' condition of dilution of the black vote resulting from intentional state legislative inaction...."

What the District Court may have meant by this statement is uncertain. In any event the analogy to the racially exclusionary jury cases appears mistaken. Those cases typically have involved a consistent pattern of discrete official actions that demonstrated almost to a mathematical certainty that Negroes were being excluded from juries because of their race.

If the District Court meant by its statement that the existence of the at-large electoral system was, like the systematic exclusion of Negroes from juries, unexplainable on grounds other than race, its inference is contradicted by the history of the adoption of that system in Mobile. Alternatively, if the District Court meant that the state legislature may be presumed to have "intended" that there would be no Negro Commissioners, simply because that was a foreseeable consequence of at-large voting, it applied an incorrect legal standard. "Discriminatory purpose ... implies more than intent as volition or intent as awareness of consequences.... It implies that the decisionmaker ... selected or reaffirmed a particular course of action at least in part 'because of,' not merely 'in spite of,' its adverse effects upon an identifiable group." *Personnel Administrator of Mass. v. Feeney* [442 U.S. 256 (1979)].

which the District Court and the Court of Appeals relied were most assuredly insufficient to prove an unconstitutionally discriminatory purpose in the present case.

First, the two courts found it highly significant that no Negro had been elected to the Mobile City Commission. From this fact they concluded that the processes leading to nomination and election were not open equally to Negroes. But the District Court's findings of fact, unquestioned on appeal, make clear that Negroes register and vote in Mobile "without hindrance," and that there are no official obstacles in the way of Negroes who wish to become candidates for election to the Commission. Indeed, it was undisputed that the only active "slating" organization in the city is comprised of Negroes. It may be that Negro candidates have been defeated, but that fact alone does not work a constitutional deprivation.

Second, the District Court relied in part on its finding that the persons who were elected to the Commission discriminated against Negroes in municipal employment and in dispensing public services. If that is the case, those discriminated against may be entitled to relief under the Constitution, albeit of a sort quite different from that sought in the present case. The Equal Protection Clause proscribes purposeful discrimination because of race by any unit of state government, whatever the method of its election. But evidence of discrimination by white officials in Mobile is relevant only as the most tenuous and circumstantial evidence of the constitutional invalidity of the electoral system under which they attained their offices.[20]

Third, the District Court and the Court of Appeals supported their conclusion by drawing upon the substantial history of official racial discrimination in Alabama. But past discrimination cannot, in the manner of original sin, condemn governmental action that is not itself unlawful. The ultimate question remains whether a discriminatory intent has been proved in a given case. More distant instances of official discrimination in other cases are of limited help in resolving that question.

Finally, the District Court and the Court of Appeals pointed to the mechanics of the at-large electoral system itself as proof that the votes of Negroes were being invidiously canceled out. But those features of that electoral system, such as the majority vote requirement, tend naturally to disadvantage any voting minority. They are far from proof that the at-large electoral scheme represents purposeful discrimination against Negro voters.[21]

---

20. Among the difficulties with the District Court's view of the evidence was its failure to identify the state officials whose intent it considered relevant in assessing the invidiousness of Mobile's system of government. To the extent that the inquiry should properly focus on the state legislature, see n. 21, *infra*, the actions of unrelated governmental officials would be, of course, of questionable relevance.

21. According to the District Court, voters in the city of Mobile are represented in the state legislature by three state senators,

B

We turn finally to the arguments advanced in Part I of MR. JUSTICE MARSHALL'S dissenting opinion. The theory of this dissenting opinion . . . appears to be that every "political group," or at least every such group that is in the minority, has a federal constitutional right to elect candidates in proportion to its numbers.[22] Moreover, a political group's "right" to have its candidates elected is said to be a "fundamental interest," the infringement of which may be established without proof that a State has acted with the purpose of impairing anybody's access to the political process. . . .

Whatever appeal the dissenting opinion's view may have as a matter of political theory, it is not the law. The Equal Protection Clause of the Fourteenth Amendment does not require proportional representation as an imperative of political organization. The entitlement that the dissenting opinion assumes to exist simply is not to be found in the Constitution of the United States.

It is of course true that a law that impinges upon a fundamental right explicitly or implicitly secured by the Constitution is presumptively unconstitutional. But plainly "[it] is not the province of this Court to create substantive constitutional rights in the name of guaranteeing equal protection of the laws." Accordingly, where a state law does not impair a right or liberty protected by the Constitution, there is no occasion to depart from "the settled mode of constitutional analysis of [legislation] . . . involving questions of economic and social policy."

. . . The dissenting opinion erroneously discovers the asserted entitlement to group representation within the "one person, one vote" principle

---

any one of whom can veto proposed local legislation under the existing courtesy rule. Likewise, a majority of Mobile's 11-member House delegation can prevent a local bill from reaching the floor for debate. Unanimous approval of a local measure by the city delegation, on the other hand, virtually assures passage.

There was evidence in this case that several proposals that would have altered the form of Mobile's municipal government have been defeated in the state legislature, including at least one that would have permitted Mobile to govern itself through a Mayor and City Council with members elected from individual districts within the city. Whether it may be possible ultimately to prove that Mobile's present governmental and electoral system has been retained for a racially discriminatory purpose, we are in no position now to say.

22. The dissenting opinion seeks to disclaim this description of its theory by suggesting that a claim of vote dilution may require, in addition to proof of electoral defeat, some evidence of "historical and social factors" indicating that the group in question is without political influence. Putting to the side the evident fact that these gauzy sociological considerations have no constitutional basis, it remains far from certain that they could, in any principled manner, exclude the claims of any discrete political group that happens, for whatever reason, to elect fewer of its candidates than arithmetic indicates it might. Indeed, the putative limits are bound to prove illusory if the express purpose informing their application would be, as the dissent assumes, to redress the "inequitable distribution of political influence."

of *Reynolds v. Sims* and its progeny.²⁵ Those cases established that the Equal Protection Clause guarantees the right of each voter to "have his vote weighted equally with those of all other citizens." The Court recognized that a voter's right to "have an equally effective voice" in the election of representatives is impaired where representation is not apportioned substantially on a population basis. In such cases, the votes of persons in more populous districts carry less weight than do those of persons in smaller districts. There can be, of course, no claim that the "one person, one vote" principle has been violated in this case, because the city of Mobile is a unitary electoral district and the Commission elections are conducted at large. It is therefore obvious that nobody's vote has been "diluted" in the sense in which that word was used in the *Reynolds* case.

The dissenting opinion places an extraordinary interpretation on these decisions, an interpretation not justified by *Reynolds v. Sims* itself or by any other decision of this Court. It is, of course, true that the right of a person to vote on an equal basis with other voters draws much of its significance from the political associations that its exercise reflects, but it is an altogether different matter to conclude that political groups themselves have an independent constitutional claim to representation.²⁶ And the Court's decisions hold squarely that they do not....

25. The dissenting opinion also relies upon several decisions of this Court that have held constitutionally invalid various voter eligibility requirements: *Dunn v. Blumstein* (length of residence requirement); *Evans v. Cornman* (exclusion of residents of federal property); *Kramer v. Union School District* (property or status requirement); *Harper v. Virginia Bd. of Elections* (poll tax requirement). But there is in this case no attack whatever upon any of the voter eligibility requirements in Mobile. Nor do the cited cases contain implicit support for the position of the dissenting opinion. They stand simply for the proposition that "if a challenged state statute grants the right to vote to some bona fide residents of requisite age and citizenship and denies the franchise to others, the Court must determine whether the exclusions are necessary to promote a compelling state interest." It is difficult to perceive any similarity between the excluded person's right to equal electoral participation in the cited cases, and the right asserted by the dissenting opinion in the present case, aside from the fact that they both in some way involve voting.

26. It is difficult to perceive how the implications of the dissenting opinion's theory of group representation could rationally be cabined. Indeed, certain preliminary practical questions immediately come to mind: Can only members of a minority of the voting population in a particular municipality be members of a "political group"? How large must a "group" be to be a "political group"? Can any "group" call itself a "political group"? If not, who is to say which "groups" are "political groups"? Can a qualified voter belong to more than one "political group"? Can there be more than one "political group" among white voters (e. g., Irish–American, Italian–American, Polish–American, Jews, Catholics, Protestants)? Can there be more than one "political group" among nonwhite voters? Do the answers to any of these questions depend upon the particular demographic composition of a given city? Upon the total size of its voting population? Upon the size of its governing body? Upon its form of government? Upon its history? Its geographic location? The fact that even these preliminary questions may be largely unanswerable suggests some of the conceptual and practical fallacies in the constitutional theory espoused by the dissenting opinion, putting to one side the total absence of support for that theory in the Constitution itself.

The judgment is reversed, and the case is remanded to the Court of Appeals for further proceedings.

Mr. Justice Blackmun, concurring in the result.

Assuming that proof of intent is a prerequisite to appellees' prevailing on their constitutional claim of vote dilution, I am inclined to agree with Mr. Justice White that, in this case, "the findings of the District Court amply support an inference of purposeful discrimination." I concur in the Court's judgment of reversal, however, because I believe that the relief afforded appellees by the District Court was not commensurate with the sound exercise of judicial discretion.

It seems to me that the city of Mobile, and its citizenry, have a substantial interest in maintaining the commission form of government that has been in effect there for nearly 70 years. The District Court recognized that its remedial order, changing the form of the city's government to a mayor-council system, "raised serious constitutional issues." Nonetheless, the court was "unable to see how the impermissibly unconstitutional dilution can be effectively corrected by any other approach."

Contrary to the District Court, I do not believe that, in order to remedy the unconstitutional vote dilution it found, it was necessary to convert Mobile's city government to a mayor-council system. In my view, the District Court at least should have considered alternative remedial orders that would have maintained some of the basic elements of the commission system Mobile long ago had selected—joint exercise of legislative and executive power, and citywide representation. In the first place, I see no reason for the court to have separated legislative and executive power in the city of Mobile by creating the office of mayor. In the second place, the court could have, and in my view should have, considered expanding the size of the Mobile City Commission and providing for the election of at least some commissioners at large. Alternative plans might have retained at-large elections for all commissioners while imposing district residency requirements that would have insured the election of a commission that was a cross section of all of Mobile's neighborhoods, or a plurality-win system that would have provided the potential for the effective use of single-shot voting by black voters. In failing to consider such alternative plans, it appears to me that the District Court was perhaps overly concerned with the elimination of at-large elections per se, rather than with structuring an electoral system that provided an opportunity for black voters in Mobile to participate in the city's government on an equal footing with whites.

■ Mr. Justice Stevens, concurring in the judgment.

... While I agree with Mr. Justice Stewart that no violation of respondents' constitutional rights has been demonstrated, my analysis of the issue proceeds along somewhat different lines.

In my view, there is a fundamental distinction between state action that inhibits an individual's right to vote and state action that affects the political strength of various groups that compete for leadership in a democratically governed community. That distinction divides so-called vote dilution practices into two different categories "governed by entirely different constitutional considerations."

In the first category are practices such as poll taxes or literacy tests that deny individuals access to the ballot. Districting practices that make an individual's vote in a heavily populated district less significant than an individual's vote in a smaller district also belong in that category. Such practices must be tested by the strictest of constitutional standards, whether challenged under the Fifteenth Amendment or under the Equal Protection Clause of the Fourteenth Amendment.

This case does not fit within the first category. The District Court found that black citizens in Mobile "register and vote without hindrance" and there is no claim that any individual's vote is worth less than any other's. Rather, this case draws into question a political structure that treats all individuals as equals but adversely affects the political strength of a racially identifiable group. Although I am satisfied that such a structure may be challenged under the Fifteenth Amendment as well as under the Equal Protection Clause of the Fourteenth Amendment, I believe that under either provision it must be judged by a standard that allows the political process to function effectively....

[The equal protection standard to be applied to claims of group vote dilution must apply equally to racial, ethnic, political, religious, economic, and all other groups.] My conclusion that the same standard should be applied to racial groups as is applied to other groups leads me also to conclude that the standard cannot condemn every adverse impact on one or more political groups without spawning more dilution litigation than the judiciary can manage. Difficult as the issues engendered by *Baker v. Carr* may have been, nothing comparable to the mathematical yardstick used in apportionment cases is available to identify the difference between permissible and impermissible adverse impacts on the voting strength of political groups....

In my view, the proper standard is suggested by three characteristics of the gerrymander condemned in *Gomillion*: (1) the 28–sided configuration was, in the Court's word, "uncouth," that is to say, it was manifestly not the product of a routine or a traditional political decision; (2) it had a significant adverse impact on a minority group; and (3) it was unsupported by any neutral justification and thus was either totally irrational or entirely motivated by a desire to curtail the political strength of the minority. These characteristics suggest that a proper test should focus on the objective effects of the political decision rather than the subjective motivation of the decisionmaker. In this case, if the commission form of government in Mobile were extraordinary, or if it were nothing more than a vestige of history, with no greater justification than the grotesque figure in *Gomillion*, it would surely violate the Constitution. That conclusion would follow simply from its adverse impact on black voters plus the absence of any legitimate justification for the system, without reference to the subjective intent of the political body that has refused to alter it.

Conversely, I am also persuaded that a political decision that affects group voting rights may be valid even if it can be proved that irrational or invidious factors have played some part in its enactment or retention. The standard for testing the acceptability of such a decision must take into account the fact that the responsibility for drawing political boundaries is generally committed to the legislative process and that the process inevitably involves a series of compromises among different group interests. If the process is to work, it must reflect an awareness of group interests and it must tolerate some attempts to advantage or to disadvantage particular segments of the voting populace. Indeed, the same "group interest" may simultaneously support and oppose a particular boundary change. The standard cannot, therefore, be so strict that any evidence of a purpose to disadvantage a bloc of voters will justify a finding of "invidious discrimination"; otherwise, the facts of political life would deny legislatures the right to perform the districting function. Accordingly, a political decision that is supported by valid and articulable justifications cannot be invalid simply because some participants in the decisionmaking process were motivated by a purpose to disadvantage a minority group.

■ Mr. Justice Brennan, dissenting.

I dissent because I agree with Mr. Justice Marshall that proof of discriminatory impact is sufficient in these cases. I also dissent because, even accepting the plurality's premise that discriminatory purpose must be shown, I agree with Mr. Justice Marshall and Mr. Justice White that the appellees have clearly met that burden.

■ Mr. Justice White, dissenting.

* * *

II

In the instant case the District Court and the Court of Appeals faithfully applied the principles of *White v. Regester* in assessing whether the maintenance of a system of at-large elections for the selection of Mobile City Commissioners denied Mobile Negroes their Fourteenth and Fifteenth Amendment rights. Scrupulously adhering to our admonition that "[the] plaintiffs' burden is to produce evidence to support findings that the political processes leading to nomination and election were not equally open to participation by the group in question," the District Court conducted a detailed factual inquiry into the openness of the candidate selection process to blacks. The court noted that "Mobile blacks were subjected to massive official and private racial discrimination until the Voting Rights Act of

1965" and that "[the] pervasive effects of past discrimination still substantially [affect] black political participation." Although the District Court noted that "[since] the Voting Rights Act of 1965, blacks register and vote without hindrance," the court found that "local political processes are not equally open" to blacks. Despite the fact that Negroes constitute more than 35% of the population of Mobile, no Negro has ever been elected to the Mobile City Commission. The plaintiffs introduced extensive evidence of severe racial polarization in voting patterns during the 1960's and 1970's with "white voting for white and black for black if a white is opposed to a black," resulting in the defeat of the black candidate or, if two whites are running, the defeat of the white candidate most identified with blacks. Regression analyses covering every City Commission race in 1965, 1969, and 1973, both the primary and general election of the county commission in 1968 and 1972, selected school board races in 1962, 1966, 1970, 1972, and 1974, city referendums in 1963 and 1973, and a countywide legislative race in 1969 confirmed the existence of severe bloc voting. Nearly every active candidate for public office testified that because of racial polarization "it is highly unlikely that anytime in the foreseeable future, under the at-large system, . . . a black can be elected against a white." After single-member districts were created in Mobile County for state legislative elections, "three blacks of the present fourteen member Mobile County delegation have been elected." Based on the foregoing evidence, the District Court found "that the structure of the at-large election of city commissioners combined with strong racial polarization of Mobile's electorate continues to effectively discourage qualified black citizens from seeking office or being elected thereby denying blacks equal access to the slating or candidate selection process."

The District Court also reviewed extensive evidence that the City Commissioners elected under the at-large system have not been responsive to the needs of the Negro community. The court found that city officials have been unresponsive to the interests of Mobile Negroes in municipal employment, appointments to boards and committees, and the provision of municipal services in part because of "the political fear of a white backlash vote when black citizens' needs are at stake." The court also found that there is no clear-cut state policy preference for at-large elections and that past discrimination affecting the ability of Negroes to register and to vote "has helped preclude the effective participation of blacks in the election system today." The adverse impact of the at-large election system on minorities was found to be enhanced by the large size of the citywide election district, the majority vote requirement, the provision that candidates run for positions by place or number, and the lack of any provision for at-large candidates to run from particular geographical subdistricts.

. . . After noting that "whenever a redistricting bill of any type is proposed by a county delegation member, a major concern has centered around how many, if any, blacks would be elected," the District Court concluded that there was "a present purpose to dilute the black vote . . . resulting from intentional state legislative inaction." . . .

[T]he Court of Appeals reviewed the District Court's findings of fact, found them not to be clearly erroneous and held that they "compel the inference that [Mobile's at-large] system has been maintained with the purpose of diluting the black vote, thus supplying the element of intent necessary to establish a violation of the fourteenth amendment." . . . The court observed that the District Court's "finding that the legislature was acutely conscious of the racial consequences of its districting policies," coupled with the attempt to assign different functions to each of the three City Commissioners "to lock in the at-large feature of the scheme," constituted "direct evidence of the intent behind the maintenance of the at-large plan." . . .

III

A plurality of the Court today agrees with the courts below that maintenance of Mobile's at-large system for election of City Commissioners violates the Fourteenth and Fifteenth Amendments only if it is motivated by a racially discriminatory purpose. . . . The plurality nonetheless casts aside the meticulous application of the principles of these cases by both the District Court and the Court of Appeals by concluding that the evidence they relied upon "fell far short of showing" purposeful discrimination.

The plurality erroneously suggests that the District Court erred by considering the factors articulated by the Court of Appeals in *Zimmer v. McKeithen* to determine whether purposeful discrimination has been shown. This remarkable suggestion ignores the facts that *Zimmer* articulated the very factors deemed relevant by *White v. Regester* . . .—a lack of minority access to the candidate selection process, unresponsiveness of elected officials to minority interests, a history of discrimination, majority vote requirements, provisions that candidates run for positions by place or number, the lack of any provision for at-large candidates to run from particular geographical subdistricts—and that both the District Court and the Court of Appeals considered these factors with the recognition that they are relevant only with respect to the question whether purposeful discrimination can be inferred.

. . . The plurality apparently bases [its] conclusion on the fact that there are no official obstacles barring Negroes from registering, voting, and running for office, coupled with its conclusion that none of the factors relied upon by the courts below would alone be sufficient to support an inference of purposeful discrimination. The absence of official obstacles to registration, voting, and running for office heretofore has never been deemed to insulate an electoral system from attack under the Fourteenth and Fifteenth Amendments. In *White v. Regester*, there was no evidence that Negroes faced official obstacles to registration, voting, and running for office, yet we upheld a finding that they had been excluded from effective participation in the political process in violation of the Equal Protection Clause because a multimember districting scheme, in the context of racial voting at the polls, was being used invidiously to prevent Negroes from being elected to public office. ... Thus, even though Mobile's Negro community may register and vote without hindrance, the system of at-large election of City Commissioners may violate the Fourteenth and Fifteenth Amendments if it is used purposefully to exclude Negroes from the political process....

Because I believe that the findings of the District Court amply support an inference of purposeful discrimination in violation of the Fourteenth and Fifteenth Amendments, I respectfully dissent.

■ MR. JUSTICE MARSHALL, dissenting.

... The plurality would require plaintiffs in vote-dilution cases to meet the stringent burden of establishing discriminatory intent within the meaning of *Washington v. Davis, Arlington Heights v. Metropolitan Housing Dev. Corp.,* and *Personnel Administrator of Mass. v. Feeney*. In my view, our vote-dilution decisions require only a showing of discriminatory impact to justify the invalidation of a multimember districting scheme, and, because they are premised on the fundamental interest in voting protected by the Fourteenth Amendment, the discriminatory-impact standard adopted by them is unaffected by *Washington v. Davis* and its progeny.... Even if, however, proof of discriminatory intent were necessary to support a vote-dilution claim, I would impose upon the plaintiffs a standard of proof less rigid than that provided by *Personnel Administrator of Mass. v. Feeney*.

I

A

... [I]n *White v. Regester*, we invalidated the challenged multimember districting plans because their characteristics, when combined with historical and social factors, had the discriminatory effect of denying the plaintiff Negroes and Mexican–Americans equal access to the political process....[7]

---

7. *White v. Regester* makes clear the distinction between the concepts of vote dilution and proportional representation. We have held that, in order to prove an allegation of vote dilution, the plaintiffs must show more than simply that they have been unable to elect candidates of their choice.... When all that is proved is mere lack of success at the polls, the Court will not presume that members of a political minority have suffered an impermissible dilution of political power. Rather, it is assumed that these persons have means available to them through which they can have some effect on governmental decisionmaking. For example, many of these persons might belong to a variety of other political, social, and economic groups that have some impact on officials. In the absence of evidence to the contrary, it may be assumed that officials will not be improperly influenced by such factors as the race or place of residence of persons seeking governmental action. Furthermore, political factions out of office often serve as watchdogs on the performance of the government, bind together into coalitions having enhanced influence, and have the respectability necessary to affect public policy.

Unconstitutional vote dilution occurs only when a discrete political minority whose

It is apparent that a showing of discriminatory intent in the creation or maintenance of multimember districts is as unnecessary after *White* as it was under our earlier vote-dilution decisions. Under this line of cases, an electoral districting plan is invalid if it has the effect of affording an electoral minority "less opportunity than ... other residents in the district to participate in the political processes and to elect legislators of their choice." It is also apparent that the Court in *White* considered equal access to the political process as meaning more than merely allowing the minority the opportunity to vote. *White* stands for the proposition that an electoral system may not relegate an electoral minority to political impotence by diminishing the importance of its vote. The plurality's approach requiring proof of discriminatory purpose in the present cases is, then, squarely contrary to *White* and its predecessors....

B

The plurality fails to apply the discriminatory-effect standard of *White v. Regester* because that approach conflicts with what the plurality takes to be an elementary principle of law. "[Only] if there is purposeful discrimination," announces the plurality, "can there be a violation of the Equal Protection Clause of the Fourteenth Amendment." That proposition is plainly overbroad. It fails to distinguish between two distinct lines of equal protection decisions: those involving suspect classifications, and those involving fundamental rights.

We have long recognized that under the Equal Protection Clause classifications based on race are "constitutionally suspect," and are subject to the "most rigid scrutiny," regardless of whether they infringe on an independently protected constitutional right. Under *Washington v. Davis*, a showing of discriminatory purpose is necessary to impose strict scrutiny on facially neutral classifications having a racially discriminatory impact. Perhaps because the plaintiffs in the present cases are Negro, the plurality assumes that their vote-dilution claims are premised on the suspect-classification branch of our equal protection cases, and that under *Washington v. Davis*, they are required to prove discriminatory intent. That assumption fails to recognize that our vote-dilution decisions are rooted in a different strand of equal protection jurisprudence.

Under the Equal Protection Clause, if a classification "impinges upon a fundamental right explicitly or implicitly protected by the Constitution, ... strict judicial scrutiny" is required, regardless of whether the infringement was intentional.[9] As I will explain, our cases recognize a fundamental right

voting strength is diminished by a districting scheme proves that historical and social factors render it largely incapable of effectively utilizing alternative avenues of influencing public policy. In these circumstances, the only means of breaking down the barriers encasing the political arena is to structure the electoral districting so that the minority has a fair opportunity to elect candidates of its choice....

9. *See Shapiro v. Thompson* (right to travel); *Reynolds v. Sims* (right to vote);

to equal electoral participation that encompasses protection against vote dilution. Proof of discriminatory purpose is, therefore, not required to support a claim of vote dilution.[10] The plurality's erroneous conclusion to the contrary is the result of a failure to recognize the central distinction between *White v. Regester* and *Washington v. Davis, supra*: the former involved an infringement of a constitutionally protected right, while the latter dealt with a claim of racially discriminatory distribution of an interest to which no citizen has a constitutional entitlement.

Nearly a century ago, the Court recognized the elementary proposition upon which our structure of civil rights is based: "[The] political franchise of voting is ... a fundamental political right, because preservative of all rights." *Yick Wo v. Hopkins.* We reiterated that theme in our landmark decision in *Reynolds v. Sims*, and stated that, because "the right of suffrage is a fundamental matter in a free and democratic society[,] ... any alleged infringement of the right of citizens to vote must be carefully and meticulously scrutinized." We realized that "the right of suffrage can be denied by a debasement or dilution of the weight of a citizen's vote just as effectively as by wholly prohibiting the free exercise of the franchise." Accordingly, we recognized that the Equal Protection Clause protects "[the] right of a citizen to equal representation and to have his vote weighted equally with those of all other citizens." ...

Indeed, our vote-dilution cases have explicitly acknowledged that they are premised on the infringement of a fundamental right, not on the Equal Protection Clause's prohibition of racial discrimination.... If the Court had believed that the equal protection problem with alleged vote dilution was one of racial discrimination and not abridgment of the right to vote, it would not have accorded standing to the plaintiffs [in earlier dilution cases], who were simply registered voters ... alleging that the state

Douglas v. California and *Griffin v. Illinois* (right to fair access to criminal process). Under the rubric of the fundamental right of privacy, we have recognized that individuals have freedom from unjustified governmental interference with personal decisions involving marriage, *Zablocki v. Redhail*, procreation, *Skinner v. Oklahoma ex rel. Williamson*, contraception, Carey v. *Population Services International, Eisenstadt v. Baird, Griswold v. Connecticut*, abortion, *Roe v. Wade*, family relationships, *Prince v. Massachusetts*, and child rearing and education, *Pierce v. Society of Sisters, Meyer v. Nebraska.*

10. As the present cases illustrate, a requirement of proof of discriminatory intent seriously jeopardizes the free exercise of the fundamental right to vote. Although the right to vote is indistinguishable for present purposes from the other fundamental rights our cases have recognized, see n. 9, supra, surely the plurality would not require proof of discriminatory purpose in those cases. The plurality fails to articulate why the right to vote should receive such singular treatment. Furthermore, the plurality refuses to recognize the disutility of requiring proof of discriminatory purpose in fundamental rights cases. For example, it would make no sense to require such a showing when the question is whether a state statute regulating abortion violates the right of personal choice recognized in *Roe v. Wade, supra.* The only logical inquiry is whether, regardless of the legislature's motive, the statute has the effect of infringing that right.

apportionment plan, as a theoretical matter, diluted their voting strength because of where they lived....

Our vote-dilution decisions, then, involve the fundamental-interest branch, rather than the antidiscrimination branch, of our jurisprudence under the Equal Protection Clause. They recognize a substantive constitutional right to participate on an equal basis in the electoral process that cannot be denied or diminished for any reason, racial or otherwise, lacking quite substantial justification. They are premised on a rationale wholly apart from that underlying *Washington v. Davis*....

III

If it is assumed that proof of discriminatory intent is necessary to support the vote-dilution claims in these cases, the question becomes what evidence will satisfy this requirement.[34]

The plurality assumes, without any analysis, that these cases are appropriate for the application of the rigid test developed in *Personnel Administrator of Mass. v. Feeney*, requiring that "the decisionmaker ... selected or reaffirmed a particular course of action at least in part 'because of,' not merely 'in spite of,' its adverse effects upon an identifiable group." In my view, the *Feeney* standard creates a burden of proof far too extreme to apply in vote-dilution cases.

This Court has acknowledged that the evidentiary inquiry involving discriminatory intent must necessarily vary depending upon the factual context. One useful evidentiary tool, long recognized by the common law, is the presumption that "[every] man must be taken to contemplate the probable consequences of the act he does." The Court in *Feeney* acknowledged that proof of foreseeability of discriminatory consequences could raise a "strong inference that the adverse effects were desired," but refused to treat this presumption as conclusive in cases alleging discriminatory distribution of constitutional gratuities.

I would apply the common-law foreseeability presumption to the present cases. The plaintiffs surely proved that maintenance of the challenged multimember districting would have the foreseeable effect of perpetuating the submerged electoral influence of Negroes, and that this discriminatory effect could be corrected by implementation of a single-member districting plan. Because the foreseeable disproportionate impact was so severe, the burden of proof should have shifted to the defendants, and they should have been required to show that they refused to modify the districting schemes in spite of, not because of, their severe discriminatory effect.

---

34. The statutes providing for at-large election of the members of the two governmental bodies involved in these cases, see n. 33, supra, have been in effect since the days when Mobile Negroes were totally disenfranchised by the Alabama Constitution of 1901. The District Court in both cases found, therefore, that the at-large schemes could not have been adopted for discriminatory purposes. The issue is, then, whether officials have maintained these electoral systems for discriminatory purposes.

Reallocation of the burden of proof is especially appropriate in these cases, where the challenged state action infringes the exercise of a fundamental right. The defendants would carry their burden of proof only if they showed that they considered submergence of the Negro vote a detriment, not a benefit, of the multimember systems, that they accorded minority citizens the same respect given to whites, and that they nevertheless decided to maintain the systems for legitimate reasons....

NOTES AND QUESTIONS

1. *The meaning of Bolden.* As evidenced by the fragmented and passionately expressed opinions within the Court, *Bolden* was a controversial and contested decision. The question is what the proper focus of this controversy ought to be. Several possibilities exist, all of which were invoked in subsequent academic and congressional responses to the decision.

    a. Some criticized *Bolden* as a dramatic change in the governing legal standard under the Fifteenth Amendment. By requiring proof of discriminatory purpose, *Bolden* was said to overturn the approach of cases like *Whitcomb* and *White*, as well as to be inconsistent with well-established lower court decisions like *Zimmer*. Which side has the better of this fidelity to precedent argument? Is there a clearly right answer? The same argument could be focused on Section 2 of the VRA, rather than the Fifteenth Amendment: was the Court correct to read the original VRA and Section 2 as requiring proof of discriminatory purpose?

Note that the District Court and the Court of Appeals, both of which found the at-large election system unconstitutional, also both applied a discriminatory purpose analysis.

    b. Instead of focusing on whether the Fifteenth Amendment standard ought to require proof of discriminatory purpose, the criticism might focus on the way the Court *applied* the purpose standard. Assuming that *White* also required a finding of discriminatory purpose, is the Court consistent in the two cases with respect to what facts are necessary and sufficient to proving purpose? If the facts here are not sufficient to establish discriminatory purpose, what factual findings would suffice? Does the Court's decision preclude development of a fuller factual record in the lower courts on Mobile's at-large elections? Note that Justice White, author of *Washington v. Davis,* 426 U.S. 229 (1976), the case that constitutionalized the intent standard for the Fourteenth Amendment, agrees in *Mobile* that the Fifteenth Amendment should similarly be interpreted to require proof of discriminatory purpose. But unlike the plurality, he believes a showing of that purpose has been made here.

Critics of *Bolden* would soon turn to Congress and ask it effectively to "overturn" the Court's decision through amendments to the VRA. We have seen that there are two quite different ways of focusing criticisms of *Bolden*; the choice between these two critical interpretations would have profound implications for the direction of legislative response. If the problem is that the decision adopts the wrong legal standard, then Congress might be urged to adopt a different standard; Congress will be asked to reject the need to show purpose. But if the problem is not with the purpose test per se, but the way the Court applies it, then Congress might be asked to specify the kind and weight of evidence that should be sufficient to justify a legal conclusion of discriminatory purpose.

c. Four Justices would not find discriminatory purpose in Mobile. Four would. Justice Stevens thus becomes the decisive vote; his opinion is significant, however, not just here, but for the general jurisprudential approach it takes to political rights.

First, he argues that equal protection must apply the same way to all claims that the voting power of some identifiable group has been diluted—whether the group is defined racially, politically, religiously, or economically. Second, and as a result, adverse impact alone on the voting power of any group cannot be sufficient to establish a constitutional violation. Third, constitutional doctrine should not focus on the subjective motivations of decision makers, which is what the discriminatory purpose doctrine does. Fourth, the Court should instead focus on whether the political decision at issue (1) is consistent with traditional practices or aberrational; (2) whether it is supported by any neutral justification; (3) whether it has an adverse impact on an identifiable group.

This approach is one Justice Stevens takes consistently to cases involving vote dilution claims. Consider whether it provides a more appropriate framework than other alternatives for dealing with these issues. As we confront other problems involving political rights, such as racial redistricting and the doctrine of *Shaw v. Reno*, return to the Stevens approach and ask how it would deal with the particular issue. For an overview of Justice Stevens's jurisprudence in this area, which argues that he provides a more coherent answer to certain central questions than does the Court, see Pamela S. Karlan, Cousins' *Kin: Justice Stevens and Voting Rights*, 27 Rutgers L.J. 3 (1996).

d. The plurality argues that the approach of Justice Marshall's dissent would require that every political group, or every minority political group have the right to elect candidates in proportion to its numbers. Is this a correct reading of the dissent? If so, what if anything is so troubling about such a principle?

2. *The reaction to Bolden.* Voting rights lawyers responded to *Bolden* with despair and outrage. The decision was said to be "devastating. Dilution cases came to a virtual standstill; existing cases were overturned and dismissed, while plans for new cases were abandoned." Armand Derfner, *Vote Dilution and the Voting Rights Act Amendments of 1982* in Minority Vote Dilution 161 (Chandler Davidson ed. 1984).

Turning to academic forums, critics lambasted the decision. *Mobile* purportedly "broke with precedents in vote dilution cases, it failed to reflect traditional solicitude for the right to vote, it established a difficult discriminatory intent standard with little direction as to how it should be applied, and it mandated judicial inquiry into discriminatory intent of public bodies—an exercise which is inherently divisive." Frank R. Parker, *The 'Results' Test of Section 2 of the Voting Rights Act: Abandoning the Intent Standard*, 69 Va. L. Rev. 715, 737 (1983). With respect to proving intent, "the *Bolden* plurality made the possibility of proving racial purpose by circumstantial evidence in vote dilution cases remote . . . the *Bolden* plurality clearly implied that circumstantial evidence of discriminatory purpose would not suffice to prove discriminatory intent." *Id.* at 743.

Sections 4 and 5 of the VRA were due to expire in 1982, and Congress had to reauthorize them to keep the statute alive. This proved to be a fortuitous opportunity for critics of *Bolden*, because the 1982 re-authorization process became a vehicle for seeking amendments to the Act that would, in effect, overturn *Bolden*. The 1982 congressional hearings became a stage on which critics of *Bolden* could parade its failings before Congress. Many witnesses testified as to how difficult, perhaps impossible, it now was to win vote dilution claims. For example, Benjamin Hooks, Executive Director of the NAACP, testified that "Congress never intended that an impossible burden of proving 'intent' to discriminate be placed on persons denied the right of franchise." Similarly, Robert Krueger, a former member of Congress, testified that "[m]odern discrimination against racial and ethnic minorities is likely to be subtle and unexpressed rather than stated in the press and in the chambers of government. As a result, it becomes extremely difficult and in some cases nearly impossible to prove subjective intent to discriminate, even where the facts fairly and clearly indicate that intentional discrimination might have been in the minds of the officials in charge of voting practices." Extension of the Voting Rights Act, 1981: Hearings Before the Subcommittee on Civil and Constitutional Rights of the House Comm. on the Judiciary, 97th Cong., 1st Sess. 906 (1981). The mayor of Richmond, Virginia, Henry Marsh, testified that "[s]hould the intent standard prevail, however, it would be extremely difficult to prove voter discrimination absent a confession of intent by a voter official." *Id.* at 365. Are these views reasonable interpretations of what *Mobile* required? Plausible ones? Exaggerated ones?

3. *Subsequent judicial applications of Bolden*. In light of the outcry about how difficult *Bolden* would make vote dilution litigation, what should be made of the following decisions:

a. On remand, the District Court held additional factual hearings and then struck down Mobile's at-large elections as having been originally adopted for racially discriminatory purposes. *Bolden v. City of Mobile*, 542 F.Supp. 1050 (S.D.Ala.1982). The court held that while the move to at-large elections early in the century had been motivated, as in many local governments in the North, by the aim of placing the business and professional classes in control of city government and excluding the lower classes, invidious racial reasons had also "played a substantial and significant part." This original purpose, combined with the present effects of the at-large elections (primarily the failure of black candidates to be elected and the non-responsiveness of elected officials to the black community) were sufficient to strike down the at-large elections. *Compare Hunter v. Underwood,* 471 U.S. 222 (1985) (striking down criminal disenfranchisement provisions dating back to 1901 Alabama Constitution).

The opinion is an extensive, and fascinating, history of local government in Mobile, aided by the expert testimony of professional historians. Before the Civil War, the city used ward-based elections. After the War, when white Democrats were not eligible to vote because they hadn't taken a required loyalty oath, the Governor used his appointment power to appoint over time at least 10 blacks to a 24 member Board of Aldermen that governed Mobile. In response, a coalition of moderate Republicans and conservative Democrats agreed to at-large elections to avoid election of black officials. In 1874, with increasing return of white control, this agreement was codified and at-large elections adopted. When the at-large system was re-adopted in 1911, the justifications included minimizing black influence, even though only 193 blacks were registered to vote while 7,104 whites were.

Consider the time and cost involved in litigating vote dilution cases on the basis of such testimony. The retrial featured the testimony of four expert academic witnesses for the plaintiffs—three historians and one sociologist. Graduate students spent hundreds of hours reading old newspapers on microfilm, going over the records of city government, and examining personal correspondence in the state archives. For an account of this process of preparing for the re-trial, see Peyton McCrary, *The Significance of Mobile v. Bolden*, in Minority Vote Dilution 47, 48–49 (Chandler Davidson ed. 1984). Conceptually, is the best understanding of policy or constitutional doctrine in this arena one in which dilution questions turn on elaborate historical inquiries into events this long ago? If not, what is the best alternative?

b. As another application of *Bolden*'s intent standard, consider the decision in *Rogers v. Lodge,* 458 U.S. 613 (1982), handed down two days after the 1982 VRA Amendments were signed into law. Blacks were 53.6 percent of the population of Burke County, Georgia and 38 percent of its registered voters. Since 1911, the county had been governed by a five-member Board of Commissioners elected at-large. Candidates had to run for designated seats, but could reside anywhere in the county, and had to receive a majority of votes in the primary or general election (with a runoff election if needed).

The Court found that voting was polarized along racial lines. Whites voted overwhelmingly for white candidates, while blacks did likewise for black candidates. As a result of the at-large election system, the cohesive white majority could get all its candidates elected to office and thereby control the entire Board of Commissioners. Consequently, no black candidate had ever been elected to the Board.

The lower courts found that the at-large system, which had been adopted in 1911, had not been adopted for a discriminatory purpose. But those courts found that it had been *maintained* for such purposes. Applying *Bolden*, the Supreme Court affirmed in an opinion by Justice White.

The Court noted that the District Court had found the presence of polarized voting, the absence of black elected officials, and the presence of many of the *Zimmer* factors. While these factors could not, standing alone, establish a violation, the Court held that they could be used as evidence to prove discriminatory purpose. The trial court had pointed to the county's history of discrimination in education and voting, the depressed socio-economic status of blacks in the county, and the nonresponsiveness of elected officials to the needs of the black community—manifested in infrequent appointment of black officials to public bodies and discriminatory patterns of road paving. The trial court also concluded that the large size of the county made it more difficult for blacks to get to polling places or campaign for office, and that the majority-vote requirement and the requirement that candidates run for specific seats further bolstered the conclusion that the at-large system was being maintained for discriminatory purposes. The Court thus upheld orders that the at-large system be replaced with five single-member districts.

Are these factual circumstances about Burke County, Georgia sufficiently different from those in Mobile, Alabama to produce such different constitutional results? In dissent, Justices Powell and Rehnquist argued that *Rogers* was flatly inconsistent with *Bolden*; in their view, *Bolden* had ruled out appeal to this kind of "sociological evidence" to prove vote dilution. Note that seven Justices considered the two cases to require the same result, though they differed on what that result was. Other critics argued that *Rogers* demonstrated that the Court itself could not adhere to the intent standard. Abigail M. Thernstrom, Whose Votes Count? Affirmative Action and Minority Voting Rights 76 (1987) (*Rogers* with a "new label had rescued a discarded product."). Do *Bolden* and *Rogers* seem consistently decided?

c. Do *Rogers* and the result on remand in *Bolden* suggest that the outcry over the Supreme Court's decision in *Bolden* was exaggerated, and that the intent standard would not be so difficult to meet in practice? Or does it suggest that the outcry, bolstered by congressional action to reject *Bolden*, caused the Court to water down the intent standard? For the suggestion that *Rogers* was the product of the Court having been "stung by nationwide criticism of the *Mobile* decision," see Armand Derfner, *Vote Dilution and the Voting Rights Act Amendments of 1982* in Minority Vote Dilution 161 (Chandler Davidson ed. 1984).

C. THE 1982 AMENDMENTS TO SECTION 2 OF THE VRA

In the wake of *Bolden*, Congress re-entered center stage in the development of voting-rights policy. One theme this book emphasizes throughout is the dynamic and complex institutional relationships in the creation, interpretation, and implementation of civil-rights policy. Perhaps nowhere is the complexity of those relationships better displayed than in the political response to the Supreme Court's *Bolden* decision—and then in the next iteration of this process, covered in the following Chapter, in which the courts return to center stage as they assume the role of giving shape to Congress' response to the Court's decision.

We do not seek to approach these institutional issues through more abstract and formal discussions of "institutional competence," the "proper role" of courts versus legislatures, and the like. One advantage of studying a specific field in depth, such as voting rights, is that it becomes possible to explore the fine-grained details of how the federal courts and Congress (and, to a lesser extent, the executive branch) respond to these issues and to each other's responses. In addition, we can examine these institutional questions from the broader historical perspective that sustained examination of one area of policy offers. As you study the following materials, consider what light they and previous materials shed on these institutional issues. What moves Congress to act in this arena? When it does, is there anything characteristic about the forms that legislative action tends to take? What, if anything, tends to differ about the ways courts and Congress address voting-rights issues? More generally, how are one's views about the abstract issues that are the typical staple of theory about these institutional questions—issues of institutional competence, proper judicial role, the role of democratic politics—affected by knowledge of the concrete details of judicial and legislative action over long periods of time? Does historical experience undermine more "traditional" views about the role of courts? Or confirm those views?

One reason these questions are often discussed in ways that seem unduly formal is that course materials frequently present only enacted statutes. But focusing on statutory language alone leaves discussion too unmoored from the confused and contentious details of actual legislative processes. In 1982, Congress amended the VRA in dramatic ways. We take the unusual step here of including not just the enacted provisions, but also an extensive account of the legislative developments behind the 1982 amendments. We also include a particularly authoritative document from the legislative history, which the courts have relied on heavily in interpreting these amendments: the Senate Judiciary Committee Report. Presenting legislative history in a casebook is difficult; we do so here by including the following: (a) the amended version of Section 2, the aspect of the 1982 amendments we will study; (b) a narrative of the legislative history; (c) the Senate Committee Report.

Before turning to these materials, a word about context: recall that a central element of the VRA, section 5, was first enacted in 1965 as a temporary provision scheduled to expire in 1970. When this provision came up for re-consideration, the statute was amended in 1970 and 1975 to extend and expand its reach. The 1975 amendments extended section 5 for seven additional years, until August 1982; seven years was chosen to avoid having section 5 up for re-consideration in the midst of the 1980s reapportionment. *Bolden* was decided close to the time when Congress would have to re-visit the VRA because section 5 would expire.

As you study these materials, focus on whether Congress had a clear and coherent conception of vote dilution in mind when it sought to "reverse" *Bolden*. What did Congress think it meant to "reverse" *Bolden*? What did Congress think *Bolden* itself meant?

1. SECTION 2 AS AMENDED IN 1982:

> (A) No voting qualification or prerequisite to voting or standard, practice, or procedure shall be imposed or applied by any State or political subdivision in a manner which results in a denial or abridgement of the right of any citizen of the United States to vote on account of race or color, or in contravention of the guarantees set forth in section 1973b(f)(2) of this title [which protects certain "language minorities"], as provided in subsection (b) of this section.
>
> (B) A violation of subsection (a) of this section is established if, based on the totality of circumstances, it is shown that the political processes leading to nomination or election in the State or political subdivision are not equally open to participation by members of a class of citizens protected by subsection (a) of this section in that its members have less opportunity than other members of the electorate to participate in the political process and to elect representatives of their choice. The extent to which members of a protected class have been elected to office in the State or political subdivision is one circumstance which may be considered: *Provided,* That nothing in this section establishes a right to have members of a protected class elected in numbers equal to their proportion in the population.

2. THE LEGISLATIVE PROCESS LEADING TO SECTION 2

What follows is a relatively lengthy summary of the legislative history behind the adoption of the 1982 Amendments to Section 2. This history is worth studying in detail not just for what it reveals about the ideas surrounding Section 2, but for what it reveals about the legislative process and the relationship of judicial decisions to politics. For other perspectives on the Section 2 amendments, see Abigail M. Thernstrom, Whose Votes Count? Affirmative Action and Minority Voting Rights (1987); Armand Derfner, *Vote Dilution and the Voting Rights Act Amendments of 1982* in Minority Vote Dilution 161 (Chandler Davidson ed. 1984). These excerpts are taken from an extensive and balanced summary of the legislative history of the 1982 Amendments, edited to emphasize the debates over Section 2.

Thomas M. Boyd and Stephen J. Markman, The 1982 Amendments to the Voting Rights Act: A Legislative History, 40 Wash. & Lee L. Rev. 1347 (1983)

... As the expiration date for the preclearance provisions neared, groups within the institutional civil rights community began to organize for what they anticipated would be a difficult political fight. The Leadership Conference on Civil Rights, to which 165 organizations belonged, hired its first full-time executive director in preparation for the legislative campaign which lay ahead. Moreover, elements of the Leadership Conference, most notably the National Urban League, began to mobilize their local affiliates for the purpose of contacting congressional offices in affected states and applying political and media pressure designed to achieve a voting majority on the House and Senate floors. Seventy-five percent of all League affiliates did so during 1981–82.

Two other members of the conference, the National Education Association (NEA) and the NAACP, would become instrumental in transmitting local sentiment to the Congress. For this purpose, the NEA organized mailings to two contact members in each of the country's 435 congressional districts, and the NAACP set up telephone banks so that local members could notify their representatives of their feelings. These banks were set up for a week prior to action in the House subcommittee, full committee, and on the floor. In all, the banks were available to local members for nearly nine months....

The portion of the Act that generated the most intense interest during congressional consideration of the 1982 amendments was section 2, a little-used provision that tracked the language of the Fifteenth Amendment. The nationwide applicability of section 2 was originally designed to appease Southerners who felt that their constituencies were being singled out for extraordinary federal action. Section 2, however, had never been successfully used as the basis for litigation. When the Supreme Court issued its 1980 plurality opinion in *Mobile v. Bolden* nine months preceding the start of the 97th Congress, new and important issues surrounding the Act came into focus for the first time....

II. HOUSE OF REPRESENTATIVE CONSIDERATION

[As introduced in the House by Congressman Peter W. Rodino, Jr., the longtime chairman of the House Judiciary Committee, the bill to amend the VRA had three important provisions. The first extended the life of the Section 5 provisions another ten years; the second similarly extended the Act's bilingual requirements. The third proposed amending section 2 in response to *Mobile;* if adopted, it would have deleted the words "to deny or abridge" in the existing Section 2 and substituted in their place "in a manner which results in a denial or abridgement of."

In the House, the hearings and legislative debate focused almost exclusively on these first two issues, primarily on how the preclearance provisions should be structured and the conditions under which covered jurisdictions should be able to "bailout" of coverage once they had been included. In the House, very little attention was focused on Rodino's proposed amendment to Section 2. It was noteworthy that the Department of Justice and the White House did not get involved during the House proceedings, declining to appear before the Subcommittee to express its views on any of the bills being considered.]

[...] On June 24, the Subcommittee gathered for the only day of hearings devoted exclusively to the section 2 issue. In preparation for this day, Mr. Edwards requested that Chairman Rodino and Congressman Hyde state their positions on section 2 before the witnesses appeared. Hyde's response, dated June 23, supported the intent standard articulated in *Mobile*, contending that it was totally consistent with the Court's earlier ruling in *White v. Regester*. Congressman Hyde also endorsed the *White* requirement that the political process be "equally open" to all and suggested a disclaimer which "specifically states that proportional representation is not necessarily required as a result of statistical imbalance and polarized voting.' " Rodino's original letter, in response to Edwards' request, was shelved in favor of another, dated July 14, after the Hyde submission and after the June 24 testimony. Chairman Rodino again claimed that what Congress had intended in 1965 was a broader standard than the Court had interpreted in *Mobile*. Rodino argued that the test for identifying discrimination in section 2 should be governed by the extent to which racial and language minority groups are denied "access" to the political process "through vote dilution and other discriminatory devices and practices." ... The focus of much of the testimony was on the meaning of the Court's 1973 decision in *White v. Regester*....

[In the full Committee, an amendment added a disclaimer to the original Rodino language. The disclaimer provided that "[t]he fact that members of a minority group have not been elected in numbers equal to the group's proportion of the population shall not, in and of itself, constitute a violation of this section." The new language was intended to cool apprehensions about the use of proportional representation as a remedy for section 2 violations].

[...] H.R. 3112 then was passed by the House of Representatives by the one-sided vote of 389 to twenty-four, with thirty members not voting. The extraordinary efforts of the civil rights lobby had achieved its purpose. The long hours of planning and congressional contact had borne fruit. As one NAACP representative said:

> Whatever I asked for that I needed I got: money, executive director's and staff time.... We normally have a variety of issues we work on, but in this case I had all my staff working on it.

Said another:

> [A]s long as I have been in Washington, this [has been] one of the most amazing, most historical events of my career.... It was beautiful, I'm happy I had the chance to participate and be instrumental in this; I'll never forget this in my life, never....

IV. THE SENATE

A. Pre–Committee

The Senate bill [originally S. 895, then changed to S.1992] was introduced by Senator Edward M. Kennedy of Massachusetts and Senator Charles Mathias, Jr. of Maryland.... Apart from the principal sponsors of S. 895, Senator Kennedy and Mathias, the key participants in the extension debate were conservative Senators, Strom Thurmond of South Carolina and Orrin Hatch of Utah. Both occupied leadership positions on the Judiciary Committee, with Thurmond serving as Chairman of the Committee and Hatch serving as Chairman of the Judiciary Subcommittee on the Constitution. S. 895 and related voting rights legislation had been referred to this Committee.

The civil rights records of Thurmond and Hatch differed considerably from those of Kennedy and Mathias. Senator Thurmond had only ascended to the chairmanship of the Judiciary Committee at the beginning of the year when the Republicans won control of the Senate. However, he had been in the Senate for nearly three decades and had developed a reputation in some quarters as an opponent of most federal civil rights legislation, although more recently he had cast a critical vote in support of a constitutional amendment providing for voting representation in Congress for the predominantly minority population of the District of Columbia. As one of the most dedicated advocates of the doctrine of state's rights, the South Carolinian had voted against the passage of the original Voting Rights Act in 1965, as well as the 1970 and 1975 amendments. Senator Hatch, in his first term of office, had never before cast a vote on the Voting Rights Act but already had acquired a reputation as an articulate critic of many of the initiatives of the civil rights leadership. He had been the leading congressional critic of "affirmative action" and racial quota programs on constitutional grounds, and had led a successful filibuster during the ninety-sixth Congress, that blocked efforts to expand Title VIII of the Fair Housing Act of 1968. His objection had been to efforts to establish a standard of defining housing discrimination that focused upon the statistical "effects" of an allegedly discriminatory action rather than upon the motivation of the alleged discriminator. Kennedy and Mathias, on the other hand, had each been in Congress for approximately twenty years and had cast "aye" votes on the original Voting Rights Act and both extensions. Both consistently endorsed the legislative objectives of the civil rights leadership and often had led fights on their behalf.

Following final House action on H.R. 3112, the strategies of both sides began to emerge. The supporters' principle objective was the perpetuation of the momentum that had been built up in the House.... The most significant fact about S. 1992, however, was that it was co-sponsored by sixty-one Senators.

... In the meantime, the strategy of those who had misgivings about HR 3112 included the enlistment of active participation by the Administration in the form of support for an alternative. They attempted to slow down the legislative process so that they could inform their colleagues about what they perceived as difficulties with the House version. To a far greater extent than is normally the case with congressional hearings, the Senate hearings on S. 1992 seemed designed to highlight defects in the legislation through debate between some of the most articulate civil rights academics and lawyers in the country.

Critics of H.R. 3112 were nearly as successful in achieving their short term objectives prior to the outset of Senate hearings as were proponents.... The Administration had played virtually no role in House deliberations on the extension of the Voting Rights Act....

On October 2, three days before the House vote, Attorney General William French Smith forwarded a private report to the President summarizing the development of the Voting Rights Act and setting forth five alternatives for consideration. In retrospect, the most striking aspect of the recommendations, which were prepared in close collaboration with the office of Assistant Attorney General for Civil Rights, William Bradford Reynolds, was its cursory reference to the issue of section 2. Under the heading "Other Considerations," a single paragraph in the twenty-one page report addressed the section 2 controversy. Most significantly, it concluded "we are opposed to including in the Administration proposal any amendment of section 2 that suggests the incorporation of an 'effects' test." The report focused almost exclusively on the issue of bailout.

On November 6, following more than a month of debate within the White House, President Reagan issued a highly ambiguous statement. The statement expressed support for a ten-year extension.... Finally, Reagan stated that the Act should retain the intent test rather than incorporating a "new and untested" effects or results standard.

The President's announcement served as a beacon for Senate skeptics of the House legislation, most of whom had been urging opposition to H.R. 3112, in its various forms, for many months. Critics quickly accelerated efforts to build a case in favor of alternatives to the House measure and to communicate them to their colleagues. Well before hearings even had been scheduled, large amounts of literature were distributed to Senate offices by both sides.

An imbalance in lobbying resources characterized the entire Senate debate on the Voting Rights Act much as it had in the House. On the proponents' side, an impressive array of organizations such as MALDEF, the NAACP, and the ACLU, coordinated efforts to secure Senate adoption of the House bill. Spearheaded by the Leadership Conference on Civil Rights, supporters of the House bill included virtually all significant civil rights, labor, civil liberties, public interest, and religious organizations. These organizations were effective in lobbying Senators, just as they had been in the House, communicating to them strong civil rights support for adoption of a mirror image of H.R. 3112.... The imbalance in lobbying resources was more apparent in the context of these amendments than in any major civil rights legislation to come before the Congress in recent years. The Administration proved not only to be the most valuable ally of those with apprehensions about the House bill, but virtually their only ally....

B. *The Subcommittee*

On January 27, 1982, shortly after the start of the second session of Congress, and after several initial delays, the Subcommittee on the Constitution began the first of eight scheduled days of hearings; a ninth was later added. The opening statement of Chairman Hatch made clear that the focal point of Senate hearings would be the results test contained in the amended section 2. In a lengthy statement, Hatch sought to dispel what he referred to as "myths" surrounding the extension of the Act. He observed, "The debate beginning in the Senate today will focus upon a proposed change in the Act that involves one of the most important constitutional issues ever to come before this body. Involved in this debate will be the most fundamental issues involving the nature of American representative democracy, federalism, civil rights, and the separation of powers." Hatch went on to argue that the proposed change in section 2, from an intent test to a results test, would redefine the concept of "discrimination" and would "transform the Fifteenth Amendment and the Voting Rights Act from provisions designed to ensure equal access and equal opportunity in the electoral process to those designed to ensure equal outcome and equal success."

For the first time during congressional consideration of the Voting Rights Act extension, the issue of the proposed change to section 2 was moved to the forefront of debate. In this regard, Senators Thurmond and

Hatch differed in their emphases during committee consideration. Thurmond, since he represented a state that had been covered since the inception of the Act in 1965, was now principally concerned with what he perceived as a need for a more effective bailout procedure for covered jurisdictions of the South. As a result, Senator Thurmond directed his primary attention toward a reform of section 5....

Senator Hatch, though, was preoccupied with section 2. Because of his involvement with the amendments to Title VIII of the 1968 Civil Rights Act, he had become sensitive to the abandonment of intent as a basis for identifying racial discrimination. His efforts in re-evaluating affirmative action programs represented similar apprehensions about the recent evolution of national civil rights policy.

The two leading Senatorial proponents of S. 1992, Mathias and Kennedy, delivered opening statements after Hatch, with Mathias speaking from the witness stand rather than from the committee podium. Hatch closely questioned both Senators.

Senator Mathias chose to concentrate his remarks on the question of section 2:

> The House amendment is needed to clarify the burden of proof in voting discrimination cases and to remove the uncertainty caused by the failure of the Supreme Court to articulate a clear standard in the *City of Mobile v. Bolden*.... We are not trying to overrule the Court. The Court seems to be in some error about what the legislative intent was.... Prior to *Bolden*, a violation in voting discrimination cases [could] be shown by reference to a variety of factors that, when taken together, added up to a finding of illegal discrimination. But in *Bolden,* the plurality appears to have abandoned this totality of circumstances approach and to have replaced it with a requirement of specific evidence of intent ... this is a requirement of a smoking gun, and I think it becomes a crippling blow to the overall effectiveness of the Act.

Hatch then initiated a line of questioning that was to be repeated on a number of occasions throughout the hearings. He requested that Mathias be more specific concerning the overall objectives of the new section 2 test:

> SENATOR MATHIAS: The purpose of the bill is to provide for fair and just access to the electoral process.
>
> SENATOR HATCH: Is [it] the most fair and just access-if 55% of Baltimore is black, that 55% ought to be represented as sole black districts or at least majority black districts.
>
> SENATOR MATHIAS: A fair and just operation of the electoral process is to give all citizens equal access to vote, run, or otherwise participate in the process.
>
> SENATOR HATCH: What does "equal access" mean?

SENATOR MATHIAS: You are well aware of what it means.

SENATOR HATCH: I want to know what you think it means, because I know what it means under the effects test. I think it means, as the Attorney General of the United States does, proportional representation.

SENATOR MATHIAS: You look at the totality of circumstances; that is what we have been doing.

SENATOR HATCH: That is what we do under the intent standard. I am quite confused as to relevance of these circumstances that you are considering in their totality.... I do not understand what the question is that the court asks itself in evaluating the totality of circumstances under the results test? What precisely does the court ask itself after it has looked to the totality of circumstances and what is the standard for evaluation under the results test?

SENATOR MATHIAS: Look at the results.

SENATOR HATCH: That is all? And if there was absolutely no intent to discrimination, as they found in the *Mobile* case, if the results looked like discrimination, then would the court be able to come down on that jurisdiction—on Baltimore, for example?

Senator Hatch inquired throughout the hearings about the significance of the "totality of circumstances" description of the proposed results test. Hatch's chief goal seemed to create a distinction between the scope of permissible evidence under a test for discrimination and the standard for evaluating such evidence. The distinction normally was couched in terms of what threshold question should judges ask in attempting to evaluate evidence before them in a section 2 proceeding. It was not until much later in the hearing process that proponents of the House bill seemed prepared to respond to this query. In Hatch's view, however, a reasonable and comprehensible response was never forthcoming.

... The themes highlighted by Hatch, as well as by proponents of the House measure, were restated frequently during the remaining eight days of hearings. Although occasional discussion of the merits of the new bailout standard relating to section 5 occurred, the consistent focus of the hearings remained upon the meaning and wisdom of the proposed results test in section 2. The principle elements of controversy regarding section 2 were as follows:

(1) *Whether the results standard was reflective of the law existing prior to the Mobile decision.* This question was important in determining whether Hatch's predictions of proportional representation were credible. If the results standard merely reflected the understanding of the law prior to *Mobile*, Hatch would have difficulty demonstrating that an explicit restatement of the results standard in section 2 to overturn *Mobile* would lead to proportional representation. While Hatch occasionally argued that some of

the decisions interpreting the effects standard of section 5 established a remedy of proportional representation, his principal argument was that the law on section 2, prior to *Mobile*, had never been anything other than an intent standard. Thus, the absence of proportional representation requirements in the past was largely irrelevant. In this regard, Hatch frequently quoted Justice Stewart's comments in *Mobile*....

To the extent that Hatch was successful in demonstrating that the results test represented a new test, one that had not existed prior to the *Mobile* decision, he was far more likely to be credible in suggesting that the impact of this test would be unwise public policy or, at best, uncertain.

In contrast, supporters of H.R. 3112 took issue with both Hatch and Justice Stewart. Laughlin McDonald, the Director of the Southern Regional Office of the American Civil Liberties Union, argued that *Mobile* required proof of intent and, therefore, was a "change in the law." McDonald continued, "Prior to *Mobile*, it was understood by lawyers trying these cases and by the judges who were hearing them that a violation of voting rights could be made out upon proof of a bad purpose or effect ... *Mobile* had a dramatic effect on our cases." ...

(2) *Whether the results standard would inevitably lead to proportional representation.* Although virtually all witnesses on both sides of the debate claimed to reject the notion of proportional representation as desirable public policy, the critical issue in the entire debate was whether the results test would lead to a political regime in which proportional representation of racial and ethnic groups became the standard on which voting rights violations would be predicated. Critics of H.R. 3112 repeatedly attacked the results test as one which could lead to such a situation. Assistant Attorney General for Civil Rights Reynolds remarked that the proposed amendment to section 2 might lead to the use of "quotas" in the election process, and that local units of government would be required to "present compelling justification for any voting system which does not lead to proportional representation." Dr. Berns similarly concluded that the amendment would reverse *Mobile* and authorize "[f]ederal courts to require States to change their laws to ensure that minorities will be elected in proportion to their numbers." Defenders of the amendment assumed that the results test represented a restatement of the law prior to *Mobile*. They argued that proportional representation had not resulted from federal court decisions during this period. As McDonald observed, "I cannot ... think of a single case in which we have won, in which we have settled, in which the courts have ruled for us under the Constitution or under section 2 ... which have resulted in proportional representation.... As an actual matter, we have never gotten proportional representation." To a large extent, the common rejection of proportional representation by proponents and critics of H.R. 3112 masked more fundamental problems of definition.

(3) *What was meant by the results test if not proportional representation.* Hatch argued that the test either would lead to proportional represen-

tation or that the test had no comprehensible meaning. If the test had no such meaning, he felt it was likely to invest the federal courts with sharply enhanced authority to substitute their own policy preferences on voting practices and electoral structures for the policies of state legislatures and local elected bodies.

Hatch asked of witnesses what the "core value" was of the results test. In the absence of any clearly defined value, Hatch argued that the totality of circumstances response, relied on by proponents of the House measure, was "unsatisfactory." To speak of the scope of permissible evidence in the context of the totality of circumstances missed the point, in his judgement. Any test, including the intent test, encouraged consideration of the totality of circumstances. The crucial inquiry involved determining the threshold question asked by a court in evaluating evidence; in other words, the standard by which the totality of circumstances would be judged. [Hatch] further complained that efforts to elicit greater guidance on the meaning of the test had degenerated into "wholly uninstructive statements of the sort that 'you know discrimination when you see it,'" or else "increasingly explicit references to the numerical and statistical comparisons that are tools of proportional representation." Initial difficulties on the part of supporters in either understanding or responding to inquiries about the "core value" of the results test soon changed. Supporters responded to such inquiries by referring either to the specific factors outlined by the Court in *White v. Regester* or by the lower federal courts in *Zimmer v. McKeithen*. Professor Norman Dorsen, of the New York University School of Law and President of the American Civil Liberties Union, was among the first to concede that the totality of circumstances description of the results test was inadequate. He relied on Justice White's remarks in *White* to provide a more useful description of the new test. In *White*, Justice White stated that "[t]he plaintiffs' burden is to produce evidence to support findings that the political processes leading to nomination and election were not equally open to participation by the group in question." Justice White's language eventually was debated in the context of the compromise offered as an alternative to the House language after the completion of Senate hearings.

(4) *Whether the disclaimer of proportional representation contained in the House proposal was effective.* Supporters of H.R. 3112 constantly argued that the amendment would not result in proportional representation because of the "disclaimer" in the new section 2.... Critics of the test were concerned that the disclaimer posed no serious barrier to a mandate of proportional representation. They, however, also recognized the internal political difficulties that the disclaimer posed. A casual observer of these amendments, several Senators noted, could not help but assume that the disclaimer language established at least some significant obstacle to the judicial transformation of the results test into a test of proportional representation....

(5) *The meaning of the intent test.* Just as critics and proponents differed on the proper meaning of the proposed results test, the two sides in the Voting Rights Amendments debate repeatedly disagreed about the meaning of the intent test, which Hatch, Thurmond and the Reagan Administration wished to preserve. Proponents of the results test repeatedly characterized the intent standard as requiring direct evidence of discriminatory purpose or intent such as overt statements of bigotry or evidence of a "smoking gun." Proponents also felt that the intent test required courts to "mind read" in order to discern the intentions of "long-dead" legislators. Dr. Arthur Fleming, Chairman of the United of States Commission on Civil Rights, and an outspoken opponent of the intent test, contended that "inquiries [into intent] can only be divisive, threatening to destroy any existing racial progress in a community. It is the intent test, not the results test, that would make it necessary to brand individuals as racist in order to obtain judicial relief." ...

(6) *What was Congress' original intent in passing section 2 of the Voting Rights Act.* The final major issue related to whether Congress' intent in 1965 was compatible with the newly proposed results test. Critics of the test argued that even if the lower federal courts had adopted a results test in their pre-*Mobile* interpretation of section 2 (which they declined to concede), the original intent of Congress had been the establishment of a test in section 2 premised upon the traditional standard of intent or purpose. The Subcommittee Report found it particularly persuasive that Congress chose not to utilize the effects language in section 2 that Congress had expressly incorporated into sections 4 and 5. Congress also had exhaustively debated the concept of an effects standard in the context of sections 4 and 5, but had not in the context of section 2.

Proponents of the results test responded by pointing to the sparse legislative history existing on the meaning of section 2. Relying upon statements by former Attorney General Nicholas Katzenbach, they concluded that Congress was aware of the competing definitions of "discrimination" and intended that section 2 cover voting rights violations established under either. Ironically, critics of the results test also relied upon the former Attorney General's remarks in 1965 to establish their case as to the original legislative intent....

Concluding the March 1 hearing, as well as the entire sequence of hearings on Voting Rights Act Amendments, Senator Hatch reaffirmed his commitment to the idea of nondiscrimination and perhaps in anticipation of forthcoming legislative events, remarked that:

> Whatever the outcome of this debate, I personally hope that we will be able to say a decade from now that we did what was right; I personally hope that we will not have to say a decade from now that no one really appreciated at the time what section 2 was all about.

[The Subcommittee then reported a version of the bill to the full Senate Judiciary Committee].

C. *The Full Committee*

During a thirty day hiatus between Subcommittee and full Committee action, intensive lobbying and negotiations took place within the Judiciary Committee, much as it had in the House, between members and judiciary Committee and outside organizations, notably the Leadership staff of the Committee Administration and the leadership of the Conference on Civil Rights....

As final Committee action approached, a general feeling seemed to exist among members of the Committee that they wished to remain supportive of the mass of outside organizations lobbying for the House version, while at the same time responding to the potentially explosive issue of proportional representation and electoral quotas.

On April 24, Senator Robert Dole of Kansas, one of the few remaining undecided members of the Committee, accorded them this opportunity by proposing a compromise on both sections 2 and 5 that was designed to reconcile the two competing viewpoints on the Committee. Formulated in coordination with representatives of the Leadership Conference, the new language on section 2 proposed to retain the results language of H.R. 3112, but to append a new subsection attempting to describe its parameters in greater detail....

Since Senator Dole was in a politically critical position in the center of the Committee, the proposed compromise effectively resolved any remaining doubts about the fate of the Voting Rights Act in the Senate and in the entire Congress....

Since the Dole compromise had been coordinated with leaders of the civil rights community, it carried with it the support of the original sponsors of S. 1992, Senators Kennedy and Mathias. In addition, the Dole compromise attracted the support of each of the other Committee co-sponsors as well as Senator Heflin. Faced with this show of bipartisan support, several Republican conservatives who had been leaning toward the Subcommittee version rather than the original also opted for the compromises.

On May 3, one day before the Judiciary Committee was finally to consider S. 1992, the Administration, unsuccessful in brokering alternative compromises, also joined in support of the compromise. President Reagan announced then that "the compromise would greatly strengthen the safeguards against proportional representation while also protecting the basic right to vote." Attorney General Smith and Assistant Attorney General Reynolds followed with similar statements.

The Dole proposal effectively supplied a political resolution to misgivings about section 2. It did not, however, put to rest the considerable confusion over what the compromise ultimately was intended to mean. During most of the remaining debate in the Senate, each side attempted to explain the reach of the Dole provision. When the full Committee commenced debate on the extension on April 28, Senator Dole explained the purpose of his language in the following manner:

> Proponents of the results standard in the Mathias–Kennedy bill persuasively argue that intentional discrimination is too difficult to prove to make enforcement of the law effective. Perhaps, more importantly, they have asked if the right to exercise a franchise has been denied or abridged, why should plaintiffs have to prove that the deprivation of this fundamental right was intentional. On the other hand, many on the Committee have expressed legitimate concerns that a results standard could be interpreted by the courts to mandate proportional representation.... The supporters of this compromise believe that a voting practice or procedure which is discriminatory in result should not be allowed to stand regardless of whether there exists a discriminatory purpose or intent.... However, we also feel that the legislation should be strengthened with additional language delineating what legal standard should apply under the results test and clarifying that it is not a mandate for proportional representation. Thus, our compromise adds a new subsection to section 2 which codifies language from the 1973 Supreme Court decision of *White v. Regester*.

The compromise was met with sharp criticism from Senator Hatch, who recognized that the Dole provision inevitably would replace the Subcommittee language. He raised a number of points designed to demonstrate that the Dole compromise was largely an "illusory" one, and that the impact of the provision was not likely to be different from the unamended House provision. Hatch made the following points with regard to the compromise: (1) the emphasis upon the totality of circumstances perpetuated the confusion that proponents of the results test had generated between the scope of the permissible evidence and the standard by which such evidence would be evaluated in a court; (2) in Hatch's view, no "core value" existed by which a results test could judge discriminatory conduct other than by a proportional representation analysis, and nothing in the compromise language established any alternative; (3) the compromise also perpetuated confusion between proportional representation as a right and proportional representation as a remedy; (4) as with the original results language, the flaw was not with an inadequately strong disclaimer of proportional representation, but with the central notion itself of a results test; (5) the concept of an "equally open" system did nothing to address the problem of legislative guidance to the courts; and (6) the concept of "protected groups" within the language of the compromise was inconsistent with the Act's original intent to protect the right of individuals, not groups, to cast their votes.

Immediately prior to final Judiciary Committee consideration of amendments to the Subcommittee bill, Hatch engaged Dole in a series of questions designed further to draw out Dole's intent in developing the compromise language.... When Hatch asked about the relationship between Dole's compromise and the *White v. Regester* test, Senator Dole said that the compromise carried forth the *White v. Regester* test. He argued that the *White v. Regester* test did not require proportional representation nor did it invalidate at-large election systems. Dole subsequently reiterated that the existence of an at-large system would not, in and of itself, give rise to a violation in circumstances where there would not otherwise have been a violation. Finally, in probably the most ambiguous exchange between the two, Senator Dole was asked whether the compromise was designed to preclude courts from imposing proportional representation as a remedy for a section 2 violation. After first responding that the compromise did not so prohibit a court, Dole stated that such concerns were unwarranted because "it is a well established legal principle that remedies must be commensurate with the violation established."

[The Committee approved the Dole compromise amendment, which became part of the enacted version of the VRA, and issued the Senate Committee Report, excerpts of which are printed below].

V. Conclusion

... The 1982 Amendments to the Voting Rights Act were significant in what they failed to say, in addition to what the new statute finally contained. The alterations to sections 5 and 2 will be litigated for years to come, with the apparent legislative intent to broaden both sections at the fulcrum of the debate.

... As so often happens in complex legislative matters, particularly where highly charged emotional issues are involved, the federal judiciary will ultimately have to tell Congress what it intended to achieve in its 1982 Amendments to sections 2 and 5. Indeed, the very constitutionality of these provisions will be the subject of considerable debate in the courts in the years ahead. While some compromises promote stability of the law, others merely postpone difficult policy decisions. The undeniably substantial controversies involved in the Voting Rights Act debate must finally be resolved; when they are, they will contribute in great measure toward a definition of the objectives of civil rights policy in the United States for the next generation....

3. Excerpts From the Senate Judiciary Committee Report

Apart from the text of a statute itself, courts typically view the formal committee reports, which accompany the referral of a bill from committee to the full House or Senate, as the most authoritative documents concerning the purposes of legislation. Because Section 2 received so little focus in the House, and only became the center of attention in the Senate, the most extensive discussion from the legislative history on Section 2 was that provided in the Senate Judiciary Committee Report. This Report has been invoked frequently by courts construing Section 2, and we reproduce the most important excerpts, including majority, dissenting and concurring views.

Senate Report No. 97–417 (1982)

S. 1992 amends Section 2 of the Voting Rights Act of 1965 to prohibit any voting practice, or procedure [that] results in discrimination. This amendment is designed to make clear that proof of discriminatory intent is not required to establish a violation of Section 2. It thereby restores the legal standards, based on the controlling Supreme Court precedents, which applied in voting discrimination claims prior to the litigation involved in *Mobile v. Bolden*. The amendment also adds a new subsection to Section 2 which delineates the legal standards under the results test by codifying the leading pre-*Bolden* vote dilution case, *White v. Regester*.

This new subsection provides that the issue to be decided under the results test is whether the political processes are equally open to minority voters. The new subsection also states that the section does not establish a right to proportional representation.

* * *

VI. AMENDMENT TO SECTION 2 OF THE VOTING RIGHTS ACT

A. Overview: Proposed Amendment to Section 2

The proposed amendment to Section 2 of the Voting Rights Act is designed to restore the legal standard that governed voting discrimination cases prior to the Supreme Court's decision in *Bolden*.

In pre-*Bolden* cases plaintiffs could prevail by showing that a challenged election law or procedure, in the context of the total circumstances of the local electoral process, had the result of denying a racial or language minority an equal chance to participate in the electoral process. Under this results test, it was not necessary to demonstrate that the challenged election law or procedure was designed or maintained for a discriminatory purpose.

In *Bolden*, a plurality of the Supreme Court broke with precedent and substantially increased the burden on plaintiffs in voting discrimination cases by requiring proof of discriminatory purpose. The Committee has concluded that this intent test places an unacceptably difficult burden on plaintiffs. It diverts the judicial inquiry from the crucial question of whether minorities have equal access to the electoral process to a historical question of individual motives.

In our view, proof of discriminatory purpose should not be a prerequisite to establishing a violation of Section 2 of the Voting Rights Act.

B. THE ORIGINAL LEGISLATIVE INTENT AS TO SECTION 2

The Committee amendment rejecting a requirement that discriminatory purpose be proved to establish a violation of Section 2 is fully consistent with the original legislative understanding of section 2 when the Act was passed in 1965.

Advocates of an intent requirement for Section 2 cite statements in the legislative history of the 1965 Act to the effect that Section 2 was designed to track the Fifteenth Amendment, whose wording it follows. They suggest that the Fifteenth Amendment has always been understood to require proof of discriminatory purpose. They claim that, inasmuch as Congress chose to track the Fifteenth Amendment, Congress also must have sought to impose an intent standard in section 2. [Thus] they argue that the Committee amendment is not consistent with the original understanding of Section 2.

Whether the Fifteenth or Fourteenth Amendment were understood by Congress in 1965 to embody an intent requirement is ultimately of limited relevance. However, the Committee has examined the legislative history of the 1965 enactment, relevant legislative history from the 1970 extension of the Act, and the general understanding in 1965 of what is required to establish a Fifteenth Amendment violation. We find no persuasive evidence to support the argument outlined above that Congress made proof of discriminatory purpose an essential requirement of Section 2 when it was first enacted....

The *Bolden* Case

... A fair reading of *Bolden* reveals that the plurality opinion was a marked departure from earlier Supreme Court and lower court vote dilution cases. As Judge Goldberg wrote in *Jones v. City of Lubbock*, 640 F.2d 777 (5th Cir.1981), "the Supreme Court (in *Bolden*) completely changed the mode of assessing the legality of electoral schemes alleged to discriminate against a class of citizens."

In *Bolden*, the plurality abandoned the clear and workable totality of circumstances test of *White*, but in doing so it failed to articulate a substitute standard to guide federal courts in the future. As Justice White noted in his dissent in *Bolden*, the plurality's rejection of the *White* test, "leaves the courts below adrift on uncharted seas ..."

The impact of *Bolden* upon voting dilution litigation became apparent almost immediately after the Court's decision was handed down on April 22, 1980. As the Subcommittee heard throughout its hearing, after *Bolden* litigators virtually stopped filing new voting dilution cases. Moreover, the decision had a direct impact on voting dilution cases that were making their way through the federal judicial system.

* * *

D. THE OPERATION OF AMENDED SECTION 2

The amendment to the language of Section 2 is designed to make clear that plaintiffs need not prove a discriminatory purpose in the adoption or maintenance of the challenged system or practice in order to establish a violation. Plaintiffs must either prove such intent, or, alternatively, must show that the challenged system or practice, in the context of all the circumstances in the jurisdiction in question, results in minorities being denied equal access to the political process.

The "results" standard is meant to restore the pre-*Mobile* legal standard which governed cases challenging election systems or practices as an illegal dilution of the minority vote. Specifically, subsection (b) embodies the test laid down by the Supreme Court in *White*.

If the plaintiff proceeds under the "results test," then the court would assess the impact of the challenged structure or practice on the basis of objective factors, rather than making a determination about the motivations which lay behind its adoption or maintenance.

As the Supreme Court has repeatedly noted, discriminatory election systems or practices which operate, designedly or otherwise, to minimize or cancel out the voting strength and political effectiveness of minority groups, are an impermissible denial of the right to have one's vote fully count, just as much as outright denial of access to the ballot box.

In adopting the "result standard" as articulated in *White v. Regester*, the Committee has codified the basic principle in that case as it was applied prior to the *Mobile* litigation.

The Committee has concluded that *White*, and the decisions following it, made no finding and required no proof as to the motivation or purpose behind the practice or structure in question. Regardless of differing interpretations of *White* and *Whitcomb*, however, and despite the plurality opinion in *Mobile* that ... *White* involves an "ultimate" requirement of proving discriminatory purpose, the specific intent of this amendment is that the plaintiffs may choose to establish discriminatory results without proving any kind of discriminatory purpose.

Section 2 protects the right of minority voters to be free from election practices, procedures or methods, that deny them the same opportunity to participate in the political process as other citizens enjoy.

If as a result of the challenged practice or structure plaintiffs do not have an equal opportunity to participate in the political processes and to elect candidates of their choice, there is a violation of this section. To establish a violation, plaintiffs could show a variety of factors, depending upon the kind of rule, practice, or procedure called into question.

Typical factors include:

1. The extent of any history of official discrimination in the state or political subdivision that touched the right of the members of the minority group to register, to vote, or otherwise to participate in the democratic process;

2. The extent to which voting in the elections of the state or political subdivision is racially polarized;

3. The extent to which voting in the elections of the state or political subdivision has used unusually large election districts, majority vote requirements, anti-single shot provisions, or other voting practices or procedures that may enhance the opportunity for discrimination against the minority group;

4. If there is a candidate slating process, whether the members of the minority group have been denied access to that process;

5. The extent to which members of the minority group in the state or political subdivision bear the effects of discrimination in such areas as education, employment and health, which hinder their ability to participate effectively in the political process;

6. Whether political campaigns have been characterized by overt or subtle racial appeals;

7. The extent to which members of the minority group have been elected to public office in the jurisdiction.

Additional factors that in some cases have had probative value as part of plaintiff's evidence to establish a violation are: whether there is a significant lack of responsiveness on the part of elected officials to the particularized needs of the members of the minority group, and whether the policy underlying the state or political subdivision's use of such voting qualification, prerequisite to voting, or standard, practice or procedure is tenuous. While these enumerated factors will often be the most relevant ones, in some cases other factors will be indicative of the alleged dilution.

The cases demonstrate, and the Committee intends, that there is no requirement that any particular number of factors be proved, or that a majority of them point one way or the other.

* * *

DISCLAIMER

When a federal judge is called upon to determine the validity of a practice challenged under Section 2, as amended, he or she is required to act in full accordance with the disclaimer in Section 2 which reads as follows:

The extent to which members of a protected class have been elected to office in the State or political subdivision is one "circumstance" which may be considered, provided that nothing in this section establishes a right to have members of a protected class elected in numbers equal to their proportion in the population.

Contrary to assertions made during the full Committee mark-up of the legislation, this provision is both clear and straightforward.

This disclaimer is entirely consistent with the above mentioned Supreme Court and Court of Appeals precedents, which contain similar statements regarding the absence of any right to proportional representation. It puts to rest any concerns that have been voiced about racial quotas.

The basic principle of equity that the remedy fashioned must be commensurate with the right that has been violated provides adequate assurance, without disturbing the prior case law or prescribing in the statute mechanistic rules for formulating remedies in cases which necessarily depend upon widely varied proof and local circumstances. The court should exercise its traditional equitable powers to fashion the relief so that it completely remedies the prior dilution of minority voting strength and fully provides equal opportunity for minority citizens to participate and to elect candidates of their choice.

* * *

E. Responses to Questions Raised about the Results Test

Opponents of the "results test" codified by the Committee have made numerous allegations as to the potential dangers of its adoption. At bottom, all of these allegations proceed from two assumptions, both of which are demonstrably incorrect.

First, these allegations assume that the "results test" is a radically new and untested standard for voting discrimination suits, with unknown contours and unforeseeable consequences. Opponents nonetheless are somehow confident enough of the implications of this allegedly new standard to predict that it will: inevitably lead to a requirement of proportional representation for minority groups on elected bodies; make thousands of at-large election systems across the country either *per se* illegal or vulnerable on the basis of the slightest evidence of underrepresentation of minorities; and be a divisive factor in local communities by emphasizing the role of racial politics.

They specifically list a number of states and cities whose election systems they allege would be vulnerable under the Committee bill.

The second assumption, equally incorrect, is that the only way to safeguard against these dangers is to make proof of discriminatory intent an essential element of establishing violations of Section 2.

* * *

The Subcommittee Report claims that the results test *assumes* "that race is the predominant determinant of political preference." The Subcommittee Report notes that "in many cases racial bloc voting is not so monolithic, and that minority voters do receive substantial support from white voters."

That statement is correct, but misses the point. It is true with respect to most communities, and in those communities it would be exceedingly difficult for plaintiffs to show that they were effectively excluded from fair access to the political process under the results test.

Unfortunately, however, there still are some communities in our Nation where racial politics do dominate the electoral process.

In the context of such racial bloc voting, and other factors, a particular election method can deny minority voters equal opportunity to participate meaningfully in elections.

To suggest that it is the results test, carefully applied by the courts, which is responsible for those instances of intensive racial politics, is like saying that it is the doctor's thermometer which causes high fever.

The results test *makes no assumptions one way or the other* about the role of racial political considerations in a particular community. If plaintiffs assert that they are denied fair access to the political process, in part, because of the racial bloc voting context within which the challenged election system works, they would have to prove it.

Proponents of the "intent standard" however, do presume that such racial politics no longer affect minority voters in America. This presumption ignores a regrettable reality established by overwhelming evidence at the Senate and House hearing.

These conclusions, based on a careful review of the existing track record under the "results test" in the Committee amendment have convinced us that the questions raised by some about that test are satisfactorily answered by that record.

F. The Limitations of the Intent Test

The intent test is inappropriate as the exclusive standard for establishing a violation of Section 2. This is so for several reasons. During the hearing, there was considerable discussion of the difficulty often encountered in meeting the intent test, but that is not the principal reason why we have rejected it.

The main reason is that, simply put, the test asks the wrong questions. In the *Bolden* case on remand, the district court after a tremendous expenditure of resources by the parties and the court, concluded that officials had acted more than 100 years ago for discriminatory motives. However, if an electoral system operates today to exclude blacks or Hispanics from a fair chance to participate, then the matter of what motives were in an official's mind 100 years ago is of the most limited relevance. The standard under the Committee amendment is whether minorities have equal access to the process of electing their representative. If they are denied a fair opportunity to participate, the Committee believes that the system should be changed, regardless of what may or may not be provable about events which took place decades ago.

Second, the Committee has heard persuasive testimony that the intent test is unnecessarily divisive because it involves charges of racism on the part of individual officials or entire communities.... Third, the intent test will be an inordinately difficult burden for plaintiffs in most cases. In the case of laws enacted many decades ago, the legislators cannot be subpoenaed from their graves for testimony about the motive behind their actions. Further, whatever the uneven extent of the legislative records for State legislative session of 50 or 100 years ago, it is clear that most counties and smaller cities will not have available the kind of official records and newspaper files which the plaintiffs were able to procure for the retrial of *Mobile*.

In the case of more recent enactments, the courts may rule that plaintiffs face barriers of "legislative immunity," both as to the motives involved in the legislative process and as to the motives of the majority electorate when an election law has been adopted or maintained as the result of a referendum.

Moreover, recent enactments, and future ones, are those most likely to pose the fundamental defect of relying exclusively on an intent standard, namely, the defendant's ability to offer a non-racial rationalization as the result of a referendum.

This defect cannot be cured completely even though plaintiffs are allowed to establish discriminatory intent by use of a wide variety of circumstantial and indirect evidence, including proof of the same factors used to establish a discriminatory result. The inherent danger in exclusive reliance on proof of motivations lies not only in the difficulties of plaintiffs establishing a prima facie case of discrimination, but also in the fact that the defendants can attempt to rebut that circumstantial evidence by planting a false trail of direct evidence in the form of official resolutions, sponsorship statements and other legislative history eschewing any racial motive, and advancing other governmental objective. So long as the court must make a separate ultimate finding of intent, after accepting the proof of the factors involved in the *White* analysis, that danger remains and seriously clouds the prospects or eradicating the remaining instances of racial discrimination in American elections....

* * *

ADDITIONAL VIEWS OF SENATOR ORRIN G. HATCH OF UTAH
Section 2 "Compromise"

The proposed amendment to section 2 contains two provisions. The first provision [adopts the results test].... For all the reasons outlined in the subcommittee report, I believe this provision to be dangerously misconceived.

The question then is whether or not the second provision—a new disclaimer of proportional representation—would mitigate any of these difficulties and improve upon the House disclaimer provision.... The "compromise" disclaimer refers to violation being established on the basis of the "totality of circumstances." This, I gather, is supposed to be helpful language. It is not. There is little question that, under either a results or an intent test, a court would look to the "totality of circumstances." The difference is that under the intent standard, unlike under the results standard, there is some ultimate core value against which to evaluate this "totality." Under the intent standard, the totality of evidence is placed before the court which must ultimately ask itself whether or not such evidence raises an inference of intent or purpose to discriminate. Under the results standard, there is no comparable and workable threshold question for the court. As one witness observed during subcommittee hearings

> Under the results test, once you have aggregated out those factors: what do you have? Where are you? You know it is the old thing we do in law school: you balance and you balance, but ultimately how do you balance? What is the core value?

There is no core value under the results test other than election results. There is no core value that can lead anywhere other than toward proportional representation by race and ethnic group. There is no ultimate or threshold question that a court must ask under the results test that will lead in any other direction.

* * *

More fundamentally, however, the purported "disclaimer" language in the amended section 2 is illusory for other reasons as protection against proportional representation.... It is illusory because the precise "right" involved in the new section 2 is not to proportional representation *per se* but to political processes that are "equally open to participation by members of a class of citizens protected by subsection (a)." The problem, in short, is that *this* right is one that can be intelligently defined only in terms that partake largely of proportional representation. This specific right—political processes "equally open to participation"—is one violated where there is a lack of proportional representation *plus* the existence of what have been referred to as "objective factors of discrimination." Such factors are described in greater detail in the subcommittee report, but the most significant of these factors is clearly the at-large electoral system. The at-large system is viewed by some in the civil rights community as an "objective factor of discrimination" because they believe that it serves as a "barrier" to minority electoral participation.

* * *

I would note, however, that in one important respect the provision is even more objectionable than the House provision. It refers expressly to the "right" of racial and selected ethnic groups to "elect representatives of their choice." This is little more than a euphemistic reference to the idea of a right in such groups to the establishment of safe and secure political ghettoes so that they can be assured of some measure of proportional representation. In this regard, I note the recent statement of Georgia State Senator Julian Bond with reference to a redistricting proposal in that State,

> I want this cohesive black community to have an opportunity to elect a candidate *of their choice*. White people see nothing wrong with having a 95% white district. Why can't we have a 68% black district?

That ultimately is what the so-called right to "elect candidates of one's choice" amounts to—the right to have established racially homogeneous districts to ensure proportional representation, through the election of specific number of Black, Hispanic, Indian, Aleutian, and Asian–American officeholders.

* * *

ADDITIONAL VIEWS OF SENATOR ROBERT DOLE

The Committee Report is an accurate statement of the intent of S. 1992, as reported by the Committee. However, I would like to add a few further comments concerning the language of the substitute amendment which I offered and the Committee adopted as it relates to Section 2 of the Voting Rights Act, and in particular, what I intended that the substitute accomplish and why it was needed.

* * *

While convinced of the inappropriateness of the "intent standard," however, I was also convinced that in order for this legislation to garner the broad bipartisan support which it deserved, the codification of the "results" test had to accompanied by language which alleviated fears that the standard could be interpreted as granting a right of proportional representation. During the hearing, this was a concern expressed by many and opposition to the results test was based primarily on this fear. Yet, during the hearings a unanimous consensus was established, among both the opponents and proponents of the results test, that the test for Section 2 claims should not be whether members of a protected class have achieved proportional representation. It was generally agreed that the concept of certain identifiable groups having a right to be elected in proportion to their voting potential was repugnant to the democratic principle upon which our society is based. Citizens of all races are entitled to have an equal chance of electing candidates of their choice, but if they are fairly afforded that opportunity, and lose, the law should offer no redress.

* * *

NOTES AND QUESTIONS ON THE SUBSTANCE OF THE 1982 AMENDMENTS

1. The 1982 amendments marked a significant shift in the nature of litigation under the Voting Rights Act. Between 1965 and 1982, virtually all litigation raised claims under section 5. Private plaintiffs challenged a variety of measures on the grounds that they constituted changes "with respect to voting" and therefore could not be implemented unless and until they had received preclearance from either the Department of Justice or the United States District Court for the District of Columbia. The objective of the litigation was thus to channel the assessment of the challenged practices into the administrative process. Section 2 was virtually never used. Prior to *Washington v. Davis*, 426 U.S. 229 (1976), and *Nevett v. Sides*, 571 F.2d 209 (5th Cir.1978), *cert. denied*, 446 U.S. 951 (1980), there was little reason to suppose the statutory standard was more protective than the constitutional one, and the plurality opinion in *Bolden* found that section 2 merely restated the constitutional prohibition. The 1982 amendments, however, squarely decoupled the statutory standard under section 2 from the constitutional standard under the Fourteenth or Fifteenth Amendments by rejecting the requirement that plaintiffs show a discriminatory purpose. The 1982 amendments dramatically changed the nature of racial vote dilution litigation, and since then, most of that litigation has taken place under section 2, rather than under either section 5 or the Constitution.

2. In the next chapter, we will see how courts gave content to the amended Section 2 through the process of statutory interpretation. Before seeing that process, consider your own understanding of what Congress did in 1982.

Did Congress develop a clear conception of vote dilution or discriminatory "results" when enacting the 1982 Amendments? It does seem clear that Congress understood itself to be effectively "overturning" or rejecting *Mobile v. Bolden*; but was there a consensus within Congress as to what *Bolden* meant, or what it meant for Congress to overturn it?

Rather than developing its own concept of vote dilution, Congress might perhaps instead be seen as simply incorporating into the statute the prior judicial caselaw that had been developing, case by case, on this question. On this view, Section 2 as amended simply sought to restore the pre-*Bolden* status quo on vote dilution. To the extent that is the way the 1982 Amendments should be seen, was that prior status quo itself clear enough to provide coherent content to the concept of vote dilution? Did Congress jump into the fray and seek to "codify" the judicial approach before the courts themselves had worked out a consistent and clear approach? Should Congress be seen as having essentially delegated the task to the courts of defining vote dilution and discriminatory "results" on a case-by-case basis? If so, would that be troubling or appropriate?

Some theorists of the legislative process argue that those in Congress are motivated to legislate in ways that enable them to gain credit among those who perceive legislation to be doing something good while avoiding responsibility for things that will be perceived as bad among other constituencies. *See generally* David Mayhew, Congress: The Electoral Connection (1974). One manifestation these incentives can take is for Congress to enact symbolic legislation; this is legislation that signals something positive to some constituents while not actually imposing any concrete costs. Another manifestation is for Congress to enact broadly worded legislation that postpones the difficult decisionmaking to agencies or courts; Congress can then claim credit for having addressed an issue while blaming agencies or courts when they make the inevitable difficult decisions, which impose real costs, that filling in the blank statutory terms will entail. For work developing these views, see, e.g., David Schoenbrod, Power without Responsibility: How Congress Abuses the People Through Delegation (1993); Michael Hayes, Lobbyists and Legislators: A Theory of the Political Process (1981).

Are these general theoretical claims about the legislative process borne out by the 1982 Amendments? If so, what implications, if any, follow?

3. Consider the Senate Report and the seven factors it lays out as guideposts for finding discriminatory results. Note that the Report then identifies two additional factors, and ultimately concludes that "there is no requirement that any particular number of factors be proved, or that a majority of them point one way or the other."

First, consider each factor alone and what kinds of difficulties it might pose for courts seeking to implement the congressional mandate. Which particular factors are most likely to be ones courts are likely to find manageable? Second, when courts try to look at these factors in the aggregate, how would they go about putting them together? That is, what kind of guidance has Congress provided when it lists a multitude of factors for courts to consider, then goes on to state that no one factor is necessary nor are any particular factors taken together sufficient? Are multi-factor tests like that in the Senate Report evidence that vote dilution can be determined only after a sophisticated, nuanced inquiry that will turn on subtle variables from case to case? Or are such tests evidence that Congress failed to develop any coherent concept of vote dilution, and simply threw a laundry list of factors at the courts?

Most importantly, recall the history of *Baker v. Carr, supra* Chapter 3, and the development of the one-vote, one-person doctrine. There the Court began doctrinal development with a recognition of the multitude of interests that districting might be thought to implicate; within a short time, however, the doctrine quickly came to give strict mathematical equality of district populations an absolute priority over any of these other interests (at least with respect to congressional districts). Recall the discussion there about the institutional and intellectual forces that might drive courts to take complex social problems and devise simple, rigid, easy-to-administer formulas for resolving them. Should one anticipate that a similar process will take place as the courts seek to transform Congress' multi-factor approach into administrable judicial doctrine? If so, around what factors do you think the judicial doctrine would likely coalesce?

Note that one factor that emerges as central in the Senate Report is the extent to which voting is "racially polarized." This factor is nowhere directly mentioned in the *White/Zimmer* line of cases; it starts to emerge in the Senate debates when proponents are forced to respond to Senator Hatch's argument that the amended Section 2 will guarantee proportional representation along racial lines. Does the emergence of this factor (or others) in the Senate debates reveal that *White/Zimmer* lacked a clear operational core, and that Congress would have to provide that core in amending the statute? Or should this be seen as a signal to the courts that Congress found the pre-*Bolden* case law an insufficient guide to vote dilution?

4. Is Section 2 constitutional? Under what source of constitutional power does Congress have the capacity to "overturn" *Mobile v. Bolden* and enact legislation that invalidates state and local electoral arrangements that have discriminatory "results" even if not motivated by discriminatory purposes? The Supreme Court has not yet addressed the constitutionality of the new Section 2, although the lower courts that have are unanimous in finding it constitutional. *See, e.g., United States v. Marengo County Comm'n*, 731 F.2d 1546, 1556–1563 (11th Cir.), *cert. denied*, 469 U.S. 976 (1984); *Jones v. Lubbock*, 727 F.2d 364, 372–75 (5th Cir.1984). Until recently, many had taken this uniformity, and the failure of the Court to intervene, as a clear indication that the constitutionality of Section 2 was settled. However, some Justices have begun to raise this question explicitly as a reminder that the Court has not confronted it; these signals might suggest that at least some Justices view the constitutional question as open and difficult. *See, e.g., Chisom v. Roemer*, 501 U.S. 380, 418 (1991) (Kennedy, J., dissenting). For a fuller discussion, see *Bush v. Vera*, 116 S.Ct. 1941 (1996) (O'Connor, J., concurring) (political bodies are entitled to assume Section 2 is constitutional "unless and until current lower court precedent is reversed and it is held unconstitutional").

The leading precedents on the constitutionality of the VRA and on the general scope of Congress' powers to effectively "overturn" by statute Supreme Court voting rights decisions are *South Carolina v. Katzenbach*, 383 U.S. 301 (1966) (upholding the original VRA as a valid exercise of Congress' power under Section 2 of the Fifteenth Amendment); *Katzenbach v. Morgan*, 384 U.S. 641 (1966); *Oregon v. Mitchell*, 400 U.S. 112 (1970) (which uphold Congress' ban on literacy tests despite *Lassiter*); and *City of Rome v. United States*, 446 U.S. 156 (1980) (upholding the Section 5 "results" test). A full discussion of these cases appeared in Chapter 5. Particularly in light of the recent decision in *City of Boerne v. Flores*, 117 S.Ct. 2157 (1997)—discussed in more detail in Chapter 5, Section A—consider whether the "results" tests of amended section 2 is constitutional. Does amended section 2 raise the same issues as those involved in the earlier challenges to the 1965 version of the VRA? Or must the congressional justifications for using its Fourteenth Amendment enforcement power to enact the 1982 amendments rest on different kinds of arguments? Are the 1982 amendments exercises of Congress' "remedial" powers to enforce the Fourteenth Amendment, as the courts have construed the Amendment? Or are the 1982 amendments an attempt by Congress to redefine the "substantive meaning" of the Fourteenth or Fifteenth Amendments? In the area of voting rights, how is the Court to draw the line, which *City of Boerne* makes crucial, between remedial and substantive legislation when Congress regulates voting practices? See generally Pamela S. Karlan, *Two Section Twos and Two Section Fives: Voting Rights and Remedies After Boerne*, 39 Wm. & Mary L. Rev. ___ (1998).

NOTES AND QUESTIONS ON THE POLITICAL PROCESS AND THE 1982 AMENDMENTS

What more general insights into the political economy of civil-rights legislation might be drawn from the specific story of these major amendments? Consider the following:

1. A standard assumption of much post–1937 constitutional theory is that majoritarian political processes can systematically fail to protect or will actively exploit the interests of "discrete and insular" minorities. The role of courts applying constitutional law is considered most justified when courts act to protect such groups. A further assumption is that racial minorities are the quintessential "discrete and insular" political group. Do the 1982 Amendments challenge that conventional wisdom at all?

a. In addition to the description above of the lobbying dynamics surrounding the 1982 Amendments, consider the following account from a larger study of congressional lobbying, taken from Michael Pertschuk, Giant Killers 148 (1986):

> In mobilizing grass roots; in structuring the media; in formulating and implementing legislative strategy; in substantive expertise and legislative draftsmanship; in building and sustaining a close and trusting relationship with its congressional leaders; in seeking out, packaging, and coaching a knockout array of witnesses at a hearing—the Leadership Conference was unmatched.... When the arms control community sought to organize to fight the MX missile, they turned to the Leadership Conference on Civil Rights as a model.

b. Why was there so little organized interest-group resistance to the 1982 Amendments? Those who have documented the legislative process consistently report "the absence of any organized opposition to the legislation." Abigail M. Thernstrom, Whose Votes Count? 113 (1987). But note that the 1982 Amendments occur at the start of Ronald Reagan's first term as President; Reagan was skeptical of race-conscious public policies in other arenas. Is it odd that in such a political context the Congress should have overwhelmingly and with bipartisan support have adopted the "results" test of Section 2? Why might there be less resistance to such policies in the voting arena than in other areas, such as employment or housing discrimination?

Consider the interests affected when policies such as these are adopted in different domains. If employment discrimination laws banned discriminatory "results," what interests or individuals would bear the most immediate burden of these heightened protections for minority workers? If voting-rights law incorporates a "results" test, are there comparable interests or individuals so palpably and immediately affected? The most obvious group made directly worse-off by the 1982 Amendments would probably be politicians who would be elected to office under the pre–1982 regime; indeed, one view is that it is liberal white Democratic politicians, in particular, who will be most disadvantaged by the changes the 1982 Amendments make.

If politicians are the principal "losers" from the 1982 Amendments, how easy is it likely to be to mobilize public opinion to resist those Amendments? If it is white liberal Democratic politicians who pay the greatest personal cost, what additional complexities do they face in leading the charge to resist the Amendments?

What does all this suggest about the political economy of enacting civil-rights legislation in different domains? That the organization of interests is likely to vary dramatically from area to area? Should that affect the way courts interpret statutes or apply the Constitution with respect to different issues involving civil rights, or should the Courts nonetheless take the same approach across all areas of civil-rights policy?

c. Bruce Ackerman has suggested that the post–1937 consensus in constitutional law on the need for courts to protect "discrete and insular" minorities needs rethinking, in light of more sophisticated insights into the political economy behind the enactment of legislation. Thus, Ackerman argues it is often "discrete and insular" groups as defined in the famous *Carolene Products* footnote, that have the *most* clout in politics:

> In fact, for all our *Carolene* talk about the powerlessness of insular groups, we are perfectly aware of the enormous power such voting blocs have in American politics. The story of the protective tariff is [the] classic illustration of insularity's power in American history. Over the past half-century, we have been treated to an enormous number of welfare-state variations on the theme of insularity by

the farm bloc, the steel lobby, the auto lobby, and others too numerous to mention. In this standard scenario of pluralistic politics, it is precisely the diffuse character of the majority forced to pay the bill for tariffs, agricultural subsidies, and the like, that allows strategically located Congressmen to deliver the goods to their well-organized constituents. Given these familiar stories, it is really quite remarkable to hear lawyers profess concern that insular interests have too little influence in Congress.

Bruce Ackerman, *Beyond* Carolene Products, 98 Harv. L. Rev. 713, 728 (1985).

Does Ackerman's argument, along with the case study of the 1982 Amendments, suggest that racial minorities effectively have more political power than the *Carolene Products* approach assumes? Or do racial minorities remain "discrete and insular" politically in ways that distinguish such minorities from economic minorities like "the farm bloc?" Does the answer vary from policy area to policy area; might racial minorities be "discrete and insular" for some issues and not others?

2. Abner Mikva, a former congressman and federal judge (as well as White House counsel to the President), has offered informed and unconventional observations on the dynamic of judicial and congressional relationships. Abner J. Mikva and Jeff Bleich, *Civil Rights Legislation in the 1990s: When Congress Overrules the Court*, 79 Calif. L. Rev. 729 (1991). Mikva argues that when the Supreme Court interprets certainly highly visible statutes narrowly, such as civil-rights statutes, Congress has a well-documented record of revisiting the issue and often overturning the Court. Moreover, when Congress is forced back into the policy arena, it not only reverses the Court, but enacts even more aggressive legislation than its initial efforts. Thus, as Mikva and Bleich put it:

> [P]arties who seek to win in the Court what they lost in Congress must be wary of what they pray for. Frequently, these parties win the battle but lose the war by galvanizing congressional forces to overrule the Court and advance to an even higher policy ground.... When Congress believes the Court is needlessly obstructing legislative policy, it tends to harden and harshen its position unnaturally.... [In the civil-rights area in general,] the Supreme Court's decisions seem to have produced a conservative defeat. Narrow civil rights decisions prompted Washington lobbyists to assemble an aggressive campaign, which may have encouraged Congress to include stronger, less ambiguous language than the political process normally tolerates.

How well does this account describe the relationship between *Mobile v. Bolden* and the 1982 Amendments to Section 2?

3. How responsive is Congress to Supreme Court decisions, particularly those in the civil-rights area, whether they involve constitutional or statutory issues (recall that *Bolden* involved both)? Many commentators assume Congress is too inertial or too busy to be particularly responsive. But the most thorough study concludes otherwise, at least today. See William N. Eskridge, *Overriding Supreme Court Statutory Interpretation Decisions*, 101 Yale L.J. 331 (1991). Between 1967 and 1974, each Congress overrode on average about six Supreme Court decisions; between 1975 and 1990, each Congress overrode an average of twelve Supreme Court decisions. According to Mikva, *supra*, between 1982 and 1988, "Congress overruled seven Supreme Court decisions concerning interpretation of antidiscrimination provisions; in each instance, Congress increased the ability of plaintiffs to bring and prevail in suits compared to the rights recognized by the court." Mikva, *supra*, at 740. The Eskridge study concludes that Congress was most likely to override the Court between 1967–1990 first in criminal law areas, then in antitrust, and then in civil rights. In the 1991 Civil Rights Act, Congress overrode numerous Supreme Court decisions interpreting civil-rights statutes.

What does the pattern of congressional response to court decisions in this area suggest, if anything, about how both the courts and Congress ought to understand their institutional roles in enacting and interpreting statutory provisions like Section 2?

4. Eskridge also provides a provocative predictive theory, based on his study of past experience, of how courts and congress will interact in the area of statutory interpretation. Consider whether this theory explains the pattern of institutional relationships in the development of voting-rights policy—and what it suggests about how the courts will interpret Section 2. Eskridge argues that courts face incentives that drive them to be less responsive to the Congress that originally enacts legislation than to the Congress (and President) in power at the time the courts interpret the statute. Thus, "current legislative expectations are usually more important to the Court than original legislative expectations ... Congress should be aware that judicial interpretations of statutes it enacts are not going to be faithful to its original expectations...." Eskridge, *supra*, at 415. *See also* William M. Eskridge, *Reneging on History? Playing the Court/Congress/President Civil Rights Game*, 79 Calif. L. Rev. 613 (1991).

If this prediction is right, what does it suggest about how courts will interpret Section 2? If the prediction is right, what steps might Congress take to make it more likely that the judicial interpretation of Section 2 will remain closer to the intent of the enacting Congress?

CHAPTER 7

Racial Vote Dilution Under the Voting Rights Act

As we saw in previous chapters, neither one-person, one-vote nor constitutional constraints on race discrimination in voting fully integrated racial minorities into the political process. One-person, one-vote was simultaneously too majoritarian and too individualistic. The majoritarian aspect of one-person, one-vote set ceilings on (numerical) minorities' political power. It did very little to provide a floor, especially given districting techniques (including the decision to use multimember districts or at-large elections) that allowed for winner-take-all elections. And while the Court's vision of voting as a fundamental, personal right reinforced the struggle for black enfranchisement described in Chapter 2, it focused on the formal right to participate, rather than on electoral outcomes.

As for the constitutional prohibition on racial vote dilution, the discriminatory purpose test delineated in *Washington v. Davis*, 426 U.S. 229 (1976), and applied to vote dilution claims beginning with *Nevett v. Sides*, 571 F.2d 209 (5th Cir.1978), *cert. denied*, 446 U.S. 951 (1980), and *City of Mobile v. Bolden*, 446 U.S. 55 (1980), threw a substantial obstacle in the path of minority plaintiffs. As we saw in the preceding chapter, proving intentional discrimination, particularly with regard to longstanding, widespread practices such as at-large elections, was time-consuming, costly, and often well-nigh impossible since it was hard to show that a particular election scheme was adopted precisely because it minimized minority voting strength rather than despite its dilutive effects. In the South, for example, at-large elections often came into being (or their enabling legislation came into being) as part of the post-Reconstruction legal overhaul. Often, at-large elections were adopted as part of a larger package. *See* J. Morgan Kousser, *The Undermining of the First Reconstruction: Lessons for the Second*, in Minority Vote Dilution 27, 32–33 (Chandler Davidson ed. 1984). Years later, it might be hard to distill out a specific intent with regard to the at-large provisions, and their continuing effect was masked for many years by the outright disenfranchisement of black voters.

After the Supreme Court decided *Bolden*, vote dilution litigation virtually shut down. Even before the Supreme Court closed off the constitutional avenues for attacking electoral practices, the Voting Rights Act had offered an alternative tool for attacking qualitative vote dilution. Beginning with the Supreme Court's decision in *Allen v. State Board of Elections*, 393 U.S. 544 (1969), the Justice Department and, to a lesser extent, the courts used the preclearance provisions in section 5 of the Voting Rights Act of 1965 to reach election practices, particularly the use of at-large elections, multi-member districts, and decennial redistricting plans that minimized minority political clout. As you may remember, section 5 was a temporary provision. Originally, it was scheduled to expire in 1970, but amendments in 1970 and 1975 extended and expanded its reach. The 1975 amendments extended section 5 for seven additional years, essentially through the 1980 reapportionment season. *Bolden* was announced just as Congress was gearing up for hearings on whether to extend section 5 again and the states were preparing to redistrict. The decision affected both processes. In 1982, Congress not only extended section 5, this time for 25 years, but also amended section 2 to prohibit voting practices or procedures that resulted in a denial of equal electoral opportunity, regardless of the intent behind the enactment or maintenance of the challenged system. Chapter 6 contains a fuller account of the 1982 amendments. But while the federal legislative process was underway, states reapportioned, and obtained preclearance of new congressional and state legislative plans that once again kept minority representation to markedly low levels. Several of these plans were precleared by the Department of Justice. Chapter 5 contains a case study of one of those apportionments, the Louisiana congressional plan ultimately invalidated in *Major v. Treen*, 574 F.Supp. 325 (E.D.La.1983) (three-judge court).

The 1982 amendments marked a significant shift in the nature of litigation under the Voting Rights Act. Between 1965 and 1982, virtually all the litigation raised claims under section 5. Private plaintiffs challenged a variety of measures on the grounds that they constituted changes "with respect to voting," and therefore that they could not be implemented unless and until they received preclearance from either the Department of Justice or the United States District Court for the District of Columbia. The objective of the litigation was thus to flush the actual assessment of the challenged practices into the essentially administrative process. Section 2 was virtually never used: prior to *Washington v. Davis* and *Nevett v. Sides*, there was little reason to suppose the statutory standard was more protective than the constitutional one, and the plurality opinion in *Bolden* found that section 2 merely restated the constitutional prohibition. The 1982 amendments, however, squarely decoupled the statutory standard under section 2 from the constitutional standard under the Fourteenth or Fifteenth Amendments, by rejecting the requirement that plaintiffs show a discriminatory purpose. Since 1982, the bulk of racial vote dilution litigation has taken place under section 2, rather than under either section 5 or the Constitution.

A. Judicial Modulation of the "Results" Standard: The Three-Part Test for Challenges to Multimember Districts

The first case under amended section 2 to receive plenary consideration from the Supreme Court involved the North Carolina General Assembly. In April 1982, the General Assembly enacted a legislative redistricting plan. That plan used a combination of single-member and multimember districts. Black voters in several of the multimember districts filed suit, claiming that within those districts there were concentrations of black citizens that were sufficiently large and contiguous to constitute effective voting majorities in single-member districts lying wholly within the boundaries of the multimember districts. (They also challenged the way in which the lines between two single-member state senatorial districts were drawn, but that issue was not addressed by the Supreme Court.) The relief they sought was the disaggregation of the multimember districts into single-member districts, some of which would have black effective voting majorities.

Thornburg v. Gingles
478 U.S. 30 (1986).

■ JUSTICE BRENNAN announced the judgment of the Court and delivered the opinion of the Court with respect to Parts I, II, III–A, III–B, IV–A, and V, an opinion with respect to Part III–C, in which JUSTICE MARSHALL, JUSTICE BLACKMUN, and JUSTICE STEVENS join, and an opinion with respect to Part IV–B, in which JUSTICE WHITE joins.

* * *

I

* * *

The District Court applied the "totality of the circumstances" test set forth in § 2(b) to appellees' statutory claim, and, relying principally on the factors outlined in the Senate Report [that accompanied the 1982 amendments to the Voting Rights Act], held that the redistricting scheme violated § 2 because it resulted in the dilution of black citizens' votes in all seven disputed districts.

* * *

First, the court found that North Carolina had officially discriminated against its black citizens with respect to their exercise of the voting franchise from approximately 1900 to 1970 by employing at different times a poll tax, a literacy test, a prohibition against bullet (single-shot) voting, and designated seat plans for multimember districts. The court observed that even after the removal of direct barriers to black voter registration, such as the poll tax and literacy test, black voter registration remained relatively depressed; in 1982 only 52.7% of age-qualified blacks statewide were registered to vote, whereas 66.7% of whites were registered. The District Court found these statewide depressed levels of black voter registration to be present in all of the disputed districts and to be traceable, at least in part, to the historical pattern of statewide official discrimination.

Second, the court found that historic discrimination in education, housing, employment, and health services had resulted in a lower socioeconomic status for North Carolina blacks as a group than for whites. The court concluded that this lower status both gives rise to special group interests and hinders blacks' ability to participate effectively in the political process and to elect representatives of their choice.

Third, the court considered other voting procedures that may operate to lessen the opportunity of black voters to elect candidates of their choice. It noted that North Carolina has a majority vote requirement for primary elections.... The court also remarked on the fact that North Carolina does not have a subdistrict residency requirement for members of the General Assembly elected from multimember districts, a requirement which the court found could offset to some extent the disadvantages minority voters often experience in multimember districts.

Fourth, the court found that white candidates in North Carolina have encouraged voting along color lines by appealing to racial prejudice. It noted that the record is replete with specific examples of racial appeals, ranging in style from overt and blatant to subtle and furtive, and in date from the 1890's to the 1984 campaign for a seat in the United States Senate....

Fifth, the court examined the extent to which blacks have been elected to office in North Carolina, both statewide and in the challenged districts. It found, among other things, that.... the overall rate of black electoral success has been minimal in relation to the percentage of blacks in the total state population....

With respect to the success in this century of black candidates in the contested districts, the court found that [there too, black electoral success had been quite minimal prior to 1982]....

The court did acknowledge the improved success of black candidates in the 1982 elections, in which 11 blacks were elected to the State House of Representatives, including 5 blacks from the multimember districts at issue here. However, the court pointed out that the 1982 election was conducted after the commencement of this litigation. The court found the circumstances of the 1982 election sufficiently aberrational and the success by black candidates too minimal and too recent in relation to the long history of complete denial of elective opportunities to support the conclusion that black voters' opportunities to elect representatives of their choice were not impaired.

Finally, the court considered the extent to which voting in the challenged districts was racially polarized. Based on statistical evidence presented by expert witnesses, supplemented to some degree by the testimony of lay witnesses, the court found that all of the challenged districts exhibit severe and persistent racially polarized voting.

* * *

II

Section 2 and Vote Dilution Through Use of
Multimember Districts

* * *

A.

Section 2 and Its Legislative History

* * *

The Senate Report which accompanied the 1982 amendments elaborates on the nature of § 2 violations and on the proof required to establish these violations. First and foremost, the Report dispositively rejects the position of the plurality in *Mobile v. Bolden,* 446 U.S. 55 (1980), which required proof that the contested electoral practice or mechanism was adopted or maintained with the intent to discriminate against minority voters....

The Senate Report specifies factors which typically may be relevant to a § 2 claim: [1] the history of voting-related discrimination in the State or political subdivision; [2] the extent to which voting in the elections of the State or political subdivision is racially polarized; [3] the extent to which the State or political subdivision has used voting practices or procedures that tend to enhance the opportunity for discrimination against the minority group, such as unusually large election districts, majority vote requirements, and prohibitions against bullet voting; [4] the exclusion of members of the minority group from candidate slating processes; [5] the extent to which minority group members bear the effects of past discrimination in areas such as education, employment, and health, which hinder their ability to participate effectively in the political process; [6] the use of overt or subtle racial appeals in political campaigns; and [7] the extent to which members of the minority group have been elected to public office in the jurisdiction. The Report notes also that evidence demonstrating [8] that elected officials are unresponsive to the particularized needs of the members of the minority group and [9] that the policy underlying the State's or the political subdivision's use of the contested practice or structure is tenuous may have probative value. The Report stresses, however, that this list of typical factors is neither comprehensive nor exclusive. While the enumerated factors will often be pertinent to certain types of § 2 violations, particularly to vote dilution claims, other factors may also be relevant and may be considered. Furthermore, the Senate Committee observed that "there is no requirement that any particular number of factors be proved, or that a majority of them point one way or the other." Rather, the Committee determined that "the question whether the political processes are 'equally open' depends upon a searching practical evaluation of the 'past and present reality,'" and on a "functional" view of the political process.

* * *

B.
Vote Dilution Through the Use of Multimember Districts

[The plaintiffs] contend that the legislative decision to employ multimember, rather than single-member, districts in the contested jurisdictions dilutes their votes by submerging them in a white majority, thus impairing their ability to elect representatives of their choice.[12]

The essence of a § 2 claim is that a certain electoral law, practice, or structure interacts with social and historical conditions to cause an inequality in the opportunities enjoyed by black and white voters to elect their preferred representatives. This Court has long recognized that multimember districts and at-large voting schemes may "operate to minimize or cancel out the voting strength of racial [minorities in] the voting population." The theoretical basis for this type of impairment is that where minority and majority voters consistently prefer different candidates, the majority, by virtue of its numerical superiority, will regularly defeat the choices of minority voters. Multimember districts and at-large election schemes, however, are not per se violative of minority voters' rights. Minority voters who contend that the multimember form of districting

---

12. The claim we address in this opinion is one in which the plaintiffs alleged and attempted to prove that their ability to elect the representatives of their choice was impaired by the selection of a multimember electoral structure. We have no occasion to consider whether § 2 permits, and if it does, what standards should pertain to, a claim brought by a minority group, that is not sufficiently large and compact to constitute a majority in a single-member district, alleging that the use of a multimember district impairs its ability to influence elections.

We note also that we have no occasion to consider whether the standards we apply to respondents' claim that multimember districts operate to dilute the vote of geographically cohesive minority groups that are large enough to constitute majorities in single-member districts and that are contained within the boundaries of the challenged multimember districts, are fully pertinent to other sorts of vote dilution claims, such as a claim alleging that the splitting of a large and geographically cohesive minority between two or more multimember or single-member districts resulted in the dilution of the minority vote.

violates § 2 must prove that the use of a multimember electoral structure operates to minimize or cancel out their ability to elect their preferred candidates.

While many or all of the factors listed in the Senate Report may be relevant to a claim of vote dilution through submergence in multimember districts, unless there is a conjunction of the following circumstances, the use of multimember districts generally will not impede the ability of minority voters to elect representatives of their choice.[15] Stated succinctly, a bloc voting majority must usually be able to defeat candidates supported by a politically cohesive, geographically insular minority group. These circumstances are necessary preconditions for multimember districts to operate to impair minority voters' ability to elect representatives of their choice for the following reasons. First, the minority group must be able to demonstrate that it is sufficiently large and geographically compact to constitute a majority in a single-member district.[16] If it is not, as would be the case in a substantially integrated district, the multimember form of the district cannot be responsible for minority voters' inability to elect its

---

15. Under a "functional" view of the political process mandated by § 2, the most important Senate Report factors bearing on § 2 challenges to multimember districts are the "extent to which minority group members have been elected to public office in the jurisdiction" and the "extent to which voting in the elections of the state or political subdivision is racially polarized." If present, the other factors, such as the lingering effects of past discrimination, the use of appeals to racial bias in election campaigns, and the use of electoral devices which enhance the dilutive effects of multimember districts when substantial white bloc voting exists—for example antibullet voting laws and majority vote requirements, are supportive of, but not essential to, a minority voter's claim.

In recognizing that some Senate Report factors are more important to multimember district vote dilution claims than others, the Court effectuates the intent of Congress. It is obvious that unless minority group members experience substantial difficulty electing representatives of their choice, they cannot prove that a challenged electoral mechanism impairs their ability "to elect." § 2(b). And, where the contested electoral structure is a multimember district, commentators and courts agree that in the absence of significant white bloc voting it cannot be said that the ability of minority voters to elect their chosen representatives is inferior to that of white voters. Consequently, if difficulty in electing and white bloc voting are not proved, minority voters have not established that the multimember structure interferes with their ability to elect their preferred candidates. Minority voters may be able to prove that they still suffer social and economic effects of past discrimination, that appeals to racial bias are employed in election campaigns, and that a majority vote is required to win a seat, but they have not demonstrated a substantial inability to elect caused by the use of a multimember district. By recognizing the primacy of the history and extent of minority electoral success and of racial bloc voting, the Court simply requires that § 2 plaintiffs prove their claim before they may be awarded relief.

16. In this case appellees allege that within each contested multimember district there exists a minority group that is sufficiently large and compact to constitute a single-member district. In a different kind of case, for example a gerrymander case, plaintiffs might allege that the minority group that is sufficiently large and compact to constitute a single-member district has been split between two or more multimember or single-member districts, with the effect of diluting the potential strength of the minority vote.

candidates.[17] Second, the minority group must be able to show that it is politically cohesive. If the minority group is not politically cohesive, it cannot be said that the selection of a multimember electoral structure thwarts distinctive minority group interests. Third, the minority must be able to demonstrate that the white majority votes sufficiently as a bloc to enable it—in the absence of special circumstances, such as the minority candidate running unopposed—usually to defeat the minority's preferred candidate. In establishing this last circumstance, the minority group demonstrates that submergence in a white multimember district impedes its ability to elect its chosen representatives.

* * *

III
Racially Polarized Voting

* * *

B
The Degree of Bloc Voting that is Legally Significant Under § 2

* * *

2
The Standard for Legally Significant Racial Bloc Voting

The Senate Report states that the "extent to which voting in the elections of the state or political subdivision is racially polarized" is relevant to a vote dilution claim....

The purpose of inquiring into the existence of racially polarized voting is twofold: to ascertain whether minority group members constitute a politically cohesive unit and to determine whether whites vote sufficiently as a bloc usually to defeat the minority's preferred candidates. Thus, the question whether a given district experiences legally significant racially polarized voting requires discrete inquiries into minority and white voting practices. A showing that a significant number of minority group members

---

17. The reason that a minority group making such a challenge must show, as a threshold matter, that it is sufficiently large and geographically compact to constitute a majority in a single-member district is this: Unless minority voters possess the potential to elect representatives in the absence of the challenged structure or practice, they cannot claim to have been injured by that structure or practice. The single-member district is generally the appropriate standard against which to measure minority group potential to elect because it is the smallest political unit from which representatives are elected. Thus, if the minority group is spread evenly throughout a multimember district, or if, although geographically compact, the minority group is so small in relation to the surrounding white population that it could not constitute a majority in a single-member district, these minority voters cannot maintain that they would have been able to elect representatives of their choice in the absence of the multimember electoral structure....

usually vote for the same candidates is one way of proving the political cohesiveness necessary to a vote dilution claim, and, consequently, establishes minority bloc voting within the context of § 2. And, in general, a white bloc vote that normally will defeat the combined strength of minority support plus white "crossover" votes rises to the level of legally significant white bloc voting. The amount of white bloc voting that can generally "minimize or cancel" black voters' ability to elect representatives of their choice, however, will vary from district to district according to a number of factors, including the nature of the allegedly dilutive electoral mechanism; the presence or absence of other potentially dilutive electoral devices, such as majority vote requirements, designated posts, and prohibitions against bullet voting; the percentage of registered voters in the district who are members of the minority group; the size of the district; and, in multimember districts, the number of seats open and the number of candidates in the field.

Because loss of political power through vote dilution is distinct from the mere inability to win a particular election, a pattern of racial bloc voting that extends over a period of time is more probative of a claim that a district experiences legally significant polarization than are the results of a single election.[25]

* * *

C

Evidence of Racially Polarized Voting

1

Appellants' Argument

.... [The State and the United States] argue that the term "racially polarized voting" must, as a matter of law, refer to voting patterns for which the principal cause is race. They contend that the District Court utilized a legally incorrect definition of racially polarized voting by relying on bivariate statistical analyses which merely demonstrated a correlation between the race of the voter and the level of voter support for certain candidates, but which did not prove that race was the primary determinant of voters' choices. According to appellants and the United States, only multiple regression analysis, which can take account of other variables which might also explain voters' choices, such as "party affiliation, age, religion, income[,] incumbency, education, campaign expenditures," "media

---

25. .... One important circumstance is the number of elections in which the minority group has sponsored candidates. Where a minority group has never been able to sponsor a candidate, courts must rely on other factors that tend to prove unequal access to the electoral process. Similarly, where a minority group has begun to sponsor candidates just recently, the fact that statistics from only one or a few elections are available for examination does not foreclose a vote dilution claim.

use measured by cost, ... name, identification, or distance that a candidate lived from a particular precinct," can prove that race was the primary determinant of voter behavior.

Whether appellants and the United States believe that it is the voter's race or the candidate's race that must be the primary determinant of the voter's choice is unclear; indeed, their catalogs of relevant variables suggest both. Age, religion, income, and education seem most relevant to the voter; incumbency, campaign expenditures, name identification, and media use are pertinent to the candidate; and party affiliation could refer both to the voter and the candidate. In either case, we disagree: For purposes of § 2, the legal concept of racially polarized voting incorporates neither causation nor intent. It means simply that the race of voters correlates with the selection of a certain candidate or candidates; that is, it refers to the situation where different races (or minority language groups) vote in blocs for different candidates....

2

Causation Irrelevant to Section 2 Inquiry

The first reason we reject appellants' argument that racially polarized voting refers to voting patterns that are in some way caused by race, rather than to voting patterns that are merely correlated with the race of the voter, is that the reasons black and white voters vote differently have no relevance to the central inquiry of § 2.... It is the difference between the choices made by blacks and whites—not the reasons for that difference—that results in blacks having less opportunity than whites to elect their preferred representatives. Consequently, we conclude that under the "results test" of § 2, only the correlation between race of voter and selection of certain candidates, not the causes of the correlation, matters.

* * *

3

Race of Voter as Primary Determinant of Voter Behavior

Appellants and the United States contend that the legal concept of "racially polarized voting" refers not to voting patterns that are merely correlated with the voter's race, but to voting patterns that are determined primarily by the voter's race, rather than by the voter's other socioeconomic characteristics.

The first problem with this argument is that it ignores the fact that members of geographically insular racial and ethnic groups frequently share socioeconomic characteristics, such as income level, employment status, amount of education, housing and other living conditions, religion, language, and so forth. Where such characteristics are shared, race or ethnic group not only denotes color or place of origin, it also functions as a shorthand notation for common social and economic characteristics. Appellants' definition of racially polarized voting is even more pernicious where shared characteristics are causally related to race or ethnicity. The opportunity to achieve high employment status and income, for example, is often influenced by the presence or absence of racial or ethnic discrimination. A definition of racially polarized voting which holds that black bloc voting does not exist when black voters' choice of certain candidates is most strongly influenced by the fact that the voters have low incomes and menial jobs—when the reason most of those voters have menial jobs and low incomes is attributable to past or present racial discrimination—runs counter to the Senate Report's instruction to conduct a searching and practical evaluation of past and present reality, and interferes with the purpose of the Voting Rights Act to eliminate the negative effects of past discrimination on the electoral opportunities of minorities.

* * *

Second, appellants' interpretation of "racially polarized voting" creates an irreconcilable tension between their proposed treatment of socioeconomic characteristics in the bloc voting context and the Senate Report's statement that "the extent to which members of the minority group ... bear the effects of discrimination in such areas as education, employment and health" may be relevant to a § 2 claim. We can find no support in either logic or the legislative history for the anomalous conclusion to which appellants' position leads—that Congress intended, on the one hand, that proof that a minority group is predominately poor, uneducated, and unhealthy should be considered a factor tending to prove a § 2 violation; but that Congress intended, on the other hand, that proof that the same socioeconomic characteristics greatly influence black voters' choice of candidates should destroy these voters' ability to establish one of the most important elements of a vote dilution claim.

4

Race of Candidate as Primary Determinant of Voter Behavior

* * *

[B]oth minority and majority voters often select members of their own race as their preferred representatives.... Thus, as a matter of convenience, we ... may refer to the preferred representative of black voters as the "black candidate" and to the preferred representative of white voters as the "white candidate." Nonetheless, the fact that race of voter and race of candidate is often correlated is not directly pertinent to a § 2 inquiry. Under § 2, it is the status of the candidate as the chosen representative of a particular racial group, not the race of the candidate, that is important.

* * *

[A]ppellants' suggestion that racially polarized voting refers to voting patterns where whites vote for white candidates because they prefer members of their own race or are hostile to blacks, as opposed to voting patterns where whites vote for white candidates because the white candidates spent more on their campaigns, utilized more media coverage, and thus enjoyed greater name recognition than the black candidates, fails for another, independent reason. This argument, like the argument that the race of the voter must be the primary determinant of the voter's ballot, is inconsistent with the purposes of § 2 and would render meaningless the Senate Report factor that addresses the impact of low socioeconomic status on a minority group's level of political participation.

Congress intended that the Voting Rights Act eradicate inequalities in political opportunities that exist due to the vestigial effects of past purposeful discrimination. Both this Court and other federal courts have recognized that political participation by minorities tends to be depressed where minority group members suffer effects of prior discrimination such as inferior education, poor employment opportunities, and low incomes. The Senate Report acknowledges this tendency and instructs that "the extent to which members of the minority group ... bear the effects of discrimination in such areas as education, employment and health, which hinder their ability to participate effectively in the political process" is a factor which may be probative of unequal opportunity to participate in the political process and to elect representatives. Courts and commentators have recognized further that candidates generally must spend more money in order to win election in a multimember district than in a single-member district. If, because of inferior education and poor employment opportunities, blacks earn less than whites, they will not be able to provide the candidates of their choice with the same level of financial support that whites can provide theirs. Thus, electoral losses by candidates preferred by the black community may well be attributable in part to the fact that their white opponents outspent them. But, the fact is that, in this instance, the economic effects of prior discrimination have combined with the multimember electoral structure to afford blacks less opportunity than whites to participate in the political process and to elect representatives of their choice. It would be both anomalous and inconsistent with congressional intent to hold that, on the one hand, the effects of past discrimination which hinder blacks' ability to participate in the political process tend to prove a § 2 violation, while holding on the other hand that, where these same effects of past discrimination deter whites from voting for blacks, blacks cannot make out a crucial element of a vote dilution claim.

5

Racial Animosity as Primary Determinant of Voter Behavior

Finally, we reject the suggestion that racially polarized voting refers only to white bloc voting which is caused by white voters' racial hostility toward black candidates....

In amending § 2, Congress rejected the requirement announced by this Court in *Bolden* that § 2 plaintiffs must prove the discriminatory intent of state or local governments in adopting or maintaining the challenged electoral mechanism. Appellants' suggestion that the discriminatory intent of individual white voters must be proved in order to make out a § 2 claim must fail for the very reasons Congress rejected the intent test with respect to governmental bodies.

The Senate Report states that one reason the Senate Committee abandoned the intent test was that "the Committee ... heard persuasive testimony that the intent test is unnecessarily divisive because it involves charges of racism on the part of individual officials or entire communities."

* * *

The grave threat to racial progress and harmony which Congress perceived from requiring proof that racism caused the adoption or maintenance of a challenged electoral mechanism is present to a much greater degree in the proposed requirement that plaintiffs demonstrate that racial animosity determined white voting patterns. Under the old intent test, plaintiffs might succeed by proving only that a limited number of elected officials were racist; under the new intent test plaintiffs would be required to prove that most of the white community is racist in order to obtain judicial relief. It is difficult to imagine a more racially divisive requirement.

A second reason Congress rejected the old intent test was that in most cases it placed an "inordinately difficult burden" on § 2 plaintiffs. The new intent test would be equally, if not more, burdensome. In order to prove that a specific factor—racial hostility—determined white voters' ballots, it would be necessary to demonstrate that other potentially relevant causal factors, such as socioeconomic characteristics and candidate expenditures, do not correlate better than racial animosity with white voting behavior.

* * *

The final and most dispositive reason the Senate Report repudiated the old intent test was that it "asks the wrong question." Amended § 2 asks instead "whether minorities have equal access to the process of electing their representatives."

Focusing on the discriminatory intent of the voters, rather than the behavior of the voters, also asks the wrong question. All that matters under § 2 and under a functional theory of vote dilution is voter behavior, not its explanations. Moreover, as we have explained in detail, requiring proof that racial considerations actually caused voter behavior will result—contrary to congressional intent—in situations where a black minority that functionally has been totally excluded from the political process will be unable to establish a § 2 violation.

* * *

6
Summary

In sum, we would hold that the legal concept of racially polarized voting, as it relates to claims of vote dilution, refers only to the existence of a correlation between the race of voters and the selection of certain candidates. Plaintiffs need not prove causation or intent in order to prove a prima facie case of racial bloc voting and defendants may not rebut that case with evidence of causation or intent.

IV
The Legal Significance of Some Black Candidates' Success
A

North Carolina and the United States maintain that the District Court failed to accord the proper weight to the success of some black candidates in the challenged districts. Black residents of these districts, they point out, achieved improved representation in the 1982 General Assembly election. They also note that blacks in House District 23 have enjoyed proportional representation consistently since 1973 and that blacks in the other districts have occasionally enjoyed nearly proportional representation. This electoral success demonstrates conclusively, appellants and the United States argue, that blacks in those districts do not have "less opportunity than other members of the electorate to participate in the political process and to elect representatives of their choice." 42 U.S.C. § 1973(b). Essentially, appellants and the United States contend that if a racial minority gains proportional or nearly proportional representation in a single election, that fact alone precludes, as a matter of law, finding a § 2 violation.

Section 2(b) provides that "[the] extent to which members of a protected class have been elected to office . . . is one circumstance which may be considered." 42 U.S.C. § 1973(b). The Senate Committee Report also identifies the extent to which minority candidates have succeeded as a pertinent factor. However, the Senate Report expressly states that "the election of a few minority candidates does not 'necessarily foreclose the possibility of dilution of the black vote,'" noting that if it did, "the possibility exists that the majority citizens might evade [§ 2] by manipulating the election of a 'safe' minority candidate.". . . .

[I]n conducting its "independent consideration of the record" and its "searching practical evaluation of the past and present reality," the District Court could appropriately take account of the circumstances surrounding recent black electoral success in deciding its significance to appellees' claim. In particular, . . . the court could properly notice the fact that black electoral success increased markedly in the 1982 election—an election that occurred after the instant lawsuit had been filed—and could properly consider to what extent "the pendency of this very litigation [might have] worked a one-time advantage for black candidates in the form of unusual organized political support by white leaders concerned to forestall single-member districting."

Nothing in the statute or its legislative history prohibited the court from viewing with some caution black candidates' success in the 1982 election, and from deciding on the basis of all the relevant circumstances to accord greater weight to blacks' relative lack of success over the course of several recent elections. Consequently, we hold that the District Court did not err, as a matter of law, in refusing to treat the fact that some black candidates have succeeded as dispositive of appellees' § 2 claim. Where multimember districting generally works to dilute the minority vote, it cannot be defended on the ground that it sporadically and serendipitously benefits minority voters.

B

The District Court did err, however, in ignoring the significance of the sustained success black voters have experienced in House District 23. In that district, the last six elections have resulted in proportional representation for black residents. This persistent proportional representation is inconsistent with appellees' allegation that the ability of black voters in District 23 to elect representatives of their choice is not equal to that enjoyed by the white majority.

In some situations, it may be possible for § 2 plaintiffs to demonstrate that such sustained success does not accurately reflect the minority group's ability to elect its preferred representatives, but appellees have not done so here. Appellees presented evidence relating to black electoral success in the last three elections; they failed utterly, though, to offer any explanation for the success of black candidates in the previous three elections. Consequently, we believe that the District Court erred, as a matter of law, in ignoring the sustained success black voters have enjoyed in House District 23, and would reverse with respect to that District.

V

Ultimate Determination of Vote Dilution

* * *

A

.... Appellants and the United States argue that because a finding of vote dilution under amended § 2 requires the application of a rule of law to a particular set of facts it constitutes a legal, rather than factual, determination. Neither appellants nor the United States cite our several precedents in which we have treated the ultimate finding of vote dilution as a question of fact subject to the clearly-erroneous standard of Rule 52(a). *See, e.g.,*

Rogers v. Lodge, 458 U.S. [613 (1982)]; *City of Rome v. United States*, 446 U.S. 156 (1980); *White v. Regester*, 412 U.S. [755 (1973)].

* * *

We reaffirm our view that the clearly-erroneous test of Rule 52(a) is the appropriate standard for appellate review of a finding of vote dilution. . . .

B

The District Court in this case carefully considered the totality of the circumstances and found that in each district racially polarized voting; the legacy of official discrimination in voting matters, education, housing, employment, and health services; and the persistence of campaign appeals to racial prejudice acted in concert with the multimember districting scheme to impair the ability of geographically insular and politically cohesive groups of black voters to participate equally in the political process and to elect candidates of their choice. It found that the success a few black candidates have enjoyed in these districts is too recent, too limited, and, with regard to the 1982 elections, perhaps too aberrational, to disprove its conclusion. Excepting House District 23, with respect to which the District Court committed legal error, we affirm the District Court's judgment. We cannot say that the District Court, composed of local judges who are well acquainted with the political realities of the State, clearly erred in concluding that use of a multimember electoral structure has caused black voters in the districts other than House District 23 to have less opportunity than white voters to elect representatives of their choice.

* * *

■ JUSTICE WHITE, concurring.

I join Parts I, II, III–A, III–B, IV–A, and V of the Court's opinion and agree with Justice Brennan's opinion as to Part IV–B. I disagree with Part III–C of Justice Brennan's opinion.

Justice Brennan states in Part III–C that the crucial factor in identifying polarized voting is the race of the voter and that the race of the candidate is irrelevant. Under this test, there is polarized voting if the majority of white voters vote for different candidates than the majority of the blacks, regardless of the race of the candidates. I do not agree. Suppose an eight-member multimember district that is 60% white and 40% black, the blacks being geographically located so that two safe black single-member districts could be drawn. Suppose further that there are six white and two black Democrats running against six white and two black Republicans. Under Justice Brennan's test, there would be polarized voting and a likely § 2 violation if all the Republicans, including the two blacks, are elected, and 80% of the blacks in the predominantly black areas vote Democratic. I take it that there would also be a violation in a single-member district that is 60% black, but enough of the blacks vote with the whites to elect a black candidate who is not the choice of the majority of black voters. This is interest-group politics rather than a rule hedging against racial discrimination. I doubt that this is what Congress had in mind in amending § 2 as it did, and it seems quite at odds with the discussion in *Whitcomb v. Chavis*. Furthermore, on the facts of this case, there is no need to draw the voter/candidate distinction. The District Court did not and reached the correct result except, in my view, with respect to District 23.

■ JUSTICE O'CONNOR, with whom THE CHIEF JUSTICE, JUSTICE POWELL, and JUSTICE REHNQUIST join, concurring in the judgment.

* * *

In construing this compromise legislation, we must make every effort to be faithful to the balance Congress struck. This is not an easy task. We know that Congress intended to allow vote dilution claims to be brought under § 2, but we also know that Congress did not intend to create a right to proportional representation for minority voters. There is an inherent tension between what Congress wished to do and what it wished to avoid, because any theory of vote dilution must necessarily rely to some extent on a measure of minority voting strength that makes some reference to the proportion between the minority group and the electorate at large.

* * *

I

In order to explain my disagreement with the Court's interpretation of § 2, it is useful to illustrate the impact that alternative districting plans or types of districts typically have on the likelihood that a minority group will be able to elect candidates it prefers, and then to set out the critical elements of a vote dilution claim as they emerge in the Court's opinion.

Consider a town of 1,000 voters that is governed by a council of four representatives, in which 30% of the voters are black, and in which the black voters are concentrated in one section of the city and tend to vote as a bloc. It would be possible to draw four single-member districts, in one of which blacks would constitute an overwhelming majority. The black voters in this district would be assured of electing a representative of their choice, while any remaining black voters in the other districts would be submerged in large white majorities. This option would give the minority group roughly proportional representation.

Alternatively, it would usually be possible to draw four single-member districts in two of which black voters constituted much narrower majorities of about 60%. The black voters in these districts would often be able to elect the representative of their choice in each of these two districts, but if even 20% of the black voters supported the candidate favored by the white minority in those districts the candidates preferred by the majority of black voters might lose. This option would, depending on the circumstances of a particular election, sometimes give the minority group more than proportional representation, but would increase the risk that the group would not achieve even roughly proportional representation.

It would also usually be possible to draw four single-member districts in each of which black voters constituted a minority. In the extreme case, black voters would constitute 30% of the voters in each district. Unless approximately 30% of the white voters in this extreme case backed the minority candidate, black voters in such a district would be unable to elect the candidate of their choice in an election between only two candidates even if they unanimously supported him. This option would make it difficult for black voters to elect candidates of their choice even with significant white support, and all but impossible without such support.

Finally, it would be possible to elect all four representatives in a single at-large election in which each voter could vote for four candidates. Under this scheme, white voters could elect all the representatives even if black voters turned out in large numbers and voted for one and only one candidate. To illustrate, if only four white candidates ran, and each received approximately equal support from white voters, each would receive about 700 votes, whereas black voters could cast no more than 300 votes for any one candidate. If, on the other hand, eight white candidates ran, and white votes were distributed less evenly, so that the five least favored white candidates received fewer than 300 votes while three others received 400 or more, it would be feasible for blacks to elect one representative with 300 votes even without substantial white support. If even 25% of the white voters backed a particular minority candidate, and black voters voted only for that candidate, the candidate would receive a total of 475 votes, which would ensure victory unless white voters also concentrated their votes on four of the eight remaining candidates, so that each received the support of almost 70% of white voters.

* * *

Although § 2 does not speak in terms of "vote dilution," I agree with the Court that proof of vote dilution can establish a violation of § 2 as amended. The phrase "vote dilution," in the legal sense, simply refers to the impermissible discriminatory effect that a multimember or other districting plan has when it operates "to cancel out or minimize the voting strength of racial groups." *White [v. Regester]*. This definition, however, conceals some very formidable difficulties. Is the "voting strength" of a racial group to be assessed solely with reference to its prospects for electoral success, or should courts look at other avenues of political influence open to the racial group? Insofar as minority voting strength is assessed with reference to electoral success, how should undiluted minority voting strength be measured? How much of an impairment of minority voting strength is necessary to prove a violation of § 2? What constitutes racial bloc voting and how is it proved? What weight is to be given to evidence of actual electoral success by minority candidates in the face of evidence of racial bloc voting?

The Court resolves the first question summarily: minority voting strength is to be assessed solely in terms of the minority group's ability to elect candidates it prefers....

In order to evaluate a claim that a particular multimember district or single-member district has diluted the minority group's voting strength to a degree that violates § 2, however, it is also necessary to construct a measure of "undiluted" minority voting strength. "[The] phrase [vote dilution] itself suggests a norm with respect to which the fact of dilution may be ascertained." Put simply, in order to decide whether an electoral system has made it harder for minority voters to elect the candidates they prefer, a court must have an idea in mind of how hard it "should" be for minority voters to elect their preferred candidates under an acceptable system.

Several possible measures of "undiluted" minority voting strength suggest themselves. First, a court could simply use proportionality as its guide.... Second, a court could posit some alternative districting plan as a "normal" or "fair" electoral scheme and attempt to calculate how many candidates preferred by the minority group would probably be elected under that scheme. There are, as we have seen, a variety of ways in which even single-member districts could be drawn, and each will present the minority group with its own array of electoral risks and benefits; the court might, therefore, consider a range of acceptable plans in attempting to estimate "undiluted" minority voting strength by this method. Third, the court could attempt to arrive at a plan that would maximize feasible minority electoral success, and use this degree of predicted success as its measure of "undiluted" minority voting strength. If a court were to employ this third alternative, it would often face hard choices about what would truly "maximize" minority electoral success. An example is the scenario described above, in which a minority group could be concentrated in one completely safe district or divided among two districts in each of which its members would constitute a somewhat precarious majority.

The Court today has adopted a variant of the third approach, to wit, undiluted minority voting strength means the maximum feasible minority voting strength. In explaining the elements of a vote dilution claim, the Court first states that "the minority group must be able to demonstrate that it is sufficiently large and geographically compact to constitute a majority in a single-member district." If not, apparently the minority group has no cognizable claim that its ability to elect the representatives of its choice has been impaired.[1] Second, "the minority group must be able to

---

1. I express no view as to whether the ability of a minority group to constitute a majority in a single-member district should constitute a threshold requirement for a

show that it is politically cohesive," that is, that a significant proportion of the minority group supports the same candidates. Third, the Court requires the minority group to "demonstrate that the white majority votes sufficiently as a bloc to enable it—in the absence of special circumstances ...— usually to defeat the minority's preferred candidate." If these three requirements are met, "the minority group demonstrates that submergence in a white multimember district impedes its ability to elect its chosen representatives." That is to say, the minority group has proved vote dilution in violation of § 2.

The Court's definition of the elements of a vote dilution claim is simple and invariable: a court should calculate minority voting strength by assuming that the minority group is concentrated in a single-member district in which it constitutes a voting majority.... If this is indeed the single, universal standard for evaluating undiluted minority voting strength for vote dilution purposes, the standard is applicable whether what is challenged is a multimember district or a particular single-member districting scheme.

* * *

To appreciate the implications of this approach, it is useful to return to the illustration of a town with four council representatives given above. Under the Court's approach, if the black voters who constitute 30% of the town's voting population do not usually succeed in electing one representative of their choice, then regardless of whether the town employs at-large elections or is divided into four single-member districts, its electoral system violates § 2. Moreover, if the town had a black voting population of 40%, on the Court's reasoning the black minority, so long as it was geographically and politically cohesive, would be entitled usually to elect two of the four representatives, since it would normally be possible to create two districts in which black voters constituted safe majorities of approximately 80%.

claim that the use of multimember districts impairs the ability of minority voters to participate in the political processes and to elect representatives of their choice. Because the plaintiffs in this case would meet that requirement, if indeed it exists, I need not decide whether it is imposed by § 2. I note, however, the artificiality of the Court's distinction between claims that a minority group's "ability to elect the representatives of [its] choice" has been impaired and claims that "its ability to influence elections" has been impaired. *Ante*, n.12. It is true that a minority group that could constitute a majority in a single-member district ordinarily has the potential ability to elect representatives without white support, and that a minority that could not constitute such a majority ordinarily does not. But the Court recognizes that when the candidates preferred by a minority group are elected in a multimember district, the minority group has elected those candidates, even if white support was indispensable to these victories. On the same reasoning, if a minority group that is not large enough to constitute a voting majority in a single-member district can show that white support would probably be forthcoming in some such district to an extent that would enable the election of the candidates its members prefer, that minority group would appear to have demonstrated that, at least under this measure of its voting strength, it would be able to elect some candidates of its choice.

To be sure, the Court also requires that plaintiffs prove that racial bloc voting by the white majority interacts with the challenged districting plan so as usually to defeat the minority's preferred candidate. In fact, however, this requirement adds little that is not already contained in the Court's requirements that the minority group be politically cohesive and that its preferred candidates usually lose....

As shaped by the Court today, then, the basic contours of a vote dilution claim require no reference to most of the "*Zimmer* factors" that were developed by the Fifth Circuit to implement *White [v. Regester]*'s results test and which were highlighted in the Senate Report.... Of course, these other factors may be supportive of such a claim, because they may strengthen a court's confidence that minority voters will be unable to overcome the relative disadvantage at which they are placed by a particular districting plan, or suggest a more general lack of opportunity to participate in the political process. But the fact remains that electoral success has now emerged, under the Court's standard, as the linchpin of vote dilution claims, and that the elements of a vote dilution claim create an entitlement to roughly proportional representation within the framework of single-member districts.

II

* * *

I would reject the Court's test for vote dilution.... The Court's standard for vote dilution, when combined with its test for undiluted minority voting strength, makes actionable every deviation from usual, rough proportionality in representation for any cohesive minority group as to which this degree of proportionality is feasible within the framework of single-member districts. Requiring that every minority group that could possibly constitute a majority in a single-member district be assigned to such a district would approach a requirement of proportional representation as nearly as is possible within the framework of single-member districts.... This approach is inconsistent with the results test and with § 2's disclaimer of a right to proportional representation.

.... [The results test] requires an inquiry into the extent of the minority group's opportunities to participate in the political processes. While electoral success is a central part of the vote dilution inquiry, ... "it is not enough that the racial group allegedly discriminated against has not had legislative seats in proportion to its voting potential" and [we have] flatly rejected the proposition that "any group with distinctive interests must be represented in legislative halls if it is numerous enough to command at least one seat and represents a majority living in an area sufficiently compact to constitute a single member district." To the contrary, the results test ... requires plaintiffs to establish "that the political processes leading to nomination and election were not equally open to participation by the group in question—that its members had less opportunity than did other residents in the district to participate in the political processes and to elect legislators of their choice."

* * *

I would adhere to the approach outlined in *Whitcomb* and *White* and followed, with some elaboration, in *Zimmer* and other cases in the Courts of Appeals prior to *Bolden*. Under that approach, a court should consider all relevant factors bearing on whether the minority group has "less opportunity than other members of the electorate to participate in the political process and to elect representatives of their choice." 42 U.S.C. § 1973. The court should not focus solely on the minority group's ability to elect representatives of its choice. Whatever measure of undiluted minority voting strength the court employs in connection with evaluating the presence or absence of minority electoral success, it should also bear in mind that "the power to influence the political process is not limited to winning elections." *Davis v. Bandemer* [478 U.S. 109 (1986)]....[a]

III

Only three Justices of the Court join Part III–C of Justice Brennan's opinion, which addresses the validity of the statistical evidence on which the District Court relied in finding racially polarized voting in each of the challenged districts. Insofar as statistical evidence of divergent racial voting patterns is admitted solely to establish that the minority group is politically cohesive and to assess its prospects for electoral success, I agree that defendants cannot rebut this showing by offering evidence that the divergent racial voting patterns may be explained in part by causes other than race, such as an underlying divergence in the interests of minority and white voters. I do not agree, however, that such evidence can never affect the overall vote dilution inquiry. Evidence that a candidate preferred by the minority group in a particular election was rejected by white voters for reasons other than those which made that candidate the preferred choice of the minority group would seem clearly relevant in answering the question whether bloc voting by white voters will consistently defeat minority candidates. Such evidence would suggest that another candidate, equally preferred by the minority group, might be able to attract greater white support in future elections.

I believe Congress also intended that explanations of the reasons why white voters rejected minority candidates would be probative of the likelihood that candidates elected without decisive minority support would be willing to take the minority's interests into account. In a community that is polarized along racial lines, racial hostility may bar these and other indirect avenues of political influence to a much greater extent than in a community where racial animosity is absent although the interests of racial groups

a. *Davis v. Bandemer*, a political gerrymandering case, was decided the same day as *Gingles*. It is discussed at length in Chapter 8.

diverge.... Similarly, I agree with Justice White that Justice Brennan's conclusion that the race of the candidate is always irrelevant in identifying racially polarized voting conflicts with *Whitcomb* and is not necessary to the disposition of this case.

In this case, ... in view of the specific evidence from each district [regarding the refusal of white voters to support black candidates], ... I cannot say that its conclusion that there was severe racial bloc voting was clearly erroneous with regard to any of the challenged districts. Except in House District 23, where racial bloc voting did not prevent sustained and virtually proportional minority electoral success, I would accordingly leave undisturbed the District Court's decision to give great weight to racial bloc voting in each of the challenged districts.

IV

.... I agree with Justice Brennan that consistent and sustained success by candidates preferred by minority voters is presumptively inconsistent with the existence of a § 2 violation. Moreover, I agree that this case presents no occasion for determining what would constitute proof that such success did not accurately reflect the minority group's actual voting strength in a challenged district or districts.

* * *

V

When members of a racial minority challenge a multimember district on the grounds that it dilutes their voting strength, I agree with the Court that they must show that they possess such strength and that the multimember district impairs it. A court must therefore appraise the minority group's undiluted voting strength in order to assess the effects of the multimember district. I would reserve the question of the proper method or methods for making this assessment. But once such an assessment is made, in my view the evaluation of an alleged impairment of voting strength requires consideration of the minority group's access to the political processes generally, not solely consideration of the chances that its preferred candidates will actually be elected. Proof that white voters withhold their support from minority-preferred candidates to an extent that consistently ensures their defeat is entitled to significant weight in plaintiffs' favor. However, if plaintiffs direct their proof solely towards the minority group's prospects for electoral success, they must show that substantial minority success will be highly infrequent under the challenged plan in order to establish that the plan operates to "cancel out or minimize" their voting strength.

Compromise is essential to much if not most major federal legislation, and confidence that the federal courts will enforce such compromises is indispensable to their creation. I believe that the Court today strikes a different balance than Congress intended to when it codified the results test and disclaimed any right to proportional representation under § 2. For that reason, I join the Court's judgment but not its opinion.

■ JUSTICE STEVENS, with whom JUSTICE MARSHALL and JUSTICE BLACKMUN join, concurring in part and dissenting in part.

In my opinion, the findings of the District Court, which the Court fairly summarizes, adequately support the District Court's judgment concerning House District 23 as well as the balance of that judgment.

I, of course, agree that the election of one black candidate in each election since 1972 provides significant support for the State's position. The notion that this evidence creates some sort of a conclusive, legal presumption is not, however, supported by the language of the statute or by its legislative history. I therefore cannot agree with the Court's view that the District Court committed error by failing to apply a rule of law that emerges today without statutory support. The evidence of candidate success in District 23 is merely one part of an extremely large record which the District Court carefully considered before making its ultimate findings of fact, all of which should be upheld under a normal application of the "clearly erroneous" standard that the Court traditionally applies.

* * *

To paraphrase the Court's conclusion about the other districts, I cannot say that the District Court, composed of local judges who are well acquainted with the political realities of the State, clearly erred in concluding that use of a multimember electoral structure has caused black voters in House District 23 to have less opportunity than white voters to elect representatives of their choice.[4] Accordingly, I concur in the Court's opinion except Part IV–B and except insofar as it explains why it reverses the judgment respecting House District 23.

NOTES AND QUESTIONS

1. The lead appellant in *Gingles* was Lacy Thornburg, the elected attorney general of North Carolina. Thornburg was a Democrat. James G. Martin, the governor, filed an *amicus* brief in support of the black appel-

---

4. Even under the Court's analysis, the decision simply to reverse—without a remand—is mystifying. It is also extremely unfair. First, the Court does not give appellees an opportunity to address the new legal standard that the Court finds decisive. Second, the Court does not even bother to explain the contours of that standard, and why it was not satisfied in this case. *Cf. ante*, n.38 ("We have no occasion in this case to decide what types of special circumstances could satisfactorily demonstrate that sustained success does not accurately reflect the minority's ability to elect its preferred representatives"). Finally, though couched as a conclusion about a "matter of law," the Court's abrupt entry of judgment for appellants on District 23 reflects an unwillingness to give the District Court the respect it is due, particularly when, as in this case, the District Court has a demonstrated knowledge and expertise of the entire context that Congress directed it to consider.

lees. See *Gingles*, 478 U.S. at 34 n.*. Martin was a Republican. Democrats had controlled both houses of the General Assembly during the reapportionment process; the lack of a veto (North Carolina was apparently unique in this respect) left the governor a bystander to the apportionment process. Consider the ways in which racial and partisan politics might overlap in the decision whether to draw majority-black districts in areas where blacks are the most reliable Democratic voters. Compare the litigation postures taken by state officials in *Gingles* with the approaches taken by various players in the post–1990 North Carolina congressional reapportionment litigation, *Shaw v. Reno*, discussed in Chapter 8. The interaction of racial and political factors in North Carolina's reapportionment process is hardly a new phenomenon. For a detailed historical account, see J. Morgan Kousser, Shaw v. Reno *and the Real World of Redistricting and Representation,* 26 Rutgers L.J. 625, 670–91 (1995).

2. In general, Justice Brennan has been one of the justices most solicitous of voting rights claims by racial minorities. In *Gingles*, though, he parts company with Justices Marshall, Blackmun, and Stevens on whether to strike down House District 23. To what extent was his decision strategic? If he had not voted to uphold the district, Justice O'Connor would have announced the judgment of the Court. Would that have given her opinion more influence than his? Might a desire to keep Justice White on board for most of his opinion also have played a role?

3. Justice Brennan derives the three-part test he announces for determining dilution through submergence neither from the legislative history of section 2, nor even from pre-amendment cases (since, as both he and Justice O'Connor point out, the factors identified in the Senate Report are distilled from the case law, specifically *White v. Regester*, 412 U.S. 755 (1973), and *Zimmer v. McKeithen*, 485 F.2d 1297 (5th Cir.1973) (en banc), *aff'd on other grounds sub nom. East Carroll Parish School Bd. v. Marshall*, 424 U.S. 636 (1976)). Instead, he distilled the test from several scholarly articles, most notably James U. Blacksher & Larry T. Menefee, *From* Reynolds v. Sims *to* City of Mobile v. Bolden: *Have the White Suburbs Commandeered the Fifteenth Amendment?,* 34 Hastings L.J. 1 (1982). Blacksher and Menefee were the lawyers for the plaintiffs in *Mobile v. Bolden*.

What accounts for the Court's substitution of the three-pronged "*Gingles* test" (as it has come to be known)—which looks at (1) the size and geographic location of the minority group; (2) its political cohesion and (3) the level of white bloc voting—for the nine "typical factors" identified in the Senate Report? Are the three *Gingles* factors more "objective" in some sense than the Senate Report factors? If they are, is *Gingles* yet another manifestation of the Court's preference for bright-line tests? Consider the following observation by a court of appeals:

> *Gingles* is a reasonable exercise of the Court's authority in statutory interpretation. The Court's approach, by focusing up front on

whether there is an effective remedy for the claimed injury, promotes ease of application without distorting the statute or the intent underlying it. It reins in the almost unbridled discretion that section 2 gives the courts, focusing the inquiry so that plaintiffs with promising claims can develop a full record. The creation of preconditions—a choice of clear rules over muddy efforts to discern equity—shields the courts from meritless claims and ensures that clearly meritorious claims will survive summary judgment. That might not always have been true had courts been allowed to consider all of the *White/Zimmer* factors at the early stages of the proceedings. Thus, although ... the *Gingles* criteria might conceivably foreclose a meritorious claim, in general they will ensure that violations for which an effective remedy exists will be considered while appropriately closing the courthouse to marginal cases. In making that trade-off, the *Gingles* majority justifiably sacrificed some claims to protect stronger claims and promote judicial economy. The Voting Rights Act is a crucially important piece of national legislation, but it is subject to the same considerations of effective administration as other similar statutes.

McNeil v. Springfield Park District, 851 F.2d 937 (7th Cir.1988), cert. denied, 490 U.S. 1031 (1989). *See also, e.g.*, Samuel Issacharoff, *Polarized Voting and the Political Process: The Transformation of Voting Rights Jurisprudence*, 90 Mich. L. Rev. 1833 (1992); Blacksher & Menefee, *supra*, at 14 (contrasting the Court's willingness to intervene to prohibit malapportionment, where there was an easily quantifiable standard, with its reluctance to protect racial minorities from qualitative vote dilution through the use of at-large elections); Jan G. Deutsch, *Neutrality, Legitimacy, and the Supreme Court: Some Intersections Between Law and Political Science*, 20 Stan. L. Rev. 169, 248 (1968) (claiming that a formula like one-person, one-vote was virtually inevitable given the Court's institutional constraints and its desire for apparent neutrality); *cf.* Sanford Levinson, *Gerrymandering and the Brooding Omnipresence of Proportional Representation: Why Won't It Go Away?*, 33 UCLA L. Rev. 257 (1985) (claiming that a similar simplifying imperative would drive the Court toward a mathematical proportionality measure in gerrymandering cases).

4. "*Gingles* brought the racially polarized voting inquiry into the undisputed and unchallenged center of the Voting Rights Act," making proof of racial bloc voting the touchstone of a section 2 claim of dilution through submergence. Issacharoff, *supra*, at 1851. Later in the chapter, we shall return to one central area of disagreement among Justices Brennan, White, and O'Connor—namely, when legally sufficient racial bloc voting exists. But it is worth understanding throughout our consideration of the post-*Gingles* case law how social scientists and courts go about estimating voter behavior. For more extensive discussions of the social science methodologies, *see generally* Bernard Grofman, Lisa Handley, & Richard G. Niemi, Minority Representation and the Quest for Voting Equality 82–108 (1992);

Richard L. Engstrom & Michael McDonald, *Quantitative Evidence in Vote Dilution Litigation: Political Participation and Polarized Voting*, 17 Urb. Law. 369 (Summer 1985); Bernard Grofman, Michael Migalski, & Nicholas Noviello, *The "Totality of Circumstances Test" in Section 2 of the 1982 Extension of the Voting Rights Act: A Social Science Perspective*, 7 Law & Policy 199 (1985). For a comprehensive discussion of the general issues posed by attempting to estimate individual voter behavior, see Gary King, A Solution to the Ecological Inference Problem: Reconstructing Individual Behavior from Aggregate Data (1997).

The concept of racial bloc voting had long played some role in judicial review of election systems, although the more empirical emphasis did not emerge until the 1980's. For example, in *United States v. Louisiana,* 225 F.Supp. 353 (E.D.La.1963), *aff'd*, 380 U.S. 145 (1965), a case challenging Louisiana's discriminatory use of a literacy test, the court recounted the white supremacist Citizens' Council's drive to purge the registration rolls "of 'the great numbers of unqualified voters who have been illegally registered' ", and who " 'invariably vote in blocks and constitute a menace to the community.' " *Cf. United States v. Association of Citizens Councils of Louisiana*, 196 F.Supp. 908 (W.D.La.1961) (noting that "[i]n elections held prior to [1956], the Negro voters [in Bienville Parish, Louisiana, where 86% of the white community but only 13% of the black community were registered to vote] had engaged in the reprehensible practice of 'bloc voting,' i.e., all or most of their votes were cast one way or another."). The concept of racial bloc voting often played out in racial appeals in campaigns, as with the claim by white candidates who played on the linguistic similarity between "bloc" voting and "black voting" to make the point that black voters would prefer different candidates, and that if enough black voters managed to cast ballots, those candidates would prevail. The first reported racial vote dilution case, *Smith v. Paris*, 257 F.Supp. 901 (M.D.Ala.1966), *modified*, 386 F.2d 979 (5th Cir.1967), struck down a switch from districted to at-large elections for the Barbour County, Alabama, Democratic Executive Committee as intentionally discriminatory because the change responded to racial bloc voting by submerging the votes of the black community. Blacks had been entirely disenfranchised prior to the passage of the Voting Rights Act, but a massive post-Act registration effort made them the majority in four of the county's sixteen "beats" (i.e., districts). Six black candidates ran for election to the committee:

> The tabulation of the election returns reflects that if the election had been held under the [single-member district] system that had previously been in force ... three of the plaintiffs would very likely have been elected [since they received a majority of the votes cast in the predominantly black beats]. Under the county-wide vote system established by this resolution, all plaintiffs were defeated by substantial majorities.

The district court noted "the anomalous twist that predominantly Negro beats now have their representatives determined for them by the predominantly white majority of voters in the county as a whole."

In these early cases, the courts' allusions to bloc voting were largely anecdotal or commonsensical. They simply assumed, based on their familiarity with local politics, that voting was racially polarized. Not until *City of Petersburg v. United States*, 354 F.Supp. 1021 (D.D.C.1972), *aff'd*, 410 U.S. 962 (1973), did a court "appl[y] the concepts of 'block voting' and 'polarization' as part of a formal analysis of evidentiary data." Joseph P. Viteritti, *Unapportioned Justice: Local Elections, Social Science, and the Evolution of the Voting Rights Act*, 4 Cornell J.L. & Pub. Pol'y 199, 232 (1994). The *Petersburg* court used a relatively simple methodological approach—"homogeneous precinct analysis" (referred to in *Gingles* as "extreme case analysis"). Basically, homogeneous precinct analysis looks at the returns from precincts whose population is overwhelmingly (more than 90 percent) of one race. In *Petersburg*, the court found that "[i]n recent Council elections, in which both black and white candidates have participated, the vote in [the four] precincts which are racially identifiable as being almost completely black or white has been overwhelmingly along racial lines." From this the court inferred "that the same type of voting occurs throughout the City of Petersburg in elections affecting local issues."

Homogeneous precinct analysis remains a widespread tool in voting rights cases. It is easy to perform: it requires only census data (or voter registration data in jurisdictions that keep registration statistics by race) and a set of election returns. It is also conceptually easy to understand: if one precinct contains only black voters, while two others contain only white ones, then the election returns will definitively reveal whether voters of different races prefer different candidates.

There are two potential problems with homogeneous precinct analysis, however. The first is practical: in many jurisdictions, most of the precincts will not be racially homogeneous (even if they are racially identifiable); thus, a homogeneous precinct analysis will have to ignore much of the available data. In some jurisdictions, homogeneous precinct analysis may be impossible; even if there are, for example, a few 90 percent-or-more white precincts, there may be no comparable black ones. The second problem involves the sort of inference made by the *Petersburg* court—that the behavior of voters in racially homogeneous communities is typical of the behavior of voters in more racially mixed ones. There are reasons, perhaps, to doubt an exact correspondence: blacks in overwhelmingly black precincts, for example, may often have lower income and education levels than blacks who live in integrated settings and thus may have different political preferences; whites who choose to live in racially integrated neighborhoods may be more open to crossover voting and biracial coalition building than those who choose to live in all-white communities. *Cf. Major v. Treen*, 574 F.Supp. 325 (E.D.La.1983) (three-judge court) (finding, with regard to the racial bloc voting inquiry, that whites who had fled from New Orleans to overwhelmingly white suburbs to avoid school integration were less likely than whites within New Orleans to support black candidates in congressional races for seats containing both the city and suburbs). Thus, homogeneous precinct analysis might overestimate the overall level of racial bloc voting within a jurisdiction, particularly if voters living in homogeneous precincts are a relatively small share of the overall population.

The other common social science technique for estimating voter behavior is bivariate ecological regression. The word "bivariate" refers to the fact that the analysis looks at two variables: the racial composition of the precincts and the votes garnered by particular candidates. The adjective "ecological" refers to the kind of data used in the analysis: election returns reflect aggregate activity (they are usually reported on a precinct-by-precinct basis), rather than the direct observation of individual behavior. "Regression" is a statistical technique for measuring the relationship between two or more variables: it determines how much one variable changes as the other variable (or variables, in a "multivariate" analysis) changes. In the context of section 2 cases, the two variables are the racial composition of a precinct and the share of the vote received by a given candidate. To understand how the process works, let us consider the data in a hypothetical community where all the voters are either black or white and there are two candidates running for election, one black candidate and one white candidate. Some data can be acquired directly: census or registration data will give us a pretty good idea of how many black voters and how many white voters there are in each precinct.[b] Election returns will tell us how many votes each candidate received in each precinct. The information we wish to derive involves the percentage of black voters and white voters who voted for each candidate. Secret ballots prevent us from obtaining that information directly, and exit polls, particularly in racially charged election contests, may be inaccurate. *See, e.g.,* Leslie Phillips, *Sick of Polls? There's Just One More*, USA Today, Nov. 3, 1992, at 12A (reporting that "[r]aces with minority candidates have confounded exit pollsters, because some respondents seem to believe revealing their vote says something about their racial bias"; in 1989, for example, in the Virginia governor's race and the New York mayor's race, exit polls showed black candidates Douglas Wilder

---

b. This represents a slight simplification, since often the data are not quite this precise. The least precise data set would be one providing only the overall number of black and white residents within each precinct. (The Census Bureau can virtually always provide this data.) If that were the data being used, adjustments would be necessary to account for the fact that a higher percentage of the minority population is likely to be ineligible to vote because of youth and, in the case of Asian–Americans and Hispanics, alienage, as well as for the fact that minority turnout is often significantly lower than white turnout. In the ideal, and only infrequently realized case, the available data will consist of actual sign-in records and registration figures kept by race, which allows for a fair degree of certainty about how many blacks and whites voted in each precinct. (There are statistical techniques for estimating turnout as well. *See* Grofman, Handley & Niemi, *supra*, at 88.)

and David Dinkins holding significant leads but both candidates actually won by only a tiny margin).

Ecological regression tries to get around these problems by inferring individual behavior from the observed data. To understand how the technique works, imagine a scattergram. The horizontal axis measures the independent variable, the percentage of voters in each precinct who are black. The vertical axis measures the dependent variable, the percentage of votes received by the "black" candidate.

The following figure is a scattergram generated from a 1980 Norfolk, Virginia, city councilmanic election studied by Engstrom & MacDonald, *supra*.

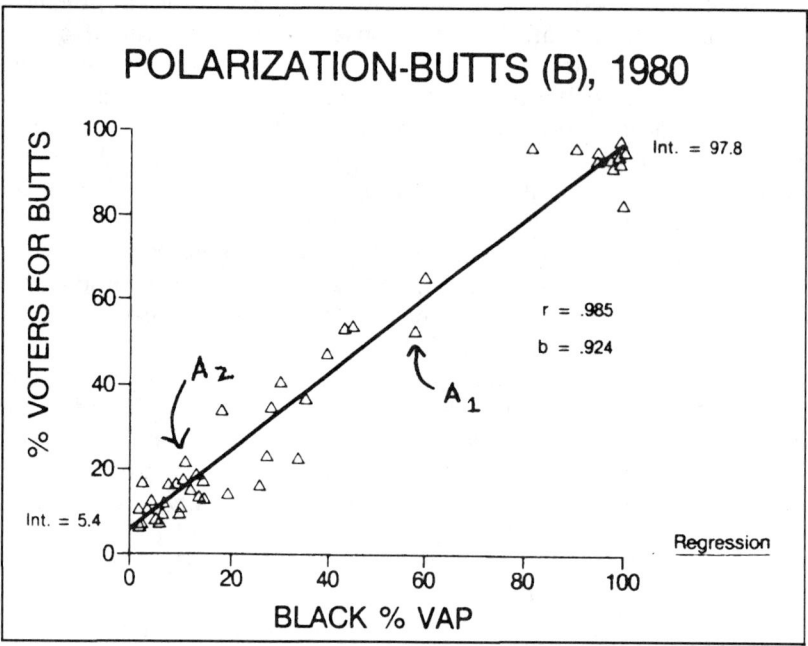

Every precinct within the community can be located on the scattergram. For example, a precinct that is 58 percent black and where the black candidate received 50 percent of the votes cast would be located at point A_1. A precinct that is 10 percent black and where the black candidate received 22 percent of the vote would be located at point A_2.

Regression is a technique for fitting a straight line through the data points. The regression line is the straight line that best fits the observed data points, meaning the line that minimizes the combined distances between each of the points and the line. It is also referred to as the "least squares" method because it seeks to minimize the aggregate distance of all the points on the graph to the regression line—as measured by squaring all the distances from the line and then adding them together. The slope and intercepts of the line enable us to draw some important conclusions about voting behavior. The slope of the line tells us how strongly the two variables are related: the greater the slope the stronger the relationship. If the regression coefficient (normally referred to as "b") is, for example, .924, then "it is estimated that every increase of 1.0 percent in the black portion of the [voting age population] across precincts tended to result in a .924 increase in the percentage of voters supporting [the black candidate]. In other words, if the black proportion of the [voting age population] in one precinct was 50 percentage points higher than in a second precinct, the percentage of voters supporting [the black candidate] in that precinct would be expected to be about 46.2 percentage points higher (50 x .924) than in the second precinct." *Id.* at 376.

Where the regression line intercepts the two vertical axes enables us to estimate the actual percentage of black and white voters who supported the black candidate. The left vertical axis of the scatterplot represents the percentage of white votes received by the black candidate; the right axis represents the percentage of black votes she received. In our scattergram, the left intercept is 5.4; this means that the regression technique estimates that 5.4 percent of the white voters supported the black candidate. The right intercept is 97.8; thus, it is estimated that 97.8 percent of black voters voted for the black candidate. In the current double regression technique, statisticians perform a second regression to determine voting behavior with regard to the white candidate as well. Notice, however, that in communities with significant residential segregation the regression analysis is heavily determined by the extreme precincts that "anchor" the regression line. For example, in Norfolk, notice how many of the precincts are heavily segregated. In such communities, extreme case analysis and bivariate regression analysis can generally be expected to produce comparable estimates of black and white voting patterns.

In addition to deriving the regression coefficient, regression analysis can also provide both a correlation coefficient (commonly reported as "r"), which measures how consistently the scores for the dependent variable vary with the independent variable, and a measure of statistical significance, that is, how likely a pattern that looks like a straight line is simply the product of chance. The correlation coefficient tells us how close to the line the various data points fall. An "r" of +1.0 would indicate a perfectly consistent positive relationship; an "r" of –1.0 would indicate a perfectly consistent negative relationship; and an "r" of 0 would indicate no relationship whatsoever between the two variables. An "r" above 0.5 is normally viewed as indicative of a real positive relationship; an "r" of 0.9 would be viewed as extremely high. The correlation coefficients for the elections studied in *Gingles* ranged from .70 to .98, meaning that between 70 and 98 percent of the variation in support for the black candidate could be ascribed to the racial composition of the electorate. In the 1980 Norfolk contest, the value of r is quite high: .985, meaning that 98.5 percent of the variation in how Butts fared in different precincts can be explained by the racial composition of the precincts.

Justice Brennan's opinion in *Gingles* endorsed a *bivariate* regression analysis, that is, one that looked at *two* variables: race of the voters and share of the votes received by each candidate. Justice O'Connor's approach, by contrast, seemed more hospitable to a *multivariate* analysis—one that looked at additional factors. We shall return to the issue below. For summaries of the various arguments that have raged in the social science literature over regression analysis, see, e.g., Grofman, Handley, & Niemi, *supra*; Bernard Grofman, *The Use of Ecological Regression to Estimate Racial Bloc Voting*, 27 U.S.F.L. Rev. 593 (1993).

1. *GINGLES'* FIRST PRONG: "SUFFICIENTLY LARGE AND GEOGRAPHICALLY COMPACT"

Gingles held that "the minority group must be able to demonstrate that it is sufficiently large and geographically compact to constitute a majority in a single-member district." Precisely how large is large enough?

Suppose that plaintiffs show that it would be possible to draw a district that is 51 percent black in total population. For a variety of demographic and sociological reasons, it is unlikely that such a district's actual electorate on election day will be majority black. First, nonwhite populations tend to be disproportionately young. According to the 1980 census, while 69.7% of the white population was of voting age, only 60% of blacks and 57.0% of Hispanics were. This disparity may be exacerbated in cases involving Hispanic communities, where many of the adults will be ineligible to vote because they are not U.S. citizens. *Cf. Garza v. Los Angeles County Board of Supervisors*, 918 F.2d 763 (9th Cir.1990), *cert. denied*, 498 U.S. 1028 (1991) (districts with less than 0.7% deviations in total population varied from 707,651 to 1,098,663 in the number of voting age citizens they contained). Second, minority communities also historically have had lower voter registration and turnout characteristics than white communities. For example, 70.1% of whites reported that they were registered to vote, and 63.6% claimed actually to have voted in the 1992 presidential elections; the comparable numbers for blacks were 63.9% and 54.0%, respectively. For Hispanics (many of whom are not citizens), they were even lower: 35.0% and 28.9%, respectively. Statistical Abstract of the United States 1994, tbl. 448. And there is some evidence that nonwhite voters tend to overreport registration and participation at a greater rate than whites. See Allan J. Lichtman & Samuel Issacharoff, *Black/White Voter Registration Disparities in Mississippi: Legal and Methodological Issues in Challenging Bureau of Census Data*, 7 J.L. & Pol. 525 (1991) (explaining the methodological flaws in census surveys that tend to overestimate registration and turnout). Thus, plaintiffs may realistically be no more likely to elect a candidate of their choice from a 51% black district than from a 40% one.

While *Gingles* did not expressly hold that plaintiffs must show that blacks are a majority of the voting-age population, the lower courts have generally adopted this requirement. *See, e.g., Romero v. City of Pomona*, 883 F.2d 1418 (9th Cir.1989); *Overton v. City of Austin*, 871 F.2d 529 (5th Cir.1989); *McNeil v. Springfield Park District*, 851 F.2d 937 (7th Cir.1988), *cert. denied*, 490 U.S. 1031 (1989); *Latino Political Action Committee v. City of Boston*, 609 F.Supp. 739 (D.Mass.1985), *aff'd*, 784 F.2d 409 (1st Cir. 1986). As the Fifth Circuit explained in *Overton*:

> [T]he raison d'etre of *Thornburg* and of amended § 2 is to facilitate participation by minorities in our political processes, by preventing dilution of their votes. Only voting age persons can vote. It would be a Pyrrhic victory for a court to create a single-member district in which a minority population dominant in absolute, but not in voting age numbers, continued to be defeated at the polls. *Thornburg* implicitly recognized this fact:
>
>> Unless minority voters possess the potential to elect representatives in the absence of the challenged structure or practice, they cannot claim to have been injured by that practice.

Is this reasoning entirely correct? Note that the North Carolina electoral scheme at issue in *Gingles* contained a majority-vote requirement. Thus, a group had to constitute a majority of the electorate to win an election. In jurisdictions with first-past-the-post, plurality-win systems, should the plaintiffs still be required to constitute an electoral *majority*? Suppose, for example, that a city council is elected in nonpartisan elections (as many are), that there are usually three candidates running for each available seat, and that the winning candidate normally garners 45% of the vote. Should a minority group be able to satisfy the first prong of *Gingles* by showing that it could constitute 45% of the electorate in a fairly drawn single-member district?

Or should the threshold be even higher? In a somewhat different context, a number of courts have relied on the so-called "65 percent rule" developed in *United Jewish Organizations of Williamsburgh (UJO) v. Carey*, 430 U.S. 144 (1977), which is reprinted in Chapter 8. In *UJO*, the Supreme Court upheld the Attorney General's insistence that New York draw some state legislative districts that were 65 percent nonwhite because a district with a smaller nonwhite majority would not offer nonwhite voters a realistic chance to elect the candidate of their choice. If, at the remedial stage, courts often find it necessary to create districts with nonwhite "supermajorities," should plaintiffs be required to show that such supermajority districts can be drawn, that is, that there will be an actual nonwhite voter majority in the proposed district on election day?

Some plaintiffs have sought to escape *Gingles'* first prong altogether by relying on footnote 12 of Justice Brennan's opinion, which expressly reserved the question "whether § 2 permits, and if it does, what standards should pertain to, a claim brought by a minority group, that is not sufficiently large and compact to constitute a majority in a single-member district, alleging that the use of a multimember district impairs its ability to influence elections." The Supreme Court has repeatedly sidestepped the question whether, and how, such "influence district" claims can be brought. See *Johnson v. De Grandy*, 512 U.S. 997, 1009 (1994); *Voinovich v. Quilter*, 507 U.S. 146, 152 (1993); *Growe v. Emison*, 507 U.S. 25, 40 n. 5 (1993). Most lower courts have rejected claims that section 2 entitles minority groups to an influence district even if they cannot satisfy the first *Gingles* precondition. *See, e.g. Latino Political Action Committee v. Boston*, 784 F.2d 409 (1st Cir.1986); *DeBaca v. County of San Diego*, 794 F.Supp. 990 (S.D.Cal.1992), *aff'd*, 5 F.3d 535 (9th Cir.1993); *Hastert v. State Bd. of Elections*, 777 F.Supp. 634 (N.D.Ill.1991).

One court, in an opinion subsequently vacated on unrelated grounds, did recognize influence district claims. *Armour v. Ohio*, 895 F.2d 1078 (6th Cir.1990), *vacated on granting of rehearing en banc*, 925 F.2d 987 (6th Cir.1991). The case involved a challenge to the Ohio State House of Representatives. The plaintiffs were black voters who lived in the area around Youngstown. Some of them lived in the 52nd District, which was 11 percent black; the rest lived in the 53rd District, which was 25 percent black. They sought to redraw the boundary lines between the districts so that virtually all the black voters would be placed in one district, which would then be 36 percent black. The district court dismissed the plaintiffs' complaint, due to the plaintiffs' failure to meet the first prong of the *Gingles* test.

The court of appeals reversed. It noted that success in the Democratic primary seemed to be the most significant factor in winning House seats within the region, and accordingly directed the district court to revisit the plaintiffs' claims under a more fluid totality of the circumstances test that would consider:

(1) whether a greater percentage of blacks than whites are Democrats in the relevant region;

(2) the extent of the difference in the respective proportions of black and white Democrats in the particular region;

(3) whether a substantial number of elections have involved more than two candidates;

(4) whether the projected black voter turnout in the proposed district would exceed the number of votes usually needed to win the Democratic primary; and if so, whether the black voter turnout in the current district has generally been less than the number of votes needed to win the primary;

(5) whether there is evidence that white cross-over voting for a black candidate could assist blacks in electing candidates of their choice.

In particular, the court of appeals directed the district court to consider whether white crossover voting would be sufficient to enable blacks to elect the candidate of their choice from an influence district:

> Such an examination acknowledges that the vote dilution claim is concerned with the ability of black voters to exert political influence over issues that concern them as voters. While voting in many elections is influenced by the race of the candidate, such polarization should not overshadow the significant number of voters who vote for candidates who are not members of their race, but who represent their interests. The analysis of cross-over voting moves away from using the candidate's race alone as a proxy for black political influence and attempts to utilize a more accurate measure of black voting power by analyzing the fulfillment of black voter preferences. By utilizing this mode of analysis, it is not necessary for black voters to be in the majority in the proposed district in order to exert political influence. Through the coalition of black voters and white voters who support black-preferred candidates, blacks may be able to elect the candidate of their choice from a majority-white single-member district.

Does *Armour* blur the distinction between the first and third *Gingles* factors? A later case involving the concept of influence districts, *Rural West Tennessee African–American Affairs Council v. McWherter*, 836 F.Supp. 453 (W.D.Tenn.1993) (three-judge court), *vacated*, 512 U.S. 1248 (1994), *on remand*, 877 F.Supp. 1096 (W.D.Tenn.). *summarily aff'd*, 116 S.Ct. 42 (1995), fuses the first and third prongs in the opposite direction. We discuss *Rural West* later in this Chapter. For more extensive discussion of the relationship between the minority's ability to elect, white crossover voting, and the first prong of *Gingles*, see J. Morgan Kousser, *Beyond* Gingles: *Influence Districts and the Pragmatic Tradition in Voting Rights Law*, 27 U.S.F. L. Rev. 551 (1993); Stanley Pierre Louise, Comment, *The Politics of Influence: Recognizing Influence Dilution Claims Under Section 2 of the Voting Rights Act*, 62 U.Chi.L.Rev. 1215 (1995).

A more limited recognition of influence district claims appears in *Garza v. Los Angeles County Board of Supervisors*, 918 F.2d 763 (9th Cir.1990), *cert. denied*, 498 U.S. 1028 (1991). The plaintiffs in *Garza*, Hispanic voters in Los Angeles, challenged the district boundaries created in the 1981 decennial reapportionment. At the time the districts were drawn, it was arguably impossible to have drawn a district with a majority of Hispanic voters, although, by the time the case was filed, such a district could be drawn. The county argued as a matter of law that the 1981 districts were lawful, "regardless of any intentional or unintentional dilution of minority voting strength, because at the time they were drawn there could be no single-member district with a majority of minority voters." The court of appeals disagreed, on the grounds that the first prong of *Gingles* was irrelevant in light of the district court's finding of *intentional* vote dilution. Is *Garza*'s implicit distinction between intent and non-intent claims faithful to section 2? Given Congress' rejection of a discriminatory purpose requirement for statutory claims, should a showing of discriminatory purpose nonetheless have special weight?

The second aspect of *Gingles*' first prong is the requirement that the minority group be "compact." *Gingles* seems to treat the compactness inquiry as entirely causal in nature—stating that "in a substantially integrated district, the multimember form of the district cannot be responsible for minority voters' inability to elect its candidates"—but consider whether the compactness prong of *Gingles* is also related to the concept of "discrete and insular" minority groups introduced in *Carolene Products*' footnote 4 and lying at the heart of contemporary process theory. Does the compactness of a minority group increase the likelihood that officeholders will ignore its distinctive interests?

Gingles nowhere defines "compactness." There are a variety of different definitions used in social science literature, statutes, and judicial opinions.

Dillard v. Baldwin County Board of Education
686 F.Supp. 1459 (M.D.Ala.1988).

■ MYRON H. THOMPSON, DISTRICT JUDGE:

* * *

II. Factual Background

Baldwin County is located in the southwest part of Alabama, and is bordered in part by Mobile Bay to the west and Florida to the east. It has a population, according to the 1980 census, of 78,556 people; of that figure, 12,716 or 16.19%, are black, and 65,840, or 83.81% are white. However, during this decade the county has experienced a population boom, with most of the boom being made up of whites. It is estimated that by 1990, the population will have increased to 98,820, with the white population having increased by 19,280 to 85,120 or 86.14% of the population, but with the black population having increased by only 984, to 13,700 and with a percentage point decrease 13.86%. Most of the black population is concentrated in neighborhoods on a strip along the county's western border.

III. Discriminatory Results

* * *

C.

* * *

2.

[T]he plaintiffs have met the *Thornburg* precondition that they be sufficiently large and geographically compact to constitute a majority in a single-member district. They have submitted a districting plan with seven single-member districts, one of which, district one, has a black voting-age majority.

The Baldwin County Board of Education argues that the plaintiffs' plan is unacceptable because it is too elongated and curvaceous and thus fails to meet the requirement of "compactness." By compactness, *Thornburg* does not mean that a proposed district must meet, or attempt to achieve, some aesthetic absolute, such as symmetry or attractiveness. An aesthetic norm, by itself, would be not only unrelated to the legal and social issues presented under § 2, it would be an unworkable concept, resulting in arbitrary and capricious results, because it offers no guidance as to when it is met. It is apparent from the *Thornburg* opinion that compactness is a relative term tied to certain practical objectives under § 2; the requirements is not that a district be compact, but that it be "sufficiently" compact under § 2. The term is a "practical" or "functional" concept, which must be considered in relation to § 2's laudatory national mission of opening up the political process to those minorities that have been historically denied such.... The degree of geographical symmetry or attractiveness is therefore a desirable consideration for districting, but only to the extent it aids or facilitates the political process, and only as one among many considerations a court should include, the principal one being § 2's vote dilution prohibition, in determining whether there is sufficient compactness for a majority black district.

The court therefore believes, especially in light of § 2's strong national mandate, that a district is sufficiently geographically compact if it allows for effective representation. For example, a district would not be sufficiently compact if it was so spread out that there was no sense of community, that is, if its members and its representative could not effectively and efficiently stay in touch with each other; or if it was so convoluted that there was no sense of community, that is, if its members and its representative could not easily tell who actually lived within the district. Also of importance, of course, is the compactness of neighboring districts; obviously, if, because of the configuration of a district, its neighboring districts so lacked compactness that they could not be effectively represented, the *Thornburg* standard of compactness would not be met. These are not, however, the only factors a court should consider in assessing a proposed district; because compactness is a functional concept, the number and kinds of factors a court should consider may vary with each case, depending on the local geographical, political, and socio-economic characteristics of the jurisdiction being sued.

The seven-member redistricting plan proposed by the plaintiffs meets this functional standard. In response to direct questions from the court, the superintendent of the Baldwin County Board of Education testified that he saw no administrative or other problems with the configuration of the proposed majority-black district in the plaintiffs' plan, and that the district could be effectively represented; in his words, the district is "manageable." The evidence also reflected that there would be a strong sense of community within the proposed black district. Moreover, and perhaps most telling, the five-member plan the school board proposed in settlement of this lawsuit has a single-member district—district five, which the board contends is majority black—that is just as elongated and curvaceous as the majority black district in the plaintiffs' plan; at the time they submitted their plan, the school board and its superintendent did not consider it to be unacceptable. The Baldwin County Board of Education's contention that the majority-black district in plaintiffs' plan lacks sufficient compactness is disingenuous.

* * *

NOTES AND QUESTIONS

1. The plan adopted by the district court not only created a majority-black district, but increased the number of seats on the county school board from five to seven. The school board proposed a five-district plan in which one district would be majority black, but the court rejected that plan as an inadequate remedy. It pointed out that census estimates suggested that by 1990, a population boom would render the proposed majority-black district majority white in voting age population. Thus, it concluded, the defendant's plan would "continue [the plaintiffs'] submersion in a majority-white population, which, because of racially polarized voting and other socioeconomic and historical conditions in the county, would still be able regularly to defeat the choices of black voters and to ignore their interest without fear of political consequences.... [T]he board's plan would itself violate § 2." By contrast, "the selection of a plan with seven, rather than five, single-member districts reflects a conservative remedy limited to only those measures necessary to cure the violation."

Does the court's analysis of the need for seven rather than five districts survive *Holder v. Hall*, where a plurality of the Court held that the size of a governing authority is not subject to a vote dilution challenge under § 2 of the Voting Rights Act? (*Holder* appears *infra*, pp. 519–35). Is there a difference between establishing liability by showing that if there were more districts plaintiffs would be able to satisfy the first prong of *Gingles* and requiring that a jurisdiction increase the number of seats as part of a remedy?

2. Compare *Dillard*'s "functional" definition of compactness with the definitions of compactness offered by Colorado and Iowa, *see* Colo. Const. art. V, § 47 (defining compactness in terms of the sum of the perimeters of district boundaries); Iowa Code Ann. § 42.4(1)(c) (West 1991) (defining

compactness as "the ratio of dispersion of population about the population center of the district to the dispersion of population about the geographic center of the district"). For more thorough discussions of compactness, see Bernard Grofman, *Criteria for Districting: A Social Science Perspective*, 33 U.C.L.A.L. Rev. 77 (1985); Richard H. Pildes & Richard G. Niemi, *Expressive Harms, "Bizarre Districts," and Voting Rights: Evaluating Election-District Appearances After* Shaw v. Reno, 92 Mich. L. Rev. 483 (1993).

3. How, if at all, does *Dillard*'s analysis of compactness correspond to the analysis of compactness offered in the *Shaw* line of cases, discussed in Chapter 8?

4. Does compactness have a different meaning in the context of local elections with relatively small districts than in congressional elections with districts that often stretch across counties or contain more than 500,000 people?

5. To what extent is it important that the minority community be "large" in a physical sense, as opposed to a numerical one? How common is the Court's model of a large, geographically discrete and isolated minority community? Particularly in the rural and small-town south, residential patterns may be racially identifiable without producing sizeable concentrations or "ghettoes" of the northern urban variety. *See* Chandler Davidson, Biracial Politics: Conflict and Coalition in the Metropolitan South 19-20 (1972) (explaining three types of racial residential patterns: (1) "back yard"—where black residences are scattered throughout the city; (2) the "ghetto" involving a "single intense concentration of Negro residences"; and (3) " 'urban clusters' involving one to three large concentrations of Negroes, as well as up to twenty smaller clusters scattered across the city").

Washington County, Florida, the jurisdiction involved in *Potter v. Washington County*, 653 F.Supp. 121 (N.D.Fla.1986), offers an example of the potential disjunction between size and segregation. Washington County was a rural county whose voting-age population was 13.1 percent black. The black community lived largely in three distinct neighborhoods, but those neighborhoods were so separated that they could not easily be combined into one geographic district. Still, by stringing some of the neighborhoods together it was possible to create a 55.8 percent black district. The district court rejected that option, even though the defendants conceded liability under section 2, because the district "arbitrarily cuts diagonally through the center of the county." *Potter* rests on a distinction between black communities that are sufficiently large and *contiguous* to form majority-black single-member districts and black communities that are geographically large and *compact*. (The proposed district would have included roughly 70 percent of Washington County's black residents in the 55.8 percent black district.) Thus, although the *district* was perhaps not compact, in that it extended from one end of the county to the other, the black *community* was fairly concentrated.

6. Does *Gingles'* first prong require some particular level of concentration of minority voters within the illustrative districts? Consider *Gomez v. City of Watsonville,* 863 F.2d 1407 (9th Cir.1988) *cert. denied,* 489 U.S. 1080 (1989). Watsonville was governed by a six-member city council and mayor. According to the 1980 census, 48.9 percent of the City's population was Hispanic, although due to demography and differential rates of citizenship, only 37.0 percent of Watsonville's voting-age citizens were.

Roughly two-thirds of the city's Hispanic population lived in three census tracts. But the district court held that that Watsonville's Hispanics were not sufficiently compact because the illustrative plans offered by the plaintiffs to meet the first prong of *Gingles* placed only one-third of the Hispanic electorate in the two majority-Hispanic districts. (The remainder of the Hispanic community was dispersed among the five majority non-Hispanic districts.)

The court of appeals reversed:

The district court erred in considering that approximately 60% of the Hispanics eligible to vote in Watsonville would reside in five districts outside the two single-member, heavily Hispanic districts in appellants' plan. Districting plans with some members of the minority group outside the minority-controlled districts are valid.... The fact that the proposed remedy does not benefit all of the Hispanics in the City does not justify denying any remedy at all.

The appellants' plan proposes two districts in which Hispanics would constitute a majority of the voters and would be able to elect representatives of their choice. It is sadly ironic that the district court concluded that because many Hispanic voters would still not be able to elect representatives of their choice under the proposed plan, no Section 2 claim could be maintained, thereby relegating all Hispanic voters to having no political effectiveness. The district court's finding is premised on a misunderstanding of the applicable legal standard.

Ought plan drawers seek to maximize the number of nonwhite voters placed in majority nonwhite districts in order to increase the number of individual voters who are able to elect a candidate of their choice? Remember, in a jurisdiction with severe racial bloc voting, voters who are in the racial minority within a district will essentially waste their votes. To what extent does increasing each *individual*'s ability to vote for a winning candidate decrease the influence of the *group* to which that voter belongs on the overall composition of the legislature? Is there simply an inherent tension between maximizing individual voters' influence and dilutive "packing"?

2. *GINGLES'* SECOND PRONG: "POLITICAL COHESION": THE SPECIAL PROBLEM OF COALITION LAWSUITS

For the most part, *Gingles*'s second prong—that "the minority group ... show that it is politically cohesive"—has occasioned little litigation. In part, this is a function of the ease with which cohesion can be shown. As Justice Brennan's opinion explained it, "[a] showing that a significant number of minority group members usually vote for the same candidates is one way of proving the political cohesiveness necessary to a vote dilution claim, and, consequently, establishes minority bloc voting within the context of § 2." Thus, the statistical techniques discussed above can easily show that the minority community throws overwhelming support behind a few candidates. In part also, the paucity of reported cases may be a function of litigation decisions. Lawyers may be reluctant to bring suit on behalf of deeply divided minority communities because the benefits from victory would be so illusory: if the minority community is unable to unite behind a candidate, even a majority-black district may be unable to elect a minority-preferred candidate. And to the extent that voting rights lawyers rely on community involvement in the litigation process, the time and trouble of litigating a case on behalf of a fractured community may be too high.

Gingles presented a textbook example of one sort of racial politics: the black-white split of the Deep South. Litigation regarding political cohesiveness has focused largely on a quite different context: the multi-racial, multi-ethnic jurisdictions of the Southwest, Florida, and the urban north. In these jurisdictions, courts must confront a definitional problem absent from *Gingles*, namely, what counts as a minority "group." Must all the members share a single racial, ethnic, or linguistic identification or can minority groups be "aggregated"? When the Supreme Court was presented with this issue, in *Growe v. Emison*, 507 U.S. 25, 41 (1993), it sidestepped the question by assuming the permissibility of combining distinct ethnic and language groups—in that case, African and Native Americans in Minneapolis—but observing that there was no statistical or anecdotal evidence in the record to show minority political cohesion. The lower courts have been sharply divided.

Nixon v. Kent County

76 F.3d 1381 (6th Cir.1996) (en banc).

■ SUHRHEINRICH, delivered the opinion of the court, in which MERRITT, KENNEDY, MILBURN, NELSON, RYAN, BOGGS, NORRIS, SILER, and BATCHELDER, joined. KEITH, delivered a separate dissenting opinion, in which JONES and DAUGHTREY, joined and in which MARTIN and MOORE joined in Parts I, II, and IIIA. MARTIN, JONES, and DAUGHTREY delivered separate dissenting opinions, with JUDGE MARTIN also joining in JUDGE JONES' dissent.

I. INTRODUCTION

.... The question before the en banc court in this interlocutory appeal is whether members of two protected minority groups, each of insufficient numbers individually to make a prima facie case of voting dilution under the Voting Rights Act, may collectively seek § 2 protection by forming a "coalition" of minorities.

Plaintiffs, three African Americans and three persons of Hispanic national origin, brought a class action suit against defendant Kent County and the individual members of the Kent County Apportionment Committee alleging that the redistricting plan the committee proposed following the 1990 census violated § 2 of the Voting Rights Act by diluting minority influence.

* * *

II. FACTS

Kent County, Michigan, is governed by a Board of Commissioners, and each member is elected from a single-member district. The Board has consisted of twenty-one members since its inception in 1968....

African Americans and Hispanic Americans make up 9.2% of the voting age population in Kent County. Although the population of Kent County increased between censuses, the Apportionment Committee approved a plan that reduced the number of districts, and therefore Board members, from twenty-one to nineteen. The new plan established one district made up of a 78.3% minority population, district 17, which included 66.5% African Americans and 11.8% Hispanic Americans. No other district included significant numbers of both....

Plaintiffs charged defendants of packing district 17 with an excessive percentage of minority voters and of splitting the remaining minority voters among districts dominated by large white majorities. Plaintiffs proposed instead a plan that retained twenty-one districts, two of which contained a majority population of minorities, at 68% and 65%, respectively. One of the districts included both African Americans and Hispanic Americans in order to establish sufficient numbers and satisfactory geographical compactness.

* * *

IV. ANALYSIS

A. The Text

* * *

Even the most cursory examination reveals that § 2 of the Voting Rights Act does not mention minority coalitions, either expressly or conceptually. Moreover, § 2 consistently speaks of a "class" in the singular....

Nothing in the clear, unambiguous language of § 2 allows or even recognizes the application of the Voting Rights Act to coalitions as urged by plaintiffs.

If Congress had intended to sanction coalition suits, the statute would read "participation by members of the classes of citizens protected by subsection (a)" or more simply, "participation by citizens protected by subsection (a)." Moreover, the central element necessary to establish a violation is a showing that "*its* members have less opportunity than other members of the electorate . . . ," not that "their members have less opportunity." Finally, Congress declared in subsection (b) that "the extent to which members of *a* protected class have been elected" is one circumstance which may be considered. As in prior instances, if Congress had intended to authorize coalition suits, the phrase would more naturally read: "the extent to which members of the protected classes have been elected."

* * *

D. Policy Concerns

Policy considerations underscore the conclusion that Congress did not authorize coalition lawsuits under the Voting Rights Act. First, the Voting Rights Act is premised upon congressional "findings" that each of the protected minorities is, or has been, the subject of pervasive discrimination and exclusion from the electoral process. Thus, many minorities in society, e.g., Eastern European immigrants or minorities from the Indian subcontinent, are not protected under the Act. The remedies of the Act only extend to members of a minority specifically protected by Congress. Everyone else must proceed under the more difficult, "one person, one vote," constitutional test and its required element of intentional discrimination.

A coalition of protected minorities is a group of citizens about which Congress has not made a specific finding of discrimination, but who nevertheless seek to avoid the more difficult constitutional burden by proceeding under § 2. Simply because Congress has found that African Americans have been discriminated against and because Congress has made the same finding regarding Hispanic Americans, there is no basis for presuming such a finding regarding a group consisting of a mixture of both minorities. This is even more true when the findings were made a decade apart and the bases for the two findings are different (i.e., Congress found that African Americans had been disadvantaged specifically by reason of race, while Hispanic Americans had been disadvantaged by reason of language and education).

Second, . . . a coalition theory could just as easily be advanced as a defense in Voting Rights Act cases, a position that courts would be logically bound to accept if plaintiff coalitions were allowed, yet a position at odds with congressional purpose. The possibility of defendants drawing district lines so as to "pack" districts with African Americans and Hispanic

Americans, thereby submerging the distinct interests of the two groups, casts further doubt on the majority's conclusion that Congress intended to protect coalitions of minorities.

Not only would acceptance of the coalition theory give an additional tool to legislators bent on furthering an invidious intent, it would also serve to frustrate those who, in good faith, seek to draw district lines according to the Voting Rights Act's nebulous requirements. If district lines are drawn pursuant to a plan to enhance the political impact of minorities separately, the plan faces potential challenge by a coalition of minorities claiming that greater influence could have been achieved had the minorities been "lumped" together. If, on the other hand, the lines are drawn to accommodate all minorities together, the plan faces potential challenge by an individual minority group on the ground that its influence could have been enhanced had it been treated separately. In both situations, courts and legislatures would be forced to "choose" between protected groups when drawing district lines. For this court to give the states, under the Voting Rights Act, a puzzle which is difficult to solve is one thing. To give the states, under the guise of "construction," a puzzle which is impossible to solve is quite another. Yet an impossible puzzle is precisely the result urged by plaintiffs.

Third, ... the test enacted by Congress in the 1982 Voting Rights Act amendments requires a showing that the minority is sufficiently numerous and geographically compact to constitute a majority in a single-member district. This necessarily recognizes that, in some cases, a minority will not be numerous enough to prove a violation of the Voting Rights Act because it fails to "constitute a majority in a single member district." Permitting coalition suits effectively eliminates this obstacle, or, at the very least, limits it to cases in which the total of all the protected minorities is less than a majority in any one district.

Finally, and most persuasively, when members of various protected minorities "join forces," they do so for the same reason that any two groups coalesce, i.e., to further their mutual political goals. Thus, an African–American/Hispanic–American coalition might elect an African–American representative, or a Hispanic–American one, or some other person, depending upon whom the members of the coalition believe will best protect their shared interests. Permitting such political coalitions the advantage of Voting Rights Act protection, however, risks wrenching the Act from its ideological and constitutional foundations. . . .

* * *

Groups whose ideas or candidates do not obtain a majority of votes lose. That is not an unfortunate by-product of democracy, but is rather the purpose of democracy. The Equal Protection Clause, the Fifteenth Amendment and the Voting Rights Act are aimed only at ensuring equal political opportunity: that every person's chance to form a majority is the same, regardless of race or ethnic origin. Coalition suits provide minority groups with a political advantage not recognized by our form of government, and not authorized by the constitutional and statutory underpinnings of that structure.

* * *

■ DAMON J. KEITH, CIRCUIT JUDGE, dissenting.

Today, in its zeal to create a circuit split, the majority holds that minority groups cannot collectively file a complaint seeking protection from vote dilution under Section 2 of the Voting Rights Act.

* * *

Although no case law supports their position, the majority ... [holds that] African–Americans and Hispanic–Americans lack the same "statutory disability," and therefore are no more than a political alliance or coalition. I disagree.

The majority opinion mistakenly focuses upon the origins of discrimination plaguing African–Americans and Hispanic–Americans, rather than the results of such discrimination. Past motives behind discriminatory treatment are of limited relevance. The question is not how to distinguish between majoritarian society's discriminatory motives regarding African–Americans and Hispanic–Americans.... The majority's ruling that in all cases voters historically denied access to the political process, protected under the Voting Rights Act, and sharing identical interests must be ethnically classified and segregated from one another denigrates the spirit and the language of the constitution.

Racial homogeneity, which divides victimized Americans and conquers any opportunity they have to participate in democracy, is not a requirement under the Voting Rights Act....

* * *

While it is true that all African–Americans do not " 'think alike, share the same political interests, [or] prefer the same candidates at the polls,' " African–Americans and other minorities share a place in history that often translates into shared political goals.

* * *

Perhaps what is most disturbing is that the practical effect of the majority's holding requires the adoption of some sort of racial purity test, so that minority group members can be properly identified and kept in their place. If we are to make these distinctions, where will they end? Must a community that would be considered racially both Black and Hispanic be segregated from other Blacks who are not Hispanic? Should the dwindling numbers of Native Americans be further decimated by a parsing of Navaho from Apache? Must Puerto–Ricans and Dominicans in the same neighborhood be separated based on their separate cultural and historical backgrounds? Perhaps we will return to a time of classifying African–Americans as quadroons and octoroons for the purposes of racial classification.

.... Non-white Americans, those generally considered minorities by their fellow white Americans, are today denied the right to free and meaningful political participation if they live next to and with one another. Do we make these distinctions between whites of Italian, German or Yugoslavian descent who constitute a voting bloc? No. That is not the way this country works. Many have been able to blend into the melting pot which is America and claim full entitlement to the fruits and opportunities which make this land great. Some, as the legislative histories demonstrate, are constantly and consistently kept on the outside due to their phenotypic differences. These are our communities of color.... Today, the majority further discriminates by compartmentalizing the discriminated against into segregated boxes from which their potential to participate fully in political life is significantly diminished.

* * *

NOTES AND QUESTIONS

1. Prior to *Nixon*, most courts had either assumed without deciding or had explicitly permitted coalition suits under section 2. *See, e.g., Badillo v. City of Stockton*, 956 F.2d 884 (9th Cir.1992); *Concerned Citizens v. Hardee County*, 906 F.2d 524 (11th Cir.1990); *Campos v. City of Baytown*, 840 F.2d 1240 (5th Cir.), *cert. denied*, 492 U.S. 905 (1989); *Knox v. Milwaukee County Bd. of Election Comm'rs*, 607 F.Supp. 1112 (E.D.Wis.1985). By contrast, the scholarly commentary on coalition lawsuits was largely negative. *See, e.g.,* Katharine I. Butler & Richard Murray, *Minority Vote Dilution Suits and the Problem of Two Minority Groups: Can a "Rainbow Coalition" Claim the Protection of the Voting Rights Act?*, 21 Pac. L.J. 619 (1990); Rick G. Strange, *Application of Voting Rights Act to Communities Containing Two or More Minority Groups—When is the Whole Greater Than the Sum of the Parts?*, 20 Tex. Tech L. Rev. 95 (1989); Sebastian Geraci, Comment, *The Case Against Allowing Coalitions to File Section 2 Dilution Claims*, 1995 U. Chi. Leg. For. 389. *But see* Aylon M. Schulte, Note, *Minority Aggregation Under Section 2 of the Voting Rights Act: Toward Just Representation in Ethnically Diverse Communities*, 1995 U. Ill. L. Rev. 441.

2. *Nixon* is surely wrong when it observes that the original voting rights act "offered legislative protection to African–American voters only." The act speaks in terms of "race," rather than identifying black Americans specifically. Certainly, white voters in a majority-black jurisdiction are not barred from bringing section 2 lawsuits. For example, white voters in Birmingham, Alabama challenged the city's continued use of at-large elections. *See White Minority Wins Right to Challenge At–Large Voting,*

Chi. Trib., June 18, 1988, at 7. And other sections of the 1965 version of the Act contemplated protection for non-black groups. Section 4, for example, also expressly protected the ability of Puerto Ricans to participate regardless of English literacy requirements. *See Katzenbach v. Morgan*, 384 U.S. 641 (1966).

Moreover, *Nixon* rests on a controversial vision of "race." The Supreme Court has interpreted 42 U.S.C. §§ 1981 and 1982, which give all citizens the same right as "white citizens" with regard to contracting, access to the courts, and real property to prohibit discrimination against persons who were Arab Americans or Jews. *See Saint Francis College v. Al-Khazraji*, 481 U.S. 604 (1987); *Shaare Tefila Congregation v. Cobb*, 481 U.S. 615 (1987). And discrimination on the basis of ancestry generally has been treated as race discrimination under the Equal Protection Clause. *See, e.g., Hernandez v. Texas*, 347 U.S. 475 (1954); *Oyama v. California*, 332 U.S. 633 (1948); *Hirabayashi v. United States*, 320 U.S. 81 (1943).

Al-Khazraji noted the plasticity of notions of "race." The statute at issue, 42 U.S.C. § 1981, was the modern-day version of a provision in the Civil Rights Act of 1866, and the Court revisited the nineteenth-century understanding of race, showing that "race" and "ethnicity" were somewhat interchangeable, as they remain today: "[M]odern dictionaries still include among the definitions of race 'a family, tribe, people, or nation belonging to the same stock.' Webster's Third New International Dictionary 1870 (1971); Webster's Ninth New Collegiate Dictionary 969 (1986)." And the Court noted the way in which race, like ethnicity more generally, was as much a social construction as a biological fact:

> There is a common popular understanding that there are three major human races—Caucasoid, Mongoloid, and Negroid. Many modern biologists and anthropologists, however, criticize racial classifications as arbitrary and of little use in understanding the variability of human beings.... [S]ome, but not all, scientists [have concluded] that racial classifications are for the most part sociopolitical, rather than biological, in nature. S. Molnar, Human Variation (2d ed. 1983); S. Gould, The Mismeasure of Man (1981); M. Banton & J. Harwood, The Race Concept (1975); A. Montagu, Man's Most Dangerous Myth (1974); A. Montagu, Statement on Race (3d ed. 1972); Science and the Concept of Race (M. Mead, T. Dobzhansky, E. Tobach, & R. Light eds. 1968); A. Montagu, The Concept of Race (1964); R. Benedict, Race and Racism (1942); Littlefield, Lieberman, & Reynolds, Redefining Race: The Potential Demise of a Concept in Physical Anthropology, 23 Current Anthropology 641 (1982); Biological Aspects of Race, 17 Int'l Soc. Sci. J. 71 (1965); Washburn, The Study of Race, 65 American Anthropologist 521 (1963).

In light of these considerations, is *Nixon*'s distinction between racial and language minorities tenable? Do the section 1981 and 1982 cases have broader implications for voting rights law?

3. The *Nixon* majority explains its reasoning in part as a function of the first prong of *Gingles*, as well as the second. Given that perspective, would the Sixth Circuit also foreclose influence district claims? Can *Nixon* be squared with *Armour v. State of Ohio*, a Sixth Circuit decision discussed above at pages 474–75?

4. The definitional provision of the Act, section 14(c)(3) contains the following provision:

> The term "language minorities" or "language minority group" means persons who are American Indian, Asian American, Alaskan Natives, or of Spanish heritage.

42 U.S.C. § 1973*l*(c)(3).

How would *Nixon*'s textual exegesis accommodate this provision? For example, suppose a coalition of Native Americans and Hispanics were to bring a lawsuit. Is that coalition permissible since the triggering mechanism for both groups is the same and the language of section 14(c)(3) can be read literally to make them members of a "language minority group"? Conversely, would Japanese Americans and Vietnamese Americans be permitted to bring a lawsuit together because they are undifferentiated Asian Americans within the statute? What about Cuban Americans and Puerto Ricans? If these two latter groups can be aggregated, despite the fact that they have quite different historical experiences, is there anything left of the Sixth Circuit's analysis beyond a formalistic textualism?

5. There are many jurisdictions in which two distinctive ethnic groups are *not* cohesive. For example, African Americans and Cuban Americans have fought bitterly over how to allocate political power in South Florida. *See, e.g., Johnson v. DeGrandy*, 512 U.S. 997 (1994) (which appears later in this Chapter); *Meek v. Metropolitan Dade County*, 908 F.2d 1540 (11th Cir. 1990), *cert. denied*, 499 U.S. 907 (1991); Larry Rohter, *A Black–Hispanic Struggle Over Florida Redistricting*, N.Y. Times, May 30, 1992 (quoting a black state representative from Miami as saying "if the basis of an extra minority seat is the Voting Rights Act, then we ought to look and see who it was standing on the Edmund Pettus Bridge in Selma getting trampled.").

Moreover, there are some jurisdictions which experience conflict within groups that are aggregated by the statutory language of the Voting Rights Act. *See, e.g., Arizonans for Fair Representation v. Symington*, 828 F.Supp. 684 (D.Ariz.1992) (three-judge court) (discussing conflict between Navajo and Hopi tribes in Arizona that resulted in their placement in separate congressional districts), *aff'd*, 507 U.S. 981 (1993); *Guy v. Hickel*, Case No. A–92–494 CIV (JKS) (D. Alaska 1995) (rejecting a claim by Yupiq Eskimos who sued under § 2 because Eskimos as a whole were fairly represented within the Alaskan legislature). *See also* Samuel Issacharoff, *Race and*

Redistricting, 2 Reconstruction 118 (1994) (referring to the tensions competing Latino communities may experience if they are combined in the same congressional district, as was done in with Mexican Americans and Puerto Ricans in Chicago); Frank J. Macchiarola & Joseph G. Diaz, *The 1990 New York City Districting Commission: Renewed Opportunity for Participation in Local Government or Race–Based Gerrymandering?*, 14 Cardozo L. Rev. 1175 (1993) (discussing councilmanic redistricting in New York and the conflict between Dominicans and Puerto Ricans in upper Manhattan and between American-born and Caribbean-born blacks in Brooklyn).

Is the answer to such internecine conflicts to conclude that the minority group is not sufficiently "politically cohesive" or should claims by distinctive subgroups be cognizable under the Voting Rights Act?

3. *GINGLES'* THIRD PRONG: "WHITE BLOC VOTING"

The disagreement between Justices Brennan and O'Connor in *Gingles* as to the precise contours of the racial bloc voting inquiry has largely been played out with regard to the third *Gingles* factor: does "the white majority vot[e] sufficiently as a bloc to enable it . . . usually to defeat the minority's preferred candidate"?

League of United Latin American Citizens (LULAC) v. Clements

999 F.2d 831 (5th Cir.) (en banc), *cert. denied*, 510 U.S. 1071 (1994).

■ PATRICK HIGGINBOTHAM, CIRCUIT JUDGE:

Over the past fifty years, the steady march of civil rights has been to New Orleans and this court. It continues but the demands have changed. Relatively clear lines of legality and morality have become more difficult to locate as demands for outcomes have followed the cutting away of obstacles to full participation. With our diverse ethnic makeup, this demand for results in voting has surfaced profound questions of a democratic political order such as the limits on rearranging state structures to alter election outcomes, and majority rule at the ballot box and even in legislative halls, questions Congress has provoked but not answered. All this can make a simple voting rights case seem difficult, certainly so with state judges elected on a partisan ballot. . . .

I. Facts

On July 11, 1988, ten individual voters and the League of United Latin American Citizens sued in federal district court alleging that Texas' system of electing state trial judges violated § 2 of the Voting Rights Act and the Fourteenth and Fifteenth Amendments in several Texas counties. . . .

As they have throughout Texas history, Texas voters elect their trial judges in county-wide elections. A voter may vote for all of the trial courts of general jurisdiction in her county. At the same time, each trial court is a distinct court, such as the 134th judicial district court of Dallas County, with county-wide jurisdiction and its own history of incumbents. A candidate runs for a particular court. Plaintiffs contend that electing trial judges county-wide violates § 2 of the Voting Rights Act by impermissibly diluting the voting power of Hispanics and blacks. Plaintiffs proceed on behalf of language and ethnic minorities in different combinations in different counties. Depending on the county—more specifically, the numbers—they argue that Hispanic voters, black voters, or the combination of both Hispanic and black voters "have less opportunity than other members of the electorate to participate in the political process and elect representatives of their choice."

* * *

III. Racial Bloc Voting

* * *

A central issue here, one that divided the panel and one over which the parties vigorously disagree, concerns *Gingles*' white bloc voting inquiry and the closely related *Zimmer* factor directing courts to examine "the extent to which voting ... is racially polarized.".... As the Court in *Gingles* held, the question here is not whether white residents tend to vote as a bloc, but whether such bloc voting is "legally significant." In finding a violation of § 2 in each of the nine challenged counties, the district court held that plaintiffs need only demonstrate that whites and blacks generally support different candidates to establish legally significant white bloc voting. Because "it is the difference between choices made by blacks and whites alone ... that is the central inquiry of § 2," the court excluded evidence tending to prove that these divergent voting patterns were attributable to factors other than race as "irrelevant" and "legally incompetent."

On appeal, defendants contend that the district court erred in refusing to consider the nonracial causes of voting preferences they offered at trial. Unless the tendency among minorities and whites to support different candidates, and the accompanying losses by minority groups at the polls, are somehow tied to race, defendants argue, plaintiffs' attempt to establish legally significant white bloc voting, and thus their vote dilution claim under § 2, must fail. When the record indisputably proves that partisan affiliation, not race, best explains the divergent voting patterns among minority and white citizens in the contested counties, defendants conclude, the district court's judgment must be reversed.

We agree. The scope of the Voting Rights Act is indeed quite broad, but its rigorous protections, as the text of § 2 suggests, extend only to defeats experienced by voters "on account of race or color." Without an inquiry into the circumstances underlying unfavorable election returns, courts lack the tools to discern results that are in any sense "discriminatory," and any distinction between deprivation and mere losses at the polls becomes untenable. In holding that the failure of minority-preferred candidates to receive support from a majority of whites on a regular basis, without more, sufficed to prove legally significant racial bloc voting, the district court loosed § 2 from its racial tether and fused illegal vote dilution and political defeat.

* * *

The principles announced and applied in *Whitcomb [v. Chavis]* and *White [v. Regester]* are instructive and, we believe, controlling. As Justice White, the author of these opinions, recently indicated, the central "theme" of *Whitcomb* and *White* is "that it is not mere suffering at the polls but discrimination in the polity with which the Constitution is concerned.".... [F]ailures of a minority group to elect representatives of its choice that are attributable to "partisan politics" provide no grounds for relief. Section 2 is "a balm for racial minorities, not political ones—even though the two often coincide.".... Rather, § 2 is implicated only where Democrats lose because they are black, not where blacks lose because they are Democrats.

* * *

Justice Brennan's discussion of the first and second *Gingles* factors received majority support. With respect to the third element, however, five justices rejected Justice Brennan's proposed standard for proving racial bloc voting. For this reason, we believe that it is to [Justice White's and Justice O'Connor's concurrences], not Justice Brennan's [opinion], that we should look in attempting to define the contours of the inquiry into legally significant bloc voting.

* * *

As courts and commentators alike have noted, Justice White and Justice O'Connor were united in their fidelity to *Whitcomb's* distinction between vote dilution and partisan politics and in their opposition to Justice Brennan's attempt to expunge this teaching from the bloc voting inquiry.

* * *

Both Justice Brennan and Justice O'Connor recognized that racial bloc voting is intimately related to the responsiveness of elected officials to the interests of minorities, one of the factors considered as part of the "totality of circumstances.".... The close tie between bloc voting and representatives' responsiveness ... rests on common sense: Public officials need not address concerns expressed by minorities so long as white bloc voting ensures that they will remain minority concerns.... [But] this close identification [is] warranted only where racial political considerations [are] present, that is, where white bloc voting cause[e] "minority candidates [to] lose elections solely because of their race." Justice Brennan's approach, [however], assumes that political leaders may safely ignore minority concerns even where black and white voters are separated only by differing interests. Put another way, Justice Brennan's bloc voting test accords governing majorities linked only by the perception of common interests the same permanence and thus relevance under § 2 as white blocs cemented by racial prejudice.

Justice O'Connor not only rejected Justice Brennan's polarized voting standard but was also unwilling to join in the questionable assumption that minorities are unable to influence elections and secure the attention of public officials where these groups have been unsuccessful in their efforts to elect their preferred representatives. Unlike Justice Brennan, she argued that "Congress also intended that explanations of the reasons why white voters rejected minority candidates would be probative of the likelihood that candidates elected without decisive minority support would be willing to take the minority's interests into account.".... Justice O'Connor believed that a minority group's prospects for future electoral success and the likelihood that elected officials will take account of their interests differ materially "in a community where racial animosity is absent although the interests of racial groups diverge." A tendency among whites to cast their votes on the basis of race presents a far more durable obstacle to the coalition-building upon which minority electoral success depends than disagreements over ideology for, as Professor Ely observes, "prejudice blinds us to overlapping interests that in fact exist." John Hart Ely, Democracy and Distrust 153 (1980). Representatives who owe their office to the support of majorities bound by prejudice need not attend to the interests of minorities, since the bias uniting their constituents ensures that these issues will remain minority concerns. Where, on the other hand, voting patterns correlate with partisan affiliation or perceived interest, the open channels of communication facilitate a recognition of points of common ground that might otherwise go undetected. Elected officials in these communities cannot ignore minority interests because this group might be part of the winning coalition that votes them out of office.

* * *

[T]here are many other possible non-racial causes of voter behavior beyond partisan affiliation. A rule conditioning relief under § 2 upon proof of the existence of racial animus in the electorate would require plaintiffs to establish the absence of not only partisan voting, but also all other potentially innocent explanations for white voters' rejection of minority-preferred candidates. Factors that might legitimately lead white voters to withhold support from particular minority candidates include, for example, limited campaign funds, inexperience, or a reputation besmirched by scandal. Because these additional factors map only imperfectly onto partisan affiliation, detailed multivariate analysis might then be the evidence of choice....

This argument possesses considerable force.... [But today we need not decide whether additional factors are relevant, since our conclusion rests on] the fundamental division between "partisan politics" and "racial vote dilution" set out by the Court in *Whitcomb* and *White* and confirmed by Congress.

* * *

[The evidence in this case shows that] white voters constitute the majority of not only the Republican Party, but also the Democratic Party, even in several of the counties in which the former dominates. In Dallas County, for example, 30–40% of white voters consistently support Democrats, making white Democrats more numerous than all of the minority Democratic voters combined. The suggestion that Republican voters are galvanized by a "white" or "anti-minority" agenda is plausible only to the extent that the Democratic Party can be viewed as a vehicle for advancing distinctively minority interests, which clearly is not the case. At the same time, white Democrats have in recent years experienced the same electoral defeats as minority voters. If we are to hold that these losses at the polls, without more, give rise to a racial vote dilution claim warranting special relief for minority voters, a principle by which we might justify withholding similar relief from white Democrats is not readily apparent.

Second, both political parties, and especially the Republicans, aggressively recruited minority lawyers to run on their party's ticket. Consequently, white as well as minority voters found themselves not infrequently voting against candidates sharing their respective racial or ethnic backgrounds in favor of their party's nominee. In particular, the undisputed evidence discloses that white voters in most counties, both Republican and Democratic, without fail supported the minority candidates slated by their parties at levels equal to or greater than those enjoyed by white candidates, even where the minority candidate was opposed by a white candidate.

* * *

■ CAROLYN KING, CIRCUIT JUDGE, with whom HENRY POLITZ, CHIEF JUDGE, joins, dissenting:

* * *

(ii) Social science problems

Even without the legal problems inherent in the majority's approach to legally significant white bloc voting and racially polarized voting, the majority's approach is severely flawed from a social science perspective. Regardless of whether the majority requires a multivariate regression analysis, which would seek to eliminate all causes of voting behavior other than race, or only a trivariate regression analysis, which would attempt to eliminate partisan affiliation, there is a problem with requiring this type of evidence as an integral part of the vote dilution inquiry: it ignores the critical distinction between experimental research and non-experimental research. Specifically, it ignores the warning of most respected social scientists, including the experts who testified in this case, that the causes of voting behavior cannot be determined from the use of any kind of regression analysis—whether bivariate, trivariate, or multivariate.

It is important to recognize that the kind of evidence that the majority requires minority plaintiffs to introduce will involve no experimental manipulation of independent variables. The plaintiffs will not be able to manipulate the race or party affiliation of the candidate to determine which one had the greater effect on election outcomes. Rather, the plaintiffs will have to take existing election results and work backwards. This kind of real world research has been labelled "non-experimental research" by social scientists.

.... [One critical problem with inferring causation on the basis of regression analyses is that] variables in nonexperimental research tend to be intercorrelated. Since more often than not researchers neither understand the causes of the interrelations nor attempt to study them, implications of regression coefficients for policy decisions are questionable.

Requiring minority plaintiffs to come forward with a multivariate regression analysis to determine the causes of racially divergent voting patterns [suffers from this problem].... The independent variables listed by Judge Higginbotham—including incumbency, campaign expenditures, party identification, income, media use measured by cost, religion—"tend to be correlated, sometimes substantially." Therefore, "it [becomes] difficult, if not impossible, to untangle the effects of each variable." By inferring causation from such analysis, we would undoubtedly be engaging in what amounts to an "almost mindless interpretation[] of regression analysis in nonexperimental research." In short, we would be importing "junk science" into the Voting Rights Act while rejecting it in other contexts.

Requiring minority plaintiffs to only come forward with a trivariate regression analysis, as the majority seems to do in this case, does not alleviate the social science problems; it only multiplies them. Not only does such a requirement ignore the fact that the two independent variables (i.e., race and partisan affiliation) are substantially correlated, it also runs the risk that the two variables being studied are only proxies for causal variables that are not included in the regression equation....

The trivariate regression analyses offered in this case undoubtedly demonstrate that the party affiliation of a candidate is a better predictor of electoral success than the race of the candidate. Because we are dealing with non-experimental research, however, I cannot take the leap that the majority makes—namely, that the party affiliation of a candidate is the best, or the single most powerful, explanation of electoral success. The evidence in this case also demonstrates that, in many of the counties, race is substantially correlated with party affiliation, and the trivariate regression analyses offered in this case did not determine, and could not have determined, why people join certain parties. In my view, then, they can no more explain why people vote the way they do than a bivariate regression analysis. Significantly, for purposes of the Voting Rights Act, they could not negate "race or color" as an explanation for election outcomes.

(iii) The practical problem

The majority's approach to legally significant white bloc voting and racially polarized voting places an almost insurmountable hurdle in front of minority groups proceeding under section 2. Unless minority plaintiffs can successfully establish that voters in the controlling political party are racially motivated—either through the use of questionable voting statistics or by calling people from that party and asking them why they voted the way they did[58]—their claim will fail. In fact, they will not even be able to make out a prima facie case.

The typical section 2 vote dilution case ... has two prominent features: One is a politically cohesive minority group (e.g., blacks or Hispanics) whose members share political interests and vote together, usually in a single political party that also includes whites. The other is the existence of a white majority, generally in a different political party, whose voting strength is sufficient usually to defeat the combined strength of minority votes plus white "crossover" votes. The problem for minority voters in the typical section 2 case is that they have been submerged in a white majority—unable to forge a coalition with enough whites to elect representatives of their choice. Thus, the Voting Rights Act, as interpreted in *Gingles* and succeeding cases, presupposes partisan voting and asks whether politically cohesive minority voters have an unequal opportunity to participate in the political process—a partisan political process—and to elect representatives of their choice on account of race or color.

Under the majority's reasoning, this typical scenario, the scenario specifically contemplated by the *Gingles* framework, will now preclude a finding of vote dilution. As long as some whites vote with minorities in the Democratic Party, partisan affiliation will always be a better predictor of election outcomes than race (even if a few minorities vote Republican). Such circumstances, under the majority's framework, will preclude a finding of vote dilution. In short, the majority has effectively eviscerated section 2 of the Voting Rights Act in communities where there is any

---

58. *But see Kirksey v. City of Jackson,* 663 F.2d 659, 662 (5th Cir. Unit A Dec.1981) (holding that, because of First Amendment concerns, voters' motivations are not subject to searching scrutiny by plaintiffs in a voting

measurable crossover voting by whites.[60]

* * *

NOTES AND QUESTIONS

1. Does *LULAC*'s approach reinstate a requirement that plaintiffs prove a racially discriminatory intent, this time of individual voters? In an earlier case, the Fifth Circuit had held that First Amendment concerns precluded the plaintiffs in a vote-dilution lawsuit from inquiring directly into the motivation behind individual citizens' votes. *Kirksey v. City of Jackson*, 663 F.2d 659, 662 (5th Cir.1981).

2. *LULAC* marks a reinvigoration of the *Whitcomb v. Chavis* analysis of partisanship, discussed in Chapter 6. It should be noted that the early challenges to at-large elections (except for *Whitcomb*) were either in the one-party Democratic South or the one-party Democratic city. *LULAC* grew out of a relatively recent phenomenon: the emergence of a heavily white southern Republican Party. *See* Pamela S. Karlan, *Loss and Redemption: Voting Rights at the Turn of a Century*, 50 Vand. L. Rev. 291, 314–20 (1997) (discussing the relationship between the Voting Rights Act and the rise of Southern Republicanism).

3. It is important to recognize that arguments over racial bloc voting involve both normative and empirical premises, and to keep clear whether particular arguments are prescriptive or descriptive. In particular, "[i]n the freighted arena of race and public policy, abstract principles often founder on uncomfortable facts." Richard H. Pildes, *The Politics of Race*, 108 Harv. L. Rev. 1359, 1381 (1995). In the wrongful districting cases, the Supreme Court has declared that the assumption that black voters "think alike, share the same political interests, and will prefer the same candidates at the polls" is "offensive and demeaning." *Miller v. Johnson*, 515 U.S. 900, 912 (1995); *Shaw v. Reno*, 509 U.S. 630, 647–48 (1993). We consider these cases more fully in Chapter 8.

It is important to understand that the Court's position is prescriptive, that is, that the Court is making a value judgment, rather than saying that

---

rights case), *clarified,* 669 F.2d 316 (5th Cir. 1982).

60. The majority implies that interest group politics did not begin in Texas until the 1980's, when the Republican Party emerged as a force to be reckoned with. The majority ignores that, even when Texas was a one party state, there were still different factions, or interest groups, within the Democratic party. Thus, partisan or interest group politics has always been a feature of Texas' colorful political landscape. To hold otherwise is to ignore the past reality. As noted previously, the evidence in this case reflects that, before 1980, minority-preferred candidates lost in Democratic primary elections, generally to white Democrats; after 1980, minority-preferred candidates may make it to the general election, but only to lose to white Republicans. "From the vantage point of minority voters—which is the vantage point of section 2—it is difficult to see how the arrival of a two party system in Texas has altered their ability to participate in the political process and elect candidates of their choice."

the assumption of shared interests is factually false. There is substantial evidence of systematic racial differences in political attitudes, policy preferences, and actual voting behavior. For extensive documentation of these differences, see Donald R. Kinder and Lynn M. Sanders, Divided by Color: Racial Politics and Democratic Ideals (1996), and David Lublin, The Paradox of Representation 72–78 (1997). For example, between 1964 and 1992, no Democratic candidate for President won a majority of white votes, while every Democratic candidate received a majority of the black vote cast. *See* Pildes, *supra*, at 1379 n.84. In House elections from 1980 to 1994, on average 87% of blacks voted Democratic, whereas 49% of Whites did so. This racial disparity in partisan preferences has increased in recent years. Between 1990 and 1994, the Democratic Party's share of the white vote in the South declined 15 points (from 50% to 35%), although its share of the black vote increased 11 points (from 80% to 91%). *See Portrait of the Electorate: Who Voted for Whom in the House*, N.Y. Times, Nov. 13, 1994, at 24. For disparities with regard to policy preferences, see, e.g., Lee Sigelman & Susan Welch, Black Americans' Views of Racial Inequality 143 (1991) (reaching the general conclusion that, "on issues where government action is contemplated, blacks as a group are more activist than whites"); *see also* An American Profile—Opinions and Behavior, 1972–1989, at 572, 710, 729 (Floris W. Wood ed. 1990) (showing differences in white and black responses over time to questions concerning the responsibility of government for aiding the poor, providing welfare, and solving big-city problems); Michael C. Dawson, Behind the Mule 183 tbl. 8.1 (1994) (reporting that, in 1988, 63% of blacks but only 33% of whites supported increased spending on government services; 57% of blacks but only 21% of whites believed government should provide jobs and a good standard of living; 82% of blacks but only 53% of whites supported increased federal spending on Social Security; 83% of but only 61% of whites supported increased federal spending on public schools); Thomas B. Edsall with Mary D. Edsall, Chain Reaction: The Impact of Race, Rights, and Taxes on American Politics 130 (1992) (in 1978, 67% of whites but only 29% of blacks supported California's Proposition 13); *id.* at 153 (in 1980, 70% of blacks and 38% of whites believed government should guarantee everyone a job); *id.* at 186 (in 1986, 81% of whites reported opposing preferences for blacks in hiring and job promotion and 69% reported opposing the reservation of openings for blacks at colleges; 57% and 73% of blacks reported favoring these programs, respectively); *id.* at 258 (citing data showing that 64% of blacks but only 34% of whites believe it is the responsibility of the federal government to guarantee a job and good standard of living and that 77% of blacks favor increased spending for improved public services although whites are evenly split).

4. Does a distinction between racial and political motivations make sense? To what extent do such attempts muddy the distinction between correlation and causation? As the previous note suggested, repeated public opinion surveys reveal that race in contemporary America is highly correlated with

views on a number of politically salient issues. For some issues, race may be only a proxy for other shared characteristics such as residence, religion, or socioeconomic status. But what if race is a causal factor in disparities regarding these characteristics? For example, suppose black voters in a particular city all voted for candidates who vowed not to approve a dumpsite in a particular neighborhood, while white voters supported their opponents. If blacks live in the affected neighborhood in part as a result of intentional government-sponsored or-condoned racial discrimination in the housing market, is voting racially polarized? If the discrimination were more attenuated, and blacks lived in the neighborhood not because of discrimination in the housing market, but because their relatively lower incomes restricted their housing choices, would the disparity in voting behavior be purely political? For some issues, race may be more of a causal factor. For example, suppose black voters all supported a candidate who pledged to sponsor fair housing legislation while whites backed her opponent. *Cf. Hunter v. Erickson*, 393 U.S. 385 (1969) (striking down a city charter provision that required approval by referendum of any housing ordinance that sought to regulate discrimination on "the basis of race, color, religion, national origin or ancestry" but not other housing ordinances on the ground that the provision was racially discriminatory).

5. There is yet another problem with an attempt to require something beyond simple correlation:

> The many difficulties with [the] attempt to disaggregate race and politics ... all result from the fact that race and political affiliation are, in fact, substantially correlated. It is thus impossible to determine which of the two is a better *explanation*—as opposed to a *predictor*—of voting patterns. A hypothetical example may clarify this point. Suppose that the two dominant political parties were the Antiblacks and the Problacks, each advocating a platform consistent with its name. If, as we might expect, virtually all black voters were members of the Problack party and voted for Problack candidates, then political affiliation would be nothing more than a proxy for race. Race clearly would be a better explanation of voting patterns than political affiliation, and there would hardly be room for doubt as to the existence of racial bloc voting. In contemporary American politics a similar (though, of course, weaker) causal relationship obtains between race and political party, with most blacks finding their interests better represented by the Democratic party. As a consequence, statistical tests such as the multivariate regression analyses of voting patterns offered by the LULAC defendants will necessarily be indeterminate with respect to the causal role of race in affecting voting behavior.... [A] typical section 2 scenario involves a politically cohesive group of nonwhite voters, usually Democrats, who have been unable to elect their preferred candidates because their votes, combined with white Democratic "crossover" votes, have consis-

tently been submerged by the votes of an overwhelmingly white, largely Republican majority. In other words, the black or Hispanic voters have not been able to form a coalition with enough white voters to overcome the white majority bloc vote. In this scenario, as long as some whites vote with minorities for the Democratic candidate, political affiliation will *always* be a better predictor of election outcome than will race; accordingly, under Judge Higginbotham's approach, the nonwhite voters will have no remedy. Yet this is precisely the sort of racial exclusion that section 2 and *Gingles* sought to remedy.

Pamela S. Karlan and Daryl J. Levinson, *Why Voting Is Different*, 84 Cal. L. Rev. 1201, 1223–24 (1996).

B. THE REEMERGENCE OF A "TOTALITY OF THE CIRCUMSTANCES APPROACH"

After *Gingles*, there was some disagreement in the lower courts about the extent to which the three *Gingles* factors supplanted the Senate factors altogether, as opposed to simply providing a threshold inquiry. *See, e.g., Solomon v. Liberty County*, 899 F.2d 1012 (11th Cir.1990) (en banc), *cert. denied*, 498 U.S. 1023 (1991), where the Eleventh Circuit was evenly split on the issue. As a practical matter, however, much section 2 litigation became routinized. Plaintiffs would present some illustrative proposed districts to satisfy the first prong of the *Gingles* test; the testimony of an expert witness who had examined election returns to satisfy the two other prongs; census data, judicial opinions, and statutes to show the presence of many of the relatively cut-and-dried Senate Report factors such as a prior history of discrimination, socioeconomic differences, the presence of electoral features that enhanced the dilutive effect of at-large elections; and some lay testimony to round out the picture. Much of the litigation involved municipal and county governments which were both financially and functionally ill-equipped to defend the lawsuits: they lacked access to the expertise developed by the small but specialized plaintiffs'-side voting rights bar. For a description of that bar, see Gregory A. Caldeira, *Litigation, Lobbying, and the Voting Rights Law* in Controversies in Minority Voting 230 (Bernard Grofman and Chandler Davidson eds. 1992).

The section 2 lawsuits that followed the 1990 census differed in some important respects. Much of the "easy" litigation had been accomplished in the half-decade between *Gingles* and the enactment of the new plans. There were far fewer lawsuits involving jurisdictions with large, geographically compact minority communities, at-large elections, and virtually no minority elected officials. In their place, plaintiffs brought challenges to single-member districting plans and in jurisdictions where although minorities had achieved some representation, they had not achieved the greatest possible amount. Moreover, many of the lawsuits involved statewide apportionment schemes, and the defendants were better financed and had access to lawyers with greater expertise.

Johnson v. De Grandy
512 U.S. 997 (1994).

■ JUSTICE SOUTER delivered the opinion of the Court.

* * *

I

[In April 1992, the Florida legislature adopted Senate Joint Resolution 2–G (SJR 2–G). SJR 2–G divided Florida into 40 single-member Senate, and 120 single-member House, districts based on population data from the 1990 census.] The De Grandy and NAACP plaintiffs [who had previously challenged the post–1980 plan on one-person, one-vote grounds] responded to SJR 2–G by amending their federal complaints to charge the new reapportionment plan with violating § 2. They claimed that SJR 2–G "'unlawfully fragments cohesive minority communities and otherwise impermissibly submerges their right to vote and to participate in the electoral process,'" and they pointed to areas around the State where black or Hispanic populations could have formed a voting majority in a politically cohesive, reasonably compact district (or in more than one), if SJR 2–G had not fragmented each group among several districts or packed it into just a few.

The Department of Justice filed a similar complaint, naming the State of Florida and several elected officials as defendants and claiming that SJR 2–G diluted the voting strength of.... the Hispanic population in an area largely covered by Dade County (including Miami)....

.... [The District Court] held the plan's provisions for state House districts to be in violation of § 2 because "more than [SJR 2–G's] nine Hispanic districts may be drawn without having or creating a regressive effect upon black voters," and it imposed a remedial plan offered by the De Grandy plaintiffs calling for 11 majority-Hispanic House districts. As to the Senate, the court found that a fourth majority-Hispanic district could be drawn in addition to the three provided by SJR 2–G, but only at the expense of black voters in the area. The court was of two minds about the implication of this finding, once observing that it meant the legislature's plan for the Senate was a violation of § 2 but without a remedy, once saying the Plan did not violate § 2 at all. In any event, it ordered elections to be held using SJR 2–G's senatorial districts.

In a later, expanded opinion the court reviewed the totality of circumstances as required by § 2 and *Thornburg v. Gingles*. In explaining Dade County's "tripartite politics," in which "ethnic factors ... predominate over all others ...," the court found political cohesion within each of the Hispanic and black populations but none between the two, and a tendency of non-Hispanic whites to vote as a bloc to bar minority groups from electing their chosen candidates except in a district where a given minority makes up a voting majority.[6] The court further found that the nearly one million Hispanics in the Dade County area could be combined into 4 Senate and 11 House districts, each one relatively compact and with a functional majority of Hispanic voters, whereas SJR 2-G created fewer majority-Hispanic districts; and that one more Senate district with a black voting majority could have been drawn. Noting that Florida's minorities bore the social, economic, and political effects of past discrimination, the court concluded that SJR 2-G impermissibly diluted the voting strength of Hispanics in its House districts and of both Hispanics and blacks in its Senate districts. The findings of vote dilution in the senatorial districts had no practical effect, however, because the court held that remedies for the blacks and the Hispanics were mutually exclusive; it consequently deferred to the state legislature's work as the "fairest" accommodation of all the ethnic communities in South Florida.

* * *

III

On the merits of the vote dilution claims covering the House districts, the crux of the State's argument is the power of Hispanics under SJR 2-G to elect candidates of their choice in a number of districts that mirrors their share of the Dade County area's voting-age population (i.e., 9 out of 20 House districts); this power, according to the State, bars any finding that the plan dilutes Hispanic voting strength....

The State's argument takes us back to ground covered last Term in two cases challenging single-member districts. *See Voinovich v. Quilter*; *Growe v. Emison*. In *Growe*, we held that a claim of vote dilution in a single-member district requires proof meeting the same three threshold conditions for a dilution challenge to a multimember district [announced in *Gingles*]....

In *Voinovich* we explained how manipulation of district lines can dilute the voting strength of politically cohesive minority group members, whether by fragmenting the minority voters among several districts where a bloc-voting majority can routinely out-vote them, or by packing them into one or a small number of districts to minimize their influence in the districts next door. Section 2 prohibits either sort of line-drawing where its result, " 'interacting with social and historical conditions,' impairs the ability of a

---

6. The Court recognizes that the terms "black," "Hispanic," and "white" are neither mutually exclusive nor collectively exhaustive. We follow the practice of the District Court in using them as rough indicators of South Florida's three largest racial and linguistic minority groups.

protected class to elect its candidate of choice on an equal basis with other voters."

.... [T]he District Court found, and the State does not challenge, the presence of both th[e] Gingles preconditions [relating to racial bloc voting]. The dispute in this litigation centers ... [instead on] whether, even with all three *Gingles* conditions satisfied, the circumstances in totality support a finding of vote dilution when Hispanics can be expected to elect their chosen representatives in substantial proportion to their percentage of the area's population.

* * *

B

We ... part company from the District Court in assessing the totality of circumstances. The District Court found that the three *Gingles* preconditions were satisfied, and that Hispanics had suffered historically from official discrimination, the social, economic, and political effects of which they generally continued to feel. Without more, and on the apparent assumption that what could have been done to create additional Hispanic super-majority districts should have been done, the District Court found a violation of § 2. But the assumption was erroneous, and more is required, as a review of *Gingles* will show.

1

* * *

Gingles provided some structure to the statute's "totality of circumstances" test in a case challenging multimember legislative districts.... But if *Gingles* so clearly identified [three preconditions] as generally necessary to prove a § 2 claim, it just as clearly declined to hold them sufficient in combination, either in the sense that a court's examination of relevant circumstances was complete once the three factors were found to exist, or in the sense that the three in combination necessarily and in all circumstances demonstrated dilution.... To be sure, some § 2 plaintiffs may have easy cases, but although lack of equal electoral opportunity may be readily imagined and unsurprising when demonstrated under circumstances that include the three essential *Gingles* factors, that conclusion must still be addressed explicitly, and without isolating any other arguably relevant facts from the act of judgment.

2

If the three *Gingles* factors may not be isolated as sufficient, standing alone, to prove dilution in every multimember district challenge, *a fortiori* they must not be when the challenge goes to a series of single-member districts, where dilution may be more difficult to grasp. Plaintiffs challenging single-member districts may claim, not total submergence, but partial submergence; not the chance for some electoral success in place of none, but the chance for more success in place of some. When the question thus comes down to the reasonableness of drawing a series of district lines in one combination of places rather than another, judgments about inequality may become closer calls. As facts beyond the ambit of the three *Gingles* factors loom correspondingly larger, factfinders cannot rest uncritically on assumptions about the force of the *Gingles* factors in pointing to dilution.

* * *

[In this case,] the District Court was not critical enough in asking whether a history of persistent discrimination reflected in the larger society and its bloc-voting behavior portended any dilutive effect from a newly proposed districting scheme, whose pertinent features were majority-minority districts in substantial proportion to the minority's share of voting-age population. The court failed to ask whether the totality of facts, including those pointing to proportionality,[11] showed that the new scheme would deny minority voters equal political opportunity.

Treating equal political opportunity as the focus of the enquiry, we do not see how these district lines, apparently providing political effectiveness in proportion to voting-age numbers, deny equal political opportunity. The record establishes that Hispanics constitute 50 percent of the voting-age population in Dade County and under SJR 2-G would make up supermajorities in 9 of the 18 House districts located primarily within the county. Likewise, if one considers the 20 House districts located at least in part within Dade County, the record indicates that Hispanics would be an effective voting majority in 45 percent of them (i.e., nine), and would constitute 47 percent of the voting-age population in the area. In other words, under SJR 2-G Hispanics in the Dade County area would enjoy substantial proportionality. On this evidence, we think the State's scheme would thwart the historical tendency to exclude Hispanics, not encourage or perpetuate it. Thus in spite of that history and its legacy, including the racial cleavages that characterize Dade County politics today, we see no grounds for holding in this case that SJR 2-G's district lines diluted the votes cast by Hispanic voters.

* * *

11. "Proportionality" as the term is used here links the number of majority-minority voting districts to minority members' share of the relevant population. The concept is distinct from the subject of the proportional representation clause of § 2, which provides that "nothing in this section establishes a right to have members of a protected class elected in numbers equal to their proportion in the population." 42 U.S.C. § 1973b. This proviso speaks to the success of minority candidates, as distinct from the political or electoral power of minority voters. And the proviso also confirms what is otherwise clear from the text of the statute, namely that the ultimate right of § 2 is equality of opportunity, not a guarantee of electoral success for minority-preferred candidates of whatever race.

3

It may be that the significance of the facts under § 2 was obscured by the rule of thumb apparently adopted by the District Court, that anything short of the maximum number of majority-minority districts consistent with the *Gingles* conditions would violate § 2.... But reading the first Gingles condition [this way] ... causes its own dangers, and they are not to be courted.

Assume a hypothetical jurisdiction of 1,000 voters divided into 10 districts of 100 each, where members of a minority group make up 40 percent of the voting population and voting is totally polarized along racial lines. With the right geographic dispersion to satisfy the compactness requirement, and with careful manipulation of district lines, the minority voters might be placed in control of as many as 7 of the 10 districts. Each such district could be drawn with at least 51 members of the minority group, and whether the remaining minority voters were added to the groupings of 51 for safety or scattered in the other three districts, minority voters would be able to elect candidates of their choice in all seven districts.[12] The point of the hypothetical is not, of course, that any given district is likely to be open to such extreme manipulation, or that bare majorities are likely to vote in full force and strictly along racial lines, but that reading § 2 to define dilution as any failure to maximize tends to obscure the very object of the statute and to run counter to its textually stated purpose. One may suspect vote dilution from political famine, but one is not entitled to suspect (much less infer) dilution from mere failure to guarantee a political feast. However prejudiced a society might be, it would be absurd to suggest that the failure of a districting scheme to provide a minority group with effective political power 75 percent above its numerical strength indicates a denial of equal participation in the political process. Failure to maximize cannot be the measure of § 2.

4

* * *

[On the other hand, an] inflexible rule [that proportionality is always a defense to a section 2 claim] would run counter to the textual command of § 2, that the presence or absence of a violation be assessed "based on the totality of circumstances." 42 U.S.C. § 1973(b).

* * *

Even if the State's safe harbor were open only in cases of alleged dilution by the manipulation of district lines, however, it would rest on an

---

12. Minority voters might instead be denied control over a single seat, of course. Each district would need to include merely 51 members of the majority group; minority voters fragmented among the 10 districts could be denied power to affect the result in any district.

unexplored premise of highly suspect validity: that in any given voting jurisdiction (or portion of that jurisdiction under consideration), the rights of some minority voters under § 2 may be traded off against the rights of other members of the same minority class. Under the State's view, the most blatant racial gerrymandering in half of a county's single member districts would be irrelevant under § 2 if offset by political gerrymandering in the other half, so long as proportionality was the bottom line....

Finally, we reject the safe harbor rule because of a tendency the State would itself certainly condemn, a tendency to promote and perpetuate efforts to devise majority-minority districts even in circumstances where they may not be necessary to achieve equal political and electoral opportunity. Because in its simplest form the State's rule would shield from § 2 challenge a districting scheme in which the number of majority-minority districts reflected the minority's share of the relevant population, the conclusiveness of the rule might be an irresistible inducement to create such districts. It bears recalling, however, that for all the virtues of majority-minority districts as remedial devices, they rely on a quintessentially race-conscious calculus aptly described as the "politics of second best." If the lesson of *Gingles* is that society's racial and ethnic cleavages sometimes necessitate majority-minority districts to ensure equal political and electoral opportunity, that should not obscure the fact that there are communities in which minority citizens are able to form coalitions with voters from other racial and ethnic groups, having no need to be a majority within a single district in order to elect candidates of their choice. Those candidates may not represent perfection to every minority voter, but minority voters are not immune from the obligation to pull, haul, and trade to find common political ground, the virtue of which is not to be slighted in applying a statute meant to hasten the waning of racism in American politics.

* * *

IV

* * *

SJR 2-G creates 40 single-member Senate districts, five of them wholly within Dade County. Of these five, three have Hispanic super-majorities of at least 64 percent, and one has a clear majority of black voters. Two more Senate districts crossing county lines include substantial numbers of Dade County voters, and in one of these, black voters, although not close to a majority, are able to elect representatives of their choice with the aid of cross-over votes.

Within this seven-district Dade County area, both minority groups enjoy rough proportionality. The voting-age population in the seven-district area is 44.8 percent Hispanic and 15.8 percent black. Hispanics predominate in 42.9 percent of the districts (three out of seven), as do blacks in

14.3 percent of them (one out of seven). While these numbers indicate something just short of perfect proportionality (42.9 percent against 44.8; 14.3 percent against 15.8), the opposite is true of the five districts located wholly within Dade County.[19]

The District Court concentrated not on these facts but on whether additional districts could be drawn in which either Hispanics or blacks would constitute an effective majority. The court found that indeed a fourth senatorial district with an Hispanic super-majority could be drawn, or that an additional district could be created with a black majority, in each case employing reasonably compact districts. Having previously established that each minority group was politically cohesive, that each labored under a legacy of official discrimination, and that whites voted as a bloc, the District Court believed it faced "two independent, viable Section 2 claims." Because the court did not, however, think it was possible to create both another Hispanic district and another black district on the same map, it concluded that no remedy for either violation was practical and, deferring to the State's plan as a compromise policy, imposed SJR 2–G's senatorial districts.

We affirm the District Court's decision to leave the State's plan for Florida State Senate districts undisturbed. As in the case of the House districts, the totality of circumstances appears not to support a finding of vote dilution here, where both minority groups constitute effective voting majorities in a number of state Senate districts substantially proportional to their share in the population, and where plaintiffs have not produced evidence otherwise indicating that under SJR 2–G voters in either minority group have "less opportunity than other members of the electorate to participate in the political process and to elect representatives of their choice."

* * *

NOTES AND QUESTIONS

1. The *Gingles* test responded well to "classical" claims of racial vote dilution—those brought by black voters challenging the use of at-large elections in predominantly white jurisdictions. The context in which *De Grandy* arose differed in at least two salient respects. First, it raised a challenge to an existing single-member district plan; second, it involved a three-way struggle for electoral power among Anglo whites, Cuban Ameri-

---

19. In the five districts wholly within Dade County, where Hispanics are concentrated, the voting-age population is 53.9 percent Hispanic and 13.5 percent black. Sixty percent of the districts are Hispanic-majority (three out of five), and 20 percent are black-majority (one out of five), so that each minority group protected by § 2 enjoys an effective voting majority in marginally more districts than proportionality would indicate (60 percent over 53.9; 20 percent over 13.5).

cans, and African Americans. Consider the argument that both of these differences exposed difficulties with the *Gingles* test:

> *Gingles* proved tremendously useful in challenges to at-large electoral systems because of the confined nature of the inquiry.... The choice of districting arrangement, should the plaintiffs prevail, was left to a highly obscure remedial process in which district courts were directed to yield as much as possible to the policy choices of the affected jurisdiction.... The liability determination was therefore a straightforward binary inquiry: the at-large status quo or some potential alternative. The ultimate resolution of a successful plaintiffs' claim—the actual shape of the new voting scheme in a successful VRA action—was left to vaguely worded remedial standards under the highly discretionary authority of a district court judge.
>
> .... Since the majority of voting rights challenges were initially brought in circumstances where blacks had not been elected to office since the demise of Reconstruction, the vote dilution inquiry could presume under-representation without having to define a baseline of proportionality. Under such circumstances, "dilution" was a functional proxy for exclusion, plain and simple.
>
> Constructing a model of minority vote dilution in the redistricting context is far more problematic. To begin with, the choice of electoral alternatives, particularly after the computer revolution of the 1980s made the process accessible to all interested parties, was anything but binary.... In the redistricting context ... the issue inherited from *Gingles*—whether a superior arrangement could have been selected—does not answer the question whether it should have been selected. This, in turn, implicates the ultimate question of what should serve as the baseline in determining whether minority voting strength has been "diluted" through the choice of one or another redistricting configuration.

* * *

> It is not only the *Gingles* presumption that fails with regard to Cuban–Americans, but the entire *Carolene Products* edifice. The *Carolene Products* premise that discreteness and insularity in the political process should be disabling has been significantly challenged by the emergence of public choice theory. Under public choice theory, the combination of freerider problems in holding together broad coalitions, together with transactions costs in drawing together broad, diffuse majorities, should provide cohesive minorities with superordinate power in the political arena.

* * *

> What happens, however, when the presumptions underlying *Gingles* and *Carolene Products* are wrong? What happens if the insularity of Cuban–Americans is simply a reflection of normal patterns of healthy immigration, ones that bespeak no long-term disabilities? Shouldn't the cohesiveness of the community provide preferential access into the halls of political power, as occurred in prior periods with, for example, the Irish of Boston or the Eastern European immigrants of Chicago? If that is the case, then we should see evidence of political muscle in the Cuban–American community as the rate of citizenship and eligibility for voting increases.
>
> In fact, every indication is that this is precisely the pattern of Cuban–American political participation. Not only are there no significant indicators of Cuban–Americans being systematically shut out of the political or economic processes of Dade County, but precisely the opposite seems to be the case. . . .
>
> Without a palpable claim of second-class status, without self-perception of disabling discrete and insular status, and with ready recourse to redress in the political process, the Cuban–Americans of Miami defy the grounds for judicial intervention into the political process that are critical for both *Gingles* and *Carolene Products*. As increasing numbers of Central Americans, Asians, and other recent immigrants establish themselves in this country and begin to test the political waters, the arguments over what justifies intervention into the ordinary workings of the political process will resurface.

Samuel Issacharoff, *Groups and the Right to Vote*, 44 Emory L.J. 869 (1995).

2. One of the most notable aspects of *De Grandy* is that, although the majority relies on two of the voting rights cases decided the previous Term, *Voinovich v. Quilter* and *Growe v. Emison*, it entirely ignores the third, and most well-known, *Shaw v. Reno*. Lani Guinier initially suggested that "[i]f *Shaw v. Reno* marks the voting rights precipice, the Court blinked in its 1993 Term" by holding in *De Grandy* "that society's racial and ethnic cleavages sometimes necessitate majority-minority districts to ensure equal political and electoral opportunity". Lani Guinier, *[E]racing Democracy: The Voting Rights Cases*, 108 Harv. L. Rev. 109 (1994). In light of the more recent wrongful districting cases discussed in Chapter 8, was this interpretation of *De Grandy* wishful thinking? Has compactness become an even more indispensable element of any claim for majority non-white districts?

3. In *Voinovich*, the Supreme Court unanimously rejected the claim of a group of plaintiffs characterized by the district court as "Democratic electors and state legislators, some of whom are members of a protected class under the Voting Rights Act," who claimed that Ohio's bitterly partisan state legislative apportionment violated section 2 because it unlawfully "packed" black voters into a few overwhelmingly black districts, wasting minority votes in the packed districts and diluting minority voting strength in surrounding areas where black voting strength had concomitantly been diminished.

Justice O'Connor's opinion for the Court observed that the choice between spreading a minority community among several districts or concentrating them in a few is normally left to the political process (a process that her opinion in *Shaw v. Reno* acknowledged was always *aware* of the racial composition of alternative districts). "Section 2 contains no *per se* prohibitions against particular types of districts.... Only if the apportionment scheme has the *effect* of denying a protected class the equal opportunity to elect its candidate of choice does it violate § 2; where such an effect has not been demonstrated § 2 simply does not speak to the matter." Because the district court had found that Ohio politics was not characterized by racial bloc voting, the choice between dispersal and concentration did not implicate section 2. (The constitutional litigation over Ohio's plan is ongoing still. *See Quilter v. Voinovich*, 912 F.Supp. 1006 (N.D.Ohio 1995) (three-judge court) (striking down the apportionment on *Shaw v. Reno* grounds as an impermissible racial classification), *vacated and remanded in light of Bush v. Vera and Shaw v. Hunt*, 116 S.Ct. 2542 (1996).)

Pamela Karlan has suggested that "the relatively favorable treatment accorded racial vote dilution claims creates an incentive for partisan groups either to recast their claims to fall under the Voting Rights Act or to use plaintiffs protected by the Act as stalking horses to get into federal court." Pamela S. Karlan, *All Over the Map: The Supreme Court's Voting Rights Trilogy*, 1993 Sup. Ct. Rev. 245; *see also* Pamela S. Karlan, *The Rights To Vote: Some Pessimism About Formalism*, 71 Tex. L. Rev. 1705 (1993). To what extent do recent section 2 cases reflect this dynamic? Is this what Professor Issacharoff and Justice Souter mean when they contrast normal interest-group politics with the special case posed by classical voting rights claims?

4. To what extent ought the totality of the circumstances inquiry look into post-electoral influence as well as the ability to form winning coalitions? Consider the somewhat tortuous history of Tennessee's 1992 state legislative apportionment. *Rural West Tennessee African–American Affairs Council v. McWherter*, 836 F.Supp. 453 (W.D.Tenn.1993) (three-judge court), *vacated*, 512 U.S. 1248 (1994), *on remand*, 877 F.Supp. 1096 (W.D.Tenn.) (three-judge court), *summarily aff'd*, 116 S.Ct. 42 (1995).

The voting-age population in Tennessee is 14.4 percent black, with most blacks clustered in a few areas of the state. The Tennessee General Assembly has a thirty-three member Senate elected from single-member districts. Under the 1992 reapportionment plan, three of the thirty-three Senate districts were majority black. Two of the three majority-black Senate districts were in Shelby County (Memphis) in southwest Tennessee.

The plaintiffs in *Rural West* brought suit under section 2, alleging that black voters in Shelby County were unnecessarily "packed" into the two majority-black districts although they were sufficiently numerous to form three 60 percent black districts, and that voters in six rural west Tennessee counties were improperly split among several districts although it would have been possible to place them in a 55 percent black district.

The district court found that various illustrative plans presented by the plaintiffs satisfied the first prong of the *Gingles* test. The court also found legally significant bloc voting: no black from a majority-white district had won a seat in the state Senate during this century.

The state argued nonetheless that it should not be required to create additional majority-black districts because while the creation of one or more majority black districts in west Tennessee would likely increase the number of black state senators, such a change would reduce the overall influence of black voters in the State Senate. In its 1993 opinion, the district court rejected this argument:

> Conceptually it may be true, at least in some instances, that black influence in the legislative process on a statewide basis could be reduced by the creation of one or more additional majority black districts. Black voters may join like-minded white voters to elect a white representative favorable to black interests. By spreading the black vote out in several districts, the influence of black voters, but not their visible black representation, may be enhanced.
>
> * * *
>
> .... Whatever may be the wisdom of the Congressional policy, it appears that the language of § 2 and its legislative purposes strongly favor the creation of majority black districts and visible black representation, instead of "influence" districts, when block voting is racially polarized and there is a history of racial discrimination. The language of the statute creates a "results" test and states that districts should be created in which racial minorities have an "opportunity ... to elect representatives of their choice." The evidence in the present case, as in many cases, shows that blacks prefer to elect black representatives when they have a choice. The Senate report explaining the language of § 2 says "the presence of minority elected officials is a recognized indicator of access" to the political process under the "results" test. It also says that "the extent to which members of the minority group have been elected to public office in the jurisdiction" in question is a major factor in determining a violation of § 2. In light of this language, it appears that § 2 opts in favor of visible black representation over other forms of political influence when racial block voting and a history of prior racial discrimination are present, as

here. In such instances, § 2 as we interpret it opts for black control of some districts rather than spreading out black "influence" in more districts likely to be represented by white elected officials.

As for the appropriate remedy, the district court applied a rough proportionality measure:

> We reject the contention that a "complete and full" remedy means drawing districts to achieve maximum possible black representation in the legislature. The explicit rejection in the text of the statute of any right to proportional representation indicates that Congress did not intend to require maximum representation. The evidence before us indicates that one more majority-black Senate district must be drawn in west Tennessee. A second majority black district would provide slightly more representation than the state's black voting age population require. It would create five black Senate districts in the state or more than 15% of the districts when the black voting age population is 14.4% The issue of creating a fifth black Senate district should be left to the political judgment of the legislature. It is not required by federal law.

On appeal, the Supreme Court vacated the district court's judgment and remanded the case in light of *De Grandy*. The second time around, the district court reached a diametrically different conclusion.

Rural West Tennessee African–American Affairs Council v. McWherter

877 F.Supp. 1096 (W.D.Tenn.) (three-judge court), *summarily aff'd*, 116 S.Ct. 42 (1995).

■ GILBERT MERRITT, CHIEF CIRCUIT JUDGE

* * *

In light of *De Grandy*, we now believe that we erred in two respects in considering the "totality of the circumstances" in *Rural West I*. First, we deliberately, but improperly, excluded consideration of "influence districts" when we weighed the "totality of the circumstances." Second, in evaluating the seventh factor listed in the Senate Report, "the extent to which members of the minority group have been elected to public office in the jurisdiction," as well as in fashioning a remedy, we did not correctly apply the concept of "proportionality." We now address each of these issues in turn.

III. Influence Districts

In our prior decision, we gave extensive consideration to the defendants' argument that we should consider as part of the totality of the circumstances the several influence districts which exist under the 1992 Plan. Ultimately we decided that the Voting Rights Act does not recognize influence districts. Upon reconsideration, we now reach a different conclusion....

The issue of influence districts may arise in voting-rights jurisprudence in two distinct contexts. It will be useful to distinguish these two situations before proceeding further.

Most commonly, plaintiffs have contended that § 2 may mandate the creation of influence districts in certain situations. Frequently this argument has been advanced in cases in which the minority group in question does not have sufficient population to comprise a majority in a majority-minority district, but nonetheless wants to be part of an influential minority in a single district. If the members of a minority group taken together can only comprise 35% of the voting-age population of one district, no matter how the district is drawn, then it is clear that they do not satisfy the first *Gingles* precondition that requires that "the plaintiffs must be able to demonstrate that the protected group is sufficiently large and geographically compact that it could constitute an effective majority in a single member district." This issue of whether § 2 may require the creation of an influence district can also arise when a minority group does have sufficient population to satisfy the first *Gingles* precondition but that population is already largely included within majority-minority districts. In such a case, plaintiffs may argue that the remainder population, not included in a majority-minority district, and not numerous enough to form an additional majority-minority district must be grouped together to form an influence district rather than be divided in small numbers among other districts. Again, members of this remainder population cannot satisfy the first *Gingles* precondition.

* * *

Influence districts may also arise in the context of § 2 cases when a court evaluates the "totality of the circumstances." In this posture, the question is not whether the Voting Rights Act requires the creation of influence districts, but whether the voluntary creation of influence districts by a legislature should be counted as a factor weighing against finding a § 2 violation. To date, other than our own previous decision, there have been no cases that explicitly address this issue. Because it arises in the case now before us, we extrapolate from Supreme Court precedent to determine whether influence districts should be counted in evaluating the totality of the circumstances.

As a threshold matter, we note that the *De Grandy* Court reemphasized that the inquiry into the "totality of the circumstances" must be based on "a searching practical evaluation of the past and present reality." Thus, the Court has instructed that the inquiry should be quite broad and take into account as many relevant factors as possible in evaluating the "totality of the circumstances." It should not be limited merely to the factors listed in the Senate Report. Therefore, the degree to which minority voters can claim strong or weak influence in districts other than majority-minority districts certainly should be included in the calculus.

In addition, the Supreme Court has suggested in several instances that considering influence districts is appropriate.

* * *

[In *Voinovich v. Quilter*, the Supreme Court recognized] that in some cases the creation of majority-minority districts can actually weaken the influence a minority group has on the legislative process.

Furthermore, in *Chisom v. Roemer*, the Supreme Court rejected "the erroneous assumption that a small group of voters can never influence the outcome of an election.".... In making this argument, the Court explicitly recognized that at least in the *Chisom* context the phrase "elect representatives of their choice" may be read as meaning having the ability to influence the outcome of an election.

Finally, in *Gingles*, Justice O'Connor's concurrence raised the issue of whether influence districts may be considered by courts together with majority-minority districts in assessing a voting rights claim. She asked, "Is the 'voting strength' of a racial group to be assessed solely with reference to its prospects for electoral success, or should courts took at other avenues of political influence open to the racial group?" The Court's jurisprudence since *Gingles* has not answered this question explicitly, but, to remain consistent with recent cases, we believe that courts should consider the existence of "other avenues of political influence" besides majority-minority districts.

* * *

Before analyzing the role that influence districts play in the 1992 reapportionment of the Tennessee Senate, it is necessary to define at what point a minority group gains sufficient influence in an electoral district for recognition under § 2. Some have argued for a highly particularized definition of an "influence district" that takes into account the degree of racial polarization in a specific district, the outcome of individual elections and the actual ability of minority voters to build coalitions within a district. While such inquiries might provide the most precise measurements of the degree of influence exercised by a minority group within a particular district, they will vary from election to election. In a close election between two candidates in a predominantly white district in which each had the support of 49% of the population, a 2% minority population could decide the election by throwing its support to one of the two candidates. In such a situation, that minority group would have tremendous influence on the outcome of the election. But in the same district in another election, the same 2% of the population might be entirely irrelevant to the outcome if the contest were not as close. Thus courts would be obliged to engage in a new analysis every election. This would effectively make evaluation of influence districts unworkable.

Instead, we favor adoption of a standard rule that any district in which a minority group composes 25% to 55% of the voting-age population be considered an influence district.[4] Standard rules enhance consistency, manageability, predictability and uniformity. Cases that involve elections and voting patterns often may require complex calculations which integrate many factors....

We are confident that a minority population that votes as a bloc (as required by the second *Gingles* precondition) and comprises at least 25% of the voting-age population in an electoral district will have significant influence on candidates in virtually every election. A serious candidate for office cannot ignore 25% of the population that tends to vote as a bloc. An analysis of the two Tennessee Senate elections conducted under the 1992 Plan supports this conclusion. In the 1992 and 1994 elections combined there were twenty-one contested senate races. In every contested race, if 25% of those who voted had changed their votes from the winning candidate to the losing candidate, they would have reversed the results of the election. Furthermore, in fifteen of the twenty-one contested races, if 25% of those who voted and also cast ballots for the winning candidate withdrew their support and did not vote at all, they would have changed the outcome of the election. Realities such as these are difficult for candidates to ignore.

Testimony from two senators who represent districts with black populations over 20% reinforces the conclusion that a minority group does not need a majority to have influence on an election or a particular senator. Senator John Wilder, who is white, represents District 26 which has a 21% black voting-age population. Senator Wilder testified convincingly that he has sought to further the interests of his black constituents by sponsoring and supporting particular projects of interest to them. He also observed that in one recent primary election, he defeated two black challengers, receiving substantial support even in predominantly black communities. In addition, Senator Wilder recounted how as Speaker of the Senate he had used his authority to ensure that black senators became chairmen of committees. Regardless of whether he is opposed by a white candidate or a black candidate, Senator Wilder testified that he always works hard for the support of the black community and is strongly influenced by their interests. Even though the 21% black population in District 26 does not suffice to meet our definition of an influence district, it is clear that his black constituents have great influence on Senator Wilder and on the outcome of

---

4. We do not address whether a district in which minorities comprise less than 25% of the voting-age population can never be considered an influence district, even when proof presented by the parties leads to the opposite conclusion. Although two districts that might be called "weak influence districts" exist under the 1992 Plan, we have no need to include them in our calculation of the totality of the circumstances.

elections in his district nonetheless. Without the support of black voters he could not be assured of reelection.

Senator Stephen Cohen represents District 30 which has a 33% black voting-age population. Senator Cohen, who is white, testified that without the support of black voters he most likely would have lost races in 1988 and 1992, both of which he won. He described how he has received support from prominent black leaders in his district and how he campaigns in black communities within his district. Like Senator Wilder, it is clear that black voters choose to vote for Senator Cohen, actively support him, and in turn can expect that he will represent their interests in the Tennessee Senate.

The most probative aspect of Senator Cohen's testimony, however, concerned the role that senators elected from influence districts play in the political dynamics of the Senate. Specifically Senator Cohen persuasively testified that adding an additional majority-minority district in western Tennessee would actually reduce the influence of black voters in the Tennessee Senate. He cited as an example the legislative proposal to make the birthday of Martin Luther King a state holiday, a bill which passed the Senate by only one vote (17 to 16). Senator Cohen and another senator who represents a district with a substantial black population in west Tennessee both voted for the bill. Senator Cohen argued that by removing the black voters from the influence districts to create a new majority-minority district, at least one more conservative white senator would also be elected. This new conservative senator, elected from an overwhelmingly white district, would be uninfluenced by black voters and would have been inclined to vote against the Martin Luther King holiday, a measure strongly favored by black voters but opposed by many white voters in west Tennessee. As a consequence the measure would not have passed.

In addition, Senator Cohen named several other issues of interest to the black community which would not have passed if his influence district and another district with significant black population had been eliminated to form a majority-minority district. In particular, he cited a gambling bill and several funding bills of special concern to his district.

Based on the statistical results of the 1992 and 1994 elections, as well as the testimony of two members of the senate, when a minority group comprises 25% or more of the voting-age population, members of that group will have sufficient political influence to deem that district an influence district. A serious political candidate cannot ignore such a sizable portion of the electorate. Furthermore, Senator Cohen's testimony reveals that black voters in west Tennessee will be able to achieve their political aims more effectively with a combination of majority-minority districts and influence districts as opposed to only majority-minority districts. The voting patterns within the influence districts also reveal cross-racial support for candidates, which means that racial polarization has been reduced somewhat in those districts, a result that comports with the goals of the Voting Rights Act.

The 1992 Plan creates three majority-minority districts in which blacks comprise at least 55% of the voting-age population. In addition, the Plan provides three influence districts in which the voting-age population is at least 30% black. Finally, there are another two districts in which the voting-age population is over 20% black, but less than 25% black. Considering only the three majority-minority districts and the three influence districts, we cannot say based on the totality of the circumstances that the 1992 Plan violates § 2 of the Voting Rights Act. Together these six districts comprise 18.2% of all districts. We reach this decision even though the plaintiffs have demonstrated that the 1992 Plan does not result in proportionality, that the *Gingles* preconditions have been met, and that several factors listed in the Senate Report exist.

Black voters in the influence districts have not necessarily been deprived of the opportunity to vote for candidates of their choice, even if they do not always have the opportunity to elect what some consider a perfect candidate, i.e., a candidate of their own race. Furthermore, the plaintiffs have not demonstrated that replacing two of the influence districts with one majority-minority district would reduce vote dilution. To the contrary, it appears as though black voters might have more influence on the legislative process with two strong influence districts than they would with one additional majority-minority district.[11] Thus, when it is not demonstrated by the evidence that a reapportionment plan violates federal law, we must defer to the political decisions made by the elected legislature. Consequently, we hold that the 1992 Plan does not violate § 2 of the Voting Rights Act.

IV. Proportionality

Our decision on influence districts is reinforced by a reanalysis of the role of proportionality in § 2 cases. We conclude that § 2 of the Voting Rights Act does not require proportionality. In this case to require proportionality would be tantamount to violating the Dole Proviso because of the particular nature of racial polarization in Tennessee, as discussed below.

Voting rights doctrine has produced two distinct, but often confused concepts to measure the degree to which members of a minority group have been denied a fair opportunity to participate in electoral processes: "proportional representation" and "proportionality." The *De Grandy* Court clarified for us the difference between them.... [W]ere it not for the language of the Dole Proviso, a requirement of proportional representation would mean that because blacks comprise 14.4% of the voting-age population, 14.4% of the elected senators must also be black. On the other hand, an obligation to create proportionality would mean that the percentage of

---

11. We do not imply that the legislature could adopt a plan under current circumstances with no majority-minority districts at all if it created a sufficient number of influence districts. Under current doctrine the facts in this case require some majority-minority districts.

blacks in the voting-age population would require 14.4% of the districts to be majority-minority districts.

.... [T]he *De Grandy* Court made clear that the Voting Rights Act requires neither proportional representation nor proportionality.

* * *

The Court's decision to interpret the Voting Rights Act as not requiring proportionality makes eminent sense. The Dole Proviso in the Voting Rights Act establishes that the Act does not create a right to proportional representation. But when extreme racial polarization exists, as in the case before us, there is no practical difference between proportional representation and proportionality. Technically, § 2 only requires that a court determine that white voters will refuse to vote for black-preferred candidates. Therefore, theoretically one could find a Voting Rights Act violation without holding that black voters will almost always choose to vote for a black candidate rather than a white candidate, if given the choice. As a practical matter, however, in most racially polarized districts where white voters prefer white candidates (as is effectively required by the third Gingles precondition to find a § 2 violation), black voters will choose to vote for black candidates. This is certainly true in Tennessee. Thus, in effect, a majority-minority district in which the voting-age population is at least 55% black virtually always will elect a black representative. Requiring a proportional number of majority-minority districts when racial polarization exists, therefore, essentially results in the election of a proportional number of black representatives. To mandate proportionality under the Voting Rights Act when the Act in its own terms clearly states that it does not require proportional representation would be nonsensical.

* * *

Lack of proportionality certainly plays a role in evaluating the "totality of the circumstances." Were there no influence districts included in the 1992 Plan, the lack of proportionality in this case combined with other factors would be sufficient to find that § 2 had been violated. But once we include influence districts in the calculus, the lack of proportionality is not significant enough to compel a holding that the 1992 Plan violates the Voting Rights Act.

* * *

NOTES AND QUESTIONS

1. How ought a court to measure "influence"? Does *Rural West*'s analysis essentially adopt an understanding of influence that parallels the discussion in *Davis v. Bandemer*, 478 U.S. 109 (1986), discussed in Chapter 8? In *Bandemer*, the plurality opinion noted, in the context of political gerrymandering claims, that

[T]he mere fact that a particular apportionment scheme makes it more difficult for a particular group in a particular district to elect the representatives of its choice does not render that scheme constitutionally infirm. This conviction, in turn, stems from a perception that the power to influence the political process is not limited to winning elections. An individual or a group of individuals who votes for a losing candidate is usually deemed to be adequately represented by the winning candidate and to have as much opportunity to influence that candidate as other voters in the district. We cannot presume in such a situation, without actual proof to the contrary, that the candidate elected will entirely ignore the interests of those voters.

2. Does the analysis in *Rural West* relieve Tennessee of the obligation to create *any* majority-black districts? Consider a state like Mississippi, where blacks constitute something around 30 percent of the population. Would *Rural West* permit the state to spread blacks evenly among all five of the state's congressional districts, rather than creating a majority-black district, on the premise that black voters would enjoy more influence that way? Does the fact that since 1988 the state has elected two exceedingly conservative Republican senators shed any light on this question? Conversely, do blacks enjoy too much influence in Tennessee?

3. At what level of the political process ought influence to be measured? In *Rural West*, the court places great reliance on the testimony of two white Democratic legislators. Leaving aside the question whether this evidence is entirely reliable, their statements raise the question whether influence involves descriptive, or substantive, representation. Senator Wilder, for example, described how he had used his authority to ensure that black senators became chairmen of committees; Senator Cohen claimed that the creation of a majority-black district would result in the election of more conservative white senators from newly created adjacent districts and thus change the partisan balance in the Tennessee Senate.

Several voting rights scholars have focused on this question of whether, and to what extent, there is a tradeoff between direct black representation and the enactment of the legislative package favored by black voters.

[T]he election of representatives represents only an intermediate point along the path to the determination of policies that are voted on within the legislature. And with regard to that determination, the critical question for an individual cannot simply be whether *she* can elect *her* preferred candidate. Rather, it must focus on whether the system for selecting a governmental *body* gives her an effective opportunity to participate in policymaking.

* * *

That larger question embodies a ... conception of voting rights [as governance].... Because the voter's horizon extends beyond the moment of representative-selection to various opportunities for collective decisionmaking by assembled legislators, she necessarily will be concerned not merely with who serves as the representative(s) of her district, but, just as centrally, with the overall composition of the governing body. She will, in short, be interested in the degree of both her direct and her virtual representation.

Pamela S. Karlan, *The Rights to Vote: Some Pessimism About Formalism*, 71 Tex.L.Rev. 1705 (1993); *see also* Richard H. Pildes, *The Politics of Race*, 108 Harv. L. Rev. 1359, 1381 (1995). Some scholars have gone even further, to claim that "preferences over assemblies, not candidates, are fundamental." Jean–Pierre Benoit & Lewis A. Kornhauser, *Social Choice in a Representative Democracy*, 88 Am. Pol. Sci. Rev. 185 (1994). There is also an emerging positive and normative literature on whether the Voting Rights Act and the creation of majority-nonwhite districts is responsible for the decline of the Democratic Party. *See, e.g.*, Mark F. Bernstein, *Racial Gerrymandering*, Pub. Int., Winter 1996, at 59; Richard L. Engstrom, *Voting Rights Districts: Debunking the Myths*, Campaigns & Elections, Apr. 1995; Kevin A. Hill, *Does the Creation of Majority Black Districts Aid Republicans? An Analysis of the 1992 Congressional Elections in Eight Southern States*, 57 J. Pol. 384 (1995); David I. Lublin, *The Paradox of* Representation (1997); John J. Miller, *Race to Defeat: How the Black Caucus Elected Newt Gingrich Speaker*, Reason, Feb. 1995, at 23.

C. Beyond Dilution Through Submergence

Most litigation under amended section 2 has challenged districting decisions—either the use of multi-member (and at-large) election systems or the location of district lines. There have, however, been some challenges to other electoral practices, and the courts' treatment of these have illuminated a number of important doctrinal, practical, and theoretical issues.

Holder v. Hall

512 U.S. 874 (1994).

■ JUSTICE KENNEDY announced the judgment of the Court and delivered an opinion, in which THE CHIEF JUSTICE joined, and in all but Part II–B of which JUSTICE O'CONNOR joined.

This case presents the question whether the size of a governing authority is subject to a vote dilution challenge under [section 2.]

I

The State of Georgia has 159 counties, one of which is Bleckley County, a rural county in central Georgia. Black persons make up nearly 20% of the eligible voting population in Bleckley County. Since its creation in 1912, the county has had a single-commissioner form of government for the exercise of "county governing authority." Under this system, the Bleckley County Commissioner performs all of the executive and legislative functions of the county government, including the levying of general and special taxes, the directing and controlling of all county property, and the settling of all claims. In addition to Bleckley County, about 10 other Georgia counties use the single-commissioner system; the rest have multi-member commissions.

* * *

II

A

.... In a § 2 vote dilution suit, along with determining whether the *Gingles* preconditions are met and whether the totality of the circumstances supports a finding of liability, a court must find a reasonable alternative practice as a benchmark against which to measure the existing voting practice. As Justice O'Connor explained in *Gingles*: "The phrase vote dilution itself suggests a norm with respect to which the fact of dilution may be ascertained.... In order to decide whether an electoral system has made it harder for minority voters to elect the candidates they prefer, a court must have an idea in mind of how hard it should be for minority voters to elect their preferred candidates under an acceptable system."

In certain cases, the benchmark for comparison in a § 2 dilution suit is obvious. The effect of an anti-single-shot voting rule, for instance, can be evaluated by comparing the system with that rule to the system without that rule. But where there is no objective and workable standard for choosing a reasonable benchmark by which to evaluate a challenged voting practice, it follows that the voting practice cannot be challenged as dilutive under § 2.

As the facts of this case well illustrate, the search for a benchmark is quite problematic when a § 2 dilution challenge is brought to the size of a government body. There is no principled reason why one size should be picked over another as the benchmark for comparison. Respondents here argue that we should compare Bleckley County's sole commissioner system to a hypothetical five-member commission in order to determine whether the current system is dilutive. Respondents and the United States as amicus curiae give three reasons why the single commissioner structure should be compared to a five-member commission (instead of, say, a 3–, 10–, or 15–member body): (1) because the five-member commission is a common form of governing authority in the State; (2) because the state legislature had authorized Bleckley County to adopt a five-member commission if it so chose (it did not); and (3) because the county had moved from a single superintendent of education to a school board with five members elected from single-member districts.

These referents do not bear upon dilution. It does not matter, for instance, how popular the single-member commission system is in Georgia in determining whether it dilutes the vote of a minority racial group in Bleckley County. That the single-member commission is uncommon in the State of Georgia, or that a five-member commission is quite common, tells us nothing about its effects on a minority group's voting strength. The sole commissioner system has the same impact regardless of whether it is shared by none, or by all, of the other counties in Georgia. It makes little sense to say (as do respondents and the United States) that the sole commissioner system should be subject to a dilution challenge if it is rare—but immune if it is common.

That Bleckley County was authorized by the State to expand its commission, and that it adopted a five-member school board, are likewise irrelevant considerations in the dilution inquiry. At most, those facts indicate that Bleckley County could change the size of its commission with minimal disruption. But the county's failure to do so says nothing about the effects the sole commissioner system has on the voting power of Bleckley County's citizens. Surely a minority group's voting strength would be no more or less diluted had the State not authorized the county to alter the size of its commission, or had the county not enlarged its school board. One gets the sense that respondents and the United States have chosen a benchmark for the sake of having a benchmark. But it is one thing to say that a benchmark can be found, quite another to give a convincing reason for finding it in the first place.

B

To bolster their argument, respondents point out that our § 5 cases may be interpreted to indicate that covered jurisdictions may not change the size of their government bodies without obtaining preclearance from the Attorney General or the federal courts....

Under § 5 ... [a] proposed voting practice is measured against the existing voting practice to determine whether retrogression would result from the proposed change. The baseline for comparison is present by definition; it is the existing status. While there may be difficulty in determining whether a proposed change would cause retrogression, there is little difficulty in discerning the two voting practices to compare to determine whether retrogression would occur.

Retrogression is not the inquiry in § 2 dilution cases. Unlike in § 5 cases, therefore, a benchmark does not exist by definition in § 2 dilution cases. And as explained above, with some voting practices, there in fact may be no appropriate benchmark to determine if an existing voting practice is dilutive under § 2. For that reason, a voting practice that is subject to the preclearance requirements of § 5 is not necessarily subject to a dilution challenge under § 2.

* * *

JUSTICE O'CONNOR, concurring in part and concurring in the judgment.

[Omitted]

■ JUSTICE THOMAS, with whom JUSTICE SCALIA joins, concurring in the judgment.

* * *

While the practical concerns Justices Kennedy and O'Connor point out can inform a proper construction of the Act, I would explicitly anchor analysis in this case in the statutory text. Only a "voting qualification or prerequisite to voting or standard, practice, or procedure" can be challenged under § 2. I would hold that the size of a governing body is not a "standard, practice, or procedure" within the terms of the Act. In my view, however, the only principle limiting the scope of the terms "standard, practice, or procedure" that can be derived from the text of the Act would exclude, not only the challenge to size advanced today, but also challenges to allegedly dilutive election methods that we have considered within the scope of the Act in the past.

I believe that a systematic reassessment of our interpretation of § 2 is required in this case.... A review of the current state of our cases shows that by construing the Act to cover potentially dilutive electoral mechanisms, we have immersed the federal courts in a hopeless project of weighing questions of political theory—questions judges must confront to establish a benchmark concept of an "undiluted" vote. Worse, in pursuing the ideal measure of voting strength, we have devised a remedial mechanism that encourages federal courts to segregate voters into racially designated districts to ensure minority electoral success. In doing so, we have collaborated in what may aptly be termed the racial "balkanization" of the Nation.

I can no longer adhere to a reading of the Act that does not comport with the terms of the statute and that has produced such a disastrous misadventure in judicial policymaking. I would hold that the size of a government body is not a "standard, practice, or procedure" because, properly understood, those terms reach only state enactments that limit citizens' access to the ballot.

I

If one surveys the history of the Voting Rights Act, one can only be struck by the sea change that has occurred in the application and enforcement of the Act since it was passed in 1965. The statute was originally perceived as a remedial provision directed specifically at eradicating discriminatory practices that restricted blacks' ability to register and vote in the segregated South. Now, the Act has grown into something entirely different. In construing the Act to cover claims of vote dilution, we have converted the Act into a device for regulating, rationing, and apportioning political power among racial and ethnic groups. In the process, we have read the Act essentially as a grant of authority to the federal judiciary to develop theories on basic principles of representative government, for it is only a resort to political theory that can enable a court to determine which electoral systems provide the "fairest" levels of representation or the most "effective" or "undiluted" votes to minorities.

* * *

A

As it was enforced in the years immediately following its enactment, the Voting Rights Act of 1965 was perceived primarily as legislation directed at eliminating literacy tests and similar devices that had been used to prevent black voter registration in the segregated South....

The Act was immediately and notably successful in removing barriers to registration and ensuring access to the ballot. For example, in Mississippi, black registration levels skyrocketed from 6.7% to 59.8% in a mere two years; in Alabama the increase was from 19.3% to 51.6% in the same time period. By the end of 1967, black voter registration had reached at least 50% in every covered State.

The Court's decision in *Allen v. State Bd. of Elections*, 393 U.S. 544 (1969), however, marked a fundamental shift in the focal point of the Act.... [There, t]he Court reasoned that § 5's preclearance provisions should apply, not only to changes in electoral laws that pertain to registration and access to the ballot, but to provisions that might "dilute" the force of minority votes that were duly cast and counted....

As a consequence, *Allen* also ensured that courts would be required to confront a number of complex and essentially political questions in assessing claims of vote dilution under the Voting Rights Act. The central difficulty in any vote dilution case, of course, is determining a point of comparison against which dilution can be measured. As Justice Frankfurter observed several years before *Allen*, "talk of 'debasement' or 'dilution' is circular talk. One cannot speak of 'debasement' or 'dilution' of the value of a vote until there is first defined a standard of reference as to what a vote should be worth." *Baker v. Carr*, 369 U.S. 186, 300 (1962) (Frankfurter, J., dissenting).... But in setting the benchmark of what "undiluted" or fully "effective" voting strength should be, a court must necessarily make some judgments based purely on an assessment of principles of political theory....

Perhaps the most prominent feature of the philosophy that has emerged in vote dilution decisions since *Allen* has been the Court's preference for single-member districting schemes, both as a benchmark for measuring undiluted minority voting strength and as a remedial mechanism for guaranteeing minorities undiluted voting power....

It should be apparent, however, that there is no principle inherent in our constitutional system, or even in the history of the Nation's electoral practices, that makes single-member districts the "proper" mechanism for electing representatives to governmental bodies or for giving "undiluted" effect to the votes of a numerical minority. On the contrary, from the earliest days of the Republic, multimember districts were a common feature of our political systems. The Framers left unanswered in the Constitution the question whether congressional delegations from the several States should be elected on a general ticket from each State as a whole or under a districting scheme and left that matter to be resolved by the States or by Congress. *See* U.S. Const., Art. I, § 4, cl. 1. It was not until 1842 that Congress determined that Representatives should be elected from single-member districts in the States. Single-member districting was no more the rule in the States themselves, for the Constitutions of most of the 13 original States provided that representatives in the state legislatures were to be elected from multimember districts. Today, although they have come under increasing attack under the Voting Rights Act, multimember district systems continue to be a feature on the American political landscape, especially in municipal governments.

The obvious advantage the Court has perceived in single-member districts, of course, is their tendency to enhance the ability of any numerical minority in the electorate to gain control of seats in a representative body. But in choosing single-member districting as a benchmark electoral plan on that basis the Court has made a political decision and, indeed, a decision that itself depends on a prior political choice made in answer to Justice Harlan's question in *Allen*. Justice Harlan asked whether a group's votes should be considered to be more "effective" when they provide influence over a greater number of seats, or control over a lesser number of seats. In answering that query, the Court has determined that the purpose of the vote—or of the fully "effective" vote—is controlling seats. In other words, in an effort to develop standards for assessing claims of dilution, the Court has adopted the view that members of any numerically significant minority are denied a fully effective use of the franchise unless they are able to control seats in an elected body. Under this theory, votes that do not control a representative are essentially wasted; those who cast them go unrepresented and are just as surely disenfranchised as if they had been barred from registering. Such conclusions, of course, depend upon a certain theory of the "effective" vote, a theory that is not inherent in the concept of representative democracy itself.[6]

6. Undoubtedly, one factor that has prompted our focus on control of seats has

In fact, it should be clear that the assumptions that have guided the Court reflect only one possible understanding of effective exercise of the franchise, an understanding based on the view that voters are "represented" only when they choose a delegate who will mirror their views in the legislative halls.[7] But it is certainly possible to construct a theory of effective political participation that would accord greater importance to voters' ability to influence, rather than control, elections. And especially in a two-party system such as ours, the influence of a potential "swing" group of voters composing 10%–20% of the electorate in a given district can be considerable. Even such a focus on practical influence, however, is not a necessary component of the definition of the "effective" vote. Some conceptions of representative government may primarily emphasize the formal value of the vote as a mechanism for participation in the electoral process, whether it results in control of a seat or not. Under such a theory, minorities unable to control elected posts would not be considered essentially without a vote; rather, a vote duly cast and counted would be deemed just as "effective" as any other. If a minority group is unable to control seats, that result may plausibly be attributed to the inescapable fact that, in a majoritarian system, numerical minorities lose elections.

* * *

But the political choices the Court has had to make do not end with the determination that the primary purpose of the "effective" vote is controlling seats or with the selection of single-member districting as the mechanism for providing that control. In one sense, these were not even the most critical decisions to be made in devising standards for assessing claims of dilution, for in itself, the selection of single-member districting as a benchmark election plan will tell a judge little about the number of minority districts to create. Single-member districting tells a court "how" members of a minority are to control seats, but not "how many" seats they should be allowed to control.

---

been a desire, when confronted with an abstract question of political theory concerning the measure of effective participation in government, to seize upon an objective standard for deciding cases, however much it may oversimplify the issues before us. If using control of seats as our standard does not reflect a very nuanced theory of political participation, it at least has the superficial advantage of appealing to the "most easily measured indicia of political power."

7. Indeed, the assumptions underpinning the Court's conclusions largely parallel principles that John Stuart Mill advanced in proposing a system of proportional representation as an electoral reform in Great Britain. See J. S. Mill, Considerations on Representative Government (1861). In Mill's view, a just system of representative government required an electoral system that ensured "a minority of the electors would always have a minority of the representatives." To Mill, a system that allowed a portion of the population that constituted a majority in each district to control the election of all representatives and to defeat the minority's choice of candidates was unjust because it operated to produce a "complete disfranchisement of minorities."

But "how many" is the critical issue. Once one accepts the proposition that the effectiveness of votes is measured in terms of the control of seats, the core of any vote dilution claim is an assertion that the group in question is unable to control the "proper" number of seats—that is, the number of seats that the minority's percentage of the population would enable it to control in the benchmark "fair" system. The claim is inherently based on ratios between the numbers of the minority in the population and the numbers of seats controlled.... As a result, only a mathematical calculation can answer the fundamental question posed by a claim of vote dilution. And once again, in selecting the proportion that will be used to define the undiluted strength of a minority—the ratio that will provide the principle for decision in a vote dilution case—a court must make a political choice.

The ratio for which this Court has opted, and thus the mathematical principle driving the results in our cases, is undoubtedly direct proportionality....

B

The dabbling in political theory that dilution cases have prompted, however, is hardly the worst aspect of our vote dilution jurisprudence. Far more pernicious has been the Court's willingness to accept the one underlying premise that must inform every minority vote dilution claim: the assumption that the group asserting dilution is not merely a racial or ethnic group, but a group having distinct political interests as well. Of necessity, in resolving vote dilution actions we have given credence to the view that race defines political interest. We have acted on the implicit assumption that members of racial and ethnic groups must all think alike on important matters of public policy and must have their own "minority preferred" representatives holding seats in elected bodies if they are to be considered represented at all.

* * *

[The Court has adopted] a working assumption that racial groups can be conceived of largely as political interest groups. And operating under that assumption, we have assigned federal courts the task of ensuring that minorities are assured their "just" share of seats in elected bodies throughout the Nation.

To achieve that result through the currently fashionable mechanism of drawing majority-minority single-member districts, we have embarked upon what has been aptly characterized as a process of "creating racially 'safe boroughs.'" We have involved the federal courts, and indeed the Nation, in the enterprise of systematically dividing the country into electoral districts along racial lines—an enterprise of segregating the races into political homelands that amounts, in truth, to nothing short of a system of "political apartheid."... Worse still, it is not only the courts that have taken up this project. In response to judicial decisions and the promptings of the Justice Department, the States themselves, in an attempt to avoid costly and disruptive Voting Rights Act litigation, have begun to gerrymander electoral districts according to race. That practice now promises to embroil the courts in a lengthy process of attempting to undo, or at least to minimize, the damage wrought by the system we created.

* * *

As a practical political matter, our drive to segregate political districts by race can only serve to deepen racial divisions by destroying any need for voters or candidates to build bridges between racial groups or to form voting coalitions. "Black-preferred" candidates are assured election in "safe black districts"; white-preferred candidates are assured election in "safe white districts." Neither group needs to draw on support from the other's constituency to win on election day.

* * *

C

While the results we have already achieved under the Voting Rights Act might seem bad enough, we should recognize that our approach to splintering the electorate into racially designated single-member districts does not by any means mark a limit on the authority federal judges may wield to rework electoral systems under our Voting Rights Act jurisprudence. On the contrary, in relying on single-member districting schemes as a touchstone, our cases so far have been somewhat arbitrarily limited to addressing the interests of minority voters who are sufficiently geographically compact to form a majority in a single-member district. There is no reason a priori, however, that our focus should be so constrained. The decision to rely on single-member geographic districts as a mechanism for conducting elections is merely a political choice—and one that we might reconsider in the future. Indeed, it is a choice that has undoubtedly been influenced by the adversary process: in the cases that have come before us, plaintiffs have focused largely upon attacking multimember districts and have offered single-member schemes as the benchmark of an "undiluted" alternative.

But as the destructive effects of our current penchant for majority-minority districts become more apparent, courts will undoubtedly be called upon to reconsider adherence to geographic districting as a method for ensuring minority voting power. Already, some advocates have criticized the current strategy of creating majority-minority districts and have urged the adoption of other voting mechanisms—for example, cumulative voting or a system using transferable votes—that can produce proportional results without requiring division of the electorate into racially segregated districts.

Such changes may seem radical departures from the electoral systems with which we are most familiar. Indeed, they may be unwanted by the people in the several States who purposely have adopted districting systems in their electoral laws. But nothing in our present understanding of the Voting Rights Act places a principled limit on the authority of federal courts that would prevent them from instituting a system of cumulative voting as a remedy under § 2, or even from establishing a more elaborate mechanism for securing proportional representation based on transferable votes.[17] As some Members of the Court have already recognized, geographic districting is not a requirement inherent in our political system.... Like other political choices concerning electoral systems and models of representation, it too is presumably subject to a judicial override if it comes into conflict with the theories of representation and effective voting that we may develop under the Voting Rights Act.

Indeed, the unvarnished truth is that all that is required for districting to fall out of favor is for Members of this Court to further develop their political thinking. We should not be surprised if voting rights advocates encourage us to "revive our political imagination," and to consider "innovative and nontraditional remedies" for vote dilution, for under our Voting Rights Act jurisprudence, it is only the limits on our "political imagination" that place restraints on the standards we may select for defining undiluted voting systems. Once we candidly recognize that geographic districting and other aspects of electoral systems that we have so far placed beyond question are merely political choices, those practices, too, may fall under suspicion of having a dilutive effect on minority voting strength. And when the time comes to put the question to the test, it may be difficult indeed for a Court that, under *Gingles*, has been bent on creating roughly proportional representation for geographically compact minorities to find a principled reason for holding that a geographically dispersed minority cannot challenge districting itself as a dilutive electoral practice. In principle, cumulative voting and other non-district-based methods of effecting proportional representation are simply more efficient and straightforward mechanisms for achieving what has already become our tacit objective: roughly proportional allocation of political power according to race.

* * *

II

.... [I believe that section 2 covers only] practices that affect minority citizens' access to the ballot. Districting systems and electoral mechanisms

---

17. Such methods of voting cannot be rejected out-of-hand as bizarre concoctions of Voting Rights Act plaintiffs. The system of transferable votes was a widely celebrated, although unsuccessful, proposal for English parliamentary reform in the last century. And while it is an oddity in American political history, cumulative voting in an at-large system has been employed in some American jurisdictions.

that may affect the "weight" given to a ballot duly cast and counted are simply beyond the purview of the Act.

A

In determining the scope of § 2(a), as when interpreting any statute, we should begin with the statutory language. Under the plain terms of the Act, § 2(a) covers only a defined category of state actions. Only "voting qualifications," "prerequisites to voting," or "standards, practices, or procedures" are subject to challenge under the Act. The first two items in this list clearly refer to conditions or tests applied to regulate citizens' access to the ballot. They would cover, for example, any form of test or requirement imposed as a condition on registration or on the process of voting on election day.

* * *

[W]e have already stretched the terms "standard, practice, or procedure" beyond the limits of ordinary meaning. We have concluded, for example, that the choice of a certain set of district lines is a "procedure," or perhaps a "practice," concerning voting subject to challenge under the Act, even though the drawing of a given set of district lines has nothing to do with the basic process of allowing a citizen to vote—that is, the process of registering, casting a ballot, and having it counted.

* * *

[N]othing in the language used in § 2(a) to describe the protection provided by the Act suggests that in protecting the "right to vote," the section was meant to incorporate a concept of voting that encompasses a concern for the "weight" or "influence" of votes. On the contrary, the definition of the terms "vote" and "voting" in § 14(c)(1) of Act focuses precisely on access to the ballot. Thus, § 14(c)(1) provides that the terms "vote" and "voting" shall encompass any measures necessary to ensure "registration" and any "other action required by law prerequisite to voting, casting a ballot, and having such ballot counted properly and included in the appropriate totals of votes cast."

It is true that § 14(c)(1) also states that the term "voting" "includes all action necessary to make a vote effective," and the Court has seized on this language as an indication that Congress intended the Act to reach claims of vote dilution. But if the word "effective" is not plucked out of context, the rest of § 14(c)(1) makes clear that the actions Congress deemed necessary to make a vote "effective" were precisely the actions listed above: registering, satisfying other voting prerequisites, casting a ballot, and having it included in the final tally of votes cast.... [20]

* * *

20. .... Contrary to Justice Stevens' suggestions, *Gomillion v. Lightfoot*, 364 U.S.

Of course, this interpretation of the terms "standard, practice, or procedure" effectively means that § 2(a) does not provide for any claims of what we have called vote "dilution." But that is precisely the result suggested by the text of the statute. Section 2(a) nowhere uses the term "vote dilution" or suggests that its goal is to ensure that votes are given their proper "weight." And an examination of § 2(b) does not suggest any different result. It is true that in construing § 2 to reach vote dilution claims in *Thornburg v. Gingles*, 478 U.S. 30 (1986), the Court relied largely on the gloss on § 2(b) supplied in the legislative history of the 1982 amendments to the Act. But the text of § 2(b) supplies a weak foundation indeed for reading the Act to reach such claims.

.... [Section] 2(b) incorporates virtually the exact language of the "results test" employed by the Court in *White v. Regester*, and applied in constitutional voting rights cases before our decision in *Bolden*. The section directs courts to consider whether "based on the totality of circumstances," a state practice results in members of a minority group "having less opportunity than other members of the electorate to participate in the political process and to elect representatives of their choice."

But the mere adoption of a "results" test, rather than an "intent" test, says nothing about the type of state laws that may be challenged using that test. On the contrary, the type of state law that may be challenged under § 2 is addressed explicitly in § 2(a).... [T]he incorporation of a results test into the amended section does not necessarily suggest that Congress intended to allow claims of vote dilution under § 2. A results test is useful to plaintiffs whether they are challenging laws that restrict access to the ballot or laws that accomplish some diminution in the "proper weight" of a group's vote. Nothing about the test itself suggests that it is inherently tied to vote dilution claims. A law, for example, limiting the times and places at which registration can occur might be adopted with the purpose of limiting black voter registration, but it could be extremely difficult to prove the discriminatory intent behind such a facially neutral law. The results test would allow plaintiffs to mount a successful challenge to the law under § 2 without such proof.

.... The most natural reading of [§ 2(b)] would suggest that citizens have an equal "opportunity" to participate in the electoral process and an equal "opportunity" to elect representatives when they have been given the

339 (1960), does not indicate that the Fifteenth Amendment, in protecting the right to vote, incorporates a concern for anything beyond securing access to the ballot. The *Gomillion* plaintiffs' claims centered precisely on access: their complaint was not that the weight of their votes had been diminished in some way, but that the boundaries of a city had been drawn to prevent blacks from voting in municipal elections altogether. *Gomillion* thus "maintains the distinction between an attempt to exclude Negroes totally from the relevant constituency, and a statute that permits Negroes to vote but which uses the gerrymander to contain the impact of Negro suffrage." *Allen v. State Bd. of Elections*, 393 U.S. 544, 589 (Harlan, J., concurring in part and dissenting in part).

same free and open access to the ballot as other citizens and their votes have been properly counted.

* * *

C

"Stare decisis is not an inexorable command[.]" Our interpretation of § 2 has ... proved unworkable. As I outlined above, it has mired the federal courts in an inherently political task—one that requires answers to questions that are ill-suited to principled judicial resolution. Under § 2, we have assigned the federal judiciary a project that involves, not the application of legal standards to the facts of various cases or even the elaboration of legal principles on a case-by-case basis, but rather the creation of standards from an abstract evaluation of political philosophy.

Worse, our interpretation of § 2 has required us to distort our decisions to obscure the fact that the political choice at the heart of our cases rests on precisely the principle the Act condemns: proportional allocation of political power according to race. Continued adherence to a line of decisions that necessitates such dissembling cannot possibly promote what we have perceived to be one of the central values of the policy of stare decisis: the preservation of "the actual and perceived integrity of the judicial process."

* * *

Few words would be too strong to describe the dissembling that pervades the application of the "totality of circumstances" test under our interpretation of § 2. It is an empty incantation—a mere conjurer's trick that serves to hide the drive for proportionality that animates our decisions. As actions such as that brought in *Shaw v. Reno* have already started to show, what might euphemistically be termed the benign "creation of majority-minority single-member districts to enhance the opportunity of minority groups to elect representatives of their choice" might also more simply and more truthfully be termed "racial gerrymandering.". . . .

In my view, our current practice should not continue. Not for another Term, not until the next case, not for another day. The disastrous implications of the policies we have adopted under the Act are too grave; the dissembling in our approach to the Act too damaging to the credibility of the federal judiciary. . . . I cannot subscribe to the view that in our decisions under the Voting Rights Act it is more important that we have a settled rule than that we have the right rule. When, under our direction, federal courts are engaged in methodically carving the country into racially designated electoral districts, it is imperative that we stop to reconsider whether the course we have charted for the Nation is the one set by the people through their representatives in Congress. I believe it is not.

* * *

■ JUSTICE BLACKMUN, with whom JUSTICE STEVENS, JUSTICE SOUTER, and JUSTICE GINSBURG join, dissenting.

* * *

II

* * *

By all objective measures, the proposed five-member Bleckley County Commission presents a reasonable, workable benchmark against which to measure the practice of electing a sole commissioner. First, the Georgia Legislature specifically authorized a five-member commission for Bleckley County. Moreover, a five-member commission is the most common form of governing authority in Georgia. Bleckley County, as one of a small and dwindling number of counties in Georgia still employing a sole commissioner, markedly departs from practices elsewhere in Georgia. This marked "departure . . . from practices elsewhere in the jurisdiction . . . bears on the fairness of [the sole commissioner's] impact." Finally, the county itself has moved from a single superintendent of education to a school board with five members elected from single-member districts, providing a workable and readily available model for commission districts. Thus, the proposed five-member baseline is reasonable and workable.

In this case, identifying an appropriate baseline against which to measure dilution is not difficult. In other cases, it may be harder. But the need to make difficult judgments does not "justify a judicially created limitation on the coverage of the broadly worded statute, as enacted and amended by Congress." Vote dilution is inherently a relative concept, requiring a highly "flexible, fact-intensive" inquiry, and calling for an exercise of the "court's overall judgment, based on the totality of the circumstances and guided by those relevant factors in the particular case," as mandated by Congress. Certainly judges who engage in the complex task of evaluating reapportionment plans and examining district lines will be able to determine whether a proposed baseline is an appropriate one against which to measure a claim of vote dilution based on the size of a county commission.

* * *

■ JUSTICE GINSBURG, dissenting.

I join the dissenting opinion by Justice Blackmun and the separate opinion of Justice Stevens, and add a further observation about the responsibility Congress has given to the judiciary.

. . . . [As Justice O'Connor observed in her concurrence in *Gingles*, "t]here is an inherent tension between what Congress wished to do and what it wished to avoid"—between Congress' "intent to allow vote dilution claims to be brought under § 2" and its intent to avoid "creating a right to proportional representation for minority voters." Tension of this kind is hardly unique to the Voting Rights Act, for when Congress acts on issues on which its constituents are divided, sometimes bitterly, the give-and-take of legislative compromise can yield statutory language that fails to reconcile conflicting goals and purposes.

* * *

When courts are confronted with congressionally-crafted compromises of this kind, it is "not an easy task" to remain "faithful to the balance Congress struck.".... However difficult this task may prove to be, it is one that courts must undertake because it is their mission to effectuate Congress' multiple purposes as best they can.

■ Separate opinion of JUSTICE STEVENS, in which JUSTICE BLACKMUN, JUSTICE SOUTER, and JUSTICE GINSBURG join.

Justice Thomas has written a separate opinion proposing that the terms "standard, practice, or procedure" as used in the Voting Rights Act should henceforth be construed to refer only to practices that affect minority citizens' access to the ballot. Specifically, Justice Thomas would no longer interpret the Act to forbid practices that dilute minority voting strength. To the extent that his opinion advances policy arguments in favor of that interpretation of the statute, it should be addressed to Congress, which has ample power to amend the statute. To the extent that the opinion suggests that federal judges have an obligation to subscribe to the proposed narrow reading of statutory language, it is appropriate to supplement Justice Thomas' writing with a few words of history.

I

Justice Thomas notes that the first generation of Voting Rights Act cases focused on access to the ballot. By doing so, he suggests that the early pattern of enforcement is an indication of the original meaning of the statute. In this regard, it is important to note that the Court's first case addressing a voting practice other than access to the ballot arose under the Fifteenth Amendment. In *Gomillion v. Lightfoot*, the Court held that a change in the boundaries of the city of Tuskegee, Alabama, violated the Fifteenth Amendment.

* * *

Because *Gomillion* was decided only a few years before the Voting Rights Act of 1965 was passed, and because coverage under the Voting Rights Act is generally coextensive with or broader than coverage under the Fifteenth Amendment, it is surely not unreasonable to infer that Congress intended the Act to reach the kind of voting practice that was at issue in that case....

During the years between 1965 and 1969 the question whether the Voting Rights Act should be narrowly construed to cover nothing more than impediments to access to the ballot was an unresolved issue. What

Justice Thomas describes as "a fundamental shift in the focal point of the Act," occurred in 1969 [in *Allen v. State Board of Elections*,] when the Court unequivocally rejected the narrow reading, relying heavily on a broad definition of the term "voting" as including " 'all action necessary to make a vote effective.' "

Despite *Allen*'s purported deviation from the Act's true meaning, Congress one year later reenacted § 5 without in any way changing the operative words. During the next five years, the Court consistently adhered to *Allen*, and in 1975, Congress again reenacted § 5 without change.

When, in the late seventies, some parties advocated a narrow reading of the Act, the Court pointed to these Congressional reenactments as solid evidence that *Allen*, even if not correctly decided in 1969, would now be clearly correct.

* * *

If the 1970 and 1975 reenactments had left any doubt as to congressional intent, that doubt would be set aside by the 1982 amendments to § 2. Between 1975 and 1982, the Court continued to interpret the Voting Rights Act in the broad manner set out by *Allen*.... In the 1982 amendment to § 2 of the Voting Rights Act, Congress substituted a "results" test for an intent requirement. It is crystal clear that Congress intended the 1982 amendment to cover non-access claims like those in *Bolden* and *Gomillion*.

II

Justice Thomas' narrow interpretation of the words "voting qualification ... standard, practice, or procedure," if adopted, would require us to overrule *Allen* and the cases that have adhered to its reading of the critical statutory language.... The large number of decisions that we would have to overrule or reconsider, as well as the congressional reenactments discussed above, suggests that Justice Thomas' radical reinterpretation of the Voting Rights Act is barred by the well-established principle that stare decisis has special force in the statutory arena.

* * *

Throughout his opinion, Justice Thomas argues that this case is an exception to stare decisis, because *Allen* and its progeny have "immersed the federal courts in a hopeless project of weighing questions of political theory." There is no question that the Voting Rights Act has required the courts to resolve difficult questions, but that is no reason to deviate from an interpretation that Congress has thrice approved. Statutes frequently require courts to make policy judgments. The Sherman Act, for example, requires courts to delve deeply into the theory of economic organization. Similarly, Title VII of the Civil Rights Act has required the courts to formulate a theory of equal opportunity. Our work would certainly be much easier if every case could be resolved by consulting a dictionary, but when Congress has legislated in general terms, judges may not invoke judicial modesty to avoid difficult questions.

III

When a statute has been authoritatively, repeatedly, and consistently construed for more than a quarter century, and when Congress has reenacted and extended the statute several times with full awareness of that construction, judges have an especially clear obligation to obey settled law. Whether Justice Thomas is correct that the Court's settled construction of the Voting Rights Act has been "a disastrous misadventure" should not affect the decision in this case. It is therefore inappropriate for me to comment on the portions of his opinion that are best described as an argument that the statute be repealed or amended in important respects.

NOTES AND QUESTIONS

1. The Supreme Court remanded *Holder* to the lower courts on the question whether, if plaintiffs could show that the jurisdictional intentionally retained the single-commissioner form of government, the scheme would violate the Fourteenth Amendment. If such a showing could be made, what would the injury be? Does that injury shed any light on how to assess whether the scheme violates the Voting Rights Act?

2. The Court distinguished between section 2 and section 5 because section 5 contains its own baseline—the pre-existing practice. Suppose Bleckley County had had a five-member county commission, elected from five single-member districts, one of which was majority black. If the County were to reduce the number of seats to three, and if blacks were now no longer sufficiently numerous to form a majority in a fairly drawn single-member district, then the Justice Department might well refuse to preclear the new plan on the ground that it diluted black voting strength, and in a judicial preclearance proceeding it would likely prevail if there was any substantial evidence of bloc voting. Now consider the Kent County (Michigan) Board of Commissioners. After the 1990 census, the board reduced the number of seats from 21 to 19. If the county had retained a 21–seat plan, it would have been possible to draw two majority-nonwhite districts while under a 19–seat plan, only one could be drawn. *See Nixon v. Kent County*, 76 F.3d 1381 (6th Cir.1996) (en banc). Is Kent County immune from all scrutiny under the Voting Rights Act because Michigan is not subject to preclearance?

3. Justice Thomas's concurrence in *Holder* is in some ways the most extraordinary voting rights opinion of modern times. Under what theory of statutory interpretation can section 2 be read not to cover vote dilution?

One scholar claims that "Justice Thomas's project—to shrink the statutory meaning of voting to the single act of casting a ballot—was not a conventional attempt at statutory construction, but a radical reconstruction of the law." Lani Guinier, *[E]racing Democracy*, 108 Harv.L.Rev. 109 (1994). Professor Guinier comments:

> The professed jurisprudential virtue of Justice Thomas's formulation is that it avoids "immers[ing] the federal courts" in the "hopeless project" of choosing between competing political theories and limits federal judicial intervention in local election matters. Justice Thomas's interpretation of the statute, however, itself rests on a particular political theory. Justice Thomas's political theory, or at least the theory he imputed to the Congress that enacted the Voting Rights Act, is that political equality is satisfied by the simple condition of universal suffrage. His position—that the statute should be limited to claims that challenge direct denial of the right to cast a ballot—rests on a political theory of individualized democracy.

Does Justice Thomas's approach go even beyond Justice Frankfurter's views in *Colegrove v. Green* and *Baker v. Carr*, discussed in Chapter 3?

Although she disagreed with most of the factual and philosophical premises of Justice Thomas's opinion, Professor Guinier nonetheless viewed the opinion as pivotal:

> Despite the gaps in its reasoning, Justice Thomas's opinion is important for two reasons. First, Justice Thomas demonstrated the centrality of political theory to an understanding of minority vote dilution. As Justice Thomas argued, vote dilution claims require the federal judiciary to develop theories of the basic principles of democratic self-government. The question of defining minority vote dilution can only be answered by reference to a theory that defines effective participation in representative government. Second, Justice Thomas provided an enduring rationale for future challenges to the Act. Although the dissents in *Holder* and the majority in *De Grandy* recognized the broad remedial goal of the statute, none of the other opinions in those cases took Justice Thomas's challenge to articulate a theory of democratic representation from which a principled and workable strategy for enforcing the Act might emerge.

What might the contours of such a theory be?

4. *The question of how to apply the Voting Rights Act to single-member offices has remained a vexing one.* Holder can be read to say that challenges to such offices are cognizable, but it shed little light on how to assess such suits. For two examples of the lower courts' approach consider *Butts v. City of New York*, 779 F.2d 141 (2d Cir.1985), *cert. denied*, 478 U.S. 1021 (1986), and *LULAC v. Clements*, 999 F.2d 831 (5th Cir.) (en banc), *cert. denied*, 114 S.Ct. 878 (1994), discussed in another context earlier in this Chapter.

C. BEYOND DILUTION THROUGH SUBMERGENCE

Butts concerned a challenge to a New York statute providing for a runoff primary if no candidate receives 40 percent or more of the votes cast in a party primary for Mayor or other citywide office in New York City. According to the court of appeals, "[p]olitical observers [were] agreed that the adoption of the run-off law was prompted by the unusual results of the 1969 New York City mayoral election. In the Democratic primary that year, two candidates—Herman Badillo and Robert Wagner—split the votes of the party's mainstream (Badillo receiving 28 percent, and Wagner 29 percent); as a result, the nomination went to Mario Proccacino (with 33 percent of the votes), who had run on a "safe streets" platform. Proccacino lost in the general election to incumbent John Lindsay, the nominee of the Independent and Liberal parties."

When a bill to require runoff primaries was introduced in the state senate, opponents argued that it could have the effect of preventing blacks and Hispanics from electing their own candidates to the offices covered by the bill, since the 40 percent threshold figure was just above the combined percentage of blacks and Hispanics in New York City at the time.

A class of black and Hispanic plaintiffs brought a challenge against the law. Although the district court ruled in their favor, finding the enactment intentionally discriminatory, the Second Circuit reversed.

> The events leading up to passage of the bill clearly support an inference of legitimate motive. The Proccacino nomination badly hurt the Democratic party in New York City, and such fluke results were likely to recur as the party system further deteriorated and a broader field of candidates emerged. The application of [the law] solely to citywide offices in New York speaks primarily to the ideological diversity within the City and the importance of those offices. The 40% threshold, which [the district court judge] called "diabolic," was obviously chosen because Proccacino received 33% of the vote in 1969, not because of the minority population figures in New York. Finally, the speed with which the bill passed both houses demonstrates its broad-based support rather than any "nefarious" motives; this broad support is also evident from the strong minority legislative vote in favor of the bill.

The Second Circuit also concluded that the runoff could not be challenged under the results test of section 2.

> Our central disagreement with the district court's interpretation of the Voting Rights Act concerns the kind of electoral arrangements that can violate the Act. There are two basic ways in which members of a class of citizens may have "less opportunity ... to participate in the electoral process." There may either be restrictive practices that deter members of the class from voting, or electoral arrangements that diminish a class's opportunity to elect representatives in proportion to its numbers. Although the

Act makes clear that a class has no right to elect its members by numerical proportion, the class does have a right to an opportunity, equal to that of other classes, to obtain such representation.

In the context of elections for multi-member bodies, equal opportunity can be denied in a variety of ways.... A run-off requirement can exacerbate the unfair effect of at-large voting for a multi-member body, and has been invalidated in that context.

We cannot, however, take the concept of a class's impaired opportunity for equal representation and uncritically transfer it from the context of elections for multi-member bodies to that of elections for single-member offices. These can be no equal opportunity for representation within an office filled by one person. Whereas, in an election to a multi-member body, a minority class has an opportunity to secure a share of representation equal to that of other classes by electing its members from districts in which it is dominant, there is no such thing as a "share" of a single-member office.... [S]o long as the winner of an election for a single-member office is chosen directly by the votes of all eligible voters, it is unlikely that electoral arrangements for such an election can deny a class an equal opportunity for representation. We need not determine whether such opportunity could ever be denied in the context of an election to a single-member office. It suffices to rule in this case that a run-off election requirement in such an election does not deny any class an opportunity for equal representation and therefore cannot violate the Act. The rule in elections for single-member office has always been that the candidate with the most votes wins, and nothing in the Act alters this basic political principle. Nor does the Act prevent any governmental unit from deciding that the winner must have not a merely a plurality of the votes, but an absolute majority (as where run-offs are required when no candidate in the initial vote secures a majority) or at least a substantial plurality, such as the 40% level required by [this law.]

In contrast to *Butts*, a district court in Arkansas concluded that the state's adoption of runoff primary laws was tainted by a discriminatory purpose. *See Jeffers v. Clinton*, 740 F.Supp. 585 (E.D.Ark.1990) (three-judge court). According to the court:

Traditionally, municipal offices, including mayor, council member, and municipal judge, were filled by nonpartisan election, conducted at the general election in November. The person receiving the highest number of votes won. A majority was not required. This situation began to change in 1973. In November 1972 P.A. (Les) Hollingsworth, a black lawyer who later served as an Associate Justice of the Supreme Court of Arkansas, was elected to the Little Rock City Board of Directors by a plurality. The General

Assembly responded in its next session, enacting Act 168 of 1973, requiring a majority vote for such offices.

In 1975, a vacancy occurred in the office of Mayor of Pine Bluff, and Robert Handley announced his candidacy. The Rev. Mr. Handley, a black man, appeared to be a strong contender. The Legislature acted promptly. In advance of the special election for Mayor of Pine Bluff, it passed Act 269 of 1975, requiring a majority vote. Mr. Handley was defeated in a run-off.

In November of 1982, Leo Chitman became the first black person to be elected Mayor of West Memphis. He ran first among five candidates but did not get a majority of the votes. He unseated a white incumbent. White candidates had won by a plurality in the past, and no legislative reaction occurred. But when Mr. Chitman was elected Mayor in the same way, the Legislature promptly responded. It passed Act 909 of 1983, to require a majority vote for election to both county and municipal offices.

And finally, in 1988 the Rev. Marion Humphrey, a black lawyer, was elected Municipal Judge of Little Rock by a plurality. Little Rock had not been subject to a majority-vote requirement. But after Judge Humphrey's election, the Legislature reacted quickly. It passed Act 905 of 1989, subjecting municipal offices in all cities and towns to a majority-vote requirement.

We cannot ignore the pattern formed by these enactments. Devotion to majority rule for local offices lay dormant as long as the plurality system produced white officeholders. But whenever black candidates used this system successfully—and victory by a plurality has been virtually their only chance at success in at-large elections in majority-white cities—the response was swift and certain. Laws were passed in an attempt to close off this avenue of black political victory. This series of laws represents a systematic and deliberate attempt to reduce black political opportunity. Such an attempt is plainly unconstitutional. It replaces a system in which blacks could and did succeed, with one in which they almost certainly cannot. The inference of racial motivation is inescapable.

Jeffers imposed a novel remedy. Section 3(c) of the Voting Rights Act provides that a court that finds constitutional voting rights violations may impose a kind of preclearance requirement:

> [T]he court, in addition to such relief as it may grant, shall retain jurisdiction for such period as it may deem appropriate and during such period no voting qualification or prerequisite to voting or standard, practice, or procedure with respect to voting different from that in force or effect at the time the proceeding was commenced shall be enforced unless and until the court finds that [the new practice] does not have the purpose and will not have the

effect of denying or abridging the right to vote on account of race or color....

Using this provision, the *Jeffers* court required that "any further statutes, ordinances, regulations, practices, or standards imposing or relating to a majority-vote requirement in general elections in this State must be subjected to the preclearance process."

For a more detailed discussion of the so-called single-member office exception, see, Pamela S. Karlan, *Undoing the Right Thing: Single-Member Offices and the Voting Rights Act*, 77 Va. L. Rev. 1 (1991); for discussion of runoff primaries more generally, see *Voting Rights Act: Runoff Primaries and Registration Barriers: Oversight Hearings before the Subcomm. on Civil and Constitutional Rights of the House Comm. on the Judiciary*, 98th Cong., 2d Sess. (1984); Katherine I. Butler, *The Majority Vote Requirement: The Case Against Its Wholesale Elimination*, 17 Urb. Law. 441 (1985); Laughlin McDonald, *The Majority Vote Requirement: Its Use and Abuse in the South*, 17 Urb. Law. 429 (1985); Matthew G. McGuire, Note, *Assessing the Legality of Runoff Elections Under the Voting Rights Act*, 88 Colum. L. Rev. 876 (1986).

LULAC v. Clements, 999 F.2d 831 (5th Cir.) (en banc), *cert. denied*, 510 U.S. 1071 (1994), a case discussed earlier in this Chapter with regard to its treatment of racially polarized voting, also considered this remedial question in the context of the single-member office doctrine. *LULAC* involved a challenge to Texas's method of electing state-court trial judges. Judges were elected at large, in county-wide elections that used a numbered-post system: that is, although each judge was elected by all the voters within a judicial district, each judge ran for a designated position. The en banc opinion concluded that Texas's interest in "linkage"—that is, in having the electoral base of a district judge correspond to the area over which he or she exercises primary jurisdiction—outweighed the evidence that the at-large structure diluted black voting strength in Harris County (Houston).

> The electoral bases of district judges are linked to the area over which they exercise primary jurisdiction. This linkage has been in place throughout the 143 year history of judicial elections in Texas. By making coterminous the electoral and jurisdictional bases of trial courts, Texas advances the effectiveness of its courts by balancing the virtues of accountability with the need for independence. The state attempts to maintain the fact and appearance of judicial fairness that are central to the judicial task, in part, by insuring that judges remain accountable to the range of people within their jurisdiction. A broad base diminishes the semblance of bias and favoritism towards the parochial interests of a narrow constituency. Appearances are critical because "the very perception of impropriety and unfairness undermines the moral authority of the courts." The fear of mixing ward politics and state trial courts of general jurisdiction is widely held. It is not surprising

then that states that elect trial judges overwhelmingly share this structure and electoral scheme.

* * *

The totality of circumstances inquiry that occurs after a showing of the *Gingles* prerequisites is not limited to factors listed in the legislative history of the Voting Rights Act. The weight, as well as tenuousness, of the state's interest is a legitimate factor in analyzing the totality of circumstances. As we have explained, the Voting Rights Act largely codifies Fourteenth Amendment jurisprudence embodied in *White v. Regester*. The substantiality of the state's interest has long been the centerpiece of the inquiry into the interpretation of the Civil War Amendments and their interplay with the civil rights statutes.

* * *

[T]he people of Texas have at least a substantial interest in defining the structure and qualifications of their judiciary. Indeed, Texas' Attorney General has submitted to this court that linkage is a "fundamental right" that "serves [a] compelling interest" of the State of Texas. Linking electoral and jurisdictional bases is a key component of the effort to define the office of district judge. That Texas' interest in the linkage of electoral and jurisdictional bases is substantial cannot then be gainsaid.

The decision to make jurisdiction and electoral bases coterminous is more than a decision about how to elect state judges. It is a decision of what constitutes a state court judge. Such a decision is as much a decision about the structure of the judicial office as the office's explicit qualifications such as bar membership or the age of judges. The collective voice of generations by their unswerving adherence to the principle of linkage through times of extraordinary growth and change speaks to us with power. Tradition, of course, does not make right of wrong, but we must be cautious when asked to embrace a new revelation that right has so long been wrong. There is no evidence that linkage was created and consistently maintained to stifle minority votes. Tradition speaks to us about its defining role—imparting its deep running sense that this is what judging is about.

On the other hand, plaintiffs' interests are not well-served by destroying linkage. The inescapable truth is that the result sought by plaintiffs here would diminish minority influence. Minority voters would be marginalized, having virtually no impact on most district court elections. Given that district judges act alone in exercising their power, that use of the Voting Rights Act is perverse. After subdistricting, a handful of judges would be elected from subdistricts with a majority of minority voters. Creating "safe" districts would leave all but a few subdistricts stripped of nearly all minority members. The great majority of judges would be elected entirely by white voters. Minority litigants would not necessarily have their cases assigned to one of the few judges elected by minority voters. Rather, the overwhelming probability would be that the minority litigant would appear "before a judge who has little direct political interest in being responsive to minority concerns." Under the totality of circumstances, we must recognize that breaking the link between the electoral base and the jurisdiction of this single-member office would perversely lessen minority influence on the conduct of most litigation.

* * *

Plaintiffs urge that the linkage interest can be accommodated even if the existing scheme were found to be illegal.... [Linkage] might be accommodated by remedies other than subdistricting. In particular, plaintiffs point to the use of limited voting or cumulative voting. The Supreme Court, of course, "strongly prefers single-member districts for federal court-ordered reapportionment." In any event, we do not agree that this argument undermines the substantiality of the state's interest.

The allegedly illegal facet of the existing electoral scheme is that it employs at-large elections. Both plaintiffs' amended complaint and plaintiff-intervenors' complaint-in-intervention assert that the existing "at large scheme" violates § 2, and pray for a court order "that district judges in the targeted counties be elected in a system which contains single member districts." By employing at-large elections, the people of Texas have linked the electoral and jurisdictional base of the district judge.

Limited and cumulative voting are election mechanisms that preserve at-large elections. Thus, they are not "remedies" for the particular structural problem that the plaintiffs have chosen to attack. At trial, plaintiffs attempted to prove the three *Gingles* prerequisites. This test establishes "that the minority has the potential to elect a representative of its own choice in some single-member district" and "that the challenged districting thwarts a distinctive minority by submerging it in a larger white voting population." Plaintiffs then tried to supplement that evidence with proof of *Zimmer* factors, such as past discrimination and anti-single shot voting rules. The question presented by this lawsuit is whether Texas' at-large election of district judges violates § 2. To answer that question, we must determine the weight of the state's linkage interest. We will not discount that interest based upon purported remedies that preserve the challenged at-large scheme. Plaintiffs cannot attack at-large voting as a violation of § 2, and then ignore the special characteristics of the judicial office by

insisting that they will embrace a remedy that preserves that scheme. To do so would completely shunt consideration of the interest to the remedy stage.

* * *

In finding that Texas' interest is substantial, we recognize that it will not always defeat § 2 liability. Substantiality is not quantifiable, and we translate its force in the practical world of trials to the burden required to overcome it. As we see it, plaintiffs cannot overcome a substantial state interest by proving insubstantial dilution. We hold that proof of dilution, considering the totality of the circumstances, must be substantial in order to overcome the state's interest in linkage established here. As a matter of law, Texas' interest cannot be overridden by evidence that sums to a marginal case. It will take more to create a fact issue for trial....

We do not now attempt to define in detail what sort of proof of dilution would be substantial enough to override the state's linkage interest. We do not change the nature or usual means of proof. The *Gingles* prerequisites and *Zimmer* factors remain. Two facts are especially relevant to assessing the substantiality of the plaintiffs' proof of dilution. One is the willingness of the racial or ethnic majority—in this case, white voters—to give their votes to minority candidates. The other critical fact is the ability of minority voters to elect candidates of their choice even when opposed by most voters from the majority. Among the *Zimmer* factors, proof of racial appeals in elections, non-responsiveness of elected officials to minority voters, and persistent lack of electoral success by minority candidates are most important.

To what extent is *LULAC* internally inconsistent in its treatment of the relationship between voters and elected judges? Would *LULAC*'s analysis apply equally to a multimember court, such as a court of appeals or state supreme court?

Finally, consider *Ortiz v. City of Philadelphia*, 28 F.3d 306 (3d Cir. 1994). *Ortiz* involved a challenge to a Pennsylvania law that removed voters from the rolls for failing to vote. (After passage of the NVRA [the "Motor Voter" law], such "nonvoter purges" cannot be used to prevent individuals from voting in federal elections.)

The court of appeals rejected the plaintiffs' claims. Its starting point was the statement in *Gingles* that "the essence of a § 2 claim is that a certain electoral law, practice, or structure interacts with social and historical conditions to cause an inequality in the opportunities enjoyed by black and white voters to elect their preferred representatives." According to the Third Circuit, this formulation meant that "there must be some causal connection between the challenged electoral practice and the alleged discrimination that results in a denial or abridgement of the right to vote." And no such causal connection had been demonstrated:

> Here, however, it is not the State which prevents citizens from exercising their right to vote, from participating in the political process, and from electing representatives of their own choosing. We are not confronted with an electoral device—such as "race-neutral" literacy tests, grandfather clauses, good-character provisos, racial gerrymandering, and vote dilution—which discriminates against minorities, which has no rational basis, and which is beyond the control of minority voters. Rather, we are faced with the fact that, for a variety of historical reasons, minority citizens have turned out to vote at a statistically lower rate than white voters.
>
> As we read Ortiz's complaint, the entire document is drawn to allege that Pennsylvania's purge statute "caused" the disparate purge rates between Philadelphia's white and minority communities. Yet, there is nothing before us, not even one iota of evidence introduced at trial or present in the record, which would establish that fact....

* * *

> [T]the individuals to whom the purge law applies apparently have surmounted and overcome [whatever socioeconomic disadvantages they face] and have registered to vote at least once, if not more often. Had they continued to do so, the purge law could not have affected them, inasmuch as the purge law operates against only those who have registered to vote at least once, but then do not vote or register again. Conversely, if individuals have never registered and have never voted, the purge law still could not be applied to them because, as stated, the purge law affects only those who have once registered to vote.

* * *

> [On the other side of the balancing of various relevant factors] review of the record and present reality demonstrates that the City's purge statute meets an important and legitimate civic interest and is needed to prevent electoral fraud.
>
> Notably, and of recent date, Philadelphia's Senate election, in which the Democratic candidate ostensibly had prevailed, was invalidated on the basis of findings that absentee votes cast by non-residents and deceased voters had been fraudulently obtained and counted.... [A]t least twenty-two individuals were "purged" because they either had died or no longer lived in the district but had, nevertheless, cast votes in the most recent election—the very fraudulent acts which the purge statute was designed to over-

come.[22] ... [E]lectoral fraud has been a part of Philadelphia's landscape for over 100 years.

* * *

[A] focus on societal disadvantages might be entitled to somewhat greater weight in a suit challenging, not Philadelphia's purge act, but, perhaps, more generally, Philadelphia's voter registration procedures themselves.

Of what relevance are the following facts: each year, the percentages of the black and Latino electorate to be purged exceeded the percentages of the white electorate, and each year purged white voters were reinstated at higher rates than blacks and Latinos?

How persuasive is the majority's assertion that purge laws differ from constitutionally suspect restrictions such as literacy tests and poll taxes because the latter sort of practice "has no rational basis, and ... is beyond the control of minority voters"? If the Voting Rights Act had not banned literacy tests nationwide what would distinguish a section § 2 challenge to a fairly administered literacy test from *Ortiz*? Isn't literacy equally within the control of individuals?

> **22.** [A recent] article recited in part:
>
> The Board of Elections has begun purging the Second Senate District voting rolls of people who no longer live there—including a woman whose vote was recorded after she died and another whose vote was cast while she lived on a Greek island.
>
> Election officials said the 22 names—including an individual who city investigators found living in New Jersey—would immediately be purged from computerized voting rolls and notification would be delivered to the addresses on their voter registration.
>
> Among the 22 people being purged in the Sixth Division of the 42d Ward is one individual who has been living in Las Vegas for two years, though a vote was cast in her name in the November election without her knowledge, and a second individual who said he did not vote in any of the five Philadelphia elections in which ballots were cast for him since 1988.
>
> Between 1988 and 1993, for example, at least 60 improper ballots were cast in the Sixth Division of the 42d Ward, 27 by machine and 33 by absentee ballot.
>
> Mark Fazlollah, *City Purging 2d District Voter Rolls*, Phila. Inquirer, April 13, 1994, at A1, A7.

CHAPTER 8

REDISTRICTING AND REPRESENTATION

The post–1990 round of redistricting plunged state officials and the courts into an unprecedented confrontation with the most basic question of the objectives of representational opportunity in a democratic electoral system. Undoubtedly, the most salient issue was the creation of minority-dominated electoral districts. The combination of the preclearance requirements under Section 5 of the Voting Rights Act, the threat of litigation under Section 2 of the Act, and the formal race-neutrality of the Equal Protection Clause proved potently destabilizing. The repeated Supreme Court confrontations with claims of racial gerrymandering in the mid–1990's reflect the fact that as courts move beyond the initial application of the one-person, one-vote rule, they increasingly confront multiple conceptions of fair representation in the electoral arena. The debates in this area turn along two competing axes. First, there are demands for effective group representation for a variety of specially-defined interests. Second, there are recurring attempts to mediate among these competing concerns by turning to additional neutral factors beyond the requirement of equipopulational districts. Accordingly, factors such as compactness and contiguity of electoral districts are designed to constrain redistricting authorities so as to avoid the increasing temptation to gerrymander.

This chapter will focus heavily on the decennial redistricting process that follows the Census enumeration of population. Because of the need to conform to new distributions of population, these redistricting battles throw the established political order into disarray and force a reexamination of the aims of representation in each state and subordinate political jurisdiction. We will explore the contested right of political opportunity by examining the diverse and competing claims for representation along racial, ethnic, partisan, and incumbent lines. These competing claims call into question the very purpose of elections in a democratic order, which the Supreme Court has identified as selecting "the free and uncorrupted choice of those who have the right to take part in that choice." *Ex parte Yarbrough*, 110 U.S. 651, 662 (1884). According to *United States v. Classic*, 313 U.S. 299, 319 (1941), elections turn on a principle of "popular choice of representatives," which has subsequently been held to be "the foundation of our representative society." *Kramer v. Union Free School District*, 395 U.S. 621, 626 (1969). Ultimately, the popular choice can be deemed to have not been selected when electoral outcomes represent a "frustration of the will of a majority of voters of a fair chance to influence the political process." *Davis v. Bandemer,* 478 U.S. 109, 132–33 (1986).

But districting necessarily imposes a filtering device on the popular choice of the voters. In their aggregate, voters may have a prescribed set of choices. When those votes are broken down into territorially-based subunits, however, substantially different results may obtain, even with the equipopulational constraint on districts. The enormous resources devoted to redistricting battles reflect the understanding that different configurations of voters may yield different electoral outcomes, even with the same distribution of total votes. A ready example may be found in the 14 contested congressional elections that occurred in Texas in 1990. The Democratic candidates in these races received a total of 3,000 votes more than the Republican candidates, out of more than 2 million cast. Yet the Democrats won 10 of the 14 congressional races—proving not only that district lines matter, but strongly indicating that control of the line drawing process yields tangible rewards. Even the Supreme Court has recognized that districting of necessity is not coextensive with insuring fidelity to popular choices:

> The very essence of districting is to produce a different—a more politically fair—result than would be reached with elections at large, in which the winning party would take 100% of the legislative seats. Politics and political considerations are inseparable from districting and apportionment. *Gaffney v. Cummings,* 412 U.S. 735, 752–53 (1973).

This chapter will explore some of the most controversial issues in determining when and under what circumstances districting authorities may seek a "more politically fair" outcome through the manipulation of electoral configurations. The Court has been careful not to treat all ends-oriented districting as constitutionally infirm gerrymandering. However, the Court's attempt to distinguish the permissible from the impermissible has run into grave difficulties. As will become evident, it is not so simple to distinguish the workaday processes of districting from "the deliberate and arbitrary distortion of district boundaries and populations for partisan or personal political purposes." *Kirkpatrick v. Preisler,* 394 U.S. 526, 538 (1969)(Fortas, J. concurring).

A. PARTISAN GERRYMANDERING

Recall that in *Reynolds v. Sims,* 377 U.S. 533, 579 (1964), the Court identified imprecise election rules as "an open invitation to partisan gerrymandering." One of the reasons given for courts to enter the "political thicket" was to provide meaningful constraints on the temptation to engage in gerrymanders of all kinds. Unfortunately, the Court's experiences post-*Baker/Reynolds* showed that one-person, one-vote was itself an insufficient constraint on gerrymandering. We turn now to the emergent threat of the equipopulational gerrymander.

Gaffney v. Cummings
412 U.S. 735 (1973).

■ Mr. Justice White delivered the opinion of the Court.

The questions in this case are whether the population variations among the election districts provided by a reapportionment plan for the Connecticut General Assembly, proposed in 1971, made out a prima facie case of invidious discrimination under the Equal Protection Clause and whether an otherwise acceptable reapportionment plan is constitutionally vulnerable where its purpose is to provide districts that would achieve "political fairness" between the political parties.

* * *

The record abounds with evidence, and it is frankly admitted by those who prepared the plan, that virtually every Senate and House district line was drawn with the conscious intent to create a districting plan that would achieve a rough approximation of the statewide political strengths of the Democratic and Republican Parties, the only two parties in the State large enough to elect legislators from discernible geographic areas. Appellant insists that the spirit of "political fairness" underlying this plan is not only permissible, but a desirable consideration in laying out districts that otherwise satisfy the population standard of the reapportionment cases. Appellees, on the other hand, label the plan as nothing less than a gigantic political gerrymander, invidiously discriminatory under the Fourteenth Amendment.[18]

We are quite unconvinced that the reapportionment plan offered by the three-member Board violated the Fourteenth Amendment because it attempted to reflect the relative strength of the parties in locating and defining election districts. It would be idle, we think, to contend that any political consideration taken into account in fashioning a reapportionment plan is sufficient to invalidate it. Our cases indicate quite the contrary. The very essence of districting is to produce a different—a more "politically fair"—result than would be reached with elections at large, in which the winning party would take 100% of the legislative seats. Politics and political considerations are inseparable from districting and apportionment.

---

18. Appellees also maintain that the shapes of the districts would not have been so "indecent" had the Board not attempted to "wiggle and joggle" boundary lines to ferret out pockets of each party's strength. That may well be true, although any plan that attempts to follow Connecticut's "oddly shaped" town lines is bound to contain some irregularly shaped districts. But compactness or attractiveness has never been held to constitute an independent federal constitutional requirement for state legislative districts.

The political profile of a State, its party registration, and voting records are available precinct by precinct, ward by ward. These subdivisions may not be identical with census tracts, but, when overlaid on a census map, it requires no special genius to recognize the political consequences of drawing a district line along one street rather than another. It is not only obvious, but absolutely unavoidable, that the location and shape of districts may well determine the political complexion of the area. District lines are rarely neutral phenomena. They can well determine what district will be predominantly Democratic or predominantly Republican, or make a close race likely. Redistricting may pit incumbents against one another or make very difficult the election of the most experienced legislator. The reality is that districting inevitably has and is intended to have substantial political consequences.

It may be suggested that those who redistrict and reapportion should work with census, not political, data and achieve population equality without regard for political impact. But this politically mindless approach may produce, whether intended or not, the most grossly gerrymandered results; and, in any event, it is most unlikely that the political impact of such a plan would remain undiscovered by the time it was proposed or adopted, in which event the results would be both known and, if not changed, intended.

It is much more plausible to assume that those who redistrict and reapportion work with both political and census data. Within the limits of the population equality standards of the Equal Protection Clause, they seek, through compromise or otherwise, to achieve the political or other ends of the State, its constituents, and its officeholders. What is done in so arranging for elections, or to achieve political ends or allocate political power, is not wholly exempt from judicial scrutiny under the Fourteenth Amendment. As we have indicated, for example, multimember districts may be vulnerable, if racial or political groups have been fenced out of the political process and their voting strength invidiously minimized. Beyond this, we have not ventured far or attempted the impossible task of extirpating politics from what are the essentially political processes of the sovereign States. Even more plainly, judicial interest should be at its lowest ebb when a State purports fairly to allocate political power to the parties in accordance with their voting strength and, within quite tolerable limits, succeeds in doing so. There is no doubt that there may be other reapportionment plans for Connecticut that would have different political consequences and that would also be constitutional. Perhaps any of appellees' plans would have fallen into this category, as would the court's, had it propounded one. But neither we nor the district courts have a constitutional warrant to invalidate a state plan, otherwise within tolerable population limits, because it undertakes, not to minimize or eliminate the political strength of any group or party, but to recognize it and, through districting, provide a rough sort of proportional representation in the legislative halls of the State.

Reversed.

■ [Dissenting opinion of JUSTICE BRENNAN omitted.]

Karcher v. Daggett

462 U.S. 725 (1983).

[In *Karcher*, the Supreme Court, per Justice Brennan, ruled that New Jersey's post–1980 congressional redistricting plan unconstitutionally violated the one-person, one-vote rule. Although the disparity in district size was less than the margin of error of the Census enumeration, the Court nonetheless held that any unjustified departure from exact equipopulational redistricting would doom a congressional election plan. Justice Stevens in concurrence and Justice Powell in dissent invited the Court to reexamine the basis for its ruling.]

■ JUSTICE STEVENS, concurring.

* * *

II

[...] I am convinced that judicial preoccupation with the goal of perfect population equality is an inadequate method of judging the constitutionality of an apportionment plan. I would not hold that an obvious gerrymander is wholly immune from attack simply because it comes closer to perfect population equality than every competing plan. On the other hand, I do not find any virtue in the proposal to relax the standard set forth in *Wesberry* and subsequent cases, and to ignore population disparities after some arbitrarily defined threshold has been crossed.... Rather, we should supplement the population equality standard with additional criteria that are no less "judicially manageable." In evaluating equal protection challenges to districting plans, just as in resolving such attacks on other forms of discriminatory action, I would consider whether the plan has a significant adverse impact on an identifiable political group, whether the plan has objective indicia of irregularity, and then, whether the State is able to produce convincing evidence that the plan nevertheless serves neutral, legitimate interests of the community as a whole.

* * *

As a threshold matter, plaintiffs must show that they are members of an identifiable political group whose voting strength has been diluted. They must first prove that they belong to a politically salient class, one whose geographical distribution is sufficiently ascertainable that it could have been taken into account in drawing district boundaries[12]. Second, they

---

12. Identifiable groups will generally be based on political affiliation, race, ethnic group, national origin, religion, or economic status, but other characteristics may become

must prove that in the relevant district or districts or in the State as a whole, their proportionate voting influence has been adversely affected by the challenged scheme.[13] Third, plaintiffs must make a prima facie showing that raises a rebuttable presumption of discrimination.

One standard method by which members of a disadvantaged political group may establish a dilution of their voting rights is by reliance on the "one person, one vote" principle, which depends on a statewide statistical analysis. But prima facie evidence of gerrymandering can surely be presented in other ways. One obvious type of evidence is the shape of the district configurations themselves. One need not use Justice Stewart's classic definition of obscenity—"I know it when I see it"—as an ultimate standard for judging the constitutionality of a gerrymander to recognize that dramatically irregular shapes may have sufficient probative force to call for an explanation.

Substantial divergences from a mathematical standard of compactness may be symptoms of illegitimate gerrymandering.... To some extent, geographical compactness serves independent values; it facilitates political organization, electoral campaigning, and constituent representation. A number of state statutes and Constitutions require districts to be compact and contiguous. These standards have been of limited utility because they have not been defined and applied with rigor and precision.[18] Yet ... scholars have set forth a number of methods of measuring compactness that can be computed with virtually the same degree of precision as a population count.[19] It is true, of course, that the significance of a particular

politically significant in a particular context....

13. The difficulty in making this showing stems from the existence of alternative strategies of vote dilution. Depending on the circumstances, vote dilution may be demonstrated if a population concentration of group members has been fragmented among districts, or if members of the group have been overconcentrated in a single district greatly in excess of the percentage needed to elect a candidate of their choice.

In litigation under the Voting Rights Act, federal courts have developed some familiarity with the problems of identifying and measuring dilution of racial group voting strength. Some of the concepts developed for statutory purposes might be applied in adjudicating constitutional claims by other types of political groups. The threshold showing of harm may be more difficult for adherents of a political party than for members of a racial group, however, because there are a number of possible base-line measures for a party's strength, including voter registration and past vote-getting performance in one or more election contests.

18. One state statute and 21 State Constitutions explicitly require that districts be compact; two state statutes and 27 Constitutions explicitly provide that districts be formed of contiguous territory.

19. The scholarly literature suggests a number of different mathematical measures of compactness, each focusing on different variables. One relatively simple method is to measure the relationship between the area of the district and the area of the smallest possible circumscribing circle. This calculation is particularly sensitive to the degree of elongation of a given shape. Another simple method is to determine the ratio of a figure's perimeter to the circumference of the smallest possible circumscribing circle, a measurement that is well suited to measuring the degree of indentation. Other measures of compactness are based on the aggregate of

compactness measure may be difficult to evaluate, but as the figures in this case demonstrate, the same may be said of population disparities. In addition, although some deviations from compactness may be inescapable because of the geographical configuration or uneven population density of a particular State, the relative degrees of compactness of different district maps can always be compared. As with the numerical standard, it seems fair to conclude that drastic departures from compactness are a signal that something may be amiss.

Extensive deviation from established political boundaries is another possible basis for a prima facie showing of gerrymandering.... Subdivision boundaries tend to remain stable over time. Residents of political units such as townships, cities, and counties often develop a community of interest, particularly when the subdivision plays an important role in the provision of governmental services. In addition, legislative districts that do not cross subdivision boundaries are administratively convenient and less likely to confuse the voters. Although the significance of deviations from subdivision boundaries will vary with the number of legislative seats and the number, size, and shape of the State's subdivisions, the number can be counted and alternative plans can be compared.

A procedural standard, although obviously less precise, may also be enlightening. If the process for formulating and adopting a plan excluded divergent viewpoints, openly reflected the use of partisan criteria, and provided no explanation of the reasons for selecting one plan over another, it would seem appropriate to conclude that an adversely affected plaintiff group is entitled to have the majority explain its action. On the other hand, if neutral decisionmakers developed the plan on the basis of neutral criteria, if there was an adequate opportunity for the presentation and consideration of differing points of view, and if the guidelines used in selecting a plan were explained, a strong presumption of validity should attach to whatever plan such a process produced.

* * *

If a State is unable to respond to a plaintiff's prima facie case by showing that its plan is supported by adequate neutral criteria, I believe a court could properly conclude that the challenged scheme is either totally irrational or entirely motivated by a desire to curtail the political strength of the affected political group. This does not mean that federal courts

---

the distances from the district's geometrical or population-weighted center of gravity to each of its points; the degree of indentation of the boundaries of a nonconvex district; the aggregate length of district boundaries; and the ratio of the maximum to the minimum diameters in a district. In each case, the smaller the measurement, the more compact the district or districts. See also 1980 Iowa Acts, ch. 1021, § 4b(3)c (setting forth alternative geometrical tests for determining relative compactness of alternative districting plans: the absolute value of the difference between the length and width of the district, and the "ratio of the dispersion of population about the population center of the district to the dispersion of population about the geographic center of the district").

should invalidate or even review every apportionment plan that may have been affected to some extent by partisan legislative maneuvering. But I am convinced that the Judiciary is not powerless to provide a constitutional remedy in egregious cases.[28]

III

In this case it is not necessary to go beyond the reasoning in the Court's opinions in *Wesberry v. Sanders, Kirkpatrick v. Preisler,* and *White v. Weiser,* 412 U.S. 783 (1973), to reach the correct result. None of the additional criteria that I have mentioned would cast any doubt on the propriety of the Court's holding in this case. Although I need not decide whether the plan's shortcomings regarding shape and compactness, subdivision boundaries, and neutral decisionmaking would establish a prima facie case, these factors certainly strengthen my conclusion that the New Jersey plan violates the Equal Protection Clause.

A glance at the map shows district configurations well deserving the kind of descriptive adjectives—"uncouth" and "bizarre"—that have traditionally been used to describe acknowledged gerrymanders. I have not applied the mathematical measures of compactness to the New Jersey map, but I think it likely that the plan would not fare well. In addition, while disregarding geographical compactness, the redistricting scheme wantonly disregards county boundaries. For example, in the words of a commentator: "In a flight of cartographic fancy, the Legislature packed North Jersey Republicans into a new district many call 'the Swan.' Its long neck and twisted body stretch from the New York suburbs to the rural upper reaches of the Delaware River." That district, the Fifth, contains segments of at least seven counties. The same commentator described the Seventh District, comprised of parts of five counties, as tracing "a curving partisan path through industrial Elizabeth, liberal, academic Princeton and largely Jewish Marlboro in Monmouth County. The resulting monstrosity was called 'the Fishhook' by detractors."

Such a map prompts an inquiry into the process that led to its adoption. The plan was sponsored by the leadership in the Democratic Party, which controlled both houses of the state legislature as well as the Governor's office, and was signed into law the day before the inauguration of a Republican Governor. The legislators never formally explained the guidelines used in formulating their plan or in selecting it over other available plans. Several of the rejected plans contained districts that were more nearly equal in population, more compact, and more consistent with subdivision boundaries, including one submitted by a recognized expert . . .

---

28. See *Gomillion v. Lightfoot,* 364 U.S. 339, 341 (1960) (noting that allegations would "abundantly establish that Act 140 was not an ordinary geographic redistricting measure even within familiar abuses of gerrymandering"). If the Tuskegee map in *Gomillion* had excluded virtually all Republicans rather than blacks from the city limits, the Constitution would also have been violated. . . .

whose impartiality and academic credentials were not challenged. The District Court found that [that] Plan "was rejected because it did not reflect the leadership's partisan concerns." . . .

NOTES AND QUESTIONS

1. *Karcher* represents the Court's unresolved confrontation with the purposes of the one-person, one-vote rule of apportionment. As political operatives became more accustomed to the strictures of the equipopulational rule, and as computer technology improved, the one-person, one-vote rule at best inconvenienced would-be gerrymanderers. Recall, however, the difficulties the Court had in articulating the basis for intervening to protect equally-weighted voting. How likely is the Court to develop the foundations for evaluating whether the electoral system has been infected by partisan gerrymandering?

2. How would plaintiffs go about proving a claim of partisan vote dilution? Justice Stevens identifies a three part test: a) proof of belonging to a politically salient class; b) proof of less than proportionate voting influence; c) prima facie proof that raises the presumption of discrimination. Do any of these factors have readily apparent meaning? Are any of them comparable to the presumptions raised in racial vote-dilution claims?

Davis v. Bandemer

478 U.S. 109 (1986).

■ JUSTICE WHITE announced the judgment of the Court and delivered the opinion of the Court as to Part II and an opinion as to Parts I, III, and IV, in which JUSTICE BRENNAN, JUSTICE MARSHALL and JUSTICE BLACKMUN join.

[This case involves a challenge to the post–1980 districting of the Indiana state legislature. As presented in the Court's opinion, the combination of districting arrangements and the use of multimember districts significantly underrepresented statewide Democratic voting strength. The Court in *Davis* for the first time held that claims of partisan gerrymandering were justiciable and then determined that such claims could be proven as follows.]

* * *

III

Having determined that the political gerrymandering claim in this case is justiciable, we turn to the question whether the District Court erred in holding that the appellees had alleged and proved a violation of the Equal Protection Clause.

A

Preliminarily, we agree with the District Court that the claim made by the appellees in this case is a claim that the 1981 apportionment discriminates against Democrats on a statewide basis. Both the appellees and the District Court have cited instances of individual districting within the State which they believe exemplify this discrimination, but the appellees' claim, as we understand it, is that Democratic voters over the State as a whole, not Democratic voters in particular districts, have been subjected to unconstitutional discrimination. Although the statewide discrimination asserted here was allegedly accomplished through the manipulation of individual district lines, the focus of the equal protection inquiry is necessarily somewhat different from that involved in the review of individual districts.

We also agree with the District Court that in order to succeed the Bandemer plaintiffs were required to prove both intentional discrimination against an identifiable political group and an actual discriminatory effect on that group. Further, we are confident that if the law challenged here had discriminatory effects on Democrats, this record would support a finding that the discrimination was intentional. Thus, we decline to overturn the District Court's finding of discriminatory intent as clearly erroneous.

Indeed, quite aside from the anecdotal evidence, the shape of the House and Senate Districts, and the alleged disregard for political boundaries, we think it most likely that whenever a legislature redistricts, those responsible for the legislation will know the likely political composition of the new districts and will have a prediction as to whether a particular district is a safe one for a Democratic or Republican candidate or is a competitive district that either candidate might win....

B

We do not accept, however, the District Court's legal and factual bases for concluding that the 1981 Act visited a sufficiently adverse effect on the appellees' constitutionally protected rights to make out a violation of the Equal Protection Clause. The District Court held that because any apportionment scheme that purposely prevents proportional representation is unconstitutional, Democratic voters need only show that their proportionate voting influence has been adversely affected. Our cases, however, clearly foreclose any claim that the Constitution requires proportional representation or that legislatures in reapportioning must draw district lines to come as near as possible to allocating seats to the contending parties in proportion to what their anticipated statewide vote will be.

[...] These holdings rest on a conviction that the mere fact that a particular apportionment scheme makes it more difficult for a particular group in a particular district to elect the representatives of its choice does not render that scheme constitutionally infirm. This conviction, in turn, stems from a perception that the power to influence the political process is not limited to winning elections. An individual or a group of individuals who votes for a losing candidate is usually deemed to be adequately represented by the winning candidate and to have as much opportunity to influence that candidate as other voters in the district. We cannot presume in such a situation, without actual proof to the contrary, that the candidate elected will entirely ignore the interests of those voters. This is true even in a safe district where the losing group loses election after election. Thus, a group's electoral power is not unconstitutionally diminished by the simple fact of an apportionment scheme that makes winning elections more difficult, and a failure of proportional representation alone does not constitute impermissible discrimination under the Equal Protection Clause.

[...] Rather, unconstitutional discrimination occurs only when the electoral system is arranged in a manner that will consistently degrade a voter's or a group of voters' influence on the political process as a whole. Although this is a somewhat different formulation than we have previously used in describing unconstitutional vote dilution in an individual district, the focus of both of these inquiries is essentially the same.... In both contexts, the question is whether a particular group has been unconstitutionally denied its chance to effectively influence the political process. In a challenge to an individual district, this inquiry focuses on the opportunity of members of the group to participate in party deliberations in the slating and nomination of candidates, their opportunity to register and vote, and hence their chance to directly influence the election returns and to secure the attention of the winning candidate. Statewide, however, the inquiry centers on the voters' direct or indirect influence on the elections of the state legislature as a whole.... In this context, such a finding of unconstitutionality must be supported by evidence of continued frustration of the will of a majority of the voters or effective denial to a minority of voters of a fair chance to influence the political process.

* * *

C.

The District Court's findings do not satisfy this threshold condition to stating and proving a cause of action. In reaching its conclusion, the District Court relied primarily on the results of the 1982 elections: Democratic candidates for the State House of Representatives had received 51.9% of the votes cast statewide and Republican candidates 48.1%; yet, out of the 100 seats to be filled, Republican candidates won 57 and Democrats 43. In the Senate, 53.1% of the votes were cast for Democratic candidates and 46.9% for Republicans; of the 25 Senate seats to be filled, Republicans won 12 and Democrats 13. The court also relied upon the use of multimember districts in Marion and Allen Counties, where Democrats or those inclined to vote Democratic in 1982 amounted to 46.6% of the population of those counties but Republicans won 86%—18 of 21—seats allocated to the districts in those counties....

Relying on a single election to prove unconstitutional discrimination is unsatisfactory. The District Court observed, and the parties do not disagree, that Indiana is a swing State. Voters sometimes prefer Democratic candidates, and sometimes Republican. The District Court did not find that because of the 1981 Act the Democrats could not in one of the next few elections secure a sufficient vote to take control of the assembly. Indeed, the District Court declined to hold that the 1982 election results were the predictable consequences of the 1981 Act and expressly refused to hold that those results were a reliable prediction of future ones.... The appellants argue here, without a persuasive response from the appellees, that had the Democratic candidates received an additional few percentage points of the votes cast statewide, they would have obtained a majority of the seats in both houses. Nor was there any finding that the 1981 reapportionment would consign the Democrats to a minority status in the Assembly throughout the 1980's or that the Democrats would have no hope of doing any better in the reapportionment that would occur after the 1990 census. Without findings of this nature, the District Court erred in concluding that the 1981 Act violated the Equal Protection Clause.

* * *

■ JUSTICE O'CONNOR, with whom THE CHIEF JUSTICE and JUSTICE REHNQUIST join, concurring in the judgment.

[...] I would hold that the partisan gerrymandering claims of major political parties raise a nonjusticiable political question that the judiciary should leave to the legislative branch as the Framers of the Constitution unquestionably intended. Accordingly, I would reverse the District Court's judgment on the grounds that appellees' claim is nonjusticiable.

There can be little doubt that the emergence of a strong and stable two-party system in this country has contributed enormously to sound and effective government. The preservation and health of our political institutions, state and federal, depends to no small extent on the continued vitality of our two-party system, which permits both stability and measured change. The opportunity to control the drawing of electoral boundaries through the legislative process of apportionment is a critical and traditional part of politics in the United States, and one that plays no small role in fostering active participation in the political parties at every level. Thus, the legislative business of apportionment is fundamentally a political affair, and challenges to the manner in which an apportionment has been carried out—by the very parties that are responsible for this process—present a political question in the truest sense of the term.

To turn these matters over to the federal judiciary is to inject the courts into the most heated partisan issues. It is predictable that the courts will respond by moving away from the nebulous standard a plurality of the Court fashions today and toward some form of rough proportional representation for all political groups. The consequences of this shift will be as immense as they are unfortunate. I do not believe, and the Court offers not a shred of evidence to suggest, that the Framers of the Constitution intended the judicial power to encompass the making of such fundamental choices about how this Nation is to be governed. Nor do I believe that the proportional representation towards which the Court's expansion of equal protection doctrine will lead is consistent with our history, our traditions, or our political institutions.

I

* * *

Clearly, members of the Democratic and Republican Parties cannot claim that they are a discrete and insular group vulnerable to exclusion from the political process by some dominant group: these political parties are the dominant groups, and the Court has offered no reason to believe that they are incapable of fending for themselves through the political process. Indeed, there is good reason to think that political gerrymandering is a self-limiting enterprise. In order to gerrymander, the legislative majority must weaken some of its safe seats, thus exposing its own incumbents to greater risks of defeat—risks they may refuse to accept past a certain point. Similarly, an overambitious gerrymander can lead to disaster for the legislative majority: because it has created more seats in which it hopes to win relatively narrow victories, the same swing in overall voting strength will tend to cost the legislative majority more and more seats as the gerrymander becomes more ambitious. More generally, each major party presumably has ample weapons at its disposal to conduct the partisan struggle that often leads to a partisan apportionment, but also often leads to a bipartisan one. There is no proof before us that political gerrymandering is an evil that cannot be checked or cured by the people or by the parties themselves. Absent such proof, I see no basis for concluding that there is a need, let alone a constitutional basis, for judicial intervention.

The plurality ... is willing to presume that elected candidates will not ignore the interests of voters for the losing candidate, and it correctly observes that "the power to influence the political process is not limited to winning elections." But these propositions support my position—that the costs of judicial intervention will be severe and that political gerrymandering simply does not cause intolerable harm to the ability of major political groups to advance their interests.

Moreover, the new group right created by today's decision is particularly unjustifiable in the context of the claim here, which is founded on a supposed diminution of the statewide voting influence of a political group. None of the elections for the Indiana Legislature are statewide. Voters in each district elect their representatives from that district. To treat the loss of candidates nominated by the party of a voter's choice as a harm to the individual voter, when that voter cannot vote for such candidates and is not represented by them in any direct sense, clearly exceeds the limits of the

Equal Protection Clause. On the Court's reasoning, members of a political party in one State should be able to challenge a congressional districting plan adopted in any other State, on the grounds that their party is unfairly represented in that State's congressional delegation, thus injuring them as members of the national party.

■ JUSTICE POWELL, with whom JUSTICE STEVENS joins, concurring in part and dissenting in part.

* * *

In *Karcher v. Daggett,* Justice Stevens, echoing the decision in *Reynolds v. Sims,* described factors that I believe properly should guide both legislators who redistrict and judges who test redistricting plans against constitutional challenges. The most important of these factors are the shapes of voting districts and adherence to established political subdivision boundaries. Other relevant considerations include the nature of the legislative procedures by which the apportionment law was adopted and legislative history reflecting contemporaneous legislative goals. To make out a case of unconstitutional partisan gerrymandering, the plaintiff should be required to offer proof concerning these factors, which bear directly on the fairness of a redistricting plan, as well as evidence concerning population disparities and statistics tending to show vote dilution. No one factor should be dispositive.

In this case, appellees offered convincing proof of the ease with which mapmakers, consistent with the "one person, one vote" standard, may design a districting plan that purposefully discriminates against political opponents as well as racial minorities. Computer technology now enables gerrymanderers to achieve their purpose while adhering perfectly to the requirement that districts be of equal population. Relying on the factors correctly described by Justice Stevens in *Karcher v. Daggett,* the District Court carefully reviewed appellees' evidence and found that the redistricting law was intended to and did unconstitutionally discriminate against Democrats as a group....

A court should look first to the legislative process by which the challenged plan was adopted. Here, the District Court found that the procedures used in redistricting Indiana were carefully designed to exclude Democrats from participating in the legislative process.... The conferees, all Republicans, were responsible for designing the voting districts and were entitled to vote on the result of their own efforts. The advisers, Democrats, were excluded from the mapmaking process and were given no Committee vote....

Next, the District Court found that the maps "conspicuously ignore[d] traditional political subdivisions, with no concern for any adherence to principles of community interest." The court carefully described how the mapmakers carved up counties, cities, and even townships in their effort to draw lines beneficial to the majority party. Many districts meander through several counties, picking up a number of townships from each....

In addition to the foregoing findings that apply to both the House and Senate plans, the District Court also noted the substantial evidence that appellants were motivated solely by partisan considerations. There is no evidence that the public interest in a fair electoral process was given any consideration by appellants. Indeed, as noted above, the mapmakers' partisan goals were made explicitly clear by contemporaneous statements of Republican leaders who openly acknowledged that their goal was to disadvantage Democratic voters. As one Republican House member concisely put it, "[t]he name of the game is to keep us in power."....

NOTES AND QUESTIONS

1. *Bandemer* for the first time recognized a cause of action for unconstitutional partisan dilution. However, the Court rejected the proof in the case as insufficient to establish that Indiana's districting scheme "consistently degrade[d] a voter's or a group of voters' influence on the political process as a whole." What evidence would establish such "consistent degradation"? How would a prospective litigant establish the requisite consistency in light of the fact that district lines must be redrawn every ten years to conform to the one-person, one-vote requirement? Could a litigant ever prove that any particular group would have "no hope of doing any better" after the next decennial census?

2. The Court in *Bandemer* appears uncertain as to how to define the harm in gerrymandering claims. If it is true, as the Court posits, that individuals who vote for winning or losing candidates can equally be presumed to be fairly represented, then why enter this thicket at all? Typically there are two forms of benefits to be obtained from gerrymandered districts. First, parties in power can enhance their electoral opportunities by displacing incumbents of the other party from their established constituents, thus denying those incumbents the benefits obtained from name recognition, past delivery of constituent services, and prior social investment in the district. The second advantage comes with altering the mix of expected partisan votes. By controlling the redistricting process, swing seats can be weakened for the opposing party or strengthened through the addition or subtraction of predictable blocs of voters. Ideally, party strength is maximized by winning each seat with one vote over the minimum required. Control over redistricting allows a party to tailor districts so that a safe cushion is created in districts that can be captured, without wasting loyal votes through the overpacking of those districts. Conversely, the ideal victory for the opponent party comes in districts that are as close to 100 percent packed as possible, thereby "wasting" as many votes as possible. Does the Court's opinion recognize such harms? How persuasive is Justice O'Connor's claim that such gerrymandering is inherently unstable?

3. In dissent, Justice O'Connor argues that recognizing a claim of partisan vote dilution will accelerate a push toward proportional representation, which in turn, threatens to undermine the current two-party system. Should the privileged position of the Democratic and Republican parties be given constitutional protection? There appears a significant danger of insider manipulation of the political process when the majority political parties are given license to engage in what political scientist Bruce Cain terms a "bipartisan gerrymander." In *Gaffney*, the Court found that such an apportionment of electoral opportunity between the major parties justified aberrantly drawn district lines. Does *Bandemer* call into question the constitutionality of a bipartisan power-sharing arrangement? Does *Bandemer* overrule *Gaffney*?

4. *Bandemer* serves as a curious sequel to the reapportionment cases that began with *Baker v. Carr* and *Reynolds v. Sims*. Recall that *Baker* announced only that claims of malapportionment were constitutionally cognizable. It was left to *Reynolds* to provide any operational content to *Baker* by the introduction of the one-person, one-vote rule. In a similar fashion to *Baker*, *Bandemer* establishes only the justiciability of partisan gerrymandering claims. What would follow? Despite the similarity between the new partisan gerrymandering cause of action and the concept of "fair and effective representation" identified in *Reynolds v. Sims*, *Bandemer* is a decisive step beyond the *Baker/Reynolds* line of cases. In the one-person, one-vote line of cases, the Court attempted to police the electoral processes leading up to the actual casting of ballots. This approach kept the Court at a safe remove from having to assess the propriety of the *outcome* of elections. By contrast, any claim made under *Bandemer* necessarily embroils courts in the messy business of comparing challenged electoral outcomes with a court's conception of what a proper electoral system would have yielded. The Supreme Court provides very little guidance of how this inquiry is to be handled. Indeed, *Bandemer* itself offers only the elliptical language of needing proof of continued frustration of the will of a majority of voters or effective denial to a minority of a fair chance to influence the political process. Consider the facts in *Badham v. Eu* to determine whether the *Bandemer* approach is workable.

Badham v. Eu

694 F.Supp. 664 (N.D.Cal.1988), *aff'd*, 488 U.S. 1024 (1989).

■ POOLE, CIRCUIT JUDGE, with whom ZIRPOLI, DISTRICT JUDGE, concurs:

This case involves a constitutional challenge by plaintiffs, Republican congressional representatives and certain registered Republican voters of California, to Assembly Bill 2X, Chapter 6, 1st Extraordinary Session of the

1983–84 California Legislature ("A.B. 2X"), which effected the redistricting of congressional districts in California following the 1980 Census.

* * *

In the 1984 election, Republicans received 50.1% of the vote statewide, but received only 40% of the congressional seats (18 of 45). This disparity narrowed somewhat in 1986, when Republicans received 46.9% of the vote and retained the same 18 seats. Plaintiffs have alleged that these results are the direct consequence of A.B. 2X and that they are a reliable prediction of future elections.

The parties disagree over whether these allegations are sufficient to satisfy the first prong of *Bandemer*'s "effects" test. Plaintiffs contend that the only deficiency in *Bandemer* was that the plaintiffs there relied solely on the results of a single election, whereas plaintiffs here have alleged that "the 1981 reapportionment would consign the [Republicans] to a minority status throughout the 1980's." Defendants argue that plaintiffs must show much more serious deficiencies, such as those shown in the racial gerrymandering cases, and in addition must show that "the [Republicans] would have no hope of doing any better in the reapportionment that would occur after the 1990 census." We need not resolve this dispute, however, because in any case it is clear that plaintiffs cannot satisfy the second prong of the "effects" test. In order to satisfy the second prong, plaintiffs must show "strong indicia of lack of political power and the denial of fair representation." The *Bandemer* plurality specifically based this requirement on its prior "cases relating to challenges by racial groups to individual multi-member districts," and noted that "[i]n those case, the racial minorities ... had essentially been shut out of the political process."

It is on this second prong of the "effects" threshold that plaintiffs' complaint falters. Specifically, there are no factual allegations regarding California Republicans' role in "the political process as a whole." There are no allegations that California Republicans have been "shut out" of the political process, nor are there allegations that anyone has ever interfered with Republican registration, organizing, voting, fundraising, or campaigning. Republicans remain free to speak out on issues of public concern; plaintiffs do not allege that there are, or have ever been, any impediments to their full participation in the "uninhibited, robust, and wide-open" public debate on which our political system relies.

* * *

[W]e also may take judicial notice of other facts which demonstrate that California Republicans are far from being effectively "shut out" of the political process. Instead, California Republicans represent so potent a political force that it is unnecessary for the judiciary to intervene, as we would be constrained to do to protect the trampled rights of a disadvantaged political or racial minority.

Chief among our observations is our undisputed knowledge that California Republicans still hold 40% of the congressional seats, a sizeable bloc that is far more than mere token representation. It simply would be ludicrous for plaintiffs to allege that their interests are being "entirely ignore[d]" in Congress when they have such a large contingent of representatives who share those interests. We also note that California has a Republican governor, and one of its two senators is a Republican. Given also that a recent former Republican governor of California has for seven years been President of the United States, we see the fulcrum of political power to be such as to belie any attempt of plaintiffs to claim that they are bereft of the ability to exercise potent power in "the political process as a whole" because of the paralysis of an unfair gerrymander.

* * *

NOTES AND QUESTIONS

1. Is this a proper reading of *Bandemer*? Could either the Democrats or Republicans ever make out a claim under the court's test in *Badham*? For a captivating description of the California state legislative redistricting battles of the 1980s, see Bruce E. Cain, The Reapportionment Puzzle 81–103 (1984).

2. Throughout its subsequent history, *Bandemer* has served almost exclusively as an invitation to litigation without much prospect of redress. To date, only one case has actually found an unconstitutional partisan gerrymander. *See Republican Party of North Carolina v. Martin*, 980 F.2d 943 (4th Cir.1992). In *Martin*, the Court of Appeals, after finding that the complaint alleged the requisite intent to gerrymander, further found that the plaintiff Republican Party had stated a cause of action based on the following alleged facts:

> [I]n order to claim an effect sufficient to state a violation of the Equal Protection Clause, RPNC must allege that the North Carolina voting scheme produces disproportionate results in elections for superior court judges and consistently degrades the influence of Republican voters "on the political process as a whole." Clearly, its complaint alleges disproportionate results. RPNC claims that throughout the twentieth century, it has been, and continues to be, virtually impossible for a qualified candidate for a superior court judgeship to prevail, if running as a Republican. Specifically, RPNC states that only one Republican superior court judge has been elected in the approximately 220 elections held to fill this office since 1968. Yet, registered Republicans comprise approximately 27 percent of the voting population in North Carolina. Moreover, RPNC claims that consistency of voter habits combined with the geographical distribution of party affilia-

tion throughout the state renders it likely that this trend will continue into the foreseeable future....

RPNC's complaint sets forth data to support its allegations that not only are the election results disproportionate, but also that the nomination and slating of candidates is affected. Claiming that the method of electing superior court judges inhibits potential Republican candidates from seeking this office, RPNC points to data revealing that in the 1984 and 1986 general elections of 40 judgeships up for election, only four were contested by Republican candidates, and that since 1968, of approximately 220 judgeships up for election, a Republican candidate offered for election in only ten. RPNC maintains that these data demonstrate that few Republicans will offer to run since the chance of success is almost nonexistent. RPNC also asserts that the method of electing superior court judges diminishes campaign contributions for these elections because potential contributors are unwilling to donate money or other resources to a candidate who is perceived to be an almost certain loser. Thus, the complaint does contain allegations of an effect that goes beyond mere disproportionate election results.

Contests for superior court judgeships ... involve statewide elections even though the office is essentially a local one and with very few exceptions, candidates are known only within their local areas. This combination of factors—the status as a statewide candidate for a local office, the requirement to run in a statewide election, and the placement on a ballot with numerous other candidates seeking the same office but from different local districts—encourages, and as history has demonstrated, results in straight-party voting. Voters have little incentive to focus on individual candidates who reside in other districts and thus will discharge their duties in areas of the state distant from the voters' local area.

We recognize that RPNC has not alleged that Republicans have been "excluded from participating in the affairs of their own party or from the processes by which candidates are nominated and elected," *Bandemer,* 478 U.S. at 137, and that to the extent *Bandemer* might be read to require such allegations in order for a political group to allege exclusion from the political process as a whole, RPNC's claims would fail. However, we cannot conclude that a political party that has clearly alleged an effect that amounts to more than disproportionate election results must also allege and ultimately prove this type of exclusion. To do so would hold, in effect, that regardless of the specific allegations of its complaint an identifiable political group could not survive a motion to dismiss or prevail on the merits of its claim. We decline to adopt a construction of *Bandemer* that would render nugatory its holding that political groups may bring claims of partisan gerrymandering.

Subsequently, the Court of Appeals upheld a preliminary injunction ordering computation of votes on both a state-wide and single-district basis. In case of a disparity in electoral outcomes, the court ordered that the sitting judge be held over until the final merits of the case were resolved. *Republican Party of North Carolina v. North Carolina State Board of Elections*, 27 F.3d 563 (4th Cir.1994). Following a trial on a stipulated record, the district court then ordered that elections be held from judicial districts rather than statewide. Prior to the entry of the final order, however, the political dynamics of the state shifted. In the 1994 election, all eight Republicans seeking statewide election to superior court were elected. This prompted the latest tale in the saga: the Court of Appeals vacated the injunction and ordered the case remanded for reconsideration of the facts in light of the 1994 elections. *Republican Party of North Carolina v. Hunt*, 77 F.3d 470 (4th Cir.1996).

3. Are the factual allegations accepted in *Martin* sufficient to state a claim under *Bandemer*? Does the 1994 victory of Republican candidates show that a claim of exclusion by one of the two major parties is difficult to maintain? Should such claims be so difficult to maintain? Or, perhaps, should the *Bandemer* experiment be abandoned?

4. Should the difficulty courts have had in applying *Bandemer* call into question the premise of judicial review of political gerrymandering between the major parties? Or should courts accept that redistricting is an inherently political contest for which judicial review is inappropriate? *See* Daniel H. Lowenstein & Jonathan Steinberg, *The Quest for Legislative Districting in the Public Interest: Elusive or Illusory?*, 33 UCLA L. Rev. 1, 74 (1985). In trying to determine whether *Bandemer* was "a predictable sequel to *Baker*," should courts examine whether some easily administered variant of one-person, one-vote could be fashioned that could quantify the amount of distortion caused by partisan gerrymandering? *See* Peter H. Schuck, *The Thickest Thicket: Partisan Gerrymandering and Judicial Regulation of Politics*, 87 Colum. L. Rev. 1325, 1327 (1987). Social scientists have attempted to address this issue, but with a lack of consensus as to the appropriate measure of gerrymandering. One approach would use statewide races for secondary state office as a standard for measuring actual partisan support for each party, and then calibrate the results of districted elections against the votes obtained. Another would impose some kind of compactness criterion on redistricting, while yet another would attempt to measure the susceptibility of the political system to change if voters were to shift party allegiances. *See* Charles Backstrom *et al.*, *Establishing a Statewide Electoral Effects Baseline, in* Political Gerrymandering and the Courts 145–62 (Bernard Grofman, ed., 1990) (using bellwether statewide races); Thomas Hofeller & Bernard Grofman, *Comparing the Compactness of California Congressional Districts Under Three Different Plans: 1980, 1982 and 1984*, *in* Political Gerrymandering, *supra*, at 281–88 (using compactness models); Richard G. Niemi, *The Swing Ratio as a Measure of Partisan Gerrymandering, in* Political Gerrymandering, *supra*, at 171–77 (using the swing ratio as a measure of the immunity from change of a particular electoral arrangement).

Other alternatives would constrain the discretion of redistricting authorities by forcing them to "precommit" to a mechanism to redistrict in advance of the actual redistricting decision. This approach is summarized in Samuel Issacharoff, *Judging Politics: The Elusive Quest for Judicial Review of the Political Process*, 71 Tex. L. Rev. 1643 (1993)(proposing the use of a precommitment to computer modeled redistricting plans before census data are available to partisan actors). Among the possible mechanisms to take redistricting out of partisan hands are either computer models that redistrict automatically or redistricting commissions that operate at one remove from partisan interests. For a discussion of various computer programs that pick an arbitrary point, such as the northwest corner of a state, and then redistrict based on contiguity, compactness, and population equality, as well as more sophisticated approaches, see Michelle H. Browdy, Note, *Computer Models and Post-*Bandemer *Redistricting*, 99 Yale L.J. 1379 (1990). For a discussion of various state experiences with non-partisan redistricting commissions, see Jeffrey C. Kubin, Note, *The Case for Redistricting Commissions*, 75 Tex L. Rev. 837 (1997).

B. RACIAL GERRYMANDERING

There can be no doubt that drawing district lines to insure minority electoral strength emerged as the most controversial voting rights issue of the 1990s. Let us begin by putting the discussion of this issue in some perspective. All districting is a purposive attempt to achieve some preconceived notion of what proper avenues of representation should look like. District-based elections have an additional problem that is generally referred to as the "wasting" of votes. Imagine a two-candidate race in which the winner prevails by a margin of 501 to 499 votes. In terms of casting a winning vote, the losers "wasted" their 499 votes. Districting authorities are subject to the exquisite temptation to try to get their opponents as close to such an optimal number of wasted votes as possible without sacrificing the electability of their candidates. But allowing such a 501-to-499 split is not the only way to waste votes. It is equally possible to waste 499 votes by creating a district that elects a candidate with 1,000 votes. In such a district, partisans of the preferred candidate will have all voted for the winner, but will have wasted the opportunity to leverage the value of the extra 499 votes in other districts. In redistricting lingo, the former type of wastage is termed "dilution," while the latter is termed "packing."

Because of the prevalence of racially polarized voting, redistricting authorities face tremendous pressures in districting to allow for minority representation. There is simply no escaping the role of state authorities in creating majority-black electoral districts. First, the state must assign black voters to compact, majority-black districts on the basis of their race. Second, the state must assign some group of voters to nondiluted, nonpacked districts to balance out the numerical mandates of one-person, one-vote. These additional individuals must not be of the relevant demographic group (in order to avoid claims of packing), and, in the interest of minority representation, they should not be expected to compete in any genuine sense for electoral representation in the district to which they are assigned, lest they undo the redistricting assignment of that district to the specified minority group. It is the status of this precarious group—the "filler people"—that raises extraordinarily troubling problems under current voting rights jurisprudence, regardless of the geographic configuration of the districts. As the following cases reveal, it is the precarious status of the "filler people" and of state awareness of the racial consequences of redistricting that proves such a conundrum in the racial gerrymandering claims. The concept of the filler people is developed in T. Alexander Aleinikoff & Samuel Issacharoff, *Race and Redistricting: Drawing Constitutional Lines After* Shaw v. Reno, 92 Mich. L. Rev. 588, 628–34 (1993).

United Jewish Organizations of Williamsburgh v. Carey
430 U.S. 144 (1977).

■ MR. JUSTICE WHITE announced the judgment of the Court and filed an opinion in which MR. JUSTICE STEVENS joined; Parts I, II, and III of which are joined by MR. JUSTICE BRENNAN and MR. JUSTICE BLACKMUN; and Parts I and IV of which are joined by MR. JUSTICE REHNQUIST.

Section 5 of the Voting Rights Act of 1965 prohibits a State or political subdivision subject to § 4 of the Act from implementing a legislative reapportionment unless it has obtained a declaratory judgment from the District Court for the District of Columbia, or a ruling from the Attorney General of the United States, that the reapportionment "does not have the purpose and will not have the effect of denying or abridging the right to vote on account of race or color...."

The question presented is whether, in the circumstances of this case, the use of racial criteria by the State of New York in its attempt to comply with § 5 of the Voting Rights Act and to secure the approval of the Attorney General violated the Fourteenth or Fifteenth Amendment.

I

Kings County, N.Y. [Brooklyn], together with New York (Manhattan) and Bronx Counties, [are] subject to § 5 of the Act.... On January 31, 1974, the provisions of the [1972] statute districting these counties for ...

state senate and state assembly seats were submitted to the Attorney General.... On April 1, 1974, the Attorney General concluded that, as to certain districts in Kings County covering the Bedford–Stuyvesant area of Brooklyn, the State had not met the burden placed on it by § 5 and the regulations thereunder to demonstrate that the redistricting had neither the purpose nor the effect of abridging the right to vote by reason of race or color.[6]

Under § 5, the State could have challenged the Attorney General's objections to the redistricting plan by filing a declaratory judgment action in a three-judge court in the District of Columbia. Instead, the State sought to meet what it understood to be the Attorney General's objections and to secure his approval.... A revised plan, submitted to the Attorney General on May 31, 1974, in its essentials did not change the number of districts with nonwhite majorities, but did change the size of the nonwhite majorities in most of those districts. Under the 1972 plan, Kings County had three state senate districts with nonwhite majorities of approximately 91%, 61%, and 53%; under the revised 1974 plan, there were again three districts with nonwhite majorities, but now all three were between 70% and 75% nonwhite. As for state assembly districts, both the 1972 and the 1974 plans provided for seven districts with nonwhite majorities. However, under the 1972 plan, there were four between 85% and 95% nonwhite, and three were approximately 76%, 61%, and 52%, respectively; under the 1974 plan, the two smallest nonwhite majorities were increased to 65% and 67.5%, and the two largest nonwhite majorities were decreased from greater than 90% to between 80% and 90%.

One of the communities affected by these revisions in the Kings County reapportionment plan was the Williamsburgh area, where about 30,000 Hasidic Jews live. Under the 1972 plan, the Hasidic community was located entirely in one assembly district (61% nonwhite) and one senate district (37% nonwhite); in order to create substantial nonwhite majorities in these districts, the 1974 revisions split the Hasidic community between two senate and two assembly districts. A staff member of the legislative reapportionment committee testified that in the course of meetings and telephone conversations with Justice Department officials, he "got the feeling ... that 65 percent would be probably an approved figure" for the nonwhite population in the assembly district in which the Hasidic commu-

---

6. The basis for the Attorney General's conclusion that "the proscribed effect may exist" as to certain state assembly and senate districts in Kings County was explained in a letter to the New York State authorities as follows:

"Senate district 18 appears to have an abnormally high minority concentration while adjoining minority neighborhoods are significantly diffused into surrounding districts. In the less populous proposed assembly districts, the minority population appears to be concentrated into districts 53, 54, 55 and 56, while minority neighborhoods adjoining those districts are diffused into a number of other districts.... [W]e know of no necessity for such configuration and believe other rational alternatives exist." ...

nity was located, a district approximately 61% nonwhite under the 1972 plan. To attain the 65% figure, a portion of the white population, including part of the Hasidic community, was reassigned to an adjoining district.

Shortly after the State submitted this revised redistricting plan for Kings County to the Attorney General, petitioners sued on behalf of the Hasidic Jewish community of Williamsburgh, alleging that the 1974 plan "would dilute the value of each plaintiff's franchise by halving its effectiveness," solely for the purpose of achieving a racial quota and therefore in violation of the Fourteenth Amendment. Petitioners also alleged that they were assigned to electoral districts solely on the basis of race, and that this racial assignment diluted their voting power in violation of the Fifteenth Amendment.

* * *

Whether or not the plan was authorized by or was in compliance with § 5 of the Voting Rights Act, New York was free to do what it did as long as it did not violate the Constitution, particularly the Fourteenth and Fifteenth Amendments; and we are convinced that neither Amendment was infringed.

There is no doubt that in preparing the 1974 legislation, the State deliberately used race in a purposeful manner. But its plan represented no racial slur or stigma with respect to whites or any other race, and we discern no discrimination violative of the Fourteenth Amendment nor any abridgment of the right to vote on account of race within the meaning of the Fifteenth Amendment.

It is true that New York deliberately increased the nonwhite majorities in certain districts in order to enhance the opportunity for election of nonwhite representatives from those districts. Nevertheless, there was no fencing out of the white population from participation in the political processes of the county, and the plan did not minimize or unfairly cancel out white voting strength. *Compare White v. Regester,* 412 U.S., at 765–767, and *Gomillion v. Lightfoot,* 364 U.S. 339 (1960), *with Gaffney v. Cummings,* 412 U.S. 735, 751–754 (1973). Petitioners have not objected to the impact of the 1974 plan on the representation of white voters in the county or in the State as a whole. As the Court of Appeals observed, the plan left white majorities in approximately 70% of the assembly and senate districts in Kings County, which had a countywide population that was 65% white. Thus, even if voting in the county occurred strictly according to race, whites would not be underrepresented relative to their share of the population.

In individual districts where nonwhite majorities were increased to approximately 65%, it became more likely, given racial bloc voting, that black candidates would be elected instead of their white opponents, and it became less likely that white voters would be represented by a member of their own race; but as long as whites in Kings County, as a group, were provided with fair representation, we cannot conclude that there was a cognizable discrimination against whites or an abridgment of their right to vote on the grounds of race.... Furthermore, the individual voter in the district with a nonwhite majority has no constitutional complaint merely because his candidate has lost out at the polls and his district is represented by a person for whom he did not vote. Some candidate, along with his supporters, always loses. *See Whitcomb v. Chavis,* 403 U.S., at 153–160.

Where it occurs, voting for or against a candidate because of his race is an unfortunate practice. But it is not rare; and in any district where it regularly happens, it is unlikely that any candidate will be elected who is a member of the race that is in the minority in that district. However disagreeable this result may be, there is no authority for the proposition that the candidates who are found racially unacceptable by the majority, and the minority voters supporting those candidates, have had their Fourteenth or Fifteenth Amendment rights infringed by this process. Their position is similar to that of the Democratic or Republican minority that is submerged year after year by the adherents to the majority party who tend to vote a straight party line.

It does not follow, however, that the State is powerless to minimize the consequences of racial discrimination by voters when it is regularly practiced at the polls. In *Gaffney v. Cummings,* the Court upheld a districting plan "drawn with the conscious intent to ... achieve a rough approximation of the statewide political strengths of the Democratic and Republican Parties." 412 U.S., at 752. We there recognized that districting plans would be vulnerable under our cases if "racial or political groups have been fenced out of the political process and their voting strength invidiously minimized"; but that was not the case there, and no such purpose or effect may be ascribed to New York's 1974 plan. Rather, that plan can be viewed as seeking to alleviate the consequences of racial voting at the polls and to achieve a fair allocation of political power between white and nonwhite voters in Kings County....

■ MR. JUSTICE BRENNAN, concurring in part.

* * *

[I]t is instructive to consider some of the objections frequently raised to the use of overt preferential race-assignment practices.

First, a purportedly preferential race assignment may in fact disguise a policy that perpetuates disadvantageous treatment of the plan's supposed beneficiaries. Accordingly courts might face considerable difficulty in ascertaining whether a given race classification truly furthers benign rather than illicit objectives. An effort to achieve proportional representation, for example, might be aimed at aiding a group's participation in the political processes by guaranteeing safe political offices, or, on the other hand, might be a "contrivance to segregate" the group, thereby frustrating its potentially successful efforts at coalition building across racial lines....

Indeed, even the present case is not entirely free of complaints that the remedial redistricting in Brooklyn is not truly benign. Puerto Rican groups, for example, who have been joined with black groups to establish the "nonwhite" category, protested to the Attorney General that their political strength under the 1974 reapportionment actually is weaker than under the invalidated 1972 districting. A black group similarly complained of the loss of a "safe" seat because of the inadequacy of the 65% target figure. These particular objections, as the Attorney General argued in his memorandum endorsing the 1974 reapportionment, may be ill advised and unpersuasive. Nevertheless, they illustrate the risk that what is presented as an instance of benign race assignment in fact may prove to be otherwise. This concern, of course, does not undercut the theoretical legitimacy or usefulness of preferential policies. At the minimum, however, it does suggest the need for careful consideration of the operation of any racial device, even one cloaked in preferential garb. And if judicial detection of truly benign policies proves impossible or excessively crude, that alone might warrant invalidating any race-drawn line.

Second, even in the pursuit of remedial objectives, an explicit policy of assignment by race may serve to stimulate our society's latent race consciousness, suggesting the utility and propriety of basing decisions on a factor that ideally bears no relationship to an individual's worth or needs. *See, e.g.,* Kaplan, *Equal Justice in an Unequal World: Equality for the Negro—The Problem of Special Treatment,* 61 Nw.U.L.Rev. 363, 379–380 (1966). Furthermore, even preferential treatment may act to stigmatize its recipient groups, for although intended to correct systemic or institutional inequities, such policy may imply to some the recipients' inferiority and especial need for protection. Again, these matters would not necessarily speak against the wisdom or permissibility of selective, benign racial classifications. But they demonstrate that the considerations that historically led us to treat race as a constitutionally "suspect" method of classifying individuals are not entirely vitiated in a preferential context.

Third, especially when interpreting the broad principles embraced by the Equal Protection Clause, we cannot well ignore the social reality that even a benign policy of assignment by race is viewed as unjust by many in our society, especially by those individuals who are adversely affected by a given classification. This impression of injustice may be heightened by the natural consequence of our governing processes that the most "discrete and insular" of whites often will be called upon to bear the immediate, direct costs of benign discrimination. *See, e.g.,* Kaplan, *supra,* at 373–374; *cf.* Ely, *The Constitutionality of Reverse Racial Discrimination,* 41 U.Chi.L.Rev. 723, 737–38 (1974). Perhaps not surprisingly, there are indications that this case affords an example of just such decisionmaking in operation. For example, the respondent-intervenors take pains to emphasize that the mandated 65% rule could have been attained through redistricting strategies that did not slice the Hasidic community in half. State authorities, however, chose to localize the burdens of race reassignment upon the petitioners rather than to redistribute a more varied and diffused range of whites into predominantly nonwhite districts. I am in no position to determine the accuracy of this appraisal, but the impression of unfairness is magnified when a coherent group like the Hasidim disproportionately bears the adverse consequences of a race-assignment policy.

In my view, if and when a decisionmaker embarks on a policy of benign racial sorting, he must weigh the concerns that I have discussed against the need for effective social policies promoting racial justice in a society beset by deep-rooted racial inequities. But I believe that Congress here adequately struck that balance in enacting the carefully conceived remedial scheme embodied in the Voting Rights Act. However the Court ultimately decides the constitutional legitimacy of "reverse discrimination" pure and simple, I am convinced that the application of the Voting Rights Act substantially minimizes the objections to preferential treatment, and legitimates the use of even overt, numerical racial devices in electoral redistricting.

* * *

Moreover, the obvious remedial nature of the Act and its enactment by an elected Congress that hardly can be viewed as dominated by nonwhite representatives belie the possibility that the decisionmaker intended a racial insult or injury to those whites who are adversely affected by the operation of the Act's provisions.[7] Finally, petitioners have not been deprived of their right to vote, a consideration that minimizes the detrimental impact of the remedial racial policies governing the § 5 reapportionment. True, petitioners are denied the opportunity to vote as a group in accordance with the earlier districting configuration, but they do not press any legal claim to a group voice as Hasidim. In terms of their voting interests, then, the burden that they claim to suffer must be attributable solely to their relegation to increased nonwhite-dominated districts. Yet, to the extent that white and nonwhite interests and sentiments are polarized in Brooklyn, the petitioners still are indirectly "protected" by the remaining white assembly and senate districts within the county, carefully preserved in accordance with the white proportion of the total county population. While these considerations obviously do not satisfy petitioners, I am persuaded that they reinforce the legitimacy of this remedy.

Since I find nothing in the first three parts of Mr. Justice White's opinion that is inconsistent with the views expressed herein, I join those parts.

7. In this regard, it is important that, notwithstanding the worrisome implications of the intervenors, *supra*, at 174–175, petitioners themselves do not protest that their treatment under the 1974 plan was motivated by anti-Semitism. See, e.g., Brest, The Supreme Court, 1975 Term, Foreword: In Defense of the Antidiscrimination Principle, 90 Harv. L. Rev. 1, 17 (1976). Indeed, it is undeniable that the Hasidic community is contiguous to several nonwhite neighborhoods, and, therefore, understandably is a candidate for redistricting given the goal of creating 10 viable nonwhite voting majorities.

■ MR. CHIEF JUSTICE BURGER, dissenting.

* * *

The result reached by the Court today in the name of the Voting Rights Act is ironic. The use of a mathematical formula tends to sustain the existence of ghettos by promoting the notion that political clout is to be gained or maintained by marshaling particular racial, ethnic, or religious groups in enclaves. It suggests to the voter that only a candidate of the same race, religion, or ethnic origin can properly represent that voter's interests, and that such candidate can be elected only from a district with a sufficient minority concentration. The device employed by the State of New York, and endorsed by the Court today, moves us one step farther away from a truly homogeneous society. This retreat from the ideal of the American "melting pot" is curiously out of step with recent political history—and indeed with what the Court has said and done for more than a decade. The notion that Americans vote in firm blocs has been repudiated in the election of minority members as mayors and legislators in numerous American cities and districts overwhelmingly white. Since I cannot square the mechanical racial gerrymandering in this case with the mandate of the Constitution, I respectfully dissent from the affirmance of the judgment of the Court of Appeals.

Shaw v. Reno
509 U.S. 630 (1993).

■ JUSTICE O'CONNOR delivered the opinion of the Court.

This case involves two of the most complex and sensitive issues this Court has faced in recent years: the meaning of the constitutional "right" to vote, and the propriety of race-based state legislation designed to benefit members of historically disadvantaged racial minority groups....

I

The voting age population of North Carolina is approximately 78% white, 20% black, and 1% Native American; the remaining 1% is predominantly Asian.... The black population is relatively dispersed; blacks constitute a majority of the general population in only 5 of the State's 100 counties.... The largest concentrations of black citizens live in the [eastern] Coastal Plain, primarily in the northern part.... The General Assembly's first redistricting plan contained one majority-black district centered in that area of the State.

* * *

The Attorney General ... interposed a formal objection [under § 5 of the Voting Rights Act] to the General Assembly's plan. The Attorney General specifically objected to the configuration of boundary lines drawn in the south-central to southeastern region of the State. In the Attorney General's view, the General Assembly could have created a second majority-minority district "to give effect to black and Native American voting strength in this area" by using boundary lines "no more irregular than [those] found elsewhere in the proposed plan," but failed to do so for "pretextual reasons." . . .

Under § 5, the State remained free to seek a declaratory judgment from the District Court for the District of Columbia notwithstanding the Attorney General's objection. It did not do so. Instead, the General Assembly enacted a revised redistricting plan, . . . that included a second majority-black district. The General Assembly located the second district not in the south-central to southeastern part of the State, but in the north-central region along Interstate 85. . . .

The first of the two majority-black districts contained in the revised plan, District 1, is somewhat hook shaped. Centered in the northeast portion of the State, it moves southward until it tapers to a narrow band; then, with finger-like extensions, it reaches far into the southern-most part of the State near the South Carolina border. District 1 has been compared to a "Rorschach ink-blot test," . . . and a "bug splattered on a windshield". . . .

The second majority-black district, District 12, is even more unusually shaped. It is approximately 160 miles long and, for much of its length, no wider than the I-85 corridor. It winds in snake-like fashion through tobacco country, financial centers, and manufacturing areas "until it gobbles in enough enclaves of black neighborhoods." . . . Northbound and southbound drivers on I-85 sometimes find themselves in separate districts in one county, only to "trade" districts when they enter the next county. Of the 10 counties through which District 12 passes, five are cut into three

APPENDIX
NORTH CAROLINA CONGRESSIONAL PLAN
Chapter 7 of the 1991 Session Laws (1991 Extra Session)

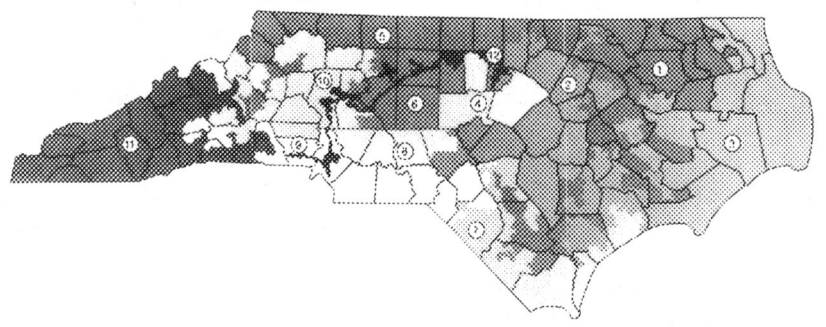

different districts; even towns are divided. At one point the district remains contiguous only because it intersects at a single point with two other districts before crossing over them.... One state legislator has remarked that " 'if you drove down the interstate with both car doors open, you'd kill most of the people in the district.' "

* * *

III

B

Appellants contend that redistricting legislation that is so bizarre on its face that it is "unexplainable on grounds other than race," ... demands the same close scrutiny that we give other state laws that classify citizens by race. Our voting rights precedents support that conclusion.

In *Guinn v. United States,* the Court invalidated under the Fifteenth Amendment a statute that imposed a literacy requirement on voters but contained a "grandfather clause".... The determinative consideration for the Court was that the law, though ostensibly race-neutral, on its face "embodied no exercise of judgment and rested upon no discernible reason" other than to circumvent the prohibitions of the Fifteenth Amendment.... In other words, the statute was invalid because, on its face, it could not be explained on grounds other than race.

The Court applied the same reasoning to the "uncouth twenty-eight-sided" municipal boundary line at issue in *Gomillion*. Although the statute that redrew the city limits of Tuskegee was race-neutral on its face, plaintiffs alleged that its effect was impermissibly to remove from the city virtually all black voters and no white voters. The Court reasoned:

> "If these allegations upon a trial remained uncontradicted or unqualified, the conclusion would be irresistible, tantamount for all practical purposes to a mathematical demonstration, that the legislation is solely concerned with segregating white and colored voters by fencing Negro citizens out of town so as to deprive them of their pre-existing municipal vote." ...

The majority resolved the case under the Fifteenth Amendment.... Justice Whittaker, however, concluded that the "unlawful segregation of races of citizens" into different voting districts was cognizable under the Equal Protection Clause.... This Court's subsequent reliance on *Gomillion* in other Fourteenth Amendment cases suggests the correctness of Justice Whittaker's view.... *Gomillion* thus supports appellants' contention that district lines obviously drawn for the purpose of separating voters by race require careful scrutiny under the Equal Protection Clause regardless of the motivations underlying their adoption.

The Court extended the reasoning of *Gomillion* to congressional districting in *Wright v. Rockefeller*.... Every member of the Court assumed that the plaintiffs' allegation that the statute "segregated eligible voters by race and place of origin" stated a constitutional claim.... The Justices disagreed only as to whether the plaintiffs had carried their burden of proof at trial. The dissenters thought the unusual shape of the district lines could "be explained only in racial terms." ... The majority, however, accepted the District Court's finding that the plaintiffs had failed to establish that the districts were in fact drawn on racial lines. Although the boundary lines were somewhat irregular, the majority reasoned, they were not so bizarre as to permit of no other conclusion. Indeed, because most of the nonwhite voters lived together in one area, it would have been difficult to construct voting districts without concentrations of nonwhite voters....

Wright illustrates the difficulty of determining from the face of a single-member districting plan that it purposefully distinguishes between voters on the basis of race. A reapportionment statute typically does not classify persons at all; it classifies tracts of land, or addresses. Moreover, redistricting differs from other kinds of state decisionmaking in that the legislature always is *aware* of race when it draws district lines, just as it is aware of age, economic status, religious and political persuasion, and a variety of other demographic factors. That sort of race consciousness does not lead inevitably to impermissible race discrimination. As *Wright* demonstrates, when members of a racial group live together in one community, a reapportionment plan that concentrates members of the group in one district and excludes them from others may reflect wholly legitimate purposes. The district lines may be drawn, for example, to provide for compact districts of contiguous territory, or to maintain the integrity of political subdivisions....

The difficulty of proof, of course, does not mean that a racial gerrymander, once established, should receive less scrutiny under the Equal Protection Clause than other state legislation classifying citizens by race. Moreover, it seems clear to us that proof sometimes will not be difficult at all. In some exceptional cases, a reapportionment plan may be so highly irregular that, on its face, it rationally cannot be understood as anything other than an effort to "segregate ... voters" on the basis of race. *Gomillion,* in which a tortured municipal boundary line was drawn to exclude black voters, was such a case. So, too, would be a case in which a State concentrated a dispersed minority population in a single district by disregarding traditional districting principles such as compactness, contiguity, and respect for political subdivisions. We emphasize that these criteria are important not because they are constitutionally required—they are not, *cf. Gaffney v. Cummings* ...—but because they are objective factors that may serve to defeat a claim that a district has been gerrymandered on racial lines. *Cf. Karcher v. Daggett,* 462 U.S. 725, 755 (1983) (Stevens, J., concurring) ("One need not use Justice Stewart's classic definition of obscenity—'I know it when I see it'—as an ultimate standard for judging the constitutionality of a gerrymander to recognize that dramatically irregular shapes may have sufficient probative force to call for an explanation")....

Put differently, we believe that reapportionment is one area in which appearances *do* matter. A reapportionment plan that includes in one district individuals who belong to the same race, but who are otherwise widely separated by geographical and political boundaries, and who may have little in common with one another but the color of their skin, bears an uncomfortable resemblance to political apartheid. It reinforces the perception that members of the same racial group—regardless of their age, education, economic status, or the community in which the live—think alike, share the same political interests, and will prefer the same candidates at the polls. We have rejected such perceptions elsewhere as impermissible racial stereotypes.... By perpetuating such notions, a racial gerrymander may exacerbate the very patterns of racial bloc voting that majority-minority districting is sometimes said to counteract.

The message that such districting sends to elected representatives is equally pernicious. When a district obviously is created solely to effectuate the perceived common interests of one racial group, elected officials are more likely to believe that their primary obligation is to represent only the members of that group, rather than their constituency as a whole. This is altogether antithetical to our system of representative democracy.

* * *

For these reasons, we conclude that a plaintiff challenging a reapportionment statute under the Equal Protection Clause may state a claim by alleging that the legislation, though race-neutral on its face, rationally cannot be understood as anything other than an effort to separate voters into different districts on the basis of race, and that the separation lacks sufficient justification. It is unnecessary for us to decide whether or how a reapportionment plan that, on its face, can be explained in nonracial terms successfully could be challenged. Thus, we express no view as to whether "the intentional creation of majority-minority districts, without more" always gives rise to an equal protection claim.... We hold only that, on the facts of this case, plaintiffs have stated a claim sufficient to defeat the state appellees' motion to dismiss.

* * *

■ JUSTICE WHITE, with whom JUSTICE BLACKMUN and JUSTICE STEVENS join, dissenting.

* * *

[T]he notion that North Carolina's plan, under which whites remain a voting majority in a disproportionate number of congressional districts, and pursuant to which the State has sent its first black representatives since Reconstruction to the United States Congress, might have violated appellants' constitutional rights is both a fiction and a departure from settled equal protection principles. Seeing no good reason to engage in either, I dissent.

I

A

The grounds for my disagreement with the majority are simply stated: Appellants have not presented a cognizable claim, because they have not alleged a cognizable injury. To date, we have held that only two types of state voting practices could give rise to a constitutional claim. The first involves direct and outright deprivation of the right to vote, for example by means of a poll tax or literacy test. See, e. g., *Guinn v. United States,* 238 U.S. 347 (1915). Plainly, this variety is not implicated by appellants' allegations and need not detain us further. The second type of unconstitutional practice is that which "affects the political strength of various groups," *Mobile v. Bolden,* 446 U.S. 55, 83 (1980) (Stevens, J., concurring in judgment), in violation of the Equal Protection Clause. As for this latter category, we have insisted that members of the political or racial group demonstrate that the challenged action have the intent and effect of unduly diminishing their influence on the political process. Although this severe burden has limited the number of successful suits, it was adopted for sound reasons.

The central explanation has to do with the nature of the redistricting process. As the majority recognizes, "redistricting differs from other kinds of state decisionmaking in that the legislature always is aware of race when it draws district lines, just as it is aware of age, economic status, religious and political persuasion, and a variety of other demographic factors." "Being aware," in this context, is shorthand for "taking into account," and it hardly can be doubted that legislators routinely engage in the business of making electoral predictions based on group characteristics—racial, ethnic, and the like.

* * *

With these considerations in mind, we have limited such claims by insisting upon a showing that "the political processes ... were not equally open to participation by the group in question—that its members had less opportunity than did other residents in the district to participate in the political processes and to elect legislators of their choice." ... Indeed, as a brief survey of decisions illustrates, the Court's gerrymandering cases all carry this theme—that it is not mere suffering at the polls but discrimination in the polity with which the Constitution is concerned.

In *Whitcomb v. Chavis,* we searched in vain for evidence that black voters "had less opportunity than did other ... residents to participate in the political processes and to elect legislators of their choice." More generally, we remarked:

"The mere fact that one interest group or another concerned with the outcome of [the district's] elections has found itself outvoted and without legislative seats of its own provides no basis for invoking constitutional remedies where ... there is no indication that this segment of the population is being denied access to the political system."

Again, in *White v. Regester,* the same criteria were used to uphold the district court's finding that a redistricting plan was unconstitutional. The "historic and present condition" of the Mexican–American community, a status of cultural and economic marginality, as well as the legislature's unresponsiveness to the group's interests, justified the conclusion that Mexican–Americans were " 'effectively removed from the political processes,' " and "invidiously excluded ... from effective participation in political life." Other decisions of this Court adhere to the same standards....

I summed up my views on this matter in the plurality opinion in *Davis v. Bandemer....* Because districting inevitably is the expression of interest group politics, and because "the power to influence the political process is not limited to winning elections," the question in gerrymandering cases is "whether a particular group has been unconstitutionally denied its chance to effectively influence the political process." Thus, "an equal protection violation may be found only where the electoral system substantially disadvantages certain voters in their opportunity to influence the political process effectively." ... By this, I meant that the group must exhibit "strong indicia of lack of political power and the denial of fair representation," so that it could be said that it has "essentially been shut out of the political process." ... In short, even assuming that racial (or political) factors were considered in the drawing of district boundaries, a showing of discriminatory effects is a "threshold requirement" in the absence of which there is no equal protection violation, ... and no need to "reach the question of the state interests ... served by the particular districts."

[...] To distinguish a claim that alleges that the redistricting scheme has discriminatory intent and effect from one that does not has nothing to do with dividing racial classifications between the "benign" and the malicious—an enterprise which, as the majority notes, the Court has treated with skepticism.... Rather, the issue is whether the classification based on race discriminates against anyone by denying equal access to the political process.

* * *

Part of the explanation for the majority's approach has to do, perhaps, with the emotions stirred by words such as "segregation" and "political apartheid." But their loose and imprecise use by today's majority has, I fear, led it astray.... The consideration of race in "segregation" cases is no different than in other race-conscious districting; from the standpoint of the affected groups, moreover, the line-drawings all act in similar fashion.

A plan that "segregates" being functionally indistinguishable from any of the other varieties of gerrymandering, we should be consistent in what we require from a claimant: Proof of discriminatory purpose and effect.

The other part of the majority's explanation of its holding is related to its simultaneous discomfort and fascination with irregularly shaped districts. Lack of compactness or contiguity, like uncouth district lines, certainly is a helpful indicator that some form of gerrymandering (racial or other) might have taken place and that "something may be amiss." . . . Disregard for geographic divisions and compactness often goes hand in hand with partisan gerrymandering. . . .

But while district irregularities may provide strong indicia of a potential gerrymander, they do no more than that. In particular, they have no bearing on whether the plan ultimately is found to violate the Constitution. Given two districts drawn on similar, race-based grounds, the one does not become more injurious than the other simply by virtue of being snake-like, at least so far as the Constitution is concerned and absent any evidence of differential racial impact. The majority's contrary view is perplexing in light of its concession that "compactness or attractiveness has never been held to constitute an independent federal constitutional requirement for state legislative districts." *Gaffney* . . . . It is shortsighted as well, for a regularly shaped district can just as effectively effectuate racially discriminatory gerrymandering as an odd-shaped one. By focusing on looks rather than impact, the majority "immediately casts attention in the wrong direction—toward superficialities of shape and size, rather than toward the political realities of district composition." . . .

Limited by its own terms to cases involving unusually-shaped districts, the Court's approach nonetheless will unnecessarily hinder to some extent a State's voluntary effort to ensure a modicum of minority representation. This will be true in areas where the minority population is geographically dispersed. It also will be true where the minority population is not scattered but, for reasons unrelated to race—for example incumbency protection—the State would rather not create the majority-minority district in its most "obvious" location.[10] When, as is the case here, the creation of a

---

10. This appears to be what has occurred in this instance. In providing the reasons for the objection, the Attorney General noted that "for the south-central to southeast area, there were several plans drawn providing for a second majority-minority congressional district" and that such a district would have been no more irregular than others in the State's plan. . . . North Carolina's decision to create a majority-minority district can be explained as an attempt to meet this objection. Its decision not to create the more compact southern majority-minority district that was suggested, on the other hand, was more likely a result of partisan considerations. Indeed, in a suit brought prior to this one, different plaintiffs charged that District 12 was "grossly contorted" and had "no logical explanation other than incumbency protection and the enhancement of Democratic partisan interests. . . . The plan . . . ignores the directive of the [Department of Justice] to create a minority district in the southeastern portion of North Carolina since any such district would jeopardize the reelection of . . . the Democratic incumbent." . . . With respect

majority-minority district does not unfairly minimize the voting power of any other group, the Constitution does not justify, much less mandate, such obstruction....

■ JUSTICE STEVENS, dissenting.

[...] The duty to govern impartially is abused when a group with power over the electoral process defines electoral boundaries solely to enhance its own political strength at the expense of any weaker group. That duty, however, is not violated when the majority acts to facilitate the election of a member of a group that lacks such power because it remains underrepresented in the state legislature—whether that group is defined by political affiliation, by common economic interests, or by religious, ethnic, or racial characteristics. The difference between constitutional and unconstitutional gerrymanders has nothing to do with whether they are based on assumptions about the groups they affect, but whether their purpose is to enhance the power of the group in control of the districting process at the expense of any minority group, and thereby to strengthen the unequal distribution of electoral power. When the assumption that people in a particular minority group (whether they are defined by the political party, religion, ethnic group, or race to which they belong) will vote in a particular way is used to benefit that group, no constitutional violation occurs. Politicians have always relied on assumptions that people in particular groups are likely to vote in a particular way when they draw new district lines, and I cannot believe that anything in today's opinion will stop them from doing so in the future.

Finally, we must ask whether otherwise permissible redistricting to benefit an underrepresented minority group becomes impermissible when the minority group is defined by its race. The Court today answers this question in the affirmative, and its answer is wrong. If it is permissible to draw boundaries to provide adequate representation for rural voters, for union members, for Hasidic Jews, for Polish Americans, or for Republicans, it necessarily follows that it is permissible to do the same thing for members of the very minority group whose history in the United States gave birth to the Equal Protection Clause....

NOTES AND QUESTIONS

1. The racial gerrymandering cases, beginning with *Shaw*, confirmed Justice O'Connor's pivotal role at the center of a deeply divided Court. Not once in the 1990s did she cast a dissenting vote in an equal protection case, despite the numerous five-to-four divisions on the Court. For Justice O'Connor, *Shaw* recognized an "analytically distinct" cause of action that turned neither on the dilution of voting strength of a cognizable group of

to this incident, one writer has observed that "understanding why the configurations are shaped as they are requires us to know at least as much about the interests of incumbent Democratic politicians, as it does knowledge of the Voting Rights Act." ...

voters nor on a claim of exclusion from the political process. The hallmark of this new cause of action was excessive reliance on race as evidenced by a marked departure from "traditional districting principles."

Despite the recognition of this new cause of action, the Court stopped short of constitutionalizing its evidentiary factors. While excessive reliance on race is constitutionally impermissible, O'Connor appears careful not to condemn all race-conscious districting. Similarly, while contorted districts are evidence of impermissible purposes behind districting arrangements, Justice O'Connor refuses to make compact districts a constitutional requirement. As this casebook goes to press, the most that can be said is that the Court has apparently set about "reviewing challenged districts one by one and issuing opinions that depend so idiosyncratically on the unique facts of each case that they provide no real guidance to either lower courts or legislatures." Pamela S. Karlan, *Still Hazy After All These Years: Voting Rights in the Post–Shaw Era*, 26 Cumb. L. Rev. 287, 288 (1996).

2. A number of factors combined to place great pressure on the redistricting process in the 1990s. In the first place, claims for minority representation were more robust in the aftermath of the 1982 amendments to the Voting Rights Act and *Thornburg v. Gingles*. Second, the Department of Justice played a more interventionist role after the 1990 Census, demanding in many instances that the number of potential minority districts be "maximized" (the Supreme Court's term) as a condition of Section 5 preclearance. Ironically, this policy did not change between the Republican Bush administration and the Democratic Clinton administration. Republicans were delighted to pack pro-Democratic minority voters into new majority-minority districts, thereby drawing away from the electoral strength of Democratic incumbents. By the time the Clinton administration assumed office in 1993, the battles over redistricting were waged in terms of preserving the districts of newly elected Democratic minority representatives—not a group a Democratic administration was likely to abandon. Third, and perhaps most significantly, the emerging computer technology of the 1990s allowed for far more careful district lines to be drawn within the parameters of the equipopulation principle. In Texas, for example, the state made available to all interested parties a powerful computer program that would automatically readjust district lines to maintain population equality while providing detailed racial and partisan data on each newly created district. The computer program contained all Census data down to the precinct level, and contained racial and ethnic data at the block by block level in many areas. This computer program also contained extensive voting data from past elections, allowing even novices to project the likely electoral outcomes in each new district. Consider the Court's description of the redistricting process in Texas from its opinion in *Bush v. Vera*, 116 S.Ct. 1941 (1996), holding three congressional districts drawn for minority representation to be unconstitutional under *Shaw*:

> The means that Texas used to make its redistricting decisions provides further evidence of the importance of race. The primary tool used in drawing district lines was a computer program called "REDAPPL." REDAPPL permitted redistricters to manipulate district lines on computer maps, on which racial and other socioeconomic data were superimposed. At each change in configuration of the district lines being drafted, REDAPPL displayed updated racial composition statistics for the district as drawn. REDAPPL contained racial data at the block-by-block level, whereas other data, such as party registration and past voting statistics, were only available at the level of voter tabulation districts (which approximate election precincts). The availability and use of block-by-block racial data was unprecedented; before the 1990 census, data were not broken down beyond the census tract level.... By providing uniquely detailed racial data, REDAPPL enabled districters to make more intricate refinements on the basis of race than on the basis of other demographic information. The District Court found that the districters availed themselves fully of that opportunity: "In numerous instances, the correlation between race and district boundaries is nearly perfect.... The borders of Districts 18, 29, and 30 change from block to block, from one side of the street to the other, and traverse streets, bodies of water, and commercially developed areas in seemingly arbitrary fashion until one realizes that those corridors connect minority populations."
>
> These findings—that the State substantially neglected traditional districting criteria such as compactness, that it was committed from the outset to creating majority-minority districts, and that it manipulated district lines to exploit unprecedentedly detailed racial data—together weigh in favor of the application of strict scrutiny.

However, the Court also found that other factors contributed as well to the odd line-drawing in Texas:

> More significantly, the District Court found that incumbency protection influenced the redistricting plan to an unprecedented extent: "[A]s enacted in Texas in 1991, many incumbent protection boundaries sabotaged traditional redistricting principles as they routinely divided counties, cities, neighborhoods, and regions. For the sake of maintaining or winning seats in the House of Representatives, Congressmen or would-be Congressmen shed hostile groups and potential opponents by fencing them out of their districts. The Legislature obligingly carved out districts of apparent supporters of incumbents, as suggested by the incumbents, and then added appendages to connect their residences to those districts. The final result seems not one in which the people select their representatives, but in which the representatives have select-

ed the people".... This finding receives inferential support from the fact that all but one of Texas' 27 incumbents won in the 1992 elections.

How significant is the actual shape of districts if, as appears in Texas, intricate district designs are more the norm than the exception? Consider the following description by Justice Stevens of a non-minority district in Texas:

> District 6 has far less an identifiable core than any of the majority-minority districts struck down by the District Court. To the extent that it "begins" anywhere it is probably near the home of incumbent Rep. Barton in Ennis, located almost 40 miles southwest of Downtown Dallas. From there, the district winds across predominantly rural sections of Ellis County, finally crossing into Tarrant County, the home of Fort Worth. It skips across two arms of Joe Pool Lake, noses its way into Dallas County, and then travels through predominantly republican suburbs of Fort Worth. Nearing the central city, the borders dart into the downtown area, then retreat to curl around the city's northern edge, picking up airport and growing suburbs north of town. Worn from its travels into the far northwestern corner of the county (almost 70 miles, as the crow flies, from Ennis), the district lines plunge south into Eagle Mountain Lake, traveling along the waterline for miles, with occasional detours to collect voters that have built homes along its shores. Refreshed, the district rediscovers its roots in rural Parker county, then flows back toward Fort Worth to the southwest for another bite at Republican voters near the heart of the city. As it does so, the district narrows in places to not much more than a football field in width. Finally, it heads back into the rural regions of its fifth county—Johnson—where it finally exhausts itself only 50 miles from its origin, but hundreds of " 'miles apart in distance and worlds apart in culture.' " (quoting *Miller v. Johnson*).

Justice Stevens concluded his dissent in *Vera* by drawing attention to the gulf between the Court's treatment of racial considerations in redistricting and other forms of ends-oriented manipulations of district lines:

> By minimizing the critical role that political motives played in the creation of these districts, I fear that the Court may inadvertently encourage this more objectionable use of power in the redistricting process. Legislatures and elected representatives have a responsibility to behave in a way that incorporates the "elements of legitimacy and neutrality that must always characterize the performance of the sovereign's duty to govern impartially".... That responsibility is not discharged when legislatures permit and even encourage incumbents to use their positions as public servants to

protect themselves and their parties rather than the interests of their constituents.

What justifications, if any, can be put forward for treating race differently from other goal-oriented manipulations of the redistricting process? What do the appearances of the following districts indicate?

APPENDIX A TO OPINION OF STEVENS, J.

TEXAS CONGRESSIONAL DISTRICT 3

586 CHAPTER 8 REDISTRICTING AND REPRESENTATION

If you were not aware that District 6 was a non-minority district and that districts 18, 19 and 20 were majority-minority districts, would the differences be apparent to you? Is it true, as Justice Stevens argues in dissent, that "[f]or every geographic atrocity committed by District 30, District 6 commits its own and more"? Would the presence of strangely configured

APPENDIX B TO OPINION OF O'CONNOR, J.

TEXAS CONGRESSIONAL DISTRICT 18

non-minority districts establish a different baseline for defining departures from "traditional districting principles"? For criticism of the way in which the Court uses maps in its racial-redistricting opinions, see Hampton Dellinger, *Words are Enough: The Troublesome Use of Photographs, Maps, and Other Images in Supreme Court Opinions*, 110 Harv.L.Rev. 1704 (1997).

APPENDIX C TO OPINION OF O'CONNOR, J.

TEXAS CONGRESSIONAL DISTRICT 29

APPENDIX A TO OPINION OF O'CONNOR, J.

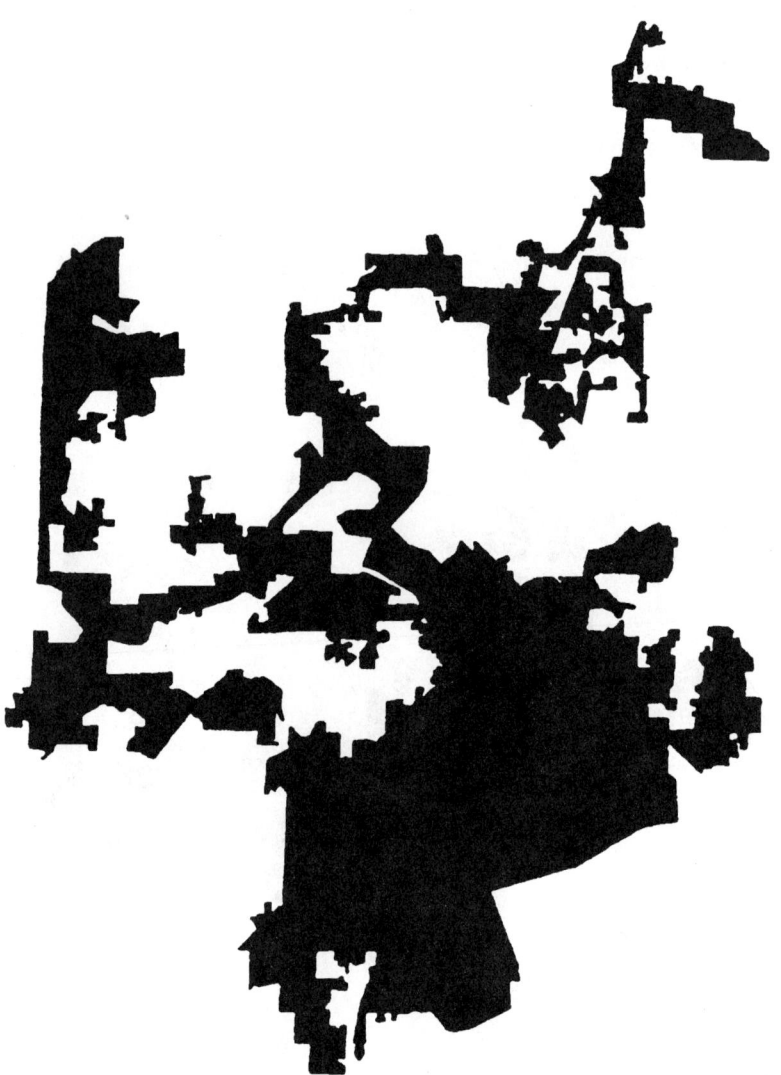

TEXAS CONGRESSIONAL DISTRICT 30

3. The result of an increasingly contested redistricting process was that district lines drawn for congressional representation after the 1990 Census were significantly more contorted than in previous decades. One study shows that about half the most extravagant district lines were in districts designed to elect a minority representative. *See* Richard Pildes & Richard Niemi, *Expressive Harms, "Bizarre Districts," and Voting Rights: Evaluat-*

ing Election–District Appearances After Shaw v. Reno, 92 Mich. L.Rev. 483 (1993). Even in these cases, as in *Shaw*, the ultimate district lines were a product of a complex interaction of desires for minority representation together with partisan and incumbent protection. Should the Court in *Shaw* have imposed a *per se* compactness requirement to constrain the temptation to use ever more elaborate computer-drawn districts?

4. In *Miller v. Johnson*, 115 S.Ct. 2475, 2486 (1995), a five-member majority of the Court, per Justice Kennedy, refashioned *Shaw* as follows:

> Our observation in *Shaw* of the consequences of racial stereotyping was not meant to suggest that a district must be bizarre on its face before there is a constitutional violation. Nor was our conclusion in *Shaw* that in certain instances a district's appearance (or, to be more precise, its appearance in combination with certain demographic evidence) can give rise to an equal protection claim, ... a holding that bizarreness was a threshold showing, as appellants believe it to be. Our circumspect approach and narrow holding in *Shaw* did not erect an artificial rule barring accepted equal protection analysis in other redistricting cases. Shape is relevant not because bizarreness is a necessary element of the constitutional wrong or a threshold requirement of proof, but because it may be persuasive circumstantial evidence that race for its own sake, and not other districting principles, was the legislature's dominant and controlling rationale in drawing its district lines. The logical implication, as courts applying *Shaw* have recognized, is that parties may rely on evidence other than bizarreness to establish race-based districting.

Accordingly, under *Miller*, all redistricting is presumptively constitutionally infirm when race has served as the "predominant" factor in the drawing of district lines. Curiously, Justice O'Connor joined Justice Kennedy's opinion in *Miller*, but then filed a concurrence reinterpreting the majority opinion:

> Application of the Court's standard does not throw into doubt the vast majority of the Nation's 435 congressional districts, where presumably the States have drawn the boundaries in accordance with their customary districting principles. That is so even though race may well have been considered in the redistricting process.... But application of the Court's standard helps achieve *Shaw*'s basic objective of making extreme instances of gerrymandering subject to meaningful judicial review. I therefore join the Court's opinion.

Are these two statements reconcilable? Does Justice Kennedy's "predominance" standard help elucidate the constitutional harm in a complex fact pattern such as that found in the Texas congressional redistricting case? For the argument that this predominant motive test cannot be implemented intelligibly in the redistricting context, see Richard H. Pildes, *Principled*

Limitations on Racial and Partisan Redistricting, 106 Yale L.J. 2505 (1997).

5. The subsequent history of Georgia's congressional apportionment suggests some of the practical and doctrinal problems with implementing the Court's new doctrine.

Having struck down the Eleventh Congressional District, the Supreme Court remanded the case to the district court to supervise the adoption of a remedy. Longstanding remedial doctrine required that Georgia be given an additional opportunity for self-apportionment even in the face of a voting rights violation. *See, e.g., Wise v. Lipscomb,* 437 U.S. 535, 540 (1978); *Chapman v. Meier,* 420 U.S. 1, 27 (1975). Although the next scheduled election was more than a year away, the district court gave the state roughly a month to get the redistricting process underway and the governor called the general assembly into special session over the summer. As you might expect, three-way wrangling among white Democrats, black Democrats, and Republicans ensued. According to a longstanding advocate of minority districting, who served as one of the lawyers representing the defendant-intervenors in *Miller* (citizens who sought to preserve the Eleventh District), one proposed plan would not only have protected the three black Democratic incumbents, but would also have created three additional districts which the Democrats would have a reasonable chance to capture. (At the time, the Democrats held only three of Georgia's eleven seats, the one white Democrat who had been elected in 1994 having switched parties after the election.) Nonetheless, "even though the Democrats controlled both houses of the general assembly, the legislature deadlocked and adjourned without enacting a plan. Some white Democrats refused to join with black Democrats in support of a pro-Democratic/incumbent protection plan because they thought the party would damage itself among conservative whites by appearing to give in to black demands or because they had no commitment to protecting black Democratic incumbents." Laughlin McDonald, *The Counterrevolution in Minority Voting Rights,* 65 Miss. L.J. 271, 296 n. 113 (1995).

Faced with a legislative stalemate, the district court drew its own plan. *Johnson v. Miller,* 922 F. Supp. 1556 (S.D. Ga. 1995) (three-judge court). Not only did the court reconfigure the Eleventh District, which the Supreme Court had held unconstitutional, but it declared the majority-black Second District unconstitutional as well. The court's plan drew only one majority-black district—in the Atlanta area where the state's 1982 reapportionment plan had previously created such a district.

The district court explained its decision about where to locate Georgia's newly acquired seat this way:

> We placed the new Eleventh District in the Northeast Atlanta corridor out to the northeast Georgia state line. The Eleventh district now contains counties which are becoming more urban with the population growth, notably Walton County and Newton

County. The Eleventh also contains the Athens–Clarke County area which has become a metropolitan area in its own right, and locating it in the Eleventh is consistent with the new Eleventh's urban/suburban flavor.

The resulting Eleventh District is a relatively compact grouping of counties which follow a suburban to rural progression and have Interstate Eighty–Five as a very real connecting cable. The road net, the area's commerce, its recreational aspect, and other features produce a district with a palpable community of interests. As a "radius" district reaching from suburban Atlanta to the state line, the new Eleventh has an analogous resemblance to the Third, Seventh, and Ninth Districts.

Id. at 1563–64. Notice that the court-created district stretches from Atlanta to the northeast Georgia state line, contains an urban to rural progression, and ties together faraway urban areas. Are the only differences between this district and the unconstitutional prior district its shape and racial composition? Does the court's reliance on Interstate 85 as the "connecting cable" of a district recall the fact that the North Carolina Twelfth Congressional District struck down in the *Shaw* litigation also used I–85 as its "connecting cable" to string together distant urban areas? To what extent does the "new" Eleventh reflect any traditional districting principles, such as respecting communities of interest?

On appeal, the Supreme Court upheld the Georgia district court's remedial plan. *Abrams v. Johnson,* 117 S. Ct. 1925 (1997). It affirmed the district court's conclusion that it was impossible to draw more than one majority-black district "without allowing that one consideration [i.e., race] to predominate over other traditional and neutral districting principles, principles which were a valid expression of legislative policy." *Id.* at 1934. In particular, the Supreme Court concluded that the two unprecleared plans the state had proposed prior to drawing the plan struck down in *Miller*— each of which had contained two majority-black districts—did not reflect the state's traditional redistricting principles because they were the product of "steady," and improper, Justice Department coercion in the section 5 preclearance process. *Id.* at 1944. Thus, they could not serve as remedial baselines:

The testimony of several legislators indicated that any such understanding was arrived at in the shadow of the Justice Department's max-black goal, and that all other policies were to give way to this racial consideration.... Thomas Murphy, Speaker of the Georgia House of Representatives in 1990 and now, said in his deposition that the initial 1991 reapportionment plan was based on "what we at least perceived to be the direction and instructions of the Justice Department." This evidence all refers to development of the original 1991 legislative plan, not the 1992 precleared plan, and thus undermines the contention that the legislature's original plan should have been controlling on the District Court.

Id. at 1934.

Consider what reliance on Georgia's *actual* "traditional" districting principles—as opposed to the set of idealized principles identified by the Supreme Court in *Miller, Shaw,* and *Vera*—would mean. After 1931, Georgia refused to redraw its congressional districts for over thirty years despite massive and growing population inequalities. Not until the Supreme Court struck down the state's existing congressional lines in *Wesberry v. Sanders,* 376 U.S. 1 (1964), did Georgia abandon its unconstitutional malapportionment. The policy of not splitting counties—whose disregard formed part of the evidentiary basis for the conclusion that the Eleventh District "subordinated traditional race-neutral districting principles, including ... respect for political subdivisions," *Miller,* 115 S.Ct. at 2488— was part and parcel of Georgia's illegitimate pro-rural bias. Given its derivation, how much deference ought to be paid to the tradition of not splitting counties?

When Georgia redrew its congressional districts following the 1970 census, the Attorney General rejected its first effort on the grounds that the plan discriminated against black voters. *See* Laughlin McDonald, *Can Minority Voting Rights Survive Miller v. Johnson?,* 1 Mich. J. Race & L. 119, 124 (1996). The state did not contest that determination, but redrew its plan and in 1974, Andrew Young was elected as the first black Representative from Georgia since Reconstruction.

After the 1980 census, the state's initial plan created no majority-black districts and split Atlanta's growing black population. This plan, like its post–1970 predecessor, prompted an objection under section 5. This time, the state sought preclearance in a declaratory judgment action in the United States District Court for the District of Columbia. That court concluded Georgia's 1981 reapportionment was purposefully discriminatory, relying in part on a statement by the Chairman of the Georgia House Reapportionment Committee, Joe Mack Wilson that "I don't want to draw nigger districts." *Busbee v. Smith,* 549 F. Supp. 494, 501 (D.D.C. 1982), *aff'd,* 459 U.S. 1166 (1983). Moreover, the district court found that Georgia House Speaker Thomas Murphy—on whom the *Miller* Court relied in finding that Georgia's creation of a second majority-black district in 1991 subverted state policy—had "racial attitudes" that led him to "purposefully discriminat[e]" throughout the 1981 redistricting process. *Id.* at 510. Only in the face of federal executive and judicial approval did Georgia ever draw a majority-black district. In light of this history of overt resistance to providing blacks with equal electoral opportunity, how accurate is the Court's comment about the "Justice Department's thorough 'subversion of the redistricting process' since the 1990 census"? *Abrams,* 117 S.Ct. at 1932.

6. The racial gerrymandering cases exposed three distinct viewpoints on the Court. First, there emerged a strong core of proponents of race neutrality in state line-drawing. This group had the consistent votes of Chief Justice Rehnquist, Justice Scalia, and Justice Thomas. The claim of race neutrality drew both from the suspect nature of race consciousness in all official activities and the presumed stigma that flowed from race-labelling: "the assumption that the group asserting dilution is not merely a racial or ethnic group, but a group having distinct political interests as well. Of necessity in resolving vote dilution actions we have given credence to the view that race defines political interest." *Holder v. Hall*, 512 U.S. 874, 902 (1994)(Thomas, J., dissenting). At the other pole emerged the proponents of racial pluralism, whose current exponents are Justices Breyer, Ginsburg, Souter and Stevens. This wing of the Court is less concerned with how the election lines are drawn than with the representativeness of the resulting legislative bodies. Repeatedly this group has expressed its concern with the risk of shutting out or diluting cognizable social constituencies as the primary evil to be avoided in the redistricting process. Finally, the center, as defined by Justice O'Connor and to some extent Justice Kennedy, seems to be searching for racial opacity—a means by which to constrain or obscure the deep racial chasms that emerge in the political arena.

7. At the time of *Shaw,* there was much debate as to the precise nature of the constitutional harm that the *Shaw* doctrine recognized. In traditional cases involving the constitutional right to vote, as discussed in Chapter 2, the harm alleged was to the individual voters who were being denied the ability to participate in particular elections. In traditional vote-dilution cases under the Constitution, as discussed in Chapter 6, the harm alleged was to the group of voters whose voting power was being diluted. Precisely who is being injured, and in what specific way, in *Shaw*-type cases? Is it all voters in the state? All voters whose race is taken into account in the redistricting process? Only those voters whose race is used to place them into black-majority districts? Only white voters whose race is used to place them in such districts?

In the wake of *Shaw,* Professors Pildes and Niemi argued that the best understanding of the doctrine was that it did not recognize individualized, material harms to specific voters or even groups of voters. Instead, it recognized what the authors called "expressive harms." In subsequent cases, both majority and dissenting Justices have embraced this characterization of the nature of the constitutional injury in the racial-redistricting cases. Thus, in *Bush v. Vera,* Justice O'Connor, writing for the Court, described the injury in these cases as an "expressive harm," as did Justice Souter, writing the principal dissent in *Bush v. Vera*.

Professor Pildes and Niemi characterized the concept of "expressive harms" in terms the following excerpt conveys. Consider whether this is the best account of the harms, if harms they be, in the racial-redistricting cases. Is it appropriate for constitutional law to acknowledge such non-individualized harms? Would the recognition of such harms be unique to the racial-redistricting context, or does constitutional law already recognize similar injuries elsewhere, such as in cases involving impermissible state "endorsement" of religion under the Establishment Clause:

> One can only understand *Shaw*, we believe, in terms of a view that what we call *expressive* harms are constitutionally cognizable. An expressive harm is one that results from the ideas or attitudes expressed through a governmental action, rather than from the more tangible or material consequences the action brings about. On this view, the *meaning* of a governmental action is just as important as what that action *does*. Public policies can violate the Constitution not only because they bring about concrete costs, but because the very meaning they convey demonstrates inappropriate respect for relevant public values. On this unusual conception of constitutional harm, when a governmental action expresses disrespect for such values, it can violate the Constitution.
>
> [*Shaw*] becomes intelligible only if one recognizes that it rests on just this concern for expressive harms. *Shaw* validates such harms as constitutionally cognizable, along with more familiar, concrete, material injuries. Indeed, close attention to the language of Justice O'Connor's opinion reveals a constant struggle to articulate exactly these sorts of expressive harms. Thus, the opinion is laden with references to the social perceptions, the messages, and the governmental reinforcement of values that the Court believes North Carolina's districting scheme conveys. There is simply no way to make sense of these references, which give the opinion its character and are central to its holding, without recognizing that the decision is grounded in concern for expressive harms. This conception of constitutionally cognizable harms explains why the Court is adamant that "reapportionment is one area in which appearances do matter." If they do, it must be because, even apart from any concrete harm to individual voters, such appearances themselves express a value structure that offends constitutional principles.
>
> *Shaw* therefore rests on the principle that, when government appears to use race in the redistricting context in a way that subordinates all other relevant values, the state has impermissibly endorsed too dominant a role for race. The constitutional harm must lie in this endorsement itself: the very expression of this king of value reductionism becomes the constitutional violation.

Richard Pildes & Richard Niemi, *Expressive Harms, "Bizarre Districts," and Voting Rights: Evaluating Election–District Appearances After* Shaw v. Reno, 92 Mich. L.Rev. 483 (1993).

Even if expressive harms are genuine injuries worth worrying about, is the concept of expressive harms judicially manageable? Consider Justice Souter's summary of the alternative paths of development for the racial redistricting caselaw in his dissent in *Bush v. Vera*:

> If the Court's first choice is to preserve *Shaw* in some guise with the least revolutionary effect on districting principles and practice, the Court could give primacy to the principle of compactness and define the limits of tolerance for unorthodox district shape by imposing a measurable limitation on the bizarre, presumably chosen by reference to historical practice (adjusted to eliminate the influence of any dilution that very practice may have caused in the past, cf. Pildes & Niemi, 92 Mich. L.Rev., at 573–574, n. 246 (discussing the egregious racial gerrymanders of the 19th century)) and calculated on the basis of a district's dispersion, perimeter, and population. This alternative would be true to *Shaw I* in maintaining that a point can be reached when the initially lawful consideration of race becomes unreasonable and in identifying appearance as the expression of undue consideration; and it would eliminate *Miller*'s impossible obligation to untangle racial considerations from so-called "race-neutral" objectives (such as according respect to community integrity and protecting the seats of incumbents) when the racial composition of a district and voter behavior bar any practical chance of separating them. The incongruities of *Shaw*'s concept of injury when considered in light of our customary equal protection analysis, our remedial practice, and traditional respect for state districting discretion would, of course, persist, but if *Shaw* were defined by measures that identified forbidden shape as the manifestation of unreasonable racial emphasis, we would at least provide the notice and guidance that are missing from the law today.
>
> The other alternative for retaining a *Shaw* cause of action in some guise would be to accept the fact that, in the kind of polarized multiracial societies that will generate *Shaw* actions as presently understood, racial considerations are inseparable from many traditional districting objectives, making it impossible to speak of race as predominating....
>
> While such is the direction in which *Shaw* and *Miller* together point, the objections to following any such course seem insurmountable. The first is the irony that the price of imposing a principle of colorblindness in the name of the Fourteenth Amendment would be submerging the votes of those whom the Fourteenth and Fifteenth Amendments were adopted to protect, precisely the problem that necessitated our recognition of vote dilution as a constitutional violation in the first place. Eliminating districting in the name of colorblindness would produce total

submersion; random submersion (or packing) would result from districting by some computerized process of colorblind randomness. Thus, unless the attitudes that produce racial bloc voting were eliminated along with traditional districting principles, dilution would once again become the norm. While dilution as an intentional constitutional violation would be eliminated by a randomly districted system, this theoretical nicety would be overshadowed by the concrete reality that the result of such a decision would almost inevitably be a so-called "representative" Congress with something like 17 black members.... In any event, the submergence would violate the prohibition of even non-intentional dilution found in Sec. 2 of the Voting Rights Act. The only way to avoid this conflict would be to declare the Voting Rights Act unconstitutional, a prospect hardly in harmony with the Court's readiness to assume today that compliance with the Voting Rights Act qualifies as a compelling state interest for purposes of litigating a *Shaw* claim.

The second objection is equally clear. Whatever may be the implications of what I have called *Shaw*'s failings, the Court has repeatedly made it plain that *Shaw* was in no way intended to effect a revolution by eliminating traditional districting practice for the sake of colorblindness....

[T]he Court's options for dealing with *Shaw*'s unworkability are in truth only these: to confine the cause of action by adopting a quantifiable shape test or to eliminate the cause of action entirely. Because even a truncated *Shaw* would rest on the untenable foundation I have described, and the supposed, expressive harm *Shaw* seeks to remedy is unlikely to justify the disruption that even a modified *Shaw* would invite, there is presently no good reason that the Court's withdrawal from the presently untenable state of the law should not be complete. While I take the commands of stare decisis very seriously, the problems with *Shaw* and its progeny are themselves very serious. The Court has been unable to provide workable standards, the chronic uncertainty has begotten no discernible reliance, and the costs of persisting doubt about the limits of state discretion and state responsibility are high.

8. The imprecise contours of the Court's definition of harm in the racial gerrymandering cases has yielded a peculiar foray into the realm of identifying who has standing to complain of such harms. In *Shaw v. Reno*, for example, none of the plaintiffs lived in the majority-black First Congressional District and only two of five lived in the much-maligned majority-black Twelfth. This apparent lack of contact with the districts caused the Court no evident concern. In an about-face, however, the Court in *United States v. Hays*, 515 U.S. 737 (1995), overturned a district court's invalida-

tion of Louisiana congressional districting for lack of plaintiff standing. The Court unanimously held that the fact that the plaintiffs did not live in the challenged black-majority district precluded them from meeting the "irreducible constitutional minimum" of a concrete, particularized "injury in fact." To establish this, Justice O'Connor writing for the Court held, plaintiffs must show that they "personally [were] denied equal treatment." Plaintiffs who "do not live in the district that is the primary focus of their racial gerrymandering claim, and [who] have not otherwise demonstrated that they, personally, have been subjected to a racial classification" fail that test. Someone who does not live in the district, the Court observed, "assert[s] only a generalized grievance against governmental conduct of which he or she does not approve." By contrast, plaintiffs who allege that they reside within a racially gerrymandered district have "been denied equal treatment because of the legislature's reliance on racial criteria" and they "may suffer the special representational harms racial classifications can cause in the voting context." In the same vein, the Court awakened the sleeping standing inquiry in its second confrontation with the post–1990 North Carolina congressional districts. Unlike its ruling in the first *Shaw* opinion, the Court held that the district lines of the Twelfth congressional district violated constitutional standards, but dismissed the claims against the First district for lack of plaintiff standing. *Shaw v. Hunt*, 116 S.Ct. 1894 (1996).

Does the Court's conception of harm match its restrictive standing rule? It is hard to reconcile a notion of an expressive harm issuing from improper governmental consideration of race with a narrow injury-in-fact requirement for standing. Consider, for example, a hypothetical problem of two white farmers having adjacent land-holdings and seeking common representation to further their interest in agricultural subsidies. Assume further that a district line is drawn between their respective farms and that it can be established that the particular decision to district in that fashion was the product of an impermissible reliance on race, as defined by *Shaw* and *Miller*. Finally let us assume that Farmer A is now in a majority black district, while Farmer B is in a majority white district. On what basis can the injury suffered to the shared political aspirations of the two farmers be found to differ? Only in that Farmer A is likely to be represented by a black elected official, while Farmer B will be represented by someone of his own race. Does the injury-in-fact requirement of *Hays* turn on the fact that Farmer A will be represented by someone of another race? Can the Constitution possibly be read to identify that as an injury?

9. Do the Court's standing rules in *Hays* properly fit the kind of constitutional injury that the *Shaw* doctrine recognizes substantively? If those injuries are the kind of "expressive harms" that Justice O'Connor identifies in *Bush v. Vera*, why should standing be limited only to those within a particular district? Do not all voters in the State experience these expressive harms in the same way? If expressive harms are harms to the political culture from the excessive use of race, rather than discrete harms to specific individuals, why shouldn't the Court recognize standing for any voter—or any resident—within the State? Does the narrow standing rule adopted in *Hays* reveal a fundamental lack of conviction on the Court's part about the kind of injury that it seems to acknowledge in *Shaw*? Or if it seems odd to recognize a cause of action the logic of which ought to permit anyone in the State to have standing, does that suggest there is something flawed in judicial recognition of *Shaw*-type injuries, or in the capacity of courts to meaningfully implement such a broad-gauged standard? More charitably, perhaps the tension between the substantive harm and the standing rules reflects a more deep-seated tension between constitutional law as the protection of individual rights versus constitutional law as the enforcement of constraints against government acting on the basis of impermissible justifications. Are these problems any different in litigation to enforce the Establishment Clause of the First Amendment? Compare *Valley Forge Christian College v. Americans United,* 454 U.S. 464 (1982) (sharply divided Court debating standing rules for such claims). The treatment of this issue by the Supreme Court has to date been inconclusive. This is also an issue on which the authors of this book are in disagreement. *Compare* Pamela S. Karlan, *Still Hazy After All These Years,* 26 Cumb. L. Rev. 287, 294 (1996)(defending stricter standing requirements to establish "necessary causal connection between racial classification *of the individual plaintiff* and ... representational harms"); *with* Samuel Issacharoff & Thomas C. Goldstein, *Identifying the Harm in Racial Gerrymandering Claims,* 1 Mich. J. of Race & Law 47, 65 (arguing that there is a mismatch between *Shaw's* conception of "noninstrumental harms" flowing from the fact of state use of racial classifications and the strict standing requirement of *Hays*) and Pildes and Niemi, *supra,* at 513 ("when courts recognize expressive harms, this traditional requirement of individualized harm comes under considerable pressure").

10. With the Republican Party's capture of both houses of Congress in the 1994 elections came an extensive debate about the role of creating majority-minority districts in disrupting traditional Democratic Party bases of support. Both political parties wavered on this issue. The Republican Party, under the leadership of Lee Atwater and Benjamin Ginsburg, at first actively supported the creation of minority districts as a way of undermining the electoral base of Democratic incumbents. In *Shaw*, however, the Republican Party filed an amicus brief urging that the black-majority districts be struck down. Does this shift reflect a change in principles? For the argument that the optimal partisan strategy for Republicans is to support minority districts, but require that they be compact, see David Lublin, *The Paradox of Representation* 98–119 (1997). For descriptions of the political meanderings underlying *Shaw, see* Timothy G. O'Rourke, Shaw v. Reno: *The Shape of Things to Come,* 26 Rutgers L.J. 723 (1995); Richard Briffault, *Race and Representation after* Miller v. Johnson, 1195 U.Chi. Legal F. 23, 35–37.

The Democratic Party was divided over the question of majority-minority districts as well. There is substantial evidence that the creation of majority-minority districts was an indispensible element in laying the foundation for significant minority legislative representation. The early studies on the role of minority districting in providing for black and Hispanic representation in Congress are summarized in Richard H. Pildes, *The Politics of Race*, 108 Harv. L. Rev. 1359 (1995)(reviewing Quiet Revolution in the South: The Impact of the Voting Rights Act, 1965–1990 (Chandler Davidson & Bernard Grofman, eds., 1994.)) While the Democratic Party drew considerable support from minority voters and welcomed the expanded minority congressional delegation, there was significant rumbling that the creation of heavily-minority districts was responsible for the Republican rise to power in Congress. The most recent and technically sophisticated studies of congressional elections largely confirm these earlier results. Thus, for congressional elections, the creation of majority-minority districts continues to be necessary to elect minorities to Congress in all but token numbers. In a study of all congressional elections between 1972 and 1994, David Lublin finds that in districts without Hispanic voters, the probability of the district electing a black congressperson is 8% when the district is 40% black in total population, 28% when the district is 45% black, 60% when the district is 50% black, and 86% when the district is 55% black. The addition of Hispanic voters typically changes these figures considerably; thus, when a district is 45% black and 20% Hispanic, the probability of electing a black representative goes up to 59%. In terms of the election of Hispanic representatives, a crucial factor is what portion of the Hispanic residents have lived in the state for at least five years; length of residence affects citizenship, registration, and actual turnout to vote. When 95% of the residents have lived in the state for at least five years, a district with 45% Hispanic population has a 61% probability of electing a Hispanic representative. Thus, Hispanics find it easier to get elected than blacks, although polarized voting is significant with respect to both groups, David Lublin, *The Election of African Americans and Latinos to the U.S. House of Representatives, 1972–1994,* 25 Am. Pol. Q. 269 (1997). Another recent and more limited study provides additional insight into racial polarization in voting, but is marred by its failure to separate out Hispanic voters from Anglo voters. *See* Charles Cameron, David Epstein, and Sharyn O'Halloran, *Do Majority–Minority Districts Maximize Substantive Black Representation in Congress,* 90 Am. Pol. Sci. Rev. 794 (1996). This study, which examines only congressional elections in 1992, concludes that to get to the 50 percent probability level of electing a black Democratic congressional candidate, districts in the South need a black voting-age population (BVAP) of 40.3 percent; in the Northwest, a BVAP of 47.3 percent; and in the Northeast, a BVAP of 28.3 percent. These data are consistent with Lublin's, but by grouping Anglo and Hispanic voters together, they fail to signal the crucial role of Hispanic voters in the election prospects of black candidates (note that while blacks and Hispanics have often been coalitional partners in national politics, such as for congressional races, recent developments suggest that in major cities for local elections, Hispanic and black voters now vote antagonistically. Peter Beinart, *New Bedfellows,* The New Republic 22 (Aug. 11/18, 1997)).

Even more interesting are the results of the tradeoff between descriptive, representation (the number of blacks in office) and substantive representation (the likelihood of a representative seeking to advance what are perceived to be the policy preferences of black voters). Although subject to methodological criticism, the easiest measure of substantive representation is the recorded votes of a representative on civil rights legislation. The potential tradeoff requires addressing two issues that can be framed in the following way. Suppose we start with two districts each represented by a typical white Democratic legislator. If one of those districts is transformed into a majority-minority district, which will tend to elect a minority, then (1) does that make it more likely that the second district will become a Republican one, and if so, (2) what is the net effect of taking two districts represented by white Democrats and making one of them a district represented by a black or Hispanic Democrat, while making the other district one represented by a Republican?

Lublin's work concludes that there are significant regional variations in the extent to which creating more minority districts leads to electing more conservative representatives in surrounding districts. He finds that "[r]acial redistricting tends to make surrounding districts more conservative and likely to elect Republicans in the South, but not the North"—due to the different geographic dispersion of black voters in the two regions and differing ideology of white voters. He also finds that the net policy effect of replacing two white Democratic congresspersons with one Republican and one minority Democrat is to make the overall representation more conservative; the typically greater liberalism of minority representatives compared to white Democratic ones is more than offset by the greater conservativism of Republicans over white Democrats. Lublin further finds that above a 40% black population, congressional representatives do not become significantly more liberal as the black population is increased further. Therefore, Lublin concludes that "[m]apmakers desiring solely to maximize black substantive representation should give priority to protecting Democratic seats over drawing additional districts greater than 40 percent black ... maximizing the number of Democratic seats, and thus black substantive representation, would entail dismantling many black majority districts." Lublin, *Paradoxes of Representation,* at 99.

Cameron's study also notes the importance of regional variation. That study concludes that, outside the South, the best circumstance for maximizing the political influence of black voters is when black voters are distributed equally across all districts. That is, two districts with 25 percent BVAP will be better, in terms of influence on civil rights legislation, than one district that is 50 percent BVAP and one that is 0 percent BVAP. "Majority-minority districts make little sense in this context, unless they confer significant nonpolicy benefits, as they create greater possibilities for electing Republicans in other districts." Cameron, et al., at 808. Within the South, this study confirms that the relationship between BVAP and political influence is more complex. While representatives are generally more liberal as the BVAP of their districts goes up, Cameron argues that this responsiveness flattens out when the BVAP is between 25–35 percent. Above those levels, significant improvements in responsiveness do occur. Thus, in terms of influence on policy, their suggestion is there is no reason to construct districts with BVAP between 25–35 percent. Note though that by 1992, there are few districts with BVAP in this range, particularly in the South, so the analysis here depends less on direct data than statistical inferences. Putting these effects together, the study concludes that in the South, the approach that maximizes the influence of black voters is to construct as many districts as possible that are around 47 percent black, with the remaining black voters distributed as evenly as possible over other districts.

The aggregate effect of racial redistricting in the 1990s on Democrats in the House is much disputed, Lublin estimates that the 1990s redistricting cost the Democrats around 11 seats that they would have won had the party distributed black voters across districts in the way most efficient for Democratic interests, rather than creating majority-minority districts. Lublin, *Paradoxes of Representation*, at 114. Grofman and Handley conclude that of the seats lost by Democrats from 1990 to 1994, between 2–5, on the low side, and 10–11 on the high side, could have been maintained as Democrat seats but for the imperatives of creating majority-black districts. Bernard Grofman and Lisa Handley, *1990s Issues in Voting Rights,* 65 Miss. L. J. 205, 263–65 (1995). A study by Kevin Hill, which focuses only on the 1992 elections and only on seats previously held by Democrats (thus leaving aside open seats and those held by Republicans) concludes that Democrats lost four seats in 1992 in consequence of the creation of majority-minority districts. Kevin A. Hill, *Does the Creation of Majority Black Districts Aid Republicans? An Analysis of the 1992 Congressional Elections in Eight Southern States*, 95 J.Pol. 384 (1995). Note that after the 1996 elections, Republicans held a 20 seat majority over the Democrats in the House.

The views noted above on the tradeoff between descriptive and substantive representation are not without controversy. Thus, Professor Karlan argues that:

> A ... critical feature of the political landscape involves the mechanism by which black Southerners in majority-white districts have their policy preferences actually "represented." Leaving aside direct constituent services ... the major benefit southern blacks receive from being in white Democratic, as opposed to white Republican, districts often comes from a sort of *virtual,* rather

than direct, representation. One especially powerful reason for southern black voters to support the Democratic candidate is not really because he personally will be a staunch advocate for their policy preferences,[52] but because when there is a partisan divide the Democrat will align with the party most sympathetic to black interests.... When it comes to policy, rather than territorially allocated pork, the "real" representatives of black southerners who live in majority-white districts are Democrats from districts where a majority of the electorate supports those policies—usually districts that are themselves majority black or are northern, liberal, and Democratic.

Pamela S. Karlan, *Loss and Redemption: Voting Rights at the Turn of a Century* 50 Vand. L. Rev. 291, 304, 305, 307–08 (1997).

Scholars of Southern politics have long observed a form of racial backlash, in which Southern whites become more conservative as the black population around them rises. Professor Karlan suggests that black political influence today within an election district might be curvilinear:

> A great deal of historical and contemporary evidence suggests the presence of an influence "tipping point": blacks are more likely to occupy a pivotal position when they are a relatively small share of the electorate, because white voters are then less likely to perceive them as a threat. As the possibility that blacks might be a dominant component of a biracial coalition grows, white backlash increases as well. The backlash hypothesis suggests that the influence of black voters "is not a linear continuum along which responsiveness increases as the minority population percentage in

---

52. The most powerful illustration of this point was made by Morgan Kousser. He graphed the *Congressional Quarterly* Conservative Coalition scores of North Carolina's representatives for the period from 1970 to 1993. Until 1992, there was *no* systematic difference between the votes of the two congressmen from the most heavily black districts—districts that were nonetheless majority white—and the votes of the representatives from districts with substantially lower black populations. A few times, the two representatives from the "blackest" districts were more conservative than even the Republicans. By contrast, there was an immense gap between the two representatives' voting behavior and the voting behavior of *black* southern Democratic representatives. (The North Carolinians' scores were, with one exception, always above 60; the black Democrats' scores were always below 20.)

After 1992, the CQ scores for the two representatives serving the two most heavily black districts in North Carolina dropped from roughly 60 to roughly 10, pulling them essentially in line with representatives from predominantly-black districts. The difference? The, post-1990 reapportionment created two majority-black districts which elected black Representatives. *See The Supreme Court, Racial Politics, and the Right to Vote: Shaw v. Reno and the Future of the Voting Rights Act,* 44 Am.U.L.Rev. 1, 60–61 (1994) (comments of Morgan Kousser). *See also* A. Leon Higginbotham, Jr., Gregory A. Clarick, & Marcella David, Shaw v. Reno: *A Mirage of Good Intentions With Devastating Racial Consequences,* 62 FORDHAM L. REV. 1593, 1653–57 (1994) (reprinting tables showing the voting records of white and black southern Democratic representatives in the 103d Cong., 1st Sess., that show huge disparities between the two groups)....

a district increases." Instead, it seems as if influence might almost be *curvilinear:* black influence grows as blacks increase to roughly 30 percent of the electorate; black voters face increasing resistance when they constitute between 30 and 50 percent of the electorate; and beyond 50 percent, the relationship between presence and influence is again positive because in William Keech's sardonic observation, "a Negro voting majority can overcome a lot of white-resistance."

Id. at 314-15. *See also* Richard H. Pildes, *The Politics of Race* 1381-83 (1995) (analyzing data on racial-backlash hypothesis). Recent scholarship, however, questions whether this traditional hypothesis still holds across all elections for contemporary Southern politics. Thus, Lublin finds for congressional elections since the Voting Rights Act was passed that the data "firmly refute the hypothesis that white backlash forms a solid barrier to black representation." He acknowledges that white backlash might make representatives less responsive to increases in black population than they otherwise would be, but "[i]ncreases in black support offset any rise in white conservatism." Lublin, *Paradoxes of Representation,* at 88. Similarly, a recent study of white support for David Duke in Louisiana found that white support was not consistent with the backlash thesis; whites were less likely, not more, to support Duke as the black population in the area increased. D. Stephen Voss, *Beyond Racial Threat: Failure of an Old Hypothesis in the New South,* 58 J. Pol. 1156 (1996).

11. Was Congress likely to have been aware of these tradeoffs between descriptive and substantive representation when it enacted the 1982 VRA Amendments? Of the magnitude of the tradeoffs? If Congress had been, would Congress have nonetheless enacted those Amendments in the same form? If these studies are right, would black voters be better off if Congress repealed the 1982 Amendments? If the Supreme Court overruled *Thornburg v. Gingles*?

12. Congressional redistricting in the 1990s was the first to take place in the wake of the 1982 VRA Amendments and their interpretation in the *Gingles* decision. As a result of greater focus on creating majority-black (and Latino) congressional districts, the number of black congressmen increased from 25 in 1989 to 38 in 1992; the Latino increase was from 10 to 17 in the same period. This increase necessitated the redrawing of many other congressional districts at the same time. As with all such realignments, the consequences extended beyond the creation of minority-controlled districts. This process brought the tension between descriptive and substantive representation to a new level.

The 1990's redistricting of Alabama illustrates concretely the interrelationship between racial and partisan considerations in recent redistricting. Consider the maps of Alabama's congressional delegation after 1980 and then after the 1990 redistricting. The most significant difference between the two maps is the creation of new District 7 to create a solidly black-majority district.

1980 CONGRESSIONAL DISTRICTS

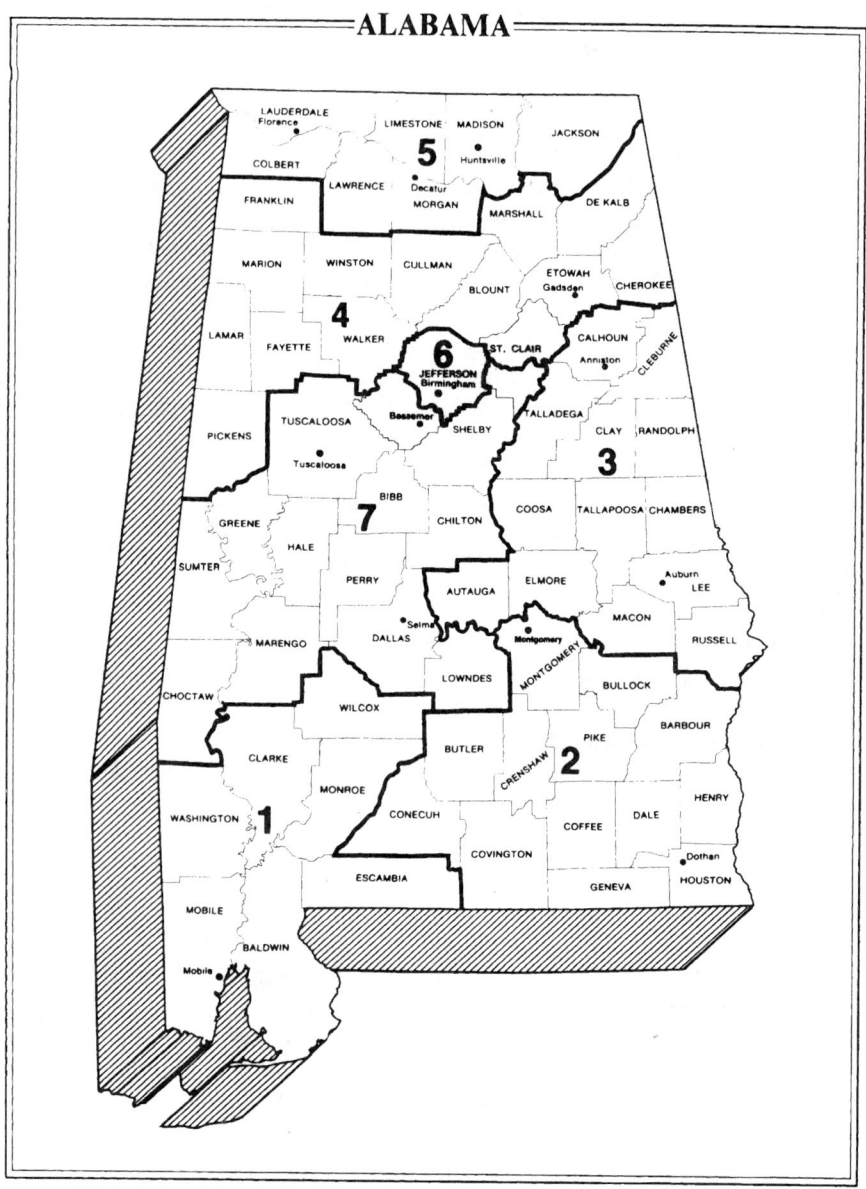

The creation of District 7 required that thousands of black voters be moved from District 2 and District 6 to expand the black population of District 7.

1990 CONGRESSIONAL DISTRICTS

Alabama

For example, the part of Montgomery County that was moved from District 2 to District 7 was 80 percent black. Now consider the partisan distribution of Alabama's congressional delegation before and after the post–1990 redistricting, and a comparison of the black percentage of each congressional district. As the Table indicates, the immediate result of the redistricting is the replacement of two white Democratic congressmen from Districts 6 and 7 with a black Democratic congressman from District 7 and a white Republican congressman from District 6. Notice as well, the near even distribution of black voters prior to 1990 and the concentration of black voters after 1990. Consider whether this result is mandated by the Voting Rights Act after *Thornburg v. Gingles* and whether it is constitutionally permissible after *Shaw v. Reno*.

Table 1

	1990		Black Total Population		1992		Black Total Population
1.	Callahan	R	31%	1. Callahan	R	28%	
2.	Dickinson	R	31%	2. Everett	R	24%	
3.	Browder	D	28%	3. Browder	D	26%	
4.	Bevill	D	7%	4. Bevill	D	7%	
5.	Cramer	D	14%	5. Cramer	D	15%	
6.	**Erdreich**	**D**	**34%**	6. **Bachus**	**R**	**9%**	
7.	**Harris**	**D**	**33%**	7. **Hilliard**	**D**	**67%**	
						[64% black VAP]	

Does the fact that this plan was proposed by the State Republican party change your assessment of the permissibility or desirability of this form of districting? Political scientist David Lublin raises this question directly:

> Redistricting in Alabama worked exactly as the Republicans hoped. Since the Alabama lines are the product of a plan suggested by the Republicans and imposed by a federal court, this outcome is not altogether surprising.... The net result of these changes was to shift the partisan balance of the Alabama delegation and diminish substantive black representation. Thanks virtually entirely to favorable redistricting, Republicans won one new seat in 1992 and held on to one seat that they otherwise would have lost. Packing black voters into the Seventh District wasted Democratic voting strength and cost Democrats their hold on the Sixth District as well as an opportunity to win the open Second District. Instead of electing three moderate white Democrats, the Second, Sixth, and Seventh Districts now send one liberal black Democrat and two conservative white Republicans to Washington.... After redistricting, Alabama blacks can count on one sure vote on the floor of the House in the form of African American Earl Hilliard, but African Americans will find it exceedingly difficult to gain the vote of Sixth District Republican Spencer Bachus. Having few blacks in his district, Bachus has little reason to worry about black concerns. In effect, redistricting increased the size of the opposition to legislation supported by African Americans by one vote.

David Ian Lublin, *Race, Representation, and Redistricting*, in Classifying By Race 111, 116 (Paul Petersen ed. 1996). Does the experience of Alabama suggest that descriptive and substantive representation must necessarily be traded off? Suppose Democrats had been in control of redistricting. Would the same tradeoff necessarily have to have been made? If you need additional facts to be able to answer, what facts would you need?

13. To what extent is any individual's conception of political community likely to remain tied to geographic boundaries? For an argument that residency within the geographic territory of local governments has become

1990 CONGRESSIONAL DISTRICTS

For example, the part of Montgomery County that was moved from District 2 to District 7 was 80 percent black. Now consider the partisan distribution of Alabama's congressional delegation before and after the post–1990 redistricting, and a comparison of the black percentage of each congressional district. As the Table indicates, the immediate result of the redistricting is the replacement of two white Democratic congressmen from Districts 6 and 7 with a black Democratic congressman from District 7 and a white Republican congressman from District 6. Notice as well, the near even distribution of black voters prior to 1990 and the concentration of black voters after 1990. Consider whether this result is mandated by the Voting Rights Act after *Thornburg v. Gingles* and whether it is constitutionally permissible after *Shaw v. Reno*.

Table 1

	1990		Black Total Population		1992		Black Total Population
1.	Callahan	R	31%	1. Callahan	R	28%
2.	Dickinson	R	31%	2. Everett	R	24%
3.	Browder	D	28%	3. Browder	D	26%
4.	Bevill	D	7%	4. Bevill	D	7%
5.	Cramer	D	14%	5. Cramer	D	15%
6.	**Erdreich**	**D**	**34%**	**6. Bachus**	**R**	**9%**
7.	**Harris**	**D**	**33%**	**7. Hilliard**	**D**	**67%**
						[64% black VAP]

Does the fact that this plan was proposed by the State Republican party change your assessment of the permissibility or desirability of this form of districting? Political scientist David Lublin raises this question directly:

> Redistricting in Alabama worked exactly as the Republicans hoped. Since the Alabama lines are the product of a plan suggested by the Republicans and imposed by a federal court, this outcome is not altogether surprising.... The net result of these changes was to shift the partisan balance of the Alabama delegation and diminish substantive black representation. Thanks virtually entirely to favorable redistricting, Republicans won one new seat in 1992 and held on to one seat that they otherwise would have lost. Packing black voters into the Seventh District wasted Democratic voting strength and cost Democrats their hold on the Sixth District as well as an opportunity to win the open Second District. Instead of electing three moderate white Democrats, the Second, Sixth, and Seventh Districts now send one liberal black Democrat and two conservative white Republicans to Washington.... After redistricting, Alabama blacks can count on one sure vote on the floor of the House in the form of African American Earl Hilliard, but African Americans will find it exceedingly difficult to gain the vote of Sixth District Republican Spencer Bachus. Having few blacks in his district, Bachus has little reason to worry about black concerns. In effect, redistricting increased the size of the opposition to legislation supported by African Americans by one vote.

David Ian Lublin, *Race, Representation, and Redistricting*, in Classifying By Race 111, 116 (Paul Petersen ed. 1996). Does the experience of Alabama suggest that descriptive and substantive representation must necessarily be traded off? Suppose Democrats had been in control of redistricting. Would the same tradeoff necessarily have to have been made? If you need additional facts to be able to answer, what facts would you need?

13. To what extent is any individual's conception of political community likely to remain tied to geographic boundaries? For an argument that residency within the geographic territory of local governments has become an outmoded basis for assigning political rights, see Gerald Frug, *Decentering Decentralization*, 60 U. Chi. L. Rev. 253 (1993). Given the nature of contemporary residential, work, social, and commercial patterns, Frug suggests that "[w]e must treat people not as located in one jurisdiction, but as switching center[s] for all the networks of influence within the region that affect their lives."

> Perhaps this emphasis on residency was justifiable when, once upon a time, home, work, family, friends, market, past, present, and future (so we imagine) linked together in one community. But these days some people do not even live at their place of residence: students who spend full-time out-of-state, people who are serving in the military, and business-people who are assigned abroad are residents of the town they are never in. And those people who do live in the area are not found solely at home. Most people spend most of their day in other parts of the region. If the neighborhood where people work deteriorates or their mall closes down, it would affect their lives just as much as an event three blocks away from their residence. In an era when people often do not even know the names of neighbors who live a block away, a person's territorial identity should not be reduced to his or her address.

As a response, Frug offers this novel proposal:

> Consider a plan, for example, in which everyone gets five votes that they can cast in whatever local elections they feel affect their interest ("local" still being defined by the traditional territorial boundaries of city, suburb, or neighborhood). They can define their interests differently in different elections, and any for of connection that they think expresses an aspect of themselves at the moment will be treated as adequate. Under such an electoral system, mayors, city council members, and neighborhood representatives in the regional legislature would have a constituency made up not only of residents but of workers, shoppers, property owners in neighboring jurisdictions, the homeless, and so forth. People are unlikely to vote in a jurisdiction they do not care about, but there are a host of possible motives for voting (racial integration, racial solidarity, redistribution of wealth, desire for gratification, etc.). Indeed, there is no reason to think that the constituency would be limited solely to those who live in the region.

What do you think of this idea in theory? In practice, what kind of difficulties do you foresee in implementing such a proposal?

14. In the 1996 congressional elections, five incumbent black Representatives who had originally won election from majority-black districts retained their seats despite having had their districts reconfigured in the wake of wrongful districting challenges. *See Vera v. Bush*, 933 F.Supp. 1341 (S.D.Tex.1996); *Johnson v. Miller*, 922 F.Supp. 1556 (S.D.Ga.1995). In two of the Texas districts, the black voting age population of the districts was reduced by a relatively small amount: from 48 percent to 44 percent in District 18, and from 47 percent to 42 percent in District 30. Both of these districts remained plurality black, and majority non-Anglo, due to substantial concentrations of Hispanic voters. In Georgia, by contrast, the alteration of the district alignments was far more dramatic. The court's redistricting plan reduced the black percentage of District 2 from 52 to 35 percent, and District 11 from 60 to 33 percent. Should the victories of these five black incumbents be seen as evidence that the racial divide in politics is lessening or that incumbency yields such distinct advantages that such cases should be treated as being *sui generis*? *See* Charles S. Bullock, *Incumbency, Not Race, Wins in the South,* Newsday, Nov. 13, 1996, at A41. The black incumbent candidates would still have suffered defeat at the hands of white voters, but the numbers are far less dramatic than those reported in cases such as *Thornburg v. Gingles*: for example, in Georgia, Cynthia McKinney received approximately 33 percent of the white vote, while Sanford Bishop received around 36 percent.

15. As of the end of its 1996 Term, the Supreme Court had reached the merits and upheld two plans against *Shaw* claims. *Lawyer v. Department of Justice,* 117 S. Ct. 2186 (1997); *DeWitt v. Wilson,* 515 U. S. 1170 (1995), *summarily aff'g* 856 F. Supp. 1409 (E.D. Cal. 1994) (three-judge court). Notably, neither plan involved district lines drawn by overtly political actors: the Florida State Senate district challenged in *Lawyer* was the product of a federal court settlement; the California state legislative reapportionments challenged in *DeWitt* were the product of three retired California judges appointed by the California Supreme Court as special masters.

The district challenged in *Lawyer* had a somewhat tangled provenance. Following a legislative impasse, the Florida Supreme Court drew a state senatorial district reminiscent of the districts struck down in *Shaw, Miller,* and *Vera:*

> [The original plan] called for an irregularly shaped Senate District 21, with a voting-age population 45.8% black and 9.4% hispanic and comprising portions of four counties in the Tampa Bay area. The district included the central portions of Tampa in Hillsborough County, the eastern shore of Tampa Bay running south to Bradenton in Manatee County, central portions of St. Petersburg in Pinellas County, a narrow projection eastward through parts of Hillsborough and Polk Counties, and a narrow finger running north from St. Petersburg to Clearwater. Although the State Supreme Court acknowledged that the district was "more contorted" than other possible plans and that black residents in different parts of the district might have little in common besides their race, it decided that such concerns "must give way to racial and ethnic fairness."

Lawyer, 117 S. Ct. at 2190. After the U. S . Supreme Court's decision in *Shaw,* six residents of Hillsborough County, including the felicitously named C. Martin Lawyer, III, filed a lawsuit in federal district court challenging District 21 as a racial gerrymander. The other parties to the lawsuit were the State of Florida, its attorney general, the U.S. Department of Justice (all original defendants) and the State Senate, the State House of

Representatives, Florida's Secretary of State, the senator from District 21, and a group of black and hispanic voters residing in the district (defendant-intervenors).

Ultimately, all the parties but Lawyer reached a settlement. The new proposed District 21 had a boundary length of roughly half the old district, eliminated the "finger," and contained parts of three counties rather than four. But the district still included land on both sides of Tampa Bay. Finally, the black voting age population was decreased to 36.2 percent.

After a fairness hearing, at which Lawyer objected and proposed a remedial District 21 contained entirely within one county, the district court approved the proposed settlement. *Scott v. Department of Justice,* 920 F. Supp. 1248 (M.D. Fla.1996). It found that "[i]n its shape and composition, proposed District 21 is, all said and done, demonstrably benign and satisfactorily tidy, especially given the prevailing geography." *Id.* at 1255.

On appeal, the Supreme Court affirmed. It first rejected Lawyer's procedural argument that the district court should not have approved the settlement—which overturned the plan drawn by the Florida Supreme Court—without first finding that the original plan violated the Constitution. The various state actors who participated in the litigation, the Court held, were entitled to decide to settle the case and to use it as a vehicle for redrawing District 21. As for Lawyer's substantive challenge to the redrawn District 21, the Court held:

> The District Court concluded that Plan 386 did not subordinate traditional distracting principles to race. That finding is subject to review for clear error, *see Miller,* of which we find none.
>
> .... The district is located entirely in the Tampa Bay area, has an end-to-end distance no greater than that of most Florida Senate districts, and in shape does not stand out as different from numerous other Florida House and Senate districts. While District 21 crosses a body of water and encompasses portions of three counties, evidence submitted showed that both features are common characteristics of Florida legislative districts, being products of the State's geography and the fact that 40 Senate districts are superimposed on 67 counties.[9]
>
> Addressing composition, the District Court found that the residents of District 21 "regard themselves as a community." Evidence indicated that District 21 comprises a predominantly urban, low-income population, the poorest of the nine districts in the Tampa Bay region and among the poorest districts in the State, whose white and black members alike share a similarly

---

9. The Supreme Court of Florida has held that the presence in a district of a body of water, even without a connecting bridge and even if such distracting necessitates land travel outside the district to reach other parts of the district, "does not violate this Court's standard for determining contiguity under the Florida Constitution."

depressed economic condition, and interests that reflect it. The fact that District 21 under Plan 386 is not a majority black district, the black voting-age population being 36.2%, supports the District Court's finding that the district is not a "safe" one for black-preferred candidates, but one that "offers to any candidate, without regard to race, the opportunity" to seek and be elected to office.

Based on these and other considerations, the District Court concluded that traditional distracting principles had not been subordinated to race in drawing revised District 21. Appellant calls this finding clearly erroneous, charging that District 21 encompasses more than one county, crosses a body of water, is irregular in shape, lacks compactness, and contains a percentage of black voters significantly higher than the overall percentage of black voters in Hillsborough, Manatee, and Pinellas counties. Appellant's first four points ignore unrefuted evidence showing that on each of these points District 21 is no different from what Florida's traditional distracting principles could be expected to produce. As to appellant's final point, we have never suggested that the percentage of black residents in a district may not exceed the percentage of black residents in any of the counties from which the district is created, and have never recognized similar racial composition of different political districts as being necessary to avoid an inference of racial gerrymandering in any one of them.

In short, the evidence amply supports the trial court's views that race did not predominate over Florida's traditional distracting principles in drawing Plan 386.

Lawyer, 117 S. Ct. at 2195. The majority opinion was signed by the dissenting Justices from *Shaw, Miller,* and *Vera,* as well as Chief Justice Rehnquist. The other four Justices dissented on the question whether the district court could approve the settlement without first finding liability and never reached the *Shaw* issue.

Is there anything about the Court's description that necessarily distinguishes it from the districts struck down in the Court's other *Shaw* cases? To what extent is the Court's decision a product of an unwillingness to hold that plans drawn under judicial auspices are invidiously motivated? Does *Lawyer* also suggest that a minority "opportunity" district, as opposed to a majority-nonwhite district, cannot be the product of a predominant racial purpose?

Consider the systemic incentives that the Court's decisions in *DeWitt* and *Lawyer* might create. If race-conscious districting is effectively permissible when done by courts but not by legislatures, does this turn the Court's original reluctance to enter the political thicket on its head? *Cf.* Samuel Issacharoff, *Judging Politics: The Elusive Quest for Judicial Review of Political Fairness,* 71 Tex. L. Rev. 1643, 1689–90 (1993) (pointing out that roughly 1/3 of all redistricting after the 1980 census was done either directly by federal courts or under federal supervision but that there were virtually no successful challenges to reapportionments performed by nonpolitical actors, such as distracting commissions); Jeffrey C. Kubin, Note, *The Case for Redistricting Commissions,* 75 Tex. L. Rev. 837, 861–72 (1997) (suggesting that federal courts are more likely to uphold the products of commission-run reapportionments).

16. Does the Supreme Court's deference to judicially created districts extend more generally to districts approved as remedies in section 2 cases? In this light, consider the recent opinion in *Addy v. Newton County,* Civ. Act. No. 4:95CV39LN (S.D. Miss. July 18, 1997). As a result of an earlier Voting Rights Act lawsuit, Newton County, Mississippi, was ordered to draw a majority-black district for its Board of Supervisors. James Addy, who had previously served on the Board of Supervisors, brought a *Shaw* challenge. The district court dismissed his complaint:

> Race undeniably and necessarily played a role in the drawing of the districts since the goal and purpose of the County's redistricting process was, first and foremost, the creation of a district with a substantial minority majority....
>
> With respect to the plaintiffs' contention that the County's ... plans failed to respect defined communities of interest by dividing each of two of the County's three major towns among two or more districts, the court would observe that the County's prior plan ... likewise split two of the towns.... In light of this fact, it would be difficult to say that the County has seen these towns as having any "community of interest" relative to County government or that it has traditionally respected the integrity of town boundaries.... Moreover, there was substantial evidence presented that those persons comprising the black populations from each of the towns that were included in ... District One have a community of shared political interests which warranted their collective inclusion in a single district.

> * * *

> ... [T]he County, in view of the geographics and demographics of the county, had two choices: it could create an east-west district in the southern part of the county, or it could do what it did, which was to draw a north-south district .... No one disputes that an east-west district ... would have been more compact .... But neither is it disputed that a north-south configuration was selected because three members of the Board—a majority—saw that it could be drawn to accomplish something that an east-west district could not, namely, to protect their own seats and to

undermine the chance of James Addy's reelection to the Board by placing him in the majority-minority district. It is easily seen, therefore, that to the extent the County may have sacrificed a degree of compactness . . . , it did so exclusively for political, not racial reasons.

Slip op. at 4–5. *Cf. Theriot v. Parish of Jefferson,* 966 F.Supp. 1435 (E.D.La. 1997) (rejecting a *Shaw* challenge to a remedial parish councilmanic district because its failure to achieve optimum compactness could be explained by political factors).

Is the difference between *Vera* and *Addy* a product of different facts or a different perspective on the relative importance of various "traditional" districting factors?

C. A REDISTRICTING EXERCISE

Imagine yourself in the position of having to redistrict a state in light of the competing concerns of the *Shaw* line of cases and the constraints of the Voting Rights Act. In order to illustrate the difficulties facing well-intentioned redistricting authorities, consider the following problem involving the hypothetical state of New Columbia.

The first map shows the districting of New Columbia after the 1980 Census. This is followed by the revised demographic distributions of the state after the 1990 Census and a map showing the black population concentrations within the state. Your task is to redistrict the state to conform to the applicable law of one-person, one-vote, the Voting Rights Act, and equal protection law. You should be prepared to defend your districting decisions as if they were to be challenged in court.

Keep in mind that this is a streamlined exercise. You are not provided with any data in any form below the county level. Your choices are accordingly constrained to moving around the county building blocks. In the real world, potential redistricters would have information broken down by precincts or census blocks, either of which would dramatically expand the universe of potential districting arrangements.

C. A Redistricting Exercise

© Jerry Wilson
by permission of author

STATE OF NEW COLUMBIA
1980 Plan

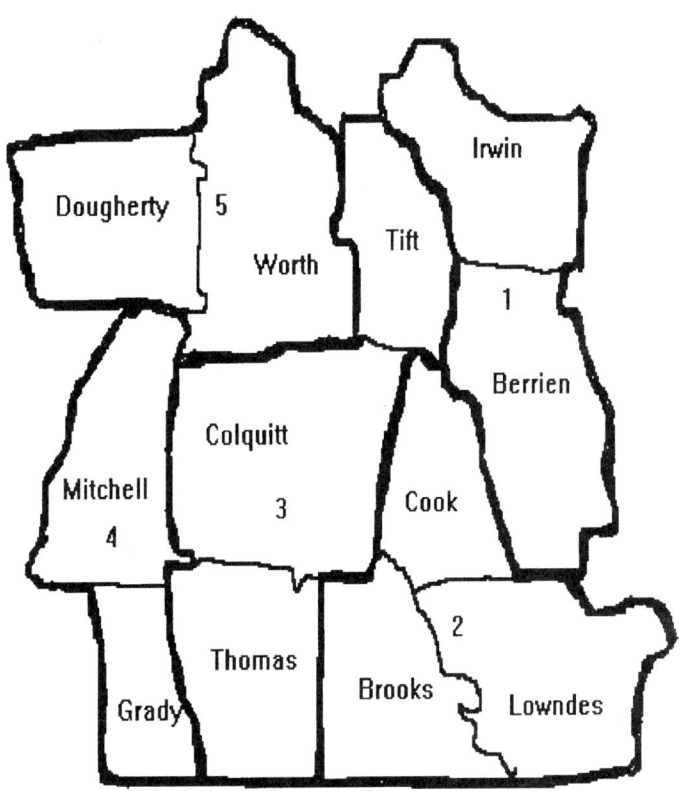

District 1 = Irwin, Berrien = 27.50% Black
District 2 = Cook, Lowndes, Brooks = 24.05% Black
District 3 = Tift, Colquitt, Thomas = 17.38% Black
District 4 = Mitchell, Grady = 30.40% Black
District 5 = Dougherty, Worth = 10.20% Black

STATE OF NEW COLUMBIA
Redistricting Worksheet for 1990

Total Population = 1,000,000

Black Population = 206,500 (20.65%)

White Population = 792,000 (79.2%)

Other Population = 1,500 (.15%)

TVAP (Total Voting Age Population) = 680,850

BVAP (Black Voting Age Population) = 132,773

Number of Seats = 5

Ideal Population = 200,000

STATE OF NEW COLUMBIA
Population

County	TP	BP	TVAP	BVAP
Berrien	75,000	48,750	49,500	32,175
Brooks	135,000	27,000	91,800	17,010
Colquitt	50,000	31,500	32,500	21,450
Cook	25,000	13,750	16,250	8,250
Dougherty	25,000	750	17,250	510
Grady	100,000	8,000	70,000	5,280
Irwin	200,000	20,000	138,000	12,800
Lowndes	65,000	9,750	43,550	6,338
Mitchell	50,000	30,000	34,000	18,000
Thomas	100,000	2,000	68,000	1,300
Tift	100,000	3,000	69,000	1,980
Worth	75,000	12,000	51,000	7,680
Total	1,000,000	206,500	680,850	132,773

C. A Redistricting Exercise   615

STATE OF NEW COLUMBIA
Majority Black Areas Shaded

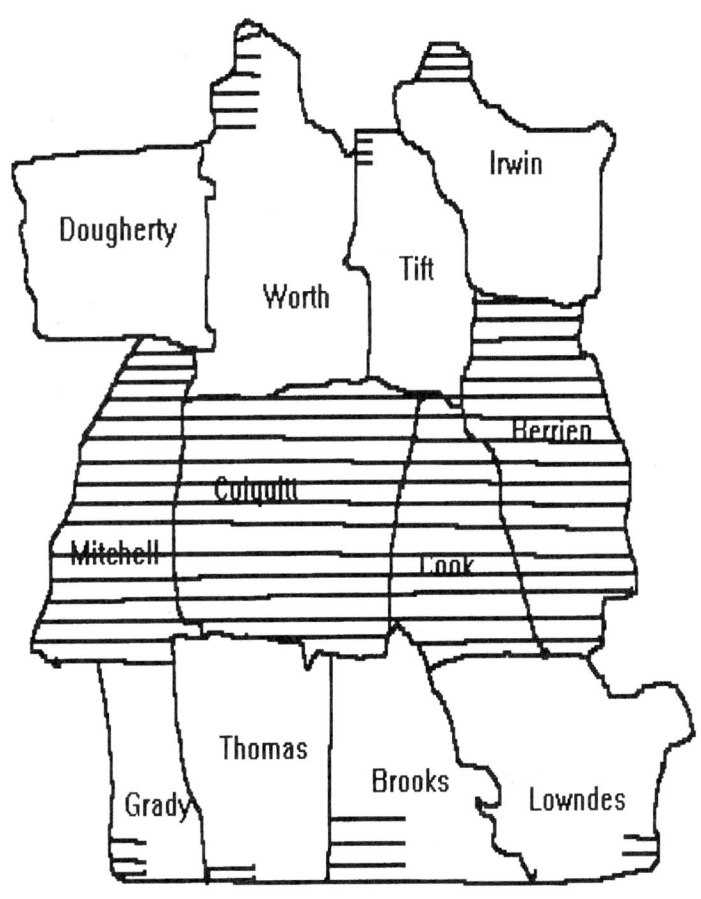

CHAPTER 9

MONEY AND POLITICS

One of the most salient features of the American political system is the sheer quantity of elective offices at all levels of government. At present, there are more than half a million government positions that are filled by popular election. Although candidates for these offices may be endorsed by a political party, they typically run for office as individuals independent of a formal party electoral slate. To be heard above the crowd, candidates need access to organization, paid publicity, and the media. These considerations point to the role of campaign financing as a determinant of who will serve in office. Correspondingly, the amount of money involved in electoral politics is staggering. For example, the total bill for the 1996 presidential and congressional campaigns was estimated to be $1.6 billion.

This chapter will address the difficult issues concerning the influence of money on the political system in general and on political speech in particular. Both the political and the legal dimensions of these issues are increasingly prominent; public pressure to reform the political system makes it possible that Congress will pass campaign finance reform legislation of at least some form in the foreseeable future. Prospective legislation will be shaped not only by political forces, but by contestable views concerning the forms that the First Amendment and Supreme Court decisions permit such legislation to take.

The modern era of regulating the role of money in electoral politics dates from the period of reform following Watergate. Although the events themselves have left their mark mostly as a suffix appended to all manner of government misdeeds (e.g., Irangate, Travelgate), the break-in at the Democratic National Committee headquarters triggered a concerted effort to reform the political order. In turn, much of the reform effort was directed at the role of money—both as a potential source of corruption in politics and as a filter on which viewpoints could be effectively aired.

Since the time of Watergate and the publication of Charles Lindblom's 1977 book, *Politics and Markets*, the issue of the role of contributions and money has taken on a life of its own in the law. This is an extremely complicated area of legal regulation because of the competing claims of government's right to regulate the functions of the political marketplace and the inevitable association between the right to contribute and the First Amendment rights of association and participation in politics. We will begin the chapter by discussing the most important of the regulatory efforts, the 1974 Amendments to the Federal Election Campaign Act of 1971, 2 U.S.C.

§ 441 *et seq.*, and then attempt to sort through the various concerns in campaign finance regulation.

Although this area is strewn with First Amendment concerns, our focus will remain on the central issues of the legal and policy rationales for regulation of the political process. Three different approaches are central to the arguments over campaign finance regulation. For introductory purposes, these may be thought of as follows:

1. *Regulation of political markets:* There is a long tradition of viewing political speech from the vantage point of a marketplace of ideas. In the words of John Milton, "Let Truth and Falsehood grapple; whoever knew Truth put to the worse, in a free and open encounter." John Milton, *Areopagitica*, reprinted in The Tradition of Freedom 28 (Milton Mayer ed. 1957). The First Amendment has accordingly long been held to guarantee debate on public issues that is "uninhibited, robust, and wide-open." *New York Times v. Sullivan*, 376 U.S. 254, 270 (1964). As against the presumption of unfettered political speech, the argument for legal oversight of campaign finance incorporates the central features of arguments for regulatory oversight of markets generally. Viewing the political arena as a market for electoral gain implies a corresponding role for the state in preserving the openness of the market. By analogy to the role of antitrust regulation in commercial markets, the argument for regulation of campaign finance speaks to the dangers of monopoly concentration of power. Without some guarantee that competitors will be able to reach the consuming public, the argument runs, there is a danger that the political market will simply collapse. A second regulatory argument warns of the contamination of the political process not by the overbearing presence of a few political actors, but by the risk that such powerful market players may be able to extort special favors from vulnerable public officials. According to these arguments, campaign finance regulations preserve the functioning of an open political market either by limiting the concentration of economic power in the political arena, or by limiting the kinds of governmental decisions that concentrated economic power might induce.

2. *Equality*: Recall that in *Reynolds v. Sims*, the Court spoke of the Constitution as guaranteeing that "each citizen have an *equally effective* voice in the election of members of his ... legislature." 377 U.S. 533, 565 (1964)(emphasis added). While this guarantee of equality has not been fully elucidated in the one-person, one-vote arena, the same conception of effectiveness comes into play with campaign finances. An argument can be mounted that the post-*Baker/Reynolds* line of cases represents a democratic vision that would assure all citizens a meaningful, and indeed equal, chance to influence the political process. On this view, the regulation of the power of money is an indispensable part of the guarantee of meaningful equality in the

electoral arena, lest the concentration of wealth simply drown out alternative voices. Professor Ronald Dworkin thus argues that, "each citizen must have a fair and equal opportunity not only to hear the views of others, as these are published or broadcast, but to command attention for his own views, either as a candidate for office or as a member of a politically active group committed to some program or convictions." Ronald Dworkin, *The Curse of American Politics,* New York Review of Books, Oct. 17, 1996, at 23.

3. *Liberty*: This view champions freedom from state restriction on expressive activity in the political arena. Regulations, directed either at speech or the expenditure of funds, necessarily implicate the state in restricting access to those who desire additional participation in electoral activity. Advocates of limiting state regulation typically compare campaign contributions and expenditures to other forms of protected political speech in arguing for a general First Amendment skepticism toward governmental restraints.

A. REGULATING CONTRIBUTIONS AND EXPENDITURES

The legal regulation of campaign finance is dominated by the great analytic divide created by *Buckley v. Valeo,* 424 U.S. 1 (1976)(per curiam). In reviewing the 1974 reforms to FECA, *Buckley* defined the current approach to legal regulation of campaign finance. The 1974 amendments tried to curb the perceived deleterious impact of money on elections through a variety of restrictions. The amendments limited the amount of contributions that could be given in federal elections by individuals, political parties, or political action committees ("PACs"). The amendments also placed ceilings on total spending by candidates in federal elections and limited personal spending by candidates. In exchange, the 1974 amendments created the first system of public funding for presidential elections through the use of matching funds for primary candidates and general federal funding of the presidential election. Finally, the amendments created elaborate reporting and disclosure requirements for candidates to federal office. The entire regulatory structure was overseen by the Federal Election Commission, a federal agency comprised of six political appointees, no more than three from any one party, together with the House Clerk and Senate Secretary *ex officio*. In practice, the FEC has always been comprised of three Democrats and three Republicans.

Only part of the regulatory regime survived Supreme Court review. In a long and oftentimes rambling opinion, the Supreme Court tried to distinguish between First Amendment-protected political speech and permissible regulation by focusing on the form of campaign finance limitations. The Court openly acknowledged that all "contribution and expenditure limitations operate in an area of the most fundamental First

Amendment activities." 424 U.S. at 14. Moreover, "The First Amendment denies government the power to determine that spending to promote one's political views is wasteful, excessive, or unwise. In the free society ordained by our Constitution it is not the government, but the people individually as citizens and candidates and collectively as associations and political committees who must retain control over the quantity and range of debate on public issues in a political campaign." *Id.* at 55.

However, the Court found a basic First Amendment distinction between expenditures by candidates who sought to advocate their positions and promote their aspirations for office, on the one hand, and contributions by supporters of these candidates or political positions, on the other:

> A restriction on the amount of money a person or group can spend on political communication during a campaign necessarily reduces the quantity of expression by restricting the number of issues discussed, the depth of their exploration, and the size of the audience reached. This is because virtually every means of communicating ideas in today's mass society requires the expenditure of money. The distribution of the humblest handbill or leaflet entails printing, paper, and circulation costs. Speeches and rallies generally necessitate hiring a hall and publicizing the event. The electorate's increasing dependence on television, radio, and other mass media for news and information has made these expensive modes of communication indispensable instruments of effective political speech....
>
> By contrast with a limitation upon expenditures for political expression, a limitation upon the amount that any one person or group may contribute to a candidate or political committee entails only a marginal restriction upon the contributor's ability to engage in free communication. A contribution serves as a general expression of support for the candidate and his views, but does not communicate the underlying basis for the support. The quantity of communication by the contributor does not increase perceptibly with the size of his contribution, since the expression rests solely on the undifferentiated, symbolic act of contributing. At most, the size of the contribution provides a very rough index of the intensity of the contributor's support for the candidate. A limitation on the amount of money a person may give to a candidate or campaign organization thus involves little direct restraint on his political communication, for it permits the symbolic expression of support evidenced by a contribution but does not in any way infringe the contributor's freedom to discuss candidates and issues. While contributions may result in political expression if spent by a candidate or an association to present views to the voters, the transformation of contributions into political debate involves speech by someone other than the contributor. 424 U.S. at 19–21.

As a general matter, the Court has extended broad constitutional protection to all expenditures by candidates for office. Reasoning that this form of "money is speech," the Court has applied strict scrutiny to any regulatory efforts aimed at limiting the use of money to express the views or positions of candidates. On the other hand, the Court has generally allowed content-neutral restrictions on campaign contributions. Contributions, unlike expenditures, have been viewed as standing at one remove from political speech and have accordingly been subject to lesser standards of judicial scrutiny. The resulting patchwork of regulation is summarized as follows:

> We shall never know what kind of regulatory regime the FECA amendments of 1974 created because they were so drastically altered by the Supreme Court in *Buckley v. Valeo*. What was intended to be a closed system in which the major flows of money into and out of campaigns were fully controlled emerged as an open system of uncontrolled outlets when the Court struck down all limits on direct spending in the campaign by candidates, PACs, and individuals. A tightly constrained regulatory system became a more relaxed, open-ended one. The modifications in *Buckley* meant that the original 1974 plan would never have to meet its two severest tests: the administration of spending limits in hundreds of races and the accommodation of excess money in a system with no effective outlets. Instead, the crippled FECA affected chiefly the recruitment of money, ending the freedom of the fat cats and encouraging the development of PACs.

Frank J. Sorauf, Inside Campaign Finance 238 (1992). After *Buckley*, campaign finance regulation survived in a form that no legislature ever voted to create and, one may surmise, no legislature would ever have voted to create. Nonetheless, the contributions/expenditures divide inherited from *Buckley* continues to be the key to current campaign finance regulation.

Colorado Republican Federal Campaign Committee v. Federal Election Commission

116 S.Ct. 2309 (1996).

■ JUSTICE BREYER announced the judgment of the Court and delivered an opinion, in which JUSTICE O'CONNOR and JUSTICE SOUTER join.

In April 1986, before the Colorado Republican Party had selected its senatorial candidate for the fall's election, that Party's Federal Campaign Committee bought radio advertisements attacking Timothy Wirth, the Democratic Party's likely candidate. The Federal Election Commission (FEC) charged that this "expenditure" exceeded the dollar limits that a provision of the Federal Election Campaign Act of 1971 (FECA) imposes upon political party "expenditure[s] in connection with" a "general election campaign" for congressional office. 90 Stat. 486, as amended, 2 U.S.C. § 441a(d)(3). This case focuses upon the constitutionality of those limits as applied to this case. We conclude that the First Amendment prohibits the application of this provision to the kind of expenditure at issue here—an expenditure that the political party has made independently, without coordination with any candidate.

To understand the issues and our holding, one must begin with FECA as it emerged from Congress in 1974. That Act sought both to remedy the appearance of a "corrupt" political process (one in which large contributions seem to buy legislative votes) and to level the electoral playing field by reducing campaign costs. *See Buckley v. Valeo,* 424 U.S. 1, 25–27 (1976)(per curiam). It consequently imposed limits upon the amounts that individuals, corporations, "political committees" (such as political action committees, or PAC's), and political parties could contribute to candidates for federal office, and it also imposed limits upon the amounts that candidates, corporations, labor unions, political committees, and political parties could spend, even on their own, to help a candidate win election.

This Court subsequently examined several of the Act's provisions in light of the First Amendment's free speech and association protections.... Most of the provisions this Court found unconstitutional imposed expenditure limits. Those provisions limited candidates' rights to spend their own money, ... limited a candidate's campaign expenditures, ... limited the right of individuals to make "independent" expenditures (not coordinated with the candidate or candidate's campaign), ... and similarly limited the right of political committees to make "independent" expenditures.... The provisions that the Court found constitutional mostly imposed contribution limits—limits that apply both when an individual or political committee contributes money directly to a candidate and also when they indirectly contribute by making expenditures that they coordinate with the candidate, § 441a(a)(7)(B)(i).

Consequently, for present purposes, the Act now prohibits individuals and political committees from making direct, or indirect, contributions that exceed the following limits:

(a) For any "person": $1,000 to a candidate "with respect to any election"; $5,000 to any political committee in any year; $20,000 to the national committees of a political party in any year; but all within an overall limit (for any individual in any year) of $25,000. 2 U.S.C. §§ 441a(a)(1), (3).

(b) For any "multicandidate political committee": $5,000 to a candidate "with respect to any election"; $5,000 to any political committee in any year; and $15,000 to the national committees of a political party in any year. § 441a(a)(2).

FECA also has a special provision, directly at issue in this case, that governs contributions and expenditures by political parties. § 441a(d). This special provision creates, in part, an exception to the above contribution limits. That is, without special treatment, political parties ordinarily would be subject to the general limitation on contributions by a "multicandidate political committee" just described. See § 441a(a)(4). That provision, as we said in (b) above, limits annual contributions by a "multicandidate political committee" to no more than $5,000 to any candidate. And as also mentioned above, this contribution limit governs not only direct contributions but also indirect contributions that take the form of coordinated expenditures, defined as "expenditures made . . . in cooperation, consultation, or concert, with, or at the request or suggestion of, a candidate, his authorized political committees, or their agents." § 441a(a)(7)(B)(i). Thus, ordinarily, a party's coordinated expenditures would be subject to the $5,000 limitation.

However, FECA's special provision, which we shall call the "Party Expenditure Provision," creates a general exception from this contribution limitation, and from any other limitation on expenditures. It says:

> Notwithstanding any other provision of law with respect to limitations on expenditures or limitations on contributions, . . . political party [committees] . . . may make expenditures in connection with the general election campaign of candidates for Federal office. . . . § 441a(d)(1).

After exempting political parties from the general contribution and expenditure limitations of the statute, the Party Expenditure Provision then imposes a substitute limitation upon party "expenditures" in a senatorial campaign equal to the greater of $20,000 or "2 cents multiplied by the voting age population of the State," § 441a(d)(3)(A)(i), adjusted for inflation since 1974, § 441a(c). The Provision permitted a political party in Colorado in 1986 to spend about $103,000 in connection with the general election campaign of a candidate for the United States Senate. . . .

In January 1986, Timothy Wirth, then a Democratic Congressman, announced that he would run for an open Senate seat in November. In April, before either the Democratic primary or the Republican convention, the Colorado Republican Federal Campaign Committee (Colorado Party), the petitioner here, bought radio advertisements attacking Congressman Wirth. The State Democratic Party complained to the Federal Election Commission. It pointed out that the Colorado Party had previously assigned its $103,000 general election allotment to the National Republican Senatorial Committee, leaving it without any permissible spending balance. *See Federal Election Comm'n v. Democratic Senatorial Campaign Comm.*, 454 U.S. 27 (1981)(state party may appoint national senatorial campaign committee as agent to spend its Party Expenditure Provision allotment). It argued that the purchase of radio time was an "expenditure in connection with the general election campaign of a candidate for Federal office," § 441a(d)(3), which, consequently, exceeded the Party Expenditure Provision limits.

The FEC agreed with the Democratic Party....

II

The summary judgment record indicates that the expenditure in question is what this Court in *Buckley* called an "independent" expenditure, not a "coordinated" expenditure that other provisions of FECA treat as a kind of campaign "contribution".... So treated, the expenditure falls within the scope of the Court's precedents that extend First Amendment protection to independent expenditures. Beginning with *Buckley*, the Court's cases have found a "fundamental constitutional difference between money spent to advertise one's views independently of the candidate's campaign and money contributed to the candidate to be spent on his campaign." *Federal Election Commission v. National Conservative Political Action Comm.*, 470 U.S. 480, 497 (1985)("*NCPAC*"). This difference has been grounded in the observation that restrictions on contributions impose "only a marginal restriction upon the contributor's ability to engage in free communication," because the symbolic communicative value of a contribution bears little relation to its size ... and because such limits leave "persons free to engage in independent political expression, to associate actively through volunteering their services, and to assist to a limited but nonetheless substantial extent in supporting candidates and committees with financial resources." At the same time, reasonable contribution limits directly and materially advance the Government's interest in preventing exchanges of large financial contributions for political favors.

In contrast, the Court has said that restrictions on independent expenditures significantly impair the ability of individuals and groups to engage in direct political advocacy and "represent substantial ... restraints on the quantity and diversity of political speech." And at the same time, the Court has concluded that limitations on independent expenditures are less directly related to preventing corruption, since "[t]he absence of prearrangement and coordination of an expenditure with the candidate ... not only undermines the value of the expenditure to the candidate, but also alleviates the danger that expenditures will be given as a quid pro quo for improper commitments from the candidate."

Given these established principles, we do not see how a provision that limits a political party's independent expenditures can escape their controlling effect. A political party's independent expression not only reflects its members' views about the philosophical and governmental matters that bind them together, it also seeks to convince others to join those members in a practical democratic task, the task of creating a government that voters can instruct and hold responsible for subsequent success or failure. The independent expression of a political party's views is "core" First Amendment activity no less than is the independent expression of individuals, candidates, or other political committees.

We are not aware of any special dangers of corruption associated with political parties that tip the constitutional balance in a different direction. When this Court considered, and held unconstitutional, limits that FECA had set on certain independent expenditures by political action committees, it reiterated *Buckley*'s observation that "the absence of prearrangement and coordination" does not eliminate, but it does help to "alleviate," any "danger" that a candidate will understand the expenditure as an effort to obtain a "quid pro quo." The same is true of independent party expenditures.

We recognize that FECA permits individuals to contribute more money ($20,000) to a party than to a candidate ($1,000) or to other political committees ($5,000). 2 U.S.C. § 441a(a). We also recognize that FECA permits unregulated "soft money" contributions to a party for certain activities, such as electing candidates for state office, see § 431(8)(A)(i), or for voter registration and "get out the vote" drives, see § 431(8)(B)(xii). But the opportunity for corruption posed by these greater opportunities for contributions is, at best, attenuated. Unregulated "soft money" contributions may not be used to influence a federal campaign, except when used in the limited, party-building activities specifically designated in the statute. See § 431(8)(B). Any contribution to a party that is earmarked for a particular campaign, is considered a contribution to the candidate and is subject to the contribution limitations. § 441a(a)(8). A party may not simply channel unlimited amounts of even undesignated contributions to a candidate, since such direct transfers are also considered contributions and are subject to the contribution limits on a "multicandidate political committee." § 441a(a)(2). The greatest danger of corruption, therefore, appears to be from the ability of donors to give sums up to $20,000 to a party which may be used for independent party expenditures for the benefit of a particular candidate. We could understand how Congress, were it to conclude that the potential for evasion of the individual contribution limits was a serious matter, might decide to change the statute's limitations on contributions to political parties. But we do not believe that the risk of corruption present here could justify the "markedly greater burden on basic freedoms caused by" the statute's limitations on expenditures. Contributors seeking to avoid the effect of the $1,000 contribution limit indirectly by donations to the national party could spend that same amount of money (or more) themselves more directly by making their own independent expenditures promoting the candidate. If anything, an independent expenditure made possible by a $20,000 donation, but controlled and directed by a party rather than the donor, would seem less likely to corrupt than the same (or a much larger) independent expenditure made directly by that donor. In any case, the constitutionally significant fact, present equally in both instances, is the lack of coordination between the candidate and the source of the expenditure. This fact prevents us from assuming, absent convincing evidence to the contrary, that a limitation on political parties' independent expenditures is necessary to combat a substantial danger of corruption of the electoral system. . . .

We therefore believe that this Court's prior case law controls the outcome here. We do not see how a Constitution that grants to individuals, candidates, and ordinary political committees the right to make unlimited independent expenditures could deny the same right to political parties. Having concluded this, we need not consider the Party's further claim that the statute's "in connection with" language, and the FEC's interpretation of that language, are unconstitutionally vague.

III

The Government does not deny the force of the precedent we have discussed. Rather, it argued below, and the lower courts accepted, that the expenditure in this case should be treated under those precedents, not as an "independent expenditure," but rather as a "coordinated expenditure," which those cases have treated as "contributions," and which those cases have held Congress may constitutionally regulate.

While the District Court found that the expenditure in this case was "coordinated," it did not do so based on any factual finding that the Party had consulted with any candidate in the making or planning of the advertising campaign in question. Instead, the District Court accepted the Government's argument that all party expenditures should be treated as if they had been coordinated as a matter of law. . . . The question, instead, is whether the Court of Appeals erred as a legal matter in accepting the Government's conclusive presumption that all party expenditures are "coordinated." We believe it did.

* * *

■ JUSTICE THOMAS, concurring in the judgment and dissenting in part, with whom THE CHIEF JUSTICE and JUSTICE SCALIA join in Parts I and III.

* * *

II

* * *

A

[. . .] Contributions and expenditures both involve core First Amendment expression because they further the "[d]iscussion of public issues and debate on the qualifications of candidates . . . integral to the operation of the system of government established by our Constitution." When an individual donates money to a candidate or to a partisan organization, he enhances the donee's ability to communicate a message and thereby adds to political debate, just as when that individual communicates the message himself. Indeed, the individual may add more to political discourse by giving rather than spending, if the donee is able to put the funds to more productive use than can the individual.

[...] I can discern only one potentially meaningful distinction between contributions and expenditures. In the former case, the funds pass through an intermediary—some individual or entity responsible for organizing and facilitating the dissemination of the message—whereas in the latter case they may not necessarily do so. But the practical judgment by a citizen that another person or an organization can more effectively deploy funds for the good of a common cause than he can ought not deprive that citizen of his First Amendment rights. Whether an individual donates money to a candidate or group who will use it to promote the candidate or whether the individual spends the money to promote the candidate himself, the individual seeks to engage in political expression and to associate with likeminded persons. A contribution is simply an indirect expenditure; though contributions and expenditures may thus differ in form, they do not differ in substance. As one commentator cautioned, "let us not lose sight of the speech." L. Powe, *Mass Speech and the Newer First Amendment*, 1982 S.Ct. Rev. 243, 258....

The other justification in *Buckley* for the proposition that contribution caps only marginally restrict speech—that is, that a contribution signals only general support for the candidate but indicates nothing about the reasons for that support—is similarly unsatisfying. Assuming the assertion is descriptively accurate (which is certainly questionable), it still cannot mean that giving is less important than spending in terms of the First Amendment. A campaign poster that reads simply "We support candidate Smith" does not seem to me any less deserving of constitutional protection than one that reads "We support candidate Smith because we like his position on agriculture subsidies." Both express a political opinion. Even a pure message of support, unadorned with reasons, is valuable to the democratic process.

In sum, unlike the *Buckley* Court, I believe that contribution limits infringe as directly and as seriously upon freedom of political expression and association as do expenditure limits. The protections of the First Amendment do not depend upon so fine a line as that between spending money to support a candidate or group and giving money to the candidate or group to spend for the same purpose. In principle, people and groups give money to candidates and other groups for the same reason that they spend money in support of those candidates and groups: because they share social, economic, and political beliefs and seek to have those beliefs affect governmental policy. I think that the *Buckley* framework for analyzing the constitutionality of campaign finance laws is deeply flawed. Accordingly, I would not employ it, as Justice Breyer and Justice Kennedy do.

B

Instead, I begin with the premise that there is no constitutionally significant difference between campaign contributions and expenditures:

both forms of speech are central to the First Amendment. Curbs on protected speech, we have repeatedly said, must be strictly scrutinized....

The formula for strict scrutiny is, of course, well-established. It requires both a compelling governmental interest and legislative means narrowly tailored to serve that interest. In the context of campaign finance reform, the only governmental interest that we have accepted as compelling is the prevention of corruption or the appearance of corruption, and we have narrowly defined "corruption" as a "financial quid pro quo: dollars for political favors." As for the means-ends fit under strict scrutiny, we have specified that "[w]here at all possible, government must curtail speech only to the degree necessary to meet the particular problem at hand, and must avoid infringing on speech that does not pose the danger that has prompted regulation."

In *Buckley*, we expressly stated that the means adopted must be "closely drawn to avoid unnecessary abridgment" of First Amendment rights. But the *Buckley* Court summarily rejected the argument that, because less restrictive means of preventing corruption existed—for instance, bribery laws and disclosure requirements—FECA's contribution provisions were invalid....

Buckley's rationale for the contrary conclusion is faulty. That bribery laws are not completely effective in stamping out corruption is no justification for the conclusion that prophylactic controls on funding activity are narrowly tailored. The First Amendment limits Congress to legislative measures that do not abridge the Amendment's guaranteed freedoms, thereby constraining Congress' ability to accomplish certain goals. Similarly, that other modes of expression remain open to regulated individuals or groups does not mean that a statute is the least restrictive means of addressing a particular social problem. A statute could, of course, be more restrictive than necessary while still leaving open some avenues for speech.[9]

III

[...T]here is only a minimal threat of "corruption," as we have understood that term, when a political party spends to support its candidate or to oppose his competitor, whether or not that expenditure is made in concert with the candidate. Parties and candidates have traditionally worked together to achieve their common goals, and when they engage in that work, there is no risk to the Republic. To the contrary, the danger to

---

9. [...] There is good reason to think that campaign reform is an especially inappropriate area for judicial deference to legislative judgment. *See generally* L. BeVier, *Money and Politics: A Perspective on the First Amendment and Campaign Finance Reform*, 73 Cal. L. Rev. 1045, 1074–1081 (1985). What the argument for deference fails to acknowledge is the potential for legislators to set the rules of the electoral game so as to keep themselves in power and to keep potential challengers out of it.... Indeed, history demonstrates that the most significant effect of election reform has been not to purify public service, but to protect incumbents and increase the influence of special interest groups.

the Republic lies in Government suppression of such activity. Under *Buckley* and our subsequent cases, § 441a(d)(3)'s heavy burden on First Amendment rights is not justified by the threat of corruption at which it is assertedly aimed.

* * *

■ JUSTICE STEVENS, with whom JUSTICE GINSBURG joins, dissenting.

In my opinion, all money spent by a political party to secure the election of its candidate for the office of United States Senator should be considered a "contribution" to his or her campaign. I therefore disagree with the conclusion reached in Part III of the Court's opinion.

I am persuaded that three interests provide a constitutionally sufficient predicate for federal limits on spending by political parties. First, such limits serve the interest in avoiding both the appearance and the reality of a corrupt political process. A party shares a unique relationship with the candidate it sponsors because their political fates are inextricably linked. That interdependency creates a special danger that the party—or the persons who control the party—will abuse the influence it has over the candidate by virtue of its power to spend. The provisions at issue are appropriately aimed at reducing that threat. The fact that the party in this case had not yet chosen its nominee at the time it broadcast the challenged advertisements is immaterial to the analysis. Although the Democratic and Republican nominees for the 1996 Presidential race will not be selected until this summer, current advertising expenditures by the two national parties are no less contributions to the campaigns of the respective front-runners than those that will be made in the fall.

Second, these restrictions supplement other spending limitations embodied in the Act, which are likewise designed to prevent corruption. Individuals and certain organizations are permitted to contribute up to $1,000 to a candidate. 2 U.S.C. § 441a(a)(1)(A). Since the same donors can give up to $5,000 to party committees, § 441a(a)(1)(C), if there were no limits on party spending, their contributions could be spent to benefit the candidate and thereby circumvent the $1,000 cap. We have recognized the legitimate interest in blocking similar attempts to undermine the policies of the Act.

Finally, I believe the Government has an important interest in leveling the electoral playing field by constraining the cost of federal campaigns. As Justice White pointed out in his opinion in *Buckley,* "money is not always equivalent to or used for speech, even in the context of political campaigns." It is quite wrong to assume that the net effect of limits on contributions and expenditures—which tend to protect equal access to the political arena, to free candidates and their staffs from the interminable burden of fund-raising, and to diminish the importance of repetitive 30-second commercials—will be adverse to the interest in informed debate protected by the First Amendment.

Congress surely has both wisdom and experience in these matters that is far superior to ours. I would therefore accord special deference to its judgment on questions related to the extent and nature of limits on campaign spending.

* * *

■ [Opinion of JUSTICE KENNEDY, with whom THE CHIEF JUSTICE and JUSTICE SCALIA join, concurring in the judgment and dissenting in part, omitted.]

NOTES AND QUESTIONS

1. At the bottom of the Court's ongoing division over campaign finance regulation is the basic question posed twenty years ago by Judge J. Skelly Wright, "Is Money Speech?" J. Skelly Wright, *Politics and the Constitution: Is Money Speech?,* 85 Yale L.J. 1001 (1976). The Court in *Colorado Republican Committee* finds that the independent expenditures of a political party are "core" activities that reflect the party's views on matters of philosophy and government. How convincing is the distinction between such expenditures by a political party and the contributions of a committed partisan to further a campaign reflecting his or her views on matters of philosophy and government?

2. In earlier opinions, Justice White made two arguments about the attempt to cordon off contributions from expenditures for First Amendment purposes. First, he challenged the analytic category that draws expenditures within the concept of speech:

> The First Amendment protects the right to speak, not the right to spend, and limitations on the amount of money that can be spent are not the same as restrictions on speaking. I agree with the majority that the expenditures in this case "produce" core First Amendment speech. But that is precisely the point: they produce such speech; they are not speech itself. At least in these circumstances, I cannot accept the identification of speech with its antecedents. Such a house-that-Jack-built approach could equally be used to find a First Amendment right to a job or to a minimum wage to "produce" the money to "produce" the speech. *FEC v. Nat'l Conservative Political Action Comm.*, 470 U.S. 480, 508–09 (1985) (White, J. dissenting).

Second, Justice White challenged the administrability of the contributions/expenditures analytic scheme:

> Let us suppose that each of two brothers spends $1 million on TV spot announcements that he has individually prepared and in which he appears, urging the election of the same named candidate in identical words. One brother has sought and obtained the approval of the candidate; the other has not. The former may validly be prosecuted under § 608(e); under the Court's view, the

latter may not, even though the candidate could scarcely help knowing about and appreciating the expensive favor. For constitutional purposes it is difficult to see the difference between the two situations. I would take the word of those who know that limiting independent expenditures is essential to prevent transparent and widespread evasion of the contribution limits. *Buckley v. Valeo*, 424 U.S. 1, 261–62 (1976) (per curiam) (White, J., concurring in part and dissenting in part).

Insofar as a concern about corruption forms a major part of the Court's rationalization for upholding limits on contributions, is there any reason to believe a candidate will not be "just as beholden" to a supporter who purchases advertisements with private funds as one who contributes money to the candidate directly? Moreover, to the extent that donors may direct their contributions to party coffers that are, in turn, used to promote the party's candidate, does the knowledge by the candidate of such contributions not open the door to the same *quid pro quo* concerns that were used to uphold limits on contributions?

3. As applied, the contribution/expenditure distinction has faced rough sledding. In *California Medical Association v. Federal Election Commission*, 453 U.S. 182 (1981), the Court upheld a $5,000 contribution limit by individual and groups to PACs. The Court ran into difficulty with the argument that the California Medical Association would be free to expend as much money as it wished independently to promote its views, but faced restrictions only when it pooled its funds into a PAC for greater effectiveness. Only four members of the Court accepted that the fact of aggregating resources allowed for a contribution ceiling. Justice Blackmun provided the concurring fifth vote on the grounds that contributions have a greater capacity for corruption than do independent expenditures.

The Court's attempt to segregate contributions from expenditures broke down in *Citizens Against Rent Control v. City of Berkeley*, 454 U.S. 290, 299 (1981), in which a clear majority of the Court held unconstitutional a limitation of $250 on contributions to committees formed to support or oppose ballot measures submitted to popular vote:

> Apart from the impermissible restraint on freedom of association, but virtually inseparable from it in this context, § 602 imposes a significant restraint on the freedom of expression of groups and those individuals who wish to express their views through committees. As we have noted, an individual may make expenditures without limit under § 602 on a ballot measure but may not contribute beyond the $250 limit when joining with others to advocate common views. The contribution limit thus automatically affects expenditures, and limits on expenditures operate as a direct restraint on freedom of expression of a group or committee desiring to engage in political dialogue concerning a ballot measure.

Subsequently, in *Federal Election Commission v. National Conservative Political Action Committee*, 470 U.S. 480 (1985), the Court struck down provisions of the Presidential Election Campaign Fund Act that used criminal sanctions to prohibit PACs from contributing more than $1,000 to any presidential candidate who had accepted public campaign financing. The Court, per Justice Rehnquist, clearly indicated its frustration with the workability of the contributions/expenditures divide:

> The PACs in this case, of course, are not lone pamphleteers or street corner orators in the Tom Paine mold; they spend substantial amounts of money in order to communicate their political ideas through sophisticated media advertisements. And of course the criminal sanction in question is applied to the expenditure of money to propagate political views, rather than to the propagation of those views unaccompanied by the expenditure of money. But for purposes of presenting political views in connection with a nationwide Presidential election, allowing the presentation of views while forbidding the expenditure of more than $1,000 to present them is much like allowing a speaker in a public hall to express his views while denying him the use of an amplifying system.

4. *Colorado Republican Committee* shows the tremendous tension created by the incomplete regulatory regime inherited from FECA, but significantly reduced by *Buckley*. The purpose behind the 1974 Amendments to FECA was to limit the overall impact of money on political campaigns. As the Act survived Court review, however, the combination of unrestricted expenditures and constrained contributions placed more pressure than ever on ingenious systems of fund-raising that did not run afoul of the Act. This pressure on "creative" fund-raising increased as a result of the introduction of public financing that attempted to condition the receipt of public funds on voluntary limitations on expenditures. In *Buckley,* the Supreme Court approved this regulatory device: "Congress may engage in public financing of election campaigns and may condition acceptance of public funds on an agreement by the candidate to abide by specified expenditure limitations. Just as a candidate may voluntarily limit the size of the contributions he chooses to accept, he may decide to forgo private fundraising and accept public funding." *Colorado Republican Committee* reflects the determined efforts of major parties to circumvent both contribution limitations and conditions for the receipt of public funding by shifting an increased level of fundraising and campaign direction to nominally independent political parties. Whereas the candidate-controlled and more tightly regulated contributions and expenditures are referred to as "hard money," the funds spent by the parties are termed "soft money." Among the reasons for the emergence of soft money is the FECA restriction on corporations and unions making direct financial contributions. These groups can circumvent FECA by donating exempted soft money in the form of "get out the vote drives," volunteer travel expenses, consulting, polls, "ordinary course of business loans," and office construction expenses. As reflected in Table 1, the emerging strategy of shifting campaign activities to the uncontrolled arena has occasioned an explosion in the use of "soft money" between the 1992 and 1996 election cycles:

Table 1

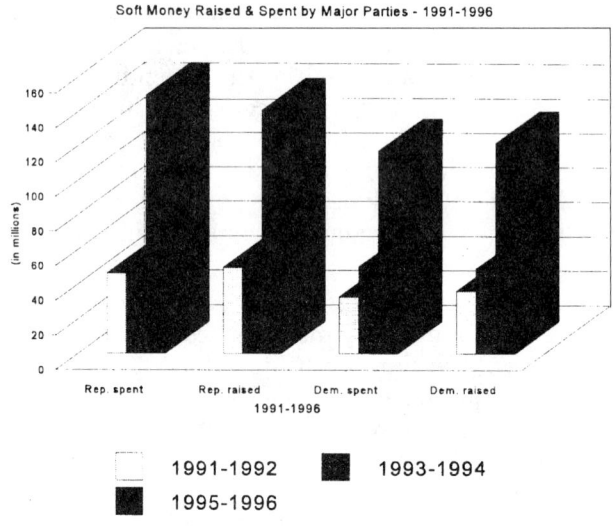

Source: Federal Election Commission

Does the distinction between "hard money" and "soft money" make sense? Is there a meaningful distinction in the risk of corruption posed by hard money as opposed to soft money contributions?

B. Do Concerns Over Corruption Justify Campaign Finance Regulation?

After *Buckley*, it appeared that the sole legitimate government interest in regulating campaign finance lay in removing the temptation for corruption. If so, could any governmental restriction on expenditures or contributions survive First Amendment scrutiny in referenda or initiatives? In such elections, the salient feature is that the decision is one of policy and not of candidate preference. Accordingly, there is no direct beneficiary of contributions who can provide some form of illicit *quid pro quo* service to the campaign contributor.

First National Bank of Boston v. Bellotti

435 U.S. 765 (1978).

■ Mr. Justice Powell delivered the opinion of the Court.

* * *

The statute at issue, Mass. Gen. Laws Ann., ch. 55, § 8 (West Supp. 1977), prohibits appellants, two national banking associations and three business corporations, from making contributions or expenditures "for the purpose of . . . influencing or affecting the vote on any question submitted to the voters, other than one materially affecting any of the property, business or assets of the corporation." The statute further specifies that "[n]o question submitted to the voters solely concerning the taxation of the income, property or transactions of individuals shall be deemed materially to affect the property, business or assets of the corporation." A corporation that violates § 8 may receive a maximum fine of $50,000; a corporate officer, director, or agent who violates the section may receive a maximum fine of $10,000 or imprisonment for up to one year, or both.

Appellants wanted to spend money to publicize their views on a proposed constitutional amendment that was to be submitted to the voters as a ballot question at a general election on November 2, 1976. The amendment would have permitted the legislature to impose a graduated tax on the income of individuals. After appellee, the Attorney General of Massachusetts, informed appellants that he intended to enforce § 8 against them, they brought this action seeking to have the statute declared unconstitutional. . . .

Appellants argued that § 8 violates the First Amendment, the Due Process and Equal Protection Clauses of the Fourteenth Amendment, and similar provisions of the Massachusetts Constitution. They prayed that the statute be declared unconstitutional on its face and as it would be applied to their proposed expenditures. The parties' statement of agreed facts reflected their disagreement as to the effect that the adoption of a personal income tax would have on appellants' business; it noted that "[t]here is a division of opinion among economists as to whether and to what extent a graduated income tax imposed solely on individuals would affect the business and assets of corporations." Appellee did not dispute that appellants' management believed that the tax would have a significant effect on their businesses.

* * *

III

The court below framed the principal question in this case as whether and to what extent corporations have First Amendment rights. We believe that the court posed the wrong question. The Constitution often protects interests broader than those of the party seeking their vindication. The First Amendment, in particular, serves significant societal interests. The proper question therefore is not whether corporations "have" First Amendment rights and, if so, whether they are coextensive with those of natural persons. Instead, the question must be whether § 8 abridges expression that the First Amendment was meant to protect. We hold that it does.

A

The speech proposed by appellants is at the heart of the First Amendment's protection.

> "The freedom of speech and of the press guaranteed by the Constitution embraces at the least the liberty to discuss publicly and truthfully all matters of public concern without previous restraint or fear of subsequent punishment.... Freedom of discussion, if it would fulfill its historic function in this nation, must embrace all issues about which information is needed or appropriate to enable the members of society to cope with the exigencies of their period." *Thornhill v. Alabama*, 310 U.S. 88, 101–102 (1940).

The referendum issue that appellants wish to address falls squarely within this description. In appellants' view, the enactment of a graduated personal income tax, as proposed to be authorized by constitutional amendment, would have a seriously adverse effect on the economy of the State. The importance of the referendum issue to the people and government of Massachusetts is not disputed. Its merits, however, are the subject of sharp disagreement.

As the Court said in *Mills v. Alabama*, 384 U.S. 214, 218 (1966), "there is practically universal agreement that a major purpose of [the First] Amendment was to protect the free discussion of governmental affairs." If the speakers here were not corporations, no one would suggest that the State could silence their proposed speech. It is the type of speech indispensable to decisionmaking in a democracy, and this is no less true because the speech comes from a corporation rather than an individual. The inherent worth of the speech in terms of its capacity for informing the public does not depend upon the identity of its source, whether corporation, association, union, or individual.

The court below nevertheless held that corporate speech is protected by the First Amendment only when it pertains directly to the corporation's business interests. In deciding whether this novel and restrictive gloss on the First Amendment comports with the Constitution and the precedents of this Court, we need not survey the outer boundaries of the Amendment's protection of corporate speech, or address the abstract question whether corporations have the full measure of rights that individuals enjoy under the First Amendment. The question in this case, simply put, is whether the corporate identity of the speaker deprives this proposed speech of what otherwise would be its clear entitlement to protection. We turn now to that question....

B

[... A]ppellee suggests that First Amendment rights generally have been afforded only to corporations engaged in the communications business or through which individuals express themselves, and the court below apparently accepted the "materially affecting" theory as the conceptual common denominator between appellee's position and the precedents of this Court. It is true that the "materially affecting" requirement would have been satisfied in the Court's decisions affording protection to the speech of media corporations and corporations otherwise in the business of communication or entertainment, and to the commercial speech of business corporations. In such cases, the speech would be connected to the corporation's business almost by definition. But the effect on the business of the corporation was not the governing rationale in any of these decisions. None of them mentions, let alone attributes significance to, the fact that the subject of the challenged communication materially affected the corporation's business.

The press cases emphasize the special and constitutionally recognized role of that institution in informing and educating the public, offering criticism, and providing a forum for discussion and debate.... But the press does not have a monopoly on either the First Amendment or the ability to enlighten.... Similarly, the Court's decisions involving corporations in the business of communication or entertainment are based not only on the role of the First Amendment in fostering individual self-expression but also on its role in affording the public access to discussion, debate, and the dissemination of information and ideas.... Even decisions seemingly based exclusively on the individual's right to express himself acknowledge that the expression may contribute to society's edification....

Nor do our recent commercial speech cases lend support to appellee's business interest theory. They illustrate that the First Amendment goes beyond protection of the press and the self-expression of individuals to prohibit government from limiting the stock of information from which members of the public may draw. A commercial advertisement is constitutionally protected not so much because it pertains to the seller's business as because it furthers the societal interest in the "free flow of commercial information." *Virginia State Bd. of Pharmacy v. Virginia Citizens Consumer Council, Inc.,* 425 U.S. 748, 764 (1976)....

C

We thus find no support in the First or Fourteenth Amendment, or in the decisions of this Court, for the proposition that speech that otherwise would be within the protection of the First Amendment loses that protection simply because its source is a corporation that cannot prove, to the satisfaction of a court, a material effect on its business or property. The "materially affecting" requirement is not an identification of the boundaries of corporate speech etched by the Constitution itself. Rather, it amounts to an impermissible legislative prohibition of speech based on the identity of the interests that spokesmen may represent in public debate over controversial issues and a requirement that the speaker have a sufficiently great interest in the subject to justify communication.

Section 8 permits a corporation to communicate to the public its views on certain referendum subjects—those materially affecting its business—but not others. It also singles out one kind of ballot question—individual taxation—as a subject about which corporations may never make their ideas public. The legislature has drawn the line between permissible and impermissible speech according to whether there is a sufficient nexus, as defined by the legislature, between the issue presented to the voters and the business interests of the speaker.

In the realm of protected speech, the legislature is constitutionally disqualified from dictating the subjects about which persons may speak and the speakers who may address a public issue.... If a legislature may direct business corporations to "stick to business," it also may limit other corporations—religious, charitable, or civic—to their respective "business" when addressing the public. Such power in government to channel the expression of views is unacceptable under the First Amendment. Especially where, as here, the legislature's suppression of speech suggests an attempt to give one side of a debatable public question an advantage in expressing its views to the people, the First Amendment is plainly offended. Yet the State contends that its action is necessitated by governmental interests of the highest order. We next consider these asserted interests.

IV

The constitutionality of § 8's prohibition of the "exposition of ideas" by corporations turns on whether it can survive the exacting scrutiny necessitated by a state-imposed restriction of freedom of speech. Especially where, as here, a prohibition is directed at speech itself, and the speech is intimately related to the process of governing, "the State may prevail only upon showing a subordinating interest which is compelling," *Bates v. City of Little Rock,* 361 U.S. 516, 524 (1960).

[...] Appellee nevertheless advances two principal justifications for the prohibition of corporate speech. The first is the State's interest in sustaining the active role of the individual citizen in the electoral process and thereby preventing diminution of the citizen's confidence in government. The second is the interest in protecting the rights of shareholders whose views differ from those expressed by management on behalf of the corporation. However weighty these interests may be in the context of partisan candidate elections, they either are not implicated in this case or are not served at all, or in other than a random manner, by the prohibition in § 8.

A

* * *

Appellee advances a number of arguments in support of his view that these interests are endangered by corporate participation in discussion of a referendum issue. They hinge upon the assumption that such participation would exert an undue influence on the outcome of a referendum vote, and—in the end—destroy the confidence of the people in the democratic process and the integrity of government. According to appellee, corporations are wealthy and powerful and their views may drown out other points of view. If appellee's arguments were supported by record or legislative findings that corporate advocacy threatened imminently to undermine democratic processes, thereby denigrating rather than serving First Amendment interests, these arguments would merit our consideration.... But there has been no showing that the relative voice of corporations has been overwhelming or even significant in influencing referenda in Massachusetts, or that there has been any threat to the confidence of the citizenry in government....

Nor are appellee's arguments inherently persuasive or supported by the precedents of this Court. Referenda are held on issues, not candidates for public office. The risk of corruption perceived in cases involving candidate elections ... simply is not present in a popular vote on a public issue. To be sure, corporate advertising may influence the outcome of the vote; this would be its purpose. But the fact that advocacy may persuade the electorate is hardly a reason to suppress it: The Constitution "protects expression which is eloquent no less than that which is unconvincing." *Kingsley Int'l Pictures Corp. v. Regents,* 360 U.S. 684, 689 (1959). We noted only recently that "the concept that government may restrict the speech of some elements of our society in order to enhance the relative voice of others is wholly foreign to the First Amendment...." *Buckley,* 424 U.S. at 48–49. Moreover, the people in our democracy are entrusted with the responsibility for judging and evaluating the relative merits of conflicting arguments. They may consider, in making their judgment, the source and credibility of the advocate. But if there be any danger that the people cannot evaluate the information and arguments advanced by appellants, it is a danger contemplated by the Framers of the First Amendment.... In sum, "[a] restriction so destructive of the right of public discussion [as § 8], without greater or more imminent danger to the public interest than existed in this case, is incompatible with the freedoms secured by the First Amendment."

B

Finally, appellee argues that § 8 protects corporate shareholders, an interest that is both legitimate and traditionally within the province of state law.... The statute is said to serve this interest by preventing the use of corporate resources in furtherance of views with which some shareholders may disagree. This purpose is belied, however, by the provisions of the statute, which are both underinclusive and overinclusive.

The underinclusiveness of the statute is self-evident. Corporate expenditures with respect to a referendum are prohibited, while corporate activity with respect to the passage or defeat of legislation is permitted, even though corporations may engage in lobbying more often than they take positions on ballot questions submitted to the voters. Nor does § 8 prohibit a corporation from expressing its views, by the expenditure of corporate funds, on any public issue until it becomes the subject of a referendum, though the displeasure of disapproving shareholders is unlikely to be any less.

The fact that a particular kind of ballot question has been singled out for special treatment undermines the likelihood of a genuine state interest in protecting shareholders. It suggests instead that the legislature may have been concerned with silencing corporations on a particular subject. Indeed, appellee has conceded that "the legislative and judicial history of the statute indicates ... that the second crime was 'tailor-made' to prohibit corporate campaign contributions to oppose a graduated income tax amendment."

Nor is the fact that § 8 is limited to banks and business corporations without relevance. Excluded from its provisions and criminal sanctions are entities or organized groups in which numbers of persons may hold an interest or membership, and which often have resources comparable to those of large corporations. Minorities in such groups or entities may have interests with respect to institutional speech quite comparable to those of minority shareholders in a corporation. Thus the exclusion of Massachusetts business trusts, real estate investment trusts, labor unions, and other associations undermines the plausibility of the State's purported concern for the persons who happen to be shareholders in the banks and corporations covered by § 8.

The overinclusiveness of the statute is demonstrated by the fact that § 8 would prohibit a corporation from supporting or opposing a referendum proposal even if its shareholders unanimously authorized the contribution or expenditure. Ultimately shareholders may decide, through the procedures of corporate democracy, whether their corporation should engage in debate on public issues. Acting through their power to elect the board of directors or to insist upon protective provisions in the corporation's charter, shareholders normally are presumed competent to protect their own interests. In addition to intracorporate remedies, minority shareholders generally have access to the judicial remedy of a derivative suit to challenge corporate disbursements alleged to have been made for improper corporate purposes or merely to further the personal interests of management....

V

Because that portion of § 8 challenged by appellants prohibits protected speech in a manner unjustified by a compelling state interest, it must be invalidated. The judgment of the Supreme Judicial Court is Reversed.

■ [Concurring opinion of CHIEF JUSTICE BURGER omitted.]

■ MR. JUSTICE WHITE, with whom MR. JUSTICE BRENNAN and MR. JUSTICE MARSHALL join, dissenting.

The Massachusetts statute challenged here forbids the use of corporate funds to publish views about referenda issues having no material effect on the business, property, or assets of the corporation. The legislative judgment that the personal income tax issue, which is the subject of the referendum out of which this case arose, has no such effect was sustained by the Supreme Judicial Court of Massachusetts and is not disapproved by this Court today. Hence, as this case comes to us, the issue is whether a State may prevent corporate management from using the corporate treasury to propagate views having no connection with the corporate business. The Court commendably enough squarely faces the issue but unfortunately errs in deciding it. The Court invalidates the Massachusetts statute and holds that the First Amendment guarantees corporate managers the right to use not only their personal funds, but also those of the corporation, to circulate fact and opinion irrelevant to the business placed in their charge and necessarily representing their own personal or collective views about political and social questions. I do not suggest for a moment that the First Amendment requires a State to forbid such use of corporate funds, but I do strongly disagree that the First Amendment forbids state interference with managerial decisions of this kind.

By holding that Massachusetts may not prohibit corporate expenditures or contributions made in connection with referenda involving issues having no material connection with the corporate business, the Court not only invalidates a statute which has been on the books in one form or another for many years, but also casts considerable doubt upon the constitutionality of legislation passed by some 31 States restricting corporate political activity, as well as upon the Federal Corrupt Practices Act, 2 U.S.C. § 441b. The Court's fundamental error is its failure to realize that the state regulatory interests in terms of which the alleged curtailment of First Amendment rights accomplished by the statute must be evaluated are themselves derived from the First Amendment. The question posed by this case, as approached by the Court, is whether the State has struck the best possible balance, i.e., the one which it would have chosen, between competing First Amendment interests. Although in my view the choice made by the State would survive even the most exacting scrutiny, perhaps a rational argument might be made to the contrary. What is inexplicable, is for the Court to substitute its judgment as to the proper balance for that of Massachusetts where the State has passed legislation reasonably designed to further First Amendment interests in the context of the political arena where the expertise of legislators is at its peak and that of judges is at its very lowest. Moreover, the result reached today in critical respects marks a drastic departure from the Court's prior decisions which have protected against governmental infringement of the very First Amendment interests which the Court now deems inadequate to justify the Massachusetts statute.

I

[...] The self-expression of the communicator is not the only value encompassed by the First Amendment. One of its functions, often referred to as the right to hear or receive information, is to protect the interchange of ideas. Any communication of ideas, and consequently any expenditure of funds which makes the communication of ideas possible, it can be argued, furthers the purposes of the First Amendment. This proposition does not establish, however, that the right of the general public to receive communications financed by means of corporate expenditures is of the same dimension as that to hear other forms of expression. In the first place, as discussed *supra*, corporate expenditures designed to further political causes lack the connection with individual self-expression which is one of the principal justifications for the constitutional protection of speech provided by the First Amendment. Ideas which are not a product of individual choice are entitled to less First Amendment protection. Secondly, the restriction of corporate speech concerned with political matters impinges much less severely upon the availability of ideas to the general public than do restrictions upon individual speech. Even the complete curtailment of corporate communications concerning political or ideological questions not integral to day-to-day business functions would leave individuals, including corporate shareholders, employees, and customers, free to communicate their thoughts. Moreover, it is unlikely that any significant communication would be lost by such a prohibition. These individuals would remain perfectly free to communicate any ideas which could be conveyed by means of the corporate form. Indeed, such individuals could even form associations for the very purpose of promoting political or ideological causes....

The governmental interest in regulating corporate political communications, especially those relating to electoral matters, also raises considerations which differ significantly from those governing the regulation of individual speech. Corporations are artificial entities created by law for the purpose of furthering certain economic goals. In order to facilitate the achievement of such ends, special rules relating to such matters as limited liability, perpetual life, and the accumulation, distribution, and taxation of assets are normally applied to them. States have provided corporations with such attributes in order to increase their economic viability and thus strengthen the economy generally. It has long been recognized however, that the special status of corporations has placed them in a position to control vast amounts of economic power which may, if not regulated, dominate not only the economy but also the very heart of our democracy, the electoral process. Although *Buckley v. Valeo* provides support for the position that the desire to equalize the financial resources available to candidates does not justify the limitation upon the expression of support which a restriction upon individual contributions entails, the interest of Massachusetts and the many other States which have restricted corporate political activity is quite different. It is not one of equalizing the resources of opposing candidates or opposing positions, but rather of preventing institutions which have been permitted to amass wealth as a result of special advantages extended by the State for certain economic purposes from using that wealth to acquire an unfair advantage in the political process, especially where, as here, the issue involved has no material connection with the business of the corporation. The State need not permit its own creation to consume it. Massachusetts could permissibly conclude that not to impose limits upon the political activities of corporations would have placed it in a position of departing from neutrality and indirectly assisting the propagation of corporate views because of the advantages its laws give to the corporate acquisition of funds to finance such activities. Such expenditures may be viewed as seriously threatening the role of the First Amendment as a guarantor of a free marketplace of ideas. Ordinarily, the expenditure of funds to promote political causes may be assumed to bear some relation to the fervency with which they are held. Corporate political expression, however, is not only divorced from the convictions of individual corporate shareholders, but also, because of the ease with which corporations are permitted to accumulate capital, bears no relation to the conviction with which the ideas expressed are held by the communicator.

The Court's opinion appears to recognize at least the possibility that fear of corporate domination of the electoral process would justify restrictions upon corporate expenditures and contributions in connection with referenda but brushes this interest aside by asserting that "there has been no showing that the relative voice of corporations has been overwhelming or even significant in influencing referenda in Massachusetts," and by suggesting that the statute in issue represents an attempt to give an unfair advantage to those who hold views in opposition to positions which would otherwise be financed by corporations. It fails even to allude to the fact, however, that Massachusetts' most recent experience with unrestrained corporate expenditures in connection with ballot questions establishes precisely the contrary. In 1972, a proposed amendment to the Massachusetts Constitution which would have authorized the imposition of a graduated income tax on both individuals and corporations was put to the voters. The Committee for Jobs and Government Economy, an organized political committee, raised and expended approximately $120,000 to oppose the proposed amendment, the bulk of it raised through large corporate contributions. Three of the present appellant corporations each contributed $3,000 to this committee. In contrast, the Coalition for Tax Reform, Inc., the only political committee organized to support the 1972 amendment, was able to raise and expend only approximately $7,000. Perhaps these figures reflect the Court's view of the appropriate role which corporations should play in the Massachusetts electoral process, but it nowhere explains why it is entitled to substitute its judgment for that of Massachusetts and other States, as well as the United States, which have acted to correct or prevent similar domination of the electoral process by corporate wealth....

II

[...] In my view, the interests in protecting a system of freedom of expression, set forth *supra*, are sufficient to justify any incremental curtailment in the volume of expression which the Massachusetts statute might produce. I would hold that apart from corporate activities ... which are integrally related to corporate business operations, a State may prohibit corporate expenditures for political or ideological purposes. There can be no doubt that corporate expenditures in connection with referenda immaterial to corporate business affairs fall clearly into the category of corporate activities which may be barred. The electoral process, of course, is the essence of our democracy. It is an arena in which the public interest in preventing corporate domination and the coerced support by shareholders of causes with which they disagree is at its strongest and any claim that corporate expenditures are integral to the economic functioning of the corporation is at its weakest.

I would affirm the judgment of the Supreme Judicial Court for the Commonwealth of Massachusetts.

■ Mr. Justice Rehnquist, dissenting.

[...] The question presented today, whether business corporations have a constitutionally protected liberty to engage in political activities, has never been squarely addressed by any previous decision of this Court. However, the General Court of the Commonwealth of Massachusetts, the Congress of the United States, and the legislatures of 30 other States of this Republic have considered the matter, and have concluded that restrictions upon the political activity of business corporations are both politically desirable and constitutionally permissible. The judgment of such a broad consensus of governmental bodies expressed over a period of many decades is entitled to considerable deference from this Court....

There can be little doubt that when a State creates a corporation with the power to acquire and utilize property, it necessarily and implicitly guarantees that the corporation will not be deprived of that property absent due process of law. Likewise, when a State charters a corporation for the purpose of publishing a newspaper, it necessarily assumes that the corporation is entitled to the liberty of the press essential to the conduct of its business. . . .

It cannot be so readily concluded that the right of political expression is equally necessary to carry out the functions of a corporation organized for commercial purposes. A State grants to a business corporation the blessings of potentially perpetual life and limited liability to enhance its efficiency as an economic entity. It might reasonably be concluded that those properties, so beneficial in the economic sphere, pose special dangers in the political sphere. Furthermore, it might be argued that liberties of political expression are not at all necessary to effectuate the purposes for which States permit commercial corporations to exist. So long as the Judicial Branches of the State and Federal Governments remain open to protect the corporation's interest in its property, it has no need, though it may have the desire, to petition the political branches for similar protection. Indeed, the States might reasonably fear that the corporation would use its economic power to obtain further benefits beyond those already bestowed. I would think that any particular form of organization upon which the State confers special privileges or immunities different from those of natural persons would be subject to like regulation, whether the organization is a labor union, a partnership, a trade association, or a corporation. . . .

It is true, as the Court points out, that recent decisions of this Court have emphasized the interest of the public in receiving the information offered by the speaker seeking protection. The free flow of information is in no way diminished by the Commonwealth's decision to permit the operation of business corporations with limited rights of political expression. All natural persons, who owe their existence to a higher sovereign than the Commonwealth, remain as free as before to engage in political activity. . . .

I would affirm the judgment of the Supreme Judicial Court.

NOTES AND QUESTIONS

1. The Supreme Court strikes down the Massachusetts restriction on corporate speech, in part, because of the absence of clear legislative findings that corporate advocacy threatened the functioning of the democratic process. Given the Court's staunch hostility to the legislature trying to give one side of a debate any electoral advantage, what would a legislative record that could satisfy the Court's scrutiny look like?

2. Should the prospect of corruption be the sole concern of campaign regulation—or even a concern at all? If corruption is "understood as implicit exchanges of campaign contributions for official actions," it is not clear that this should be a rationale for campaign finance reform. *See* David A. Strauss, *Corruption, Equality, and Campaign Finance Reform*, 94 Colum. L. Rev. 1369, 1389 (1994). Rather, Professor Strauss argues, campaign contributions are a way of cementing the bond between elected representatives and their constituents. If responsiveness to the interests of constituents is one mark of effective representation, then the difference between contributions and promise of votes in the future begins to blur. Strauss then argues that the real issue is a concern that certain groups have greater influence because of their greater wealth, a rationale for campaign finance regulation that is distinct from the narrower claim of corruption that the *Buckley* Court endorsed. *See also* Bruce E. Cain, *Moralism and Realism in Campaign Finance Reform*, 1995 U. Chi. Legal F. 111, 112 ("The core problem in campaign finance is not corruption in the traditional sense. Rather, it is how far equity considerations can and should be carried in a democracy").

3. Closely related to regulating the funding of political campaigns is the question of regulating the content of what candidates for office may say. The Court's concern for corruption does not carefully distinguish between the trade-off of legislative action for campaign money and the perhaps equally problematic trade-off of legislative action for votes during the campaign. In *Brown v. Hartlage,* 456 U.S. 45 (1982), the Court struck down the Kentucky Corrupt Practices Act, which prohibited candidates from making an "expenditure, loan, promise, agreement, or contract as to action when elected, in consideration for a vote." In the context of a pledge of performance once in office, the Court ruled, "so long as the hoped for personal benefit is to be achieved through the normal processes of government, and not through some private arrangement, it has always been, and remains, a reputable basis upon which to cast one's ballot." *Id.* at 57. Under this rationale, should campaign contributions given in support of open public promises of anticipated legislative action be constitutionally protected? For the argument that actual promises made to voters during campaigns should be legally enforceable, see Note, *Read My Lips: Examining False Campaign Promises*, 90 Mich.L.Rev. 428 (1991). On the question of vote buying, see Pamela S. Karlan, *Not By Money But By Virtue Won? Vote Trafficking and the Voting Rights System*, 80 Va.L.Rev. 1455 (1994).

4. To what extent should the Court consider the effects that financial pressures have on the quality of governance, as opposed to the election process? Currently, an incumbent Senator raises, on average, more than $4 million in a six-year term, or more than $12,000 per week over the six-year election cycle. Kenneth J. Levit, *Campaign Finance Reform and the Return of Buckley v. Valeo,* 103 Yale L.J. 469 (1993). As reported by former congressman Bob Edgar, "Eighty percent of my time, 80 percent of my staff's time, 80 percent of my events and meetings were fundraisers. Rather than go to a senior center, I would go to a party where I could raise $3,000 or $4,000." *Quoted in*, Phillip M. Stern, Still the Best Congress Money Can

Buy 119 (1992). Professor Vincent Blasi argues that "certain forms of campaign finance legislation can be justified, even against First Amendment challenge, by resort to the constitutionally ordained value of representation." Could legislative findings that the time of elected representatives is being redirected to endless fund raising satisfy the Supreme Court's invitation for actual evidence "that corporate advocacy threatened imminently to undermine democratic processes"? Consider the form of regulation that would follow from the argument put forward by Professor Blasi as an alternative to the narrow focus on anti-corruption:

> If candidate time protection is the objective, the principal regulatory measure must be a limit on the overall amount of money that can be spent in an election campaign. From this perspective, it is a matter of secondary importance what restrictions are placed on the size of contributions to candidates, parties, and political action committees; on the sources of funds collected by candidates; and on independent expenditures in support of candidates. Even the availability of public financing of some election expenses, or of a voucher system designed to equalize the opportunity to contribute, pales in significance compared to the need to limit overall spending. Candidates facing or fearing tight racers will be preoccupied with fund-raising (or voucher raising) under any system that does not restrict total spending. If candidates are permitted to spend vast amounts of money in pursuit of votes, they will inevitably spend vast amounts of time in pursuit of money. Spending limits are the sine qua non of candidate time protection.
>
> The centrality of candidate spending limits was not so apparent when Congress passed its major campaign finance reforms in 1971 and 1974, nor when the Supreme Court in 1976 held several provisions of that legislation unconstitutional, including the mandatory ceilings on overall campaign spending by congressional candidates. At that time, what has come to be known as the war chest mentality had not yet seized the Congress.... One indication of how dramatically the war chest mentality has altered the regulatory landscape is the fact, startling in retrospect, that the Supreme Court in *Buckley* never considered how spending limits might be justified as a means of preventing candidates from spending excessive amounts of time on fund-raising. In 1976, candidate time protection was not seen as a major objective of campaign finance reform. Corruption, disproportionate influence, the fencing out of impecunious candidates, and the alienation of the electorate were the dominant concerns....

Vincent Blasi, *Free Speech and the Widening Gyre of Fund–Raising: Why Campaign Spending Limits May Not Violation the First Amendment After All*, 94 Colum. L. Rev. 1281, 1283 (1994). Is Professor Blasi correct in asserting that absent restrictions on expenditures, there can be no effective campaign finance regulation?

5. Justice White's dissents from the post-*Buckley* line of cases raise a separate issue concerning who should decide whether the structure of campaign financing threatens harm to the electoral process. The Court's decisions establish that campaign regulations potentially infringe upon critical First Amendment rights and must accordingly be subject to strict scrutiny. This in turn requires that governmental regulations be justified both by a compelling state interest and by a narrow tailoring to limit the scope of potential First Amendment impact. Repeatedly, Justice White questions the capacity of the Court to second-guess Congress and state legislatures in determining both the extent of the compelling state interest and the precision of the fit between regulation and the state concern. For Justice White, beginning with *Buckley*, a critical issue is whether courts should defer to the superior fact-gathering abilities of legislatures in this arena:

> Despite its seeming struggle with the standard by which to judge this case, this is essentially the question the Court asks and answers in the affirmative with respect to the limitations on contributions which individuals and political committees are permitted to make to federal candidates. In the interest of preventing undue influence that large contributors would have or that the public might think they would have, the Court upholds the provision that an individual may not give to a candidate, or spend on his behalf if requested or authorized by the candidate to do so, more than $1,000 in any one election. This limitation is valid although it imposes a low ceiling on what individuals may deem to be their most effective means of supporting or speaking on behalf of the candidate, i.e., financial support given directly to the candidate. The Court thus accepts the congressional judgment that the evils of unlimited contributions are sufficiently threatening to warrant restriction regardless of the impact of the limits on the contributor's opportunity for effective speech and in turn on the total volume of the candidate's political communications by reason of his inability to accept large sums from those willing to give.
>
> The congressional judgment, which I would also accept, was that other steps must be taken to counter the corrosive effects of money in federal election campaigns. One of these steps is § 608(e), which, aside from those funds that are given to the candidate or spent at his request or with his approval or cooperation limits what a contributor may independently spend in support or denigration of one running for federal office. Congress was plainly of the view that these expenditures also have corruptive potential; but the Court strikes down the provision, strangely enough claiming more insight as to what may improperly influence

candidates than is possessed by the majority of Congress that passed this bill and the President who signed it. Those supporting the bill undeniably included many seasoned professionals who have been deeply involved in elective processes and who have viewed them at close range over many years.

Buckley v. Valeo, 424 U.S. 1, 260–61 (1976) (White, J., concurring in part and dissenting in part).

In *Citizens Against Rent Control v. City of Berkeley,* 454 U.S. 290, 310–11 (1981), Justice White applies the same rationale to state and local determinations of threats to the integrity of the political process:

> Perhaps, as I have said, neither the city of Berkeley nor the State of California can "prove" that elections have been or can be unfairly won by special interest groups spending large sums of money, but there is a widespread conviction in legislative halls, as well as among citizens, that the danger is real. I regret that the Court continues to disregard that hazard.

Does the First Amendment require independent judicial examination of both the compelling state interest and the specific tailoring of all campaign finance regulations? Should courts defer to the determinations of threats to the political process made by incumbent political powers?

C. EQUALITY AND LIBERTY IN POLITICAL CAMPAIGNS

Buckley and its companion cases drew tremendous criticism as part of the *"Lochnerization"* of the First Amendment. *See* Morton J. Horwitz, *Foreword: The Constitution of Change: Legal Fundamentality Without Fundamentalism,* 107 Harv. L. Rev.30, 111–16 (1993); Cass R. Sunstein, Democracy and the Problem of Free Speech 97 (1993). For critics of the campaign finance case law, this was a struggle in which "Capitalism almost always won." Owen M. Fiss, *Free Speech and Social Structure,* 71 Iowa L. Rev. 1405–07 (1986). Once the issue of campaign finance regulation is taken beyond the narrow rationale of preventing *quid pro quo* corruption of the political process, the difficulties in defining a coherent regulatory structure multiply. The inescapable question must be whether government can equalize the voices of all citizens consistent with a democratic ordering of politics. The Court's initial reaction was decidedly hostile. In *Buckley,* for example, the Court stated, "the concept that government may restrict the speech of some elements of our society in order to enhance the relative voice of others is wholly foreign to the First Amendment. . . ." 424 U.S. at 48–49. Subsequently, the Court added a first amendment freedom of association argument to its concerns about campaign finance regulation. In *Citizens Against Rent Control v. City of Berkeley,* 454 U.S. 290, 294 (1981), a case striking down a limitation of $250 on contributions to committees formed to support or oppose ballot measures submitted to a popular vote, the Court wrote:

> We begin by recalling that the practice of persons sharing common views banding together to achieve a common end is deeply embedded in the American political process. The 18th-century Committees of Correspondence and the pamphleteers were early examples of this phenomena and the Federalist Papers were perhaps the most significant and lasting example. The tradition of volunteer committees for collective action has manifested itself in myriad community and public activities; in the political process it can focus on a candidate or on a ballot measure. Its value is that by collective effort individuals can make their views known, when, individually, their voices would be faint or lost.

However, this view was qualified even under the terms of *Buckley* itself in which the Court describes the First Amendment as having been "designed to secure the widest possible dissemination of information from diverse and antagonistic sources." 424 U.S. at 428–29. As Professor Julian Eule argued, the Court appeared to invite a requirement that the public be exposed to the widest possible diversity of views. Julian Eule, *Promoting Speaker Diversity:* Austin *and* Metro Broadcasting, 1990 Sup. Ct. Rev. 105, 109. In *Federal Election Commission v. Massachusetts Citizens for Life*, 479 U.S. 238, 257–58 (1986), the Court then took the critical step of allowing some restrictions on expenditures by distinguishing between funds amassed directly for purposes of political expression, and those that were generated as a byproduct of unrelated commercial activity:

> Political "free trade" does not necessarily require that all who participate in the political marketplace do so with exactly equal resources. Relative availability of funds is after all a rough barometer of public support. The resources in the treasury of a business corporation, however, are not an indication of popular support for the corporation's political ideas. They reflect instead the economically motivated decisions of investors and customers. The availability of these resources may make a corporation a formidable political presence, even though the power of the corporation may be no reflection of the power of its ideas.

This then set the stage for a much more expansive view of the power of the legislature to regulate the political marketplace. Professor Owen Fiss in turn argues that such an approach, far from being prohibited under the First Amendment analysis of *Buckley,* should be compelled:

> [W]hat the first amendment requires in these cases is not indifference, but a commitment on the part of the Court to do all that it can possibly do to support and encourage the state in efforts to enrich the public debate, to eliminate those restrictions of its subsidy programs that would narrow and restrict public debate,

and if need be even to require the state to continue and embark on programs that enrich debate.

Free Speech and Social Structure, 71 Iowa L. Rev. at 1424.

Austin v. Michigan Chamber of Commerce
494 U.S. 652 (1990).

■ JUSTICE MARSHALL delivered the opinion of the Court.

* * *

I

Section 54(1) of the Michigan Campaign Finance Act prohibits corporations from making contributions and independent expenditures in connection with state candidate elections.[1] The issue before us is only the constitutionality of the State's ban on independent expenditures. The Act defines "expenditure" as "a payment, donation, loan, pledge, or promise of payment of money or anything of ascertainable monetary value for goods, materials, services, or facilities in assistance of, or in opposition to, the nomination or election of a candidate." § 169.206(1). An expenditure is considered independent if it is "not made at the direction of, or under the control of, another person and if the expenditure is not a contribution to a committee." § 169.209(1); see § 169.203(4) (defining "committee" as a group that "receives contributions or makes expenditures for the purpose of influencing or attempting to influence the action of the voters for or against the nomination or election of a candidate"). The Act exempts from this general prohibition against corporate political spending any expenditure made from a segregated fund. § 169.255(1). A corporation may solicit contributions to its political fund only from an enumerated list of persons associated with the corporation. See §§ 169.255(2), (3).

The Chamber, a nonprofit Michigan corporation, challenges the constitutionality of this statutory scheme. The Chamber comprises more than 8,000 members, three-quarters of whom are for-profit corporations. The Chamber's general treasury is funded through annual dues required of all members. Its purposes, as set out in the bylaws, are to promote economic conditions favorable to private enterprise; to analyze, compile, and disseminate information about laws of interest to the business community and to publicize to the government the views of the business community on such matters; to train and educate its members; to foster ethical business practices; to collect data on, and investigate matters of, social, civic, and economic importance to the State; to receive contributions and to make

---

1. Section 54(1) is modeled on a provision of the Federal Election Campaign Act of 1971, 86 Stat. 11, as amended, 2 U.S.C. §§ 431–455, that requires corporations and labor unions to use segregated funds to finance independent expenditures made in federal elections. § 441b.

expenditures for political purposes and to perform any other lawful political activity; and to coordinate activities with other similar organizations.

In June 1985 Michigan scheduled a special election to fill a vacancy in the Michigan House of Representatives. Although the Chamber had established and funded a separate political fund, it sought to use its general treasury funds to place in a local newspaper an advertisement supporting a specific candidate. As the Act made such an expenditure punishable as a felony, see § 169.254(5), the Chamber brought suit in District Court for injunctive relief against enforcement of the Act, arguing that the restriction on expenditures is unconstitutional under both the First and the Fourteenth Amendments.

* * *

II

* * *

B

The State contends that the unique legal and economic characteristics of corporations necessitate some regulation of their political expenditures to avoid corruption or the appearance of corruption.... State law grants corporations special advantages—such as limited liability, perpetual life, and favorable treatment of the accumulation and distribution of assets— that enhance their ability to attract capital and to deploy their resources in ways that maximize the return on their shareholders' investments. These state-created advantages not only allow corporations to play a dominant role in the Nation's economy, but also permit them to use "resources amassed in the economic marketplace" to obtain "an unfair advantage in the political marketplace." *FEC v. Massachusetts Citizens for Life, Inc. (MCFL)*, 479 U.S. 238, 257 (1986). As the Court explained in *MCFL*, the political advantage of corporations is unfair because

> [t]he resources in the treasury of a business corporation ... are not an indication of popular support for the corporation's political ideas. They reflect instead the economically motivated decisions of investors and customers. The availability of these resources may make a corporation a formidable political presence, even though the power of the corporation may be no reflection of the power of its ideas.

We therefore have recognized that "the compelling governmental interest in preventing corruption support[s] the restriction of the influence of political war chests funneled through the corporate form." *NCPAC*, 470 U.S. at 500–501....

The Chamber argues that this concern about corporate domination of the political process is insufficient to justify a restriction on independent expenditures. Although this Court has distinguished these expenditures from direct contributions in the context of federal laws regulating individual donors ... it has also recognized that a legislature might demonstrate a danger of real or apparent corruption posed by such expenditures when made by corporations to influence candidate elections.... Regardless of whether this danger of "financial quid pro quo" corruption ... may be sufficient to justify a restriction on independent expenditures, Michigan's regulation aims at a different type of corruption in the political arena: the corrosive and distorting effects of immense aggregations of wealth that are accumulated with the help of the corporate form and that have little or no correlation to the public's support for the corporation's political ideas. The Act does not attempt "to equalize the relative influence of speakers on elections" ... ; rather, it ensures that expenditures reflect actual public support for the political ideas espoused by corporations. We emphasize that the mere fact that corporations may accumulate large amounts of wealth is not the justification for § 54; rather, the unique state-conferred corporate structure that facilitates the amassing of large treasuries warrants the limit on independent expenditures. Corporate wealth can unfairly influence elections when it is deployed in the form of independent expenditures, just as it can when it assumes the guise of political contributions. We therefore hold that the State has articulated a sufficiently compelling rationale to support its restriction on independent expenditures by corporations.

C

We next turn to the question whether the Act is sufficiently narrowly tailored to achieve its goal. We find that the Act is precisely targeted to eliminate the distortion caused by corporate spending while also allowing corporations to express their political views. Contrary to the dissents' critical assumptions, ... the Act does not impose an absolute ban on all forms of corporate political spending but permits corporations to make independent political expenditures through separate segregated funds. Because persons contributing to such funds understand that their money will be used solely for political purposes, the speech generated accurately reflects contributors' support for the corporation's political views.

* * *

III

The Chamber contends that even if the Campaign Finance Act is constitutional with respect to for-profit corporations, it nonetheless cannot be applied to a nonprofit ideological corporation like a chamber of commerce. In *MCFL,* we held that the nonprofit organization there had "features more akin to voluntary political associations than business firms, and therefore should not have to bear burdens on independent spending solely because of [its] incorporated status." In reaching that conclusion, we enumerated three characteristics of the corporation that were "essential" to our holding. Because the Chamber does not share these crucial features, the Constitution does not require that it be exempted from the generally applicable provisions of § 54(1).

The first characteristic of Massachusetts Citizens for Life, Inc., that distinguished it from ordinary business corporations was that the organization "was formed for the express purpose of promoting political ideas, and cannot engage in business activities." Its articles of incorporation indicated that its purpose was "[t]o foster respect for human life and to defend the right to life of all human beings, born and unborn, through educational, political and other forms of activities," and all of the organization's activities were "designed to further its agenda." MCFL's narrow political focus thus "ensure[d] that [its] political resources reflect[ed] political support."

In contrast, the Chamber's bylaws set forth more varied purposes, several of which are not inherently political. For instance, the Chamber compiles and disseminates information relating to social, civic, and economic conditions, trains and educates its members, and promotes ethical business practices. Unlike MCFL's, the Chamber's educational activities are not expressly tied to political goals; many of its seminars, conventions, and publications are politically neutral and focus on business and economic issues....

We described the second feature of MCFL as the absence of "shareholders or other persons affiliated so as to have a claim on its assets or earnings. This ensures that persons connected with the organization will have no economic disincentive for disassociating with it if they disagree with its political activity." Although the Chamber also lacks shareholders, many of its members may be similarly reluctant to withdraw as members even if they disagree with the Chamber's political expression, because they wish to benefit from the Chamber's nonpolitical programs and to establish contacts with other members of the business community. The Chamber's political agenda is sufficiently distinct from its educational and outreach programs that members who disagree with the former may continue to pay dues to participate in the latter.... Thus, we are persuaded that the Chamber's members are more similar to shareholders of a business corporation than to the members of MCFL in this respect.

The final characteristic upon which we relied in *MCFL* was the organization's independence from the influence of business corporations. On this score, the Chamber differs most greatly from the Massachusetts organization. MCFL was not established by, and had a policy of not accepting contributions from, business corporations. Thus it could not "serv[e] as [a] condui[t] for the type of direct spending that creates a threat to the political marketplace." In striking contrast, more than three-quarters of the Chamber's members are business corporations, whose political contributions and expenditures can constitutionally be regulated by the State.... Business corporations therefore could circumvent the Act's restriction by funneling money through the Chamber's general treasury.

Because the Chamber accepts money from for-profit corporations, it could, absent application of § 54(1), serve as a conduit for corporate political spending. In sum, the Chamber does not possess the features that would compel the State to exempt it from restriction on independent political expenditures.

IV

The Chamber also attacks § 54(1) as underinclusive because it does not regulate the independent expenditures of unincorporated labor unions. Whereas unincorporated unions, and indeed individuals, may be able to amass large treasuries, they do so without the significant state-conferred advantages of the corporate structure; corporations are "by far the most prominent example of entities that enjoy legal advantages enhancing their ability to accumulate wealth." The desire to counterbalance those advantages unique to the corporate form is the State's compelling interest in this case; thus, excluding from the statute's coverage unincorporated entities that also have the capacity to accumulate wealth "does not undermine its justification for regulating corporations."

* * *

VI

Michigan identified as a serious danger the significant possibility that corporate political expenditures will undermine the integrity of the political process, and it has implemented a narrowly tailored solution to that problem. By requiring corporations to make all independent political expenditures through a separate fund made up of money solicited expressly for political purposes, the Michigan Campaign Finance Act reduces the threat that huge corporate treasuries amassed with the aid of favorable state laws will be used to influence unfairly the outcome of elections. The Michigan Chamber of Commerce does not exhibit the characteristics identified in *MCFL* that would require the State to exempt it from a generally applicable restriction on independent corporate expenditures. We therefore reverse the decision of the Court of Appeals.

■ [Concurring opinions of JUSTICE BRENNAN and JUSTICE STEVENS, omitted.]

■ JUSTICE SCALIA, dissenting.

"Attention all citizens. To assure the fairness of elections by preventing disproportionate expression of the views of any single powerful group, your Government has decided that the following associations of persons shall be prohibited from speaking or writing in support of any candidate: _____." In permitting Michigan to make private corporations the first object of this Orwellian announcement, the Court today endorses the principle that too much speech is an evil that the democratic majority can proscribe. I dissent because that principle is contrary to our case law and incompatible with the absolutely central truth of the First Amendment: that government cannot be trusted to assure, through censorship, the "fairness" of political debate.

* * *

■ JUSTICE KENNEDY, with whom JUSTICE O'CONNOR and JUSTICE SCALIA join, dissenting.

* * *

II

Our cases acknowledge the danger that corruption poses for the electoral process, but draw a line in permissible regulation between payments to candidates ("contributions") and payments or expenditures to express one's own views ("independent expenditures"). Today's decision abandons this distinction and threatens once-protected political speech. The Michigan statute prohibits independent expenditures by a nonprofit corporate speaker to express its own views about candidate qualifications. Independent expenditures are entitled to greater protection than campaign contributions. . . .

The majority almost admits that, in the case of independent expenditures, the danger of a political quid pro quo is insufficient to justify a restriction of this kind. Since the specter of corruption, which had been "the only legitimate and compelling government interest[s] thus far identified for restricting campaign finances," is missing in this case, the majority invents a new interest: combating the "corrosive and distorting effects of immense aggregations of wealth," accumulated in corporate form without shareholder or public support. The majority styles this novel interest as simply a different kind of corruption, but has no support for its assertion. While it is questionable whether such imprecision would suffice to justify restricting political speech by for-profit corporations, it is certain that it does not apply to nonprofit entities. . . .

With regard to nonprofit corporations in particular, there is no reason to assume that the corporate form has an intrinsic flaw that makes it corrupt, or that all corporations possess great wealth, or that all corporations can buy more media coverage for their views than can individuals or other groups. There is no reason to conclude that independent speech by a corporation is any more likely to dominate the political arena than speech by the wealthy individual, protected in *Buckley v. Valeo,* or by the well-funded PAC, protected in *NCPAC* (protecting speech rights of PAC's against expenditure limitations). . . .

The Act, as the State itself says, prevents a nonprofit corporate speaker from using its own funds to inform the voting public that a particular candidate has a good or bad voting record on issues of interest to the association's adherents. Though our era may not be alone in deploring the lack of mechanisms for holding candidates accountable for the votes they cast, that lack of accountability is one of the major concerns of our time. The speech suppressed in this case was directed to political qualifications. The fact that it was spoken by the Michigan Chamber of Commerce, and not a man or woman standing on a soapbox, detracts not a scintilla from its validity, its persuasiveness, or its contribution to the political dialogue.

* * *

IV

The Court's hostility to the corporate form used by the speaker in this case and its assertion that corporate wealth is the evil to be regulated is far too imprecise to justify the most severe restriction on political speech ever sanctioned by this Court. . . .

By constructing a rationale for the jurisprudence of this Court that prevents distinguished organizations in public affairs from announcing that a candidate is qualified or not qualified for public office, the Court imposes its own model of speech, one far removed from economic and political reality. It is an unhappy paradox that this Court, which has the role of protecting speech and of barring censorship from all aspects of political life, now becomes itself the censor. In the course of doing so, the Court reveals a lack of concern for speech rights that have the full protection of the First Amendment. I would affirm the judgment.

NOTES AND QUESTIONS

1. In *Austin,* the Court identifies "a different type of corruption in the political arena" caused by disparities of wealth. Can this concern really be considered as a type of corruption at all? Professor Julian Eule argues to the contrary:

> Nobody ought to be fooled. This is simply a repackaging of the equalization goal. The corporate voice is being contained in order to "equalize the relative ability of all citizens to affect the outcome of elections." Once the definition of corruption is enlarged to encompass the corruption of the electoral process as well as the elected candidate, the distinction between the corruption rationale and the equalization one is obliterated.

Julian N. Eule, *Promoting Speaker Diversity: Austin and Metro Broadcasting,* 1990 S.Ct. Rev. 105, 109–10.

2. Can *Austin* be reconciled with the solicitude of prior cases for independence from state regulation? In *Meyer v. Grant,* 486 U.S. 414 (1988), for example, the Court struck down a Colorado law that made it a felony to use paid petition gatherers in conjunction with trying to get an initiative on a state-wide ballot. Writing for a unanimous Court, Justice Stevens held that the Colorado restriction unconstitutionally limited the right of political expression of groups seeking to leverage their resources by using paid petition gatherers:

> The circulation of an initiative petition of necessity involves both the expression of a desire for political change and a discussion of the merits of the proposed change. Although a petition circulator may not have to persuade potential signatories that a particular proposal should prevail to capture their signatures, he or she will at least have to persuade them that the matter is one deserving of the public scrutiny and debate that would attend its consideration by the whole electorate. This will in almost every case involve an explanation of the nature of the proposal and why its advocates support it. Thus, the circulation of a petition involves the type of interactive communication concerning political change that is appropriately described as "core political speech."
>
> The refusal to permit appellees to pay petition circulators restricts political expression in two ways: First, it limits the number of voices who will convey appellees' message and the hours they can speak and, therefore, limits the size of the audience they can reach. Second, it makes it less likely that appellees will garner the number of signatures necessary to place the matter on the ballot, thus limiting their ability to make the matter the focus of statewide discussion....
>
> That appellees remain free to employ other means to disseminate their ideas does not take their speech through petition circulators outside the bounds of First Amendment protection. Colorado's prohibition of paid petition circulators restricts access to the most effective, fundamental, and perhaps economical avenue of political discourse, direct one-on-one communication. That it leaves open "more burdensome" avenues of communication does not relieve its burden on First Amendment expression.... The First Amendment protects appellees' right not only to advocate their cause but also to select what they believe to be the most effective means for so doing.

Id. at 422–24. Does *Meyer* survive *Austin*? Can the Court's concern in *Austin* over the distorting effect of wealth coexist with the general schema from *Buckley*, which draws a First Amendment line between contributions and expenditures? Consider the argument of Professor David Cole:

> [*Austin* reflects] the Court's first serious acknowledgment of the structural problem underlying the campaign spending issue: capitalism and democracy are an uneasy mix. Free market capitalism threatens the free marketplace of ideas by giving certain voices inordinate influence, not because of the power of their ideas, but because of the volume they can generate for their voices with

dollars earned through commercial activities. Because even "free speech" costs money, those who succeed in the economic marketplace are able to purchase far more speech opportunities than those who do not. Absent government intervention of some kind, the marketplace of ideas, and in turn the election of our representatives, threatens to go to the highest bidder. The threat posed by concentrated wealth is not merely the aberration of a bribed official, but the structural threat of a monopolized marketplace of ideas.

[...] Where the laissez-faire model had focused almost exclusively on the threats to free expression posed by public actors, the First Amendment antitrust model recognized that a robust and wide-open debate could also be undermined by powerful private actors. This recognition requires a wholesale rethinking of the role of the government in the marketplace of ideas.... Once "corruption" is understood to encompass the systemic distorting effects of wealth, expenditures are just as corrupting as contributions and referenda elections are just as subject to being corrupted as candidate elections. Even the distinctions relied upon in *Austin* are undermined by the "New Corruption": distortion can be caused not only by for-profit corporations, but also by wealthy individuals, nonprofit corporations, associations, and the media. Thus, every distinction the Court has erected in the field of campaign finance is called into question by the Court's belated recognition that economic power can skew democratic speech.

David Cole, *First Amendment Antitrust: The End of Laissez–Faire in Campaign Finance*, 9 Yale L. & Pol'y Rev. 236, 237, 266, 272 (1991); *see also* Jamin Raskin & John Bonifaz, *The Constitutional Imperative and Practical Superiority of Democratically Financed Elections*, 94 Colum. L. Rev. 1160, 1163 (1994)(arguing that inequality of resources produces a "massive structural bias in government which favors the parochial interests and personal wealth over the interests of those citizens lacking access to wealth"). Once down this path, however, there is no clear point of demarcation that separates disparities in wealth from other differential distribution of resources that bear on the political process. For example, Professor Lucas Powe argues that the logic of campaign finance reform pushes in two quite dramatic directions. L.A. Powe, Jr., *Mass Speech and the Newer First Amendment*, 1982 Sup. Ct. Rev. 243. First, the greatest potential concentration of extra-governmental power may be the mass media, but extensive content regulation of the media would run afoul of core First Amendment concerns. Second, if the real concern is the distortive effect of unequal wealth on the marketplace of ideas, would not the better argument be for attacking the source of the problem by redistributing wealth? Do the market reform arguments of *Austin* offer a stopping point short of Professor Powe's slippery slope? Would Professor Powe's concern be met by a system that guaranteed each voter equal financial resources for the purpose of supporting or opposing any candidate or position in an election? *See* Edward B. Foley, *Equal-Dollars–Per–Voter: A Constitutional Principle of Campaign Finance*, 94 Colum. L. Rev. 1240 (1994).

3. The attempt to regulate campaign expenditures may also be criticized as encroaching on fundamental political liberties. For example, Professor Bradley Smith argues that the effect of regulation is to make it harder to challenge incumbents:

> Campaign finance reform measures, in particular limits on contributions and overall spending, insulate the political system from challenge by outsiders, and hinder the ability of challengers to compete on equal terms with those already in power.
>
> Contribution limits tend to favor incumbents by making it harder for challengers to raise money and thereby make credible runs for office. The lower the contribution limit, the more difficult it becomes for a candidate to raise money quickly from a small number of dedicated supporters. The consequent need to raise campaign cash from a large number of small contributors benefits those candidates who have in place a database of past contributors, an intact campaign organization, and the ability to raise funds on an ongoing basis from PACs. This latter group consists almost entirely of current officeholders. Thus, contribution limits hit political newcomers especially hard because of the difficulties candidates with low name recognition have in raising substantial sums of money from small contributors.

Bradley A. Smith, *Faulty Assumptions and Undemocratic Consequences of Campaign Finance Reform*, 105 Yale L. J. 1049, 1072–73 (1996). There is significant empirical support for Professor Smith's argument. In the 1992 elections, for example, PAC contributions to incumbents exceeded those to challengers by a 10.5 to 1 margin; in the Senate it was 6 to 1. By contrast, individual contributions favored House incumbents by a significantly smaller 2.7 to 1 margin. In sum, PAC contributions constituted 47 percent of the total contributions to incumbents running for the House of Representatives. Fred Wertheimer & Susan Weiss Manes, *Campaign Finance Reform: a Key to Restoring the Health of Our Democracy,* 94 Colum. L. Rev. 1126, 1137 (1994). In addition there is the concern expressed by the Eighth Circuit in striking down a Missouri law limiting contributions to $100–300 per voter, that at some level contributions could be so low they "prevented candidates and political committees from amassing the resources necessary for effective advocacy." *Carver v. Nixon*, 72 F.3d 633, 642 (8th Cir.1995).

D. HAS CAMPAIGN FINANCE REGULATION WORKED?

Perhaps the most striking feature of the post–1974 campaign finance reform efforts has been the dramatic increase in election spending that accompanied the rise of federal regulation. Estimates of total spending on American elections topped $3 billion for the 1996 election cycle. As reflected in Table 2, campaigns for federal office, the most regulated area of elections, show an unmistakable rise in spending accompanying the post-reform period.

Table 2

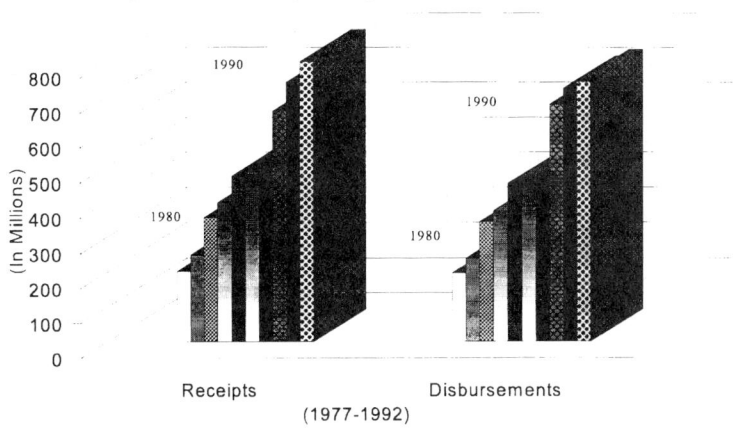

Congressional Campaign Money, House & Senate, 1977-1996

Source: Federal Election Commission

The failure of FECA reforms to check the escalating spiral of spending and solicitation of contributions has led to calls for state funding of elections. This is already done in countries such as Japan, Germany, France, Spain and Belgium, in which public money is given to political parties in proportion to either their parliamentary representation or their percentage of votes obtained; Canada also reimburses parties and candidates for part of their campaign expenditures. However, there is a real concern that Americans will not accept public responsibility for campaign funding at levels adequate to sustain informed political debate. For example, only about one-third of Americans check off the box on their federal tax returns allowing for a one dollar contribution to federal campaign funding.

In addition to federal reforms, more than 20 states now provide at the state level for either public financing of campaigns or for restricting campaign expenditures for state and local office. For examples of case law governing these regulatory schemes, *see, e.g.* the statutes discussed in the following cases: *Shrink Missouri Government v. Maupin,* 71 F.3d 1422, (8th Cir.1995)(striking down a Missouri statute requiring candidates to sign an affidavit stating whether they will comply with certain spending limits; candidates who chose not to comply with the limits were required to submit daily disclosure reports and only allowed to accept contributions from individuals, not PACs, corporations, etc.; the statute also prohibited the carryover of contributions between elections); *Day v. Holahan,* 34 F.3d 1356 (8th Cir.1994)(striking down a Minnesota statute which provided an increase in a candidates' expenditure limit to the extent an expenditure is made expressly advocating defeat of the candidate or election of an opposing candidate; prohibited independent expenditures by certain corporations and limited contributions to PACs to $100); *Virginia Society for Human Life v. Caldwell,* 906 F.Supp. 1071 (W.D.Va.1995)(certifying to state court an interpretation of a Virginia statute requiring individuals and PACs who contribute or expend more than $100 to file a statement of organization, maintain records, and file disclosure reports; but striking down a statutory provision requiring persons and PACs spending certain amounts to identify the person or group responsible for any campaign literature).

E. A Caution on Public Financing

Does public funding actually curb expenditures? Or does it serve as an additional source of income to the established political parties? Consider the history of public financing of political conventions as a cautionary tale. In 1974, Congress mandated public funding of presidential nominating conventions and presidential elections as part of its post-Watergate federal campaign finance reform effort. Congress was persuaded to prohibit private contributions to the parties' nominating conventions in the wake of a scandal in which ITT was believed to have donated $400,000 to the 1972 Republican National Convention in exchange for favorable treatment in an antitrust suit brought by the Department of Justice. Following the 1974 federal campaign finance reforms, nominating conventions were considered federal elections for the purposes of federal regulations. As such, nominating conventions fell under 1974 federal regulations prohibiting corporations and labor organizations from making contributions or expenditures in connection with a general election. 2 U.S.C. § 441b.

Under these regulations, each major party is now entitled to $4 million in public funding, plus a cost-of-living adjustment. Rather than serve as a cap on convention funding, however, public financing has served as the down payment on increasingly lavish affairs. Since 1974, the FEC has approved numerous exceptions that allow the Republican and Democratic National Parties to circumvent the ban on private contributions to defray expenses from their nominating conventions, while still accepting full public funding of them. In a series of advisory opinions, the FEC progressively loosened restrictions on convention funding to "enable commercial vendors and local corporate and labor organizations to engage in various activities in connection with a Presidential nominating convention held in their city." In so doing, the FEC explicitly presumed that business and donors "are motivated by civic and commercial purposes rather than by election-influencing objectives" or policy-influencing objectives once the federal elections are decided. Federal Election Commission, *Presidential Nominating Conventions: Permissible Corporate/Labor Activity,* Record, February 1996, Vol. 22, No.2, 7–8. Federal election regulations now permit private individuals, corporations and commercial vendors to contribute both to such municipal funds, set up by local government agencies and municipal corporations, and to non-profit funds managed by the convention city's "host committee" organizations.

Table 3

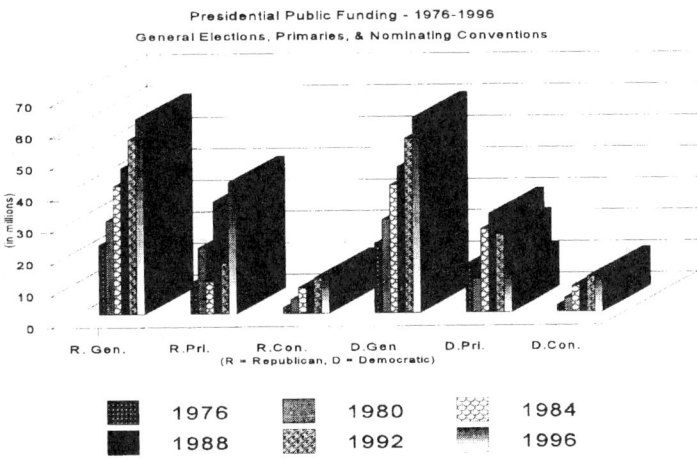

Source: Federal Election Commission

As reflected in Table 3, the pressure for increased public funding of conventions yielded an escalation of costs similar to the public funding of the presidential primaries and general elections. But public funding was only part of the story. By 1996, the amount of private money filtering to the conventions dwarfed public funding. In 1996, the Chicago and San Diego Host Committees spent a combined $40.9 million on their respective conventions, over and above the $12.4 million in public funding each party received for its convention. Overall, the reports filed by these host committees with the Federal Election Commission reveal that the majority of funding comes from corporations that would otherwise be restricted in showing their largesse. The record further suggests that the presumption of disinterested private giving may not be warranted. For example, through promotional considerations, donated services, cash payments and the like, AT & T donated $2,653,226 to the Republican convention through the San Diego Host Committee and $558,741 to the Democratic convention through the Chicago Host Committee. As explained by J. Michael Brown, AT & T Vice President for Federal Legislation, the reason for the contributions was as follows:

> There's a political positioning that is important to us for our business. We are regulated at both the state and federal level. We participate actively in the government process. This year, in particular, as the communications industry is being restructured, we want to be present and visible and let people know we're a good company.

Congressional Quarterly, Vol. 54, Supp. to No. 31, August 3, 1996, at 31. Is this development predictable in light of the composition of the FEC as appointed representatives of the Democratic and Republican parties? Does the experience with convention financing call into question the claim by Justice White that the federal courts should adopt a deferential attitude toward the political branches in the regulation of campaign financing?

F. Proposals for Reform

On January 21, 1997, S. 25, the Bipartisan Campaign Finance Bill of 1997 (the "McCain–Feingold–Thompson bill") was introduced in the Senate. As originally introduced, this bill would attempt to limit the amount of money spent on federal campaigns by combining inducements to candidates who agree to limit their expenditures, together with greater restrictions on contributions, particularly toward soft money. The critical provisions are:

1) Voluntary limitations on expenditures with caps based upon the voting age population of each state. The caps would restrict the total amount each candidate could spend, the amount of personal wealth each candidate could spend, and would require that 60 percent of all contributions come from within the home state of the candidate. The caps would be increased in any election in which a challenger exceeds the voluntary limitations.

2) All candidates complying with the voluntary limitations would received postage discounts for mailings equal to two times the relevant voting-age population, 30 minutes of free television advertising time (available in 30 second to five-minute increments) and a 50 percent discount on their other television advertising 60 days before the general and 30 days before the primary election.

3) A ban on all soft money contributions to political parties.

4) A requirement that hard money be used for all "express advocacy," which is defined to include any general public communication that advocates the election or defeat of a clearly identified candidate for federal office.

5) A ban on PAC contributions to federal candidates. In case this provision is deemed to be unconstitutional, a "back-up" provision lowering PAC contributions from $5,000 to $1,000 and limiting Senate candidates to accepting no more than 20 percent of the allowable spending limit in total PAC contributions.

The express purpose of the Bill, according to its chief sponsor Senator McCain is that

> Passage of campaign finance reform is necessary if we are to curb the public's growing cynicism for politics and Congress in particular.... Twenty-five years after Watergate, the electoral system is out of control. Our elections are awash in money which is flowing into the system at record levels.... Something must be done.

Congressional Record, S384, Jan. 21, 1997. In light of *Buckley* and *Colorado Republican Committee*, is S. 25 constitutional in whole? In part? Is S. 25 an improvement from a public policy perspective? What will be the likely effect of S. 25 if its constitutionality is upheld in whole? What if it is only upheld in part?

S. 25 builds upon various state initiatives to induce candidates to voluntarily limit the role of campaign contributions in the electoral process. For example, in December, 1996, the Eighth Circuit upheld the constitutionality of Minnesota's campaign finance law which provides partial public financing by granting candidates a subsidy in exchange for voluntary campaign expenditure limits. *See Rosenstiel v. Rodriguez*, 101 F.3d 1544 (8th Cir.1996), *cert. denied* 117 S.Ct. 1820 (1997).

The most far-reaching state initiative is the Maine Clean Elections Act of 1996. Under this Act, candidates are eligible for public funding once they have raised a threshold number of $5 contributions from constituents. If the candidate elects to follow the public funding route, she must turn over all these funds (referred to as "seed money") to the Clean Elections Fund and she is in turn barred from any further private private fundraising. In exchange for giving up all collected funds and eschewing all further private fundraising, the Act holds out the promise of full public financing for state elections. The amount of funding is set by averaging the amount spent by candidates in the previous two elections. One of the central goals of the Act was to level the playing field for all candidates, particularly between incumbents and challengers. Another objective was to keep candidates who opted for public funding competitive with privately funded candidates by pegging the level of the state subsidy to the amounts that had previously been spent in prior elections for the same positions. Proponents of the Act argue that it survives *Colorado Republican Committee* and *NCPAC* by ensuring that participation is voluntary and that receipt of public funding is conditioned on the voluntary limitation on the acceptance of private funding.

Could the Maine Clean Elections Act be applied to federal elections? Would the purposes of the Act be undermined if campaign reliance on soft money continued to escalate as projected in Table 1 of this Chapter? Would an accompanying restriction on soft money survive challenge under *Colorado Republican Committee?*

CHAPTER 10

DIRECT DEMOCRACY

From the Greek city-states to the Roman plebiscites to the New England town meetings, direct democratic participation in political decisions has served as an alternative to government by elected representatives. In the last 20 or so years, there has been a revival of direct democratic participation at the state level on major issues of statewide importance. This revival has come in the form of increasing use of the two most prevalent forms of direct democracy in contemporary America: the initiative and the referendum. Professor David Magleby has offered a brief description of the two processes:

> Using the initiative, voters may write statutes, and in some states constitutional amendments, which will go to the ballot if sufficient valid petition signatures are gathered.... Initiatives that meet the signature requirement go either directly to the voters (the direct initiative) or are placed on the state legislature's agenda (the indirect initiative), where, if the legislature does not enact the initiative within a specified time, the proponents have the option to gather additional signatures and place the measure on the ballot. Five states permit both the indirect and direct initiative, and not surprisingly when they do, initiative sponsors prefer taking their issue directly to the voters.
>
> In contrast, citizens may use the popular referendum to place laws previously enacted by local or state legislative bodies before the voters for approval. As with the initiative, citizen petitions qualify a popular referendum for the ballot. Initiatives are sometimes used as referendums, as in the case of a 1964 California measure that overturned an open-housing law passed by the state legislature.... Referendums can also be called by local or state legislatures. For instance, all states except Delaware require that constitutional changes go before the voters in a referendum, and many state legislatures place measures on the ballot for voter approval.

David B. Magleby, *Governing by Initiative: Let the Voters Decide? An Assessment of the Initiative and Referendum Process*, 66 U. Colo. L. Rev. 13, 13–14 (1995).

This chapter considers several questions that arise from the increasing role of direct popular decisionmaking in democratic government. We begin by asking whether such decisionmaking is consistent with the constitutional structure and the framers' theory of government. We then turn to the way popular decisionmaking interacts with the voting rights system more generally.

A. Constitutional Underpinnings and Concerns

The constitutional system reflects a Madisonian design of institutional checks and balances to avoid the risk of majority factions having untrammeled power. In *The Federalist Papers* No. 10, Madison clearly distinguishes between "pure Democracy" in which citizens jointly administer the state, and a "Republic" based on government by representatives:

> From this view of the subject it may be concluded that a pure democracy, by which I mean a society consisting of a small number of citizens, who assemble and administer the government in person, can admit of no cure for the mischiefs of faction. A common passion or interest will, in almost every case, be felt by a majority of the whole; a communication and concert result from the form of government itself; and there is nothing to check the inducements to sacrifice the weaker party or an obnoxious individual. Hence it is that such democracies have ever been spectacles of turbulence and contention; have ever been found incompatible with personal security or the rights of property; and have in general been as short in their lives as they have been violent in their deaths. Theoretic politicians who have patronized this species of government, have erroneously supposed that by reducing mankind to a perfect equality in their political rights, they would, at the same time, be perfectly equalized and assimilated in their possessions, their opinions, and their passions.
>
> A republic, by which I mean a government in which the scheme of representation takes place, opens a different prospect, and promises the cure for which we are seeking. Let us examine the points in which it varies from pure democracy, and we shall comprehend both the nature of the cure and the efficacy which it must derive from the Union.
>
> The two great points of difference between a democracy and a republic are: first, the delegation of the government, in the latter to a small number of citizens elected by the rest; secondly, the greater number of citizens, and greater sphere of country over which the latter may be extended.
>
> The effect of the first difference is, on the one hand, to refine and enlarge the public views, by passing them through the medium of a chosen body of citizens, whose wisdom may best discern the true interest of their country, and whose patriotism and love of

justice will be least likely to sacrifice it to temporary or partial considerations. Under such a regulation, it may well happen that the public voice, pronounced by the representatives of the people, will be more consonant to the public good than if pronounced by the people themselves, convened for the purpose....

The other point of difference is, the greater number of citizens and extent of territory which may be brought within the compass of republican than of democratic government; and it is this circumstance principally which renders factious combinations less to be dreaded in the former than in the latter. The smaller the society, the fewer probably will be the distinct parties and interests composing it; the fewer the distinct parties and interests, the more frequently will a majority be found of the same party; and the smaller the number of individuals composing a majority, and the smaller the compass within which they are placed, the most easily will they concert and execute their plans of oppression. Extend the sphere, and you take in a greater variety of parties and interests; you make it less probable that a majority of the whole will have a common motive to invade the rights of other citizens; or if such a common motive exists, it will be more difficult for all who feel it to discover their own strength, and to act in unison with each other.

Technological change has made the process of citizen consultation far easier. Some have pointed to recent technological advances as a justification for embracing more direct democratic participation and decisionmaking. *See, e.g.*, Lawrence Grossman, The Electronic Republic (1995). But the key to Madisonian Republicanism rested in government at one remove from the direct wishes (and passions) of the populace: a republic is "a government which derives all its powers directly or indirectly from the great body of the people; and is administered by persons holding offices during pleasure, for a limited period, or during good behavior." By contrast, "[l]awmaking by popular vote on an initiated proposal of course bypasses the committee study, hearings, amendments, and compromises of legislative deliberation; that was and is its purpose." Hans A. Linde, *When Initiative Lawmaking Is Not "Republican Government": The Campaign Against Homosexuality*, 72 Ore. L. Rev. 19, 34 (1993).

Despite the concerns of the Founders, direct democracy came to be seen as an antidote to the entrenched power of political machines and the powers of moneyed interests at the legislative level. The major expansion of direct democracy in this country occurred in the Progressive Period at the turn of the twentieth century. Initiatives and referenda were touted at the time as a means of overcoming the capture of legislatures by special interests, such as the railroads, mining companies, and other industrial interests, and of circumventing the power of ward-based political machines, in much the same way as the system of at-large elections of city and county officials was promoted during that same period. Direct participation was also thought to educate and improve the civic virtue of citizens. In addition, in Oregon itself—the font of direct decisionmaking—the legislature had become so deadlocked that the normal processes of legislation by representatives had ground to a halt. *See generally* Nathaniel Persily, *The Peculiar Geography of Direct Democracy: Why The Initiative, Referendum and Recall Developed in the American West*, 2 Mich. L. & Pol'y Rev. 11 (1997). One prominent proponent of direct lawmaking, Senator Jonathan Bourne, Jr., of Oregon put his case this way, in speaking to an academic audience:

> Always there are a few intellectual leaders who are in advance of the masses of the people; but the practical workings of delegated government are such that the masses of the people are always in advance of those individuals who secure political but not intellectual leadership. "Practical politics," under a system of delegated government, brings into power men who are guided more by selfish interest than by general welfare. Popular government reverses this condition and gives power to intellectual leaders rather than to men whose success is due to skill as "practical politicians."

XLIII Annals of the American Academy of Political and Social Science 7 (1912).

In response to the arguments of initiative proponents, 23 states enacted the initiative, the referendum, or both between 1898 and 1918. During the early decades of the 20th century, these new devices were invoked quite frequently; but from the 1940s to the 1960s, direct lawmaking declined. K.K. DuVivier, *By Going Wrong All Things Come Right: Using Alternative Initiatives to Improve Citizen Lawmaking*, 63 U. Cinn. L. Rev. 1185, 1188 (1995). But there has recently been a resurgence in use of these devices, which began in the late 1960s and then took off with the success in 1978 of California's Proposition 13, the symbol of the "property tax revolt," which capped property taxes. Today, these direct lawmaking devices are being used for statewide lawmaking at rates comparable to when the process was first created early in the century. In California itself, for example, voters passed only two initiatives in the 1950; three in the 1960s; seven in the 1970s; and then 21 in the 1980s and 15 between 1990 and 1996. Peter Schrag, *Take the Initiative, Please: Referendum Madness in California*, 28 Am. Prospect 61 (1996). For discussion of the use of direct lawmaking for local government issues, see Clayton Gillette, *Plebiscites, Participation, and Collective Action in Local Government Law*, 86 Mich. L. Rev. 930 (1988). The statewide initiative remains largely, though not exclusively, a phenomenon of western politics, where it began: California and Oregon accounted for nearly one-third of all statewide initiatives in the 1980s.

The Supreme Court confronted the question whether direct democracy was constitutionally permissible in a challenge brought by Pacific States Telephone & Telegraph to an Oregon gross revenue tax enacted by initiative in 1906. As with its early forays into reapportionment, *see supra* Chapter 3, the Court avoided the issue.

Pacific States Telephone & Telegraph Company v. Oregon

223 U.S. 118 (1912).

■ Mr. Chief Justice White delivered the opinion of the Court:

* * *

The case is this: In 1902 Oregon amended its Constitution. This amendment, while retaining an existing clause vesting the exclusive legislative power in a general assembly consisting of a senate and a house of representatives, added to that provision the following: "But the people reserve to themselves power to propose laws and amendments to the Constitution, and to enact or reject the same at the polls, independent of the legislative assembly, and also reserve power at their own option to approve or reject at the polls any act of the legislative assembly." [Art. 4, sec. 1.] Specific means for the exercise of the power thus reserved was contained in further clauses authorizing both the amendment of the Constitution and the enactment of laws to be accomplished by the method known as the initiative and that commonly referred to as the referendum. As to the first, the initiative, it suffices to say that a stated number of voters were given the right at any time to secure a submission to popular vote for approval of any matter which it was desired to have enacted into law, and providing that the proposition thus submitted, when approved by popular vote, should become the law of the state. The second, the referendum, provided for a reference to a popular vote, for approval or disapproval, of any law passed by the legislature, such reference to take place either as the result of the action of the legislature itself, or of a petition filed for that purpose by a specified number of voters.... By resort to the initiative in 1906, a law taxing certain classes of corporations was submitted, voted on, and promulgated by the governor in 1907 as having been duly adopted....

The Pacific States Telephone & Telegraph Company, an Oregon corporation engaged in business in that state, made a return of its gross receipts, as required by the statute, and was accordingly assessed 2 per cent upon the amount of such return. The suit which is now before us was commenced by the state to enforce payment of this assessment and the statutory penalties for delinquency.... [The corporation's legal challenges] are all based upon the single contention that the creation by a state of the power to legislate by the initiative and referendum causes the prior lawful state government to be bereft of its lawful character as the result of the provisions of Section 4 of article 4 of the Constitution, that "the United States shall guarantee to every state in this Union a republican form of government, and shall protect each of them against invasion; and on application of the legislature, or of the executive (when the legislature cannot be convened), against domestic violence." This being the basis of all the contentions, the case comes to the single issue whether the enforcement of that provision, because of its political character, is exclusively committed to Congress, or is judicial in its character.

* * *

It was long ago settled that the enforcement of [the republican form of government clause in Article IV, Sec. 4] belonged to the political department. In [*Luther v. Borden*, 48 U.S. 1 (1849)], it was held that the question, which of the two opposing governments of Rhode Island, namely, the charter government or the government established by a voluntary convention, was the legitimate one, was a question for the determination of the political department; and when that department had decided, the courts were bound to take notice of the decision and follow it.... [T]he settled distinction which the doctrine just stated points out between judicial authority over justiciable controversies and legislative power as to purely political questions ... distinguish[es] between things which are widely different; that is, the legislative duty to determine the political questions involved in deciding whether a state government republican in form exists, and the judicial power and ever-present duty whenever it becomes necessary, in a controversy properly submitted, to enforce and uphold the applicable provisions of the Constitution as to each and every exercise of governmental power....

As the issues presented, in their very essence, are, and have long since by this court been, definitely determined to be political and governmental, and embraced within the scope of the powers conferred upon Congress, and not, therefore, within the reach of judicial power, it follows that the case presented is not within our jurisdiction, and the writ of error must therefore be, and it is, dismissed for want of jurisdiction.

NOTES AND QUESTIONS

1. State and federal courts have struck down the *results* of many initiatives and referenda on federal constitutional grounds. *See, e.g., U.S. Term Limits v. Thornton*, 514 U.S. 779 (1995) (striking down on Qualifications Clause grounds Arkansas' imposition of term limits on its congressional delegation); *Evans v. Romer*, 882 P.2d 1335 (Colo.1994), *aff'd*, 116 S.Ct. 1620 (1996) (striking down Colorado's anti-gay rights constitutional amendment on equal protection grounds). But they have not seriously revisited the question whether the very *process* of lawmaking through initiative and referendum is constitutional. Perhaps as a result, federal courts have also not considered in any meaningful way important subsidiary questions. For example, should the fact that a law emerges from direct democratic processes as opposed to the ordinary legislative process influence the techniques the courts use to interpret the law? Are there certain kinds of laws whose constitutionality should turn on whether they are enacted by voters rather than legislatures? We pursue this question below. Should the courts develop techniques of working with the products of direct lawmaking that differ from those the courts use to deal with ordinary legislation?

2. What would or should have happened had the Supreme Court reached the merits in *Pacific States*? Is lawmaking by direct democracy consistent with the concerns for "majority faction" so central in *The Federalist Papers* No. 10? If one "great point of difference between a democracy and a republic" is that in the latter, representative government produces one check on the tendency of popular government to sacrifice to its ruling passion or interest both the public good and the rights of other citizens, should the Court have held the initiative process unconstitutional, or at least applied special scrutiny to policies adopted through initiatives? One answer to these questions might be that *Pacific States* involved the choice at the state level between different forms of lawmaking. Perhaps the Constitution and *The Federalist Papers* should not be understood to articulate any general conception of self-government, but only one applicable to national lawmaking institutions. In that case, consider whether Congress could *by statute* create a national initiative referendum mechanism. Could such a mechanism be created only by a constitutional amendment? Consider these two proposals for a national referendum process, the second of which was introduced as a proposed constitutional amendment in the late 1970s with more than 50 congressional supporters:

> a) Whenever the president and Congress are in conflict or deadlock on domestic legislation, either or both may submit the question at issue to a referendum vote of the electorate. The people of the United States may petition for referendum on national legislation, after passage by Congress ... When 10 percent of registered voters in more than one-third of all states sign a legal petition for referendum, the proposed law shall be put to majority decision of the electorate at the next regularly scheduled election.
>
> b) A national initiative would be held when advocates of a policy proposal, in an 18–month period, gathered signatures equal to 3% of the ballots cast in the last presidential election, including 3% in each of at least ten states (about 3 million signatures). At the next regularly scheduled national election, if a majority of those voting approved, the measure would take effect in 30 days (or as otherwise specified). Congress could amend or repeal by a two-thirds vote in both houses within two years of adoption and by a simple majority vote after that. The initiative could not be used to amend the Constitution, call up troops, or declare war.

For discussion, see Thomas E. Cronin, Direct Democracy 157–95 (1989).

3. *Pacific States* explicitly distinguishes the question whether a particular state's government is "republican in form"—a question it holds to be nonjusticiable—from the question whether a particular "exercise of governmental power" by a state's government is permissible—the ordinary matter of constitutional adjudication. Should the state's form of government shed any light on judicial evaluation of the latter sorts of questions? Put more concretely, suppose the Court had reached the merits in *Pacific States* and had upheld the initiative form of lawmaking on the merits. Would that mean that courts faced with federal constitutional challenges to a state law or state constitutional provision should review the challenged measure without regard to its provenance? Or should courts pay particularly close attention to the differences between representative institutions and popular lawmaking in assessing popular lawmaking's use in specific cases and its compliance with constitutional standards—particularly those designed to insure that the *process* of lawmaking facilitates focused and thoughtful deliberation? *Compare* Julian N. Eule, *Judicial Review of Direct Democracy*, 99 Yale L.J. 1503 (1990) (arguing that judicial review is especially important because the initiative process gives full sway to majority preferences without any Madisonian checks and balances) *with* Robin Charlow, *Judicial Review, Equal Protection and the Problem with Plebiscites*, 79 Cornell L. Rev. 527 (1994) (arguing that those pressing for more aggressive judicial review of initiatives are wrong and are more often frustrated with the substantive content of current equal protection doctrine) *and* Mark Tushnet, *Fear of Voting: Differential Standards of Judicial Review of Direct Legislation*, 1996 NYU Ann. Surv. Am. L. ___ (1997) (forthcoming) (arguing against differential judicial review for popularly enacted laws as compared to ordinary legislation). For a case study of the role of constitutional arguments in initiative processes, see David A. Sklansky, *Proposition 187 and the Ghost of James Bradley Thayer*, 17 Chicano-Latino L. Rev. 24 (1995) (documenting that in the process of adopting California's Proposition 187, which barred aliens from a variety of social services, supporters urged the disregard of constitutional concerns on the assumption that judicial review would take care of any problems). We shall return to these questions below. But consider for the moment some of the purely interpretive problems. As summarized by Professor Jane Schacter:

> The case of direct democracy tests the limits of judicial willingness to deploy intentionalist methodology. There are reasons to suspect that a search for "popular intent" will be even more problematic than the traditional search for legislative intent. Consider, for example, the mass size of the electorate; the absence of legislative hearings, committee reports, or other recorded legislative history; and the inability of citizen lawmakers to deliberate about, or to amend, proposed ballot measures. In addition, voters are not professional lawmakers, so it is problematic to impute to the electorate the same knowledge about law, legal terminology, and legislative context that courts routinely ascribe—if sometimes only as aspiration—to legislators. These structural dynamics of the direct lawmaking process should further burden what is in any circumstance a problematic quest for the single intent underlying a law.

Jane S. Schacter, *The Pursuit of "Popular Intent": Interpretive Dilemmas in Direct Democracy*, 105 Yale L.J. 107 (1995). For a sophisticated argument as to how courts should go about the process of interpreting the products of direct lawmaking, see Philip P. Frickey, *Interpretation on the Borderline: Constitution, Canons, Direct Democracy*, 1996 NYU Ann. Surv. Am. L. ___ (1997) (forthcoming). To the general problems of legal interpretation of texts enacted popularly—rather than through formal legislative means—can be added the problems caused by initiatives whose language is overwhelmingly long or hopelessly obscure. In addition, it is not uncommon for voters to approve two apparently conflicting initiatives in the same election—a process that sometimes results because once one initiative gets underway, others will seek to qualify an "alternative" initiative on the same topic. For endorsement of this process of generating competing, alternative initiatives, see K.K. DuVivier, *By Going Wrong All Things Come Right: Using Alternative Initiatives to Improve Citizen Lawmaking*, 63 U. Cinn. L. Rev. 1185 (1995). Under California law, when such a conflict occurs, the provision that has received the most votes prevails. In *Taxpayers to Limit Campaign Spending v. Fair Political Practices Commission*, 799 P.2d 1220 (1990), this had the ironic effect of leading to invalidation of both of the two campaign finance reform initiatives that voters had approved; the court held the two in conflict, declared the one with the most votes to be the one adopted, but struck that one down as unconstitutional. As a result, voters got no campaign finance reform in any form.

4. Does the Guarantee Clause critique of direct democracy embody an overly romantic notion of the legislative process? Critics of direct democracy argue that it tends to inflame passions on single issues, thereby undermining the processes of reasoned deliberation that should hold sway in a legislative setting. Others, however, argue that the contrast is between direct democracy and "an idealized construct of the legislative process" that fails to take into account the real infirmities of legislative deadlock and interest group capture. *See* Richard Briffault, *Distrust of Democracy*, 63 Tex. L. Rev. 1347, 1350 (1985). Briffault emphasizes that the existence of initiative provisions can serve as an indirect check on legislative policy even when initiatives are not directly used to make law. The fact that voters can turn to the initiative to overturn legislative policies can cast a shadow over the dynamics of legislative policymaking. For analysis of this possible role of initiatives, see Elisabeth R. Gerber, *Legislative Response to the Threat of Popular Initiatives*, 40 Am. J. Pol. Sci. 99 (1996).

In thinking about the relationship between direct democracy and representative institutions, keep in mind that direct democracy has been structured in a number of different ways in different states. Some states permit only the initiative; some states permit only the referendum; some states permit both. In Michigan, initiatives must first be submitted to the legislature and are voted on only if the legislature fails to enact the measure within a specified time. Florida and North Carolina permit initiatives only for constitutional amendments, while other states permit the initiative also for statutes. Some states prohibit the initiative or referendum for certain subjects, such as appropriations, special legislation, or laws on health and safety. Other states prohibit direct lawmaking on more precisely defined subjects: in Massachusetts, for issues involving religion; in Montana, for issues involving support for state government; in Colorado, for matters dealing with property classifications. For a general overview of state practices, see ABA Task Force on Initiatives and Referenda, *The Challenge of Direct Democracy in a Republic: Report and Recommendations of the Task Force on Initiatives and Referenda* 8–9 (1992).

The effect of the shadow of direct lawmaking processes on legislatures presumably depends on the precise form direct lawmaking is required to take in different states. Should any of the constitutional issues surrounding direct lawmaking depend on which particular form is used? For example, is there less of a "republican form of government" concern with direct lawmaking that involves a specific role for the legislature? Some states permit initiative advocates to choose whether to seek a constitutional amendment or a statutory initiative on the same subject; constitutional amendments can only be changed through subsequent popular vote, but statutory initiatives can be amended either through popular vote or legislative action. Magleby, *supra,* at 13. For an argument that in such states, voters are unlikely to perceive the consequences of the difference, and that therefore courts should adopt strong presumptions that difficult to characterize initiatives will be treated as statutory rather than constitutional, see Elizabeth Garrett, *Who Directs Direct Democracy?*, 4 U. Chi. Roundtable ___ (forthcoming, 1997).

5. The arguments for and against the proposition that direct democracy is inconsistent with the Guarantee Clause are well summarized in *Symposium: Guaranteeing a Republican Form of Government*, 65 Colo. L. Rev. 709 (1994). For a review of litigation in state courts, see Hans A. Linde, *When Initiative Lawmaking Is Not "Republican Government": The Campaign Against Homosexuality*, 72 Or. L. Rev. 19 (1993).

6. To what extent does *Pacific States* resemble *Colegrove v. Green*, 328 U.S. 549 (1946), in which the Court declined to exercise jurisdiction over claims of quantitative malapportionment in Illinois' congressional delegation, or *Giles v. Harris*, 189 U.S. 475 (1903), in which the Court declined to exercise jurisdiction over challenges by black voters to provisions of Alabama's disenfranchising convention? Here, presumably, there would be no major enforcement problem. That is, if the Supreme Court had simply declared initiatives unconstitutional, it is hard to imagine that states would have continued to hold them, whereas administrability problems loomed large in both *Colegrove* and *Giles*. On the other hand, any line drawing short of outright approval or rejection of initiatives and referenda might be very tricky to police. Consider, for example, what would have happened if the Court had upheld initiatives or referenda regarding the enactment or amendment of a state *constitution*, while requiring lawmaking once a constitution is established to be done legislatively. Would this be easily circumvented by constitutionalizing everything? In this light, consider the vast difference between the U.S. Constitution, which is short and largely structural in nature, and many state constitutions which are lengthy documents that regulate large substantive areas.

NOTE ON MONEY AND THE INITIATIVE PROCESS

In *Meyer v. Grant*, 486 U.S. 414 (1988), discussed in Chapter 9, the Supreme Court unanimously held unconstitutional on First Amendment grounds state efforts to prohibit the use of paid signature gatherers in the initiative process. Colorado had defended this policy with the argument, among others, that it was necessary to protect "the integrity of the initiative process." The Court construed this defense in an exceedingly narrow way, taking it to mean that the state was concerned paid signature gatherers were more likely to take fraudulent signatures. Having construed the state's justification this way, the Court held that there was no evidence to support this speculation, and that the state had other means of prohibiting such fraud. Ironically, in the aftermath of *Meyer*, Colorado has found that paid signature collection does result in greater fraud. Richard Collins and Dale Oesterle, *Structuring the Ballot Initiative: Procedures that Do and Don't Work*, 66 U. Colo. L. Rev. 47, 74 (1995); Magleby, *supra*, at 23. Recall also that the Court's decision that corporations have the same First Amendment rights as voters to engage in political campaigning arose in the initiative context, where a Massachusetts statute had made it criminal for corporations to make donations in initiative campaigns (except where the measure materially affected corporate property, business, or assets). *First National Bank of Boston v. Bellotti*, 435 U.S. 765 (1978). Before *Bellotti*, 18 states had limited corporate spending in initiative campaigns. *See also Citizens Against Rent Control v. Berkeley*, 454 U.S. 290 (1981) (striking down on First Amendment grounds a $250 cap on contributions individuals or corporations could make to committees formed to support or oppose ballot measures).

But was protecting the integrity of direct lawmaking at issue in *Meyer* in only the limited sense the Court viewed as at stake? *Meyer* and *First National Bank of Boston* also raise more general questions about the actual and appropriate role of money and interest groups in direct lawmaking processes. *Meyer* enabled the rise of an initiative industry of paid signature gatherers. For a critique of *Meyer*, see Daniel H. Lowenstein and Robert Stern, *The First Amendment and Paid Initiative Circulators: A Dissenting View and a Proposal*, 17 Hast. Const. L.Q. 175 (1989). States vary, but typically require valid signatures from about 8 percent of those who voted for governor in the previous election to qualify an initiative for the ballot. In California, this means around one million signatures. Most signatures must be gathered under tight deadline pressures, typically 90-150 days. According to recent studies, professional agencies charge up to $1.50 per name in California, and as low as 30 cents per name in North Dakota. Between signature gathering and the other costs associated simply to qualify a measure for the ballot, the cost of doing so is estimated for California to be around one million dollars. *See, e.g.,* Dan Morain, *1996 Expected to be Boon Year for Initiatives*, L.A. Times, Dec. 9, 1995 at A1; Briffault, *supra*, at 1352.

The cost of the actual campaign on the merits is much greater and has reached stunning levels in recent years. Interest groups hire consultants to poll voters and gauge their response to different words and messages that might be used; they launch advertising and promotion efforts; they seek to line up coalitions to support the initiative and do door-to-door campaigning or use direct-mail and other fund-raising techniques. In 1988, the California ballot contained five different initiatives on automobile insurance; the insurance industry reportedly spent $88 million campaigning on these measures—more than either Presidential candidate directly spent that year on his Presidential campaign. Peter Schrag, *Take the Initiative, Please: Referendum Madness in California*, 28 Am. Prospect 61 (1996). The average spending for four statewide initiatives in Michigan in 1992 was more than $5 million. Proponents of an initiative in Washington to approve financing for a new football stadium reportedly spent more than $3 million on the campaign, breaking the state's previous record of $2.1 million spent on an unsuccessful initiative to legalize slot machines on tribal reservations. David Scoffer, *Stadium Foes Chide Allen for Not Voting: Campaign to Set Spending Record*, The Seattle Times, May 28, 1997, B1.

Many commentators now believe that the direct lawmaking process is at least as driven by "special interests" as ordinary lawmaking, and that the image of direct lawmaking as a means for citizen control over special-interest captured legislatures is largely an illusion. *See, e.g.,* Garrett, *Who Directs Direct Democracy?, supra;* Daniel H. Lowenstein, *Campaign Spending and Ballot Propositions: Recent Experience, Public Choice Theory and the First Amendment*, 29 UCLA L. Rev. 505 (1982); Randy M. Mastro et. al., *Taking the Initiative: Corporate Control of the Referendum Process through Media Spending and What to do About It*, 32 Fed. Comm. L.J. 315 (1981); John S. Shockley, *Direct Democracy, Campaign Finance, and the Courts: Can Corruption, Undue Influence, and Declining Voter Confidence Be Found*, 39 U. Miami L. Rev. 377 (1985). But studies of the relationship between spending and success suggest that the link is complex rather than deterministic. One study found that campaign spending was the decisive factor in about one-eighth of the ballot measures held between 1976–1984. David D. Schmidt, Citizen Lawmakers: The Ballot Initiative Revolution 35 (1989). Several studies conclude that heavy spending is much more effective in defeating measures than in getting them enacted. *See, e.g.,* Lowenstein, *Campaign Spending*, at 511. Consider whether the considerations in favor and against limitations on expenditures in candidate contests discussed in Chapter 9 are the same or different in the context of direct lawmaking.

On the other hand, direct democracy may be the only mechanism for contesting what Professor Klarman has called "legislative entrenchment," that is, the tendency of legislators to act to retain their hold on their offices. *See* Michael Klarman, *Majoritarian Judicial Review: The Entrenchment Problem*, 85 Georgetown L.J. 491 (1997). Campaign finance law—the subject of Chapter 9—is especially susceptible to legislative entrenchment, since incumbents are in a good position to pass laws that help them keep their seats and to block laws that would open the process up to more competitive challenges. *See id.* at 522–23, 536–37. Despite concerns about the role of money in the direct lawmaking process, though, many political reforms not capable of being legislatively adopted have succeeded through this alternative route. It is significant how many states have recently approved ballot initiatives dealing with campaign finance. The Maine Clean Election Act, discussed in Chapter 9, is a particularly sweeping example of citizen-initiated campaign finance reform. And voters in five other states also approved ballot measures in 1996 intended to reduce money's influence on the election process. We return at the end of this Chapter to another example of popular lawmaking that responds in part to an entrenchment problem: term limits.

B. Direct Democracy and Rights of Political Participation

In recent times, the initiative process has been used to take on some of the most controversial political issues of the day. In this section, we focus on areas where the courts' treatment of the products of direct democracy intersects with judicial regulation of the political process more generally.

1. Popular Lawmaking and Unpopular Groups

Hunter v. Erickson
393 U.S. 385 (1969).

■ Mr. Justice White delivered the opinion of the Court.

The question in this case is whether the City of Akron, Ohio, has denied a Negro citizen, Nellie Hunter, the equal protection of its laws by amending the city charter to prevent the city council from implementing any ordinance dealing with racial, religious, or ancestral discrimination in housing without the approval of the majority of the voters of Akron.

The Akron City Council in 1964 enacted a fair housing ordinance premised on a recognition of the social and economic losses to society which flow from substandard, ghetto housing and its tendency to breed discrimination and segregation contrary to the policy of the city to "assure equal opportunity to all persons to live in decent housing facilities regardless of race, color, religion, ancestry or national origin." Akron Ordinance No. 873–1964 § 1.

* * *

[Subsequently, the Akron City Charter was amended to provide that]

Any ordinance enacted by the Council of The City of Akron which regulates the use, sale, advertisement, transfer, listing assignment, lease, sublease or financing of real property of any kind or of any interest therein on the basis of race, color, religion, national origin or ancestry must first be approved by a majority of the electors voting on the question at a regular or general election before said ordinance shall be effective. Any such ordinance in effect at the time of the adoption of this section shall cease to be effective until approved by the electors as provided herein.

Akron City Charter § 137. The proposal for the charter amendment had been placed on the ballot at a general election upon petition of more than 10% of Akron's voters, and the amendment had been duly passed by a majority.

* * *

.... Here ... there was an explicitly racial classification treating racial housing matters differently from other racial and housing matters.

By adding § 137 to its Charter the City of Akron ... not only suspended the operation of the existing ordinance forbidding housing discrimination, but also required the approval of the electors before any future ordinance could take effect. Section 137 thus drew a distinction between those groups who sought the law's protection against racial, religious, or ancestral discriminations in the sale and rental of real estate and those who sought to regulate real property transactions in the pursuit of other ends. Those who sought, or would benefit from, most ordinances regulating the real property market remained subject to the general rule: the ordinance would become effective 30 days after passage by the City Council, or immediately if passed as an emergency measure, and would be subject to referendum only if 10% of the electors so requested by filing a proper and timely petition. Passage by the Council sufficed unless the electors themselves invoked the general referendum provisions of the city charter. But for those who sought protection against racial bias, the approval of the City Council was not enough. A referendum was required by charter at a general or regular election, without any provision for use of the expedited special election ordinarily available. The Akron charter obviously made it substantially more difficult to secure enactment of ordinances subject to § 137.

* * *

Like the law requiring specification of candidates' race on the ballot, *Anderson v. Martin,* 375 U.S. 399 (1964), § 137 places special burdens on racial minorities within the governmental process. This is no more permissible than denying them the vote, on an equal basis with others. *Cf. Gomillion v. Lightfoot,* 364 U.S. 339 (1960); *Reynolds v. Sims,* 377 U.S. 533 (1964); *Avery v. Midland County,* 390 U.S. 474 (1968).... Because the core of the Fourteenth Amendment is the prevention of meaningful and unjustified official distinctions based on race, racial classifications are constitutionally suspect, and subject to the most rigid scrutiny. They bear a far heavier burden of justification than other classifications.

We are unimpressed with any of Akron's justifications for its discrimination. Characterizing it simply as a public decision to move slowly in the delicate area of race relations emphasizes the impact and burden of § 137, but does not justify it. The amendment was unnecessary either to implement a decision to go slowly, or to allow the people of Akron to participate in that decision.[1] Likewise, insisting that a State may distribute legislative power as it desires and that the people may retain for themselves the power over certain subjects may generally be true, but these principles furnish no justification for a legislative structure which otherwise would violate the Fourteenth Amendment. Nor does the implementation of this change through popular referendum immunize it. *Lucas v. Colorado General Assembly,* 377 U.S. 713, 736–737 (1964). The sovereignty of the people is itself subject to those constitutional limitations which have been duly adopted and remain unrepealed. Even though Akron might have proceeded by majority vote at town meeting on all its municipal legislation, it has instead chosen a more complex system. Having done so, the State may no more disadvantage any particular group by making it more difficult to enact legislation in its behalf than it may dilute any person's vote or give any group a smaller representation than another of comparable size. *Cf. Reynolds v. Sims,* 377 U.S. 533 (1964); *Avery v. Midland County,* 390 U.S. 474 (1968).

We hold that § 137 discriminates against minorities, and constitutes a real, substantial, and invidious denial of the equal protection of the laws.

* * *

■ MR. JUSTICE BLACK, dissenting.

* * *

[One] argument used by the Court supposedly to support its holding is that we have in a number of our cases supported the right to vote without discrimination. And we have. But in no one of them have we held that a

---

1. The people of Akron had the power to initiate legislation, or to review council decisions, even before § 137. The procedural prerequisites for this popular action are perfectly reasonable, as the gathering of 10% of the voters' signatures in the course of passing § 137 illustrates.

State is without power to repeal its own laws when convinced by experience that a law is not serving a useful purpose. Moreover, it is the Court's opinion here that casts aspersions upon the right of citizens to vote. I say that for this reason. Akron's repealing law here held unconstitutional, provides that an ordinance in the fair housing field in Akron "must first be approved by a majority of the electors voting on the question at a regular or general election before said ordinance shall be effective." The Court uses this granted right of the people to vote on this important legislation as a key argument for holding that the repealer denies equal protection to Negroes. Just consider that for a moment. In this Government, which we boast is "of the people, by the people, and for the people," conditioning the enactment of a law on a majority vote of the people condemns that law as unconstitutional in the eyes of the Court! There may have been other state laws held unconstitutional in the past on grounds that are equally as fallacious and undemocratic as those the Court relies on today, but if so I do not recall such cases at the moment. It is time, I think, to recall that the Equal Protection Clause does not empower this Court to decide what ordinances or laws a State may repeal. I would not strike down this repealing ordinance.

NOTES AND QUESTIONS

1. *Hunter* illustrates some of the difficulties the Court has had in applying "tiers of scrutiny" equal protection analysis to voting rights claims. As Justice Marshall argued in his dissent in *City of Mobile v. Bolden*, 446 U.S. 55 (1980), strict scrutiny can be triggered either by the use of a racial classification in providing a state benefit, or by state impairment of a fundamental right of citizenship. In *Hunter,* the Court characterized the ordinance as involving "an explicitly racial classification." But in exactly what way was that so? The Akron charter amendment did single out regulation "on the basis of race, color, religion, national origin or ancestry" for different treatment than regulation directed at, for example, discrimination on the basis of age. But a large proportion of contemporary antidiscrimination law does exactly the same thing. For example, Title VII of the 1964 Civil Rights Act forbids discrimination in employment on the basis of race, religion, national origin, and sex, but not on the basis of political affiliation. Is Title VII "an explicitly racial classification" that is presumptively invalid and must be justified under strict scrutiny? If not—and no court has ever subjected standard antidiscrimination ordinances to strict scrutiny—this suggests that it is not the mere mention of race that makes for a racial classification.

In *Hunter*, the Court focused on the effects of the Akron ordinance to explain why it was a racial classification. First, the Court suggested that the charter amendment would have disproportionate effects on racial minorities because "the reality [was] that the law's impact [fell] on the minority." But in contemporary equal protection doctrine, disparate impact alone would not be enough; *Washington v. Davis,* 426 U.S. 229 (1976), would undermine *Hunter* unless plaintiffs could also establish that the charter amendment had been adopted for a discriminatory purpose.

Moreover, if *Hunter* is an ordinary disproportionate impact case, why did the Court find it either necessary or desirable to rely on its apportionment decisions as well? This suggests a different theory underlying *Hunter*: that the amendment was unconstitutional because it restructured the political process selectively for different groups. Those who supported certain kinds of regulations of housing could pursue change through the city council; those who sought regulation of housing to protect against racial, religious, or ancestral discriminations had to get the voters of Akron to approve. Perhaps this selective restructuring of the political process for certain groups was the constitutional defect. In a concurring opinion, Justices Harlan and Stewart offered what might be considered a third theory: that the *purpose* of the charter amendment was to make it more difficult for certain racial and religious minorities to achieve legislation in their interest. Is that an alternative rationale for finding that although the Akron charter amendment was facially neutral it had a discriminatory purpose? Is it persuasive?

2. *The problem of issues versus groups.* Any substantive constitutional provision restructures the political process with respect to the issue involved. When abortion is recognized as a constitutional right, those who desire to see abortion restricted or prohibited cannot appeal to the ordinary political process, but are left with only the recourse of seeking constitutional amendment to transform their preferences into policies. Whether the relevant provision explicitly says so or not, any substantive issue dealt with constitutionally is necessarily an issue that can no longer be addressed in the ordinary political process. Does that mean that the equal protection rights of pro-life voters have been violated when the Constitution is read to recognize that pregnant women have a constitutional right to make decisions regarding continuation of their pregnancies? But suppose pro-lifers were to succeed in having the Constitution amended to prohibit abortion. At that point, those who are pro-choice would not be able to resort to the ordinary legislative process; they would now have to seek a constitutional amendment if they were to transform their preferences into policies.

If *Hunter* rests on an impermissible restructuring of the political process, the problem then is to distinguish between restructuring that makes it more difficult for one side to achieve success *on an issue* and restructuring that makes it more difficult for *a relevant group* to participate in the political process. Had the charter amendment in Akron permitted black voters to participate only in direct lawmaking but not lobby the city council, that would obviously have been an unconstitutional group-disadvantaging gerrymandering of the political process. But the charter amendment did not classify voters by race; on its face, it classified issues. For what reasons, then, is the amendment to be understood as regulating groups rather than issues? Is it because the Court perceives there to be a strong correlation between one's stance on fair-housing legislation and one's race? But what if a significant number of white voters supported such legislation in Akron, even if not enough to defeat the charter amendment? Is it because the Court perceives the beneficiaries of such legislation to be overwhelming racial or religious minorities? In that event, would it make any difference to the constitutional issue—to whether the charter amendment was treated as "an explicitly racial classification"—if minorities in Akron were actually somewhat divided over whether fair-housing legislation was in their interest?

3. Is the Court's approach in *Hunter* reminiscent of its perspective in *Gomillion v. Lightfoot*, 364 U.S. 339 (1960), discussed *supra* in Chapter 2? Given the Court's statement that "we do not hold that mere repeal of an existing ordinance violates the Fourteenth Amendment," *Hunter*, 393 U.S. at 390 n.5, does the Court's measure of appropriate political power here depend on its acceptance of the pre-existing baseline of lawmaking authority as fair? *See generally* Pamela S. Karlan, *Just Politics?: Five Not So Easy Pieces of the 1995 Term*, 34 Houston L. Rev. 289, 298–304 (1997) (discussing this aspect of *Hunter*). Why does the Court mistrust Akron's popular legislation process if the same result could be obtained by getting the city council simply to repeal the fair housing ordinance?

4. The permissibility of popular repeal of pre-existing state policy perceived to involve racial questions, and the restructuring of governmental processes for such questions, was revisited in a pair of Supreme Court decisions in 1982, in which the Court reached diametrically opposite results. In *Crawford v. Board of Education*, 458 U.S. 527 (1982), the Court upheld a voter initiated amendment to the California Constitution (Proposition I) that forbade state courts from ordering busing to achieve desegregation unless a federal court would do so to remedy a violation of the Equal Protection Clause of the Fourteenth Amendment of the United States Constitution. But in *Washington v. Seattle School District No. 1*, 458 U.S. 457 (1982), the Court struck down a Washington State initiative (Initiative 350) that prohibited school boards from requiring any student to attend a school other than the one geographically nearest or next nearest to his home.

Justice Powell's opinion for the Court in *Crawford* rejected, as "destructive of a State's democratic processes and of its ability to experiment" the claim that "once a State chooses to do 'more' than the Fourteenth Amendment requires, it may never recede." *Id.* at 535. *Hunter*, in contrast to Proposition I, "involved more than a 'mere repeal' of the fair housing ordinance; persons seeking antidiscrimination housing laws—presumptively racial minorities—were singled out for mandatory referendums while no other group ... [faced] that obstacle."

> [Proposition I neither] distorts the political process for racial reasons [nor] allocates governmental or judicial power on the basis

of a discriminatory principle. The Constitution does not require things which are different in fact or opinion to be treated in law as though they were the same.... Surely it was constitutional for the.... people of the State to determine that the standard of the Fourteenth Amendment was more appropriate for California courts to apply in desegregation cases than the standard repealed by Proposition I.

By contrast, the *Seattle School District* Court relied heavily on *Hunter* in identifying "a simple but central principle":

> [State action that] explicitly us[es] the racial nature of a decision to determine the decisionmaking process ... places special burdens on racial minorities within the governmental process, thereby making it more difficult for certain racial and religious minorities [than for other members of the community] to achieve legislation that is in their interest. Such a structuring of the political process ... [is] no more permissible than [is] denying [members of a racial minority] the vote, on an equal basis with others.... [T]he practical effect of Initiative 350 is to work a reallocation of power of the kind condemned in *Hunter*. The initiative removes the authority to address a racial problem—and only a racial problem—from the existing decisionmaking body, in such a way as to burden minority interests. Those favoring the elimination of de facto school segregation now must seek relief from the state legislature, or from the statewide electorate. Yet authority over all other student assignment decisions, as well as over most other areas of educational policy, remains vested in the local school board.... As in *Hunter*, then, the community's political mechanisms are modified to place effective decisionmaking authority over a racial issue at a different level of government.

* * *

> [It is true that t]he State might have vested all decisionmaking authority in itself.... [But] until the passage of Initiative 350, Washington law in fact had established the local school board, rather than the State, as the entity charged with making decisions of the type at issue here.... Given this statutory structure, we have little difficulty concluding that Initiative 350 worked a major reordering of the State's educational decisionmaking process. Before adoption of the initiative, the power to determine what programs would most appropriately fill a school district's educational needs—including programs involving student assignment and desegregation—was firmly committed to the local board's discretion. The question whether to provide an integrated learning environment rather than a system of neighborhood schools surely involved a decision of that sort. After passage of Initiative 350, authority over all but one of those areas remained in the hands of

the local board. By placing power over desegregative busing at the state level, then, Initiative 350 plainly differentiates between the treatment of problems involving racial matters and that afforded other problems in the same area. The District Court and the Court of Appeals similarly concluded that the initiative restructured the Washington political process, and we see no reason to challenge the determinations of courts familiar with local law.

* * *

[Initiative 350] burdens all future attempts to integrate Washington schools in districts throughout the State, by lodging decisionmaking authority over the question at a new and remote level of government. Indeed, the initiative, like the charter amendment at issue in *Hunter*, has its most pernicious effect on integration programs that do not arouse extraordinary controversy. In such situations the initiative makes the enactment of racially beneficial legislation difficult, though the particular program involved might not have inspired opposition had it been promulgated through the usual legislative processes used for comparable legislation. This imposes direct and undeniable burdens on minority interests.

5. Can *Crawford* and *Seattle School District* be reconciled simply by pointing to the standards for appellate review—in the California case, the lower courts declined to find a racially discriminatory purpose, while in the Washington State case, they found such an impermissible intent? In *Crawford*, the Court pointed to Proposition I's statement of purpose:

> [The] Legislature and people of the State of California find and declare that this amendment is necessary to serve compelling public interests, including those of making the most effective use of the limited financial resources now and prospectively available to support public education, maximizing the educational opportunities and protecting the health and safety of all public school pupils, enhancing the ability of parents to participate in the educational process, preserving harmony and tranquility in this state and its public schools, preventing the waste of scarce fuel, resources, and protecting the environment.

The Court found that voters might have been motivated by any of these purposes, as well as by a belief that mandatory busing was actually "aggravating rather than ameliorating the desegregation problem," and quoted with approval the California state court's characterization of "petitioners' claim of discriminatory intent on the part of millions of voters as but 'pure speculation.' "

> In this case the Proposition was approved by an overwhelming majority of the electorate. It received support from members of all races. The purposes of the Proposition are stated in its text and are legitimate, nondiscriminatory objectives. In these circum-

stances, we will not dispute the judgment of the Court of Appeal or impugn the motives of the State's electorate.

In *Seattle School District*, however, the lower court had reached a different conclusion about the popular intent behind Initiative 350:

> Neither the initiative's sponsors, nor the District Court, nor the Court of Appeals had any difficulty perceiving the racial nature of the issue settled by Initiative 350. Thus, the District Court found that the text of the initiative was carefully tailored to interfere only with desegregative busing. Proponents of the initiative candidly "represented that there would be no loss of school district flexibility other than in busing for desegregation purposes." ... The Washington electorate surely was aware of this, for it was "assured" by CiVIC officials [the people who had drafted the initiative] that "99% of the school districts in the state"—those that lacked mandatory integration programs—"would not be affected by the passage of 350." It is beyond reasonable dispute, then, that the initiative was enacted because of, not merely in spite of, its adverse effects upon busing for integration.

Is this account of *Seattle School District* persuasive? Unlike *Hunter*, the regulation under challenge does not expressly refer to racial or ethnic groups. Even if busing is characterized as an issue of a "racial nature," why is taking a position on that issue tantamount to being motivated by constitutionally discriminatory purposes? Is strict scrutiny necessary to ferret out the underlying racial motive in *Seattle School District*? If so, does the opinion suffer from circular reasoning in that exacting scrutiny is necessary to ferret out an unarticulated racial purpose, which in turn provides the evidence of a racial classification, which in turn justifies the initial application of strict scrutiny?

6. Does the difference between the cases turn on the fact that *Crawford* involved restrictions on the remedial powers of courts, while *Seattle School District* involved school boards, an entity more conventionally conceived as a policymaking body? Note that the *Seattle* Court, as in *Hunter*, invoked the Court's precedents from the apportionment area—precedents that do not apply to courts.

7. Opponents of direct democracy charge that the initiative and referendum processes overreward voting majorities and threaten minority rights. *See* Derrick A. Bell, Jr., *The Referendum: Democracy's Barrier to Racial Equality*, 54 Wash. L. Rev. 1 (1978). Think about the reasons why a majority might be able to enact discriminatory legislation through the popular processes even when such legislation is not enacted by its representatives. To what extent do anonymity, the lack of any requirement for giving reasons, and the inability to logroll account for the difference in outcomes? On the other hand, an argument can be made that legislators rarely can devote themselves to systematic attention to any particular issue, no matter how pressing, and that deliberation among citizens on an issue of public moment may be of higher quality that legislative debate. *See* Lynn A. Baker, *Direct Democracy and Discrimination: A Public Choice Perspective*, 67 Chi.-Kent L. Rev. 707, 744–52 (1992).

Evans v. Romer
882 P.2d 1335 (Colo.1994).

■ CHIEF JUSTICE ROVIRA delivered the opinion of the court

* * *

["Amendment 2"—a proposal to amend article II, section 30 of the Colorado constitution—was approved by the state's voters in November 1992 by a vote of 813,966 to 710,151 (53.4% to 46.6%).]

Amendment 2 provides:

> No Protected Status Based on Homosexual, Lesbian, or Bisexual Orientation. Neither the State of Colorado, through any of its branches or departments, nor any of its agencies, political subdivisions, municipalities or school districts, shall enact, adopt or enforce any statute, regulation, ordinance or policy whereby homosexual, lesbian or bisexual orientation, conduct, practices or relationships shall constitute or otherwise be the basis of or entitle any person or class of persons to have or claim any minority status, quota preferences, protected status or claim of discrimination. This Section of the Constitution shall be in all respects self-executing.

* * *

[In our decision reviewing the trial court's entry of a preliminary injunction,] we held that the Equal Protection Clause of the United States Constitution protects the fundamental right to participate equally in the political process, and that any legislation or state constitutional amendment which infringes on this right by fencing out an independently identifiable class of persons must be subject to strict judicial scrutiny.

The right to participate equally in the political process is clearly affected by Amendment 2, because it bars gay men, lesbians, and bisexuals from having an effective voice in governmental affairs insofar as those persons deem it beneficial to seek legislation that would protect them from discrimination based on their sexual orientation. Amendment 2 alters the political process so that a targeted class is prohibited from obtaining legislative, executive, and judicial protection or redress from discrimination absent the consent of a majority of the electorate through the adoption of a constitutional amendment.

Rather than attempting to withdraw antidiscrimination issues as a whole from state and local control, Amendment 2 singles out one form of discrimination and removes its redress from consideration by the normal political processes.

* * *

A legislative enactment which infringes on a fundamental right or which burdens a suspect class is constitutionally permissible only if it is "necessary to promote a compelling state interest," *Dunn v. Blumstein,* [405 U.S. 330 (1972)], and does so in the least restrictive manner possible.... Defendants ... argue that Amendment 2 "promotes the compelling governmental interest of allowing the people themselves to establish public social and moral norms." In support of this proposition, defendants define two related norms which are promoted by Amendment 2: Amendment 2 preserves heterosexual families and heterosexual marriage and, more generally, it sends the societal message condemning gay men, lesbians, and bisexuals as immoral.... [But d]efendants have cited no authority to support the proposition that the promotion of public morality constitutes a compelling governmental interest, and we are aware of none. At the most, this interest is substantial. However, a substantial governmental interest is not sufficient to render constitutional a law which infringes on a fundamental right—the interest must be compelling.

Furthermore, even recognizing the legitimacy of promoting public morals as a governmental interest, it is clear to us that Amendment 2 is not necessary to preserve heterosexual families, marriage, or to express disapproval of gay men, lesbians, and bisexuals. First, we reject defendants' suggestion that laws prohibiting discrimination against gay men, lesbians, and bisexuals will undermine marriages and heterosexual families because married heterosexuals will "choose" to "become homosexual" if discrimination against homosexuals is prohibited. This assertion flies in the face of the empirical evidence presented at trial on marriage and divorce rates....

Defendants also argue that the "endorsement" of homosexuality undermines marriage and heterosexual families because antidiscrimination laws implicitly endorse that conduct which is deemed an improper basis for discrimination. We are of the opinion, however, that antidiscrimination laws make no assumptions about the morality of protected classes—they simply recognize that certain characteristics, be they moral or immoral—have no relevance in enumerated commercial contexts. For instance, it is difficult to imagine how a law which prohibits employers from discriminating against anyone engaged in off-duty, legal conduct such as smoking tobacco, see § 24–34–402.5, 10A C.R.S. (1994 Supp.), constitutes an endorsement of smoking.

In short, prohibitions on discrimination against gay men, lesbians, and bisexuals do not imply an endorsement of any particular sexual orientation or practices. To the contrary, prohibitions on discrimination imply at most that termination of employment, eviction or denial of rental opportunities, denial of insurance coverage, and other sanctions in commercial contexts based on sexual orientation are not appropriate ways of advancing even valid moral beliefs.

* * *

Defendants contend that Amendment 2 "prevents government from supporting the political objectives of a special interest group." ... [D]efendants offer no authority to support the rather remarkable proposition that the government has a compelling interest in seeing that the state does not support the political objectives of a "special interest group." The state exists for the very purpose of implementing the political objectives of the governed so long as that can be done consistently with the constitution. The fact that some political objectives are promoted by "special interest groups" is utterly inconsequential. Indeed, virtually any law could be regarded as a benefit to a "special interest group." If defendants' argument had any merit at all, the compelling state interest defined would justify striking down almost any legislative enactment imaginable. This is clearly not the law. No citation of authority is needed to make the point.

* * *

Defendants claim that Amendment 2 "serves to deter factionalism through ensuring that decisions regarding special protections for homosexuals and bisexuals are made at the highest level of government." More specifically, they argue that "Amendment 2 is intended, not to restrain the competition of ideas," but "seeks to ensure that the deeply divisive issue of homosexuality's place in our society does not serve to fragment Colorado's body politic." Amendment 2 accomplishes this end by eliminating "city-by-city and county-by-county battles over this issue."

We reject the argument that the interest in deterring factionalism, as defined by defendants, is compelling. Political debate, even if characterized as "factionalism," is not an evil which the state has a legitimate interest in deterring but rather, constitutes the foundation of democracy. "There is no significant state or public interest in curtailing debate or discussion of a ballot measure." *Citizens Against Rent Control v. City of Berkeley*, 454 U.S. 290, 299 (1981). We fail to see how the state, which is charged with serving the will of the people, can have any legitimate interest in preventing one side of a controversial debate from pressing its case before governmental bodies simply because it would prefer to avoid political controversy or "factionalism."

* * *

NOTES AND QUESTIONS

1. We focus on the opinion of the Colorado Supreme Court because it found Amendment 2 unconstitutional on the basis of the "fundamental right to participate in the political process" that had been the rationale for *Hunter*. The United States Supreme Court reached the same result as the

Colorado Supreme Court, but on different grounds that made no mention of any right to participate in the political process. *See Romer v. Evans*, 116 S.Ct. 1620 (1996). Instead, the United States Supreme Court held that Amendment 2 violated the rational basis scrutiny of conventional equal protection analysis.

But can Amendment 2 be held unconstitutional without invoking the same concerns about restructuring the political process that the Court invoked in Hunter? Compare the following passages from *Hunter*, which the United States Supreme Court did not rely upon, and *Romer*:

ROMER v. EVANS 116 S.Ct. 1620 (1996)	HUNTER v. ERICKSON 393 U.S. 385 (1968)
"Central both to the idea of the rule of law and to our own Constitution's guarantee of equal protection is the principle that government and each of its parts remain open on impartial terms to all who seek its assistance.... A law declaring that in general it shall be more difficult for one group of citizens than for all others to seek aid from the government is itself a denial of equal protection of the laws in the most literal sense."	"A state may no more disadvantage any particular group by making it more difficult to enact legislation in its behalf than it may dilute any person's vote or give any group a smaller representation than another of comparable size."
"[T]he protections Amendment 2 withholds.... are protections taken for granted by most people either because they already have them or do not need them."	"The majority needs no protection against discrimination and if it did, a referendum might be bothersome but no more than that."

Given these parallels, why did the U.S. Supreme Court so assiduously avoid relying on *Hunter*? Why did the Court not see the case as raising issues about the structure of the political process? For one extensive explanation, see Pamela S. Karlan, *Just Politics?: Five Not So Easy Pieces of the 1995 Term*, 34 Houston L. Rev. 289 (1997). Would reliance on *Hunter* have suggested that classifications involving sexual orientation were suspect or quasi-suspect, thus warranting heightened judicial scrutiny?

2. Justice Scalia's vigorous dissent in *Romer* quite clearly views the case as a political process case:

> The central thesis of the Court's reasoning is that any group is denied equal protection when, to obtain advantage (or, presumably, to avoid disadvantage), it must have recourse to a more general and hence more difficult level of political decisionmaking than others. The world has never heard of such a principle, which is why the Court's opinion is so long on emotive utterance and so short on relevant legal citation. And it seems to me most unlikely

that any multilevel democracy can function under such a principle. For whenever a disadvantage is imposed, or conferral of a benefit is prohibited, at one of the higher levels of democratic decisionmaking (i.e., by the state legislature rather than local government, or by the people at large in the state constitution rather than the legislature), the affected group has (under this theory) been denied equal protection. To take the simplest of examples, consider a state law prohibiting the award of municipal contracts to relatives of mayors or city councilmen. Once such a law is passed, the group composed of such relatives must, in order to get the benefit of city contracts, persuade the state legislature—unlike all other citizens, who need only persuade the municipality. It is ridiculous to consider this a denial of equal protection, which is why the Court's theory is unheard-of.

The Court might reply that the example I have given is not a denial of equal protection only because the same "rational basis" (avoidance of corruption) which renders constitutional the substantive discrimination against relatives (i.e., the fact that they alone cannot obtain city contracts) also automatically suffices to sustain what might be called the electoral-procedural discrimination against them (i.e., the fact that they must go to the state level to get this changed). This is of course a perfectly reasonable response, and would explain why "electoral-procedural discrimination" has not hitherto been heard of: a law that is valid in its substance is automatically valid in its level of enactment. But the Court cannot afford to make this argument, for ... there is no doubt of a rational basis for the substance of the prohibition at issue here. The Court's entire novel theory rests upon the proposition that there is something special—something that cannot be justified by normal "rational basis" analysis—in making a disadvantaged group (or a nonpreferred group) resort to a higher decisionmaking level. That proposition finds no support in law or logic.

According to Justice Scalia, Amendment 2 was a response to the "problem (a problem, that is, for those who wish to retain social disapprobation of homosexuality) ... that, because those who engage in homosexual conduct tend to reside in disproportionate numbers in certain communities, have high disposable income, and of course care about homosexual-rights issues much more ardently than the public at large, they possess political power much greater than their numbers, both locally and statewide. Quite understandably, they devote this political power to achieving not merely a grudging social toleration, but full social acceptance, of homosexuality."

To what extent is Justice Scalia making a process failure argument here, that is, an argument that Amendment 2 was designed to correct a failure in Colorado's political process that had given gays and their allies disproportionate political power? Consider his explanation:

> [Amendment 2] sought to counter both the geographic concentration and the disproportionate political power of homosexuals by (1) resolving the controversy at the statewide level, and (2) making the election a single-issue contest for both sides. It put directly, to all the citizens of the State, the question: Should homosexuality be given special protection? They answered no. The Court today asserts that this most democratic of procedures is unconstitutional.

How might the majority respond to Justice Scalia's attack?

3. It seems implausible that the Colorado Supreme Court would have reached the same decision in *Romer* if the state legislature had simply pre-empted all local anti-discrimination ordinances. Is the fact that Amendment 2 is a *constitutional* provision or the fact that it was *popularly enacted* more salient? In this regard, consider the possible array of lawmaking techniques. Laws might be enacted either popularly or through representatives; they might be either constitutional provisions or statutes.

4. *Romer* reflects a growing trend toward placing some of the most controversial issues of the day directly before the electorate. Oftentimes, as in *Romer*, the proposed referendum or initiative would remove from governmental consideration certain social programs that are thought to fare better legislatively. Courts have had a difficult time with these "hand-tying" referenda since the object appears to be to prevent the duly elected representatives of the majority of the population from enacting legislation. In particular, courts have had difficulty reconciling the attack on referenda which remove certain issues from legislative control with the very notion of constitutionalism, which is by nature a decision to remove certain matters from popular sovereignty. Beginning with *Lucas v. Colorado* and continuing through *Gordon v. Lance, Hunter, Crawford,* and *Seattle School District No. 1,* the caselaw has treated with perhaps understandable uncertainty initiatives and referenda that appear both to be intended to place barriers on minority demands on the political process *and* to operate by restricting only the operation of majoritarian processes. Perhaps the most controversial of such recent initiatives is the California Civil Rights Initiative, presented to the voters as Proposition 209. This initiative sought to end all public affirmative action programs in California by decreeing that the state and its subdivisions may not grant preferential treatment to any individual or group on the basis of "race, sex, color, ethnicity, or national origin..."
A district court entered a preliminary injunction against the operation of Proposition 209 on the grounds, *inter alia,* that the statewide effect of the Proposition would impose a substantial political burden on minorities and women seeking redress through the political process, a burden apparently condemned by *Hunter* and *Seattle School District No. 1. See Coalition for*

Economic Equity v. Wilson, 946 F.Supp. 1480 (N.D.Cal.1996). On appeal, the Ninth Circuit reversed and held:

> Plaintiffs allege that Proposition 209 places procedural burdens in the path of women and minorities, who together constitute a majority of the California electorate. Is it possible for a majority of voters impermissibly to stack the political deck against itself? The Supreme Court leaves us, quite frankly, a little perplexed as to the answer.
>
> The "political structure" equal protection cases, namely *Hunter* and *Seattle*, addressed the constitutionality of political obstructions that majorities had placed in the way of minorities to achieving protection against unequal treatment. *Hunter*, holding that the Akron amendment denied minorities equal protection of the laws, observed that "[t]he majority needs no protection against discrimination and if it did, a referendum might be bothersome but no more than that." *Hunter*, 393 U.S. at 391. *Seattle* addressed a political structure held "to place special burdens on the ability of minority groups to achieve beneficial legislation." *Seattle*, 458 U.S. at 467. In *Romer v. Evans*, 116 S.Ct. 1620 (1996), the most recent "political structure" case, Colorado's Amendment 2 left homosexuals to "obtain specific protection against discrimination only by enlisting the citizenry of Colorado." *Id.* at 1627. It would seem to make little sense to apply "political structure" equal protection principles where the group alleged to face special political burdens itself constitutes a majority of the electorate....
>
> When the electorate votes up or down on a referendum alleged to burden a majority of the voters, it is hard to conceive how members of the majority have been denied the vote.

Coalition for Economic Equity v. Wilson, 110 F.3d 1431, 1441–42 (9th Cir. 1997). Should majoritarian alterations of political *procedures*, as in *Lucas v. Colorado*, be more suspect than majoritarian alterations of *substantive* rights? Can the procedures and the substantive implications of referenda such as Proposition 209 or Amendment 2 really be kept effectively separate? Are the outcomes in *Coalition of Economic Equity* and *Romer* reconcilable?

5. What explains the increasing recourse to referenda and initiatives to address highly controversial social issues? One theory is suggested by Justice Scalia's public-choice critique of the majority in *Romer*. On this view, public referenda serve as healthy antidotes to the ability of highly motivated, self-interested minorities to leverage their political strength either in local governance or in the legislative process. For just the reasons suggested by Madison in *Federalist Papers* No. 10, popular ballots may provide for greater appeals to inflamed passion than legislative bodies constrained by deliberative processes and subject to institutional checks and balances. At the same time, an argument can be made that such extralegislative processes may serve as a check on the inherent limitations of elected legislative bodies:

> [An] important function of the substitutive plebescite is the "safety valve" it provides for particularly volatile issues that state legislators, concerned with reelection, might not want to handle. It is noteworthy that many landmark reforms that were highly controversial at the time of enactment began as initiatives in various states: women's suffrage, the abolition of poll taxes, prohibition and antiprohibition measures, the eight-hour work day, campaign finance regulations, and establishment of the nation's first presidential primary system, to name but a few.

Lynn A. Baker, *Direct Democracy and Discrimination: A Public Choice Perspective*, 67 Chi.-Kent L. Rev. 707, 754–55 (1992). Initiatives also serve other political functions than simply seeking to have enacted into law a particular policy in a particular state, and advocates have become increasingly aware of additional aims initiative campaigns can realize. Success in one state often becomes a catalyst for similar ballot propositions elsewhere. Candidates for political office now sponsor or endorse initiatives in an effort to bring more supporters to the polls. Political parties sometimes hope that voters can be more mobilized to turn out for certain highly visible initiative battles, and will then vote for candidates from the party supporting the initiative. For a survey of different motivations underlying the revival of initiatives, see Magleby, *supra*, at 28–29.

NOTE ON IMPROVING THE PROCESSES OF DIRECT LAWMAKING

The language in Colorado Amendment 2 appears exceptionally ambiguous: it bans "any minority status, quota preferences, protected status, or claim of discrimination" on the basis of homosexual, lesbian, or bisexual orientation. Does this Amendment ban protection against discrimination of any sort against people based on their sexual orientation? Or does it only ban the granting of "special preferences" to people on the basis of sexual orientation? As is the case with many initiatives today, a lawsuit was filed seeking to enjoin Amendment 2 immediately after it passed. Thus, both the Colorado Supreme Court and the United States Supreme Court were asked to decide significant constitutional questions involving major social policy issues when the relevant legal provision was ambiguous and vague and had never been applied in any concrete case. Is there anything troubling about substantive constitutional decisions being made in such contexts?

The problem of vague and obscure initiative language might be thought worse than problems of vagueness in ordinary legislation. In the latter case, there are often authoritative sources of interpretive intent to which courts can look to give content to seemingly unclear language: committee reports, debates on the floor of the legislature, and the like. But as noted above, the problems of looking outside the text of an initiative to other sources to give the language content is fraught with problems when the process involves several million voters and no sources of authoritative statements analogous to committee reports. In addition, when courts interpret unclear statutes, legislatures can more easily re-enter the process and respond than voters can when they enact constitutional amendments through direct lawmaking. There might also be greater incentives for professionals in the initiative process to deploy vague or even misleading language because voters might be more easily manipulated than professional legislators. Because the courts have not focused much attention on the differences between direct lawmaking and legislative enactments, they have not yet addressed whether they should develop doctrines specifically designed to deal with the process of direct lawmaking and the distinct interpretive problems it raises.

Several possible reforms have, however, been suggested. One already on the books in some states is the "single-subject rule." For example, in California during the 1940s, initiative sponsors began to load them up with an array of diverse subjects; one initiative included provisions relating to pensions, taxes, the right to vote for Indians, gambling, oleomargarine, the health professions, reapportionment of the state Senate, fish and game, and surface mining. In response, the California Constitution was amended in 1948 to limit initiatives to a single subject. For an overview of how courts there have applied this provision, see Daniel H. Lowenstein, *California Initiatives and the Single-Subject Rule*, 30 U.C.L.A. L. Rev. 936 (1983). Similar regulations apply to direct lawmaking and have been the subject of judicial interpretation in Arizona, Florida, Massachusetts, and Montana. Single-subject requirements might be considered to serve either of at least two purposes. First, they encourage the use of direct lawmaking as a response to specific failings in the legislature. When direct lawmaking is limited to addressing a single subject, as opposed to a list of unrelated policies, it might be more likely to be invoked only when the legislature has been given an opportunity to address the particular policy. Second, single-subject rules discourage a logrolling sort of strategy in which different provisions are included to appeal to different interest groups.

More broadly, an ABA Task Force recently completed a detailed study of the initiative process that concluded with several recommendations. ABA Taskforce on Initiatives and Referenda, *The Challenge of Direct Democracy in a Republic: Report and Recommendations of the Task Force on Initiatives and Referenda* 8–9 (1992). Some of these focused on the means by which measures qualified to appear on the ballot. The Task Force emphasized the capacity of pre-ballot review by courts or administrative agencies to address misleading or confusing language in ballot titles and propositions. Thus, the Task Force recommended that state officials be available to assist in drafting; that state officials should have the power to draft the title for the measure; and that courts should be permitted to determine before a measure appears on the ballot whether the submitted language was misleading or confusing. With respect to the process of voter decisions on the merits, the Task Force also had recommendations. Thus, to increase voter comprehension of the issues, the Task Force suggested that all states provide voters with a pamphlet at least 30 days before the vote that would include the ballot title of the provision; a summary of it; an explanation of the effects of a vote either way; and advocacy statements from proponents and opponents. Several states already have such requirements. In addition, the Task Force recommended that states should sponsor and moderate hearings or debates on initiative proposals; no state currently requires such hearings.

Would some or all of these process oriented proposals enhance the deliberative character of direct lawmaking? Or should they be seen as efforts by legal elites to so legalize the process of popular lawmaking that such lawmaking would be drained of its role as a vehicle for popular challenges to professional politics?

In this light, consider political scientist James Morone's argument that the history of democratic reforms shows how they quickly come to reproduce the very problems they were designed to cure. Professor Morone points to direct democracy as one example of this phenomenon:

> The other contrivances of Progressive democracy bore similar consequences. The people were swamped rather than strengthened by the referendum. In Oregon, for example, voters were asked to judge forty-one amendments and sixty-one laws in twelve years. The ostensibly democratic device clearly favored educated voters who could fathom the complex questions being put to them. It took organization and money to organize referenda, launch an initiative, or circulate recall petitions.

James A. Morone, The Democratic Wish 124 (1990).

2. POPULAR LAWMAKING AND PROBLEMS OF ENTRENCHMENT

The preceding cases suggested a rationale for more skeptical judicial review of certain products of popular lawmaking: those that target discrete and insular minorities who are particularly unlikely to be able to protect themselves in an unmediated political process. But is there ever an argument that courts should be especially deferential to popular lawmaking, that is, that courts should be especially reluctant to strike down a provision because it was enacted by the people directly? In this regard, consider the term limits controversy.

U.S. Term Limits, Inc. v. Thornton
514 U.S. 779 (1995).

■ JUSTICE STEVENS delivered the opinion of the Court.

* * *

Today's cases present a challenge to an amendment to the Arkansas State Constitution that prohibits the name of an otherwise-eligible candidate for Congress from appearing on the general election ballot if that candidate has already served three terms in the House of Representatives or two terms in the Senate.... Such a state-imposed restriction is contrary to the "fundamental principle of our representative democracy," embodied in the Constitution, that "the people should choose whom they please to govern them." *Powell v. McCormack*, 395 U.S. 486, 547 (1969). Allowing individual States to adopt their own qualifications for congressional service would be inconsistent with the Framers' vision of a uniform National Legislature representing the people of the United States. If the qualifications set forth in the text of the Constitution are to be changed, that text must be amended.

I

At the general election on November 3, 1992, the voters of Arkansas adopted Amendment 73 to their State Constitution. Proposed as a "Term Limitation Amendment," its preamble stated:

"The people of Arkansas find and declare that elected officials who remain in office too long become preoccupied with reelection and ignore their duties as representatives of the people. Entrenched incumbency has reduced voter participation and has led to an electoral system that is less free, less competitive, and less representative than the system established by the Founding Fathers. Therefore, the people of Arkansas, exercising their reserved powers, herein limit the terms of the elected officials."

The limitations in Amendment 73 apply to three categories of elected officials.... Section 3, the provision at issue in these cases, applies to the Arkansas Congressional Delegation. It provides:

"(a) Any person having been elected to three or more terms as a member of the United States House of Representatives from Arkansas shall not be certified as a candidate and shall not be eligible to have his/her name placed on the ballot for election to the United States House of Representatives from Arkansas.

"(b) Any person having been elected to two or more terms as a member of the United States Senate from Arkansas shall not be certified as a candidate and shall not be eligible to have his/her name placed on the ballot for election to the United States Senate from Arkansas."

* * *

II

[T]he constitutionality of Amendment 73 depends critically on the resolution of two distinct issues. The first is whether the Constitution forbids States from adding to or altering the qualifications specifically enumerated in the Constitution. The second is, if the Constitution does so forbid, whether the fact that Amendment 73 is formulated as a ballot access restriction rather than as an outright disqualification is of constitutional significance....

Twenty-six years ago, in *Powell v. McCormack,* 395 U.S. 486 (1969), we reviewed the history and text of the Qualifications Clauses in a case involving an attempted exclusion of a duly elected Member of Congress. The principal issue was whether the power granted to each House in Art. I, § 5, to judge the "Qualifications of its own Members" includes the power to impose qualifications other than those set forth in the text of the Constitution. In an opinion by Chief Justice Warren for eight Members of the Court, we held that it does not.... In *Powell,*.... [w]e noted that allowing Congress to impose additional qualifications would violate that "fundamental principle of our representative democracy ... 'that the people should choose whom they please to govern them.' "

Our opinion made clear that this broad principle incorporated at least two fundamental ideas.[2] First, we emphasized the egalitarian concept that the opportunity to be elected was open to all. We noted in particular Madison's statement in *The Federalist* that " 'under these reasonable limitations [enumerated in the Constitution], the door of this part of the federal government is open to merit of every description, whether native or adoptive, whether young or old, and without regard to poverty or wealth, or to any particular profession of religious faith.' "

Second, we recognized the critical postulate that sovereignty is vested in the people, and that sovereignty confers on the people the right to choose freely their representatives to the National Government. Thus, in *Powell*, we agreed with the sentiment expressed on behalf of Wilkes' admission to Parliament: " 'That the right of the electors to be represented by men of their own choice, was so essential for the preservation of all their other rights, that it ought to be considered as one of the most sacred parts of our constitution.' "

* * *

III

Our reaffirmation of *Powell* does not necessarily resolve the specific questions presented in these cases. For petitioners argue that whatever the constitutionality of additional qualifications for membership imposed by

---

2. The principle also incorporated the more practical concern that reposing the power to adopt qualifications in Congress would lead to a self-perpetuating body to the detriment of the new republic. *See* 2 Farrand 250 (Madison) (" 'If the Legislature could regulate [the qualification of electors or elected], it can by degrees subvert the Constitution. A Republic may be converted into an aristocracy or oligarchy as well by limiting the number capable of being elected, as the number authorised to elect' ")....

Congress, the historical and textual materials discussed in *Powell* do not support the conclusion that the Constitution prohibits additional qualifications imposed by States. In the absence of such a constitutional prohibition, petitioners argue, the Tenth Amendment and the principle of reserved powers require that States be allowed to add such qualifications.... Contrary to petitioners' assertions, the power to add qualifications is not part of the original powers of sovereignty that the Tenth Amendment reserved to the States. Petitioners' Tenth Amendment argument misconceives the nature of the right at issue because that Amendment could only "reserve" that which existed before. As Justice Story recognized, "the states can exercise no powers whatsoever, which exclusively spring out of the existence of the national government, which the constitution does not delegate to them.... No state can say, that it has reserved, what it never possessed."

* * *

With respect to setting qualifications for service in Congress, no such right existed before the Constitution was ratified. The contrary argument overlooks the revolutionary character of the government that the Framers conceived.... [T]he Framers envisioned a uniform national system, rejecting the notion that the Nation was a collection of States, and instead creating a direct link between the National Government and the people of the United States. In that National Government, representatives owe primary allegiance not to the people of a State, but to the people of the Nation.... Our conclusion that States lack the power to impose qualifications vindicates the same "fundamental principle of our representative democracy" that we recognized in *Powell*, namely that "the people should choose whom they please to govern them."

As we noted earlier, the *Powell* Court recognized that an egalitarian ideal—that election to the National Legislature should be open to all people of merit—provided a critical foundation for the Constitutional structure. This egalitarian theme echoes throughout the constitutional debates. In *The Federalist No. 57,* for example, Madison wrote:

> "Who are to be the objects of popular choice? Every citizen whose merit may recommend him to the esteem and confidence of his country. No qualification of wealth, of birth, of religious faith, or of civil profession is permitted to fetter the judgment or disappoint the inclination of the people."

.... Additional qualifications pose the same obstacle to open elections whatever their source. The egalitarian ideal, so valued by the Framers, is thus compromised to the same degree by additional qualifications imposed by States as by those imposed by Congress.

Similarly, we believe that state-imposed qualifications, as much as congressionally imposed qualifications, would undermine the second critical idea recognized in *Powell*: that an aspect of sovereignty is the right of the people to vote for whom they wish. Again, the source of the qualification is of little moment in assessing the qualification's restrictive impact.

Finally, state-imposed restrictions, unlike the congressionally imposed restrictions at issue in *Powell,* violate a third idea central to this basic principle: that the right to choose representatives belongs not to the States, but to the people. From the start, the Framers recognized that the "great and radical vice" of the Articles of Confederation was "the principle of LEGISLATION for STATES or GOVERNMENTS, in their CORPORATE or COLLECTIVE CAPACITIES, and as contradistinguished from the INDIVIDUALS of whom they consist." The Federalist No. 15 (Hamilton). Thus the Framers, in perhaps their most important contribution, conceived of a Federal Government directly responsible to the people, possessed of direct power over the people, and chosen directly, not by States, but by the people. The Framers implemented this ideal most clearly in the provision, extant from the beginning of the Republic, that calls for the Members of the House of Representatives to be "chosen every second Year by the People of the several States." Art. I, § 2, cl. 1. Following the adoption of the 17th Amendment in 1913, this ideal was extended to elections for the Senate. The Congress of the United States, therefore, is not a confederation of nations in which separate sovereigns are represented by appointed delegates, but is instead a body composed of representatives of the people.

* * *

Consistent with these views, the constitutional structure provides for a uniform salary to be paid from the national treasury, allows the States but a limited role in federal elections, and maintains strict checks on state interference with the federal election process. The Constitution also provides that the qualifications of the representatives of each State will be judged by the representatives of the entire Nation. The Constitution thus creates a uniform national body representing the interests of a single people.

Permitting individual States to formulate diverse qualifications for their representatives would result in a patchwork of state qualifications, undermining the uniformity and the national character that the Framers envisioned and sought to ensure. Such a patchwork would also sever the direct link that the Framers found so critical between the National Government and the people of the United States.[3]

* * *

---

3. There is little significance to the fact that Amendment 73 was adopted by a popular vote, rather than as an act of the state legislature. In fact, none of the petitioners argues that the constitutionality of a state law would depend on the method of its adoption. This is proper, because the voters of Arkansas, in adopting Amendment 73, were acting as citizens of the State of Arkansas, and not as citizens of the National Government. The people of the State of Arkansas have no more power than does the Arkansas Legislature to supplement the qualifications for service in Congress....

V

The merits of term limits, or "rotation," have been the subject of debate since the formation of our Constitution, when the Framers unanimously rejected a proposal to add such limits to the Constitution. The cogent arguments on both sides of the question that were articulated during the process of ratification largely retain their force today. Over half the States have adopted measures that impose such limits on some offices either directly or indirectly, and the Nation as a whole, notably by constitutional amendment, has imposed a limit on the number of terms that the President may serve. Term limits, like any other qualification for office, unquestionably restrict the ability of voters to vote for whom they wish. On the other hand, such limits may provide for the infusion of fresh ideas and new perspectives, and may decrease the likelihood that representatives will lose touch with their constituents. It is not our province to resolve this longstanding debate.

We are, however, firmly convinced that allowing the several States to adopt term limits for congressional service would effect a fundamental change in the constitutional framework. Any such change must come not by legislation adopted either by Congress or by an individual State, but rather—as have other important changes in the electoral process—through the Amendment procedures set forth in Article V. The Framers decided that the qualifications for service in the Congress of the United States be fixed in the Constitution and be uniform throughout the Nation. That decision reflects the Framers' understanding that Members of Congress are chosen by separate constituencies, but that they become, when elected, servants of the people of the United States. They are not merely delegates appointed by separate, sovereign States; they occupy offices that are integral and essential components of a single National Government. In the absence of a properly passed constitutional amendment, allowing individual States to craft their own qualifications for Congress would thus erode the structure envisioned by the Framers, a structure that was designed, in the words of the Preamble to our Constitution, to form a "more perfect Union."

* * *

■ JUSTICE THOMAS, with whom THE CHIEF JUSTICE, JUSTICE O'CONNOR, and JUSTICE SCALIA join, dissenting.

It is ironic that the Court bases today's decision on the right of the people to "choose whom they please to govern them." Under our Constitution, there is only one State whose people have the right to "choose whom they please" to represent Arkansas in Congress. The Court holds, however, that neither the elected legislature of that State nor the people themselves (acting by ballot initiative) may prescribe any qualifications for those representatives. The majority therefore defends the right of the people of Arkansas to "choose whom they please to govern them" by invalidating a provision that won nearly 60% of the votes cast in a direct election and that carried every congressional district in the State.

I dissent. Nothing in the Constitution deprives the people of each State of the power to prescribe eligibility requirements for the candidates who seek to represent them in Congress. The Constitution is simply silent on this question. And where the Constitution is silent, it raises no bar to action by the States or the people.

* * *

[T]he majority infers from the Framers' "democratic principles" that the [Constitution] must have been generally understood to preclude the people of the States and their state legislatures from prescribing any additional qualifications for their representatives in Congress. But the majority's evidence on this point establishes only two more modest propositions: (1) the Framers did not want the Federal Constitution itself to impose a broad set of disqualifications for congressional office, and (2) the Framers did not want the Federal Congress to be able to supplement the few disqualifications that the Constitution does set forth. The logical conclusion is simply that the Framers did not want the people of the States and their state legislatures to be constrained by too many qualifications imposed at the national level. The evidence does not support the majority's more sweeping conclusion that the Framers intended to bar the people of the States and their state legislatures from adopting additional eligibility requirements to help narrow their own choices.

* * *

The fact that the Framers did not grant a qualification-setting power to Congress does not imply that they wanted to bar its exercise at the state level. One reason why the Framers decided not to let Congress prescribe the qualifications of its own members was that incumbents could have used this power to perpetuate themselves or their ilk in office. As Madison pointed out at the Philadelphia Convention, Members of Congress would have an obvious conflict of interest if they could determine who may run against them. But neither the people of the States nor the state legislatures would labor under the same conflict of interest when prescribing qualifications for Members of Congress, and so the Framers would have had to use a different calculus in determining whether to deprive them of this power.

As the majority argues, democratic principles also contributed to the Framers' decision to withhold the qualification-setting power from Congress. But the majority is wrong to suggest that the same principles must also have led the Framers to deny this power to the people of the States and the state legislatures. In particular, it simply is not true that "the source of the qualification is of little moment in assessing the qualification's restrictive impact." There is a world of difference between a self-imposed constraint and a constraint imposed from above.

Congressional power over qualifications would have enabled the representatives from some States, acting collectively in the National Legislature, to prevent the people of another State from electing their preferred candidates. The John Wilkes episode in 18th-century England illustrates the problems that might result. As the majority mentions, Wilkes's district repeatedly elected him to the House of Commons, only to have a majority of the representatives of other districts frustrate their will by voting to exclude him. Americans who remembered these events might well have wanted to prevent the National Legislature from fettering the choices of the people of any individual State (for the House of Representatives) or their state legislators (for the Senate).

Yet this is simply to say that qualifications should not be set at the national level for offices whose occupants are selected at the state level.... Indeed, the invocation of democratic principles to invalidate Amendment 73 seems particularly difficult in the present case, because Amendment 73 remains fully within the control of the people of Arkansas. If they wanted to repeal it (despite the 20-point margin by which they enacted it less than three years ago), they could do so by a simple majority vote.

* * *

Amendment 73 is not the act of a state legislature; it is the act of the people of Arkansas, adopted at a direct election and inserted into the state constitution. The majority never explains why giving effect to the people's decision would violate the "democratic principles" that undergird the Constitution. Instead, the majority's discussion of democratic principles is directed entirely to attacking eligibility requirements imposed on the people of a State by an entity other than themselves.

The majority protests that any distinction between the people of the States and the state legislatures is "untenable" and "astonishing." In the limited area of congressional elections, however, the Framers themselves drew this distinction: they specifically provided for Senators to be chosen by the state legislatures and for Representatives to be chosen by the people. In the context of congressional elections, the Framers obviously saw a meaningful difference between direct action by the people of each State and action by their state legislatures.

* * *

III

It is radical enough for the majority to hold that the Constitution implicitly precludes the people of the States from prescribing any eligibility requirements for the congressional candidates who seek their votes. This holding, after all, does not stop with negating the term limits that many States have seen fit to impose on their Senators and Representatives.[4]

---

4. Going into the November 1994 elections, eight States had adopted "pure" term limits of one sort or another. *See* Colo. Const., Art. XVIII, § 9a; Mich. Const., Art. II,

Today's decision also means that no State may disqualify congressional candidates whom a court has found to be mentally incompetent, *see, e.g.,* Fla. Stat. §§ 97.041(2), 99.021(1)(a) (1991), who are currently in prison, see, e.g., Ill. Comp. Stat. Ann., ch. 10, §§ 5/3–5, 5/7–10, 5/10–5 (1993 and West Supp. 1995), or who have past vote-fraud convictions, *see, e.g.,* Ga. Code Ann. §§ 21–2–2(25), 21–2–8 (1993 and Supp. 1994). Likewise, after today's decision, the people of each State must leave open the possibility that they will trust someone with their vote in Congress even though they do not trust him with a vote in the election for Congress. *See, e.g.,* R. I. Gen. Laws § 17–14–1.2 (1988) (restricting candidacy to people "qualified to vote").

In order to invalidate § 3 of Amendment 73, however, the majority must go farther.... Amendment 73 does not actually [prescribe "genuine, unadulterated, undiluted term limits."].... It says only that if they are to win reelection, they must do so by write-in votes.

* * *

The majority suggests that this does not matter, because Amendment 73 itself says that it has the purpose of "evading the requirements of the Qualifications Clauses.".... [I]nquiries into legislative intent are even more difficult than usual when the legislative body whose unified intent must be determined consists of 825,162 Arkansas voters.

The majority nonetheless thinks it clear that the goal of § 3 is "to prevent the election of incumbents." In reaching this conclusion at the summary-judgment stage, however, the majority has given short shrift to petitioners' contrary claim. Petitioners do not deny that § 3 of Amendment 73 intentionally handicaps a class of candidates, in the sense that it decreases their pre-existing electoral chances. But petitioners do deny that § 3 is intended to (or will in fact) "prevent" the covered candidates from winning reelection, or "disqualify" them from further service. One of petitioners' central arguments is that congressionally conferred advantages have artificially inflated the pre-existing electoral chances of the covered candidates, and that Amendment 73 is merely designed to level the playing field on which challengers compete with them.

§ 10; Mo. Const., Art. III, § 45(a); Mont. Const., Art. IV, § 8; Ohio Const., Art. V, § 8; Ore. Const., Art. II, § 20; S.D. Const., Art. III, § 32; Utah Code Ann. § 20A–10–301. Eight other States had enacted "ballot access" provisions triggered by long-term incumbency or multiple prior terms in Congress. *See* Ariz. Const., Art. VII, § 18; Ark. Const., Amdt. 73, § 3; Calif. Elec. Code Ann. § 25003 (West Supp. 1994); Fla. Const., Art. VI, § 4(b)(5), (6); N.D. Cent. Code § 16.1–01–13.1 (Supp. 1993); Okla. Const., Art. II, § 12A; Wash. Rev. Code §§ 29.68.015, 29.68.016 (1994); Wyo. Stat. § 22–5–104 (Supp. 1994). In the 1994 elections, six more States—Alaska, Idaho, Maine, Massachusetts, Nebraska, and Nevada—enacted term-limit or ballot-access measures, bringing to 22 the total number of States with such provisions. *See* Pear, *The 1994 Elections*, N. Y. Times, Nov. 10, 1994, p. B7, Col. 4. In 21 of these States, the measures have been enacted by direct vote of the people.

To understand this argument requires some background. Current federal law (enacted, of course, by congressional incumbents) confers numerous advantages on incumbents, and these advantages are widely thought to make it "significantly more difficult" for challengers to defeat them. For instance, federal law gives incumbents enormous advantages in building name recognition and good will in their home districts. *See, e.g.,* 39 U.S.C. § 3210 (permitting Members of Congress to send "franked" mail free of charge); 2 U.S.C. §§ 61–1, 72a, 332 (permitting Members to have sizable taxpayer-funded staffs); 2 U.S.C. § 123b (establishing the House Recording Studio and the Senate Recording and Photographic Studios). At the same time that incumbent Members of Congress enjoy these in-kind benefits, Congress imposes spending and contribution limits in congressional campaigns that "can prevent challengers from spending more ... to overcome their disadvantage in name recognition." App. to Brief for State of Washington as Amicus Curiae A–4 (statement of former 10–term Representative William E. Frenzel, referring to 2 U.S.C. § 441a). Many observers believe that the campaign-finance laws also give incumbents an "enormous fund-raising edge" over their challengers by giving a large financing role to entities with incentives to curry favor with incumbents. In addition, the internal rules of Congress put a substantial premium on seniority, with the result that each Member's already plentiful opportunities to distribute benefits to his constituents increase with the length of his tenure. In this manner, Congress effectively "fines" the electorate for voting against incumbents.

Cynics see no accident in any of this. As former Representative Frenzel puts it: "The practice ... is for incumbents to devise institutional structures and systems that favor incumbents." In fact, despite his service from 1971 to 1989 on the House Administration Committee (which has jurisdiction over election laws), Representative Frenzel can identify no instance in which Congress "changed election laws in such a way as to lessen the chances of re-election for incumbents or to improve the election opportunities for challengers."

At the same time that incumbents enjoy the electoral advantages that they have conferred upon themselves, they also enjoy astonishingly high reelection rates. As Lloyd Cutler reported in 1989, "over the past thirty years a weighted average of ninety percent of all House and Senate incumbents of both parties who ran for reelection were reelected, even at times when their own party lost control of the Presidency itself.".... [I]n the 100th Congress, as many Representatives died as were defeated at the polls. Even in the November 1994 elections, which are widely considered to have effected the most sweeping change in Congress in recent memory, 90 percent of the incumbents who sought reelection to the House were successful, and nearly half of the losers were completing only their first terms. Only 2 of the 26 Senate incumbents seeking reelection were defeated, and one of them had been elected for the first time in a special election only a few years earlier.

The voters of Arkansas evidently believe that incumbents would not enjoy such overwhelming success if electoral contests were truly fair—that is, if the government did not put its thumb on either side of the scale. The majority offers no reason to question the accuracy of this belief. Given this context, petitioners portray § 3 of Amendment 73 as an effort at the state level to offset the electoral advantages that congressional incumbents have conferred upon themselves at the federal level.

* * *

I do not mean to suggest that States have unbridled power to handicap particular classes of candidates, even when those candidates enjoy federally conferred advantages that may threaten to skew the electoral process. But laws that allegedly have the purpose and effect of handicapping a particular class of candidates traditionally are reviewed under the First and Fourteenth Amendments rather than the Qualifications Clauses. Term-limit measures have tended to survive such review without difficulty.

To analyze such laws under the Qualifications Clauses may open up whole new vistas for courts. If it is true that "the current congressional campaign finance system ... has created an electoral system so stacked against challengers that in many elections voters have no real choices," are the Federal Election Campaign Act Amendments of 1974 unconstitutional under (of all things) the Qualifications Clauses? If it can be shown that nonminorities are at a significant disadvantage when they seek election in districts dominated by minority voters, would the intentional creation of "majority-minority districts" violate the Qualifications Clauses even if it were to survive scrutiny under the Fourteenth Amendment? More generally, if "district lines are rarely neutral phenomena" and if "districting inevitably has and is intended to have substantial political consequences," will plausible Qualifications Clause challenges greet virtually every redistricting decision?

* * *

NOTES AND QUESTIONS

1. Virtually every state whose constitution provides for direct democracy passed some form of term limit initiative during the 1990's. What conclusions can we draw from this phenomenon? Consider Professor Klarman's analysis:

> The term limits issue reveals legislative entrenchment at its worst. Contemporary public opinion polls reveal strong support for legislative term limits. Yet state legislatures generally have refused to do their constituents' bidding on this issue. Twenty-two of the twenty-four states that had enacted legislative term limits as of 1994 acted through popular initiative and referendum. By contrast, of those states whose constitutions lack any mechanism for

amendment that permits circumvention of the legislature, only one—New Hampshire—has adopted legislative term limits. In other words, the correlation between adoption of term limits and the existence of state constitutional mechanisms for bypassing the legislature is nearly perfect; virtually every state possessing a popular initiative and referendum mechanism has adopted legislative term limits through that process, while every state but one lacking such a mechanism has failed to do so. This could be a coincidence, but I doubt it. More likely, this is legislative entrenchment par excellence.

Michael J. Klarman, *Majoritarian Judicial Review: The Entrenchment Problem*, 85 Georgetown L.J. 491, 510 (1997).

2. Conceptions of democratic politics are central to the Court's decision in *Thornton*. The Court found many of the legally relevant sources to which it looked to be ambiguous, but then justified its result by appeal to what it called "the fundamental principle of our representative democracy ... that the people should choose whom they please to govern them." Indeed, the Court characterized that principle as the "most importan[t] factor" in its decision, more important than "the text and structure of the Constitution" and "the relevant historical materials." *Thornton* thus turns in part on underlying assumptions about how the relationship between representative institutions and popular will should be conceived.

Are the Court's assumptions correct? For the argument that term limits foster democracy and enable more accurate expression of voters' preferences, see Einer Elhauge, *Are Term Limits Undemocratic*, 64 U. Chi. L. Rev. 83, 193 (1997). Elhauge argues that term limits "reduce collective action pressures to vote for a senior incumbent to gain a higher share of legislative clout. And term limits lower entry barriers that keep out challengers. Both effects would likely reduce the ideological divergence between electorates and their representatives." Do term limits undermine or actually further "the fundamental principle of our representative democracy?" For further analysis of the policy and political consequences of term limits, see Matthew Spitzer and Linda Cohen, *Term Limits*, 80 Geo. L.J. 477 (1992). For further discussion of the historical materials, see Polly J. Price, *Term Limits on Original Intent? An Essay on Legal Debate and Historical Understanding*, 82 Va. L. Rev. 493 (1996).

3. *Thornton* might be thought to address only state efforts to regulate qualifications for service in the federal government, or for those offices the Constitution specifically creates and for which it defines qualifications. For this view, see Kathleen M. Sullivan, *Dueling Sovereignties: U.S. Term Limits, Inc. v. Thornton*, 109 Harv. L. Rev. 78 (1995). But a federal district court relied on *Thornton* to hold unconstitutional a voter initiative in California that imposed lifetime terms limits on *state* legislators. *Bates v. Jones*, 958 F.Supp. 1446, 1997 WL 199477 (N.D.Cal.1997). Proposition 140 limited state senators to two four-year terms and state lower-house members to three two-year terms. The district court held that the "fundamental principle of our representative government" the Supreme Court invoked in *Thornton*, as well as the fact that Proposition 140 purportedly burdened "fundamental rights to vote on an equal basis with others" made lifetime state term limits a violation of the Constitution. In reaching this conclusion, the district court relied on the reapportionment cases, see Chapter 3, for the principle that voters must be provided an equal basis for political participation. Is this a correct application of *Thornton*? Of the one-person, one-vote cases?

4. To what extent is the pressure for term limits the outgrowth either of the Court's campaign finance jurisprudence or its hands-off approach to claims of political gerrymandering? Are these three forms of regulation substitutes for one another? *See generally* Richard L. Hasen, *Clipping Coupons for Democracy: An Egalitarian/Public Choice Defense of Campaign Finance Vouchers*, 84 Cal. L. Rev. 1, 3 (1996) (linking dissatisfactions with incumbency to push for term limits); Kristen Silverberg, Note, *The Illegitimacy of the Incumbent Gerrymander*, 74 Tex. L. Rev. 913 (1996). Could demands for term limits be satisfied if redistricting power were removed from incumbent control and served to genuinely "reshuffle" the political deck every ten years? Would such active redistricting be a less intrusive mechanism for unsettling the incumbent edge identified in Justice Thomas's dissent? Both term limits and more aggressive redistricting policies are examples of "precommitment strategies." Although voters are free to vote incumbents out of office, or free to reject incumbents running from gerrymandered districts, there are credible reasons to believe that these policy preferences might be disregarded when a particular election is held. A precommitment strategy is one by which an actor chooses to restrict options *ex ante* for fear of temptation to yield at a later point of decision. The classic example from literature is the decision of Ulysses to have himself bound to the mast of this ship in order that he not give in to the temptations of the song of the Sirens. *See* Jon Elster, Ulysses and the Sirens: Studies in Rationality and Irrationality 37-47 (1979); *see also* Samuel Issacharoff, *Judging Politics: The Elusive Quest for Judicial Review of Political Fairness*, 71 Tex. L. Rev. 1643, 1664-69 (1993) (providing examples of contemporary uses of precommitment strategies); Michael Fitts, *Can Ignorance Be Bliss? Imperfect Information as a Positive Influence in Political Institutions*, 88 Mich. L. Rev. 917 (1990) (discussing congressional uses of such strategies).

5. *Thornton* relies heavily on *Powell v. McCormack*, 395 U.S. 486 (1969) both for the latter's historical analysis and its evocation of "democratic principles." Quoting *Powell*, Justice Stevens sums up the Court's holding by stating that state-imposed restrictions on legislative qualifications, such as term limits, are contrary to the "fundamental principle of our representative democracy ... that the people should choose whom they please to govern them."

Is the context of *Powell* the same as that in *Thornton*? At stake in *Powell* was the desire of voters in Adam Clayton Powell's congressional district to return him to office despite well-known allegations that he had acted improperly and perhaps illegally in his previous term in the House. Thus, when the House of Representatives acted to deprive Powell of his seat, he was being excluded not because the voters in his district imposed a barrier to his continued service, but because a political body, the United States House, sought to exclude him *despite* the manifested desire of his constituents that he represent them.

In this respect, *Powell* is remarkably similar to the famous Wilkes episode, which was so central to the consciousness of the Framing generation regarding democratic elections. Wilkes was expelled from Parliament for taking political positions the majority in the House of Commons opposed; despite being re-elected by his constituents, Parliament again expelled him and barred him from re-election. When Wilkes finally prevailed, the episode came to stand in both England and the United States for the principle that the people had the right to elect members of their choice, free of political control.

By contrast, in *Thornton* no outside political institution imposed constraints on the voters of Arkansas. Instead, the people of Arkansas themselves voted to adopt a general policy concerning whom they would let represent them. Justice Stevens asserts that *Powell* recognized "the critical postulate that sovereignty is vested in the people, and that sovereignty confers on the people the right to choose freely their representatives to the National Government." In what way is this "critical postulate" violated when the people of Arkansas exercise their sovereignty by deciding not to permit anyone to represent them more than a certain number of terms? Note that, as Justice Thomas's dissent points out, a substantial majority of voters in every congressional district in Arkansas voted to endorse term limits. Thus, one cannot even say in this context that a statewide majority was constraining the preferences of the voters in any particular district.

Consider another possible difference between *Powell*, the Wilkes episode, and term limits. In the first two, political bodies were not applying general qualifications policies, established in advance of specific cases; they were making more particularistic, ad hoc decisions about specific cases. In *Thornton*, term limits were being established as a general policy. Are not the dangers of political manipulation of purported "qualifications" standards much greater in the former context? Should this matter?

6. Is it realistic to expect a national constitutional amendment for congressional term limits? In this regard, consider the provisions in Article V for proposing a constitutional amendment. Article V sets out two paths: first, Congress can propose such amendments if two thirds of each Chamber agrees; second, the state legislatures of two thirds of the states can call a constitutional convention, which can then propose amendments. In either event, the amendment then goes to the states for ratification. Recent experience suggests that even explicit congressional promises to follow the former path are unlikely to succeed. *See* Klarman, *supra*, at 511–12. As for the latter path, note that no such constitutional convention has ever been called. *See* Ronald D. Rotunda and Stephen J. Safranek, *An Essay on Term Limits and a Call for a Constitutional Convention*, 80 Marq. L. Rev. 227 (1996).

7. Is Justice Stevens' approach a contemporary manifestation of the principles announced in *Lucas v. Forty–Fourth General Assembly of Colorado*, 377 U.S. 713 (1964), regarding a majority's inability to bind itself with regard to political rights? Is Justice Thomas's approach reminiscent of Justice Frankfurter's perspective in *Colegrove v. Green*, 328 U.S. 549 (1946), that Illinois' congressional delegation represents Illinois as a polity rather than individual Illinois citizens? For an interesting discussion of these issues, see Henry P. Monaghan, *We the Peoples, Original Understanding, and Constitutional Amendment*, 96 Colum. L. Rev. 121 (1996).

8. For further discussion of *Thornton*, see, e.g., Elizabeth Garrett, *Term Limitations and the Myth of the Citizen–Legislator*, 81 Cornell L. Rev. 623 (1996); Ronald D. Rotunda, *The Aftermath of Thornton*, 13 Const. Commentary 201 (1996); Harry H. Wellington, *Term Limits: History, Democracy, and Constitutional Interpretation*, 40 N.Y.L. Sch. L. Rev. 833 (1996); Mark R. Killenbech and Steve Sheppard, *Another Such Victory? Term Limits, Section 2 of the Fourteenth Amendment, and the Right to Representation*, 45 Hastings L.J. 1121 (1994).

9. Starting in 1842, Congress required that States elect congressional representatives from single-member districts, rather than at-large from the state as a whole. Before then, some states elected their congressional delegations at-large; other states had already shifted to single-member districts. For the complete history of congressional districting, see Chapter 11. *Thornton* prohibits both Congress and state legislatures from imposing new "qualifications" for the House and Senate. Is the congressional imposition of districting for House elections a violation of this holding? Before Congress imposed this requirement, were States that voluntarily adopted districted elections in violation of the Qualifications Clauses, as interpreted in *Thornton*? Which is the appropriate baseline, at-large or districted elections, for determining whether congressional elections comply with "the fundamental principle" that the people have a right to choose their representatives? Does a "fundamental principle" put in such sweeping terms make any sense at all in this context; that is, is there a general, universal principle of democracy that should be understood to require *either* districted elections or at-large elections—or should voters be able to impose either upon themselves without violating democracy's "fundamental principles"? If so, how do term limits differ?

10. Through the Twenty–Second Amendment, the people of the United States imposed term limits on their choice of potential Presidents. Does this constraint, although clearly constitutional, violate any "fundamental principle" of democracy? If not, is the situation any different when similar limits are imposed on Senators or Representatives?

11. Even if there are good reasons that neither Congress nor state legislatures should be granted the power to impose additional qualifications for representatives, do those reasons apply with the same force when "the people" impose these constraints through direct initiative?

The Court dismisses this possibility with the comment that "We are aware of no case that would even suggest that the validity of a state law under the Federal Constitution would depend at all on whether the state law was passed by the state legislature or by the people directly through amendment of the state constitution." This view that for constitutional analysis, all law is the same, regardless of its source, is as the Court says, a position the Court has generally taken. But does this only show that the Court continues to fail to think carefully about the difference between different lawmaking processes? In terms of either the general philosophy of democracy or constitutional analysis, should the source of additional representative qualifications, such as term limits, be irrelevant?

Consider the alternative view:

> ... Madison made an often-quoted speech in which he "opposed ... the Section [a proposal in the Constitutional Convention that would have given Congress power to add additional qualifications for election to the House or Senate] as vesting an improper and dangerous power in the legislature. The qualifications of the electors and elected were fundamental articles in a Republican Govt ... and ought to be fixed by the Constitution. If the legislature could regulate those of either, it can by degrees subvert the Constitution. A Republic may be converted into an aristocracy or oligarchy as well as by limiting the number capable of being elected, as the number authorized to elect. In all cases where the representatives of the people will have a personal interest distinct from their Constituents, there was the same reason for being jealous of them...."
>
> This passage is worth noting because it shows that Madison, like others at the convention, was opposed to additions of qualifications by the legislature, not to additions of qualifications in general. Madison was not the only delegate to hold this belief: Benjamin Franklin also "did not think the elected had any right in any case to narrow the privileges of the electors," through specifying additional qualifications for either electors or elected. Madison's objection in both cases, which he repeated when participating in Virginia's Constitutional Convention of 1829, was specifically directed against legislatures, for the protection of the electors. Madison felt that the legislature could not be trusted to prescribe qualifications, because such a "fundamental article of Republican gov[ernment]" was beyond the power of a mere agent to alter....

[T]he national people, according to Madison, can delegate powers to the state peoples without delegating that power to the state governments. This distinction between state people and state government is the foundation on which this article's argument rests. The "states"—meaning the state peoples—have powers that no state government possesses. The power of the state peoples can extend to "a fundamental article" of Republican government like electoral and legislators' qualifications. The power of the state governments cannot extend so far.

The text of Article I, Section 2 gives explicit support for such an exclusive delegation to the state peoples alone: the provision specifically refers to the "people of the several states" as choosing representatives. Assuming that the framers of the Constitution meant what they said, the duty of choosing representatives, and the correlative duty of excluding some from being representatives, is delegated exclusively to the people of the several states rather than to the state governments.

It would be a singular perversion of Madison's reasoning to interpret his argument against legislative control of qualifications as a justification for excluding the electors themselves from adding extra qualifications for the elected through state constitutions. Madison's argument was a defense of the elector's power, not a limitation of it. His argument was premised on the power of the electors, the state peoples, to control the elected.

Roderick M. Hills, Jr., *A Defense of State Constitutional Limits on Federal Congressional Terms*, 53 U. Pitt.L.Rev. 97, 120–22 (1991).

12. At the end of its opinion, the Court drew a distinction between permissible state regulation of the conditions a candidate must meet to get onto the ballot and the unconstitutional imposition of new qualifications for officeholding. This distinction might bear on the constitutionality of various pre-conditions that can be imposed for candidates seeking to get onto the ballot. These conditions are particularly important for candidates seeking to challenge the dominance of the two major political parties— independent candidates or candidates seeking to run under the banner of new parties. Ballot-access restrictions include requirements that candidates collect a specific number of signatures on nominating petitions; that these signatures be distributed across the relevant jurisdiction in particular ways; that the candidates not have lost in a party primary for the seat in question. We saw in Chapter 4 that in general the Court has permitted a wide variety of restrictive ballot access measures. Could the decision in *Thornton* be used to attack the Court's prior precedents?

Take "sore loser" statutes as an example. In Texas, a candidate who runs for President in the primary of a party and loses cannot run in the general election as an independent candidate for President. Thus, if someone like Colin Powell had run as a Republican in the Texas primaries and lost, he would not have been able to get on the Texas ballot as an independent in the general election for President. Is this Texas statute a permissible regulation of access to the ballot, or an impermissible addition of new qualifications for the office of the Presidency (that the candidate not have lost a party primary) beyond those specified in the Qualifications Clause for that office, Art. II, Sec. 5? What is the difference *Thornton* suggests between new qualifications and legitimate ballot-access restrictions?

DOES DIRECT LAWMAKING CONTRIBUTE TO GOOD POLICY-MAKING?

We have considered the constitutional questions initiatives raise, as well as certain procedural reforms that some suggest might improve the process, including a more aggressive judicial role. We have also raised questions about whether the same interest group processes that characterize ordinary lawmaking also characterize direct lawmaking in the age of the initiative industry. But even apart from these specific questions and the issues particular initiatives raise, what has been the general and cumulative effect of the recent revival of direct lawmaking? In the state in which the initiative has been invoked the most frequently, California, one estimate is that by 1990, only eight percent of the state budget was controlled by the legislature; voters controlled the remainder through the voter initiative process. DuVivier, *supra*, at 1189 n.23.

> But the more important development is the way the initiative, which for a half century was regarded as an extraordinary expedient available in the rare cases of serious legislative failure or abuse, has not just been integrated into the regular governmental-political system, but has begun to replace it. Some students of California government think it's easier to amend the state constitution by initiative than to approve budgets or raise taxes, both of which require two-thirds votes in the legislature. Whether or not that's correct, the initiative has by general agreement become the principal driver of policy in California, sometimes for the good, but more often not. The cumulative effect of the plebiscitary reforms of the past two decades has been to strip cities, school districts, and especially counties of their ability to generate their own funds; to divide authority and responsibility uncertainly between state and local government and among scores of agencies; and to make it increasingly unclear who is ultimately accountable for the results of all these changes.

Peter Schrag, *Take the Initiative, Please: Referendum Madness in California*, 28 Am. Prospect 61 (1996). Was Madison right?

CHAPTER 11

ALTERNATIVE DEMOCRATIC STRUCTURES

At the beginning of this book, in Chapter 1, we asked whether "democracy" could really be said to pre-exist, or remain autonomous from, the specific laws and institutions that construct it in particular contexts. Through historical, legal, and theoretical perspectives, we have tried to show that the democracy we now experience is, indeed, something *constructed*—the outcome of legal rules and institutional frameworks, rather than some entity such as "We the People" that pre-exists these structural choices.

In this chapter, we turn to dramatically different ways of constructing democratic institutions, particularly voting rules. We examine alternatives to the traditional Anglo–American electoral structure of territorially-based election districts, particularly the single-member district. One possibility is what are called alternative voting systems, which have become of increasing interest recently in the United States: these include cumulative voting, preference voting (or single-transferrable voting, STV), and limited voting. Another option is the kind of electoral system that dominates in European democracies and nearly all Latin American ones, which is one form or another of proportional representation. As material in the previous chapters shows, controversies today over concepts of representation, the Voting Rights Act, racial redistricting, and the like raise challenges to long taken-for-granted foundations of American democracy. Contemporary struggles in such areas return us to first principles, and the flourishing of interest in alternative democratic structures results from this renewed encounter with the fundamental principles of democratic institutional design.

As you examine these alternative approaches to voting and elections, consider them along several dimensions. First, what is the theory of political representation and democratic politics implied in different electoral structures? Second, to what extent would various problems we have dealt with earlier in the casebook be better addressed, not through the constitutional or policy approaches discussed there, but through wholly different electoral structures such as those presented here? Rather than trying to work within the taken-for-granted constraints imposed by a continuing commitment to current electoral structures in the United States, would the problems previous chapters address be more appropriately dealt with through more radical institutional reconfigurations? Finally, the choice of voting systems cannot be debated only in terms of theories of representation and democracy; all voting systems should be seen as packages of potential advantages and disadvantages. From a pragmatic perspective, try to analyze what tradeoffs are presented by the various electoral systems we explore here. What incentives do different systems give candidates? political parties? voters? Even if the current system has the kind of costs exposed throughout this casebook, might that system remain preferable to the plausible alternatives?

In addition to examining alternative voting structures, we will look at the historical development of territorial districting in the United States. How much do current electoral practices reflect, not so much deliberative policy choices among the competing alternatives, but the path dependency of democratic institutions—that is, the fact that particular institutions were chosen at one point in time and then endured in the face of new possibilities primarily because they had already been chosen and were set in place? As a leading scholar of election systems puts it, "one of the best-known generalizations about electoral systems is that they tend to be very stable and to resist change." Arend Lijphart, Democracies 52 (1994). After you understand the alternative possibilities, consider whether you think the United States would choose its current electoral structures were that choice being confronted for the first time today, on a clean slate.

Before examining the details of alternative democratic structures, read this quiz. It is designed to provide an initial perspective on how the legal framework of politics can strongly influence the substantive outcomes of elections. How much is the kind of democracy different countries experience a function of profound cultural and historical differences between them, and how much is it instead a function of the choice of legal rules different countries use for constructing their politics (which might, of course, be influenced by these other differences)?

VOTING QUIZ
[answers can be found at p. 717]

International Elections

1. Of the 36 democracies in the world with at least two million people and with a high human-rights rating of "1" or "2" from the organization Freedom House, how many use a plurality, winner-take-all, single-member district election system such as in the United States? How many use forms of proportional representation?

2. In the most recent elections in the United Kingdom, where the Labour Party won a "landslide" and became the governing majority for the first time in 18 years, what percentage of the vote did Labour get? What percentage of the seats in the Parliament did Labour get?

The second principal party is the Conservative Party, while a third party, the Liberal Party, regularly attracts votes in United Kingdom elections. What percent of the votes did this third party get in the most recent election? What percent of the seats in Parliament?

3. Germany and New Zealand use proportional representation to elect some of their legislators and a plurality, winner-take-all, single-member district system, as in the United States, to elect others. How much more likely is a woman to be elected under these proportional representation systems than in U.S-style districted elections?

4. How many times has a political party in the United Kingdom won a majority of the popular vote in elections since World War II?

5. In 1993, candidates for the Liberal Party in Canada won 53% of the popular vote in Ontario. What percentage of Ontario's 99 seats did they win?

United States

6. Of 103 U.S. House Members who were first elected between 1980 and 1988 and who ran for re-election in 1996, how many won? How many won by a margin of more than 10%? How many won by more than 30%?

7. Since 1952, which two elections in the United States have had the highest rate of "straight ticket" voting (meaning voters supporting candidates of the same party) for president and Congress?

8. What percentage of Americans rate the job Congress does as excellent? What percentage approve of its job?

9. Of the 200 state legislative seats in Massachusetts, how many were contested by both major parties in 1996? What percentage of the 5,958 state legislative seats elected in 1996 around the nation were contested?

10. Of 211 state legislative seats in New York, how many were won by margins of at least 10% in 1996?

Duverger's Law, Duverger's Hypothesis

In 1951, the French political scientist, Maurice Duverger, formulated what he called "a true sociological law" concerning the effects of different electoral systems on the structure of politics. This "law" was that systems in which office is awarded to a candidate who receives the most votes (with two candidates, a majority, but with more than two, a plurality) in a single-ballot election will produce a two-party political system, rather than a multi-party one. Maurice Duverger, Political Parties: Their Organization and Activity in the Modern State (1954). This plurality, winner-take-all system is used for nearly all American elections, as it is for British elections. Other political scientists had reached similar conclusions: "single-member district-system-plus-plurality-elections ... discriminate *moderately* against the second party; but against the third, fourth, and fifth parties the force of this tendency is multiplied to the point of extinguishing their chances of winning seats altogether." Elmer E. Schattschneider, Party Government 75 (1942).

More modern studies essentially confirm this view. *See generally* Douglas Rae, Political Consequences of Electoral Laws (1971). A few qualifications have been added to the general law based on countries, like Canada and India, that use plurality voting but nonetheless have more than two significant parties. In countries with strong decentralized government, like Canada, local parties can be the main parties in certain provinces, which leads to their ability to capture enough votes at the national level to be viable third parties. But with minor qualifications, most political scientists accept in one form or another Duverger's "law"—particularly if it is viewed as describing a strong tendency, rather than a deterministic view on the influence of institutions on politics. For a good survey of debates between institutionalist and more culturally-oriented explanations of politics, along with a sophisticated reevaluation of Duverger's Law, see Gary Cox, Making Votes Count: Strategic Coordination in the World's Electoral Systems (1997).

Duverger proposed two causal mechanisms to explain this pattern. Both implicitly derive from what today are called rational-choice models for how politicians and voters behave. One mechanism focused on voters: they were assumed not to want to "waste" their votes on candidates who stood little chance of being elected. Rather than voting for a third-party candidate who might be the voter's first choice, that voter in a plurality, winner-take-all system will vote for a candidate from one of the two major parties who has a "realistic" chance to win. Voters do not vote sincerely, but strategically, in the sense that they do not vote their true first preference. Notice that this view, which empirical studies bear out, means that voters are motivated in particular ways when voting—they vote not primarily as a means of expressing their political values, but as a means of influencing the choice between the two candidates with the most likely chance of winning (recall the discussion of whether constitutional doctrine should recognize an expressive dimension of voting in Chapter 4, where we discussed *Burdick v. Takushi*, 504 U.S. 428 (1992)).

The second mechanism focuses on politicians and the way the plurality, winner-take-all system exaggerates the votes of large parties and diminishes the influence of small ones. If candidates from two parties face each other in this system, the one who wins 51 percent of the vote gains office, meaning a candidate with 49 percent of the vote gets nothing. The system has the "balloon effect" of transforming 51 percent of the votes into 100 percent of the political power at issue. Unless a third party can come close to capturing 33 percent of the votes, with the rest evenly divided between the two major parties, it stands little chance of winning office. As a result, Duverger argued that politicians did not consider forming or joining third parties in this system.

Duverger also proposed another generalization about electoral systems, which he termed a "hypothesis" rather than a law. This hypothesis is that systems that use proportional representation will tend to lead to the formation of many independent parties. This, too, stems from the rational-choice model of what motivates voters and politicians; because parties receive seats in proportion to their total votes, votes for smaller parties are not "wasted." While many systems that use proportional representation do have multiple parties, there are notable exceptions: Austria, Ireland, and, until recently, Germany all were countries that were dominated by two principal parties despite using forms of proportional representation. For data correlating the effective number of political parties in different countries with the type of electoral system used, see David M. Farrell, Comparing Electoral Systems 146–47 (1997) (generally showing that countries with plurality, winner-take-all voting have around 2 effective parties, while those using forms of proportional representation tend to have 3–5 parties).

Given the strong influence of electoral laws on the shape of democratic politics, re-consider the question posed at the beginning of this book in Chapter 1: how much does law *construct* democracy, rather than democracy pre-exist specific institutional arrangements? How much is the kind of democracy different countries experience a function of cultural and historical differences, and how much is it a function of the technical details of their different electoral institutions? Some historians have famously argued for the proposition of "American exceptionalism," the view that America is distinct from European democracies because there is less ideological disagreement on fundamental questions. *See, e.g.*, Louis Hartz, The Liberal Tradition in America (1955). But how much is America's perceived ideological consensus, either in the 1950s or today, a function of institutions, rather than culture or politics? Would the United States quickly become a Western–European style multi-party democracy if it shifted to proportional representation? *See, e.g.*, Daniel Lazare, The Frozen Republic: How the Constitution is Paralyzing Democracy 295-96 (1995) (arguing that the "Republican–Democratic duopoly" since the mid–19th century reflects "a record of political stagnation without parallel in virtually any other country" and that if House elections were to be based on proportional representation, it would open the door to multi-party political competition).

For two interesting, recent, brief perspectives on Duverger's Law, see William H. Riker, *Duverger's Law Revisited* and Maurice Duverger, *Duverger's Law: Forty Years Later*, both in Electoral Laws and Their Political Consequences (Bernard Grofman & Arend Lijphart eds. 1986).

ANSWERS TO QUIZ

International

1. Only four of these 36 countries do not use proportional representation (PR) for at least some national elections. Those four countries are the United Kingdom and its former colonies Canada, Jamaica, and the United

States. Both Canada and the United Kingdom have many influential voices calling for proportional representation; the recently elected Labour Party in the United Kingdom has pledged while in office to hold a referendum on PR.

2. The Labour Party won the election with only 44.4% of the vote but gained 65.2% of the seats. Tony Blair captured only 0.5% more votes than Margaret Thatcher had in 1979, but his party won 12.2% more seats than her party had won in 1979. The Conservative Party gained 31.5% of the vote, but won only 25.7% of the seats. The Liberal Democrats gained 17.2% of vote but won only 7.2% of the seats.

3. In the most recent elections in Germany and New Zealand, women were three times as likely to be elected in the half of seats elected by PR than in the half elected by single-member districts. The ratio was 39% to 13% in Germany in 1994 and 45% to 15% in New Zealand in 1996. Women consistently win more seats in PR elections than winner-take-all elections.

4. No political party in the United Kingdom has won a majority of the popular vote in elections since World War II. The Conservative party never won more than 44% of the vote—which is less than the percentage won by Democratic presidential candidate Michael Dukakis in 1988—in its 18 years of government from 1979–1996.

5. In 1993, candidates for the Liberal Party in Canada won 98 of 99 Ontario's seats with only 53% of the popular vote. The province-by-province results in the 1993 elections in Canada were classic examples of distortions of majority rule and minority representation.

United States

6. In 1996, of the 103 Members in the House of Representatives who were first elected in the 1980–1988: all 113 won; 109 won by at least 10% (e.g., more than 55%–45%); and 75 won by at least 30% (e.g., more than 65%–35%). Districts won by less than 10% are considered "marginal" districts that have some chance of changing hands in the next election.

7. The two elections in the United States that have had the highest rate of "straight ticket" voting in elections in the last 44 years for President and Congress are 1992 (highest) and 1996 (second highest).

8. Percentage of Americans who rate the job Congress does as excellent: 2%. Percentage who approve of its job: 32%. (April 1997 poll by Louis Harris and Associates).

9. Of the 200 state legislative seats in Massachusetts, only 63 (31.5%) were contested by both major parties in 1996. Nationwide, 32.8% of state legislative seats were not contested—actually down from 36% in the last two presidential elections in 1988 and 1992. Few state legislative districts are competitive.

10. Of 211 state legislative seats in New York, 201 were won by more than 10% in 1996. As the New York Times editorialized, in state races, due to gerrymandered district lines, New Yorkers have "no more voting options than North Koreans have." As additional evidence of New York state's noncompetitive democracy, more than half of all U.S. House races in New York were won by more than 40% (e.g., 70%–30%) in elections from 1982 to 1996.

A. TYPES OF ELECTORAL SYSTEMS

A recent work, on which this Note draws, suggests there are at least 2,500 works dealing with electoral structures and their consequences. David M. Farrell, Comparing Electoral Systems 1 (1997). Here we provide a brief and simple overview of the basic electoral systems, which we divide into three. Later discussions will provide more detail on several of these different systems.

1. Majoritarian Systems. These are the systems used in the United Kingdom and several countries that inherited their institutions from it, including the United States, Canada, Australia, and, until recently, New Zealand. It is also used for some elections in India, Bangladesh, the Philippines, Zambia, Nepal, Thailand, and Chile. There are two common forms of this system, and a third used only in Australia.

The first form is often called "First Past the Post," (FPTP) or the plurality-vote system. Here, the candidate who receives the most votes in a territorial district is elected, regardless of how many votes the candidate receives. In a study of all elections in 27 democracies between 1945–1990, which includes the 24 most durable democracies since 1945, five countries used FPTP in nearly all their elections: Canada, India, New Zealand, the United Kingdom, and the United States. Arend Lijphart, Electoral Systems and Party Systems 18 (1994). Historically, the movement has been away from this system and toward systems of proportional representation. Thus, New Zealand replaced its FPTP system, and none of the newly emerging democracies in the 1970s in Mediterranean Europe (Greece, Portugal, Spain) nor those in eastern and central Europe or the former Soviet Union in the 1980s and 1990s adopted it.

The second form is a more strictly majoritarian one. This is called the second-ballot or runoff system. If no candidate receives an absolute majority in the first round, a second round of elections is held. Rules vary as to how well candidates have to fare in the first round to make it to the second ballot; in some elections, only the top two candidates make it to the second round. The aim of this system is to make it more likely that the candidate elected will have an actual majority of the votes cast in the second round, thus avoiding plurality-elected candidates. This system is used for some elections in the United States, particularly in the South, and has been challenged as a violation of the Voting Rights Act. *See* Chapter 7. This system is most commonly associated with France during the Fifth Republic, but it is used for presidential elections in many countries. For extensive discussion of FPTP and runoff systems in different countries, see Arend Lijphart, Democracies: Patterns of Majoritarian and Consensus Government in Twenty–One Countries 150–169 (1984).

Australia uses what is called the alternative vote system, or "instant run-off," invented in the 1870s by a professor at the Massachusetts Institute of Technology, W.R. Ware. *See* Farrell, *supra*, at 45. The Irish Republic also uses this system for presidential and some other elections, and parts of Canada used it in the 1950s (Ann Arbor, Michigan used it for one mayoral election in the 1970s), but the system is used far more in Australia than anywhere else. Voters rank all the candidates running in order of preference; in Australia, the failure to do so invalidates the ballot. A candidate must receive more than 50 percent of the actual vote to be elected. Thus, if no candidate reaches this level in the initial count, the candidate with the least votes is eliminated, and all his or her votes transferred to the second choice those voters marked. The process continues until a candidate emerges with more than 50 percent of the votes. Notice that this system avoids multiple rounds of elections to generate a majority-supported candidate; voters rank all candidates at once and the vote transfers take place until a winning candidate emerges. This system resembles STV, discussed below, but unlike STV, which is used to elect a representative body as a whole, the instant run-off is used to elect one candidate to represent a district.

2. Proportional Representation Systems. Majoritarian systems are based on geographic constituencies (candidates are elected from districts), and voters vote directly for individual candidates. Proportional representation systems come in many forms, but in general, voting tends to focus on parties, not candidates, and the districts involved are much larger—often extending to the entire country. The basic idea of PR is that parties should end up with a number of seats roughly proportional to the number of votes they receive. All European countries other than Great Britain, France, and Ireland use PR.

The origins of PR provide insight into the justifications for it. PR arose in the late 19th century, with the extension of the suffrage and the development of mass political parties. Pressure for adopting it was greatest in Belgium and Switzerland; both had sharp cleavages along religious and ethnic lines, which in turn generated pressure for "fairer representation." In 1899, Belgium became the first country to adopt the system of list PR. Finland followed in 1906, Sweden in 1907, and by 1920, most European countries had made the switch.

a. *List-PR.* In list-PR systems, voters vote for a party, which puts on the ballot a list of candidates. Parties then receive seats in proportion to their votes. To avoid representation of "fringe" parties, most countries establish an electoral threshold, below which a party receives no seats. This threshold ranges from 1 percent in Israel (raised to 1.5 percent in 1992) to 5 percent in Germany. A few countries, such as the Netherlands and Israel, use the entire nation as the relevant election unit; representation is closest to precise proportionality in these systems. Other countries are divided into regions or constituencies; the smallest of these are found in Greece, where each elects five representatives, and the largest in Portugal, where regions elect 24 candidates. These "districts" are not at all like those in single-member district systems; voters do not vote for individual candidates, and the units are much larger than typical single-member districts. The more regions or constituencies, the greater the likely departure in the national legislature from precise proportionality. Diverse technical formulas are used in various countries for determining exactly how seats should be allocated to parties. For a survey of these formulas, see Arend Lijphart, Electoral Systems and Party Systems (1994).

The most important difference is between *closed list* and *open list* systems. In closed-list PR, the parties decide in which order to list their candidates and voters can only vote for the party list as it is presented to them. Thus, if the region will send 20 candidates to the parliament, the party will list its candidates from 1 to 20. If the party gets 25 percent of the vote, its top 5 candidates would win office. This system of PR is used in many newer democracies, such as Argentina, Columbia, Costa Rica, Israel, Portugal, Spain, Turkey, and Uruguay. Germany also employs it for those seats filled by PR (see below for more on Germany's system). Few countries have dropped this system once they adopted it (Italy and France are exceptions), while several countries have abandoned FPTP for it. Of course, this system grants great power to internal party processes and party elites. But one potential advantage of party control is that it can be used to generate a desired mix of candidates representing the party in office. For example, in the first democratic elections in South Africa, held under closed-list PR, many parties presented ethnically mixed lists that they hoped would appeal to broad constituencies. Woman and minorities can do well under this system, if parties support them, because voters cast ballots for parties not individual candidates, which makes practices like racially-polarized voting more difficult. Farrell, *supra*, at 73.

Open-list PR systems vary in detail and are now used in Austria, Belgium, the Netherlands, Norway, Sweden, France, Luxembourg, and Switzerland. One version allows voters to vote either for a party or one specific candidate; the latter counts as a vote for moving that candidate up in the party's rank-ordering. In the most open systems, voters receive as many votes as there are seats to fill; they can vote for a party; give up to two votes to a candidate; and even cast votes for candidates on different lists.

b. *The Two-Vote System of PR* (also, The German System; or additional-member PR; and other names). Many countries seek some hybrid structure that combines the seeming best of PR and majoritarian systems.

In this system, voters cast two votes: one goes for a party list, and the other for a candidate elected from a single-member district. Thus, the effort is to capture the benefits both of individual representatives accountable to specific geographic constituencies, as well as the fair representation benefits of a PR system. The longest use of this system has been in Germany, but countries forming democracies today are often drawn to it.

In Germany, half the seats in the Bundestag are filled by election of candidates from single-member districts. The second vote is a closed-list PR ballot, the totals from which are aggregated on a national level to determine the overall proportion of seats each party ought to receive. Candidates from the party lists are then added to that party's candidates elected through the single-member districts up to the point at which the level of proportionality, as measured by the second vote, is attained. Thus, if there were 100 total seats to fill, and Party X elected 20 individual candidates from individual districts in the first vote, and received 40 percent of the vote in the list-PR phase, Party X would then have the first 20 of its candidates on the list also added to office (20+20=40, which means 40 percent of the seats). The list-PR election is based on geographic regions, analogous to states, known as *Landër*. The system tries to encourage the sense of having individual legislators from districts by calling this phase "the primary vote," but given the electoral structure, the list-PR phase is actually more important in terms of political power. If this system appears a mixture of British and Continental electoral systems, that reflects its origins: after World War II, the British pressed the Germans to adopt districted elections, and to emphasize the role of the *Landër,* in order to enhance the stability of the electoral system. As you will soon learn, in this period, it was widely believed that Germany's pre-WWII system of PR had fractionalized the government and enhanced its instability by enabling minor parties to gain too great representation. This history of Weimar Germany also explains why the threshold for parties to gain seats is set unusually high in Germany (5 percent or three constituency seats).

Other countries also use hybrids of single-member districts and PR elections, including several that have chosen their electoral systems recently. These mixed systems include Japan, Mexico, Russia, and Italy.

3. *Semi–Proportional Representation Systems.* These systems include cumulative voting, preference voting (also known as single-transferrable voting, STV), and limited voting. They can be viewed as occupying an intermediate position between majoritarian and proportional representation systems. These semi-proportional systems are discussed in detail in the following material.

B. Cumulative Voting

1. The alternative voting system that has received the most attention in the United States recently is cumulative voting (CV). The reason for this

interest is that CV is offered as an alternative to address the specific problem of racial and ethnic underrepresentation to which so much recent energy has gone under the Voting Rights Act. *See* Chapter 7. The approach taken under the Act, the creation of "safe" black and Hispanic election districts, has come under challenge from both constitutional and other directions. *See* Chapter 8. In the midst of the intense controversies now surrounding this approach, CV has been offered as a means of enhancing minority representation without requiring districts to be set aside on a specific racial or ethnic basis.

For a description of how cumulative voting works, and what its purported advantages might be over the current way of addressing minority underrepresentation, consider the following excerpt from Richard H. Pildes, *Gimme Five: Non-gerrymandering Racial Justice*, The New Republic (March 1, 1993):

> [...] Cumulative voting is a simple concept: each voter is given as many votes to cast as there are seats to be filled. Voters are free to distribute their votes among candidates in any way they choose. This approach enables voters to express not just their raw preferences, but the intensity with which those preferences are held. In a five-way race, for example, a voter can cast one vote for each candidate, vote three times for one candidate and twice for a second, or cast all his votes for one candidate. In this way, minority groups with common interests and strong preferences for a particular candidate can ensure her election, even in the face of a hostile majority.
>
> This represents a radically different alternative to the current Voting Rights Act. Rather than breaking up the at-large electoral system into five smaller territorial districts, cumulative voting has the advantage of leaving the original electoral system intact; yet it produces outcomes similar to those under the current laws. Under either approach, a 20 percent black population that chooses to vote cohesively would be able to elect one of the five council members.
>
> And cumulative voting offers striking advantages. Most obviously, it avoids the drawing of radically defined political districts that so trouble the Act's critics. It might also diminish conflicts between minority groups struggling over district boundary lines, such as between blacks and Hispanics in many places. In fact, cumulative voting reduces gerrymandering opportunities in general. Because it relies on several candidates competing in at-large elections, it requires geographically broad electoral units. The fewer district lines to be drawn, the fewer the invitations to gerrymander.
>
> But the appeal of cumulative voting runs deeper. It is a way of pursuing the goals of the Voting Rights Act within the framework of political liberalism. Voters voluntarily define their own interests

and the voting affiliations that best promote them. Adopting this approach thus avoids any assumption that black or Hispanic voters are monolithic groups with unitary political values and interests. Under the current approach, black voters of widely varying socioeconomic status are sometimes grouped together. Cumulative voting would enable these voters to decide for themselves whether their political values are better defined by what they have in common or by what they do not. The current law, moreover, singles out particular minority groups for distinct legal status. Cumulative voting reduces these moral and political conflicts by minimizing the need for judgments about which minority groups warrant distinct protection. Any group that feels the need to vote cohesively is able to do so. "Redistricting," in effect, is done by voters themselves, not by politicians. Moreover, it takes place with each new election, instead of once a decade in the wake of a new census.

The most common concern about cumulative voting is that it is too confusing. But this reflects an instinctive fear of new voting procedures rather than informed experience. Cumulative voting is already used by some corporations in electing boards of directors. Illinois began using cumulative voting to elect its lower house in the aftermath of the Civil War. (Voters were given several chances to abolish the system, but it lasted until 1980, when the overall structure of the Illinois House was changed.) In New Mexico the city council for Alamogordo was elected in 1987 through cumulative voting, the first such local government election this century. Each voter had three votes to use in filling three city council seats; 70 percent of the voters seized this advantage and cast more than one vote for a particular candidate. Although the city's population was 24 percent Hispanic and 5 percent black, it had been nearly twenty years since either a Hispanic or black politician had been elected at-large. But in the 1987 election, one Hispanic official was elected. She was only fourth in the number of voters who supported her, but because her support was particularly intense, she finished third in total votes. Of Hispanics who voted for her, 80 percent gave her more than one vote. They thus relinquished some influence over two seats in order to ensure the election of the one candidate they strongly preferred. Similarly, in Sisseton, South Dakota, members of the Sisseton Wahpeton Sioux tribe recently used cumulative voting to elect their candidate of choice to the local school board.

Cumulative voting is not a panacea. Voters must be knowledgeable about a larger number of candidates; political campaigns might become more expensive as candidates pursue votes through a larger region; representatives would have ties to a broader constituency, but perhaps not as strong ones to a specific, local political base; political parties might try to influence the results by taking control over the number of candidates they slate for office; and, of greatest concern, political bodies might become more fractured and less effective in governing as more officials come into office with the support of less than 50 percent of voters. These are genuine potential costs that warrant discussion... .But the status quo has its costs as well. We might therefore begin to test cumulative voting incrementally. The Voting Rights Act could be amended so that courts could consider cumulative voting as one option for redressing violations of existing law. It may turn out that the system is not practical on a large scale. But the Voting Rights Act is here to stay, and we should consider new approaches that protect civil rights while easing political, ideological and racial tensions.

2. Cumulative voting received widespread national attention when President Clinton nominated Professor Lani Guinier to be head of the Civil Rights Division of the Department of Justice. Professor Guinier had been a leading advocate for greater use of cumulative voting to address minority representation issues currently addressed through the "safe" districting approach under the Voting Rights Act. Consider some of the arguments she offers for CV in Lani Guinier, The Tyranny of the Majority 16,152 (1994):

> As a solution that permits voters to self-select their identities, cumulative voting also encourages cross-racial coalition building. No one is locked into a minority identity. Nor is anyone necessarily isolated by the identity they choose. Voters can strengthen their influence by forming coalitions to elect more than one representative.... Women too can use cumulative voting to gain greater representation. Indeed, in other countries with similar, alternative voting systems, women are more likely to be represented in the national legislature ... cumulative voting serves many of the same ends as periodic elections or rotation in office, a solution that Madison and others advocated as a means of protecting against permanent majority factions.... [What CV] does is to transform the unit of representation from a territorial one or racial constituency to a political or psychological one.

3. *Technical properties*: The strategy of choice for a cohesive minority group with intense preferences for a particular candidate is, under cumulative voting, to "plump" all the available votes on one candidate. If five seats on a city council are to be filled, voters would have five votes each to distribute as they saw fit. The pure majoritarianism of traditional single-member districts is constrained because the same majority cannot dominate the election for all five city-council seats. If the voters in a sufficiently large minority group concentrate all their votes on the same candidate, they can assure that candidate's election regardless of how other voters, including a majority of voters, cast their ballots. Even with extensive racially polarized voting, for example, a cohesive minority group that constituted at least one-sixth of the electorate would be able through cumulative voting to control one of the five city-council seats. The concept of the "threshold of exclusion" describes the minimum size a minority group must reach under various voting rules to have effective control over at least one seat. The formula for the threshold of exclusion under cumulative voting is $1/(1+N)+1$, where N is the number of seats to be filled. Thus, with five seats at stake and five votes to cast, a minority that casts one vote more than $1/(1+5)$, or one vote more than one-sixth of the total vote can control the outcome of one seat. This assumes that the minority group votes perfectly cohesively: all members cast all five of their votes for the same minority-preferred candidate. By contrast, the threshold of exclusion of FPTP systems is $1/2 + 1$.

4. CV is increasingly being used as a remedy in voting-rights litigation, particularly in the rural South where it is more difficult to devise districts that concentrate black voters into a majority in particular districts. One of the earliest developments of CV as an alternative remedy came in the massive *Dillard* litigation, discussed earlier in Chapter 7, which challenged the structure of county commissions and boards of education throughout Alabama. Note that the court here did not impose CV against the preferences of the defendant jurisdiction; the parties entered into a consent decree, which the court approved. After reading the case, you will then read a detailed case study of how CV has worked out in practice in Chilton County, Alabama.

John Dillard v. Chilton County Board of Education and Chilton County Commission

699 F.Supp. 870 (M.D.Ala.1988).

■ Myron H. Thompson, District Judge:

The plaintiffs have brought these two lawsuits on behalf of all black citizens in Chilton County, Alabama. They charge that the "at-large" system used to elect the Chilton County Commission and Board of Education violates § 2 of the Voting Rights Act of 1965. The commission and the school board have admitted that their at-large system violates § 2. The issue before the court is whether a settlement proposed by the parties, incorporating a "cumulative voting" scheme for the county's commission and school board, is acceptable. Several members of the plaintiff class have objected to the settlement, claiming that it does not adequately remedy the § 2 violation. After conducting a hearing, in which the objectors as well as plaintiff class members favoring the settlement testified, the special master in this case, United States Magistrate John L. Carroll, recommended in each of these two cases that the court approve the settlement. For the reasons that follow, the court concludes that the magistrate's recommendations should be adopted.

I.

According to the 1980 census, Chilton County has a total population of 30,610. Of that number, 11.86% are black. The black population is dispersed throughout the county.

Chilton County and its school system are currently governed by a five-member commission and a five-member board, respectively.... To remedy the admitted § 2 violation, the plaintiffs, the commission and the school board have proposed a seven-member commission and a seven-member board of education elected by cumulative voting. Under this system, each voter has seven votes to cast among the candidates. However, a voter may distribute his or her votes in any way he or she desires. For example, a voter could vote all seven votes for one candidate, four votes for one candidate and three for another, one vote for each of the seven different candidates, or in various other combinations. There are no majority-vote or numbered-post requirements.

Several members of the plaintiff class argue that the proposed settlement does not cure the § 2 violation, and they have proposed a single-member districting plan in its place.

II.

* * *

A.

* * *

[T]he critical issue for the court, in its assessment of the settlement proposed by the parties, is whether the black voters in the county have under the settlement the potential to elect representatives of their choice, even in the face of [severe racial polarization.] In determining whether the settlement offers such, the court will apply a concept known as "threshold of exclusion."

The threshold of exclusion "is the percentage of the vote that will guarantee the winning of a seat even under the most unfavorable circumstances." The worst case scenario that defines the threshold of exclusion is based on two assumptions. The first is that the majority sponsor only as many candidates as there are seats to be filled; for example, in a seven-seat jurisdiction, only seven majority-preferred candidates would run. The second is that the majority spread its votes evenly among its candidates, with no "crossover voting" for the minority-preferred candidate. If either of these assumptions is relaxed, then it is entirely possible for the minority candidate to win even if the minority does not constitute more than the threshold of exclusion in turnout.

There is a calculable threshold of exclusion for any election scheme. For example, in an at-large system, such as the one [now] used in Chilton

County, the threshold of exclusion is more than 50%. Any group that constitutes more than 50% of the electorate in that district—that is, a group of "50% plus"—is guaranteed that its preferred candidate will win. Of course, in a plurality-win at-large district, as opposed to a district with a majority-vote requirement, a group with less than 50% plus of the electorate can elect its preferred candidate in certain cases. For example, a group constituting 40% of the electorate might elect its candidate in a three-way contest where the other 60% of the electorate spreads its votes between the other two candidates, each of whom receives 30%. However, although a group that constitutes less than 50% plus of the population in an at-large jurisdiction may, in some cases, elect its preferred candidate, the threshold of exclusion remains 50% plus; that is, a group of 50% plus, by voting strategically—sponsoring only as many candidates as there are seats and voting for the entire majority-sponsored slate—can totally shut out the minority.

In a cumulative voting system, however, the threshold of exclusion is dependent on the number of seats to be filled in a given election. It can be expressed as "1/1 + #of seats plus." Thus, in a jurisdiction with seven seats, the threshold of exclusion would be 12.5% plus. If 1000 electors vote for seven positions, and if there is a worst case scenario, only seven candidates preferred by the majority, with an evenly split vote, a minority would need only 876, or 12.51% of the 7000 votes, to elect the candidate of their choice.

The threshold of exclusion concept should not, however, be applied in a vacuum. Section 2 requires that, in evaluating vote dilution claims, a court must engage in "a searching practical evaluation of 'past and present reality.'" *Gingles*. A court must look not to just the worse case scenario or the best scenario, but to the totality of the circumstances, to the social and economic as well as the political circumstances of the jurisdiction in which the election system has been, or will be, used. In actual settings, the above two assumptions will exist in varying degrees; and, more than likely, there will be other factors that impede or facilitate the access of minorities to the political process. Therefore, based on a particular jurisdiction's totality of circumstances, a questioned election system may very well not be adequate for the jurisdiction, even though the percentage of black voters in the jurisdiction exceeds the threshold of exclusion for the system; and, conversely, the system may very well be fully adequate in another jurisdiction, even though the percentage of black voters in that jurisdiction is less than the system's threshold of exclusion. The threshold of exclusion concept is therefore not an automatic cut-off point, but rather is a broad guideline which may be helpful in assessing the impact on minorities of present and proposed election systems.

Under the present at-large system used to elect the Chilton County Commission and Board of Education, the threshold of exclusion is 50% plus. Because the percentage of blacks in the county, 11.86, does not even approach this threshold and because there is extensive racial polarization in the county, black voters in the county do not have a realistic opportunity to participate in the political process and elect candidates of their choice.

In contrast, the cumulative voting system proposed by the parties does offer black voters in the county such an opportunity. Admittedly, the percentage of blacks, 11.86, in the county is less than the threshold and, admittedly, if the black voters cumulate their votes, they will not be able to elect a representative under the worse case scenario. But it also cannot be overlooked that the percentage of black citizens in the county approaches the threshold of exclusion. Looking at the totality of the circumstances in Chilton County, the parties urge, and the court agrees, that the system does offer black voters in the county the potential to elect candidates of their choice to the county commission and school board, even in the face of substantial racially polarized voting.

* * *

IV.

Finally, the six members of the plaintiff class, who objected to the cumulative vote proposal, have submitted a single-member districting scheme of their own. The objectors ignore the demographics of Chilton County. As previously noted, black persons comprise only 11.86% of the population of Chilton County, and they are dispersed throughout the county. It is impossible to draw a five or seven single-member district plan which both has a majority black district and satisfies the one-person-one-vote requirement. For example, the objectors presented a five single-member district plan to the court, with most of the black citizens included in one district. However, that district would have a total population of approximately 11,000, making it roughly twice the size of an ideal district. The plan obviously fails to satisfy the one-person-one-vote requirement. *See, e.g., Chapman v. Meier*, 420 U.S. 1, 27 (1975) (court-ordered plans must normally meet the goal of population equality with little more than de minimis variation).

* * *

NOTES AND QUESTIONS

1. *Case study: Chilton County, Alabama.* The political science literature has thoroughly explored the theoretical advantages and disadvantages of different voting systems. But there are few concrete studies of alternative voting systems in operation, in part because until recently, few American jurisdictions used anything other than the traditional system of plurality, winner-take-all voting rules. Rather than debate the abstract merits of alternative voting systems, however, it is now possible to study local governments in the United States, such as Chilton County, that have quietly been using such systems for nearly a decade.

Does actual experience with cumulative voting raise new issues beyond those identified in the theoretical literature, or does it largely confirm academic predictions? What follows are excerpts from a detailed case study of the aftermath of the *Dillard* litigation in Chilton County:

Richard H. Pildes and Kristen A. Donoghue, Cumulative Voting in the United States
1995 U. Chi. Leg. Forum 241.

* * *

4. *The Chilton County settlement.*

[T]he County stipulated to findings that voting was racially polarized" and to substantive liability." On the same day, it filed a proposed settlement agreement that had been reached with the plaintiffs. Conceiving the terms of settlement, however, had proven difficult. The County had been willing to convert to a districted system and to draw a majority-minority district. But, unless the County Commission and Board of Education were increased to at least fifteen members each (an option the County leaders viewed as unwieldy and unduly expensive), the geographic dispersion of black voters in the County made the drawing of a contiguous, relatively compact majority-black district impossible.

In settlement discussions, a private attorney assisting in the settlement process for *Dillard v. Baldwin County Board of Education* proposed moving to an alternative voting system. Alternative voting systems are increasingly common at the local level in Alabama, in part because the leading statewide black political organization understood the concept early and has been a consistent supporter of it. Between twenty and twenty-three jurisdictions in Alabama use limited voting, primarily for municipal elections; indeed, Alabama is the national leader in the use of limited voting.

Chilton County, however, decided instead to opt for cumulative voting. After a "long, long series of discussions" of both cumulative voting and limited voting, the lawyer representing Chilton County, John Hollis Jackson, concluded that cumulative voting would be preferable. Those negotiating the settlement for the County feared that limited voting would be perceived as interfering with principles of equality and fair voting because voters would not be permitted to cast a vote for all the seats being filled. Indeed, when the ADC [the Alabama Democratic Conference, the major black political organization in the State] proposed limited voting, the leading local paper editorialized that "being allowed to vote for only one candidate borders on forbidding residents to have the Constitutionally given right to elect those who govern." In opting for cumulative voting, Chilton County became the only Alabama jurisdiction to do so. The motivating force for the decision to accept an alternative voting system was, without a doubt, the fear of what the federal court might impose instead.

Once Jackson agreed to consider a cumulative-voting remedy, he had to persuade the County's political officials to accept it. Initially, they were incredulous. As Jackson put it, they "acted like I was insane to even bring it to them." Jackson held several meetings with the existing County Commission and Board of Education in which various options, including pursuing the litigation, were discussed. As he put it, one day there would be agreement to accept the cumulative voting solution, the next day, the political leaders would be "totally opposed." Eventually, both bodies became persuaded that, as alien as the idea of cumulative voting had seemed initially, it was the best option. After formally voting to adopt the cumulative voting scheme, the two bodies held a joint press conference to begin the process of persuading the County's citizens to accept it. Once the political leaders endorsed cumulative voting as the best alternative under the circumstances, they remained committed to their decision; thus steadfastness played a considerable role in the eventual, begrudging public acceptance of cumulative voting. The parties drafted a formal settlement agreement and the district court approved it, over the objection of some members of the plaintiff class.

5. *Selling cumulative voting to the citizens of Chilton County.*

One of the most interesting aspects of the Chilton County experience was the self-conscious way public efforts were made to explain and justify the new system....

The official announcement of the settlement came at a news conference led by Jackson in February of 1988, with the first cumulative voting elections to take place in that summer's primaries. Thus, there was little time to prepare for the new system. Both the County Commission and Board of Education, which had been five-member bodies with residency requirements, would become seven-member bodies, elected at large with no residency requirements. The move from five to seven members was necessary for the cumulative voting system to work as intended.... With a black population of around 11.8 percent, a five-member body would not ensure Chilton County's black population of control over even one seat in the face of extreme racially polarized voting. With a seven-member board, a cohesive minority just above 12.5 percent would effectively control one seat....

In the news conference explaining the new system, the County's attorney, John Hollis Jackson, told voters, "I can confidently say that not one single member of either board like[d] what he had to do." The same issue of the *Independent Advertiser* that reported the press conference included an editorial entitled "Making the Best of a Bad Situation," indicating that the paper had switched positions and was now reconciled to cumulative voting. While saying that the federal court order would "anger many residents," and that "We are angry too," the editorial also said that cumulative voting was "the better of the evils" and that it was "time to make the best of a bad situation. Learn the new system and exercise your right to vote."

The cumulative voting system apparently was met with contempt and disbelief by the general public. Sue Smith, a Republican elected to the Board of Education in 1988, remembered:

> When the idea was first proposed, as far as the public reaction, we thought it was a joke, because the idea that one person could vote seven times in one particular race was just really unheard of at that time, and many people thought it was just something that they were grasping at straws kind of a thing, and it would not ever come into effect here. Once it became the law under the settlement of this court case, a lot of people still didn't believe it.

Nor was this skepticism confined to whites. Bobby Agee, Chilton County's first black County Commissioner, who was elected under cumulative voting, recalled that "I didn't see how it would work.... Everybody kept saying it would work, but in the back of my mind I just could not figure out with the white population being as large as it is and the minority population being as small as it is, I kept thinking we're still going to lose no matter what." As the summer primaries approached, the educational efforts of both local government officials and other, more partisan forces, accelerated....

B. Results to Date under the Cumulative Voting System

* * *

a. Black representation.

In fact, cumulative voting has worked just as predicted ex ante with respect to enhancing black representation even in the face of racially polarized voting. In elections for the powerful County Commission in 1988, the first held under cumulative voting, Bobby Agee became the first black representative to be elected to the Chilton County Commission since Reconstruction. Indeed Agee, the only black candidate in the general election, not only was elected, but received more total votes than any other candidate in the fourteen-candidate field.

Statistical analysis of the 1988 election reveals that Agee was not the leading vote getter due to cross-racial support. Instead, black voters effectively used the cumulative voting system to concentrate their support for Agee despite almost no white crossover support. Only 1.5 percent of white voters appear to have cast even a single vote for Agee, while virtually all black voters voted for him. More importantly, most black voters gave Agee multiple votes, including many who cast all seven votes for Agee. One means of testing this is by examining the number of precincts in which various candidates received more votes ("bonus votes") than the number of actual voters. Agee received bonus votes in more precincts than any other candidate, indicating that voters were casting more multiple votes for him than for other candidates.

b. Representation of other minorities.

Advocates of cumulative voting assert that, in contrast to race-conscious districting, which enhances the electoral opportunities only of racial minorities, cumulative voting—as a neutral means of enhancing minority representation more generally—ought to enhance minority representation of other groups as well. Cumulative voting has indeed had this effect in Chilton County.

Republicans

Republicans were dramatically underrepresented on the County Commission prior to the 1988 election. In 1988, however, Republicans won three of the seven commission seats. This sudden transformation occurred before the dramatic shift toward the Republican party at the local level in the South. Sue Smith, then Chairperson of the Chilton County Republican Party, believes that cumulative voting contributed to the Republican breakdown of the Democratic monopoly on local political power. In 1992, Republicans again were successful, this time winning two seats on the County Commission....

Women

... In Chilton County, women have been elected to the Board of Education since cumulative voting began. Only one woman was on the Board before 1988, but in the cumulative voting election that year, two women, both Republicans, were elected. A third woman, a Democrat, was nearly elected but placed eighth, one position away from a seat. One of the successful women candidates in the 1988 election commented that she was not sure cumulative voting had played a role in the sudden success of women candidates. She did, however, note that more women were running because more women had decided that they could get elected—which might be associated with the use of cumulative voting. Still, women have not been successful in County Commission elections, even since cumulative voting began. The one woman who has run in a primary or general election for the County Commission was defeated.

In sum, since cumulative voting began, groups that previously had not been represented—blacks, Republicans, and women—have been elected in significant numbers to both the County Commission and the Board of Education.

2. Effects on minority representation: substantive representation.

Descriptive representation—the actual presence of minorities in political office—is the immediate test of alternative voting systems. Descriptive representation might in and of itself bring about several desirable results: among other effects, it might enhance the legitimacy of political bodies within the community as a whole and foster a greater sense of civic inclusion among political minorities. But a major question is whether more minorities in office translates into substantive representation that is more responsive to the minority community. Previous scholarship concludes that verifiable, material changes in local government policy do occur when racial minorities begin to assume public office. Nonetheless, some continue to question the link between descriptive and substantive representation: whether the increased presence of black public officials translates into tangible policy and other benefits for minority voters. Is minority representation of primarily symbolic importance? Do white officials represent the actual substantive interests of black constituents just as effectively? Indeed, white members of the Chilton County Commission questioned whether there was any need for minority representation on the County's various administrative bodies.

In Chilton County, we found at least three significant changes in local government—two policy oriented and one attitudinal—in the wake of the cumulative voting system and the first election of a black County Commissioner. First, the most significant function of the County Commission is to make road-paving decisions. Of the various functions within the Commission's jurisdiction, none occupies more time or matters more to the residents of Chilton County than petitions to have roads paved. The County still has about six hundred miles of unpaved roads, which become muddy in the frequent rains, but financial resources sufficient to pave only eight miles per year.

Before Agee was elected, the County Commission granted road-paving petitions in an *ad hoc* and informal way. At Agee's urging, the Commission adopted a more formal point system with neutral criteria that eliminated the potential for favoritism. The point system depends on the number of houses on a road, whether the mail carrier travels it, if there is a church present, and the like. According to Agee, he was motivated by several problems in the old system and not solely by the aim of ensuring that road-paving services were distributed more equitably in the black community. But one consequence of adopting general, neutral criteria is that more roads now are being paved where black residents live than were under the system that existed before Agee was elected.

Second, Agee's presence has led to the appointment of more minorities to important administrative boards. One of the Commission's principal tasks is appointing, by majority vote, these administrative officials. Agee thus cannot appoint anyone directly, but as he says, "the mere fact of me being there and recommending a minority goes a long way." These administrative boards wield considerable power because they operate independently of the County Commission. Agee has succeeded in appointing a minority to the Hospital Board and the Water Board, both of which previously had not had minority members....

The third benefit observers attributed to Agee's presence was more intangible. Many people, including Agee himself, said that black residents in Chilton County "definitely" took a lot of pride in Agee's presence and felt more connected to local government as a result. As the County's attorney put it, "I do think that the black community is really proud of having elected [black] officials. I think that makes a difference." As the reporter who covers local politics put it, black residents like the cumulative voting system "because it works, and for the longest time they had no voice in government and now they do...."

One of the more dramatic long-term consequences of the emergence of black representation on the County Commission, in the wake of cumulative voting, is that Bobby Agee eventually became Chairperson of the Commission. The Chairperson normally is elected by the other commissioners. An unusual clause in the litigation settlement, however, had entitled Agee to serve as Chairperson. The settlement provided that black officials elected to the County Commission or Board of Education could serve as Chairperson for eight months any time they chose to do so during their initial term in office. Agee, however, did not feel prepared to assume the duties of Chairperson during his first term and did not want to invoke this special clause if unnecessary.

After being in office for one full term, Agee had established enough credibility and expertise that the other commissioners elected him Chairperson for one year and then reelected him for a second year. We found no evidence that the other commissioners were motivated by the specter of Agee invoking his right to serve as Chairperson under the settlement agreement. In any event, even if that motivation played a role in Agee's initial election (in the sense that the settlement was understood to entitle him to serve as Chairperson once), it could not have played any role in his reelection. Instead, the commissioners we interviewed regularly remarked on Agee's judgment, temperament, and ability as the reasons they voted him Chairperson of the Commission. As one put it, "Agee is the most intelligent and most educated man on the commission."

Agee's elevation to Chairperson of the most powerful local government political body in Chilton County illustrates the integrative role cumulative voting can play. Given racially polarized voting patterns, Agee could not have come close to being elected in an at-large election, even after he had served his first term. Yet given the opportunity to serve that cumulative voting created, he earned sufficient respect from his fellow commissioners to be elected Chairperson twice....

3. *Public satisfaction with cumulative voting?*

One of the striking discoveries we made was that cumulative voting was widely disliked in Chilton County. Virtually everyone we interviewed reported this fact. Even more interesting were the reasons for this dislike. The principal reason was the widely shared view that cumulative voting was undemocratic and unconstitutional because it violated the one person, one vote principle. As one observer put it, "they feel it violates their sense of governmental propriety somehow. They keep saying it's unconstitutional, 'I just know it's unconstitutional.' I hear that all the time." Indeed, one person reportedly refused to cast more than one of his seven votes "because the system is unconstitutional." Some attributed this view to the uniqueness of the system: "[I]t goes away from practically the rest of the country and how they vote." Others attributed this view to the fact that "[o]lder people are just stuck in their ways and they don't want to change." ...

Yet more irony emerged when we explored whether dislike of cumulative voting was a cover for resistance to minority political power. We ultimately rejected this explanation. We consistently were told—and came to believe—that, whatever complaints people had about cumulative voting, there was general acceptance of the need for minority representation. Many people stated that they understood the importance of minority representation but would have preferred drawing majority-black districts had that been possible. Indeed, one prominent member of the Board of Education who thought cumulative voting was a terrible system said that he had thought for a long time about what Chilton County could have done instead. He concluded that the County should have set aside one seat on the relevant bodies as a "minority seat," for which all voters would vote but which a minority candidate would have to win. Thus, he preferred a blatantly unconstitutional means—the setting aside of a seat for minority officeholders—to a clearly constitutional one—cumulative voting—because of his strong convictions that the latter violated the fundamental, though relatively recent, principle of one person, one vote. Such is constitutional law in action, rather than on the books.

Nonetheless, the widespread dislike of cumulative voting is not to be interpreted as disapproval of the system. Even people who did not like the system appeared to accept it because "it works." By working, people meant that it did produce the intended result of black elected officials roughly representative of the black population. Based on our interviews, there seemed to be a consensus that cumulative voting was effective, necessary to achieve minority representation, and therefore begrudgingly accepted even while being disliked.

5. *Statistical analysis of recent cumulative voting elections.*

[...] For the 1992 election, voting was polarized heavily along racial lines: a strong proportional relationship exists between the percentage of black voters and support for black candidates in any given district. Racial voting patterns are more difficult to interpret in the 1994 election, but black candidates continued to poll significantly better in districts with large numbers of black voters.... racial crossover voting appears limited in both elections, especially in 1992....

Our analysis of racial voting patterns in the 1992 County Commission election is confirmed by exit-poll data others have gathered. The validity of these exit polls is confirmed by the close fit between the self-reports of the 702 voters surveyed and the actual election outcomes. Thus, Agee received at least one vote from 67 percent of blacks who voted in this election; among these black voters, 85.4 percent reported casting all seven votes for Agee. On average, then, black voters who supported Agee did so intensely and took advantage of the "plumping" option cumulative voting creates:

Agee received an average of 6.28 votes from each black voter who supported him. In contrast, the exit-poll data confirms that Agee received little white crossover support. Among white voters, Agee came in twelfth among all candidates, ranking ahead only of the other black candidate and one white Republican. Only 13.4 percent of whites cast even a single vote for Agee. In other words, only the use of cumulative voting made Agee's election possible. Had the at-large system remained in place, Agee would not have stood a chance....

   6. *Partisan side effects and fringe candidates.*

Interestingly, cumulative voting in Chilton County has indirectly weakened partisan campaigning in ways we did not see predicted in the literature. In a general election under the cumulative voting system to fill the seven-seat County Commission, each party runs seven candidates. When the parties distribute sample ballots or otherwise provide advice about how their supporters should vote, the major parties recommend casting one vote each for the party's seven candidates.

For any individual candidate, however, the optimal strategy is different. Each candidate would like to have as many total votes cast for him or her as possible. Thus, the interests of parties and their candidates diverge under cumulative voting. In the first cumulative voting election, most candidates asked for only one vote and followed the party strategy of recommending that voters distribute the remainder of their votes for the party's other candidates. But by subsequent elections, candidates learned the importance of concentrated support. Many candidates therefore began to distribute their own sample ballots in which they asked voters for all seven votes. In turn, political parties have cut back on sample ballots that recommend vote dispersion; in 1994, the Republican party urged voters to pick one Republican candidate and to give that candidate all seven of their votes. Several County leaders reported that in ways like this, cumulative voting has begun to erode traditional party politics. Candidates increasingly tend to run as individuals, rather than as representatives of parties. Those who noticed this effect of cumulative voting viewed it as a benefit at the local-government level; the new system was perceived to be leading voters to elect candidates based more on individual qualities than in previous elections. Of course, in another sense cumulative voting has revitalized party politics by helping Republicans to break the monopoly on local political power that Democrats long held under the traditional majority-rule system.

A longstanding concern about cumulative voting is that it enables the election of extremist or fringe candidates.... After seven years, there is no evidence of this problem arising in Chilton County. While the potential for election of fringe candidates exists in theory, it has not occurred in practice. Whether there is any general lesson in Chilton County's failure to elect extremist candidates must be left to speculation. Perhaps political and cultural forces particular to Chilton County make it a generally moderate area; some observers reported that most people, white and black, were "in the middle" and "rather conservative." On the other hand, it might result from structural features concerning the nature of local-government politics and elections, in which case Chilton County's experience might be of greater predictive value for other local governments contemplating alternative voting systems. Local-government elections tend to be pragmatic, rather than ideological, and local office seekers have numerous incentives to fit themselves within the existing party structure—whether for reasons of financial and other support, future political prospects for higher office, or other considerations. Thus, although cumulative voting theoretically does give fringe candidates better electoral prospects, other structural features of local elections might moderate this possibility....

7. Problems with cumulative voting's at-large feature.

Before cumulative voting was adopted, Chilton County used at-large elections for the County Commission and Board of Education. This at-large system retained, however, one attribute of a districted system: residency requirements for candidates. Voters throughout the County voted for each seat, but candidates were required to run for specific seats from specific residency districts. Cumulative voting replaces districted elections and necessarily does away with residency districts. As a result, a concern is whether the move toward at-large elections has entailed any significant costs associated with the loss of individual districts.

One specific fear, expressed at the time the system was introduced, was that elected representatives would be disproportionately concentrated in more densely populated parts of the County, such as the city of Clanton. In practice, however, this problem has not materialized. Candidates have continued to be elected from all parts of the County. Perhaps voters in different areas concentrate their votes on candidates from their areas, or perhaps candidates tend to focus their campaigning on different areas. Whatever the dynamics, the different areas of the County all continue to be represented under the cumulative voting system.

A more significant cost, however, has been the decline in specific geographic links between constituents and elected representatives. Legislators often serve an "ombudsman" role in which they serve as intermediaries in conflicts between their constituents and government agencies. The poor and minorities tend to be most dependent on legislators for this role, for they typically lack the traditional alternative mechanisms, such as lobbyists, lawyers, or personal contacts for resolving these conflicts. Political scientists have concluded that constituents more easily identify representatives from single-member districts than at-large systems, although the studies do not examine legislators elected through alternative voting systems, such as cumulative voting. We discovered, however, that cumulative voting does create problems of this sort. The lack of a direct tie between an individual representative and constituents was perhaps the most serious disadvantage of the shift to cumulative voting that we discovered.

Several individuals cited the abandonment of residency requirements as the major problem they had experienced under cumulative voting. A number of people commented that they did not know whom to call on either the County Commission or the Board of Education when they had an issue to discuss. In the former system of residency districts, the representative from a particular "district" was understood to be the person to turn to for local problems. Sue Smith, former member of the Board of Education, remarked:

> [Y]ou lose the feeling of "this is my representative on this Board." And I feel that way on the County Commission now. If I had a problem to speak with the County Commission about I would call two or three of them because I don't really know which one I ought to make contact with. I think that's a sense of frustration for the general population....

Representatives also described some costs in moving to at-large elections. For better or worse, they now feel a general sense of responsibility to citizens of the entire County. When asked about the disadvantages of cumulative voting, Agee cited the at-large feature, because "you've got more people to satisfy ... where, if you had a district you'd be concerned with just satisfying those people in that district...."

8. *The dynamics of racial politics.*

... Our long conversations with Bobby Agee left the impression that cumulative voting has provided a thoughtful advocate for the black community and has begun to decrease racial polarization in politics. Agee reported that in his first campaign, he felt he was considered "the black candidate." He was the only candidate who campaigned in black neighborhoods and when he was elected, the other representatives viewed him as "the black representative." By the second election, however, many white candidates had gained an appreciation for the power of the black vote, and actively campaigned in black neighborhoods. In addition, Agee reported that he now receives more phone calls and requests from white constituents than black constituents, in line with the demographics of Chilton County. Agee's final comment sounds almost quaint in its resonance with the civil-rights discourse of the 1960s: people in Chilton County, he says, are starting to "get away from race, creed[,] and color." They are "[looking] at [the] ability of [the] person."

NOTES AND QUESTIONS

1. The ideological resistance of Chilton County voters to casting multiple votes, on the ground that doing so violates the constitutional "principle" of one-person, one-vote, suggests an interesting framing question about cumulative voting. Rather than structuring the system so that each voter has seven votes to cast, should each voter be presented as having one vote, *parts* of which they could cast for different candidates? Thus, voters could be told that they could cast one-seventh of a vote for each candidate, or that they could give their one vote to one candidate. Would shifting the frame from "seven votes" to "one vote" that could be parceled out into fractions of one-seventh be likely to reduce the kind of discomfort with multiple voting experienced in Chilton County? If not, is this concern significant enough to suggest that limited voting, discussed *infra*, in which voters cannot cast more than one vote for any one candidate, should be seen as preferable to cumulative voting?

2. Note that the loss of direct accountability of individual representatives to constituents that some Chilton County residents complain of might be felt most significantly by the poor and the very minorities CV is designed to benefit. One important function local politicians play is to work out conflicts between constituents and various governmental agencies. This role of local representatives, characterized in the excerpt as the function of "ombudsman," is particularly important for those who are least likely to have other resources for resolving these conflicts, such as lawyers, lobbyists, or personal contacts. The demand for constituent services also generally tends to be greatest in districts below average in socioeconomic characteristics.

At least three possible questions are raised by noticing this important ombudsman function of local representation. First, is there reason to think that over time with a CV system, representatives and constituents would find ways to construct similar personal service relationships to those currently existing in the system of districted elections? Recall that many at-large systems for local government elections required candidates to identify specific residency districts from which they were running; would a similar structure be desirable for CV elections? Second, if not, should the effort be to create, if possible, hybrid forms of CV, in which at least some representatives would be elected from districts, and some through CV, in a kind of mixed electoral system? For example, the settlement in *Bencomo v. Phoenix Union High School Dist. No. 10* CV90–0369–PHX–EHC (D. Ariz. July 3, 1990), replaced a pure at-large electoral system with a system using five single-member districts and two seats elected through limited voting. Mixed at-large/districted systems are quite common at the local level in the United States. Third, if CV does compromise the capacity of poor voters to find assistance in negotiating their way through government bureaucracies, should that be a reason sufficient to maintain districted elections? For discussion of this ombudsman function in the context of CV, see Samuel Issacharoff, *Supreme Court Destabilization of Single–Member Districts*, 1995 U. Chi. Legal F. 205, 237–38.

3. How likely is it that courts will be comfortable accepting novel voting systems, such as cumulative voting, as remedies in litigation? In *Dillard, supra*, the parties agreed upon a CV or limited voting remedy for many of the local government bodies being challenged, and the court approved all the consent decrees that provided for alternative voting systems. But will courts be prepared to impose CV against the objections of defendant jurisdictions? Does the Voting Rights Act give them the power to do so? Note that in *Dillard*, some jurisdictions could not easily create black-majority single-member districts, but also did not agree to the use of alternative voting systems. Many years after liability was found, the district judge has still not acted on the plaintiffs' efforts to impose alternative voting on recalcitrant jurisdictions. If the VRA is viewed as not giving judges the power to impose alternative voting, should the statute be amended to expressly authorize CV as one remedial option? If so, under what circumstances should it be appropriate for courts to order CV as a remedy?

In litigation that lasted several rounds involving Worcester County, Maryland, the federal district court initially imposed a CV scheme that plaintiffs had proposed as a remedy for VRA litigation under Section 2. The Fourth Circuit then reversed on the ground that the court first had to give the county adequate opportunity to propose its own remedy. On remand, the district court then once again imposed CV, for the reasons given in the following opinion. Once again, the Fourth Circuit overturned the CV scheme, this time on the ground that neither of the parties supported it. *Cane v. Worcester County, Md.*, 59 F.3d 165 (4th Cir. 1995). How persuasive is the district court's rationale? Would CV be preferable to creating single-member "safe" minority districts in contexts like that presented here?

Cane v. Worcester County, Md.

874 F.Supp. 687 (D.Md.1995).

■ JOSEPH H. YOUNG, DISTRICT JUDGE:

In *Cane v. Worcester County*, 35 F.3d 921 (4th Cir.1994), the Fourth Circuit affirmed the Court's finding that the at-large electoral system used by Worcester County ("County") for election of the County Board of Commissioners ("Board") was violative of § 2 of the Voting Rights Act, 42 U.S.C. § 1973, and reversed and remanded the Court's imposition of a remedial system based upon cumulative voting with instructions to afford the County an opportunity to submit a plan to remedy the § 2 violation. In accordance with the remand, the County proffered three alternative proposals and the plaintiffs submitted one plan, and a hearing was held on the merits.

The County, afforded the first opportunity to devise an electoral plan to remedy the § 2 violation, now claims it was not afforded a meaningful opportunity to respond because of the allegedly strict deadlines imposed by the Court. The County, however, did not begin consideration of potential alternatives until after the denial by the Fourth Circuit of the County's petition for a rehearing en banc. This was six weeks after the panel's opinion and almost two years after the legality of the County's voting scheme was first challenged in court. Moreover, the testimony of County officials suggests that they believe that the plans presented were the best that could be developed and that additional time would not allow for meaningful improvements in the plans. The Court finds the County has been afforded an adequate opportunity to remedy the § 2 violation. Accordingly, the three plans submitted will be considered by the Court.

A plan proffered by a legislative body to remedy a § 2 violation must provide the protected minority group with a "realistic opportunity to elect a representative of their choice." At a minimum, a remedial plan must not itself be violative of the Voting Rights Act. Therefore, a threshold question when evaluating such a plan is whether it violates the standards announced in *Thornburg v. Gingles*, 478 U.S. 30 (1986).

First, it should be noted that it has been established that the African–American community in Worcester County is politically cohesive and sufficiently large and compact to constitute a majority in a single-member district. Further, the Fourth Circuit accepted the Court's findings that the white community has typically voted as a bloc to defeat the minority's preferred candidate, and that, considering the totality of the circumstances, African–Americans have not had the same opportunity as whites to participate in the electoral process and to elect representatives of their choice.

The remaining issue, therefore, is whether any of the proposed remedial plans preclude the majority from voting as a bloc to defeat the minority's preferred candidate. The County insists that its three plans are due great deference, but the Court can be deferential only if it finds that one of the plans remedies the § 2 violation. The County's plans cannot be accepted if they continue to allow white candidates to control all of the seats on the Board.

PROPOSED REMEDIAL PLANS

The County's Plan #2 has been the primary focus of the attention of the parties, and it will be considered first. This scheme divides the County into five single-member districts for both the primary and general elections. The County has attempted to remedy the § 2 violation with the creation of District 3 in which African–American voters comprise 44.68% of the voting age population. The County asserts that in this district, " ... black voters in Worcester County [would] enjoy a functional majority[9] ... and an equal opportunity to elect the representative of their choice."

The County bases this assertion largely on the work of Dr. Allan Lichtman and Gerald Hebert in *A General Theory of Vote Dilution*, 6 La Raza L.J. 1 (1993). The authors do argue that, in principle, "[a] remedial district may include a white population majority if coalition voting is

9. A functional majority district in this context would be one in which blacks, although a minority of voters, could nonetheless typically elect the candidate of choice as a result of white cross-over votes.

sufficient to elect minority-preferred candidates." It should also be noted that the authors state that the party asserting the adequacy of a remedial district based upon a functional majority should "have the burden of showing that minority cohesion and turnout, as well as white 'crossover' voting are sufficiently high to enable minorities to elect candidates of their choice."

The creation of a functional majority district would, in theory, negate the third prong of the *Gingles* test. If a minority community is sufficiently large and a white community is sufficiently fractious, then the majority will be unable to vote as a bloc to enable it usually to defeat the minority's preferred candidate.

The Supreme Court has held that a finding of vote dilution in a multi-member districting plan generally requires remediation by the creation of super-majority districts. *Growe v. Emison*, 507 U.S. 25 (1993). Remedial districts have been required to contain more than a " ... mere majority even of [minority] voting age population ..." unless there is specific evidence on the record to overcome the accepted presumption that a super-majority is necessary for electoral success. Further, courts have been reluctant to even consider crossover voting when adjudicating § 2 remedies. Indeed, a remedial plan has never been accepted when its success was dependent entirely upon the effectiveness of functional majorities.

The County nonetheless insists that the 44.68% "functional majority" in District 3 remedies the § 2 violation because the cross-over of white voters will give an equal chance of electoral success to African–Americans. This position is unsupported by the record, however, and the data in fact suggests that District 3 will be dominated by whites. Thus the County has failed to sustain the burden, as described by Lichtman and Hebert ... and placed on the proponent of a functional majority district. Assuming that all eligible voters do vote,[10] white voters will still control the electoral outcome in District 3 whether predictions of future voting behavior and electoral outcomes are based upon the average cross-over rates or individual elections. The average white cross-over rate in Worcester County is 19%, while the data for African–American cross-over is less certain. The Court found minority cohesion to be at least 60%, but for the purposes of this analysis it will be assumed to be 80%. Applying those percentages to future elections in the proposed District 3, the candidate preferred by white voters would win with 54% of the vote.

10. In Worcester County, 77% of white voters register to vote while only 32% percent of eligible African–American voters register. (A large and relatively equal percentage of registered African–American and white voters actually vote). Such patterns are, of course, precisely the reason that a super-majority is typically required in remedial districts, and Dr. Ronald Weber, the County's expert, concedes Lichtman and Hebert's assertion that participation levels are crucial to an evaluation of the effectiveness of a functional majority district.

If, alternatively, the Court uses the 1986 District 3 election to predict future voting behavior as urged by the County, the projected rate of African–American cross-over voting would be 38.2% and 32.2% for white cross-over voting. Again, if such numbers are applied to the County's proposed District 3, the white candidate would win with 54% of the vote....

ALTERNATIVE REMEDIES

If a municipality fails to proffer an acceptable remedy following a finding of a § 2 violation, a court must exercise its discretion to fashion a "near optimal" plan. In doing so, the court's remedy "must include consideration of both racial fairness and traditional districting principles." *Bridgeport Coalition for Fair Representation v. City of Bridgeport*, 26 F.3d 271, 278 (2d Cir. 1994). Thus, while the Court need not defer to the County's specific proposals if they are violative of § 2, it must nonetheless effectuate "to the greatest extent possible the policy judgments expressed by the County" which underlie those proposals. ...

The Circuit Court found, quoting Justice Thomas in *Holder v. Hall*, 114 S. Ct. 2581 (1994), that there is nothing inherently radical or inappropriate about the judicial imposition of cumulative voting pursuant to a finding of a § 2 violation. It acknowledged that cumulative voting would "promote the County's desire to have commissioners serve the collective interest of the County by requiring the candidates to appeal to all of the voters in the County." Further, cumulative voting would obviously not require the division of municipalities.

In light of the Fourth Circuit's decision, and in strong deference to the County's expressed policy judgments, the Court will not impose the plaintiffs' plan but rather will exercise its discretion to attempt to fashion a "near optimal" plan for the County. The County's primary elections for Board of Commissioners will be by single-member district based upon the district maps designed by the County for Plans #1 and #2. The general election will be by cumulative voting. The use of cumulative voting in the general elections will provide the benefits previously described by the Court, while a single-member district primary will ensure substantial geographic diversity on the Board.

The Court's plan will provide a substantial remedy for African–American citizens of Worcester County. The record suggests that African–Americans in the County are primarily Democrats, while whites are split relatively evenly between the parties. This being so, African–Americans will comprise a significant majority of Democrats in District 3 and should be able to elect their preferred candidate in the primaries. A cumulative voting regime for the general election would then allow African–Americans voters county-wide to elect the nominated Democrat from District 3 if they so chose.

The Court's plan would also address the County's concerns with geographic diversity. The use of single-member district guarantees that all regional interests, as defined by the County's districting scheme, will have candidates standing in the general election. After a general election based upon cumulative voting, at least three of the five districts will be represented on any given Board. Moreover, if a particular region or municipality desires representation, it is assured of two candidates in the general election and it will be able to successfully elect a Commissioner as long as at least 17% of the County electorate is so committed.

The plan imposed by the Court best achieves the Fourth Circuit's mandate and adheres to the requirements of the Voting Rights Act and the political will of Worcester County. African–American voters of the County will have an opportunity to elect a candidate of their choice, but that opportunity will not come at the expense of geographical diversity, the division of municipalities, or racial segregation. Coalitions of voters will be free to cast their ballots on the basis of race, region, political issue, or any other consideration and have a real chance of electoral success while Board members will still be beholden to every County citizen.

NOTES AND QUESTIONS

1. *Other uses of cumulative voting:*

a. The most significant use of CV in American politics was in Illinois, where in the aftermath of the Civil War, election laws were changed to use CV to elect members of the lower house from three-member election districts. The system was adopted in 1870 and retained until 1980. Illinois had been bitterly riven during the Civil War, and the aim of CV was to provide representation to restore unity in the state by ensuring seats for minority parties within each district, and to help ensure more proportional representation statewide of the different parties. With CV, Republicans would gain some representation in the overwhelmingly Democratic portions of southern Illinois, while Democrats would likewise gain some seats in the Republican northern regions of the state. For House elections, the state was divided in 59 districts, each of which filled three seats, and voters could give one vote each to three candidates; three votes to one candidate; or one and one-half vote to two candidates. In 1970, Illinois voters voted to retain CV in a specific ballot question presented as part of a referendum on a new state constitution, but voted to abolish CV in 1980 when they approved a ballot measure, presented as a cost-saving device, that reduced the size of the state legislature. For the history of the Illinois experience, see Leon Weaver, *Semi-Proportional and Proportional Representation Systems in the United States*, in Choosing an Electoral System: Issues and Alternatives 197 (Arend Lijphart & Bernard Grofman eds., 1984); *see also* Richard Wiste, *Cumulative Voting and Legislative Performance,* in Illinois: Political Processes and Government Performance 119–120 (G. Crane, Jr. ed. 1980);

Charles W. Dunn, *Cumulative Voting Problems in Illinois Legislative Elections*, 9 Harv. J. Legis. 627 (1972); George S. Blair, Cumulative Voting: An Effective Device in Illinois Politics (1960); George S. Blair, *Cumulative Voting: Patterns of Party Allegiance and Rational Choice in Illinois State Legislative Contests*, 52 Am. Pol. Sci. Rev. 123 (1958).

The system did achieve its principal goals of reducing geographic divisions between the parties and increasing minority party representation. Only about 1.5 percent of the districts were represented by three figures from the same party from 1920–1980. But a problem was that voters ended up with few actual choices because the political parties would effectively collude; where Democrats were dominant, they would agree to run only two candidates and Republicans one, while where Republicans were dominant, they would agree to run only two candidates and Democrats one. As a result, elections were typically a foregone conclusion. For example, of 1,776 House elections between 1902 and 1969, only 17 districts ever had as many as five candidates run for the three contested seats. Dunn, *supra*, at 646. At the same time, though, CV did increase competition in the primaries, particularly within the minority party because there was much greater incentive to fight for nomination from a minority party. Charles Wiggins and Janice Petty, *Cumulative Voting and Electoral Competition*, 7 Am. Pol. Q. 345, 350–53 (1979).

One possible solution to the problems of diminished competition is to legally mandate that parties run a specified number of candidates in each district. Illinois did modify its rules a bit in this direction in 1970. For a thoughtful assessment of this approach, see Michael E. Lewyn, *When is Cumulative Voting Preferable to Single-Member Districting*, 25 N. Mex. L. Rev. 197, 220–224 (1995).

b. The first adoption of CV this century was in Alamogordo, New Mexico (site of the first test of the atomic bomb) in 1987. Since then, elections there have been the subject of careful study. *See, e.g.*, Richard Engstrom, Delbert A. Taebel, and Richard L. Cole, *Cumulative Voting as a Remedy for Minority Vote Dilution: The Case of Alamogordo, New Mexico*, V J. Law & Pol. 469 (1989). Although minorities constituted nearly 30 percent of the population, no minority had been elected to the city council since 1970. Under the CV system, to elect the city council, three members were selected at-large by CV and four were elected from districts. An Hispanic woman was elected the first time the system was used, with her election being due to 75 percent of her voters casting more than one vote for her—thus taking advantage of the CV system. Turnout was high in the first election, and nearly all voters used all three of their votes. Despite conclusions of academics that the system had worked well to enhance minority representation, voters in 1997 voted 850–596 to switch to all district elections by 2000.

c. In Texas, at least twenty-six small cities and school districts now use cumulative voting; one Texas jurisdiction uses limited voting. Robert

Brischetto, *Cumulative Voting at Work in Texas: A 1995 Exit Survey of Sixteen Communities*, in Voting and Democracy Report: 1995, at 61, 62 (The Center for Voting and Democracy, 1995). Cumulative voting was introduced first in 1991 in settlement of voting-rights litigation challenging the Lockhart Independent School District. Preliminary studies of these Texas elections reach results similar to those in the Chilton County study: cumulative voting in Texas appears to be working largely as predicted, without significant or unexpected disadvantages.

In what circumstances is CV likely to work best? Lewyn, *supra*, at 226–27 argues that CV is best for small cities, for nonpartisan elections (where political parties cannot control slates as they did in Illinois), and for jurisdictions with a stable, dominant majority faction or party. He argues that CV is not a good approach for big-city or statewide elections, in part because the problems of voter coordination that effective use of the CV option requires are too great in large jurisdictions.

d. For other works advocating cumulative voting, particularly as a tool under the Voting Rights Act, see Lani Guinier, The Tyranny of the Majority 99–101 (1994); Pamela S. Karlan, *Maps and Misreadings: The Role of Geographic Compactness in Racial Vote Dilution Litigation*, 24 Harv. CR–CL L. Rev. 173 (1989). For other studies of cumulative voting in operation, see Richard L. Engstrom, Jason F. Kirksey, and Edward Still, *One Person, Seven Votes: The Cumulative Voting Experience in Chilton County, Alabama*, in Affirmative Action and Representation (Anthony Peacock ed. 1997); Richard L. Engstrom and Charles J. Barrilleaux, *Native-Americans and Cumulative Voting: The Sisseton–Wahpeton Sioux*, 72 Soc. Sci. Q. 389 (1991).

e. Corporations have a long history of using cumulative voting for shareholder votes, although that practice appears to be waning. For a good history of cumulative voting in the corporate context, see Jeff Gordon, *Institutions as Relational Investors: A New Look at Cumulative Voting*, 94 Colum. L. Rev. 124 (1994).

f. Legislative cumulative voting? Lani Guinier has also proposed that CV might be used, not just in the selection of officeholders, but within governing bodies themselves to vote on policy. She offers this suggestion as a response to situations like that in *Presley v. Etowah County Commission*, 502 U.S. 491 (1992), discussed in Chapter 5. Consider whether her argument is persuasive:

> Legislative cumulative voting would discourage voting up or down on individual proposals. Rather, over a period of time and a series of legislative proposals, votes on multiple bills would be aggregated or linked. By linking votes on several issues to allow both weighted and split issue voting, the black representatives could more reliably participate in the legislative process, plumping votes to express the intensity of constituent preferences on some issues and trading votes on issues of constituent indifference.

Lani Guinier, The Tyranny of the Majority 108 (1994).

In response, Professor Karlan has argued that "Guinier's procedural solution is a two-edged sword":

> [Guinier's idea] would be impossible to implement: in most legislatures, the form bills take is so subject to manipulation that a minority could be forced to expend all its votes simply to block a few objectionable proposals, thereby both making it impossible for the group to affirmatively enact anything and stripping its members of an effective voice on the remaining items on the agenda. No legislature uses internal cumulative voting, although many engage in the sort of legislative drafting and logrolling that it might resemble.

* * *

> [The sorts of changes in legislative voting Guinier suggests] may give a black legislative caucus a "veto" over truly objectionable legislation, but it may do little to fortify an affirmative legislative strategy. Indeed, supermajority rules might actually impede such a strategy by denying progressive majorities the ability to overcome the resistance of a conservative, or even racist, minority. Supermajority rules tend to favor the status quo by making change difficult to achieve.

Pamela S. Karlan, *Democracy and Dis–Appointment*, 93 Mich. L. Rev. 1273, 1285, 1287 (1995).

C. Preference Voting or the Single-Transferrable Vote (STV)

Many who are sympathetic to the goals of cumulative voting nonetheless believe that another system better realizes those goals. The more colloquial phrase for this alternative is preference voting, although in the academic literature it is typically called single-transferrable voting (STV). "Many political scientists consider STV the 'best' electoral system because it enables voters to vote for any mix of candidates they prefer, for whatever reason they prefer them." Rein Taagepera and Matthew Shugart, Seats and Votes: The Effects and Determinants of Electoral Systems 27 (1989). The system was invented by an Englishman, Thomas Hare, in 1857, who was worried about rising class antagonisms and sought to promote better political representation. The philosopher and candidate for Parliament, John Stuart Mill, learned of Hare's system and thought it one of the great inventions in democratic government. Mill became the leading advocate for the system, but he was unsuccessful in persuading England to adopt it. For the full historical account, see Jenifer Hart, Proportional Representation: Critics of the British Electoral System 1820–1945 (1992).

STV is thought particularly attractive for countries with traditions of constituents electing individual legislators because, unlike the typical PR system, STV permits voters to vote for individual candidates yet bring about more proportional representation. Thus, STV has been called the "Anglo–Saxon method of securing proportional representation." Vernon Bogdanor, What is Proportional Representation? A Guide to the Issues 76 (1984). The reason is that STV enables a voter "to choose between candidates on personal as well as party grounds, and his choice overrides that of any party organization." Enid Lakeman, How Democracies Vote: A Study of Majority and Proportional Electoral Systems 140 (3d ed. 1970).

The following excerpt provides a lucid summary of how this alternative works and the arguments in favor of it. For those interested in alternatives to districting, would preference voting be better than cumulative voting? As you read, consider whether the choice of voting systems can depend only on their theoretical properties, or whether it must inevitably depend in a democracy on what the social perceptions about different voting systems will likely be. With preference voting, that is a particular concern because while the system is easy to use, explaining how votes are counted in this system is quite difficult. The excerpt comes from a book review of Lani Guinier, The Tyranny of the Majority (1994), in which Guinier advocates cumulative voting, and the excerpt refers to her work throughout:

Richard Briffault, Lani Guinier and the Dilemmas of American Democracy, 95 Colum. L. Rev. 418 (1995)

[T]here is another form of proportional representation, known as single transferable voting (STV), which is well-suited to a nonpartisan setting, and would enhance the proportionate representation of minority interests, would allow voters to form their own constituencies, and in general, would appear likely to perform at least as well as cumulative voting . . .

Like cumulative voting, STV dispenses with single-member districting and returns to multi-member districts or at-large elections. But instead of allowing voters to cumulate votes behind one candidate, STV provides a preference voting system. The voter casts one ballot but can rank candidates to reflect the voter's relative preferences among them. Ranking candidates in order of preference enables votes that would be "wasted" on one candidate to be transferred to another candidate. A vote can be "wasted" if it is "surplus"—that is, a vote cast for a candidate who would win without it—or if it is cast for a losing candidate. STV saves "wasted" votes by providing for their transfer to the next ranked candidate on a voter's ballot. STV thus increases the proportion of voters who vote for a winning candidate, and increases the likelihood that the voter will be represented by a legislator of his or her choosing.

The vote-transfer feature of STV benefits electoral minorities, even in the face of the firm opposition of the majority.[11] In a jurisdiction with a five-seat legislature, a candidate with slightly more than one-sixth of the vote will be able to win a seat under either a cumulative voting or STV electoral system. But STV would appear to be superior to cumulative voting [in achieving these goals]: (a) the representation of minority groups in proportion to their numbers; (b) the representation of the greatest diversity of viewpoints; (c) more competitive elections; and (d) the creation of cross-racial alliances.

(a) *STV and proportional representation.* STV may be more likely than cumulative voting to assure a minority group representation in proportion to its votes. Cumulative voting works best when a group focuses its votes on one candidate. If there are two or more minority candidates, the minority risks the prospect of splitting its vote and failing to elect any of its choices. If the minority constitutes a large proportion of the population and might reasonably seek two or more seats, cumulative voting might result in only one minority seat if minority voters do not divide their votes evenly between the candidates but, instead, give one candidate more votes than she needs for victory while failing to provide the other candidate with sufficient votes to win.

Guinier presents a scenario of a jurisdiction with 1,000 voters, 250 of whom are black, and a ten-member legislative body ... If such a jurisdic-

---

11. Like cumulative voting, STV relies on the concept of a threshold of exclusion. The threshold for winning a legislative seat in an STV election is $V/(N+1) + 1$, where V is the total number of votes and N is the number of seats to be filled. In a jurisdiction with 10,000 voters and five seats, 1,667 votes will be sufficient to elect a candidate, and any candidate receiving that many first-place votes will be deemed elected (no more than five candidates can win 1,667 first-place votes). If one or more candidates (but fewer than five) cross the electoral threshold on first-place votes, their "surplus" votes—that is, the votes above the threshold which were unnecessary to elect them—will be redistributed to the second choices named by those voters, so that additional winners may be determined. If no candidate crosses the threshold on the initial count, the last-place candidate is dropped, and his or her votes are transferred to the candidates listed as the second preference on those ballots which listed the losing candidate as the first preference. If any candidate now has reached the threshold, that candidate is elected. If not, the next lowest candidate is dropped and the process of ballot transfers continues until all the seats are filled.

Transferring the votes of losing candidates is straightforward. All of the ballots of an eliminated candidate are simply transferred to the voters' next choices. The transfer of the surplus votes of winning candidates, however, is more complicated, and several methods are used. One is simply to declare a candidate elected once his or her vote crosses the threshold of exclusion and to treat all subsequently counted ballots as surplus, to be applied to the second choices listed on those ballots. A second method, used in Ireland where STV is the basic election system, is to select randomly among the winning candidate's ballots. A third method, probably the preferable one now that computers can be used to count votes, is to distribute a winning candidate's surplus votes according to the percentage of second choice preferences registered on the winning candidate's ballots. See generally Richard L. Engstrom, *The Single Transferable Vote: An Alternative Remedy for Minority Vote Dilution*, 27 U.S.F. L. Rev. 781, 790 (1993) (describing alternative versions of STV).

tion used cumulative voting, the minority would need only 91 votes to win a seat.[12] Guinier assumes that the black electorate would divide itself up into two groups of 91, with 68 voters left over. The two groups of 91 would each take a seat, and the group of 68 would be able to "join with 23 sympathetic whites to elect a third candidate who is also electorally accountable." In this manner, blacks would win their proportionate share of the legislative seats.

But Guinier's example appears to rest on an unduly optimistic appraisal of the ability of a large group of ordinary voters to organize itself and to assign different specific voters to different candidates. It also makes the rosy assumption that an individual black candidate will be content to win just 91 votes and will direct potential supporters to the other black candidate in order to enhance the number of blacks elected. Few candidates are so confident of election or so committed to the advancement of their group in addition to their own success that they believe there are "surplus" votes that can be given to a potential competitor. Thus, although cumulative voting makes it easier to elect one minority candidate, it is unlikely to produce "full proportional representation" for the minority. That is why political scientists refer to it as a semiproportional system....

STV's vote transfer mechanism may be more likely to produce a proportionate result. Where a group has more than two candidates, and one receives enough first-place votes to be elected, STV would transfer her "surplus" ballots to the next choices on those ballots. If the second-choices are the candidates of the minority group, then the group may elect a second candidate. Moreover, if no minority candidate wins on first-place votes, the vote transfer mechanism could reallocate votes from the weaker minority candidate to the stronger, thus reducing the possibility that competition among minority candidates would deny the minority a seat.[13]

12. Applying the formula of $1/(1+N) +1$, with $N=10$, in a jurisdiction of 1000 voters, the minimum number of votes necessary to win a seat is $1/(1 + 10)$ or $1/11$ of 1000, or 90, plus 1, which is 91.

13. For example, assume an election with 1000 voters, 300 minority voters and 700 majority voters; three seats to be filled; two minority-preferred candidates, and three majority-preferred candidates. Assume that the majority votes only for majority-preferred candidates; that it spreads its first-place votes evenly across its candidates (233 or 234 per candidate); and that majority voters' subsequent preferences are also only for majority candidates. Assume that minority voters split, 170 first-place votes for candidate A and 130 first-place votes for candidate B, and that voters for candidate B list candidate A as their second choice.

In order to win, a candidate needs $1000/(3+1) + 1$, or 251, votes. On the first count, candidate B would be eliminated. But B's voters would have listed A as their second choice, and on the second round B's votes would go to A, giving him 300 votes and a seat. Subsequently, the weakest majority candidate would be eliminated and the other two elected.

If this scenario had been played out in a cumulative voting election, all three majority candidates might have been elected if minority voters had split their cumulated votes among two candidates. Alternatively, only one minority candidate might have run, thereby denying the supporters of the other minority candidate the opportunity to express their strongest preference and the opportunity to identify themselves as a political

(b) STV and diversity of representation. STV may increase the prospects for minority representation without suppressing divergent points of view within the minority group. With STV, there could be multiple candidates from a group, and the concomitant expression of a variety of viewpoints, without undermining the group's opportunity to elect a candidate of its choice. A conservative black voter, for example, could give her first-place vote to a conservative black candidate and then, if race dominates ideology in her political priorities, give her second-place vote to a more liberal black candidate. In this way, STV could function as both a primary election and a general election in a single ballot, with minority voters participating in an intragroup election without jeopardizing their chances for electoral success in the intergroup election.

Similarly, STV may better advance Guinier's agenda of representing "voluntary constituencies that self-identify their interests" than would cumulative voting. Like districting, cumulative voting rewards only first-place votes. This discourages voters from voting for those candidates who may best represent their views but who, the voters think, are unlikely to garner enough votes to win election. As a result, the ballots cast may understate the real level of support for those candidates among the electorate. This, in turn, serves to discourage candidates who represent groups that do not approach a plurality in a single-member district system or the threshold of exclusion in a cumulative voting jurisdiction from even running. This denies their potential supporters the opportunity to vote for them and denies the community the awareness of the existence and size of such a political group. In practice, much as districting favors local majorities, cumulative voting is likely to help only the largest minority and "not the full range of minority political groups." Like districting, cumulative voting tends to hold down the number of parties or groups that can win representation, even if cumulative voting is less restrictive.

STV can remove this disincentive to vote for candidates perceived to have less chance of winning, since the voter can give her first-choice vote to the long-shot who is her most preferred candidate, while choosing among the perceived front-runners for her second-place selection. If the first-choice candidate fails to win election, and the front-runners have not won enough votes to fill all the seats at issue, the ballot can be counted in the contest among the front-runners. Moreover, if enough voters are no longer discouraged from voting for the long-shot by the fear that their ballots will be wasted, then the long-shot might actually win. Alternatively, the voter could list the long-shot in second place. If the first-place winner wins easily, and a sufficient number of other voters also list the long-shot as a second choice, then the transfer of "surplus" votes could also transform the long-shot into a winner. Even if the long-shot is unable to capture a legislative

group, and denying the community useful information concerning the existence and strength of candidate B's supporters.

seat, the existence of the group, and the extent of its political support, will be more clearly known, and the long-shot, and the long-shot's constituency, may become more of a factor in local politics.

(c) STV and competitive elections. For these reasons, STV may also be more likely than cumulative voting to promote competitive elections. Cumulative voting requires group solidarity, discourages intragroup competition, and may lead to de facto deals among the major groups to allocate seats.... Like districting, cumulative voting can produce "safe seats" and uncontested elections. With its built-in incentive to vote for more candidates, STV may be more likely to increase electoral competitiveness.

(d) STV and cross-racial alliances. Finally, STV would appear to be better than cumulative voting in achieving Guinier's other goal—reducing racial polarization in the legislature. By eliminating racially homogeneous black and white districts and using jurisdiction-wide electoral units, both cumulative voting and STV at least make it possible for some candidates to achieve electoral success by putting together a platform that appeals to some blacks and some whites. STV's preferential voting mechanism, however, offers an additional incentive for reducing racial polarization.

Cumulative voting enables minorities to cumulate their votes for one candidate so that the intensity of the group's preference overcomes the group's minority status. Cumulative voting's structural incentive in racially polarized jurisdictions for cumulating votes behind the most intensely preferred candidate is, thus, in deep tension with cumulative voting's potential for cross-racial voting. STV could mute that tension, although not eliminate it, by enabling voters to register several degrees of preference, thus giving them an opportunity to support their own group's candidate and the most attractive candidates of other groups without undermining the prospects of their own-group's first choice. This, in turn, gives candidates an even stronger incentive to campaign across group lines. With STV, candidates might appeal to the voters of groups who would be unlikely to give them first-place votes but might provide them crucial second-place votes. For example, black voters could give their highest preferences to black candidates and their lower-ranked preferences to the white candidates most attractive to them. If the successful black candidate or candidates win more votes than they need to be assured of their seats, their "surplus" would be transferred to the black-preferred white candidates. This could induce some white candidates to campaign for black votes, and ultimately increase the legislature's attention to black political concerns.

It is not clear why Guinier gave no attention to STV and instead focused exclusively on cumulative voting. STV is a more complicated system than cumulative voting, and it works a greater departure from districting. There is relatively little experience with STV in the United States and it could be that its theoretical advantages will fail to materialize in practice. Perhaps Guinier feared that STV is so different from districting that it is, as a practical matter, a nonstarter. On the other hand, STV may have greater potential than cumulative voting to advance Guinier's goals of proportionate minority interest representation, the representation of smaller groups and dissidents within existing groups, and appeals across group lines. Certainly, whatever the strengths and weaknesses of STV, any consideration of the process of electing a democratic legislature ought to examine the full range of options, not just cumulative voting.

NOTES AND QUESTIONS

1. *Uses of Preference Voting or STV.*

   a. Given the continuing academic enthusiasm for STV, it is particularly noteworthy that so few democratic systems have opted to use it. Does that suggest anything about the practicalities, as opposed to theoretical advantages, of STV?

   STV systems had something of a heyday in municipal elections in the United States from 1915–1945 or so. It was used in about two dozen cities, for city councils, school boards, and local school committees. For a good general survey of this history, see Leon R. Weaver, *The Rise, Decline, and Resurrection of Proportional Representation in Local Governments in the United States* in Electoral Laws and Their Political Consequences 139 (Bernard Grofman & Arend Lijphart eds. 1986). Between the 1920s and 1940s, 22 local governments adopted STV; but nearly all abandoned these systems in subsequent years, with the exception of Cambridge, Mass., which continues to use it today. In addition, in 1969, mandated by state statute, New York City began using STV to elect its 32 community school boards as part of the theory that devolving authority to local community groups would improve public education.

   Weaver concludes that (1) the city councils elected under STV were more diverse, with greater representation of minority parties, significant ethnic groups, and perhaps other segments of the community; (2) that STV affected campaigning style by decreasing the incentives for candidates to engage in personal attacks against others, lest they alienate those candidates' first-choice supporters; (3) that STV even when used with nonpartisan ballots tended to induce the use of parties or party-like groups because programmatic politics and disciplined voting by party was an advantage. As far as the abandonment of these alternative voting systems, Weaver concludes that (1) they were frequently opposed by party organizations and their leaders because they typically lost influence over nominations, since STV was usually accompanied with the right to nominate by petition; (2) party leaders often worked against STV because STV was often enacted by reform forces seeking to bypass party leaders and appeal to the electorate directly; (3) concerns often voiced by skeptics over whether STV would lead to factionalism, extremist candidates, or political paralysis of governing bodies do not appear to have been reasons for the decline of STV; (4) the decline also cannot be attributed to STV not being usable by voters; (5)

repeal was made easy by the fact that STV was typically adopted through local referenda, rather than statute, and hence was subject to repeal by the same method. Weaver concludes that more general lessons from this experience are difficult to draw because so much of the political argument pro and con was motivated more by concern for its political consequences than the kinds of questions political scientists debate about STV.

b. From 1937–1945, New York City used preference voting to elect the New York City Council. The system was adopted through a citywide vote, with overwhelming support, in 1936, and used for five elections. Some argue that the system brought about a "golden age" of council politics, because officeholders were formidable challengers to existing party politics who could not have been elected in district system, and because the "system institutionalized the representation of a wide number of political parties with differing viewpoints." Martin Gottlieb, *The "Golden Age" of the City Council*, N.Y. Times (Aug. 11, 1991). In the 1945 elections, in heavily Democratic New York, Democrats won 15 of the 25 seats, with the rest split among Republicans, Liberals, Communists, and American Labor Party members. After the STV system was eliminated, Democrats obtained a virtual monopoly on power, winning 24 of the 25 seats in the 1949 election.

Why did voters repeal the system in 1947? According to a leading study, "the one issue above all others responsible for the repeal of PR in 1947 was Communism." Belle Zeller and Hugh Bone, *The repeal of P.R. in New York City—Ten Years in Retrospect*, 42 Am. Pol. Sci. Rev. 1127 (1948). One or two Communists were regularly elected, but after World War II, anti-Communist sentiment was easier to mobilize against the system. The Democratic and Republican party organizations fought aggressively against the system because it proved a "real benefit" to independent Democrats and Republicans; the system deprived the party machines of complete control. The black community also fought strongly against repeal, given its success under STV. This study found that turnout was exceptionally high under STV and that, despite fears the system would encourage voting along ethnic and religious lines, political party remained the most important factor in voting patterns.

c. While Cambridge, MA continues to use STV, it has become controversial in the one other place STV is used in the United States, for New York community school board elections. On the other hand, in the 1996 elections, voters in San Francisco had on the ballot a proposition to adopt STV to elect the Board of Supervisors, the governing body of San Francisco. The ballot measure was endorsed by many leading political organizations, including the Democratic Party, but it lost 56 percent to 44 percent. Instead, voters opted to return to district-based elections.

d. Internationally, STV is used for national elections in Australia (the Senate), the Republic of Ireland (for all legislative elections), and Malta (for the unicameral parliament). It is also used for some states in Australia, and for local and European Parliament elections in Ireland. Of the new democracies that formed in recent years in eastern and central Europe and the former Soviet Union, only Estonia, from 1989–1992, used STV. For analyses of the effects of STV on elections in Malta and Ireland, see Arend Lijphart, Electoral Systems and Party Systems, 144–46 (1994).

e. Notice that all these countries are relatively small in population. Does STV make the most sense only for small jurisdictions? If so, why? Scholars consider there to be a tradeoff with STV systems, as with any electoral system. To achieve the desired level of proportionality, the electoral unit must be large enough to have the requisite number of seats being contested (recall the "threshold of exclusion" analysis). But if the number of seats and candidates grows too large, voters will have to choose between an overwhelming number of candidates. The common view among students of STV is that the optimal size is a system in which between 5–7 seats are at issue. In general, scholars of electoral systems argue that district magnitude—the number of seats being filled—is perhaps the most important variable in constructing the forms of a country's politics, such as how many parties it has. *See* Rein Taagepera and Matthew Shugart, Seats and Votes: The Effects and Determinants of Electoral Systems Ch.11 (1989).

f. Consider the incentives STV gives candidates as to how they should conduct their campaigns. Consider the incentives it gives political parties as to how they should choose candidates and structure campaigning. Would these incentives produce better or worse election campaigns?

g. In addition to the works already cited, for further writings on preference voting or STV, see George H. Hallett, Jr., *Proportional Representation with the Single Transferable Vote: A Basic Requirement for Legislative Elections*, in Choosing an Electoral System: Issues and Alternatives (Arend Lijphart & Bernard Grofman, eds., 1984); Peter Mair, *Districting Choices under the Single-Transferable Vote*, in Electoral Laws and Their Political Consequences 289 (Bernard Grofman & Arend Lijphart eds. 1986).

D. LIMITED VOTING

A third alternative voting system also being used more frequently among local governments these days in the United States is limited voting (LV). This is another form of semi-proportional representation. Limited voting works by giving voters fewer votes to cast than the total number of seats at issue. Thus, if five seats on a city council are to be filled, voters throughout the city might each be permitted to cast only three votes. The effect of limiting each voter to three votes is, as with other semi-proportional systems, to prevent the same majority from dominating each and every seat. Well-organized minority groups that are sufficiently large are thereby enabled to control the outcome of at least one seat. In limited voting, the formula for calculating the threshold of exclusion is $V/(V+N) + 1$, where V is the number of votes a voter may cast and N is the number of seats to be filled. Thus, with three votes to cast in a five-member election, the threshold would be $3/(3+5)+1$, so that any group that is 37.5 percent or more of the voting pool could, in principle, effectively control the outcome with respect to at least one seat. Notice that, unlike CV, where minorities must vote cohesively by plumping all or most of their votes for the same candidate, LV requires less strategic coordination among minority voters. With fewer votes to cast, and with only one vote going to any one candidate, LV requires fewer decisions—and hence requires fewer decisions in tandem—from minority voters.

Consider in general the variations between STV, CV, and LV. What distinguishes the systems in terms of their effects on voters, candidates, and parties? In what circumstances might it make most sense to use one or another of these alternatives? For example, CV might require more successful coordination among minority voters than LV does; with CV, the minority group must all concentrate its multiple votes on the same candidate to make most effective use of the system. If members of the minority group do not all follow this path, the candidate most group members prefer might still not be elected. Effective political organizations might thus be required to mobilize minority voters and signal the proper voting strategy. With LV, in contrast, the mechanism by which the majority's power is fragmented is by giving each voter fewer votes to cast than there are seats to fill. LV thus requires less coordination of large numbers of votes among minority voters; voters simply have to decide whether to vote for a candidate, without having to decide as well precisely *how many* votes to give that candidate. As a result, one consideration in deciding whether LV or CV is most appropriate as a means of ensuring minority representation perhaps should be how substantial the difficulties of effective coordination of votes among the relevant minority group might be in particular circumstances. That, in turn, could depend on factors like whether the particular election is a high-visibility or low-visibility one; CV might be well suited to the former, such as city council elections, while LV might be more suited to the latter, such as judicial elections. Another factor might be whether there are existing political organizations with the resources and sophistication to mobilize the relevant minority community to use CV effectively; one reason voting-rights litigators have been willing to endorse CV in Alabama is that the state has a longstanding and effective political organization for black voters that was willing and able to take on the responsibility of educating black voters to make effective use of CV.

There is less discussion in the literature of alternative voting in the United States on LV. As one scholar put it a decade ago, but which still remains true today, "LV systems have been more widely adopted and have shown greater capability to survive, but have been written about very little as compared to [CV and STV]." Leon Weaver, *Semi-Proportional and Proportional Representation Systems in the United States*, in Choosing an

Electoral System: Issues and Alternatives 191, 201 (Arend Lijphart & Bernard Grofman, eds., 1984). Limited voting has been approved by courts in many states; the Fourth Circuit, for example, has recognized at least four consent decrees in settlement of voting-rights litigation in North Carolina in which limited voting elections were adopted. For discussion of the local jurisdictions that have used LV, and for a survey of the VRA cases that have used LV as a remedy, see Pamela S. Karlan, *Maps and Misreadings: The Role of Geographic Compactness in Racial Vote Dilution Litigation*, 24 Harv. CR–CL L. Rev. 173, 223–31 (1989); *see also* Richard L. Engstrom, *Modified Multi–Seat Election Systems as Remedies for Minority Vote Dilution*, 31 Stetson L. Rev. 743, 758–60 (1992); Joseph F. Zimmerman, *The Federal Voting Rights Act and Alternative Election Systems*, 19 Wm. & Mary L. Rev. 621, 652–54 (1978).

Most of the limited-voting schemes that have gone into effect at the local level have come in response to actual or potential voting-rights litigation. In voluntary settlements, some jurisdictions have agreed to adopt LV. This approach, like that involving CV, typically occurs when geographic constraints prevent effective use of the conventional "safe" minority districting approach as a remedy. And as with CV, the courts of appeals have been reluctant—much more so than district courts, which have been willing to be more experimental—to uphold lower-court decisions imposing LV on a resistant jurisdiction. Does this reluctance reflect a sound appreciation of the policies of the VRA? The limits that should be recognized on the power of federal courts to restructure the basic democratic process of local governments? Apart from those concerns, would LV be a desirable policy tool for dealing with VRA problems, so that Congress should amend the statute to make explicit the power of courts to order it as a remedy? Consider those questions as you study a specific context in which the courts of appeals have overturned a LV alternative:

McGhee v. Granville County Board of Commissioners
860 F.2d 110 (4th Cir.1988).

■ DICKSON PHILLIPS, CIRCUIT JUDGE:

* * *

I

* * *

The Board [of Commissioners] is the governing body of Granville County. At the time the plaintiffs brought this action, the Board consisted of five members, [elected] on a county-wide at-large basis, but required to reside in particular residence districts. Each member was elected for a four-year term. The terms of the various Board members were staggered, with elections being held in even numbered years. Three of the five incumbent members were serving terms which expired in 1988. The remaining two incumbent members were serving terms which expire in 1990.

Black citizens make up 43.9 percent of the county's total population (1980 data), 40.8 percent of its voting age population (1980 data), and 39.5 percent of its registered voters (1987 data). Despite these population numbers, and despite the fact that a number of black residents have run for election to the Board, no black has ever been elected to the Board.

[After the parties stipulated that the existing electoral structure violated § 2 of the Voting Rights Act, the County proposed as a remedy a single-member districting plan containing seven districts, with members serving staggered terms, thereby both abandoning the at-large election method and expanding Board membership from five to seven. The parties agreed that the best plan of this sort would only be able to create one "safe" black-majority district and one more in which black voters would have "a fighting chance." Because the total black voting-age population in the County was nearly 41 percent, while the single-member districting plan would give blacks no more than 14–28 percent representation on a seven member Board, the plaintiffs objected that the plan would not provide black citizens "a chance to elect a number of commissioners that is commensurate with their portion of the population and with their voting strength." Plaintiffs argued that single member districting was inadequate in Granville County and instead proposed a limited voting plan. The Board would be composed of seven members elected concurrently on a county wide at-large basis, with voters allowed to vote for any three or fewer candidates as they chose. Plaintiffs asserted that this plan would give black voters a fair chance of electing three commissioners, 42 percent of the Board. The district court rejected the County's plan as inadequate. Instead, that court adopted a modified version of the plaintiffs' limited voting plan.]

The [district] court's plan was specific and detailed:

1. The Board shall be expanded to seven members at the 1988 election, and shall remain at that number indefinitely. All terms shall be for four years except as otherwise stated in this order. In all elections, the candidates who receive the highest number of votes shall be deemed elected.

2. The two Commissioners not up for re-election in 1988 shall retain their seats until their terms expire in 1990.

3. In all elections, except as specifically noted herein, voters shall be limited to voting for a maximum of two candidates to fill the available seats.

4. Five Commissioners shall be elected in 1988, with the Commissioner receiving the fewest votes to serve a two-year term to expire in 1990.

5. Starting in 1990, an election shall be had every four years, in even years not divisible by four, to fill the three expiring terms;

starting in 1992, an election shall be had every four years in even years divisible by four, to fill the other four expiring terms.

    6. Beginning with the election in the year 2000, and in all elections and subsequently in even years divisible by four, voting shall be at large. In subsequent elections, in years not divisible by four, voters shall continue to be limited to voting for a maximum of two candidates to fill the available seats.[14]

[During the one election for which the district court's plan was in effect, black candidates won nomination to three of the five seats being contested, and all the primary winners were running uncontested for the general election at the time of this appeal].

II

The dispositive issue, put in broadest terms, is whether the district court properly could reject the County's remedial single-member district plan and impose instead its own modified version of the plaintiffs' limited voting plan. [... Where] the legislative body does respond with a proposed remedy, a court may not thereupon simply substitute its judgment of a more equitable remedy for that of the legislative body; it may only consider whether the proffered remedial plan is legally unacceptable because it violates anew constitutional or statutory voting rights—that is, whether it fails to meet the same standards applicable to an original challenge of a legislative plan in place. If the remedial plan meets those standards, a reviewing court must then accord great deference to legislative judgments about the exact nature and scope of the proposed remedy, reflecting as it will a variety of political judgments about the dynamics of an overall electoral process that rightly pertain to the legislative prerogative of the state and its subdivisions.

* * *

III

* * *

The judicial and legislative process of putting principled bounds upon the vote dilution concept has now culminated in the Supreme Court's exhaustive analysis of the concept as codified in amended § 2, in *Thornburg v. Gingles*.... Further, and of particular importance to our analysis,

---

    14. Within its premises, the district court's plan is an admirably thoughtful and creative one. By rejecting the plaintiffs' concurrent-election proposal and continuing the extant staggered-term feature, the court deliberately sought to guard against massive board turnovers during what inevitably was to be a sensitive transition period. By scaling down the limited voting plan's impact over time, the court sought to take into account an anticipated change in racial polarization voting patterns which the court thought would occur as black representatives allayed traditional white voter concerns about fitness and voting propensities.

the Court noted that the "size and compactness" requirement confines dilution claims to situations where diminution of voting power is "proximately caused by the districting plan," and thus "would not assure racial minorities proportional representation." Finally, in defining the "essence of a § 2 claim," the Court made plain that the adverse "result" for which such a claim seeks a remedy must be traceable ultimately to the impact of "a certain electoral law, practice or structure interact[ing] with social and historical conditions."

IV

* * *

If these principles be accepted—as we do—they of course reveal the fallacy of the plaintiffs' position and the error of the district court's rejection of the County's proposed remedial plan. Within those principles, the plaintiffs' concession that the County plan provided the maximum remedy possible by redistricting establishes the plan as a legally adequate one that should have been accepted in deference to the affected local government's primary jurisdiction to ordain its electoral processes.

The plaintiffs' principal contentions to the contrary deserve some discussion.

A

Their primary contention, expressly accepted by the district court, is that the districting remedy, though concededly maximum by that means, was not the "complete" one legally required. Though not made explicit, it is obvious that this view of "completeness" of remedy has to assume one of two legally erroneous standards against which to measure "completeness."

The first standard necessarily looks to the plight of those minority voters not included within one of the remedial plan's "safe" districts. As to those included within those districts, the remedy is manifestly "complete," both legally and practically. It is only as to those voters not included that the plan might be considered in any sense an incomplete eradication of the "submergence" caused by the at-large voting system. For some, possibly all of these voters, the remedial plan "submerges" their voting power—at least in direct terms—to a greater degree in their new constituencies than did the challenged system in the old. This, of course, is simply an unavoidable mathematical consequence of the demographics that will constrain practically all single-member district remedial plans. It is undoubtedly to some extent an ironic consequence. But it is a consequence that has not been thought to invalidate remedial plans by those courts that have considered the matter directly. Those courts have instead, apparently without exception, simply accepted it as a necessary concomitant of the inevitably rough-hewn, approximate redistricting remedy.

* * *

The other standard implicit in plaintiffs' contention, and in the district court's reasoning, is even more plainly inappropriate. Despite the disavowals of both, it is obvious that ultimately the plaintiffs urged and the district court accepted a proportional representation standard. This directly violates the § 2(b) proviso expressly disclaiming any such "right."

Plaintiffs apparently seek to avoid the proviso's effect, as we understand their position, by insisting that vote dilution violation and vote dilution remedy are to be separately considered in assessing the proviso's intended effect. On this view, the proviso only prohibits finding a violation based solely upon a lack of proportional representation; where a violation properly traceable to a specific voting mechanism is found, the proviso does not then prohibit a court from rejecting a proposed remedy that does not assure approximate proportional representation and imposing one that does. Here the violation established was vote dilution specifically caused by an at-large electoral system, not simply the lack of proportional representation....

This contention seizes upon and seeks to exploit the undoubted logical problem created by Congress' simultaneous allowance of vote dilution claims, which necessarily require some consideration of population proportions, and the disclaimer of any "right" to proportional representation. The problem of statutory interpretation is certainly there, but we are satisfied that to adopt the plaintiffs' position and affirm the district court's reasoning and judgment would simply negate the proviso, and defeat Congress' intention in adopting this disclaimer as the ultimate back-stopping principle of this "compromise" legislation.

The practical consequence of uncoupling violation from remedy in this way would necessarily be to allow proportional representation to become in practical effect the "right" protected by § 2. *Ubi jus, ibi remedium*, and vice versa. Certainly implicit in the *Gingles* Court's analysis of the nature of § 2 vote dilution claims is the notion that, so far as those claims are concerned, right and remedy are inextricably bound together, for to prove vote dilution by districting one must prove the specific way in which dilution may be remedied by redistricting....

Whatever its other effects, we therefore believe that the § 2 proviso prevents a court from rejecting a remedial legislative districting plan which provides the maximum opportunity for representation possible by that means for the sole reason that the representation possible does not sufficiently approximate proportionality.

* * *

NOTES AND QUESTIONS

1. As a matter of either public policy or of the legislative purposes and history of the Voting Rights Act, why should the existing system of territorial districting be the baseline against which claims of minority vote dilution are measured?

2. Does the adoption of alternative voting systems, such as limited voting, for the purpose of enhancing representation of black voters run afoul of the constitutional constraints on the role of race in the design of political institutions that *Shaw v. Reno*, 509 U.S. 630 (1993) and subsequent cases establish? For discussion of *Shaw*, see Chapter 8. In *Cleveland County Ass'n for Govt. By the People v. Cleveland County Bd. Of Comm'rs*, 965 F.Supp. 72 (D. D.C.1997), Cleveland County, North Carolina entered into a consent decree in which it agreed to move to limited voting to elect its Board of Commissioners. Before litigation began, the Board consisted of five members elected at-large throughout the County, and no black had ever been elected. Plaintiffs and the County agreed to settle a voting-rights lawsuit by increasing the Board to seven members, with each voter to have only four votes to cast. Represented by the same lawyer who filed *Shaw*, another group of plaintiffs then brought an action alleging that this settlement violated the Constitution. They argued that the decision to adopt limited voting was "race conscious" and that race had been "the predominant factor" for the decision. The district court acknowledged that the move to limited voting had been race conscious, but held that strict scrutiny was nonetheless not required because limited voting did not involve any racial classifications or distinguish voters along racial lines.

3. Should the congressional statute that now requires states to use single-member districts to elect members of Congress, 2 U.S.C. § 2 (1994), be amended to give states *the option* of using alternative voting systems, such as CV, preference voting, or limited voting, to elect congresspersons? The statute currently permits states to use at-large elections only in certain narrowly specified circumstances, such as when the state is entitled to an additional seat in Congress but the state has not yet been redistricted to take account of the increase in representation. In 1995, Rep. Cynthia McKinney (an African American representative whose then-existing majority-black district was declared unconstitutional by the Supreme Court in *Miller v. Johnson*, 515 U.S. 900 (1995)), introduced the "Voters' Choice Act" (H.R. 2545), which provided, in pertinent part:

Sec. 2. Multi-member Districts Permitted for Election of Representatives for States with Certain Voting Systems.

(A) In General.—Notwithstanding Public Law 90–196 (2 U.S.C. 2c), a state that is entitled to more than one representative in Congress may establish a number of districts for election of representatives that is less than the number of representatives to which the state is entitled, if and only if that state uses a system of limited voting, a system of cumulative voting, or a system of preference voting in its multi-member districts.

(B) Limited Voting Described.—Limited voting is a system in which a voter may not cast a number of votes that is more than one-half the number of representatives to be elected.

(C) Cumulative Voting Described.—Cumulative voting is a system in which a voter may cast a number of votes up to the number of representatives to be elected, and the voter may distribute those votes, including fractions of votes, in any combination, including all votes for one candidate.

(D) Preference Voting Described.—Preference voting is a system in which a voter ranks the candidates and candidates win by reaching a required threshold of votes. After totaling first-place votes, all candidates who have reached the threshold are declared elected. Votes in excess of the threshold are transferred to the voters' next-choice candidates: either some votes at full value or all votes at an equally reduced value. When no candidate is above the threshold and all seats have yet to be filled, the candidate with the fewest top-ranked votes is eliminated, and all of the candidate's votes are transferred to the next-choice candidates at full value. Voters may rank candidates equally. When candidates are so ranked, the value of the ballot is divided equally among such candidates. The threshold is calculated as–

(1) votes divided by the number of representatives to be elected;

(2) votes divided by the number of representatives to be elected plus one, plus one vote; or

(3) any number between the number calculated under paragraph (1) and the number calculated under paragraph (2).

(E) Equality Requirement.—In a state that uses districts in a system of limited voting, a system of cumulative voting, or a system of preference voting, the number of residents per representative in a district shall be equal for all representatives elected.

(F) Single–Member Districts Allowed.—A state may use single-member districts alone or in combination with multi-member districts.

Sec. 3. Relation to Voting Rights Act of 1965.

The rights and remedies established by this Act are in addition to all other rights and remedies provided by law, and the rights and remedies established by this Act shall not supersede, restrict, or limit the application of the Voting Rights Act of 1965 (42 U.S.C. 1973 et seq.). Nothing in this Act authorizes or requires conduct that is prohibited by the Voting Rights Act of 1965 (42 U.S.C. 1973 et seq.).

What are the advantages and disadvantages of the Voters' Choice Act? The proposal was referred to the House Judiciary Committee, where no action was taken. Is there any realistic possibility that Congress would voluntarily alter the single-member district requirement?

E. THE LOT VERSUS THE ELECTION

What about lotteries as an alternative system of election, at least in some contexts? Throughout both the practice and political theory of republican government, until the American and French Revolutions, the lot was considered an integral tool of republican self-government. Indeed, the lot was considered the quintessential democratic selection device, while elections were considered a means of ensuring more aristocratic rule. From today's vantage point, the idea of selecting public officials through some form of lottery likely seems fanciful or absurd, raising the specter of incompetent officeholders and random politics (although lotteries do sometimes play a role in selecting jurors). But in practice, the lot was always used within a broader institutional context that might be thought to have minimized these concerns.

Are there contexts today in which lotteries might be an appropriate alternative voting technique? What values might lottery voting help realize? In what contexts might such a device be a pragmatically useful tool? Consider those questions as you reflect on the theory and practice of lots rather than elections as a means of selecting public officials.

1. Democratic lotteries, aristocratic elections: Many leading political theorists of republican government, including Montesquieu, Harrington, Rousseau, and Aristotle, believed the lot was *the* democratic selection device, while elections were intrinsically aristocratic in nature. Indeed, the leading historical study on this issue calls it "a paradox that has hitherto gone unnoticed" that at the same time American and French Revolutions proclaimed the equality of all citizens, they led to elections becoming the only form of selecting officeholders. Bernard Manin, The Principles of Representative Government 79 (1997).

These thinkers all believed that elections selected for preexisting elites, in part on the view that people will tend to recognize and choose their betters. In contrast, selection by lot had the following advantages: it avoided disgracing those who lost elections; it minimized envy and jealousy of those selected; it reduced the intense factional fighting and intrigue that would surround elections. Most important, the lot would distribute public officeholding in egalitarian and hence democratic terms. Thus, the lot was closely linked to another principle that some republicans considered crucial, that of rotation in office. Rotation both distributed offices in more egalitarian terms and was a check on too great a separation between rulers and ruled. *See* Gordon S. Wood, The Creation of the American Republic 140–141 (1969) (on rotation being a "cardinal tenet" of republican thought in 1776).

These views about the different social and political effects of different selection systems had their analogues in debates over the Constitution. Anti–Federalists, who opposed ratification, "made the size of the House the leading point in their indictment of the national scheme of representation." Jack N. Rakove, Original Meanings: Politics and Ideas in the Making of the Constitution 228 (1996). They argued that the structure of national elections would ensure that the government would have "the soul of aristocracy," dominated by "the few men of wealth and abilities." The "middle and lower classes" who formed "the democracy" of the American people would not be present. Although the Anti–Federalists did not urge the use of lots, they did endorse a theory of representation that emphasized the need for representatives to mirror their constituencies. Their principal objection was that the proposed ratio between electors and representatives was too small to allow the proper "likeness," "resemblance," and "closeness;" they argued that representation should be a "true picture" of "the people." Manin, *supra*, at 109. As a leading Anti–Federalist put it: "The very term representative, implies, that the person or body chosen for this purpose, should resemble those who appoint them—a representation of the people of America, if it be a true one, must be like the people." II The Complete Anti–Federalist 9, 42 Brutus, Essay III (Herbert J. Storing ed. 1981). This true picture conceived "likeness" in a social or economic sense: "the farmer, merchant, mechanick and other various orders of people, ought to be represented according to their respective weight and numbers." *Id.* Note the similarity to contemporary concerns over descriptive representation, discussed for example, in Chapter 8.

The Constitution specifically rejected the Anti–Federalist theory of political representation. Madison and those defending the Constitution justified many of its structural features on grounds that representation should not be a mirror of the constituents. In *The Federalist Papers* No. 35, Hamilton rejected as "altogether visionary" the claim that "all classes of citizens should have some of their own number in the representative body, in order that their feelings and interests may be the better understood and attended to." The structural features of the Constitution were designed, essentially, to accentuate the elite effects elections had long been thought to have. Thus, the Constitution was designed to ensure that those with the "most wisdom" and "most virtue" would hold office. *The Federalist Papers* No. 57. Representative government itself was to be preferred over direct democracy because the "small number of citizens elected by the rest [would] refine and enlarge the public views by passing them through the medium of a chosen body of citizens...." *The Federalist Papers* No. 10. Most importantly, the Constitution's defenders argued for a large republic and for election from large districts precisely because these devices were thought more likely to select for representatives of a certain type of distinction and character. Thus, "the larger the district of election, the better the representation.... Nothing but real weight of character can give a man real influence over a large district." As Madison put it, "large districts are manifestly favorable to the election of persons of general respectability, and of probable attachment to the rights of property, over competitors depending on the personal solicitations practicable on a contracted theatre." *See also* Rakove, *supra*, at 222 (describing the "key hypothesis" of Madison as "that elections held in districts larger than the county and township units used to choose state legislators would encourage a superior class of lawmakers to gain national office, thereby enabling national law to be framed with a deliberation rarely found in the states."). Regular elections, rather than social likeness, would be the link between representatives and constituents.

Consider whether the historical debates over lots versus elections sheds light on the debates over theories of representation underlying the Constitution. Manin concludes his study with this provocative thought: "The fundamental fact about elections is that they are *simultaneously* and indissolubly egalitarian and inegalitarian, aristocratic and democratic." Is that right? Does it shed any light on how to think about the design of democratic institutions?

2. The historical practice of selection by lot. The lot was an important element in the earlier democratic systems on which the Framers drew in developing their own political theory. Thus, in the classical democracy of Athens and in the centers of republicanism and civic humanism, the republics of Venice and Florence, lottery selection was used under various circumstances and justified by several considerations. The influence of these systems in so many other areas of the Constitution's design makes the absence of any role for selection by lot all the more intriguing. The following history is taken from Manin, *supra*, at 79–94.

In Athens, the principal political body, the Popular Assembly, was elected. But lots were used to fill numerous other public offices, including important administrative and executive posts. The principal justification seems to have been ensuring rotation in office and widespread political participation. Most interesting, selection by lot was integrated into a much more complex system of institutional arrangements. Thus, for magistrates (who among other things conducted preliminary investigations before lawsuits and presided over courts) the term of office was one year; a citizen could not hold the same position more than once and had to be over 30; and only those who volunteered to be considered were among the pool from which lots were picked. Those selected by lot still had to meet various qualifications: to have paid taxes; performed military service; have behaved properly toward their parents; and to not have had oligarchic sympathies. There was also aggressive ex post monitoring of performance while in office; those selected by lot had to render account on leaving office, and during their terms, any citizen can bring a vote of no confidence against them. These structures might suggest that lottery voting should not be considered in isolation, but in the context of other structures which might surround it.

In Venice and Florence, the justifications for lots were to avoid ruling cliques perpetuating themselves in office and to ensure equal access to public office. The most interesting feature of these experiments is the way Florence combined elections with the lot. Thus, for certain important posts, a nominating committee would first select a large number of citizens deemed potentially qualified for office; the electorate would then vote in secret among those selected. Those who received more than a certain number of votes would then have their names placed in bags, from which the names of those who would assume office were drawn at random. Thus, among those considered qualified and worthy of holding office, the most equitable distribution of office was considered to be by lot.

3. Contemporary proposals for lottery voting. Until recently, there have been few proposals to reinvigorate the tradition of using lots as elements in democratic choice. Akhil Amar has suggested the following structure as a thought experiment about the possible benefits of incorporating lots into choosing public representatives. Voters would vote over competing candidates, but the votes would not directly determine outcomes. Instead, the votes determine the probability that candidate will be elected, but the actual selection then occurs through drawing a single ballot at random. Thus, if A receives 60 percent of the votes and B 40 percent, then A would have a 60 percent probability of being chosen when the random ballot was drawn to determine who would hold office. Among the benefits Amar offers for this proposal is that it would make rotation in office more likely; it would provide a means of enabling minorities to win some of the time; it would minimize wasted votes because each additional vote a candidate received would increase his or her probability of being elected. See Akhil Reed Amar, *Lottery Voting: A Thought Experiment*, 1995 U.Chi.L. Forum 193.

Similarly, Jon Elster suggests the following advantages of lottery voting: it "reconciles honesty with self-interest" in the sense that lottery voting is the only means of ensuring that voters genuinely vote for their most preferred alternative. The reason they have an incentive to do so is related to reasons just noted: because each additional vote increases the likelihood the candidate will be elected, and because even a candidate who only receives 25 percent of the vote still has a 25 percent chance of being elected, voters will vote for the option they genuinely prefer. Elster further argues lottery voting would block the emergence of professional politicians and would ensure that there be no permanently unrepresented minorities. Jon Elster, Solomonic Judgements 78–92 (1989). For the argument that lottery might be an appropriate way to set the legislative agenda, given modern insights into how much the order in which issues are considered can influence substantive outcomes, see Richard H. Pildes and Elizabeth S.

Anderson, *Slinging Arrows at Democracy: Social Choice Theory, Value Pluralism, and Democratic Politics*, 90 Colum. L. Rev. 2121, 2196–97 (1990).

Elster notes at least three other contexts in which introducing randomness has been offered as a means to improve the design of political institutions. First, the economist Richard Thaler has suggested that members of Congress might be assigned to committees through a random process; among other aims, the purpose here would be to break up entrenched powers of seniority. Second, Elster proposes that redistricting might be done through random redesign, which he asserts would be "clearly superior to the current American system." Third, elections might be randomly timed; the aim here would be to avoid the tendency of governments to manipulate policy to coincide with election dates known long in advance.

Are the advantages offered on behalf of lottery voting persuasive? In what electoral contexts are they most convincing?

With respect to randomness more generally, would any of these particular uses Elster suggests be attractive? Are there perhaps other contexts in which lots or the features of randomness associated with lots might be a better way of structuring aspects of politics?

F. THE HISTORY OF TERRITORIAL DISTRICTING

To gain perspective on the current system of congressional representation in order to consider alternative possibilities, it is useful to consider the history by which the single-member geographic district came to be the form used for congressional elections. As you analyze the alternative voting systems described above, consider whether the current electoral system in the United States can be said to result from a deliberative choice to reject these alternatives. Instead, are the justifications originally offered for single-member districts ones that would better be realized today by the use of the alternative voting systems described above, or the proportional representation systems described below?

Frequently, it is assumed that the United States has always used single-member districts to elect members of Congress. *See, e.g.,* Steven G. Calabresi, *Beyond the Public/Private Distinction: Political Parties as Mediating Institutions*, 61 U. Chi. L. Rev. 1479, 1507 (1994) ("Today, as in 1789 ... Representatives represent single-member geographical districts...."). But this is inaccurate. Only after a lengthy struggle did Congress eventually come in 1842 to use its powers under Art I, sec. 4 of the Constitution to legislate and require single-member districts. As we examine this history, consider whether the justifications for districts would be better realized today by structures other than geographic districts, such as the alternative voting systems this Chapter explores.

At the time the Constitution was adopted, "[m]ost legislators saw the problem as a choice between two alternatives: at-large or district elections." Rosemarie Zagarri, The Politics of Size 105 (1987). *See also* Andrew Hacker, Congressional Districting: The Issue of Equal Representation 8–10 (1963). Other possibilities, including what we now call alternative voting systems or forms of proportional representation, were not discussed because the mechanics for PR and these other systems had not yet been developed. Both sides in the debates over representation tended to assume that districts would be used. The arguments for districts emphasized that they would protect minority interests within a state, ensuring for example that the "mercantile interest" would not "swallow up the agricultural." Zagarri, *supra*, at 111 (quoting debates in New Jersey). Districts would reflect the heterogeneity of interests within states, and would ensure more connection between local interests and representatives. Writing in *The Federalist Papers* No. 56, Madison argued that if large states were split into several districts, "it will be found that there will be no peculiar local interest in either, which will not be within the knowledge of the representative of the district." The decision was reached, however, not to resolve the method of election in the Constitution itself, but to leave it to each state to choose its own method of selection—subject to the potential congressional override of Art. I, sec. 4.

Initially states experimented, some switching back and forth between systems. The majority of states held at-large congressional elections initially; only Massachusetts, New York, Maryland, Virginia, and South Carolina used districts. Pennsylvania's experience is particularly noteworthy. In the east, Federalists dominated, while in the western part of the state, Antifederalist sentiment was strong. Because the Federalists controlled the state legislature, the state adopted at-large congressional elections. In the first federal elections, all eight congressmen elected were Federalists who lived in the eastern part of the state. As one outraged critic put it, "I am sure that Pennsylvania will never again suffer eight representatives to be elected out of a mere corner of the state." Enough pressure was put on the state legislature that by the next elections, it had divided the state into eight congressional districts. In general, most states settled on either districts or at-large elections by this second round of congressional elections and kept that system until Congress intervened in 1842.

The significant fact, though, is the stark pattern regarding which states chose districts. Consistently, the large states employed districted elections while small states used at-large elections. These differences stemmed from both diverse circumstances and distinct conceptions of representation and its relationship to geography.

Small states conceived of representation in traditional geographic terms. "The residents of states with limited territory and relatively small populations continued to think about representation in spatial terms. They presumed that geography represented the most fundamental variable in constructing representative institutions." Zagarri, *supra*, at 147. In their state legislatures, representation was typically by town or county, not population, and they argued that the state was a territorial community that should be represented that way in the House of Representatives.

In the large states, representation was conceived more in demographic than geographic terms. The state was viewed "as an amalgam of diverse interests that an accident of history had united into a single unit." *Id.* at 123. Representation was thought of "in terms of randomly associated individuals rather than communities, in terms of population rather than territory." *Id.* at 143. In these states, geographic boundaries were viewed as malleable, subject to change as population changed. They moved their state capitals to the demographic centers of their states, adopted population-based schemes of representation in their lower houses, and supported districted rather than at-large elections for Congress.

A fascinating set of strategic interactions eventually led to Congress's actions in 1842. Because small states used at-large elections, they tended to elect unified congressional delegations. Within a small state, the representatives tended to come from the same party. But the large-state delegations, elected through individual districts, were more fractured, reflecting the partisan divisions within the state. As a result, congressional delegations from the small states were more effective in the House. As the large states began to recognize this consequence of the different electoral systems, they began to talk about shifting back to at-large elections. This, in turn, prompted the small states to fear that if large states too went to at-large elections, they would soon dominate the small states; unified delegations that would then vote as a bloc would be more likely to represent each of the large states. By 1842, 9 of the 26 states used at-large elections (to get a sense of the magnitude of at-large elections at the time, the largest state using them was Georgia, which was entitled to eight representatives and had a total population of 691,392). But enough of the small states feared the large states switching to at-large elections that there was sufficient support for Congress to step in and require all states to adopt single-member geographic districts. Districting was preferable, in the view of some small states, to universal use of at-large congressional elections.

In 1842, there were enough votes for Congress to pass the Reapportionment Act of 1842, ch. 47, 5 Stat. 491. That Act required, for the first time, that "In every case where a State is entitled to more than one Representative, the number to which each state shall be entitled ... shall be elected by districts composed of contiguous territory equal in number to the number of Representatives to which said State may be entitled, no one district electing more than one Representative." But despite the Act, New Hampshire, Georgia, Mississippi, and Missouri conducted their 1842 elections under at-large systems; over protests, Congress seated all the members of these states, *Congressional Quarterly Inc., Jigsaw Politics: Shaping the House After the 1990 Census* 18 (1990). The 1842 Act lasted ten years, but it began a regular practice of congressional enactments requiring districted elections for the House.

In 1901, Congress added a compactness requirement to the Act, Reapportionment Act of 1901, ch. 93, § 3, 31 Stat. 733, 734. In 1929, Congress enacted a combined census-reapportionment bill that established a permanent method for apportioning House seats after each Census. Reapportionment Act of 1929, ch. 28, section 22, 46 Stat. 21, 26–27. This legislation contained no statement of whether previous requirements, such as districting, compactness, or contiguity, continued to apply. Three years later, the Supreme Court held that these requirements from earlier legislation had lapsed with the passage of the Reapportionment Act of 1929. *Wood v. Broom*, 287 U.S. 1 (1932). *See also Franklin v. Massachusetts*, 505 U.S. 788, 791 (1992) (discussing the passage of the Reapportionment Act of 1929). Not until 1967 did Congress enact legislation once again requiring that states elect House members from single-member districts. Act of December 14, 1967, Pub. L. No. 90–196, 81 Stat 581. During the interim period, from 1929–1967, several states, including some large ones, did elect at least some of their delegation at large. Interestingly, a primary motivation for the 1967 legislation reinstituting the requirement of single-member districts was the Voting Rights Act of 1965: Congress feared Southern states might resort to multimember congressional districts to dilute minority voting power. Today, only the seven states that are entitled to a single representative—Alaska, Delaware, Montana, North Dakota, South Dakota, Vermont, and Wyoming—hold at-large congressional elections. Occasionally, states have returned to at-large congressional elections for temporary reasons; Alabama, for example, lost a congressional seat after the 1960 Census and the legislature could not agree on how to redistrict, which led to the state's 1962 and 1964 congressional elections being held on at-large basis. For a good overview of congressional reapportionment acts, see Emanuel Celler, *Congressional Apportionment—Past, Present, and Future,* 17 Law & Contemp. Probs. 268 (1952).

Does this history suggest that the Constitution did not originally resolve the struggle between geographic and demographic views of representation? Does it suggest that by 1842 the demographic conception had become dominant? Consider whether the arguments for districts are best realized today by that system or some alternative system not available or discussed in 1842. Note also the problems with individual states seeking to make independent decisions about how to structure their congressional selection methods. Given that states are not just trying to construct an internally appropriate system, but also to enhance their effectiveness in the House, can congressional election procedures only be effectively regulated at the national level? Does this suggest that if congressional term limits are to be adopted, for example, they should be adopted nationally rather than on a state-by-state basis?

Recall that most alternative voting systems, like CV, were not invented at the time the Constitution was created, nor were they yet recognized when Congress enacted the 1842 districting statute. Would those who supported districting have favored one of these alternative systems had it been known at the time? Consider the views of United States Senator Charles Buckalew of Pennsylvania, at first a leading proponent of districting, who became the leading advocate of cumulative voting and proportional representation by the 1860s. In a speech in Philadelphia in 1867, he described why he would have supported cumulative voting, rather than single-member districts, had the former system been known at the time he campaigned successfully to replace at-large elections with single-member districts:

> I drew the amendment to the Constitution of our State by which your city is broken into districts .... What was the idea of that amendment? ... The idea was to break up the political community, and allow the different political interests which compose it, by choosing in single districts, to be represented in the Legislature of the State. Unfortunately, when that arrangement was made for your city (and for Pittsburgh also, to which it will soon apply), this just, equal, almost perfect system of voting [cumulative voting], which I have spoken of tonight, was unknown; it had not then been announced abroad or considered here, and we did what best we could.

Charles R. Buckalew, Proportional Representation 62–63 (1872).

Does this statement from a leading advocate of districted elections support the view that the United States has not really had a debate between single-member districts and these alternatives?

G. THE DEBATE BETWEEN MAJORITARIAN SYSTEMS AND PROPORTIONAL REPRESENTATION

Ever since the well-known debates between John Stuart Mill, an advocate of proportional representation, and the English political writer, Walter Bagehot, political scientists have debated the merits of Anglo–American majoritarian systems and PR. For a good overview of the debate, see the essays in Choosing an Electoral System: Issues and Alternatives (Arend Lijphart & Bernard Grofman eds. 1984). The central argument for PR is that it produces fairer political representation: representation that more accurately mirrors the range of opinions and party preferences in the political community. The central argument for majoritarian alternatives, which give a candidate who receives 51 percent of the vote 100 percent of the political power by awarding him or her the seat at issue, is that the system enables more effective and stable governance. Representation versus effectiveness are the fundamental lines along which the battle is usually drawn; as the conflict is sometimes cast, "either you can have a representative parliament, or you can have strong and stable government." David M. Farrell, Comparing Electoral Systems 153 (1997). We will examine some of the more specific points of conflict in a moment.

In this country, PR has never been a serious matter of public debate, with the exceptions of the limited local government experiments discussed above. This reluctance was only heightened in the aftermath of World War II, when PR was blamed as one of the causes that enabled the rise of German and Italian fascism. The causal mechanism offered to support this view was that PR led to governments that were so representative that they were unable to govern effectively; the paralysis that resulted generated clamors for effective leadership to address the countries' problems, thus opening the road to dictatorship. In a famous, highly detailed, and widely noticed book published in 1941, Democracy or Anarchy? A Study of Proportional Representation, Professor Ferdinand Hermens of Notre Dame developed this argument. In a chapter entitled "Proportional Representation and the Triumph of Hitler," Hermens began this way: "Nowhere have the consequences of P.R. so demonstrated the utter senselessness of the system as in Germany." Hermens went on to purport to show, through detailed election analyses, that the Nazis' rise to power could be attributed to Weimar Germany's PR system: "P.R. was an essential factor in the breakdown of German democracy." So, too, Hermens argued that fascism had failed in France but succeeded in Italy because the former used majoritarian election systems and the latter used PR. But whether these powerful claims are factually accurate has been disputed. *See, e.g.,* Vernon Bogdanor, What is Proportional Representation 123 (1984). Nonetheless, Hermens' arguments have continued to exert a presence in the limited American debates over PR.

1. Stability. A common and powerful charge against PR systems is that they produce unstable governments. But as one leading election-systems scholar puts it: "There is no evidence whatsoever that proportional representation is likely to lead to instability." Vernon Bogdanor, What is Proportional Representation 147 (1984). As another remarks, "the charge of instability is one of the great myths surrounding PR." Douglas Amy, Real Choices, New Voices 159 (1993). For example, in a study of the number of governments various democracies have had between 1945–1992, the United Kingdom predictably fares well, with only 19, compared to countries like France and Italy, which have had 53 and 51. But the United Kingdom is only the sixth most stable on the list, with the five more stable systems all using PR (including Austria, Ireland, and the Netherlands).

The question of stability also depends on what one focuses on. Majoritarian systems can produce great fluctuations in policies even when public opinion shifts only slightly. The system tends to produce two principal parties, for reasons Duverger's Law explains, and small changes in votes from one of the two principal parties to the other can lead to a change in control of the government. If the two parties have widely differing ideologies, this can lead to massive changes in policy with only small shifts in actual voter preferences. Some believe this was manifested in the politics of Great Britain during the 1970s, when the Labour Party was oriented toward more socialist economic approaches and the Conservative Party toward free-market ones. Because the two parties alternated as the majority under the FPTP systems, government policy cycled between more socialist and more free-market systems, with industries being nationalized and de-nationalized. Segments of the business community joined the effort to move Great Britain to a PR system to avoid these dramatic swings in policy that made business planning difficult. The perceived advantage of PR is that governments are typically coalitions, which require greater consensus and compromise for policy changes; that coalitions tend to encourage greater continuity between governments when governments do shift; and that PR systems translate incremental changes in voter preferences into incremental changes in seats allocated to parties, rather than the dramatic shifts that can take place with majoritarian systems.

2. Coalition Governments and Electoral Mandates. Critics of PR sometimes argue that it tends to produce coalition governments between several parties, which is viewed as troubling, in part because such governments are said to lack a clear electoral mandate. This is another reason why PR is argued to produce ineffective governments, in addition to purportedly unstable ones. The critique of coalition governments is that voters do not know what policies they are voting for, because coalitions are put together by party leaders after electoral results are in. In addition, because no one party gains majority control, typically, voters cannot as readily hold "the government" responsible for failing to live up to campaign commitments. Majoritarian systems, by contrast, are said to empower one party to govern, which enables voters to hold that party accountable for government policies.

PR elections sometimes lead to one dominant party, but they do tend to produce coalition governments far more often than majoritarian systems. Amy, *supra*, at 157–160. But defenders of PR respond that voters frequently know in advance which coalitions are likely to emerge, either because parties declare so in advance or because it is clear which parties will work together should neither receive a decisive majority. As far as clear mandates go, the assumptions about majoritarian systems are subject to at least two challenges. First, how clear is it in countries like the United States that the party that wins control of the House, the Senate, and/or the Presidency, has a clear electoral mandate? Second, the seeming mandates that dominant parties win is often "manufactured" under majoritarian systems. A manufactured majority is one in which the party that gets a majority of seats does not receive a majority of the actual votes, but becomes a governing majority because of the way majoritarian systems overreward the dominant parties.

Manufactured majorities occur often in majoritarian systems but rarely in PR ones. Lijphart, *Democracies, supra*, at 166–68. As Question 4 in our Voting Quiz indicates, during the time the Conservative Party governed the United Kingdom from 1979–1996, it never won more than 44 percent of the actual vote. In 1992, it received only 41.9 percent of the vote. Most of the other votes went to the main party on the left, Labour, as well as to the Liberal Democrats, a third party also to the left of the Conservatives. Hence, the "mandate" of the Conservative Party was perhaps rejected by a majority of voters, yet without PR, the Conservative Party was able to control government policy.

3. *Extremist and Fringe Parties.* Because PR does enable smaller parties to win seats, the concern arises that extremist parties will gain office, thus legitimating their views through the public platform officeholding provides. Indeed, one of the causes of the demise of PR in local governments in the United States was that during the 1930s and 1940s, some Communists began to win office in PR systems. One response might be that, to the extent marginal viewpoints do have some level of support, they ought to be represented; but that does not address the legitimation point. A somewhat more responsive argument advocates of PR make is that bringing such groups into formal politics actually moderates their views. Raising the threshold of exclusion is one structural way of combating this tendency of PR systems. But perhaps the most significant response is an empirical one: as a practical matter, PR does not appear to have facilitated the rise of extremist parties in European countries. France, for example, now uses a majoritarian system for its direct elections for president, employing a second ballot or runoff system; under this system, the extreme right-wing National Front garnered about 6.5 percent of the vote. Farrell, *supra*, at 157. In a study of such parties in European democracies, the authors found that these parties had achieved comparable levels of support in both majoritarian countries and in PR countries, and that the level of support did not vary with the type of PR system used, thus making it difficult to see a connection between the PR system and the rise of such parties. *See* Michael Gallagher et. al., Representative Government in Modern Europe (2d ed. 1995). Nonetheless, PR systems by their very structure do enable smaller parties to gain office. The potential costs and benefits of that tendency, as well as the other advantages and disadvantages of PR, need to be compared in choosing an electoral structure.

Note also that the concern that PR provides "kingmaker" power to small parties might be of less concern in the United States. PR can produce this kind of result in parliamentary systems "in which not only legislative majorities but also executive power are reconstituted with each shift of electoral preferences." Samuel Issacharoff, *Supreme Court Destabilization of Single-Member Districts*, 1995 U. Chi. Legal F. 205, 237–38. To the extent versions of PR would be adopted in the United States in conjunction with direct elections for President or Governors, the power of coalitional partners in the legislature would be diminished.

4. Election of Women. PR systems enhance representation of women as compared to majoritarian systems. In a study of the number of women legislators in the lower house of a number of democracies, those using PR averaged 20 percent women, while those using majoritarian systems averaged 10.4 percent. Farrell, *supra*, at 151 (though the most recent elections in Great Britain in 1996 did see a dramatic surge in the number of women MPs). In another study of Western democracies from 1970–1991, those using majoritarian systems elected on average 5.8 percent women, while the comparable figure for PR systems was 14.7 percent women. Amy, *supra*, at 102–03. One confirmation that these differences reflect the differing electoral structures, rather than cultural differences, comes from elections within the same country. Thus, Australia, Japan, and Germany use both PR and single-member or small districts for some elections; the PR elections compared to the districted elections resulted in three times as many women winning office in Australia, ten times as many in Japan, and twice as many women officeholders in Germany between 1987–1993. Wilma Rule, *Why Women Should be Included in the Voting Rights Act*, National Civil Review 355, 363 (1995). For other studies reaching similar conclusions, see Pippa Norris, Politics and Sexual Equality: The Comparative Position of Women in Western Democracies (1987); R. Darcy et. al., *Election Systems and the Representation of Black Women in American State Legislatures*, 13 Woman & Politics 73 (1993) (arguing that the problem of black political descriptive underrepresentation is primarily a problem of underrepresentation of black women officeholders).

The mechanism involved turns on the willingness of parties to nominate and support various candidates. In PR systems, parties do not run individual candidates; they put up a slate of candidates upon whom voters vote as a group (this is particularly true in closed-list PR systems). The parties thus face incentives to offer a slate that represents the diverse constituencies to which the party seeks to appeal. In some PR countries, particular parties have adopted quotas for the percentage of their candidates that should be women. For a survey and critical analysis of this approach, see Anne Phillips, The Politics of Presence 58–83 (1995). In single-member district elections, parties put up the individual candidates they believe are most likely to prevail; this often means candidates who appear uncontroversial, and often the safest candidate is perceived to be a man. Moreover, polarized voting against women or minority candidates can occur in a candidate-based election system, but not as readily in a PR system when voters must choose a party's slate as a whole.

Indeed, so strong is the tendency of alternative voting systems, such as cumulative, limited, and preference voting, as well as PR systems, to enhance descriptive representation of women compared to the tendency of single-member district systems, that some have argued the Voting Rights Act as amended in 1982 has undermined women's representation. On this view, the very device emphasized in the 1982 amendments—single-member districts to replace at-large and multi-member elections—is precisely the device least likely to enhance women's representation. This argument concludes that the VRA should be amended to emphasize alternative voting systems and PR, and to move away from single-member districts, in order to "include" women in the VRA. Rule, *supra,* at 366.

5. *Deliberation.* Which electoral system facilitates the appropriate kind of democratic deliberation? A recent work defends PR, not just on the traditional ground that it brings about fairer representation, but that elections under PR are more consistent with the aims of deliberative democracy. Consider whether this view is persuasive:

> Defenders of single-member district representation argue that "government by majority is government by persuasion".... The trouble with these arguments, however, is that they ignore the strong tendency towards vagueness and ambiguity that is generated by these systems. Thus, the persuasion of ordinary citizens is of a superficial sort that leaves much of the decisionmaking to party leaders and leaders of interest groups who are at liberty to bargain with each other in the background. Often this bargaining on the basic points of the legislative agenda is done out of the sight of ordinary citizens and undermines their capacity to control the state. Furthermore, the system of single-member district representation puts a straitjacket on the kinds of issues that are discussed by citizens and parties. In general, the discussion in electoral campaigns tends to take place on a one-dimensional issue space. Discussion in proportional representation elections tends to involve more issues in a number of different dimensions. The single-member district system simplifies unnecessarily the process of social discussion. Some may argue that the multidimensionality of issues for discussion demonstrates that there is greater fragmentation in the public at large than when the issues are very simple. But surely this kind of fragmentation is precisely what we should expect from discussion amongst equals who have very different experiences and roles in the society. And such fragmentation should have the beneficial effect of getting all citizens to understand the diverse interests and points of view that exist in their society and deepening their understanding of how to fairly accommodate these interests.
>
> Overall, a scheme of proportional representation is superior to other electoral schemes in promoting rational social deliberation on the overall aims of society.

Thomas Christiano, The Rule of the Many: Fundamental Issues in Democratic Theory 261 (1996).

6. *Voter Turnout.* Advocates of PR argue that more voters will vote because fewer votes are wasted under PR. Seats are more closely tied to percentages of votes received; hence even voters who prefer a minor party have an incentive to turn out and vote for it. In a recent, comprehensive

study, Lijphart appears to confirm this claim: he concludes that average voter turnout is about 9 percent points higher in PR systems than in non-PR ones. Arend Lijphart, *Democracies: Forms, Performance, and Constitutional Engineering*, 26 European J. of Pol. Research 6–7 (1994).

7. Gerrymandering. The problems of gerrymandering within a single-member district system are ones that by now should be familiar to readers of this casebook. With PR, the problems of gerrymandering are significantly diminished. If the country as a whole is the electoral unit, no lines need to be drawn; if the country is divided into a few regions, only those lines must be defined. Moreover, the absence of the winner-take-all feature of majoritarian systems makes gerrymandering far less important, even where opportunities exist. Consider, though, whether the same forces that drive gerrymandering would appear elsewhere in the PR systems. Where might those pressures be channeled—into which choices, made by whom?

8. Examples of PR failings in specific countries. Critics of PR frequently point to particular countries whose governments are thought to bear out the critics' predictions. That most Western democracies use PR is less salient than that some countries using it are purportedly dominated by small, extremist parties and that effective governing coalitions are difficult to construct. *See, e.g.*, Sanford Levinson, *Gerrymandering and the Brooding Omnipresence of Proportional Representation: Why Won't It Go Away?*, 33 U.C.L.A. L. Rev. 257, 272 (1985) (using example of Israel to raise such concerns about PR). But the examples offered up in this way are frequently distinguished by the extreme versions of PR they use. Whatever their problems, they can be seen not as stemming from PR per se, but the peculiar versions of it they use. Thus, Israel, where small parties do wield exceptional power in the governing coalition, elects all 120 members of its Knesset in one, nationwide election. There are no regions, districts, or states. With 120 seats up for grabs at any one time, a party with as little as 1/120th of the vote (less than 1 percent) could win a seat. In addition, Israel has had one of the lowest thresholds of exclusion of any PR country. Until 1992, any party that managed to get 1 percent of the vote would get a seat; in 1992, the threshold was raised to 1.5 percent, still one of the lowest. Thus, the enormous magnitude of the election district, combined with such low thresholds, has made the Israeli PR system an extreme one—exceptionally prone to the traditional concerns about PR, including the power of small parties and the difficulty of establishing governing coalitions. To enable more decisive government, Israel recently moved to direct elections for its Prime Minister.

Of course, for every country that suffers from political problems that might be associated with PR (Italy was another frequently offered example, before recent reforms in its electoral laws), there are other countries, such as Germany and Austria, that have had strong and stable governments since World War II while using forms of PR.

H. Consociational Democracy

A theme through much of the law and theory of democracy has been that of ensuring adequate representation of, and attention to, the interest of minorities within democratic regimes. Proportional representation and alternative voting systems such as cumulative voting, STV, and limited voting are designed to enhance the political representation of such groups. Depending on the particular cultural, historical, and political context, these forms of representation might be sufficient to ensure a well-functioning democratic system when viewed from the vantage point of the different groupings in the society. But if the cleavages between various groups are profound and enduring enough, even these alternatives might be insufficient. The kind of cleavages that have tended to work this way have been at times religious, tribal, ethnic, racial, linguistic, cultural, or some combination of these. After all, even greater presence inside the institutions of political power does not prevent minority groups from still being political minorities, capable of being outvoted by hostile political majorities.

When territories are riven with such conflicts, one possibility is that the relevant groups should be separated and not made to co-exist within the same, single nation-state. Writing in the 19th century, the liberal political philosopher John Stuart Mill famously asserted: "Free institutions are next to impossible in a country made up of different nationalities. Among a people without fellow-feeling, especially if they read and speak different languages, the united public opinion, necessary to the working of representative government, cannot exist." John Stuart Mill, Considerations on Representative Government 230 (C. Shields ed. 1958). But another possibility is that creative engineering of democratic institutions might enable stability and a sufficient level of cooperation to emerge even in the midst of these kinds of conflicts. Consociational democracy is the name that has been given to the institutional structures devised in several countries to attempt to sustain democracy in the midst of powerful differences. Are these structures the last frontier in democratic institutional design?

Consider in what circumstances existing or newly forming countries should consider adopting some of these features. Are there any circumstances in the United States today in which it would be worth contemplating using consociational structures?

1. Theory and Structure. The basic focus of consociational structures is to foster cooperation among political elites. Countries can adopt one or more element of consociational structures, but the classic work on these systems identifies the four common elements as (1) government by a grand coalition of all significant segments; (2) a mutual veto or concurrent-majority voting rule for some or all issues; (3) proportionality as the principle for allocating political representation, public funds, and civil service positions; (4) considerable autonomy for various segments of the society to govern their internal affairs. Arend Lijphart, Democracy in Plural Societies: A Comparative Exploration 25 (1977).

Grand coalitions aim to replace the model of a governing majority and an opposition that, roughly, take turns in office over time. The stakes in politics are considered too high in the divided societies involved; being part of the government is designed to provide some security and protection. Grand coalitions can take several forms. The four European countries that have used forms of consociationalism and that are the focus of Lijphart's study are Austria, Belgium, the Netherlands, and Switzerland. The apogee of consociationalism in these countries, when they were most divided, was the late 1950s; since then, consociationalism has declined because, according to Lijphart, it succeeded. In Switzerland, the federal executive branch was governed by a seven-member body, according to a "magic formula:" the seats were set aside for the four main parties, 2–2–2–1, roughly proportional to their nationwide support, and the seven members also represented the different regions and languages of the country. Post–World War II Austria was governed from 1945–1966 by a coalition cabinet with balanced delegations from the two dominant parties. Temporary grand coalitions of party leaders were created to resolve the same, exceptionally divisive issue in the Netherlands in 1917 and Belgium in 1958: state aid to religious schools.

Minority vetoes can be formal or informal. They hearken back to John C. Calhoun's unsuccessful pre-Civil War advocacy of a concurrent majority system for the United States Congress, in which a majority from each section of the country, North and South, would have to approve legislation concurrently for it to become law. In contemporary times, an example of a formal minority veto is the Constitution of Belgium, amended in 1970 to require that any bill affecting the "cultural autonomy" of the country's two principal linguistic groups—a Dutch-speaking majority and a French-speaking minority—requires not only the approval of two-thirds majorities in each chamber of the legislature, but also approval of a majority of the legislators from each linguistic group.

The proportionality principle for allocating positions and funds involves group-preference policies and is relatively straightforward; note that in some systems, minority groups get overrepresentation in office or employment or funding. Finally, segmental autonomy seeks to give distinct groups large degrees of autonomous power, particularly over such issues as affect the groups with little spillover to other groups. This autonomy is facilitated by geographical concentration of the relevant groups, in which case autonomy can be territorially based—the strong independent role of the Swiss cantons being one example (federalism can be one form of such autonomy, depending on how it is applied)—but segmental autonomy can also be "personality" based where the segments are too geographically intermingled. In cultural affairs, Belgium, the Netherlands, and Austria all provide substantial decisional autonomy to their different cultural groups, but through power-sharing and voting rules, rather than through territorial allocations of power.

2. *Favorable Conditions.* Austria, Belgium, and the Netherlands are viewed as the most divided of Western democracies, with Switzerland in the middle of the spectrum. In Belgium, for example, about half the population is French speaking, about half Dutch speaking, with strong religious and cultural divides as well.

Consociationalism rests on the hope that elite leaders of the various divided groups can cooperate and compromise. It thus requires that these leaders be committed to maintaining the unity of the country and to democratic politics. Success depends on "the extent to which party leaders are more tolerant than their followers" and "are yet able to carry them along." Hans Daalder, *Parties, Elites, and Political Developments in Western Europe*, in Political Parties and Political Development 69 (Joseph LaPalombara & Myron Weiner eds. 1966). In addition, Lijphart concludes that the following conditions make success more likely with consociational structures for divided societies: (1) a multiple balance of power among three or more groups; (2) small country size; (3) territorial isolation of the various segments; (4) overarching loyalties; (5) prior traditions of elite accommodation; (6) crosscutting cleavages.

The balance of power point is particularly interesting. If one segment has a clear majority, it is likely to seek to govern through majoritarian forms. If there are two principal groups of roughly equal size, they may engage in continual struggle to become the sole, dominant governing power. Thus, consociationalism is thought to work best when there are multiple groups, without the prospect of one becoming dominant (too many groups, however, can make governing more difficult). Note the similarity to Madison's defense in *The Federalist Papers* No. 10 of a large republic precisely because it will contain so many factions that they will cancel each other out. Isolation of the different segments, such as geographic concentration of different groups in specific regions, helps because in societies to which this model extends, closer contact among the different groups has already been judged to increase rather than diminish conflict and hostility. Thus, isolation can facilitate devolution of more autonomy to each group without imposing as many externalities on other groups. Finally, the more that the relevant cleavages are crosscutting—so that religious divides do not map perfectly onto linguistic divides, or ethnic divides onto cultural ones—the more likely accommodation and compromise appear to be. When the same cleavages track each other recurrently, consociationalism is apparently less likely to succeed.

The question of whether the consociational forms from these few Western European countries are likely to extend successfully to other divided societies, with a focus on African countries, is comprehensively explored in Donald L. Horowitz, Ethnic Groups in Conflict (1985). He argues that, compared to the group conflicts within modern African states, the ones in the European countries are "less ascriptive in character, less severe in intensity, less exclusive in their command of the loyalty of participants, and less preemptive of other forms of conflict." *Id.* at 572. Thus, he concludes that finding democratic arrangements to stabilize these divisions is both more necessary and more difficult. Horowitz also provides case studies of consociationalism in several other countries, including Lebanon, Nigeria, Sri Lanka, and Guyana.

3. Costs. The most difficult calculus with consociationalism is whether the divisions are so deeply entrenched as to justify this approach. As even defenders of this system acknowledge, in the short run, consociational structures more deeply entrench the relevant divisions. Thus, a prior judgment is required that these divisions are profound enough that efforts to overcome them are less promising than efforts "to recognize them and to turn the segments into constructive elements of stable democracy." Lijphart, *supra*, at 42. Note the parallel with debates over whether race-conscious districting in the United States merely recognizes the reality of racially-polarized voting or accentuates race-consciousness.

Other potential concerns are that government can become paralyzed or unable to act efficiently because consociational structures require such widespread agreement before action is possible. There is also the problem that, these systems focus more on ensuring equality among the relevant groups, rather than a focus on equal treatment of individuals; indeed, to the extent they grant autonomy to specific groups, such systems might enable groups to exert more conformist pressures over their members. In addition, the vision of democracy is more elite oriented than mass oriented. The question must be whether these costs are worth bearing in light of the alternatives in deeply divided societies. Finally, as Horowitz points out, the very question of how to measure whether consociational systems have been effective is uncertain; is mere stability and preservation of the state sufficient, or should success be understood to require more? Absence of violence? Economic prosperity? The reduction of differences? *See* Horowitz, *supra*, at 570–71.

4. American Consociationalism? Should any features of consociationalism be brought into American structures for democracy at either the local or national level? Lijphart argues that contrasts between countries using these structures and those that do not are overdrawn: "The fundamental error ... is to exaggerate the degree of homogeneity of the Western democratic states." Lijphart, *supra*, at 21. Are the problems of racial polarization really profound and intractable enough in the United States that features of consociationalism would be appropriate? What about the cultural, religious, and linguistic conflicts between Quebec and other parts of Canada?

Lani Guinier has raised the possibility of employing some consociational features to address problems of race in the United States: " 'A minority veto' for legislation of vital importance to minority interests would respond to evidence of gross 'deliberative gerrymanders.' [These are means majority legislators might use to undermine the power of minority legislators]. Alternatively, depending on the proof of disproportionate majority power, plaintiffs might seek minority assent through other supermajority arrangements, concurrent legislative majorities, consociational arrangements, or rotation in office." See Lani Guinier, *The Triumph of Tokenism: The Voting Rights Act and the Theory of Black Electoral Success*, 89 Mich. L. Rev. 1077, 1140 (1991). Would any of these structural changes be desirable? In what circumstances? There are some examples already in place: after the district court (on remand from the Supreme Court's decision in *City of Mobile v. Bolden* 446 U.S. 55 (1980)) found the at-large electoral structure for city commissioners in Mobile, Alabama, to be unconstitutionally enacted and maintained for discriminatory purposes, the black and white political leaders negotiated a supermajority voting requirement for the reformed City Commission. This provision requires affirmative votes from five of the seven commissioners to pass any rules or "transact any business;" three of the seven single-member electoral districts have black voter majorities. For discussion of this provision, see Guinier, Tyranany of the Majority, *supra*, at 17.

Some states routinely use supermajority requirements. For example, California requires a two-thirds vote in each house of the legislature to enact a state budget or approve appropriations. In addition, several of the important initiatives voters have adopted there in recent years impose supermajority voting requirements for certain legislation; for example, Proposition 13, which capped property tax increases, requires a two-third legislative vote to raise most taxes. For the view that California policymaking has become paralyzed as a result of the minority veto these voting requirements give powerful groups, particularly the cumulative effect of all the various supermajority requirements under which the State now operates, see Peter Schrag, *California's Elected Anarcy: A Government Destroyed by Popular Referendum*, Harper's Magazine 50 (Nov. 1994). Schrag notes that tax breaks can be approved through a simple majority vote, but can only be abolished through a supermajority vote because ending a tax break is treated as a "tax increase."

5. For other important works on consociationalism, see Brian Barry, *The Consociational Model and Its Dangers*, 3 European Journal of Political Research 405 (1975); Hans Daalder, *The Consociational Democracy Theme*, 26 World Politics 616 (1974); H. Daalder, *Parties, Elites, and Political Developments in Western Europe*, in Political Parties and Political Development (Jospeph LaPalombara & Myron Weiner eds. 1966); Robert Dahl, Political Oppositions in Western Democracies (1966).

INDEX

References are to Pages.

Alternative Voting Systems, Congressional proposals for, 763–65
Annexations (See Voting Rights Act, Section 5)
Anti–Federalists, 766–67
Argentina, 721
Association, Freedom of (See First Amendment)
At–large representation, 388–409, 770
Australia, 719–20, 755–56
Australian ballot system, 190–93
Austria, 782–83
Ballot access, 203–12, 242–63, 711–12
Ballot, secret, 189–93
Bangladesh, 719
Belgium, 719, 782–83
Bicameral legislatures (See also One person–one vote, local governments; Senate), 3–15, 177–85
Bipartisan gerrymandering, 561
Bizarrely shaped districts, 581–89
Black disenfranchisement, 29–31, 38–39, 68–107, 264–66
Blanket primaries, 249–53
Bullet voting, 202–03
California Civil Rights Initiative, 691–92
Campaign expenditures, 1996 elections, 616
Campaign financing
    and corruption concerns, 632–47, 649–55
    and incumbents, 658
    equal access concerns, 617–18, 647–58
    liberty concerns, 618, 647–58
    marketplace theory of, 617
    public financing, 660–62
    reform
        genesis of, 616
        proposals, 662–64
Canada, 719
Census (see also population assessment), 546
Chile, 719
City council elections, 388–405
Columbia, 721
Compactness, 719
Consociational democracy, 780–84
Constitutional power of Congress to regulate voting, 54–56, 266–74, 277–85, 436–40
Contributions, 618–64, 675–77
    corporate, 649–64, 675–77
Corruption and campaign financing, 632–47, 649–55
Costa Rica, 721

Cross–filing, 254–63
Crossover voting, 607–08
Cumulative voting, 722–48
Deannexation, 172–73
Democratic party, 599–603
Demographic representation, 766–67
Direct lawmaking devices
    ABA Taskforce on Initiatives and Referenda, 694
    alternative initiatives, 673
    and the Constitution, 669–75
    and ballot qualification, 711–12
    and corporate involvement, 675–76
    and legislative entrenchment, 695–712
    and minority rights and interests, 677–93
    and role of money, 675–77
    and special interest groups, 675–77, 712
    as tool to restructure democratic institutions, 3–15
    history, 665–68
    limiting judicial action, 682–86
    limiting legislative action, 677–82
    signature requirements, 675–77
    single–subject rule, 694
    state variations and limitations, 674
Discriminatory effects, 387–88, 429–31, 507
Discriminatory intent, 387–88, 506–07, 538–39, 496–99
Duke, David, 218–20, 223–24
Duverger's Law, 715–17
English–only election materials, 275
Equal Protection Clause, 677–93
Equipopulation principle (See one–person / one–vote)
Estonia, 755–56
Expenditures
    candidate, 619–20
    political party, 620–32
Expressive harms, 593–98
Extremist parties, 776
Federal Election Commission, 618
Federal Election Commission Act, 1974 Amendments, 618, 631
Fourteenth Amendment, 21–185, 332, 387–409, 548–98, 609–23, 686–89
Fifteenth Amendment, 68, 77, 106–07, 387–409, 568–73
    Congressional enforcement / remedial powers (See Constitutional power of Congress to regulate)
Filing fees, 204–12

Finland, 720
First Amendment
    generally, 237–44
    and initiative process, 675–77
    campaign financing, 616–64
First–Past–the–Post systems, 261, 719
France, 720–21
Freeholders, 31–32, 172
Fringe parties, 776
Fundraising, impact on candidates, 644–45
Fusion candidates, 254–63
Geographic districting (see territorial districting)
Germany, 721–22
Gerrymandering (See partisan, racial gerrymandering)
    Tuskegee, 103–07
Gingles **test,** 441–519
    and "Totality of the Circumstances", 499–519
    "Geographically compact", 476–80
    "Political Cohesion", 481–89
    "Sufficiently large", 472–76
    "White Bloc Voting" (See also Racial bloc voting), 489–99
Great Britain, 774–75
Greece, 719
Hard money, 631
Homogeneous precinct analysis, 468–69
Incumbency protection (see also Campaign financing), 155, 583–89
Independent candidates, 244–62
India, 719
Influence district claims, 474–76, 509–19
Initiatives (See Direct lawmaking devices)
Instant run–off systems, 720
Interest representation, 177–85
International elections, 717–22
Ireland, 719–20, 755–56
Israel, 721
Judges, elected, 163, 540–43, 563–65
Judicial review of political rights, 69–77, 117–35
Language minorities, 488
Limited voting, 756–65
Literacy tests, 40–42, 75–77, 95–102, 277–85
Litigation
    prior to Voting Rights Act of 1964, p. 264–66
    trends, 499–500
Log Cabin Republicans, 94, 220–23
Lottery voting, 765–69
Loyalty oaths, 216–17
Madisonian Republicanism, 189, 666
Majoritarian systems, 773–79, 719–20
    Minority rights within (See also Proportional representation systems), 14–16, 55–57, 691–92
Majority–minority districts, definition of majority, 472–73
Malta, 755–56

Matching funds, 618
Minority coalition lawsuits, 481–89
Minority representation, descriptive vs. substantive, 598–603
Money as political speech (See Campaign Financing, First Amendment)
Motor–Voter Act, 113–15, 543
Multimember districts, 367–409, 443–99
Multiple–party nomination, 254–63
Nepal, 719
Netherlands, 782–83
New Zealand, 719
Nineteenth Amendment (See also Women), 21, 32–33
Non–population based bodies (See Senate)
Nonresidents, 61–65
Nonretrogression (See also Voting Rights Act, Section 5), 313–24
O'Connor, Justice Sandra Day, 581–82
One–person / one–vote
    generally, 135–86
    Art. I sec. 2, p. 144
    deviations, 147–57, 547–54
    justiciability, 116–35
    local governments (as applied to), 157–77
    population assessment, 145–50
    public perception, 739–40
    Senate / political fairness, 3–15, 147–50
    state governments (as applied to), 3–15
    used for political gain, 150–55
Open primaries, 224–30
Overseas voters, 65–66
Partisan gerrymandering, 547–66
Party slating, 384–85
Petition requirements, 210–12, 249–52
Philippines, The, 719
Political Action Committees (PACs), 618–31
Political parties
    and the Constitution, 187–89
    history, 187–89
    internal affairs, 237–44
    nominating process, 212–20
    participation
        activist organizations, 220–24
        candidates, 218–20, 223–24
        voters, 79–95, 212–18, 224–37
    third parties (see Third parties)
Poll taxes, 42–47, 78–79, 275
Population Assessments
    Census, 155
    for equipopulational purposes, 144–50
Portugal, 719, 721
Preclearance (See Voting Rights Act, Section 5)
Precommitment strategies, 95, 707
Preference voting, 748–56
Primaries
    blanket (See Blanket primaries)
    white (See White primary cases)
Property owners, 31–32, 172

Proportional representation systems, 720–22, 773–79
Proposition 209 (See California Civil Rights Initiative)
Public campaign Financing, 660–62
Puerto Rico, 66, 277–80
Qualification Clauses (See candidate qualifications)
Race and political parties, 465, 494–99
Race conscious districting
   as expressive harm, 593–98
   impact on political parties, 598–606
Race
   as predominant factor in redistricting, 589–92
   Definition under Voting Rights Act, 486–89
Race–conscious districting
Racial bloc voting, 386–87, 436, 489–99
Racial gerrymandering claims
   generally, 566–612
   standing, 597–98
Racially polarized voting (see also racial bloc voting), 386–87, 436
Reapportionment (See One–person / one–vote)
REDAPPL, 583–84
Redistricting computer software, 583–84
Redistricting, student exercise, 612–15
Referendum (See Direct lawmaking devices)
Registration, 66, 69–77, 95–102, 107–15, 264–65
   purge laws (See also Motor–Voter Act), 543–45
Regression, 469–72, 493–95, 497–98
Republican party, 599–603
Residency requirements, 53, 56–67
Retrogression (See Nonretrogression)
Reynolds, William Bradford, 348–59
Right to vote
   black disenfranchisement (see Black disenfranchisement)
   children, 54–56
   citizenship, 29–31, 53–54
   Congressional power to regulate (See Constitutional power of Congress to regulate)
   criminals, 33–42
   geographic boundaries, 102–07
   homeless, 60–61
   nonresidents, 61–65
   property restrictions, 31–32, 172
   special purpose elections, 157–77
   transient residents, 58–60
   women (see Women)
Run–off elections, 536–40
School Board elections, 47–54, 173–77, 536–40, 682–85
School systems, 173–77
Secret ballot, 189–93
Selma, Alabama, 265–66

Senate (See also Bicameral legislatures), 3–15, 148, 177–85
Seventeenth Amendment, 21
Signature requirements, 248
Single–member districts, 519–45, 709, 769–73
Single–shot voting, 202–03
Single–Transferrable voting, 748–56
Sixty–five percent rule, 473
Soft money, 620–32
Sore–loser statutes, 247–48, 711–12
South Africa, 721
Southern Christian Leadership Conference, 265
Spain, 719, 721
Special purpose elections, 157–77
Stevens, Justice John Paul, 406
Student Nonviolent Coordinating Committee, 265
Substantive minority representation (see Minority representation)
Supermajorities, 155–57, 473–74
Sweden, 720–21
Term limits, 695–712
Territorial districting, 13, 606–08
   history of, 769–73
Thailand, 719
Third parties, 715–17
   candidates, 244–62
Totality of the circumstances, 499–519
Traditional districting principles, 581–92
Turkey, 721
Turnout (See Voter turnout)
Twenty–fourth Amendment (See Poll Tax), 275–76
Twenty–second Amendment, 709–10
Twenty–sixth Amendment 21, p. 55–56
Two–party systems, 715–17
Uruguay, 721
Vote Dilution claims (See also *Gingles* test)
   discriminatory effects, 387–88, 429–31
   discriminatory intent, 387–409
   justiciability, 368–80
   litigation of, 408
   multimember districts, 368–409
   nature of the harm, 368–87
Voter turnout, 107–15, 778
Voting Rights Act
   Section 2 (1982 Amendments) (See also *Gingles* test)
      and Legislative process, 437–10
      and *Mobile v. Bolden*, 407–11
      Congressional Power to enact, 436–40
      Impact on litigation, 434
      Legislative History, 411–34
      Legislative intent, 603
      Section 2 compromise, 431–33
      Section 2 results test, 429–30
      Senator Charles Mathias, Jr., 414–24
      Senator Edward Kennedy, 414–24
      Senator Orrin Hatch, 414–24, 431–33

Voting Rights Act—Cont'd
  Section 2 (1982 Amendments) (See also *Gingles* test)—Cont'd
    Senator Robert Dole, 422–24, 433–34
    Substance, 434–36
  Section 3(c), 539–40
  Section 4(e), 277–80
  Section 5
    amendments, 275, 442
    and Equal Protection Clause, 322–24
    and Judicial decrees, 276, 308–12
    and Section 2 of the Act 321–24 Judicial Review, 325–29
    and 3–judge courts, 293
    annexations, 294, 317–21
    bailout, 276–77
    burden of proof, 294
    candidate qualification restrictions, 295–99
    case study, 336–66
    changes in decisionmaking authority of elected officials, 299–305
    Constitutionality of, 277–85
    covered changes, 285–312
    discriminatory purpose or effect, 313–24
      regulations, 305–06

Voting Rights Act—Cont'd
  Section 5—Cont'd
    municipalities, 275–77
    preclearance
      administrative process, 324–59
      number of requests, 294
    private suits, 293–94
    "standard or practice with respect to voting", 288–90, 295–307
    "Test or device", 274–76
    triggering formula and covered jurisdictions, 274–76, 307–09
  Size of government body and liability, 519–45
  Tradeoff between substantive and descriptive representation, 600–03
Voting
  as political speech (See also First Amendment), 201
  assistance in, 192
Water districts, 164–71
White Primary cases, 79–95, 224
Women, 22–33
  representation under different electoral systems, 777
Write–in voting, 193–202
Zambia, 719
Zero deviation, 144–45, 150–54
Zimmer factors, 385–87, 436